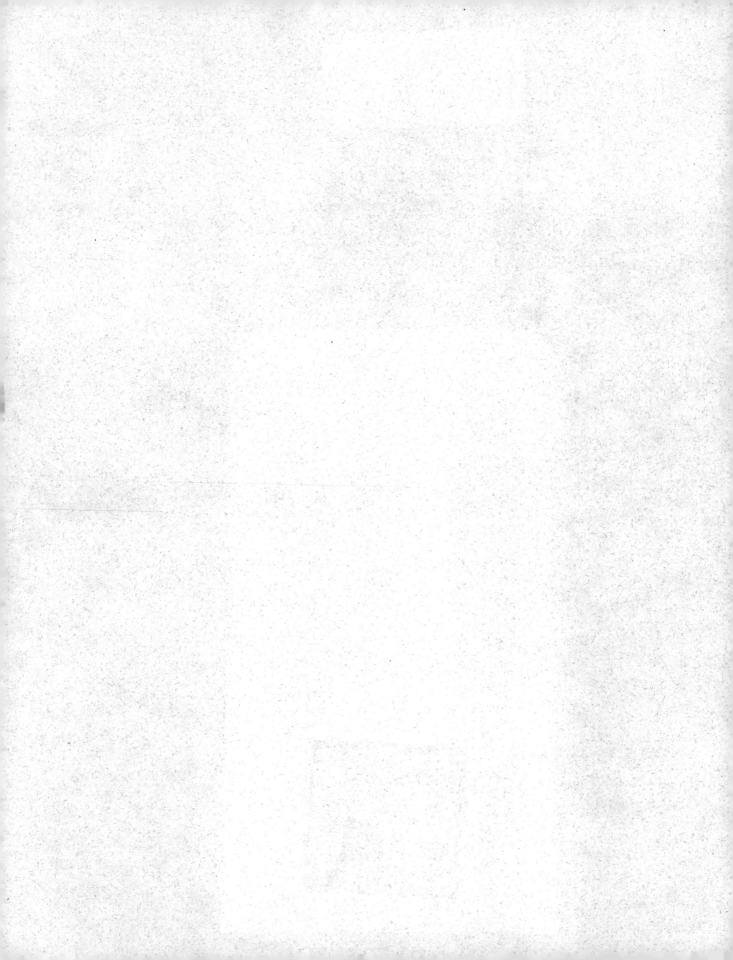

Children's Books and Their Creators

Children's Books and Their Creators

Anita Silvey, EDITOR

Houghton Mifflin Company BOSTON · NEW YORK

For information about permission to reproduce selections from this book, write to Permissions, Houghton Mifflin Company, 215 Park Avenue South, New York, New York 10003.

For information about this and other Houghton Mifflin trade and reference books and multimedia products, visit The Bookstore at Houghton Mifflin on the World Wide Web at http://www.hmco.com/trade/.

Library of Congress Cataloging-in-Publication Data

Children's books and their creators / Anita Silvey, editor.
p. cm.
Includes indexes.
ISBN 0-395-65380-0
1. Children's literature — Bio-bibliography — Dictionaries.
2. Children's literature, English — Bio-bibliography — Dictionaries. 3. Children's literature — History and criticism.
4. Children's literature, English — History and criticism.
I. Silvey, Anita
Z1037.C5424 1995
[PN1009.A1]
028.1'62'03 — dc20 95-19049 CIP

Printed in the United States of America

DOW 10 9 8 7 6 5 4 3 2 1

FOR MY COLLEAGUES:
the women and men who have created,
published, purchased, sold, promoted,
and championed children's and
young adult books in this century.
They have loved and nurtured the books
described in these pages — and have
taught me all that I know.

Contents

Introduction

Life is a banquet — and most of us starve. This adage is especially true of readers of children's books. Despite the wealth, the complexity, the beauty of children's books, so few readers have the time, or the resources, to experience the full richness offered. *Children's Books and Their Creators* attempts, under one cover, to bring the banquet to everyone.

I have spent many years in the children's book field, and often when seeking basic information, I found myself searching through a dozen reference volumes. Gradually I formed a mental image of the reference book on children's literature that I frequently reached for but had not yet found. First, it would concentrate on the books created for children over the last one hundred years and particularly on the last fifty years in the United States. Although many fine reference books about the history of children's and young adult books have been published, few have included publishing in the latter part of the twentieth century. Second, it would treat its subjects broadly. Some reference books provide biographical material and some provide critical overviews: *Children's Books and Their Creators* would provide both. Entries would include essential names, titles, and dates, but not at the expense of neglecting to offer thoughtful evaluations. Third, in addition to presenting a vast array of information, the entries would also attempt to entertain, to bring some of the joy contained in children's books to each adult who reads about them, whether they were learning about books and authors entirely new to them or revisiting books they had loved as children. Finally, my ideal reference would include a wide range of critical perspectives, but it would also invite children's book authors and artists to speak for themselves about the origins and meaning of their work. With these objectives in mind, I conceived of this book.

Children's Books and Their Creators, an illustrated, alphabetically arranged encyclopedia, covers children's and young adult books of the twentieth century. The three types of entries are biographies about the creators; overviews of history, issues, and genres; and "Voices of the Creators," written by the authors and illustrators themselves. The biographical essays provide basic information about the full scope of a creator's work, including the time period and genres in which the creator worked, some of the titles produced, an overall assessment of the work, and some sense of the themes, strengths, and, if appropriate, weaknesses of the books. The longer essays explore books dealing with the Holocaust, preschool books, Latino books, animal stories, mysteries, and alphabet books, as well as genre overviews. Juxtaposed with the critical entries are entries written by seventy-five of the finest contemporary creators themselves, providing a taste of the writing and thinking found in contemporary children's books. Critical volumes can sound lifeless when compared to the literature that inspires them; the "Voices of the Creators" bring into the encyclopedia some of the spontaneity that permeates fine books for children.

Among the satisfactions of editing this book has been the opportunity to review the accomplishments of the last century of publishing for young adults and children, to sift and sort and evaluate as the twentieth century draws to a close. This re-evaluation has shaped the content of this book, perhaps taking it in some surprising directions. Clearly, although many books from the turn of the century have vanished completely, some, like *Anne of Green Gables*, are experiencing a newfound popularity. Generally, only the survivors are included here, favoring continuing vitality over historical interest. Some of the entries, therefore, cover nineteenth-century works that continue to be read in the twentieth century. Because of their importance to young readers, it would have been shortsighted, in a volume of this size, to exclude Mark Twain, Louisa May Alcott, and Lewis Carroll simply because they happened to write in another century. But, proportionally, this volume is weighted to emphasize the books of the latter half of the twentieth century, the books published after World War II. And rather than stop when wading into the murky waters of contemporary literature, as most reference books do, I was particularly intent on including current books and issues. I wanted the volume to explore books that actually speak to contemporary children; consequently, I've included entries on creators of the 1990s.

Like any sane human being undertaking such a massive project, I immediately recognized my limitations. But I was reminded of the classic statement by the children's book editor Ursula Nordstrom, one of the great geniuses of the twentieth century, when she was grilled on her qualifications for her job: "I was once a child." I am particularly comfortable with post–World War II children's books because those are the books of my childhood, my young adult years, and my twenty-five years of professional work. For sixteen of those years I have worked at *The Horn Book Magazine,* the last eleven as editor, and I spend most days reading as many as possible of the two to five thousand children's books published each year, trying to determine which are the best and which will stand the test of time.

In selecting the entries for this volume, I kept several criteria in mind, including the historical importance, popularity, current interest in, and availability of the books, and the overall contribution of the author or artist. I was also concerned that entries reflect the wide variety of cultural backgrounds represented in children's books. But when I had to make my final choices, I held the quality of artistry as most important. All my sympathies lie with those trying to fashion the best children's books; I keep those immortal words of Walter de la Mare at the front of my consciousness: "Only the rarest kind of best in anything is good enough for the young."

In selecting the contributors for this volume, I was able to call upon many people with extensive experience reading and evaluating books for children, and their qualifications can be found in the "Notes on the Contributors." I am drawn to those passionate about children's books, and many entries by children's book enthusiasts appear in these pages. The entries bear the names or initials of their authors, and the opinions and evaluations represent the views of those who have written the pieces. As the entry on controversial books notes, children's books often engender strong opinions — wide ranging and often conflicting opinions. In the mid 1960s, for instance, people argued about whether Maurice Sendak's *Where the Wild Things Are* was a masterpiece or was bad for children's psychological health; they fought over whether Dr. Seuss was a genius or someone who undermined children's reading skills. Such issues and perspectives, both yesterday's and today's, will be found in this volume. As editor, I believe that it is far more important for writers to have freedom of expression than for me to agree with all their stated beliefs.

Children's Books and Their Creators has been fashioned for all who seek information about children's and young adult books: parents, teachers, librarians, booksellers — anyone with an interest in children's books. Readers of all ages are, by nature, inquisitive. Many readers are curious about the authors and artists whose books they enjoy, and this volume can satisfy that curiosity, whether the person is seeking a particular fact or simply wants to read more about favorite books and the context in which they were created and received. The encyclopedia can be used as a quick reference or can be read in depth, using the extensive subject index and cross-references to follow a line of research about a particular author, illustrator, title, or topic.

Large as it is, this volume could easily have been twice the size. So many possible entries were, for one reason or another, excluded, and so much more could be said about all of the people and topics that do appear on these pages. But this book is published with the hope that it will intrigue readers and lead them to additional sources and to the books themselves. It is my hope that *Children's Books and Their Creators* will bring many to the books explored here. In the end, I hope that these pages will serve as an invitation to all to the banquet of children's books.

This book would not have come to be without the work of hundreds of people. To begin with, several hundred contributors created these entries, and my chief pleasure in compiling the volume has been working with them. Books are written by authors and published by houses, and the entire staff at Houghton Mifflin, especially Susan Boulanger, my editor, and Brook Matzell, editorial assistant, took a manuscript and made an idea a published book. Special thanks are also due to my colleagues Mary Burns and Barbara Bader for their suggestions and questions about the overall scope of the work. Peter Sieruta exhibited enthusiasm at the beginning, wrote for two years, and aided and abetted me in the final weeks of the project by his willingness to take on impossible deadlines. My husband, Bill Clark, did say one night, wistfully, at what passed for a dinner at our home, that he now understood what authors meant when they mentioned their spouses in a book. For his understanding, his support throughout this project, and his friendship, I am particularly grateful.

ANITA SILVEY

Getting Started: A Basic Reading List

The books listed here, drawn from major articles in this volume, represent some of the finest works produced for children.

Books for Every Age

BOARD BOOKS

Tana Hoban
Helen Oxenbury
"Max" series, Rosemary Wells

CHAPTER BOOKS

The Courage of Sarah Noble (1954), Alice Dalgliesh
Little House in the Big Woods (1932), Laura Ingalls Wilder
The Lucky Stone (1979), Lucille Clifton
Sarah, Plain and Tall (1985), Patricia MacLachlan
Stone Fox (1980), John Reynolds Gardiner

EASY READERS

"Amelia Bedelia" series, Peggy Parish
The Cat in the Hat (1957), Dr. Seuss
"Frog and Toad" series, Arnold Lobel
"Henry and Mudge" series, Cynthia Rylant
Little Bear (1957), Else Holmelund Minarik
"Nate the Great" series, Marjorie Sharmat

MIDDLE-GRADE FICTION

A Hero Ain't Nothin' but a Sandwich (1973), Alice Childress
Are You There, God? It's Me, Margaret (1970), Judy Blume
Bridge to Terabithia (1977), Katherine Paterson
Harriet the Spy (1964), Louise Fitzhugh
Hatchet (1987), Gary Paulsen
Homer Price (1943), Robert McCloskey
It's Like This, Cat (1964), Emily Neville
M. C. Higgins, the Great (1974), Virginia Hamilton
"Moffats" series, Eleanor Estes
The Pinballs (1977), Betsy Byars
"Ramona" series, Beverly Cleary

PICTURE BOOKS

And to Think that I Saw It on Mulberry Street (1937), Dr. Seuss
Andy and the Lion (1938), James Daugherty
The Carrot Seed (1945), illustrated by Crockett Johnson, and *A Hole Is to Dig* (1952), illustrated by Maurice Sendak and Ruth Krauss
Clever Bill (1926), William Nicholson
Make Way for Ducklings (1941), Robert McCloskey
Mike Mulligan and His Steam Shovel (1939), Virginia Lee Burton
Millions of Cats (1928), Wanda Gág
The Snowman (1978), Raymond Briggs
The Snowy Day (1962), Ezra Jack Keats
The Story of Ferdinand (1936), Munro Leaf, illustrated by Robert Lawson
The Very Hungry Caterpillar (1969), Eric Carle
Where the Wild Things Are (1964), Maurice Sendak

PRESCHOOL BOOKS

Goodnight Moon (1947), Margaret Wise Brown, illustrated by Clement Hurd
Have You Seen My Duckling? (1984) and *Spots, Feathers, and Curly Tails,* (1988), Nancy Tafuri
Holes and Peeks (1984), Ann Jonas
How Do I Put It On? (1984), Shigeo Watanabe
"More More More," Said the Baby (1990), Vera Williams

YOUNG ADULT NOVELS

The Catcher in the Rye (1951), J. D. Salinger
The Chocolate War (1974), Robert Cormier
The Contender (1967), Robert Lipsyte
Dinky Hocker Shoots Smack (1972), M. E. Kerr
The Ghost Belonged to Me (1975), *Ghosts I Have Been* (1977), and *The Dreadful Future of Blossom Culp* (1983), Richard Peck

The Moves Make the Man (1984), Bruce Brooks
The Outsiders (1967), S. E. Hinton
The Pigman (1968), Paul Zindel
Weetzie Bat (1989), *Witch Baby* (1990), *Cherokee Bat and the Goat Guys* (1991), and *Missing Angel Juan* (1993), Francesca Lia Block
Where the Lilies Bloom (1969), Vera and Bill Cleaver

Books for Every Interest

ALPHABET BOOKS

Aardvarks, Disembark! (1990), Ann Jonas
Alphabatics (1986), Suse MacDonald
Anno's Alphabet (1975), Mitsumasa Anno
Brian Wildsmith's ABC (1963)
Chicka Chicka Boom Boom (1989), Bill Martin, Jr., and John Archambault
The Cow Is Mooing Anyway (1991), Laura Geringer
I Spy: An Alphabet in Art (1992), Lucy Micklethwait
On Beyond Zebra! (1955), Dr. Seuss
Pigs from A to Z (1986), Arthur Geisert
Potluck (1991), Anne Shelby

ANIMAL STORIES

Animal Family (1965), Randall Jarrell
The Black Stallion (1941), Walter Farley
Charlotte's Web (1952), E. B. White
Incredible Journey (1960), Sheila Burnford
Julie of the Wolves (1972), Jean Craighead George
Martha Speaks (1992), Susan Meddaugh
One-Eyed Cat (1984), Paula Fox
Sounder (1969), William Armstrong
The Wind in the Willows (1908), Kenneth Grahame

AMERICAN FOLKLORE

All Night, All Day: A Child's First Book of African-American Spirituals (1991), Ashley Bryan
The Girl Who Loved Horses (1979), Paul Goble
The Jack Tales (1943), Richard Chase
Keepers of the Earth (1989), Joseph Bruchac and Michael J. Caduto
The Naked Bear: Folktales of the Iroquois (1987), John Bierhorst
Paul Bunyan (1984), Steven Kellogg
Pecos Bill (1983), Ariane Dewey
The People Could Fly: American Black Folktales (1985), Virginia Hamilton
Rainbow People (1989) and *Tongues of Jade* (1991), Laurence Yep

BIOGRAPHY

America's Paul Revere (1946), Esther Forbes
The Glorious Flight, Across the Channel with Louis Blériot (1983), Alice and Martin Provensen
Indian Chiefs (1987) and *Lincoln: A Photobiography* (1987), Russell Freedman
Paul Robeson: The Life and Times of a Free Black Man (1974), Virginia Hamilton
Unconditional Surrender: U. S. Grant and the Civil War (1994), Albert Marrin
What's the Big Idea, Ben Franklin? (1976), and *Traitor, the Case of Benedict Arnold* (1981), Jean Fritz

COMIC BOOKS AND GRAPHIC NOVELS

"Bloom County" series, Berke Breathed
"Calvin and Hobbes" series, Bill Watterson
The Dark Knight Returns (1989), Frank Miller
"Doonesbury" series, Garry Trudeau
"The Far Side" series, Gary Larson
"Life in Hell" series, Matt Groening
Maus (1986) and *Maus II* (1991), Art Spiegelman
The Watchman (1987), Alan Moore

COUNTING BOOKS

Anno's Counting Book (1975), Mitsumasa Anno
In Ten Black Dots (1986), Donald Crews
Moja Means One: Swahili Counting Book (1971), Muriel and Tom Feelings
One, Five, Many (1990), Kveta Pacovska
1, 2, 3 (1985), Tana Hoban
1 Hunter (1982), Pat Hutchins
One Was Johnny (1962), Maurice Sendak
Pigs from 1 to 10 (1992), Arthur Geisert
Ten, Nine, Eight (1983), Molly Bang
Who's Counting (1986), Nancy Tafuri

CLASSICS

Alice's Adventures in Wonderland (1865), Lewis Carroll
A Christmas Carol (1843), Charles Dickens
The Hobbit (1937), J. R. R. Tolkien
Johnny Tremain (1943), Esther Forbes
Just So Stories (1902), *The Jungle Books* (1894), and *Second Jungle Book* (1895), Rudyard Kipling
The Lion, the Witch and the Wardrobe (1950), C. S. Lewis
Mary Poppins (1934), P. L. Travers
The Merry Adventures of Robin Hood (1883), Howard Pyle
Peter Pan (1905), J. M. Barrie
Pinocchio (1927), Carlo Collodi
The Reluctant Dragon (1938), Kenneth Grahame

Roll of Thunder, Hear My Cry (1976), Mildred Taylor
The Secret Garden (1911), Frances Hodgson Burnett
The Tale of Peter Rabbit (1901), Beatrix Potter
Tom Sawyer (1876) and *Huckleberry Finn* (1884), Mark Twain
Treasure Island (1883), Robert Louis Stevenson
The Wonderful Wizard of Oz (1900), L. Frank Baum

FAMILY STORIES

Anastasia Krupnik (1979) and sequels and *The Giver* (1993), Lois Lowry
Arthur, for the Very First Time (1980) and *Baby* (1993), Patricia MacLachlan
Caddie Woodlawn (1935), Carol Ryrie Brink
Dragonwings (1975) and *Child of the Owl* (1977), Laurence Yep
Fly Away Home (1991), Eve Bunting
The Great Brain (1972), John Fitzgerald
The Great Gilly Hopkins (1978) and *Jacob Have I Loved* (1980), Katherine Paterson
The Homecoming (1981), *Dicey's Song* (1982), *Sons from Afar* (1987), and *Seventeen Against the Dealer* (1989), Cynthia Voigt
It's Like This, Cat (1963), Emily Neville
Journey to Topaz (1971), Yoshiko Uchida
Little Women (1867), Louisa May Alcott
Maniac Magee (1990), Jerry Spinelli
Understood Betsy (1917), Dorothy Canfield Fisher
Up a Road Slowly (1966), Irene Hunt
Zeely (1967) and *The Planet of Junior Brown* (1971), Virginia Hamilton

FAMILY STORIES, ALTERNATIVE

Celine (1989), Brock Cole
Changeover: A Supernatural Romance (1984) and *Memory* (1988), Margaret Mahy
Dear Mr. Henshaw (1983), Beverly Cleary
Lizard (1991), Dennis Covington
Missing May (1992), Cynthia Rylant
Monkey Island (1991), Paula Fox
Rabble Starkey (1987), Lois Lowry
Sentries (1986), Gary Paulsen
Somewhere in the Darkness (1992), Walter Dean Myers
The True Confessions of Charlotte Doyle (1990), Avi
Unlived Affections (1989), George Shannon
What Hearts (1992), Bruce Brooks

FANTASY

The Blue Sword (1982) *and The Hero and the Crown* (1985), Robin McKinley
The Chronicles of Narnia (1950–1956), C. S. Lewis
Chronicles of Prydain (1964–1967), Lloyd Alexander
The Dark Is Rising Quintet (1965–1977), Susan Cooper
The Dragon's Boy (1990), Jane Yolen
The Earthsea Trilogy (1968–1972), Ursula K. Le Guin
Five Children and It (1902), E. Nesbit
"Green Knowe" series (1954–1976), Lucy M. Boston
The Mouse and His Child (1967), Russell Hoban
The Story of Dr. Dolittle (1920), Hugh Lofting
Tom's Midnight Garden (1958), Philippa Pearce
Tuck Everlasting (1975), Natalie Babbitt
Winnie-the-Pooh (1926), A. A. Milne

HISTORICAL FICTION

Across Five Aprils (1964), Irene Hunt
Bull Run (1993), Paul Fleischman
Cecil's Story (1991), George Ella Lyon
Fallen Angels (1988), Walter Dean Myers
The Friendship (1987), Mildred Taylor
Island of the Blue Dolphins (1960) and *Sing Down the Moon* (1970), Scott O'Dell
Johnny Tremain (1943), Esther Forbes
Kidnapped (1886), Robert Louis Stevenson
Lyddie (1991), Katherine Paterson
Morning Girl (1992), Michael Dorris
My Brother Sam Is Dead (1974), James and Christopher Collier
One Bad Thing About Father (1970), F. N. Monjo
The Ox-Cart Man (1979), Donald Hall
The Slave Dancer (1973), Paula Fox
The Strange Affair of Adelaide Harris (1971), Leon Garfield

HOLOCAUST LITERATURE

Anne Frank: The Diary of a Young Girl (1952)
The Endless Steppe (1968), Esther Hautzig
Kindertransport (1992), Olga Levy Drucker
Michling Second Degree (1977), Ilse Koehn
My Enemy My Brother (1969) and *The Traitors* (1968), James Forman
Never to Forget: The Jews of the Holocaust (1976), Milton Meltzer
Number the Stars (1989), Lois Lowry
On the Other Side of the Gate (1975) and *Uncle Micha's Partisans,* Yuri Suhl
Rose Blanch (1984), Christophe Gallaz and Roberto Innocenti
Smoke and Ashes (1988), Barbara Rogasky
The Upstairs Room (1972) and *Journey Back* (1986), Johanna Reiss

INFORMATION BOOKS

Boys' War (1990), Jim Murphy
Exploring the Titanic (1988), Robert Ballard
From Hand to Mouth: Or, How We Invented Knives, Forks, Spoons, and Chopsticks and the Table Manners to Go with Them (1987), James Cross Giblin
The Great Dinosaur Atlas (1991), William Lindsay
Magic School Bus at the Waterworks (1986), Joanna Cole
Neptune (1992), Franklyn M. Branley
Our Solar System (1992), Seymour Simon
Outside and Inside You (1991), Sandra Markle
Predator (1991) and *Nature by Design* (1991), Bruce Brooks
Surtsey: The Newest Place on Earth (1992), Kathryn Lasky
Volcano (1986), Patricia Lauber
Working Frog (1992), Nancy Winslow Parker
The Wright Brothers (1991), Russell Freedman

MYSTERIES

Basil of Baker Street (1958), Eve Titus
The Bodies in the Bessledorf Hotel (1986), Phyllis Reynolds Naylor
Bunnicula, A Rabbit Tale of Mystery (1979), Deborah and James Howe
The Case of the Baker Street Irregulars (1978), Robert Newman
The Case of the Cackling Ghost (1981), Sid Fleischman
The December Rose (1987), Leon Garfield
The Egypt Game (1967), Zilpha Keatley Snyder
"Encyclopedia Brown" series, Donald Sobol
Goody Hall (1971), Natalie Babbitt
The House of Dies Drear (1968) and *The Mystery of Drear House* (1987), Virginia Hamilton
The House with a Clock in Its Walls (1973), John Bellairs
Jane Martin, Dog Detective (1984), Eve Bunting
The Man Who Was Poe (1989), Avi
Piggins (1987), Jane Yolen
The Way to Sattin Shore (1983), Philippa Pearce
The Westing Game (1978), Ellen Raskin
Who Really Killed Cock Robin? (1971), Jean Craighead George

NURSERY RHYMES

Book of Nursery and Mother Goose Rhymes (1954), Marguerite De Angeli
Brian Wildsmith's Mother Goose (1964)
Hector Protector and As I Went Over the Water (1965), *I Saw Esau* (1992), and *We Are All in the Dumps with Jack and Guy* (1993), Maurice Sendak
London Bridge Is Falling Down (1967), Peter Spier
Mother Goose's Little Misfortunes (1990), Amy Schwartz
The Mother Goose Treasury (1966), Raymond Briggs
Ring O'Roses (1922), L. Leslie Brooke
The Tall Book of Mother Goose (1942), Feodor Rojankovsky

PHOTOGRAPHY

Bridges (1991), Ken Robbins
The Dream Is Alive (1990), Barbara Embury
A Gathering of Garter Snakes (1993), Bianca Lavies
How Was I Born? (1975), Lennart Nilsson
Look Again (1971), *Count and See* (1972), and *Of Colors and Things* (1989), Tana Hoban
Pablo Remembers: The Fiesta of the Day of the Dead (1993), George Ancona
Photos That Made U.S. History (1993), Edward Wakin and Daniel Wakin
Seeing Earth from Space (1990), Patricia Lauber
Small Worlds Close Up (1978), Lisa Grillone and Joseph Gennaro
To the Top of the World: Adventures with Arctic Wolves (1993), Jim Brandenburg

POETRY

All Small (1986), David McCord
Alligator Pie (1974), Dennis Lee
Bronzeville Boys and Girls (1956), Gwendolyn Brooks
Don't You Turn Back (1969), Langston Hughes
Finding a Poem (1970), Eve Merriam
I Met a Man (1961), John Ciardi
Joyful Noise: Poems for Two Voices (1988), Paul Fleischman
Knock at a Star: A Child's Introduction to Poetry (anthology, 1982), X. J. Kennedy
The New Kid on the Block (1984), *Something Big Has Been Here* (1990), and *Poems of A. Nonny Mouse* (anthology, 1989), Jack Prelutsky
Night on Neighborhood Street (1991), Eloise Greenfield
Peacock Pie (1917) and *Come Hither* (anthology, 1923), Walter de la Mare
Reflections on a Gift of Watermelon Pickle (1966) and *The Place My Words Are Looking For* (1990), Paul B. Janeczko
Roomrimes: Poems (1987), Sylvia Cassedy
Side by Side: Poems to Read Together (anthology, 1988), Lee Bennett Hopkins
This Same Sky: A Collection of Poems from Around the World (1992), Naomi Shihab Nye
The Trees Stand Shining (1971), Hettie Jones
A Visit to William Blake's Inn (1981), Nancy Willard

Where the Sidewalk Ends (1974) and *The Light in the Attic* (1974), Shel Silverstein

SCIENCE FICTION

Childhood's End (1953), Arthur C. Clarke
The Delikon (1977), H. M. Hoover
Devil on My Back (1984) and *The Dream Catcher* (1987), Monica Hughes
Dragonsong (1976) and *Dragonsinger* (1977), Anne McCaffrey
Eva (1988), Peter Dickinson
Moon-Flash (1984), Patricia McKillip
Mrs. Frisby and the Rats of NIMH (1971) and *Z for Zachariah* (1975), Robert C. O'Brien
Pebble in the Sky (1950), Isaac Asimov
Rocket Ship Galileo (1947), Robert Heinlein
Step to the Stars (1954), Lester del Rey
A Wrinkle in Time (1962), Madeleine L'Engle

SPORTS STORIES

The Contender (1967), Robert Lipsyte
Hoops (1981) and *The Outside Shot* (1984), Walter Dean Myers
The Kid from Tompkinsville (1940), John Tunis Matt
Running Loose (1983), Chris Crutcher
The Team That Couldn't Lose (1967), Matt Christopher
There's a Girl in My Hammerlock (1991), Jerry Spinelli
Winning (1977), Robin Brancato
Zanbanger (1977), R. R. Knudson

SURVIVAL STORIES

The Cay (1969), Theodore Taylor
Deathwatch (1972), Robb White
The Goats (1987), Brock Cole
Hatchet (1986), Gary Paulsen
Maus (1986) and *Maus II* (1991), Art Spiegelman
Robinson Crusoe (1719), Daniel Defoe
Slake's Limbo (1974), Felice Holman

WORLD WAR II BOOKS

Along the Tracks (1991), Tamar Bergman
Behind the Secret Window: A Memoir of a Hidden Childhood during World War Two (1993), Nelly S. Toll
The Devil in Vienna (1978), Doris Orgel
Don't You Know There's a War On? (1992), James Stevenson
Good Night, Mr. Tom (1981), Michelle Magorian
The Hidden Children (1993), Howard Greenfeld
A Nightmare in History (1987), Miriam Chaiken
Paper Faces (1993), Rachel Anderson
Shadow of the Wall (1990), Christa Laird
Stepping on the Cracks (1991), Mary Downing Hahn
Twenty and Ten (1952), Claire Huchet Bishop

Multicultural Perspectives

AFRICAN AMERICAN LITERATURE

The Dream Keeper (1932), Langston Hughes
Every Man Heart Lay Down (1970), Lorenz Graham
My Lives and How I Lost Them (1941) and *The Lost Zoo* (1940), Countee Cullen
Roll of Thunder, Hear My Cry (1975), *Let the Circle Be Unbroken* (1981), and *Road to Memphis* (1990), Mildred Taylor
Stevie (1964), John Steptoe
Walk Together Children (1971), Ashley Bryan
You Can't Pet a Possum (1934) and *Sad-Faced Boy* (1937), Arna Bontemps
Zeely (1964) and *M. C. Higgins the Great* (1974), Virginia Hamilton

CHINESE AMERICAN LITERATURE

City Kids in China (1991), Peggy Thomson
Dragonwings (1975), *Child of the Owl* (1977) and *Star Fisher* (1991), Laurence Yep
El Chino (1990), Allen Say
Fifth Chinese Daughter (1950), Jade Snow Wong
The Five Chinese Brothers (1938), Claire Huchet Bishop
Lon Po Po: A Red Riding Hood Story from China (1990), Ed Young
The Story about Ping (1933), Marjorie Flack
Tales from Gold Mountain (1989), Paul Yee

JAPANESE AMERICAN LITERATURE

Baseball Saved Us (1993), Ken Mochizuki
The Coming of the Bear (1992), Lensey Namioka
Faithful Elephants: A True Story of Animals, People, and War (1988), Yukio Tsuchiya
The Journey: Japanese Americans, Racism, and Renewal (1990), Sheila Hamanaka
Sadako and the Thousand Paper Cranes (1977), Eleanor Coerr
Samurai of Gold Hill (1972) and *The Bracelet* (1993), Yoshiko Uchida
Tales from the Bamboo Grove (1992), Yoko Kawashima Watkins
Tree of Cranes (1991) and *Grandfather's Journey* (1993), Allen Say
Umbrella (1958), Taro Yashima

LATINO LITERATURE

Baseball in April and Other Stories (1990) and *Local News* (1993), Gary Soto
El diablo inglés y otros cuentos (*The English Devil and Other Stories,* 1969), María Elena Walsh
Un diente se mueve (*A Loose Tooth,* 1990), Daniel Bardot
Going Home (1986) and *El Bronx Remembered: A Novella and Stories,* Nicholasa Mohr
Miguel y el pastel (*Miguel and the Cake,* 1992), Maribel Suárez
Teo en un día de fiesta (*Teo during a Holiday,* 1987), Violeta Denou

International Perspectives

AUSTRALIAN LITERATURE

All We Know (1986), Simon French
Far Out, Brussel Sprout! (1983), June Factor
Firestorm! (1985), Roger Vaughan Carr
The Giant Devil Dingo (1973), Dick Roughsey
Hating Alison Ashley (1984), Robin Klein
The Nargun and the Stars (1974) and the Wirrun Trilogy (1977–1981), Patricia Wrightson
Waltzing Matilda (1971), Desmond Digby
The Watcher in the Garden (1982) and *The Way Home* (1973), Joan Phipson

BRITISH LITERATURE TO WORLD WAR II

Book of Nonsense (1846), Edward Lear
Puck of Pook's Hill (1906), Rudyard Kipling
The Silver Sword (1956), Ian Serraillier
The Story of the Treasure-Seekers (1899) and *The Wouldbegoods* (1901), E. Nesbit
"Swallows and Amazons" series (1930), Arthur Ransome
The Sword in the Stone (1938), T. H. White
Tom Brown's Schooldays (1857), Thomas Hughes

CANADIAN LITERATURE IN ENGLISH

Angel Square (1984) and *Spud Sweetgrass* (1992), Brian Doyle
Anne of Green Gables (1908), L. M. Montgomery
Beautiful Joe (1894), Marshall Saunders
Hunter in the Dark (1982) and *Keeper of the Isis Light* (1980), Monica Hughes
In Search of April Raintree (1983), Beatrice Culleton
The Kindred of the Wild (1902), Charles G. D. Roberts
Lost in the Barrens (1956), Farley Mowat
Shadow in Hawthorn Bay (1986), Janet Lunn
The Story of Canada (1992), Janet Lunn and Christopher Moore
Wild Animals I Have Known (1898), Ernest Thompson Seton

CANADIAN LITERATURE IN FRENCH

Ciel d'Afrique et pattes de gazelles (1989), Robert Soulieres
Le dernier des raisins (1986), Raymond Plante
L'été enchanté (1962), Paule Daveluy
Mon ami Pichou (1976), Ginette Anfousse
Le premier voyage de Monsieur Patapoum (1993), François Vaillancourt and Gilles Tibo

TRANSLATION

Crutches (1988), Peter Härtling
Hiroshima no Pika (1980), Toshi Maruki
Linnea in Monet's Garden (1987), Christina Björk and Lena Anderson
The Man from the Other Side (1991), Uri Orlev
Phenomenal Phone (1989), Milos Macourek and Adolf Born

A

Adams, Adrienne

American illustrator and author, b. 1906. Adrienne Adams was one of the most distinguished and prolific illustrators in the fifties and sixties. Her books were often on American Library Association Notable lists, and she was twice the runner-up for the Caldecott Medal for her illustrations for *Houses from the Sea* (1959) and *The Day We Saw the Sun Come Up* (1961), both written by Alice E. Goudey. Her pictures are simply but skillfully drawn and display a wealth of authentic detail. She is known for her design and decoration, often in exquisite color, sometimes pastel, sometimes darkly luminescent, sometimes glowing with warmth. Her work is charming, but neither cloying nor trite.

Her illustrated work includes a child's first experiences with nature, reinterpretations of folk and fairy tales, and popular stories about holidays, all of which have been enjoyed by successive generations of young children. *Houses from the Sea* is the classic first introduction to shell collecting and identification. The experiences of a beautiful summer day from predawn to bedtime in *The Day We Saw the Sun Come Up* also stimulate enjoyment of the natural world. Similarly, the collaborations with Aileen Fisher, *Going Barefoot* (1960) and *Where Does Everyone Go?* (1961), project childlike pleasures in the changing seasons and offer a close look at a variety of animals. The endpapers of paw prints in *Going Barefoot* are a captivating addition.

Adams has been cited for her straightforward interpretations of stories by the Brothers Grimm. *The Shoemaker and the Elves* (1960) with its large, clear pictures and deft characterizations has great appeal for young children. Her rendering of *Hansel and Gretel* (1975) avoids psychological subtleties, relying instead on the traditional setting and elements of the folktale in which two children solve their problems with logic.

Among the many books written by other authors that Adams illustrated were several for her husband, Lonzo Anderson. The first, *Bag of Smoke,* launched her career in 1942; another was the sprightly tale *Two Hundred Rabbits* (1968). Later, she wrote and illustrated her own books, including *A Woggle of Witches* (1971), *The Easter Egg Artists* (1976), *The Christmas Party* (1978), and *The Great Valentine's Day Balloon Race* (1980).

Technical craftsmanship was a high priority for Adams, who often did her own color separations, a painstaking chore. This gave the artist the greatest possible control over her design in the transfer process from original drawing to book page. An example of the success of this process was *The Easter Bunny That Overslept* (1959) by Priscilla Friedrich and Otto Friedrich, where there is arresting contrast between white paper and watercolor.

For Adams, as she described it in a 1964 article, the high point in the process was not when the finished book arrived—she could always see ways that it could be improved—it was the moment of beginning a new book, a time of high optimism, when she could say, "Now, given another chance, I will do a better book."

Adrienne Adams received the 1973 Rutgers University Award for her contributions to children's literature. Her work was exhibited by the American Institute of Graphic Arts and received citations from the New York Society of Illustrators.

Adrienne Adams's most productive years coincided fortuitously with the time of marked increase in government subsidies for school library book collections. Many of her titles fit the demand as publishers expanded their lists to include introductory science experiences. With the increase in child care centers, Headstart, and public library preschool programs in the latter decades of the twentieth century, Adams's seasonal and holiday books continue to be staples in most book collections for children. § E.C.H.

Adams, Richard

British author, b. 1920. *Watership Down* (1972) was published as a novel for all ages. In England, it won two of that country's most prestigious awards for children's books; in the United States, it stayed atop the adult best-seller lists for nearly a year. Critics on both sides of the Atlantic were equally enthusiastic about this enthralling and well-written FANTASY. The novel's success was especially surprising because the author was a middle-aged government employee who had never before written a book.

Richard Adams was born in Newbury, Berkshire, England, the son of a surgeon. He attended Bradfield College in Berkshire and received a master's degree from Oxford's Worcester College. A civil servant for more than twenty-five years, Adams wrote his first book for the enjoyment of his daughters. Epic in both length and scope, *Watership Down* concerns a group of rabbits who leave their warren and find a new home, which they must protect during a war with a rival warren. The author brilliantly depicts a complex rabbit society, which has its own laws, language, and mythology and is populated by a cast of well-defined anthropomorphic animals. Filled with suspense and adventure, the novel won the Carnegie Medal and the Guardian Award and was made into a 1978 animated film.

Adams has written rhyming texts for picture books such as *The Ship's Cat* (1977) and several more epic fantasies for all ages, including *Shardik* (1974) and *The Plague Dogs* (1977). Although their length and complexity may be daunting to some young readers, Adams's novels continue to be enjoyed for their intrigue, adventure, and detailed presentation of fully believable fantasy worlds. P.D.S.

ADOFF, ARNOLD

AMERICAN AUTHOR, B. 1935. Arnold Adoff has earned a fine reputation as a poet and anthologist whose works often celebrate racial pride and harmony. Born in the Bronx, New York City, he was raised in a close-knit, liberal immigrant family that valued assimilation but also honored its European Jewish heritage. A voracious reader, Adoff began writing poetry in his teens and continued to write while attending City College of New York and graduate school at Columbia University. He then embarked on a teaching career in Harlem, where he discovered that school textbooks often neglected ethnic literature.

The African American poetry Adoff collected to share with his students formed the basis of his first book, *I Am the Darker Brother: An Anthology of Modern Poems by Negro Americans* (1968), which contains works by LANGSTON HUGHES, Gwendolyn Brooks, Richard Wright, and many other important writers. Adoff's other well-received African American collections are *Black Out Loud: An Anthology of Modern Poems by Black Americans* (1970) and *My Black Me: A Beginning Book of Black Poetry* (1974), which is geared toward a somewhat younger audience and includes such poets as NIKKI GIOVANNI and Sonia Sanchez. *It Is the Poem Singing into Your Eyes: Anthology of New Young Poets* (1971) contains the work of teenage writers, which was solicited through newspaper and magazine queries.

Beginning with a simply written biography, *Malcolm X* (1970), Adoff moved away from anthologies to concentrate on his own writing. *MA DA LA* (1971) uses the repetition of syllables to represent moments in the life of an African family, but, unfortunately, because the meaning of the sounds is not revealed within the text, the book remains fairly inaccessible, despite its evocative rhythms.

Race is a central issue in much of the author's own poetry. Married to the acclaimed children's author VIRGINIA HAMILTON, who is African American, Adoff is the father of two children. *Black Is Brown Is Tan* (1973) presents biracial family life in a series of cheerful poems, while *All the Colors of the Race* (1982) contains comforting, sensitive poems that address family heritage, prejudice, and self-acceptance in a mixed family.

Adoff's poetry is fluid and musical, although usually unrhymed. He disdains the term "free verse" but experiments with structure, nonsense sounds, punctuation, capitalization, and the layout of a poem on the page. In *Make a Circle, Keep Us In: Poems for a Good Day* (1975), the joys of family life are described in a text that uses a variety of typefaces, with lines that form unusual patterns, words that bump into each other, and individual letters that break apart.

Many of Adoff's books revolve around a theme, such as two food-centered volumes, *Eats: Poems* (1979) and *Chocolate Dreams* (1988). Other books present a continuous story through a series of related poems. *Tornado! Poems* (1977) shows the effects of a tornado on a Midwestern family, from the first radio warnings to the repair of storm-damaged buildings. *In for Winter, Out for Spring* (1991) follows a loose narrative structure in a cycle of first-person poems told by young Rebecca and set against the changing of the seasons. JERRY PINKNEY's beautiful illustrations provide the perfect complement to the beauty of the writing.

Adoff is one of the few contemporary American poets who consistently publishes for children; his work is notable for its challenging themes, evocative language, and beautiful rhythms. P.D.S.

Aesop

Traditional Greek author of fables, b. mid sixth century b.c.(?) Almost nothing about Aesop is certain except the universal and unfading popularity of the fables associated with his name. We do not know exactly when or where he lived or what he did. We have no evidence that he put any of the fables he told into writing and only a few clues as to which fables were actually his. Twentieth-century research has established, moreover, that fables identical to Aesop's in form, and sometimes in substance, existed much earlier, in Mesopotamia. Yet the testimony of Aristophanes, Plato, Herodotus, and other eminent Greeks is firmly in accord on the fame of Aesop as a fable-maker, or fabulist.

His life quickly took on legendary dimensions—the eloquent Aesop, it was said, was once a despised, mute slave—and fables from here and there attached to his name. Originally, they were not meant for children, but first as examples of pithy composition and later as lessons in wise conduct, fables entered the curriculum of young nobles and gentlemen, while young peasants picked up phrases from the fables—"the lion's share," "sour grapes," and "crying wolf," for example—as common wisdom.

The spread of popular education in the nineteenth century, along with advances in printing and graphic reproduction, brought forth schoolbooks and storybooks with selections from Aesop, often vividly illustrated. To parents and pedagogues, fables were instructive tales that children actually enjoyed. Graphic artists appreciated their clear-cut, concentrated action and the scope they allowed for interpretation.

Illustrated collections of the fables especially designed for children became a regular feature of publishers' lists. Walter Crane entitled his elaborate, proto–Art Nouveau presentation (somewhat inaccurately) *The Baby's Own Aesop* (1887). In the relatively static, traditionalist world of early-twentieth-century children's literature, Crane's Aesop held their place into the 1950s, along with two other vintage British editions, folklorist Joseph Jacobs's embroidered retelling of the fables (1894), valued for its historical introduction, and the Arthur Rackham *Aesop* (1912), an odd pairing of Rackham's visual theatrics with lean, shapely new translations by V. S. Vernon Jones.

The one strong American entry was an undisguised artist's showcase, Boris Artzybasheff's *Aesop's Fables* (1933), based on wood engravings and intended for both adults and children. In many quarters, however, a subtler, more far-reaching exploitation of Aesopica was getting under way. Alexander Calder (1931), Antonio Frasconi (1954, 1964), and Joseph Low (1963) produced a motley of broadsides, albums, and portfolios for cultural sophisticates and the occasional questing child.

Illustration by Thomas Bewick for Aesop's fable "The Crow and the Pitcher" from *Bewick's Select Fables of Aesop and Others* (1784).

Early in the picture-book explosion, James Daugherty contrived out of Aesop, Roman legend, and frontier Americana a sentimental blockbuster, *Andy and the Lion* (1938). The widening, unceasing search for picture-book texts brought multiple versions of some of the more anecdotal, folktale-like fables ("The Country Mouse and the City Mouse"; "The Miller, His Son, and the Donkey") as well as attention to some of the little-known ones. There were outright dazzlers, too, most prominently Brian Wildsmith's *The Lion and the Rat* (1963) and *The North Wind and the Sun* (1964), from Aesop via Jean de La Fontaine.

The fables themselves were adapted, grouped, and packaged in a multitude of ways. For beginning readers, Eve Rice retold ten fables in fluent primerese and, under the title *Once in a Wood* (1979), supplied them with emblematic animal close-ups. The single, climactic year of 1992 produced, indicatively, two disparate, unorthodox Aesops: Barbara McClintock's rendering of nine *Animal Tales from Aesop* as a courtly theatrical performance and, from Barbara Bader and Arthur Geisert, *Aesop & Company*, which presents the fables in their original terse form (and in a historical setting), with freely interpretive, graphically American illustrations.

For the twentieth century, clearly, there is no end of Aesops. ❧ B.B.

Afanasyev, Aleksandr

Russian ethnographer and compiler of Russian folk and fairy tales, 1826–1871. Between 1855 and 1864 the literary world was enriched through the diligent efforts of a young man trained in law whose quest for knowledge of Russian history, legend, and folk tales led him to compile and publish over six hundred Russian folk and fairy tales. His monumental accomplishment has been compared to that of the Brothers Grimm. While it is said he only recorded about a dozen tales himself, he collected chapbook publications from the late eighteenth and early nineteenth centuries and selected stories from the vast collections of Russian physician and writer Vladimir Dahl and the Russian Geographical Society.

Aleksandr Nikolayevich Afanasyev was born into the large family of a notary in Voronezh province in Central Russia. Since his family was not wealthy, he was educated by local parish priests and by a teacher at a regional college. At eleven he entered the Voronezh gymnasium. It is said his schooling was not the best. Afanasyev compensated for this deficit through his curiosity and insatiable love of reading. His perseverance enabled him to pass the difficult admission examinations for Moscow University's law school, where he graduated with honors. His interests, however, steered him toward writing, and he became a notable member of the literary community and an affiliate of a literary movement known as the "mythological school." Afanasyev is best remembered for his *Russian Popular Fairy Tales* (8 vols., 1855–1863; trans. 1945), *Russian Folk Legends* (1859; trans. as *Russian Folk Tales,* 1915), and *Beloved Fairy Tales.* Through these the world was introduced to magical wolves, horses, and bears and to the unique turns of phrase that distinguish Russian tales: "Beyond the thrice-nine land, in the thrice-ten kingdom"; "Mornings are wiser than evenings"; "Whether the journey was little or long"; "All of them braver and more handsome than story teller can tell or pen can write." Tales often end with the storyteller's request for recompense: "And now a pot of butter for my tale, friend."

Characters unique to Russian tales are Baba Yaga, Koshchey the Deathless, and The Firebird. Baba Yaga, a crone, lives in the woods in a wooden hut built on chicken legs. While she threatens to eat anyone who visits her, she also feeds and helps those who request her aid, thereby personifying a duality of good and evil. She flies around in a mortar while beating it with a pestle and sweeping away her tracks with a broom. Koshchey the Deathless is an ancient, vengeful, villainous character who can only be killed if the hero finds his external soul, which is ingeniously hidden inside an egg. The Firebird with its flaming feathers is an elusive, mischievous creature greatly coveted for its beauty by kings and tsars. Unlike the Firebird of the ballet, the fairy-tale Firebird does not grant boons. His significance and origins are as elusive as he is. Two additional Russian features, the "water of death" and the "water of life," restore life to a slain hero. His severed head and limbs join together with a sprinkling of the water of death, while the water of life resurrects him. Both waters are fetched by a bird (usually a falcon or a raven). Bladders or vials tied to the bird's legs hold the magical fluids. Among the many stories children enjoy from Afanasyev's collections are "The Magic Ring," "Baba Yaga and the Brave Youth," "The White Duck," "Vasilisa the Beautiful," "Marya Morévna," "Koshchey the Deathless," and "Prince Ivan, the Firebird, and the Grey Wolf." S.R.

African American Children's Literature

It is indeed a misconception to believe that little material was published for or about the African American child in the first sixty years of the twentieth century. There were many books by white authors and illustrators whose final products exemplified two schools of thought. There were those whose portrayal of the Negro in words and visuals showed a sensitivity to and a respect for this minority culture. Their creations seemed to subscribe to the criteria suggested in 1944 by the noted librarian Augusta Baker:

> When considering language, the most important point is to eliminate books which describe Negroes in terms of derision . . . Another language consideration is the use of heavy dialect. It is too difficult for the child to read and understand and since often it is not authentic, but has been created by the author, it is misleading. The use of regional vernacular is acceptable. . . . [Another] factor is illustrations. An artist can portray a Negro child—black skin, crinkly hair and short nose—and make him attractive.

Among those whose artwork exemplified Baker's criteria was Erick Berry, who illustrated Paul Laurence Dunbar's poetry collection *Little Brown Baby* (1941) and Arna Bontemps's *You Can't Pet a Possum* (1934). Caldecott Medal winner Lynd Ward achieved appealing, dramatic figures with which to accompany Hildegarde Swift's stirring biographical sketches in *North Star Shining* (1947). In her novel *Zeke* (1931), set in the area of

Tuskegee, Alabama, the white civil-rights activist Mary White Ovington demonstrated her ability to use Negro dialect in a manner that was realistic without being offensive. FLORENCE CRANNELL MEANS carved a niche in literary history for the Negro child with her novel *Shuttered Windows* (1938). This appears to be the first novel by a white author in which all the characters are black.

From another perspective, there were those white writers and illustrators who, within a most accepting society, enjoyed great popularity with stories and pictures that would contribute little to the Negro child's self-esteem. Elvira Garner's "Ezekiel" series, set in rural Florida, Lynda Graham's *Pinky Marie* (1939), with her "ink black" parents, and Inez Hogan's highly praised *Nicodemus* tales, include many of the characteristics against which Baker spoke. The works of these authors—who were not alone—were replete with the exaggerated use of dialect and illustrations that showed the Negro child with heavy lips, bulging eyes, night-black skin, and woolly hair. Too often the "pickaninny" protagonist was portrayed as a youngster who saw his color as less than acceptable.

By far, much of the best literature was created by blacks themselves, some of whom are familiar in contemporary literary history and others, now forgotten, who should be rediscovered. Arna Bontemps is most often thought of as addressing an adult audience, yet he wrote such fun-filled juvenile novels as *You Can't Pet a Possum* and *Sad-Faced Boy* (1937). In this last title there is one scene to which librarians of any era can relate. The protagonist, Slumber, coming to New York from Alabama, takes his brothers on their first trip to a public library. Slumber reads aloud from a book that sends the group into gales of laughter, and the boys find themselves summarily dismissed by the librarian. As Slumber leaves, he muses about what one is supposed to do with a funny book in the library! With journalist Jack Conroy, Bontemps also wrote a picture book, *The Fast Sooner Hound* (1942) in which a dog outruns a train. In a poetry anthology for young readers, *Golden Slippers* (1941), Bontemps selected poems from the pens of not only those who had gained name recognition, such as Claude McKay and Sterling Brown, but also pieces from such lesser known yet talented writers as Frank Davis, Beatrice Murphy, and Georgia Johnson. The book was enriched with the inclusion of biographical sketches of each of the contributors.

In these early years, even as today, Countee Cullen was considered to be writing for an adult audience. But at least two pieces were written with young people in mind. Collaborating with his pet cat, Christopher, Cullen wrote *My Lives and How I Lost Them* (1941). The eight rollicking tales describe how Christopher, living gingerly on his ninth life, lost the others. The first life, he related, was lost almost immediately after birth when out of curiosity he leaned too far over the edge of the top hat in which he was born. The fall to the floor unceremoniously ended life number one. Other lives were lost under such circumstances as an encounter with a rat and trying to survive the results of a fast brought on by a case of unrequited love. As a public school teacher in Harlem, Cullen is said to have written the animal fantasy *The Lost Zoo* (1940) as an innovative way to teach students certain life lessons. He made his point through the poetic description of the misadventures of the animals who never made it onto the ark. He warned against teasing in the tragic tale of the Squililili-gee who drowned rather than live with the constant taunting that came as a result of his strange name. The fate of the Snake-That-Walked-Upon-His-Tail was an admonishment against false vanity. Snobbishly proud of his tiny feet, the snake planned to be the last to enter the ark. But those same feet became entangled in a vine. With no help available, the walking snake sank beneath the waters, never to be seen again. The thoughtful reader might well see these humorous images philosophically as more truth than fantasy.

Like many of his peers whose work had a multilevel appeal, the noted poet LANGSTON HUGHES selected from his own works some pieces he felt would speak to young people and put them together in The *Dream Keeper* (1932). The selections were tastefully embellished with black-and-white illustrations by HELEN SEWELL. In addition to the poetry, Hughes also wrote a series of "First Books" on such topics as rhymes, jazz, and the history of the Negro, all for early readers. With MILTON MELTZER he organized the still-valuable *Pictorial History of the Negro in America* (1953).

But there were many African American creators whose primary audience was young people. Held in high esteem among those whose novels spoke with quiet forcefulness against racism was Jesse Jackson. He earned a place in the world of children's literature with the publication of two school stories: *Call Me Charley* (1945) and its sequel, *Anchor Man* (1947).

Heartbreak and repeated rejection preceded the acceptance of many African American authors' and illustrators' manuscripts by major publishers. A case in point is the work of LORENZ GRAHAM. It was not until 1958, nine years after the novel had been completed, that Graham's *South Town* was printed. The story, whose basic theme descried the injustices that resulted from racist principles in the Deep South, was considered too controversial. To the surprise of many, however, the book's popularity led to a series continuing the saga of the Williams family in *North Town* (1965), *Whose Town* (1969), and *Return to South Town* (1976). During the time that Graham served as United States Ambassador to Liberia, he became enthralled with the rhythmic patois speech of the West Africans. This fascination was translated into a collection of Bible stories in *How God Fixed Jonah* (1946). At a later date some of the selections were published as individual volumes, the most popular of which was the Nativity story, *Every Man Heart Lay Down* (1970). Graham's work spanned four decades. His last publication was the biography *John Brown* (1980), nine years before his death.

While Lorenz Graham wrote only one children's biography, his sister, Shirley Graham, was a leader among those who saw the form as a driving force to record with truth and accuracy the story of a Negro so often omitted from or distorted in available texts. Her biography *George Washington Carver* (1944) was the first of several designed to tell African American readers and others about the achievements of such figures as Booker T. Washington, Benjamin Banneker, and Julius Nyerere. Graham's marriage to the often castigated civil-rights leader W. E. B. Du Bois unfortunately had adverse consequences for her writing career. But her work may have been inspirational for other writers, such as Chicago librarian Charlemae Rollins, who wrote collections of brief biographies about African American poets, entertainers, and leaders in the world of political action, science, and business.

Just as it is the major job of biography to report life within a historical context, by contrast folklore reports life from the perspective of an ethnic group's social structure. Through the tales of a people, passed down from one generation to another, one learns of government structure, customs, mores, taboos, and even something of the language. Early in this century a major folklorist was Alphonso O. Stafford. In addition to his collection of animal stories, Stafford was a regular writer for *The Brownies Book* (1920–1922). In almost every issue he had African stories, riddles and, sometimes, songs. *The Brownies Book,* founded by W. E. B. Du Bois, was a periodical for "children of the sun." Its contents included, in addition to the folklore, biographical sketches of famous African Americans, poetry, games, and even a bit of international news!

Although the purist might question the inclusion of reading textbooks in a study of children's literature, in this circumstance it seems appropriate. The correlation between relevancy and motivation to learn is not really a new concept. In the early years of the twentieth century many African American educators in public school systems were aware of the exclusion of information about African Americans in material in their general texts. The result was the design of readers that incorporated, along with the techniques for teaching reading, historical, biographical, and cultural information. As an example, Emma Akin, in her primer for first graders, included a simplified story of the life of Paul Laurence Dunbar. Elizabeth Cannon, in her introduction to *Country Life Stories* (1938), stated that she made no attempt to "check the vocabulary with foundation word lists" because so many of those words were of little meaning to the rural children for whom she was writing. The book goes on to describe the works of the Jeanes Supervisor, the role of the County Agents, and the regulations under which the Rolling Store functioned! Stella Sharpe's photographic reader, *Tobe* (1939), was in answer to a little African American boy's query as to why he never saw anyone who looked like him in a book.

Finally, in this glimpse into the history of literature for the African American child, it seems appropriate to include the contribution not of an author or an illustrator, but of a publishing house. Around 1915 Carter G. Woodson organized the Associated Publishers in Washington, D.C. Through this avenue, many little-known yet capable writers and illustrators found an outlet for their works. Books from Associated Publishers included Helen Whiting's easy reader folk tales, such as the collection *Negro Folk Tales for Pupils in Primary Grades* (1938); Parthenia McBrown's *Picture Poetry Book* (1935), designed with the hope that it would inspire children to love poetry; and Altona Trent-Johns's *Play Songs of the Deep South* (1944), well reviewed in some newspapers.

As the first half of the twentieth century drew to a close, the children's literature world was witness to what some describe as a "literary explosion" of works by African American authors and illustrators. Perhaps such outside factors as the growing voice of the civil-rights movement and the legal decision in the Brown vs. Board of Education Supreme Court case contributed to this phenomenon. But surely the greatest credit must go to the creative talent of the authors and illustrators whose names at this time were becoming better and better known.

VIRGINIA HAMILTON's ever popular *Zeely* (1964) was only the first in a list of quality books for children and young adults that led to her becoming the first African American to win the Newbery Medal, for *M.C. Higgins the Great* (1974). In *Zeely* Hamilton has crafted a deceptively simple plot with a subtle blend of fantasy and reality. Underlying the quiet action is a deep sense of family, a characteristic that permeates later works by this creative storyteller. Elizabeth Perry, a city-raised child, renames herself Geeder and her brother Toeboy, when they go to spend the summer on a farm with their Uncle Ross. Life changes for Geeder on the day she first sees Zeely. With her fertile imagination, Geeder is *positive* that this stately figure must be a Watutsi queen! Who but a queen could stand "six and a half feet tall, thin, and as deeply dark as a pole of Ceylon ebony"? Talking with Zeely, Geeder learns who Zeely really is, something of the history of slavery, and a bit of African American lore and legend. Through Zeely's wise counsel, Hamilton shows not only Geeder but also her readers the importance of recognizing and accepting one's identity. Hamilton's skillful use in this book of dialect and unusual sentence structures have since become the hallmark of her distinctive writing style. Beyond these technical attributes, other constants in this writer's works are the persistent message about positive self-image and the importance of family history, the unobtrusive inclusion of ethnic history, and the admonition never to give up hope.

To date, the only African American other than Hamilton to receive the Newbery Medal is MILDRED TAYLOR for her book *Roll of Thunder, Hear My Cry* (1975). *Roll of Thunder, Hear My Cry* is a well-crafted story of an African American family surviving in Deep South Mississippi during the Depression years of the 1930s. There is a sense of family unity strongly supported by the father, Mr. David Logan, who never let his children forget the value of ownership: He owned acres of land while others, white and black, struggled to survive as sharecroppers. With quiet deliberation Taylor makes the reader aware of the ravages of racism in education, in economics, in the justice system, and in frequently humiliating social interactions. Deftly woven into the story is an aspect of racism sometimes overlooked—its effect on some young white people, represented here by Jeremy Simms. Stacey Logan asks him, "Why don't you leave us alone? How come you always hanging 'round us anyway?" There is pathos in Jeremy's stammered reply: "C-cause I just likes y'all." The mood is sustained as Cassie reports the end of this meeting: "When we reached the crossroads he looked hopefully at us as if we might relent and say good-bye. But we did not relent and as I glanced back at him standing alone in the middle of the crossing, he looked as if the world itself was slung around his neck."

With purposeful selection of words and clearly delineated characters, with honesty and perception, Taylor introduces readers to a family whose strength is built on positive self-esteem, courage, and a steadfast belief in holding on to what is yours, no matter what it takes. With Cassie Logan as the protagonist, Taylor continues the saga of the Logan family in two other titles, *Let the Circle Be Unbroken* (1981) and *Road to Memphis* (1990), which through the passage of time show what can be accomplished when a family is determined not to be beaten down by any outside forces.

From an understated beginning in the world of children's literature with the drawings for Joyce Arkhurst's *Adventures of Spider* (1964), JERRY PINKNEY has gone on to receive many honors for his illustrations which recognize the beautiful uniqueness and individuality of members of the black race. Among his citations, Pinkney has six times received the Coretta Scott King Award for illustration in books by both black and white writers. ASHLEY BRYAN's talents as an illustrator were introduced in *Moon, for What Do You Wait?* (1964). As an artist, musician, and historian, Bryan saw the need to preserve for *all* children, but especially for black children, the beauty and significance of the Negro Spiritual. Over the years he has illustrated and provided musical notations for several volumes of spirituals, the first of which was *Walk Together Children* (1971). A young JOHN STEPTOE came on the scene with *Stevie* (1964). Over the years Steptoe showed amazing versatility in style and medium, culminating in his achieving both a Caldecott Honor and the Coretta Scott King Illustrator Award for the brilliant paintings in *Mufaro's Beautiful Daughters* (1987).

As one continues to view the world of children's literature, it can be observed that not only are the doors of major publishing houses opening wider to African American authors and illustrators, but smaller houses, minority-owned houses, are providing yet another avenue of visibility for an ever increasing list of talented African American artists and writers. And surely the primary beneficiaries of these signs of progress are the children and young adults for whom the books are produced. ❧ HENRIETTA M. SMITH

AGEE, JON

AMERICAN AUTHOR AND ILLUSTRATOR, B. 1960. There is nothing ordinary about Jon Agee's PICTURE BOOKS. This Brooklyn artist, who was trained in painting and filmmaking at Cooper Union, depends heavily on graphic visual images and short but well-composed texts in books that are witty, ludicrous, and satirical. His most boldly graphic paintings appear in *Ludlow Laughs* (1985), in which the opening vision of a thick, black semicircle—a frown—leads into a story about a mean-spirited man who is mysteriously transformed; thus, the book's last image is another thick, black semicircle—a smile. The illustrations, using large areas of intense, slightly muddied primary colors, and the spare text play off each other expertly, each enlarging rather than repeating the effect of the other. Reflecting an oft-used theme in Agee's work, *Ludlow Laughs* shows a man being used and discarded by society. While this daytime grump laughs infectiously in his sleep, the whole world laughs along as a radio crew broadcasts his guffaws. When Ludlow's funny dreams end, his fickle fans move on to other entertainments.

Ellsworth (1983) centers on a similar theme. Ellsworth, a dog, is quite content to be a stuffy economics professor, well respected by his human "peers." But he cuts loose at night, chasing cars and digging up bones, until he is discovered and fired. He hangs around the park, miserably jobless, until he becomes inspired to be a dog. The absurdity of the fable works on the surface, while the satire of human values works on a slightly deeper level.

The Incredible Painting of Felix Clousseau (1988) also shows the main character turning his back on society. Clousseau, a painter, places his small, stylized portrait of a duck next to the gargantuan, elaborate portraits entered in a Parisian competition. His painting reaps ridicule until the duck quacks and walks away. Clousseau becomes famous, but not for long, because his painted tornado erupts and other such tragedies ensue. In a twist of fate, he is released from prison and quietly "return[s] to his painting" by literally disappearing into the empty streets of the town on one of his canvases. Clousseau's viewpoint is never explored, and he never seems to be more than glasses, beard, and nose. Yet while he appears to be a misfit, the reader knows that it is society's routines and habits that are in question.

Agee's artistic approach changes to suit each story, but *Clousseau* represents his most familiar style. Using thick black outlines on the stylized figures and few contextual details, the paintings consist of large flat areas of subdued colors, often in murky browns and grays. The muddied palette reflects the darker subtexts of Agee's work, which suggest that all is not as pure—or as funny—as it appears. The flat subjects are given depth through mass, shadow, and perspective. Often objects will have a grainy, almost tactile texture. In *Clousseau* each page is like a cartoon on its own, largely because of the concise text and the unrelenting comedy. In *Go Hang a Salami! I'm a Lasagna Hog!* (1991), Agee moves completely to the single-panel comic format. Filled with palindromes, this book highlights Agee's absurd wit, as his zany pen-and-ink drawings elaborate on such statements as "Elsie's on a nose isle" and "Put Eliot's toilet up." Agee's distinctive style and outlook provide for interesting and provocative picture books. His work says to the reader, "Dare to be different." And Agee practices what he preaches. ❧ S.S.

Ahlberg, Janet
Ahlberg, Allan

Janet: British illustrator, 1944–1994; Allan: British author, b. 1938. The publication of the *Brick Street Boys* (1975), a series of five humorous, comic-strip-style books that describe the activities of a group of multiethnic children in a working-class neighborhood, firmly established the Ahlbergs as creators of highly popular books for young readers. Their body of fresh, lighthearted work includes ingenious toy books, joke books, short stories, and picture books. Many have been designated *School Library Journal* Best Books and American Library Association Best Books for Children.

Both Janet and Allan attended Sunderland College of Education. Janet worked as a layout artist and freelance designer before illustrating children's books, and Allan worked variously as a letter carrier, plumber's helper, and teacher before becoming a full-time children's book author. While Janet was primarily the illustrator and Allan the writer of this team, they considered themselves first and foremost bookmakers, deciding together on all aspects of production, from the book size and typeface to the endpapers, cover, and jacket copy. Their ease of collaboration is reflected in books that display a flawless integration of words and pictures.

The Ahlbergs claimed there are "no deep philosophies" in their work, preferring instead to stress the playful elements of their books. They often made use of the conventions of storytelling, including morals and happy endings. "Once upon a time there were three bears" begins *Jeremiah in the Dark Woods* (1977), the story of a boy detective who sets out to find the robber who has stolen his grandma's tarts. Rhyming couplets introduce readers to fairy-tale and nursery-rhyme characters as they search for Mother Hubbard, Cinderella, and others hiding in the whimsical, humorous pictures of the Kate Greenaway Medal winner *Each Peach Pear Plum* (1978). Allowing preschoolers both the fun of an "I Spy" game and the pleasure of reexperiencing the familiar in an inventive new way, the book is considered a contemporary classic. Other books that exhibit the Ahl-

Illustration by Janet and Allan Ahlberg from their book *The Jolly Postman; or, Other People's Letters* (1986).

bergs' keen awareness of the child's psyche are *Peek-a-Boo!* (1981), *The Baby's Catalogue* (1982), and *Starting School* (1988). The innovative *The Jolly Postman; or, Other People's Letters* (1986) again reinforces and builds on previous literary knowledge. Warm, witty illustrations depict a postman cycling on his rounds, delivering letters between fairy-tale characters. Each real, removable letter, contained in its own envelope, reveals a different form of correspondence—a postcard, a party invitation, an advertisement. Published in eleven countries to critical and popular acclaim, the book is the Ahlbergs' best-known work and received the Emil Award in England, the Book Key Prize in Holland, and the Prix du Livre pour la Jeunesse in France. Its companion book, *The Jolly Christmas Postman* (1991), is a Kate Greenaway Medal recipient.

Warm, entertaining, and involving stories convey a sense of joy in reading and have earned the Ahlbergs a place among the best-loved contemporary children's authors and illustrators. ❧ C.S.

Aiken, Joan

British author, b. 1924. Versatility and a soaring imagination are the hallmarks of the work of Joan Aiken, an accomplished writer who has few equals in the contemporary children's book world. Aiken is noted primarily for her inventive novels and masterly short stories, but her opus also includes poetry, picture books, plays, and retellings of folktales. Aiken was born in Rye, Sussex. As the daughter of the American poet Conrad Aiken and the stepdaughter of the English writer Martin Armstrong, she grew up immersed in a literary environment. At the age of five she made up her mind that she, too, would become a writer. During her schooling at Wychwood, Oxford, Aiken had two poems published by the *Abinger Chronicle,* edited by E. M. Forster and others. Aiken married the journalist Ron Brown; after his death she wrote short stories to augment her income. These stories make up Aiken's first published books, *All You've Ever Wanted* (1953) and *More Than You've Bargained For* (1955).

Her second published novel, *The Wolves of Willoughby Chase* (1962), recipient of the Lewis Carroll Bookshelf Award, began her loosely linked series of adventures set in a historical time that never was—the imaginary reign of King James III of England. Aiken makes use of real historical detail, but the book and its successors—*Black Hearts in Battersea* (1964), *Nightbirds on Nantucket* (1966), *The Whispering Mountain* (1968), *The Cuckoo Tree* (1971), *The Stolen Lake* (1981), *Dido and Pa* (1986), and *Is Underground* (1993)—brim with outrageous improbability, wild exaggeration, lavish melodrama, and humor. These "unhistorical" books are often termed *Dickensian* for their intricate plots and colorful characters. Feisty, smart, and courageous child protagonists—like the resourceful waif Dido Twite—populate Aiken's fictional world. Aiken has said that her "books are concerned with children tackling the problem of an adult world," but, reassuringly, good always triumphs over evil. Aiken's story collections, many of them horror and suspense, have garnered as much acclaim as her adventures, ably demonstrating the scope and variety of her craft. *The Kingdom Under the Sea* (1971), winner of the Kate Greenaway Medal for JAN PIENKOWSKI's brilliant illustrations, draws together new versions of favorite Russian folktales. Stories ranging from the whimsical to the eerie constitute *Up the Chimney Down* (1984). *Past Eight o'Clock* (1987) meshes traditional and contemporary elements by basing each story on a well-known folktale. The atmospheric stories included in *A Whisper in the Night* (1982), *Give Yourself a Fright* (1989), and *A Foot in the Grave* (1992) portray a modern world in which the fantastic and the supernatural are commonplace. Other notable books include *The Shadow Guests* (1980), a novel with a family curse as its premise, and *Arabel's Raven* (1972), the first of several funny books about preschooler Arabel and her raucous, trouble-making pet raven, Mortimer.

A lively, headlong style energizes Aiken's books, which have been honored with the Guardian Award, the Edgar Allan Poe Award, and the Carnegie Medal Honor. Complete command over, and delight in, language evidences itself in her books through delicious wordplay, sly parody, and vivid imagery. Poetic richness and striking originality aside, Aiken's work is wholeheartedly entertaining. ❧ C.S.

ALCOCK, VIVIEN

BRITISH AUTHOR, B. 1924. With the publication of her first book, *The Haunting of Cassie Palmer* (1980), Vivien Alcock immediately established her reputation as a successful author of supernatural FANTASY. Later books would prove that she could write MYSTERIES and adventure stories with equal ease. Her training as an artist at the Ruskin School of Drawing and Fine Arts, Oxford, may have heightened her keen awareness of the powerful interplay between dark and light and the importance of detail, while her service as a British Army ambulance driver during World War II may account in part for the underlying theme of compassion basic to all her plots, no matter the genre.

Vivien Alcock has a flair for creating sinister and eerie moods, building on readers' repressed but ever-present fear of the unknown. In spite of the alarming situations in which her protagonists find themselves, they manage to deal with the forces which threaten them. The heroines—usually Alcock's central characters are girls—may exhibit uncertainty and confusion, but they do not lack pluck. This conflicting capacity for self-doubt and resoluteness builds a strong bond of sympathy with her readers. While many of Alcock's books fall within the supernatural/mystery genre, she demonstrated her ability to write a straightforward adventure story in *Travelers by Night* (1983), a book which contains plenty of action but no chilling overtones. This engaging account follows the adventures of a boy and girl determined to rescue an aged elephant destined for the slaughterhouse.

Ghostly Companions (1987), a collection of imaginative ghost stories, displays Alcock's facility to make the ordinary extraordinary. These taut, fast-paced tales also reveal her deliciously piquant sense of humor. In such books as *The Sylvia Game* (1982) and *A Kind of Thief* (1992), Alcock proves herself to be a master mystery writer. In both stories flawed family relationships result in misperceptions. Alcock uses this device to provide a deeper understanding of her characters. She adheres to the best mystery tradition by lacing her well-constructed plots with tantalizing clues which keep readers engrossed in trying to separate truth from sleight-of-hand. Alcock's protagonists grow and develop in the process of untangling the threads of the mystery; this important feature sets Alcock's books apart from others in the genre which merely supply thrills. Forced to make hard decisions, her heroines take significant steps toward maturity. Perhaps the best example is *The Trial of Anna Cotman* (1990). In this gripping story Anna breaks free from a club in which one calculating member sets out to corrupt the group.

In a complete departure from her usual contemporary setting, *Singer to the Sea God* (1993), a hero tale, takes place in mythic Greece. This imaginative story is a further demonstration of Alcock's versatility as a storyteller. Her polished command of the English language provides all of her books with both wit and depth, making them a joy to read. Vivien Alcock and her husband, author LEON GARFIELD, make their home in London. ❧ P.S.

ALCOTT, LOUISA MAY

AMERICAN NOVELIST, 1832–1888. After considering several careers, including acting, Louisa May Alcott learned that her talent and her earning power lay in writing; and though she had aspirations of writing serious novels for adults, she was in demand for the melodramatic, sensational tales she wrote under a pseudonym and for the hugely successful books for children for which she is best known today.

Louisa May Alcott had an unusual upbringing. Her father, Bronson Alcott, was a penniless philosopher, one

Voices of the Creators

Vivien Alcock

I am always flattered when I'm invited to write about my own work: when the time comes and it is too late to back out, I panic. I feel I am the wrong person to do it. For one thing, I am biased in favor of my books, even the worst of them. I am no Frankenstein to turn against my own creations. So I try to think of a way of blowing my own trumpet, while at the same time remaining becomingly modest. It is not easy. I am a timid person. I prefer to write from behind the masks of fiction. If I were a film star, I should wear large dark glasses all the time, even in the bath.

Then I have a bad memory for names and dates. I remember unimportant things clearly and sometimes inaccurately. For instance, I can remember, quite vividly, walking to school past bleached seaside houses, with the salt wind blowing through my long red hair. The houses and the wind are true enough. I lived for the first ten years of my life in a small seaside town in the south of England. But my hair at that time was dark and straight, and very short owing to my sister's passion for scissors. (She had already turned all our dolls into monks.) It was inside my head, not on the outside, that I had long red hair.

I think we all tell stories to ourselves. We take in hard facts through our senses and promptly start knocking corners off them in case we get hurt, changing them to suit our needs, or simply embroidering them to make people listen. If Coleridge's ancient Mariner had just said, "I had a run of bad luck recently," the Wedding Guest would have passed him by.

I try and make my books as exciting as I can because, like the ancient Mariner, I want to be listened to. I don't write just for the money. Nobody would. As John Steinbeck said, "The profession of book writing makes horse racing seem like a solid, stable business." Nor do I write because I have an important message I feel I must give the world. I just love telling stories. I like to entertain and amaze. When I talk in schools, I like watching the young faces, so bright and responsive. Perhaps I'm just a show-off.

However, when I'm actually writing, I don't think of an audience at all. I live in the world I've made up. Whether it's a fantasy, complete with ghosts and monsters, or a straight adventure story, it becomes equally real to me. I don't mean I lose myself in it or that the characters take over. I'm both the playwright and the player. I find an idea that interests me, choose the scenery, and set the action in motion. Then I move in alternative childhoods, looking out through the eyes of the various characters, trying to discover . . . I don't know what. An answer to something? Or merely the right ending to the story?

Some of my friends ask me when I am going to start writing for adults, as if they thought there was something odd in a person of my age getting stuck with writing for young people. I tell them that I find it exciting to go back to a time when the world was new to me. I tell them that by trying to look once again through the eyes of a child, ridding myself of the prejudices and dusty opinions I've acquired through the years, I can see more clearly. Then I remember uneasily what my friends and I were like at, say, twelve or thirteen. Our eyes were brighter and more observant, it's true. Very little of what went on around us went unnoticed—but what a muddle we made of the things we saw. We discovered the prejudices and absurdities of our elders, and rejected them, leaving ourselves free to choose our own. This is the time I love writing about; the shifting balance between childhood and maturity. Some of us never quite get it right. I know a man who often sounds and acts like a child of ten. I know a sad child who acts and sounds like a woman of fifty. It is an exciting and dangerous time, and it fascinates me.

of many New England thinkers who wished to effect social reform. During Louisa's childhood he founded a "consociate family" on a fruit farm, where people came and went, contributing ideas as well as depleting the meager supply of food. Louisa and her three sisters, Anna, Elizabeth, and May, were given linen clothing to wear, because linen did not exploit the slaves who picked cotton or deprive sheep of their wool. The commune was a miserable failure, as were many of Bronson Alcott's other ventures, and the Alcotts often had to rely on the charity of Louisa's mother's wealthy Boston relatives. But the family was a close and loving one, and their neighbors and friends in Concord, Massachusetts, included great writers and activists such as Henry David Thoreau and Ralph Waldo Emerson. The Alcotts were also staunch abolitionists, sometimes harboring escaped slaves making their way north on the Underground Railroad.

Louisa and her sisters were taught from early childhood to read philosophy and to keep diaries, recording their shortcomings and resolving to improve upon them. Louisa saw her faults as her temper and impatient nature—traits she later gave to Jo in *Little Women*. She began writing poetry at age eleven, and was soon adapting fairy tales for the dramatic performances she and her sisters produced in their barn. Then followed original plays, stories, and fables. In 1852 she sold her first story and became aware that she might be able to support her family—a lifelong concern of Louisa's—through writing. She invented lurid, dramatic, sensational stories that were published in various magazines under pseudonyms like A. M. Barnard. Her first book, a collection called *Flower Fables*, which she wrote as a girl to amuse Emerson's daughter Ellen, was published in 1854.

The year 1858 was a difficult one for Louisa. Her beloved younger sister Elizabeth died of scarlet fever after an illness of many months, and her older sister, Anna, announced her engagement. Anna married and left home in 1860. Although Louisa continued to work at her parents' house in Concord, she would occasionally rent a room in Boston, where she could write. It was an invigorating time to be in Boston: there were lectures on social and prison reform, abolitionism, and women's education. Louisa was in favor of women's suffrage and was one of the first women to vote in Concord. It was during this period that she wrote *Moods* (1864). The book departs from the potboiler style of her pseudonymous stories. This was Louisa's first attempt at serious writing. Two other books, also written for adults, like *Moods*, never sold well; they are *Work: A Story of Experience* (1873) and *A Modern Mephistopheles* (1877). She revised and republished *Moods* in 1882 and liked it best of all her work.

During the Civil War, Louisa volunteered to work as a nurse in a hospital in Washington, D.C., but after just a few weeks contracted typhoid and was sent home. She was treated with a mercury-based medicine and as a result suffered ill health for the rest of her life. Over the next few years, however, she wrote a series of lighthearted pieces about her nursing experiences. They were first serialized in a newspaper under Louisa's own name, but were so popular that they were published as a book, *Hospital Sketches* (1863). Soon her work was in demand.

In 1867 she was asked to write a book for girls. Part One of *Little Women, or Meg, Jo, Beth, and Amy* was written in two and a half months and published in 1868. Essentially it was the story of her own family, in which the girls enjoy the loving devotion of their thoughtful parents and strive to improve their small faults through their trials and pleasures. The book includes the death of Beth and the marriage of Meg, but Louisa made light of the poverty the family endured. The partner and manager of the publishing house suggested that she take a royalty rather than a flat fee for *Little Women*, and as the book was an immediate and immense success, Louisa's fortune was made.

At the request of her publishers, Louisa wrote the book's sequel the following year, resisting the pressure from the girls who wrote to her by refusing to "marry Jo to Laurie to please anyone." (The two books were later published together in one volume under the title *Little Women.*) Louisa became such a celebrity that her picture was mounted on cards and sold to fans. On more than one occasion, she climbed out of a back window to escape the reporters who hounded her parents' door. She was asked to write more lurid stories under her own name, but she refused and never again wrote this type of story after her success.

Little Women not only brought financial stability to the entire Alcott family, but allowed Louisa to indulge them with comforts and pleasures, including travel to Europe. But while abroad, Louisa received word of Anna's husband's death and immediately began to write *Little Men* (1871) specifically to provide for Anna's children. The book features Jo March as a married woman, running Plumfield School with her husband, Professor Bhaer. In the book, orphaned or abused boys are directed to their home and taken in. A strong, swaggering boy named Dan is sent away after introducing the other boys to poker-playing and beer but returns, drawn by his affection for a baby in the household. Though the Bhaers' goodness and love permeate the book, Louisa lent the work a few thrills through her portrayal of the rough Dan and his daring ways. Some of her subsequent books include *Eight Cousins* (1875), *Rose in Bloom* (1876), and *Jo's Boys* (1886).

Louisa hosted her nephews and nieces in Nonquitt, Maine, for the happiest times of her later years, which were plagued with ill health. She died in 1888, only two days after her father. Louisa May Alcott saw a million copies of her books sold during her lifetime. *Little Women* remains her most popular and enduring work.

SALLY HOLMES HOLTZE

Alexander, Lloyd

American author, b. 1924. When Lloyd Alexander decided at age fifteen that he wanted to be a writer, he

Voices of the Creators

Lloyd Alexander

At fifteen, in my last year of high school, I horrified my family. I told them I wanted to be an author. My parents strongly suggested that I would be better off doing something useful. What that might be, I had no idea. In fact, I had no idea how to become an author. If reading offered preparation for writing, there were grounds for hope. I had been reading as long as I could remember. I loved all the world's fairy tales and mythologies. King Arthur was one of my great heroes, but I began to fear that not even Merlin himself could transform me into a writer.

As for doing something useful, I found a job as a bank messenger, hardly an occupation that would teach me to be an author. Adventure, I decided, was the best way. World War II had begun; I eagerly joined the army only to become, in discouraging succession, an artilleryman, a cymbal player in the band, a medic, and an organist in the post chapel. Finally, I was assigned to something more venturesome: a special combat intelligence team. To finish training, we were stationed briefly in Wales. Wild, rough-hewn, with rugged crags and ancient castles, Wales appeared truly a realm of bards and heroes. I expected to see King Arthur and his companions gallop from the mountains. Without knowing it then, I had been given a glimpse of another enchanted kingdom.

From Wales, we were sent to Alsace-Lorraine, the Rhineland, and southern Germany. When the war ended, I was assigned to a counter-intelligence unit in Paris. Later, I was discharged to attend the University of Paris, and I met a beautiful Parisian girl, Janine; we soon married. Life in Paris was fascinating, but I knew that, if I were to write anything worthwhile, I would have to be closer to my own roots, to where I was born and raised.

We went home to Drexel Hill, near Philadelphia. Writing anything worthwhile, however, seemed more and more unlikely. I produced manuscript after manuscript, which every publisher quite wisely turned down. Meantime, I worked as a cartoonist, copywriter, layout artist, and associate editor for a small magazine. After seven years, when I was about to give up hope altogether, my first novel was published.

During the next ten years, I wrote happily for adults. I still have no clear idea why, at that point, I felt an urge to write for young people. Perhaps I sensed that whatever it was that I now wanted to say could best be said through the form of a children's book. My instinct was sound. Writing for young people became the most creative and liberating experience of my life.

Time Cat was my first fantasy novel. Doing research for it renewed my love of Welsh mythology. It was as if all the hero tales, dreams, and imaginings of my childhood had suddenly come back to me. The result was *The Book of Three* and the following Chronicles of Prydain; that imaginary kingdom being something of the land of Wales that had so enchanted me twenty years before.

Since then, most of my books have been in the form of fantasy. *The Remarkable Journey of Prince Jen*, for example, is unquestionably a fantasy; so, too, *The First Two Lives of Lukas-Kasha.* Yet, the Vesper Holly adventures pretend to be straightforward realism. In the Westmark trilogy, there is no fantasy in a technical sense, but the world of Westmark is a world of the imagination, a world that never existed. Whether writing realism or fantasy, however, my concerns are the same: how we learn to be genuine human beings. To me, fantasy is one of the many ways to express whatever truths we manage to perceive about our own human condition, not there-and-then but here-and-now.

Writing for children—nothing has given me greater joy. Children, of course, grow to be adults, and my hope is that my books may have some part in their journey. No author could wish for more.

had no plans to write for children; in fact, for seventeen years he wrote books for adults before producing his first work for children, *Time Cat: The Remarkable Journeys of Jason and Gareth* (1963). With the publication of the "Chronicles of Prydain" in the 1960s, Alexander emerged as one of the foremost American writers of fantasy for young people.

Based loosely on Welsh mythology, which fascinated Alexander from a young age, the "Prydain" series consists of five fantasy novels: *The Book of Three* (1964); *The Black Cauldron* (1965), a Newbery Honor Book; the *Castle of Llyr* (1966); *Taran Wanderer* (1967); and *The High King* (1968), winner of the Newbery Medal. The books trace the development of Taran from a headstrong Assistant Pig-Keeper with a desire for adventure to a humble man with a challenging but realistic vision of

Jacket illustration by EVALINE NESS for *The High King* (1968), by Lloyd Alexander.

rebuilding the war-ravaged land. Filled with quests, romance, magic, and humor, the classic tales deal with some of the more difficult matters that challenge every individual, including personal identity, pride, justice, decision-making, failure, friendship, and death. Heroic but very human figures face villains ranging from the merely misguided to the purely evil. Each of Taran's faithful companions possesses memorable gifts and peculiarities as well as a distinctive voice: Fflewddur Fflam, whose harp strings break whenever he stretches the truth, puts aside his royal crown to travel as a bard, while Princess Eilonwy scorns traditional feminine activities and insists on taking part in the adventures.

Alexander undeniably possesses a flair for characterization, using lively description and expressive speech patterns in all of his work. Vesper Holly, the brilliant, resourceful protagonist of *The Illyrian Adventure* (1986) and other adventure novels, fairly overflows with vitality. Her less confident, very proper guardian narrates the escapades, a perfect counterpoint to Vesper's unconventional personality. Other noteworthy feisty, intelligent female characters in Alexander's work include Mickle and Voyaging Moon. Alexander's frequent use of feline characters reflects his fondness for cats, which are featured in the "Chronicles of Prydain," *The Marvelous Misadventures of Sebastian* (1970), *The Cat Who Wished to Be a Man* (1973), *The Town Cats and Other Tales* (1977), and *The Remarkable Journey of Prince Jen* (1991). Music, another of the writer's passions, is also a recurrent theme in his work. An amateur violinist, Alexander took pleasure in writing about a gifted musician and his magic violin in *The Marvelous Misadventures of Sebastian*. The "Chronicles of Prydain" feature a lovable bard, while Voyaging Moon fills *The Remarkable Journey of Prince Jen* with beautiful music from a perfectly crafted flute.

Alexander brings more to his work from his personal life than his joyful preoccupations, however. Having had no idea as a young man of how to go about becoming a writer, he entered the military to persue adventure. His service gave him the background needed to write *Westmark* (1981), *The Kestrel* (1982), and *The Beggar Queen* (1984), a series of novels recounting the political struggles of a country at war internally and with its neighbors. Alexander spares the reader little of the brutality of war and its effect on the human spirit, but the element of hope—an integral part of his work—remains.

Lloyd Alexander's fiction challenges all readers to be true to themselves and to face the struggles of life seriously, while maintaining the ability to laugh and enjoy living. ♣ A.E.D.

ALGER, JR., HORATIO

AMERICAN AUTHOR, 1832–1899. While growing up in Chelsea, Massachusetts, Horatio Alger, Jr., was groomed to follow his father into the Unitarian ministry. The young Alger began studying Latin and Greek at age six, and not long afterward he was accompanying his father on pastoral visits.

Upon graduation from Harvard in 1852, Alger was more interested in writing than the ministry, and it was only after several failed attempts to live by his pen that he reluctantly entered Harvard Divinity School. Alger's desire to write remained strong, however, and during his divinity school period he published poems, short stories, and his first boy's novel, *Frank's Campaign* (1864). In 1864 Alger took up duties as a Unitarian minister in Brewster, Massachusetts, but abruptly quit his post in March 1866. Some eighty years after Alger's death church records revealed that he left Brewster because he had been caught having sexual relations with boys in his congregation. From Brewster, Alger went directly to New York City, where he took up writing full-time and acquainted himself with the lives of the urban newsboys, bootblacks, and street musicians who would populate his novels.

Alger's first New York novel, *Ragged Dick* (1867), tells the story of a boy bootblack's rise to prosperity. Like most Alger novels, *Ragged Dick* first appeared as a magazine serial before seeing print as a book. Besides being a huge success, the work set the tone for the rest of Alger's boys' novels. Typically, an Alger hero is a poor boy struggling either to make a living or to save his family's mortgaged property from foreclosure. If the boy is not living in New York at the beginning of the novel, the plot will often contrive to place him there. The Alger hero is usually conspired against by either a man of middling wealth (often a squire) or a young, aristocratic snob. Though these squires and snobs frequently cheat, kidnap, shanghai, or frame the Alger hero, their evil actions always prove futile, for in the end the hero wins out and ascends to middle-class prosperity, if not outright riches.

Contrary to the "Horatio Alger myth," the Alger hero's improvement in station is not brought about by hard work; rather, success invariably comes through the intervention of a wealthy gentleman for whom he happens to perform some act of bravery—stopping a runaway horse, foiling an armed robbery, preventing a train wreck. While it is astonishing that Alger successfully reused his hackneyed formula in over one hundred novels, it is no more astonishing than the sheer awfulness of his prose. Heavy on stock figures, improbable action, and stilted dialogue, Alger's novels lack description and character development and frequently contain major plot errors. Nonetheless, Alger was perhaps the best-selling author of his time, and his novels remained a powerful popular culture phenomenon into the 1920s. The Alger novel only faded from the scene when, in the end, America could no longer share the author's notions of class boundaries easily leapt and just rewards coming to all who remain cheerful, honest, and hard-working. § D.B.

Aliki

AMERICAN AUTHOR AND ILLUSTRATOR, B. 1929. Illustrator of her own works as well as those of other authors, Aliki has contributed to over a hundred books in the past three decades.

Aliki aspired to be an artist since kindergarten, when she first won special recognition from her teacher and her parents for her artistic talent. After graduating from the Philadelphia College of Art, she worked in advertising and taught art and ceramics. On a trip to Europe, where she explored her Greek roots, she met and married Franz Brandenberg, a children's book author; inspired by their life in Switzerland, she wrote and illustrated her first book, *The Story of William Tell* (1960). After she and her family returned to New York, Aliki began a career illustrating children's books, which she continued after the family's move to London in 1977.

With the publication of *The Listening Walk* (1961) by Paul Showers and of *My Five Senses* (1962) and *My Hands* (1962), both of which she wrote as well as illustrated, Aliki embarked on a long association with the Let's-Read-and-Find-Out Science Books series. Her many contributions to the field of nonfiction for children have been especially notable. She treats complex topics clearly and succinctly while providing lively pictures, with informative details and humorous elements often appearing in "balloons." By including people and humor in her informational books, she makes the subjects palatable and refreshing. Her books about dinosaurs—*Digging Up Dinosaurs* (1981), *My Visit to the Dinosaurs* (1969), and *Dinosaurs Are Different* (1985)—are extremely popular with young readers, while *Mummies Made in Egypt* (1979) and *A Medieval Feast* (1983) are about historical subjects that appeal to older children. In *Feelings* (1984) and *How a Book Is Made* (1986), books that delight both adults and children, she cleverly uses a comic-strip style to explain both intangible states of mind and emotion and a complicated, multi-stage process. Recently Aliki was asked to reillustrate in full color many of her earlier nonfiction books; she used this opportunity to make textual revisions and to include multi-ethnic, nonsexist scenes that are characteristic of her later works.

In addition to nonfiction, Aliki writes fiction that draws on her personal interests and experiences or those of her family. Her devotion to her Greek heritage finds an outlet in nonfiction such as *Diogenes: The Story of the Greek Philosopher* (1969) and in editions of tales such as *The Gods and Goddesses of Olympus* (1994). Her own stories include *The Two of Them* (1979), a book with an intergenerational theme, and *We Are Best Friends* (1982), a book about moving. She also illustrates stories written by others, most notably by her husband, who enjoys their collaboration because, he says, she "understands me better than anyone else"; typical of their joint efforts are *Aunt Nina and Her Nephews and Nieces* (1983) and *Leo and Emily* (1984). In all her works, Aliki ably varies

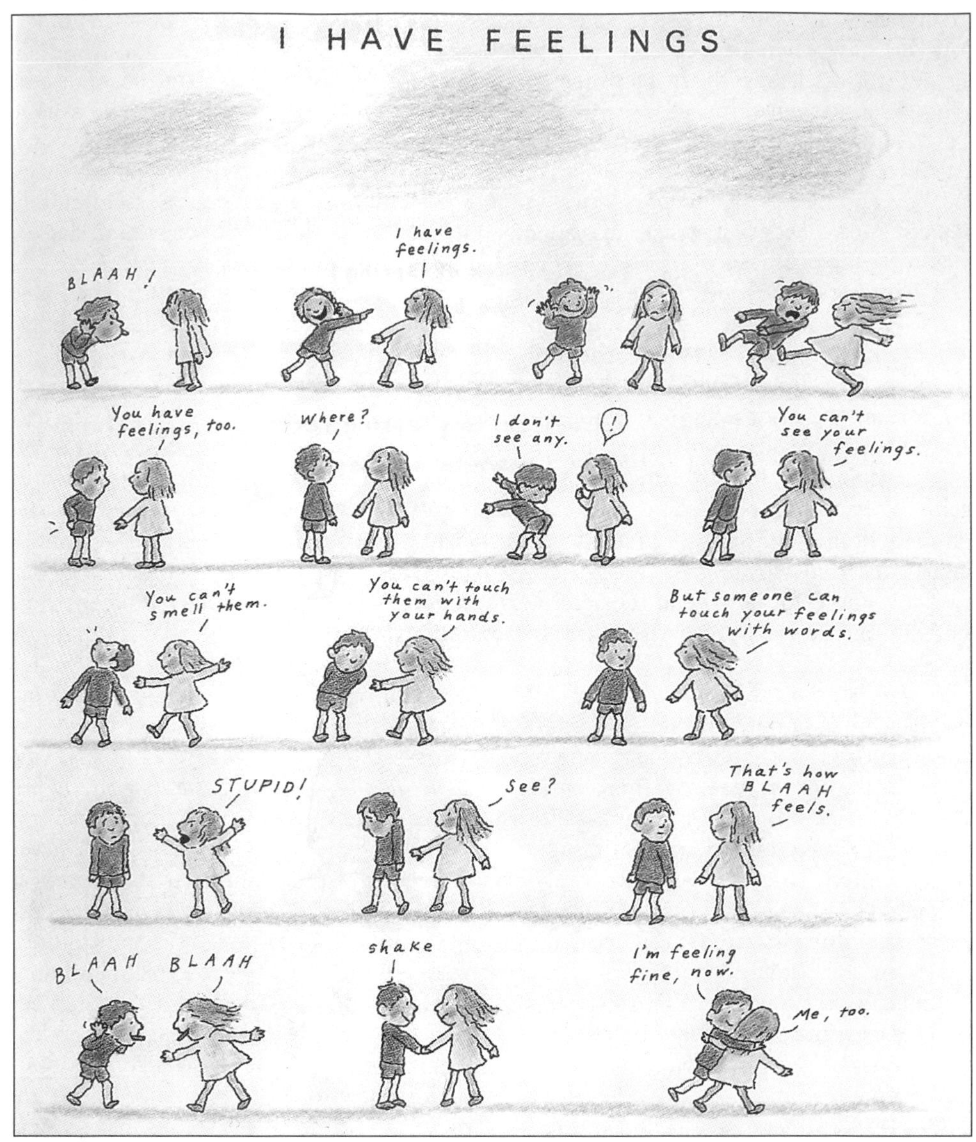

Illustration by Aliki from her book *Feelings* (1984).

her artistic style to suit the need of her subject. She likes to include details that will cause the reader to look at a book again and again, discovering things not seen before. Obviously she has fun being an artist. As she says, "I write fiction out of a need to express myself. I write nonfiction . . . out of curiosity and fascination. And I draw in order to breathe." ❧ H.G.N.

Alphabet Books

Move the clock back two hundred and fifty years to Colonial America. A few solemn children sit in wooden desks and begin their schoolwork, chanting in unison, "In Adam's fall / We sinned all." Their serious rhyme begins one of the first alphabet books, an early instructional tool that provided youngsters with a formal introduction to reading, coupling the letters and sounds of language with moral instruction.

Compare this scene with a modern classroom. Children in one corner respond to Bert Kitchen's *Animal Alphabet* (1984) by cutting out magazine pictures of creatures whose names begin with particular letters. Others roll their tongues over those glorious words in *Hosie's Alphabet* (1972): the "quintessential quail," the "omnivorous swarming locust," and the "ghastly, garrulous gargoyle." Still another group sprawls on the floor, reciting *Potluck* (1991), Anne Shelby's story of a potluck supper: "Acton appeared with asparagus soup. Ben brought bagels. Christine came with carrot cake and corn on the cob. Don did dumplings." Like their historical counterparts, these youngsters are learning to read with alphabet books, but this time the learning crackles with both excitement and joy.

For more than two centuries, what has remained constant in classrooms and nurseries is children and alphabet books. What has changed is how the number and variety in the latter motivate and educate the former.

Children's greatest growth in language comes during the preschool years. Infants make sounds. These sounds translate into words, the words into sentences, the sentences into stories. When they learn to read, youngsters link their oral language to its written counterpart. Their first alphabet books begin this transition.

The very youngest child needs simple, uncluttered books. Words should represent familiar, concrete objects, with "A" beginning apple rather than atom. First alphabet books typically pair initial sounds with words, and these associations should depict regular phonographs. Pages that proclaim "K is for knife" or "G is for gnu" bewilder rather than educate. These key words should also have unambiguous names; "B for bow-wow," in a book peopled with nouns rather than verbs, will confuse the child who identifies the animal as a dog.

In addition, illustrations must be obvious and straightforward. Complications in naming lead to misunderstandings. One preschooler, upset because she had read an alphabet book incorrectly, sadly pointed out this problem: "I said 'R for rope,' but the book meant 'S for snake!'"

While the above criteria represent important considerations in evaluation, they must not create static prescriptions for mass producing similar texts. Artists and authors frequently break traditional rules; often they do so brilliantly. *Brian Wildsmith's ABC* (1963), for example, designates *I* for iguana, a word and sound less obvious to youngsters than the more standard *I* for ice cream. Yet, when readers encounter WILDSMITH's iguana, a glorious, multicolored reptile with its quivering, scarlet throat, they simply must know more about this strange and wondrous creature.

Children interacting with their first texts are not reading in the traditional sense of relying solely on the printed word. Instead, they depend on illustrations to create meaning. Consequently, in initial alphabet books, only one or two objects should appear on the page, acknowledging a child's immature perceptual and spatial skills. There's plenty of time later on to hunt for hidden pictures, sort out numerous nouns, or locate obscure objects after letter-sound correspondence has been mastered.

Although text is of lesser importance than illustrations, it nonetheless deserves attention. Predictable patterns, such as *A* is for apple, *B* is for bear, restate a letter-is-for-noun sequence that lets children imitate reading each time they turn and identify an illustration within the established motif. In addition, text that includes both upper- and lower-case letters gives youngsters a true picture of our written language.

Once children familiarize themselves with the basics, they can be challenged to apply their newfound knowledge to other texts. Lucy Micklethwait's *I Spy: An Alphabet in Art* (1992), for example, not only introduces readers to twenty-six handsome reproductions, but also directs them to find appropriate symbols on each canvas, alternating the obvious umbrellas from Rembrandt's signature painting to Miró's stars in the more abstract *Woman and Bird in the Moonlight.*

Not all alphabet books concentrate on naming; some deal with the positioning of letters. BILL MARTIN, JR., and John Archambault's *Chicka Chicka Boom Boom* (1989) treats youngsters to a jazzy alternative to the traditional "Alphabet Song," which for generations has led children to wonder just what letter "el-em-en-o-pee" really is. Here they chant "A told B, and B told C, I'll meet you at the top of the alphabet tree." For a show-stopping alternative to reading aloud, pair the book with Ray Charles's classy audiocassette and let children explore the alphabet with a musical master.

In real words, letters appear out of sequence, so children need practice in identifying them without their traditional orthographic neighbors. Laura Geringer's *The Cow Is Mooing Anyway* (1991) combines this skill with a slight story line and more advanced, busy illustrations. A mother initiates a morning ritual when she brings her daughter breakfast. But once she leaves the scene, all sorts of wacky diners join the little girl. First a horseshoe crab "drives up in a taxicab," accompanied by the iguanas, who "come in their pajamas." They are joined, in turn, by other combinations of animals who enter the double-page spreads: a dragonfly/goose, a quail/albatross/x-ray fish, and a kangaroo/eel. Each alphabetic entry is noted in a repeating lettered border that positions the letters in their traditional slots, while frenetic scenes call for multiple readings, since details, such as the wall paintings, change along with the story.

Expanding on letter play, Suse MacDonald manipulates shape rather than position. In *Alphabatics* (1986) she takes each letter, twisting and enlarging and altering the form until the letter becomes a visual representation of a key word. *A*, for instance, turns upside down, adds a watery base, grows two animals, and becomes an ark, while *b* rotates on its side, rounds its former base, and floats across the page as a balloon. ARTHUR GEISERT introduces more text in his *Pigs from A to Z* (1986), while encouraging pictorial detectives to locate the numerous examples of a specific letter, along with both preceding and succeeding ones, hidden in his clever illustrations of swine in motion.

Additional visual and verbal sophistication awaits readers of *Anno's Alphabet* (1975) by MITSUMASA ANNO. Each bordered page introduces a single letter, an improbable Mobius strip of twisted wood, and a full-color, slyly implausible illustration: a typewriter types only *T*s, an umbrella rains inside itself, and a rocking horse rests on crossed runners. Delicate pen-and-ink borders frame the wordless text, introducing animals and plants beginning with the appropriate letter. The naming of these creatures and flora requires, or begins to cultivate, an extended vocabulary, while locating them becomes an optical treasure hunt.

As children's language develops, so does their need for story, and more advanced alphabet books provide simple narration within their familiar pattern. ANITA and ARNOLD LOBEL's *On Market Street* (1981), for example, takes a shop-till-you-drop youngster to Market Street, where he discovers all sorts of wondrous wares to sample. Anita Lobel's unusual illustrations depict each product (from apples to zippers) as a costume, while the simple text provides the sparest of frames for naming the twenty-six objects. Two cumulative pages recap the shopping expedition, first in alphabetic sequence, and second in random order.

ANN JONAS's *Aardvarks, Disembark!* (1990) makes use of this sophisticated narrative pattern. Couching her alphabet book within the story of Noah and the Ark, Jonas outlines events of the Great Flood. As the waters recede, Noah must empty his vessel and, showing a real flair for organization, does so in alphabetical order. His biological roll call allows the most conventional creatures to emerge, but Noah soon discovers all sorts of less familiar animals aboard. He "didn't know their names, so he could only call, 'Disembark, everyone! Everyone disembark!'" They start down Mount Ararat, in familiar alphabetical order, taking an entire day to reach the bottom. Who are these forgotten animals, the aye-ayes, the dingos, the tarpans, and the wombats? Most are either endangered or extinct, and, in an informative appendix, Jonas gives the status and environmental location of each.

This pattern, which uses the alphabet as an organizing structure for presenting like information, defines a subculture of alphabet books that explore finite subjects, introduce concepts, and organize literary forms for older children. LOIS EHLERT's *Eating the Alphabet* (1989), for example, highlights fruits and vegetables, often including the less obvious varieties, such as *X* for xigua or *U* for Ugli fruit, along with nonstandard sounds, such as *J* for jalapeño or jicama. Intended to introduce subject rather than letters, this book concludes with a picture glossary, which for many provides an appropriate introduction to the dictionary. Mary Beth Owens's *A Caribou Alphabet* (1988) narrows the subject to one species of animal, including such entries as lichen, predator, and *xalibu*, the Indian word meaning "one who scrapes or paws snow," from which the word *caribou* derives.

Betsy Bowen introduces a sequential structure along with the alphabet in *Antler, Bear, Canoe: A Northwoods Alphabet Year* (1991). From January to January she takes readers through activities, terms, and situations native to her Minnesota environment, covering fishing in March, loons in June, and zero temperatures in December.

Many such subject-driven alphabet books cover less concrete, and consequently more sophisticated, topics. Ann Whitford Paul's *Eight Hands Round: A Patchwork Alphabet* (1991), for instance, represents American history through twenty-six quilting patterns. Each highlights a specific characteristic, introducing games (kite flying), handicrafts (Yankee puzzle), living conditions (log cabin), and events (underground railroad). Similarly, Jim Aylesworth's Pennsylvania Dutch alphabet book, *The Folks in the Valley* (1992), outlines a daily way of life that begins with *A* for alarm clocks, continues with *H* for pitched hay, and concludes with *Z* for "the sound / Of their well-earned rest."

Other alphabet books depend heavily on text and thus expand their audience to older children. Individual volumes, such as *Alligators to Zooplankton: A Dictionary of Water Babies* (1991), resemble mini-encyclopedias, combining the traditional format of letter/word identification with expository text, informative charts, handsome illustrations, a detailed bibliography, and a cross-index. Similar in form but more idiosyncratic in execution, Tim Arnold's *Natural History from A to Z: A Terrestrial Sampler* (1991) employs varied entries (from specific animals such as *C* for coatimundi to the more general classifications such as *U* for ungulates) as convenient points of departure for all kinds of far-ranging discussions on natural history.

Literary forms, as well as informational subjects, will occasionally depend on ABC order for organization. SYLVIA CASSEDY's *Roomrimes* (1987) explores twenty-six spaces in verse, taking the reader from attics to elevators to parlors to zoos. Assonance and alliteration appropriately mark Jeanne and WILLIAM STEIG's alphabetic POETRY (*Alpha Beta Chowder,* 1992), introducing such memorable creatures as the irksome and irascible Ivan the Terrible and Adorable Daphne, who dresses divinely, unlike Deplorable Dora, who is "definitely dowdy" in "that dismal dirndl."

Alphabet books not only use the basic structure of language for reading readiness, subject exploration, and organizational patterns, but sometimes introduce early wordplay. Cathi Hepworth's *Antics!* (1992) spotlights twenty-six words, all with "ant" hidden in the syllables. There's the philosophical Kant, the artistic "Rembrant," and the worldly Nonchalant, who appear with several clever linguistic creations: a Xanthophile, worshiping yellow bananas, and Your Ant Yetta, relaxing with tea and bonbons.

But leave it to DR. SEUSS to find the standard twenty-six letters limiting. In *On Beyond Zebra!* (1955) his young narrator declares: "In the places I go there are things that I see / That I never could spell if I stopped with the Z." His lingua franca includes creatures like Yuzz-a-ma-Tuzz, Umbus ("A sort of a Cow, with one head and one tail . . . [and] ninety-eight faucets that give milk quite nicely"), and Jogg-oons ("Who doodle around in the far desert dunes / Just doodle around, crooning very sad tunes"), which require letters such as YUZZ, UM, and JOGG just to spell them. A few readings of On Beyond Zebra!, and a creative child might just agree with the good doctor: "This is really great stuff! / And I guess the old alphabet / ISN'T enough!" ❧ BETTY CARTER

AMERICAN CHILDREN'S LITERATURE, 1620–1960

If we define children's literature as including only books written to entertain rather than to instruct, and if we further confine our attention to those books both written and published in the United States, our selection of works from the colonial period through the mid-nineteenth century is very limited indeed. Yet, examining the past, however briefly, is important for tracing the development of those attitudes, themes, and ideas in children's books that seem today particularly "American." Many of these were derived from notions of a limitless frontier, realization that ingenuity and hard work were requirements for survival, and awareness that, in a new land, settlers, like latter-day Adams and Eves, had opportunities to create a society different from that left behind.

In comparison with those earlier times, our own seems rich with choice, given the thousands of books now available, including many classics written before 1900. But that is getting ahead of the story, which begins with the arrival of the *Mayflower* in 1620 and the coming of the Puritans a decade later.

Devoted to the Bible, concerned with salvation for themselves and their children, the Puritans brought to the New World books that they admired in the Old. Yet, it was not long before several were adapted or renamed and new ones written specifically for the colonies. Of these, two were particularly significant as representing the attitude of the times: *Spiritual Milk for Boston Babes* by John Cotton (1656), the first book for children printed in the New World, and *The New England Primer* (1686–90), which included genres such as poetry, Biblical verses, prayers, and a rhyming alphabet based on religious subjects.

This didactic trend continued throughout the eighteenth century, tempered occasionally with reprints or revisions of more lighthearted European works such as *Mother Goose's Melodies* (1786), a pirated edition of a work originally published in England, probably around 1780, by John Newbery. The Puritan concept of honesty appears not to have extended to literary ventures!

The notion of writing or adapting books for American audiences is also apparent in the early nineteenth century. The American Revolution had created a new country; the War of 1812 created a strong sense of nationalism, reaffirmed by the Monroe Doctrine in 1823 and reflected in efforts to celebrate the American experience. The approximately 120 works of Samuel Griswold Goodrich (Peter Parley) exemplify this approach, beginning with *The Tales of Peter Parley about America* (1827) and *The Tales of Peter Parley about Europe* (1828). Supposedly factual, they included, and probably perpetuated, many stereotypical concepts about American Indians as well as inhabitants of other continents.

But despite the pervasive influence of Goodrich and others of his ilk, familiar today primarily to literary or social historians the nineteenth century marked the beginning of a genuine American literature for children—conceived, written, and published in the United States. Yet, that literature seems at times ambivalent—searching for a past as it celebrates the present.

Still popular, the long story-poem by CLEMENT CLARKE MOORE, *A Visit from St. Nicholas,* more familiarly known as *The Night before Christmas,* was composed in 1822 and published in 1823. Although the jolly saint may resemble his European antecedents, narrator and setting suggest a new locale. NATHANIEL HAWTHORNE, who drew on the dark side of the Puritan soul for his great novel *The Scarlet Letter,* turned to classical themes when writing for children, retelling Greek myths and legends in *A Wonder Book* (1852) and *Tanglewood Tales* (1853). Framing them in the context of a New England landscape and introducing as narrator a young college student and as listeners a lively group of children, Hawthorne ensured that for his young readers the ancient gods and heroes would find a home in the Berkshire Hills of Massachusetts.

Despite political separation from Europe, Americans were still enamored of its culture and tradition. Consequently, the Grand Tour became a necessary adjunct to the education of the well-to-do. For those unable to afford a continental junket, several authors provided alternatives through travelogue storybooks in which young persons, accompanied by omniscient adults, were led to one historic site after another and treated to informative, frequently moralizing, lectures.

Most of these travelogues were closely related to the didactic writings of Samuel Goodrich, but one survived the genre's limitations: *Hans Brinker, or the Silver Skates* (1865) by MARY MAPES DODGE, later the visionary editor of *St. Nicholas* magazine. Her decision to tell the story from a Dutch child's perspective rather than a tourist's was as notable as her ability to design an intriguing plot through which to impart information about Holland.

Significant as *Hans Brinker* was, however, more distinctively American contributions to children's literature were *Little Women* (1868–69) by LOUISA MAY ALCOTT and *The Adventures of Tom Sawyer* (1876) by Samuel Langhorne Clemens (MARK TWAIN), followed by *The Adventures of Huckleberry Finn* (1885). Although Concord, Massachusetts, the genteel setting of *Little Women,* contrasts sharply with Hannibal, Missouri, where Tom and Huck explored the environs of the Mississippi, both Alcott and Clemens introduced important elements into writing for children, most notably descriptions of the lives and concerns of ordinary people; Clemens went further, introducing likable but not quite respectable protagonists. Beginning with these authors, realism rather than fantasy emerged as a major strength of American children's literature, coexisting, at least until the 1960s, with an idealized romanticism.

Like Clemens, but less earthy, Lucretia Hale employed several conventions of American humor in *The Peterkin Papers* (1880), short stories about a problem-prone family rescued from self-induced dilemmas by the no-nonsense "Lady from Philadelphia." Their antecedents may be found in the noodlehead tales of folklore, but the characters, rooted in New England soil, still have audience appeal.

Another nineteenth-century interest manifested itself in the success of JOEL CHANDLER HARRIS's *Nights with Uncle Remus* (1883), reintroduced in the late 1980s with the omission of objectionable stereotypical elements. Like the tall tale heroes, the animal characters of these stories, drawn from the oral traditions of black slaves, were ordinary individuals empowered by wit to succeed where the less imaginative failed. These and other folkloric figures, derived from the disparate experiences of various minority groups, became still another indication that American literature has many voices—"the varied carols" celebrated by that most American of American poets, Walt Whitman.

Like Nathaniel Hawthorne, illustrator and author HOWARD PYLE turned to the past for inspiration. But his interest was in medieval rather than classical times as demonstrated in books such as *The Merry Adventures of Robin Hood* (1883). His masterful use of black and white, sense of page design, and interest in the narrative potential of illustration strongly influenced succeeding generations of artists, as can be observed in the American preference for narrative rather than abstract art—the pictorial equivalent, perhaps, of the tendency to produce better realistic novels than fantasies. By extension, America's contribution to nonfiction in recent years is a logical development of the reportorial strand running through its publishing for children.

Thus, by the early years of the twentieth century, definite patterns could be discerned. The establishing of children's rooms in public libraries in the late 1800s, the awarding of the first Newbery Medal in 1922 and the Caldecott Medal in 1938, the founding of *The Horn Book Magazine* in 1924 all focused attention on children's books to an extent never before experienced, confirmed by the creation of specialized departments within major publishing houses. With larger numbers of books available, the patterns already mentioned became more obvious: development of realism both as a genre and as a distinct element in fantasy; emphasis on the narrative quality of illustration; interest in regional and ethnic folklore; a sense of national pride; the value of information; the celebration of ordinary folk.

Two books, still in print, confirm many of these premises: *The Wonderful Wizard of Oz* (1900), by L. FRANK BAUM, and *Rebecca of Sunnybrook Farm* (1903), by KATE DOUGLAS WIGGIN. For young Dorothy, transported by a tornado to the magical land of Oz, nothing quite equals Kansas. Nor is she a Victorian English child but rather a forthright, inventive young American used to hard work and plain living. Similarly, Rebecca, sent to live with her strait-laced aunt in Maine, is both formed by and informs her environment with ingenious and ingenuous charm.

This faith in strength of character nurtured by farm life, life on the frontier, or life in small towns where similar values prevailed is a continuing motif throughout the first six decades of the twentieth century echoed in the "Little House" books, by LAURA INGALLS WILDER, the first of which was published in 1932; *Caddie Woodlawn* (1935), by CAROL RYRIE BRINK; *The Moffats* (1941), by ELEANOR ESTES; and *Henry Huggins* (1950), by BEVERLY CLEARY, first of an enduring series and a remarkable example of genuine literature for seven- to ten-year-old readers. Regard for the drama of daily life is also reflected in one of the finest fantasies ever produced, *Charlotte's Web,* by E. B. WHITE (1952). That a spider and a pig should achieve greatness is surely a tribute to the homely virtues thought to be products of a bucolic environment!

Between the end of World War I and the close of the 1950s, interest in the past, particularly the American past, produced several historical novels, period stories, and information books. The "Little House" books and *Caddie Woodlawn* not only reflected the influence of the pioneer spirit but were based on personal or family reminiscences. In contrast, novels like ESTHER FORBES's *Johnny Tremain* (1943) and ELIZABETH GEORGE SPEARE's *Witch of Blackbird Pond* (1958) suggest considerable research into the backgrounds against which their plots unfold. The former, the story of a feisty silversmith's apprentice who witnesses the beginnings of the American Revolution, was published during World War II. Its memorable passage—"We fight, we die, for a simple thing. Only that a man can stand up"—would have been readily appreciated at that time. Similarly, Elizabeth Speare's heroine Kit, by challenging the narrow-minded Puritans of 1697, emphasizes the belief in freedom supposedly guaranteed by the New World. Although some authors turned to other historical pasts, as did MARGUERITE DE ANGELI in *The Door in the Wall* (1949) and HENDRIK VAN LOON in *The Story of Mankind* (1921)—winner of the first Newbery Medal and a model for later writers of information books—most of the more enduring historical re-creations were those rooted in the American experience.

The storytelling tradition in illustration, noted earlier, produced many classic picture books in the first half of the twentieth century. Some, like WANDA GÁG's *Millions of Cats* (1928), suggest the folklore of the Old World. Others, like VIRGINIA LEE BURTON's *Mike Mulligan and His Steam Shovel* (1939) and ROBERT MCCLOSKEY's *Make Way for Ducklings* (1941) seem quintessentially American in settings, themes, characters, and plot resolution. But what, after all, does "quintessentially American" really mean? Picture books published in the United States have continually been enriched by the infusion of new talent from other countries and more recently by recognition of ethnic diversity within its borders: examples include LUDWIG BEMELMANS and ROGER DUVOISIN before the 1960s and LEO and DIANE DILLON, TOM FEELINGS, and ALLEN SAY from later decades.

A contemporary phenomenon, books for beginning readers, appeared in 1957 with the publication of *The Cat in the Hat,* by Theodor Seuss Geisel, known, of course, as DR. SEUSS. Not quite picture books, although illustrations are a fundamental component; not quite complete without pictorial embellishment, although text is prominently featured, these are a hybrid genre, the best of which skillfully utilize the narrative potential of both words and pictures. They have proliferated because of their popularity with children, parents, and teachers, but *The Cat in the Hat* endures mostly for its beloved hero, in whose antipathy to rules of the adult world children recognize a kindred spirit.

Many other fine writers and illustrators—including poet DAVID MCCORD, whose first book for children, *Far and Few,* was published in 1952—were among those who created a distinctive body of literature for children in the first decades of the twentieth century. This brief survey cannot adequately document the diversity of their works nor even include all of their names. Yet, beneath that diversity was a sense of unity, an optimistic view of childhood, and belief in America's promise. Probably no one captured that euphoria more than author-illustrator ROBERT LAWSON, the only individual to date to win both the Newbery and the Caldecott medal. Celebrated as the illustrator of MUNRO LEAF's *Story of Ferdinand* (1936), he began writing and illustrating his own stories in 1939 with *Ben and Me,* an iconoclastic view of Benjamin Franklin presented by his pet mouse. Attuned to the times, Lawson's humor and style of art were instantly recognizable and appreciated by his audience. Rarely has the "American dream" been more celebrated than in Lawson's Newbery winner *Rabbit Hill* (1944), the story of an animal community that coexists with humans because "there is enough for all."

That optimism began to fade as the first half of the twentieth century waned and the realization dawned that many Americans would never share in the dream without dramatic economic and social changes—changes that would also affect the course of children's literature in the 1960s and beyond.

MARY MEHLMAN BURNS

American Folklore

Folklore, that combination of myth, legend, folktales, anecdotes, sayings, and songs that have been passed down from one generation to the next, reflects a people's concept of themselves—their beliefs, hopes and fears, courage and humor, sense of delight in the odd, fascination with the supernatural. By its nature, folklore incorporates the traditional with a society's changing view of itself. In America, we are in the midst of great change and an ever-expanding sense of who "we" are. Our understanding of the term *American folklore* has therefore expanded also.

American folklore includes stories and legends that have been so influenced by this land and its peoples' histories that no matter where some of the plot lines originated, they now belong to our own traditions. A ghost story first told in Scotland, for instance, is transformed into a New England story with a Massachusetts setting, common settlers' names, and New Englanders' speech mannerisms. Or a Spanish tale, brought to Santa Fe with a seventeenth-century governor's entourage, is retold by a Pueblo from an entirely different perspective, in his own language, and passed down until it is translated again and printed in a collection of his tribe's stories to be shared in English with a larger audience.

The American experience differed by group and condition from the very beginning. The hundreds of Native American tribes established distinct cultures. Then, with the coming of Europeans and slaves and later immigrants from a broad range of countries, even more variety was introduced. Though we can point to distinct periods in this nation's history and say that major events had an impact on all of its peoples, what that impact was depended on who the people were.

Free men immigrated with the expectation of making their way in the wilderness and told exaggerated tales of pioneer heroism to bolster their courage. Slaves imported talking-beast tales from various African regions and developed a wryly humorous view of their own survival in a foreign land where they were prisoners, unable to follow their own dreams. Certainly, there are distinct philosophical differences between the swaggering of a Paul Bunyan willing to cut down half the trees in the country and Native American lore about humanity's connection with the land they share with all other living things. Chinese immigrants remained almost invisible because of barriers of language and outlook as they worked in mining camps and on the transcontinental railroad, telling tales that are only now being made available.

This continent's oldest stories, and its only indigenous religions and mythologies, come from the various Native American tribes who crossed the Bering Strait centuries before the first Europeans arrived. But for myths to be vital, they must still be told within the culture. In some places that vitality holds and is being encouraged by a new awareness in the society as a whole, particularly concerning humans' role in the environment. Appreciation of these earliest tales may reflect a more holistic approach to survival in the modern world.

Indian agent Henry Rowe Schoolcraft is credited with being one of the first to purposefully collect and translate Indian myths and stories into English; his two volumes of Chippewa tales (*Algic Researches*, 1839), though romanticized and rewritten, are still mined for folkloric gold. After him came more serious ethnologists and collectors, who convinced tribal traditionalists that their heritage could be preserved in books no matter what happened in their struggle with the U.S. government and white value systems. Franz Boas and others who were creating the science of anthropology at the turn of the century realized that folklore would be one of their greatest resources, and as they collected and compared their findings, the patterns of influence and change among tribes became apparent. But their emphasis on what was common among the tribes was changed in the 1930s by anthropologist Ruth Benedict, who insisted that in spite of commonalities, it was a tribe's specific selection of tales to tell that gave the greatest insights into its culture. Later still, collectors began to showcase individual storytellers. One of the most exciting recent developments has been the growing number of Native Americans who are publishing their own narratives as well as being published as authors and illustrators in the mainstream book trade. The result is a growing respect for sources, an understanding that the rhythms of narrative often differ between the Native American and European models, and that many of the earlier retellings in English have strayed from the heart of the original stories.

In earlier times (and even now where storytellers still pass on a tribe's traditions), some stories served to educate as well as to entertain, teaching what a person needed to know about survival, explaining the natural and spiritual worlds, and reinforcing the culture's sense of order and balance. In some tribes, certain stories are sacred, a reflection of the people's spiritual view of the universe, and told only in certain situations and at certain times of the year.

Native American folklore, as varied as it is from tribe to tribe, includes many similar types of stories, among them a large body of *pourquoi* tales, or "why" stories explaining natural phenomena—why possum has a naked tail, for instance, or why constellations are shaped as they are, or why birds are different colors. There are quest stories or hero tales, transformation tales, and, of course, the popular trickster tales.

The same trickster figures can be godlike or greedy or foolish. In MARGARET HODGES's adaptation of *The Firebringer: A Paiute Indian Legend* (1972) Coyote heroically brings fire to the first men, while in Shonto Begay's rendition of the Navajo traditional story *Maii and Cousin Horned Toad* (1992), he tries to cheat virtuous Horned Toad out of his corn and is soundly beaten. Such tales typically include ghosts, riddles, laughter, and a great many moral lessons.

Among those works available to children, JOHN BIERHORST has provided several impeccably documented collections, including *The Naked Bear: Folktales of the Iroquois* (1987), PAUL GOBLE has written and illustrated some striking PICTURE BOOKS, several of them transformation tales, such as *Buffalo Woman* (1984) and the Caldecott Medal–winning *The Girl Who Loved Wild Horses* (1979), in which a girl finally becomes a fine mare in the herd. More recently, he has published several picture books about the Plains trickster figure Iktomi. Christie Harris's collections—*Once Upon a Totem* (1963), *Mouse Woman and the Vanished Princesses* (1967), and others—highlight tales from the tribes of the North Pacific. Joseph Bruchac, storyteller and gatherer of his grandfather's Abenaki tales as well as those of many other tribes, has published individual stories and several collections, including his well-known *Keepers of the Earth* (1989), written with Michael J. Caduto.

In the seventeenth and eighteenth centuries, colonists came from Northern Europe and Britain to settle the East Coast, bringing their desire for religious freedom and their belief that they must make a community of Saints in the wilderness of the New World. Puritans, with their deep resolve to live with clear consciences, hoped to govern themselves through their theology; their culture heroes were godly men. Their storytelling derived from those concerns, emphasizing providences, witchcraft, and diabolical possessions, such as the tales published in Boston by Increase Mather in his 1684 publication *An Essay for the Recording of Illustrious Providences*, in which God sent great storms, saved ships, or destroyed sinners according to His divine will. New England is still famous for its witches and ghost stories along with later tall tales about giant codfish and an abiding reputation for retaining a "puritan conscience" and adding a dry, understated wit.

Southern Appalachia has provided a wonderful opportunity to hear what happened to many of the less religious and lighthearted settlers' tales when they met another way of life. Because some people who moved into this mountain country remained there for generations, virtually cut off from much of the rest of the world, their oral traditions remained strong and their use of language rich and humorous, often mixing down-home dialect with an Elizabethan turn of phrase that delights the ear. RICHARD CHASE produced the first collections of these stories in *The Jack Tales* (1943), and this and his later collection, *Grandfather Tales* (1973), provide endless enjoyment for children and resources for storytellers. Jack the trickster hero outwits his foes with great insouciance, and the combination of giants, unicorns, bean trees, and kings with hams, turkeys, colloquial mountain sayings, and common sense brings laughter and satisfaction to the listener. GAIL HALEY's collection *Mountain Jack Tales* (1992) gives a fresh voice to the well-known stories, as do her *Jack and the Bean Tree* (1986) and William Hooks's *Three Little Pigs and the Fox* (1989), which have come out as single picture books with unexpected mountain language giving old tales new charm.

While those who stayed in the mountains transformed a group of folktales from England, Scotland, and Ireland, the pioneers who moved on and out into other areas of the new nation in the early 1800s began to create a new group of stories. They celebrated their young country with democratic culture heroes who had been willing to stand up to tyranny in the Old World and fight for independence. From George Washington to that true man of the people, Honest Abe Lincoln, legends grew up about political heroes. Side by side came even more exaggerated stories about common folk with great courage, like the woodsman Daniel Boone and daredevil Davy Crockett, as well as one of our quietest heroes, Johnny Appleseed.

Daniel Boone was born in Pennsylvania in 1735, but he and his fast-moving wife, Rebecca—who was first mistaken for a deer by the mighty hunter—moved to Kentucky, where Daniel became a model for the perfect folk hero, his exploits exaggerated into near impossibility as the legends grew. Interestingly, Davy Crockett's wife was also known for streaking through the woods faster than a deer, though Sally Ann Thunder Ann Whirlwind Crockett is credited with much more now that heroines are sought after by anthologists and storytellers. Born in the mountains of Tennessee in 1786, Davy Crockett wrote much of his own press when he ran for Congress. He was known as a sharpshooter, trapper, bear wrestler, humorist, the perfect match for Mike Fink the Keelboatman on the Mississippi, and, at the end, a man who died at the Alamo. The numerous stories about him were collected in the Davy Crockett Almanacks, which began to circulate not long after his death.

Paperbound books, magazines, and newspapers may also have been the source of most of our tall-tale heroes, though their creators insisted that they came originally from oral tradition. Wherever they came from, they matched the American mood of the nineteenth century perfectly—and they reflected the nation's rising industries. Here were heroes so much larger than life that they could solve any problem—even physically reshape the land itself, pushing mountains into place and moving rivers where they liked, as the cowboy's hero, Pecos Bill, did. Or, in the case of the Eastern seasalt's answer to pioneer bravado, soap the cliffs of Dover white when Old Stormalong sailed the biggest Yankee clipper in existence through the English Channel. Paul Bunyan, the greatest lumberjack who ever lived, was born in Maine and felled giant forests from there through Michigan and on to the Pacific Northwest, accompanied by the gigantic blue ox, Babe. There was even a consummate Swedish farmer named Febold Feboldson who could make it rain in Nebraska. STEVEN KELLOGG's *Paul Bunyan* (1984) and Ariane Dewey's *Pecos Bill* (1983) are part of a small but growing number of picture-book editions available. There are work heroes among the stories coming from the African American heritage as well, such as the great steel-driving John Henry, but he came after the Civil War and the end of slavery (if not racial prejudice).

Brought here against their wills and held prisoner in a land where as slaves they were forbidden to learn to read and given few opportunities for leisure, many African Americans maintained a strong oral tradition, importing African animal stories that were transformed into familiar folk tricksters like Brer Rabbit and passing on secret messages through songs and stories about Moses (Harriet Tubman) and the Drinking Gourd that gave encoded directions on how to flee north to freedom. A legendary trickster hero who could always outsmart the Master is presented in Steve Sanfield's *The Adventures of High John the Conqueror* (1989). VIRGINIA HAMILTON's beautifully written collection *The People Could Fly: American Black Folktales* (1985) displays the variety and range of African American tales, including as it does talking-beast tales, supernatural stories to chill the spine, and moving tales of freedom won. ASHLEY BRYAN has selected songs from slavery days in his *All Night, All Day: A Child's First Book of African-American Spirituals* (1991).

Perhaps the best-known animal character is Brer Rabbit, who first appeared in print through the journalist JOEL CHANDLER HARRIS in the nineteenth century. These stories about talking animals show the underdog's shrewd understanding of human nature and a heartening ability to outwit those who seem more powerful. Harris's original work, though a rich resource, is less accessible than William Faulkner's *The Days When the Animals Talked* (1977) or recent adaptations by Van Dyke Parks in *Jump!: The Adventures of Brer Rabbit* (1986) and its sequels. JULIUS LESTER's four scholarly yet readable editions, beginning with *The Tales of Uncle Remus: The Adventures of Brer Rabbit* (1987), shed new light on the stories' many hidden meanings for the slaves who told and heard them.

Children can now read stories told by Chinese workers who helped lay the tracks for the Central Pacific Railroad across the Sierra Nevada, such as Kathleen Chang's retelling of "The Iron Moonhunter" in compiler Amy Cohn's invaluable resource, *From Sea to Shining Sea: A Treasury of American Folklore and Folk Songs* (1993), and in *Rainbow People* (1989) and *Tongues of Jade* (1991) by LAURENCE YEP. Yep, in his introduction to *Tongues of Jade*, tells about large numbers of men from southern China who could not easily bring their wives and children to this country because of immigration laws and who told each other stories to "show how a wise man could survive in a strange, often hostile land." There it is again: survival, with wisdom and humor.

As the collections and single picture-book folktales continue to be published, that sense of ourselves continues to grow. We learn a lot about those who came before us by hearing the tales they shared; we learn a great deal about ourselves when we look at which stories most touch our hearts, carry our ideals, or make us laugh out loud today. We add stories to the general storehouse. We subtract—at least in the telling—those that jar our current sensibilities. We change. Stories change. Even now, in this age of print, the author/illustrator/storyteller makes an impact on our folklore, re-visioning an old tale for us in a familiar setting, carrying on the ancient tradition of honing and personalizing a tale to its audience. We are rich—and growing richer. ❧ SARA MILLER

ANDERSEN, HANS CHRISTIAN

DANISH POET AND WRITER, 1805–1875. A prolific writer best known for his fairy tales, Hans Christian Andersen wrote and published numerous plays, novels, travel books, and an autobiography. Written between 1835 and 1872, Andersen's fairy tales are among the most anthologized and retold literary works in children's literature. Many of his 156 fairy tales and stories have been translated into more than one hundred languages. What ensured Andersen's fairy tales their widespread popularity was their universality—rags-to-riches themes and characters with recognizable human traits and foibles who overcome adversity through their determination, goodwill, and humor. Yet his tales have been described as paradoxical, revealing a dark side of life and human nature and presenting themes of unrequited love, poverty, selfishness, and vanity.

Andersen's early years influenced his work as a writer. About his works Andersen wrote, "Most of what I have written is a reflection of myself. Every character is from life. I know and have known them all." Like the heroine in "The Princess and the Pea" (1835), Andersen was extremely sensitive. Although he realized his talents, he suffered self-doubt and loneliness. He endured persecution before fame, just like the hero in "The Ugly Duckling" (1845), while "The Little Mermaid" (1837) reflected his unhappy love life and his lifelong struggle as an outsider in society. He has been described as hypochondriacal, because of his recurring anxiety that he would suffer the same fate as his mentally disturbed paternal grandfather. But Andersen was witty and considered good company; perhaps these contrasts formed the basis for Andersen's genius as a writer.

Born and raised in Odense, on an island off the coast of Denmark, Andersen was the only child of a poor shoemaker and a washerwoman. Although the Andersen household lacked money, Hans was allowed the freedom to dream, play with his puppet theater, and wander about the countryside at will. His father loved to tell stories and often read aloud from *The Arabian Nights*, LA FONTAINE, and Danish dramatic works. Andersen's first volume of stories for children, *Fairy Tales Told for Children* (1835), contained four tales, three of which were based on Danish folktales he had heard as a child: "The Tinder Box," "Little Claus and Big Claus," and "The Princess and the Pea." Only "Little Ida's Flowers" was completely original.

Although Andersen's childhood town had a small population of 7,000, Odense represented a miniature version of Danish society. The crown prince of Denmark lived in Odense. Therefore, royalty and the royal court, merchants and tradesmen lived in close proximity to the unskilled and journeymen. Andersen had ample opportunity to observe and even to visit members of the royal court, where he sang songs and recited scenes from the plays of Danish playwright Ludwig Holberg. Later, he used the insights derived from these experiences to write "The Tinder Box" and "The Emperor's New Clothes" (1837). Although Andersen received an uneven education in Odense, he learned to read and developed a passion for books, borrowing them whenever he could. After his confirmation at the age of fourteen, Andersen left home for Copenhagen to seek his fortune, not unlike the hero in his tale "The Traveling Companion" (1836).

Practically penniless but ambitious, Andersen tried unsuccessfully to become an actor and singer. Eventually, friends from the Royal Theater persuaded King Friedrich VI to fund Andersen's education, enabling him to receive a few years of schooling at Slagelse and Elsinore. In 1822, he wrote his first book, *Youthful Attempts*—only seventeen copies sold, and the remaining 283 copies served as wrapping paper for a local grocer. Andersen published a more successful volume in 1829, a fantasy entitled *A Journey on Foot from Copenhagen to the Eastern Point of Amager.* Six years later he wrote his first novel, *The Improvisator,* and, more important to his subsequent career, he published *Fairy Tales Told for Children.* Thereafter he published a fairy tale almost every year until his death. He discovered that the form of the fairy tale, rather than plays or novels, allowed him the freedom to break away from the more staid parameters of Victorian literature.

Andersen enjoyed reading his works aloud, and he infused his fairy tales with an intimacy that quickly pulls the reader into the story. About his first tales, Andersen wrote to a friend, "I have set down a few of the fairy tales I myself used to enjoy as a child and which I believe aren't well known. I have written them exactly as I would have told them to a child." Andersen had an intuitive understanding of children; he conveyed abstract words by using straightforward images that children understood. In "The Little Mermaid," for instance, Andersen described the depth of the sea this way: "Many church steeples would have to be piled up one above the other to reach from the bottom of the sea to the surface." He achieved his realistic style through simple colloquial language. Andersen exploited the characteristics of inanimate objects. He brought to life doorknobs, broomsticks, teacups, darning needles, and fire-tongs, always deriving their attributes from a realistically restricted realm of experience. Among his most famous tales are "The Ugly Duckling," "Thumbelina," "The Nightingale," "The Snow Queen," "The Little Match-Girl," "The Steadfast Tin Soldier," and "The Little Fir Tree."

Continuously popular since the middle of the nineteenth century, Andersen's fairy tales have been translated and illustrated by writers and artists from around the world. The first English translation of his stories was published in 1846. *Wonderful Stories for Children,* rendered by Mary Howitt, featured a selection of ten tales. The Danish translators, however, are often hailed as the most accurate interpreters of Andersen's colloquial diction. Considered highly representative of Andersen's inimitable style, *Hans Christian Andersen's Complete Tales,* translated by the Danish scholar and children's book author ERIK CHRISTIAN HAUGAARD, was published in 1974. *Hans Christian Andersen's Eighty Fairy Tales* (1976), translated by Danish author R. P. Keigwin, incorporates the classic black-and-white line drawings of Andersen's most notable early Danish illustrators, Vilhelm Pedersen and Lorenz Frolich.

Andersen's words best describe the enduring function of the literary genre he mastered so well: "In the whole realm of poetry no domain is so boundless as that of the fairy tale. It reaches from the blood-drenched graves of antiquity to the pious legends of a child's picture book; it takes in the poetry of the people and the poetry of the artist." S.M.G.

ANDERSON, C. W.

AMERICAN AUTHOR AND ILLUSTRATOR, 1891–1971. Clarence William Anderson's many fine horse stories for preschoolers have earned him a place alongside such thoroughbreds as MARGUERITE HENRY and WALTER FARLEY. Like Henry's *Misty of Chincoteague* and its sequels and Farley's "Black Stallion" series, the adventures of Billy and Blaze, the "beautiful bay pony with four white feet and a white nose," have been entertaining young horse lovers for generations. With their attention to detail and exciting, involving plots, the "Billy and Blaze" series, along with Anderson's many excellent titles for older readers, have kept young riders enthusiastic fans.

From the opening sentence in *Billy and Blaze* (1936)—"Billy was a little boy who loved horses more than anything else in the world"—the reader knows it is only a matter of time before Billy's wish will come true, and, indeed, "one birthday morning" brings the pony destined to become Billy's most loyal companion. With simple language, coupled with finely detailed black-and-white illustrations, Anderson teaches many lessons about proper equine care. For example, the meaning of the term *blaze* is introduced early in *Billy and Blaze*: "After thinking for a long time about many names, Billy decided to call the pony Blaze because he had a white blaze down his face." The accompanying illustration clearly shows the pony's face, making it easy for the beginner to identify this characteristic marking. Each Blaze adventure incorporates the details of proper horsemanship, as well as providing the reader with an exciting adventure. Whether Billy is exploring new territory in *Blaze Finds the Trail* (1950), hunting mountain lions out west in *Blaze and the Mountain Lion* (1959), or mourning the loss of Blaze stolen in *Blaze and the Gypsies* (1937), the reader is swept along as the excitement mounts.

Anderson's love of horses and the reputation he built as a fine equestrian illustrator began early. He was born in Wahoo, Nebraska, finished high school, and became a country schoolteacher for two years in order to finance his studies at the Art Institute of Chicago. He next began working as a freelance artist in New York and eventually focused on drawing horses. With the publication of *Billy and Blaze,* Anderson began to produce a series of horse stories for young readers, as well as some excellent nonfiction collections. Titles like *Deep Through the Heart* (1940), *Thoroughbreds* (1942), and *Twenty Gallant Horses* (1965) all contain portraits of the greatest champions of the equestrian world, and Anderson mixes information and anecdotes to give the reader a comprehensive look at some of history's most famous horses.

Illustration by C. W. Anderson from his book *Billy and Blaze* (1936).

Many readers of the "Billy and Blaze" stories who have sustained their love of horses into the elementary years have come to know Anderson's fiction for an older audience, and books like *Afraid to Ride* (1957) and *A Filly for Joan* (1960) continue to be favorites today. In *Afraid to Ride*, a riding accident causes Judy to withdraw from the world of horses completely. The attention of a caring horseman, who gives her the job of restoring the spirit of a badly abused horse, brings Judy back to the sport she has loved so much. The character of Joan in *Filly* is similarly drawn; both girls love and care for their horses, and Anderson provides plenty of accurate detail.

Anderson says, "Especially important to me is the idea that any information that a child may get about horses from the books must be correct and that a horseman could read them to his child without wincing." Readers have come to expect and appreciate Anderson's attention to accuracy, adding to the enduring popularity his books have enjoyed. ❧ E.H.

Animal Stories

Nearly every baby shares its crib with an assortment of teddy bears, flop-eared dogs, and calico cats, beginning an association with animals that for many children continues to grow and deepen with the years. Infants, like puppies, kittens, and other young animals, not only share a diminutive size and appealing "cuteness," but are also alike in their innocence and dependence on larger creatures. This early identification between child and animal often leads to a lifelong respect and love for both household pets and the entire animal kingdom. Certainly children's literature reflects this interest, as animal stories are among the most popular and enduring books published for young people. There are folktales in which animals enact universal truths about humanity, PICTURE BOOKS filled with bunnies and mice, child-and-dog stories, ambitious fantasies about animal communities, and naturalistic portraits of wild animals. Stories about animals cross a wide spectrum of genres and intended age groups, providing evidence that these books are popular with readers of nearly every age and taste.

More than two thousand years ago, AESOP used animal characters to convey moral lessons in fables such as "The Town Mouse and the Country Mouse" and "The Fox and the Grapes." This tradition predates Aesop, however, and is in reality as old as storytelling itself. Most cultures have folktales and myths in which animals represent human characteristics. Talking animal stories, a staple of folklore, have also inspired many original books for children. This genre, however, which includes some of the most brilliant works of the twentieth century, also includes some of the worst. Too many authors have tried to make a hackneyed, sugary, or moralistic story palatable to children by slapping a tail, paws, or a cold, wet nose on the protagonist. A prime example is the regrettably popular "Berenstain Bears" series, created by STAN and JAN BERENSTAIN. These stories of a humanized bear family offer trite, didactic writing and cartoonlike illustrations to an audience of beginning readers. Fortunately, the same age group can enjoy one of the finest talking animal series ever produced: the "Frog and Toad" books by ARNOLD LOBEL. Beginning with *Frog and Toad Are Friends* (1970) and including the Newbery Honor Book *Frog and Toad Together* (1972), the books follow the pair as they go swimming, bake cookies, and tell each other stories. Distinguished for both their gentle prose and amusing illustrations, the books present a portrait of true friendship accessible to most young readers.

Frog and Toad spring from a literary tradition that allows animal characters to think, behave, and sometimes even dress as human beings, although they remain animals in many other respects. Thus, Lobel's Frog wears a bathing suit and rides a bicycle, yet hibernates all winter. BEATRIX POTTER, beloved by generations of readers for her charming illustrated stories, also utilized this technique. In her classic *The Tale of Peter Rabbit* (1901), the young rabbit wears a jacket and shoes, but also has a craving for carrots and a fear of being caught by Mr. McGregor and cooked into a pie.

Humanized animals inhabit a number of important FANTASY novels for intermediate readers. KENNETH GRAHAME's classic *The Wind in the Willows* (1908) contains an evocative portrait of nature as several animals travel through the English countryside. The novel depicts the friendship of Mole and Water Rat, as well as the comic adventures of Toad, who lives in a mansion and covets motorcars. Published near the century's midpoint, *Charlotte's Web* (1952) immediately established itself as a benchmark by which all twentieth-century animal fantasies must be measured. E. B. WHITE's unforgettable tale of Wilbur the pig, whose life is saved by the spider Charlotte, is filled with memorable animal characters, features important themes of life, death, and friendship, and is written in crystalline prose. Critics continue to express shock that this distinguished book failed to win the Newbery Medal, but nearly twenty years later, another strong animal fantasy did capture the prize. *Mrs. Frisby and the Rats of NIMH* (1971), by ROBERT C. O'BRIEN, mixes a domestic story of a mouse who must relocate her family with scientific speculation about escaped super-intelligent laboratory rats who live in a sophisticated rodent community.

Two British animal fantasies must also be noted. *Watership Down* (1972), by RICHARD ADAMS, is an epic novel about rabbits who leave their warren to find a new home. The book succeeds as both an exciting adventure and a wonderfully complex portrait of a rabbit society. Young readers and adults continue to enjoy this lengthy, ambitious novel. Although lacking the philosophical depth of a great animal fantasy, Dodie Smith's *Hundred and One Dalmatians* (1956) is an immensely popular farce of kidnapped puppies, vicious villains, and harrowing rescues. The style is tongue-in-cheek, but the suspense is real.

While most talking animal stories are presented in a matter-of-fact tone, another type of fantasy, which dates back to the nursery rhyme "Old Mother Hubbard and Her Dog," derives its humor from animals that display human characteristics. DR. SEUSS's time-tested classic *The Cat in the Hat* (1957) uses a minimal vocabulary and bouncing rhyme to tell the story of a boisterous cat who visits two bored children on a rainy day. One of the funniest canines in children's literature appears in *Martha Speaks*, SUSAN MEDDAUGH's 1992 picture book about a dog who develops the ability to talk. At first Martha's family of humans is charmed by her new skill, because she can now explain such long-pondered questions as "Why don't you come when we call?" and "Why do you drink out of the toilet?" Less charming is Martha's tendency to tattle, make rude remarks, and tell her life story in excruciating detail. How Martha traps a burglar and learns to control her talking makes a thoroughly delightful story.

A final category of animal fantasy combines everyday behavior with fantastic happenings. RANDALL JARRELL's *Animal Family* (1965), illustrated by MAURICE SENDAK, features a bear and a lynx. Although perhaps tamer than most wild animals, the pair does not talk, dress up, or emulate human behavior in any way. Yet these animals are integral to the plot of this fantasy about a mermaid who leaves the sea to join a hunter in starting a family. Exploring issues of loneliness, love, and family, this poetic and lyrical story speaks directly to the heart.

Conversely, Catherine Cate Coblentz places a mystical animal within a fact-based story of colonial history in *The Blue Cat of Castletown* (1949), the beautifully written tale of a cat who inspires a Vermont girl to create a rug that was later to be displayed in the Metropolitan Museum of Art. Few modern readers are familiar with this Newbery Honor Book, but it deserves rediscovery as one of the most magnificent depictions of creativity and the power of art ever explored in a children's book.

Realistic fiction that examines the connections between humans and animals is consistently popular with children. Many stories concern a child's longing for a pet, or the pleasure that an animal can bring to a young person's life. MEINDERT DEJONG writes with intensity of Davie's longing for, and eventual attachment to, a small black rabbit in *Shadrach* (1956), an exceptionally sensitive novel highlighted by Maurice Sendak's illustrations. WALTER FARLEY's *The Black Stallion* (1941) is the exciting story of young Alec Ramsey, who, along with a wild horse, is shipwrecked on a desert island. Alec gentles the horse and, after their rescue, rides him to victory in a race. The boy-and-dog stories of Jim Kjelgaard are also appealing. His best-known, *Big Red* (1945), depicts the relationship between a rural teenager and a neighbor's prize-winning Irish setter. Danny travels to New York for Big Red's dog show, then returns to Smokey Creek, where he teaches the dog to hunt game and track the marauding bear that is killing local livestock. MARGUERITE HENRY has explored the bond between child and animal in a number of realistic novels, including *Misty of Chincoteague* (1947) and *King of the Wind* (1948), which are based on historical horses. The vivid background material provides authenticity to her always exciting story lines.

Many children list animal stories and funny stories as their favorite types of reading. Realistic books that combine the two are especially welcome, as proven by the popularity of BEVERLY CLEARY's work. Beginning with *Henry Huggins* (1950), in which Henry finds a stray dog and takes him home, through *Henry and Ribsy* (1954), which concerns Henry's efforts to keep his dog out of trouble for two months, the series presents the warm relationship between boy and dog as they become involved in numerous comic situations.

Even in an uncomplicated, humorous story, the relationship between child and animal usually serves as a catalyst for positive change in the young person's life. Similarly, animals often help guide a child through a crisis or personal problem in a serious novel. LYNN HALL's realistic animal stories are written with conviction, integrity, and heart. *Halsey's Pride* (1990) concerns a thirteen-year-old girl who learns to accept her epilepsy through her relationship with a collie. A lonely boy who shoots a stray feline confronts issues of guilt and responsibility in PAULA FOX's moving and elegantly written *One-Eyed Cat* (1984). Arctic wolves help a troubled Eskimo girl sort out her problems and survive the North Slope of Alaska in JEAN CRAIGHEAD GEORGE's *Julie of the Wolves* (1972), a Newbery Medal–winning novel distinguished by evocative writing and deep understanding of both human and animal behavior. Another Newbery Medal–winner, *Sounder* (1969), by William Armstrong, tells the story of an African American family in which the father is arrested and his "coon dog" is wounded. The dog is both a presence and a metaphor in this stark, Depression-era novel that has the power of an American myth.

Realistic animal stories do not always concern a child's interactions with a pet or wild animal. Some books focus on the animal itself, giving a naturalistic account of its life experiences. Anna Sewell's nineteenth-century novel *Black Beauty* (1877) was a forerunner of this type. Although the reader must first accept the premise of a first-person story narrated by a horse, the text is firmly grounded in the animal's perceptions and observations. Albert Payson Terhune collected a number of stories about his own collie in *Lad: A Dog* (1919), a volume that realistically records a dog's varied adventures. An even better known collie is featured in *Lassie-Come-Home* by Eric Knight (1940). Knight takes assiduous care to avoid humanizing Lassie in this story of her four-hundred-mile journey from Scotland to Yorkshire; the dog's actions are consistently guided by instinct or simple thought processes. *The Incredible Journey* (1960), by Canadian author Sheila Burnford, tells of a lengthy trek made by an English bull terrier, a Labrador retriever, and a cat, and also ascribes few human emotions or thoughts to the trio of animals. Felix Salten's *Bambi* (1926) presents a naturalistic portrait of life in the wild. There is savagery, bloodshed, and fear of the human "He." As Bambi grows into adulthood, an almost ineffable sadness hangs over the story, as he begins to behave in instinctive ways he does not completely understand. Yet for all its realism, the animals of this tale converse with one another, making the novel a hybrid between an animal-centered realistic story and a fantasy.

Stories that adopt the viewpoint of a dog or deer are based on the author's perceptions and conjectures and may not be an accurate representation of an animal's experience, yet there is little question that these books increase understanding of the natural world and cause many readers to view animals in a different light. Realistic fiction detailing the love between a child and an animal, whether through comic situations or through personal drama, is also engaging and enlightening. Fantasies in which animal communities symbolize human society or individual animals represent human traits may be the most illuminating of all. Sometimes the most important thing about an animal story is what it teaches us about ourselves. ❧ PETER D. SIERUTA

Anno, Mitsumasa

Japanese author and illustrator, b. 1926. Mitsumasa Anno was a teacher for ten years, and his books reflect an understanding of how children learn. He is both an artist and a mathematician and has won many awards, including the Golden Apple Award given by the Biennale at Bratislava and the First Prize for Graphic Excellence in Books for Children conferred by the jury at the Bologna Children's Book Fair.

The first Anno book published in the United States was *Topsy-Turvies: Pictures to Stretch the Imagination* (1970), and a companion volume, *Upside-Downers: More Pictures to Stretch the Imagination*, appeared the following year. *Topsy-Turvies* is an amazing collection of improbable constructions filled with impossible perspectives and angles in the watercolor paintings peopled by tiny figures in ingenious confusion. There are no words in the trompe-l'oeil first book; its companion volume has a text in which playing-card characters argue about which way is up.

In *Anno's Alphabet* (1975) the letters are shown as solid pieces of rough-grained wood and the facing pages have delicately drawn black-and-white frames filled with plant and animal forms. Centered objects are in strong but muted colors, and the book is as much an art lesson as an alphabet book. In *Anno's Animals* (1979) the inventive artist adds a new element: creatures hidden in leafy forest scenes. This is a device used in some other Anno books, which he deliberately includes because he feels that children are interested in challenges. *The King's Flower* (1979) is one of the few Anno books that has a story line; it's an amusing if minatory tale about a foolish king who wants everything he possesses to be the biggest of its kind in the world.

Several of this innovative author's books focus on mathematics: *Anno's Counting Book* (1977), *Anno's Counting House* (1982), and *Anno's Mysterious Multiplying Jar* (1983), written jointly with his son Masaichiro Anno. The first book adroitly incorporates concepts (including "zero") so that they reinforce each other via a landscape in which details accumulate. The second book introduces the first ten numbers, plus such concepts as addition, subtraction, sets, and group theory in the form of a game in which ten little people move from one house to another. The book can be read backward or forward. The third book is for somewhat older readers, as it blends a story with the concept of factorials and moves into fantasy.

One of a set of books about other countries, *Anno's Journey* (1978), moves from an open landscape to a town and then to a city with visual delights everywhere: a Van

Gogh bridge or a building marked "Anno 1976." This was followed by *Anno's Italy* (1980) and *Anno's Medieval World* (1980), and, to the delight of his fans in the United States, *Anno's USA* (1983). The pictures, meticulously drawn, show familiar landscapes and many historical personages as well as some surprises: Laurel and Hardy, for example, or the ducks from ROBERT MCCLOSKEY's *Make Way for Ducklings*.

Anno's draftsmanship and composition are always impressive and his use of color restrained. He is both entertaining and informative: he informs with wit and offers his readers both humor and beauty. ❧ Z.S.

ARDIZZONE, EDWARD

BRITISH AUTHOR AND ILLUSTRATOR, 1900–1979. With the publication of *Little Tim and the Brave Sea Captain* in 1936, Edward Ardizzone launched the successful PICTURE-BOOK series that was to assure his international reputation as an eminent children's author and illustrator. Although he had little art school training, he illustrated over one hundred and seventy books. Ardizzone's vigorous pen-and-ink sketches and watercolor illustrations make distinctive use of line to express movement, form, character, and atmosphere. Illustrator MAURICE SENDAK wrote that Ardizzone's art "harks back to the great nineteenth-century watercolorists" and to the innovative picture books of British author and illustrator WILLIAM NICHOLSON. Incorporating humor and drama, Ardizzone developed a style uniquely his own.

Born in Indochina at the turn of the century, at age five Ardizzone moved to England, traveling by sea with his mother and siblings. Time spent living in Ipswich, a busy seaport town, allowed young Ardizzone and his cousin Arthur to spend many hours roaming the docks and exploring the holds of the small coastal steamers and barges anchored there. Years later, Ardizzone drew upon these adventures for *Little Tim and the Brave Sea Captain,* first told to his own two small children. He discovered that the story improved with each retelling, as he perfected the timing and rhythm and his children "added those wonderful inconsequential details" which can enrich a narrative. Tim, the intrepid young hero, lives in a small seaside cottage ideally situated for his numerous seafaring adventures; it was, in fact, the same house that Ardizzone had once lived in as a child. Endearingly modest, Tim bravely encounters shipwrecks, storms, fire, and villains. Ardizzone sparingly used word balloons in his illustrations to help convey the personalities of characters and to lend humor, familiarity, and at times drama to his narrative.

In the four decades that followed, Ardizzone went on to create ten more picture books, which make up the Tim adventure series. The first volume was published in a large format with watercolor illustrations throughout and a text hand-lettered by Ardizzone. A few years later the book was reissued. This edition set the standard for the other books in the series with its smaller size and alternating pages of watercolor and black-and-white illustrations. In his books Ardizzone created what he termed a "visual background" for his characters by including detailed settings in his drawings. In *Little Tim and the Brave Sea Captain,* for example, Captain McFee entertains Tim with seafaring yarns one cold, blustery afternoon. Ardizzone pictures the pair comfortably seated before a cozy fire, teakettle boiling and Captain McFee's rum tucked conveniently at his side. With apparent ease and a quick scratch of the pen, Ardizzone achieved movement and tone through intricate crosshatch patterns and beautifully animated curves. He preferred sketching the whole human figure and thought the back view of his protagonists revealed more about character than did their faces. Ardizzone was among the first authors to break with the traditional picture-book format of alternating pages of picture and text; he incorporated his straightforward prose over, around, and under the soft-edged illustrations, a technique that added energy and excitement to the narrative. In 1956, *Tim All Alone* was awarded the first Kate Greenaway medal—England's most prestigious award for illustration.

In addition to his own books, Ardizzone illustrated works for children and adults by ELEANOR FARJEON, James Reeves, WALTER DE LA MARE, and others. Ardizzone once said that a good picture book author-artist "must create a world in which, in spite of all sorts of improbabilities from an adult point of view, he can believe in one part of himself, the childish part." Edward Ardizzone, in creating the Little Tim books, gave children such a world. ❧ S.M.G.

ARMSTRONG, WILLIAM

AMERICAN AUTHOR, B. 1914. William Armstrong was born in Lexington, Virginia. He credits the fact that he rode his horse in the Shenandoah Valley where Robert E. Lee once rode and attended the same church where Stonewall Jackson once taught for his love of the land and its history. Armstrong says he grew up reading Bible stories and listening to those told by "a black man around [his family's] Virginia farmhouse table." He attended Hampden-Sydney College, where he was editor in chief of the college's literary magazine; after graduation he decided to teach rather than pursue a career in journalism. He became a history master at the Kent School in Connecticut in 1945. Walking down a moonlit road one autumn night, Armstrong heard a noise that reminded him of the "faint, distant voice of Sounder, the great coon dog" he had heard about years before from the storyteller at his table.

That memory grew into Armstrong's first children's book, *Sounder* (1969), a deceptively simple story about a poor black sharecropper's family and his hunting dog. When Sounder's master, the father, steals a ham to feed his starving family, the sheriff arrives at the family's shack to take the father away. In an act of defiance, Sounder attacks the lawman and is shot; he crawls off to die. The boy is abandoned, bereft of both his father and Sounder. He grows to manhood and learns to read but never stops waiting for the return of his father and Sounder. Both do return—wounded and tired—and the boy must accept the changes in his loved ones.

The critical reaction to *Sounder* was extreme. Awarded the Newbery Medal, the book was praised for its "epic quality" and "guaranteed a long life in the memories of all readers." The starkness of the writing, almost poetic at times, contrasts with the complex philosophical nature of the story; the slow narrative pace masks the depth of the emotions displayed by the main characters. Not all criticism was full of praise, however. "The style of *Sounder* is white fundamentalist; deep-seated prejudice . . . denies human individualization," reads one of the more scathing reviews. The complaint most often expressed questions why none of the characters but Sounder are named. While some claim that this raises the issue of white supremacy, leaving the characters nameless puts such strong emphasis on their universality that this could be any poor family in any small town. *Sounder* may be a bleak book, but it speaks honestly about cruelty, suffering, and enduring love.

Armstrong did eventually name his young hero in his sequel, *Sour Land* (1971); the boy—Moses Waters—has become a schoolteacher who is befriended by the white Stone family. The beautiful descriptions of nature and the peaceful tone with which Armstrong charts the passing of time and seasons is marred by the lackluster personalities of the main characters.

Armstrong continued to write children's books, but the critical response has been harsh. *Barefoot in the Grass* (1970), a biography of Grandma Moses, includes eight full-color plates that unfortunately fail to make up for the heavy writing. *Hadassah: Esther the Orphan Queen* (1972), a retelling of the Biblical story of Esther and Mordecai, was overburdened with long passages of Jewish history that hid the romantic quality of the tale. *The MacLeod Place* (1972) is an allegory about Good and Nature that contains unnatural dialogue and a slow-moving plot. Such criticism is ironic considering that Armstrong never intended to write children's books. He says, "I didn't even know *Sounder* was a children's book until it was published." Nevertheless, the haunting wail of the wounded coon dog, Sounder, is one children and adults alike cannot easily forget. ❧ M.I.A.

Arnosky, Jim

AMERICAN AUTHOR AND ILLUSTRATOR, B. 1946. Naturalist and artist Jim Arnosky shares his enthusiasm for the natural world through his books about drawing, fishing, and investigating wild places. His books provide information, but they are not instructional manuals; instead, they take the reader on an exploration of the outdoors, encouraging awareness and personal discovery. Arnosky's books reflect his experiences in the surroundings of his rural northern Vermont home, a long way from his native New York City.

Arnosky had no formal art training, but learned techniques from his father, a draftsman. Initially, he worked as a freelance artist, illustrating stories for magazines such as *Cricket, Jack & Jill,* and *Ranger Rick.* After five years, he started illustrating children's books, and shortly thereafter began to write and illustrate his own books. His books have won many awards, including the American Nature Study Society's Eva L. Gordon Award for his contribution to children's literature.

Jim Arnosky's greatest contributions to children's literature are his nature books. His first book, *I Was Born in a Tree and Raised by Bees,* published in 1977, introduces Crinkleroot, a wise and cheerful forest dweller who invites the reader to walk with him as he meanders through the forest, poking among the leaves, listening for sounds, and following animal tracks. In *Crinkleroot's Guide to Walking in Wild Places* (1990), readers learn about both potential hazards—such as ticks, poison ivy, and bees—but also about the pleasures of discovering a clear stream or imitating a raccoon's walk. Arnosky savors details, and he invites his reader to do the same. In *Secrets of a Wildlife Watcher* (1983), he shares his experience in using clues to find animals and their habitats. In his picture books, such as *Come Out, Muskrats* (1989); *Deer at the Brook* (1986); and *Raccoons and Ripe Corn* (1987), the precise but warm drawings add intriguing detail to the simple text. His illustrations provide specific information about animals and plants, but they also evoke the mood of these wild places, allowing readers to sense the sparkling brilliance of a pond or the darkness of the forest.

Skillfully weaving instruction with personal reflection, Arnosky engages the reader as a wise grandparent might. In his books about fishing and in his four books about sketching outdoors, beginning with *Sketching Outdoors in Spring* (1987), Arnosky explains techniques but also reveals the excitement and quiet pleasure that can be found walking in the woods and observing nature. Although he writes from his experiences amid woodlands and streams, the appeal of his books is not limited to children who live in the country. His suggestions for drawing birds and mammals in *Drawing from Nature* (1982), for example, apply to pigeons and house cats as well as to hawks and bobcats. His honest and positive depiction of the natural world offers great encouragement to future naturalists, artists, and writers. ✥ A.E.Q.

Aruego, José

Filipino-born American author-illustrator, b. 1932. After being born and raised in Manila and earning B.A. and law degrees from the University of the Philippines, José Aruego moved to New York City, where he still lives, to attend the Parsons School of Design. He worked in advertising and graphic design until he started illustrating children's books in 1969.

Aruego chooses humorous stories aimed at toddlers and preschoolers, and he illustrates them with simple line drawings and wash that portray fanciful, endearing animal characters who express the immediacy of children's emotions. Aruego has illustrated books by himself, but the bulk of his work he has illustrated with his former wife, Ariane Dewey (also Ariane Aruego). In their continuing collaborations, Aruego designs the page and draws the outlines and Dewey fills in the wash. The color is often flat, but occasionally shaded or textured, and the palettes range from subtle earth tones to creamy sherbet hues.

Typical of Aruego's story matter is a lesson hidden beneath the rollicking effervescence of the characters' antics. In *Rockabye Crocodile* (1988), written and illustrated by Aruego and Dewey, a mean, selfish boar learns the delights of being kind, but the story is all fun and frolic along the way. The boars, with their dainty, curved tusks, stand on tiny two-toed feet with bulky, fluffy bodies seemingly lighter than air. As in his other books, Aruego's active, almost balletic characters, often buoyed by a flat background, have expressive postures and revealing facial expressions executed with minimal use of line.

Aruego and Dewey have illustrated several of Mirra Ginsburg's simple adaptations of Russian tales. *Mushroom in the Rain* (1974) shows a chain of animals taking shelter under a little mushroom. They all fit because the rain makes the mushroom grow. Aruego designs many of the pages in a frameless, comic-strip format, so the reader can follow the struggle as each animal squeezes under the dome. The brown mushroom is lumpy and cushionlike, its form and function implying the softness and caring of a mother. Aruego's curvilinear drawing style imparts this comforting beanbag look to all his characters and landscapes.

Both alone and with Dewey, Aruego has collaborated on many books with Robert Kraus. In *Herman the Helper* (1974), a young octopus spends his whole day helping friends and family and then gets to "help himself" to mashed potatoes. This story reflects a common theme in Aruego's books: The animals convey toddler and preschooler traits, such as Herman's eagerness to help and the mastery of language that allows him to enjoy a different kind of helping—helping himself.

The unbounded enthusiasm of toddlers and preschoolers is the crux of the plot in *We Hide, You Seek* (1979), written and illustrated by Aruego and Dewey, in which a young rhinoceros seeks his camouflaged friends. The distracted rhino accidentally startles them out of hiding by sneezing or stumbling or stepping on a tail. His exuberant expressions and jubilant movements reveal the essence of childhood joy. And for children, the recognition of their own spontaneous feelings is what leads them to take Aruego's books into their hearts. ✥ S.S.

Asbjörnsen, Peter
Moe, Jörgen

Asbjörnsen: Norwegian folklorist, 1812–1885; Moe: Norwegian folklorist, 1813–1882. When Peter Christen Asbjörnsen was fifteen, he was sent away to school, where he met a fellow named Jörgen Moe. They were opposite in temperament—Moe was brooding and sensitive, and Asbjörnsen was lighthearted and relaxed. The two discovered a mutual interest in collecting folklore that soon became more than just a hobby.

Illustration by Theodor Kittelsen for "The Bear and the Fox" from *A Book of Fairytales for Children* (vol. II, 1884), a collection by Peter Christen Asbjörnsen and Jörgen Moe.

They took fishing and walking tours together through the verdant valleys and the raw Norwegian mountains, listening to country folk telling their traditional tales. Even after they were established in their professions, they kept up this passion. Moe was a lyric poet and theologian; he became the bishop of Kristiansand in 1875. Asbjörnsen was a zoologist, and as he collected specimens in remote areas he also collected tales. Together the friends spent all their spare time writing down the stories. In 1838, the first set of stories was printed in a children's publication called *Nor.* These were followed in 1841 by a full-length book: *Norwegian Folk and Fairy Tales* (trans. 1923). Soon thereafter came two volumes of stories about the nymphs and elves who grace the Norwegian woods. The characters in these Northern tales are not those of aery fantasy but rougher characters—giants, trolls, hags, and talking animals. Some of the tales are obscure now, but many have become household favorites, such as "The Three Billy Goats Gruff." This short, simple tale affirms the parable of the weak overpowering the strong when the biggest billy goat says to the ugly troll: "I've got two spears—I'll poke your eyeballs out your ears!" Perhaps their best-known story is the more lyrical "East of the Sun and West of the Moon," a variation of "Beauty and the Beast" and the Greek myth Cupid and Psyche. A poor man gives his daughter to a great white bear for a promise of riches. The bear is really a bewitched prince who only comes to her in human form at night. The daughter, overcome by curiosity, lights a candle and falls instantly in love with the sleeping prince. But when she bends to kiss him, dripping candle wax awakens him. Their luck is broken, he tells her, for had she only waited one year to find him out, he would have been free of the spell of his stepmother. Now he must be off to her castle which stands East of the Sun and West of the Moon, where a troll-princess waits to marry him. This tale of a maiden finding her prince is long, rhythmic, and fully satisfying. "Peer Gynt," which Ibsen later used as the basis for his famous play, was originally collected by Asbjörnsen, and he also discovered the rollicking tale of "The Pancake," a version of "The Gingerbread Man."

While Asbjörnsen had a nose for a good tale, it was Moe who had the ear of a poet. He gave each story its particular voice. A tale about royalty, such as "The Princess on the Glass Mountain," has a smooth, lyrical text, while a story about Boots, a classic younger son, is more rugged. Although Asbjörnsen and Moe used methods similar to those of the Brothers GRIMM in collecting their stories, there is a difference in the product due to the nature of the tales' locations. These stories have a rough elegance that reflects their birth in the jagged fjords, the dense forests, and the majestic mountain peaks of Norway. J.A.J.

ASHABRANNER, BRENT

AMERICAN AUTHOR, B. 1921. *People Who Make a Difference,* the title of Brent Ashabranner's 1989 book describing the actions of ordinary citizens involved in helping others, is a designation which could well be applied to the author himself, for he has taken on the difficult role of America's conscience. After graduating from Oklahoma Agricultural and Mechanical College, where he helped finance his education by selling stories to Western magazines, Ashabranner found that his interest in people, especially those at risk, resulted in his entering a career in public service. While working for the Agency for International Development and the Peace Corps, Ashabranner continued his writing, but his vocation as spokesperson for the underprivileged did not achieve full stride until his retirement. He was then able to devote all of his efforts to addressing the issues that troubled him.

Having lived in many countries around the globe, Ashabranner acquired an interest in differing cultures, which he now applies to peoples of varying backgrounds living largely within the United States. In books such as *To Live in Two Worlds: American Indian Youth Today* (1991) and *Morning Star, Black Sun* (1982), Ashabranner ponders the concerns of Native Americans. Whether interviewing refugees from Central America or newly arrived young Asian immigrants, he creates complete and sympathetic portraits from his thoughtful, probing conversations. Ashabranner's travels—often in the company of photographer Paul Conklin, whose excellent work illuminates many of his accounts—may take him to Western farms and ranches or to a small town in Florida. But no matter what the destination may be, Ashabranner is there to meet people and to listen. He found that the objective writing style of the investigative reporter is the one best suited to the complicated subjects he examines. Ashabranner's intuitive sense of what makes a good story, coupled with his even-handed approach, allows him to write about hardships and survival and to turn the information into highly readable accounts. Perhaps the best example is *Gavriel and Jemal: Two Boys of Jerusalem* (1984). This journey, which took Ashabranner and Conklin to Israel, provided an opportunity to write about two youths—one Arab, one Jewish—living parallel lives in a city separated by religious and racial barriers. The book stands as a significant statement on behalf of peace and understanding. When Ashabranner turns his attention to national monuments, as in *Always to Remember: The Story of the Vietnam Veterans Memorial* (1988), he does far more than recount the history of the structure.

Ashabranner's perceptive investigation brings to light poignant anecdotes that make his books memorable. His award-winning human interest accounts are concise, balanced, and well documented. But of equal importance is his ability to increase the reader's understanding of others, and this he does with authority and grace. ❧ P.S.

Asimov, Isaac

AMERICAN AUTHOR, 1920–1992. Isaac Asimov has been called one of the most prolific writers in America; at the time of his death, he had written or edited almost five hundred books. But it is not just the quantity of his work that is overwhelming but the quality of it as well. His writing is witty and colorful, encyclopedic and explanatory, concise and complex.

Born in Russia, Asimov emigrated to the United States with his family at age three. As a child, he was allowed to read only educational books; he began reading science books and was immediately hooked. He received his Ph.D. in biochemistry from Columbia University and taught at the Boston University School of Medicine. When he was thirty-one, Asimov published the first book in a trilogy, *Foundation* (1951) and followed it with *Foundation and Empire* (1952) and *Second Foundation* (1953), and this trilogy is considered to be the cornerstone of modern science fiction. Earlier science-fiction writers told of man's attempt to journey toward the stars; in Asimov's books, men, rulers of the Galaxy for generations, have begun to lose their hold, and Galactic civilization is collapsing, just as the Roman Empire, Asimov's model, had. Hari Seldon, patriarch of the Foundation, uses the science of psychohistory to prove that the behavior of the masses can be predicted; in other words, humanity follows patterns. In 1966 the Foundation Trilogy won Asimov the Hugo for the best all-time science fiction series. Asimov believed that science fiction was not only bound to fascinate children—"Science fiction is modern fairy tales. Kids may think giants, ogres, and wicked witches are babyish, but not Darth Vader!"—but also could serve as a learning device in that it stimulates curiosity and the desire to question.

Using the pseudonym Paul French, Asimov began his career as a children's writer with the publication of the first of his six Lucky Starr books, *David Starr: Space Ranger* (1952). This series told of the adventures of David "Lucky" Starr and his friend/cohort John Bigman Jones as they traveled from Venus to Mercury, from Jupiter to Saturn, in order to solve the puzzles of the universe: intergalactic conspiracies, scientists who used telepathic animal extensions for strength, and computers misused to control and gain power. These books, full of suspense and humor, sparkling with complexities of plot, and bound to fascinate, provided readers with an introduction to science fiction that educated as well as excited.

Asimov's ability to present clear, readable explanations of complex material, to synthesize vast amounts of factual information into a logical, condensed format, made him an ideal writer of nonfiction books for children. His thirty-volume "How Do We Find Out About" series covers the history of scientific discovery from dinosaurs to DNA. In these books, Asimov offered what textbooks do not: a sense of the history of science. *How Do We Find Out About Genes?* (1983), starts with Gregor Mendel's pea-breeding experiments and ends with Hermann Muller's irradiation and mutation theories. Similarly, *How Do We Find Out About Computers?* (1984), begins with finger counting and the abacus and concludes with modern electronic devices. In another series, he focused on the planets in the Milky Way; in *Saturn and Beyond* (1979), he pointed out the fallacies in the various theories of the origin of the solar system but didn't espouse any one theory or push his reader toward any particular belief.

Displaying the same passionate enthusiasm he did when sharing his scientific knowledge, Asimov also wrote dozens of historical nonfiction books for children. *The Roman Republic* (1965) and *The Roman Empire* (1967) point out the impact and importance of Roman rule on the later history of Roman law and government, *The Story of Ruth* (1972) explores the laws and customs of this Biblical era and the historical antecedents of the story, and *The Golden Door: The United States from 1865 to 1918* (1977) probes the motivations of the people who shaped the events rather than just cataloguing dates and facts. In 1985 Asimov received the Washington Post/Children's Book Guild Nonfiction Award for his total contribution to the quality of nonfiction for children. Asimov has left an enduring legacy—a lifetime of writing—that has educated, amazed, and amused readers for years. M.I.A.

Atwater, Richard
Atwater, Florence

RICHARD: AMERICAN AUTHOR, 1892–1948; FLORENCE: AMERICAN AUTHOR, 1896–1979. Richard Atwater, born Frederick Mund Atwater, graduated with honors from the University of Chicago in 1910 and continued graduate study until 1917. For a time, he taught Greek there, but his main career was as a journalist, book editor, and columnist for various newspapers. He wrote a humor column under the pseudonym "Riq" for two Chicago newspapers, first the *Evening Post* and then the *Daily News*, and a book of verse, *Rickety Times of Riq* (1925), came from these columns. He also published an operetta and a translation from Greek. In 1931, he wrote a children's book, *Doris and the Trolls*. After seeing a film of Richard Byrd's first Antarctic Expedition, Atwater wrote another story for children. The story of Mr. Popper was completed but unsubmitted when Atwater suffered a stroke from which he never fully recovered, in 1934.

Florence Carroll Atwater earned bachelor's and master's degrees in French literature at the University of Chicago. She and Richard Atwater had married in 1921; following his stroke, she worked to support herself, her husband, and their two children. She earned three Chicago teaching certificates and taught high school English, French, and Latin. As a writer, she published in *The New Yorker* and *The Atlantic*. After two publishers turned down her husband's manuscript about Mr. Popper, she did some editing and rewriting, primarily of the beginning and ending chapters. One of her daughters, Carroll Atwater Bishop, remembers that the story was originally very fanciful and that her mother's changes added reality to it.

Mr. Popper's Penguins (1938) received a Newbery Honor, was named a Pacific Northwest Library Association Young Reader's Choice in 1941, and was awarded a Lewis Carroll shelf designation in 1958. In the more than

Illustration by ROBERT LAWSON from *Mr. Popper's Penguins* (1938), by Richard and Florence Atwater.

fifty years since its original publication, the book has been translated into several languages. Rarely has a book for ages seven to ten years stood the test of time so well, especially one that is not part of a large body of work or a series. This story of a house painter and dreamer about world travel who receives a gift of a penguin and soon has twelve captures children's hearts. Although filled with absurdities, such as the basic one of penguins as pets, the story has a no-nonsense base in reality that makes the reader want to believe. To be sure, some of the so-called reality is not—penguins don't lay ten eggs at a time and drilling holes in the refrigerator to keep penguins comfortable is unlikely, but everything is explained in a matter-of-fact fashion. Robert Lawson's black-and-white drawings help the reader believe the tale and further the droll humor. The book has an easy style, straight-faced and never coy, and the Atwaters never preach any lessons. The adventure and the characters, especially kindly, dedicated Mr. Popper and his penguins, are what readers enjoy as much today as when the book was first published. ❧ B.J.P.

Australian Children's Literature

Australian literature for children reflects the country's social history. It records, as no history book could, the changing relationship of Australians to their land, to their institutions, and to one another. Australian literature for children has always reflected a growing national identity.

The first book in the infant colony of New South Wales to be written expressly for children was *A Mother's Offering to Her Children*, published in Sydney in 1841 and written by Charlotte Barton, a governess. It was narrated in dialogue form, very much in the English and European educational tradition inspired by the work of Rousseau. Mrs. Saville and her children have frequent discussions about the "remarkable trees" of the countryside, but, on the insistence of the children, Mrs. Saville also narrates episodes of high adventure, shipwreck, and cannibalism. This and other books of the same genre, such as *Tasmanian Friends and Foes* (1880) by Louisa Anne Meredith, saw the land through alien English eyes and portrayed aboriginals as benighted heathens. The pervading attitudes were fervently moralistic.

Quickly in Australia a strain of robust boys' adventure literature developed in the tradition of G. A. Henty and R. M. Ballantyne. The harsh Australian climate, the demands of a hostile land, an inability to understand the culture of aboriginal tribes, and the threat from outlaws and escaped convicts provided a challenge to the survival and manhood of young boys straight from Britain. Many of the early children's books were in essence exotic travelers' tales enjoyed by adults. *A Boy's Adventures in the Wilds of Australia* (1854) by William Howitt and other books, such as *From Squire to Squatter* (1888) by William G. Stables, were inducements to stalwart Britishers to immigrate to the colonies, to rough it, toughen up, and make their fortune.

The gold rush of the 1850s added conflict and romance to books like *Tom's Nugget* (1880) by Professor Hodgetts—and also gave the author an opportunity for social comment: "A fouler sink of iniquity than Melbourne in 1852 cannot be imagined." Australian adventure literature of survival is still being published, but contemporary writers such as Ivan Southall have added a psychological dimension. Physical ordeal frequently uncovers feelings of personal guilt or inadequacy. In *Firestorm!* (1985) by Roger Vaughan Carr, a disastrous bush fire tests individual adults as well as children and the community itself.

Along with adventure stories, fantasy literature came early to Australia. However, it did not always fare well. Early attempts to import English elves and fairies—providing "the merry children of the fair South Land" with "dreams of their own Fairy Lore"—in books such as Atha Westbury's *Australian Fairy Tales* (1897) were rejected by Australian children. But while the English were trying to intrigue children with English fairies, the theme of caring for Australia's bushland heritage was becoming embedded in the Australian folktale tradition of storytelling and in a developing, indigenous fantasy. In *Dot and the Kangaroo* (1899) by Ethel Pedley, Dot eats berries of understanding and then converses with bush creatures and rides in the pouch of a kangaroo; the book offers a fantasy adventure, but it also makes a plea for kindness to animals and the preservation of the Australian bush—themes which endure to the present day. And it was the bush itself—the gum trees and banksias, the hardy wildflowers and unique bird and animal life—which provided the inspiration for a true Australian genre of fantasy. Ida Rentoul Outhwaite's beautifully executed and lavishly produced *Elves and Fairies* (1916) has become a collector's item. However, while Outhwaite depicted English sprites inhabiting Australian glens and glades, May Gibbs created from her lively imagination true bush creatures—the bold and bad Banksia man and gumnut cherubs who personified the Australian bush. Norman Lindsay's *The Magic Pudding* (1918) combined magic, satire, realism, and sheer tomfoolery with childhood's perennial preoccupation with food. The episodic adventures of Bunyip Bluegum and his battle with the Puddin' Thieves has become one of the country's most acclaimed children's books.

In 1933 Dorothy Wall created *Blinky Bill,* a mischievous but lovable koala of lasting appeal, and in 1935 Pixie O'Harris produced an Australian sea fantasy, *Pearl Pinkie and Sea Greenie.* However, Frank Dalby Davison's *Children of the Dark People* (1936) pointed the direction of future Australian fantasy. In this book the aboriginal spirit world reaches out to engulf two children, who are pursued by the forces of fear, personified by the Witch Doctor. They are aided by the Spirits of the Bush, including the venerable Mr. Bunyip. Many of the finest contemporary Australian fantasy writers delve into our rich aboriginal vein—Nan Chauncy, JOAN PHIPSON, Bill Scott, and PATRICIA WRIGHTSON. Patricia Wrightson's books—*The Nargun and the Stars* (1974) and her Wirrun trilogy—are far more than literary fairy tales using aboriginal spirit creatures. They are sagas of the indestructibility of the land. They state implicitly that those who live in harmony with the land and follow its laws are the strong—that true heroes belong to, and are at one with, the land which gave them birth.

Another important genre, the "story of family life," developed in Australia only after Australians, feeling that they had partly conquered and tamed the bushland, began to live in cities and to enjoy holidays in the mountains and excursions to beaches. The novel of domestic adventure began with Ethel Turner's famous *Seven Little Australians* (1894). Staged, filmed, and still widely read, it is regarded as an Australian classic. This essentially happy family—along with numerous other families created by Ethel Turner and her sister Lilian—provided the prototype of Australian family life that was to endure into the 1970s in novels by writers such as Joan Phipson and Eleanor Spence.

School provided the environment for Louise Mack's *Teens* (1897) and *Girls Together* (1898), in which personal relationships are tested and cemented. Although the novels precede ROBIN KLEIN's *Hating Alison Ashley* (1984) by almost a hundred years, the loves, hates, fears, and enthusiasms are much the same—they are merely more freely expressed in the later novels.

Between 1894 and 1942 Ethel Turner and Mary Grant Bruce, whose Billabong series has a cult following even today, published over eighty titles and helped provide Australian children with a sense of national identity. These books gave a sense of belonging to a country and a society that was based on enduring, rock-like values: the work ethic, the solidity of family life, and the worth of the individual.

By the 1950s Australians felt that they had conquered and subdued the land, and they were determined to provide a rosy future for their children. With the development of school and children's libraries and the establishment of organizations such as the Children's Book Council, children's books came to be taken seriously in Australia. Local writers could at last forsake English models and write of family life on the land and in the city as they knew and experienced it. In the next decade, Nan Chauncy, Patricia Wrightson, Joan Phipson, Eleanor Spence, Margaret Paice, Mavis Thorpe Clark, and Hesba Brinsmead began portraying almost ideal Australian families. Life might bring its troubles in these books, but problems could be overcome with initiative and creative activity.

It was these established writers, later joined by many new ones, who were to leave the well-traveled paths of children's books and give their stories a new relevance for the children of the 1960s. From the middle sixties through the seventies and into the eighties, writers began in Australia, as they did in the United States, to break new ground in children's books by dealing with problems such as drunkenness and physically handicapped children. Although these problems are personal, they also belong to the family and to society. Since 1970 Australia has incurred the stresses to and distresses of social and family life that technological advance always brings. Australian books have simply mirrored those problems. During this period writers also became socially aware and active; they began to explore more vigorously themes such as conservation, race relations, migrants in Australia, and poverty and hardship. Aboriginal voices also surfaced in the literature. Writers such as Oodgeroo Noonuccal and Daisy Utemorrah have been joined by artists like Miriam-Rose Ungunmer and Arone David Meeks to help bridge the gulf between white and black ways of seeing.

So the subject matter of children's books has widened to include practically every aspect of life as Australians experience it. At the same time the style of writing for children has moved from formal nineteenth-century English to Australian English with all its registers and colloquialisms. The point of view adopted has become increasingly that of the child protagonist; Simon French's *All We Know* (1986), for example, is a personal, nonjudgmental record of a girl's thoughts and feelings during the last year at primary school.

Since the 1970s, when technological developments made color printing much more accessible and less costly, artists have adopted the picture book as an art form of self-expression. Desmond Digby's *Waltzing Matilda* (1971) was the first of a line of bush ballads and early Australian songs preserved in picture-book form. Then came a series of aboriginal stories by Dick Roughsey and later Percy Tresize, beginning with *The Giant Devil Dingo* (1973). Today a vast range of picture books are available—alphabet and counting books, wordless stories, concept books, and picture books for mature readers. Ron Brooks, JULIE VIVAS, ROBERT INGPEN, Jane Tanner, PATRICIA MULLINS, and JEANNIE BAKER have gained an international following for their highly evocative and subtle art.

Apart from C. J. Dennis, whose *A Book for Kids* was published in 1921, few Australian poets wrote specifically for children. In 1958 Lydia Pender published *Marbles in My Pocket,* a collection of gentle poems for young children. Her work and that of poets such as Irene Gough began to appear in anthologies, but even as late as 1975 Alf Mappin's collection *Sing in Bright Colours* consisted largely of adult poems considered suitable for children.

Then Doug MacLeod and Max Fatchen began to publish humorous, sometimes satirical, verse written from a sardonic child's point of view. These books became instant favorites in the classroom, and anthologies of humorous verse quickly became popular. At about the same time, June Factor began to publish her collections of children's playground rhymes—many of them rude—beginning with *Far Out, Brussel Sprout!* (1983), and a new liveliness entered Australian children's poetry.

The state of Australian literature for children has never been better. In 1986 Patricia Wrightson won the Hans Christian Andersen Award for writing, and Robert Ingpen received the award for illustrating. It was the only time in the history of the Andersen awards that both medals had gone to the same country. After one hundred and fifty years, Australian children's literature has come into its own. MAURICE SAXBY

AVI

AMERICAN AUTHOR, B. 1937. In 1991, Avi's seafaring adventure, *The True Confessions of Charlotte Doyle,* was first named a Newbery Honor Book and then went on to win the Boston Globe–Horn Book Award for fiction. The following year, his novel *Nothing but the Truth* was chosen as an Honor Book for both those awards. Critics and readers began to re-evaluate this author, who had served a lengthy apprenticeship in children's and young-adult books. Although he had long been considered a dependable, solid writer, it had taken twenty years of published work before he was recognized as one of the most talented and inventive authors of his generation.

Born and raised in New York, Avi Wortis was such a poor writer during high school that he required a private

VOICES OF THE CREATORS

AVI

One aspect of my work that seems to attract particular attention is the variety of my books—from picture books to young adult novels. It is also the *form* my books take, ranging from traditional descriptive narrative to books that contain nothing but dialogue, from documentary novels that try to represent stark reality to comic-book novels which offer fantasy.

While this range is nothing I set out to achieve, I'm happy to confess that I've come to enjoy the great freedom it allows me to answer the question every writer asks: *How* shall I tell this story? Some writers ask the question but once, and find an answer that serves them—and their readers—wonderfully for all they do. There are times I envy that. I just seem to ask the question often.

Archibald MacLeish once wrote, "[Writers] write to give reality to experience." It is my belief that books for young people convey experience in more than words, that their reading is greatly aided by the *way* a story is told and indeed the way a story *looks.* Too often we forget that narrative form is in itself an integral part of the story. As the French writer Flaubert wrote, "Style is a way of seeing."

Of course I also believe that there is never one way of seeing anything—certainly no right way.

These beliefs liberate me when it comes to deciding how I am going to write my story. There is no form, voice, or even style to which I am bound. I feel quite free to invent new ways.

Still, before I get to sounding excessively profound, let me hasten to say that perhaps the key part of this narrative design process is that it's enormous *fun* for me, too. Maybe that's reason enough.

tutor. He credits this tutor with awakening his desire to become a writer. Avi received degrees in theater and history from the University of Wisconsin and attended library school at Columbia University. He worked as a full-time librarian during much of his writing career. Avi began writing for the stage, without great success, but this early experience is evident in his terse, dramatic style. In fact, his novel *"Who Was That Masked Man, Anyway?"* (1992) is written entirely in unattributed dialogue without a single word of conventional narration.

Avi began writing for young people only after he had children of his own. Starting with the publication of his first book, *Things That Sometimes Happen* (1970), he has become one of the most prolific creators in the field, producing works for all age groups and spanning numerous genres, including historical novels, fantasies, thrillers, and light comedies. Avi has been acclaimed for this diversity, although his audience has sometimes been limited since his works cannot easily be slotted into a single category.

Despite their diversity, however, Avi's books share a number of common traits. Most begin with a strong, attention-grabbing chapter that immediately captures the reader; they are often written in an episodic style, with short, tightly written scenes; the multileveled storytelling offers a plot strong in incident and action, yet with a thematically rich subtext. *Wolf Rider* (1986) is a riveting suspense novel in which Andy searches for a possible killer, but the book contains an equally strong subtext about trust and communication in the unfolding of the strained relationship between Andy and his father.

The True Confessions of Charlotte Doyle is a wonderfully entertaining, finely detailed depiction of the 1832 ocean voyage during which Charlotte abandons the principles of her prim background and joins the ship's crew in mutiny. On a deeper level, the novel is about Charlotte's liberation from a family and a society that have very restrictive and rigid expectations for a thirteen-year-old girl.

Perhaps the most innovative Avi novel is *Nothing but the Truth.* Presented as a pastiche of memos, journal entries, newspaper articles, and dialogue blocks, it is the story of a teenager's disruptive classroom behavior and its snowballing consequences. There are no simple answers in this novel, and each reader may come away with a different perception—but almost every reader will find the novel thought-provoking and the final scene overwhelmingly powerful.

As Avi's books continue to grow in power and depth, readers will continue to await each new book with high expectations. ❧ P.D.S.

Awards and Prizes

According to the 1992 edition of *Children's Books Awards and Prizes,* published by the Children's Book Council, there are at least 191 children's book prizes. Awards for children's books—by their sheer numbers, marked increase in recent years, and variety—have sometimes been confusing to parents and others concerned with children's reading. Yet they need not be. By becoming aware of the basic trends and categories in the field, concerned adults can become familiar with the awards that will best serve to lead them to good books for the readers they guide. There are four basic categories: major awards given by organizations; awards selected by children; awards chosen by state or regional groups; and international awards.

In the first category, the Newbery and Caldecott medals are the oldest, best-known, and most prestigious awards given by an organization in the United States. The Newbery, established in 1922, was donated and named by Frederic G. Melcher, editor of *Publishers Weekly,* as a tribute to the first English publisher of books for children, John Newbery (1713–1767). The award is given annually and is selected by an awards committee of the Association for Library Services to Children (ALSC) of the American Library Association (ALA) to honor the author, a resident or citizen of the United States, who has made the most distinguished contribution to literature for children published in the United States during the preceding year. In 1937, Melcher donated a parallel award for picture-book illustration, naming it the Caldecott in honor of the nineteenth-century English illustrator Randolph Caldecott. By establishing these two awards, Melcher made an inestimable contribution to the validation and prestige of the field of children's literature.

The Laura Ingalls Wilder Award, also administered by a committee of ALSC, was first awarded in 1954 to the author for whom it was named. From 1960 to 1980 the honor was given every five years to an author or illustrator whose books, published in the United States over a period of years, had made a significant contribution to children's literature. Beginning in 1983, the bronze medal has been bestowed every three years.

In 1966 the ALA established the Mildred L. Batchelder Award to honor the former executive director of the ALSC. A citation is given annually to the publisher of a trade book for children considered to be the most outstanding of those books originally published in a foreign language in a foreign country and translated for publication in the U.S.

Other U.S. organizations offer equally influential

awards. Since 1967 the Boston Globe–Horn Book awards have been awarded annually by the *Boston Globe* and *The Horn Book Magazine.* In 1976 the awards categories were expanded from two (text and illustration) to three; the current categories are Outstanding Fiction or Poetry, Outstanding Nonfiction, and Outstanding Illustration.

The Coretta Scott King Award was established in 1970 to honor Martin Luther King and his wife. Recognition is given annually to an African American author and to an African American illustrator whose books, published in the preceding year, are inspirational and educational contributions to children's literature. The Social Responsibilities Round Table and the ALSC select the winners and make the presentations.

The Jane Addams Book Award is presented to the author of a children's book that helps to promote peace, social justice, and equality of the sexes and of all races. This award has been given annually since 1953 by the Women's International League for Peace and Freedom and the Jane Addams Peace Association.

The Scott O'Dell Award for Historical Fiction was instituted and donated by SCOTT O'DELL, himself an honored children's book author, in 1981. First awarded by the selection committee in 1984, the O'Dell award is an annual prize for a distinguished work of historical fiction for children or young adults, published in English by a U.S. publisher and set in North, Central, or South America.

An increasing number of awards are selected each year by children. In 1986 there were twenty-eight such statewide awards; in 1992 the number had risen to forty-one. Child-selected awards counter the complaint made by some that the winners of the prestigious children's book awards often appeal to the adult readers who made the selections but not to the very readers for whom the books are intended. Sponsored by state departments of education, universities, or library associations, these awards are usually organized for the express purpose of encouraging children to read more and better books. Candidates for child-chosen awards are most often initially nominated by teachers and librarians before being voted on by young readers. The oldest such program is the Pacific Northwest Young Reader's Choice Awards, established in 1940 and covering students from Alaska, Idaho, Montana, Oregon, and Washington in the United States and from Alberta and British Columbia in Canada. Other awards selected by young readers include: The Texas Bluebonnet Award; Minnesota's Maud Hart Lovelace Book Award; and Wyoming's Indian Paintbrush Book Award.

Currently twenty-four state and regional awards recognize the work of resident authors or illustrators or books about or taking place in the specified state or region. These awards are often sponsored by state library associations, as in the case of the Lupine Award, sponsored by the Children's and Young Adult's Services Section of the Maine Library Association (begun in 1990 to recognize an outstanding contribution to children's literature from or about Maine), or by a local organization, as in the case of the Society of Midland Authors Book Awards (established in 1961 to honor the outstanding book of the year written by a native or resident of the Midwest).

Of the awards made in other countries, the most useful for American readers are those from the primarily English-speaking countries, especially Australia, Canada, and Great Britain. The international awards selections are made from among candidates from a select list or from all countries of the world. The Carnegie and Kate Greenaway medals are major British awards. The former, established in 1937, is presented annually by the British Library Association to the outstanding children's book written in English and first published in the United Kingdom during the preceding year. The Kate Greenaway Medal, also given annually by the British Library Association, honors the most distinguished illustrated children's book of the preceding year.

In Canada the most prestigious award is the Canadian Library Association Book of the Year for Children Award. First presented in 1947, this annual award honors a children's book of outstanding literary merit written by a Canadian. Between 1954 and 1973 two awards were made: one for a work in English and the second for a work in French. The Prix Alvine-Belisle, established in 1975 and administered by the Association pour l'avancement des sciences et des techniques de la documentation, is awarded annually to the author or illustrator of the best children's book by a Canadian national published in Canada in French. The Amelia Frances Howard-Gibbon Medal has been presented annually since 1971 by the Canadian Library Association to honor the outstanding illustrated book published in Canada by a Canadian native or resident.

The Australian Children's Books of the Year Awards, begun in 1946, recognize books in three categories: Book of the Year for Older Readers, Book of the Year for Younger Readers, and Picture Book of the Year. The winners, selected by the Children's Book Council of Australia, must be Australians or residents of Australia. A short list of finalists is announced in March, and these books are the subject of much attention and speculation before the winners are announced at the beginning of Children's Book Week in July or August. The BILBY

Awards (Books I Love Best Yearly) are child-selected awards, named for the bilby, a rare species of bandicoot. First presented in 1990, the award has three categories: Read Alone (Primary), Read Alone (Secondary), and Read Aloud.

The world's most prestigious award in children's literature, often referred to as the "little Nobel Prize," is the Hans Christian Andersen Award, the first international children's book award. Established in 1956 by the International Board on Books for Young People (IBBY), the medal is given every two years to an author whose body of work has made an important international contribution to children's literature. Since 1966 an artist's medal has been conferred on the same basis. Winners are selected by a jury composed of the jury president, the president of IBBY, and eight children's literature experts elected by an executive committe of IBBY.

The sheer number of awards, and their recent increase, expresses the strength and vitality of children's literature and its place as a major genre in contemporary literature. That so many prize programs, honoring so many titles, are available is a sign of the health of children's literature and the support it receives from readers as well as professionals in the field. Trends toward more child-selected awards, more state and regional awards, and stronger contenders from Canada and Australia serve not to diminish the genre, but rather to enhance it. By learning to navigate the confusing shoals of children's book awards, adults can get good books into children's hands. ❧ CONSTANCE BURNS

B

Babbitt, Natalie

American author and illustrator, b. 1932. With *Tuck Everlasting* (1975), Natalie Babbitt created an enduring classic of American children's literature. The thought-provoking story of ten-year-old Winnie Foster, who discovers a fountain of youth, raises profound questions of morality and immortality. Winnie learns of the magical effects of a spring hidden in the woods on her family's property when she discovers Jesse Tuck, an eternal seventeen-year-old, drinking from it. As she encounters the rest of the Tucks—a gentle pioneering family who haven't aged since drinking from the spring more than eighty years before—she comes to understand the complex combination of blessings and curses their secret holds.

Angus Tuck, the father, provides strength to his family, though he has grown tired of their eternal existence; Mae, the mother, is accepting and wise; Miles, the older brother who had once married, is full of sorrow from having had to leave his wife and children, who aged while he remained unchanged. Only young Jesse, handsome and lively, revels in what he believes is a gift.

A suspenseful interplay comes with the foreboding presence of the villainous "man in the yellow suit," a shady, opportunistic fellow who intends to profit from the power of the spring. The momentum increases when Mae Tuck inadvertently kills this man and faces a death sentence; since she cannot die, this would make their secret public, opening the spring to exploitation. Winnie, showing her inner strength and resourcefulness, chooses to help the Tucks escape, thereby keeping the spring secret. Before the Tucks set off to continue their endless roaming, Jesse leaves Winnie a tempting bottle of the spring water, encouraging her to wait to drink it until she is seventeen and then to come find them.

Babbitt successfully parallels events in the text with symbolic use of weather to create tension. The writing is economical, straightforward, and unassuming, like the Tucks, yet the result is a mysterious, subtle evocation of emotion for this family and their fate. Here, as in most of Babbitt's fiction, sophisticated ideas are presented with simplicity. Never doubting that her concepts are within the grasp of children, Babbitt never succumbs to didacticism or condescension.

While some adults have objected to what they consider the unnecessary death of the man in the yellow suit, most young readers focus on Winnie's ultimate decision not to drink from the spring. Her choice is revealed when, many years later, the Tucks again pass through Winnie's town, Treegap, and find a tombstone that reads: "In Loving Memory / Winifred Foster Jackson / Dear Wife / Dear Mother / 1870–1948." Pa Tuck is moved. "Good girl," he says.

Much of Babbitt's work displays a unique combination of folklore, fairy tale, myth, and legend, as in the allegorical tale *The Search for Delicious* (1969). To settle a disagreement among members of the court, a twelve-year-old Prime Minister's assistant, Gaylen, is sent out to poll the kingdom on the correct definition of the word *delicious*. From its beginnings in folly, the quest develops into a dangerous and politically significant mission. Exposed to a great variety of opinions, and to eccentric characters and supernatural beings such as the worldweller (a tree dweller), a group of dwarfs, and a mermaid, Gaylen is finally faced with the unexpected challenge of saving the kingdom. The main character evolves believably through his mythical quest, and the fanciful, satirical tale is distinguished by Babbitt's lyrical writing, as well as its adventures and humor.

Another beautifully written allegory is *Kneeknock Rise* (1970), a Newbery Honor Book. This story about man's desire to believe in the mysterious is a delightfully entertaining fable of a town's fear of the Megrimum, a mythical creature that resides on the top of a neighboring mountain. A boy, Egan, who is visiting his relatives one day, ventures to seek out the Megrimum and discovers, of course, that there is no such beast. The book's philosophy is conveyed through Egan's itinerant Uncle Ott, who postulates: "Is it better to be wise if it makes you solemn and practical, or is it better to be foolish so you can go on enjoying yourself?"

Voices of the Creators

Natalie Babbitt

I became a writer more or less by accident. It was certainly not part of my plan, a plan quite settled when I was nine. That year, my mother sent away for a very nice edition of Lewis Carroll's *Alice in Wonderland,* and I fell in love at once with John Tenniel's pictures because they were beautiful and funny both at once. I was used to pictures that were beautiful and sweet, or cartooned and funny, but this was a new combination. It made a deep impression on me. I had already decided to be an artist, and now, thanks to Tenniel, I knew what sort of artist: I would be an illustrator of children's books, and I would draw funny, beautiful pictures in pen and ink.

In this country we believe it is our right to choose the kind of seeds we will plant in the gardens of our lives—a cloying metaphor, but useful. We have the right to choose the seeds, but whether or not they will flourish depends upon a lot of things beyond our control: weather conditions, the chemistry of the soil, and whether or not the head gardeners are vigilant. I was lucky. The soil and the weather were adequate, and the head gardeners, my mother and father, were not only vigilant, they were also good role models. My mother was a beautiful, though nonprofessional, artist, and my father was funny.

I don't know how common it is to decide on a future career in the fourth grade and then to stick firmly to that decision and bring it to fruition nearly a quarter of a century later. Most of the people I know changed their minds a number of times while they were growing up. But for me it seemed reasonable, by the age of nine, to settle the question. I had wanted, as a preschooler, to be a pirate, and then, in second grade, to be a librarian. I might have made a pretty good librarian, but with my distaste for heavy exercise, I would probably have made a poor pirate. No matter; an illustrator I soon decided to be, and an illustrator I have, in part, become.

I chose to plant that particular seed in my garden, but my mother planted a few of her own choosing, and it is from these, I guess, that the writing part came. For she read aloud to my sister and me for years, thereby creating a love for stories and reading. My father planted a seed, too, though I know he didn't do so on purpose: he loved the language and used it in the most inventive and hilarious ways, thereby creating in me an ear for words. Plagued as we were by the 1930s Depression, there were many things we didn't have. Looking back, I know, now, that we had all the things that really matter.

When my first illustrations were published, to accompany a story written by my husband, it felt natural and preordained. But then my husband had other fish to fry, and I had to try to create my own stories. This felt decidedly *un*natural. Nothing in my growing up, it seemed, had prepared me to be a professional writer. But now I see that we all have stories to tell and we all use words every day of our lives. And if we have also grown up with books, there's no reason why a writing career shouldn't be possible, assuming we have a taste for the life. The writing I've done—though it's certainly been hard work—has seemed pretty simple. There's always one best word, if you listen for it, and there are always a few ideas about which you feel passionate enough to turn them into stories. Writing is a left-brain exercise, and insofar as ideas come from the subconscious, can even be seen as a kind of therapy. But picture-making is a right-brain exercise. To me it is mysterious, and I have no idea at all how it can happen, even though I've been doing it all my life. Watching my preschool grandson at work with crayons, I am awe-struck to see how, one day, he suddenly does not merely scribble but makes a creature with legs and neck and one large eye. Something has all at once clicked into place in his brain, and a message, sent down to his little hand, has told him how to draw.

All this is not a value judgment on my part about pictures as opposed to stories. I would always rather read a book than visit an art museum. And a picture book with a bad story is a bad picture book, no matter how beautiful the pictures may be. Still, picture-making is a kind of kinetic marvel, poorly understood—and poorly understood marvels are for me the most interesting things in life.

Though Babbitt's wit is evident in all her stories, nowhere is it more prevalent or immediate than in her collections of short stories about the devil as he attempts to stir up trouble on earth and to increase the population of his southern realm. *The Devil's Storybook* (1974) and *The Devil's Other Storybook* (1987) feature a devil who is less evil and daunting than he is merely mischievous and cantankerous. His plans are often thwarted, and he is frequently outsmarted, resulting in folktale-like stories riddled with comical error and whimsy.

Most of Babbitt's works are complemented by her own expressive pen-and-ink drawings. Her original intention was to become an illustrator, and to that end she studied art at the Laurel School in Cleveland and at Smith College. Her first book, *The Forty-Ninth Magician,* was written by her husband, Samuel Fisher Babbitt, and published in 1966. Babbitt also provided the simple, but elegant, drawings for several collections of small poems by VALERIE WORTH. She began writing primarily to have stories to illustrate. With the publication of the picture books *Nellie: A Cat on Her Own* (1989) and *Bub: Or the Very Best Thing* (1994), she comes full circle as an illustrator, providing full-color illustrations for her own texts.

Other notable works include *Goody Hall* (1971), a period piece with Gothic elements, about young Willet Goody, the heir to the great mansion Goody Hall, who, with the help of his new tutor, Hercules Feltwright, uncovers the mystery of his father's disappearance; and *The Eyes of the Amaryllis* (1977), a fantasy involving a young girl, Jenny, who visits her grandmother and learns of her romantic and potentially dangerous enchantment with the sea.

Natalie Babbitt's work is known for its haunting, ethereal quality as well as its clear, poetic writing. Her stories are infused with ideas from myth, folklore, and legend, and, though the concepts they contain are far from simple, they are accessible to young readers while still intriguing to adults. Each is an insightful, wise offering in a timeless body of work. ❧ EDEN EDWARDS

BAGNOLD, ENID

BRITISH AUTHOR, 1889–1981. Enid Bagnold's reputation as an author for children is based solely on her 1935 novel, *National Velvet.* Born in Rochester, Kent, England, Bagnold spent her early years in Jamaica, where she first began writing. She attended schools in England, France, Germany, and Switzerland and worked as a journalist before serving in a hospital and driving ambulances during World War I—experiences she fictionalized in her first adult novels, *A Diary without Dates* (1918) and *The Happy Foreigner* (1920). Bagnold's other works include poetry collections and *Serena Blandish* (1924), a novel published under the pseudonym "A Lady of Quality." The author achieved her greatest success writing for the theater. *The Chalk Garden* (1955) and *A Matter of Gravity* (1976), which starred Katharine Hepburn, were among her Broadway productions.

Bagnold published only two children's books, the long-forgotten *Alice and Thomas and Jane* (1930) and *National Velvet,* the story of a fourteen-year-old butcher's daughter who wins a piebald horse in a raffle, then disguises herself as a boy to ride in the Grand National. Considering its era of publication, the novel is surprisingly adult in language and attitude. The interactions of Velvet and her siblings are generally based on Bagnold's own children, resulting in refreshingly pithy characterizations and dialogue. Strangely, the piebald is not a particularly memorable literary horse and the important race is neither exciting nor well observed. Yet the novel succeeds as a wish-fulfillment story in which a girl's most cherished dreams come true. The popular 1944 film adaptation featured Elizabeth Taylor, Mickey Rooney, and Angela Lansbury in juvenile roles. Children still enjoy reading this story of a young girl with a passion for horses. ❧ P.D.S.

BAILEY, CAROLYN SHERWIN

AMERICAN AUTHOR OF FICTION AND NONFICTION, 1875–1961. Carolyn Sherwin Bailey, best known for her timeless fantasy *Miss Hickory,* was born in Hoosick Falls, New York, and educated at home until she reached age twelve. She trained as a teacher at Teachers College, Columbia University, and studied at both the Montessori School in Rome and the New York School of Social Work. She worked as a teacher and social worker before becoming a writer and editor of books for children. Bailey's first published work for children, *The Peter Newell Mother Goose* (1905), began her long career, which included more than seventy books for children. She wrote and collected short stories, publishing several compilations of stories and plays, and wrote many craft and activity books for children.

Bailey lived much of her adult life in Temple, New Hampshire, and drew on her love of rural New England and her own childhood for the 1947 Newbery Medal winner *Miss Hickory.* This charming story, illustrated with pencil drawings by RUTH CHRISMAN GANNETT, tells of the adventures of a doll made from the twig of an apple tree and with a hickory nut for her head. Miss Hickory is left behind when her owner, Ann, moves to Boston for the winter, and she must survive the harsh

New Hampshire winter with the help of the woodland animals. Miss Hickory is rather hardheaded, and many of her adventures are a direct result of the difficulty she has with the drastic changes in her life. After a winter of misadventures Miss Hickory loses her head to a hungry, absent-minded squirrel. Without her head she climbs up an apple tree and becomes grafted onto it. When Ann returns to New Hampshire, her doll is missing but an old apple tree has new blossoms. Bailey uses a conspiratorial tone to involve her reader in the story from the first sentence, and Miss Hickory is an endearing, childlike character.

Although most of Bailey's books have gone out of print and are no longer read, *Miss Hickory* and *The Little Rabbit Who Wanted Red Wings* (1945), the story of a rabbit who is dissatisfied with himself, address universal themes and continue to appeal to readers. ❧ M.V.K.

Baker, Jeannie

Australian illustrator, b. 1950. "As long as I can remember I was fascinated with peeling plaster on an old wall. I could see the natural effects of erosion: the cracks, the frayed edges. . . . I have always thought deeply about materials." A preoccupation with peeling plaster may sound like a rather eccentric start to a career as a children's book illustrator, but for Jeannie Baker it could scarcely have been more appropriate. This talented author-illustrator, one of the world's finest collage artists, incorporates seemingly everything into her marvelously detailed collage constructions—from real leaves and grass to cloth, ground-up sponge, and human hair. She builds trees from cardboard and clay and uses real feathers to lend authenticity to a bird's plumage. Her artwork hypnotizes readers.

Jeannie Baker grew up in London in the 1950s and studied graphic design at the Croydon College of Art and the Brighton College of Art. Her embarkation on an artistic career initially involved her in freelance illustration for various journals and the preparation of visual material for animated children's programs on Thames Television. But soon the books began. Once she had illustrated Elaine Moss's story *Polar* in 1975, she began producing her own books—first *Grandfather,* followed by *Grandmother:* both portraits of elderly people and of places, as seen through a child's eyes. After moving to Australia, Jeannie Baker began work on a book called *Millicent,* a celebration of the people and creatures in Sydney's Hyde Park. Impressed by the creativity she displayed in that work, the Australia Council granted her residency in its New York studio, where she formulated her ideas for *Home in the Sky.*

Although Baker is not an "especially political person," she does consider herself an environmentalist as well as an artist and likes to make people question what's going on around them. "When it comes down to it in the end," she says, "communication is more important than my personal vision." That intention becomes piercingly clear in her award-winning *Where the Forest Meets the Sea* and her wordless book *Window.* Both of these environmentally linked picture books compel readers' attention to their intricately illustrated worlds. While each contains what can be interpreted as a simple story line, many other layers can be peeled away as well. Baker built three-dimensional panoramas that were then photographed for the books. Each page offers viewers a wealth of fascinating, often provocative details. In *Window,* for example, Baker presents a series of views from a house over a period of twenty-four years. Her depiction of changes in the environment, both obvious and extremely subtle, draws readers irrevocably into the book and holds them spellbound as they hunt for the differences from page to page. ❧ K.J.

Bang, Molly

American author and illustrator, b. 1943. Molly Garrett Bang's picture books draw from the legends of many cultures and reflect her belief in the importance and power of folktales.

Born in Princeton, New Jersey, Bang lived in Japan, India, and Mali and holds degrees in French and Oriental studies. She has said that she was inspired as a child to become an illustrator by looking at the work of Arthur Rackham. After illustrating health manuals overseas, Bang began to collect and illustrate folktales. Her first book, *The Goblins Giggle* (1973), is a compilation of stories that she illustrated with frightening black-and-gray paintings. The stories are filled with mystery and suspense, and the collection is notable for the fluency of its retelling.

Both *The Grey Lady and the Strawberry Snatcher* (1980) and *Ten, Nine, Eight* (1983) were named Caldecott Honor Books. *Grey Lady* is a suspenseful, wordless picture book painted in rich gouache colors. The Grey Lady is pursued through the story by a frightening blue figure who attempts to steal her strawberries. The Grey Lady blends into the gray of the background until at times only her face, hands, and strawberries are discernible. The striking, unusual illustrations are, like her folktales, full of surprises. *Ten, Nine, Eight* is a very different book, a rhythmic bedtime story that has been much compared to MARGARET WISE BROWN's *Goodnight Moon.* Bang wrote the text for her adopted Bengali daughter because she was concerned about the paucity of positive images of brown children in picture books. The gentle countdown to bed stars a happy girl surrounded by people, objects, and love.

Bang's many retellings of folktales have earned her a devoted readership and acclaim for her attention to detail and authenticity. *Wiley and the Hairy Man* (1976), a folktale from the southern United States, is the exciting story of a young boy and his mother who together outwit the frightening Hairy Man. Like *The Goblins Giggle*, it is illustrated entirely in black and gray paint, and Bang skillfully uses white space as another element in the page design. *The Paper Crane* (1988) was awarded the Boston Globe–Horn Book Award for illustration. The Japanese tale of a beggar who rewards a man for his generosity and gives him a magic paper crane is illustrated with remarkable cut-paper collage. The three-dimensional artwork suits the text in which an origami crane turns into a live dancing bird. Bang achieves the same transformation in her art—a folded paper bird becomes a rounded, delicate crane in a series of cut and folded paper images.

Bang's illustration style always matches the particular story and the sound of the text. Her illustrations for SYLVIA CASSEDY's collection of Japanese haiku, *Red Dragonfly on My Shoulder* (1992), are created from collages that include objects such as a carrot, a bolt, and grains of rice. Bang's tutorial on design and visual composition, *Picture This: Perception and Composition* (1992), leads the reader through exercises to understand the art of illustration and how meaning is created through images.

Although she began as an artist, Bang retells many of her own stories and exhibits an awareness of the sounds of language, so her stories read aloud particularly well. Bang has made a place for herself through her willingness to experiment with illustration, her understanding of the power of traditional stories, and her skills as an artist and storyteller. ❧ M.V.K.

BANKS, LYNNE REID

See REID BANKS, LYNNE.

BARRIE, SIR J. M.

SCOTTISH DRAMATIST AND AUTHOR, 1860–1937. "Children have the strangest adventures without being troubled by them," wrote James Matthew Barrie. It is apt that Barrie penned this phrase, because with the publication of his masterpiece, *Peter Pan and Wendy* (1911), he introduced the children of England to the strangest adventure they would ever experience—a world of fairies, mermaids, a one-armed pirate, and a flying boy who refused to grow up. Barrie's fantasy land had its roots in real-life events; the sudden death of his older brother and the attention Barrie lavished on his grieving mother manifest themselves in his veneration for mother figures and his interest in little boys who do not age.

The history of *Peter Pan* is one of the most complex in children's literature. Peter began as a minor character in one of Barrie's adult novels, *The Little White Bird* (1902), and later became the hero of his popular play, *Peter Pan* (first performed in 1904 and published in 1928), created for the amusement of the five Davies brothers, children with whom Barrie walked in Kensington Gardens. The version that has been passed down through generations combined the dramatic tale with its sequel, *Peter Pan: An Afterthought; or, When Wendy Grew Up* (1908). Peter, the leader of a band of children known as the Lost Boys, escorts a trio of London siblings—Wendy, Michael, and John Darling—through the clouds to Never Never Land, where they meet the villainous Captain Hook, the beautiful Tiger Lily, and the jealous Tinker Bell.

The literary history of *Peter Pan* is rivaled by its critical history. Soon after its publication, it was compared to a "breath of fresh air . . . a bit of pure phantasy" and was recommended for the "imaginative, the eternally youthful, and the pure in heart." It was considered "the best thing [Barrie] has done—the thing most directly from within himself." The critical tide turned in the second half of the century as Barrie's work met with a different response; critics believed it portrayed incestuous and homosexual relationships and hinted at castration. It was said that the story was "one of the most fragmented and troubled works in the history of children's fiction." Some may continue to think that the images in *Peter Pan* are unsettling to young readers, but it seems best to follow advice written in 1920: "The most intelligent attitude to take toward *Peter Pan* is unconditional surrender. If one unreservedly yields one's mind and heart to its enfolding charm, then one will understand." Understand and, perhaps, fall in love with it over and over. ❧ M.I.A.

Barton, Byron

American author and illustrator, b. 1930. Since 1969, when his ink drawings appeared in Constance Greene's *A Girl Called Al,* Byron Barton has created striking illustrations and picture books with his skilled use of bold lines and flat shapes. Barton grew up in Los Angeles and studied art at the Chouinard Art Institute. He worked in television animation before becoming interested in children's books.

Most of Barton's excellent picture books are works of nonfiction for the very youngest child. Many of them focus on technology: *Trucks* (1986), *Wheels* (1979), *I Want to Be an Astronaut* (1988), and *Machines at Work* (1987) are just a few of his well-received titles. These books use few words and dramatic line and color to convey the excitement of machines and technology to preschool children. Barton's information books do include a story. For example, they may show the drama of a train arriving and leaving again or the joy of finding a dinosaur skeleton and then reconstructing the dinosaur. Barton uses black line and bold colors and shapes to define his subjects. The people he draws are representative rather than realistic, but both objects and people are clearly recognizable. Barton includes a multiethnic population of men and women in both conventional and nontraditional occupations throughout his books. He uses the whole book, including covers and endpapers, to create his story.

When he illustrates the work of other authors, Barton varies his style and use of color. In *Truck Song* (1984) by Diane Siebert, Barton defines objects with shadow and shades of color as well as with his characteristic bold lines. *Gila Monsters Meet You at the Airport* (1980), by Marjorie Weinman Sharmat, is illustrated with predominantly brown and green tones, suited to the protagonist's imaginary vision of the West. The hilarious story about misconceptions is aptly illustrated with childlike drawings accentuating the ridiculous aspects of the real and mythical West.

In addition to his nonfiction, Barton has also illustrated nursery stories and folktales for very young children. His retelling of *The Three Bears* received attention for its refreshingly childlike art and spare story. Here, again, Byron Barton's work is exemplary for his use of simple, flat shapes and for his ability to capture the essence of a story or subject for very young children. He approaches his subject matter first from a visual perspective; illustration is more important than text in the books he writes and illustrates.

Barton's books have gained a wide readership among young children, who are attracted to his powerful images and simple stories. His books embody an understanding of the drama inherent in information, and he makes nonfiction subjects available and attractive to the youngest readers. ❧ M.V.K.

Base, Graeme

Australian author and illustrator, b. 1958. Well over a million copies of *Animalia* (1986) perch on bookshelves around the world. The creator of this strikingly successful picture book lives in Victoria, Australia, where he continues to write and illustrate widely acclaimed children's titles.

Graeme Base spent the first eight years of his life in England. His family then moved to Australia, where his foreignness, he says, made him an outcast as far as his young peers were concerned. Since the only time he could impress his schoolmates was in art class, he threw himself into the challenge, deciding then and there to become a professional artist. So off he went to study graphic design at Swinburne College of Technology in Melbourne, which he enjoyed immensely. He then began a job in advertising, which he did not enjoy and escaped as quickly as possible. He began drawing for some literary magazines, which allowed him far more creative freedom than had advertising. He also published his first work, a large picture book called *My Grandma Lived in Gooligulch.*

In the early 1980s, Base began spending his free hours working on an alphabet book, which he called "An Animal Alphabet." Three years later he published it as *Animalia,* and Graeme Base's career was off and running. The large, colorful, detailed illustrations mesmerized young readers. In Australia the book met with immediate success—it was named as an Honor Book in the Children's Book Council Book of the Year Awards—and it quickly developed a huge following overseas as well. After its publication, Base spent a year traveling in Europe, using some of that time to develop scenes and characters for a new idea, his equally popular mystery *The Eleventh Hour.*

While Graeme Base has illustrated books written by others—including Lewis Carroll's *Jabberwocky*—he has acquired the largest readership for the titles he has both written and illustrated. *The Eleventh Hour,* with its engaging mystery elements, has also attracted huge numbers of readers in other countries, particularly the United States. They seem captivated by the author-artist's imaginative sense of fun and story and love to pore over his detailed, frequently humorous paintings.

Although some critics consider his artwork somewhat cluttered and garish, this children's book creator remains enormously popular, attracting throngs of fans at conferences throughout the world. Their eagerness attests to the powerful imagination and artistic skill that enables Base to achieve an almost magical hold over readers young and old. ❧ K.J.

Baskin, Leonard

American illustrator and author, b. 1922. Beginning with the provocative watercolor illustrations in *Hosie's Alphabet* in 1972, Leonard Baskin added another art form to his already highly recognized body of work, which includes sculpture, graphics—woodcuts in particular—book design, and printing. Although the animals and birds for the alphabet were chosen by then three-year-old Hosea, his brother, Tobias, and Baskin's wife, Lisa, they are not conventional alphabet fare for small children, as, for instance, "D is for Demon" and "V The cadaver-haunted vulture" proclaim. Yet with memorable epithets such as "P A primordial protozoa" and "G A ghastly garrulous gargoyle" as inspiration, the artist, with sometimes spirited, sometimes mystic, always creative, imaginative paintings, brought an exciting, edgy quality to the art in children's books: he created an art that demands attention and reaction, that is professionally astute and visually memorable. In 1973 *Hosie's Alphabet* was named a Caldecott Honor Book.

In his work for *Season Songs* (1975), poems by Ted Hughes for young adult readers, Baskin carried on his uncompromising approach with dramatic illustrations, his paintings growing out of the poem's moods and the qualities and possibilities of watercolor as a medium. His line drawings for another collection of poems by Hughes, *Moon-Whales and Other Moon Poems* (1976), presented powerful images in black-and-white. No matter the medium, Baskin's unique and provocative birdman is a common theme in all his work, from the bronze statue on the Smith College campus in Northampton, Massachusetts, through many of his graphics, to "C The Carrion Crow" of his alphabet paintings. A variety of birds appeared in *Hosie's Aviary* (1979); the text again was by the artist's family, and Baskin used full-page watercolors to illustrate it.

Baskin himself wrote and illustrated *Imps, Demons, Hobgoblins, Witches, Fairies & Elves* (1984). Once more his long experience with printing and bookmaking led him to design the pages using a variety of type sizes and styles and lines of text that often reflected the shape of a painting. Although some subjects are as familiar as Rumpelstiltskin and the Billy Goats Gruff, others are his own invention, such as the Demon of Energy, who exhorts the artist to "a frenzy of work." *A Book of Dragons* (1985), with text by Hosie Baskin, was a mature collaboration by author son and artist father. Monstrous creatures of literature, from Biblical account to folktale, epic to modern fantasy, and several Hosie originals provided the impetus for bravura interpretations, unique forms, and striking juxtapositions of color.

Baskin attended the Yale School of Art and the New School for Social Research in New York City, as well as studying in Paris and Florence. His sculpture and graphics are in major museums and collections of American modern art. Since 1953 he has been a professor of graphics and an artist in residence at Smith College. As founder of the Gehenna Press in Northampton, Baskin has designed and printed small editions of his own books, which are now collectors' items. His illustrations for Richard Lattimore's translation of the *Iliad* (1962) brought him his first high praise and wide acclaim in the bookmaking field, and his paintings and drawings for children's books have established the highest standards for uncompromising quality and exceptional vision. ❧ L.K.

Bauer, Marion Dane

American author, b. 1938. Through absorbing stories, Marion Dane Bauer confronts her own internal conflicts while engaging young people in comparable psychological and moral challenges. In her insightful *What's Your Story: A Young Person's Guide to Writing Fiction* (1992), she emphasizes that "the secret is to find that place within yourself where feelings are strong and then to ask, What if . . . ?"

Having struggled through her own maturing years with a father who was "argumentative and neurotic" yet brilliant and a mother who tried to keep her socially isolated, Bauer frequently focuses her writing on young adolescent characters who face various harsh realities of growing up. It is no surprise that adult/child relationships are the frank focal point in a number of her works. Although Bauer's characters must take personal responsibility for their own decisions and actions, in doing so they inevitably move toward some meaningful connection with others. *On My Honor*, a widely acclaimed novel chosen as a 1987 Newbery Honor Book, epitomizes the best of Bauer's work. Here she provokes the reader to explore with twelve-year-old Joel a myriad of emotions, including fear, guilt, and blame, and reconciliation with his father, as Joel struggles with the drowning of his friend, Tony, and with his own decision on whether to tell the truth about his part in it. *Shelter from the Wind* (1976), Bauer's first published novel, brought her immediate positive attention and was selected as an American Library Association Notable Book. Praiseworthy are Bauer's respectful, straightforward writing and her forceful, precise imagery as she describes a young adolescent's quest for her mother in the hot, desolate Oklahoma panhandle.

A fine-tuned sense of place and time characterizes this and other of the author's novels set primarily in her native Midwest. Powerfully evoking her own experience in central Illinois of the 1940s, *Rain of Fire* (1983), the revealing exploration of a young boy's shame and his lies to cover up his soldier brother's refusal to claim heroism in World War II, earned Bauer the Jane Addams Peace Association Children's Book Award. Bauer's experiences as both a biological and a foster parent provided background for her novel *Foster Child* (1977), recipient of the Golden Kite Honor Book Award of the Society of Children's Book Writers. Through her straightforward treatment of sexual abuse in this novel, psychological abuse in *Face to Face* (1991), gay and lesbian issues in her short story collection, *Am I Blue? Coming Out from the Silence* (1994), and similar candor in other works, Bauer demonstrates the courage she expects of her characters. On occasion she explores her themes through fantasy as well as realism, especially when her intended audience is the preadolescent child, as it is in *Ghost Eye* (1992).

Forthright in life as in fiction, Bauer openly discusses reasons she considers some of her works less effective than others. Her keen analysis of the art of writing reflects the many years she has taught writing to adults. The impact of Bauer's literature has been extended through the *ABC Afterschool Special* "Rodeo Red and the Runaway," loosely based on *Shelter from the Wind*, and the videocassette *On My Honor*. E.T.D.

Baum, L. Frank

AMERICAN AUTHOR, 1856–1919. With more than one hundred and fifty books, plays, songs, poems, and essays to his credit—many written under pseudonyms—Lyman Frank Baum is best known as the creator of *The Wonderful Wizard of Oz* (1900), which has been called "America's first fairy tale." His place in the history of children's books is firm; in the realm of children's literature it is less so. Whatever strengths the best of his work for children possesses, whatever flashes of humor and storytelling genius shine through, however popular his books may have been, his prose style remains ordinary. It is not his words but the land of Oz and its characters that endure in the affectionate memories of long-ago readers and that are immortalized in the classic 1939 film *The Wizard of Oz*, an ironic yet fitting tribute to Baum's own theatrical vision.

Baum was a man of many talents and accomplishments whose direction in life took many turns before ending in the world of books. Born and raised in upstate New York, he lived briefly in South Dakota and for many years in Chicago and finally in Hollywood. In his lifetime he was a journalist, poet, playwright, actor, composer, salesman, business manager, theater manager, filmmaker, showman, master storyteller, prodigious author, and happy family man who has been compared to P. T. Barnum, WALT DISNEY, and his own creation, the Wizard of Oz.

It was to amuse his children that he elaborated on familiar Mother Goose rhymes, resulting in *Mother Goose in Prose* (1897), illustrated by MAXFIELD PARRISH and the first book for both men. *Father Goose, His Book* followed in 1899 to become the best-selling book of the year. Baum's friend W. W. DENSLOW did the colored illustrations that appeared on every page—an innovation in children's books of the time, author and artist sharing the high cost of reproduction. Baum much admired the work of the cartoonists of his day, wanting the pictures for his books to be colorful and humorous. Denslow also illustrated *The Wonderful Wizard of Oz*, which tells of practical, honest, kind-hearted Dorothy Gale (her name itself typical of Baum's penchant for punning), who is swept away by a cyclone from her beloved Kansas home into the magical land of Oz and who journeys to the Emerald City to seek the wizard's help in getting home again. In a land filled with magic, talking animals, witches good and bad, winged monkeys, and friendly characters such as the Scarecrow, the Tin Woodman, and the Cowardly Lion, Oz the Great and Terrible turns out to be merely a humbug wizard whose "magic" is based on technology and psychology. In the end, magical silver shoes take Dorothy and her dog, Toto, back home to Aunt Em and Uncle Henry, while a real gas-filled balloon carries the wizard off to his native Omaha and Dorothy's friends remain behind, happy to believe that through the wizard's magic they now possess the things they thought they had lacked: a brain, a heart, and courage. *The Wonderful Wizard of Oz* is not a literary masterpiece, but it is a highly original, imaginative, and enduring story for children, laced with humor and excitement.

Baum's approach to writing was strongly visual, and after the publication of *The Wonderful Wizard of Oz*, his theatrical bent took over. His musical extravaganza of 1902, *The Wizard of Oz,* was a great success, but it was written and staged for adults. The writing of the thirteen Oz sequels (all illustrated by John R. Neill) was influenced by Baum's simultaneous absorption with the stage and the new technology of film. It was through his investment in film that he lost the modest fortune he had earned with his early books, forcing him to concentrate on turning out SERIES BOOKS for children. Written under various pseudonyms, these included *The Boy Fortune Hunters in Alaska* (1908) by "Floyd Akers," *The Flying Girl* (1911) and *Mary Louise* (1916) by "Edith Van Dyne," and *Sam Steele's Adventures on Land and Sea* (1906) by "Capt. Hugh Fitzgerald."

The best books in the "Oz" series—after the first—are considered to be *The Marvelous Land of Oz* (1904), *Ozma of Oz* (1907), and the last one, *Glinda of Oz* (1920), which some regard, along with his 1901 story for boys, *The Master Key: An Electrical Tale,* as early SCIENCE FICTION. His wildly popular series of ten adventure stories for girls (1906–1915), which began with *Aunt Jane's Nieces,* was written under the pseudonym Edith Van Dyne and, like the "Oz" books, was continued by others after his death.

Baum set out to do two things in his writing for children: to entertain them and to write "modern" fairy tales, merging magic with technology in a world without violence or any emphasis on romantic love—a world solidly based on American idealism, virtues, and homely realism. In this he succeeded. S.L.R.

Bawden, Nina

BRITISH AUTHOR, B. 1925. Nina Bawden started writing at an early age. She recalls that her first efforts included "an epic poem in blank verse about a beautiful orphan with curly golden hair." Later Bawden gave up writing temporarily; she wanted to become a farmer. This desire lasted throughout her stint as an evacuee from World War II London until she went to Somerville College at Oxford. In 1953 Bawden published the first of her many adult novels. She created her first children's book ten years later and has continued to write for both children and adults. To her list of novels for children, many of them well received by critics, Bawden has added several picture books: *William Tell* (1981); *St. Francis of Assisi* (1983); and *Princess Alice* (1985), a story about an adopted child.

Perhaps Bawden never forgot that orphan in her poem; certainly her own father was away in the merchant navy much of the time, and she still remembers her wartime lack of a real home. *Carrie's War* (1973) and *Henry* (1988) are both based on her experiences as an evacuee. *Carrie's War* tells the story of a twelve-year-old and her younger brother, who are sent from London to Wales and placed in the home of the stern Mr. Evans. As Bawden herself has noted, many of her characters find themselves on the "outside." Like Jane in *The Outside Child* (1989), a novel inspired by family history, these children, isolated by circumstances, often live in nontraditional families. Bawden removes one or both parents from the scene, leaving the children to cope with the events that follow. In *Kept in the Dark* (1982) these events proved so suspenseful that the book was named a runner-up for the Edgar Allan Poe Award.

Psychological tensions and moral dilemmas have increasingly added another distinctive dimension to Bawden's storytelling. Thrust from the security of a safe childhood, the children in her stories encounter the injustices and ambiguities of the adult world. At the end of *Humbug* (1992) a girl decides between telling a lie and hurting the people she loves. To remedy a predicament he considers unfair, and to remain loyal to a friend, the protagonist in *The Robbers* (1979) becomes a thief. Bawden consistently demonstrates her respect for children by acknowledging the seriousness of the conflicts that trouble them. Her characters chafe against the powerlessness inherent in youth, yet they make momentous decisions that affect their lives and the lives of others.

Bawden populates this imperfect but exciting world with a wide array of people and, occasionally, an animal, such as young Poll's doomed pig in *The Peppermint Pig* (1975) and the squirrel cared for by the evacuated family in *Henry.* Readers encounter a number of women who are single, widowed, or have absent husbands—like Poll in *The Finding* (1985), who shelters street children. Bawden's stories contain elderly characters as well, many of whom feel the same sense of powerlessness that the children do. And always there exists the push and pull of family dynamics, involving siblings, parents, and other relatives in turbulent relationships. Bawden frequently concludes her novels with a gathering or reunion of family and friends: in *Squib* (1971), a once-abused child joins a new family; at the end of the award-winning *Peppermint Pig,* Poll's father returns to his family, who have lived in reduced circumstances since he left for America. While often bittersweet with the awareness of inevitable change, these meetings communicate love and warmth. Though life may prove difficult and complex, even "outside children" can find a way to come inside. M.F.S.

Voices of the Creators

Nina Bawden

Writers write for themselves and others like themselves—for kindred spirits of whatever age. When I began to write novels, it did not occur to me that I might write for children. Or, indeed, that I *could.* I had written *about* children. There was a nine-year-old in my fourth novel, *Devil by the Sea* (1957), a little girl in danger from a murderer. But to use a child to provide an extra turn of the screw in a thriller was not the same thing as writing a story that would engross a person of that age. I thought—insofar as I did think about it—that children's writers were likely to be specialists of one sort or another.

I had children of my own, two boys and a baby girl. I told them the kind of stories my grandmother had told me; bloodthirsty tales, like the story of the old woman who had had her finger chopped off at the butcher's when she was buying half a leg of lamb. That is the story that opens *The Peppermint Pig,* but at the time I told it to my little boys I had no notion of writing it down. They had listened eagerly. Well, I thought, all children will listen to their mothers.

I wrote my first children's book by chance. I had just finished my seventh novel. We were moving house. "Why not write a children's book?" my husband said. "It won't take you so long."

It took a year. And no one wanted to publish it. It was "unsuitable for children." The mother died at the beginning. The children were unhappy. One of the characters was old and mad. "I told you so!" I said. "Proper children's books are about rabbits wearing funny clothes."

Finally, in 1963, *The Secret Passage* (called *The House of Secrets* in America) was published and sold well. Children wrote to me. What interested them was what I had hoped would interest them. Not the plot, although they seemed to find it exciting, but the emotions of the child characters. "I didn't know," my readers wrote, "that other people felt like that."

This is the true magic of fiction. Although children need story—the gossipy power of what happens next to draw them into the world of the book—what will hold them there, what their imaginations will respond to, is its emotional landscape: the inner lives of the characters, not their external circumstances. Urban children do not necessarily want to read about urban children. But to meet someone in a book who shares your feelings, especially if they are shameful ones like jealousy or anger, is a comfort at any age. And for children it is particularly important to be reassured, told that they are not alone.

Although my first books for children were conventional adventure stories with kidnappings, mysteries, and treasure found in caves on remote Scottish islands, I was determined that the children in them should feel and think as children do. I wanted to write solid, grown-up novels for children; books that treated them seriously, respecting their opinions and acknowledging the turbulent strength of their feelings—grief and hate as well as love and joy. And, perhaps as a result, the plotting of the later books became less adventitious. *Carrie's War* (1973) is my own wartime story of separation and loss that depends on a sequence of real events for its excitement. And when the young heroine of *The Outside Child* (1989) uses her detective powers, it is to unravel the real-life mystery of her father's second family.

For thirty years I have written an adult book one year, a novel for children the next. To my mind, they are all part of a coded autobiography: the jottings that make up a life. One leads to the other, and because of the difference between the child and the adult point of view, themes often overlap. And sometimes I am not sure at the beginning on which side a book will fall. *The Peppermint Pig* (1975) could have been a novel about family life at the turn of the century. *The Real Plato Jones* (1993), which is about a conflict of loyalties in wartime Greece and its repercussions fifty years later, could have been, with a slight shift of emphasis, a novel for adults.

It seemed to me when I was young that to be a child was to be trapped in humiliating disguise. I feel much the same now that I am old. I have no theories about writing for children. Once I begin a book, write the first sentence, all I care about is doing the best I can for this particular story.

Baylor, Byrd

AMERICAN AUTHOR, B. 1924. Texas native Byrd Baylor makes her home in Arizona. Her PICTURE BOOKS are some of the best portraits of the Southwest available for children, and her simple stories are written with poetic, rhythmic prose that conveys the particular values, people, and landscape of the southwestern part of the

United States. Although her books are regional in setting and subject, she addresses universal themes, particularly the relationship between humans and the environment, as well as aspects of the culture of various Native American groups.

Her work has been illustrated by a number of artists, but her most successful books have art by PETER PARNALL. Beginning with *Everybody Needs a Rock* (1974), Baylor's spare texts have been paired with Parnall's equally austere and dramatic pen-and-ink drawings. *Hawk, I'm Your Brother* (1976), *When Clay Sings* (1972), and *The Desert Is Theirs* (1975) were all named Caldecott Honor Books.

The strength of Baylor's work is her ability to transmit meaning and images with few words, and she turns her subjects into personal experiences for the reader. *Everybody Needs a Rock* discusses the importance of finding a personal rock that feels "easy in your hand when you close your fingers over it" as a means of connecting the reader with the earth. Baylor claims that possession of such a rock, somewhat in the tradition of worry beads, can help individuals to put their concerns in perspective, and she feels that, for her, carrying the rock becomes like carrying a friend around in her pocket. The theme that all humans need to be reminded of their connection with nature recurs in other books as well. *When Clay Sings* and *They Put On Masks* (1974) deal with ancient Native American artifacts and modern mask making and pottery, which connects Native Americans with their heritage and the cycles of nature.

Baylor does not shy away from communicating messages through her texts, using simple stories and descriptive poetry to express her views about the relationship between humans and the earth. *I'm in Charge of Celebrations* (1986) is a litany of celebrations that a young girl chooses for herself. Each of these celebrations, such as "Green Cloud Day" and "Rainbow Celebration Day," rejoices in the seasonal changes of the Southwest and the small but important changes that take place in the world around us. By creating a book of special holidays, Baylor encourages her readers to notice the changes in the world around them, whether the environment is Arizona or Maine: "You can tell what's worth a celebration because your heart will POUND and you'll feel like you're standing on the top of a mountain."

Many of Baylor's books invite the reader to participate in life—by inventing celebrations, finding a rock, or otherwise noticing and rejoicing in the world. Her gentle, direct texts express an understanding of the southwestern United States, a setting found in few other picture books. ❧ M.V.K.

BAYNES, PAULINE

BRITISH ILLUSTRATOR AND AUTHOR, B. 1922. Using simple yet expressive line drawings, Pauline Baynes began her career illustrating works by two great fantasy writers: J. R. R. TOLKIEN and C. S. LEWIS. Her drawings for her first book, Tolkien's *Farmer Giles of Ham* (1949), caught Lewis's eye. He particularly liked her dragon and decided that she would be perfect to render the variety of creatures in *The Lion, the Witch and the Wardrobe* (1950). She went on to illustrate the other six books in the "Chronicles of Narnia" series and Tolkien's *Adventures of Tom Bombadil* (1962). Her illustrations have received numerous awards, including the Kate Greenaway Medal in 1968 for *A Dictionary of Chivalry* by Grant Uden.

Born in England, Baynes went to India with her family when she was a few months old. Her mother became ill when she was five, and the family returned to England while her father stayed in India. Baynes and her older sister were placed in a convent school while her mother recuperated. Having been pampered in India, Baynes had a difficult time adjusting to the impersonal discipline of the English school. At fifteen she left school and entered Farnham School of Art. Still resenting discipline, she found courses in perspective and life drawing very difficult and turned instead to design. A strong sense of design is apparent in her books. For example, in *Let There Be Light* (1991), the Biblical story of creation, she uses swirling patterns to represent the creation process: small vague swirls in the beginning that become more distinct and expansive as God creates more and more until finally plants, fish, birds, and animals representing the infinite variety of life sweep across whole pages.

Baynes's people and animals are rarely totally realistic, three-dimensional beings. More often she emphasizes the internal patterns within flat shapes. Although her style is recognizable from book to book, it does vary somewhat to reflect the subject matter. Her illustrations for collections of folktales capture the national flavor of the stories. For instance, the title decorations for each story in *A Gift from the Heart* (1966), a collection of tales from Bulgaria by Radost Pridham, are intricate silhouettes reminiscent of Eastern European cut-paper folk art. In contrast, Baynes uses shading and detail in her illustrations for *Four Dolls* (1983) by RUMER GODDEN, their realism reflecting the contemporary setting. For Godden's *The Dragon of Og* (1981), set in the time of dragons, the drawings are simpler and the use of borders in the color illustrations gives them a medieval feel. Baynes creates the impression of an illuminated manuscript in

The Song of the Three Holy Children (1986), a hymn of praise from the Book of Daniel. The lack of perspective, the stylized figures, and the color scheme all work together to achieve the effect.

Baynes has written only a few stories of her own, among them a *pourquoi* tale, *How Dog Began* (1987). She gives the story a delightful twist at the end as she explains why a group of cave people decide to name a tame wolf "Dog." She designed the black-and-white illustrations to look like cave paintings, and although the people are merely stylized silhouettes, their body language is very expressive. With a keen sense of design and an appreciation of the material to be illustrated, Baynes consistently creates books that are beautiful and appealing. ❧ P.R.

Beatty, John
Beatty, Patricia

JOHN: AMERICAN AUTHOR OF HISTORICAL FICTION, 1922–1975; PATRICIA: AMERICAN AUTHOR OF HISTORICAL FICTION, 1922–1991. Noted for their thoroughly researched yet entertaining HISTORICAL FICTION, the prolific Beattys collaborated on eleven novels set in Britain's past. In addition to their joint work, Patricia Robbins Beatty has written over forty historical novels with American settings.

The Beattys' collaboration blends Patricia's love of history and sensitivity toward people with John's sociability and academic knowledge of seventeenth- and eighteenth-century England. "My fetish," he said, "is accuracy in fact and tone in all writing." But their accuracy of detail for dress and daily habits—especially the details of speech—never weighs down their plots, and the characters' speech is perfectly comprehensible to today's young readers. The award-winning *Campion Towers* (1965), set during the English Civil War, remains at its heart an espionage tale, and *The Royal Dirk* (1966) is an action-filled Scottish Highlands adventure.

John and Patricia Beatty met as students in the same history class at Reed College. After their marriage, John completed a Ph.D. in history and began a career as a college professor, while Patricia taught high school and then held a variety of library positions. In an effort to fill her time at a very quiet reference desk where no one asked any questions, Patricia wrote her first novel. Although set in the past, it draws on her childhood in a series of Pacific Northwest Indian villages (her father was a commander of Coast Guard stations). She had completed a second Western historical novel by the time she, John, and their young daughter Ann Alexandra moved to England for a year. There she began a story set in 1752 London. When she turned to her husband for assistance—"After all, English history is your field, isn't it?"—she gained a coauthor for *At the Seven Stars* (1963).

Together the Beattys completed about one book a year until John's death in 1975. But Patricia wrote her own books at the same time, about one a year, and continued to do so after her husband died. The historical fiction by Patricia Beatty has won praise for its well-defined sense of place and believable characters. The novels fall into two groups. The first are humor-laced, first-person narratives about the West in the late nineteenth century. Books such as *Hail Columbia* (1970) and *Lacy Makes a Match* (1979) are "sprightly books with sharp-witted girl heroines who can do just about anything a boy could." The second group includes third-person narratives about the Civil War such as *Charley Skedaddle* (1987) and *Turn Homeward, Hannalee* (1984), darker books, the author has said, "probably because I so often heard as a child the stories my mother's family told of 1860s Kansas—their fears and hardships."

Patricia Beatty once said, "I try to make the English and American 'pasts' come to life in order to convince the nine to fourteen age group that people of the past were real people." As a measure of their success, her books remain models of the genre. ❧ S.A.B.

Bellairs, John

AMERICAN MYSTERY NOVELIST, 1938–1991. The American MYSTERY writer and master storyteller John Bellairs has enthralled countless fans with his intriguing tales that pit ordinary characters against extraordinary situations. Bellairs's stories include all the trappings of the genre—haunted houses, coffins, bones, ghosts, and wizards—but they are distinguished by the use of what Bellairs calls "the common ordinary stuff—the bullies, the scaredy-cat Lewis, the grown-ups, the everyday incidents." Drawing from his own experience, Bellairs found that "writing seems to be a way of memorializing and transforming my own past. I write about the things I wish had happened to me when I was a kid."

Born in the small town of Marshall, Michigan, Bellairs turned his hometown into the setting of New Zebedee in *The House with a Clock in Its Walls* (1973), the novel that started his first series. Other places where he has lived are used as settings for later books. His characters, like the author, are intellectual, bookish loners who worry about finding friendship, and his protagonists are helped by an older relative or friend who offers wisdom, understanding, and more often than not a dose of eccentricity.

Bellairs's first frolicsome novel was the popular, well-received FANTASY *The Face in the Frost* (1969), which recounts the tale of two magicians and their attempt to stop a third sorcerer who has acquired a deadly book of spells.

With *The House with a Clock in Its Walls,* Bellairs achieved even greater popularity and established himself as one of the most compelling mystery writers for children. The book introduces Lewis, who goes to live with his Uncle Jonathan after his parents die in an accident. From the moment of his arrival, Lewis suspects that there is something strange about his uncle and Mrs. Zimmermann, the kindly next-door neighbor. When he discovers they are both witches, Lewis experiments with some magic forces, setting in motion a wild chase with two dead wizards that threatens to bring about the end of the world. In subsequent books, a common feature is the protagonists' accidental mishandling of magical properties.

Lewis returns in *The Letter, the Witch and the Ring* (1976), which also features Mrs. Zimmermann and Lewis's cohort, Rose Rita Pottinger. With his second series, the "Blue Figurine," Bellairs introduced Johnny Dixon, his grandparents, and the cantankerous Professor Childermass, who confront a slew of ghosts and evil sorcerers. Johnny Dixon and Lewis reappear in a number of his books, which have some of the qualities of a series without repeating the same format.

When asked why he chose to write for children, Bellairs responded, "I have the imagination of a ten-year-old." Bellairs's work is marked by an adroit balance between tension and humor. Spooky tales move between the insecurities and foibles of his protagonists and the chilling descriptions of apparitions and evil enemies, providing one of the key dynamics in Bellairs's writing.

Bellairs's books will forever be linked with the distinctive black-and-white artwork of EDWARD GOREY, whose illustrations capture perfectly the subtle humor and eerie nature of the author's mysteries. ❦ C.L.

BELLOC, HILAIRE

BRITISH AUTHOR AND POET, 1870–1953. The brilliance of Joseph Hilaire Pierre Belloc's literary output, which numbers upward of one hundred and fifty works of history, biography, fiction, travel, essays, serious poetry, and comic verse remains undimmed, if somewhat unknown, after nearly one hundred years. He is perhaps best remembered by the general reader for his books of humorous verse for children, which are as fresh and hilarious today as when they were first published. Written fifty years after EDWARD LEAR's *A Book of Nonsense* (1846) and thirty years after LEWIS CARROLL's *Alice's Adventures in Wonderland* (1865), Belloc's first writing for children is often spoken of in the same breath and valued, like theirs, for being unique.

In 1896 *The Bad Child's Book of Beasts* was published, followed in 1897 by *More Beasts (for Worse Children).* Both were illustrated by his friend of recent Oxford days (Belloc had graduated from Balliol College in 1895 with a first in history), Lord Basil Blackwood, or "B.T.B." Blackwood's wonderfully comic drawings were a perfect match for the witty verse. He later illustrated Belloc's *Cautionary Tales for Children* (1907) as well as his books of humorous verse for adults. Blackwood died in World War I, and the much later *New Cautionary Tales* (1930) was illustrated with equal esprit by Nicolas Bentley.

Belloc's sparkling menagerie of beasts, including "The Yak," "The Hippopotamus," and "The Frog," and his darkly funny "morality" tales illustrate the principles he himself laid down for children's verse. He felt that it should be simple, terse, of improbable and final theme, with a strong lilt and "something indelible for the memory." Who can forget the stories of Jim, who was eaten by a lion; of Rebecca, who slammed doors; of George, who played carelessly with a gas-filled balloon; and of Matilda, "who told such dreadful lies it made one gasp and stretch one's eyes"? His verses have been much anthologized, and STEVEN KELLOGG, WALLACE TRIPP, VICTORIA CHESS, and Harold Berson are among his later illustrators.

Belloc, the son of a French father and an English mother, was an extraordinary writer, an extraordinary man. Born near Paris, he became a British subject, served as a liberal in the House of Commons, edited a conservative paper, wrote on military subjects during World War I, and lectured on military history at Cambridge. He met and spoke at length with such important men of his time as Foch, Pétain, Franco, Mussolini, Franklin Roosevelt, and two popes. His staunch Roman Catholicism, a strong bond between him and his close friend G. K. Chesterton, prevented his gaining a fellowship at Oxford, which was a lifelong disappointment. In his early thirties he moved with his family to the beloved Sussex of his childhood, where he lived for the rest of his life. He sailed, he rode, he farmed, he walked alone in the American West and over Europe and the Alps. He married, fathered five children, and left behind him a literary treasure awaiting discovery by new generations. Belloc's terse and witty verse, full of surprise and mischievous delight, is as entertaining today as when it was first published. It cries out to be read aloud. ❧ S.L.R.

Bemelmans, Ludwig

American author and artist, 1898–1962. Throughout his life, Ludwig Bemelmans saw himself, first and foremost, as a painter, despite his considerable success at writing for both children and adults. He wrote short stories, novels, articles, essays, poetry, and reminiscences of all sorts, and he always wrote about what he *saw*—usually with great wit, charm, and honesty. He was forty-one years old when *Madeline* was published in 1939, but everything in the book was drawn from a child's point of view—the enormously tall and energetic teacher Miss Clavel, the twelve identically shaped little girls, the color, splash, and joy of the streets of Paris. Best of all was the simplicity and directness of his line.

Bemelmans emigrated to the United States from Germany in 1914, when he was sixteen. He had been raised in the Austrian Tyrols and in Bavaria and learned to speak French and later German. During his early childhood he lived in a hotel his father owned and managed, and later, in New York, he worked his way up in the hotel business to support himself. On the side he pursued what gave him the greatest pleasure—painting and drawing.

Bemelmans's first children's book, *Hansi* (1934), recounts a young boy's visit to his uncle's mountain home in the Austrian Tyrols; *The High World* (1954) is also an adventure set where Bemelmans grew up. These long storybooks, with half-page illustrations throughout, were similar in format to *The Golden Basket*, which was a Newbery Honor Book in 1937. In this story, two girls tour Bruges with their father, encountering one day twelve little girls out for a walk, one of whom is called Madeline. Bemelmans was an inveterate traveler, and it was a visit to Belgium with his wife, Madeline Freund, that inspired *The Golden Basket*.

His great success as an artist is that he conveys much childlike joy, energy, and spontaneity in his work. *Madeline* (1938), a Caldecott Honor Book, was followed by five other stories in a similar large, spacious format about the fearless little girl who always stepped out of line and found her way to adventure. *Madeline's Rescue* (1953) won the Caldecott Medal in 1954, and after that came *Madeline's Christmas in Texas* (1955), *Madeline and the Bad Hat* (1956), *Madeline and the Gypsies* (1959), and *Madeline in London* (1961). Of all Bemelmans's books for children, these are the ones that have stayed in print and won the loyalty of countless readers.

The original inspiration for *Madeline* was the convent where Bemelmans's mother was educated as a child, along with the author's own experience in boarding school, where he walked with his classmates in two straight lines. The story itself grew in Bemelmans's imagination as he recuperated from a biking accident in France; a little girl in the same rural hospital had just had her appendix out. The text for *Madeline* is brief, written in rhyming couplets, and the memorable opening lines are found in other "Madeline" books: "In an old house in Paris / that was covered with vines / lived twelve little girls in two straight lines."

Bemelmans wrote more than fifteen children's books and more than twenty for adults, including anecdotal collections about his years in the hotel business, diaries of his World War I experiences in the U.S. Army, and, later, writings about Paris, which he loved and which became his second home.

When Bemelmans was becoming established as a painter in New York, his work was exhibited and sold in galleries, and he found the public role of a gallery artist very unpleasant. But eventually he discovered a way to maintain his privacy and still have a wide audience for his work. In his Caldecott acceptance speech for *Madeline's Rescue*, he explained: "I looked for another way of painting, for privacy; for a fresh audience, vast and critical and remote, to whom I could address myself with great freedom. . . . I wanted to paint purely that which gave me pleasure . . . and one day I found that the audience for that kind of painting was a vast reservoir of impressionists who did very good work themselves, who were very clear-eyed and capable of enthusiasm. I addressed myself to children." ❧ K.M.K.

Benary-Isbert, Margot

German author, 1889–1979. Because she refused to join the Nazi writers' organization, Margot Benary-Isbert was not permitted to publish her work during Hitler's regime, but she later used her observations of wartime Germany in writing novels for children.

The author was born in Saabrücken, Germany, and published magazine fiction during her teenage years. While attending the University of Frankfurt, Benary-Isbert worked for the Museum of Ethnology and Anthropology, where she met her future husband. The couple moved to Thuringia and raised a daughter. Although she was not allowed to publish between 1933 and

1945, Benary-Isbert continued to write short stories and poetry. The American army liberated Thuringia in 1945, but the region was soon given to the Russians. Benary-Isbert and her family fled to West Germany, where she wrote *Die Arche Noah* (1948), one of the first postwar children's books published in Germany.

It is the moving story of a refugee family struggling to survive in West Germany, despite the death of a brother and the imprisonment of their father. The two oldest children, Matthias and Margret, find work as stable hands on a farm, where they convert an old railway car into living quarters that they call The Ark. Although leisurely paced, the book presents a vivid picture of postwar Germany. Subtle details reveal the ultimate cost of war, as when the children idly wonder if their grandparents have survived the conflict, then quickly dismiss the idea. Similarly, the family does not belabor the wartime death of Margret's twin brother, though for the reader this emotional issue always remains at the story's periphery.

Published in the United States in 1953 as *The Ark,* the novel received critical acclaim, despite its then controversial sympathetic treatment of Germans. Perhaps the book's greatest strength is in showing the common threads of humanity that unite children of all nationalities. Nevertheless, it can be faulted for depicting only innocent German victims. Neither Nazism nor the Holocaust is acknowledged, although they are briefly addressed in the sequel, *Rowan Farm* (1954), which follows the Lechow family as they continue to rebuild their lives on the farm. *Dangerous Spring* (1961), however, provides an unflinching look at the Hitler Youth Movement and its impact on a German family.

Benary-Isbert immigrated to the United States in 1952 and became a naturalized citizen, although she continued to write in her native language. Among her other works is a trilogy (*The Shooting Star,* 1954; *Blue Mystery,* 1957; and *A Time to Love,* 1962), which follows a German girl from her lighthearted days as a nine-year-old to war involvement at age fifteen. The author has also written fantasy, *The Wicked Enchantment* (1955); *The Long Way Home* (1959), which concerns a German war orphan who immigrates to the United States and includes brief appearances by two of the Lechow children, who provide updates on their family; and a romance set in nineteenth-century Germany, *Under a Changing Moon* (1964).

The slow pace and relative length of Benary-Isbert's novels have limited their audience among modern readers, but the books remain notable for their realism, three-dimensional characterizations, and unique depiction of an important place and time in world history. ❧

P.D.S.

Benchley, Nathaniel

American author, 1915–1981. Nathaniel Benchley was a well-established writer long before he entered the field of children's literature. Benchley, a Harvard University graduate, was the son of the renowned humorist Robert Benchley and the father of Peter Benchley, author of *Jaws* and *The Deep.* Nathaniel began his career as a feature columnist for the *Connecticut Nutmeg* but soon became a city reporter for the *New York Herald Tribune.* From 1941 to 1945, he served as public relations officer in the U.S. Navy, a position that led to duty on destroyers and P.C. boats (Patrol Craft) and in convoys, for a time in the Pacific. Returning to civilian life in New York City, he became assistant drama editor for *Newsweek.* From there he branched out into freelance work: short stories and articles (all published in prestigious national magazines), a play, a movie, a biography of his father, and several adult novels.

It was not until he moved from New York City to Nantucket in the 1960s that Benchley started writing for children. He wanted "to get young people in the habit of reading instead of staring at the tube." Benchley's "personal battle with TV" led him to write twenty-four books for children and young adults. He was one of the early contributors to Harper's I Can Read series of easy readers. While these books constitute the bulk of his work for children, his juvenile and young adult novels are more powerfully written. Two of his I Can Read books, *Sam the Minuteman* (1969) and *George the Drummer Boy* (1977), are exceptional. In these Benchley respectively portrayed the initiations of an American boy and a British boy into the realities of war via the American Revolution. Both are extraordinary tales told in a limited format, yet each has all the immediacy of Benchley's young adult novels.

Benchley, a strong proponent of young adult fiction, felt that some teens needed transitional books to entice them to read. Toward this end, he researched historic events, enlivened them with first-person narratives, enriched them with fascinating details, and brought history to life. His penchant for writing historical novels won him two awards for young adult fiction: the 1973 Western Writers of America Spur Award for *Only Earth and Sky Last Forever* and the 1974 American Library Association notable book award for *Bright Candles: A Novel of the Danish Resistance,* which concerns seventeen-year-old Jens Hansen's defiance of German authority. Benchley wrote *Only Earth and Sky Last Forever* after reading a Native American survivor's account of the Battle of Little Big Horn, in which Custer was killed. Amazingly, he found that when this young man rode into battle with Crazy Horse, he "only wanted to make a good impression on his girl. He had no idea it was [a stand against] Custer or anything like that." His other novels, *Gone and Back* (1971), Obediah Taylor's story about his hapless family's involvement in the Oklahoma Land Rush, *Beyond the Mists* (1975), a young Viking's adventures with Leif Eriksson, and *A Necessary End: A Novel of World War II* (1976), a young seaman's journal based on Benchley's own experiences in the navy, are also grounded in history.

In all his writing, Benchley held to his theory that children like suspense, humor, and a reason to turn the page: "Each right-hand page has to have a what-will-happen-next to it"—a solid formula to which this polished writer was committed. S.R.

Berenstain, Jan
Berenstain, Stan

Jan: American author and illustrator, b. 1923; Stan: American author and illustrator, b. 1923. Jan and Stan Berenstain, who met as students at the Philadelphia College of Art, are among the most familiar names in children's literature. Their first collaborative efforts were as magazine cartoonists, but when they decided that there weren't enough humorous books for their sons to read, they began to write for the groundbreaking "Beginner Books" series published by Random House. The Berenstains wrote many books for this series, which was originated by Theodor Geisel (Dr. Seuss), to help children learn to read through humor and a controlled vocabulary and by matching illustrations to text. The Berenstains created the Bear family for this series—a bungling but loving father, a determined but wise mother, and a brother and, later, a sister who get into trouble but learn from their mistakes.

The first of the Berenstains' Beginner Books, *The Big Honey Hunt*, was published in 1962; it was followed by other Bear books, such as *The Bike Lesson* (1964) and *The Bear Scouts* (1967). The Bear family was also seen in some of the "Bright and Early" series books for even younger readers, such as *The Berenstain Bears and the Spooky Old Tree* (1978). Then, in 1981, the Berenstains began a new series, "First Time Books," which shows the Bear family in new situations of dealing with contemporary problems. *The Berenstain Bears Go to the Doctor* (1981) was the first, but in other volumes the family copes with messy rooms, pollution, strangers, and Mama Bear's new job. The "Big Chapter Books" series was launched in 1993 with books such as *The Berenstain Bears and the Drug Free Zone* and *The Berenstain Bears and the Female Fullback*. This series is for children who are ready for longer books but not ready to leave the Bears.

There is no denying the popularity of the Berenstain Bears books, which often win Children's Choice awards, and of the Bears' television programs and merchandise. Children love this familiar, humorous family and the reassuring happy endings. The quality of the books, however, is frequently questioned by some critics, who find the cartoon illustrations uninspired, the stories heavy-handed, and Papa Bear's ineptness offensive. Still, it appears that the Berenstains will continue to appear on the best-seller lists for years to come. P.O.B.

Berry, James

Jamaican-British poet and author of fiction, b. 1925. In the title story of James Berry's *A Thief in the Village and Other Stories*, a 1988 Coretta Scott King award honor book, a London schoolgirl's English teacher overhears her telling a story to her classmates about an incident from her father's childhood in Jamaica. The teacher persuades her to write down how the people of her father's village wrongly suspected Big-Walk, "the tall, ragged man with knotted beard and matted-looking hair," of stealing their livestock and vegetables. Then, proud of her work, he makes her read it to the class "in her Jamaican voices."

Having taught in the British school system before he began writing for children, Berry had noticed that there were few Caribbean voices in British children's literature. He had not always cherished his native speech as a child in Jamaica. He wanted to "talk like books" that he read in school, to talk the way his headmaster talked. But after moving to England in 1948, Berry maintained literary ties with his heritage, writing poetry in Jamaican Creole and editing *Bluefoot Poetry by West Indians in Britain* (1981, revised from a 1976 book).

The stories in *A Thief in the Village* are filled with children driven by their deep desires—from Becky, who longs for a bike so the "Wheels-and-Brake Boys" cannot keep riding away without her, to Fanso, who has never known his father and who cannot understand why, when a man calling himself his father appears, his Granny-Flo drives him away "like a mangey dog." But they are also filled with a celebration of the wealth of life in Jamaica. Sundays remind the narrator of one story of how much he has to celebrate. On Sunday, according to custom, Jamaican men and boys bring their animals down to the ocean for a weekly bath: "It's like a village baptism of people and animals."

Like most Jamaicans, Berry grew up around animals, some of which—Dog, Puss, Jackass, Goat—became characters in the Anancy stories, folktales brought to Jamaica from Ghana that feature a spiderman trickster who survives by his wits. In *Anancy-Spiderman* (1988), Berry retells tales of, as he says in his introduction, "the African Anancy showing his new Caribbean roots." The poems of *When I Dance,* winner of the Signal Poetry Award in 1989, give glimpses into teen life in both Britain and the Caribbean. A motivating force behind this collection is to help teenagers accept "each other's similarity with difference."

As a black man living in mostly white London, Berry knows firsthand that perceived differences can cause human beings to shun, even deny one another. His wrenching novella, *Ajeemah and His Son,* which won the Boston Globe–Horn Book Award in 1993, shows how this denial leads to evil in the form of the African slave trade. It tells of Ajeemah and his teenage son Atu, captured by slave traders in the early nineteenth century as they walk to deliver a dowry of gold to Atu's bride-to-be and subsequently shipped to Jamaica. Sold to different masters, although only a few miles apart, the two never see each other again. While Atu, his escape attempt cruelly thwarted, commits suicide, Ajeemah hides and protects the bridal gift as he painfully carves a new life for himself in Jamaica. Berry endows this father and son, as he does all his characters, with a universality that radiates out from their very personal sorrows and joys—a "similarity with difference." ❧ C.H.

Beskow, Elsa

Swedish author and illustrator, 1874–1953. For generations of Swedes, Elsa Beskow has defined childhood. At her best, Beskow is considered the Swedish Beatrix Potter. Like Potter, she has an obvious delight in nature, and the realistic detail of her paintings make the fantasy of her stories all the more believable. Her mushroom paintings, for example, are so accurate they could be used as a field guide to edible fungi. This preciseness was always a focus for her: "I remember how delighted I was," she says, "even at the age of four or five, every time I discovered a new and more correct way of drawing a face or figure."

When she grew up, Beskow continued her study at the art academy in Stockholm. While there, she saw an exhibit of Walter Crane's work. Walking through those art nouveau paintings of tiger lily ladies and flower fairies, she felt such a connection with his work that it helped define her own style. Personifying the various wood and meadow life was a natural extension for her. But in contrast to Crane's elegant, otherworldly ladies, Beskow's flower fairies are realistic characters that children respond to. There is a bustling buttercup mama, a bristly old thistle man, and blueberry boys whose cheeks and knees are stained with purple juice. In Beskow's enchanted woods, the mythic creatures—elves and trolls, and the Scandinavian Tomte—are as real as the birch branch they swing from.

In *Children of the Forest* (1970, but first published under a different title in 1932), Beskow shows a year in the lives of the little-seen Tomte. The Tomte children, wearing red-spotted caps, gather canterella mushrooms larger than themselves, sled with a snowshoe hare, and

Illustration by Elsa Beskow from her book *Children of the Forest* (1966).

run from an old mountain troll who looks like he is made from the mossy stone he hides behind. In *Clever Annika* (1960), a little girl quite matter-of-factly meets a Tomte family and gives permission for the Tomte mother to milk their cow. "But don't fill the pail all the way full," says Annika. The title, *Clever Annika,* suggests the didacticism that was so popular early in the century, and Beskow's best-known book in the United States, *Pelle's New Suit* (1929), is one of her most educational. Bank Street College praised it for its simplicity, and May Hill Arbuthnot said, "Here is a story as spare of ornamentation as a loaf of bread, but like bread, it is good to the taste, plain, wholesome, and nourishing." In 1952, Beskow was awarded the Nils Holgersson Plaque for her body of work, and in 1958 the Elsa Beskow Award was established for the best Swedish picture-book illustrator of the year.

Recently, Beskow's books are enjoying a resurgence of interest in the United States, the United Kingdom, and Europe. Though she has been criticized for her idealism, and some of her English texts have lost the Swedish lilt in translation, Beskow must be recognized as one who worked not for the critics but for the children themselves. In her simple voice and bright and charming paintings, she created a world that children recognize: a summer meadow, full of adventure, void of fear, with home safe around the corner. ❧ J.A.J.

Bierhorst, John

American folklorist, editor, and adapter of American Indian literature for children; linguist and translator, b. 1936. John Bierhorst holds a unique and respected position in the field of children's literature as an editor and a translator of stories, poems, and songs of American Indians. His reverence for his material and penchant for accuracy result in the impeccable presentation of the culture of a people in all its beauty, mystery, and humor.

Bierhorst was born in Boston, Massachusetts, and grew up in Ohio. He never encountered American Indian culture in any of the books he had as a child. In fact, his boyhood passion was his study of botany, and he spent countless hours classifying plants. He discovered he wanted to write when he was at Cornell University. His first writing job eventually earned him the money to travel, and it was in Peru that he heard the Quechua language and became aware of American Indian life. He began to study native cultures of America and was encouraged by his wife, Jane, a children's book designer, to edit his first collection of stories. The material in the book, *The Fire Plume* (1969), was collected by Henry Rowe Schoolcraft. One of his early books, *In the Trail of the Wind* (1971), is an anthology of songs, prayers, orations, and chants from forty languages of tribes of the Americas. As always, Bierhorst provides admirable notes on the tribes and languages represented.

In *The Hungry Woman: Myths and Legends of the Aztecs* (1984), his versions of the myths and legends are taken directly from the Nahuatl texts or from the earliest Spanish or French adaptations. Bierhorst compiled an Aztec-English dictionary in the course of his work for his research on Aztec literature. He also translated *Spirit Child: A Story of the Nativity from the Aztec* (1984). In 1985, *The Mythology of North America* was published, delineating the mythology described into eleven regions in the Americas. Bierhorst also concentrates on the Mayan people, in *The Monkey's Haircut and Other Stories Told by the Maya* (1986); and he published a source book on South America in *The Mythology of South America* in 1988. He concentrates on the Iroquois in *The Woman Who Fell from the Sky: The Iroquois Story of Creation* (1993), a picture book.

Many of his books have been recognized as Notable Books by the American Library Association. Bierhorst is a member of the American Folklore Society and the American Anthropological Association. He has had scholarly articles published in such publications as the *Journal of American Folklore* and the *Bulletin of Research in the Humanities.* He has also received grants from several agencies, including the National Endowment for the Humanities. His translation of eight Charles Perrault tales from the 1697 text in *The Glass Slipper,* published in 1981, was praised as another example of accuracy in translation, research, and documentation. He has also written a study of American Indian music, *A Cry from the Earth* (1992). ❧ S.H.H.

Biography

Carlyle observed that "A well-written Life is almost as rare as a well-spent one." Emerson maintained that "There is properly no history; only biography." And George Eliot commented that "Biographies generally are a disease of English literature." All three quotations could well describe the evolving nature of biography for children.

Probably the earliest biographical efforts were inscriptions on some type of monument, still a popular device, carried to gargantuan proportions on Mount Rushmore. Later, storytellers, minstrels, and poets celebrated heroes through the oral tradition. Commemorating greatness dictated certain conventions in style and content: repetition of key phrases is typical of ballads; preternatural circumstances of the subject's birth, lack of information about his adolescence, and mysterious elements attendant on his demise are characteristic of hero stories. Although one of the precursors of biography, the art of storytelling—of narrative construction—often ignored in formulaic treatments, is a significant element in literary biography.

The move from commemoration to didacticism seems inevitable. If legends of heroes indicated virtues peculiar to a particular nation, legends of saints, recorded in medieval monasteries, offered scope for teaching ethical concepts and numerous subjects for emulation. The Victorian period saw renewed emphasis on exemplary lives and avoidance of the unseemly—a view that dominated selection of subjects for children's books until the postsixties period. These two impulses, the commemorative and the didactic, are still functioning, particularly in the children's book field.

Until the mid-nineteen seventies, biography was the stepchild among the genres of children's literature. Not that there were too few but rather that there were too few that qualified as literature, let alone as good biography. In various manifestations such as fictionalized accounts of famous childhoods, encyclopedic compilations of facts about "worthy" lives, or cut-and-paste versions of books written originally for adults, these so-called biographies enjoyed a kind of half-life. Adults found them useful; children read them. After all, they were harmless—or so popular theories had it—and they were inspirational. But, as children's literature came under scrutiny as an academic discipline in the sixties, shortcomings in biographical writing for the young became more apparent. In 1973, writing in *Top of the News,* Patrick Groff entitled an article on the misuses of biography for educational or bibliotherapeutic purposes, "Biography: The Bad or the Bountiful." Emphasis on nonliterary applications of biography, he maintained, encouraged the proliferation of contrived, poorly written books, unacceptable as literature. Earlier, in 1972, in *A New Look at Children's Literature,* written with William Anderson, Groff not only critically examined biography but also included an annotated bibliography, compiled by Ruth Robinson, of acceptable books. Among these were *Abraham Lincoln* by INGRI and EDGAR PARIN D'AULAIRE (1939), a picture book and winner of the 1940 Caldecott Medal; ALIKI Brandenberg's *A Weed Is a Flower* (1965), an introduction to the life of George Washington Carver for the primary grades; *The Walls of Windy Troy: The Biography of Heinrich Schliemann* (1960) by Marjorie Braymer; *Tom Paine, Revolutionary* by OLIVIA COOLIDGE (1969); *George Washington's World* (1941) a comparative history by GENEVIEVE STUMP FOSTER; and *Langston Hughes: A Biography* (1968) by MILTON MELTZER. William L. Shirer's *The Rise and Fall of Adolf Hitler* (1961) was included, a "World Landmark" biography that demonstrates that not all books in a series should be categorically dismissed. Absent from Robinson's compilation were two Newbery medalists: CORNELIA MEIGS'S *Invincible Louisa* (1933), considered dull by some critics because it failed to re-create the subject's personality, and *Daniel Boone* by JAMES DAUGHERTY (1939), criticized for stereotyping American Indians. Among the selections, however, were two titles castigated by others for racist elements, both Newbery medalists: *Amos Fortune, Free Man* (1950) by ELIZABETH YATES, the story of an eighteenth-century New England slave who later bought his own freedom, and *I, Juan de Pareja* (1965) by ELIZABETH BORTON DE TREVINO, a fictionalized account of the relationship between the Spanish painter Velázquez and the slave who longed to be an artist.

Most titles on the bibliography in Groff's book were for older readers; some, such as Ann Petry's *Tituba of Salem Village* (1964) might be more accurately classified as historical fiction. Clearly, there were not many examples of well-written biography, particularly for younger readers. Few books for this audience approached the integrity of ESTHER FORBES'S *America's Paul Revere,* illustrated by LYND WARD (1946), a reconstruction of her Pulitzer Prize–winning work.

Then came JEAN FRITZ, and the picture changed dramatically. Already praised for her historical novels *Brady* (1960) and for *The Cabin Faced West* (1958), Fritz combined the storyteller's art with the discipline of the historian in writing biography for preadolescents as well as for readers in their early teens. She launched a new era in approaching the past—not as a maker of myths or perpetuator of stereotypes—but as a joyous explorer, keenly interested in the human condition, certainly a prime requisite for a biographer and historian. In books such as *What's the Big Idea, Ben Franklin?* (1976) and *Traitor, the Case of Benedict Arnold* (1981), she provided examples in books for children not only of what biography is but of what it could be. That biography has now become one of the more exciting genres in children's book publishing is due in large part to her influence. We still have the made-for-school-projects textbook-style accounts of famous lives, but there is now a considerable body of biographical writing worthy to be examined by literary standards and in relation to the historical development of the genre.

Another factor may be renewed interest in and heightened standards for biography in general. Because children's books tend to reflect rather than originate literary trends, quite likely the art of biographical writing as practiced by Lytton Strachey in *Eminent Victorians* (1918), further developed by Leon Edel in his study *Literary Biography* (1973), and currently manifested in David McCulloch's *Truman* (1992) has created a climate in which writers like RUSSELL FREEDMAN, Jean Fritz, and Albert Marrin can be appreciated. Biographies such as Tamara Hovey's *A Mind of Her Own: A Life of the Writer George Sand* (1977) would have been considered too risqué in the nineteen forties and fifties. VIRGINIA HAMILTON's *Paul Robeson: The Life and Times of a Free Black Man* (1974) required a freer political climate than prevailed in earlier decades.

To reach a wider audience while acknowledging differences in experience and interest as well as the relatively limited number of competent practitioners, Jo Carr in her essay "What Do We Do about Bad Biographies?" (1982) advocated, among other approaches, using autobiographies, historical fiction, diaries, and journals. From a practical perspective, she is correct. But strictly speaking, these are not biographies. Discussion of literary genres as literature requires that definitions be clear and distinctions drawn. There are many forms of writing related to biography, including autobiographies, diaries, and letters—and yet, they differ from the observations and interpretations of a third person. Wonderful as they are, books such as ERIK BLEGVAD's *Self-Portrait* (1979), *The Endless Steppe* (1968), ESTHER HAUTZIG's memoirs of growing up as an exile in Siberia during World War II, and FERDINAND MONJO's *Letters to Horseface: Being the Story of Wolfgang Amadeus Mozart's Journey to Italy, 1769–1770, When He Was a Boy of Fourteen* (1975) require somewhat different criteria for evaluation than Albert Marrin's *Unconditional Surrender: U. S. Grant and the Civil War* (1994). Although biography and its associated forms are frequently treated as equivalent to historical documents, this blurs valuable distinctions and is a disservice to young readers.

A brief overview of format, subject, text components, and style affords insight into some of the current trends in biography for children. Picture-book biographies focusing on a specific event and brief, copiously illustrated lives suggest appeal to a generation accustomed to visual presentations. Both *The Glorious Flight, Across the Channel with Louis Blériot* (1983), written and illustrated by ALICE and MARTIN PROVENSEN, and *Flight: The Journey of Charles Lindbergh* (1991), written by Robert Burleigh and illustrated by Mike Wimmer, stress pivotal episodes in the subjects' lives. DIANE STANLEY's *Peter the Great,* (1986) and with Peter Vennema, *Shaka: King of the Zulus* (1988) present accessible portraits of personalities not usually found in children's books. Collective biographies, the best of which have a thematic organization, are exemplified by Russell Freedman's stunning *Indian Chiefs* (1987). Already mentioned are the proliferation of series on specific themes. Although many are poor, others deserve attention. Particularly interesting are a number of series about artists: "Portraits of Women Artists for Children," which includes Robyn Montana Turner's *Mary Cassatt* (1992), a picture-book biography; "First Impressions: Introductions to Art," for preadolescents, which, as in Avis Berman's lively *James McNeill Whistler* (1993), incorporate a considerable amount of art history into readable narratives; and "A Weekend With . . . ," featuring such diverse personalities as Picasso, Renoir, and Velázquez. The "weekend" books interweave factual material into imagined monologues with which the subject entertains a young visitor; not strictly biography in the classic sense, they offer creatively constructed interpretations of their subjects' lives. As these series indicate, the range of topics for biography has expanded considerably since the 1970s.

Given the possibilities in form and content, what should be expected of biographies? While biographies for children may be selective in the years of a life to be chronicled, certainly accuracy, honest interpretation, and insight should be no less in biographies for the young than in those for adults. Softening reality to the point of distortion is unacceptable. Nor should these works be stylistically inferior. Given the resources available, we expect documentation as thorough as Albert Marrin's; we applaud the skill with which Russell Freedman allows details to reveal the subject as in *Lincoln: A Photobiography* (1987); and we celebrate Jean Fritz's remarkable ability to transform facts into an engrossing narrative. Above all, the biography, whatever the subject, should suggest that it was written with passionate attention and intense curiosity for, as Jean Fritz states: "We cannot afford to forget that the past is not just a series of events; it is *people* doing things."

MARY MEHLMAN BURNS

BISHOP, CLAIRE HUCHET

FRENCH-BORN AMERICAN STORYTELLER AND AUTHOR, 1899?–1993. Claire Huchet Bishop helped to establish L'Heure Joyeuse, the first children's library in France. Later, her own books would reside in children's libraries around the world.

Born in Brittany, in France, Bishop was raised in a family of storytellers. Her own gift for storytelling, however, lay dormant until she began telling tales to young library patrons. After her marriage to an American, Bishop immigrated to the United States and joined the staff of the New York Public Library, where she continued to develop her storytelling skills. Her first book was based on one of her most popular recitations. Illustrated by KURT WIESE, *The Five Chinese Brothers* (1938) is a humorous picture book account of five brothers who evade execution because of their unusual physical traits. The book was a major success, although modern critics have complained about its violent plot and negative portrayal of Asians.

Bishop also wrote a number of acclaimed works for middle-grade readers, including the Newbery Honor Book *Pancakes-Paris* (1947), the story of a boy who is given a box of pancake mix in post–World War II France. Another book about that war, *Twenty and Ten* (1952), concerns a group of students who protect some Jewish children from the Nazis. The story is exciting and touching; the use of the metaphor of children's pretend games as mirrors for reality is particularly accomplished. Bishop's second Newbery Honor Book, *All Alone* (1953), tells of a French boy tending cattle in the mountains. His kindness in assisting a fellow herder causes his townspeople to abandon their isolationist ideology and to develop a sense of community.

Bishop's stories set in France are especially representative of her work and noteworthy for their authentic atmosphere, warm characterizations, and a simple yet impor-tant humanitarian philosophy. ❧ P.D.S.

BLAKE, QUENTIN

BRITISH ILLUSTRATOR AND AUTHOR OF FICTION AND POETRY, B. 1932. Quentin Blake began drawing for *Punch* and other British magazines while still in his teens. After attending Downing College in Cambridge and the London University Institute of Education, he took life classes at the Chelsea School of Art and soon after began to illustrate children's books. As an award-winning illustrator of close to two hundred books, Blake is a visiting tutor at the Royal College of Art in London, where he was head of the Illustration Department for ten years.

Among the many esteemed writers and poets whose books Blake has illustrated are JOAN AIKEN, RUSSELL HOBAN, MARGARET MAHY, Michael Rosen, and John Yeoman. Blake and Hoban received the Whitbread Literary Award for the PICTURE BOOK *How Tom Beat Captain Najork and His Hired Sportsmen* (1974), in which Blake's jaunty illustrations perfectly suit the story about Tom, whose aunt summons Captain Najork and his hired sportsmen to teach the boy to stop fooling around. Another made-in-heaven pairing was Blake's illustrations and Margaret Mahy's text in *Nonstop Nonsense* (1989), a collection of comic poems and stories enhanced by Blake's madcap drawings. In Yeoman's *Wild Washerwomen* (1979), Blake's art extends the understated humor of the narrative about seven discontented washerwomen who go on a rowdy rampage until they meet their match in seven woodcutters. They all then marry and share a contented life in which both men and women wash clothing and cut wood with gusto.

Blake is perhaps most widely recognized among young readers for his long-term collaboration with the popular but sometimes controversial author ROALD DAHL, with whom he produced a number of books, including *The Enormous Crocodile* (1978), *The Twits* (1980), *The B.F.G.* (1982), and another Whitbread Award winner, *The Witches* (1983).

Blake's accomplishments as an author-illustrator have also been highly praised by critics and appreciated by children. The Kate Greenaway Medal was given to *Mister Magnolia* (1980), in which the utter absurdity of Blake's nonsense poem about a man with one shoe is further magnified by his hilarious color illustrations. In another picture book, *Mrs. Armitage on Wheels* (1987), Blake tells a cumulative story about an elderly woman who continues to add accessories to her bicycle until, inevitably, it crashes in a riotous ending. The art depicts a proper-looking Mrs. Armitage, who sits primly atop her bike and then, following its sad demise, dons a pair of roller skates.

The unique appeal of Blake's art lies in his ability to create pictures that provide information not explicit in the story. The physical stances, facial expressions, and actions of his characters go beyond the text to tell the reader even more about their individual attitudes and personalities. Blake's spare sketches are deceptive, for their appearance of having been hastily scribbled in a helter-skelter manner conceals the many hours spent in their planning. The exaggerated and zany sense of humor conveyed in all of Blake's art is something no reader, child or adult, can fail to see and appreciate. ❧ J.M.B.

Voices of the Creators

Quentin Blake

Like other artists and writers I get letters, both from children and adults, from many countries in the world. I like getting these letters, but I have to admit that I prefer them when they tell me something rather than when, as often, they are full of questions. Some of these questions are easy to answer. Do you have any children? (No.) Are you married? (No.) Do you have any pets? (No.) Will you draw a picture of my brother, he has freckles and his ears stick out? (Unfortunately, no.) But some are difficult; at least, they call for quite long and complicated answers. For instance, some people ask: Which illustrators have influenced you? I can do part of the answer to this question straightaway. Honoré Daumier, the French illustrator and cartoonist who drew for humorous newspapers in Paris nearly a hundred and fifty years ago, has always been one of my heroes. One of the first art books I ever bought was about Daumier. That was about forty-five years ago, and it cost two *guineas* (two pounds two shillings), which seemed a tremendous amount to me as a schoolboy, though I've probably never spent money better. I still look at that book now.

And then there were more recent artists. About the time that I bought that Daumier book I started publishing drawings in the humorous magazine *Punch*. They were very small drawings, and very much influenced by the artists who drew for the magazine at that time. One in particular: another French artist, André François. His work has always been valued by graphic artists in America as well as in Europe. I didn't actually want to make my drawing look like his. It was that his way of drawing—free, energetic, scratchy, inventive—made me realize how exciting drawing could be; and that because a drawing was going to be printed it didn't necessarily mean that it had to be well behaved.

Another hard question, and a familiar one: where do you get your ideas from? *Quite* where ideas come from is a mysterious business, and perhaps no one really knows the full explanation. However, the first part of my answer is: I get them from authors. Some illustrators are really only happy when they are working on a book which they have entirely invented themselves; but I enjoy working with other people's words and ideas as much as my own. It's like being given a ticket to visit someone else's imagination, and you never quite know what you will find there.

The beginning of the process of working with someone else's manuscript has to begin with reading—reading and rereading, becoming familiar with the character of the story. This is just what any other reader does, except that right from the beginning I'm on the lookout for good drawing opportunities, and making marks in the margin so that I can easily find them again when I need them. Then I begin to draw, and in the early stages this is really two activities. One is to make very rapid rough sketches for the individual drawings. If I do this almost as quickly as I can, it isn't because I'm in a rush to get the job done but because I want to get down as instinctively as possible my response to each incident and the way the sequence of them follows through a book. The other activity is working on what the finished drawings will actually look like. Part of this is deciding on the appearance of the characters, their features and expressions, the way they move, what they are going to wear. This in its turn may also influence the way the pictures are drawn and what you draw them with. Take the Twits, for instance. Such a dirty and degraded pair seemed to call for quite a coarse pen-nib and a rough, angular way of drawing. I needed to be able to show clearly their deplorable tricks and antics, and at the same time to suggest the atmosphere of the crazy world they live in; one that isn't quite the same as ours.

I don't ever try my books out on children; it's the infant in myself that I try them out on. At the same time, however, part of my mind has before it the social situation of reading and what happens between words and pictures and people, and I make sure that words and pictures aren't performing exactly the same function. We need (my young readers need, I need) the reassurance of cross-checking—that what is mentioned in the text can be found in the pictures—and that in its turn opens up the possibility of laying in a few moments of thought and discussion. The short statement can be expanded in the illustration, and sometimes even contradicted. *Cockatoos* is largely based in the pictures telling a different story than the words; Professor Dupont and the text know that there aren't any cockatoos in the attic, but we can see them lined up behind the suitcases. Words and pictures can give us a story that not only exists, but is enacted; and is ready to happen again whenever we want it to.

Blegvad, Erik

Danish artist, b. 1923. "Illustrating a children's book gives me a role which seems natural, accompanist rather than soloist," Erik Blegvad once wrote. While other illustrators sometimes act like divas—with their art so overpowering that it sometimes drowns out the text—Blegvad has had another sort of career altogether. His art, seldom showy, always expert, has subtly served scores of novels and picture-book texts by some of the most distinguished children's writers, including Judith Viorst, Charlotte Zolotow, Mary Stolz, Jane Langton, and Margery Sharp. Seemingly modest, his ambition to be the best accompanist possible is, in fact, grandly ambitious. For his goal, which he has achieved again and again in his long career, is to create books in which text and art combine into one voice.

Born in Copenhagen, the son of a marine biologist and the grandson of a schoolmaster, he grew up in a house full of paintings, drawings, and art books. During the German occupation of Denmark, he attended art school. After World War II ended, he eked out a living contributing drawings to a friend's newspaper. In 1947 he moved to Paris with his bike, his savings, his art portfolio, and, at the advice of his mother, ten pounds of butter. The butter soon melted away, as did his savings, but he began to find illustrating jobs. In time, he found a wife as well, Lenore, who later became a writer and his collaborator on a number of books. In 1951 they moved to her native New York City. The following year, he won his first children's book assignment and was able to support his growing family by illustrating books and magazine pieces, including, notably, Mary Norton's *The Borrowers,* which first appeared in the United States as a serial in *Woman's Day.*

His picture books include the classic *The Tenth Good Thing about Barney* (1976) by Judith Viorst. Here finely detailed crosshatched drawings support the story's wistful melancholy. The little boy and his family, whose cat has just died, are drawn with affection and sympathy. The book's design is simple and spare, an unaffected presentation for a tale of ordinary life, gently and tellingly observed.

His own *Self-Portrait: Erik Blegvad* (1979) is an especially engaging portfolio of his work. Illustrated with art created just for the book, including depictions of his boyhood haunts in Copenhagen, and with previously published work, it offers an appealing view of life happily and busily spent developing a craft. He generously acknowledges the friends and colleagues who helped him along the way and takes special pleasure in his good fortune at being able to earn a living by his pen, "which to my delight, proceeds to create people, objects, and worlds I never knew existed." ❧ A.Q.

Bloom, Lloyd

American illustrator, b. 1947. Born in New York City and graduated from Hunter College in 1972, Lloyd Bloom received an M.F.A. degree from Indiana University at Bloomington in 1975. He also studied at the Art Students League in New York and at the New York Studio School.

Bloom has illustrated books that have gained both a wide audience and critical acclaim. An example of his early work, Patricia MacLachlan's *Arthur, for the Very First Time* (1980), named a 1980 Notable Book by the American Library Association, shows sinewy human figures that recall the style of Reginald Marsh. The ALA also named one of the books he illustrated, *Like Jake and Me* (1984) by Mavis Jukes, a Newbery Honor Book. The illustrations boldly portray the relationship between the strikingly different personalities of a young man and his stepfather. *Poems for Jewish Holidays* (1986), selected by Myra Cohn Livingston, won a 1987 National Jewish Book Council Award for Illustration from the Jewish Book Council. In the picture book *Yonder* (1988) by Tony Johnston, Bloom paints a lush countryside landscape in oils. The fluid movements and powerful stances of people are portrayed with undetailed, broad brush strokes, but the details of the landscape, especially the featured plum tree, are painted individually, to the smallest bud and leaf, with ingeniously repetitious patterns. One of Bloom's most powerful visions is the fantasy world in *The Green Book* (1982) by Jill Paton Walsh, in which a commune fleeing from the doomed earth colonizes a world they call Shine, where the vegetation is crystalline and translucent. The novel is interpreted thematically, with Bloom's rounded shapes, from the ship's porthole to the moon framed inside the porthole to a field of moth-creatures ordered across the landscape in their chrysalis stage. The stylized landscape of the strange world recalls Grant Wood's geometric farmlands, and Bloom's use of light and shadow conveys beautifully the startling aspect of luminous plants, which are used to build houses that one can almost see through, lit from within by hearth fires. The human population has a statuesque sameness, the figures exhibiting the sinewy grace typical of Bloom's style, and they are arranged in groups on a page in a way that frames the action with their bodies, composition lending strength to the novel's fable quality. Bloom also added his powerful illustrations to *Hear O Israel: A Story of the Warsaw Ghetto* (1990) by Terry Walton Treseder, the bleak first-person Holocaust story of a boy who, before he dies in the Treblinka concentration camp, relates his family's terrible experiences and how their suffering affects the faith of different family members. § S.H.H.

Blos, Joan W.

AMERICAN AUTHOR, B. 1928. In her Newbery Medal acceptance speech in 1980, Joan W. Blos said that she strives for truth in her writing—not just factual accuracy but a sense of social, psychological, and literary truthfulness. *A Gathering of Days: A New England Girl's Journal, 1830–1832,* the book for which she received the medal, succeeds on all these levels. Catherine Hall, the fourteen-year-old protagonist, is firmly rooted in the nineteenth century through the well-researched details Blos provides and the language Catherine uses as she writes in her journal. In addition, these entries reveal her inner growth and development as she copes with the challenges of the times and of growing up, of adjusting to a new stepmother and to the death of her best friend.

Blos was raised in New York City, attended Vassar College, and received a master's degree in psychology from City College of New York. She taught children's literature at Bank Street College of Education and the University of Michigan. *A Gathering of Days* began as research about her husband's New Hampshire house more than twelve years before it was published. Initially, she was intrigued with the history of the 140-year-old house and its several owners. Gradually, her interest expanded to the time period of its construction and early history, and she decided to write a nonfiction history of New Hampshire. But, as she said, "The book decided for itself that fiction would serve the content better," for she found that the thoughts, actions, and motivations of people were more interesting than facts alone.

Although Blos also had intended her second novel, *Brothers of the Heart: A Story of the Old Northwest, 1837–1838* (1985), to be about New England, using some of the characters from *A Gathering of Days*, she found that the story, once again, took on a life of its own: Her characters turned out to be pioneers in Michigan. After Shem, a lame fourteen-year-old, has a quarrel with his father, he runs away and eventually joins a winter trading expedition to northern Michigan. Shem's story of survival and his return to his family is compelling, and Blos's use of letters and journal entries provides an interesting texture to the novel. The characters, however, don't have quite the depth of those in *A Gathering of Days*.

In addition to her novels, Blos has written a number of PICTURE BOOKS. Using a combination of prose and rhyme, Blos tells the story of Molly Brown in *The Heroine of the Titanic: A Tale Both True and Otherwise of the Life of Molly Brown* (1991), illustrated by Tennessee Dixon. In *Martin's Hats* (1984), illustrated by MARC SIMONT, Martin dons different hats and becomes different characters, from an explorer, to a train engineer, to a farmer, and finally, putting on a nightcap, he comes home to bed. In *Lottie's Circus* (1989), illustrated by Irene Trivas, Lottie creates a magnificent circus complete with clowns, animal acts, and trapeze artists using her dolls and stuffed toys. Grandpa, in *The Grandpa Days* (1989), illustrated by EMILY ARNOLD MCCULLY, gently encourages Philip to design something they can build together in his woodworking shop.

In her pursuit of truth in her writing, Blos demonstrates her respect for young readers and for the power of their imaginations. § P.R.

Blumberg, Rhoda

AMERICAN NONFICTION WRITER, B. 1917. When *Commodore Perry in the Land of the Shogun* (1985) received the Boston Globe–Horn Book Award for nonfiction, Rhoda Blumberg recalled how her job as scriptwriter and researcher for CBS radio had developed her taste for information: "Nonfiction proved to be as gripping as fiction—a fantastic discovery."

When Blumberg started writing INFORMATION BOOKS for children as well as for adults, her books covered a wide variety of subjects. A series of professional travel guides eventually led to the publication of two children's books—*The First Travel Guide to the Moon* (1980) and *The First Travel Guide to the Bottom of the Sea* (1983)—both of which gained recognition from science educators. Blumberg then began to focus on history. *Commodore Perry in the Land of the Shogun* traces U.S. efforts to make contact with Japan in the mid-nineteenth century, a time when the Japanese and the Americans knew very little about each other. Part of a general trend toward engaging, eye-catching nonfiction, this Newbery Honor Book was followed by *The Incredible Journey of Lewis and Clark* (1987), an account of the expedition to the Pacific Coast headed by the two explorers from 1804 to 1806. In *The Great American Gold Rush* (1989), Blumberg tells about the people who flocked to California from 1848 to 1852 in search of riches. *The Remarkable Voyages of Captain Cook* (1991) chronicles the British explorer's three journeys to the Pacific Ocean between 1768 and 1780.

Blumberg's work reveals her fascination with topics that straddle the boundary between fiction and fact; her history books show how travel and exploration have helped establish facts where only legend and speculation existed before. For instance, in Patagonia, South America, Captain Cook met normal humans, not the expected twelve-foot giants. Lewis and Clark came across numerous animals unknown to them, but they never did sight the giant sloths or live mammoths they thought they might find. Good design is a prominent feature of Blumberg's large-format history books, which have uncluttered pages abundantly illustrated with historical material selected by Blumberg herself; for example, more than seventy pictures from fourteen collections enhance *The Remarkable Voyages of Captain Cook.*

The books also demonstrate other qualities vital to good informational books. Striving for a balanced presentation, Blumberg displays an increasing sensitivity to the viewpoints of the peoples encountered by the explorers and travelers she describes. Her passion for research sends her to numerous primary and secondary sources, all recorded in thorough bibliographies and chapter notes. She has said, "I . . . willingly endure monotonous diaries and poorly written manuscripts when they reward me with surprising information about people." For *The Great American Gold Rush,* she dug through letters and diaries for more than a year. Blumberg complements her research with skilled use of the storyteller's art; she enjoys language and has the ability to select and tell audience-pleasing stories. As she remarked on receiving the John and Patricia Beatty Award for *The Great American Gold Rush,* "Stories are enchanting, and for me true stories—from history—are the most enchanting." ❧ M.F.S.

BLUME, JUDY

AMERICAN NOVELIST, B. 1938. Few authors have equaled Judy Blume's popularity, whether one judges by the sales of her books, all of which seem to stay in print *ad infinitum,* or by the number of awards chosen by children, primarily in statewide contests.

Her first two books, *The One in the Middle Is the Green Kangaroo* (1969), which deals with the problems of being a middle child, and *Iggie's House* (1970), the story of a black family that moves into a white neighborhood, were lightly humorous despite the fact that they dealt—realistically—with serious problems. Blume's third book, *Are You There God? It's Me, Margaret* (1970), brought her national attention: some raves, some disparaging frowns. It was in this story that her readers first saw the author's compassion and sympathy and her conviction that the universal problems of adolescents should be reflected, with dignity and understanding, in the books they read.

"I think I write the kind of books," she said in a statement for *Something About the Author,* "I would have liked to read when I was young." This follows a comment about the fact that there were no books that mirrored her own interests and feelings when Judy Blume was a child. Certainly eleven-year-old Margaret, in *Are You There, God?,* is a prototypical preteen, worried about how long it will be before she develops breasts and begins menstruating. She is, as the title indicates, devout—but she's not sure exactly how she should worship, with one parent who's Jewish and one who's not. The religious conflict incurred no observable wrath; the inclusion of sexual and physical concerns did upset many adults. Girls tended to be delighted at finding topics about which almost all preteens are concerned.

The same kind of percipient concern for the problems of teenage boys appears in *Then Again, Maybe I Won't* (1971). It describes thirteen-year-old Tony's adjustment to change, his realization that his parents are social climbers, and his embarrassment at showing sexual arousal (he drapes his coat over his arm and holds it in front of him—just in case). While the book deals with specific problems, it addresses Tony's growing sensitivity and maturity.

In *Deenie* (1973) and *Blubber* (1974) Blume explores young people's intense concern with their physical appearance and their reactions to their own physical limitations and those of others. Deenie's mother wants her pretty twelve-year-old daughter to become a model, and she's appalled when a test reveals the reason Deenie moves oddly, a peculiarity spotted by an agency interviewer. Deenie is also upset at learning that she has scoliosis and will have to wear a back brace for four years. She finds that her friends won't desert her just because she's "different," a predictable and happy conclusion to the secret fears of being unpleasantly set apart. But the author is realistic about the fact that such acceptance doesn't always happen, as is evident in her next story. *Blubber* is painfully honest in showing how cruel children can be to each other and in illustrating group dynamics. Linda is the fifth-grade scapegoat, even though she's not the only fat girl in the class. One classmate is sympathetic, but she's one of the few who stop persecuting Linda. In this book Blume decided to include the sometimes rough language that she heard fifth-graders using. But the author yielded to compromise: "Bad" language stayed in if it contributed to plot or character development; otherwise it was removed.

Certainly Blume's most controversial book has been *Forever . . .* (1975). Those who objected were not impressed, as were many critics and parents (and young people), by the author's advocacy of sexual responsibility and her recognition of developmental and physical needs. Katherine and Michael are in love; their feelings are passionate and romantic, and they become lovers. Kath, who tells the story, feels wholly committed—but she finds, when she takes a summer camp job at her parents' insistence, that she is attracted to another man. That's the end of "forever." Moralists felt that the lovers should have been punished; some of them felt that the book encouraged sexual activity. Other critics praised the candor of the story and its dialogue, characterization, and depiction of familial relationships.

In two novels, Blume's protagonists are affected by their parents' marital problems. In *Just as Long as We're Together* (1987) Stephanie's parents have begun a trial separation, and she's therefore particularly vulnerable when she runs into a problem with peer relationships. Parental separation also causes grief in *It's Not the End of the World* (1972), but the main character here admits to herself that the hostility would still be there if Dad did come back. Always concerned about personal relationships, Blume tells a touching and credible story of loss, adjustment, and the slow healing process that can be helped by friendship, love, and patience in *Tiger Eyes*, in which the father has been shot in a robbery at his convenience store.

While most of her books for teenage readers have moments of humor even when they deal with serious issues, it is in her books for younger readers, those in the middle grades, that Blume is at her amusing best. Many of the titles for this age range are linked: *Tales of a Fourth Grade Nothing* (1972) is a chapter-by-chapter wail of comic despair from Peter, whose two-year-old brother Fudge is his greatest trial—for example, Fudge gulps down Peter's turtle. The sequels, *Superfudge* (1980) and *Fudge-a-Mania* (1990), are equally ebullient and equally popular. In the last, Peter's parents share a summer house with the parents of Sheila, Peter's archenemy and the protagonist of *Otherwise Known as Sheila the Great* (1972).

For Judy Blume fans, there is a special appeal in *Starring Sally J. Freedman as Herself* (1977), because it seems so clearly a reflection of the author's childhood. The wildly imaginative, highly histrionic heroine is both beguiling and amusing; the book's episodic structure makes it less cohesive than most of Blume's writing, but readers have been captivated. In Sally they see the seeds of the writer who has been their advocate, who has broken barriers of taboos about what subjects and what language are appropriate for children's books. "Perceptive, funny, sad, and honest," one reviewer said. It is all those aspects that have made Judy Blume loved and defended by her readers. Contributing to her own long record of defending the right to better access to information on serious issues, she established The Kids Fund in 1981; the organization has made many grants each year to nonprofit organizations for the development of programs that address such needs. It is for that courageous honesty that she was given the CARL SANDBURG Freedom to Read Award in 1984 and the American Civil Liberties Union Award in 1986. ❧ ZENA SUTHERLAND

Board Books

Board books are a relatively new phenomenon in the world of children's trade publishing. Responding to a perceived need for books suitable for babies and toddlers, the first of a modern generation of cardboard-paged books appeared in 1979 with the publication of ROSEMARY WELLS's series about a rabbit named Max. One in a set of four, *Max's Ride* is a disarmingly simple story about Max's thrilling adventure the day his baby carriage careens out of control. The strong visual appeal of the uncluttered illustrations, which are placed on bright, solid-colored backgrounds, grabs children's attention, and the understated, economically phrased text adds humor and suspense that guarantees requests for repeated readings.

In the 1980s the trickle of books turned into a flood of newly published board books, astutely timed to coincide with the decade's baby boom, when many affluent, highly educated professionals who had postponed childbearing until later in life and had a strong interest in the future success of their children put much of their considerable disposable income into educational materials and books. A number of award-winning children's authors and illustrators, such as LEO LIONNI, PETER SPIER, and ERIC CARLE, produced board books during this time.

A large number of new titles continue to appear in the 1990s, although most resemble successful books from the plethora of board books that appeared in the previous decade. The format continues to be popular with public libraries and the book-buying public because the books can withstand repeated abuse at the hands of very young children. Echoing an earlier phenomenon, authors and illustrators who have already established their reputations in other arenas of children's book publishing continue to try their hands at board books. MARTHA ALEXANDER ("Lily and Willy Board Books," 1991), FRANK ASCH ("Moonbear Books," 1993), LUCY COUSINS ("Animal Board Books," 1991), and CYNTHIA RYLANT ("The Everyday Books," 1993) are among the writers who have made recent contributions of note to this popular field.

A new and sensible trend that began in the early 1990s is the publication in board-book format of titles that were originally successful as traditional books. Interest by babies and toddlers in books such as RUTH KRAUSS's *Carrot Seed* (1945; 1993), MARGARET WISE BROWN's *Goodnight Moon* (1947; 1991), CHARLES SHAW's *It Looked Like Spilt Milk* (1947; 1993), and BILL MARTIN, JR.'s *Chicka Chicka Boom Boom* (1989; 1993) have resulted in welcome board-book versions of these titles. ALEXANDRA DAY's nearly wordless stories about a Rottweiler named Carl, such as *Carl's Masquerade* (1993), have also been released as board books.

Some of the most frequently encountered physical features of cardboard books include rounded page corners for the safety of small children who are often unsteady on their feet and might fall while holding the book; pages that are coated so they can be wiped clean; and small size for the comfort of the tiny hands that carry them. A typical book measures no more than 6 inches square, although some titles have appeared that are as large as $8^1/_2$ by $9^1/_2$ inches.

Many board books are wordless, so that adults can use the pictures to stimulate discussion with a child. TANA HOBAN's wordless *What Is It* (1985) offers elegant color photographs of familiar objects—such as a shoe, a spoon, and a set of keys—for a child and adult to name and talk about together. Hoban makes use of recent research in the field of child development in her stylish illustrations for *Black on White* (1993) and *White on Black* (1993), which showcase high-contrast black or white shapes against the opposite color background; scientists indicate that children are able to focus on high-contrast pictures at a very young age. Other titles, such as Valerie Greeley's set about animals, feature delicate but realistic painting of animals in naturalistic settings. In *Field Animals* (1984), for example, squirrels and rabbits appear amid flowering plants and trees and provide a first introduction to nature for a young child.

Some board books for this audience do include words and a simple plot, as seen in Wells's "Max" series. Caldecott Honor Medalist NANCY TAFURI's successful introduction to colors, *In a Red House* (1987), features a narrative that is a model of economy: "A purple chair / an orange ball / a brown bear / a yellow dog / a white duck / green blocks / a pink bunny / and a gray truck / are all in my own blue room!" The uncomplicated, brightly colored objects outlined in black take up most of the space on the book's white pages. In *I Hear* (1986), HELEN OXENBURY introduces the concepts of listening and sounds as a round-faced, overall-clad toddler experiences a bird's song, a baby's wail, and a telephone's ring. One word, such as *bird, telephone,* and *baby,* accompanies each double-page spread. *Tickle, Tickle* (1987) is one in a set of four books by Oxenbury that features a multicultural cast of toddlers, a growing trend in children's books. Four young children with a variety of skin colors cavort in the mud and clean up in the bath; a delightful rhyme accompanies joyous illustrations that pulse with the energy generated by toddlers playing.

Recent research demonstrates the importance of children's early years in their future educational success. Parents, teachers, and librarians who embrace these findings begin sharing books with children when they are infants. Their continued quest for high-quality board books—books that match content with format by limiting text and using developmentally appropriate illustrations or photographs—keeps publishers, authors, and illustrators searching for fresh ideas to develop into board-book format. This push toward providing materials for infants and toddlers has also influenced traditional hardcover publishing. Books by author-illustrators such as JIM ARNOSKY and Douglas Florian incorporate some of the genre's best stylistic features, such as large print, uncomplicated illustrations, and brief stories, in books for slightly older children. Adults who choose children's books can expect to see a continuing trend of cross-fertilization among books for various ages of children, as those who produce board books heed the needs of very young children.

ELLEN G. FADER

BOBBSEY TWINS SERIES

Imagine a family, living in an idyllic town, that consists of two sets of fraternal twins who enjoy spending their time together. This may sound like a simplistic idea for a children's series, but the tales of Mary and Richard Bobbsey's children—dark and lively eight-year-old twins Nan and Bert and blond and chubby four-year-old twins Flossie and Freddie—have been an integral part of childhood for readers since 1904.

Edward Stratemeyer, founder of the series book empire, the STRATEMEYER LITERARY SYNDICATE, wrote the first book in the Bobbsey series—*The Bobbsey*

Twins, or Merry Days Indoors and Out—as an experiment to gauge the sales potential of a series for younger readers of both sexes. The book proved to be a success, and over the next five decades, forty-seven more Bobbsey Twin books—all written under the pseudonym "Laura Lee Hope"—followed. By 1981 there were seventy-six books in the series. The Bobbsey Twins had more titles and a longer run than any other Stratemeyer series.

The early Bobbsey books featured meandering, almost nonexistent plots where adventure took a back seat to family frolic. The atmosphere of these tales was pastoral, with entire chapters devoted to blissful family activities—sleigh rides, fireworks, shopping, train journeys, seashore vacations. The chapters were strung together in near-incidental fashion and would often end in a mild cliffhanger. All problems would be solved in the following chapter, and the Bobbseys would return to their carefree, happy activities. It has been said that reading the early books was akin to watching a "nursery soap-opera."

In 1950, almost fifty years after the publication of the first Bobbsey book, the Stratemeyer Syndicate began revising the books. Some changes were superficial: In 1960, for instance, the ages of the two sets of twins were increased to twelve and six. More important changes revolved around the removal of the ethnic dialect used by Dinah and Sam Johnson, the Bobbseys' maid and gardener; racist references were also deleted. The twins themselves were transformed into junior detectives (à la NANCY DREW and the HARDY BOYS) and the word *mystery* or *adventure* was inserted into most titles. Despite these changes, Nan, Bert, Flossie, and Freddie remained the same ingenuous children first introduced at the beginning of the century, possessing the same qualities they always had: decency, enthusiasm, and curiosity. § M.I.A.

BOND, MICHAEL

BRITISH AUTHOR, B. 1926. It is almost impossible to think of Michael Bond without also thinking of his most famous character, Paddington Bear, so inescapably linked are the two. Bond's first published writing, however, was not for children.

Born and raised in Berkshire, England, Bond began writing while serving with the British army in the Middle East. His first short story published, Bond decided to become a writer. As he says, "I amassed a vast quantity of rejection slips but also had articles published. I turned to writing radio plays, then television. At my agent's suggestion, I began to write things for children." Such "things" turned into a collection of short stories about a small bear named Paddington, published in 1958 in England as a book, *A Bear Called Paddington*, which chronicles the discovery by the Brown family of an English-speaking bear from Darkest Peru at the Paddington train station and Paddington's gradual assimilation into the Browns' London household.

Illustration by Peggy Fortnum from *Paddington Abroad* (1972), by Michael Bond.

Paddington's appeal came not only from the hilarious situations and mishaps in which he found himself—from being buried under groceries on his first supermarket trip to discovering cheese soufflés and pickled onions at a fancy restaurant—but also from Peggy Fortnum's pen-and-ink sketches, which capture Paddington's bewitching charm and combination "little boy/small bear" character.

Paddington's adventures continued with the publication of *More About Paddington* (1961), *Paddington Helps Out* (1961), *Paddington at Large* (1963), *Paddington at Work* (1967), *Paddington Goes to Town* (1968), *Paddington Takes the Air* (1971), *Paddington Abroad* (1972), and *Paddington on Top* (1975). In each book—actually a compilation of seven distinct stories joined by a general theme—Paddington Bear bumbles delightfully from one absurd escapade to the next. While Bond believes his bear to be a typical English character—as English as

Voices of the Creators

Michael Bond

I wrote my first children's book in 1957 and it came about largely by accident.

At that time I had been a part-time writer for about ten years, following a common progression in those days: short stories, newspaper and magazine articles, radio plays, plus a few short plays for television. I thought it was a good year if I sold one piece in ten.

Without giving the matter any great thought, I had always regarded writing for children as a lesser form of creativity—quite untrue, of course. As Gertrude Stein might have said—a book is a book is a book, and writing is perhaps even more of an agonizing process of distillation when it's for children.

There being nothing more soul-destroying than staring at a blank sheet of paper hoping something will happen (it won't unless you make it), I was sitting at the typewriter one morning when my gaze happened to alight on a toy bear I had bought my wife for Christmas. We called him Paddington, so I typed the words: "Mr. and Mrs. Brown first met Paddington on a railway platform. In fact, that was how he came to have such an unusual name for a bear, for Paddington was the name of the station."

Suddenly, I *wanted* to write more about this small character. Where had he come from? What was he doing in London? What were his reactions to life in England and the curious complications we humans make for ourselves?

Until that time I had always thought up stories and then tried to people them with characters. Suddenly, I learned a very simple fact of fictional life: If you create a believable character and you place it into a situation, events will develop naturally of their own accord.

Many of my radio and television plays had been light comedies which more often than not were returned with the comment "Sorry—no call for fantasy" written across the rejection slip. Nonsense, of course: All works of fiction are fantasy, and nothing could be more so than the concept of a bear with a penchant for marmalade sandwiches, who lives in Notting Hill Gate and speaks perfectly good English. But until then, I hadn't learned the trick of making it seem believable. That won't happen unless both you, the writer, and all the characters in the story believe in it, too.

I wrote the first chapter very quickly, instinctively putting in all the things I felt I would have wanted as a child. More followed, and in ten days I had a finished book.

In retrospect, some thirty-five years and many books later, I think most fictional characters who enjoy longevity do so because someone, somewhere, at some time wrote about them for the very simple reason that they *wanted* to.

The first book of any series is the most fun to write; everything is fresh and exciting, and you can go anywhere your fancy takes you. Recapturing the original mood in subsequent books isn't always easy. Parameters have been set which dictate future stories; what the characters can and can't do. Paddington has the best of all worlds; he combines the naiveté of a small child with the sophistication of an adult, plus ingredient "X"—his own peculiar brand of logic. Being a bear, he gets away with things without seeming precocious. The stories wouldn't work were he a small child.

Children hate being written down to or made to feel they are being patronized. They like their heroes to come out on top and the feeling of comfort that goes with a safe return to base or the comfort of a home. They also—quite rightly—dislike being sold short.

I hold the old-fashioned view that stories should have a beginning, a middle, and an end, and the hardest part with Paddington is not getting him into trouble—he does this of his own accord—but getting him out of it in a way which is morally justifiable; someone must always benefit from his misdeeds, however tenuously.

If fiction does nothing else, it provides a window on the world; perhaps showing things from a different viewpoint; even if—as in the case of another series I write about a guinea-pig called Olga da Polga—that window happens to be part of a hutch.

I once received a letter from a child who said she liked my books because they made pictures in her head. It was the nicest compliment I've ever had.

Mary Poppins and Peter Pan—the books have been translated into more than ten languages. "Obviously," Bond says, "Paddington-type situations happen to people all over."

In 1967 Bond introduced a new series and a new character in *Here Comes Thursday*. Thursday, an orphaned mouse, enters the lives of the Cupboardosities, a family of mice who live in the church organ loft and run the cheese store. His adventures continue in *Thursday Rides Again* (1969) and *Thursday in Paris* (1971). The "Thursday" series—noted for its fluent style and light humor—lacks the contrast between engaging animal behavior and realistic human behavior that adds a nonsensical note to the Paddington Bear stories.

Continuing with his tradition of orphaned animals and adoptive families, Bond introduced the guinea pig Olga da Polga in *The Tales of Olga da Polga* (1972) and continued her story in *Olga Meets Her Match* (1975), *Olga Carries On* (1977), and *Olga Takes Charge* (1983). Olga was, in fact, a real member of Bond's family—she arrived as a birthday present for Bond's daughter—and he claims that while some of Olga's tales are partly based on actual events, "others are figments of Olga's imagination." Olga's appeal lies in her exuberant zest for life, her penchant for inventing stories, and her complacent confidence in her own charms.

The enduring popularity of Bond's characters may be due to his philosophy about writing children's books: If you plan to write *for* children, "you run the risk of writing down." Rather than condescendingly treat his readers to quaint animal stories, Bond's books, specifically the "Paddington Bear" series, recognize the everyday worries of small, accident-prone children and treat their fears with compassion, wit, and laughter. ❧ M.I.A.

Bond, Nancy

AMERICAN AUTHOR, B. 1945. As a youngster, Nancy Bond roamed the countryside around Concord, Massachusetts, developing a fascination with the natural world. She earned a B.A. in English composition at Mount Holyoke, never really considering her assignments as work, since writing was—and is—a labor of love for her. After immersing herself in the Welsh culture and environment while attending library school in Wales, Bond began writing her first novel, *A String in the Harp* (1976)—which was both a Newbery Honor Book and a Boston Globe–Horn Book Honor Book. In the book, twelve-year-old Peter and his family move to Wales temporarily. The fragmented family, floundering after the death of Peter's mother, finally pulls together to help Peter, who finds a mystical ancient harp key that slowly draws him into the life of the sixth-century bard, Taliesin.

All of Bond's books are inextricably linked to distinct locales. The inclusion of intimate details about location serves several purposes. First, a specific setting gives an underlying identity to the characters. The wild dunes of Cape Cod convey the strength and individualism of the people in *The Voyage Begun* (1981). Second, such details lend credibility to the story. In *The Best of Enemies* (1978), a map displays the streets of Concord, Massachusetts (where the author still resides) and the reader always knows where the characters are, often traveling with them. Weather and geographic features as well as native wildlife often dramatically affect mood and tone. In *Country of Broken Stone* (1980), an unrelenting sun and the increasingly parched Northumberland landscape reflect the rising tensions between visiting archeologists and the local country folk. Finally, local history often plays an important role in plot. In *Another Shore* (1988), Lyn wears the garb of an eighteenth-century girl as she serves food at Louisbourg, a living museum in Nova Scotia. When she suddenly finds herself transported back to 1744, her perceptions and adaptations provide a fascinating historical comparison that is crucial to the plot.

Bond's attention to detail makes for some dense writing, requiring a certain level of reader sophistication, but one of the results is the development of believable characters. Bond has a good ear for dialogue and uses it liberally to develop recognizable relationships. Though the protagonists are always adolescents, their worlds are peopled with fully fleshed persons of all ages. Portrayed often are refreshing intergenerational friendships, like the bonds that grow between an eleven-year-old girl, a sixteen-year-old boy, two middle-aged adults, and an aged man in *The Voyage Begun*—and the reader is often led to ponder the ties that bind people of different ages, times, and cultures, despite conflicting attachments and viewpoints.

Both rich and introspective, Bond's stories contain numerous subplots and resonating themes. Common to them all is the theme of young people dealing with internal and external change. In *Country of Broken Stone*, Penelope's father has remarried, gracing her with three new siblings; she learns about being an older sister while braving her own growing pains. In *A Place to Come Back To* (1984), the sequel to *The Best of Enemies*, Charlotte and Oliver must deal with the death of Oliver's guardian and come to grips with their intensifying friendship. Bond conveys the first tugs of romance delicately and enticingly.

Nancy Bond writes with craftsmanship, integrity, and passion, and in that tradition her books' endings are actually commencements. Instead of providing absolute closure, they recognize growth and self-realization while acknowledging the challenges of the future. And these open endings ensure that the characters inhabit the reader's imagination long after the book has been shelved. ❧ S.S.

Bonsall, Crosby

American author and illustrator, 1921–1995. Beginning readers have cheerfully and enthusiastically embraced the work of Crosby Barbara Newell Bonsall, most notably her I Can Read mysteries, for many years, and her books continue to appeal to new generations of young readers.

Born in New York City, Bonsall received her professional training at the American School of Design and the New York University School of Architecture before beginning a career in advertising. Later she was to say, "All that commercial art, advertising copy, and the year I spent at New York University of School of Architecture struggling with sculpting and design were not lost. Writing copy to space teaches you a discipline which I find handy in writing books for children just learning to read. I've never used a controlled vocabulary—I just keep the consumer in mind." It is this focus on the child that has allowed Bonsall's books to retain their appeal. Her characters are real children—children who interact with humor and charm, but also with a certain amount of temper, rivalry, and frustration so commonly found at the preschool age. Whether writing about a young boy trying to overcome his fears (*Who's Afraid of the Dark,* 1980), or the gang of investigators in her I Can Read titles, Bonsall clearly has kept her "consumer" in mind.

Prior to her work in the beginning-to-read field, Bonsall collaborated on a series of books featuring the photography of Camilla Koffler, who uses the pseudonym Ylla. In works such as *Polar Bear Brothers* (1960), *Look Who's Talking* (1962), and *I'll Show You Cats* (1964), Bonsall created stories that provided a framework for a series of beautiful black-and-white animal photographs. When illustrating her own work, Bonsall used finely detailed, expressive ink drawings to capture her characters' actions. Bonsall relied primarily on black, browns, and grays, adding one or two muted shades, such as green or blue, and let the black line dominate. She used detailed cross-hatching to add dimension or to differentiate skin tones.

Bonsall's entries in the I Can Read series are appropriate for the beginning reader and can be enjoyed as read-aloud stories. Even the simple text of *Mine's the Best* (1973), which features a brief conversation between two young boys about their newly purchased balloons, sparkles with the kind of obvious humor and sight gags that young children love. The background illustrations are particularly effective. As the two boys argue, a procession of young children, all carrying identical balloons, pass by and add their own amusing antics to the scene. *The Day I Had to Play with My Sister* (1972) is equally engaging, as a young boy tries, unsuccessfully, to teach his little sister the finer points of hide-and-seek. Bonsall captured perfectly the interaction between these siblings, especially the sister's inability to follow even the simplest directions. Many young readers with younger siblings of their own will find themselves on familiar ground.

The four young crime fighters featured in Bonsall's many "Case" mysteries also capture the young reader's interest. In the first book, *The Case of the Hungry Stranger* (1963), a defiant "No Girls" sign appears on the boys' clubhouse door. As the boys, led by Wizard, the chief private eye, go about their business of solving difficult crimes—the disappearance of a blueberry pie, a lost pet, and an invisible doorbell ringer—young readers will notice that these detectives could use a little help. In *The Case of the Double Cross* (1980), the boys have joined forces with Marigold and her friends, and the "No Girls" sign has been replaced with a new clubhouse logo that combines *Wizard* and *Marigold* into the *Wizmars.* Bonsall's mysteries are excellent for beginning readers, with intriguing plots and the evidence of boy-girl rivalry that so often appears at this age.

In all Bonsall's books, her conversational style, appealing illustrations, and delightful young characters combine to entertain young readers. ❧ E.H.

Bontemps, Arna

American author, editor, and anthologist, 1902–1973. Through difficult times and into the Second, postsegregation Reconstruction, Arna Bontemps worked to bring African American history and everyday black life into the mainstream of American children's books and the standard school curriculum—with almost no company, for years, save that of his great friend and occasional collaborator, Langston Hughes.

Born in Louisiana, Bontemps grew up in Los Angeles

and in the nonracial Seventh-Day Adventist Church, where his father was a minister. Spared institutional segregation, he was sensitive to other, subtler, potentially more corrosive forms of marginalization. As a boy, Bontemps wondered "why the slave never fought for freedom" and, digging away, he discovered that they had—unbeknownst to the history texts—in Haiti and elsewhere in the Caribbean and in the antebellum South. When he was just short of twelve, he read about the celebration of the centennial of the Battle of New Orleans, "exclusively by white soldiers, white orators, and white schoolchildren," with no recognition of the role of black troops, extravagantly praised by General Andrew Jackson, which he learned about from the black press. In a milieu and a household indifferent to black culture, Bontemps became a bookish rebel with a cause.

At twenty-three Harlem beckoned—a Harlem recently launched, in 1924, on its celebrated Renaissance. Bontemps, who had entrée as a fledgling poet, quickly met Countee Cullen, the latest poetry sensation, and through him met Hughes and other writers and intellectuals. But he was also living a stable, diligent, down-to-earth personal life that set him apart—as a teacher at Harlem Academy, an Adventist high school, and as a husband and a father of the first of an eventual brood of six children. Throughout most of his subsequent career as a writer, Bontemps would have one foot in the big world of black culture, and one in the small world of teaching (or other regular employment), child rearing, and pragmatic child study.

For Bontemps, displaced from Harlem by the Depression—teaching for three unhappy years in Alabama, taking refuge under the paternal roof in Los Angeles, recouping during a Chicago stay, then settling in as librarian at Fisk University (1943–65)—the chief conduit between the two worlds was his buddy Hughes. In a constant flow of correspondence, Bontemps and Hughes swapped literary ideas and publishing tips, discussed joint projects, and proposed one another for assignments. Back from Haiti with the nub of a children's book, it was only natural for Hughes to turn to Bontemps for help in getting it into shape. Set in a pristine, paradisiacal Haiti of naked tykes and soap from trees, *Popo and Fifina, Children of Haiti* (1932) revolves around the delight a small boy and his older sister take in moving from the countryside into town, where carefree days of kite flying on the beach calmly give way to apprenticeship in a woodworking shop and the pride of accomplishment. Disarmingly illustrated by E. Simms Campbell, *Popo and Fifina* met with an appreciative reception.

In their later collaborations, Bontemps and Hughes functioned as coeditors, not coauthors, and Hughes, though the designated literary person of the pair, attempted no further fiction for children. Bontemps, on the other hand, had published one adult novel of black folklife, *God Sends Sunday* (1931), and was only just turning to historical fiction and historical writing, his area of expertise in the division of labor with Hughes. And while writing for children was mainly a welcome source of additional income for Hughes, it was that and more for Bontemps, who saw in children's books a way to let in light and sweep away misconceptions.

In the early 1930s, that called for ending the monopoly of jocose tales like *Epaminondas*. With that view Bontemps wrote a sunny story of a barefoot Southern black farm boy and his "ole, yellow, no-nation" dog, *You Can't Pet a Possum* (1934), which was undone by near caricature illustration; a picaresque yarn about three Alabama boys amid the perils, temptations, and golden opportunities of Harlem, *Sad-Faced Boy* (1937); and the haunting tale of a dreamy young trumpet player, *Lonesome Boy* (1955), that came later and endured. To Bontemps *Lonesome Boy* was "prose in the folk manner," a designation that fits all three works. As such they are akin to Gwendolyn Brooks's stories about Maud Martha and Hughes's famous anecdotes of "My Simple Minded Friend," and unique in American children's literature of the period.

Other Bontemps juvenile projects fell into more conventional categories. But just about everything he did has application elsewhere, as fodder or reinforcement. Two works of adult historical fiction, *Black Thunder* (1936), about the Gabriel Prosser insurrection, and *Drums at Dusk* (1939), about the 1794 Haitian revolt, prepared him to write antebellum African American history, notably *Story of the Negro* (1948), a landmark volume that lays out the truth about the African past and the distortions about slavery.

They Seek a City (1945), written in collaboration with proletarian writer Jack Conroy (and issued in a revised edition in 1966 as *Anyplace But Here*), drew on research into black migration, from DuSable's Chicago trading post to World War II Detroit, that Bontemps and Conroy conducted on the Chicago WPA Federal Writers' Project. That research was also utilized in a Bontemps-Hughes crossover compendium, *The Book of Negro Folklore* (1958), as well as in Bontemps's all-age history, *One Hundred Years of Negro Freedom* (1956), which recreates the immediate gains of Reconstruction and the ensuing setbacks and years of struggle through the interwoven lives of Booker T. Washington and W. E. B. Du Bois and other principals.

From industrial folklore Conroy gathered for the

WPA, Bontemps fashioned three tall tales that appeared under joint authorship: *The Fast Sooner Hound* (1942), a longtime favorite bouncily illustrated by VIRGINIA LEE BURTON, *Slappy Hooper, the Wonderful Sign Painter* (1946), and *Sam Patch, the High, Wide and Handsome Jumper* (1951). To suit the first to children, Bontemps toned down the ending—but, "I expect the truth will out." See B. A. Botkin, *Treasury of American Folklore*, 533–36. The body of black literature, familiar to Bontemps from childhood, furnished him with classics and fresh discoveries for *Golden Slippers* (1941), the first anthology of African American poetry for children.

True stories of triumphing over odds lay to hand. With typical World War II expansiveness, Bontemps wrote *We Have Tomorrow* (1945), profiles of twelve young blacks succeeding at a variety of occupations "as Americans, not as heroes." On the Fisk campus he could not help but be inspired by the Jubilee Singers, subjects of *Chariot in the Sky* (1951).

There was also a call, of course, for individual biographies of noted African Americans. Bontemps's *Story of George Washington Carver* (1954) differs from other early biographies, juvenile and adult, in making less of white encouragement to the budding scientist and more of aid and comfort from the Midwest's scattered blacks. Twice Bontemps directly took on the protean figure of Frederick Douglass. In *Frederick Douglass: Slave, Fighter, Freeman* (1958), a book for younger readers, it is the boy's effort to get an education and the youth's resolve to gain his freedom that hold center stage. *In Free at Last: The Life of Frederick Douglass* (1971), a full-length portrait for teenagers and adults, the focus is justifiably on Douglass the abolitionist.

But Bontemps, who knew his subjects inside out, did not leave off quite there: In *One Hundred Years of Negro Freedom* he takes Douglass through to his controversial remarriage, late in life and long past his heroic prime, to his young white secretary. A fascinating, fine-screened chapter baldly titled "The Second Mrs. Douglass" carries the newlyweds around the British Isles and across the European continent, attended by an odd lot of old admirers, to Egypt and the Great Pyramid, which the aged Douglass, mindful that Egyptians are persons of color by American definition, cannot but climb. "One view of the Sphinx, the River Nile, and the desert was reward enough for three score and ten years of pain and effort."

As African American history by an African American author, Arna Bontemps's books were exceptional in his time. As authoritative history, thoughtfully presented and stirringly dramatized, they are exceptional for any time. ❧ BARBARA BADER

Boston, L. M.

ENGLISH AUTHOR, 1892–1990. Of all the rich crop of midcentury books, Lucy Maria Boston's "Green Knowe" stories are notable for their perfect portrayals of a sense of place. Using her own home in rural England as a model—a place she called a "miracle" to own—Boston set her novels in a twelfth-century manor house beside a river. Its magical grounds include a maze and topiary yew trees representing various animals and a huge, vaguely human figure known as Green Noah.

Boston did not begin writing for children until she was in her sixties, stimulated by her fascination with the history of her ancient house. Using a complex story structure, she intertwined multiple themes seamlessly, allowing her stories to unfold in the dramatic climaxes that characterize her novels. Boston did not moralize. She said of writing: "In a work of art every word . . . has a reference to every other. . . . They interrelate, foreshadow, recall, enlarge, and play all over each other to produce a specific feeling—*not* a moral. . . . A word arbitrarily changed . . . could change a book." Such meticulous attention to words never became an end in itself, however, and never interfered with Boston's sense of story.

Illustration by Peter Boston from *An Enemy at Green Knowe* (1964), by L. M. Boston.

Boston not only respected the written word, she respected her audience, the children. She believed they "react to style with their whole being.... Style has an irresistible authority." She abhorred writing down to children and felt that "the young of the race continue to be born with their hope intact.... I would bring two gifts [to them]—veneration and delight, because you can't have one without the other."

Combining the realistic with the fantastic, Boston never asked readers to believe more than they could believe. The joyousness of the characters and the curiosity of the children in the stories bring the mansion's secrets and history to life and breathe story into its history. In *The Children of Green Knowe* (1954) and *The Chimneys of Green Knowe* (1958), young Toseland, known as Tolly, and old Mrs. Oldknowe experience a time gone by through the lively ghosts of three young children; in *The Stones of Green Knowe* (1976), Roger, the son of the twelfth-century builder of the mansion, slips through time to meet other children living in the mansion in centuries to come; and in *A Stranger at Green Knowe* (1961), a child named Ping, in an entirely realistic though surprising story, meets an escaped gorilla.

Boston's smooth prose is ideal for reading aloud to younger children, and children of all ages respond to the dramatic setting and characters revealed in these stories. Although Boston's own story of finding and meticulously restoring the house may be a miracle, it is her "Green Knowe" stories for children that best preserve the manor and disseminate its history. ❧ J.B.

Boutet de Monvel, Maurice

French painter and illustrator, 1850–1913. Born in Orléans, a place significant for its association with Joan of Arc, the French national heroine, saint of the Catholic Church, and the subject of his masterpiece *Jeanne d'Arc* (Joan of Arc, 1895), Louis Maurice Boutet de Monvel studied at the Ecole des Beaux-Arts in Paris under distinguished artists of his time. His dream had been to paint large canvases depicting dramatic scenes in the academic tradition. By 1878 he had had paintings exhibited at the Salon de Paris and been awarded his first medal.

At about this time, driven by the need to support his family, a chance opportunity to create forty or so pen-drawn vignettes for a history of France began his celebrated career in the field of children's books. He was the illustrator of the French edition of *St. Nicholas,* the famous magazine for boys and girls, and contributed pictures to *Century* and *Scribner's* magazines as well. In 1882 he conceived the idea of illustrating in color a collection of French children's songs. The resulting book, *Vieilles Chansons et Rondes pour les Petits Enfants* (Old songs and rounds for children), published in 1883, was followed in 1884 by *Chansons de France pour les Petits Français* (French songs for little Frenchmen). In 1886 Boutet de Monvel's illustrations for Anatole France's *Nos Enfants* (Our children) verified his genius in portraying the spirit of childhood. Other books for children followed, many of which were translated into English in the early 1900s.

His pictures of children, based on the memory of his earlier keen observations of his own young brothers and sisters at home and at play, charmed the public and were admired for his genius in capturing the moods and expressions of his subject. He was soon sought after to do portraits of the children of leading families in French and international society and continued these two careers simultaneously. At one point he considered giving up book illustration altogether because he was so busy with commissions for portraits. Fortunately for posterity, he continued to illustrate children's books and his magnificent *Jeanne d'Arc* was born.

Boutet de Monvel wrote his own text for the book, but he was neither writer nor historian, and it is his illustrations that live. The epic pictures for his artistic monument bring to mind the sort of dramatic scenes he had set out to paint early in his career, but with a difference. The muted tones and flat look associated with Japanese prints gave a soft and entirely different effect, depicting his feelings for the spirit, the essence of the story and its heroine as translated into a picture book for children. The artist himself described his colors thus: "It is not color really, it is the impression, the suggestion of color." And he expressed his disappointment that in reproduction the softness of the watercolors and the "finesse of the outline is lost." Gerald Gottlieb observes in his introduction to a modern American edition, *Joan of Arc* (1980), that the composition, the stylized backgrounds, and the rich detail of Boutet de Monvel's illustrations are reminiscent of early fifteenth-century illuminated manuscripts.

In 1899 Boutet de Monvel went to the United States to exhibit his portraits, watercolors, and other works. He was commissioned to execute a series of large-scale panels based on his illustrations for *Jeanne d'Arc* for an important room in the house of a prominent and wealthy American. Six panels originally planned for Joan of Arc's memorial chapel in Domremy are now preserved in the Corcoran Gallery in Washington, D.C.

The name Maurice Boutet de Monvel is preserved as well. His warm and sensitive style places him alongside

Without alerting Joan, the French had attacked the English bastion of Saint-Loup. The attack failed; the French were retreating in disorder. Joan rushed up, rallied them, and led them once more to the very foot of the bastion. The English, under their commander Talbot, fought back desperately for three hours, but despite their resistance the French overcame them and captured the bastion.

Illustration by Maurice Boutet de Monvel from his book *Joan of Arc* (1896).

England's RANDOLPH CALDECOTT and KATE GREENAWAY as a major figure in the nineteenth century's Golden Age of children's book illustration. ❦ S.L.R.

BOYLSTON, HELEN DORE

AMERICAN AUTHOR, 1895–1984. Helen Boylston's works are credited as among those that first defined the young adult category. Boylston's career novels include the "Sue Barton" and the "Carol Page" series, which depict the lives of young career women in, respectively, nursing and the theater.

The medical background mirrors Boylston's own working life before she started writing professionally. The daughter of a New Hampshire dentist, she graduated from Massachusetts General Hospital's nursing school at the age of twenty. Her positions varied from that of anesthetist to psychiatric care nurse. During World War I, Boylston served with the Harvard Unit assigned to assist the British army and was a nurse in field hospitals in France until the Armistice in 1918. Following the war, Boylston continued her medical career by working with the American Red Cross in Poland, Italy, Germany, Russia, and Albania. For two years she lived with author Rose Wilder Lane (daughter of LAURA INGALLS WILDER) in Albania and later lived with the Wilder family on their Mansfield, Missouri, farm.

It was at Lane's insistence that Boylston published her first book, *"Sister": The War Diary of a Nurse* (1927). Boylston worked periodically as a teaching and practicing nurse while continuing to write for a variety of magazines, including *McCall's*, *The Country Gentleman*, *The Atlantic Monthly*, and *Harper's*. In 1936 she launched the first of her vocational novels with *Sue Barton, Student Nurse*. Critics and readers found the book authentically based on medical practice and free of sentimentality. It was followed by *Sue Barton, Senior Nurse* (1937), *Sue Barton, Visiting Nurse* (1938), *Sue Barton, Rural Nurse* (1939), and *Sue Barton, Superintendent of Nurses* (1940).

In 1941 Boylston turned from medicine to the theater

as the setting for her books, researching theatrical life by observing backstage action at Eva Le Gallienne's Civic Repertory Theatre in New York City. The first of the four "Carol" books was *Carol Goes Backstage* (1941). It was followed by *Carol Plays Summer Stock* (1942) and two additional volumes that made theatrical life seem a realistic and attainable goal for teenage girls. Boylston collaborated on some of the "Sue" and "Carol" books with Jane Cobb Berry.

The "Sue Barton" books in particular enjoyed great popularity and remained vibrant until the notion of working women in America had become the norm rather than the exception. Boylston's novels are historically significant for having provided role models to girls in the 1930s, 1940s, and 1950s who wished to pursue careers. Boylston once again drew upon her own nursing background to write the biography *Clara Barton, Founder of the American Red Cross* (1955) for the Random House "Landmark" series. A journal of her years in Europe, written with Rose Wilder Lane, was published as *Travels with Zenobia: Paris to Albania by Model T Ford* (1983). ❧ W.A.

Brady, Irene

AMERICAN AUTHOR AND ILLUSTRATOR, B. 1943. Irene Brady is a respected botanist and paleontological illustrator. An ardent conservationist, Brady has, she says, a respect and love for "the beauty, perfection and rightness of nearly all things in their natural state." Brady was born in Ontario, Oregon, and spent her childhood at a farm near Caldwell, Idaho, where she developed an interest in all sorts of creatures. She graduated from the Oregon College of Art in 1975. In addition to her books for children, Brady has been a regular contributor of art and text to *Audubon* magazine and *Ranger Rick,* the nature magazine for young people. Confessing that she is primarily an "arts and crafter," she prefers illustrating to writing, which she finds difficult. Brady nonetheless communicates volumes in her intricately detailed, lifelike illustrations. She feels that illustrators have a special responsibility and maintains that "the best illustrations tell more than the text and may stay with the reader far longer than mere words."

One of Brady's most celebrated books is *Wild Mouse* (1976), named the Outstanding Science Book for Children and awarded the New York Academy of Sciences Children's Science Book Award. *Wild Mouse* is a simple, accessible diary of the birth and development of three mice born to a field mouse in Brady's home. The soft, sepia-toned drawings provide a warm and humorous minute-by-minute account of the babies' birth and progress. In *Beaver Year* (1976), soft, luminous, black-and-white drawings depict the usually unseen underwater world of a beaver family. This realistic piece of fiction finds the beavers engaging in amusing antics, often gazing or peeking from the page at the reader. While the overall tone is lighthearted, danger approaches in the form of a flood, and the terrified expressions of the young beavers as they rush to safety is remarkably moving. Brady's novel for young horse-lovers, *Doodlebug* (1977), is the story of the transformation of a scraggly, mistreated colt into a proud horse through a young girl's loving care.

Brady has also contributed her considerable skill to books by others. Both *Gorilla* (1984) and *Lili: A Giant Panda of Sichuan* (1988) by Robert M. McClung are fictionalized accounts of conservationists' attempts to save endangered species. Both contain the same realistic, almost photographic quality of illustration, and the quiet, expressive beauty of the animals portrayed. *Peeping in the Shell: A Whooping Crane Is Hatched* (1986) by Faith McNulty is yet another example of Brady's graceful technique, as she illustrates the birth of a chick who was incubated in captivity in an effort to save the species. Perhaps the most masterful example of Brady's expertise is *Living Treasure: Saving Earth's Threatened Biodiversity* (1991) by LAURENCE PRINGLE. Brady's representations of varied aspects of nature, from birds to bugs to marine life, is the perfect accompaniment to Pringle's informative, important text. Each of these four books contains a valuable index filled with helpful recommendations for further exploration and information. ❧ M.O'D.H.

Brandywine School

At his studio in the Brandywine Valley of southeastern Pennsylvania and northern Delaware, and previously in Philadelphia, HOWARD PYLE instructed and inspired a generation of notably successful illustrators who spread his influence through their own artwork and teaching. As a champion of American illustration, a believer in illustration as art, and an artist of analytical bent, Pyle had a natural calling to teach—to transmit principles as well as skills and techniques. For six years (1894–1900) he conducted large, heterogeneous classes at Philadelphia's Drexel Institute, chafing at the dullards but giving abundantly to the gifted few. MAXFIELD PARRISH, already a rising star, needed little help from Pyle. JESSIE WILLCOX SMITH and Elizabeth Shippen Green blossomed under his tutelage, adopting a softer version of

Pyle's strong outlines and broad color areas; he in turn identified and encouraged their individual aptitudes, and through his many publishing contacts arranged congenial book and magazine assignments for them. Smith, Green, and other "Brandywine women"—among them Alice Barber Stephens and Ethel Franklin Betts—were soon mainstays of children's book illustration. In 1900, with two successful summer-school ventures behind him, Pyle left Drexel to devote himself to students of similar promise.

The informal Howard Pyle School of Art was held in the summertime at a rustic Colonial enclave along the Brandywine River near Chadds Ford, Pennsylvania, where Revolutionary War history was made; winters, the students had studio and living quarters near the Pyle home in Wilmington. There was no tuition; students contributed toward school expenses and paid for their own low-cost room and board. Applicants' work had to pass rigorous scrutiny, and so did their character and motivation; Pyle wanted only the best qualified and most committed, who would graduate to full-time illustration within a year. And they came—from Drexel, a nucleus that included Frank Schoonover and Stanley Arthurs; from Pittsburgh and the University of Pennsylvania, Thornton Oakley; from South Dakota and the Chicago Art Institute, Harvey Dunn; from Needham, Massachusetts, and various Boston art schools, N. C. WYETH, the most famous of Pyle's pupils. Wyeth, in his letters, also left the fullest record of life-with-Pyle: the towering yet attentive presence of the Master; the glorious days outdoors, the student hijinks, the stellar occasions and festive celebrations, the hard work, the breakthroughs. In its original, ideal state the school lasted only through the summer of 1903; thereafter Pyle, turned fifty, cut back. But Wyeth and some of the other graduates stayed around to work with Pyle, and a corps of experienced professionals set up studios nearby to benefit from his instruction and comment.

The heart of Pyle's teaching was *dramatization*—"Project your mind into your subject until you actually live in it. Throw your heart into the picture and then jump in after it." Analogously, concretize: "Make real things, real surroundings, real backgrounds. A tone for background will not do." At Friday evening classes Pyle scrutinized and discussed student compositions; each Saturday evening the members of the class had an hour to interpret a given abstract theme—typically, "Consolation, the Fugitives, or Rebellion," reports Brandywine historian and heir Henry Pitz.

Pyle and his followers are best described as romantic realists, in contradistinction to artists working in the decorative Arts-and-Crafts and Art Nouveau modes then dominant internationally in the graphic arts. Romantic realism suited the scenes from the American past that were a Brandywine specialty, creating images of heroism and nobility that, given a documentary gloss by accurate detail, entered the American consciousness as historical fact.

Four-color process reproduction, part of the publication boom responsible for disseminating Brandywine imagery in calendars, advertisements, and color prints, permitted book illustrations to be full-color paintings. New, uniform editions of children's CLASSICS quickly appeared, the first and foremost of which, Scribner Illustrated Classics, was virtually a Brandywine fiefdom. Who, once exposed, can forget N. C. Wyeth's *Treasure Island* (1911) or Jessie Willcox Smith's *Child's Garden of Verses* (1905)?

Brandywine luster faded at mid-century under the manifold impact of modernism, though illustration courses kept the Pyle teaching-model alive. In the late 1980s, however, a countertrend set in. Many of the Scribner Illustrated Classics have been reprinted in facsimile editions; the original oils and watercolors of famous illustrations are proudly exhibited in museums; the Brandywine style, root and branch, has gained new adherents. ❧ BARBARA BADER

BRANLEY, FRANKLYN M.

AMERICAN AUTHOR AND EDITOR, B. 1915. A firm believer in exposing even preschool children to the excitement of science, Franklyn M. Branley aimed to get them interested before they became "cynical sophisticates — say twelve years old."

Born in New Rochelle, New York, he received his early education in an old-time country school complete with double desks, water pail, and potbelly stove. When he began his career in the New York State elementary school system in 1936, teaching science to younger people was a novel idea. Few course materials existed, and most instructors did not bother to teach it at all. As a result, Branley coauthored a pamphlet detailing methods for teaching science to primary school students. Besides filling a need in the curriculum, it launched his writing career as a contributor to many professional and children's magazines. His works, generally well received by the critics, includes over one hundred books plus numerous periodical articles.

Branley's writing style is simple but not simplistic. In his books he strives to give a thorough understanding of scientific theory and often suggests hands-on experiments to illustrate points. Readers can perform the experiments or merely follow the detailed instructions of each experiment; either way they gain valuable scientific information, and the books generate enthusiasm and discovery, not just routine learning.

Between 1947 and 1957, Branley and Frederick Beeler coauthored nine "Experiment" series books, exploring topics such as light, electricity, optical illusion, chemistry, airplane instruction, atomics, and microscopes. Their motto was "Try it and see for yourself," and many of the experiments could be performed using items easily found in most homes.

In 1956 Branley became an associate astronomer and director of the renowned American Museum of Natural History, Hayden Planetarium, in New York City. During this period he focused more in his writing on astronomy, the nature of the universe, and space travel. His work had always been timely, but never more so than when the United States and the U.S.S.R. were engaged in the cold war, and each was struggling to be the first in space. *Exploring by Satellite* (1957) was published one day after the U.S.S.R. launched *Sputnik* on October 4, 1957.

Branley is also the founder and coeditor of the long-running "Let's Read and Find Out" series, which began in the sixties and targets young children just starting to read. Still true to his original hypothesis, Branley says of the series, "Young children have the openmindedness to make errors, the spirit of inquiry, the courage to take a challenge—attitudes that are requisites to solid scientific investigation."

A longtime member of the American Astronomical Society, he is also the recipient of many literary awards, including the Edison Award for the outstanding child science book of 1961, *Experiments in Sky Watching*.

Branley will be best remembered as one of the first writers to recognize and fill the need for accurate and interesting scientific reading material for all ages. ❧

S.M.M.

Brenner, Anita

Mexican-born American author, 1905–1974. Mexico's contributions to American children's books have been diverse and complex—and not to be measured in numbers, as in the case of Anita Brenner. The Mexican Revolution of 1910 gave rise to the Mexican Renaissance of the 1920s, a modern affirmation of the nation's mixed Spanish-Indian heritage, nowhere better portrayed than in *Idols Behind Altars* (1929) by a Mexican-born and -domiciled American, Anita Brenner, and significantly advanced by a French-born artist, Jean Charlot, both of whom had a deep interest in Mexican folkways and a commitment to Mexican popular values, to the ungilded and unmaterialistic, that had issue in a collaborative work for children, *The Boy Who Could Do Anything and Other Mexican Folk Tales* (1942).

As a collection of tales, Mexican or not, the book is unusual in virtually every respect. Selections are not, in the ordinary sense, representative—not a roundup from all over Mexico, not an exhibit of the most popular or widely known stories. What the collection does represent, in common with adult field collections, is the lore of a particular area at a certain period, tales actually told by local storytellers. Brenner's informant, we learn, was an Indian woman named Luz, who told the "best stories" in the town of Milpa Alta.

Because this is Mexico and Milpa Alta is close to its historical heart, the tales range from Aztec and post-Conquest legends to formula tales (with worldwide analogues) and local anecdotes, from tales of black and white magic to numskull yarns. The stories are not strictly authentic, however, in the sense that they are "retold." But retold with a difference: Brenner, a natural storyteller at home in the Mexican vernacular, has not merely adapted the selections for a young audience, she has assimilated them to childhood. Thus, "The Boy Who Could Do Anything," subject of a group of stories and a transient presence elsewhere, is none other than the mighty Tepozton, lord of the mountain bearing his name, as a wee Moses at nature's mercy, then as a boy with magic powers that he clearly relishes wielding or withholding. He can be defiantly, provocatively cryptic: "I have to go and see how many different colors my white flowers are." He can be tauntingly, teasingly elusive: "How can I be Tepozton if I am Chuco?"

Life is often harsh, the rich are sometimes merciless. Yet there is ever-present an underlying sweetness of nature, an inherent goodness. Folk tales, however romantic or harrowing, seldom touch the heart as these do, especially in the black-and-white magic cycle that begins with "The Cow That Cried"—in which Florencio's solitary neighbor Margarita, bewitched and condemned to the stockyard by a mercenary priest, cries for herself because she has no one to cry for her—and ends with the downfall of the priest and the de-witchment of the cattle people by Chuco-who-might-be-Tepozton. Meanwhile, the skeptic Florencio, spellbound by the same priest and consigned to the bullring, provides a nest egg for his faithful wife—he performing as the fiercest bull, she winning the prize for best bullfighter.

Charlot, as comfortable among the living dead as Mexicans generally and old Mexico hands, depicts these goings-on with his customary combination of clear definition, subtle contouring, and ingenious composition. A second Brenner-Charlot collaboration, *A Hero by Mistake* (1953), is equally felicitous on a smaller scale—in text, typography, illustrations, and layout it is one of the most engaging small volumes extant. *The Timid Ghost* (1966), another good story, is a somewhat more elaborate, less cohesive entity; *Dumb Juan and the Bandits* (1957) is a tale from *The Boy Who Could Do Anything* illustrated in Charlot's later, brusque manner.

What Brenner and Charlot together wrought, in fidelity to the Mexican spirit, to its shifting forms and high color, could well be regarded in any case as an end product of the Renaissance and an export product of particular integrity. ❧ B.B.

Brett, Jan

American illustrator, b. 1949. A book illustrated by Jan Brett is many things: vivid, rich, lavish; filled with attention to detail; often humorous. Indeed, each page created by this artist is so lush with colorful objects, large and small, that it tells an entertaining story by itself. Born and raised in Massachusetts, Brett makes an annual summer pilgrimage with her family to a cabin in the Berkshire Mountains of western Massachusetts, where her husband plays in the Boston Symphony at Tanglewood and she finds inspiration for her children's books. Using no models, she designs her intricate pages from memory, recalling objects from her past and transferring them to paint on paper.

The majority of Brett's most successful picture books find their subjects in folklore, whether traditional or modern. Those she writes herself are based on established motifs, such as holiday stories, animal tales, or fantasy, and often employ a cumulative structure. Brett's adaptation of the Ukrainian folktale *The Mitten* (1990) is perhaps the best example of this format. Using an elaborate series of borders, the artist frames the action detailed in the text with small pictures suggesting both a simultaneous and a future event, a foreshadowing that provides the child observer with a delicious sense of anticipation. Brett plays similar artistic games in her rendition of Lear's *The Owl and the Pussycat* (1991), where a pair of fish carry on their own courtship in the waves under the pea-green boat.

Illustration by Jan Brett from *The Twelve Days of Christmas* (1986).

Voices of the Creators

Jan Brett

If I could go back in time to my kindergarten class and have someone ask me what I wanted to be when I grew up, I would have answered, "Children's book illustrator." I knew the word *illustrator* in kindergarten because of my uncle, Harold Brett. Uncle Harold was a well-known illustrator. I met him when he came to visit us and worked on portraits of the children in our family. My sister Sophie and I loved to look at the book and magazine illustrations which he had created.

I was very shy in school and had difficulty saying what I meant. Happily, when it came time to draw, everything came out right. Drawing was a way I could express my thoughts. I don't know if I first decided to be a children's book illustrator, and then tried to shape my drawings to fit this image, or if people noticed my drawings and told me that I should be an illustrator. With my drawings I'd get encouragement from adults and acceptance from my classmates. Even now, I'm best able to express myself in my artwork.

My mom thought that we should have unlimited crayons, lots of time to draw, and no art lessons. I spent hours and hours drawing imaginary stories. The fun of having a picture unfold was my best entertainment. I first noticed this at school. The art teacher was out for the day, and our substitute teacher gave us each a huge sheet of Manila paper with new boxes of crayons and said, "You have one hour to draw anything you want." At the time, I desperately wanted to go to see the circus. I started in one corner of the Manila paper and drew tigers, lions, horses, costumes, cotton candy, and the bright birds on sticks that hawkers sell. The paper was only about one-third filled when the teacher said that time was finished. I couldn't believe that the hour was over. It seemed like five minutes. Later, when our family did go to the circus, the experience gave me even more ideas, which I used in my next circus picture. Drawing the pictures became more fun than actually going to the circus.

The curious thing about all of this is that, emotionally, I feel an allegiance to a child's point of view. When I'm drawing, it's for Jan Brett, age six. Children are absorbent and complex. Their emotions are as strongly held as adults', and their minds don't always follow the well-worn paths that we expect. Because young children are just learning to read, the writing in picture books is basic. But the ideas that make up the books do not have to be simple. The pictures help release the information in the story; they are the place where the story is unlocked.

As a child, I remember reaching for a book, pulling it from the shelf, and opening it. Inside could be better than real, better than dreams. I was forever grateful when the pictures made the story leap to another reality. I promised myself to remember and to try hard to make my books create this jump.

When I work now, I remember my feelings as a child, and I recognize those feelings when a drawing takes off. There is something about the way a picture will take on a life of its own that will always be mysterious and fascinating. I love to draw and to watch my artwork grow into something that creates its own world.

While always maintaining the same recognizable style of illustration, Brett remains true to each story's individual traits, such as nationality, class, time period, and character. She is known in particular for her illustrations of Scandinavian characters and settings. For her fairy tales she carefully clothes her subjects in an accurate rendition of traditional folk costume, often including jewelry, braid, embroidery, lace, feathers, and other finery when appropriate. Dramatic backgrounds filled with tapestries, variegated outdoor landscapes, and complex architectural structures frequently reflect a specific setting or theme, but fade at moments of high drama in favor of close-ups or silhouettes.

Brett has met with occasional criticism from those reviewers who embrace a "less is more" artistic philosophy; her illustrations fall under the category of realism, and, indeed, they leave little to the imagination. Brett is seen as less gifted with words than with pictures, and her adaptations of folktales and her illustrations for books by other authors are generally considered to be the most successful of her works. Praise for her own writing, however, has been just as frequent as criticism. *The Mitten,* Brett's finest book, was named one of *Booklist*'s Best Books for the 1980s, and a number of other works have received similar, well-deserved acclaim.

C.C.B.

Bridgers, Sue Ellen

American author, b. 1942. Sue Ellen Bridgers knew nothing about the young adult field when she submitted a manuscript about a migrant family to *Redbook* magazine, yet this submission eventually resulted in the publication of her first young adult novel and established Bridgers as one of the leading authors in that field.

Born Sue Ellen Hunsucker, the author was raised in a neighborhood filled with relatives in the tobacco-farming town of Winterville, North Carolina. These strong family ties are evident in her novels, as is the rural, small-town atmosphere in which the whole community seems to be an extended family. Bridgers's family was filled with storytellers in the Southern tradition, and she grew up absorbing their tales. Bridgers had always wanted to be a writer and had several poems published in the local newspaper. She was associate editor of the literary magazine at East Carolina State College but left school in her junior year to marry Ben Bridgers. After living in Mississippi and South Dakota, they returned to North Carolina, where Bridgers, the mother of three, began publishing stories in literary and women's magazines. She also returned to college, obtaining a degree from Western Carolina University.

During this time, Bridgers wrote "Home Before Dark" and submitted it to *Redbook*, whose editor urged her to try for book publication. Bridgers was surprised in 1976, when Knopf decided to publish the manuscript as a young adult title because she had not written the novel for young readers. This story of a migrant family settling in North Carolina centers on fifteen-year-old Stella, who longs for a permanent home. Although some of Stella's observations and thoughts seem preternaturally adult, she always remains a strong protagonist, and Bridgers does an excellent job of authentically conveying the North Carolina locale. Occasionally, the adult origins of the material intrude upon the story, but the author's gift for language and storytelling is apparent on every page, and each subsequent novel has further enhanced her reputation as one of the finest literary stylists in the field.

Young adult books typically focus on a single protagonist, but Bridgers's novels are unconventional in their use of shifting viewpoint. *All Together Now* (1979) skillfully interpolates the stories of eight major characters, frequently changing focus from one to another. Twelve-year-old Casey is at the heart of the novel, but much time is spent detailing the courtship and marriage of a middle-aged couple. Bridgers consistently uses her gift for characterization to adroitly limn characters outside the usual sphere of young adult literature. *Notes for Another Life* (1981), like many of Bridgers's novels, concerns teenagers separated from their mother. Harrowing, yet life-affirming, the book examines the relationship of siblings Kevin and Wren, whose father suffers from a debilitating mental illness. Once again, older characters, here a grandmother and a kindhearted minister, provide strength and sustenance to the teens. *Sara Will* (1985), a leisurely paced novel about a middle-aged woman, was not published for teens but nevertheless was selected as an American Library Association Best Book for Young Adults, as were all Bridgers's previous novels; the paperback edition was marketed for a teenage audience. Two more young adult novels, *Keeping Christina* (1993) and *Permanent Connections* (1987), focus on troubled relationships and are written in the author's inimitable style: clear, character-driven, and ultimately concerned with the connections between individuals that every Bridgers book so artfully explores. P.D.S.

Bridwell, Norman

American author and illustrator, b. 1928. *Clifford, the Big Red Dog* first appeared as an unpretentious paperback in 1962, but grew into an extremely popular series of books for preschool readers. Clifford's creator, Norman Bridwell, was born in Kokomo, Indiana, and educated at the John Herron Art Institute and Cooper Union Art School. He worked for a filmstrip company, designed fabrics, and was a freelance artist before publishing his first book.

Clifford, the Big Red Dog is narrated by Emily Elizabeth, a little girl whose pet is so large that he bathes in swimming pools and lives in a doghouse that dwarfs his owners' home. Despite the bland writing and cartoonlike red-and-black illustrations, children were enchanted by this oversized, good-natured, but sometimes clumsy canine; further volumes include *Clifford Gets a Job* (1965), *Clifford's Halloween* (1966), and *Clifford's Tricks* (1969). Bridwell has published a series about a young witch, including *The Witch Next Door* (1965) and *The Witch's Vacation* (1973), and a few individual titles such as *Kangaroo Stew* (1979), but he is best known for the Clifford books, which later included pop-up editions and such nonstory items as *Clifford's Sticker Book* (1984). When Clifford graduated to hardcover in the 1980s, some of the earlier volumes were reissued with full-color illustrations. A series of BOARD BOOKS, "Clifford, the Small Red Puppy," concerns the dog's early years and includes *Clifford's Animal Sounds* (1991) and *Clifford Counts Bubbles* (1992).

From a critical perspective, Bridwell's contributions to children's literature appear slight. Yet the books are undeniably popular with beginning readers, who appreciate the antics of Emily Elizabeth's dog and who may use the stories as steppingstones to more challenging, rewarding reading. ❧ P.D.S.

Briggs, Raymond

English author and illustrator, b. 1934. Raymond Briggs has been providing comic joy for young readers since he first began his career in book illustration in the early 1960s. Children laugh out loud at his balding, grumpy Father Christmas, his nearsighted, stubble-faced giants, and a host of other traditional characters he has brought to life in anthologies of nursery rhymes and fairy tales.

Among his early works are two brief collections, *Ring-a-Ring o' Roses* (1962) and *Fee Fi Fo Fum* (1964), which received a commendation for the Kate Greenaway Medal. These were followed by *The Mother Goose Treasury* (1966), which won the Medal. This collection of over four hundred nursery rhymes includes almost nine hundred of Briggs's drawings and paintings. What makes the illustrations in all three books unique is Briggs's irreverent attitude. Rather than use the pastel

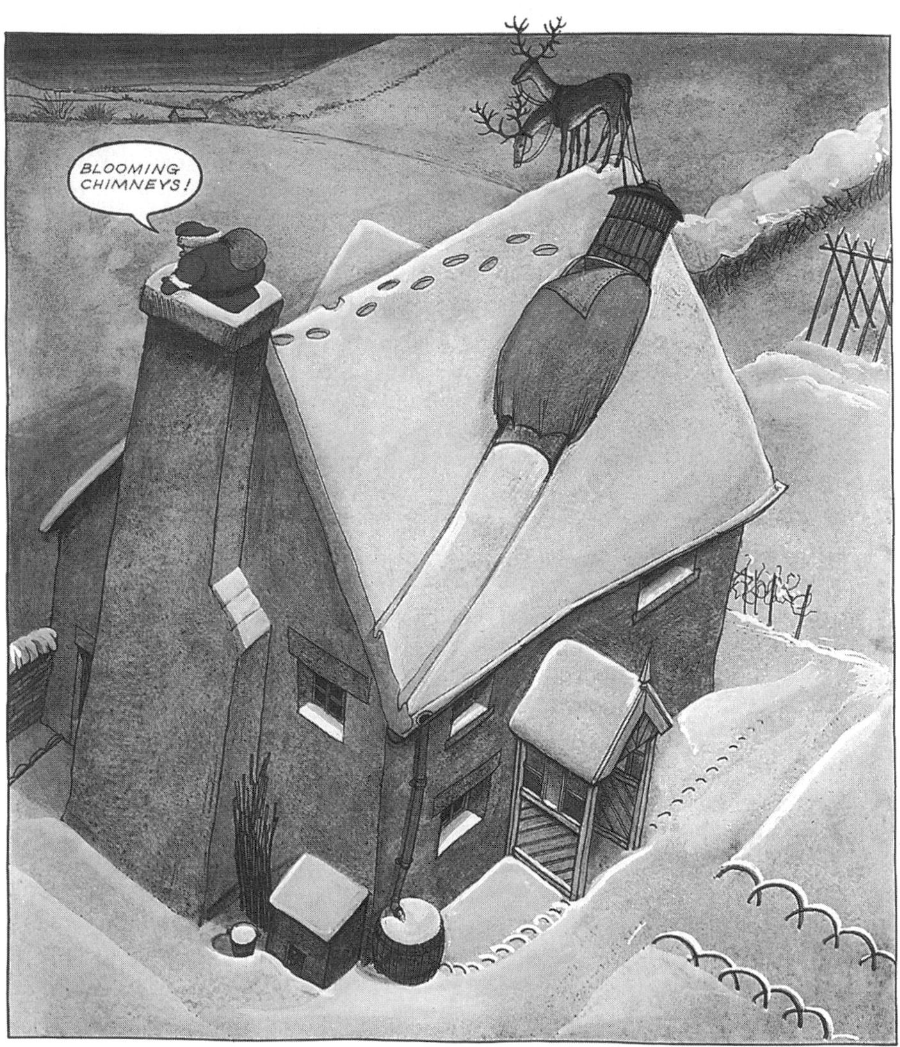

Illustration by Raymond Briggs from his book *Father Christmas* (1973).

colors and romantic treatments of earlier nursery rhyme collections, Briggs employs contemporary settings and comic, working-class characters. His plump MOTHER GOOSE has a prominent chin, a perpetual grin, and sensible shoes, and many of his characters wear rough clothes, day-old beards, and bemused expressions. The red-cheeked, redheaded giant featured in *Treasury* foreshadows the giant in his later work, *Jim and the Beanstalk* (1970). With this book Briggs came into his own as an author as well as an illustrator of children's books. This fractured tale of a giant who needs love and understanding, glasses, a wig, and false teeth appeals to young readers who wish that they, like Jim, could rescue a giant.

Another sassy, original tale, *Father Christmas,* was published in 1973 and received the Kate Greenaway Medal. While some adults were shocked at Briggs's portrayal of Santa, who punctuates almost every sentence with the word "blooming," many were delighted by the down-to-earth story, which features comic-book frames and dialogue bubbles. Briggs has said that Father Christmas's job was probably much like his father's job as a milkman, with all the early-morning deliveries. He has created a working-class Father Christmas who does not dislike his work but goes about it with a certain grouchy style. In a sequel, *Father Christmas Goes on Holiday* (1975), Father Christmas gets fed up with the cold North Pole and takes off to visit warmer climes in a caravan flown by his reindeer.

Two of Briggs's books use a similar comic-book format but appeal to older readers. *Fungus the Bogeyman* (1977) features clever language and is set in the green-and-brown slimy underground world of the bogeys. *When the Wind Blows* (1982) is Briggs's darkest work and reflects his involvement in the British Campaign for Nuclear Disarmament. Here, he tells the story of a working-class couple who don't believe that nuclear war is possible and quietly die of radiation sickness after a nuclear explosion. This book, which Briggs has rewritten for radio, the stage, and an animated film, has deeply affected young adult readers, who come to it expecting a cartoon and find themselves moved by its message. Perhaps Briggs's best-known book is *The Snowman* (1978), a wordless picture book that features soft watercolor paintings rather than the pen-and-ink outlines and bright colors of his earlier books. In this gentle story, a boy's snowman comes to vivid life for one long blissful night of fun, but the boy awakes to find him melted and gone in the morning. The book, which features the author's own house and garden, has a bittersweet quality missing from his earlier works.

Briggs has said that he doesn't necessarily write and illustrate books for children, he writes and draws to please himself. In pleasing himself Briggs uses sly humor and serious themes, twitting the world and beliefs of adults to the delight of children of all ages. ❧

B.C.

BRINK, CAROL RYRIE

AMERICAN AUTHOR, 1895–1981. "A lonely or unhappy childhood may be the greatest blessing for a writer," wrote Carol Ryrie Brink. Born in Moscow, Idaho, and orphaned by the age of eight, Carol, an only child, was raised by a maiden aunt and her maternal grandmother. Young Carol Ryrie learned to assuage her loneliness by creating her own amusements: "reading, writing, drawing, making things with my own hands." She formed a strong emotional bond with her grandmother, Caddie Woodhouse, "whose tales of her childhood in Wisconsin gave a lonely little girl many happy hours." Had she not done so, *Caddie Woodlawn,* the Newbery classic based on her grandmother's recollections, may well have never been written.

Carol Brink thought that a good writer should draw heavily from his or her own stockpile of personal experiences, "to begin laying up riches in childhood and never to cease learning and experiencing and storing away, so that the older the writer becomes the richer the hidden mine will be." Although she wrote numerous short stories, articles, plays, poems, and adult novels, it is her sixteen children's novels, inspired by her own child within, which best demonstrate her talent for characterization, her detailed sense of place, her humor, and her adventurous attitude toward life. In her novel, *Two Are Better Than One* (1968), she, herself, is the model for the protagonist, Chrystal Reese Banks, a girl growing up at the turn of the century in a small university town. The author's husband, Raymond, a mathematics professor, makes an appearance as the young Mr. Banks, a college instructor boarding at Grandmother Reese's house. In *Family Grandstand* (1952) and *Family Sabbatical* (1956), she chronicles the adventures of the Ridgeway children. Their mother is a mystery writer, and their father is a professor at the local university, mirroring the author's own family life as an aspiring writer and mother of two.

The Brink family often summered at a family cottage in northern Wisconsin, and it is there that Carol Brink gained firsthand knowledge of the vast Wisconsin backwoods, information that would prove to be of great value to her in re-creating her grandmother's childhood for *Caddie Woodlawn.* Carol Ryrie Brink dearly loved her grandmother's tales detailing the adventures of the many Woodhouse children: "I said to myself, if I loved them so much, perhaps other children would like them, too." *Caddie Woodlawn* (1935), Brink's second book, was given the Newbery Medal in 1936. In it, eleven-year-old Caddie, red-headed and spunky, is encouraged by her father to "run wild with the boys," embracing life on the Wisconsin frontier in 1864. With her brothers, Tom and Warren, Caddie embarks on a series of adventures. She explores the banks and waters of the Menomonie River, hunts with her visiting uncle, challenges the school bully, and, boldly pushing through ignorant prejudice, rides into the night to warn her Native American friends of impending danger. Like Louisa May Alcott's Jo March, Caddie Woodlawn is a spirited heroine whose courage and humanity young people can both recognize and admire.

Baby Island (1937), *Two Are Better Than One* (1968), *Louly* (1974), and *Magical Melons* (1944), which details additional adventures of the Woodlawn clan, still interest readers. However, it is *Caddie Woodlawn,* with its rich period detail and keenly drawn characters, that has become a favorite in children's literature. Readers of all ages, especially fans of LAURA INGALLS WILDER'S *Little House* series, are captivated by *Caddie Woodlawn.* It is Carol Ryrie Brink at her finest. ❧ M.B.B.

British Children's Books to World War II

The great strength of British children's books is in fantasy and nonsense, which, ironically, authority long tried to suppress. Responsible public opinion was strong against such irrational folly in the eighteenth century, and in the two centuries before, preachers and moralists denounced what one writer in 1577 called "fayned fables, vayne fantasyes, and wanton stories." These were associated with the bad old days before the Protestant movement led the church in England away from Rome. The precious gift of literacy must never be squandered thus but used to read the Bible and catechism.

But the English are a conservative and obstinate race, with much resistance to what is said in pulpits, and they clung to such medieval romances as *Guy of Warwick, Sir Bevis of Hampton, Valentine and Orson, Fortunatus,* and *Reynard the Fox* with such tenacity that chapbook versions were still being sold well into the nineteenth century. These works had been enjoyed in literary circles four centuries before, but latterly had been relegated to the poor and ignorant, and to children. In them readers might read of chivalrous knights, heroic exploits, fights with giants, dragons, and monsters, talking animals, magic, courtship, and love. Authority condemned them all as subversive and corrupting.

The stories nevertheless were cherished, especially by children. Many poets and writers, Wordsworth and Coleridge among them, singled out chapbook versions of these ancient tales, and the fairy tales which came later, as their favorite childhood reading. Even Bunyan, who groaned over his youthful addiction to such reading as "George on Horseback and Bevis of Southampton" showed in *The Pilgrim's Progress* (1678) how strongly he had been influenced by them.

For centuries ballads were an important part of popular culture. They also told stories, sometimes of folk heroes like ROBIN HOOD, sometimes of battles and historical events. Often they were love stories, which might be crude like the original version of "Where are you going to, my pretty maid?" or comic like "A Frog he would a-wooing go," or tragic like "The Children in the Wood." Abhorred by the Puritan divines, they were nevertheless kept alive by oral tradition, and many fragments from them, wrenched out of context and therefore sounding nonsensical or tantalizingly mysterious, have become incorporated into the nursery of MOTHER GOOSE rhymes, which have had so much influence on British writers and poets.

The first collection of these to have survived, *Tommy Thumb's Pretty Song Book,* was published in London in 1744. Up till then nobody had thought it worthwhile to print them, nor had there been much attempt to provide children with recreational literature of their own. Ever since the dawn of printing in the 1470s there had been schoolbooks, and among Caxton's publications were works of universal appeal such as *Le Morte d'Arthur, The Canterbury Tales,* and *Reynard the Fox.*

Caxton had also published a translation of *Aesop's Fables,* which were the only secular stories considered proper for children—but normally read in Latin, at school. The puritans in the seventeenth century had begun shaping religious books for the needs of the younger readers, who had hitherto been expected to move from their ABC straight to the Bible, and then to the same theological manuals as their elders. But though the books designed to teach small children to read became markedly lighter in tone from the 1690s onward, there was no easy reading available to follow. In the absence of milk-and-water items, children enjoyed the strong ale of *The Pilgrim's Progress, Robinson Crusoe* (1719), and *Gulliver's Travels* (1726) quite as much as adult readers.

Thomas Boreman (fl. 1730–40) seems to have been the first English bookseller to specialize in children's books. But he operated in a very small way, and it was John Newbery who was the first to make a commercial success of them. Though he published little of lasting literary merit, Newbery showed others the possibilities in the juvenile book market. One of his better-known titles was *The History of Little Goody Two-Shoes* (1765). This tale of a female Dick Whittington—an orphan who by her initiative, good sense, and good conduct achieves high rank and riches—was enormously popular and, cut down to sixteen pages or less, survived in chapbook form for a hundred years. Many of Newbery's publications were instructional, and the dominant characteristics of his books to amuse were boisterous jollity combined with much advice on how to achieve worldly success through good behavior.

Of imaginative stories there were very few. Responsible parents in the eighteenth century thought little of giving their children fairy stories. These, like the old romantic tales, were associated with the ignorant. Stories from the *Arabian Nights* like Sinbad, Aladdin, and Ali Baba had been circulating in chapbook form from about 1706, and PERRAULT's *Histories, or tales of past times,* with its stories of Little Red Riding Hood, Bluebeard, Puss in Boots, Sleeping Beauty, and Cinderella, published in France in 1697, had been translated into English in 1729. But these tales were as abhorrent to the eighteenth-century guardians of children's morals as the ancient romances had been to their predecessors. Some deplored them as deficient in moral teaching; others saw them as thoroughly irrational and providing no useful information.

Though there was a brief interlude in the early 1800s when firms such as John Harris (successors to Newbery and his heirs) were publishing lighthearted picture books, the juvenile book trade at the turn of the eighteenth century was dominated by the moral tale and by books of information. There were some protests by writers who remembered happier days, and Catherine Sinclair prefaced *Holiday House* (1839), a celebration of the exploits of two naughty children, with sad reflections on the way that play of the imagination was now carefully discouraged, while children were stuffed "like a cricket-ball, with well-known facts and ready-made opinions."

But there was the beginning of a revival of literary interest in the stories and rhymes of the past. In 1823 tales collected by the Brothers GRIMM were translated into English under the title of *German Popular Stories.* James Orchard Halliwell made the first scholarly collection of NURSERY RHYMES in 1842, and selections from HANS CHRISTIAN ANDERSEN's stories were translated in 1846, the same year that saw EDWARD LEAR's *Book of Nonsense.* The subsequent emergence of the literary fairy tale and of nonsense writing also coincided with a huge growth in religious fiction. Thackeray's farcical send-up of French fairy tales, *The Rose and the Ring* (1855), Frances Browne's Grimm-inspired *Granny's Wonderful Chair* (1856), CHARLES KINGSLEY's *The Water-Babies* (1863)—half religious allegory, half scientific manual—and the anarchic nonsense of LEWIS CARROLL's Alice books (1865 and 1871) had to compete with such religious best-sellers as Mrs. Sherwood's *Fairchild Family* (published in three parts in 1818, 1842, and 1847), which was part of most middle-class young Victorians' upbringing, and with tear-jerking stories about street waifs such as Hesba Stretton's *Jessica's First Prayer* (1867) and Mrs. O. F. Walton's *Christie's Old Organ* (1875).

In general, works of imagination, such as the nonsense of Lewis Carroll and the finely wrought religious allegories of GEORGE MACDONALD, were reserved for the child of the more leisured home. The poorer classes were provided in their Sunday schools with purposeful, improving fiction that reflected their own background. Charlotte Yonge, author of innumerable works of fiction and instruction, found in 1887 that many children in the village school where she taught had never been told the familiar fairy stories. Subversive literature now tended to be boys' "penny dreadfuls"—sensational stories of crime and violence—or, for girls, cheap novelette love stories, rather than the tales of the marvelous that had amused their ancestors.

Sunday-school prizes (a highly lucrative Victorian publishing enterprise), while they had to have a strong moral message applicable to working-class children, did also include books outside their experience, such as boys' boarding-school stories—Thomas Hughes's *Tom Brown's Schooldays* (1857), F. W. Farrar's *Eric, or Little by Little* (1858)—and hearty, patriotic adventure stories by writers such as W. H. G. Kingston and R. M. Ballantyne. Far surpassing these, though Stevenson acknowledged a debt to them, were ROBERT LOUIS STEVENSON's *Treasure Island* (1883) and *Kidnapped* (1886)—probably the best boys' stories ever written.

The infinitely complex stratification of the Victorian social classes had a blighting effect on family stories, which in Britain never had the universal appeal that *Little Women* achieved in the United States. Too many of the works of Juliana Horatia Ewing (1841–85) and all the large output of Mary Louisa Molesworth (1839–1921) could be appreciated only by upper-middle-class families, while Charlotte Yonge's family stories, steeped in the *mores* peculiar to her class and period, are even more rarefied—though she did also write vivid little tales about village children. The books of EDITH NESBIT (1858–1924) have lasted far better than any of these writers. In *The Story of the Treasure-Seekers* (1899) and *The Wouldbegoods* (1901) she described the comic efforts of the disaster-prone Bastable children, impoverished but genteel, to redeem the family fortunes. She created similarly likable and high-spirited families for her books about magical events in everyday life, such as *Five Children and It* (1902).

By the end of the nineteenth century children's publishing was at its most varied. The pleasure principle—even for the working classes—was now thoroughly accepted, and there was a huge choice of, among much else, fairy tales. ANDREW LANG's twelve *Fairy Books* were published between 1889 and 1910 and became as much a part of the privileged child's literary background as the chapbook tales had been for their less fortunate predecessors. RUDYARD KIPLING's extraordinarily varied writing included the stories of Mowgli and the animals in *The Jungle Books* (1894 and 1895); the amoral and violent school world of *Stalky and Co.* (1899); the nursery nonsense of *The Just So Stories* (1902); and the subtle and allusive historical narratives contained in *Puck of Pook's Hill* (1906) and its sequel. Picture books reached a new level of distinction in the 1880s, when the engraving firm of Edmund Evans was commissioning work from WALTER CRANE, KATE GREENAWAY, and RANDOLPH CALDECOTT, and then rose to even greater heights in 1902 when BEATRIX POTTER began an outstanding series with *The Tale of Peter Rabbit.* In these subtly ironical animal fables there is no vestige of moral; her sympathy is always with the villain, her satire directed against the conforming and well-behaved. She is the supreme stylist of children's writers, and her mordant and economic prose is set off by her exquisite draftsmanship. KENNETH GRAHAME in *The Wind in the Willows* (1908) produced one of the few children's classics that appeals to adult and child equally. Like Potter he depicted human characters in the guise of animals, but *The Wind in the Willows* is a far more personal book than she ever chose to write. Not only is it a nostalgic evocation of the English countryside and a way of life that he felt was under threat, but in the characters of Rat and Mole we can detect aspects of himself.

The turn of the century saw a new desire on the part of writers to present a child's-eye view of the world. Kenneth Grahame had started the fashion with his essays *The Golden Age* (1895) and *Dream Days* (1898). Intended for adults, they showed a world where children are locked in perpetual warfare with the adult "Olympians" who have wholly forgotten how it feels to be young. Many writers took up the theme. J. M. Barrie went further and in *Peter Pan,* first performed in London in 1904, wrote of a boy who wished never to grow up. Its huge success with the Edwardian public was part of the cult of immaturity that characterized the attitude toward children in the first decades of the century, and which lasted, in fact, right up to World War II. The poems and stories of WALTER DE LA MARE (1873–1956) reflected this preoccupation, but they are timeless and highly idiosyncratic. Nearly everything he wrote touches on either childhood or death, which he saw as just another part of the same circle.

The pre-1939 middle-class parents wished to shelter their young from the harshness of life and to present the world as a safe and pretty place. They wanted them to believe in fairyland; and fairies, pixies, and gnomes abounded in upmarket and downmarket literature alike. They were depicted by illustrators as far removed as ARTHUR RACKHAM and Mabel Lucie Attwell; they were celebrated by versifiers like Rose Fyleman; they had whole magazines, such as Enid Blyton's *Sunny Stories,* devoted to them.

Illustration by ERNEST H. SHEPARD from *The Wind in the Willows* (1931), by KENNETH GRAHAME.

The real world had little place in any children's book during those years. Hugh Lofting, seared by his experiences in the Great War, turned his back on the real world in the Doctor Dolittle books, just as the doctor himself abandoned treating humans and turned to animals. A. A. Milne in *Winnie-the-Pooh* (1926) and *The House at Pooh Corner* (1928) created a kingdom where a little boy presided over toy animal companions. Arthur Ransome, author of the "Swallows and Amazons" series, which began in 1930, wrote about capable children in a wholly benign world, sailing and camping untroubled by adult supervision, thereby starting a fashion for holiday adventure stories which lasted some thirty years. Nor did the mass-produced school stories which girls between the wars compulsively devoured attempt to describe any credible school or pupils. Two works of fantasy, however, transcended all fashion—T. H. White's witty extension of the Arthurian legend, *The Sword in the Stone* (1938), and J. R. R. Tolkien's *The Hobbit* (1937), perhaps the finest work of fantasy ever written for children. Significantly, both of them derive from the wealth of myths, legends, and ancient romance to which English literature owes so much.

World War II did little to change the style of what was offered to children. As in the previous war, adult instinct was to protect and comfort them; the tone of jolly optimism was also official policy. The first notable book to discuss the realities of war was Ian Serraillier's *The Silver Sword* (1956), but though the 1950s were the years of the Narnia (C. S. Lewis) and the Borrower (Mary Norton) chronicles, and saw the debut of William Mayne, Rosemary Sutcliff, and Philippa Pearce, it was also a period when Enid Blyton's type of emollient escapism could dominate juvenile lists. It was not until some twenty years after the war that it began to be customary to expose children to the full range of the ills of humanity. The destruction of childhood as the earlier twentieth century had seen it had begun. ❧ GILLIAN AVERY

Brittain, Bill

AMERICAN AUTHOR, B. 1930. In 1984, Bill Brittain received a Newbery Honor Award for *The Wish Giver: Three Tales of Coven Tree.* Based on folkloric themes, the novel is a highly original FANTASY spiced with homespun humor, laced with enjoyable doses of magic and mystery, and peopled with believable, engaging characters. The title is based on a sinister stranger who comes to the New England town of Coven Tree promising to make "wishes come true." Villagers of Coven Tree are well acquainted with the supernatural, for their heritage of witchcraft dates back to Colonial days. But the children who purchase wishes are ill prepared for the consequences of meddling with magic. The logical narrator for the tale is local storekeeper Stewart Meade; not only is he the village's historian, but he holds the "wish giver's" final wish.

Brittain wrote four books with roots in Coven Tree, where witches appear and Old Lucifer himself occasional "cut[s] a swath of chaos and destruction through usually everyday lives." Stewart Meade (nicknamed Stew Meat by the townsfolk) is the engaging narrative voice in each book and the hero the children call upon to set things right. He first appeared in *Devil's Donkey* (1981) recounting the story of Dan'l Pitt, who did not believe in witches until he crossed a witch who turned him into a donkey. Courage and a risky deal with the devil saved Dan'l. *Dr. Dredd's Wagon of Wonders* (1987) finds the people in Coven Tree in trouble again. Townspeople make a deal with suspicious Dr. Dredd, who offers to deliver them from a drought. He exacts a dreadful cost, and residents refuse to pay. Events escalate along with the wicked Dr. Dredd's fury, but two spunky youngsters send the villain packing. In *Professor Popkin's Prodigious Polish* (1990), Coven Tree again attracts excitement when young Luther Gilpin attempts to strike it rich by purveying the professor's polish. The polish not only animates everday objects but turns them hostile as well. Soon the whole town is battling lethal objects on a rampage. It takes Luther's mother's homemade lye soap to negate the spell. All Brittain's stories are touched with irony but are never cruelly satiric; they hold the right amount of good versus evil, are filled with crackling suspense, and bubble with humor.

Brittain spent his childhood in Spencerport, New York. After college, he began a teaching career; his first children's book was inspired by a real conversation between two students making outlandish wishes. That humorous result, *All the Money in the World* (1979), recounts the disasters that can happen when a boy wishes for untold wealth. Brittain's penchant for mystery, magic, and imagination permeates most of his books. *Who Knew There'd Be Ghosts* (1985) and its sequel, *The Ghost from Beneath the Sea* (1992), chronicle the escapades of three children and their ghostly allies. *My Buddy the King* (1989), about a boy who befriends a teenage king, is the only novel without overtones of the supernatural. Brittain's books are appealing choices for middle-grade readers. His lively blend of comedy and suspense keeps his audience hanging on every word. ❧ S.L.

Brooke, L. Leslie

British illustrator and author, 1862–1940. Leonard Leslie Brooke, whose droll pen-and-ink-line drawings, enchanting watercolor illustrations, and beloved books about Johnny Crow and his friends have delighted generations of children and the grown-ups who read to them, was educated in his native Cheshire and later in London at the Royal Academy. He received the Academy's Armitage Medal in 1888 and began his artistic career as a watercolorist and portrait painter, but when he succeeded Walter Crane in 1891 as illustrator of Mrs. Molesworth's Victorian novels for children, his career took a different course.

With the publication of *The Nursery Rhyme Book* (1897), edited by Andrew Lang, Brooke found his niche among children's book immortals. The pictures he drew with such skill and humor, that he painted with such warmth and color for his lovely books of Mother Goose rhymes and traditional nursery tales, class his art with that of Walter Crane, Beatrix Potter, Kate Greenaway, and Randolph Caldecott and his gently absurd humor with Edward Lear and Lewis Carroll. *Johnny Crow's Garden* (1903), the first book he both illustrated and wrote, earned a Lewis Carroll Shelf Award in 1960.

Johnny Crow, ever courteous, solicitous, and unassuming, plays quiet host to an intriguing assortment of fellow birds and animals in his beautiful garden. Rhymed couplets introduce his individual friends and their antics. The accompanying pictures reveal further details of their stories until at last "they all sat down together in a row in Johnny Crow's garden."

The roots of this appealing classic for young children and of its companion books, *Johnny Crow's Party* (1907) and *Johnny Crow's New Garden* (1935), lie in childhood: Brooke's own childhood, that of his sons, and that of his grandson. The clever rhyming game shared among four generations produced three books equal in wit, beauty, and spirit that are filled with the character and personality of their creator. Brooke was a kind and gentle man who loved and understood children. His sense of fun, his feelings for the English garden and countryside, and his affection for animals are apparent in all his work.

Brooke lavished his attention on portraying animals, not as an animal artist, but as a friendly observer of his fellow man. His humanized animals, though true to their kind, express in their faces and bodies an enormous range of mostly sunny human emotions that children can instantly recognize. Whether from farm or jungle, they are happy, funny, silly, serious, surprised; coy, bored, sick, embarrassed, proud, crest-fallen. To admire his animals, however, is not to slight his humans. The young kings and queens who grace his books are as royal and as beautiful as one could wish, the children as charming and innocent, but none would be recognized in the face of a neighbor. It is the lined and worn faces of his old folk that are a reminder of the artist's early interest in portraiture.

The height of Brooke's picture-book creativity was from the turn of the century to about 1916. During this period—besides the first two books about Johnny

Illustration by L. Leslie Brooke from his book *Johnny Crow's Party* (1907).

Crow—he created new illustrations for the nonsense rhymes of Edward Lear, retold and illustrated four classic nursery tales that appeared both separately and later together in *The Golden Goose Book* (1905), and illustrated a series of Mother Goose rhymes that were published in omnibus form in 1922 under the title *Ring o' Roses.*

During the 1920s Brooke illustrated several books for adults. In the thirties the world received the gift of two more inspired children's books from his hand. *A Roundabout Turn* (1930) by Robert Charles had originally appeared as a poem in *Punch* and, like Lear's nonsense verses, was in perfect tune with Brooke's own whimsical art. *Johnny Crow's New Garden* (1935), written for his grandson, was the astonishing equal of its two predecessors, written thirty years before.

Times change and tastes change, but in an age when humor, playfulness, and pictorial detail in books for the young have reached a new level of appreciation, there is much to appreciate in the world of Leslie Brooke. ❧ S.L.R.

Voices of the Creators

Bruce Brooks

When I was growing up and secretly planning to write novels one day, I was always disconcerted by a central requirement I kept hearing about writing: Writers Express Themselves. Of course, this famous feature of literary practice was never mentioned as a "task" or anything so unpleasant; quite the contrary, the opportunity for self-expression was so adoringly celebrated that I imagined it *ought* to be the reason one *wanted* to write. One ought to yearn to discharge feelings and opinions rather directly onto the page; one ought to compose stories or poems that made one's take on things clear to the reader. The stuff I read in school, and the stuff my classmates were praised for writing, was stuff that demanded exactly this sort of interpretation (if interpretation was even needed—the messages were utterly self-evident).

Well—I fled from the idea of manifesting my take on the world. For one thing, I *had* no take on the world, or at least nothing that could be neatly summarized and packaged in a message. I was ten, eleven, twelve years old—all too alert to ambiguity, and the shiftiness of perceptions and feelings. The adults around me did no better: they obviously hadn't solved life's puzzles yet, any better than I had. So when I read books in which the adults or even the children were presented as exemplars of the standard assurances I had heard so many times in Sunday school, I winced at the falseness. It all seemed almost smug. Expressive? Yes. True? No, as far as I could tell.

What finally brought me into my own as a writer was stumbling upon a character—Jerome Foxworthy—who was a child. I was intrigued with Jerome, yet also safe. There was no danger of feeling that Jerome "was" me, or represented me, or expressed me. On the surface level, we were distinct: I was a white adult in Iowa; Jerome was an African American seventh-grader in North Carolina. On deeper levels, we differed just as much. Yet the fact that *he* was a child made it okay for me to study and embody the ambiguities that had fascinated *me* when I was a kid. My adult secret was: I was *still* fascinated by this lack of storybook clarity, *still* puzzling through the shiftiness of things.

As a kid I had thought a lot like an adult. As an adult, I thought a lot like a child. In other words, I had really been pretty much the same person all my life. I believe this is true about most people; I believe we adopt poses of maturity, and presumptions of seriousness and wisdom, that we falsely imagine set us off from who we were at nine, twelve, and fifteen. We don't do this out of hypocrisy. We are simply responding to the attitudes of our culture toward the distant days of yore, childhood. For a slew of reasons, our adult culture needs to feel a safe distance from the awkwardnesses of our youth. What I discovered, by finding it so natural to write in the voice of a thirteen-year-old kid, was that we are missing more than we think. By investing in this illusion of distance, we not only push away and forget the moments of awkwardness, we also push away and forget a lot of insight, intelligence, and sensitivity. We were smarter than we remember. We were hipper.

By forgetting this about ourselves, we forget it about the kids around us now. We fail to respect what complete—if young—people we used to be (and have always been). Naturally, we then cannot extend such respect to today's children. All of this became increasingly evident to me as I wrote about Jerome and Bix and their families, and somehow it inspired my empathy tremendously. But not *too* tremendously. Because he and I were so different, writing about Jerome did not betray my desire *not* to "self-express"; but because I was basically still a smart but sometimes bewildered person who could admit my marveling lack of grasp, I could exercise all the empathy I possessed in a childhood on paper. As I wrote the book, I found myself—for the first time in my twenty years of writing—to be emotionally involved and technically thrilled. This union of feeling and technique, of empathy and detachment, grows with every book I write about kids and adults living together. I imagine it will always do so.

I've heard vague references here and there to pop-psychology doctrines that urge people to "discover the inner child." I hasten to say that I have no idea what such doctrines contain or advise; indeed, I confess that to me the phrase has a suspiciously cute and self-indulgent sound. This is all part of the adult trick of distancing one's self from one's life. I think kids are too busy living their lives to get so finicky and philosophical about interpretations or alternatives; life is reality when you are a child, not a subject for speculation. Knowing this makes it very easy for me to respect my characters, and to emphasize with them as they live *their* lives, not mine. As they express *themselves*, not me.

Brooks, Bruce

American author, b. 1950. Since making an explosive debut in young adult literature with *The Moves Make the Man* (1984), Bruce Brooks has published a succession of challenging, complex, and brilliantly crafted novels.

Born in Richmond, Virginia, the author's childhood was divided between his divorced parents' homes in Washington, D.C., and North Carolina. From his first day of school, Brooks created alternate plots for the stories he read in textbooks and soon began writing original fiction. He attended the University of North Carolina at Chapel Hill and the prestigious University of Iowa Writers' Workshop. He was employed as a teacher, a letterpress printer, and a journalist before his first book won the Boston Globe–Horn Book Award for fiction and was named a Newbery Honor Book.

The Moves Make the Man concerns the friendship between two thirteen-year-old boys in 1950s North Carolina. Jerome is a smart and savvy African American; Bix is a troubled white boy with a mentally ill mother and malevolent stepfather. Jerome teaches Bix how to play basketball, and the game serves as a stunning metaphor on several levels throughout the novel. Jerome's first-person narration is exceptionally fine, and Brooks extended his mastery of the first-person voice in *Midnight Hour Encores* (1986), whose narrator is a sophisticated sixteen-year-old cello prodigy. The story artfully explores the bonds between parent and child as Sibilance T. Spooner and her father travel from Washington, D.C., to San Francisco, where Sib meets her mother for the first time and makes some momentous decisions about her life.

Family relationships are also at the center of *No Kidding* (1989), in which fourteen-year-old Sam is forced to take on adult responsibilities in a twenty-first-century society ravaged by the effects of alcoholism. Although the book includes an unnecessary subplot involving clerics and the omniscient narration lacks the immediacy of the author's previous novels, Brooks presents a thoughtful, intriguing look at the future. An unnamed Southern boy confronts issues of mortality and love after his grandfather suffers a heart attack in *Everywhere* (1990), a small gem of a novel, which, like each of the author's books, departs from his previous work in style and content. What all the novels have in common are protagonists who, despite their vastly different backgrounds and speech patterns, share a keen awareness of their own intelligence. A particularly shrewd yet openhearted character is portrayed in *What Hearts* (1992), a volume of four short stories focusing on such crucial events in young Asa's life as leaving home at age seven and falling in love at age twelve. Rich in emotion and challenging in vision, this Newbery Honor Book contains wonderful writing, but seems to be directed at adult readers, rather than children. The author has also written several nonfiction books. The "Knowing Nature" series includes *Predator* (1989) and *Making Sense: Animal Perception and Communication* (1993). Collections of essays written especially for young readers are rare, but in *Boys Will Be* (1993) Brooks, the father of two sons, writes about baseball caps, dangerous friends, sports, and other boyhood concerns in spirited, compassionate prose.

As an author of well-received nonfiction and novels distinguished by their integrity, superb characterizations, and inspired use of language, this versatile stylist has proved himself a writer of nearly limitless possibilities. ❧ P.D.S.

Brooks, Martha

Canadian author and playwright, b. 1944. With a refreshing style and engaging characters, Martha Brooks has created terrific new additions to the young adult genre. The daughter of a surgeon and a nurse, Brooks grew up in Manitoba on the grounds of the tuberculosis sanatorium where her parents worked. She has written several plays for the Prairie Theatre Exchange in Winnipeg, the city where she lives with her husband, Brian Brooks, and her daughter, Kirsten.

Brooks's first book for young adults, *Paradise Café and Other Stories,* was selected a School Library Journal Best Book of 1990. Its fourteen stories, all written in the first person, each tell the tale of a different kind of love—familial, romantic, and even a boy's affection for his dog. *Two Moons in August* (1992), Brooks's first young adult novel, sensitively tells the story of a sixteen-year-old girl struggling to come to terms with her mother's death the previous year. By writing in the first-person present, Brooks instantly puts the reader at ease with her narrator, even though events in the novel take place in an unfamiliar setting—a tuberculosis sanatorium in 1959.

Prior to becoming a novelist, Brooks taught creative writing to high school students in Winnipeg. She has clearly learned a great deal from her students and from her teenage daughter as well as from her own experience; even though her stories are often set in other decades, her writing, especially the dialogue, consistently rings true. ❧ A.C.

BROWN, MARC

AMERICAN AUTHOR AND ILLUSTRATOR, B. 1946. The name Marc Brown is well known to most elementary-school children. The author and illustrator of the beloved Arthur books as well as many other successful works of fiction and nonfiction, Brown has secured for himself a sparkling reputation among both child readers and adult reviewers—certainly no easy task. An awareness of contemporary children and issues, combined with a bright, captivating visual artistry, are the signatures of his large and diverse body of work.

Born in Erie, Pennsylvania, Brown showed an early artistic talent that flowered under the guidance of an

VOICES OF THE CREATORS

MARC BROWN

The first drawing I remember being really excited about was one I created in second grade at Jefferson Elementary School. It was a Nativity scene on blue construction paper, and I used a silver crayon for the stars. Something very special happened in my reaction to that drawing; I knew then that drawing was something I could do well. I had feelings of elation and great self-satisfaction.

As a child, I loved telling stories and had a friend who did, too. We would find quiet places away from everyone else, where we could tell stories. Each of us might talk for an hour or so, and we would listen patiently to each other. We were good listeners; I don't know if we were good storytellers.

My parents didn't think it was a good idea for me to study art; they wanted me to do something more respectable. My art teacher surreptitiously took me to apply to art school. The most remarkable person I have ever known, my grandmother, gave me money to start college; then, after my first year, I had to get scholarships.

To support myself in college, I took a job at a television station. My first assignment was to make more people want to watch the weather report. The station wanted something different. I gave it my best shot. I decided to dress the weather reporter, Shirley, up as a weather fairy; she'd swing onto the set on a big swing with her gossamer wings flapping behind her. My boss didn't see the humor: he gave me a free Christmas ham—and fired me.

After school I started teaching and illustrating textbooks. When I began illustrating picture books, my first son was born. In sharing books with Tolon and later with my son Tucker, I could see the kinds of things they looked for in a book. I changed my ideas about illustrating because of the way they looked at the world. They had this wonderful fresh vision that I had lost. I wanted to recapture that view. I worked hard in joining them in their childhood and in their vision.

Arthur's Nose evolved out of a bedtime story I was telling my son. My editor, Emilie McLeod, at the Atlantic Monthly Press, thought it needed a lot of revision but was willing to work with me. The hardest thing for me at the beginning was to learn how to say something in a sentence or in a few words. I thought I needed three paragraphs. Emilie helped me understand how to use the pictures to do what they could do best and how to use the words to do what the pictures could not do.

Usually my story ideas come from something that is happening in real life. My sons were eating dinner one night, and they were having mashed potatoes and little peas, or rather *heaving* mashed potatoes and little peas. This prompted me to look for a good book on manners at the library. The ones I found were very stale, and I wanted a manners book that would be fun. Consequently, Stephen Krensky and I collaborated on *Perfect Pigs: An Introduction to Manners.*

When I begin working on a book, I always struggle with the writing at first and read the story aloud to hear how it sounds. I often create thirty versions of a manuscript before I show it to anyone. Sometimes I will put a manuscript away for a year before I finish it. I use pencil and paper and cut and paste. Once I have the right sequence, I start to think of picture possibilities.

For me the most satisfying part of the process is how children feel about the books. I never tire of hearing that children like what I am creating. It is also wonderful to have a partner who shares the same interests, and my wife, Laurie, and I sometimes collaborate. We are always looking for picture-book subjects to help inform children about their world, because they are increasingly thrust into complex situations and premature independence.

Every morning when I walk into my studio, I feel so lucky to be able to make a living doing what I really love.

encouraging grandmother and uncle. Trips to area museums became favorite excursions, and he went on to receive a B.F.A. in painting at the Cleveland Institute of Art. He has worked as a television art director, a professor of mechanical drawing, and a freelance illustrator.

Brown creates in several media, but he prefers pencil with watercolor, and he uses a variety of papers to produce different visual effects. Strong lines and bold colors characterize his recent work; such strong artistic statements capture the attention of young audiences, but without sacrificing a highly expressive quality that makes believable characters out of dinosaurs, monkeys, cats, and other winsome creatures.

During the mid-1970s, Brown began writing his own material. His first effort, *Arthur's Nose* (1976), began a series that would span two decades and introduced one of the most popular characters in picture-book history. Starring the enormously appealing anteater, Arthur, and his diverse and likable group of friends and relatives, each of the titles addresses a child-relevant theme or situation with an easy-to-read text, colorful illustrations, and plenty of humor. A spinoff series featuring Arthur's irrepressible sister, D. W., makes use of the same down-to-earth style and has also met with success.

Brown's ability to keep a long series fresh and innovative is a rare gift. In addition to the Arthur books, he has created several other notable series. The "Rhymes" series—*Finger Rhymes* (1980), *Hand Rhymes* (1985), *Play Rhymes* (1987), and *Party Rhymes* (1988)—is a joyfully illustrated set of fingerplays, jump-rope games, and other movement activities suitable for use with children of all ages. Aside from these books' popularity with parents, their ability to hold the attention of young children has made them indispensable tools for librarians and preschool teachers. For information on such timely topics as divorce, safety, and the environment, children and adults turn to Brown's nonfiction "Dinosaurs" series. Created in collaboration with his wife, psychologist Laurene Krasny Brown, such appealing and useful books as *Dinosaurs, Beware! A Safety Guide* (1982), *Dinosaurs Travel: A Guide for Families on the Go* (1988), and *Dinosaurs to the Rescue! A Guide to Protecting Our Planet* (1992) feature a set of charismatic green dinosaurs that cavort across the pages while they convey their important dos and don'ts. Unlike many unsuccessful theme books, the Dinosaur guides take a humorous but sincere approach that avoids stereotypes or saccharine characterizations. They are as accessible to their young audiences as are any of Brown's other favorites, and readers continue to clamor for more. Whether it's an Arthur book, a favorite seen on "Reading Rainbow," or a special fingerplay, children are always ready to revel in the words and pictures of Marc Brown. C.C.B.

Brown, Marcia

American author and illustrator, b. 1918. Of the thirty books Marcia Brown has written, translated, and illustrated, three have won Caldecott Medals and six have been named Caldecott Honor Books, an unprecedented achievement and proof of her success in portraying the spirit of a story. Brown always wanted to illustrate children's books, particularly individual folk and fairy tales. After graduating from the New York College for Teachers in 1940, she taught English and drama for three years before deciding to immerse herself in children's literature. At a time when the Central Library in New York was the seminal hub of children's literature, she was hired into the New York Public Library system. Brown worked as an assistant librarian from 1943 to 1948, telling stories, mounting exhibits, and meeting people involved in children's books from all over the world. During her tenure there, she continued taking art lessons with the hope of becoming a writer and an illustrator. This, plus her love of art, reading, and travel, provided the foundations for her stories.

Her first book, *The Little Carousel* (1946), focuses on a child's loneliness when he is left at home by himself. Barbara Bader notes that at a time when picture books addressed "archetypes and universals," Brown's book saw the "personal and circumstantial." *Stone Soup*, winner of the 1948 Caldecott Medal, was the first of many folk and fairy tales Brown would illustrate. Brown firmly believes in the power of story as one of the building blocks children need in defining their personalities and in the power that pictures have in making tales memorable. Because she believes that children need heroes with whom they can identify, she presents ordinary people who achieve extraordinary feats: a poor boy becomes Lord Mayor of London (*Dick Whittington and His Cat*, 1950); a penniless son becomes the Marquis of Carabas (*Puss in Boots*, 1952); a stepdaughter goes to the prince's ball (*Cinderella, or The Little Glass Slipper*, winner of the 1955 Caldecott Medal).

Further, Brown believes that "fairy tales are revelations of sober everyday fact. They are the abiding dreams and realities of the human soul." She also believes that an illustrator must feel the rhythm of the story in order to "interpret . . . and intensify its meaning." Brown has always been faithful to this creed; her hallmark is the originality she brings to her art. She has used wash and line, pastels and ink, gouache and watercolors, and

Voices of the Creators

Marcia Brown

I often think of illustrators as I think of performers of music. Those one can listen to longest are often those most selfless, those who are content to be a medium for the music. They put their own individualities at the service of the music, to probe its depths and reveal its spirit, rather than to display the idiosyncrasies of their own personalities. Techniques that hammer can dull the eyes as well as the ears.

Even though I may be the composer, I have come to think of the illustrator more and more as the performer of the spirit of a book. If one lives with a book from its beginning, one may be closer to that spirit. Some spirits speak so loudly their voices are unmistakable. Others are more delicate. No one way can be called the best way to interpret them to children.

Feelings appropriate to the fine arts, especially painting, are often called forward in speaking about illustration for children. Little children readily look at all kinds and styles of art. They are probably the freest and most imaginative audience in the world. But illustration is illustration, and not painting. It is communication of the idea of a book.

There seems to be very great interest in the composing process, in the *how* of making a book. It might be a good idea if we were occasionally to ask *why*. There is a great interest in the contribution of the individual artist, but perhaps we are asking him or her to talk too much about how he or she works and we are not looking hard enough at what he or she does.

Some time ago, I was asked to answer a questionnaire on the "composing process"—to try to track down what is elusive in the process of making books. The questions were intelligently thought out. But I suspect that what is elusive will remain so, since it is a subtle combination of personality, inner drive, and imagination in the author or illustrator.

Illustration and writing can be a lonely business, and artists when they get together often compare notes on ways of working. I am often asked why each of my books is apt to look different from the others. Each artist has a unique way of working. After a while an artist works in possibly the only ways that seem right, given an individual temperament.

I feel about each book very differently. My interest is in the book as a whole, not just in the illustrations. Every detail of a book should, as far as possible, reflect the intentions the artist and designer had toward the idea of the book. These intentions need not even be expressible in words, but they should be felt. That quality of the individual book which is the strongest—the simple vigor, the delicacy, the mood, the setting—should determine the color, not an arbitrary application of brilliance to whatever the subject.

The atmosphere of a book is extremely important. A story that is very traditional in feeling can often suffer from illustrations that are stylistically too different in period. When one adapts a modern technique to illustrations for a historical period, one must think of the young child looking, with little knowledge of the period. Do the costumes give the feeling of the period if they do not produce the details?

Freshness lies in the intensity of expression, not in the novelty of the technique.

In order not to drag the ideas or techniques that I have developed during work on one book into another, I try to take a good piece of time between books, painting or just taking in impressions by travel, to clear the way for the next.

In *The Little Prince*, Saint-Exupéry makes a statement in the context of one human relationship that perhaps we could apply to another: "One is forever responsible for whom one has tamed." Children walk, open arms, to embrace what we give them. Those who work with children should be encouraged to hand on to them their personal involvement with the child. A child needs the stimulus of books that are focused on individuality in personality and character if he or she is to find his or her own. A child is an individual; a book is individual. Each should be served according to its needs.

linoleum cuts in her interpretations: Each time, she let the story dictate the medium. To evoke the endurance and spirit of fable, Brown turned to woodcuts for stories such as *Once a Mouse*, winner of the 1962 Caldecott Medal, *Backbone of the King* (1966), and *The Blue Jackal* (1977). Because she believes in the vital importance of passing down folklore from generation to generation, she was enthralled by a poem by Blaise Cendrars, which became *Shadow*, winner of the 1983 Caldecott Medal and her most powerfully illustrated book. This tale,

Illustration by Marcia Brown from her book *Cinderella or the Little Glass Slipper* (1954).

inspired by African storytelling, reaches back and taps man's primal fear of the dark, hauntingly pulling ghosts, past and present, in and out of the subconscious. Through *Shadow,* Brown creates the dance of the eternal spirit of man, again, successfully weaving timelessness through her work. In 1992 she won the Laura Ingalls Wilder Award for the body of her work. S.R.

Brown, Margaret Wise

American writer, 1910–1952. In a many-faceted, brief, but remarkable career, Margaret Wise Brown pioneered in the writing of books for the nursery school ages; authored more than one hundred volumes including the classic *Runaway Bunny* (1942) and *Goodnight Moon* (1947); served as a bridge between the worlds of publishing, progressive education, and the experimental arts of the 1930s and 1940s; and did much to make children's literature a vital creative enterprise in her own time and afterward.

Born in the Greenpoint section of Brooklyn, New York, on May 23, 1910, Brown grew up the second of three children in suburban Beechurst, Long Island. Her father, Robert Bruce Brown, was an executive of the American Manufacturing Company, makers of rope and bagging for the maritime trade. Her mother, born Maude Johnson, had been Robert's childhood playmate in Kirkwood, Missouri. Both parents traced their American ancestry to pre-Revolutionary War Virginia, where Robert's forebears, in particular, had flourished in church and government service. It was a great thing to be born a Brown, young Margaret soon learned; and in the perfectionistic, emotionally chilly world of the Brown household, each child vied for distinction.

Margaret's older brother Gratz was a shrewd problem-solver like their father. Their younger sister Roberta's intellectual prowess was more broadly based; always a brilliant scholar (and dutiful daughter), Roberta would skip two grades of school on her triumphant way to Vassar. Wedged uncomfortably between these daunting paradigms of achievement, Margaret carved a dubious niche for herself as the family storyteller, trickster, and daydreamer.

At the girls' preparatory school Dana Hall, however, "Tim" Brown (as Margaret was known for the golden color, like timothy, of her long, flowing hair) at last met teachers capable of channeling her freeform, intuitive style of attention, and of making learning stick. Then, as an undergraduate at Hollins College, she received her first encouragement to write. On graduating from Hollins in 1932, however, her literary aspirations remained of the vaguest sort. Three more years passed before, lacking an alternative, she enrolled in the teacher training program of New York's progressive Bureau of Educational Experiments (called "Bank Street" for its Greenwich Village location). There, as part of the experientially based training routine, Brown composed her first children's stories and found her vocation.

From her inspired teacher, Bank Street founder Lucy Sprague Mitchell, Brown received important lessons in craft and professionalism and a thorough grounding in Mitchell's controversial ideas about writing for the young. Mitchell's study of the patterns of early childhood development had led her during the second decade of the twentieth century to ask whether there were not certain types of stories and poems that corresponded most closely to the needs and abilities of children at each developmental stage. Research into this question had prompted her to reject many of the reigning library establishment's basic assumptions about literature for the younger ages. Children under the age of six, Mitchell had found, had no special affinity for fantastic tales about castles and kings or for traditional nursery nonsense, as the librarians supposed. The very young seemed far more at home with stories about the modern-day world, which to them *was* fantastic. Mitchell laid out this and several other equally arresting ideas in the introduction and notes to her *Here and Now Story Book* of 1921, an age-graded anthology that provoked a lively debate on publication and later served as a model for Brown and others.

By the mid-1930s, with a talented protegée like "Brownie" to assist her, Mitchell was ready to advance her children's literature project several steps further. First, in 1936, she enlisted Brown and a small group of others to collaborate with her on a sequel anthology, *Another Here and Now Story Book* (1937), which reaffirmed in somewhat more flexible terms Mitchell's critique of the librarians' unscientific and, as she thought, essentially sentimental point of view. Then, in 1937, Mitchell established the Bank Street Writers Laboratory as a permanent training ground for authors in the here-and-now vein (Brown was a charter member); and, the following year, she helped launch the small publishing firm of William R. Scott, Inc. (with Brown as editor), as a vehicle for sending here-and-now-style books out into the world.

As Scott's editor, Brown was in a position to champion the innovative work of others, and to publish herself. She did both with alacrity. "I submitted it," she later recalled of *The Noisy Book*'s (1939) origin. "We"—that is, Brown again—"accepted it." From the start, her own books led the list of the fledgling firm's critical and commercial successes (limited as those successes were by the wariness of the library establishment to books cooked in the laboratory of progressive education). The roster of Brown's editorial discoveries—illustrators CLEMENT HURD, author-artists ESPHYR SLOBODKINA and CHARLES SHAW, and others—was also impressive. Her most spectacular coup, however, came with the publication of Gertrude Stein's first children's fantasy, *The World Is Round* (1939), which Scott commissioned at Brown's prompting. Stein's robust delight in wordplay and fascination with the expressive possibilities of rhythmic repetition were features of the voluble expatriate's avant-garde work that Brown found distinctly "childlike" (as defined by Mitchell's research) and thus adaptable to writing for the young.

Steinian echoes reverberate throughout Brown's own Noisy Book series (which grew to eight volumes), *Red Light Green Light* (published under the name, Golden MacDonald, 1944), *The Important Book* (1949), *Four Fur Feet* (1961), and many others. The younger author's understanding of modernist experimentation and its relevance for children's literature is equally apparent in the styles of illustration art she favored as an editor. Slobodkina and Shaw (who were charter members of the American Abstract Artists group of painters), Hurd (who had studied in Paris with Fernand Léger), JEAN CHARLOT (a dazzling printmaker with links both to the Paris avant-garde and to the Mexican muralists), and Weisgard (an illustrator influenced by Stuart Davis and the Constructivists), all created children's book art that eschewed the anecdotal realism of the day for a bolder, more graphic, and deliberately contemporary vision. Starting with elements of the modern artist's stock-in-trade—the purely expressive use of color, the ideographic distillation of representational forms, the free-flowing reorganization of pictorial space—these illustrators produced vibrant, accessible art aimed at heightening the here-and-now sensory enjoyment of young children. Inspired by their author-editor friend, Hurd, Weisgard, and the others joined Brown in an impassioned quest to make the picture book new.

Bumble Bugs and Elephants (1938), *The Little Fireman* (1938), *A Child's Good Night Book* (1943), *They All Saw It* (1944), and *Where Have You Been?* (1952) are among the many books in which, sentence by sentence or stanza by stanza, Brown presented young children with simple, gamelike structures in which to frame their own rhymes, thoughts, and perceptions. In thus extending to readers an open invitation not to hold solemnly to the author's word as final, but instead to ring their own variations on the printed text, these books epitomized the Bank Street view that children were best approached as full collaborators in learning.

Illustration by GARTH WILLIAMS from *Little Fur Family* (1946), by Margaret Wise Brown.

The Noisy Book series and *SHHhhh . . . BANG* (1943), which asked readers to produce a variety of amusing sound effects; *The Color Kittens* (1949), which offered a winsome introduction to color theory; and *Little Fur Family* (1946), in its snuggly-soft original fur-bound edition, reflected the Bank Street belief in the centrality of sensory experience for the development of children under the age of six. In *Goodnight Moon,* the one- and two-year-old's here-and-now world was shown to consist in large measure of his or her own home surroundings. *Five Little Firemen* (coauthored by EDITH THACHER HURD under the joint pseudonym Juniper Sage, 1948) was one of several books to survey a somewhat older child's expanding here-and-now awareness of modern towns and cities and their myriad doings. Mitchell had argued that once children acquired an understanding of their present-day world, a grounding rooted primarily in firsthand observation, they were ready to study the past. In *The Log of Christopher Columbus' First Voyage to America in the Year 1492* (1938) and *Homes in the Wilderness* (1939), the latter of which contained excerpts from the diaries of William Bradford and other Plymouth Colony settlers, Brown provided readers of eight and older with opportunities to glimpse the past through the firsthand observations of participants.

Mitchell's influence on Brown's writings and editorial work was thus various and immense. But Brown had too incisive an imagination, and was too fine a writer, not to have searched out the limits of her mentor's ideas, and to have ventured beyond them. Mitchell had based her model of here-and-now development on the outlines of the child's changing capacity for cognition and perception. Brown's first published book, *When the Wind Blew* (1937), a melancholy tale about an old woman living by herself, signaled its author's interest in exploring the emotional realm as well. In *The Runaway Bunny, Little Fur Family, The Little Island* (published under the name Golden MacDonald, 1946), *Wait Till the Moon Is Full* (1948), and *Mister Dog* (1952) Brown fashioned poignant fables of the shifting balance of the child's deep-seated yearnings for security and independence. And in books like *Little Fur Family, The Little Island, Fox Eyes* (1951), and *The Dark Wood of the Golden Birds* (1950), she took further exception with here-and-now orthodoxy through her whole-hearted embrace of fairy-tale elements of magic and mystery. Brown, who had relished from early childhood ANDREW LANG's Rainbow Fairy collections and the rhymes of MOTHER GOOSE, had never been altogether convinced that such open-endedly imaginative material could be inappropriate at *any* stage in a child's development.

It was in 1942, the year of *The Runaway Bunny*'s publication, that Brown ended both her editorial work for Scott and her regular participation in Bank Street activities, including the Writers Laboratory. As an extraordinarily prolific author, she continued throughout the rest of her brief career to add to the list of houses with whom she published. But from the early 1940s onward, Harper and Brothers, under the editorship of the boldly receptive Ursula Nordstrom, was Brown's creative home.

As the titles of several books—*Big Dog, Little Dog* (1943), *Night and Day* (1942), and *The Quiet Noisy Book* (1950)—suggest, Brown delighted in the play, and contemplation, of opposites. In *Goodnight Moon,* the book for which she has long been best known, she achieved her most compelling synthesis of the opposing tendencies within her imaginative vision. Brown furnished the "great green room" not only with the chairs and clocks of Bank Street actuality but with fanciful images (the three little bears, the cow jumping over the moon) of classic make-believe and with the tantalizing nonpresence of "nobody." In so doing, she accurately mirrored, and thus confirmed, the young child's experience of here-and-now reality and the land of pretend as largely overlapping territories.

On November 13, 1952, at the age of forty-two, Margaret Wise Brown died unexpectedly while visiting the south of France, of an embolism following a routine operation. She never married or had children of her own. Her private life was a whirl of glamorous friends, eccentric houses, and adventurous travel, but also of torturous bouts with self-doubt and of inconclusive, more than occasionally painful relationships, most notably her ten-year-long on-again-off-again affair with Michael Strange, the celebrity-socialite-poet and former wife of John Barrymore. Strange, who died in 1950, was old enough to have been Brown's mother; James Rockefeller, Jr., to whom Brown became engaged just months before her sudden death, was young enough to have been her son. The striking reverse symmetry in the age differences of these two relationships, whatever its significance as a clue to Brown's own internal dynamics, hints at the source of the abiding power of her work: Brown's ability simultaneously to write from a child's perspective *and* as a good provider of comforting fables and luminous, clarifying perceptions. In *Goodnight Moon,* it is that good provider who gently leads the listener into the great green room; but it is the child who then takes up the litany of "goodnights," and is thus assured, as the young are by so many Brown books, a satisfying role in the scheme of existence.

LEONARD S. MARCUS

Browne, Anthony

English author and illustrator, b. 1946. With the publication, in 1983, of his picture book *Gorilla,* Anthony Browne firmly established his ranking as one of the most highly original creators of picture books to arrive on the scene in recent years. He had already proven himself one of the most controversial.

Gorilla tells the story of a child whose loneliness is assuaged when her toy gorilla comes to life one night and provides the kind of companionship that has so far been unavailable from her usually preoccupied father. The winner of numerous awards in the United States, Britain (where it won a Kate Greenaway Medal), and elsewhere, the book exemplifies many of the qualities characteristic of Browne's work: forceful, strongly narrative watercolors that blend near-photographic realism with fantastical touches and that exert a strong emotional, often unconscious, pull; the skillful use of color, pattern, and background detail to convey mood and meaning; ingenious visual puns and surprises that frequently point to serious, often disturbing, underlying themes; and an exquisite empathy for the concerns of lonely, sensitive children.

Browne was born in Sheffield, England, where his parents ran a pub—a circumstance he credits with his affinity for simian characters, since his father, he has said, was "like a gorilla, big and potentially aggressive during his pub days." He describes himself as having been "a kid with terrors" and recalls "a lot of dark furniture which looked very menacing to me," reminiscences which open fascinating windows onto the symbolic and suggestive ways in which he employs ordinary household objects, such as a couch or a television, in his art. Although Browne's family was not especially bookish, his father was a frustrated painter and helped spark his son's artistic interest—one that, Browne says, manifested itself from the start in storytelling pictures and in visual jokes, such as a decapitated talking head he drew as a child.

Browne obtained a degree in graphic design from Leeds College of Arts. He then worked as a medical artist at the Royal Infirmary (a stint that developed his gift for visual narration, for he learned to "tell the story of an operation in pictures"), as a teacher, and as a greeting-card designer before publishing his first book, *Through the Magic Mirror,* in 1976. Many notable works followed, among them the deceptively simple but unset-

Illustration by Anthony Browne from his book *Gorilla* (1983).

tling *Bear Hunt* (1979) and the more ominous *Bear Goes to Town* (1982); *Willy the Wimp* (1984), a hilarious tale that spoofs the physical-fitness craze by profiling a chimpanzee who remains as timid as ever despite a beefed-up physique (followed a year later by *Willy the Champ*); *The Visitors Who Came to Stay* (1984), by Annalena McAfee, another title which demonstrates his remarkable ability to plumb an unhappy child's inner world; and a version of *Hansel and Gretel* (1981) that was, variously, praised for its effective use of symbol to suggest both external and psychic realities and excoriated for its grimly contemporary setting. As the controversy attending this last title implies, Browne is a boldly unconventional artist whose striking images rarely fail to elicit a powerful response. ♦ A.J.M.

Bruchac, Joseph

American author, b. 1942. Joseph Bruchac III, partially descended from Abenaki Indians, has drawn on his Native American heritage throughout his writing career. Born in Saratoga Springs, New York, Bruchac attended Cornell and Syracuse University and received his doctorate from Union Graduate School. He has taught literature and writing in West Africa, at American universities, and in a prison school. His first adult book, *Indian Mountain and Other Poems* (1971), was followed by many volumes of poetry and by novels such as *Dawn Land* (1993).

His early works for children include *Turkey Brother, and Other Tales: Iroquois Folk Stories* (1975) and *Stone Giants and Flying Heads: Adventure Stories of the Iroquois* (1978). These retold tales are written with authority but were published in unfortunately mediocre editions. Two oversized volumes, *Keepers of the Earth: Native American Stories and Environmental Activities for Children* (1988) and *Keepers of the Animals: Native American Stories and Wildlife Activities for Children* (1991), both written with Michael J. Caduto, interestingly combine stories, crafts, and scientific experiments but are directed at an adult audience of parents and educators.

Bruchac is best known for his picture book texts. Written with Jonathan London, *Thirteen Moons on Turtle's Back: A Native American Year of Moons* (1992) is a collection of evocative, yet mysterious poems, each celebrating a different Native American nation. The *First Strawberries: A Cherokee Story* (1993) is a moving folktale about marital respect. *Fox Song* (1993) weaves elements of Native American culture into the story of a contemporary child's grief over her great-grandmother's death. Illustrated by distinguished artists, these accessible, emotionally satisfying texts prove Bruchac to be a formidable talent in the field of multicultural books for children. ♦ P.D.S.

Bryan, Ashley

American author and illustrator, b. 1923. Born in the Bronx, New York City, Ashley Bryan was artistic from childhood. He considers his work as an illustrator to be a "natural outgrowth" of his love for drawing and painting and makes no distinction between the fine arts and fine illustration, "since, through the ages, artists have used themes from tales or books as a basic resource for expression."

Bryan majored in philosophy at Columbia University and also graduated from two art schools, the Cooper Union Art School and Columbia. He taught drawing and painting at Queens College, Lafayette College, the Dalton School, and other institutions around New York. He has also worked in the Head Start program and within organizations such as churches, teaching art to children. He had the idea of illustrating folktales years before he illustrated his first book, *Fablieux*, in 1964; after illustrating one more book, he began to create his own works. His first, *The Ox of the Wonderful Horns and Other African Tales* (1971), contained four tales of trickery. Bryan does extensive research into source material and adapts it for his authentic tales. Many of his books are illustrated with paintings made to resemble woodcuts; with this technique, the art in the finished book bears a closer relation to the original art.

Bryan's next book, *Walk Together Children: Black American Spirituals* (1974), grew out of an interest in that music while he was growing up. In this case, he used block prints, inspired by early religious block-print books, to illustrate the book. Music, language, and art converged again in *Beat the Story-Drum, Pum-Pum* (1980), a collection of folktales told with humor and a rhythmic, poetic use of language. The book won the 1981 Coretta Scott King award for illustration, given by the American Library Association. In addition to his books of spirituals and folktales, Bryan illustrated and introduced a volume of poetry by Paul L. Dunbar, *I Greet the Dawn* (1978). In a critical article for *The Horn Book Magazine* in 1979, he discusses not only Dunbar's poetry in dialect and in standard English, but gives an overview of African American poets that is as elegantly written as it is informative. Bryan has also written poetry; in his *Sing to the Sun* (1992), twenty-three original poems are depicted in illustrations that are composed of

Voices of the Creators

Ashley Bryan

I can't remember a time when I have not been drawing or painting. This is my nondiscursive way of speaking, the voice at the heart of all I do. Look at my paintings, the illustrations in my books. They are voices, telling you things about myself that I cannot put into words. Let me tell you what I can.

I was born in Harlem, New York, and raised in the Bronx. My book publication came early, in kindergarten, uh-huh! As we learned the alphabet, we drew pictures for each letter. When we reached *Z*, we used colored construction paper as the cover, and then we sewed the pages together. That was my first published book; I was author, illustrator, binder, and distributor as well. Number books, word books, sentence books followed.

There was a large family at home: my mother and father, three brothers, two sisters, and three cousins my parents raised when my aunt died. These one-of-a-kind "limited editions" received rave reviews from all. Encouraged, I published books as gifts to family and friends on all occasions. By the time I was in third or fourth grade, I had published hundreds of books.

That has led up to and prepared me for the books I do now. The difference is that now my books are printed in the thousands. I tell the children I meet that behind every commercially published book I do today there is that one-of-a-kind "limited edition," just like the ones I made in elementary school, like the ones they are doing now.

After graduating from high school, I went on to college at the Cooper Union art school in New York City. There I studied the art of world cultures.

My studies in African art were vital to me because that is the art of my ancestors. In a number of my books of African folktales the illustrations were inspired by my studies of African masks, sculpture, textiles, jewelry, and rock paintings. I work to develop a personal style, based on these influences.

Sometimes a text leads to another approach. This opens an exploration of other cultures for the illustrations in some of my books. Whatever the source or influences, I try to absorb them and offer visual statements that speak of myself.

I illustrated African folktales to texts that were, generally, quite brief. They documented story motifs but had little to do with the oral tradition of storytelling. When my illustrations were to be used in a book, I wanted a livelier form of story to accompany my illustrations. I began retelling the tales.

To approach the oral tradition in written form, I work from poetry. I study the work of the Black American poets.

Poetry is an oral art. Like song, it is meant to be heard, and like song, a poem requires practice before it can be shared with an audience. I practice reading poems aloud, listening for the sound of the voice in the printed word.

I then apply this practice to my writing, using the devices of poetry in my retelling of the tales. I hope, in this way, to catch the ear of the reader, to suggest the presence of the storyteller, even when one is reading silently.

My work with the Black American spirituals is very important to me. These songs come from the time of slavery and are a gift from the musical genius of the Black people. They are considered America's most distinctive contribution to world music and are loved and sung throughout the world. Over a thousand spirituals have been collected since the end of the Civil War. Though many were sung, there were no introductory books for young people devoted solely to selections of these songs. I have done five books of spirituals, and I will continue to offer selections of these songs in books for all ages.

I now live on a small island off the coast of Maine. I paint from the landscape, illustrate books, retell African tales, make puppets from things gathered on daily walks along the shore. I use beach glass to make stained-glass panels, and I play instruments.

These are different activities, but I see them all as illuminations of myself. Still, there's more to my story, as there is to yours, than all of these things put together. For my work with books, I see them interacting with the many-faceted potential of the viewer and reader as well.

In my programs to audiences on Black culture, I try to push past resistance, stereotypes, categories; the walls that separate us from others and from ourselves. I try, through my presence and work, to open audiences to feelings, revelations that may change or be included in their lives.

So I go on creating toward that end, seeking further into the realms of the unexplored.

color blocks stylized somewhat like stained glass windows.

Ashley Bryan began an association with Dartmouth College in the early 1970s, and after serving as chairman of the Art Department, he is now professor emeritus of Art and Visual Studies. Bryan exhibits his work on the island in Maine where he has spent his summers for three decades and to which he intends to move permanently. He is known for his dramatic readings of his own and others' works, using different voices and grand gestures. He creates puppets using driftwood, shells, and bones, which he uses when telling stories on the island. Ashley Bryan has exhibited his paintings in many one-man shows and has lectured extensively on his own work and on African American poets. He was invited by the American Library Association to deliver the 1990 May Hill Arbuthnot Lecture. S.H.H.

BULLA, CLYDE ROBERT

AMERICAN AUTHOR, B. 1914. When Clyde Robert Bulla was a first-grader in the tiny one-room schoolhouse in the farming town of King City, Missouri, he was asked by his teacher, "What would you buy if you had a hundred dollars?" Bulla replied that he would choose a table, though the reason behind this unusual wish was not clear to him. Later on, when he realized that his goal in life was to be a writer, his choice seemed eminently sensible.

Born on January 9, 1914, Bulla was the last child of four. His father was a frustrated scientist who supported his family through farming, and his mother "cooked, sewed, kept house, made do with little and hoped for better things," Bulla recalls. In his autobiography, *A Grain of Wheat* (1955), Bulla describes his family's indifference to his ambition to be a writer. His father maintained he could never be a writer because he had nothing to say. Though his mother was slightly more encouraging, she was discouraged by his early lack of success. Though Bulla was aware of his parents' doubts, as a schoolboy he found some hope in winning a small prize in a local essay contest. It is notable that the themes of persistence and self-reliance are prevalent in many of his stories and that his young protagonists often have to make their own way without much support from adults—striking parallels from Bulla's own efforts to become a writer.

The scope and volume of Bulla's work is a remarkable achievement for the artist, who in spite of his doubts has earned an indelible place as a writer for children. The author of more than fifty books, Bulla's subjects include history, FANTASY, Bible stories, and operas. He has written PICTURE BOOKS as well as novels, holiday stories and science books. In 1975 he published one of his best-known stories, *Shoeshine Girl,* about ten-year-old Sarah Ida, an angry and uncooperative child who is sent to visit her aunt, in another town, where she gains a sense of independence and generosity by working for a kindly shoeshine man. Bulla was awarded the Sequoyah Children's Book Award as well as the Charlie May Simon Children's Book Award in 1978 for this title.

In *White Bird* (1966) young John Thomas goes against his guardian Luke's wishes to track down his stolen bird. Though Luke has always cautioned him against venturing into the nearby town, John Thomas's search takes him away from his home and his guardian's oppressive hold. *The Chalk Box Kid* (1987), one of Bulla's most widely read books, shows the ingenuity of a young boy whose birthday is forgotten when his family moves to a new house after the father loses his factory job. Forced to share a room with his unsympathetic uncle, Gregory adjusts to his new surroundings and the loneliness of his school life by creating a magnificent chalk garden on the walls of a burnt-out building. There his art triumphs, and the adults in his life are forced to reckon with his talent. *A Lion to Guard Us* (1981) vividly describes the courage of a brother and sister as they make the perilous journey from England to Jamestown without their parents.

Like their creator, Bulla's characters have had to find hope where they could and to survive under conditions that were often challenging for physical or emotional reasons. Though their struggle is tinged with an underlying sadness, they emerge in the end as stronger versions of themselves having overcome some obstacle.

Bulla's writing style has a simple and direct appeal. His settings and characters are tightly interwoven. When writing, the author asks himself, "What kind of person is the hero? What is his environment, and how does he react to it?" A resident of Los Angeles for many years, Bulla describes himself as "someone who is not easily bored." His career, he explained once, has kept a simple rhythm: "I write. I travel. I come home to write again." C.L.L.

BUNTING, EVE

AMERICAN WRITER, B. 1928. Eve Bunting, born in Ireland, tells of the tradition of the Shanachie, who "went from house to house telling his tales of ghosts and fairies, of old Irish heroes and battles still to be won." The author says, "Maybe I'm a bit of a Shanachie myself, telling my stories to anyone who'll listen." With more than one hundred titles to her credit, this prolific author has shared her unique storytelling talents in PICTURE BOOKS, MIDDLE-GRADE NOVELS, and YOUNG ADULT NOVELS. Her stories explore the imaginary worlds of giants and ghosts as well as contemporary themes that reflect the adolescent world.

Bunting's writing career began in 1958, when she moved to California with her husband and three children. Several years after the transition to a new country, she enrolled in a writing-for-publication class at her local junior college. "All doubts vanished when I had my first published story and then my first published book," she recalls.

The sheer range and volume of Bunting's work make one speculate as to how the author generates so many new ideas. "I would definitely say that ninety percent of my story seeds come from something I've read in my daily paper or in my weekly periodical . . . and the other ten percent from what I see happening around me." Bunting's books have tackled homelessness, in the picture book *Fly Away Home* (1991); mixed-up identities, in *Sharing Susan* (1991); and responsibility, in *Our Sixth Grade Sugar Babies* (1990). In *Babies*, Bunting, with a light touch, looks at the perils of a classroom experiment in which each sixth-grader is expected to look after a five-pound bag of sugar as if it were a baby. For Vicki this is a chance to try to prove to her mother that she can be trusted to baby-sit her half sister. But when a handsome seventh-grader asks her to go bicycling, Vicki is faced with some uncomfortable choices about her charge.

Bunting's stories are well paced and engaging. *Coffin on a Case* (1992) introduces Henry Coffin, the twelve-year-old son of a private investigator who spends part of the summer helping an attractive high school student track down her missing mother. Appealing even to reluctant readers, the light-hearted book won the best Juvenile Mystery Edgar Award in 1993. In addition to this award, Bunting has received the Golden Kite Award from the Society of Children's Book Writers and Illustrators in 1976 for *One More Flight* (1976) and the Southern California Council on Literature for Children and Young People 1993 Distinguished Body of Work Award. Reaching a variety of readers is an important part of Bunting's work. She says, "One of my greatest joys as a writer is the knowledge that I do reach older, reluctant readers."

Bunting's characters wrestle with the choices that face them, and their responses are believable and genuine. Yet, without becoming didactic, the author skillfully guides her readers to responsible choices. Her adult as well as her child characters are not immune to problems or mistakes. In *The Wednesday Surprise* (1989), the father is illiterate and tries to hide the fact from his young daughter. In *Sixth-Grade Sleepover* (1986), Janey's parents help her overcome her fear of the dark, which resulted from a negative experience with a harsh baby sitter. Bunting deals with compelling issues. Her protagonists often face difficult situations and choices because, as she says, "That's life." ❧ C.L.

Burch, Robert

AMERICAN AUTHOR, B. 1925. Robert Joseph Burch displays a keen understanding of the problems children face while growing up. An idea about a struggling protagonist often motivates his writing, which begins by envisioning characters: "After I know them so well that they are real to me, I consider plot." Because he wanted to write a character study of a young person entrapped by the once widespread sharecropping system, Burch wrote *Skinny* (1964), about a self-reliant boy who has a series of spirited adventures after being orphaned by his alcoholic father's death. *Queeny Peevy* (1966) concerns the feisty motherless child of a small-town ne'er-do-well and grew out of Burch's desire to portray "a type of person who covers up deep-seated hurt with outrageous behavior." A creation in the same vein is Ida Early, a mountain Mary Poppins, who has the figure and dubious habits of a scruffy young man but who is a caring nurturer nonetheless. She endears herself to readers in *Ida Early Comes over the Mountain* (1980) and *Christmas with Ida Early* (1983). Although it has a more contemporary setting, *King Kong and Other Poets* (1986) concerns yet another misfit, Marilyn, a motherless child with a rich imagination and poetic talent.

Burch admits, "Often the setting and the economic circumstances of my stories are what I have known firsthand." He grew up on a Georgia farm during the Depression and, he has said, "I try to show there were lots of things more important than money or material wealth." Burch didn't intend to be a writer; he never kept notebooks while growing up. It was not until he was thirty years old, living in New York, that he took a writing course "for the fun of it." Dr. William Lipkind —"Will" of the author-illustrator partnership producing the Will and Nicolas picture books—was the instructor, the one who encouraged Burch to write for children.

A pioneer in the more clear-eyed realistic fiction of

the 1960s, Burch is often criticized for his less-than-perfect and highly permissive parents, but the young protagonists learn to use their independence responsibly. They may live in impoverished rural areas or be part of nontraditional families, but they are fresh and original, possessing warmth, humor, and traditional values—laced with hard-edged practicality. It is a perspective young readers have welcomed for more than thirty years. ❧ S.A.B.

Burgess, Gelett

American nonsense poet and illustrator, 1866–1951. The most quoted poem in twentieth-century America, after "The Night before Christmas," was almost certainly a four-line nonsense jingle by the irrepressible young Gelett Burgess, entitled "The Purple Cow." So well remembered that the first words follow unbidden after the title—"I never saw a purple cow, / I never hope . . . "—the famous quatrain came to haunt Burgess, hurled at him by presidents (Theodore Roosevelt, Woodrow Wilson, Franklin Delano Roosevelt) and passersby alike. His early rejoinder—"Ah, Yes, I Wrote the 'Purple Cow'— / I'm Sorry, now, I Wrote it! / But I can Tell you Anyhow, / I'll Kill you if you Quote it!"—served, if anything, to reinforce the fame of his creation.

Among children, their parents, and connoisseurs of juvenile regalements, Burgess was also renowned as the inventor of "The Goops," a tribe of rubber-limbed, balloon-headed, infantlike creatures whose offenses against mannerly behavior were cited, in *Goops and How to Be Them* (1900), as dire warnings to the young. And, entertained by Burgess's good-natured admonitions and droll illustrations, the young responded in kind: "Don't be a Goop," they said to one another.

The Goops were not born looking or acting like children. Along with the "P. Cow" (as Burgess called it) they first saw the light in the most celebrated of the decade's unruly little magazines, *The Lark*. Launched by Burgess and other young San Francisco iconoclasts in May 1895 as a sixteen-page pamphlet printed on splintery bamboo paper, *The Lark* offered a monthly repast of "essay, verse, fiction, nonsense," virtually all soon written and illustrated by Burgess, for two increasingly successful years. Then, because "I wanted it to die young and in its full freshness," he shut it down and headed east.

The *Lark* motto, said Burgess, was "Only such Humor as would be understood by your Grandfather and your Grandson." Unlike the Chicago-based *Chap-Book* and its progenitor, *The Yellow Book* of British fin-de-siècle decadence fame, *The Lark* exuded an air of lighthearted, ageless (and timeless) abandon. In this respect, Burgess was at one with Edward Lear and Lewis Carroll, his distinguished forebears in the field of nonsense. Like Lear's limericks and *Alice's Adventures in Wonderland,* "The Purple Cow" was originally composed for a child acquaintance. In the first issue of *The Lark* it took pictorial form as a sportive cow and a supplicating androgynous nude, against an art nouveau design of tendrils and loops—cause of innocent merriment, still.

And so were other nonsense rhymes and drawings in *The Lark*, which are preserved along with the "P. Cow" and oddments from other periodicals in *The Burgess Nonsense Book* (1901). A strong Little Boy—"Terrible Strong"—reaches from an upper window to stretch a puny Three-Foot lamppost to proper Second-Story height. A Giant Horse goes walking through the Town, "A-Stepping into all the Roofs, / And smashing Houses Down!" Besides a child's wild dreams come true, Burgess preferred the sheer nonsense of such as "The Window Pain": "The Window has Four Little Panes; / But One have I— / The Window Pains are in its Sash; / I Wonder Why!"

The original Goops, also preserved in *The Burgess Nonsense Book,* were sinuous, featureless, all-purpose figures ("A Co-Tangent, Harmonious Loop"). They were transformed into ill-behaved children on the pages of *St. Nicholas* magazine and, enlarged upon for *Goops and How to Be Them,* remained popular through a half-dozen sequels and spin-offs; the last, *New Goops and How to Know Them,* appeared only in 1951, a half century after the first.

Burgess's other attempt to create something especially for children, *The Lively City O'Ligg* (1899), sank with hardly a ripple. Under the subtitle "A Cycle of Modern Fairy Stories for City Children," we encounter "The Terrible Train," "The Very Grand Piano," "The House Who Walked in Her Sleep," and so on—a highly original assortment of tales animating the inanimate, in a mix of traditional nonsense ("the dish ran away with the spoon") and Hans Christian Andersen whimsy.

In addition to "Goop" as a label for the uncouth, Burgess was responsible for the expression "bromide" for a platitudinous bore, as laid out in *Are You a Bromide?* (1906), and for the term "blurb" apropos of a brief accolade on a book jacket. He wrote numerous other books for adults too—novels, short stories, serious essays, satire—without repeating his earlier success. But he will forever remain what he was for contemporaries: the poet laureate of America's all-inclusive age of nonsense. ❧ B.B.

Burgess, Thornton W.

American author, 1874–1965. For much of his adult life, Thornton W. Burgess wrote a new children's story every day of the week but Sunday. These tales, published in newspaper columns, magazines, and well over a hundred book-length volumes, combined the author's interests in nature and storytelling.

Burgess was born in the small Cape Cod village of Sandwich, Massachusetts. He attended a Boston business college for one year, but economic constraints prevented him from continuing his education. Burgess worked as a cashier and bookkeeper in a shoe store for two years before he began writing advertising copy, newspaper stories, and magazine verse. Hired as an office boy at the Phelps Publishing Company in Somerville, Massachusetts, he advanced to associate editor of one of their most popular publications, *Good Housekeeping.*

Burgess's first work was written for his son, whose mother had died during childbirth. When the boy was five years old and visiting relatives in another state, Burgess sent him stories about Peter Rabbit, Jerry Muskrat, Sammy Jay, Mr. Black Snake, and many other characters who reside in the Green Forest and Green Meadows. These anthropomorphic animals, along with Mother West Wind and her children, the Merry Little Breezes, appear in *Old Mother West Wind* (1910) and seven more volumes in the "Mother West Wind" series, including *Mother West Wind's Animal Friends* (1912) and *Mother West Wind "How" Stories* (1916).

Each book is composed of stories that fall into three main categories. There are mild adventures about jokes the animals play and parties they attend, fables purporting to explain such things as why Grandfather Frog has no tail, and moralistic stories that are clearly meant to be instructive to young readers. Although the writing style is precious and occasionally quite stilted, the books found an audience among children, who enjoyed the simple writing and whimsical humor. Burgess conveys an appreciation for the natural world and strives for accuracy in describing the physical appearance of each animal, but the characters display a broad spectrum of human emotions and behavior. It is not surprising that the author occasionally refers to his animal characters as "little people."

Among Burgess's best-known works is the twenty-volume "Bedtime Story-Books" series, which includes *The Adventures of Johnny Chuck* (1913), *The Adventures of Danny Meadow Mouse* (1915), and *The Adventures of Bob White* (1919). These books focus on individual animals, most of whom were introduced in the "Mother West Wind" series. Many of the didactic episodes drive home their moral lessons with couplets such as "Who makes an enemy a friend, / To fear and worry puts an end."

Burgess was one of the most prolific authors of his era. He wrote a number of other series, including the "Boy Scouts" series, the "Wishing Stone" series, and the "Smiling Pool" series. The "Natural History" series, which includes *The Burgess Bird Book for Children* (1919) and *The Burgess Flower Book for Children* (1923), presents factual information about nature within a fictional framework. His adult memoir, *Now I Remember: Autobiography of an Amateur Naturalist* (1960), describes the love of nature that informed most of his juvenile works.

Although his books are now dated by a sentimental writing style, they were among the most popular titles published for children in the early twentieth century.

P.D.S.

Burkert, Nancy Ekholm

American illustrator, b. 1933. Although her body of work is small, Nancy Ekholm Burkert is well known for her fine illustrations for works by such masters as Hans Christian Andersen, Edward Lear, Roald Dahl, the Brothers Grimm, and Emily Dickinson. Quality, not quantity, is clearly her motto. Meticulously detailed endpapers, informative prefaces, and her intricately detailed artwork, usually created in brush, ink, and pencil, combine to create a beautiful package. To Burkert, producing a book is a work of art in itself.

Always striving for authenticity, Nancy Ekholm Burkert researches each new project in depth so that all aspects of her illustration remain true to the text. Verisimilitude doesn't always correspond with readers' expectations, however, as in the case of Burkert's Caldecott Honor edition of the Grimm brothers' classic fairy tale *Snow-White and the Seven Dwarfs* (1972). Burkert's interpretation varies distinctively from the popular Disney version that most readers know, but most aficionados find hers infinitely superior. The clothing, furnishings, and architecture reflect the medieval setting of the story of Snow-White, an innocent girl threatened by her evil stepmother and befriended by dwarfs when she stumbles into their cabin in the woods. With illustrations true to the somber mood of this Grimm tale of greed and jealousy, Burkert respectfully depicts the dwarfs as they are in the story—working, misproportioned men, not carefree caricatures.

Burkert's concern for social issues and the environment all provides inspiration for her artwork. *Valentine*

& Orson (1989) is an epic romance about twin brothers who, after being separated at birth, meet as foes but become fast friends. With its themes of brotherly love and peaceful resolution, this book is Burkert's personal response to the threat of nuclear devastation. In *The Scroobious Pip* (1968), a nonsense poem left unfinished by Edward Lear and later completed by Ogden Nash, Burkert makes a plea for conservation. As she states in her preface, many of the creatures that Lear, writing in the nineteenth century, included in his poem are now extinct. With her exuberant illustrations, Burkert captures Lear's joyous celebration of the diversity of the animal world. An amazing variety of curious creatures, depicted with exacting attention to every feather and fin, gather together to see the Pip—part bird and beast, part insect and fish.

Burkert's feeling for the theme of the beauty and fragility of nature is clear in her decision to illustrate *The Acts of Light,* poems by Emily Dickinson, and two Hans Christian Andersen tales: the poignant holiday favorite *The Fir Tree* (1970) and the classic story *The Nightingale* (1965). In the latter, set in imperial China, the emperor and his court love the nightingale's comforting song but find the bird too plain in appearance and create a jeweled mechanized facsimile to replace it. However, the man-made bird's song is no match for the real bird's song, and the emperor learns that beauties of the natural world cannot be owned or copied.

Although often set in distant time periods and places, Nancy Ekholm Burkert's books celebrate universal truths—the need for love, peaceful coexistence among all humanity, and respect for the natural world—which she feels are important for today's children to discover. Through her beautifully produced picture books, readers will gain something else, as well—a respect for books as an art form. ❧ A.M.D.

Burnett, Frances Hodgson

English-born American writer and playwright, 1849–1924. Although now best known for her

Illustration by Nancy Ekholm Burkert from *Snow-White and the Seven Dwarfs* (1972), by the Brothers Grimm, translated by Randall Jarrell.

children's novels *Little Lord Fauntleroy* (1886), *Sara Crewe* (1888), and *The Secret Garden* (1911), Frances Hodgson Burnett first established herself as a late Victorian novelist and playwright for adults. A hardworking and prolific writer known for her use of telling details, Burnett became a self-described "pen-driving machine," using her storytelling skills in a quest for financial and social security. Much has been written of Burnett's fondness for a particular garden behind a childhood home in Manchester, England, of her fascination with the poor children who ran in the alleyways just beyond, and of her lively imagination that turned to inventing stories at a very young age. According to her autobiography, her formative years were not only full of books, but also full of experiences she would later use in her writing.

Burnett was an established American novelist and dramatist, as well as a wife and the mother of two young boys, when she began to write for children. Her first stories appeared in *St. Nicholas* magazine, but it was *Little Lord Fauntleroy,* written for her boys, that cemented her international reputation as a children's writer. It is unfortunate that Cedric Fauntleroy, the charming American grandson of a crusty English earl, has been stereotyped as a sissy, for he is a charming and resourceful child. But his characteristic velvet suit with Vandyke collar, a fashion of the day, was forced on many real-life boys who then looked upon the novel with disfavor. Nonetheless, it became one of the best-selling books of all time on both sides of the Atlantic, and spawned dozens of theatrical and film interpretations. The book's success encouraged Burnett to write more and better works, such as *Sara Crewe,* which, although another rags-to-riches story, uses a child's point of view. Burnett's dramatization of *Sara* greatly expanded on the slim story and was so successful Burnett was urged to make the expanded play back into a novel. It was given the play's American title, *A Little Princess.*

Not all Burnett's work was well written or successful. Several of her children's novels written at this time, such as *Editha's Burglar* (1888) and *The Two Little Pilgrims' Progress* (1895), have appropriately faded into obscurity. Much was rightly criticized as overly romantic and cloying. But *The Secret Garden* persists as one of the most popular children's books of all time. Begun in 1909, while Burnett was establishing a garden for her new Long Island home, its clear-eyed characterization of unattractive Mary Lennox and her hypochondriac cousin Colin Craven is compelling. The plot is original, and it incorporates much of what we now know to be sound psychology. The spoiled orphan Mary is transformed by her physical labors in a long-neglected garden and by her social efforts with peevish Colin, and both benefit from their friendship with guileless Dickon. Although the novel made no great impact when first published, it still affects readers deeply. Burnett's final major children's book, *The Lost Prince* (1915), has a highly romantic plot that does not match the power of *The Secret Garden.* Popular taste turned against all her writing for adults, but Burnett had the satisfaction of seeing some of her work for children well established. She echoed one recurring theme when she observed, "The happiest thing in the world is to feel that, after all, one's work was worthy of the doing." ❧ S.A.B.

BURNFORD, SHEILA

SCOTTISH-BORN CANADIAN WRITER (1918[8]1984). Critical debate goes on over whether *The Incredible Journey* (1961) is a model of the realistic animal novel or whether it is, like Anna Sewell's *Black Beauty,* another sentimental and anthropomorphic animal tale for children. Ironically, Burnford did not even conceive the novel as a children's book.

Sheila Burnford wrote just six books, only two for

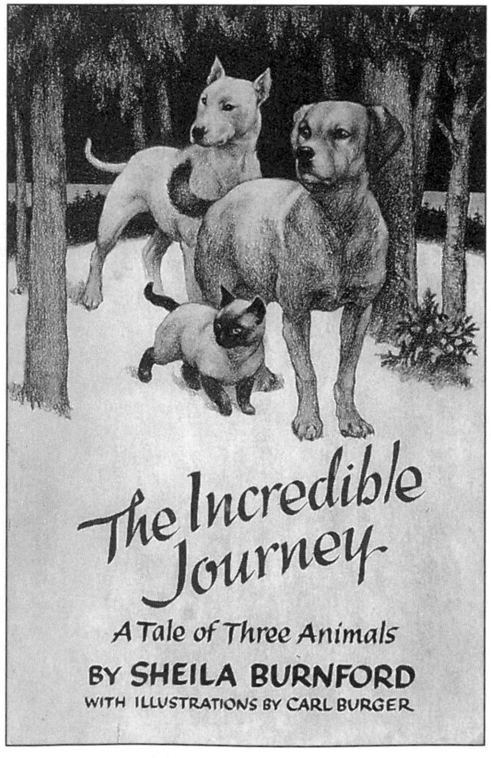

Jacket illustration by Carl Burger for *The Incredible Journey* (1961), by Sheila Burnford.

children. But *Mr. Noah and the Second Flood* (1973), which she intended for children, is not read today; *The Incredible Journey*, which has been claimed by them, outshines work by more prolific writers for children. The fictional story tells of a treacherous 250-mile journey through the Canadian wilderness made by three animal friends—an old bull terrier, a Siamese cat, and a Labrador retriever. While their owners vacation, the trio are left in the care of a family friend, but they escape and embark on the trek home. They struggle against wild animals, interfering humans, and rugged terrain, all the while fighting their domestication in order to survive and protect each other. The animals—and their relationships—were taken from life.

Born in Scotland and privately educated in England and Europe, Burnford lived in Sussex during World War II, when her children were young. She once recalled, "I came to rely upon [Bill, my English bull terrier] for comfort and security far more than one would in normal times." She talked to him, even read aloud to him for long stretches at a time. After they moved to Canada, a Siamese kitten, Simon, was added to the family "as companion and consolation for Bill, when the children were away all day at school. They were closer than any other cat-and-dog relationship I have seen." When Burnford's husband later acquired a Labrador, the aging bull terrier and young Lab developed an interdependent relationship as well. It was at this time that Burnford started writing for magazines, and, when Bill died, *The Incredible Journey* began to take shape.

The novel turns on one of Burnford's long-standing interests, the "individual and original communication that exists even between animals of diversified species when they live harmoniously with common domestic background." *The Incredible Journey* has been translated into over twenty languages and made into two WALT DISNEY films, the first (1963) using the same name, and more recently (1993) as *Homeward Bound: The Incredible Journey.* It has received numerous awards, including the Canadian Library Association's 1963 Book of the Year for Children Medal, the counterpart to the Newbery Medal. It was placed on the 1964 IBBY Honor List, named an ALA Notable Book, and in 1971 received a Lewis Carroll Shelf Award.

Fans point to the highly dramatic third-person point of view and to Burnford's care in keeping the animals true to their breeds. Critics point out the plot's heavy reliance on coincidence and the animals' human motivations. Although flaws exist, the strengths far outweigh them and the body of children's literature has no finer example of realistic animal fiction than *The Incredible Journey.* ❧ S.A.B.

BURNINGHAM, JOHN

BRITISH AUTHOR AND ILLUSTRATOR, B. 1936. John Burningham is one of the most respected author-illustrators of books for the very young. His books convey a message that children love: Though dependent on their parents in many ways, they have a rich life of their own apart from them.

Burningham was born in Farnham, Surrey, England, and his family—which included his two older sisters—moved frequently while he was growing up because his father was a salesman. Burningham attended ten different schools, including A. S. Neill's Summerhill, well known as a place where nonconformism was the norm. Burningham was an indifferent student at every school he attended—although he loved art—and he preferred to be out of doors. A conscientious objector for two years during the 1950s Burningham worked on farms, in hospitals, and on forestry projects. After his alternative service, he attended London's Central School of Art and Craft, where he met his wife-to-be, illustrator HELEN OXENBURY. After finishing art school, London Transport gave him an assignment designing posters. After a brief time in New York, Burningham returned to London and was teaching part-time in art school when his first book sold.

This first attempt at writing and illustrating was accepted when an editor saw a rough draft of *Borka, the Adventures of a Goose with No Feathers* (1963). The book won the Kate Greenaway Medal and encouraged Burningham to pursue a career in children's books. In 1973 he wrote and illustrated *Mr. Gumpy's Outing,* the story of a man who goes out for a Sunday afternoon ride on the river and ends up with a boat full of children and animals. For this book he once again won the Kate Greenaway Medal, which secured him a respected place in Great Britain's children's literature world. His version of *Around the World in Eighty Days* took him on the path of Jules Verne; the real-life charting of a fictitious journey was so hectic that Burningham had no time at all to draw and had to reconstruct the trip back home in England. *Come Away from the Water, Shirley* (1978), a favorite of many readers, exhibits his customary triumph in depicting a child's imagination, in this case, one who sees herself on a pirate ship rather than at the beach in her parents' dull, prosaic world. *Would You Rather...* (1978) presents choices that make children laugh and wonder at the same time.

Burningham works in a variety of media, including crayon, charcoal, india ink, gouache, and pastel. The Burninghams have three children, Lucy, William, and Emily, and, though John did not consciously seek their

Voices of the Creators

John Burningham

I work from my house in London in a room at garden level. I draw on a big old boardroom table, which came from The Monkey Club—a school for debutantes in Kensington—and is littered with pens, pencils, paints, paper, and roughs of drawings. I look out over our garden, which is unusually large for London. At the bottom of the garden is a row of tall trees and, beyond that, a small park—so there is a lovely sense of light and air. I feel it's very important to have that sense of space while I'm working.

When I'm not working on a book, I love collecting: furniture, statues, staircases, old curtains. I travel around England and France looking for unusual things either to put in my house or to sell to someone else. As a result, our London garden has a pagoda and a large fountain, as well as a bell tower, which I rescued from a church that was being demolished. In fact, there are about twenty-six different bits and pieces from houses and churches all over England in our garden.

My younger daughter, Emily, likes finding things, too; one of her most recent finds was a large rabbit, who came to live with us, completely took us over, and, I suppose, in a vague kind of way, was the inspiration for *Aldo.* It is always difficult when someone asks me where I find my ideas for books, as there can never be a definitive answer. If I read anything that interests me or amuses me in a magazine or newspaper, I'll tear it out and stick it on the wall. I'm surrounded by scraps of paper that eventually might be the germ of an idea for a book. I spend a lot of my time just thinking—perhaps *musing* is a better word to describe this activity. I can muse for days on end, and while I'm musing, I'm really coming up with an idea, thinking about it, exploring it, and then either discarding it or, perhaps, letting it take hold. If it takes hold, I might start drawing or writing things down. More often than not, I will eventually let an idea go. But every so often something sticks and develops and gradually grows into a book.

I've always been interested in the third dimension, and many of my drawings have to be constructed layer by layer because I enjoy painting on materials—paper, cardboard, wood—so that a variety of textures comes through the printed page. Two of the most interesting projects I've been involved with in recent years were also three-dimensional. One was the animation of my book *Grandpa,* which was turned into a film, and the second was designing a real railway with stations, trains, and carriages like the ones in *Hey! Get Off Our Train* for Japan's Expo '90. The stations are now permanent sites in Japan.

I start the day with things to look forward to: a large mug of good coffee; lunch, when my wife, Helen Oxenbury, and I discuss our work or just have a general chat; and at about six o'clock, a glass of delicious red wine, preferably French (wine is another one of my interests).

Some of my projects take a long time. I've been working on one book for over ten years. It seems to have taken forever, but I feel that I must get it exactly right, and it can take months to get the book right on the pages. At times, the way I work can be painfully slow and frustrating. At other times, when I've got a deadline to meet, it's like being on a runaway train, and that can be frightening. Ultimately, I love what I do and am generally surprised and delighted that people around the world seem to love the books, too.

opinions, the offhand critiques of his readership were available to him while he worked at home. Burningham has won many awards, including the *School Library Journal*'s Best Book Award, the Child Study Association of America's Children's Book of the Year, the Deutscher Jugend-literaturpreis—the German Youth Literature Prize—the New York Times Best Illustrated Children's Books of the Year Award, and the Boston Globe–Horn Book Award for illustration. A.C.

Burton, Hester

British author, b. 1913. Whether battling rising floodwaters in Norfolk in 1953 or the mass hysteria that seized Britain in the wake of the French Revolution, the young heroes and heroines of Hester Burton's novels refuse to be conquered by fear.

The witches and goblins of her imagination were the most fearful things in Burton's own Suffolk childhood, but she, too, felt ready to face any challenge. She half jokingly attributes her supportive upbringing to her parents' secret wish that she had been born a boy. She didn't suffer "the indignities of being a girl" as keenly as did Nell, a character in her second book for children, *Castors Away!* (1962), who could never hope to study medicine or ship off to defend England against Napoleon as did her brothers. In fact, Burton believes that her physician father gave her a typewriter for her eighteenth birthday so she could become the writer he had always hoped to be.

A graduate of Oxford, she married, had three daughters, and wrote an adult biography and some children's nonfiction before finding her niche as a writer of historical fiction for children. By showing how people in the past might have faced adversity, Burton feels she helps children face the trials of life in the present. After all, some problems—poverty, bigotry, injustice—persist from era to era. In 1801 the government's failure to provide adequate living conditions for London's poor spurs Mr. Pargeter of Burton's Carnegie Medal–winning *Time of Trial* (1964) to pen plans for "The New Jerusalem," but he discovers that even the best of intentions can't neatly solve such a complicated problem. His teenage daughter, Margaret, discovers that, while most of England considers her father at worst an enemy of the state and at best an old fool, it is more noble to live by principle than public opinion.

Despite Burton's self-proclaimed fondness for the rebel, her work encourages a coming together, a bridging of the gap between social classes. A natural disaster equalizes the villagers in *The Flood at Reedsmere* (1968) as they work to save not only themselves but one another. An orphan from the slums of London, Liz in *In Spite of All Terror* (1968), forms a bond with the aristocratic family who take her into their country home when England enters World War II. Liz comes to realize that "they were inextricably bound to one another by sadness, hope, and love."

Romance as well as high ideals beats in the hearts of many of Burton's protagonists. Strong-minded young women and men pair, stimulating instead of stifling each other's spirit and intellect. That Burton fashions such gripping adventure stories from Britain's history may have something to do with her deep affection for her country, for the very soil upon which she lives. She remembers loving her garden plot so much as a child that she filled a bucket with some of its soil and spread it across her nursery floor to keep it always near.

Burton's characters never denounce their country, only the practices that keep it from providing a nurturing home for all its citizens. ❧ C.H.

Burton, Virginia Lee

American author and illustrator, 1909–1968. The undiminished reputation of Virginia Lee Burton is embodied in a lifework of seven books of her own creation and her illustrations for seven books by other writers. Taking her cue from her small sons, Aristides and Michael, Burton chose subjects that would intrigue children: Choo Choo, the runaway engine; Mary Ann, the steam shovel who helped Mike Mulligan; Katy, the brave snowplow; the Little House, who survived a city burgeoning about her; Calico, the wonder horse of a Western adventure told in a comic-strip format. All are characters who have survived for generation after generation of readers. What also survives is the quality of the art: the strong drawings in *Choo Choo* (1937) and *Calico the Wonder Horse* (1941), full of liveliness and motion; the small telling details that children enjoy finding on the pages of *Mike Mulligan and His Steam Shovel* (1939); the satisfying integration of shaped text areas and pictures in *The Little House* (1942); the decorative borders that enhance *Katy and the Big Snow* (1943).

Elements that most distinguish Burton's work are her intricate theory of design, which she used in all her books but which was particularly effective in Anne Malcomson's *The Song of Robin Hood* (1947); her sense of the wholeness of the book, that is, the relationship of successive pages, which she showed by reprising each page in a sequence of tiny drawings on the endpapers of the 1950 edition of *Calico* and of *Maybelle the Cable Car* (1952). Over the years she kept refining her theories of design and became unhappy with her art for the 1941 edition of *Calico.* Her zeal for perfection led her to redraw every illustration, sharpening details and using subtle gradations of black and white, and, happily, to use the word she originally wanted, Stinker instead of Slinker, in the title: *Calico the Wonder Horse or The Saga of Stewy Stinker.* In *Life Story* (1962) she used the device of a stage on which various characters—an astronomer, an explorer, a lecturer, an author, and an artist (herself)—dramatically pull the curtains to reveal scenes showing the history of the universe and the development of life. Act V relied on the seasonal themes and setting of *The Little House,* but far from being repetitious, the familiar scenes fit into her overarching scheme—the story of life from cosmic bang to her own backyard.

Although she illustrated several tales by Arna Bontemps and her favorite Hans Christian Andersen story, "The Emperor's New Clothes," Burton's long labor of love was *The Song of Robin Hood.* Using with virtuosity a black-and-white scratchboard technique, she designed full-page illustrations with vignettes for

Endpaper illustration by Virginia Lee Burton for her book *The Little House* (1942).

each ballad verse that are vigorous, witty, and intricately designed and detailed. *The Song of Robin Hood* was named a Caldecott Honor Book in 1948 and *The Little House* won the 1943 Caldecott Award.

Born in Massachusetts, Burton was brought up in California. Her father was the first dean at Massachusetts Institute of Technology; her mother was a poet and painter who called herself Jeanne D'Orge. Burton intended to make dance her career, but on coming to Boston in her late teens, she studied drawing with George Demetrios, a well-known sculptor whom she married in 1931. At her home in Folly Cove, part of Gloucester, Massachusetts, she taught her theories of design to friends and neighbors. Together they organized the Folly Cove Designers, a guild-type group that for over thirty years was internationally famous for its hand-block-printed textiles.

Burton never considered herself a writer, and her ideas and their subsequent development into art provided the impetus for her texts. Once her sons were grown her inspiration to create books for children waned, and she spent her time block-printing textiles and working on *Design and How!*, a book presenting her theories of design, which she had not finished at the time of her death. Her stories may be simple and straightforward; but her books have heroes and heroines children can understand and enjoy, ingenious and satisfactory endings, and lively illustrations. The books survive because they exhibit so effectively the elements most basic to children's literature. ❧ L.K.

Butterworth, Oliver

AMERICAN AUTHOR, 1915–1990. Because humorous stories are always in demand by middle-grade readers, Oliver Butterworth's novel *The Enormous Egg* has enjoyed great popularity since it was first published in 1956. The author was born in Hartford, Connecticut, and grew up in the surrounding rural area. After attending boarding school as a teenager, he received his bachelor's degree from Dartmouth College, did graduate work at Harvard, and later earned a master's degree from Middlebury College. For most of his career, Butterworth taught English at Hartford College, but the two years he taught elementary school inspired him to write books for young readers.

Drawing on this classroom background, as well as on his experiences raising chickens with his family, Butterworth wrote the story of twelve-year-old Nate Twitchell, who helps tend an enormous egg laid by a backyard hen. When a triceratops hatches, scientists and reporters descend on the Twitchell home in Freedom, New Hampshire. As the dinosaur grows to mammoth proportions, Nate travels to Washington, D.C., for a few weeks to help his pet settle at his new home in the National Museum. Although the sudden appearance of a twentieth-century triceratops is never explained and the high comic tone of the novel is not fully sustained throughout, the zany situations and Nate's matter-of-fact narration are greatly appealing to young readers.

Butterworth's second comic FANTASY, *The Trouble*

with Jenny's Ear (1960), contains much humorous dialogue, but the unwieldy, attenuated plot lacks focus. The novel initially concerns brothers Joe and Stanley Pearson, who share a great interest in electronics and install loudspeakers, closed-circuit televisions, and telephone answering machines throughout their house. The focus of the story suddenly switches to their six-year-old sister, Jenny, when she inexplicably develops the ability to read minds and exploits her telepathic talents on television so she can earn money to stop a real-estate developer from buying up a nearby hillside. Jenny's psychic adventures and her brothers' electronics antics are both amusing, but the two strands of plot never mesh. The book also includes extraneous scenes and characters and adult-oriented humor, such as a female network employee named Miss Svelt, who works with a man named Random Groper. Nevertheless, *The Trouble with Jenny's Ear* continues to be popular with young readers due to its generally humorous writing.

Butterworth's other children's books are more serious in tone. Originally published as a bibliotherapeutic pamphlet in 1987, *A Visit to the Big House* was released by a mainstream publisher in 1993. The story concerns two children whose father is in prison for stealing. *The Narrow Passage* (1973) is a return visit with Nate Twitchell, who accompanies an archaeological expedition to France, where he and a young French friend discover a cave decorated with paintings and protected by what appears to be a prehistoric man. This intriguing premise makes for an interesting story, although the plot development remains inconclusive. In addition, fans of Nate Twitchell will be disappointed to find the narrative almost completely lacking in humor.

Butterworth continues to be best known for his first two books. Although they may now seem dated by some sex-role stereotyping, both were ahead of their time in terms of their subject matter; dinosaurs and electronic gadgetry didn't explode into the public's consciousness until many years later. The books remain humorous and entertaining for today's readers. ❧ P.D.S.

Byars, Betsy

American author, b. 1928. Reading a Betsy Byars book is like talking to a good friend: ideas and problems are taken seriously, but laughter is sure to follow. Betsy Byars has written over thirty books, among them picture books, easy readers, fantasies, and historical fiction, but she is best known for her realistic fiction in which splashes of humor brighten serious subjects. Betsy Byars started writing when her children were young, first magazine articles and then children's books. Her children's books began to receive critical mention after several years, and she has won numerous awards, including the Newbery Medal for *The Summer of the Swans* (1970).

In *The Summer of the Swans,* Sara, a young girl at odds with herself and her family, discovers the strength of both when she locates her mentally handicapped younger brother, who had become lost in the woods. Betsy Byars's protagonists are usually likable preadolescents who are seeking a sense of belonging or connection to alleviate loneliness. In *The Midnight Fox* (1968), Tom, a nonathletic city boy, is sent to his aunt and uncle's farm for the summer while his parents travel in Europe. He feels lonely and out of place until he discovers a black fox and is distracted from his sadness by her wild beauty and by the fierceness with which she protects her one remaining cub.

Betsy Byars is particularly adept at making her protagonists come alive, giving vivid form to their sadness and joy. The reader is privy to much of the characters' thoughts, and the frequent use of memory and fantasy provide further illumination of character. When we first meet Betsy Byars's characters, they are frequently being pulled along by a tide of events, with little control over the direction of their lives. But from their inevitable and brave attempts to swim the current, wisdom and maturation result. When the three children in *The Pinballs* (1977) are sent to the foster home, they initially see themselves as pinballs: they simply go wherever the adult world sends them. But as they begin to care about one another, they discover that they can make choices—and take responsibility.

Unusual families are typical in Betsy Byars's books and are often significant, if not central, to the protagonist's difficulties. Frequently one or both parents are absent, due to divorce, death, or even, as in *The Two Thousand Pound Goldfish* (1982), because they are wanted by the FBI. The remaining parent or guardian is often distracted by trying to earn a living or simply gives way to selfishness. In *The Night Swimmers* (1980), while Retta's father is consumed by his attempt to become a successful country singer, Retta must be a mother to her younger brothers—with anger and sadly predictable failure as the result. Betsy Byars's "Blossom family" and "Bingo Brown" series, both for younger children, are lighter; in them the humor mingles with simpler problems than appear in her other books. The enduring popularity of Betsy Byars's books attests to her knack for connecting with the emotions and experiences of her readers. ❧ A.E.Q.

Voices of the Creators

Betsy Byars

When I was a girl, growing up in North Carolina, I made my own clothes. My father worked at a cotton mill, and we got free cloth. I have a vague memory of not being allowed to wear the outfits out of the yard, but I could soon turn out a gathered skirt in fifteen minutes. I sewed fast, without patterns and with great hope and determination, and that is approximately the same way that I write.

There is no single moment in my writing that is more satisfying, more full of promise for a bright and interesting future, than a title page. I usually get the title for a book first, and I type it up immediately. I sit there and look at it and admire it, and I think to myself, I just need four thousand sentences to go with this and I'll have a book. It is such a pleasurable moment that I type many more title pages than I could ever use.

When I start a book, I don't have the perfect idea with all the details in place. What I look for in an idea for a book is something with possibilities, something that can go many ways: kids swimming at night in someone's pool, a character lost in the woods, kids in a foster home. Basically, what I want is an idea that will allow my imagination to go to work.

The idea itself determines whether the book will be a "one-character book" or a "three-character book." If I can choose the number of characters, I always choose three—two boys and a girl or two girls and a boy. The three-character book—such as *The Pinballs* (1977) or *The Night Swimmers* (1980)—is my favorite kind of book to write. The writing goes faster, and I get to know what's going on in everybody's head. The Blossom family books, a series that began with *The Not-Just-Anybody Family* (1986), were going to be three-character books, but then I got so interested in the Blossom family that I took the point of view of the grandfather, Mad Mary, Mud (the dog), and anybody else that came along.

If it's a one-character book, such as *Cracker Jackson* (1985) or *The 18th Emergency* (1973), I always stay with the main character, even though something more interesting may be going on across town. In these books, the plot generally concerns the main character facing a problem which becomes more critical as the book progresses but which is finally solved. I always get rid of one or both of the parents in these books, because the crisis will be more dramatic if the main character has to face it alone.

Although I started my writing career on a manual typewriter (on my kitchen table) and now use a computer (in my studio), my actual method of writing has not changed. I write as fast as I can because until I see what I've done in print, I can't tell what's wrong with it or—hopefully—what's right about it.

I print what I've written, take it somewhere else—like the living room or kitchen—and I go over it. I make changes; I smooth it out; I add; I subtract. I go back to the word processor, put in the changes, go sit somewhere else, and edit it again. I keep doing this until the writing is absolutely simple, until it looks as if I haven't worked on it at all. If it looks as if I've worked on it, I go back and work some more.

I rely a great deal on instinct. If my instinct tells me something is wrong with a manuscript, it generally is. And I will rewrite an entire manuscript—as many times as it takes—to get it right. I have also had a series of excellent editors who have helped me when my instinct failed.

When I first began to write, I thought writers were like wells, and sooner or later we would use up what had happened to us and our children and our friends and our dogs and cats, and there wouldn't be anything left. We would go dry and have to quit.

I suppose we would if it weren't for that elusive quality—creativity. I can't define it, but I have found from forty years' experience that the more you use it, the better it works.

C

Caldecott, Randolph

English illustrator and author, 1846–1886. Along with Walter Crane and Kate Greenaway, Randolph Caldecott was one of the three great illustrators to work under the auspices of the English printer Edmund Evans and to usher in a golden age of book illustration for children. His style, livelier than Crane's and more robust than Greenaway's, is still held up as a model for illustrators of children's books, for his pictures were full of energy and humor as well as mischief, and they spoke to a real rather than an idealized world of childhood.

Caldecott showed an early talent for drawing and for remodeling in clay and wood, but unlike Crane and Greenaway, whose artist fathers encouraged their talents, Caldecott's father steered him away from a career in art and into banking. Caldecott continued to draw the farms and animal life of his beloved countryside in his spare time, however, and banking colleagues recall finding sketches of horses and dogs among his bills and ledgers. When he moved from the Shropshire countryside to Manchester, he took classes at the school of art and developed a group of friends among the artists of that community. By 1872 he had had several drawings published, and when he moved to London he continued to study art and sculpture. Here, too, he established close friendships with artists and publishers who encouraged his talents. Indeed, throughout his life Caldecott's warm and unassuming manner endeared him to a wide circle of friends who sought eagerly to assist his endeavors and protect his well-being. In fact, it was because of his ill health, thought to be the result of a bout with rheumatic fever when he was a child, that his good friend, editor Henry Blackburn, suggested that he illustrate travel books. This occupation would allow him to travel to milder climates and avoid English winters. One of the first of these books, *Harz Mountains: A Tour in the Toy Country* (1872), exhibits his unique and lively view of life that would so delight children and helped to establish his reputation as an illustrator.

Following a great success with the illustrations for

Illustration by Randolph Caldecott from his book *Hey Diddle Diddle* (1882).

several chapters of WASHINGTON IRVING's *Sketch Book* called *Old Christmas* (1878) and the commission for a second Irving book, *Bracebridge Hall* (1878), Caldecott began to think seriously about illustrating children's books. He knew of Walter Crane's success with his books for children and admired their quality; he turned to Crane for advice. At about the same time, the printer Edmund Evans, having seen Caldecott's illustrations for the Irving book, called upon him to propose a collaboration. Although at this point in his career Caldecott had not done much color work, Evans's success in color printing and Crane's recommendations must have convinced him to consent. Eventually, the two agreed to produce the first of sixteen picture books for children, *The Diverting History of John Gilpin* (1878) and *The House That Jack Built* (1878). In these and others, such as *The Queen of Hearts* (1881) and *Three Jovial Huntsmen* (1880), Caldecott's delight in life, his eye for the odd detail or the ludicrous incident, and his warmth and playfulness found their true home. He was a skilled draftsman, and the exceptional and lively quality of his work can be seen in his outline sketches as much as in his full-color illustrations. Caldecott was able to bring individual characters to life, giving each their own personality. Drawn with a careful sense of composition and with as much care for the empty spaces as for the little details, Caldecott's illustrations did not simply mirror words in the text, they extended them in unique, humorous, and surprising ways. His books have offered delight to readers of all ages in his time and our own. ♠ B.K.

CALHOUN, MARY

AMERICAN AUTHOR, B. 1926. Born in Keokuk, Iowa, Mary Calhoun had a childhood rich in storytelling and books. She grew up listening to her mother's stories, and she developed a love of reading by spending time at her local library. By the age of seven, she had already decided that she wanted to be an author.

Her first book, *Making the Mississippi Shout,* was published in 1957. The many pictures and novels which were to follow reflect her interests and background. Her memories of growing up in a large, old house, built by her great-grandfather, inspired her to write the books about Katie John, one of her most popular characters. Her fascination with the folklore of European elves led her to write a series of picture books about them—but only after thoroughly researching the topic. As she wrote, "In studying folklore collected in the nineteenth century, I found a whole sociology of elfdom emerging from people's beliefs. Before I was done, I felt I could take a degree in elfology."

This attention to detail is part of what has made her picture books about Henry, a resourceful, intelligent Siamese cat, among the most popular of her books. These stories would seem to be more fantasy than realism, yet Henry is, at all times, perfectly catlike. These stories of Henry's extraordinary exploits are told with a subtle blend of humor and drama that is completely engaging. In *Cross-Country Cat* (1979), Henry goes skiing; in *High-Wire Henry* (1991), he becomes a daredevil on the high wires. Both books cause children to laugh out loud. Whether writing about a lively little girl, an adventurous cat, or a mischievous elf, Mary Calhoun loves to tell stories, and these stories have already delighted two generations of children. ♠ K.F.

CAMERON, ELEANOR

AMERICAN AUTHOR AND CRITIC, B. 1912. An astute critic as well as a writer of fiction, Eleanor Cameron has earned a respected position with her dedication to upholding the highest literary standards in the evaluation of books written for children. *The Green and Burning Tree: On the Writing and Enjoyment of Children's Books* (1969) and *The Seed and the Vision: On the Writing and Appreciation of Children's Books* (1993) serve as valuable sources for teachers, parents, and others interested in critical discussions of both classics and more contemporary works.

After working for several years as a librarian, Cameron published a novel for adults in 1950 and then, at the request of her seven-year-old son, David, began work on what became the Mushroom Planet series. Over the years, countless children have shared David's enthusiasm for these stories about children traveling to a planet named Basidium, which is just the right size for exploration, and have delighted in the adventures of David and Chuck and their friends, Tyco and Theodosius Bass. Cameron's interest in astronomy and anthropology is evident in her meticulous construction of the tiny satellite of Earth and the history of its sporelike people. Cameron explores the dangers of the blind pursuit of scientific knowledge and emphasizes the importance of protecting a society from exploitation for individual gain. Less effective is her attempt to link the history of the Mushroom People to King Arthur and Welsh mythology in *Time and Mr. Bass* (1967). The series evolves from mild science fiction into a complex, semiepic fantasy, in which the spaceship serves merely as an express airplane to Wales. Nevertheless, the Mushroom Planet books provide an entertaining introduction to the science fiction genre.

Cameron's other work for children also demonstrates the influence of her personal preoccupations, particularly in its emphasis on time and place. With few exceptions, her stories take place either in California, where Cameron has lived most of her life, or in Britain. San Francisco comes to life as the city of Cameron's 1920s childhood in the series featuring Julia Redfern and as a hectic, modern city in *The Court of the Stone Children* (1973). The events and perceptions of her youth form the foundation for these novels, though Cameron uses her memories as springboards into fiction. In *A Room Made of Windows* (1970), Julia struggles with her desire to write fiction and with her frustration about the impending remarriage of her widowed mother, as Cameron did as a child. The decision to write the succeeding novels backward through time, toward Julia's early years, allowed Cameron to explore in a unique way the effects time has on character development; her challenge was to explain events referred to in the first book from the perspective of a younger, but not simpler, character. In *The Court of the Stone Children,* she intricately weaves theories of time into the ghost and mystery story.

Cameron's characters, though introspective, possess a sometimes unexpected spunk and a refreshing inquisitiveness. Each story focuses on the extraordinary, whether it is a ghost, a secret planet, a mysterious beast similar to the Loch Ness monster, or the unusual friendships and escapades of a young girl. Cameron's achievements as an author complement her insightful critical studies of children's literature. ❧ A.E.D.

Canadian Children's Literature in English

Canadian children's books of the home-grown variety—that is, created by Canadian-born writers—did not flourish until the second half of the nineteenth century, when there was more to living than the pioneer struggle for survival. Before that, the English model of children's books can be seen in early religious and educational offerings. The gap between such publications and the beginnings of a national literature was filled by a few English writers who never set foot in Canada, by visitors, and, most importantly, by Canada's best-known literary pioneer, Catharine Parr Traill.

Although an English influence was noticeable, there were differences between books that had English backgrounds and those that were set in Canada. The first difference was the land itself. It seized the imagination of many a visitor, including Frederick Marryat, author of *Settlers in Canada* (1844), and Robert M. Ballantyne, author of *Snowflakes and Sunbeams; or, The Young Fur Traders* (1856). It is worth remembering that landscape played little or no part in English children's literature until CHARLES KINGSLEY's *The Water-Babies* (1863). Moreover, these early stories of wilderness survival showed their youthful heroes as at one with their environment. The second noticeable trait of nineteenth-century books with a Canadian setting is a spirit of youthful freedom. It is no accident that all the English boys' adventure stories of the period were set in the colonies or on exotic islands. A country as class-conscious and as devoted to primogeniture as England was no place for younger sons or for those intent on improving their lot in life. But in Canada's forests, fields, and rivers, only skill, courage, and ingenuity counted—not birth and breeding.

The third quality is concerned with independent thinking. In *Little Grace; or, Scenes in Nova-Scotia* (1846) by an otherwise unknown Miss Grove, a little girl is being taught the history of her province. However, little Grace shows more spirit (and intelligence) than most English girls of her period as she thoughtfully questions what she has been told about the expulsion of the Acadians from Nova Scotia. The twelve-year-old girl in Catharine Parr Traill's *Canadian Crusoes* (1852) acts more independently and courageously than her two older male cousins. *Canadian Crusoes* (the American title is *The Canadian Crusoes*) is considered the first Canadian novel for children.

One of the first Canadian-born writers, James De Mille, gave children an opportunity to see more of Canadian life than the forests and pioneer ways of Upper and Lower Canada. He drew upon his personal knowledge of a boys' boarding school in Nova Scotia and his own youthful adventures around the Bay of Fundy for *The "B.O.W.C."* (Brethren of the White Cross), the first of a series, published in 1869. The book is remarkable for its time in that it is completely devoid of Christian sentiment or the cult of manliness and "muscular Christianity" so prevalent in English books of the period, such as Thomas Hughes's *Tom Brown's Schooldays* (1857). De Mille wrote for entertainment. He did, however, indulge in some stereotypes of the time, notably that of the good-natured "darky."

In the first two decades of the twentieth century in England and the United States, sentimentality was the most obvious characteristic in books for the young. It was the age of what Jonathan Swift described as "sweetness and light," exemplified by the Edwardian penchant for angelic heroines. In strong contrast to books for boys of some sixty years before, there came a flood of books with girls as the chief protagonists: from the United States *Rebecca of Sunnybrook Farm* (1903), *A Girl of the Limberlost* (1909), and *Pollyanna* (1913); and from England *A Little Princess* (1905). In these rhapsodic narratives the young heroines not only solve their own serious difficulties by their goodness and charm, but eventually those of all the adults around them.

Canadians not only contributed to this wave, but, for the first time, a few produced international best-sellers. The first sentimental "hit" was about a dog rather than a child. *Beautiful Joe* (1894), by the prolific Nova Scotian writer Margaret Marshall Saunders, was cast in the format of the famous English *Black Beauty* (1877), in that a mistreated dog relates the story of his life, just as Anna Sewell's horse tells of his fortunes and misfortunes. It was first published by the American Baptist Society and did much for the prevention of cruelty to animals.

However, even its popularity was insignificant in comparison with LUCY MAUD MONTGOMERY's *Anne of Green Gables* (1908), still Canada's best-known children's book. Of all the girl heroines of the Edwardian era, Anne was to be the only one with staying power, with the possible exception of FRANCES HODGSON BURNETT's Mary Lennox, protagonist of *The Secret Garden* (1911). Eighty-five years later the red-headed orphan from Prince Edward Island has gained new audiences through television adaptations of the Anne books and is extraordinarily popular in Japan and Poland. Anne's despairs and triumphs are reenacted yearly on Prince Edward Island in a musical based on the first book. The seven sequels, written under pressure from Montgomery's publishers, never captured its freshness, originality, and humor, but they are still devoured by adoring fans around the world. Montgomery's second series—the Emily books, including *Emily of New Moon* (1923), *Emily Climbs* (1925), and *Emily's Quest* (1927)—has never achieved the popularity of the Anne books, but are generally deemed superior to them in writing craft and story line by Montgomery critics.

Two other writers of the period—Nellie McClung and Ralph Connor (pseudonym of Charles William Gordon)—also achieved fame both inside and outside of Canada. However, Nellie McClung is now best remembered as an early Canadian feminist and politician rather than for her first children's book, *Sowing Seeds in Danny* (1908), and Ralph Connor is chiefly remembered for his missionary endeavors rather than for his first great publishing success, *Glengarry Schooldays* (1902). However, McClung and Connor belong with Montgomery in two important respects. Like her, they brought to life the corner of Canada about which they wrote—McClung, the small towns and farms of Manitoba and Connor, the Ottawa Valley. They also, as did Montgomery, provided children with the then rare opportunity to gain insights into the adult world, which in most children's books of the era were seldom more than shadowy.

Illustration by M. A. and W. A. J. Claus from *Anne of Green Gables* (1908), by LUCY MAUD MONTGOMERY.

While Saunders, Montgomery, McClung, and Connor were working the rich lode of sentimentality, ERNEST THOMPSON SETON and Charles G. D. Roberts were concentrating on realistic portrayals of wild animals. With Seton's *Wild Animals I Have Known* (1898) and Roberts's *The Kindred of the Wild* (1902), a new genre was formed—the animal biography. Quite distinct from the talking-animal tales of Marshall Saunders, the new form—realistic animal biography—was to be

Canada's major contribution to world literature for many years.

For about the next forty years, Canadian children's literature was fairly static. But during this period of little noticeable change or development, a few books emerged that were excellent of their kind and which held their popularity for a long time. Excerpts from Norman Duncan's *The Adventures of Billy Topsail* (1906) were reprinted for years in Canadian Readers for elementary-school students, so that almost every child knew the story of Billy's rescue from drowning by his Newfoundland dog and of his fight with an octopus. Indian legends entered the consciousness of children with the gently retold (and romantically illustrated) tales by Cyrus Macmillan in *Canadian Wonder Tales* (1918) and *Canadian Fairy Tales* (1922). In *The Adventures of Sajo and Her Beaver People* (1935) by Archibald Stansfeld Belaney (who used the pseudonym Grey Owl), the little girl Sajo became Canada's first Native Indian heroine in a realistic story that also combined a fast-paced plot with a concern for animal life and the Indian concept of the environment. In 1946 Roderick L. Haig-Brown became the first writer to produce a survival story with a teenager who had personal problems and whose character, as well as his skills and abilities, developed under his ordeals. This trend was carried on by FARLEY MOWAT in *Lost in the Barrens* (1956) and in JAMES HOUSTON's *Tikta'Liktak* (1965) and *The White Archer* (1967) and is now the basic psychological component in all modern survival stories. In 1950 Catherine Anthony Clark became Canada's first major fantasist with the publication of *The Golden Pine Cone*. This and her other five books were deeply rooted in the landscape of the British Columbia Kootenays. These books are uniquely Canadian in their settings and incorporate West Coast Native Indian culture and values.

By the middle of the 1960s, realistic fiction for children, particularly that emanating from the United States, had undergone a dramatic and drastic change. At the root of it were the turbulent social upheavals of the decade, adult changes in attitudes toward children (they were to be liberated from the domestications of childhood), and the increased influence of television. In children's literature this eventually meant a change in themes from the convention of the adventure story to the problems of the young caused by the adult world. Indeed, the term *problem novel* came to be used for a type of fiction that concentrated on social problems without regard for background, character development, or story line.

At the time, and for about another ten years, Canadian writers stood aloof from such trends. Indeed, the period is chiefly memorable for a group of retellings of Native Indian legends by nonnative writers. Today there is a strong feeling that the reworking of such material should be left to the Natives, and, indeed, there is now much creative activity in the retelling of indigenous material. However, it should be acknowledged that without such 1960s retellers as Christie Harris, Robert Ayre, Dorothy Reid, Frances Fraser, and Kay Hill, much Native Indian material might have been lost. Also in the 1960s, William Toye introduced the concept of the presentation in picture-book form of the single Indian legend. It is another trend of the time that has been continued and expanded.

The middle of the 1970s brought major changes to writing and publishing for the young. Although there were many reasons for this, they all appeared to coalesce at once. The major reasons now appear to be a rise in Canadian nationalism; the advent of small, often regional publishing firms frequently devoted chiefly or exclusively to the publishing of children's books; and an influx of government money for Canadian-owned publishers. It should be mentioned here that many of these small publishers have lasted into the 1990s, producing books that match in production, color, and excellence the books of the major publishers. Most important, when the publishing climate for children's books brightened, there was at hand a cadre of talented writers and illustrators simply waiting in the wings to be recognized.

The most noticeable change was seen at first in the numbers of picture books published, which within a few years in the late 1970s moved from almost zero to a veritable flood. This trend now includes all types of picture books, all that had hitherto been imported, chiefly from the United States and England. Many of the authors and illustrators of these works have become internationally famous: Eric Beddows, Paulette Bourgeois, KADY MACDONALD DENTON, Phoebe Gilman, TED HARRISON, STÉPHANE POULIN, Ian Wallace, and TIM WYNNE-JONES, among many others.

The young adult novel also came into prominence in recent decades and has joined its counterparts in other English-speaking countries in concentrating on adolescents in conflict with themselves and those around them, or caught in a traumatic moment of their lives. MONICA HUGHES's *Hunter in the Dark* (1982) displays both a conventional manly quality and a sensitiveness toward wild creatures as a teenager comes to terms with his anticipated death, while Kevin Major's *Hold Fast* (1978) explores a teenager's rage when both his parents are killed in an accident. Mary Razzell's *Snow Apples* (1984) and Beatrice Culleton's *In Search of April Raintree*

(1983) deal respectively with teenage love and rejection and the problems of being born between two worlds—Native Indian and white.

Much of the new fantasy also tends to fall in the sphere of the young adult novel, but since fantasy has a wider range of readership than realistic fiction, this trend is probably not of supreme importance. What is most noteworthy in recent times is the *type* of fantasy that is being written. There is no recent creation of "other worlds" such as LEWIS CARROLL's Wonderland or C. S. LEWIS's Narnia. Writers seem to be more concerned with how their protagonists are affected when the supernatural breaks into their everyday lives in the form of witchcraft, psychic powers, second sight, or some aspect of the supernatural. JANET LUNN's *Shadow in Hawthorn Bay* (1986) is a splendid example of the use of second sight (which some readers would not consider fantasy) and has deservedly acquired a wide readership. However, most of our serious fantasies by such authors as Welwyn Katz, Michael Bedard, and Margaret Buffie have strong psychological components. Allied to fantasy is science fiction, and Canada can claim pride of place through the works of Monica Hughes. It is difficult to think of a more moving science fiction story than her *Keeper of the Isis Light* (1980).

In keeping with writing and publishing trends in the United States and England, few novels are being written for middle-aged children, that is, for those between the ages of approximately nine and twelve. Most writers appear to need the freedom of adolescent life to propound their messages; they seem unwilling or unable to maneuver within the restrictions of childhood. There are some significant exceptions: these are the many child-centered novels of JEAN LITTLE, BRIAN DOYLE's *Angel Square* (1984), Jan Truss's *Jasmin* (1982), SARAH ELLIS's *The Baby Project* (1986), and Barbara Smucker's *Jacob's Little Giant* (1987). There are, of course, books of light, humorous fiction (in the style of the American BEVERLY CLEARY's Ramona books). The traditional definition of historical fiction as a story set in a time beyond living memory may be changing. Many writers now find their inspiration in the recent past. Notable among these are KIT PEARSON's *The Sky Is Falling* (1989) and its sequels, *Looking at the Moon* (1991) and *The Lights Go On Again* (1993), stories of two English children evacuated to Canada in the early years of World War II.

Canada's multicultural society is increasingly reflected in its children's books. The largest gain has been, naturally enough, in retellings of the oral tradition. Paul Yee's *Tales from Gold Mountain: Stories of the Chinese in the New World* (1989) is a collection of original stories drawing on Chinese Canadian experience and culture. Many picture books, books of realistic fiction, and historical fiction reflect this reality of Canadian life. Here a wide and welcome divergence in authorship and plot can be seen in two recent offerings. *Spud Sweetgrass* (1992) is a multiracial story with a fast-moving plot by the well-established writer Brian Doyle; while *My Name Is Seepeetza* (1992) by Native writer Shirley Stirling is the fictionalized autobiographical account of a young Native girl at an Indian residential school. There is little doubt that this segment of writing will increase to the point where the presentation of various cultures will no longer be considered ethnic but simply Canadian.

Informational books have increased in numbers and excellence, and include such gems as *The Junior Encyclopedia of Canada* (1990) and *The Story of Canada* (1992) by Janet Lunn and Christopher Moore. The latter is an example of history that is soundly researched, exceptionally readable, and beautifully produced. At the other end of the spectrum, modern poetry and verse for children has practically been created by DENNIS LEE, whose *Alligator Pie* (1974) and later collections have won the hearts of Canadian children.

Canadian children's literature has changed, as has seemingly every other children's literature in the Western world. Today's writers are as much a part of their time as earlier writers were of theirs, and their books reflect this, being more concerned with personal crises in the lives of their protagonists than physical ones, and with emphasizing, existentially, their determination to succeed through an understanding of themselves rather than depending upon physical prowess and knowledge and a belief in the help of God. Canadian children's books have become more sophisticated and less parochial. But even though they have joined "the republic of childhood" in spirit, most of the best are as distinctively Canadian as ever. ❧ SHEILA A. EGOFF

Canadian Children's Literature in French

Children's literature in French, or Quebec's children's literature (86 percent of French-speaking Canadians living in Canada reside in Quebec province) emerged less than a century ago and very nearly perished before its astonishing revival as a robust and vibrant form in the 1970s. Today, more than one out of three books published in Quebec are written for children or teenagers.

Early Quebec children's literature, beginning with

Marie-Claire Daveluy's *Les aventures de Perrine et de Charlot* (1923), the first volume in a series of historical novels written specifically for children, was overtly moralizing and didactic. Nevertheless, the most popular authors among children managed to instruct *and* entertain young readers. Marie-Claire Daveluy, for instance, embellished her tales of the founding of the colony with extraordinary adventures, including transatlantic stowaways and kidnappings by the Iroquois.

The Second World War, which slowed the importation of European books, ushered in the first golden age for children's literature in Quebec. During the first fifty years of its existence, children's literature in Quebec quietly won over its readers, shifting slowly from an adult discourse on childhood to a more child-centered view of the world. In 1942, the Alfred Collection (*Journal de bord d'Alfred, Alfred le découvreur*) promised readers "everyday heroes, full of life and imagination with their games and their dreams, their joys and their sorrows, their qualities and also, their weaknesses." Although these books retained a didactic purpose focused on socialization and Christian education, the hero had clearly embarked on a quest of fun and adventure, more closely resembling a real child than Marie-Claire Daveluy's virtuous Perrine.

L'été enchanté, Paule Daveluy's best-seller, published in 1958, was translated as *Summer in Ville-Marie* (1962). Rosanne, the sixteen-year-old heroine, falls in love with the settlement's doctor, embodying the dreams and fantasies of contemporary teenagers rather than serving to convey adult notions of adolescence. In 1963 Suzanne Martel published one of Quebec's first science fiction novels, *Quatre Montréalais en l'an 3000,* which was translated in the United States and republished under the title *Surréal 3000.* Her sister, Monique Corriveau, is a renowned and prolific children's author whose works include the popular *Le secret de Vanille* (1959), *Le Wapiti* (1964), and *Les saisons de la mer* (1975).

By 1970 the number of children's books published in Quebec could be counted on one hand. Communication-Jeunesse was founded in 1971 to promote children's book publishing. Two works appeared in 1972—*Pleins feux sur la littérature de jeunesse au Canada français* by Louise Lemieux and *La littérature de jeunesse au Canada français* by Claude Potvin—and in 1978 two magazines, *Lurelu* and *Des livres et des jeunes,* were launched. As a result of these and many other efforts, annual production rose from half a dozen books in 1970 to 250 twenty years later.

After 1975 heroes in children's fiction turned over a new leaf, becoming stronger, more independent, and more surprising than ever. More picture books appeared as talented young illustrators turned their attention to children. The arrival of Jiji in 1976, the heroine of a series of illustrated books by Ginette Anfousse (*Mon ami Pichou, La cachette . . .*), upset the cozy little world of other contemporary heroes, whose greatest trials in life consisted in tidying up an overturned basket of blueberries or suffering indigestion after a visit to the sugar shack. Jiji and Pichou, a little girl and her stuffed anteater, experience more emotionally charged situations: a quarrel between friends, fear of the *bonhomme sept heures* (the combined equivalent, in Quebec folklore, of the sandman and a benevolent bogeyman), and the desire to have a baby sister. Jiji challenges and engages children. She is mischievous, determined, resourceful, and resolutely imperfect.

Ten years later, Raymond Plante's *Le dernier des raisins* (The big loser, 1986) immediately enthralled teenage readers with the confessions of the hero, François Gougeon, in the opening lines: "A fly! I'd swallowed a fly! Not a big green garbage fly. I was pretty sure of that. Maybe just a gnat. At the worst, a dung fly. But a fly is a fly. I felt it crash into the back of my throat. Not a pleasant feeling. I'll have to learn to keep my mouth shut when I'm on a bike." Plunging into the world of adolescence, *Le dernier des raisins* deals head on with everything from driving lessons to love at first sight, as well as a *Playboy* hidden under the mattress.

Translated into six languages, *Le dernier des raisins* won several awards, including an IBBY (International Board on Books for Young People) Honor, but its greatest accomplishment lies in the fact that it initiated so many teenagers to the pleasure of reading. Like Ginette Anfousse ten years earlier, Raymond Plante profoundly influenced children's literature in Quebec. In his wake, Quebec children's authors have been compelled to concentrate on winning the complicity of young readers.

On the eve of the twenty-first century, Quebec publishers are counting on diversity to widen their readership. All the literary genres are represented, and each has its celebrities: Daniel Sernine and Jacques Lazure for science fiction; Chrystine Brouillet for mystery; Denis Côté for horror. Other writers resist labels. Christiane Duchesne (*La Vraie Histoire du chien de Clara Vic,* 1990; *Victor,* 1992), who has won the Canadian Governor General's Award twice, invents poetic, fantastic, and comic fictional worlds peopled with extraordinary characters. Robert Soulières mixes genres and narrative levels. His full-length novel, *Ciel d'Afrique et pattes de gazelles* (1989), incorporates a song, a Western film, impromptu theater, and a passage in which the reader becomes the hero, as well as many other surprises.

Since the mid-eighties, Quebec publishers have shifted their focus to the novel. About fifty collections representing a wide range of styles have become available for children of all ages. Many illustrators have since acquired international reputations. Michèle Lemieux, Marie-Louise Gay, Pierre Pratt, Mireille Levert, Stéphane Poulin, Suzanne Duranceau, Marc Mongeau, Darcia Labrosse, Philippe Béha, Gilles Tibo, and Hélène Desputeaux are courted by some of the world's most noteworthy publishers.

Despite its short tradition, Quebec children's fiction now occupies a distinguished place at the forefront of world children's literature. The infatuation with a new literature that engages young readers because it truly reflects their experience is genuine and has triggered a groundswell of enthusiasm among publishers, writers, illustrators, and even other artists. In 1992 painter, photographer, and sculptor François Vaillancourt, known for his bold installations in Montreal's contemporary art world, devoted himself to sculpting tiny plasticine characters in miniature settings constructed of assorted materials. The photographs of his model figures illustrate *Le premier voyage de Monsieur Patapoum* (Mr. Patapoum's first trip, 1993), which he coauthored with illustrator Gilles Tibo.

Quebec children's literature appears destined to captivate an ever-expanding French-speaking readership. Daring and vital, it vies with the best works produced in countries where children's literature is firmly anchored in several centuries of literary culture. ❧

DOMINIQUE DEMERS

Carle, Eric

American illustrator and author, b. 1929. The artist and author of one of America's most popular contemporary picture books, *The Very Hungry Caterpillar* (1969), works in a studio filled with large drawers of colored tissue paper on which he has splashed, painted, or dabbed acrylic paints to create special textures and effects. Eric Carle cuts tissue paper into the desired shapes, then pastes them in layers on cardboard. He then takes full-color photographs of the artwork, to be reproduced in a picture-book format. "Ninety-nine percent of the illustration is made of paper," says Carle, "but sometimes I use a crayon or a bit of ink to accent small details."

Born of German parents in Syracuse, New York, in 1935, Carle and his family returned to Germany, where he disliked the rigid school system, except for his art classes, in which he was free to exercise his creativity. At age twenty-two, Carle returned to the United States and worked as a graphic designer for the *New York Times.* He began freelance work in commercial art in 1963.

It never occurred to Carle to write and illustrate children's books until Bill Martin, an editor at Holt, Rinehart and Winston, asked him to illustrate *Brown Bear, Brown Bear, What Do You See?* in 1967. Shortly after the publication of *Brown Bear,* Carle met Ann Beneduce, and she became his editor, a relationship that lasted almost twenty years. Carle remembers, "We discussed picture books and agreed they should be fun, bright, bold, and educational without being heavy-handed." Carle's first book for Beneduce, *1, 2, 3 to the Zoo* (1968), won first place at the Bologna International Children's Book Fair. Says Carle, "Suddenly, at age forty, I was an illustrator and author! And I knew what I wanted to do for my life's work."

The Very Hungry Caterpillar is the story of a winsome caterpillar who eats his way through holes in the book while introducing themes of counting, days of the week, and the life cycle of the butterfly. Carle was one of the first illustrators intrigued with the idea of introducing natural science concepts to young children. *The Very Hungry Caterpillar* has remained in print for twenty-five years, attesting to its popularity with preschool and elementary age children. Since that book, Carle has illustrated more than forty books for preschool and primary school children.

The underlying purpose behind the brightly colored pictures and hidden surprises in Carle's books is, he says, "to combine learning with fun and to bridge the gap for youngsters making the transition between home and school." His approach to making picture books is exemplified in *The Grouchy Ladybug* (1977), a cumulative tale about an impolite ladybug who be-comes happier when she is better behaved. Here Carle works the themes of appropriate social behavior and telling time into the entertaining plot. Also representative is *The Very Busy Spider* (1984), a story about persistence that features a raised spider web, enabling visually impaired children to feel the story's progression. In *Animals Animals* (1989) and *Dragons Dragons* (1991), the artist's vivid collages illustrate poems describing a variety of real and imagined creatures. *Today Is Monday* (1993) bears all the earmarks of its popular predecessors. The energy of its pictures combined with its spirited traditional verses offers a rollicking, good-humored romp for young listeners and readers.

A young child once called Carle "Mr. Picture Writer," a title he enjoys and one that seems highly appropriate for an illustrator whose picture books continue to entertain, teach, and spark a child's imagination. ❧ S.L.

Voices of the Creators

Eric Carle

One day in kindergarten, in Syracuse, New York, my teacher stamped a cow and a rooster into my workbook. I then drew a barnyard scene around the oddly placed animals. I harnessed the cow to a wagon loaded with hay and added a farmer with a pitchfork. Then I surrounded the rooster with a hen house, which I attached to a barn with a sliding door. It seemed to me that these two forlorn animals needed to be "explained."

My teacher asked my mother to come to school for a conference. My mother was convinced that I had behaved badly or worse. Walking down the hallway, she noticed many pictures taped to the wall; they were signed "Eric." The teacher told her that her son had drawn them, that he was good at art, and that she should nurture this talent. My mother promised that she would. A door opened that day. I formed the unshakable conviction that drawing and making pictures would be the core of my life. My teacher opened the door; my mother kept her promise; my father gave the promise shape.

My father had wanted to become an artist, but his strict father would not have a starving artist in the family. My father loved nature and animals, especially small ones. He and I, hand in hand, would walk across meadows and through the nearby forest. On our explorations, he would lift rocks to show me a worm or a salamander; he taught me that it was easier to catch a slow lizard in the cool morning than a quick lizard in the hot afternoon.

My parents went back to Germany in 1935. Because of a grade-school teacher who inflicted corporal punishment, I felt physically and emotionally so devastated that I hated school for the next ten years—until I went to art school. But while I was in Gymnasium—high school—I discovered a love of classical music. My Latin teacher, a short man with a goatee, was a lover and practitioner of classical music. He and his wife and six children each played an instrument, and some Sunday afternoons they performed at his home. From these occasions he would ask his pupils to join his friends and family for a round of Beethoven, Mozart, and Schubert.

In a strange way a door had opened again. Later I learned that picture books, too, need rhythm, that a book must flow like a symphony or quartet or duo; that it must have movements, adagios, and fortissimos. Books, like music, must be held together by a beginning, a middle, and an end.

My art teacher soon discovered my love for drawing and painting. There were few who liked art, and Herr Kraus was grateful to have found someone who took his classes seriously. As a young man he had been a Socialist and follower of the German Expressionist movement. Socialists and Expressionists, however, were out of favor under Hitler. Abstract artists were "degenerate" and forbidden to paint or show their work; often it was confiscated and even destroyed.

One day Herr Kraus asked me to his home. There he pulled from the rear of his linen closet a large box. "I like your drawings," said my art teacher. "I like their loose and sketchy quality. Unfortunately, I have instructions to teach naturalistic and realistic art. But I want to show you something else." He reached into the box and pulled out a reproduction of one of the forbidden paintings. At first I was shocked and repulsed. Never had I seen anything like this. But Herr Kraus stood there, unruffled and unafraid; he was proud of his kind of art, and his love for it shone in his eyes. He opened one more door at a most appropriate moment.

My childhood during World War II was gray. The buildings in the cities and towns of Germany were camouflaged in dull greens, dull grays, and dull browns. Clothing, now utilitarian, was cheerless and without color. Even the weather in central Europe is often gray. In art school after the war I learned about the joys of color. Ever since, I have striven for bold colors in order to counteract the grays and dark shadows of my youth. I want to celebrate color and push the range of colors to ever new heights.

Not too long ago, a child wrote to me: "We are alike in the same way; you like colors and I like colors." Another one wrote, "Dear Mr. Carle, you are a good picture writer." I would like to be remembered as a picture writer and as someone who has opened a door for children to the world of pictures and words.

Carlson, Natalie Savage

American author, b. 1906. In *The Half-Sisters* (1970) and its sequel, *Luvvy and the Girls* (1971), Natalie Savage Carlson presented a fictionalized account of her childhood. Born in Winchester, Virginia, she was raised on a Maryland farm and attended a convent boarding school much like the one described in her autobiographical novels. The author wrote stories for the *Baltimore Sun* at an early age and continued writing when her family moved to California and she began public school. After graduation, she worked as a reporter for the *Long Beach Sun*, then married and had two daughters.

Reading aloud to her children inspired Carlson to write for young readers. She took a writing course and soon began to sell her stories to children's magazines. Her first book, *The Talking Cat and Other Stories of French Canada* (1952), includes folktales she learned from relatives as a child and showcases her ability to create a strong sense of setting and culture in fiction. As the wife of a career naval officer, Carlson traveled widely and lived in a number of locations, including Hawaii, where she was an eyewitness to the bombing of Pearl Harbor. The author's firsthand observations from her travels give many of her books a sense of authenticity and atmosphere. *The Song of the Lop-Eared Mule* (1961) was written after a visit to Spain; a trip to Canada enhanced the background of *Jean-Claude's Island* (1963).

The three years that the Carlsons lived in Paris inspired some of the author's best-known works. *The Happy Orpheline* (1957) concerns the twenty girls who happily reside in a Paris orphanage and don't really want to be adopted. Focusing on the orphan Brigitte, who becomes lost in Paris during an outing, the book provides a memorable portrait of France and is filled with distinctive characters. Carlson continued this charming series with *A Brother for the Orphelines* (1959), *A Pet for the Orphelines* (1962), *The Orphelines in the Enchanted Castle* (1964), and *A Grandmother for the Orphelines* (1980). Like much of Carlson's work, these novels appear to be written in effortless prose and reveal her gift for depicting character chiefly through action and dialogue. These qualities are also evident in her Newbery Honor Book, *The Family under the Bridge* (1958), which tells of the friendship between a hobo and a homeless family during a Christmas season in Paris. The author anticipated the problems of homelessness by several decades in a novel that is warm and gently humorous.

Carlson also dealt with social issues in her subsequent novels, including *The Empty Schoolhouse* (1965), a story of desegregation in a Louisiana Catholic school. Fourteen-year-old Emma Royall, an African American school dropout and motel "scrub girl," narrates the story of her younger sister's plight at St. Joseph's School, but functions basically as an observer and never comes alive as a character. The book is interesting for its social commentary and Louisiana setting, but ultimately lacks emotional resonance. A more successful treatment of race relations is found in *Ann Aurelia and Dorothy* (1968), an episodic, humorous story of the friendship between a Caucasian foster child and an African American girl. Although it does not have the strong sense of setting found in much of Carlson's writing, this fine novel includes the usual engaging scenes and sympathetic characters that distinguish the author's best books. ❧ P.D.S.

Carrick, Carol
Carrick, Donald

Carol: American writer, b. 1935; Donald: American illustrator, 1929–1989. For more than twenty years writer Carol Carrick collaborated with her husband, Donald, to create thirty-seven outstanding children's books. Their career together began when Donald, a portrait and landscape painter who had studied in Spain, was asked by Robert Goldston to illustrate his children's history book *The Civil War in Spain* (1966). As Donald went on to illustrate other books, an editor suggested that he write and illustrate a picture book of his own. He asked Carol to help. In Vermont, Don drew sketches of a beautiful barn; Carol researched animals that lived in barns and wrote a text for his drawings. *The Old Barn* (1966) was published and was soon followed by a number of nature books, including *The Brook* (1967), *Swamp Spring* (1969), and *The Pond* (1970), which captures in poetic imagery and watercolor the atmosphere of a summer pond and the creatures that depend upon it.

Both Donald and Carol grew up playing in woods and ponds, Donald in Michigan, Carol in Queens, New York. Donald drew, and Carol collected cocoons, identified wildflowers, and wrote poems and stories. Their shared deep appreciation for nature balanced with their conscientious concern for accuracy makes their books richly sensitive and substantial and has earned them many awards, including the Outstanding Science Trade Book for Children from the National Science Teachers Association and the Children's Book Council for *The Blue Lobster* (1975) and *The Crocodiles Still Wait* (1980). Carol imagined these books visually, choosing the concepts for Donald's art. When she got an idea for a book, she would first ask Donald what he thought of it. Later, she would show him a draft of the manuscript and again ask for his opinion. They worked independently, save for their research. As Donald always worked from life, this involved crayfish living in the turkey roaster, turtles in the bathtub, and a vole and a lobster in captivity.

With the birth of their sons, Christopher and Paul, Carol rediscovered emotions from her own childhood and began to write from family experiences. They moved from New York City to Martha's Vineyard, and she wrote numerous picture-book adventures starring Christopher and his dog on the island: *Sleep Out* (1973), *Lost in the Storm* (Children's Book of the Year Award from the Library of Congress, 1974), *The Accident* (1976), and *The Foundling* (1977). In these adventures, as in all her work, the child is portrayed as an independent thinker, making important decisions alone. The writing is simple and heartfelt, sincere, with the right balance of drama and tension.

Carol's sensitivity finds it fullest expression in her books for older readers. *What a Wimp* (1979), *Some Friend* (1979), and *Stay Away from Simon* (1985) deal with the idea of outsiders and explore inner feelings with deep insight. *Stay Away from Simon*, set in the nineteenth century, is a powerful adventure story of a retarded boy, feared and shunned, who rescues two children lost in a snowstorm. Here, where lives are at risk, Carol demonstrates the great importance of understanding between people, compassion, and the ability to see beneath appearances.

During their years of collaborating, Donald was always open to opportunities for new directions for his work. He especially enjoyed writing and illustrating his own books, the first of which were *The Tree* (1971) and *Drip Drop* (1973), and he illustrated numerous books by other writers. Since her husband's death in 1989, Carol continues writing and has recently published *Whaling Days* (1993) and *Two Very Little Sisters* (1993).

In all their work together Donald and Carol's unique insight into the child's experience made them a strong creative team. Donald's skillful drawing conveys a tenderness and sensitivity that complements Carol's intuitive grasp of the child's vision, her empathy, and the strong value of human kindness. ❧ L.L.H.

Carroll, Lewis

English author and mathematician, 1832–1898. The English masterpiece *Alice's Adventures under Ground* had a modest beginning: it was handwritten and charmingly illustrated by Charles Lutwidge Dodgson as a Christmas gift for a child friend, Alice Liddell. Three years later, in 1865, at the insistence of Mrs. George MacDonald, the manuscript, retitled by the publisher *Alice's Adventures in Wonderland*, was published under the pen name of Lewis Carroll, adorned with illustrations by Sir John Tenniel. The book's droll illustrations, exuberant fun, and lunacy combined with logic captivated children, and this revolutionary fantasy, achieved immediate and rousing success. Its influence was widespread, inspiring other writers, including George MacDonald and Edith Nesbit, to write stories for children unfettered by the didacticism that had previously been the norm in British Children's books. Carroll followed *Alice* with *Through the Looking Glass and What Alice Found There*, also illustrated by Tenniel. Children so eagerly awaited the second book that 15,500 copies were presold before the book's release in 1871. Carroll's other major contributions to children's literature include the poems *Jabberwocky* (1855) and *The Hunting of the Snark: An Agony in Eight Fits* (1876).

Alice's Adventures in Wonderland begins with a bored Alice who is suddenly mesmerized by the appearance of a fully clothed white rabbit running toward a large rabbit hole and repeating "Oh dear! Oh dear! I shall be too late!" Without a moment's thought, Alice follows the rabbit down the hole and finds herself in a veritable wonderland where nothing seems to follow the logic she has learned during her proper British upbringing. So powerful has been the book's influence that memorable characters, such as the Hatter, March Hare, Dormouse, and Cheshire Cat, to name a few, have become inextricable parts of our popular culture.

Dodgson, a shy and obscure mathematician and deacon at Christ Church, Oxford, was horrified to discover that his alter ego, Lewis Carroll, was famous, praised, and sought after, even by Queen Victoria. Dodgson attempted to dissociate himself from Lewis Carroll, and he wrote, "Mr. Dodgson neither claims nor acknowledges any connection with the books not published under his name." Although Dodgson wrote mathematical treatises and invented many games of mathematics and logic under his own name, his fame was reserved for his children's books and poems written as Lewis Carroll.

Carroll's books have been analyzed by critics, and his inner life has been scrutinized by psychologists. Originally reviewed simply as nonsensical fairy tales, the stories came to be seen as symptoms indicating a disturbed mind. More likely, Carroll retained his playful and childlike perspectives as a result of a happy childhood. Apparently he was more comfortable with children because with them he did not stammer, as he did when in the company of adults. He avidly read fairy tales and nonsense rhymes and even as a boy had entertained other children with games, stories, puzzles, plays, and drawings. Carroll recognized the child's inner fears, wishes, intelligence, and imagination. He unleashed thousands of children's minds and imaginations and invited them to laugh.

His stories and poems have been translated into many languages and adapted to stage, film, television, and even rock music. In 1991–92, the British Museum exhibited Carroll's original writings and photographs in celebration of the one hundred twenty-fifth anniversary of *Alice's Adventures in Wonderland* and of the talented man who changed children's literature. B.J.B.

Caseley, Judith

AMERICAN AUTHOR AND ILLUSTRATOR, B. 1951. Since the publication of her first picture book in 1985, Judith Caseley has written realistic fiction for a number of age groups. Caseley was born in Rahway, New Jersey, and received a bachelor of fine arts degree from Syracuse University. After college, she lived in London for seven years, where she worked as a receptionist at Sotheby Parke Bernet and had the opportunity to visit France, Turkey, Greece, and many other locations. Caseley hoped to become a professional artist, and some of her work was exhibited in the United States and Europe. She also designed and sold greeting cards and provided the illustrations for an English book by Olga Norris, *The Garden of Eden* (1982). When she began writing stories for young readers, Caseley delved into her own childhood experiences. Remembering a traumatic bout with stage fright, she wrote *Molly Pink* (1985), about a little girl selected for a vocal solo at a school concert. Illustrated with stylized pastel watercolor paintings, the simple text and artwork tell the reassuring story of how Molly conquers her stage fright with a little help from her family; it was followed by a sequel, *Molly Pink Goes Hiking* (1985).

Caseley's work often depicts children growing up in Jewish families; one of her most common themes is intergenerational relationships. Both elements are present in *When Grandpa Came to Stay* (1986), which tells how Benny helps Grandpa cope with Grandma's death. The text realistically describes Benny's fears and Grandpa's grief, and the illustrations are simple and comforting. *Dear Annie* (1991) also explores the love between grandparent and grandchild, in a series of letters that Grandpa has sent Annie from the day of her birth. Caseley has written several easy-to-read books about the Kane family.

Beginning with *Hurricane Harry* (1991) and followed by *Starring Dorothy Kane* (1992), *Chloe in the Know* (1993), and *Harry and Arney* (1994), this warm and amusing series focuses on everyday events in the lives of children, such as snowball fights and class trips, as well as the larger issues: moving, a hospitalized grandmother, a new baby in the family. The strong bonds between family members are displayed in engaging scenes that are occasionally overcrowded with incident or conversation; while the dialogue is generally sprightly, the reader is sometimes overwhelmed by the characters' talkiness. Nevertheless, the books make pleasant reading for early readers.

Kisses (1990), Caseley's first young adult novel, features a strong protagonist. Hannah Gold's emotional development rings true as she dates, attends school, plays the violin, and deals with the unwanted advances of a male teacher. The book contains the same strengths and weaknesses found in Caseley's previous work. There is an authentic portrait of a modern Jewish family and an interesting relationship between Hannah and her grandparents. But the story is overcrowded with subplots and extraneous dialogue, which many readers may find distracting. A second young adult novel, *My Father, the Nutcase* (1992), realistically depicts Zoe's concern for her father's mental depression, but is also undermined by a plethora of side issues.

Caseley has published a wide range of books in a relatively short period of time. Although tighter plotting and more focused writing would improve her work, she remains a promising, evolving talent who has already produced several interesting books. P.D.S.

Cassedy, Sylvia

AMERICAN NOVELIST AND POET, 1930–1989. Sylvia Cassedy was a great believer in the power of imagination. Intrigued by a child's ability to invent make-believe worlds, she wrote about how these worlds can save their inventors. Her three novels—*Behind the Attic Wall* (1983), *M.E. and Morton* (1987), and *Lucie Babbidge's House* (1989)—explore the plight of three lonely, desperately unhappy young girls. Each, in her own unique way, turns to an inner fantasy life for affirmation and strength to survive and grow.

As a child, Cassedy remembered having friends but feeling unpopular anyway. She said that she hoarded hurts and injustices and suffered greatly. Her heroines are "re-creations not of my actual childhood but of how I perceived it at the time and remember those perceptions now." After graduating from Brooklyn College, Cassedy married and raised four children. In addition, she taught second grade and creative writing to both primary and secondary students. Based on this experience, she wrote *In Your Own Words: A Beginner's Guide to Writing* (1979), in which she encourages young people to use their imaginations, to notice the world around them, and to write about it.

Cassedy was also a poet, writing *Roomrimes: Poems* (1987), about rooms of all sorts, and *Zoomrimes: Poems about Things That Go* (1993). In both collections the poems, one for each letter of the alphabet, display Cassedy's sense of humor and joy in using language. In addition, working with native speakers, she has translated poems from India and Japanese haiku. Published first as *Birds, Frogs, and Moonlight* (1967), her haiku collection was later revised, retitled, and republished as *Red Dragonfly on My Shoulder* (1992) and enhanced with intriguing collages by MOLLY BANG.

However, Cassedy's novels are her crowning achievement. She combines a humorous yet serious storytelling style with an insightful understanding of preadolescent girls coping with rejection and self-acceptance. The main characters in two of Cassedy's novels are orphans, and all three feel isolated and excluded. Each girl creates a fantasy world in which she is able to express parts of herself that she could never show to her hostile peers or caregivers. Cassedy has a wonderful flair for capturing these inner worlds, which are at once rich and poignantly pathetic. Ultimately she throws a magical element into each story as a catalyst, enabling the girls to transform their fantasy into a workable reality. In these wonderfully complex, multilayered stories, Cassedy develops both the child and her inner world so that each comes alive in a real and believable fashion. Cassedy had a deep appreciation and respect for children, giving voice and validity to their fantasy lives. Her books stand as a monument to the power and beauty of the imagination, highlighting the importance of the inner world and the role it plays in healing us all. P.R.

CATALANOTTO, PETER

AMERICAN ILLUSTRATOR, B. 1959. For someone who has been in the children's book field a relatively short time, Peter Catalanotto has created a readily recognized and evocative style with his watercolor illustrations.

From his earliest days, he knew he wanted to be an artist. When his kindergarten teacher asked what he wanted to be when he grew up, his startled answer was "I'm an artist now!" Family influence established a presence. His mother was a Sunday painter, his father was a printer, and four of the five children attended art colleges. Artistic influences in Catalanotto's early life were EZRA JACK KEATS's sense of design, the art of Edward Hopper and Andrew Wyeth, and the multileveled humor he found in the cartoon character Bullwinkle. Catalanotto left Long Island for Pratt Institute and New York City, where he expected to paint and illustrate professionally and starve to death. His employment the first six years following college included illustrating but also bartending and working as a messenger and custodian. His paintings appeared in popular magazines like *Reader's Digest* and *Woman's Day* and on numerous book jackets. It was the cover for JUDY BLUME's *Just as Long as We're Together* (1987) that prompted an offer from a publisher to illustrate a picture book.

Catalanotto's first book, *All I See* (1988) by CYNTHIA RYLANT, received instant notice. His enjoyment in illustrating that book induced him to write his own. *Dylan's Day Out* (1989) tells the story of a Dalmatian and a soccer ball through a series of lively paintings. Making the transition from painting book jackets to illustrating picture books was difficult for Catalanotto since the picture on a jacket has to convey everything quickly in one image and a picture-book illustration must entice the reader inside to a slowly unfolding story. Mastering that transition has given him two specific strengths—subtlety and foreshadowing, which he uses effectively to meld with the story. Of the books that followed, the ones written by GEORGE ELLA LYON are especially noteworthy. *Cecil's Story* (1991), *Who Came Down That Road?* (1992), and *Dreamplace* (1993) are evocative reflections of voices past and present within a given time and place. Lyon writes with pure emotion, and Catalanotto paints that emotion. Since she uses few adjectives in her writing, he is free to create his own vision of her words. Catalanotto does not simply interpret the text but uses his soft realistic style to extend it. The emotional responsiveness that his illustrations capture is also evident in his books with Rylant: *All I See* (1988), *Soda Jerk* (1990), and *An Angel for Solomon Singer* (1992) display definite feelings of sentiment, memory, and powers of observation. The imagery throughout Catalanotto's evanescent watercolors encases emotions and reflects ruminations while enhancing the texts and adding new dimensions to the stories. J.C.

CAUDILL, REBECCA

AMERICAN AUTHOR, 1899–1985. The experiences and impressions of an early childhood in the eastern Kentucky mountains yielded three heartwarming episodic stories of Appalachian family life early in Caudill's career and three radiant tales of small-child triumph near its close. Yet neither her career nor her work is cut to a standard pattern.

This daughter of Appalachia came of age on the gentle, sunny slopes of central Tennessee, worked her way through all-female Wesleyan College in Georgia, where she was tagged "Yank" for that deviation, and took a master's degree in international relations at Vanderbilt University. Then, in her words, she "set out to see the world"—as teacher, editor, adventurous traveler. Once married, she settled into homemaking and writing for children in Urbana, Illinois. Her books included four teenage novels, two historical and two contemporary, all respectfully received for their seriousness of purpose, none actually successful as a work of fiction. One historical story, *Barrie & Daughter* (1943), and one contemporary story, *Susan Cornish* (1955), are interesting nonetheless for their reformist approach to Appalachian life, reflecting the mixed affection and anger of her memoir, *My Appalachia* (1966).

What Caudill prized about Appalachia is the far more potent unspoken message of her books for younger children. Inseparable, as *My Appalachia* makes plain, is a family legacy of independence *and* togetherness, of ceremony, ritual, celebration—and achievement.

Happy Little Family (1947), the first of the early "Fairchild" books, begins with four-year-old Bonnie, youngest of the brood, only half thrilled at going skating in a kitchen chair, because, as she says, by doing babyish things, "she would never grow as big as Debby," the next oldest child. The book's final episode finds her crossing a shaky footbridge unassisted after learning, on a school visit, to read the word "cat"—the end, Bonnie tells her father, of "being little forever and ever." Within minutes she passes a Fairchild family milestone by finding "her very first arrowhead."

In *Schoolhouse in the Woods* (1949), Bonnie starts school on her own with "a new first reader, a new slate, and a slate pencil," while Debby falls heir to Emmy's old reader, Emmy gets Chris's, and so on. At term's end Bonnie happily updates a hand-me-down reader. Crossing out Debby's name after the phrase "This book belongs to," she then inscribes her own. The highlight of the term, however, and perhaps of the entire series, is the arrival, the adoption, and the disappearance of Grandpap, an old box turtle of placid dignity and steadfast turtleness.

Caudill's work combines distinct, folkloristic plot structure and language patterns with a natural ease in human contact with animals and among humans themselves. The dichotomy is manifest in *Up and Down the River* (1951), which tells of the summer Bonnie and Debby spend peddling pictures and bluing to their mountain neighbors, thereby gaining one lamb, one duck, three kittens, and a pair of bantam chicks. A later addition to the series, *Schoolroom in the Parlor* (1959), falters on all fronts.

Caudill was not wedded to a Fairchild formula, however. In the mid-1960s, as children's books became leaner, tighter, and more intense, she responded with a trio of quietly dramatic, freestanding stories that, felicitously illustrated, scored as picture-story books. They are Appalachian but loosely contemporary and, in their lack of period emphasis, closer to timeless. Their plot development, though replete with lively incident and humor, is essentially character development. *A Pocketful of Cricket* (1964) and *Did You Carry the Flag Today, Charlie?* (1966) carry two very different little boys over the threshold of school, where a pocketed cricket gives confidence to shy, ruminative Jay, and a liking for snakes makes a student of scatterbrained, impulsive Charlie. *A Certain Small Shepherd* (1965) is the story of a mute boy and a Christmas miracle that calls for no explanation.

The child psychiatrist Robert Coles, who has studied Appalachia's children, gives Caudill the best of endorsements: her books "tell a lot about the region's terrain," and his three boys "doted on them." ❧ B.B.

Cavanna, Betty

American author, b. 1909. Betty Cavanna is the popular author of numerous light romances for young adolescent girls. Cavanna grew up in the "typical American small town" of Haddonfield, New Jersey. She claims to have been "involved with printer's ink" since age twelve. After majoring in journalism at Douglass College, Cavanna worked for a newspaper and in publicity and advertising for the Presbyterian Board of Education in Philadelphia. The setting of Cavanna's adolescence is reflected in many of her books. Cavanna's heroines are usually small-town girls who have been transplanted to a different locale and are faced with the problems of being an outsider. These moves are often combined with an upheaval in the character's personal life, presenting a double set of obstacles for the young, usually resourceful, heroines to overcome. In *The Scarlet Sail* (1959) and *Angel on Skis* (1957), the protagonists are faced not only with moving to a new state but with parental death and remarriage as well. In *Passport to Romance* (1955), *A Time for Tenderness* (1962), and *Jenny Kimura* (1964), the heroines move to a foreign country and must contend with different lifestyles and societal prejudices.

Cavanna has a keen insight into the teenage experience, a sensitivity she attributes to both an "almost total emotional recall for this particular period" of her life and the fact that, because her brother and sister were ten and twelve years younger than she, she witnessed their adolescent crises firsthand. Her most popular books, *Going on Sixteen* (1946), considered a classic, *Accent on April* (1960), and *A Date for Diane* (1946)—written under the name Elizabeth Headley—demonstrate Cavanna's clear perception of teenagers. While Cavanna's books were warmly received by critics at the time of publication in the 1950s and early 1960s, they were later criticized as unrealistic and simplistic. The girls' preoccupation with their hair, clothes, makeup, and femininity was deemed trivializing. It was also noted that her characters relied too heavily on men for salvation and that the male characters were impossibly good and charming.

One must keep in mind, however, the era in which and of which Cavanna wrote. At the time, this sort of romance novel was considered suitable young adult fiction. Authors rarely dealt with disturbing themes. When issues like divorce, racial conflict, and the emerging radical counterculture were mentioned, they were always tangential to the main story line. In later books, such as *Spice Island Mystery* (1969) and *Mystery on Safari* (1970), Cavanna introduced sensitive issues such as drug smuggling and animal poaching into her books and made her heroines less sanctimonious. In *Runaway Voyage* (1978), Cavanna wrote of America's unsettled West in the 1860s. These books, however, were not well received; still, Cavanna's books work well within the framework of another time or place, evoking a strong sense of the exotic. Regardless of the irrelevance to modern readers of the plots and frivolous concerns of her characters, Cavanna remains a good storyteller. She writes with a vivid, engaging style, and her portrayal of major characters is strong and sympathetic. ❧ M.O'D.H.

Chambers, Aidan

English author, b. 1934. Aidan Chambers's work has forwarded children's literature in many respects. As a teacher of English and drama he has helped students see literature as vital, near-spiritual sustenance. As a critic he has given illuminating readings of individual works as well as traced the complex web linking author, reader, and book. In 1978 his article "The Reader in the Book," addressing the need for the critical study of children's literature to take into account the child-as-reader, earned him recognition from the Children's Literature Association, which selected it for their first award for criticism. As an editor and publisher, notably of the British critical journal *Signal*, which he founded with his American wife, Nancy, he has helped shape the field of British children's books. And his column "Letter from England," published in the *The Horn Book Magazine* from 1972 to 1984, provided a line of connection between children's literature enthusiasts in Britain and America.

His own works of fiction, the majority of which are for young adults, reflect his commitment to writing about situations and emotions familiar to his audience while simultaneously challenging and expanding their horizons with the unfamiliar. Because he couldn't find plays for his teenage students to perform that reflected their age group's concerns—and because he felt it important that such plays exist—he wrote his own, which were subsequently published. His novels provide a challenge, as he often experiments with narrative technique, attempting to convey ideas or sensations as authentically as possible. Slipping back and forth between first- and third-person narration, including disjointed streams of consciousness, handwritten letters, even a cartoon, *Breaktime* (1978) atypically records a typical teenage rite of passage. At the same time, it sets out to disprove the assertion put forth by the protagonist, Ditto's friend Morgan, that "literature is a sham, no longer useful, effluent, CRAP." As the supposed author of the book, Ditto accepts, as does Chambers, the paradox of fiction: a lie by definition that says something true. Another of his young adult novels, *Dance on My Grave* (1982), is notable not only for its stylistic devices but for its honest treatment of a homosexual relationship between two teenage boys. Primarily a compilation of journal entries interspersed with a social worker's reports, the novel follows Hal as he tries to come to terms with his lover Barry's death and with his own propensity for obsession. Even before he became fixated with Barry, Hal had other obsessions: seeking a perfect match to his idealized vision of a best friend and contemplating death. Given the frequency with which his protagonists partake in this contemplation, Chambers himself—the son of an undertaker—must have had death frequently in mind as a boy, as he injects his characters with a philosophical curiosity about the state of being dead combined with an instinctive terror of their own mortality.

Along these same lines, Chambers has edited numerous collections of ghost stories, some of which, like *A Haunt of Ghosts* (1987), include his own writings. A belief that collections need to be "sensitively arranged ... as in the hanging of pictures" so that each story enhances and builds upon another informs his work as an anthologist. Whether editing anthologies or writing or reviewing children's books, Aidan Chambers takes his work seriously. He believes children, like adults, deserve good books written just for them. ❧ C.M.H.

Chapter Books (Transitional Readers)

Nothing is more satisfying to a new reader six, seven, or eight years old than the ability to read a book independently. Chapter books are intended to motivate these young readers by providing transitional reading that falls between controlled vocabulary books and fully developed novels. In the best of these books, the vocabulary is not limited but is clear and natural and the writing spare but rich. Relatively large type and plenty of white space create unintimidating pages; the books are usually slim, with a minimum of subplots, and the chapters often episodic. Novels attempt to be simple enough not to daunt the tentative while offering sufficient detail of character and plot to allow readers space to lose themselves in the story.

The Little House in the Big Woods (1932) by Laura Ingalls Wilder has long been one of the first choices of a child attempting a chapter book for the first time. Its homey details of pioneer life, the independent spirit of its main character, and the resourcefulness of the Ingalls family are remembered affectionately by readers long after they have moved on to more difficult books. Almost as popular are the two "Betsy" series: Maud Hart Lovelace's "Betsy-Tacy" titles, first appearing in 1940, and Carolyn Haywood's series beginning with *B Is for Betsy* (1939). Both series feature fully developed characters who grow with each succeeding book. Another perennial favorite is *The Hundred Dresses* (1944), Eleanor Estes's poignant story of prejudice that introduces Wanda Petronski, a Polish girl from the wrong side of the tracks who is the butt of her classmates' jokes.

Based on a true story, Alice Dalgliesh's *Courage of Sarah Noble* (1954) describes the adventures of an eight-year-old girl who travels with her father to the Connecticut wilderness of the eighteenth century, where they build a home in the woods. Sarah stays behind with Indian neighbors while her father leaves to collect the rest of the family. The sensitive treatment of the Native Americans in this book, as well as Sarah's plucky determination to be brave, renders it timeless. The hero in John Reynolds Gardiner's *Stone Fox* (1980) displays courage of another kind. In order to earn enough money to pay the back taxes on his and his grandfather's farm, Willy pits himself and his dog Searchlight in a dogsled race against Stone Fox, the best racer in the country. The heartbreaking ending of this exciting story is alleviated by Stone Fox's gesture of tribute to the dog and the boy.

That simplicity and brevity need not be synonymous with skimpiness in either characterization or plot was made manifestly clear in *Sarah, Plain and Tall* (1985), which won the Newbery Medal. The poetry of Patricia MacLachlan's language, rich in metaphor and imagery as it describes Sarah's attempts to acclimate herself to the prairie landscape, coupled with Anna and Caleb's palpable yearning for Sarah to become their mother, gives the book the undiluted power of a small masterpiece.

Stories about pioneers have always been popular with younger readers. One that combines that theme with the equally cherished subject of horses is Elizabeth Shub's *White Stallion* (1982), in which a young girl traveling West in a covered wagon finds herself in the midst of a herd of wild horses. Also set in the past, but in a different era entirely, is Riki Levinson's *DinnieAbbieSisterr-r!* (1987), an endearing story about a Jewish family living in Brooklyn during the Depression. Lucille Clifton's *The Lucky Stone* (1979) takes a longer, symbolic view of history as it tells the story of a pebble first found in the cotton fields by Miss Mandy during slavery days. The stone rescues, in some way, all those who possess it.

While most younger children find it comforting to read stories about everyday experiences, more adventurous readers seek to have their imaginations captured by fantasies that bridge the gap between the familiar and the exotic. An early animal fantasy still enjoyed by children is *My Father's Dragon* (1948) by Ruth Stiles Gannett. Also much admired is *A Toad for Tuesday* (1974) by Russell E. Erickson, with appealing line drawings by Lawrence Di Fiori depicting the comically perilous relationship between Warton the toad and his owl captor. Maxine Chessire's black-and-white wash drawings add depth and mystery to *My Friend the Monster* (1980) by Clyde Robert Bulla, with its themes of friendship and tolerance. Even science fiction is occasionally represented in transitional novels, one of the most notable being Lee Harding's dramatic account of an alien who falls to Earth in *The Fallen Spaceman* (1980).

For the pure, unadulterated silliness that children love, however, few can compete with the books of

DANIEL MANUS PINKWATER. One of the most accessible to newly independent readers is *Blue Moose* (1975), which describes in five brief, hilarious episodes the doings of a blue moose who appears unannounced one day at the door of Mr. Breton's restaurant. More recent novels in the same nonsensical vein are JAMES MARSHALL's *Rats on the Roof and Other Stories* (1991) and JON SCIESZKA's books about the Time Warp Trio, beginning with *Knights of the Kitchen Table* (1991). Only slightly less outlandish is *Hilary and the Troublemakers* (1992), Kathleen Leverich's amusing cautionary fable about a girl who has trouble keeping her imagination in check.

Like well-worn shoes, SERIES BOOKS are appreciated by tentative readers for the easy comfort of the instantly recognizable characters and settings. While many are unremarkable, some remain spontaneous in plot and consistently strong in style and characterization. Among the best of these are JOHANNA HURWITZ's books about the rambunctious and curious boy described in *Rip-Roaring Russell* (1983). Other popular series characters include Adam Joshua, from Janice Lee Smith's series beginning with *The Monster in the Third Dresser Drawer* (1981), and Julian from Ann Cameron's heartwarming series about an African American family that originated with *The Stories Julian Tells* (1981). Two well-drawn characters with special appeal to girls are Angel (*Back-Yard Angel*, 1983) by JUDY DELTON and Jenny (*A Job for Jenny Archer*, 1988) by ELLEN CONFORD. Slightly more sophisticated in tone is SHEILA GREENWALD's *Give Us a Great Big Smile, Rosy Cole* (1983). As the potential subject of a children's book written by her famous uncle, Rosy might find herself glorified, but her instincts are appealing and natural.

Books that focus on the familiar world of the classroom are especially popular, and some of the most widely read are Patricia Reilly Giff's stories about the Polk Street School. A strikingly independent character is the feisty heroine of *Muggie Maggie* (1990) by BEVERLY CLEARY, a writer who understands well how small issues can loom large in childhood. An especially endearing story in the younger range of transitional novels is BETSY BYARS's *Beans on the Roof* (1988), in which the Bean family becomes involved in Anna's school poetry project. This little treasure by an author who usually writes for older children portrays a loving, hardworking family in a few well-chosen words.

In recent years, some notable chapter books have been set in foreign countries. Ann Cameron's *The Most Beautiful Place in the World* (1988) is about a boy who lives with his grandmother in a small village in Guatemala, where in spite of the intense poverty he experiences, he manages to find a way to go to school. In Margaret Sacks's *Themba* (1992) a boy leaves his small South African village and embarks on a journey to the city to meet his father, who is returning from the gold mines of Johannesburg. Miriam Schlein's *The Year of the Panda* (1990) introduces an environmental theme in her story of a Chinese boy who finds and raises an abandoned baby panda.

Clearly, self-imposed limitations of vocabulary and length have not prevented the authors of chapter books from expressing largeness of imagination, feeling, and spirit. ❧ NANCY VASILAKIS

CHARLIP, REMY

AMERICAN AUTHOR AND ILLUSTRATOR, B. 1929. Drama, originality, and a vibrant design sense permeate Remy Charlip's entire body of work, which engages and entertains children and adults.

As a highly creative PICTURE BOOK author and illustrator, Charlip first entered the field of children's literature in the mid-fifties and has since crafted nearly thirty books, which differ extensively in pictures and words. Charlip's artwork, a peculiar pastiche of media, clearly demonstrates his penchant for colorful, kinetic, graphic innovation in picture-book illustration. He successfully employs line drawings, naive art, and watercolors to produce imaginative and noteworthy works. As diverse as his illustrations, Charlip's texts include an easy reader, jokes, poems, a jump-rope rhyme, plays, and a retelling of a legend.

Born in Brooklyn, Charlip brings to children's literature a diverse background especially rich in theatrical experience, which translates specifically into a unique understanding of the dramatic turning of the picture-book page. His second self-illustrated book, *Where Is Everybody?* (1957), succeeds because of such drama. Starkly simple in design and execution, the book introduces beginning readers to vocabulary as it places a word or words directly on a black-outlined image the word denotes. Sky, bird, sun, river, and cloud, each labels its respective image on separate pages; each word picture compels the reader to turn the page to reveal yet another word picture. With this onward thrust the narrative unfolds to tell of an afternoon rain shower, a story easily grasped by novice readers.

Charlip most frequently uses naive art, a childlike style of drawing characterized by simplicity and void of sentimentality, to illustrate children's books, as he did or two of MARGARET WISE BROWN's titles. In

The Dead Bird (1958), one of the first American picture books about death for very young children, Charlip's superb naive drawings, in predominant hues of green, blue, and yellow, convey the childlike fascination the young protagonists have for the dead bird they find, bury ceremoniously, and eventually forget. Simply and directly, Charlip's illustrations capture perfectly the text's tone; Charlip's whimsically naive pictures for Brown's cheerful poem *Four Fur Feet* (1961) cleverly show only the bottom half of a furry, four-legged, nameless animal who ambles around the world. To accompany the creature on his global circumnavigation, the reader literally turns the book completely around, an innovative design technique choreographed by Charlip.

Fortunately (1964), written and illustrated by Charlip, contains alluring naive artwork and page-turning drama. Alternating colorful double-page spreads with black-and-white ones—which coincide with his humorous usage of "fortunately" and "unfortunately"—Charlip tells of the good and bad luck that befalls a young boy en route to a birthday party. He solemnized and softened his naive style of art when he illustrated *Harlequin and the Gift of Many Colors* (1973), which he wrote with Burton Supree. Set in rural Italy, the legend retelling how penniless Harlequin acquired his patchwork carnival costume from compassionate, generous friends quietly glows with the love and sacrifice Harlequin's peers offer him. Equally resplendent are Charlip's naive watercolor drawings, rendered in delicate pastel hues of lavender, peach, and blue. More realistic than his previous illustrations, the drawings for *Harlequin* include details, shadows, and perspective that emphasize an exquisiteness the tender tale imparts.

A long collaboration with Jerry Joyner resulted in *Thirteen* (1975), Charlip's most intriguing, ingenious, and complex work. Winner of the 1976 Boston Globe–Horn Book Award for Outstanding Illustration, the book develops thirteen individual graphic stories simultaneously in an equal number of double-page spreads. The barest of text accompanies lovely pastel watercolors, and each image possesses narratives over which readers can pore. Brilliant in concept and form, *Thirteen* further establishes Charlip's dramatic propensity to craft picture books that distinctively dance alone. ❧ S.L.S.

Charlot, Jean

AMERICAN ILLUSTRATOR, 1898–1979. Muralist, painter, and printmaker, Jean Charlot possessed many technical talents that permeated his work as an illustrator. One of the most eminent fine artists ever to illustrate children's books, he had a masterly sense of space and design. An American citizen of Mexican descent, Charlot spent his first twenty-two years in France. Charlot's move to Mexico in the early 1920s proved instrumental in his career. He became immersed in the new Mexican muralist movement led by national artists such as Diego Rivera and José Clemente Orozco. During the late 1920s, Charlot studied and copied ancient Mayan murals while he worked at the Carnegie Institute archeological dig in the Yucatán.

These formative years studying and perfecting the technique of mural painting influenced his philosophical and practical approach to the form of the picture book. He believed creating art for children's books involved a change of scale rather than a change in point of view. In 1943 Charlot illustrated his first notable picture book, *A Child's Good Night Book* by MARGARET WISE BROWN. The drawings for Brown's book established Charlot as a new presence in the field of children's literature. His expertise as both an illustrator and a printmaker influenced the production of the book. Rather than reproducing the illustrations using a traditional photomechanical process, Charlot drew the crayon pictures directly on the lithographic plates. He chose muted color tones to evoke a sleepy mood for Brown's bedtime lullaby: yellow ocher, carmine red, cobalt blue, and gray. The book's small size, perfect for bedtime snugglers, proved unsuitable for standard library shelving. It was reissued in 1950 in a large vertical format, losing one double-page spread and the color tonality; the second edition even suffered alteration of the typeface. Fortunately, in 1992 *A Child's Good Night Book* was restored to the original format of the 1943 Caldecott Honor Book.

Charlot described his style as architectural. The "raw material," or paper, was the most important artistic consideration. He wrote, "In its thinness, its flatness, and its whiteness, paper should impose its essence in the illustration as assertively as does the mortar in the case of the fresco painter, or at that, marble or stone in that of the sculptor." Jean Charlot respected the integrity of his material most remarkably in his illustrations for Margaret Wise Brown's picture book *Two Little Trains* (1949). Drawing diagonal gray lines against a double-page white background to show rain pelting the fearless children on their cross-country journey, Charlot never allowed his art to mask the essence of the paper. Charlot's streamlined train and old locomotive move across the pages of the book just as Brown's simple rhythmic words thrust the action forward. As MAURICE

SENDAK has said, Charlot's pictures "live with the words in sweet harmony." Charlot's strong line drawings enhanced two consecutive Newbery Medal winners, *The Secret of the Andes* (1952) by ANN NOLAN CLARK and . . . *And Now Miguel* (1953) by JOSEPH KRUMGOLD. In these books, Charlot's formal Mayan sketches reflect his beginnings as a muralist. Charlot also illustrated *The Timid Ghost* (1966) by ANITA BRENNER and *The Poppy Seeds* (1955) by CLYDE ROBERT BULLA. Charlot's technical contributions to fine lithography enriched his artistic interpretation of the picture book for young children. His command of line and architectural design and his unerring touch of humor ensure his appeal to young audiences today. ❧ S.M.G.

CHASE, RICHARD

AMERICAN FOLKLORIST, 1904–1988. Richard Chase was a collector and teller of tales that had been handed down from generation to generation in the Appalachian regions of the United States. His forte was the ability to combine scholarly research on the origins of the stories and patient editing of the many versions he collected with his passion for encouraging their oral tradition of being told *spontaneously.* "Reading the printed word," he wrote in a preface to *Grandfather Tales* (1948) "is, indeed, not the same as the sound of your own voice shaping a tale as it wells up out of your memory and as your own fancy plays with all its twists and turns." His advice to storytellers was not to worry about dialect but to tell the tale in their natural common speech and let the surge of the story prevail. By the 1930s folk singers and country dancers had found a rich heritage in the songs and ballads, the steps and tunes, of Anglo-American folk music. Chase was among them, and his *Old Songs and Singing Games* appeared in 1938.

He also found that the Appalachian regions of Virginia and North Carolina were a repository of folktales, such as "Jack and the Beanstalk" and "Jack and the Giant Killer," in which the hero is stock figure, a lad generically known as Jack. But in the few generations since the tales had been brought over by emigrants from England and Scotland, the eponymous Jack, according to Chase, had been transformed from "the cocksure, dashing young hero" of the fairy tale to "an easy-going, unpretentious" rural boy and that even though mysterious forces sometimes aided Jack, he remained a "thoroughly human . . . unassuming representative of a very large part of the American people." Chase first learned the tales from R. M. Ward and his kin, descendants of Council Harmon, a renowned storyteller, and edited them into *The Jack Tales* (1943).

Illustration by Berkeley Williams, Jr., for "Jack and the Bean Tree" from *The Jack Tales* (1943), edited and retold by Richard Chase.

Chase traced stories and traditions on both sides of the Atlantic. When *Grandfather Tales* was published, the collection included Appalachian versions of European tales: Robin, in "The Outlaw Boy," learned his bow-and-arrow techniques from the Indians; in "Ashpet" the heroine went to a church meeting instead of a ball; "Like Meat Loves Salt" was a version of King Lear's story; and Hansel and Gretel, abandoned in a primeval wilderness, became Buck and Bess in "The Two Lost Babes." Chase also researched the Uncle Remus stories first collected by JOEL CHANDLER HARRIS and was the editor and compiler of *The Complete Tales of Uncle Remus* (1955). His retellings of *Jack and the Three Sillies* (1950), *Wicked John and the Devil* (1951), and *Billy Boy* (1966) were published as picture books. Chase is termed the compiler, rather than editor, of *Billy Boy* and his rhythmic retelling echoes the many rhymed versions of Lord Randall's tragic tale.

For many years Richard Chase, born in Alabama, lived near Henderson, North Carolina, and was closely associated with the Appalachian Center at Mars Hill College in Mars Hill, North Carolina. He played the recorder, enjoyed leading children and adults in songs and "play-party" games, taught American folk songs and dances, and took part in many storytelling and folk festivals. Chase has been called the man "most responsible for the renaissance of Appalachian storytelling." ❧ L.K.

Chess, Victoria

American author and illustrator, b. 1939. Born in Chicago and raised in Washington, Connecticut, Victoria Chess lived for fifteen years in Manhattan and traveled extensively before returning to rural Connecticut, where she now lives with her husband and pets. When Chess attended the Boston Museum School for art training, she was asked to leave due to her lax work habits, but she later found that the promise of money would help keep her productive through more than thirty children's books.

Chess renders her illustrations in a cartoon style with clean outlines and pages busy with pattern, decoration, and detail. She uses colored pencils, liquid watercolors, technical pens, and waterproof inks in a distinct and recognizable style. Her people have ample, pink flesh, and although they are stocky, the flat outlines filled in with light wash make them appear almost weightless. Long, toothy grins and close-set, circular eyes surrounded by heavy crosshatching create intense expressions often bordering on mania, a technique quite appropriate for some of the bizarre books Chess illustrates. Even when the subject matter is wild, however, Chess's controlled line and stable composition grant the book a mainstream acceptability and the renegade themes hold great child appeal. When a careless girl breaks all her toys in *Fables You Shouldn't Pay Any Attention To* (1978), by Florence Parry Heide and Sylvia Worth Van Clief, she gets replacements, while her good siblings, who still have their old toys, receive nothing. In *Poor Esmé* (1982), written and illustrated by Chess, Esmé learns a harsh lesson when she wishes for a playmate and ends up with a hair-pulling, diaper-soiling baby brother. David Greenberg's verse in *Slugs* (1983) describes kids torturing slugs until the creatures take revenge. Chess's drawings allow the reader to feel no sympathy for the amorphous slugs, who let themselves be victimized, or for the mean people, who are as bulbous as the slugs. According to Jim's parents in Hilaire Belloc's *Jim, Who Ran Away from His Nurse, and Was Eaten by a Lion* (1987), another gruesome book, Jim got what he deserved. The punishment seems severe, but thanks to Chess's portrayal of Jim as mean-eyed and disgustingly roly-poly, the amused reader knows Jim won't be missed.

As in *Jim* and *Slugs* and in several collaborations with Jack Prelutsky, many of Chess's books contain texts written in light verse. The combination of singsong text and comic art can defuse a scary situation, so the story is harmless yet titillating, and children can feel scared and secure simultaneously. Such is the case in Florence Parry Heide's *Grim and Ghastly Goings-on* (1992), where even the cheerful colors belie the grisly content.

With little variation in style, Chess successfully adapts her techniques to suit a range of manuscripts. With vivid colors and her strong line, Chess helps Verna Aardema retell a Mpongwe folktale in *Princess Gorilla and a New Kind of Water* (1992). In *A Hippopotamusn't* (1988) the quietly joyful illustrations capitalize on J. Patrick Lewis's witty animal poems.

Whatever the theme of the book, always present is Chess's sense of humor, as her illustrations ask the reader not to take life too seriously. ❧ S.S.

Childress, Alice

American author, 1920–1994. Alice Childress spent most of her career around the theater, but when she turned her talents to writing for young people, she produced unique and outstanding literature.

Childress was born in South Carolina but raised in Harlem in New York City. She attended public schools and remembered growing up amid love, generosity, and kindness. Her first brush with drama was hearing an actress recite Shakespeare, and she had her first role as a child. She was an actress in school plays and became one of the original members of the American Negro Theatre, acting for eleven years and serving as director for twelve. In the late 1940s, she began to write plays. She won a 1956 Obie Award for her off-Broadway play *Trouble in Mind*. She codirected her play *Wedding Band* with Joseph Papp at the Public Theatre in New York, in a production in the 1972–73 season that starred Eartha Kitt.

One of the themes Childress treated in her plays was how black people survive in contemporary America.

From her first book for young people, she elaborated on this theme. FERDINAND MONJO, a children's book editor and author, suggested that Childress write a book about drugs, because it was needed. The result was *A Hero Ain't Nothin' but a Sandwich*, the story of a black thirteen-year-old heroin user. Published in 1973 to controversy and critical acclaim, the book was nominated for a 1974 National Book Award, named a Notable Book by the American Library Association, and made into a film for which Childress wrote the screenplay. More praise came her way with the publication of *Rainbow Jordan* (1981), a novel told by three women—a fourteen-year-old girl, her unreliable mother, and a strong older woman. The characterization is exceptional, and Childress achieved her aim of showing characters who learn to deal with rejection and with other people. Her third novel for young adults, *Those Other People* (1989), also told from several points of view, addresses racism, blackmail, suicide, and sexual abuse in the story of a homosexual protagonist who witnesses a rape.

Childress said that when writing novels she used a "monologue style" recalling the 1951 Japanese film *Rashomon*, famous for presenting one story from several characters' points of view. This style, in its homage to the film, underscores Childress's roots in the dramatic arts. Childress wrote several plays for young people, including *When the Rattlesnake Sounds* (1975), a one-act play about Harriet Tubman. Among her other writing and editing were novels for adults.

Childress won many honors and awards, including the Paul Robeson Award for Outstanding Contributions to the Performing Arts, and she was a member of many organizations, including PEN, the Harlem Writers Guild, and the Dramatists Guild. In 1966 she was appointed a playwright/scholar to the Radcliffe Institute for Independent Study and was graduated from Radcliffe/Harvard in 1968. S.H.H.

CHINESE-AMERICAN BOOKS FOR CHILDREN

Published in 1950, *Fifth Chinese Daughter* by Jade Snow Wong attracted a great deal of attention; the story of a second-generation Chinese-American girl growing up in San Francisco's Chinatown in the 1930s was soon translated into several different languages and won worldwide acclaim. Never before had there been such an intimate account of a Chinese-American family as it struggled to retain and pass on its culture, while bearing hardship and discrimination and learning the many lessons necessary to become part of its new country.

Until *Fifth Chinese Daughter* children's books were mainly about China, the country left behind, and they were written by people outside the culture. Such books as Newbery winner *Young Fu of the Upper Yangtze* (1932) by E. F. Lewis; *The Story about Ping* (1933) by MARJORIE FLACK; *The Five Chinese Brothers* (1938) by CLAIRE HUCHET BISHOP; and Caldecott winner *Mei Li* (1938) by Thomas Handforth represented almost all that was available about China in children's fiction books.

It was puzzling to Chinese-American children that the clothing, food, and customs depicted in these books were not what they knew about the land from which their parents emigrated. Imagine the confusion when, each year, at Chinese New Year, well-meaning teachers and librarians read *Mei Li* to their students and talked about how the new year was celebrated in China in walled cities where people rode on camels on the frozen ground. America's largest group of Chinese immigrants came from Guangdong (Canton) province in the south of China, where the weather was temperate and where camels and snow existed only in stories.

The concepts of the vastness of China and the diversity of its population are difficult to comprehend. Language, as well as local customs, food, and clothing, reflected regional differences and differences of social class, occupation, religion, and diverse ethnic traditions. In 1949, China experienced a great upheaval that changed the lives of all the people at every level and in every region. For the first time in its long history, China was united under one government and its people shared a common language. But the China found in America's children's books continued to be exotic and anchored to the past, and the experiences of Chinese-Americans continued to be overlooked and underrepresented.

The success of Wong's *Fifth Chinese Daughter* was not to be followed by another such story for twenty-seven years. In *Dragonwings* (1975) LAURENCE YEP combined the elements of life in turn-of-the-century San Francisco Chinatown, the 1906 earthquake and fire, and the reunion of a young man with his father into a compelling story. It is based on a true account of a Chinese immigrant who built a flying machine and flew it off the Oakland hills in 1909. *Dragonwings* was selected as a 1976 Newbery Honor Book. Yep's *Child of the Owl* (1977), imbued with Chinese tradition, is the story of a young girl who is sent to live with her grandmother in San Francisco's Chinatown. The child grows to love and accept herself as a "child of the owl," akin to the dark, negative *yin* elements of the universe. A more recent book, *Star Fisher* (1991), is based on Yep's family's experiences when they moved from Ohio to West Virginia in the 1920s. In an autobiographical work, *The Lost Garden* (1991), Yep wrote about his own experiences growing up in San Francisco.

Stories of early Chinese in America include *Chang's Paper Pony* (1985) by Eleanor Coerr, in which an immigrant boy's wish for a pony is fulfilled in the gold mining country; Ruthanne Lum McCunn's *Pie Biter* (1983), a fable of success of a hard-working young Chinese pioneer; and McCunn's *Thousand Pieces of Gold* (1981), which chronicled the life of a Chinese slave girl who overcame adversity to become a respected and loved member of her Idaho community.

By far the richest stories of early immigrants are to be found in the anthologies by Paul Yee and Laurence Yep. The stories in Yee's *Tales from Gold Mountain* (1989) are stories of the Chinese in the New World. The tales are full of humor, irony, and optimism, qualities that gave strength to these early adventurers. Yep's two collections, *The Rainbow People* (1989) and *Tongues of Jade* (1991), were selected from sixty-nine folktales gathered and translated by Jon Lee as part of a WPA project in the 1930s. These stories, brought by the Chinese from their homeland, were told and retold to help sustain their bonds with the country they left. Ghost stories, tales of luck, cunning, heroism, and magic have entertained generations of Chinese immigrants and their children. These folktales, adapted to their New World settings, not only passed on the stories from China, but also included the stories of the immigrants.

Since folklore continues to account for much of what is considered "multicultural literature," demand for culturally diverse materials has resulted in the recent publication of more and more folktales; many are filtered through the minds of writers and illustrators outside the culture. Among the more successful Chinese folktales written from outside the culture are Marilee Heyer's *The Weaving of a Dream* (1986); *Ming Lo Moves the Mountain* (1982) by ARNOLD LOBEL; *The Seven Chinese Brothers* (1990) by MARGARET MAHY; Doreen Rappaport's *The Journey of Meng* (1991); Robert San Souci's *The Enchanted Tapestry* (1987); and *The Magic Wings* (1986) by DIANE WOLKSTEIN.

But the most important contributions to the literature have been made by those inside the culture. Few Chinese authors and illustrators have been as successful as ED YOUNG, who has illustrated Diane Wolkstein's *White Wave* (1979), Ai-Ling Louie's *Yeh Shen: Cinderella Story from China* (1982), Margaret Leaf's *Eyes of the Dragon* (1987), MARGARET HODGES's *The Voice of the Great Bell* (1989), and Robert Wyndhams's *Chinese Mother Goose Rhymes* (1968). Young's personal knowledge of China not only lends authenticity to these works, but his elegant artwork enhances the stories as well. Like Chinese calligraphy, Young's illustrations are simple and complex at the same time. Ed Young has been the recipient of many awards for his work. The most prestigious have been the Caldecott Honor Award for his illustrations for JANE YOLEN's *Emperor and the Kite* (1968); the Caldecott Medal for *Lon Po Po: A Red Riding Hood Story from China* (1990); and a Caldecott Honor Award for *Seven Blind Mice* (1992).

Frances Carpenter's *Tales of a Chinese Grandmother* (1937) and *Chinese Mother Goose Rhymes* (1968), compiled and edited by Robert Wyndham, continue to find new audiences as teachers, librarians, and parents, searching for material on China, encounter them in library collections and in bookstores. The stories and the translated nursery rhymes reveal much about the lives of children in China.

Biographies written about Chinese Americans have been scarce, since few have achieved national notoriety in fields traditionally selected for biographies for children: sports, entertainment, and government. *Tiffany Chin: A Dream on Ice* (1986) by Ray Buck was written at the height of interest in the Olympic ice-skating medalist. In *El Chino* (1990) ALLEN SAY chronicles the life of Bill Wong, who chose an unusual sport for a young Chinese American when he sought to become a bullfighter in Spain. Mary Malone's *Connie Chung: Broadcast Journalist* (1992) traces the life of Ms. Chung as an immigrant to her current role as one of the nation's leading television journalists.

In China, three-year-old Yani started painting and won international acclaim when she became the youngest artist to exhibit at the Smithsonian Institute. Yani's work and her early years are featured in Zheng Zhensun's *A Young Painter* (1991). There have been several biographies of Mao-Zedong and Chou En-Lai, two of China's revolutionary leaders, but few others have been selected as subjects of biographies.

JEAN FRITZ's *Homesick* (1982) is an account of what it was like to grow up as a child of American missionaries in a troubled China of the 1920s. When the family moved back to America, Fritz had to learn about living in a new country. When she was living in China she was homesick for America, and she often felt like an outsider. Once in America, she felt homesick for China, and so still felt like an outsider. On her first day at school in America, she was called a "Chinaman" by a boy. Fritz tried to explain to her classmates that the Chinese were not called "Chinks" or "Chinamen," and, in any event, she was an American. Her turmoil parallels the experience of many immigrant children, who feel that they are strangers in both the land of their birth and the land where they live. This perspective of an "outsider" is valuable to share with young readers who often think they are the only ones who feel alienated.

In *The China Year* (1991) by EMILY CHENEYL NEVILLE, a thirteen-year-old girl spends a year in Beijing after her father accepts a job teaching there. Without the usual amenities vital to the welfare of the typical American teenager, she finds her life difficult until she meets a Chinese student who speaks English. The observations of life in China through the eyes of this young girl are fresh, tough, and compassionate.

There have been few titles published about children living in modern-day China. Miriam Schlein's *Project Panda Watch* (1984) is a story of a Chinese boy who finds a baby panda and becomes a part of his country's organized effort to preserve the nearly extinct animal. These Chinese, dressed in contemporary clothing and concerned with contemporary issues such as the environment and endangered animals, enable young readers to understand that China is not a land of mythical dragons, pagodas, and people wearing elaborate silk robes.

City Kids in China (1991) by Peggy Thomson, with photographs by Paul Conklin, shows the daily lives of the children of Changsha in posed and candid black-and-white pictures. Depicted are poignant unguarded moments as well as the usual events that give readers insight into a culture—perhaps quite different from their own. *City Kids in China,* an album of one city, is not to be taken as typical of all of China, where cultural and geographical diversity is at least as extensive as that which is found in the United States.

According to the U.S. Bureau of Census, as reported in 1989, "certain minority groups, especially Asian/Pacific Islanders, are increasing far more rapidly than the population as a whole. From 1980 to 1988, when the rate of increase for the total population was 8.1 percent, the rate of increase for the Asian/Pacific Island population was seventy percent." Although Asian Americans comprise only three percent of the total United States population in the 1990 census, their presence on the West Coast, especially in California, continues to grow. In San Francisco, Asian Americans comprise twenty-two percent of the population, and all indications are that the figures will rise in the next decade.

Children's books about this diverse group of Americans need to include more than folktales. There should be more stories that focus on their experiences as immigrants, more stories that recognize the contributions of Asian Americans to the growth and strength of America, and many more stories that include Asian Americans in the fabric of American life. Only then will young readers be able to discover the remarkable wholeness in the intricately woven tapestry of American society and learn to appreciate and embrace the unique variety brought by many cultures to that intriguing fabric.

MILDRED LEE

CHRISTOPHER, JOHN

ENGLISH SCIENCE FICTION AND FANTASY WRITER, B. 1922. John Christopher, a pseudonym for Christopher Samuel Youd, was born in Lancashire, England. As a young boy he loved science, but performed poorly in his science classes. At sixteen he left school to work in a government office and spent many years working in industry before turning his full-time attention to writing. His early novels—written under the pseudonyms Hilary Ford, William Godfrey, Peter Graaf, Peter Nichols, and Anthony Rye—were for adult readers. Then a publisher asked him to write a science fiction series for boys. In 1967, as John Christopher, he wrote the enormously popular novel *The White Mountains,* the first book in the Tripods Trilogy (1967–68), and Christopher's first work for young readers. Christopher thus began a new phase in his writing career and has since said of writing for children that "it is the form of writing which I can now least imagine giving up."

In the futuristic Tripods Trilogy, Earth has been invaded and conquered by an alien species from outer space. Human beings are controlled by the mysterious tripods through the ritual of "capping," the implanting of metal caps on people's heads. But thirteen-year-old Will Parker and his companions Henry and Beanpole struggle to escape capping and search for a community of free, uncapped people living in the White Mountains. Eventually, the companions' goal becomes not only freedom for themselves, but for all humankind. Masquerading as a capped slave, Will manages to enter the aliens' secret city and discovers their plan to eradicate the human race. Henry, Beanpole, and Will lead the tiny band of free people in a courageous and ultimately successful attempt to rid the planet of the alien menace.

With the publication of the Tripods Trilogy, science fiction for children—previously the home of hack or uncreative writing—came into its own and was finally taken seriously. The high quality of Christopher's writing, his emphasis on character development, and the difficult, often troubling questions he raises in his novels make it impossible to dismiss his work as simple action/adventure stories for children.

The Guardians, published in 1970, won the Christopher and Guardian awards. Set in the year 2052, the novel describes a world divided into two rigidly controlled social classes: One class lives in overpopulated, violence-ridden cities, while the select few of the other class maintain a privileged existence reminiscent of traditional English aristocracy. The Sword of the Spirits Trilogy (1970–72) is set in the unspecified future, in a world profoundly changed by the aftereffects of a nuclear holocaust, and combines elements of medieval chivalry and the Arthurian legends with advanced technology. As in many of his other books, technology is portrayed as a double-edged sword, capable of benefiting humanity in important ways, but equally capable of wreaking destruction upon the world. In the Fireball Trilogy (1981–86), Christopher combines fast-paced adventure with a playful exploration of an alternative history when two cousins are transported to a parallel world in which the Roman Empire never fell.

A recurring theme in Christopher's books is the importance of free will. His protagonists must choose between a life of contentment and happiness and the ability to think and act freely, with all the difficulties and responsibilities this freedom entails. His protagonists are primarily young boys on the brink of manhood, but boys and girls alike respond to their courage, curiosity, and determination. His heroes, far from perfect, wrestle with and often surmount their all-too-human flaws in a way that makes them appealing to young readers. Christopher explores serious issues, giving his books added substance and interest, but he is also justly appreciated for his consistent ability to tell a good story. In a straightforward narrative style, he recounts fantastic yet strangely plausible adventures that always leave his readers spellbound from start to finish. ❧ K.T.

Christopher, Matt

AMERICAN AUTHOR, B. 1917. Matthew F. Christopher, author of dozens of sports stories for young children, was raised in a small, multi-ethnic community in upstate New York. Christopher grew up playing baseball, basketball, and football; to him, sports meant a special form of camaraderie, a sentiment prevalent in all of his books. Christopher's parents did not attend school beyond the fourth grade; there were no books in his home as a child, so Christopher frequented public libraries, where he found his favored adventure stories. Later, Christopher enjoyed a satisfactory career as a semiprofessional baseball player until forced to stop playing because of an injury. Christopher has said that he always loved to create; as a youth he built things and wrote poetry and song lyrics. He feels that writing children's books was a natural byproduct of his creativity in other areas. While supporting his family with a number of positions as a laborer, Christopher continued writing. Eventually, Christopher became a full-time writer, but it took time and perseverance before his efforts came to fruition. His first book, *The Lucky Baseball Bat,* was published in 1954. Since then, Matt Christopher has been a prolific writer, covering a wide range of sports in his books.

Christopher's books are characterized by accuracy and a vivid use of the language—the "patter"—peculiar to each sport, which he feels "heightens the realism of the book." To ensure accuracy, Christopher conducts extensive research for those sports in which he has not been personally involved. His characters are human, with human faults and emotions. In many of Christopher's early books, the game provides the main focus; there is little evidence of life outside the ballpark. Books such as *The Year Mom Won the Pennant* (1968) and *Shortstop from Tokyo* (1970) reflect the social mores of the time and, as a result, seem dated to the modern reader. In later books—for example, *Takedown* (1990), *The Fox Steals Home* (1978), and *The Hockey Machine* (1986)—Christopher incorporates the more relevant subjects of adoption, divorce, and unethical athletes. The accessibility of his books is, perhaps, the greatest praise one can confer upon Christopher. Young boys who would not otherwise be considered avid readers flock to these books, and Christopher finds this circumstance particularly satisfying. In an effort to become more "introspective" in his writing, Christopher has recently added elements of mystery, fantasy, and the supernatural to his stories.

Matt Christopher has also written screenplays, short stories, a comic strip (which ran for six years in *Treasure Chest* magazine), a one-act play, and humorous verses. He was the recipient of the Junior Book Award Certificate in 1957 for *Basketball Sparkplug.* ❧ M.O'D.H.

Chute, Marchette

AMERICAN AUTHOR, B. 1909. Born and brought up in Minnesota during the early years of this century, Marchette Chute has many qualities as a writer that strike modern readers as peculiarly—and pleasingly—

Victorian. There is no one category that suits her: She writes for children as well as adults; she writes biographies and histories, poetry and fiction; she is a scholar as well as a popularizer. Above all, she is an inveterate student and a gifted teacher. "I find myself," she once observed, "curious about something which happened in the past, and I set out to find everything I can about it. It is the reality of the past that I'm looking for."

Chute's scholarship, particularly in the field of Elizabethan literature, is distinguished for both its thoroughness and its enthusiasm. There is little equivocation or cautious circumspection in her attitude. Her books are beautifully written and gracefully shaped. They are also purposeful. She is an unabashed supporter of great thinkers, great creators, and people of courage and vision.

Chute's classic volume *Stories from Shakespeare* (1956) retells all thirty-six plays from the bard's First Folio, grouping them into the traditional categories of comedy, tragedy, and history. Making the inevitable comparison to Charles and Mary Lamb's version, *Tales from Shakespeare* (first published in 1807), the noted critic Bergen Evans succinctly phrased his opinion of Chute's achievement: "She's better." The retellings are robust and engaging, easy enough for a child in the middle years to enjoy, and satisfying for their elders as well. Equally impressive is her brief introduction to the work of Shakespeare, the times in which he lived, the language he employed, and the audience for which he wrote. Above all, she stresses that Shakespeare's plays are best appreciated inside a theater, not from an armchair, and she expresses the hope that her book "may open a door... and give a glimpse, however slight, into what lies beyond."

The Green Tree of Democracy (1971), was based on an earlier book Chute wrote for adults, *The First Liberty* (1969). From the first colonial settlements to the fight for civil rights legislation in the 1960s, she chronicles the history of voting in America. Underscoring the struggles along the way, she emphasizes what was frightening (to some) and what is important (to all) about universal suffrage in a democracy.

The middle of three sisters, all of them writers, Chute graduated from the University of Minnesota and came to New York City as a young woman to begin her career. She has lived there ever since, reading widely, writing prolifically, and regularly researching at one of the city's most important democratic institutions: the New York Public Library. Marchette Chute's books are models of intelligence and rigorous thought. They challenge readers to treasure their own curiosity and trust their talents, just as she has. ❦ A.Q.

Ciardi, John

AMERICAN POET AND CRITIC, 1916–1986. John Ciardi is credited by both poets and critics with forever changing the face of poetry for children, making it a field to be taken seriously. His poetry has wordplay, charm, wit, and surprise. It is varied and can be bitingly sophisticated, but Ciardi never loses sight of his purpose: "I want the contact [with children] to be fun."

The fourth child and only son in an Italian American family, Ciardi was already spoiled when he became the man of the family at age three, on his father's death. He used his much-increased power, he said, quite selfishly. Perhaps this accounts for his poetic references to children as *savages* and *monsters.* Ciardi has admitted an early interest in books, and his fascination with language dates from these years, for his upbringing was bilingual. "I have always felt that when you have a second language, you have three things: the first language, the second language, and the difference between them."

Ciardi's first children's collections reflect the influence of the children around him. *The Reason for the Pelican* (1959) was written as a game between himself and his nephews and nieces. Full of liveliness and humor, it focuses on animals, which pleases children, and it does so with a subtlety that pleases adults. When asked to create poetry from a first-grade reading vocabulary list, Ciardi wrote *I Met a Man* (1961), mainly because he liked the idea of creating a first book for his daughter Myra, who was then in kindergarten. The collection is full of fun and nonsense, but with the challenge of an increasingly difficult vocabulary.

Each of his collections has a distinct personality. The nonsense poems in *The Man Who Sang the Sillies* (1961) are in the Edward Lear tradition. *You Read to Me, I'll Read to You* (1962) has poetry on alternating pages of black and blue type, the black written in the vocabulary of a first grader, the blue in that of an adult. Although his poetry is never childish, later collections like *Fast and Slow: Poems for Advanced Children and Beginning Parents* (1975) and *Doodle Soup* (1985) have a satiric quality, a caustic wit best suited to older, more sophisticated, children. Often criticized for his violence, Ciardi once responded, "The language of childhood, the imagination of childhood, is naturally violent."

Ciardi's later books examine both the light and dark sides of childhood, a relatively shocking view in the 1960s. With MAURICE SENDAK and LOUISE FITZHUGH, Ciardi opened the door to much in childhood which had been hidden or denied, and he depicted it with skill. It is skill that has been acknowledged by numerous awards, including the 1982 National Council of Teachers of English Award for Excellence in Poetry for Children. Ciardi's collections for children remain well crafted and refreshingly honest treasures for both young people and adults. ❧ S.A.B.

CINDERELLA

The story of Cinderella, in all its many variations, is one of the world's best-known fairy tales. In its most familiar form, the story begins with a beloved daughter who suffers the death of her mother and, through her father's remarriage and his subsequent absence or neglect, is given over to the care of a jealous stepmother and stepsisters who condemn her to a life of drudgery and servitude. Because she often shelters by the hearth for comfort and warmth, she is tauntingly called Cinderella. In spite of the onerous demands heaped upon her and the rags she is forced to wear, Cinderella remains good and loving and far more beautiful than her stepsisters.

In the different versions of the story, Cinderella receives help from a variety of mother substitutes when her tasks become impossible. In "Aschenputtel" or "Ash Girl," told by the brothers GRIMM, a tree, watered by the girl's tears, grows from her mother's grave; a little white bird that sits in its branches grants her wishes, and birds fly to help her with her tasks. In other tales, various other animals—a cow, a goat, or a fish—are the sources of magical help. The Russian story of "Vasilissa the Beautiful" includes a magic doll, given to the heroine by her dying mother, as the instrument through which the tasks are fulfilled. In the CHARLES PERRAULT version, a magical godmother is moved by Cinderella's tears and performs the wonderfully imaginative and even humorous transformations that make it possible for Cinderella to go to the royal ball.

The ball is the turning point of the story. MARCIA BROWN in her translation from Perrault says, "Then—a deep silence fell over the room . . . all eyes turned to the great beauty of this mysterious one." Cinderella, knowing that the magic will end at midnight, runs from the enthralled prince and, in her flight, leaves behind one of her glass slippers. The prince begins a search for the owner of the slipper; and, though the wicked stepmother and sisters try to trick the prince's retainers, Cinderella is discovered, and she and the prince are wed. In Perrault's tale, Cinderella forgives her sisters and marries them to two lords of the court, whereas in the Grimm version, the sisters are punished with blindness when birds peck out their eyes.

The Cinderella theme appears in tales of many cultures, reflecting the values and setting of their sources; and, in recent years, some noteworthy versions of these have become available in English-language children's books. The Perrault version, included in a 1697 edition of *Histoires ou Contes du Temps Passé* as "Cendrillon," is the most often used source for Western texts. The 1954 edition of Marcia Brown's translation from Perrault, with her illustrations, still stands as the perfect interpretation of the tale. The flowing text is close enough to the original to maintain some flavor of its French origin while also attaining a contemporary quality that engages modern readers. At the same time, the delicate, graceful lines and soft pastel colors of the pictures convey enough splendor to satisfy the most romantic soul.

The earliest known recorded version of a Cinderella tale was written in China in the middle of the ninth century A.D. by Tuan Ch'eng-shih. This story was the inspiration for *Yeh-Shen: A Cinderella Story from China* (1982), retold by Ai-Ling Louie with subtle and evocative illustrations by ED YOUNG. The orphaned Yeh-Shen is cruelly mistreated by her stepmother but finds comfort in caring for a beautiful fish that she caught and has raised. When the jealous stepmother kills and eats the fish, the spirit of an old man tells Yeh-Shen to gather its bones, which will grant her wishes when she is in need. At spring festival time, the bones of the fish make it possible for Yeh-Shen to attend the festival by clothing her in an azure gown and golden shoes. Running down a mountainside to avoid being identified by her stepsister, Yeh-Shen loses one of the golden shoes. The shoe comes into the hands of the king of an island kingdom; fascinated by its tiny size, he begins a search for the woman whose foot will fit the golden slipper. Yeh-Shen is found and weds the king while the stepmother and stepsister are crushed to death by falling stones.

In a Vietnamese folktale retold by ANN NOLAN CLARK in *In the Land of Small Dragon* (1979), Tam, the heroine, is abused and forced to labor in a rice paddy by an envious stepmother and her daughter, Cam. During a fishing contest to see which sister will have superior status with their father, Cam steals all but one small fish from Tam's basket and wins their father's favor. Tam raises the remaining fish, which is later killed and eaten by the greedy Cam. As in the Chinese tale, the bones are gathered and become the magical source of a silken dress and jeweled *hai,* or shoes, for Tam. One of the shoes is snatched by a blackbird and brought to the emperor's son, who searches until he finds Tam and marries her.

A story from Greco-Egyptian history, based on the first century B.C. marriage between a Greek slave-girl named Rhodopis and an Egyptian pharaoh, becomes the source for Shirley Climo's *The Egyptian Cinderella* (1989). Because Rhodopis is a slave, she must endure the taunts and commands of the Egyptian master's household servants. A gift from her master of rosy-red golden slippers increases the servants' cruelty. As Rhodopis works by the river, a falcon, the symbol of the god Horus, snatches one of her slippers and flies to Memphis, where he deposits the slipper in the pharaoh's lap. Taking this as a sign, the pharaoh searches for the owner to be his queen.

In *Rough-Face Girl* (1990), an Algonquin Indian Cinderella tale retold by Rafe Martin, the youngest of three daughters has been forced for years by her two cruel older sisters to sit by the fire and keep it burning. Over time, sparks from the flames have burned and scarred her face and arms so badly that she is called Rough-Face Girl. In a wigwam set apart from the village live a powerful Invisible Being and his sister. The two vain older sisters present themselves in their finery as brides for the Invisible Being but fail to answer his sister's questions about her brother's appearance. When Rough-Face Girl asks her father for finery to present herself as a bride, there is nothing left but some large, discarded moccasins. Taking these, Rough-Face Girl makes herself clothes from birch bark and, believing in herself in spite of people's laughter, goes through the village, seeing the Invisible Being in the natural world all around her. When she is therefore able to answer all the sister's questions, the Invisible Being comes to her, saying "And oh, my sister, but she is beautiful," and they are married.

The Chinese story, with its traditional value of tiny feet for women as a symbol of beauty and status; the Vietnamese story of a Cinderella who labors in a rice paddy; the story of the Egyptian Cinderella in which the pharaoh compares his beloved's green eyes to the color of the Nile, her unruly hair to the feathery papyrus, and her pink skin to the lotus flower; and the reverence for nature at the core of the Algonquin tale of *Rough-Face Girl*—all of these portrayals are important for their insight into different cultures as well as for their differing images of beauty and goodness. These Cinderella stories of the mistreated child whose true worth is recognized and whose dream of romantic love is fulfilled will continue to speak to many generations to come.

HANNA B. ZEIGER

CLARK, ANN NOLAN

AMERICAN AUTHOR, B. 1896. For many years, Native Americans did not fare well in children's literature. With rare exceptions, their people and cultures were either vilified, sentimentalized, or ignored. Ann Nolan Clark was among the first to write about the Indians of North and South America with authenticity and respect. She was born in Las Vegas, in the territory of New Mexico. Her first published work, a poem celebrating New Mexico's statehood, appeared in the local newspaper. While still a student at New Mexico Highlands University, Clark spent two months teaching Tewa Indians at the Tesuque Pueblo in Santa Fe, where she was introduced to Native American culture. As an employee of the United States Bureau of Indian Affairs, Clark later taught at reservations and Native American boarding schools. A geography text she wrote for these students was published as *In My Mother's House* (1941), which describes the daily lives of a Native American family in simple, cadenced prose that has the indelible power of poetry. The text is remarkable for its beauty and dignity, and the evocative illustrations by Velino Herrara received Caldecott honors.

Following this, the Bureau of Indian Affairs assigned Clark to write stories that could be translated into Native American languages. Living among the Pueblo, Navajo, Dakota Sioux, and Zuni tribes, she produced such outstanding readers as *Little Herder in Autumn* (1940), which contains prose poems printed in both English and Navajo. Clark continued to write Native American stories for a mainstream audience as well. Like many of the author's books, *Little Navajo Bluebird* (1943) depicts a child torn between two cultures, as six-year-old Doli sees her older siblings leave the reservation to attend school in the outside world. Other books set in the American Southwest include *Blue Canyon Horse* (1954), the story of a mare who joins a herd of wild horses, and *Along Sandy Trails* (1969), which uses realistic color photographs to illustrate the story of a Papago Indian girl.

Several of the author's books resulted from the five years she spent training teachers in Mexico, Costa Rica, and Peru for the Inter-American Educational Foundation. *Secret of the Andes* is the story of Cusi, a contemporary Inca boy who herds llamas in the mountains above Peru. When Cusi travels from the mountains for the first time, he discovers the secret of his past and makes important decisions about his future. Winner of the 1953 Newbery Medal, the novel is often cited as an especially poor selection because it defeated E. B. WHITE's *Charlotte's Web*. The controversy may cause readers to overlook many excellent qualities found in Clark's book, including beautiful, rhythmic prose and a rich appreciation for the Incan heritage. Its minor flaws—plot elements that strain credibility and a slow, introspective tone—do not prevent *Secret of the Andes* from being a rewarding work.

Late in her career, Clark explored a number of other cultures in her fiction. *Hoofprint on the Wind* (1972) has an Irish setting; *Year Walk* (1975) is the story of a Basque teenager who comes to the United States as a sheep herder; *To Stand Against the Wind* (1978) concerns Vietnamese refugees.

But the author remains best known for her enlightened and dignified portrayal of Native American life, written in a simple, poetic style that begs to be read aloud. ❧ P.D.S.

Classics

In 1865, John Ruskin described all books as divisible into two categories: "the books of the hour, and the books of all time." Of the many juvenile stories written annually, most are "of the hour." They surface briefly, are known to a relative few, then disappear. Others, responsive to contemporary interests, enjoy temporary popularity, but their very timeliness and topicality dates them, and they vanish. Some few books have special qualities which, despite changing circumstances and literary fashions, continue to excite imaginations, stir hearts, and linger in some indelible form in memory. Such vibrant works, persisting through generations, become children's classics.

To understand how books achieve this status, three questions should be posed: What are the intrinsic qualities that give a book staying power? What persisting needs of children do such books satisfy? Which cultural beliefs, perceptions, values, and images give these stories both societal and personal worth?

Superior literary quality is frequently claimed for books described as "classics." Traditional standards are applied when stories are examined to ascertain if characters seem real and vital, if their adventures are absorbing, and their concerns important. Settings, whether real or fantastic, are expected to be vivid and the storyteller's voice irresistible and memorable. Indeed, some of the finest children's literature bears the coveted title of "classic." Contrarily, some books of superb quality have failed to survive, while others with gargantuan flaws nonetheless retain their vitality and appeal. Clearly, quality, while significant, is not the only element that needs to be considered.

Recent research suggests that reading is an interactive process whereby youngsters, using the text as a stimulus, re-create the story using their own idiosyncratic background of language and experience. This transactional theory implies that a book should not be considered only as a self-contained, discrete object, but must be assessed in conjunction with reader response. Thus, stories connecting in powerful ways to the urgent, timeless needs of developing children have the potential to become juvenile classics.

Reading, writing, and publishing exist within a particular societal context. Those books which articulate cultural values and generate potent images of society are especially significant to immature readers and, simultaneously, function to acculturate them. Through such works, children become privy to the mores of the adult world, see their roles as defined by adults, and learn linguistic codes and forms of expression that are particularly valued. Adults, functioning as publishers, critics, teachers, parents, and librarians, generally participate in this transmission of the cultural heritage by endorsing, promoting, and, most significantly, buying such books, thereby ensuring their accessibility for subsequent generations.

Traditional literary criticism, focusing exclusively on text, has examined such relevant aspects as plot, characterization, setting, and the like. However, fiction is more than the sum of its parts; each of its various aspects are organically interrelated. Plot should emerge from character; that is, the beliefs and actions of various characters precipitate crises and bring about believable resolutions. Setting should provide an environment in which action is played out to advantage. Theme ought to be manifest throughout the story, emerging naturally rather than as a didactically delivered message. Style should be harmonious with the other elements, providing pace, ambience, and tone that readers accept as genuine, even inevitable.

Which incidents make up the plot, whether interest is sustained, and whether the resolution is satisfying are all vital issues. Events, even those in the most exotic fantasies, appear credible, urgent, and ineluctable. The archetypical adventure story *Treasure Island* (Robert Louis Stevenson, 1883) remains vibrant and compelling after more than a century. Dorothy's adventures in Oz, the confrontation between Rikki-Tikki-Tavi and Nag, and Colin's rehabilitation in the secret garden continue to absorb readers as these story lines depict, in highly dramatic form, the ineffable concerns and hopes of Everychild.

Characterization is of paramount importance in story development. For any story to endure, its characters must be engrossing—vivid and unforgettable. Then the absorbed reader bonds with the hero or protagonist and is inexorably swept along by events engulfing that character. To have encountered the title character from

Charlotte's Web (E. B. WHITE, 1952) or her friend, Wilbur, is to remember them forever. Mary Poppins, Mowgli, and the self-centered, self-indulgent, irrepressible Toad from *The Wind in the Willows* (KENNETH GRAHAME, 1908), to name just a few, are creations whose luster does not diminish over time. Captain Hook, the Cheshire Cat, and Pinocchio have become so deeply etched in the language that their names are references for nonstory situations, and have become part of the adult lexicon.

Plot is what happens in a story; theme embraces plot meaning. Theme contains those impressions which persist in readers' minds long after the last page has been turned. *A Wrinkle in Time* (MADELEINE L'ENGLE, 1963) recounts the adventures of two children who zealously search the cosmos to save their father's life. Perceptive youngsters realize that the story fundamentally is about the nature of good and evil, family loyalty, the power of love, and the destructive nature of conformity. These elemental issues distinguish this narrative from lesser works of fantasy and account for its continuing appeal.

Indeed, the enduring value of many classics derives from their themes, which typically convey the authors' convictions about the nature of the human experience. These books comment on opportunity and destiny, innocence and experience, heroism and treachery, joy and sorrow—doing so in a way that extends beyond the immediacy of the text, suggesting how life should be lived. Many major works have, at their core, values and ideals that represent laudable qualities.

A number of writers of juvenile works have employed narrative constructs common to adult books, most notably forms such as the prodigal son and the quest. *Pinocchio* (CARLO COLLODI, 1883) is typical of the first motif. The little puppet, indifferent to his creator's love and to the sacrifices made on his behalf, runs away from home, is seduced into dangerous and wicked adventures by his villainous companions, repents, redeems himself, and returns home to a grand welcome.

The quest, another ubiquitous paradigm, features a protagonist launched on a dangerous mission requiring acts of intelligence, skill, and bravery. The journey's completion finds not only the mission accomplished but a transformation of the traveler into a person who is wiser, more insightful, and more self-aware. The perilous undertakings of Dorothy in Oz, Meg on Camazotz, and Bilbo Baggins in Middle-earth all result in the enlightenment of the protagonists. At minimum, such exemplars offer models for readers to contemplate as they begin the arduous developmental task of constructing their personal ethos.

Setting, often an element of major importance in children's classics, offers an arena for vicariously experiencing fantastic adventures, enchantments, heroic exploits, heart-stopping dangers, or comfort, peace, and contentment. Tom Sawyer, LEWIS CARROLL's Alice, and Laura Ingalls face and overcome dangers and challenges in milieus that make demands on character. The secret garden, initially an overgrown, neglected, but nonetheless idyllic refuge, nourishes the spirit of Mary Lennox and is transformed by her efforts. Just as the garden is revitalized, so is Colin's health restored and Mary's character transformed.

However, it is the manner in which the tale is told, that is, how the characters are developed, the plot advanced, the setting made vivid, the ideas expressed—in short, the author's style that ultimately proclaims the quality of a work of fiction.

RUDYARD KIPLING's playfulness in elucidating the elephant child's "'satiable curtiosity" or in describing the Parsee's hat as one "from which the rays of the sun were reflected in more than Oriental splendor" elicits an immediate response from readers who understand, even without knowing the precise meaning of each word, that something truly spectacular is going on. Commentator Robert MacNeil recalled the intoxicating effect of Kipling's words on him: "the exotic Indian words, like *Bandarlog* and *dhak tree* . . . seemed to have a taste as well as a sound. . . . The repetitions, the sing-song rhythms, and the exotic vocabulary were so suggestive that I imagined I could smell things like the perfumed smoke from a dung fire or the mysterious odour of sandalwood."

The enthralled reader is swept along by the power of the story, extracting cues from context, guessing meaning from cognates or roots, ignoring passages or accepting them without full understanding as simply another part of life whose meaning is yet to be revealed.

Although narrative is the most salient feature of fiction, occasionally book design contributes to a work's longevity. HOWARD PYLE's pen-and-ink drawings for *The Merry Adventures of Robin Hood* (1883) and N. C. WYETH's magnificent illustrations for *Treasure Island* are integral to the appeal of these classics. When narrative and format are inseparably united, the book in its totality is memorable.

The new interactive view of reading redefines those needs of readers which impel them to seek, absorb, and find meaning in particular books. Paradoxically, many of these needs are in opposition to each other. It may be that their resolution involves exploration along the continuum until the child achieves homeostasis, providing emotional balance and subsequent comfort.

Security, carrying the implication of stability and continuity, is the most fundamental of childhood needs. Children intuit that there are costs for this idyllic psychological environment which, for the most part, they are willing to pay: These "payments" include dependence, obedience, and conformity. Long-term acceptance of this role, however, has consequences in terms of growth, competence, and self-esteem. Moreover, the inexorable forces of maturation require that children learn to resist infantilization and simultaneously gain mastery over their own impulses and destructive desires. This dynamic tension between developing an identity and seeking self-control is difficult for children to resolve.

Books provide youngsters with surrogates who can safely explore these conflicting needs for them all along the security/risk-taking spectrum. Children find reassurance in fictional worlds where loving parents provide a protective cocoon from perils. *The Little House in the Big Woods* (LAURA INGALLS WILDER, 1932) features a loving, supportive family that projects an island of invulnerability in an uncertain world. Ironically, the dependable universe represented by such stories fosters readers' readiness for adventure. Books not only identify the kinds of temptations and dangers to be confronted and surmounted, but provide models for emulation.

The child soon ascertains that power is central to one's position in the world and, most important, that other people have it. Restive and rebellious under continual restrictions, the child fervently wishes for control over those large people who seem to dominate every dimension of existence. Again the child is conflicted: How can power be gained over often "unreasonable oppressors" without losing their protection and love? Max in *Where the Wild Things Are* (MAURICE SENDAK, 1963) and the boy who tames *The Reluctant Dragon* (KENNETH GRAHAME, 1938) solve this dilemma in radically different ways. Classic adventure stories offer vicarious experiences as children feel the rush of adrenaline and the shared thrill of facing down worthy enemies. *The Wizard of Oz* (L. FRANK BAUM, 1900), *A Wrinkle in Time,* and *The Lion, the Witch and the Wardrobe* (C. S. LEWIS, 1950) are stories which inform children, on a deeply emotional level, that attaining power is possible, even likely, in their future.

The drive to acquire knowledge accompanies and partially defines the concept of development. This urge, however, is problematic for many parents. Children seem endearing because of their innocence, their naiveté, and their lack of guile or cynicism. These qualities inevitably fade as children become more knowing, less gullible, and newly able to see contradictions, ambiguities, and paradoxes. Innocent children, like Tiny Tim or Peter Pan, are fixtures of classic children's stories, but increasingly aware children—Mowgli, Johnny Tremain, and others—offer contrasting models.

Through both action and reflection, children encounter many opportunities for knowing: stories assist in that process by providing a scaffolding for their learning experiences. Using information, analytical skills, wit, and ingenuity, characters in children's books prevail over difficulties and dangers. By sharing the perceptions and adventures of literary characters, youngsters, still in their formative years, are escorted by literary mentors who express ideas and beliefs which children are not yet able to articulate. Thus, issues of faith, or convictions about moral and ethical positions, matters critical to the development of a personal code of values, are communicated by characters with whom the reader bonds.

Society's need for both change and continuity parallels the developing child's need for adventure and stability. If a culture is to avoid stagnation, it requires rebels to keep it dynamic; its vitality depends heavily on the iconoclast. Predictably, it is the rule-breaker who is frequently the hero of classical literature. Huckleberry Finn (MARK TWAIN, 1884), Julie/Miyax in *Julie of the Wolves* (JEAN CRAIGHEAD GEORGE, 1972), and Cassie Logan in *Roll of Thunder, Hear My Cry* (MILDRED TAYLOR, 1976) assertively and deliberately defy conventional expectations. Their actions induce readers to question the validity of societal practices and constraints, setting the stage for a less passive acceptance of the status quo.

Survival is the most aggressively pursued goal of a society. To persist, each new generation must be inducted into the ceremonies, rituals, and conventions that define the culture, but above all, society must transfer its values to its children. Youngsters, often rebelling against conventions, reject advice, admonishments, and lectures by adults, but willingly embrace the ideals of admired characters in favored books. When values posed by the literature are congruent with those the culture professes to admire, acceptance and promotion of classics become a means whereby societal principles are perpetuated.

Titles once thought to be immortal may no longer connect with the values, understandings, or modes of expression of a society. These are destined to lose their place among the classics. However, each year brings the possibility that a new juvenile work of extraordinary literary quality will be so congruent with developmental and cultural imperatives that it too will become a book "of all time." ❧ BARBARA H. BASKIN AND KAREN HARRIS

Classroom, Books in

During the last part of the twentieth century, the use of children's trade books in the classroom has increased greatly. In some classrooms children's books are an integral part of both the reading program and a cross-disciplinary curriculum. Advocates of the whole language approach to teaching reading, a grass-roots movement, have promoted this use of real books in the classroom. Whole language teachers are abandoning the traditional textbook model of instruction and using children's books as an alternative. In the 1960s there was also a government-funded movement, which later diminished when funding disappeared, to increase the use of children's books in the classroom. The current movement has spread across the United States, Australia, New Zealand, and part of Canada.

Although traditional basal reading programs continue to dominate as they have for decades, today a growing body of research challenges their use. Basal programs treat reading as the identification and pronunciation of words. The whole-language approach uses trade books to teach reading as a process of constructing meaning. Frank Smith's theory that children learn to read by reading meaningful texts is documented by the success of literature-based programs. Such programs demonstrate that early experiences with the richness and variety of trade books motivate children to learn to read and to adopt the habit of reading for pleasure and information.

Research challenging basal programs comes from several areas, including reader-response theories, acquisition theories, and research about composition and literacy. Researchers have also examined instructional practices that encourage reading. Their findings provide insights into more effective ways of structuring experiences with literature. Pioneers such as Charlotte S. Huck from Ohio State University, Ken and Yetta Goodman from the University of Arizona, and Marie Clay and Don Holdaway from New Zealand have provided leadership in the move toward using trade books in the classroom. Their efforts have provided vision, models, and theories for classroom teachers to adopt.

Children's books in the classroom have become part of some official state education programs. In a survey by the Association of American Publishers in 1989–1990, twenty states were identified as being especially active in the use of trade books to teach elementary reading. California's *English–Language Arts Framework* (1987) declared that one of the three goals of the English–Language Arts curriculum should be "a systematic literature program with a meaning-centered approach based on intensive reading, writing, speaking and listening."

Teachers who incorporate children's literature into their reading programs find a wealth of materials to meet their needs. Children's book publishers are making more books available for classroom use by providing more paperback editions and Big Books (over-sized versions of texts and illustrations originally published at more usual sizes). Even basal publishers are changing their basal readers to incorporate more material originally published in trade-book format. The growth in publication of INFORMATION BOOKS provides appealing, intriguing texts with colorful illustrations or photographs that can be used for classroom lessons in all subject areas, extending the use of trade books across the curriculum.

The following description of a classroom model provides a glimpse of books in use as the core of an instructional program. The model describes the most effective contemporary practices in using children's books in the classroom, the result of many years of progress in understanding how to share literature with children. These practices will continue to evolve as research influences teacher education.

In a multi-age classroom of kindergarten through third grade, a welcome sign hangs on the door in the form of a poem chosen by the class from a current favorite poetry book. Bulletin board displays and interest centers focus on trade books. Books are displayed everywhere—Big Books, paperbacks, hardbacks—most with their colorful covers showing. A variety of genres are included with an emphasis on information books useful for subject area investigations. Displays of children's writing, artwork, and poems further demonstrate the class's involvement with books.

The teacher plans a regular time for reading aloud to the whole class each day and also finds time to read aloud to small groups. The children are attracted to the way the teacher reads—with fluency, expression, and verve. Some of the selected titles are related by genre, theme, or topic. These connections encourage the children to discover patterns, to explore interrelationships, to think more deeply, and to respond more fully to the text. As the children listen to books read aloud, they develop language and critical thinking skills that deepen their response to literature. Most importantly, they experience the pleasures of reading.

After reading aloud to the children, the teacher encourages thoughtful and appreciative discussions. Sometimes the children also respond in writing, with dramatization, or with artistic interpretations. When the children request it, which they often do, the teacher rereads a story, knowing that repeated readings promote a deeper understanding of the stories.

When the teacher finishes reading aloud a story, it is placed in the classroom library, and the children often choose to reread it on their own. During the day children have many opportunities to choose books from the classroom library for independent reading. The classroom library is an integral part of the instructional program, because the teacher understands that the children need extended periods during the day to practice their reading. Many books are featured to entice reading. The teacher rotates books so there are always new titles to stimulate the children's interest. The books, at least eight to ten per child, are purchased with school funds.

The children have named their library "The Reading Place." It is a cozy, well-lighted corner with a couch, rumpled bean bag chairs, a rocking chair, and a soft carpet. A white board, a flannel board, and puppets invite the children to retell the books they've read. During choice time at least five or six children are always in "The Reading Place." Others take their choices to other comfortable places.

Reading instruction is based on the belief that children learn to read by reading. Big books are used to instruct small groups of children just learning to read. Before reading the story, the teacher guides the children in predicting what will happen, inviting them to discover the clues in the illustrations and title. The teacher then reads the story aloud, using a pointer so the children can follow the text. After the story has been read, the children reread in unison. Then the teacher demonstrates strategies that give the children tools to become more fluent readers, showing, for example, how to unlock the meaning of a new word by using contextual clues or guiding a discussion that emphasizes the meaning of the story. Later, the students may collaborate in retelling the story. They carefully select sentences the teacher has written on strips of paper and place them in sequence in a chart with pockets to hold each strip. The teacher and the students will reread these familiar stories many times during the year.

The teacher designs other reading instructional experiences around music and the choral reading of poetry. Children gather around the piano to sing. They read the lyrics off a chart that the teacher has made and later enjoy the illustrations in a book that extends and expands the lyrics. Other groups of children share and recite poems from anthologies in choral readings. Each of these experiences gives the children opportunities to increase their fluency in reading but also demonstrates to them the pleasures of reading.

The teacher has multiple copies of a variety of books, displayed so the children may browse during choice time. Children who are fluent readers select from these sets and sign up for the title they wish to read. Children can choose to read with a partner, independently, or with a small group. Some read the parts of different characters; some read silently; some listen to an audio version of the book; still others take turns reading aloud.

While they read, the children write unfamiliar words on bookmarks. The words are shared during a group meeting with the teacher, who helps the students discover how to unlock the meaning by examining the context. When a group has finished reading their book, they collaborate on a project that demonstrates their response to it. A group reading folktales might create their own tales. A group reading about community workers may conduct interviews to find out more about other careers. A group reading historical fiction might create a mural that demonstrates the different lifestyle of that period.

The children's writing illustrates the influence of books in the classroom. Many of the children's pieces are variations on poems and stories that they have enjoyed together. The children's writing demonstrates the sense of story they have gained as they have listened to and read books. For example, their writing has structure, and they use words and phrases from favorite books. As the children write independently, they often check books for ideas and inspiration.

The teacher plans thematic units that cross the different disciplines of the curriculum and that give the children choices about topics they would like to learn about in depth. The core of the curriculum is a large selection of books with a variety of reading levels and genres. The whole class, for example, has been reading about and studying Native Americans. One group has chosen to write their own *pourquoi* or "why" stories. A pile of Native-American *pourquoi* tales is heaped on a table. As they create their own stories the children often refer to those tales. Another group is investigating the dwellings of Native Americans. They study the text and illustrations of information books that focus on that subject as they create models of the Indian dwellings. One group is creating a mural about Native Americans, studying the illustrations of PAUL GOBLE. Another group's project is a dramatization of a Native American tale. They reread the story with the teacher's support and then plan their presentation. A parent volunteer assists a group that is excitedly preparing a tasting of Native American foods they have read about. The whole class collaborates on identifying the plant specimens they gathered on a field trip to a nearby canyon. The books on native plants help them make the identifications. Next, they will explore how native people used the plants. Again, the books will provide information.

This is a classroom that promotes the love of reading and teaches children how to turn to reading for both pleasure and information. The teacher employs books as the core of the instructional reading program and fills the classroom with books to encourage the children to read in order to learn. The children thoughtfully apply the strategies of problem solving, inquiry, and higher-order thinking as they read and share a variety of books that reflect a diversity of voices, reading levels, and topics. Similar models can be incorporated in other grade levels.

What reforms need to be enacted to enable all classrooms to achieve this model? Professional associations, teacher-training institutions, leaders from business and government as well as teachers themselves are working together to bring about educational restructuring. The use of children's books as the core of the curriculum represents a vital move toward more thoughtful, meaning-centered classrooms. To enable more teachers to move toward the practices described in the model, many reforms must be enacted.

First, administrators and teachers will need to restructure teaching assignments to allow the time necessary for ongoing professional development. For teachers to acquire the knowledge and authority necessary to effectively use the practices described in the model, they will need to explore children's literature, holistic assessment, curriculum integration, language and literacy acquisition, and cooperative learning. As teachers work together to incorporate the practices described in the model, they will also need more time to develop a curriculum that meets the needs and interests of their students.

The second reform is to find or create new funding sources to pay for staff development and to purchase children's books and furniture for classroom libraries: Bookshelves, rocking chairs, comfortable chairs, and rugs are all needed. Even schools that have received no increases in funding have discovered ways of changing spending practices to fulfill their needs for staff development and more books and resources. Funds are also required to hire credentialed school librarians and to build an excellent school library collection.

The third challenge is to create lines of communication with parents to promote the reading program at school and in the home. For some schools, that will mean parent education classes that focus on reading with the child and selecting excellent books to share.

Thousands of teachers around the world are adopting or already have adopted the practices described in the model. These teachers, along with the librarians, administrators, and parents who support them, are dedicated to a "literacy of thoughtfulness." As the above-mentioned reforms are enacted, more teachers will be able to incorporate the practices described in the model. Then children will be reading more, and more children will become life-long readers.

MARILYN CARPENTER

Cleary, Beverly

AMERICAN AUTHOR, B. 1916. Henry Huggins. Ramona Quimby. Ralph S. Mouse. Ribsy. For many, the names of Beverly Cleary's best-known characters read like a list of very special friends. Since the publication of *Henry Huggins* in 1950, Cleary has been entertaining readers with simply written books filled with some of the most endearing characters in twentieth-century children's literature.

Born Beverly Atlee Bunn in McMinnville, Oregon, the author spent her earliest years on a farm in nearby Yamhill before moving to Portland at the age of six. Although her schoolteacher mother had organized the first library in Yamhill, Cleary did not enjoy reading. In her outstanding autobiography, *A Girl from Yamhill* (1988), Cleary relates how a difficult first-grade teacher made her fear the written word. Even though she loved looking at books and hearing stories read aloud, Cleary found reading a laborious and unpleasant activity. Things changed one rainy Sunday afternoon during the third grade. Out of boredom, Cleary picked up a copy of LUCY FITCH PERKINS's *The Dutch Twins* to look at the pictures but suddenly found herself reading; she was enthralled by the experience. She became a voracious reader, although she always questioned why the juvenile books of that era were predominantly set in historical times or dealt with children in foreign countries; she further wondered why events usually centered on mysteries or wild adventures. Cleary wanted to read funny stories about everyday children.

Soon after discovering the joy of reading, Cleary wrote a book review that was published in the Oregon *Journal* and later won a two-dollar prize for an essay about a beaver. A school librarian suggested that Cleary should someday write books for children. This goal was put on hold while she attended the University of California at Berkeley, library school at the University of Washington, worked as a children's librarian, married, and became the mother of twins.

Inspired by a brief job selling children's books in a department store, Cleary began writing *Henry Huggins,* the story of a third-grade boy who lives on Klickitat Street in Portland. Early on, Henry discovers a stray dog

Voices of the Creators

Beverly Cleary

I recall my pleasure upon entering the first grade at seeing above the blackboard a reproduction of Sir Joshua Reynolds's painting *The Age of Innocence.* I was filled with admiration for the pretty little girl who was wearing, to my six-year-old eyes, a white party dress. I loved that little girl, but by Thanksgiving my love had changed to resentment. There she sat under a tree with nothing to do but keep her party dress clean. There I sat itching in my navy blue serge sailor dress, the shrunken elastic of my new black bloomers cutting into my legs, struggling to learn to read.

My first grade was sorted into three reading groups—Bluebirds, Redbirds, and Blackbirds. I was a Blackbird, the only girl Blackbird among the boy Blackbirds, who had to sit in the row by the blackboard. Perhaps this was the beginning of my sympathy for the problems of boys. How I envied the bright, self-confident Bluebirds, most of them girls, who got to sit by the windows and who, unlike myself, pleased the teacher by remembering to write with their right hands—a ridiculous thing to do in my six-year-old opinion. Anyone could see that both hands were alike. One should simply use the hand nearer the task.

To be a Blackbird was to be disgraced. I wanted to read, but somehow I could not. I wept at home while my puzzled mother tried to drill me on the dreaded word charts. "But reading is fun," insisted my mother. I stomped my feet and threw the book on the floor. Reading was not fun.

By second grade I was able to plod through my reader a step or two ahead of disgrace. Although I could read if I wanted to, I no longer wanted to. Reading was not fun. It was boring. Most of the stories were simplified versions of folktales that had been read aloud to me many times. There were no surprises left.

Then, in third grade, the miracle happened. It was a dull rainy Portland Sunday afternoon when there was nothing to do but thumb through two books from the Sunday school library. After looking at the pictures, I began out of boredom to read *The Dutch Twins* by Lucy Fitch Perkins. Twins had always fascinated me. As a small child, I had searched through magazines—my only picture books—for pictures of the Campbell Soup twins. To me, a solitary child, the idea of twins was fascinating. A twin would never be lonely. Here was a whole book about twins, a boy and girl who lived in Holland but who had experiences a girl in Portland, Oregon, could share. I could laugh when the boy fell into the Zuyder Zee because I had once fallen into the Yamhill River. In this story, something happened. With rising elation, I read on. I read all afternoon and evening, and by bedtime I had read not only *The Dutch Twins* but *The Swiss Twins* as well. It was one of the most exciting days of my life. Shame and guilt dropped away from the ex-Blackbird, who had at last taken wing. I could read and read with pleasure! Grown-ups were right after all. Reading was fun.

From the third grade on, I was a reader, and when my school librarian suggested that I should write children's books when I grew up, I was ecstatic. Of course! That was exactly what I wanted to do. By now I had gone on from the twin books and was reading everything on the children's side of our branch library. I had grown critical. Why couldn't authors write about the sort of boys and girls who lived on my block? Plain, ordinary boys and girls I called them when I was a child. Why couldn't authors skip all that tiresome description and write books in which something happened on every page? Why couldn't they make the stories funny?

And so I grew up to try to create the books I had wanted to read as a child—books to make reading exciting and interesting and, most of all, enjoyable. It is my fondest hope that readers will finish a book of mine, close it, and think, "Well! Grown-ups are right after all! Reading is fun!"

and names him Ribsy; the relationship between boy and dog is at the heart of this book and all the books that follow in the "Henry" series. With *Henry Huggins,* Cleary achieved her goal of writing an amusing book about an ordinary child. The episodic plot touches on problems that sometimes seem overwhelming to Henry. Cleary's skill as an author makes the reader sympathize with Henry's concerns, but the events are also hilariously recounted. There is the time Henry's pet fish begin to multiply, resulting in "gallons of guppies." Another time Henry dusts Ribsy with talcum powder before a dog show and Ribsy turns pink from head to toe. In a moving final chapter, Ribsy's original owner appears and Henry must face the possibility of losing his pet. Later

Illustration by Alan Tiegreen from *Ramona and Her Father* (1975), by Beverly Cleary.

volumes are equally percipient and humorous but more cohesively structured around a particular event in Henry's life—his first paper route, an upcoming fishing trip, a backyard clubhouse.

As the series grew in popularity, Cleary wrote books about Henry's friends. *Ribsy* (1964) is presented from the point of view of Henry's dog. *Beezus and Ramona* (1955) concerns Henry's friend Beatrice Quimby—always known as Beezus—and her mischievous little sister. Ramona receives scant mention in *Henry Huggins,* but she can be glimpsed on the very last page of the book. In one of Louis Darling's superb illustrations, she appears as a small, ghostlike figure in overalls, standing apart from the other children as they gather around Ribsy. But as the series progresses, Ramona assumes a greater role in each of the books—destroying birthday cakes, upsetting checkerboards, following Henry on his paper route. It was almost inevitable that Cleary would publish a series of books about this boisterous yet appealing character.

Beginning with *Ramona the Pest* (1968), the stories follow Ramona from kindergarten through the third grade and contain a depth of emotion only hinted at in the "Henry" books. The reader laughs at Ramona's antics but also empathizes with the imaginative, often misunderstood girl. Cleary shows that even a child from a happy family has a strong need for understanding and love. Ramona is Cleary's most developed characterization, a child at once ordinary and extraordinary. This is most evident in *Ramona the Brave* (1975), in which the character can be viewed as both a typical first-grader and an exceptionally creative, artistic child. *Ramona Forever* (1984), the last volume in the series, deals with such monumental events as a wedding, a new baby in the Quimby family, and the death of a pet.

Cleary has written a variety of other books. *The Mouse and the Motorcycle* (1965) begins an extremely popular fantasy series about interactions between a boy and a talking mouse. Cleary's four teenage romances were published in the late 1950s and early 1960s; though they are dated, they continue to be read. Several picture books have been generally well received but lack the freshness of the author's other works. Cleary is most adept at writing simple chapter books that can be enjoyed by even the youngest readers yet are so sharply observed that readers of all ages respond to the material.

For much of her career, the stigma connected with "series books" prevented many from recognizing Cleary's remarkable achievements. The author labored in the field for over a quarter century before *Ramona and Her Father* (1977) and *Ramona Quimby, Age 8* (1981) were selected as Newbery Honor Books. Cleary finally won the Newbery Medal in 1984 for a book completely different from anything she had previously written. Employing the first-person voice in a series of letters and journal entries, *Dear Mr. Henshaw* depicts a boy's growing self-awareness and maturity, brought about through his correspondence with a favorite author. Leigh Botts is a well-rounded character in a book that contains humor, but it is a sadder, more complex work than most Cleary novels, and it marks the first time the author deals with children of divorce. Cleary received the Laura Ingalls Wilder Award for the body of her work and remains one of those rare authors who are both critically acclaimed and immensely popular with young readers. § PETER D. SIERUTA

CLEAVER, BILL
CLEAVER, VERA

BILL: AMERICAN AUTHOR, 1920–1981; VERA: AMERICAN AUTHOR, B. 1919. In writing about Appalachia, the Deep South, the Great Plains, and other rural American locales, Vera and Bill Cleaver examined a large and often overlooked segment of the population.

Vera Allen was born in Virgil, South Dakota, and Bill Cleaver was born in Seattle, but both families moved frequently and the children were educated at a variety of schools. Neither Vera nor Bill attended college or took a creative writing course, but they intended to become writers. The couple married after World War II. Bill served in the air force and worked as a jeweler and watchmaker; Vera was employed as a bookkeeper. On weekends the couple wrote short stories for a variety of periodicals. They produced nearly three hundred short stories before their first book for children was published. *Ellen Grae* (1967) concerns an inventive girl who faces a moral dilemma when entrusted with a horrible secret. This brief novel won critical acclaim for its eccentric characters, crystal-clear narration, and uncompromising look at ethical issues, yet some question exists about whether it is really a children's book. Although the heroine is eleven years old, the story seems aimed at a sophisticated adult audience. The sequel, *Lady Ellen Grae* (1968), has more child appeal but is flawed by its broad comedy.

With their next book, the Cleavers produced a masterpiece. *Where the Lilies Bloom* (1969) is the story of Mary Call Luther, an Appalachian teenager trying to hold her orphaned family together. The characterizations are three-dimensional, the setting is brilliantly realized, and Mary Call's narration is both plainspoken and beautifully lyrical. Many reference books erroneously list *Where the Lilies Bloom* as a Newbery Honor Book; the screen credits of the fine film adaptation even make this false claim. As a matter of record, the novel was not a Newbery title, although certainly a work of its caliber was deserving of the highest possible honors. The Cleavers' successive titles, including *The Whys and Wherefores of Littabelle Lee* (1973), *Me Too* (1973), and *Queen of Hearts* (1978), sustain this high degree of excellence, and *Dust of the Earth* (1975) won a Golden Spur Award for best juvenile fiction from the Western Writers of America. Even the occasional weak book, such as *Delpha Green and Company* (1972), is redeemed by its stunning conclusion and ingratiating heroine.

Most often the Cleavers write about feisty, resourceful, self-sufficient teenage girls, although one of their best novels, *Grover* (1970), concerns a boy coping with his mother's death. There is a strong affinity for nature in the well-described rural environments, and the writing contains a rare purity of thought and language. Although these similarities may suggest the Cleavers worked within a narrow framework, they employed wide variations that make each novel unique. Some titles are contemporary; others are historical. Settings range from Florida to South Dakota to the grim scenes of Chicago slum life in *The Mimosa Tree* (1970). The rural locales should not suggest sentimentality or dated issues; the Cleavers toppled taboos by writing of murder, suicide, illegitimacy, mental handicaps, and the problems of the elderly. Handling these topics in a tasteful, nonexploitative way, the authors helped advance realism in children's books.

The nature of their literary collaboration is hard to define. It is widely believed that Bill and Vera jointly created the plots and characters but that Vera did the actual writing of the books. Since Bill's death in 1981, Vera has continued to produce outstanding novels that meet the high standards of their predecessors. ❧ P.D.S.

Cleaver, Elizabeth

CANADIAN ILLUSTRATOR AND AUTHOR, 1939–1985. Elizabeth Cleaver's first book, *The Wind Has Wings* (1968), poems compiled by Mary Alice Downe and Barbara Robertson, is often cited as a turning point in CANADIAN CHILDREN'S LITERATURE. Illustrated in mixed media, it offered vibrantly colored torn-paper collage, as well as dramatic black-and-white linocuts. No less an authority than scholar and critic Sheila Egoff has called it "the first really impressive illustrated book to be published in Canada."

The Wind Has Wings led the way for a body of work that includes four Indian legends retold by William Toye: *How Summer Came to Canada* (1969), *The Mountain Goats of Temlaham* (1969), *The Loon's Necklace* (1977), and *The Fire Stealer* (1979); three stories Cleaver wrote herself: *The Miraculous Hind: A Hungarian Legend* (1973), *Petrouchka* (1980), based on Igor Stravinsky's ballet, and *The Enchanted Caribou* (1985), an Inuit transmogrification tale that she illustrated with shadow puppets; a child-sized alphabet book, *ABC* (1984); a French-Canadian folktale, Downie's *The Witch of the North* (1975); and Cyrus Macmillan's *Canadian Wonder Tales* (1974). Cleaver was working on *The Wooden Prince*, based on the Béla Bartók ballet, when she died of cancer at the age of forty-five.

Born in Montreal, Cleaver spent her teen years in Hungary and attended school at Sarospatak, where, as she would explain to her audiences in later years, seventeenth-century Czech scholar Amos Comenius created *Orbis Sensualium Pictus*, the first picture book used in schools. In 1967, after undergoing cancer surgery, she left her job with an advertising agency in Montreal to pursue a career in children's literature. Drawing on childhood memories of cutout paper dolls and the pleasure they used to bring, Cleaver turned to cut- and torn-paper collage as her preferred medium, since it allowed her "to exploit the accidental" and engage in "a form of visual play." She used mixed media, drawing on her vast store of monoprints (textured papers that she painted), incorporating linoleum cuts and adding found objects—keys, pearls, paper clips, birch bark, pine needles, and fur—to create her images.

Critics sometimes questioned Cleaver's choice of subject matter—can a child care about the complexities of *Petrouchka*, they asked, in which a clown-puppet dies for the love of a ballerina while his spirit survives? But the quality of her art raised Cleaver's books to award-winning heights. *The Wind Has Wings*, which she revised in 1984, won the Canadian Library Association's first Amelia Frances Howard–Gibbon Illustrator's Award in 1971, a prize the artist captured again in 1978 for *The Loon's Necklace*. In 1980 *Petrouchka* won the Governor General's Literary Award for Children's Literature.

Cleaver said she loved PICTURE BOOKS because they allowed her to "create a world and live twice: once when I have an experience or idea and again when I re-create it." She added that "artistically valuable books will educate the child's taste and visual sense." Cleaver's editor and collaborator, William Toye, in eulogizing her work, told how she phoned him from her hospital bed in January 1968 to ask if she might still illustrate the book he had offered her. "Much later she told me she had prayed that if she were spared, she would devote her life to making beautiful books for children." B.G.

CLEMENS, SAMUEL LANGHORNE

See TWAIN, MARK.

CLIFFORD, ETH

AMERICAN AUTHOR, B. 1915. Eth Clifford's best-known title, *Help! I'm a Prisoner in the Library* (1979), concerns a situation she would no doubt welcome. A passionate reader as a child, she became a dedicated author and editor with scores of her own titles on library shelves.

Clifford was born on Christmas Day in New York City and moved several times as a child. She remembers learning to read in a one-room schoolhouse set in an apple orchard, and she discovered the public library when her family later moved to Philadelphia. At age sixteen, she met her future husband at a poetry reading in Brooklyn, and it was he who encouraged her to begin writing while he was stationed in the South Pacific during World War II. Clifford began with short stories and soon published her first adult novel, *Go Fight City Hall* (1949), which was a *Reader's Digest* Book of the Month and was excerpted in humor anthologies. Clifford, her husband, and their daughter later moved to Indiana, where they lived for twenty years. While there, Clifford contributed to many social studies, science, and language arts textbooks for children, and this work eventually developed into her primary interest—writing children's fiction.

Clifford's books for children cover a wide range of ages and subject matter. Her youngest readers can match their sleuthing abilities against an animal detective in *Flatfoot Fox and the Case of the Missing Eye* (1990), handsomely illustrated by Brian Lies. Middle-grade readers enjoy Clifford's deft combination of suspense and humor in a mystery adventure series of five novels about Mary Rose and Jo-Beth Onetree, the sisters who were first introduced in *Help! I'm a Prisoner in the Library*, which won the 1982 Young Hoosier Award. Among the story's appealing elements are the believable relationship between the practical and responsible Mary Rose and her younger, very dramatic sister and the real sense of fear generated as the girls feel their way through the darkened rooms of the old mansion turned library. Subsequent adventures find the sisters sleuthing in such places as a ghost town and a shoe museum. All five books were illustrated by George Hughes.

Clifford often incorporates interesting factual information into her humorous works. Children reading *Harvey's Marvelous Monkey Mystery* (1987) have an opportunity to learn about the companion monkeys who are trained to perform useful services for their physically challenged owners. In *The Rocking Chair Rebellion* (1978), a book for teens that includes contemporary problems, a young girl finds herself involved with the distresses of the elderly when she volunteers to work for the aged. This book was made into an "ABC Afterschool Special." Some of Clifford's books are written with a simplicity of style coupled with an emotional resonance that appeal to readers of all ages. *The Remembering Box* (1985) is a quiet and beautifully told story of the legacy that a Jewish grandmother gives her grandson and the understanding between them that allows the boy to accept her death.

Clifford once called her ambition the desire to "rival Scheherazade and tell one thousand and one stories." She has succeeded in creating a readership that looks to her for a variety of books, all with strong characterization, sensitive treatment of relationships, authentic detail, and wonderful adventure. P.H.

Clifton, Lucille

American author of fiction and poetry for children and adults, b. 1936. Lucille Clifton was born Lucille Sayles in Depew, New York, near Buffalo. Her father told stories about her African ancestors, including her great-great-grandmother, born of Dahomey people but captured and forced into slavery. There was poetry in the household as well—her mother wrote poetry and read it aloud to her children. Later in life, Clifton wrote a memoir about her family, *Generations* (1976). When she was sixteen years old, Clifton won a full scholarship to Howard University. After spending two years there, she transferred to Fredonia State Teachers College, where she banded together with a group who liked to read and perform plays. She met the novelist Ishmael Reed, who showed her poetry to Langston Hughes. He included some of her poems in an anthology.

In 1969 Clifton won an award for her poetry and had her first book of poems published. *Good Times*, poems for adults, was chosen as one of the ten best books of the year by the *New York Times*. She went on to write several other books for adults.

Jacket illustration by Ann Grifalconi for *Everett Anderson's Year* (1974), by Lucille Clifton.

Her first work for children, *Some of the Days of Everett Anderson*, was published in 1970. It chronicles the life of a six-year-old black child who lives in the city, each day of the week described in a poem. *Everett Anderson's Christmas Coming*, which followed a year later, describes the anticipation and joy of the five days before Christmas. Evaline Ness illustrated both books. Several other Everett books followed, illustrated by Ann Grifalconi. Clifton won the 1984 Coretta Scott King Award for *Everett Anderson's Goodbye.*

In addition to these well-loved picture books, Clifton wrote *All Us Come Cross the Water*, a children's book about people being brought into slavery, in 1973. *The Time They Used to Be* (1974) is an example of her fiction for children. It is a story told in the first person, describing a period of time in 1948 in the life of two girls who observe the people around them, some of whom are recovering from the war, some who see ghosts. It ends when President Truman ends Jim Crow laws in the military. A poet's touch and a storyteller's art combine in the language and the narrative pacing to capture a moment in history and some unforgettable memories. Clifton continued to portray black experiences in *Amifika* (1977), which tells of a small boy, again a city dweller, who is fearful about his father's return from the army, since the boy does not remember him. *The Black BC's* (1970) is an ABC book that contains information on black history.

Clifton has turned her storyteller's background and her lyrical use of language into the basis for realistic and full-dimensional literature about African American characters. She was poet laureate of the state of Maryland and has been poet in residence at Coppin State College in Baltimore, Maryland. She has held positions at Columbia University School of the Arts, at George Washington University, and at the University of California at Santa Cruz. S.H.H.

Clymer, Eleanor

American author, b. 1906. Eleanor Clymer, who has written several noteworthy books about urban children, was born and raised in New York City. The daughter of Russian immigrants, she wrote from an early age but did not consider writing for children until she attended the Bank Street College of Education. Her first book, *A Yard for John* (1943), concerns a city boy who moves to the country. Clymer continued writing modest, enjoyable fiction, including *Here Comes Pete* (1944) and *Treasure at First Base* (1950), and occasional volumes of scientific nonfiction, such as *Search for a Living Fossil* (1963). Some of her most popular stories concern animals. *Harry, the Wild West Horse* (1964) is a retired farm animal who finds work in show business; *Horatio* (1968) tells of a city cat whose adventures fill several volumes, including *Horatio's Birthday* (1976) and *Horatio Goes to the Country* (1978).

Clymer wrote about the urban phenomenon of

"latch-key children" in *The Latch Key Club* (1949) and later published a number of short, strong books about city life. *My Brother Stevie* (1967) is the story of an elementary school youngster who falls in with a gang; *Me and the Eggman* (1972) concerns a fatherless city boy who runs away to a farm; *Luke Was There* (1973) is the story of two brothers living in a shelter while their mother is hospitalized. Although the plots are fairly shapeless, the first-person narratives are intense and the subject matter was unusual for the era.

Clymer has written minor children's books under the pseudonyms Janet Bell and Elizabeth Kinsey but is best known for her topical stories about the concerns and struggles of contemporary urban children. ❧ P.D.S.

Coatsworth, Elizabeth

American author and poet, 1893–1986. Recognized throughout her life as a distinguished author of children's books, Elizabeth Coatsworth first broke into print with a volume of adult poetry, *Fox Footprints* (1923). During a career that spanned several decades, Elizabeth Coatsworth wrote over ninety books of poetry and prose. She won the Newbery Medal for her book *The Cat Who Went to Heaven* (1930), a story based on a Japanese legend celebrating the transcendency of love. Although this book won critical praise and recognition, it never achieved the popularity of her classic story, *Away Goes Sally* (1934), which describes Sally's adventures as her home is moved on a sledge from Massachusetts to Maine one snowy winter. Coatsworth frequently included poems within her stories, often interspersing them between chapters. She used this device in *Away Goes Sally,* enhancing an already appealing story with lyric poems. Several of these poems are notable examples of Coatsworth's successful use of comparisons and contrasts, a technique she used to alter rhythm patterns and mood.

Of her considerable output of poetry, those which celebrate nature best demonstrate her ear for language and effective use of imagery. Her fiction also reveals her deep appreciation and understanding of the everyday world. Married to naturalist and author Henry Beston, Coatsworth shared with him a love of the out of doors, noting the wonders of each passing season. Travel, too, had a profound influence on her writing. She was born in Buffalo, New York, but even as a child she traveled widely in the United States and abroad. *Bess and the Sphinx* (1967) is based on her childhood visit to Egypt. Other countries served as settings for her stories, but the United States and Maine in particular provided her primary sources of inspiration. Elizabeth Coatsworth received her formal education at Vassar College and Columbia University, but it was her own inquiring mind and observant nature that made her a scholar.

Her writing reveals her intelligence and her pleasure in the small everyday things of life—factors which in no way impede her gift as a storyteller or poet. With her prodigious output, it is not surprising to find that each book is not of equal stature. It can be said, however, that Elizabeth Coatsworth's books were consistently a reflection of her outlook on the world in which she saw beauty, goodness, and wonder. It was a world she wanted to share with children. ❧ P.S.

Cobb, Vicki

American author, b. 1938. Forget malodorous laboratory experiments and distracted scientists in white lab coats. Vicki Cobb brings fun to books about science. For more than thirty years, this Barnard College and Columbia University graduate has brought science to the kitchen and the backyard, providing a whiff of fresh air to sometimes musty scientific tenets. "If my book is the first book on a subject that is read," Cobb admits, "it will definitely not be the last."

How many scientists suggest eating the results of an experiment, as Cobb does in *Science Experiments You Can Eat* (1972)? Or reinforce the idea that "failing is no disgrace," as she does in *Bet You Can't!* (1980, with Kathy Darling)? An attitude of adventure, unimagined possibilities, and risk taking encourages children and young adults to experiment with things around them—and with life. "What is reality, really?" this former science teacher asks in *How to Really Fool Yourself* (1981), as she describes our five senses. Readers learn about stimuli, sensation, and knowledge from Aristotle and umpires: After eating artichokes, everything tastes sweet. Illustrations in the corner of the book allow readers to create their own motion picture by flipping quickly through the pages. The French Tricolor demonstrates that brightly colored areas appear larger than darker colored ones. A thought experiment, "logic at its best," explains the concept of motion. In *How to Really Fool Yourself,* Cobb lightheartedly threads her way through physics and chemistry, demystifying principles and stressing the reality of fun.

This "hands-on" approach in *Gobs of Goo* (1983) allows readers to experience "gooey stuff . . . soft and thick and sort of wet." Scientists call it an emulsion;

Cobb defines it as mayonnaise and gives instructions on how to create a "mixture of oil and water held together by a third substance." The journey through goo begins and ends with human cells because "an important part of all living things is gooey stuff."

Cobb's descriptions make scientific concepts sing, dance, and come alive. Whether she deals with principles of matter, in *Why Can't You Unscramble an Egg?* (1990), or energy, in *Why Doesn't the Sun Burn Out?* (1990), the weightiest of complex principles become lightweight and understandable. Like an imaginary Albert Einstein sitting on the floor to discuss an experiment with a child, Cobb patiently leads readers on an entertaining journey of discovery in the scientific realm. ❧ B.C.

Cohen, Daniel

AMERICAN AUTHOR, B. 1936. A prolific writer who has published scores of nonfiction books, Daniel Cohen never considered a literary career when he was growing up. Born and raised in Chicago, Cohen was an average student who was bored by school. His childhood ambition was to become a zookeeper, so when he entered the University of Illinois in Chicago, he decided to satisfy his interest in animals by studying biology. He soon realized he was not interested in that field. He liked to hang around the school newspaper office, where he had friends. Cohen began working for the newspaper, eventually becoming editor in chief. Writing clearly and quickly to meet deadlines, he developed work habits that later enabled him to publish as many as nine books a year.

Cohen completed journalism school at the University of Illinois in Champaign-Urbana. Upon graduation, he worked for Time, Inc., then moved to New York as an editor of *Science Digest*. During his ten years with the magazine, he began writing articles that skeptically examined topics such as extrasensory perception, monsters, and UFOs. These articles, as well as new pieces, were included in his first book, *Myths of the Space Age* (1967), which was published for adults.

Cohen began writing for children with his next book, *Secrets from Ancient Graves* (1968), which concerns archeological finds. Since becoming a full-time writer, Cohen has concentrated almost exclusively on children's books. Using an extensive personal library and a wide circle of contacts, he has published books on a staggering number of topics, including computers, cars, and medicine. With his wife, Susan Cohen, he has published biographies of rock stars, wrestlers, and astronauts, as well as the more serious books *A Six-Pack and a Fake I.D.: Teens Look at the Drinking Question* (1986) and *When Someone You Know Is Gay* (1989).

But Cohen is best known for writing about monsters, ghosts, and psychic phenomena. Reluctant readers, in particular, appreciate the intriguing subject matter and fast-moving prose found in *The World of UFOs* (1978), *Everything You Need to Know about Monsters and Still Be Able to Sleep* (1981), *How to Test Your ESP* (1982), and many other works of speculative nonfiction. Cohen's adaptations of paranormal tales from historical and urban folklore are equally popular and include *The Ghosts of War* (1990) and *Phantom Animals* (1991).

Perhaps because he treats writing as a business enterprise rather than an art form, Cohen's style is not highly polished, though his prose is generally competent. His willingness to write about almost any topic has resulted in an uneven body of work that ranges from the excellent guide to museum exhibits he wrote with his wife, *Where to Find Dinosaurs Today* (1992), to ephemeral paperbacks that capitalize on popular television programs. Yet within this large and varied spectrum, there are books that are likely to be diverting or interesting to almost any reader's individual tastes. ❧ P.D.S.

Cole, Brock

AMERICAN NOVELIST AND PICTURE-BOOK AUTHOR AND ILLUSTRATOR, B. 1938. Formerly a philosophy instructor at the University of Wisconsin, Brock Cole is a self-taught illustrator who has created a number of fine picture books. His texts recall the simplicity and dignity of folktales, and the matter-of-fact tone of his smoothly flowing narratives lends plausibility to even the most extraordinary happenings. Cole's skillful art successfully portrays action, emotion, and humor through the facial expressions and body language of his characters. The protagonists in his picture books often find that appearances are deceiving. Jessie McWhistle, in *No More Baths* (1980), envies animals until she learns that, like humans, they have their own disgusting bathing practices. Preston the pig, in *Nothing but a Pig* (1981), discovers that "fine clothes do not make a man." In *The Winter Wren* (1984), young Simon finds that Spring is not, as he had believed, simply "a princess all dressed in green and gold."

Deceptive appearances are also a theme in Cole's novels for young adults. In *The Goats* (1987), a girl and a boy at a summer camp are labeled social misfits by their camp mates, stripped of their clothing, then left on a small island as a prank. Laura and Howie manage to swim back to land but instead of returning to the camp, they decide to stay in the woods together, and, using survival skills they didn't know they possessed, they find clothing, food, and shelter. On leaving the island, Laura and Howie no longer see each other as social outcasts but begin to see each other as they truly are: intelligent, caring, and honest individuals. Though in the end they return to their old world, Laura and Howie are not their old selves, having found a measure of self-worth that emboldens and empowers them. Certainly controversial when it was published, *The Goats* was hailed by some as a rare and significant publication and was criticized by

Voices of the Creators

Brock Cole

I was born in a small town in Michigan and spent my first few years there. My grandfather was a dentist and a banker who lost most of his money in the Great Depression. I remember him as old and frail in a large house with two parlors and a crack in the dining-room wall for which the railroad was held responsible. He would listen to "Mr. Keene, Tracer of Lost Persons" on a large radio that also gave us all the news about the war in Europe.

When I was young, children were generally swept out of the house in the morning and not expected to show up again before dark, except for meals. I don't think adults worried about us much. How wonderful that was! And, indeed, we seemed quite indestructible. I remember very clearly falling off a hay wagon once and having the heavy, steel-shod wheel bounce across my chest. I never told anyone. I wasn't hurt. I think miracles were more common then. I learned to swim in a dammed creek when I was four or five. There were no shallows. A person simply plunged in and dog-paddled for dear life.

In the fall, just at dusk, great flocks of migrating starlings would descend on the town. They would roost in the tall elms and make such a noise as I've never heard since. Men would take their shotguns out into the streets and slaughter hundreds of the birds, who would then be swept into the gutters and cremated under great piles of burning leaves. My mother didn't approve of this, and would call for my brother and me to come in, but we resisted as long as we dared. I can still remember very clearly the fading light, the dark figures of the men in the middle of the road pointing their guns straight up, and the derisive chorus of thousands of invisible birds overhead....

I think most writers must draw on their own experience for a sense of what childhood is like. It isn't easy. So much gets lost.

I try to write every day. To sit down in the morning about nine o'clock and to turn out a draft of new material until about twelve. Often it's very hard to get started. I want to do anything but write, but I simply try to get on with it. To fill up a page. I can always throw it out, I remind myself. That's a great comfort. Once my imagination is engaged, it gets easier.

I try not to revise until I'm sure which way a story is going. It's a mistake to revise too soon, too carefully. A writer can become enamored of a scene or passage that is absolutely useless.

At the right moment, revision is easy. I prune, primarily. I shape. If there are two adjectives, I take one out. I like a sentence to have a certain rhythm, a nice sound. I try not to polish too much. If a draft isn't right, it usually doesn't get any better if I labor over it. It's better to take a fresh run at it.

I'm an illustrator as well as a novelist. I'm not sure it was a good idea to try to be both. They are jealous trades and each resents time given over to something else.

Drawing is a wonderful thing to do. I like working with pencil especially. Editors aren't too fond of it, because it doesn't reproduce well, but it's capable of great subtlety. A good line looks like an accident. It should always be just out of control.

I like to look at the work of other illustrators. My favorites are Ardizzone and Shepard. Their work is never labored. They put down a line or two, and there is a picture full of life and light. Most people don't seem to realize how wonderful these drawings are. They prefer something with a bit more finish. Something that obviously was a bit of hard work.

Not everyone feels the way I do about drawing. Often people visit me and don't even look at what's on the drawing table! I don't understand this. When I was a child, to watch someone draw was the most exciting thing I could think of. People aren't much interested in what one can make with a pencil and a piece of paper anymore. It's surprising, but it's so.

others for its portrayal of adults as unconcerned or unable to help the children. But the novel found a readership and has proved especially effective as a book to spark classroom discussion. The raw emotion in the novel is well balanced. Cole counterposes pain with joy, shame with pride, ostracism with friendship, and impotence with competence. Primary and secondary characters are fully drawn; Laura and Howie, on the cusp of adolescence, are particularly believable, and their transformation is realistic and touching.

Cole's second young adult novel, *Celine* (1989), is quite different but just as arresting, as he juggles tragedy and comedy. It is narrated by sixteen-year-old Celine, a young artist and a true individual. The adults in Celine's world are greatly lacking in maturity and honesty and seem mainly concerned with escaping from their present lives and responsibilities. As in *The Goats*, adults often fail children, but it is ultimately heartening to witness Celine and her young neighbor, Jacob, help each other compensate for the sad lack of adult assistance. In both of Cole's novels the young protagonists initially appear to be lacking in maturity, but eventually prove themselves more responsible than many of the adults. With the publication of these novels, Cole has earned himself a place among the gifted few who have multiple talents as artists and as writers of both picture books and novels. ❧ J.M.B.

Cole, Joanna

American author, b. 1944. As the author of almost sixty fiction and nonfiction books for children, Joanna Cole is undeniably a versatile and accomplished writer. In her case, quantity is quality: Many of her books have been named ALA Notables and NSTA/CBC Outstanding Science Trade Books for Children. In 1991 Joanna Cole received the Washington Post/Children's Book Guild Nonfiction Award for her contribution to nonfiction literature for children.

In recent years she has given the term *nonfiction* new meaning with the "Magic School Bus" series. A masterly combination of scientific facts, humor, and fantasy, these books turn science class into story hour. Whether traveling through the city's waterworks as raindrops in *The Magic School Bus at the Waterworks* (1986) or coursing through a human body as red blood cells in *The Magic School Bus inside the Human Body* (1989), Miss Frizzle, the strangest teacher in school, and her sometimes disbelieving but always eager class learn firsthand about what they are studying. In the Magic School Bus books, illustrator Bruce Degen's lively artwork and comic-strip-style word balloons fully engage the reader and humorously extend Joanna Cole's fascinating text.

Her highly praised series on animals' bodies, with stunning black-and-white photographs by Jerome Wexler, is a noteworthy illustration of Joanna Cole's unique approach to her subject. Beyond merely describing and explaining the different parts of, for example, a snake's body, Cole takes the reader a step further to show how a snake's particular form relates to its environment. As she says, the books are a study of "adaptation and morphology, that is, the form and structure of a living animal as they relate to the animal's way of life."

Science has been a lifelong passion with Joanna Cole: as a child growing up in East Orange, New Jersey, she spent hours wandering around her backyard, studying insects and plants. She loved school and particularly enjoyed writing reports for science class. Her love of learning is evident in all of her work. As Cole has said, "I see it as my job to learn about something that fascinates me, to filter all I've learned through my own mind, to tell the story in the simplest, clearest way possible and then to present it as a gift to the reader." After graduating from the City College of New York with a degree in psychology, Joanna Cole began her career as a librarian in a Brooklyn elementary school. It was during that time that the idea for her first book, *Cockroaches* (1971), came to her. Many other award-winning nonfiction titles were soon to follow, and in 1980 Cole decided to become a full-time children's book writer. She has written books on parenting for parents and children to share, such as *How You Were Born* (1984; revised edition, 1993) and *Your New Potty* (1989), which clearly and matter-of-factly deal with topics to which children are sensitive.

Always keeping in mind the emotional level of her audience, Joanna Cole presents her information in a reassuring, caring tone, with great respect for children. She has also retold a number of folktales; they appeal to her because she sees in the hero's quest a parallel with the child's struggle to exist in an adult world. Joanna Cole has said that she considers it a privilege to be doing as an adult the very thing she loved doing as a child; it is, also, a privilege for her readers that she is able to share her enthusiasm for learning and for childhood in her many exciting and absorbing books. ❧ K.F.

Cole, William

American anthologist and poet, b. 1919. William Cole has been a columnist, a publicity director, an editor, and a poet in his own right, but children know him best as the compiler of many of their favorite anthologies. Following his tour of duty in the United States Army during World War II, Cole entered the publishing world, a milieu well suited to his talents. His first books were collections of cartoons for the adult audience, but his inveterate interest in poetry soon resulted in poetry anthologies for young people, the first being *Humorous Poetry for Children,* published in 1955.

From that time on Cole continued putting together collections of thoughtfully selected poems centered on a specific theme, with compilations of humorous verse leading the way. He has created poetry anthologies on such diverse subjects as eating, in *Poem Stew* (1981); holidays, in *Poems for Seasons and Celebrations* (1961), and the marine realm, in *The Sea, Ships, & Sailors* (1967). A perennial favorite is the wickedly amusing *Beastly Boys and Ghastly Girls* (1964), an American Library Association Notable Book, which recounts with glee the obnoxious behavior of recalcitrant children. Perhaps William Cole's anthologies of animal poems best demonstrate his ability to distinguish that which is fresh, challenging, and playful. *A Book of Animal Poems* (1973) and *A Zoo-ful of Animals* (1992), prime examples of such collections, are guaranteed to stretch the reader's imagination. According to Cole, "Animals are a good thing, and poetry is a good thing, and I, for one, can't get enough of either"—nor, would it seem, can his audience.

It is Cole's practice to select poems from a widely diverse group of celebrated poets, but he also goes out of his way to include versifiers of no established reputation. The process that enables Cole to come up with just the right poem may take him to libraries and bookstores as well as to his own extensive library and clipping files. Over the years his anthologies have been illustrated by an exemplary array of artists, including TOMI UNGERER, Helen Siegal, Karen Ann Weinhaus, and LYNN MUNSINGER, whose works reinforce his point of view and, where appropriate, underscore the humor. William Cole suggests that his anthologies are not to be taken "at one gulp," but when children dip into his collections, they are apt to keep right on going, for entertainment such as he has prepared is hard to resist. ❧ P.S.

Illustration by TOMI UNGERER from *Beastly Boys and Ghastly Girls* (1964), by William Cole.

COLLIER, JAMES LINCOLN COLLIER, CHRISTOPHER

JAMES LINCOLN: AMERICAN AUTHOR, B. 1928; CHRISTOPHER: AMERICAN AUTHOR, B. 1930. Individually, James Lincoln Collier and Christopher Collier have each published a number of well-regarded books. Together, the brothers have collaborated on many first-rate historical novels for young people.

The Colliers were born in New York City and grew up in rural Connecticut. Many writers were in the family, including their father, Edmund, who wrote books about the American West. Both brothers were interested in writing, but Christopher pursued a teaching career. He studied history at Clark University in Worcester, Massachusetts, and received graduate degrees from Columbia. He next taught junior and senior high school and was a history professor at Yale, Columbia, and the University of Connecticut.

James Lincoln Collier attended Hamilton College, in Clinton, New York, worked as a magazine editor, then became a freelance writer, publishing magazine articles and paperback fiction. He entered the children's book field with *Battleground: The United States Army in World War II* (1965), a nonfiction look at the battles and military personalities of that war. His first novel for young people was *The Teddy Bear Habit: Or, How I Became a Winner* (1967), the wildly humorous story of a twelve-year-old boy pursuing a rock music career, but unable to give up his teddy bear. Firmly rooted in the sixties, the book now seems dated, though George is a likable protagonist and the fast-paced story retains appeal. The author has written only a few comic novels. Most of his fiction has been quite somber, frequently focusing on troubled father-son relationships, as in *When the Stars Begin to Fall* (1986). Another central theme is music. *Give Dad My Best* (1976) is one of several novels about the music world. The author, who plays trombone professionally, has written many nonfiction books about music, including *Inside Jazz* (1973).

Christopher began publishing books much later than his brother, but he also received acclaim; *Roger Sherman's Connecticut: Yankee Politics and the American Revolution* (1971) was nominated for the Pulitzer Prize. Christopher wanted to teach young people history through fiction and persuaded James to collaborate on a book. *My Brother Sam Is Dead* (1974) is a haunting story of the American Revolution. College student Sam Meeker is a committed Patriot in a Loyalist Connecticut family. His younger brother, Tim, is unsure which side he supports in the war, but records the hardships and violence that ultimately tear his family apart. The novel was named a Newbery Honor Book and is noted for its realism, honesty, and moral ambiguity.

The Colliers have written several other historical novels, which follow a similar pattern. Meticulously researched, they are based on true events. Though famous characters appear, the focus is always on a fictional young person. The stories are told in the first person and use a modern style of language. The Colliers each contribute to the book in different ways. Christopher does the initial research, then the brothers create the characters together. James does the plotting and writing. This process has produced a number of strong novels, including the three-volume Arabus Family Saga—*Jump Ship to Freedom* (1981), *War Comes to Willy Freeman* (1983), and *Who Is Carrie?* (1984)—which concerns African Americans in eighteenth-century New England. Together, James and Christopher Collier have created an important body of HISTORICAL FICTION. ❧

P.D.S.

Illustration after Attilio Mussino from the 1926 edition of *The Adventures of Pinocchio*, by Carlo Collodi.

Collodi, Carlo

ITALIAN AUTHOR, JOURNALIST, EDITOR, AND TRANSLATOR, 1826–1890. *The Adventures of Pinocchio* is a children's classic, but Carlo Collodi's life was ordinary and his skills unremarkable. Born in Florence, Italy, Carlo Lorenzini (his mother's village provided his pen name, Collodi) grew up in poverty. His wide-ranging knowledge was gained through self-education. Collodi became a hack journalist, an undecorated soldier, and a low-level government official; he began two different idealistic magazines—which folded—and wrote a series of stiff educational texts.

Collodi's fame rests solely on *Pinocchio,* a thirty-five-episode children's serial story begun in 1881 and published as a book in 1883. In the rambling tale a disobedient marionette comes to life as he is being whittled and immediately sets about making trouble. After being lectured by a talking Cricket, Pinocchio agrees to behave and attend school but runs away instead, meeting with the first of many unsavory characters. Eventually a kindly puppet master gives Pinocchio five gold pieces and tells him to go home, but the naive puppet stumbles upon one trouble after another as he struggles to return to Gepetto, his "Daddy."

The Adventures of Pinocchio has been translated into over one hundred languages; it has been adapted for movies and filmstrips, plays, musicals, and television. James T. Teahan maintains, in *Twentieth-Century Writers for Children,* that the story has been so "bowdlerized, expurgated, abridged, adapted, dramatized, trivialized, diluted, and generally gutted" that it no longer resembles the original. In its original form (and in faithful translations), *Pinocchio* is full of inconsistencies and contradictions, evidence of careless writing. What sets it apart is not the craftsmanship but the conception. A bachelor, Collodi was clearly at his creative apex when he invented the mischievous boy-puppet and the tale's fifty-odd imaginative creatures. Of Collodi's large body of writing—liberal journalism, Perrault fairy-tale translations, technical books for adults, and numerous stories for children—only *Pinocchio* survives for readers. Scholars have found complex symbolism, classical references, and ties to traditional folklore; religious parallel, political allegory, social morality, and psychological quest. *Pinocchio* has been variously considered an animal fable, literary folktale, fantasy, and didactic tract. The episodic series of escapades has been favorably compared to Jonathan Swift's *Gulliver's Travels* and LEWIS CARROLL's "Alice" books. It is often declared superior to L. FRANK BAUM's *Wizard of Oz,* J. M. BARRIE's *Peter Pan,* and even E. B. White's *Charlotte's Web.* Scholarly assessment aside, the tale is notable for its universality, its blend of imagination and humor, its lively pace, and its ethereal charm. But it has a dark side—its honest depiction of children's fears. *Pinocchio* has been criticized for its didacticism, a characteristic of nineteenth century children's literature, but it has also been praised for its refreshingly modern, highly pragmatic morality. *Pinocchio* delicately balances fantasy and reality, and therein lies its source of greatness.

It is ironic that Carlo Lorenzini, a man of middling talent, died in 1890, while his tale was only a middling success. He never saw its international popularity or knew he was the creator of a classic. S.A.B.

COLMAN, HILA

AMERICAN AUTHOR, B. 19? Born and raised in New York City, Hila Colman readily admits that she led the life of an "over-protected girl from a well-to-do family," with a summer house on Long Island and a chauffeur-driven Cadillac. Colman refers to her mother, a fashion designer, as an early feminist who instilled the idea of independence—both financial and spiritual—in her daughters. Colman attended Radcliffe College for two years and later became involved with left-wing political causes during the late 1930s and early 1940s. Her first article, "Can a Man Have a Career and a Family, Too?" (a spoof on similarly titled articles directed at women in the late 1940s), was published in the *Saturday Evening Post;* she continued to write for a number of successful women's magazines over the next decade. Nevertheless, the experience of writing for magazines was unsatisfactory, and Colman turned to books for children and young adults.

The idea for Colman's first book, *The Big Step* (1957), developed from a family she knew in which a man with two teenage daughters married a woman with one teenage daughter. Colman returned to this theme of remarriage and its difficulties in *Weekend Sisters* (1985), which features one of the most appealing and believable mothers—honest, assertive without being obnoxious, liberated, warm, and humorous—in current young-adult fiction. While many of the ideas for Colman's books stem from people she knows and places she has visited, two of her books were drawn directly from her own life. *Rachel's Legacy* (1978), based loosely on Colman's mother, who emigrated from Russia as a child, charts Rachel Levine's progress from rags to riches. The book not only gives an authentic account of the life and traditions of turn-of-the-century American immigrants but also focuses on the framework of religious beliefs that lend strength to the family. Rachel's death and the Depression combine to force Rachel's daughter, Ellie, to claim her mother's legacy—her sturdy character—in *Ellie's Inheritance* (1979). Just as Colman herself did, Ellie meets intense young leftists who work under the shadow of the approaching Holocaust. Both books capture the laughter and the sorrow of their respective historic periods.

Colman believes that adolescence is the time "when one establishes one's identity and comes of age in a number of critical areas—social, political, cultural, sexual. Conflict prevails during these years with one's parents, teachers, peers, and, most painfully, with oneself." Her characters routinely confront painful problems but, without fail, eventually find the means necessary to survive. In *Claudia, Where Are You?* (1969), sixteen-year-old Claudia runs away from her parents' suburban community to the psychedelic East Village of New York City. Colman presents both the mortification and anguish of her parents and the excitement and perils of Claudia's bohemian existence. Colman's ability to portray sympathetically the young protagonist while exploring the conflicts and relationships that surround her heroine is seen in many of her books, including *The Parent Trap* (1982). When fifteen-year-old Becky is orphaned and left in the care of her rigid older sister, she asks the court to become an "emancipated minor." Becky gains her independence, and Colman allows the reader to think that she and her sister will have a better chance for a healthy sibling relationship.

The Diary of a Frantic Kid Sister (1973) was the subject of a censorship debate in Florida because of its language and invocation of the Lord's name. The diary in question belongs to eleven-year-old Sara, who fills the pages with her struggle for her own identity, with her good and bad fantasies, and with her need to find an adequate role model. It is her diary, reflecting her moods of humor, despair, jealousy, and sympathy, which finally convinces her that she is becoming an original and creative person in her own right. The sequel, *Nobody Has to Be a Kid Forever* (1976), was the winner of the Garden State Children's Book Award.

While Colman's writing may not be exceptional, she has the ability to speak about basic issues in a nonjudgmental voice. Her adolescent heroines look, behave, and sound like adolescents, and Colman allows them to display their true feelings honestly, realistically, and authentically. ♠ M.I.A.

Colum, Padraic

Irish author, 1881–1972. In the early part of the twentieth century, Padraic Colum belonged to the Dublin literary circle whose members included J. M. Synge and William Butler Yeats. During this time, Colum had his first poetry published, founded and edited *The Irish Review,* and also founded the Irish National Theatre—now the Abbey Theatre—where his play *The Land* enjoyed great success in 1905. Born in Longford, Ireland, Colum spent much of his childhood in County Cavan, where his family lived with a grandmother while their father sought work in the United States. This grandmother's love of traditional storytelling had a profound influence on the author's career. After working a few years as a railway clerk, he began publishing volumes of poetry and plays for adults.

Colum's first novel, however, was written for children. *A Boy in Eirinn* (1913) tells of Finn O'Donnell, an Irish boy sent to live with relatives after his father is imprisoned and his mother finds work in the United States. The depiction of an Irish childhood provides a vivid picture of that country's past, but Finn's story is frequently interrupted by chapters consisting of folktales that are related to the boy. One lengthy chapter contains the complete text of a play that Finn sees. Individually, these components are interesting, but they are detrimental to the flow of the novel.

Colum came to the United States in 1914, and tried to retain his knowledge of the Irish language by translating traditional folk stories into English. When an editor from the New York *Tribune* asked if he had any material for the children's page of the newspaper, Colum submitted one of his translations and found a new career adapting folktales and legends for young readers. *The Golden Fleece and the Heroes Who Lived before Achilles* (1921), a retelling of Greek myths, was an Honor Book for the first Newbery Medal. Colum wrote two other Newbery Honor Books: *The Voyagers: Being Legends and Romances of Atlantic Discovery* (1925) is a collection of tales about Prince Henry the Navigator, Ponce de León, Columbus, the island of Atlantis, and other matters connected with the Atlantic Ocean. *The Big Tree of Bunlahy: Stories of My Own Countryside* (1933) contains traditional Irish tales about leprechauns and magic. All three titles written in rhythmic prose are particularly suited to reading aloud, but the leisurely plots are so overcrowded with episodes that the books have a choppy, uneven quality. Dated writing also undermines some of the author's "folk romances," which include *The Girl Who Sat by the Ashes* (1925), a variation on the Cinderella story. Most of Colum's retellings have their origins in Greece and Ireland, although he also traveled to Hawaii to collect island legends, which he published in two volumes for adults, *At the Gateways of the Day* (1924) and *The Bright Islands* (1925).

Colum's other adult works include plays, poetry, novels, and nonfiction such as *Our Friend James Joyce* (1958), a memoir Colum and his wife, Mary, wrote about the great Irish writer. But Colum was best known for his children's books. The legends he retold are timeless in appeal, though a dated writing style prevents them from being widely read today. ♠ P.D.S.

Comic Books and Graphic Novels

Comic books like most popular culture are looked down upon by educators and intellectuals. Deemed too violent and without substance, comic books have been virtual symbols of lowbrow reading almost since their creation in the late 1890s. There was no such thing as a comic book in 1895, when "The Yellow Kid," the first newspaper comic strip, appeared. The American comic book evolved from early supplements of colored Sunday comics produced by competing newspapers and newspaper syndicates. Max Charles Gaines pioneered the now-familiar format in 1933, reprinting previously published strips on pulp paper with a color illustration on the cover.

Two years later, Detective Comics (DC) launched the first comic book containing original material. In 1938, with the birth of Superman, the first costumed superhero, in *Action Comics #1,* the genre was born. Combining elements from movies and pulp magazine stories, a blend of narrative and visuals, plus a low price, the comic book became instantly popular among youth. Rival companies soon produced copycat heroes, and comic-book titles abounded by the end of World War II.

In *Seduction of the Innocent* (1954), the psychologist Frederic Wertham accused the comic book industry of glorifying violence and undermining morals, prompting a Senate hearing that led to the adoption by the industry of the self-defined, self-imposed Comics Code. The industry intended that voluntary self-regulation would forestall legislation. The Code strictly governed the content of comic books sold on newsstands and sent a chill through the industry. Similar to the movie industry's

Hayes Code, the Comics Code demanded conformity and stifled experimentation. Many independent comics publishers were squeezed out of business, particularly those producing so-called "gore" titles like *Tales from the Crypt* and *Vault of Horrors,* both created by Max Gaines's son William. Ironically, this led William Gaines to create a much more subversive, yet popular, comic magazine that has for generations poked fun at the status quo—*Mad.*

DC dominated the industry into the early 1960s, when Marvel Comics raised a challenge. Their flawed heroes, such as Spiderman, the Fantastic Four, and the X-Men, appealed to adolescent readers, the primary audience, through their humor and humanness, while staying within the bounds of the Comics Code. Comic-book superheroes began to "cross over" into other entertainment, notably Saturday morning television cartoons. The long-standing connection between comics and other media, stretching back to the movie short subjects and serials of the 1940s, expanded in the 1960s, and comics became entrenched in popular culture, a trend that peaked in the late 1980s when several hit movies took their inspiration from the comics. *Batman* (1989) was the most successful; its tremendous box office clout in turn led to greater comics sales and increased overall interest in the comics, generally.

While comics were moving into mainstream culture, another type of comic was emerging in the late 1970s. With the increase in specialty comic-book stores, a number of alternative and independent publishers entered the market. The new publishers, influenced by the underground press of the 1960s and inspired by punk subculture, printed comics that flouted the guidelines of the Comics Code. Into the 1980s, titles like *Raw, Love and Rockets,* and *Weirdo* helped create an audience of mostly older readers who were interested in more sophisticated material.

This shift in marketing challenged DC and Marvel, the industry giants. To attract the new audience, they were forced to break away from assembly-line methods of comics production by allowing artists and writers more creative control. This artistic freedom, and the growing demand for more sophisticated stories, breathed fresh life into already established heroes—as in Frank Miller's grim reworking of Batman in his *The Dark Knight Returns*—and prompted a renaissance in creativity exemplified by such works as the *Watchman* by Alan Moore. No longer could the term *comics* be used to lump pictorially told stories together. Comics as literature had arrived. The most dramatic example of a break with the past was the decision to "kill off" Superman in 1992.

Yet, even as the modern comic book developed, traditional comic strips continued to be popular. Comics such as *Pogo, Peanuts,* and *Hagar the Horrible* were collected and reprinted in book form, packaged into various treasuries. In the late 1980s *Life in Hell* books by Matt Groening were extremely popular for their smart-aleck humor, while Jim Davis's bland *Garfield* franchise reached best-sellerdom. Collections of *Doonesbury* by Garry Trudeau, *The Far Side* by Gary Larson, *Bloom County* by Berke Breathed, and Bill Watterson's *Calvin and Hobbes* all gained best-seller status among a new generation of comics readers of all ages.

A further development in mass-market comic art came with the introduction of the graphic novel in the mid-1980s. The graphic novel is an extended comic-style narrative, published in trade paperback, and often showing little kinship with their comic-book cousins. Reprints of stories originally published as comic books, such as the *Greatest Batman Stories Ever Told,* are marketed as graphic novels, yet they are simply collections of previously published works. Among the first true graphic novels was *Maus* by Art Spiegelman, published in 1987. *Maus* was widely reviewed—in itself a breakthrough—and the praise it earned from critics for its literary merit enhanced the prestige of the comic form. The late 1980s resurgence of comics led to extensive mainstream press coverage, with the *New York Times, The Atlantic, Rolling Stone,* and other publications carrying articles praising comic books. Library, education, and children's literature publications also reexamined long-standing prejudices against comics. Many concluded that a serious look at comics was needed to meet the reading interests of youth.

The appeal of comics to children and adolescents is simple: comics are easy and fun to read; they have simple vocabularies, few pages, stock characters, heroes worth idolizing, and exciting, action-packed stories. Young adolescents, especially boys, find comics satisfying not only as leisure reading—the only reading some ever do—but for emotional reasons as well. As young teens attempt to figure out their place in the world, they find in comics both an escape with superhero exploits and comforting answers in simple wish-fulfillment stories. But basic good-versus-evil tales are not so simple in current comics; comic books have introduced serious subjects such as drugs, gun control, child abuse, and even AIDS. While many comics continue to deal with superheroes, more and more comics tackle the villains of everyday life, such as the 1992 *Alpha Flight* storyline concerning a gay superhero, AIDS babies, and homophobia.

This new realism has added a further dimension to

the long-standing debate about the value of comic books: Is any reading children do to be encouraged, even comic books? In contrast to television, reading a comic is still active, albeit nondemanding, reading rather than passive watching. From the Sunday funnies to the complex world of *Maus,* comics offer children an opportunity to escape, have adventures, laugh, learn, and develop reading skills. Comics have evolved from their disreputable status of the 1950s. Rather than being seen as entertainment with no redeeming value, comics are often viewed as fairy tales for adolescents . . . fairy tales that may help them cope with the changing world around them. ❧ TIM RETZLOFF AND PATRICK JONES

Cone, Molly

AMERICAN AUTHOR, B. 1918. Molly Cone has always thought of herself as a writer, and in a career of writing for children that has spanned more than three decades, she has written more than forty books and shown herself to be most versatile. She has written fiction for young readers and teens, biographies of the Ringling Brothers and Leonard Bernstein, and nonfiction books about the Jewish faith and holidays. Some of her books reflect her love of the Puget Sound area and her interest in conservation.

Born in Tacoma, Cone was educated at the University of Washington. Her first career was as an advertising copywriter. As mother of three children, she did not begin writing fiction until she was nearly forty years old. Cone is a talented writer of humor, and one of her early books, *Mishmash* (1962), is still a favorite. Mishmash is a large, lovable, and unusual dog who watches television, opens gates, and draws his own bubble bath. Cone's inspiration for this animal character came from a family pet called Tiny. Unlike Mishmash, Tiny was a small red cocker spaniel, but Tiny, like Mishmash, did favor such human comforts as sleeping in a bed, tucked under the covers with his head resting on a pillow. The Mishmash books eventually became a series of seven titles, all engagingly illustrated in black-and-white by Leonard Shortall. The books feature short chapters, dialogue, and plot episodes that readily appeal to emerging readers, and reviewers have praised the series for the positive way in which it portrays teachers.

Cone is a perceptive observer of teenagers, and several of her novels explore the dilemmas and conflicts that teens experience. In *Annie, Annie* (1969), Cone describes the longing for family rules and regulations a young girl in a liberal family feels. Annie rebels by taking a job as a live-in helper in a rigid and boringly predictable household, a step that opens the way for dialogue with her own family. In *Dance around the Fire* (1974), the heroine takes a consciousness-raising trip to Israel. In *Purim* (1967) and other books about Judaism, Cone expresses her love of storytelling and her deep interest in Jewish traditions. In 1972 she received the Shirley Kravitz Children's Book Award from the Association of Jewish Libraries for the body of her work.

Cone has a long-standing affection for the Pacific Northwest and became very intrigued when she learned that the students in an elementary school in Everett, Washington, had accepted the challenge to reclaim Pigeon Creek, a debris-filled stream that had not harbored live fish for twenty years. *Come Back, Salmon: How a Group of Dedicated Kids Adopted Pigeon Creek and Brought It Back to Life* (1992), illustrated with photographs by Sidnee Wheelwright, tells the story of the school's success in removing mountains of trash and raising tiny salmon to seed the river. The inspiring conclusion depicts the results a few years later, as the first mature salmon return to spawn. Cone's interest in all facets of the world around her has led her to share her ideas, humor, and enthusiasms with children of all ages. ❧ P.H.

Conford, Ellen

AMERICAN AUTHOR, B. 1942. Ellen Conford has employed her characteristically light touch in writing picture books as well as novels for both the intermediate and young adult audience.

Raised in Queens and Long Island, the native New Yorker began writing at an early age. During high school, she wrote for the campus newspaper and was editor of the school humor magazine. Conford attended Hofstra University, then endured several years of rejections before her poems and stories began to be published in *Reader's Digest* and other periodicals. As the mother of a young son, Conford became frustrated by the poor writing she found in many children's books and attempted her own picture-book story. *Impossible, Possum* (1971) concerns Randolph Possum, who cannot hang from his tail like the other members of his family. This amusing book was well received, although the relative length and complexity of the story gave some indication that Conford's writing was better suited for an older audience.

The author soon began writing for middle-grade readers. *Dreams of Victory* (1973) is the story of Victory Benneker, who daydreams of her triumphs as an actress, Olympic skater, and president of the United States while struggling with daily life as a sixth-grade student. The book is representative of much of Conford's writing in its focus on a suburban, middle-class girl questioning her identity, discovering boys, and gaining self-esteem. Like most of the author's protagonists, Victory is an appealing character, although not particularly memorable. The humorous tone of the first-person narration makes the familiar story move quickly.

Conford continued writing other novels for the intermediate grades, including *Felicia the Critic* (1973) and *The Luck of Pokey Bloom* (1975), but as her own son grew up, the author discovered that her characters were also moving into their teenage years. Like her middle-grade books, Conford's young adult novels contain humor and likable characters, although the romantic component is usually given greater emphasis. Unfortunately, the plotting and characterization seldom attain much complexity or depth. Conford usually ignores complicated or emotionally charged issues in favor of commercially appealing topics. One of Conford's teenagers discovers a young television star is attending her high school, another is enthralled by paperback romance novels, and others find work as disc jockeys and advice columnists. Despite this concentration on superficial concerns, the author's breezy, humorous writing makes the books readable and appealing.

Throughout her career, Conford has shown signs of experimentation and growth. Occasionally, she writes a novel with a male protagonist, including *Lenny Kandell, Smart Aleck* (1983). Books such as *And This Is Laura* (1977) and *Genie with the Light Blue Hair* (1989) contain elements of the supernatural. Conford has attempted different genres with a volume of short stories, *If This Is Love, I'll Take Spaghetti* (1983), and a series of easy-reading books about Jenny Archer, an enterprising grade school student. *To All My Fans, With Love, From Sylvie* (1982) is a significant departure from the author's other novels. Almost all of her books have been contemporary, but this novel is set in the 1950s. Sylvie is one of the few Conford characters not growing up in a stable, two-parent home. Topics such as sexual abuse and running away are among the serious issues Conford examines in this ambitious work. It is unusual, however, for a Conford novel to make many demands on a reader. She is best known for providing pleasant, light entertainment. P.D.S.

Conly, Jane Leslie

AMERICAN AUTHOR, B. 1948. The daughter of author ROBERT C. O'BRIEN entered the field of children's books by writing sequels to her father's Newbery Award–winning novel *Mrs. Frisby and the Rats of NIMH* (1971). She later won Newbery honors of her own.

Jane Leslie Conly was born in Virginia, where her family lived on a small farm, before moving to Washington, D.C. She attended Smith College and the Writing Seminars Program at Johns Hopkins University. Her first book was a continuation of her late father's best-known work, a talking-animal FANTASY about a community of intelligent laboratory rats. Using his premise and many of the same characters, Conly wrote *Racso and the Rats of NIMH* (1986), which concerns a field mouse and a young rat who help save the rodent settlement from being destroyed by developers. Conly's second sequel, *R-T, Margaret, and the Rats of NIMH* (1990), contains the first significant human characters in the series, as a brother and sister get lost in the woods and are befriended by the rat community. The novel contains adventure and humor, but is not quite as focused as its two fine predecessors.

Conly's first completely original work, *Crazy Lady!* (1993), is the well-crafted story of Vernon, a lower-class Baltimore boy failing seventh grade and grieving over his mother's death. Vernon's relationship with an alcoholic neighbor and her retarded son help him appreciate the strength of his own family's unity. Selected as a Newbery Honor Book, this unusually solid novel features sharply defined characterizations, honest emotions, and a developing sense of self and community. It also provides evidence that Conly is a strong, evolving voice in contemporary children's fiction. P.D.S.

Conrad, Pam

AMERICAN AUTHOR, B. 1947. In picture books, stories for young readers, and novels for young adults, many of Pam Conrad's characters experience loss of some kind. At times the loss results from the ordinary trials of everyday existence. Eight-year-old Nicki moves to a new house and misses her old neighborhood in *I Don't Live Here!* (1984). In a sequel, *Seven Silly Circles* (1987), Nicki worries about losing her dignity: Playing with the suction cup on a toy arrow has left her with red circles on her face. Heather, the protagonist of *Staying Nine* (1988), does not want to forsake the familiar life of a nine-year-old, so she decides to ignore her first double-digit birthday.

Conrad's books for older readers usually deal with graver losses. Simone, haunted by guilty memories of the death of her beloved caretaker, attempts suicide in *Taking the Ferry Home* (1988). Despairing over the truth

Illustration by Richard Egielski from *The Tub People* (1989), by Pam Conrad.

about her dead father, Darcie literally follows the charismatic but deeply disturbed Roman into a lion's den in *What I Did for Roman* (1987). *Holding Me Here* (1986) shows how Robin's unresolved feelings about her parents' divorce lead to her disastrous interference in another family's problems. In *My Daniel* (1989) Julia, now an old woman, recalls her childhood on the prairie and the death of her brother, to whom she was completely devoted.

In these deeply felt books, however, loss is seldom the end of the story. An accidental fire destroys the meager possessions of the solitary castaway in the picture book *The Lost Sailor* (1992), illustrated by Richard Egielski, yet this fire attracts the ship that finally rescues him. Another picture book, *The Tub People* (1989), also illustrated by Egielski, shows how two toy parents cherish their toy child even more after he has been lost and found. In the suspenseful Edgar Award–winning *Stonewords: A Ghost Story* (1990), Zoe Louise travels back in time and saves the life of the girl whose ghost has been her playmate for years. While doing so, she uses her mixed feelings about her absent, nonnurturing mother to summon the strength and love she requires to overcome her fear. She loses her ghostly companion, but she begins to heal herself. Louisa, the narrator of the evocative, highly acclaimed historical novel *Prairie Songs* (1985), witnesses the mental breakdown of a fragile newcomer to the frontier, but she also gains a new appreciation for her family.

In *Prairie Visions: The Life and Times of Solomon Butcher* (1991), Conrad demonstrates that her storytelling skills extend to nonfiction writing as she explores the life of a traveling photographer who took pictures of frontier families in Nebraska. It comes as no surprise that Butcher's story caught her eye, since he employed photographic images to preserve his visions of prairie people. Conrad, too, is concerned with capturing moments. In an "Author's Note" for *Pedro's Journal: A Voyage with Christopher Columbus, August 3, 1492–February 14, 1493* (1991), she states her main reason for writing the novel: "to sail through a brief period of history inside the mind and heart of a young boy."

Using her considerable command of language, including her talent for creating effective imagery, Conrad tells the stories of characters who stand poised at turning points in their lives. ❧ M.F.S.

Controversial Books for Children

It can be said with great assurance that everything is bound to offend someone, with controversy the usual result. Children's books most often become controversial because of political, moral, or religious convictions; portrayals of women, ethnic minorities, racial differences and stereotypes, sex and sexuality, or violence; and, of course, language considered profane or otherwise offensive.

Controversies over many children's books have little to do with their literary merit and much more to do with adults' views of what is appropriate for children. Books can be potent forces and are perceived as more permanent—hence, more powerful—than the fleeting images seen on television or movie screens. Because of this perception, children's books may stir sharper controversy than do other media. Ideologies, perceptions, and language change in a changing society, and thoughtful reassessment of children's reading can be healthy if the literature and its readers are respected.

Political and religious controversy can arise over a seemingly marginal detail in a work or over the work's central premise or theme. WILLIAM STEIG's picture book *Sylvester and the Magic Pebble* (1969) clashed with the politically charged climate of the 1960s and was harshly criticized for its portrayal of the police. Sylvester, a young donkey, happens upon a magic pebble, is transformed into a rock, and is thus separated from his loving parents. Frantic, Sylvester's parents (also donkeys) seek help from the police, depicted as concerned pink pigs in blue uniforms. Where readers today recognize a satisfying story, cleverly told and illustrated and happily resolved, readers in the 1960s were sometimes offended by a depiction that seemed to evoke the then common derogatory epithet for police officers.

Also viewed as political commentary rather than literature were *The Lorax* (1971), a fantastic, rhyming, environmental cautionary tale by DR. SEUSS, and *Eli's Songs* (1991), by Monte Killingsworth, a novel of a twelve-year-old boy's growing self-awareness, set in Oregon, where a threat to an old-growth forest parallels the dramatic changes in the boy's life. Both books were charged with bashing the timber industry and were declared inappropriate for children in some communities of rural California.

In 1993 Laurence Yep's *Dragonwings* (1975) occasioned a court case in Pennsylvania. This moving story of a Chinese immigrant and his son who dream of building a biplane in the San Francisco of the early 1900s was accused of advocating Taoism, reincarnation, and secular humanism, religious convictions to which the complainant was opposed.

Perceived challenges to mainstream social mores arouse controversy as well. The picture books *Heather Has Two Mommies* (1991), by Leslea Newman, and *Daddy's Roommate* (1991), by Michael Willhoite, consciously attempt to help children understand a potential source of anxiety for being "different" and suggest the viability of nontraditional families in their presentation of children living with gay parents. Only marginally effective in terms of plot, character development, and illustration, the mere presence of a lesbian couple and of a gay father and his lover in books for children has caused a swirling controversy. Those who argue in favor of these books contend that they depict the kind of family in which many children live. Opponents object to the books' nontraditional moral and religious values and alternative lifestyles.

A more subtle social challenge—in a more artistically effective work—can similarly arouse the ire of some adults. In *Harriet the Spy* (1964), by Louise Fitzhugh, Harriet's spy notebook, filled with her brutally honest observations, falls into her friends' hands, and under the stress of discovery, the eleven-year-old's behavior deteriorates rapidly. Harriet's busy, socialite parents cannot cope and send her to a psychologist; Old Golly, Harriet's eccentric former nanny, writes to suggest that Harriet learn to tell small lies to prevent hurting others' feelings. Harriet does, and her friendships are restored. Is Fitzhugh advocating, in this humorous, well-crafted novel, that children should lie or that well-meaning parents should seek professional help for their errant children? Not likely, but where children empathize and even identify with Harriet, laughing at her exploits, some adults are offended by Fitzhugh's portrayal of adults and this "rude" child.

Heightened sensitivity to our society's multiethnic make-up has led to close scrutiny of the portrayal of minorities in contemporary books for children as well as reexamination of earlier works. Books from earlier eras, when reexamined, may receive harsh criticism from contemporary readers who impose on them their anachronistic perspectives. Consider the seemingly endless discussion about the perceived racism in MARK TWAIN's *Adventures of Huckleberry Finn* (1884) or the sexism ascribed to Wendy's passive role in J. M. BARRIE's *Peter Pan* (1911).

Contemporary works can elicit similar concern. In *Jump Ship to Freedom* (1981), by JAMES LINCOLN COLLIER and CHRISTOPHER COLLIER, protagonist Daniel Arabus, a young slave in post–Revolutionary War America, must cope with a dishonest master and with his yearning for freedom. His trials cause him to question his own capabilities, but through his response to them, both Daniel and the reader, by novel's end, recognize his intelligence and worth. The authors' use of the hurtful language prevalent in the eighteenth century and their depiction of the character's self-doubt have caused many concerned adults to question the book's impact on contemporary African American children and, since the Colliers are not African Americans, the authenticity of the point of view.

Cultural authenticity has also been at the center of a minor controversy over Jennifer Armstrong's *Chin Yu Min and the Ginger Cat* (1993), a picture book describing how a haughty Chinese woman learns humility through friendship with a cat. Although the angular figures in the stylized artwork have been criticized as perpetuating a harmful, offensive stereotype, other critics contend that the strong form and line of the illustrations represent not stereotypes but a distinctive style.

Many adults believe that children must be protected

from the portrayal of violence and things unsettling. MAURICE SENDAK's visual interpretation of two NURSERY RHYMES in *We Are All in the Dumps With Jack and Guy* (1993) is intentionally unsettling, portraying a dark world in which thin, ill-clad children live in cardboard structures and are pursued by human-sized rats and where Jack considers knocking a "little boy with one black eye" on the head. Children may see such scenes on city streets and in television news programs, but many adults question whether they are appropriate in a children's book.

Controversy around Sendak's interpretations of a child's world is not new. Not only did Max's sassiness to his mother disturb adults who read *Where the Wild Things Are* (1963), but so did the Wild Things themselves. They were and, to some adults, still are too frightening, too unsettling, too potentially violent for young children.

Nowhere is violence in children's literature more apparent than in folktales. A troll is "crushed to bits, body and bones," in the "Three Billy Goats Gruff"; two out of three pigs become a wolf's snack in pre-Disney versions of the "Three Little Pigs"; the nasty sisters' toes and heels are mutilated as they attempt to wear the golden slipper in "Aschenputtel," the Grimm version of "Cinderella." Probably no body of literature has created the number of recurring controversies that folktales have, though no body of literature has had a greater or more lasting influence. The Grimm tale "Hansel and Gretel," despite wide distribution in picture-book editions and in story collections, remains controversial for its portrayal of stepmothers, child abuse, and violence.

Folktales have their defenders. They are satisfying stories with clear conflict, straightforward characterization, and appropriate resolutions, and they allow children—according to psychologist Bruno Bettelheim—"access to deeper meaning, and that which is meaningful to [the child] at his stage of development." Folk and fairy tales, says Bettelheim, "stimulate [the child's] imagination; help him to develop his intellect and to clarify his emotions; be attuned to his anxieties and aspirations . . . while at the same time suggest solutions."

Mother Goose rhymes, too, despite their perennial popularity as satisfying, brief stories with playful, easy-to-understand rhythm and language have been criticized as being too violent. All violence or potentially offensive references have been written out of *The New Adventures of Mother Goose: Gentle Rhymes for Happy Times* (1993), by Bruce Lansky. In this sanitized version, "three blind mice" don't chase the farmer's wife and get their tails cut off "with a carving knife"; rather, "three kind mice" run "after the farmer's wife," take "out some cheese/and they cut her a slice." The satisfying mini-adventure offered by Mother Goose has been replaced by a saccharine revision, in accordance with some adults' view that only "happy times" are appropriate for children.

Perhaps the most provocative issue in children's books is sex and sexuality. Examples of books that have violated this societal taboo include Maurice Sendak's *In the Night Kitchen* (1970), the now classic (and ever-popular) story of Mickey's fantastic nighttime adventure, with its depiction of a frontally nude Mickey, and JUDY BLUME's young adult novel of first love and sexuality, *Forever . . .* (1975).

"Dirty" or profane language can create similar controversy. The title character in KATHERINE PATERSON's novel *The Great Gilly Hopkins* (1978) is an unhappy child, moved from one foster home to another, always believing that her mother will return. Gilly's language reflects her misery and her determination to drive people away from her. Though entirely in keeping with her character, it is Gilly's occasional use of offensive language, not her isolation or unhappiness, that has frequently stirred controversy. A novel, Paterson wrote, "cannot . . . set examples, it must reflect life as it is. And if the writer tells her story truly, then readers may find in her novel something of value for their lives." The lasting value of this novel extends far beyond the words in Gilly's vocabulary.

Adult offense at the use of "dirty" words in books for children is sometimes so strong that it leads to censorship. In one example, an elementary school headmaster abruptly removed LOIS LOWRY's humorous, contemporary novel *Anastasia Krupnik* (1979) from his school when the book, which had been available to his students for more than a month, unhappily fell open in his sight to a page that contained an offensive word. His prohibition, of course, merely assured for months thereafter the constant use of the public library's copy. In another incident, the book was first removed and then returned to a school library—with the offending words whited out. Eleven-year-old Anastasia used a "dirty" word to express frustration with her parents and with the impending arrival of a new child. Her language, as well as that used by Paterson's Gilly, is appropriate within the context of the book's character, plot, and theme; only when seen in isolation does it become controversial.

Literature provides pleasure and understanding. It can inform, inspire, interpret, amuse, arouse, and more. It cannot, as C. S. LEWIS once wrote, protect a child from "the knowledge that he is born into a world of death, violence, wounds, adventure, heroism and cowardice, good and evil." But literature can help the child to clarify that world. As long as there are children and books, there will be controversy. Perhaps in the end, controversy simply indicates that adults care about the books children read because they believe in the power of literature. ❧ MARIA B. SALVADORE

COOLIDGE, OLIVIA E.

BRITISH-BORN AMERICAN AUTHOR, B. 1908. Olivia Coolidge has earned her place in the pantheon of children's literature through her retellings and biographies demonstrating meticulous scholarship and the ability to bring the past to life.

Coolidge was born in London, the daughter of Robert C. K. Ensor, an eminent newspaper columnist, lecturer, and historian, and received her education at Wycombe Abbey School and at Somerville College, Oxford University, where her major subjects were Latin, Greek, and philosophy. She taught in England and Germany and, from 1938 until her marriage in 1946, in the United States.

In Coolidge's first book, *Greek Myths* (1949), she worked from original sources to retell twenty-seven Greek myths. She wrote about the great heroes, simple villagers, immortal visitors from Olympus, and the landscape of early Greece in a vigorous and appealing way. A sequel, *The Trojan War* (1952), was equally welcomed for its simple and powerful prose. *Legends of the North* (1951) explored a different group of hero tales with spontaneity and real feeling for the effect of the harsh northern landscape on the value of courage.

From myths and epic tales, Coolidge went on to create books in which she invented characters and situations to bring to life ancient cultures. In *Egyptian Adventures* (1954) she told stories about pharaohs, soldiers, traders, and slaves set in the context of a daily life involving superstitions, ceremonies, and festivals. *Men of Athens* (1962) was an ALA Notable and Horn Book Honor Book. *Roman People* (1959) and *People in Palestine* (1965) continued this group of books that are notable for the excellence of their scholarly research and the convincing writing style.

Coolidge's next direction was to bring the lives of more contemporary figures to her young adult readers. Again, her scholarly discipline resulted in detailed, dignified, analytical work. Among her subjects were George Bernard Shaw, Joseph Conrad, and Winston Churchill. *Gandhi* (1971) was an ALA Notable and Horn Book Honor Book.

As a biographer, Coolidge paid careful attention to distinguishing fact from judgment and to the particular needs of her young readers. Consequently, her biographies provided the broader historical background that young readers might not be expected to know. Coolidge's respect for history and for her readership have set high standards for her followers. ❧ P.H.

COONEY, BARBARA

AMERICAN ILLUSTRATOR, B. 1917. In a career begun in 1940, Barbara Cooney has created more than one hundred picture books for children. She has twice received the Caldecott Medal: in 1958 for *Chanticleer and the Fox* (1957), her retelling of the Chaucer tale, and in 1979 for DONALD HALL's *Ox-Cart Man* (1978), a celebration of the cycle of working and growing on a nineteenth-century New Hampshire farm. Cooney's work reflects a strong sense of place and a love of small living things—an awareness, in her words, of "the beauty of humble flowers or tiny, peering animal faces."

Born in Brooklyn, New York, Barbara Cooney was brought up on Long Island and spent her summers on the Maine coast. Introduced to art as a child by her artist mother, Cooney became an artist herself because she had "access to materials, a minimum of instruction, and a stubborn nature." She majored in art at Smith College, graduating in 1938, and then studied lithography and etching at the Art Students League in New York. It was at this point that she began illustrating books for children—her first was Carl Malmberg's *Ake and His World* (1940)—and since then she has illustrated continuously for more than fifty years. She has lived most of her life in New England, first in Pepperell, Massachusetts, where she and her physician husband, Charles Talbot Porter, raised four children, and later—like the heroine of what is possibly her best-loved book, *Miss Rumphius* (1982)—in a house overlooking the sea, in Damariscotta, Maine.

Cooney's choice of media has changed over the years. She used scratchboard frequently in the first two decades of her career, notably in such books as MARGARET WISE BROWN's *The Little Fir Tree* (1954) and her own *The Little Juggler* (1961) and *Chanticleer and the Fox*. Cooney's etchings are clean yet intricate, set exquisitely against white space, and full of authentic detail. But after the success of *Chanticleer*—"I had always thought: once you succeed, change"—she tried a variety of media, including pen and ink, collage, watercolor, and acrylics, fitting her technique to the spirit of each book she took on. In later years she has worked almost exclusively in acrylic, now filling up the whole page with her

Voices of the Creators

Barbara Cooney

My life is in my books, in thousands of pictures, in hundreds of words. It's all there—well, at least all that I care to tell—for anyone who is interested. The places that I love are there—the fields and the hills, the mountains and the desert and the sea; the seasons are there, with snow and clouds and fog; and above all there are people, adults and children, always children. I never went to the hospital to have my babies without a sketch-book. Almost before they opened their eyes, I made pictures of them. In my many books I tried to hold on to all these wonders. But the three books, the ones I call my trilogy—*Miss Rumphius, Island Boy,* and *Hattie and the Wild Waves*—come as close to any autobiography as I will ever get.

Like my character Hattie, I was "always making pictures" on any scraps of paper that were handy. "Some of [my] happiest times were when [I] had a bad cold and Mama kept [me] in bed for two or three days running. Then [I] could make pictures from morning until night, interrupted only by bowls of milk toast and chicken broth."

Like little Alice in *Miss Rumphius,* I "got up and washed [my] face and ate porridge for breakfast. [I] went to school and came home and did [my] homework. And pretty soon [I] was grown up."

At two I had fallen in love with the coast of Maine. My heart still skips a beat when I look at the sea's horizon. Adventure, magic, all possibilities lie beyond it. Nearer at hand the sun and the moon sparkle on the water, and its reflections dance on my studio walls. I made *Island Boy* as my hymn to Maine.

How I happened into the field of illustration I cannot say. Perhaps because I am a bookworm. Shortly after college the long career of illustration began. In the beginning I worked in black and white, that being the most economical for the publisher. I yearned for color. "But," said my editor, "you have no color sense." Still yearning for color, I accepted the discouraging pronouncement. Eventually a little color was allowed—sometimes two colors, sometimes three. But each color had to be painted on a separate sheet of paper. These were called "overlays." One art director hoped to convince me that working with these separations was "the purest form of illustration." But I found it tedious.

After roughly twenty years I made a book called *Chanticleer and the Fox.* I had found the story in Geoffrey Chaucer's *Canterbury Tales.* Because I had taken a fancy to a particular hen yard full of exotic chickens glowing in late afternoon October sunlight and because I was fond of the Middle Ages, I thought to combine these in a picture book. For this I was allowed *four* color overlays plus the black key drawing. And the book won a Caldecott Medal. The first thing I did was to buy a huge old second-hand Smith-Corona typewriter for thirty dollars. The second thing was to order a wooden skiff, $185, complete with two sets of oars. A third thing happened: my editor offered me a lovely book, with a French setting, and in *full color!* So I packed up the family and went to France. My apprenticeship was now half over.

The French period was a happy one. Now with full color I could create *ambiance.* My people and animals and buildings and plants were no longer isolated in space. They became part of the scene. They were placed in landscapes and seascapes, on farms and in villages and cities and inside buildings; they were placed in Spain and in Ireland and Greece, in the Spice Islands and in New England.

Another change began to come into my work during this period: I fell in love with the art of painting with light—with photography. I even considered changing careers. I sat at the drawing table in Hermit Wood, my new studio/house in Maine, and watched the reflections from the water tremble on the white walls. And light began to flood my artwork. Twenty years after *Chanticleer,* I was illustrating Donald Hall's *Ox-Cart Man* and wondering about my career. When *Ox-Cart Man* won the Caldecott, I figured my apprenticeship was over at last. I would not change careers, after all. Still, a change was in order. I decided to write the stories for my illustrations. And in 1981 I sat down and wrote *Miss Rumphius.* Twelve years have gone by, during which some of my best work has been done. For four or five of the books I was simply the illustrator. But I have written the trilogy, which is my heart.

I can't end without saying that I started out like Hattie making pictures simply for the delight it gave me. It was selfishness. And it has brought me rewards beyond measure. Recognition is gratifying, but the love is far, far better.

luminous paintings. In the 1980s Cooney produced a trilogy of picture-book biographies featuring strong, self-determining characters—*Miss Rumphius,* about a venturesome woman who at the end of her peripatetic life returns to live by the sea and fulfills her grandfather's charge to do something to make the world more beautiful by planting lupines everywhere; *Island Boy* (1988), a historical account of Matthais Tibbetts, who grew up with his family on a remote Maine island and chose to spend his life there; and *Hattie and the Wild Waves* (1990), set in the opulent world of turn-of-the-century Brooklyn and based on the childhood of Cooney's mother. Each of these encapsulated biographies features Cooney's distinctive style and palette—flat, spacious, luminous landscapes in cool, chromatic blues and greens; quiet, detailed, warm interior scenes; children with small, pixieish faces. Cooney's gift has become even more finely honed in the nineties, as evident in such books as Alice McClerran's *Roxaboxen* (1990), an exploration of the imaginative play of a group of children in the desert of the Southwest, and *Emily* (1992), by Michael Bedard, the story of a young girl's unforgettable encounter with Emily Dickinson in Amherst, Massachusetts.

All of Cooney's work, as critic Ethel Heins has noted, exudes "an atmosphere of calm and composure that reflects the strength and serenity" of the stories she illustrates. As the artist has said, "I draw from life whenever possible, and I do not invent facts. . . . In spite of this, my pictures don't look realistic; they always look like me, which bothers me. However, they are the truth—as I see it—and my attempt to communicate about the things that matter to me." Like Miss Rumphius, who must "do something to make the world more beautiful," Barbara Cooney has adorned the world of children's books with her elegant, life-affirming illustrations. ❧ M.V.P.

Cooper, James Fenimore

American author, 1789–1851. An anecdote about James Fenimore Cooper tells us that while he was reading a British novel one evening, he threw the book down in disgust, saying he could write a better story. Responding to his wife's challenge to do so, Cooper anonymously wrote *Precaution* (1820) and privately published it. This book, which failed to do well, was believed by the public to have been written by an English gentlewoman.

In 1821 Cooper wrote *The Spy,* a book about the fictitious Harvey Birch, who helped the Americans win the Revolutionary War. This book's immediate success caused it to be pirated and sold in England. Translations in French, German, and Italian soon appeared. With its international fame, *The Spy* set the standard for romantic, historical American novels and launched Cooper's career as a writer of heroic American dramas; his historic tales soon rivaled those of England's Sir Walter Scott.

Cooper, born into a wealthy family in Burlington, New Jersey, was the eleventh of twelve children. In 1790 his father purchased land near Otsego Lake in upper New York State, built a manor for his family, and invited settlers to inhabit Cooperstown, which he founded. Cooper was tutored locally, and entered Yale at thirteen but never graduated. After leaving Yale, he spent eleven months "before the mast" experiencing many adventures before returning home and becoming commissioned an ensign in the United States Navy. Later, he drew on his knowledge of sailors, the sea, and his own adventures to write swashbuckling successes like *The Pilot* (1823), *The Red Rover* (1828), *The Water-Witch* (1830), *The Two Admirals* (1842), and *The Wing-and-Wing* (1842).

Considering Cooper's knowledge of the sea, it is ironic that he is best remembered for his "Leatherstocking Tales": *The Deerslayer* (1841); *The Last of the Mohicans* (1826), his most popular story; *The Pathfinder* (1840); *The Pioneers* (1823); and *The Prairie* (1827). In these stories, which portray the struggles of the Indians, the French, and the British to claim American land, he established the archetypal American hero, the frontiersman. The "Leatherstocking Tales," although not written sequentially, follow Natty Bumppo's adventures from his youth to his death. Natty's trusted companions and mentors are the American Indians Chingachgook and Uncas. In each adventure Natty's bravery and resourcefulness earn him a new title conferred by his Indian friends: Hawkeye, the Deerslayer, the Pathfinder, and, finally, the venerable title of Leatherstocking. Although Cooper's books were written for adults, by the turn of the century they had become standard reading for children, and illustrated editions by N. C. Wyeth remain popular classics of children's literature.

In his thirty years as an author, Cooper wrote thirty-three novels, many volumes of social commentary, a *History of the Navy of the United States* (1839), and five volumes on travel. That which started as a challenge to write a book brought Cooper a profitable career of international fame in his lifetime. By present-day standards, Cooper's books tend to be too long, tedious, and moralistic, with characters who never sweat or get muddy, tattered, or bitten by insects. They make it through all hardships as tidily as they entered. They were never meant to be thus blemished; Cooper's books were romances. It was enough that he told a well-paced, episodic tale of adventure. The mark he left on American literature was his creation of a new genre, the American story and the American hero; he firmly entrenched the sailor and frontiersman in the hearts of readers of all ages. S.R.

VOICES OF THE CREATORS

SUSAN COOPER

Whyever do I write fantasy? I haven't the right background. I began my professional writing life as a journalist, dealing in hard, unmalleable facts for seven years. I've written two sturdy nonfiction books—a biography and a study of the United States—and a novel, *Dawn of Fear,* which is not only realistic but autobiographical. I write television screenplays based, quite often, on the lives of real people. Yet whenever I start to write an original piece of fiction, the story emerges as fantasy. It's as though my imagination can only find complete freedom when it's inhabiting a metaphor.

The English writer Jill Paton Walsh once pointed out that a remarkably high proportion of English fantasy writers were educated—as she and I were—at the University of Oxford. She suggested, with tongue only partly in cheek, that we write fantasy because the Oxford English syllabus, with its stress on early and medieval literature, taught us to believe in dragons. Well . . . certainly my unconscious rings with echoes from *Beowulf* and *The Faerie Queene, Sir Gawain and the Green Knight,* and *Le Morte d'Arthur.* But I wrote my first little (very little) fantasy book when I was eight, before I'd even heard of most of those. Perhaps the crucial influences were earlier—the fairy stories and myths and nursery rhymes that I absorbed when I was so young that I can't now remember beginning to hear them.

Or perhaps my imagination was pushed toward fantasy by poetry, which I heard and read and recited in larger quantities than almost anything else. My mother, who was a teacher, had long chunks of Tennyson and Browning and the Romantic poets in her head, and even my father, who had no literary bent whatsoever (though he had the most beautiful handwriting I've ever seen), would occasionally launch with spirit into a recitation of *La Belle Dame sans Merci.* Poetry, like fantasy, uses metaphor as its language. Maybe I'm by nature a poet who writes prose.

I have to confess that I don't really care about any of this speculation, not beyond those occasional vague wonderings. Academics love it; I've read whole astonishing theses explaining the derivation of the images in *The Dark Is Rising.* (They're always very ingenious, and usually wrong.) But I don't really want to know why I write as I do; I'm just grateful that by some freak of nature I am able to write the kind of books I've always liked to read. Fantasy is my country. My imagination lives there. So, luckily for me, do the imaginations of a great many children, though some of them leave when they grow up.

Mowgli lives in that country, and Puck, in the high company of a whole panoply of gods and mythic heroes. Rat and Mole are there, Pooh, Peter Pan, the ghost of Thomas Kempe, and some small people called Borrowers. There's a secret garden there, and a midnight garden, a phoenix, a carpet, a cauldron, and a land that can only be reached through the back of a wardrobe. There are dragons and magicians and hobbits, a great deal of music, the paintings of David and Claude and Chagall, and at night a starlit sky filled with comets and auroras. And every journey through that country is a quest.

It's my refuge, this land of metaphor and enchantment. In real life, when I was twenty-seven years old I became a piece of flotsam: I married an American and left Britain, to spend the rest of my days as a permanent visitor in a foreign land, a "resident alien." Maybe the real spur for the books of the "Dark Is Rising" sequence was homesickness. Finding myself uprooted, but unable to grow new roots elsewhere, I took refuge in the country of the imagination, the home which had not been left behind but had come with me, as it will always go with any fantasy reader or writer as long as he or she may live.

In 1991 I went back to that enchanted country, after a gap of eight years, to write a book called *The Boggart.* The "Dark Is Rising" books had been written in the seventies, and I hadn't written a full-length fantasy novel since *Seaward,* published in 1983. So off I went on my new quest—and found, this time, more delight than any book has ever given me before. The reason was very simple. My imagination was happy because it, like its owner, had been away, and had come home.

This time I think I'll stay.

Cooper, Susan

English author residing in the United States, b. 1935. Raised on the ancient stories of legend and folklore, Susan Cooper instinctively turned to them when writing *Over Sea, Under Stone* (1965), her first book for children, which relates the adventures of three siblings on a quest to find the Holy Grail. A journalist, Cooper decided to try her hand at fiction when she saw a press release for a prize offered by a publishing company. Though she has produced several picture books and novels for children in addition to her award-winning fantasy sequence, "The Dark Is Rising," Cooper has not limited her audience to young readers; her achievements include newspaper columns, a biography, and plays for theater and television. Nevertheless, the power of her fantasy for children places Cooper firmly among the best of children's authors.

Challenging but accessible, "The Dark Is Rising" series draws from the legends surrounding King Arthur and other figures rooted in the mythology of Britain and Wales and depicts the struggle between the powers of the Light and the Dark. Will Stanton, who discovers on his eleventh birthday that he is one of the Old Ones, the servants of the Light, joins forces with the three siblings introduced in *Over Sea, Under Stone* and Bran Davies, who has been raised in the modern world, though he is the son of King Arthur and Guinevere. Possessing varying degrees of understanding, step by step, and with the help of Merriman Lyons—Merlin—the children fulfill the prophecies that strengthen the Light for the final defense against the Dark. Set in modern-day England and Wales, the sequence depicts the epic struggle with depth and brilliance but also conveys the message that the potential for evil is embedded in human nature; hence, the fight for that which is right is eternal. Often compared to Tolkien's work, Cooper's fantasy series is intricate and intriguing; by involving ordinary characters as well as those with supernatural powers, she explores the relationship between acts that are humane and those that are good.

Cooper brings her love of the ancient literature of her native land into all her work. *The Silver Cow: A Welsh Tale* (1983) and *The Selkie Girl* (1986) are fluid picture-book retellings of British folktales, while the novel *The Boggart* (1993) explores the collision of the Old World and the New, as two children accidentally transport a mischievous sprite called a "boggart" to Canada from the castle in Scotland that is his home.

A child of World War II who left her family and country at age twenty-seven to marry and move to Cambridge, Massachusetts, Cooper invests in her characters her feelings of displacement. The Boggart yearns intensely for home; Bran Davies is torn between his birthright as King Arthur's son and his place among modern friends and family; Will Stanton rarely forgets that he is more than an ordinary boy. In *Seaward* (1983), Cally and West travel through an unknown land, fleeing from terrors behind them and facing the uncertain future. Filled with images of life and death, the story is an allegory and more; like all of Cooper's fiction, it is deeply symbolic, multifaceted, and rewarding. The tremendous scope and intensity of Cooper's work marks her as a modern master of the high-fantasy genre. ❧ A.E.D.

Corcoran, Barbara

American author, b. 1911. A surprising number of children's book authors began their careers as playwrights. This may be a natural progression, since the basic elements of playwriting—visible action, strong dialogue, interesting characters—are especially valued in children's writing. Barbara Corcoran spent the early part of her career working in the theater and had several plays produced; this early writing experience is reflected in her novels.

The author was born in Hamilton, Massachusetts, and graduated from Wellesley College in 1933. Her varied careers include war duties as a naval electronics inspector and as a cryptanalytic aide for the Army Signal Corps; she also worked as a radio copywriter, did editorial work for the Hollywood Celebrity Service, and served on the staff of the CBS story department. After receiving an M.A. from the University of Montana in 1955, she taught college English courses in Kentucky, Colorado, and California. Although she published magazine fiction, her first novel did not appear until 1967. *Sam* is a sympathetic account of a teenage girl's relationship with family, school friends, and the dog she is training. Corcoran soon became a prolific full-time author, sometimes publishing several books a year under her own name and pseudonyms. She has written as Gail Hamilton, but her best-known pseudonym is Paige Dixon. Dixon's *May I Cross Your Golden River?* (1975), a moving story about a terminally ill teenage boy, is one of her best books.

Corcoran is adept at creating focused, fast-moving plots, well-established settings, and sympathetic, interesting characters. Certain themes run through many of the books, such as a love of nature and animals. Characters live in strong families or create new family units for themselves. But the scope of Corcoran's writing shows her versatility. She has written mysteries (*A Watery Grave*, 1982; *You're Allegro Dead*, 1981), animal stories (*A Horse Named Sky*, 1986; *Sasha, My Friend*, 1969), and problem novels concerning such topics as epilepsy (*Child of the Morning*, 1982) and hearing impairment (*A Dance to Still Music*, 1974; *Make No Sound*, 1977).

The well-traveled author has set her books in locations such as Russia, Hawaii, and all across the United States. Most of the stories are contemporary, but a few take place in earlier parts of the twentieth century. Corcoran's books are usually well received by critics at the time of publication, but, on the whole, the author has not been given the credit she deserves. She has won few awards, and her name is not often included among lists of prominent children's writers. Perhaps because she seldom experiments with literary techniques, and her writing style does not draw attention to itself, her seamless novels appear to be written with relative ease. However, books such as *The Clown* (1975), *This Is a Recording* (1971), and *Hey, That's My Soul You're Stomping On* (1978) showcase the author's ability to create highly readable novels that combine vivid, sensitive characterizations with engaging storylines. ❧ P.D.S.

Cormier, Robert

AMERICAN AUTHOR, B. 1925. In 1974 Robert Cormier entered the field of young adult fiction with *The Chocolate War.* Although the title suggests an innocuous, even humorous story, the novel's first line establishes a very different tone: "They murdered him." With these stark, uncompromising words, the reader is plunged into a dark tale of tyranny and evil played out against the background of a boys' parochial school. With its challenging themes and taut, suspenseful writing, the book made a shattering impact on the world of the YOUNG ADULT NOVEL. The author's subsequent books have continued to enhance his reputation as one of the outstanding creators in the field.

Cormier was born and raised in the French Hill section of Leominster, Massachusetts, a small, close-knit community of French Canadian immigrants. Renamed Monument, Massachusetts, his hometown is featured in several of his books, including *Fade* (1988), which evocatively describes a neighborhood where all the fathers work at the town plastics factory, all the children attend the local Catholic school, and grandparents, aunts, and uncles live just down the block. As a teenager, some of Cormier's early poems were published in the Leominster *Daily Enterprise.* He attended nearby Fitchburg State College for one year, but left school to make his living as a writer. He worked for a radio station and a newspaper before settling at the Fitchburg *Sentinel,* where he spent more than twenty years as a writer and editor. The married father of four also published stories in such magazines as *Redbook* and *The Saturday Evening Post.* His powerful first novel, *Now and at the Hour* (1960), concerns an elderly man facing death. Cormier wrote two more adult novels before his teenaged son's experiences with a school candy sale inspired a new story.

Although published as a young adult book, *The Chocolate War* is written with a complexity seldom associated with the genre. A mosaic of short, tightly written scenes, the book centers on Jerry Renault, a freshman at Trinity, a New England Catholic school. Insecure and still grieving over his mother's death, Jerry asks himself the question printed on his favorite poster: "Do I dare disturb the universe?" Archie Costello, the amoral leader of the Vigils, Trinity's secret society, gives Jerry the assignment of refusing to sell chocolates for the school fundraiser. In turn, Brother Leon, an evil and power-hungry teacher, pressures Archie into revoking Jerry's assignment. But Jerry continues not to sell the chocolates, resulting in an inevitably brutal conclusion. The novel is an explosive examination of evil and the corruption of power; each of the many characters is brilliantly defined and the writing is stark and fast-moving, yet contains penetrating images and metaphors.

In Cormier's next two books, social and political problems alter the lives of contemporary teenagers. *I Am the Cheese* (1977) is extremely complex in structure, interpolating three connected stories: Adam Farmer's first-person, present-tense account of a mysterious bicycle journey, a third-person description of his past, and a transcript of his interrogation by a strange man named Brint. The plot, which hinges on a witness-relocation program, comes to a breathtaking conclusion that causes many people to reread immediately the entire novel, looking for the clues that foreshadow the disheartening outcome. *After the First Death* (1979) also contains riveting suspense, an unusual structure, and a grim theme. The story concerns a busload of small children held hostage by terrorists, and its young adult appeal results from its focus on three teenage characters, including Kate, the young bus driver. Cormier's first female protagonist is particularly memorable for her courageous actions in this exquisitely written novel of suspense, betrayal, and bravery.

The author received the 1991 Margaret A. Edwards Award for his first three young adult novels, which remain unforgettable in their storytelling and devastating

Voices of the Creators

Robert Cormier

In a single paragraph of an article dealing with *The Chocolate War, I Am the Cheese,* and *After the First Death,* a writer listed these topics as central to the books: brutality, sadism, corruption (religious and governmental), insanity, murder, torture, personality destruction, terrorism, child murder, and suicide.

What kind of person writes about those terrible things? And why?

The name on the novels is Robert Cormier, and my name is Robert Cormier. But sometimes I don't recognize myself, either in what others say about my work or when I face questions from an audience about the violent nature of the books that bear my name.

I am a man who cries at sad movies, longs for happy endings, delights in atrocious puns, pauses to gather branches of bittersweet at the side of a highway. I am shamelessly sentimental: I always make a wish when I blow out the candles on my birthday cake, and I dread the day when there may be no one there to say "Bless you" when I sneeze. Although I aspire to be Superman, I am doomed to be Clark Kent forever, in an endless search for that magic telephone booth. I wear a trench coat, but nobody ever mistakes me for Humphrey Bogart. I hesitate to kill a fly—but people die horrible deaths in my novels.

But, of course, it's easy to kill off characters in novels or assign them tragic roles, because they are only figments of the imagination. People in books are made of print and paper, not flesh and blood, after all. They are creatures who live and die only between the covers of a book. Right?

Wrong. They also live in my mind and imagination and have the power to disturb dreams and to invoke themselves at odd, unguarded moments. Kate Forrester in *After the First Death* was a very real person to me. I cheered her brave actions as they unfolded on the page. I was moved by her sense of responsibility toward the children who were hostages on that hijacked bus. I loved the way she refused to concede defeat. And yet, I sensed a doom descending on her, a foreshadowing of failure. She was an amateur at deceit and intrigue. And amateurs often make mistakes, fatal miscalculations. In going to the limit of her dwindling resources to protect the children and then to escape, it was inevitable that she would go too far. I saw her moving in that direction with the horror that a parent feels watching a child dash into noonday traffic on a busy street, helpless to avert what must happen.

Fiction must follow an internal logic. Given the circumstances I had created, Kate had to die. That doesn't mean I didn't mourn—or that I don't wish to write happier stories, with strolling-into-sunset endings, the cavalry arriving at the last minute. How I loved the sound of bugles and those thundering hooves at Saturday movie matinees.

But I've come to realize that Saturday matinees have nothing to do with real life, that innocence doesn't provide immunity from evil, that the mugger lurking in the doorway assaults both the just and the unjust.

It is possible to be a peaceful man, to abhor violence, to love children and flowers and old Beatles songs, and still be aware of the contusions and abrasions this world inflicts on us. Not to write happy endings doesn't mean the writer doesn't believe in them. Literature should penetrate all the chambers of the human heart, even the dark ones.

A fifteen-year-old high-school sophomore sat in my living room recently and asked me, "Why do people get upset by your novels?" She was a lovely person, tender toward small animals, and she tries to be a good kid. But she knows that people like Kate Forrester don't always survive or that a boy like Adam Farmer in *I Am the Cheese* can become a victim of the times in which he lives. That doesn't mean that she is cynical or that she is not idealistic. But she has faced realities.

It's sad, of course, to face realities. But not to face them is to live in a never-never land, where struggle and growth and the possibility of triumph are absent.

This essay may not tell you what kind of person writes about terrible things—but, perhaps, it tells you why.

in their impact. Among his other young adult books are *Eight Plus One* (1980), a collection of short stories that is somewhat uneven due to the frequent use of adult protagonists; *The Bumblebee Flies Anyway* (1983), a chilling tale of terminally ill teenagers; *Beyond the Chocolate War* (1985), a strong sequel, with an even greater suspense quotient; and *We All Fall Down* (1991), a well-written story of urban violence that includes few appealing characters. One of Cormier's most talked-about novels is a vast departure from his previous works. *Fade* contains elements of the supernatural, as young Paul Moreaux discovers his ability to become invisible and, a generation later, must stop his troubled nephew from abusing the power that he, too, has inherited. The work's raw violence and sexuality push the envelope of adolescent fiction and may disturb readers of all ages. But few will deny the power of this compelling novel, which is notable for its autobiographical descriptions of 1930s "Frenchtown," its shifting viewpoints, and its terrifying plot and themes.

Much of the author's work has been informed by his strong Roman Catholic faith, a topic he addresses directly in *Other Bells for Us to Ring* (1990), his first book for younger readers. This story of Darcy, who moves to Frenchtown during World War II and becomes friends with a Catholic girl, is very well written, but may seem simplistic and sentimental to fans of Cormier's earlier novels. *Tunes for Bears to Dance To* (1992) explores the subject of evil for a juvenile audience, as a loathsome employer bribes young Henry into committing a destructive act against an elderly Holocaust survivor. Although flawed by insufficient character motivation and a truncated plot, the author's fine writing and descriptive skills remain in top form.

Cormier's novels have been adapted for films, taught in secondary schools, studied by critics, and continue to be popular with young readers. Like all important books, they have elicited controversy. The author's unwillingness to sugarcoat his themes or compromise the integrity of his stories by providing unrealistic happy endings has caused some to criticize the bleak, pessimistic view of humanity displayed in his work. Do the books portray a universe filled with only defeat and despair? Yes, they often do. But is this actually the overriding theme of the writing? No. Half of each reading experience involves the emotions and attitudes of the reader. Cormier's readers come away from his books asking serious questions of themselves. Do I have the courage of Kate in *After the First Death*? Do I have the resolve of Jerry in *The Chocolate War*? What would I do if I were one of his classmates? Do I dare disturb the universe?

In his brilliantly crafted novels, Cormier presents important ethical issues and asks tough questions. The reader is left to ponder the answers. ❧ PETER D. SIERUTA

Counting Books

The toddler calls out "one, two, fwee" and is immediately greeted with smiles, applause, and exclamations of approval by her adult audience. Their response is so satisfying that she adds this performance to her repertoire even though she does not yet know that these sounds form part of a sequence that can be expanded and reversed, can reveal a one-to-one correspondence, can be represented orthographically and symbolically, can be manipulated to reveal insights about the objective world, can be a stimulus for aesthetic experiences, and, best of all, can be a continuing source of fun and pleasure. Children's counting books help this toddler and countless others discover the possibilities inherent in the world of numbers.

Ostensibly a category of books with limited possibilities, counting books have attracted some of the most prominent names in the field of children's literature, revealing surprisingly varied approaches in content as well as aesthetics. For the youngest child, there are simple, direct books that typically employ easily identifiable, familiar objects in limited quantities. TANA HOBAN's *1, 2, 3* (1985) is a board book for the nursery set that features a birthday cake with a single candle, two baby tennis shoes, three building blocks, and, finally, ten infant toes. There is no text other than the names of the numbers, which are accompanied by numerals and a corresponding quantity of dots. Equally suitable for the preschool child is *Who's Counting* by NANCY TAFURI (1986), which follows a puppy past one squirrel, two birds, and the like until he reaches home, where his nine siblings join him for dinner.

In *Ten Black Dots* (1986), DONALD CREWS transmutes five black circles into "buttons on a coat or the portholes of a boat." This handsome little book with its vibrant colors, clear, uncluttered images, and rhyming text is a work of charm as well as practicality. MOLLY BANG counts, in *Ten, Nine, Eight* (1983), a serene bedtime book featuring an African American child and her loving father counting backward from "ten small toes all washed and warm" to "one big girl all ready for bed." *One Was Johnny* (1962), from the incomparable Nutshell Library, is anything but a bedtime book. MAURICE SENDAK's young hero is invaded by a succession of rowdies whom he evicts by counting backward until he reestablishes his preferred solitary state.

In *1 Hunter* (1982), PAT HUTCHINS dispatches her totally incompetent hunter on a safari. He marches obliviously past nine sets of wild creatures, who are only imperfectly camouflaged, finally fleeing in panic when all are assembled together. In Peter Pavey's *One Dragon's Dream* (1979), it is again the objects to be counted that are camouflaged. Embedded in busy and complex illustrations, the elements of the sets may vary in form, be partially obscured or viewed from differing angles, complicating the identification process but expanding the understanding of what may constitute a set. Brushes, all elements of a single set, are variously suitable for artists or house painters; of the three tigers, two are real and one paper. Employing both visual puns and linguistic games, the book's intellectual challenge extends far beyond just counting. Joy Hulme's *Sea Squares* (1991) can be either a simple counting book or an exercise in multiplication and division or even in squares and roots.

MITSUMASA ANNO's books are the work not only of an artist but also of a mathematician. Beginning with zero and proceeding through twelve, each page of *Anno's Counting Book* (1975) reflects a different month and different hour of the day. More complicated is *Anno's Counting House* (1982), which extends beyond sets and correspondence to include comparison, conservation, subsets, position, addition, and subtraction.

Kveta Pacovska's *One, Five, Many* (1990) defies categorization. Using cutouts, accordion foldouts, paper doors, and even a silver mirror, this spiral-bound book is more a celebration of the joys and possibilities of numbers than a straightforward counting book. It invites the child to consider, ponder, and play with numbers for the sheer glory of the experience.

Some authors have used popular media characters to introduce number concepts. Considering the emphasis on counting in *Sesame Street,* it is not surprising to see *Little Bert's Book of Numbers* (1992), by Anna Ross, utilizing the popular television muppet to introduce a simple sequence. *One Hundred and One Dalmatians* (1956) by Fran Manushkin, employs these favorite film canines to lead young readers in counting just past one hundred.

In some books, the counting aspect may be equaled or eclipsed by other elements. *Animal Numbers* (1987) by Bert Kitchen is little more than an excuse for some stunningly beautiful illustrations. A child could certainly count the three baby squirrels or the ten Irish setter puppies, or even the twenty-five garter snakes, but such usage is mere *langnaippe.* The pictures alone more than justify this lovely book. BRUCE MCMILLAN's expertly photographed wildflowers in *Counting Wildflowers* (1986) are more a celebration of nature than an excuse to move from one to twenty, and Jan Thornhill's *The Wildlife 1, 2, 3: A Nature Counting Book* (1989) reveals in its title its dual purpose. This beautifully designed book features handsome illustrations, intriguingly framed on each page, a pleasure to contemplate and incidentally offering objects to count. A notable book of this type is *Moja Means One* (1971) by Muriel and TOM FEELINGS. Primarily a book to introduce aspects of East African rural and village life and evoke a sense of rootedness in

Illustration by TOM FEELINGS from *Moja Means One* (1971), by Muriel Feelings.

African American children, it is secondarily a Swahili counting book. The eponymous heroes of ARTHUR GEISERT's *Pigs from 1 to 10* (1992) embark on a quest to locate "a lost place with huge stone configurations." In each double-page spread, the numerals from 0 to 9 are embedded. Some are readily spotted, but others take considerable study to unearth. This challenge, the sophisticated language, and the witty illustrations suggest that the intended audience is well past toddler age.

Counting is a fundamental behavior. Its exploration in children's books would seem to be relatively limited and constrained, but such is not the case. The twentieth century has witnessed an astounding variation in children's counting books, and the last few years have produced a truly surprising array of works. Just when it seems every possible aspect of this topic has been explored, a genuinely unique work appears. There is no reason to suspect this process will not continue indefinitely. ❧ KAREN HARRIS

Courlander, Harold

AMERICAN AUTHOR, B. 1908. Harold Courlander's appreciation of foreign cultures is reflected in the folktale collections he published for an American audience. Courlander was born in Indianapolis, where he lived until age six, when his family moved to Detroit. Growing up in this ethnically diverse community, Courlander became interested in the African American, Polish, and German cultures that surrounded him. After graduating from the University of Michigan, he spent five years farming, then worked for the U.S. Office of War Information in India, journeyed overseas as a historian with the Douglas Aircraft Corporation, served as an editor and a senior political analyst with Voice of America, and as an information officer with the United Nations. During his travels, Courlander collected stories and music from the indigenous cultures he encountered. Although he always felt that folktales could be enjoyed by readers of all ages, publishers believed they were best suited for young audiences.

Courlander's best-known collection of folktales, *The Cow-Tail Switch, and Other West African Stories* (1947), was written with George Herzog. This Newbery Honor Book includes humorous and thought-provoking stories about talking animals and villagers and is written in a clear, unembellished style. Liberia, Nigeria, and the former Gold Coast Colony are among the sources of these tales, some personally recorded by Courlander and Herzog, others derived from obscure publications. The trickster Anansi is depicted as a human character in two of the stories, but appears as a spider throughout *The Hat-Shaking Dance and Other Tales from the Gold Coast* (1957), a collection of folktales from the Ashanti people, who call all stories "Anansesem," in honor of this traditional character. Courlander's other collections of African folktales include *The King's Drum and Other African Stories* (1962) and *Olode the Hunter and Other Tales from Nigeria* (1968). *Son of the Leopard* (1974) is an original story Courlander wrote, based on an Ethiopian legend; this brief novel of a man shunned and cast out by his people is distinguished by its rhythmic prose.

Because the author collected folklore from a variety of cultures, readers of Courlander's work can perceive how universal concerns and themes are adapted to individual societies. Folktales from the Far East are represented in *Kantchil's Lime Pit, and Other Stories from Indonesia* (1950) and include several stories about the Indonesian trickster figure, a mouse-deer called Kantchil. Coyote is the trickster figure in *People of the Short Blue Corn: Tales and Legends of the Hopi Indians* (1970). A second, more densely written collection, *The Fourth World of the Hopis* (1971), includes music within the text.

Courlander is also noted for the record albums he made from his own field recordings in the Caribbean and Africa. Among his numerous adult works of nonfiction, *Negro Folk Music, U.S.A.* (1963), is perhaps the best known. His adult novel, *The African* (1967), received much public attention when it was revealed that Alex Haley illegally used portions of the book in writing *Roots*. Courlander received a legal settlement speculated to be more than half a million dollars. In 1980, the author was nominated for the Laura Ingalls Wilder Award.

His tightly written collections of folktales explore a wide spectrum of human culture and represent a significant contribution to children's literature. ❧ P.D.S.

Cousins, Lucy

BRITISH AUTHOR AND ARTIST OF PICTURE BOOKS, B. 1964. Lucy Cousins's introduction to children's literature began with modest forays into bookstores, where she enjoyed looking at children's books and thought about "having a go at them." Cousins first studied art at Canterbury Art College. She received her degree in graphic design at Brighton Polytechnic and continued her studies at the Royal College of Art. While a student there, Cousins produced *Portly's Hat* (1989), a small, illustrated story about a penguin in black and white, that had been inspired by a visit to the zoo. Cousins originally sent the manuscript to a competition for art students sponsored by Macmillan, and the highly original and charming submission won second prize and was subsequently published. The following year it garnered a runner-up for the Bologna Graphics Prize. So began an innovative career by an artist who has become a favorite choice for the under-five group. Her second book was *The Little Dog Laughed* (1990), a collection of NURSERY RHYMES that featured bold colors and shapes, elements now synonymous with her work. Cousins's art has a deceptively simple childlike quality that belies its sophisticated composition and style.

An exhibit of her work at her college-degree show inadvertently led to an important career move. Encouraged by others to contact a publishing house, Cousins followed this advice and was immediately taken on by one. Armed with a dummy of what was to become the best-selling *Maisy Goes to Bed*, Cousins's work impressed the art director and editor with the originality of its design.

The "Maisy" series features a small mouse who engages in familiar routines. In *Maisy Goes to Bed* (1990), the cheerful character goes through all the rituals of putting on her nightclothes and washing up before falling asleep. *Maisy Goes Swimming* (1990) follows the same format, as Maisy dons a bathing suit and tries some swimming strokes. In *Maisy Goes to School* (1992) the character dresses up as a pirate and dances like a ballerina with flailing arms and legs. A trip to the park in *Maisy Goes to the Playground* (1992) shows a contented Maisy licking a Popsicle while the wrapper goes into the litter can. Readers can follow Maisy's activities by lifting flaps and pulling tabs that show her movements as she brushes her teeth or changes her clothes. With the use of these paper mechanics, readers have an active role in her books and the pleasure of engineering the action.

Though it is Cousins's artwork that stands out, the concept behind her books shows a deep understanding and appreciation of the kinds of experiences that her young audience finds appealing. Her humor is contagious and evident in the small details. Part of her commitment to her work includes trying new techniques and taking her art in different directions, such as her cloth books and BOARD BOOKS. A series of board books thematically centered on animals—*Garden Animals*, *Farm Animals*, *Country Animals*, and *Pet Animals* (all 1991)—once again featured Cousins's distinctive style. Other books for this age group were *What Can Rabbit See?* and *What Can Rabbit Hear?* (both 1991).

Noah's Ark (1993) once again demonstrates Cousins's ability to surprise and delight her readers. With this retelling of the Biblical flood, Cousins uses a simple text that makes the story comprehensible to very young children. Noah is an appealing-looking figure, and the artist's rainbow-bright colors and toylike forms bring this adaptation to life.

As an artist Cousins has consistently provided her audience with books that possess an exuberant tone and a playful spirit that neatly matches a young child's world. ❧ C.L.L.

Cox, Palmer

CANADIAN-BORN AMERICAN WRITER CARTOONIST, 1840–1924. For two generations the antics of Palmer Cox's Brownies entertained multitudes, and the very figure of a Brownie sold consumer goods of every description. Appearing at a time of flux, the Brownies were both a wholesome, likable alternative to the new, "disgraceful" comic strips and the first of the licensed characters. History aside, their success attests to the power of an image and a concept.

At the age of forty Cox was a cartoonist of some repute with two fairly conventional strings to his bow: animals in comical situations and genial satire of American society. He might have gone on in this fashion, one among many graphic humorists, had it not been for *St. Nicholas* magazine and its hunger for fresh material. Not content with being an occasional contributor, Cox cast about for a niche of his own, a secure place in the affections of children, and bethought himself—so the oft-told story goes—of the brownies of English and Scottish Highlands folklore, companions of his own childhood in the Scottish community of Granby, in Quebec.

The Brownies of Cox's devising are no mere household helpers, however, doing chores while the family sleeps. True to tradition, they go about unseen after dark, but from their 1883 debut in "The Brownies' Ride," they are bent on a night of comradely adventure, with an occasional service to humankind factored in. In precisely rendered, cunningly detailed pictures and jingle-jangle rhyme, they ride bicycles, play baseball, canoe; they visit the seaside, the toy shop, the zoo. As the series develops their outings become not only more timely but distinctly topical. The new Brooklyn Bridge attracts daredevil jumpers: Count on the Brownies to take a leap (with due warning to mere people). Construction of the World's Columbian Exposition is behind schedule? Trust the Brownies to pitch in with paintbrush and hammer.

In appearance, too, the Brownies undergo a crucial transformation. Initially they are all alike and, like the

They were not long—for Brownies smart
At such a time display their art;
To be of service they can teach
Whatever comes within their reach—
They harnessed up the goats and pigs,
And fastened them to various rigs
So each might do
a proper share
Of all that was
progressing there.
Though goats are
seldom taught
to haul,
Like horses taken
from the stall,

Illustration by Palmer Cox from his book *The Brownies at Home* (1893).

storied brownies, slender and largely unclothed. But soon they acquire the round bellies, spindly legs, and odd-shaped heads that make them cute, comical, and unique: the Palmer Cox Brownie. By adding headgear and a few distinctive articles of clothing, Cox transformed them further into individuals—the stock characters of late-nineteenth-century popular culture. In time there was a Brownie Policeman, Soldier, Poet, Clown. An early and a perennial favorite was the Brownie Dude. There were ethnic types galore: a pigtailed Chinaman, kilted Scotsman, feathered Indian, fur-capped and -coated Eskimo, turbaned Turk. A late arrival, suggested by Teddy Roosevelt, was the Cowboy Brownie, who bore a striking resemblance to TR. In each episode the Brownies act with characteristic daring or prudence, agility or clumsiness. The fun for children, and increasingly for their elders, was in following pet characters from page to page, story to story, and, before long, book to book.

The first compilation, *The Brownies: Their Book,* appeared in 1887. In the next dozen years or so Brownie books came thick and fast, eventually reaching thirteen. Like the globe-trotting heroes of boys' SERIES BOOKS, the Brownies moved onto the world stage; the expansionist war with Spain led to *The Brownies in the Philippines* (1904). A reasonable estimate puts overall sales at a million copies; ascertainably, 100,000 were sold as early as 1895, another 100,000 as late as the 1920s.

Among the spinoffs was a "Musical Extravaganza," *Palmer Cox's Brownies,* book and lyrics by Cox, which opened in New York in 1894 and toured the United States for five years. More significantly, there were Brownie toys and games galore, licensed by Cox; Brownie dolls of wood, paper, cloth, and bisque, some designed by Cox; Brownie wallpaper, salt and pepper shakers, napkin rings. Cox also wrote and drew Brownie ads for Procter & Gamble's Ivory Soap and Cashmere Bouquet, for patent medicines, assorted beverages, and cotton thread. He designed Brownie booklets to serve as merchandise premiums. The Brownies, in fact, had no bigger fan than Cox himself. A childless bachelor, he spent his winters working in isolation, his summers at Brownie Castle, a castellated wooden house he built in Granby and fitted out with Brownie paraphernalia. All told, the Brownies and their mass audience of believers set the pace for the twentieth-century union of make-believe and merchandising. ❧ B.B.

CRAIG, HELEN

BRITISH ILLUSTRATOR AND AUTHOR, B. 1934. With the publication of *Angelina Ballerina* in 1982, illustrator Helen Craig and author Katharine Holabird introduced a spunky, winning heroine in the form of an anthropomorphic mouse. Angelina's debut heralded the beginning of a series that currently boasts eleven volumes and is extremely popular with young children. The success of these books results from their breadth and variety; Craig takes some of the stories away from the ballerina's dance floor and grounds them in the ordinary, everyday experiences of a child's world. *Angelina Goes to the Fair* (1985) finds Angelina disgruntled because she must take her cousin Henry to the fair; her annoyance turns to fright when she loses the youngster and then to joyous relief upon finding him. *Angelina's Birthday Surprise* (1989) features Angelina as a cyclist on an old bike that crashes and sends the heroine sprawling, so Angelina must start a vigorous campaign to earn money for a new bike. In *Angelina Ice Skates* (1993), the protagonist shows the neighborhood boys that girls are able to move as quickly on skates as boys.

One aspect of the "Angelina" books' appeal to all youngsters is their agreeable gender balance within text and illustrations. Although Angelina's personality is clearly the force that moves the stories within the series, the real thread that binds them securely together is Craig's artwork. Craig delineates character and expression with the slightest line. The illustrations are energetic, humorous, and alive with movement that sends the eye across the page.

Craig began illustrating children's books in 1970; the first book she both wrote and illustrated was *The Mouse House ABC* (1977). Another character created by Craig, with author Sarah Hayes, is Bear, a beguiling teddy bear who stars in three charming books that the youngest listeners have taken to heart. The appeal of the predictable stories is in the interaction between the three main characters: Bear, the young boy devoted to Bear, and a naughty, lovable dog who thinks Bear gets too much attention. *This Is the Bear* (1986) introduces the series; it is followed by *This Is the Bear and the Picnic Lunch* (1988) and *This Is the Bear and the Scary Night* (1992). The text, written in rhythmic, cumulative verse, is accompanied by word balloons that allow the Bear, the dog, and other creatures to speak as they proceed through their amusing adventures. Executed in watercolor and ink, the illustrations, perfectly attuned to a child's world, create relationships among the characters that are believable, warm, and reassuring.

Craig has illustrated three books of her own: *The Night of the Paper Bag Monsters* (1984), *The Knight, the*

Illustration by Helen Craig from *Angelina's Birthday Surprise* (1989), by Katherine Holabird.

Princess and the Dragon (1985), and *A Welcome for Annie* (1986). The stories' appeal rests in Craig's imaginative integration of text and pictures. Susie and Alfred, two close friends who happen to be piglets, cavort through simple plots laced with good-natured humor.

Whatever text Craig illustrates, her gentle, detailed watercolors and perceptive interpretations visually celebrate the wonders of friendship and the commonplace events of childhood. ❦ S.L.

Crane, Walter

English illustrator and author, 1845–1915. Walter Crane was the first of the grand triumvirate in children's book illustration who worked under the tutelage of the English printer Edmund Evans. Crane, the son of an artist, developed his artistic talents from an early age and at seventeen exhibited at London's Royal Academy. As a young teenager, he apprenticed himself to the engraver William James Linton for three years before setting out on his own to earn a living as an artist. His early books were illustrated anonymously, but he soon met Evans, who had developed and perfected a method of color printing and was looking for talented illustrators to produce books for children. Crane's first children's books, *The House that Jack Built* and *Dame Trot and Her Comical Cat*, were published in 1865 when he was twenty and were followed by more than forty books for children over the course of his career. Many of these were toy books, so called because of their small length and size.

In addition to illustrating and painting, Crane worked as a teacher and as a designer of wallpaper, textiles, ceramics, and interiors. He was a disciple of William Morris and a member of the Arts and Crafts movement, which attempted to provide an alternative to the ugliness that resulted from the Industrial Revolution by seeking to bring beautiful design and craftsmanship to everyday things. The influence of this movement can be seen in Crane's concern for the overall design of his books. He was one of the first illustrators to be concerned with the appearance of the double-page spread and often planned the entire book design, including the endpapers, title page, and lettering.

Crane took readily to illustrating for children. His strengths as an illustrator lay in his strong sense of composition and design and in his use of color, which was influenced by Japanese prints. In books such as the *Absurd ABC* (1874), the contrasting values set up by the use of large areas of black set against red and yellow convey a feeling of lively movement in spite of the flatness of the figures that resulted from his use of uniform color. In this book, the breakup of some pages into panels depicting the different letters creates an alternative rhythm to the double-page spreads and further energizes the overall effect. The illustration style is also reminiscent of the Japanese wood-block prints that Crane

Illustration by Walter Crane for "Beauty and the Beast" from Crane's book *Beauty and the Beast and Other Tales* (1875).

found so appealing. At times, Crane's admitted concern with design and detail made him lose sight of his child audience, and the storytelling qualities of his illustrations are sometimes overwhelmed by decoration. But the range of his talent as an illustrator for children is most evident in works like *The Baby's Opera* (1877) and *The Baby's Bouquet* (1879). *First of May: A Fairy Masque* (1881) has surprisingly delicate drawings and restrained page design. Another book that demonstrates Crane's versatility is *Household Stories* (1882) by the Brothers GRIMM. Here we see his true talents in the small drawings used to illustrate the beginnings and endings of the chapters. In these small spaces there is no room for fussy details, and Crane's vitality of line and composition is particularly evident.

Over the course of his career Crane set himself many artistic challenges by choosing to illustrate a variety of texts, from alphabet books and brief rhymes to fully developed fairy tales, and he strove in all of these works to bring coherence to the overall appearance of the individual book. In addition to his books for children he created illustrated books for adults and several textbooks about book design and illustration. When Crane died in 1915 he had become internationally known and admired, and his contributions to children's book illustration can still be seen in children's books of the late twentieth century. ❧ B.K.

CRESSWELL, HELEN

ENGLISH AUTHOR, B. 1934. Born in Nottinghamshire, Helen Cresswell won her first literary prize at age fourteen. "I do not remember a time when I did not know that I was to be a writer," she recalls. Cresswell is the author of more than sixty books, including books written for early readers, such as *Rainbow Pavement* (1970) and the "Two Hoots" series, beginning with *Two Hoots* (1974), as well as writing original scripts for television.

Cresswell is perhaps best known, however, for her MIDDLE-GRADE and YOUNG ADULT FICTION, from the hilarious chronicles of the eccentric but lovable Bagthorpe family, introduced in *Ordinary Jack* (1977), to the complex fantasy of *The Night Watchman* (1969) and the contemporary drama of *Dear Shrink* (1982), in which three young siblings face the challenges of living on their own. Her work has been critically acclaimed throughout Cresswell's career, and four books—*The Piemakers* (1967), *The Night Watchman* (1969), *Up the Pier* (1971), and *The Bongleweed* (1973)—were runners-up for the top British children's book award, the Carnegie Medal. Her many other honors and awards include five titles selected as Notable Children's Books by the American Library Association.

Cresswell's trademark style—an exaggerated, often slapstick humor; comedic timing; and a keen appreciation of the absurd—have garnered a devoted following among many young readers. "I have a very strong sense of childhood," she explains, "and like to be talking to human beings before they have become capable of pose or hypocrisy or prejudice." Cresswell delights in the unexpected and unpredictable; events often unfold at a dizzying pace. In *The Piemakers,* the Roller family decides to create the "biggest pie that's ever been made in the whole history of the world," enlisting the aid of the entire town of Danby Dale. They commission a pie dish so big it has to be steered, like a barge, down the river, to which they add sensational seasonings, crust, and filling—and are rewarded by winning the King's contest. When a wild weed starts growing at a remarkable rate in *The Bongleweed,* Becky Finch and her sensible father, a gardener, find themselves defending a plant that threatens to overtake their village. The Wilks family, servants in London in 1887, enjoy an unusual vacation one hundred years in the future, in *Time Out* (1990). The Pontifexes are brought from 1921 into 1971 by a magic spell in *Up the Pier,* and in *Moondial* (1987) young Minty Kane tries to rescue the spirits of abused children from long ago.

Cresswell offers an affectionate, nostalgic view of an unspoiled English countryside and memorable characters. Even their names are evocative: the proper housekeeper Mrs. Fosdyke, desperately trying to keep order among the unruly Bagthorpes; Gravella Roller of *The Piemakers;* the title character of *Lizzy Dripping* (1973). Often eccentric, always determined and spirited, these charming characters lead the reader on a "magical mystery tour" that is quite exhilarating—or sometimes just plain silly. Cresswell celebrates the value of creativity and of the individual, who is often at odds with a more stodgy society. In the more subtle and subdued fantasy of *The Night Watchman,* the offbeat characters of Josh and Caleb, two tramps who inhabit an underworld of hidden reality, transform the boring and lonely life of young Henry. Turning this theme topsy-turvy in the six-part Bagthorpe Saga, the hero of *Ordinary Jack* despairs of ever fitting into his frenetic, unconventional, talented family. In the end, Jack learns to accept himself as he is, reinforcing the Cresswell creed that "family" is a place where solace and comfort can be found, no matter how unusual that family might be. Like Jack, the reader inevitably emerges refreshed and satisfied at the conclusion of Cresswell's lively and boisterous novels. ❧ C.J.

Crews, Donald

American author and illustrator of picture books, b. 1938. Donald Crews was born in Newark, New Jersey. Long interested in drawing and sketching, he attended Arts High School, which had special classes in music and art, then went to Cooper Union School for the Advancement of Science and Art in New York City. While serving in the military in Germany, he worked on a design portfolio. There he designed his first book for children, *We Read: A to Z,* which was published in 1967. He next wrote a book called *Ten Black Dots* (1968), a companion to the first. He has illustrated many books by others, such as *Rain* (1978) and *Blue Sea* (1979) by Robert Kalan and *The Talking Stone: An Anthology of Native American Tales and Legends* (1979), retold and edited by Dorothy de Wit.

When he turned back to creating his own texts, Crews captured the imagination of critics and judges with *Freight Train* (1978). The spare text labels the different freight cars, shown in bright colors and bold shapes, and depicts the train moving across trestles and passing by cities. At first stationary, it begins to pick up speed until it is a blur, an effect achieved with airbrush technique. He based the book on childhood memories of travels south to his grandparents' farm in Cottondale, Florida, where he watched and counted trains that passed near the house. The book was named a 1979 Caldecott Honor Book by the American Library Association, and its success allowed Crews to devote himself to picture books.

Crews's next work, *Truck,* also has a simple text, in which the journey of a brightly colored tractor-trailer displays the intricate shapes of highways and geometric signs. In 1981 the American Library Association named *Truck* a Caldecott Honor Book. *Harbor* (1982) shows an active city harbor, with all manner of shipping vessels, ocean liners, and tugboats. Crews works the names of some family members into the illustrations as the names of boats, as he often works messages into his artwork in the form of signs and other lettering. In *Carousel* (1983) Crews varies his technique by photographing the artwork, which depicts children on a carousel, moving the camera so that the image appears blurred to signify movement. He explores other aspects of a child's world in books like *Light* (1981), *Parade* (1983), and *School Bus* (1984). He returns to the setting that inspired *Freight Train* in *Bigmama's* (1991), in which he portrays

Illustration by Donald Crews from his book *Parade* (1983).

a trip his family makes to visit his grandmother in Florida. *Shortcut* (1992) tells the sobering tale of a group of children who take a route home via some railroad tracks. They come so close to being struck that it frightens them deeply. Thus Crews evolves from the creator of *Freight Train*, bold, simple, and devoid of human characters, into the author of a book that re-creates an incident that has lasting emotional reverberations for its protagonists.

This innovative artist continues to experiment; he applies his fascination with elements such as light, movement, photography, and collage to invent new ways of creating a picture book. Crews has been recognized by the American Institute of Graphic Arts in several of its exhibits. S.H.H.

Cross, Gillian

English author, b. 1945. Gillian Cross was raised in London in a postwar home filled with books. She studied English literature at Oxford University and received her Ph.D. at the University of Sussex. Cross credits her doctoral thesis for turning her into a writer—she believes it taught her how to keep a specific audience in mind while writing a long piece.

Cross's early books for children were based on social and industrial history. *The Iron Way* (1979), her first published novel, tells the story of the early days of the railway in southern England and its impact on rural society; *Revolt at Ratcliffe's Rags* (1980) focuses on children caught in an industrial dispute. With the publication of *The Demon Headmaster* (1982) and its sequel, *The Prime Minister's Brain* (1985), Cross successfully bridged the gap between her historical writing and her new genre, which combined history with suspense, entertainment, fantasy, and realism. In the first book, a group of schoolchildren attempt to break a spell cast by a diabolical headmaster, who returns in the second book as the organizer of a computer contest for kids, which turns out to be a front for a scheme to figure out the computer codes that access the brain of the prime minister.

Cross may be a master of suspense, but her stories are not always easy reading; critics have said that she "reveals a certain darkness that is sometimes shown as pure evil and sometimes a symptom of human weakness." Cross herself has said that violence is "crucial to the nature of children's fiction. Death and danger and injury are hard, definite, dramatic things." She does not, however, use violence to skirt issues or ignore ethical questions; rather, she uses it as a method of highlighting the ambivalent nature of humankind and the turmoil of growing up. Cross takes the hard realities—terrorism, abandonment, irresponsible or absent parents—and spins them into gripping thrillers. *On the Edge* (1984), an Edgar Allan Poe Award and Whitbread finalist, tells the story of a London boy who is kidnapped by a terrorist group whose aim is to abolish the family unit. Tug, the son of a famous journalist, has part of his memory erased by his kidnappers, who later claim to be his parents. Tug's struggle to survive on his own terms and maintain his identity despite the brainwashing techniques raises personal and political questions about the power of an individual. In *Wolf* (1991) Cassy is sent from the comfort of her grandmother's house to the squalor of an abandoned hut where her mother lives. She asks no questions but begins to suspect that the strange figure lurking around the squat is her mysterious father and then discovers a hidden package that contains weapons for a terrorist attack. While critics have been relatively unanimous in their reaction to the overwhelming wolf symbolism—believing it to be heavy-handed and artificially belabored—they are also unanimous in their praise for the fierce, shocking climax and the rich, subtle psychological depth of the narrative.

Even though Cross features malevolent elements in her books, her stories are by no means depressing. Her heroes and heroines—strong individuals confronting difficult problems—face their fears and make intelligent, moral decisions that allow them to triumph over their desperate situations. Cross believes that much literature concerns itself with the powerlessness of ordinary people. Her books contradict this belief. "I believe that ordinary people are important people and that everyone has the power to influence his own life." In Cross's books, the ordinary do become extraordinary as each page brings an intensely thrilling adventure. M.I.A.

Crutcher, Chris

American young-adult novelist and short story writer, b. 1946. By incorporating his love and knowledge of athletics with his experiences as a mental-health professional, Chris Crutcher creates sports novels that transcend the genre. In his fast-paced contemporary novels, athletics serve as a vehicle to explore the lives of young men and women struggling to cope with their personal problems. They have turned to sports to exert control over the one thing in their lives they can control: their own bodies. Daily practice and competition give their lives structure, as teammates, coaches, and teachers provide discipline and support. The characters quickly become more than just athletes to readers.

Crutcher knows the problems and concerns of adolescents firsthand from his experience in working with troubled youths. Since graduating from Eastern Washington State University with a degree in psychology/sociology, Crutcher has worked as a teacher of high school dropouts, coordinator of a child abuse protection agency, and child and family therapist. The problems he encounters on a daily basis—substance and child abuse, runaways, suicide—provide him with plenty of material for his stories.

The logging town of Cascade, Idaho, where Crutcher grew up, was so small that he had to play on the football, track, and basketball teams in high school for want of players. He includes these experiences in his writings, and his firsthand knowledge lends his work a credible tone. In *Running Loose* (1983), his first novel, the football field is the setting for racism and an ethics issue, as the coach prompts his team to take out the opposing star quarterback, an African American player who threatens their championship position. *Stotan!* (1986) is based on an intense week of grueling practice, which Crutcher experienced as a college-level swimmer. In this novel, four members of the high school swim team face a similar week, which bonds their friendships and gives them the strength to face the even greater challenges waiting outside the pool. These include one swimmer's fight against leukemia and another's problems with an abusive father. In *The Crazy Horse Electric Game* (1987), a water-skiing accident sidelines baseball star Willie Weaver. Unable to cope, he runs away and ends up at a tough alternative school in Oakland, California, which is based on a school where Crutcher taught and was director for several years. Here, Willie learns to compensate for his lost physical abilities and regains his self-esteem with the aid of a challenging teacher and a basketball. Crutcher also used his basketball knowledge in his fourth novel, *Chinese Handcuffs* (1989). The memory of a brother who committed suicide haunts triathlete Dillon, who befriends Jennifer, a star basketball player who has her own secret of sexual abuse.

Crutcher's books have all been recognized by the American Library Association with the designation Best Book for Young Adults. Some readers feel that Crutcher includes too many problems in each book; others find his realistic style too graphic. As Crutcher comments in his short story collection, *Athletic Shorts* (1991), however, "There are a significant number of people who . . . don't believe that basic lessons are best taught by reflecting the truth. . . . They think kids should not be exposed in print to what they are exposed to in their lives. But I believe what I believe, and so I write my stories." ❧ A.M.D.

Cuffari, Richard

American illustrator, 1925–1978. Richard Cuffari was born in Brooklyn, New York, where he lived all his life. Both of his parents worked, and he spent a great deal of time caring for his brother, who was mentally retarded. Although he did not receive encouragement for his artistic talent, he spent what time he could drawing and painting and was given an expensive oil paint set by an uncle, a great luxury at the time that made a lifelong impression on him. He won awards for his artwork in high school, and after serving in World War II, Cuffari attended Pratt Institute until 1949. He spent many years working at a commercial art studio, then formed his own company. He began working as a freelance children's book illustrator in 1968.

The first book he illustrated was *The Wind in the Willows* by Kenneth Grahame, in 1966. Dorothy Aldis's *Nothing Is Impossible: The Story of Beatrix Potter,* which was published, with Cuffari's illustrations, in 1969, was named a Junior Literary Guild selection, as were several of his books. He was interested in history, in historical figures, their clothing, and how they lived. In the interests of accuracy, he kept an extensive research library. In 1973 he illustrated Martha Bacon's novel set in eighteenth-century Italy, in which an orphan boy is pictured in lively street scenes and amid the architecture of cities such as Venice. *The King's Road* (1970), by Cecelia Holland, historical fiction set in the Middle Ages, tells the story of Frederick II, Holy Roman Emperor, king of Jerusalem. In Elizabeth Pope's *Perilous Gard* (1974), he portrays the Tudor period.

The list of novelists whose work he has given his signature to include Theodore Taylor, Betsy Byars, Betty Cavanna, and Rosemary Wells. In addition to fiction and history, he has illustrated books on sports, like *Jackie Robinson* (1971), and books on science, like *Ecology* (1971) and *Water for Dinosaurs and You* (1972). He illustrated more than two hundred books in his eleven-year career, particularly books for older children. He also illustrated a great deal of nonfiction and novels. As one of his editors, James Giblin, stated in a note in one of Cuffari's last books, *Balder and the Mistletoe*

(1978), Cuffari "was well aware that the lion's share of critical attention went to the illustrators of picture books for young children." However, he did receive many prestigious awards from fellow illustrators, including two Citations of Merit from the Society of Illustrators, in 1969 and 1970, and Citations from the American Institute of Graphic Arts, in 1973 and 1974. The Christopher Award was presented to him in 1973. He has also been represented in the Children's Book Showcase in 1974 and 1975. For a time he was an instructor of book illustration at Parsons School of Design. Cuffari was also a painter and had his work exhibited in New York galleries. Cuffari had a distinctive style of a delicate line combined with selective shading and crosshatching, immediately recognizable, which comes through in his pen-and-ink line drawing with wash. His artwork on a book jacket evokes a particular era in children's book publishing. S.H.H.

CUMMINGS, PAT

AMERICAN ILLUSTRATOR, B. 1950. Variety has been a common thread in both the personal life and the work of artist Pat Cummings. She experienced variety during her years as an army brat; although born in Chicago, she spent her childhood in many places both in and out of the United States. Cummings began drawing as soon as she could hold a crayon, desiring, even then, to be an illustrator. Her parents encouraged her by keeping her well supplied with artists' materials. In 1974 she graduated from Pratt Institute and began her career as a freelance illustrator.

Cummings's interest in illustrating children's books sprang from her work with children's theater groups. Her duties ranged from creating the ads, posters, and flyers to designing the sets and even some of the costumes. The fantasy and imagery of children's theater appealed to her, and she continues to rely upon this background in creating her book illustrations. She incorporates her personal experiences into books in other ways, as well, by including people she knows, household items she uses, and places she has been.

Cummings's first children's book was *Good News* (1977), by ELOISE GREENFIELD. In 1982 her drawings for Jeannette Caines's *Just Us Women* earned her a Coretta Scott King Honorable Mention. Recognition of her artistry began to grow. She has since won the Coretta Scott King Award in 1984 for *My Mama Needs Me* (1983), by MILDRED PITTS WALTER, and received two additional Coretta Scott King Honorable Mentions for *C.L.O.U.D.S.* (1986) and for MARY STOLZ's *Storm in the Night* (1988). Cummings both wrote and illustrated two books: *Jimmy Lee Did It* (1985), which draws on children's everyday use of their imaginations; and *C.L.O.U.D.S.*, in which she returns to her love of fantasy.

In *Talking with Artists* (1992), Cummings compiles biographies of outstanding artists and illustrators by using a series of questions similar to those which she is asked by students. She conveys insight into the importance of art in the lives of her subjects and introduces her readers to the variety of careers that one may pursue with an art background. Much emphasis is placed on the art created by each artist during childhood, and the text is accompanied by examples of this art as well as by their illustrated work in children's books. Through the combination of biographies, interviews, and artwork, Pat Cummings provides a text that encourages children to appreciate their own artistic talent and to consider art careers, while it feeds the curiosity of adult readers interested in the backgrounds of these artists. Cummings has illustrated a number of other books, which vary in theme from child molestation, in *Chilly Stomach* (1986), to hugging, in *Willie's Not the Hugging Kind* (1989).

Whether the stories deal with fantasy or reality, are humorous or serious, Pat Cummings's signature of colorful illustrations and a zest for life infuse the pages of her books. C.H.S.

CURRY, JANE LOUISE

AMERICAN AUTHOR, B. 1932. Jane Louise Curry has published a variety of books for young readers, but she is best known for writing FANTASIES that explore the connections between past and present.

Growing up in East Liverpool, Ohio, Curry dreamed of becoming an actress, artist, or writer and eventually sampled all three fields. As a child she staged her own plays and, after moving to Pennsylvania with her family, joined a theater company, where she performed and used her artistic talents for set decoration. Curry studied art education at Pennsylvania State University and Indiana University of Pennsylvania, then taught junior high school in Los Angeles for several years. She later received her doctorate in English literature from Stanford and attended the University of London on a Fulbright grant. While living in England, she worked with a group of Girl Guides, whom she entertained with Native American stories. Encouraged by their response, she wrote *Down from the Lonely Mountain: California*

Indian Tales (1965). This enjoyable collection of animal and creation myths was followed by *Back in the Before-time: Tales of the California Indians* in 1987.

Curry's first fantasy, *Beneath the Hill* (1967), concerns a group of cousins who discover an ancient colony of Welsh fairies living in West Virginia mining country. It is the first in a series of loosely connected novels—including *The Change-Child* (1969), *The Daybreakers* (1970), *Over the Sea's Edge* (1971), *The Watchers* (1975), *The Birdstones* (1977), *The Wolves of Aam* (1981), and *Shadow Dancers* (1983)—that form an ambitious fantasy cycle originating in a magical prehistoric era and incorporating elements of Celtic and Native American mythology into North American civilization. Time-travel figures play a part in the series as modern-day children interact with historical characters, affecting each other's societies and experiencing personal growth through their adventures.

The mystery of time is one of the main themes of Curry's work. In *The Sleepers* (1968), teenagers discover the cave where King Arthur and his band sleep, waiting to be awakened when they are needed by Britain. A less complex tale for a younger audience, *Parsley Sage, Rosemary and Time* (1975), concerns a girl who travels back to eighteenth-century Maine. *Me, Myself and I: A Tale of Time Travel* (1987) is a fast-paced farce about a sixteen-year-old computer whiz who uses a mysterious machine to meet his younger self. Even a fine realistic novel such as *The Lotus Cup* (1986) shows how the past affects the present as seventeen-year-old Corry discovers she has inherited artistic abilities from her pottery-making ancestors.

In addition to her time-travel novels, the author's fantasies include the Lilliputian stories *Mindy's Mysterious Miniature* (1970) and *The Lost Farm* (1974). Curry has demonstrated her ability to write in a number of genres, including ghost stories (*Poor Tom's Ghost,* 1977), mysteries (*The Bassumtyte Treasure,* 1978), and adventures both contemporary (*The Big Smith Snatch,* 1990) and historical (*What the Dickens!,* 1991).

Throughout her career, she has shown continued growth as an author, writing novels for different age groups, experimenting with the first-person voice, and adding humor to her work. Curry's books are moderately successful and would likely become much more popular if paperback editions were issued and promoted. Young readers seeking historical and fantasy novels with strong characterizations and complex, finely detailed plots will find her books absorbing and rewarding. ❦ P.D.S.

D

Dahl, Roald

English author, 1916–1990. The creator of what many claim to be the most popular children's books of all time, Roald Dahl is a legend despite the enormous campaigns that have been mounted against him by the adult world. For children, to read one Dahl book is reason to read them all, and to read them all is reason to read them all again. Born in South Wales to Norwegian parents, Dahl's early life was not without difficulties. When his father died of pneumonia in 1920, the family was left with a large estate and moved to Kent, England. At age eight, Dahl was shipped off to boarding school, where he learned to cope with disciplinary procedures that bordered on the torturous. He remained there through his early teens, when he transferred to a renowned British private school. Dahl's experiences in boarding school, summer vacations in Norway, and other anecdotes from his childhood years are the subject of his first autobiography, *Boy* (1984).

Dahl joined the Royal Air Force in 1939 and suffered severe injuries when his plane was shot down over Egypt. Even after his recovery, the resulting ailments plagued him for the rest of his life, necessitating numerous spinal operations as well as a hip replacement. In 1941, while still serving in World War II, he wrote his first fiction, a collection of short stories for adults based on his experiences in the air force that were published in 1946 as *Over to You.* Dahl and his famous wife, actress Patricia Neal, had four children. The first, Olivia, died of measles at the age of seven; their only son, Theo, developed hydrocephalus after a severe car accident but was cured several years later. The well-known couple and their various misfortunes have been the subject of much fascination and scrutiny, and in 1969 a biography, *Pat and Roald,* was published and later made into a TV movie.

Dahl's first book for children, *The Gremlins,* appeared in 1943 and was later purchased by Walt Disney for a feature film, which was never completed. After 1943 Dahl penned numerous other children's favorites, creating for himself a reputation rivaled by none. These books include *James and the Giant Peach* (1961), *Charlie and the Chocolate Factory* (1964), *Danny: The Champion of the World* (1975), *The BFG* (1982), and *The Witches* (1983). Most of Dahl's stories revolve around a strict portrayal of good versus evil, and the child who embodies good is always triumphant. Evil, whether it is represented by landowners, witches, giants, or nasty children, is always severely done away with in the end by a means appropriate to the character involved, evoking a bizarre and often gruesome sense of justice that empowers the child hero and, in turn, the child reader.

The reasons for children's attraction to Dahl's books can also be found in the author's horrific descriptions of evildoers: the Twits, possibly the most disgusting couple in all of children's books (*The Twits,* 1980); the colossal creatures wreaking havoc in *The BFG;* and Dahl's version of witches, who appear to be ordinary people until they reveal their toeless feet, bald pimpled heads, teeth stained by blue saliva, and hideously long claws (all hidden by high-heeled shoes, wigs, closed-lip smiles, and gloves) are just a few of his fanciful freaks whose attempts to rid the world of goodness are repeatedly denounced and foiled. His heroes, in turn, are generally bright, patient, selfless children who are suffocating under the misguided protection of delinquent caregivers or burdened by some other penalty such as poverty, dyslexia, or shyness. By heroic effort, and sometimes some assistance from a sympathetic adult figure, they are destined to overcome their difficulties in a miraculous manner and to have plenty of deliciously harrowing escapes along the way. Using a remarkable skill with words, Dahl combines likable children, nasty villains, plenty of action, a large dose of nonsense, and deftly constructed plots to create one extraordinary tale after another.

But not all agree that Dahl's work merits praise. Critics, reviewers, teachers, and parents the world over have looked at the events of Dahl's early life and labeled them the cause of the black, violent side found in nearly all his books; but, whatever the cause, this blackness is most certainly present with a vengeance. Characterized by racial stereotyping; violent, gruesome deaths; negative portraits of parents, teachers, and other adults; extreme depictions of right and wrong; and crude and vulgar language, the books certainly provide ample material for his detractors. Dahl's *Charlie and the Chocolate Factory*, one of the most popular children's books of all time, also ranks among the most controversial. The story of a young, impoverished boy whose selflessness and luck eventually wins him the coveted Willy Wonka Chocolate Factory, *Charlie* earned for its author a cult following among child readers as well as critical condemnation for the book's racist overtones, age discrimination, and excessive violence. Leading the crusade has been ELEANOR CAMERON, a well-known author of fantasy for children and a respected critic. In her 1972 essay "McLuhan, Youth and Literature," Cameron lashed out against *Charlie and the Chocolate Factory*, calling it "one of the most tasteless books ever written for children." Cameron's remarks drew a flurry of outrage and united Dahl's fans, young and old, in a war of words. Most of his books, in turn, came under similar attack, but they did not remain undefended in the realm of professional critics. Dahl has been called a literary genius; his books have been considered modern fairy tales. But whether or not adults approve of them Dahl's fiction has found a devoted readership in children, and despite his significant contribution to adult literature (*Kiss Kiss, Switch Bitch*) and screenwriting (*You Only Live Twice, Chitty Chitty Bang Bang*), his name will be forever associated with the peaches, chocolate, and Big Friendly Giants of the children's book world that he changed forever. ❧ CHRISTINE C. BEHR

DALGLIESH, ALICE

AMERICAN AUTHOR, 1893–1979. Alice Dalgliesh contributed to the field of children's books as both author and editor.

The daughter of an English mother and Scottish father, Dalgliesh was born and raised in Trinidad and began writing at age six. Her teenage years were spent in England, where she attended school and published stories in the children's pages of a popular magazine. Dalgliesh later moved to New York City, attended Pratt Institute, and received a bachelor's degree in education from Columbia University Teachers College and a master's degree in English from Columbia. For seventeen years, Dalgliesh taught kindergarten and elementary school, as well as courses in children's literature at Teachers College.

Her early picture books reflect her teaching background by encouraging reader involvement. *The Little Wooden Farmer, and the Story of the Jungle Pool* (1930) consists of two tales that children can play along with, using toy animals to follow the stories' action. *The Choosing Book* (1932) allows readers to decide which house, toys, and pets a family should purchase. Dalgliesh began writing for somewhat older children with *The Blue Teapot: Sandy Cove Stories* (1931), a pleasant, old-fashioned book about youngsters living in a Nova Scotia community. *Relief's Rocker* (1932) and *Roundabout* (1934) also take place in Sandy Cove and feature some of the same characters.

When Dalgliesh became editor of books for young readers at Scribner's in 1934, she began publishing the works of GENEVIEVE STUMP FOSTER, MARCIA BROWN, Katherine Milhous, and many others, but also continued her own writing career, which included well-received nonfiction such as *Ride the Wind* (1956), a story about Charles Lindbergh, and *The Thanksgiving Story* (1954), which was a Caldecott Honor Book for illustrator HELEN SEWELL.

Dalgliesh's most memorable fiction was often based on historical incidents and written for an early grade school audience. *The Bears on Hemlock Mountain* (1952) is derived from a Pennsylvania tall tale about a young boy who encounters bears while delivering a large iron pot to his mother. With its rhythmic, repetitive prose, the book is excellent for reading aloud, as is *The Courage of Sarah Noble* (1954), the fact-based story of an early-eighteenth-century Connecticut girl who lives with an Indian family while her father is away from home. Both titles were Newbery Honor Books, although the latter book never quite reaches a dramatic climax and includes some rather patronizing attitudes about American Indians. A third Newbery Honor Book, *The Silver Pencil* (1944), an autobiographical novel for older readers, follows Janet Laidlaw from her childhood in Trinidad to her teaching and writing careers in the United States. A sequel, *Along Janet's Road* (1945), deals with the life of a children's book editor and lacks the panoramic vista of place and time that makes the first book so appealing. Nevertheless, anyone deeply interested in children's books will be fascinated by its portrait of publishing and will enjoy guessing the true identities of some of the characters. The book represents a merging of Dalgliesh's two worlds—publishing and writing.

As an author, she is best remembered for her pleasantly appealing stories. Although some may now seem dated and precious in tone, her best books—such as

The Silver Pencil and *The Bears on Hemlock Mountain*—remain fresh and enjoyable for today's readers. ❧ P.D.S.

Danziger, Paula

American author, b. 1944. As a teenager, Paula Danziger read *The Catcher in the Rye* repeatedly because it reassured her that she "wasn't alone." As an adult, her best-selling young adult novels have engendered that response in junior high age readers since the publication of the popular *The Cat Ate My Gymsuit* (1974). Several years as a junior high school English teacher, along with a vivid recall of her own painful adolescence, helped Danziger to forge this successful connection with her audience. Her largely first-person, female cast of narrators fight for their rights within their less-than-perfect families and schools, while simultaneously suffering the typically teenage blights of acne and awkwardly emerging sexuality. Through it all, they keep intact a sharp, occasionally pun-laden, sense of humor.

The therapeutic role literature played in her own life fostered Danziger's commitment to write about difficult situations her young readers commonly face. Her books don't shy away from ugly emotions, such as the anger Phoebe harbors for her materialistic mother in *The Divorce Express* (1982) or Cassie's comic but real fear that her dictatorial homeroom teacher will make her remove her sunglasses, exposing her overly tweezed eyebrows in *The Pistachio Prescription* (1978). Along with her best-selling status, Danziger has received numerous regional awards as well as two Parents' Choice Awards for Literature. Some critics, however, have faulted her for offering teens easily digestible clichés about themselves. Thirteen-year-old Marcy Lewis in *The Cat Ate My Gymsuit,* Danziger's self-proclaimed autobiographical novel, provides a counter to this criticism when she points out that "middle-class kids have problems too." Most of Danziger's heroines' problems stem from adults more concerned with exercising authority than with listening, although one or two sympathetic teachers or parents usually surface in each book to act as mentors, encouraging young people not to conform but to stand up for themselves. Danziger herself found such a mentor in the poet John Ciardi, who nurtured her appreciation for literature and gave her the courage to believe she could actually become a writer.

Not only issues of self-esteem but political concerns such as women's rights, the rights of young people, education reform, and environmentalism thread their way through Danziger's stories. She takes a traditionally liberal stance, mobilizing her teenage characters to work together within the system for change. Though sticking to the same types of main characters and issues, her writing has evolved over the years: her perspective has become less black and white and her humor less angry. *Everyone Else's Parents Said Yes* (1989) marks a switch to third-person narration and a male protagonist—eleven-year-old Matthew, also featured in succeeding books. But as with all of Danziger's stories, the Matthew books exist firmly within the often tumultuous realm of the everyday. ❧ C.M.H.

Daugherty, James

American illustrator and author, 1889–1974. James Daugherty is primarily remembered for his inspired expression of the American spirit in both visual and literary form, a spirit characterized by appreciation for the heroes of democracy and the affirmation of Manifest Destiny. Daugherty has confessed that his first reading of Walt Whitman, when he was a young art student in England, was life-changing for him: "I took fire from his vision of America." This fire inspired murals in public places and, later, book illustrations with swirling lines, energetic rhythm, humor, and a compassionate view of humanity. Whitman's inspiration also found

Illustration by James Daugherty from his book *Andy and the Lion* (1938).

expression in Daugherty's carefully composed dedicatory pages, his popular Random House/Landmark volumes, and lively biographical accounts of American heroes. His biographies include the winner of the 1940 Newbery Award, *Daniel Boone* (1939), *Poor Richard,* about Benjamin Franklin (1941), *Abraham Lincoln* (1943), and *Of Courage Undaunted,* about Lewis and Clark (1951). Some readers of *Daniel Boone* have commented on what they perceived as offhand treatment of American Indians and African Americans; in fact, the historical times were accurately reflected.

Daugherty began to create art for young people in the mid-twenties when Doubleday's May Massee suggested he illustrate *Daniel Boone, Wilderness Scout* (1926), by Stewart E. White. He subsequently became one of the best-known American illustrators of children's books, illustrating more than forty books by other authors. One of his most felicitous collaborations was with CARL SANDBURG in *Abe Lincoln Grows Up* (1928), which remains an outstanding example of the book as art form, a seamless integration of subject, word, and image. For Daugherty, line and design were foremost and to simplify was "the first of all the commandments." His work was exhibited in many one-man shows and is represented in a number of art collections.

Daugherty's writing career did not begin until after he was well established as an illustrator. He first created text to go with his drawings in *Andy and the Lion* (1938), an original version of the Androcles tale, which was a Caldecott Honor Book. LYND WARD praised it as a model picture book worthy of study by other writer-artists: "The interlocking relationship between the word and picture . . . has been carried several steps farther than I have seen it in any other place."

Nearly twenty years later, Daugherty's illustrations for *Gillespie and the Guards* (1957), written by Benjamin Elkin, was also a Caldecott Honor Book. This story with folktale elements is about a boy who cleverly outwits the King's sharpsighted guards. In the turbulent sixties, Daugherty chose to illustrate his own selections from the writings of Whitman and Thoreau for young people: *Walt Whitman's America* (1964) and *Henry David Thoreau, A Man for Our Time* (1967).

Daugherty's art and texts combined gusto, exuberance, and rich detail—singing, with Whitman, a song of America. In his Newbery acceptance speech in 1940, Daugherty summed up the spirit of his major lifework: "Wit and taste, beauty and joy are as much a necessary part of the democratic heritage as economics and the utilities . . . Children's books are a part of that art of joy and joy in art that is the certain inalienable right of free people." ❧ E.C.H.

D'Aulaire, Edgar Parin
D'Aulaire, Ingri

EDGAR: AMERICAN AUTHOR AND ILLUSTRATOR, 1898–1986; INGRI: AMERICAN AUTHOR AND ILLUSTRATOR, 1904–1980. The D'Aulaires established the picture-book biography for younger children as a valued staple of library-book collections; for nearly fifty years they produced more than twenty books of outstanding craftsmanship. Their favorite subjects were heroes of American history and Norwegian culture. For their biography *Abraham Lincoln* (1939), they won the Caldecott Medal. Both D'Aulaires received early art education and worked with the abstract expressionist Hans Hofmann in Munich. Edgar, who was born in Munich, had illustrated German books, and Ingri Mortenson was a portrait artist. They met in Paris and were married in 1925; immigrating to the United States in 1929, they began to create PICTURE BOOKS together.

The style of their large, colorful, impressionistic illustrations was intended to appeal to a child's eye. The figures have a large paper-doll quality, resembling folk art. To some the illustrations in *George Washington* (1936) appear stiff and lifeless, but the artists' intention was to offer drawings that would remind children of rocking horses and toy soldiers. They included a wealth of authentic detail in their books, and their pictures have the integrity of originals with their unusual depth and richness of color. They employed the lithographic process of early craftsmen, who without cameras had worked carefully by hand. This process required that each picture be completely drawn (with no erasing possible) on a large stone, with separate drawings made for each color. Their detailed illustrations expanded their carefully developed texts. One thousand hours of research in the Louvre, the New York Public Library, and the University of Norway might be compressed into one book. Extended camping and "tramping" trips enabled them to see and feel the prairies for *Abraham Lincoln,* the clear waters of the West Indies for *Columbus* (1955), and the hills of Virginia for *George Washington* and *Pocahontas* (1946). The biographies were inspired by the imaginative heroic tales Edgar had been told by his American mother in Germany, including some about his grandfather, who had enlisted in Lincoln's army. Some critics have seen excessive idealism in the Lincoln pictures; some have criticized the mention of George Washington's slaves, who "kept everything spic and span." Others note that biographies reflect the times in which they were written and provide useful information about the ideals and legends that were valued. In fact,

Illustration by Ingri and Edgar Parin D'Aulaire from their book *D'Aulaires' Trolls* (1972).

the D'Aulaires presented balanced information for young children. Columbus must face disappointment in his failure to find a passage to India, while others succeeded. In *Benjamin Franklin* (1950) a selection of Poor Richard's wise sayings adorns each page, but the reader is told that Franklin was lucky not to be electrocuted during his experiments with lightning.

The D'Aulaires Norse culture books, which include translations of folktales and two bright, oversized books, *Norse Gods and Giants* (1967) and *D'Aulaires' Trolls* (1972), are authenticated in the stories and experiences of Ingri's childhood in Norway. The large, humorous, detailed illustrations complement the subjects. A companion book to *Norse Gods and Giants* is *Ingri and Edgar Parin D'Aulaire's Book of Greek Myths* (1962).

The D'Aulaires, who were once described as "one unity with two heads, four hands, and one handwriting," were presented the Regina Medal in 1970. E.C.H.

Davis, Jenny

American author, b. 1953. In her fine teenage novels, Jenny Davis presents a realistic, often unsettling, view of adult behavior that affects, scars, and ultimately strengthens her young protagonists.

Davis was born in Louisville, Kentucky, but grew up in Pittsburgh. She wrote stories as a child, but did not aspire to become an author. As a teenager in the 1960s, she marched for civil rights, protested the Vietnam War, and rarely attended her dangerous urban school. She developed a greater appreciation for formal education when she began attending a community college; she later received bachelor's and master's degrees from the University of Kentucky. Davis has taught sex education, reading, and writing to grade school students.

In 1987, she published her first book, *Good-bye and Keep Cold*, which details the experiences of Edda Combs, an eastern Kentucky girl whose mother embarks on a prolonged grieving period after Edda's father is killed in a mining accident. Davis did not write the book specifically for a teenage audience, which may account for its unusual perspective. The story focuses on Edda's childhood, but is given a young adult sensibility because her evocative, first-person narrative is a postcollege reminiscence. The plot deals with marital discord, infidelity, venereal disease, and other issues affecting the adults in Edda's life; their behavior, in turn, influences her childhood in devastating ways. The novel is notable for its characterizations, emotional truth, and sensitive prose.

Sex Education (1988) also deals with young people embroiled in the problems of adults. Recovering from a nervous breakdown, sixteen-year-old Livvy relates the story of her intense first love for David Kincaid and how their relationship was destroyed. As part of a school sex-education unit, David and Livvy are assigned to "care about someone." They choose the Parkers, a troubled young neighborhood couple expecting their first child. Tragedy ensues when the teenagers discover that Mr. Parker is abusing his wife. The tautly written novel presents a powerful portrait of domestic violence and is equally believable in its depiction of a high school romance. The small cast of characters is well defined but, except for David's adoptive mother, most of the adults are shown to be cruel, weak, or ineffectual. Livvy displays an ambivalent attitude toward her own parents, who play a relatively minor role in the book. This ambivalence is also at the core of *Checking on the Moon* (1991), the story of thirteen-year-old Cab Jones who, with her older brother, is sent to live with a grandmother she's never met while her mother tours Europe. The author realistically records the love and anger Cab simultaneously feels toward her mother.

Lack of family unity is a consistent theme in Davis's novels. The reader never learns why Edda's family is estranged from her maternal grandparents, why Livvy has a poor relationship with her parents, or why Cab has never before met her grandmother. *Checking on the Moon,* however, provides a sense of resolution and understanding, as Cab comes to love her grandmother, begins to consider the neighbors an extended family, and learns to accept her mother.

Davis has dealt with similar themes in all her books, but there is enough variation to make each title unique. Her well-crafted prose and three-dimensional characterizations make her an exciting voice in young adult literature. § P.D.S.

DAY, ALEXANDRA

AMERICAN ILLUSTRATOR AND AUTHOR, B. 19?. Alexandra Day (the pseudonym for Sandra Darling), the founder, with her husband, of the Green Tiger Press, is best known as the creator of the Carl books, a series about a gentle rottweiler who is the baby sitter of every child's dreams. In the picture books, Carl is given the unlikely task of watching the baby while his master and mistress are away, and each time, with the infant astride his strong back, Carl heads off in search of adventure. Beginning with *Good Dog, Carl* (1985) the books develop variations of the theme, allowing the daring duo to explore a new venue each time, including the park, a daycare center, and a masquerade ball. In *Carl Goes Shopping* (1989), the rottweiler is instructed to mind the baby in a department store lobby while his owner shops. Right on cue, the toddler climbs from her carriage onto the dog's waiting back, and Carl takes his charge in search of all the fun to be found in a department store. As always, they return to their starting point in time for the competent nanny to receive his well-earned praise from his ever-trusting owner: "Good dog, Carl!" Though Carl's outings with the baby are patently impossible, Day's vivid oil paintings portray rottweiler and child realistically, enabling readers to easily suspend their disbelief. The striking art successfully carries the story line in these almost-wordless books, some of which have also been published in Spanish editions and as BOARD BOOKS for preschoolers.

Other books by Day include *The Teddy Bear's Picnic* (1983), based on the Jimmy Kennedy song, which won a special mention at the Bologna Book Fair in 1984 and was an International Reading Association Children's Choice the same year; *Paddy's Pay-Day* (1989), a picture book about an Irish terrier; and *Frank and Ernest* (1988) and *Frank and Ernest Play Ball* (1990), featuring a bear and elephant duo.

Day, a vegetarian and an animal lover, uses her pets as the models for Carl and Paddy. Her realistic paintings and straightforward texts depicting animals trotting about among the human populace and improbably engaging themselves in everyday human activities create stories filled with gentle humor. § J.M.B.

DE ANGELI, MARGUERITE LOFFT

AMERICAN AUTHOR AND ILLUSTRATOR, 1889–1987. Publishing thirty books for children over a fifty-year career, Marguerite De Angeli specialized in HISTORICAL FICTION and accounts of ethnic groups in America. Born in Lapeer, Michigan, De Angeli trained as a singer in Philadelphia, where she spent most of her life. In 1910 she married John De Angeli, and they had six children. An illustrator friend started tutoring her in art, and in 1922 De Angeli's work began appearing in leading magazines; she was also in demand as an illustrator of children's books.

Encouraged by the Doubleday Company, De Angeli combined authorship with her art and produced her first children's book, *Ted and Nina Go to the Grocery Store* (1935). Like many of her books, it was based on her family's experiences. In 1936 *Ted and Nina Have a Happy Rainy Day* appeared. Her interest in the lives of the foreign-born in America led De Angeli to write and illustrate books that became popular teaching tools, used for their accurate portrayals of the customs and folklore of America's ethnic populations. Included among them were *Henner's Lydia* (1936) and *Yonie Wondernose* (1944), Pennsylvania Dutch stories; *Petite Suzanne* (1937), set in French Canada; *Thee Hannah!* (1940), about a Quaker girl; *Elin's Amerika* (1940), about Swedes in colonial Delaware; and *Up the Hill* (1942), set in Pennsylvania, which portrays a Polish family. In 1946 De Angeli broke literary ground with *Bright April,* considered the first modern children's book to deal with a black child's encounter with racial prejudice.

In 1949 De Angeli published *The Door in the Wall,* the story of a crippled boy in thirteenth-century England, which won the Newbery Medal. The book drew attention to the difficulties of handicapped children and further established De Angeli as a meticulous creator of historically based text and illustration. The foreign setting of *The Door in the Wall* was atypical of De Angeli's work, which most often employed American locales. Books with American backgrounds, inspired by experiences of the author's relatives and friends, included *Copper-Toed Boots* (1938), *Turkey for Christmas* (1944),

Fiddlestrings (1974), and *Whistle for the Crossing* (1977). De Angeli's writing was marked by a homespun, sympathetic, and quietly humorous style. She stressed the need to instill a strong work ethic in children, the roles of supportive parents, and the importance of goals. *Copper-Toed Boots,* the story of her father's yearning for boots in pioneer Michigan, is a typical example of these values expressed in prose.

In her artwork, De Angeli employed several media, from oil painting and watercolor to pencil and pen and ink. She favored brilliant color for her carefully researched versions of the folk art, costumes, and settings of the various ethnic groups she portrayed. Some of De Angeli's best art appears in her *Book of Nursery and Mother Goose Rhymes* (1954). Full-page color plates alternate with whimsical pencil sketches and lively action dominates each picture.

De Angeli's autobiography, *Butter at the Old Price* (1971), chronicles her long career as an author-illustrator. Aimed at adults, the autobiography gives a detailed account of children's book publishing from the 1930s through the 1960s, along with De Angeli's experiences in the field. *Friendship and Other Poems* (1981) was her final book, published when she was ninety-two. In both word and picture, De Angeli effectively portrayed the world of the young. Her collective works celebrate the universality of childhood experiences, notwithstanding racial, ethnic, or historical differences. ♠ W.A.

DE BRUNHOFF, JEAN
DE BRUNHOFF, LAURENT

JEAN: FRENCH AUTHOR AND ILLUSTRATOR, 1899–1937; LAURENT: FRENCH AUTHOR AND ILLUSTRATOR, B. 1925. If there is a universal symbol for childhood, Babar the elephant is probably it. Created by Jean de Brunhoff in the 1930s, continued by his son, Laurent, in the following decades, and available now in every manner of merchandise, the character has enthralled generations of children all over the world with his Victorian rectitude and pachyderm panache.

The inspiration for Babar came from Madame de Brunhoff, Jean's wife, who told stories about a little elephant to amuse her young children. Their enthusiasm for the tales encouraged their artist father to shape them into illustrated books, beginning with *The Story of Babar* (1933). Six more Babar books by Jean de Brunhoff followed quickly, including *Babar and His Children* (1938) and *Babar and Father Christmas* (1940), which were published after his death.

The original Babar books were oversized in format, with the text printed in script. Subsequent editions have taken every imaginable shape and form, but the luxuriously large volumes are still the best way to fully appreciate Jean de Brunhoff's mastery of the picture-book form. His books, as MAURICE SENDAK once observed, "have a freedom and charm, a freshness of vision, that captivates and takes the breath away. . . . Between 1931 and 1937, he completed a body of work that forever changed the face of the illustrated book."

The elder de Brunhoff's Babar books were kind-hearted portrayals of family and community life yet, at the same time, unflinchingly direct in their depiction of tragedy. Within the first few pages of *The Story of Babar* the little elephant sees his mother killed by hunters. He cries but does not tarry in his mourning, fearful that he too might be shot. The plot then proceeds briskly, compelling the elephant and perhaps readers as well to go forward and get on with their own lives. Jean de Brunhoff's tuberculosis was diagnosed in the early 1930s, as he was beginning the books. His failing condition and the fact that he created the books with his own children in mind may well have inclined him to present sorrow in as straightforward a manner as possible, artfully offering consolation to his young audience that even the cruelest blows can be survived.

Laurent de Brunhoff was only twelve years old when his father died. He studied art and in 1945 decided that he wanted to continue the series his father had begun. "Babar was a friend to me," he once remembered. "I had lived with him for years. It occurred to me that I could follow a tradition that had been cut off too early." Over the decades, the younger de Brunhoff has written and illustrated dozens of additional Babar stories, creating new characters and often putting the elephant in the service of helping young children sharpen their skills in counting, cooking, color recognition, and the like. His books, though often more pedestrian than inspired, have indeed accomplished what he set out to do: they have kept Babar alive for children who, like Laurent de Brunhoff himself, think of the elephant as part of their family. ♠ A.Q.

DEGEN, BRUCE

AMERICAN AUTHOR AND ILLUSTRATOR, B. 1945. Armed with a sense of joy, an appreciation of silliness, a love of nature, and a passion for children's books, Bruce Degen has illustrated over forty books since 1977. Having first started to draw in elementary school, he later earned a B.F.A. at the Cooper Union and an M.F.A. at Pratt Institute and began a multifaceted artistic career. When he turned to children's book illustration, he chose a variety of manuscripts to illustrate, from POETRY to PICTURE BOOKS, from EASY READERS to NONFICTION. Degen's artwork has received occasional awards, including children's choice awards for *Little Chick's Big Day* (1981), *Jamberry* (1983), and *The Forgetful Bears Meet Mr. Memory* (1987), and a Boston Globe–Horn Book honor for *The Magic School Bus at the Waterworks* (1986). However, this artist's work has contributed most to children's literature not by drawing attention to itself but by providing strong accompaniment to the texts.

Degen generally illustrates using pencil or ink line with watercolor, but his pencil work is also strong. His artwork in JANE YOLEN's "Commander Toad" series and CLYDE ROBERT BULLA's *Dandelion Hill* (1982), for instance, displays a sinuous, almost voluptuous line and a decorative sense of design. Many of Degen's pages employ creative borders, and his illustrations can be strongly narrative. They are nearly always delightfully full, if occasionally overfull, of details extending the text. Degen's cartoon-style people tend to be stiff, but this style perfectly suits the successful "Magic School Bus" series. Usually, his main characters are animals, and bears are featured in some of his best work, such as those who prance at the nonsense verse in *Jamberry* and to the joyous rhymes in Nancy White Carlstrom's "Jesse Bear" series. Although all the bears resemble each other, Degen provides individual and endearing characteristics through facial expressions, posture, and attire. Visual gags that go beyond the literal text commonly appear in Degen's books. In the "Commander Toad" series, a takeoff on space quests like *Star Wars,* a humanoid toad and his frog crew eat "hop-corn" and drink green tea. In his strongest self-authored book, *Jamberry,* Degen depicts a boy wallowing blissfully in a train-car loaded with berries—"boys-in-berries." For that matter, the main character is a bear, an animal that not only eats berries, but whose name is a shortened aural version of *berry.* Degen's appealing treatment makes these jokes fresh and funny.

Collaborating with JOANNA COLE on the "Magic School Bus" series, Degen epitomized visual silliness. The straightfaced teacher, Ms. Frizzle, wears outlandishly thematic clothes, such as a dress printed with frogs eating flies and coordinating shoes decorated with Venus's-flytraps. The children's usual grade-school antics accompany "The Friz's" unusual teaching methods, as they travel by bus through the earth or through a child's circulatory system. The crowded pages are absorbing as they display action, text, bubble-dialogue, and school reports. The result is an endlessly entertaining set of books with a wide and loyal readership—a remarkable achievement for a science series. No doubt these books, like many of Degen's efforts, will retain their child appeal perennially. S.S.

DeJong, Meindert

AMERICAN AUTHOR, 1906–1991. In 1962 Meindert DeJong became the first American to receive the prestigious HANS CHRISTIAN ANDERSEN Medal. This international prize seemed a particularly fitting award for a European-born author who grew up in the United States and whose literary works were influenced by both his native and adopted cultures.

Born in Wierum, the Netherlands, DeJong and his family immigrated to Grand Rapids, Michigan, when he was eight years old. Educated at private Calvinist schools, Meindert and his brother David began writing while attending Calvin College. Both brothers would eventually become successful authors but had little early success. Meindert worked as a mason, tinner, sexton, and gravedigger; he taught briefly at a small Iowa college, but he hated teaching and soon turned to poultry farming. A children's librarian suggested he write a story about farm life, and *The Big Goose and the Little White Duck* was published in 1938. During his early years as a children's author, DeJong wrote animal stories, as well as several novels set in Holland. These well-received books were distinguished for their keen understanding of both animals and children.

Beginning with *The Tower by the Sea* in 1950, DeJong produced a remarkably sustained run of brilliant books that secured his reputation as an author. For DeJong, the decade was truly golden, as *The Wheel on the School* won the Newbery Medal in 1955, and four other novels were named Newbery Honor Books during the 1950s. *The Wheel on the School* is a delightful and involving story of six schoolchildren trying to lure storks to Shora, their Dutch village. There is a growing sense of community in the novel, as fellow villagers become increasingly involved in the initiative. DeJong controls suspense so masterfully that by the book's conclusion the reader is vitally concerned about the arrival of the storks. MAURICE SENDAK's excellent illustrations add great appeal to this and many other DeJong novels. The author reaped Newbery honors for two separate 1953 titles, both of which rank among his finest. *Hurry Home, Candy* is a heart-rending and unflinching novel about a stray dog who wanders alone for a year. *Shadrach* concerns

Davie's first pet, a black rabbit, and is written in the sensitive, almost breathless prose style for which DeJong is known. Other Newbery Honor Books were *Along Came a Dog* (1958), which, like several of the author's animal stories, contains no child characters, and *The House of Sixty Fathers* (1956), the story of Tien Pao's search for his family during the Japanese occupation of China. DeJong was stationed in China as a U.S. Army sergeant during World War II, and the book, considered among his best, was based on his friendship with a young Chinese boy. During the 1960s, DeJong published two strong novels about Holland, *Far Out the Long Canal* (1964) and *The Journey from Peppermint Street*, which in 1969 won the first National Book Award for children's literature.

DeJong's last books were criticized for their sentimentality, and the childless widower retired from writing in the early 1970s. Perhaps because his novels are often lengthy and leisurely paced, DeJong's work is no longer very popular. Nevertheless, the books are alive with the author's unparalleled ability to write with great empathy about children and animals. Intensity of style and integrity of stories mark the DeJong canon. ❦ P.D.S.

DE LA MARE, WALTER

ENGLISH POET, ANTHOLOGIST, STORYTELLER, WRITER, 1873–1956. Walter de la Mare was the most distinguished lyric poet writing for children in the first half of the twentieth century. His fresh original voice, noted for its astute perception and subtle imaginative vision, was elegantly balanced by his mastery of language and of the many melodies of rhythmic pattern. De la Mare's apparent indifference to "writing for the market" kept his work from period limitation, and thus it has maintained a place in the canon of children's literature. The ethereal loveliness of "Silver" in *Peacock Pie* (1913) still finds delighted listeners.

Jacket illustration by Walter Chappell for *Come Hither* (1957), by Walter de la Mare.

While poetry for both children and adults was his most natural channel of expression, de la Mare was also a master of prose. He produced retellings of traditional tales and Bible stories, original stories with folkloric elements, anthologies with remarkable prefaces and notes, a play, one long fantasy, criticism, collections of essays, and award-winning novels. De la Mare maintained the same high standard of artistic integrity whether writing for children or adults; he lived by his own dictum: "Only the rarest kind of best in anything can be good enough for the young."

Childhood was a primary topic for de la Mare, but never one for fond sentiment. Children as well as adults were to be considered authentic individuals. "The acorn is the oak . . . in mind and spirit we are most of us born . . . the age at which for the rest of our lives we are likely to remain." He observed his own four children, but more importantly, he retrieved many of his own childhood memories, dreams, and fantasies. He often fused the imaginative and the commonplace in his poems, effecting a haunting eeriness. There are glimpses of phantom children, spellbinding dreams, or dilemmas such as that of poor Jim Jay who "got stuck fast in yesterday"; there are unanswered questions posed in "Someone" or "The Little Green Orchard."

The masterpiece of anthologies is *Come Hither* (1923). An illuminating, allegorical preface introduces a collection of more than 483 poems by 260 poets, covering approximately 600 years of literature in English; the poems are accompanied by 300 pages of fascinating notes that disclose the wisdom, humanity, and scholarship of its editor. *The Three Royal Monkeys* (formerly *The Three Mulla Mulgars*, 1919) is a fantasy adventure story about the loyal and intrepid Nod Nizzaneela Ummanodda, his brothers, and the wonderstone. Inventive language, a fully realized secondary fantasy world, well-crafted suspense, and numinous poetic vision combine to create an enthralling experience. Many children today find it difficult reading, but when it is read aloud by an appreciative reader, entire classrooms may be brought under its spell.

Walter de la Mare received the Carnegie Medal of the Library Association for *Collected Stories for Children* (1947). The British Crown made him a Companion of Honor in 1948 and awarded him the Order of Merit in 1953. In a rare tribute by *The Horn Book Magazine*, the June 1957 issue was devoted to an appreciation of the art of Walter de la Mare. ❦ E.C.H.

Delessert, Etienne

Swiss-born American illustrator and author, b. 1941. Embarking on a career in graphic arts while still a teenager in Lausanne, Etienne Delessert was twenty-one and living in Paris when he published his first book, *Kafka contre l'absurde* (1962) by Joël Jakubec. Wanting a chance to break into children's literature, in 1965 he moved to the United States, where illustrator Tomi Ungerer introduced him to various publishers. Delessert found one that would allow him great freedom and published his first children's book, a Noah's ark story entitled *The Endless Party* (1967), which he wrote with Eleonore Schmid and illustrated. His suggestion that the publisher approach French-Romanian playwright Eugène Ionesco to write a children's story resulted in a collaboration that produced *Story Number 1 for Children Under Three Years of Age* (1968) and *Story Number 2 for Children Under Three Years of Age* (1970). The volumes were critically acclaimed, but some people felt that Delessert's books were beyond a child's understand-ing: too sophisticated, too avant-garde. Never one to shrink from a challenge, the artist asked famed child psychologist Jean Piaget his opinion. This led to a book about children's views on nature, written and illustrated by Delessert with a foreword by Piaget: *How the Mouse Was Hit on the Head by a Stone and So Discovered the World* (1971).

Delessert moved back to Europe in 1972, established a film studio specializing in animation, creating several segments for "Sesame Street," and launched a publishing house that produced award-winning children's books. Returning to the United States, he settled in Connecticut in 1985 with his wife, Rita Marshall, a gifted art director credited with the design of Delessert's recent books. She is also the author of *I Hate to Read!* (1992), the story of reluctant reader Victor Dickens, who is lured into the world of literature by a variety of Delessert's fantastic and playful characters.

While Delessert is something of a hero to those working in children's literature and editorial illustration on both sides of the Atlantic, his name is not familiar to the average reader in North America, perhaps because of the avant-garde nature of his work. With more than fifty volumes to his credit, he has a distinctive style that features highly detailed illustrations sometimes bordering on the surreal, often involving animal-like characters of his own creation. Working in pencil and watercolor, Delessert uses rounded lines rather than angular ones, which soften his images and make them nonthreatening without sacrificing the sense of disquiet present in much of his work. His illustrations reflect the workings of the human mind and often represent opposing forces. *Ashes, Ashes* (1990), for example, deals with life's fragility and the strength we can find to deal with it. Delessert's illustrations in *Flowers for Algernon* (1988), startling in their depth and honesty, are a perfect complement to Daniel Keyes's poignant text about a mentally retarded man who gains wisdom only to lose it again. Three of these illustrations echo Delessert's more personal artwork, some of which was included in an extensive retrospective exhibit that toured Europe and North America from 1991 to 1994. It was the artist's second retrospective; the first was held at the Louvre when he was thirty-four. ❧ B.G.

Delton, Judy

American author, b. 1931. Judy Delton's good-humored approach to life is revealed in stories about very real and ordinary children engaged in deciphering the often mysterious adult world around them. A master at creating short, amusing episodes, Delton was born in St. Paul, Minnesota, was educated at the College of Saint Catherine, and taught in the city's parochial schools. She did not begin writing until 1971, when she needed to support her four children. She has since published countless articles, stories, and over fifty books.

Her first book for children, *Two Good Friends* (1974), was a Junior Literary Guild selection and an ALA Notable Book. *Kitty in the Middle* (1979), the first of three books about a young girl growing up in the forties, was called "an Irish Catholic answer to Cleary's Ramona." Delton says that the idea for the "Kitty" books came from her own childhood: "I remember vividly not being able to find 'do' in music class and hiding in the bathroom, and being so homesick in the country that my parents had to come and get me. I can't 'make things up,' and when I exhaust my own experiences, I borrow from the lives of my friends and relatives." *Backyard Angel* (1983) began a series that reminds readers of Eleanor Estes's fine work. Delton recalls, "When I began the 'Angel' series, the only thing I had in mind was a picture of my own daughter sitting on our back steps pouting. I put her there (in the story) and things began to happen. She went from being my own daughter to being Angel, a person of her own." Both the "Angel" and "Kitty" books were written for middle-grade readers. In her next books, Delton began to write for even younger children. *Cookies and Crutches* (1988) was the first book in the "PeeWee Scouts" series, all illustrated by Alan Tiegreen. This very popular series became the object of a lawsuit brought by the Girl Scouts and Boy Scouts of America for trademark infringement, but a federal judge in New York dismissed the complaints.

Along with writing, Delton lectures at colleges, workshops, and seminars. She taught writing for publication for five years in Minnesota colleges and was given an Outstanding Teacher Award in 1977. Delton's classes are intended to be inspirational and motivational, and she is especially pleased that many of her students are now publishing books, as are her daughters, Jina and Julie. § P.H.

Denton, Kady MacDonald

CANADIAN AUTHOR AND ILLUSTRATOR, B. 1942. Kady MacDonald Denton is a sentimental picture-book artist, not in the pejorative sense of mawkish, but in the older sense of being steeped in emotion. In each of her pictures, whether illustrating her own texts or those of other writers, she captures the essential feeling of the moment—the anarchistic pleasures of jumping on the bed in *Dorothy's Dream* (1989), the excited expectation of waiting for Granny to arrive in *Granny Is a Darling* (1988), the moment of reining in a fantasy run amuck in *Janet's Horses* (1990). She invariably chooses to illustrate the one delicate gesture that speaks volumes: the cat dancing on her glockenspiel at the end of *The Travelling Musicians* (1991); a couple walking with arms interlocked through the deep snow accompanying the poem "December" in the anthology *Til All the Stars Have Fallen* (1989); little Jackie, nose to bill with his pet duck in *The Story of Little Quack* (1990).

Denton's success comes from the simultaneous sensibilities of adult and child. She is a formally trained artist with a keen interest in art history. And she is a parent. Like many picture-book creators, her interest in the genre was first sparked by her own children. The "Ned" books, a set of early readers, arose from her need to find beginning readers for her daughter. But she traces her influences to the remembered pictures from childhood books—by GARTH WILLIAMS and JEAN DE BRUNHOFF—and says of her writing and painting, "I think of how it was for me as a child, not as it is now for me as a parent."

Denton illustrates traditional material, Bible stories, poetry, folktales, and stories of the domestic lives of young children—the loss of a pet, fear of the dark, imaginary friends. Her watercolor technique has a formal, traditional look. She also chooses settings that are timeless. Her children do not wear logos on their shirts. She leaves the reader and the viewer plenty of room to develop their own interpretations.

Nowhere does this spaciousness work more effectively than in her portrayal of make-believe and dreams. In *Dorothy's Dream,* for example, her illustration to the text "Down in her covers, deep in her bed, she had cold, sour dreams" shows a gray-toned, lunarlike landscape littered with objects that are frustratingly, terrifyingly semirecognizable, the stuff of childhood nightmare. It is at her most abstract that Denton is most innovative. She takes make-believe as seriously as she takes everything else intrinsic to childhood. Her child readers recognize this authenticity. § S.E.

dePaola, Tomie

AMERICAN ILLUSTRATOR AND AUTHOR, B. 1934. Tomie dePaola is one of the country's most popular illustrators for children, who greatly enjoy his recognizable characters and clean, stylized art form and respond to the energy and empathy expressed in both his ink and watercolor art and in his lively storytelling.

Thomas Anthony dePaola was born in Meriden, Connecticut, into a mixed Irish and Italian family. His artistic talent developed early, encouraging him to pursue a bachelor's degree in art education at Pratt Institute in Brooklyn and a master's degree at California College of Arts and Crafts in Oakland. During his years in graduate school, he worked as a stage set designer and muralist, painting murals for a number of New England churches. This experience is reflected in the architectural and friezelike qualities of many of his books.

Tomie dePaola has written more than 180 books since his first publication in 1965. He has drawn on his Italian and Irish backgrounds for many folktales and for his series of autobiographical stories. His best-known book, *Strega Nona* (1975), is a retelling of the folktale of a magic pot that stops boiling only with the proper magic spell. In his version the pot spews pasta all over an Italian village square when Big Anthony fails to master Strega Nona's magic. DePaola has always been completely at ease with folktales, whether it is *Fin M'Coul: The Giant of Knockmany Hill* (1981) from Ireland, *The Legend of the Bluebonnet* (1983) from the Comanche of Texas, or his many Italian stories.

He has written several autobiographical stories in which he shares childhood experiences that are sometimes amusing, as in *Watch Out for the Chicken Feet in Your Soup* (1974), but more often deeply personal and serious, as in *Nana Upstairs and Nana Downstairs*

Voices of the Creators

Tomie dePaola

When I was a student at Pratt in the 1950s studying illustration, I remember a fellow student asking one of our instructors, "When do we learn about style?" "We won't learn about style," he replied. "Style happens naturally. If you keep on working, eventually the way you can and want to express yourself will surface. Meanwhile, do the assignments, listen to the critiques, don't miss your drawing classes, painting classes, design classes and, by all means, look at everything. Go to the galleries and the museums. Your own style will surface." Another instructor, the wonderful Richard Lindner, told us, "Observe. Observe everything around you. Observe what *you* are interested in. Observe what kind of objects you surround yourself with. That will give you the clue to your *own* vision." During the summer of 1955, I was studying at Skowhegan School of Painting and Sculpture in Maine. I was fortunate enough to work with Ben Shahn, who was an idol of mine. The wise words from this great man were similar. Style evolves. He also spoke to me at length about "the shape of content." It was Shahn's thought that "a point of view conditions the paint surface which the artist creates."

So, being a "good student," I listened to my mentors. I noticed how my devotion changed from Jon Whitcomb, who did "pretty girl" illustrations, to Shahn, Picasso, Bonnard, and Rouault. How the "candy box" religious art from my Catholic boyhood was replaced by Cimabue, Fra Angelico, Giotto, and Botticelli and all those unknown sculptors and fresco painters of the Romanesque period. How over the years my love of folk art from all cultures became and still is close to obsessive.

All these things added up and my style began to emerge. And it hasn't really changed in over thirty-five years. The roots are there in my early drawings and paintings—things done way before I began illustrating books. There are white birds, pink tiled roofs, arched doors and windows. My early love of line and strong design and stylization has grown and been refined over the years, but the seeds are all there in the early work.

My work is recognizable. I've chosen to follow my own vision rather than switch around and try what is fashionable or "au courant." It thrills and pleases me when teachers, parents, and librarians tell me that young children know when they are looking at one of my books or a piece of my art. My style is purely an outward expression of my own inner vision, further determined in its nuances by the content of the piece being visualized.

At Pratt Institute, students were also exposed to a myriad of technical skills—representational drawing, rendering, perspective, stylized drawing, use of nonrepresentational color, various painting techniques—and of mediums. Success was measured by how well one could use the various techniques and skills when called upon. But, finally in junior and senior year, favorite mediums and favorite ways of applying them became very individual and personal. Even to this day, I can do a photographic rendering if I have to. (I'd rather give up popcorn or use a camera.) Those skills and techniques are just that — methods to be called upon when needed. My preference is for strong line and design, using the medium and technique appropriate to the piece.

I personally use one of several techniques for my work. The first is very straightforward—a dark brown line with the color applied within the line. For this, I use Rotring Artists Colors, which is a liquid transparent acrylic paint. I use it because it is colorfast and permanent and totally intermixable. It reduces with water and is waterproof when dry, so I can build up thin "skins" of color. *The Art Lesson* was done in this technique.

The second technique is more painterly. I use acrylic paints opaquely. I lay down a base color, usually a golden shade. Next, I do a line drawing, again with a dark brown line. Then, I begin painting, building up layer after layer. *Bonjour, Mr. Satie* is a good example of this technique.

The third technique I employ is a combination of the two—both transparent and opaque, with the occasional use of colored pencils as well. I used this technique in *Hark!*

Unfortunately, technique can mask bad composition and bad drawing. Flashy, rendered photographic art can overwhelm the untrained eye so that mediocre expression gets undeserved attention. The personal expression that style hinges on is just that—personal. And after thirty years illustrating books, I'd need several volumes to pass on all that I think about when I create my books.

Illustration by Tomie dePaola from his book *Tomie dePaola's Mother Goose* (1985).

(1973). The poignancy of these books is also present in his series of religious stories. *The Clown of God* (1978) and *Francis, the Poor Man of Assisi* (1990) have formal compositions and serious-faced characters reminiscent of medieval Italian church paintings.

DePaola began a series of anthologies in 1985 with *Tomie dePaola's Mother Goose*, an exuberant, brightly illustrated book that has become one of the standards of the genre. It was followed by collections of nursery tales, poems, Bible stories, and Christmas carols. In addition to his own books, he has illustrated many works by other writers, most notably Tony Johnston (*The Quilt Story*, 1985) and Jean Fritz (*Shh! We're Writing the Constitution*, 1987). Recently, he broke out of his simple picture-book mold with *Bonjour, Mr. Satie* (1991), a spoof of Gertrude Stein's literary salon. It received mixed reviews, and its visual jokes appealed mainly to DePaola's adult audience.

DePaola has garnered many awards from children's literature professionals during his career: He received a Caldecott Honor Award in 1976 for *Strega Nona*, the Kerlan Award of the University of Minnesota in 1981, the Regina Medal by the Catholic Library Association in 1983, and, in 1990, he was the United States nominee for the Hans Christian Andersen Award for illustration.

Tomie dePaola's popularity and volume of work assure him prominence in the world of children's books. The variety, wit, and child appeal of his books should make a lasting contribution to the field. ♠ J.S.

DE REGNIERS, BEATRICE SCHENK

AMERICAN AUTHOR, POET, AND EDITOR, B. 1914. A prolific writer of PICTURE BOOKS, Beatrice Schenk de Regniers continually celebrates the playful, the serendipitous, and the fanciful in her work. As a child growing up in a college town, Crawfordsville, Indiana, she imagined for years that she was the special friend of the town's best-known literary personage, Lew Wallace, the author of *Ben-Hur*. Later she discovered that he had died before she was born, but somehow that didn't unhinge her in the least. The town was steeped in literary tradition, and she reveled in its creative atmosphere.

While a student at the University of Chicago, she decided she wanted to go into the theater, but her father encouraged more practical work—this was during the Great Depression—so she studied social work, none too happily, and worked at a settlement house. She also danced in a small professional group, however, and although that career never took hold, its disciplines did. "It's no accident, I think," she once wrote, "that when I write books I think in terms of choreography. That is, the story and pictures must have a pace and pattern." In time she married, moved to New York City, and juggled two very successful careers: writer and editor. She was the founding editor of *Scholastic*'s Lucky Book Club in 1961 and retired from the position twenty years later.

Her many books include *May I Bring a Friend?* (1972), for which illustrator BENI MONTRESOR won a Caldecott Medal. The story in verse of a welcoming king and queen who encourage a young guest to bring a surprising menagerie of friends over to the palace, it is an amiable and bouncy tale, with not a word out of place. Montresor's illustrations—some in black-and-white, others in color—are silly and elegant at the same time, delightfully appropriate complements to the playful text.

De Regniers is particularly expert at retelling classic tales with simple verse that beginning readers can enjoy all by themselves. *Little Red Riding Hood* (1972) is traditionally told, but with just a touch of the smart-alecky added. For example, when Grandma is released from the wolf's belly she chides her savior: "What took you so long?/I almost died/in there." EDWARD GOREY's illustrations are largely conventional, breaking out only now and again with his trademark macabre touches. His portrayal of the wolf bounding into Grandma's house, with his eager red tongue wagging, is both hilarious and revolting.

Jack and the Beanstalk (1985), illustrated by Anne Wilsdorf, tells the familiar tale using refrains, an easy vocabulary, and short phrases. Confident and very satisfying, it's clearly the work of a writer who, like Jack, is "Bold as brass / Sharp as tack."

In one of her first books, *A Little House of Your Own* (1954), de Regniers considers the pleasures of finding a special place all your own. That book, one of her personal favorites, exemplifies the characteristics that make her work so distinctive and so pleasing: crisp, uncluttered words speaking for a joyful heart. A.Q.

Design and Typography

Most readers express surprise when told that all books, including those for children, are designed. While perhaps dismaying to the practitioner of the craft, this response is really quite understandable. For, ironically, book design and typography are at their most successful when not immediately apparent to the reader. It can even be said that book design is a kind of "invisible" art.

In her book *The Crystal Goblet* (1956), British typographer Beatrice Warde likened good bookmaking to a crystal goblet of wine: "Everything about it is calculated to *reveal* rather than to hide the beautiful thing it was meant to *contain*." As she further points out in her metaphor, to pour wine into a solid goblet would be to disguise the drink—one would appreciate the vessel itself perhaps, but that is all. And so it is with good bookmaking—good design provides the form or framework within which words and images can shine through. The child who reads to herself or the adult who reads to her surely senses the feeling of delight—of appropriateness—that the fully realized book can bring. Each book—whether picture book, poetry, fiction, or nonfiction—has a personality as distinct as the individual who will read it or appreciate its illustrations. It is the special job of the designer to assemble the many diverse elements which make up a book and bring them together into a whole that is much more than the sum of its parts. It is the author who provides the words, but it is the designer, along with the illustrator, who must give the text a visual shape while remaining true to the spirit of the author's message.

The designer first encounters a book accepted for publication in the form of typewritten pages, handed over by an editor who has been working with the author to bring it to this stage. Much transpires at this initial "meeting" with the manuscript. While the designer reads the text carefully, many thoughts begin to surface as he or she tries to visualize the physical properties of the future book. Most designers are prepared for this moment by their training in several fields of the graphic arts. A children's book designer must have a thorough, working knowledge of illustration and photography, graphic design, typography, printing, paper, and binding techniques. It is also most important for anyone involved with bookmaking to love to read and to be excited by the prospect of bringing the elements of a new book together, a process which can take anywhere from six months to two years to complete. It is not unusual to work simultaneously on as many as fifty projects in various stages of completion. An ability to see the larger picture, while focusing on a myriad of details, is important.

In a true picture book, there should be a seamless mesh of words and images—one could not exist without the support of the other. Picture books are like little plays, and the illustrator must bring the characters to life, moving them across the thirty-two pages most commonly allotted the form, to tell a story which reflects and extends the author's words. Some authors are also illustrators, but if the author has provided just the words, the designer and editor look for an artist who can successfully visualize and execute the text.

Once the illustrator is chosen, the designer suggests a shape or trim size for the book. Here form most surely follows content—a book on a snake, for instance, begs to be long and horizontal to accommodate the special shape of that animal. A book for a very young child lends itself to a small trim size, perfect for tiny hands to hold. After a general trim size is agreed on, the designer, in consultation with the production manager, confirms that this is a size that fits well on the large sheets of paper, printing press, and binding machinery that are necessary to produce the book in multiple editions for publishing.

With the trim size and page count confirmed and with manuscript in hand, the illustrator can now begin work on the dummy, or rough-sketch version of the book. The illustrator considers not only which images to create, but how to break up the text and pace the story to create drama and interest. With the help of the designer, the illustrator decides which images to make large and which to make small, providing variety and tension on the page.

Frequently, at this stage, it is necessary to have the

Century Expanded
ABCDEFGHIJKLMNOPQRSTUVWXYZ
abcdefghijklmnopqrstuvwxyz
1234567890

Minion
ABCDEFGHIJKLMNOPQRSTUVWXYZ
abcdefghijklmnopqrstuvwxyz
1234567890

Palatino
ABCDEFGHIJKLMNOPQRSTUVWXYZ
abcdefghijklmnopqrstuvwxyz
1234567890

Helvetica
ABCDEFGHIJKLMNOPQRSTUVWXYZ
abcdefghijklmnopqrstuvwxyz
1234567890

A selection of text typefaces—including Minion, the font used in setting this book—available both on computer and from traditional composition houses.

words set into type galleys, to plan out how much actual space will be available for the illustrations. The selection of a typeface is another of the key decisions a designer must make, whether the book is an illustrated one or not. There are many typefaces from which to choose, and the widespread use today of the computer for typesetting has further expanded the number of types available to the designer. The challenge is to find the appropriate one for the book at hand. As with all other decisions in the design process, the clues to selecting the right typeface lie within the manuscript itself. A careful reading will yield a strong suggestion of the "feel" of the story. The designer then pores over type specimen books, searching for the style of type that fits the concept of the book in hand. Classic or modern, heavy or light, condensed or expanded—the choice can seem daunting at times. In selecting a typeface, however, there are rules and models to follow.

Legibility is the most important consideration. In keeping with the *Crystal Goblet* theory, the designer is trying to create a sense of order and clarity, making it easy for the reader to enter the world of the author. A designer, through study and experience, learns which faces look best in the larger sizes common to children's books and how certain type designs give a better fit between the letters and words when set on specific typesetting equipment. For a picture book, the text must be large enough for legibility, yet still leave plenty of room for illustrations. In a novel, on the other hand, much care must be given to the proportions of the page. Size of type, length of line (type measure), number of lines on the page, and the space between lines (leading) are only some of the elements to deal with at this stage. As elsewhere, much of the problem solving that occurs is a fine balance between the real and the ideal. While the best possible page design is surely the goal, reality dictates that the designer also be responsible for making the book come out to an acceptable number of pages. The number of characters in any given text must be counted and translated into an actual number of typeset book pages. Restrictions such as these are very much part of the collaborative process of producing a commercial product and can actually enhance and refine the process when looked on as challenges rather than as limitations.

When positioning the type on the page, consideration is given to the amount of area or margin to leave around the type block. Books are read while opened out to double-page spreads—the inner, or gutter, margin should be the narrowest because it doubles in size when the book is opened. The outer margin must leave sufficient room for thumbs to rest and not cover up text. Likewise, folios or page numbers should be placed for discreet visibility, far enough from the curve of the gutter or the edge of the page.

Basic utilitarian decisions such as these are always influenced by both historic models for page design and current design styles. Classical proportions refer back to the golden rectangle, devised from the golden section, a system first used in ancient Greece for designing architecture. Many early printed books reflected these proportions. This is, however, but one of many historic models learned when studying book design. In the end one must trust one's own instincts to determine what appears pleasing or appropriate on the page. In fact, the uniqueness of designing books for children is that all of the rules can be broken if necessary. *The Stinky Cheese Man* (1992) takes all of the elements of book design and turns them upside down, spoofing the form in the same way that the text skews traditional fairy tales. While this is rather unorthodox, it is certainly appropriate for the subject matter.

After the proper text has been designed, the other elements of the book must be addressed. All books have title pages and copyright pages, and type for these has to

Bernhard Tango

Bodoni Poster

Caslon 3

LITHOS LIGHT

Mona Lisa Recut

Remedy

A selection of display typefaces, available both on computer and from traditional composition houses.

be specified and arranged. If necessary, specifications must be made for a table of contents, index, and bibliography—whatever the author has written, the designer must style typographically. A display, or larger size, type must be chosen to feature the book's title on the title page and jacket. This display type must at once complement the text type and be bold enough to attract attention. A book title is made up of only a few words, and a book jacket must be read at considerable distance and often by someone moving past a bookstore window or library shelf. The number of display types available far exceeds that of text faces, but with the opposite effect. While a designer tends to rely on a relatively small number of dependable text types, there never seem to be enough display faces to satisfy the wide variety of subjects dealt with on children's book jackets. There are many times when either the style of the artwork itself or lack of just the right face dictates the use of handdrawn lettering or calligraphy, usually to wonderfully creative results. The use of the computer has also made it possible for designers to create their own display (and sometimes text) faces, and this has opened up very interesting possibilities, particularly in jacket design.

A book jacket is a small poster and must convey at a glance the essence of the story. In many cases the appeal of the jacket alone will be what first entices a prospective reader to pick up a book and examine it further. A children's book jacket might portray the main characters in the story in a representational way or be more abstract and convey primarily the mood of the story. Many jackets accomplish both. Some jackets are entirely typographic, and on them typography, color, size, and arrangement have to do the whole job. Most commonly, art and typography appear together, in all manner of styles. While some books are successfully designed with art and type complementing each other, another approach is to contrast typographic form with illustration style, juxtaposing a humorous illustration with a more formal type, to create a bit of tension or surprise.

After the artwork is completed and reproduction proofs of the type are in hand, the designer creates a mechanical, or camera-ready version of the book, for the printer to photograph. With the help of the production department, the book now goes through several stages of proofing, where everyone involved can preview what the artwork and text will ultimately look like when reproduced with ink on paper. In the collaborative world of children's books, illustrator, editor, designer, and production manager all have a role to play in choosing the materials used to produce the book. The production manager will suggest certain printing stocks that might produce the desired effect and the designer will make the final decision. Color proofs of the pages of a picture book arrive, and the designer and illustrator will comb them carefully, comparing the results to the original art, making adjustments where necessary. They must then rely on the expertise of the production manager to let them know if their comments can be carried out by the printer. Blueprints arrive from the printer and are checked by editor and designer to make certain all type and artwork is where it should be and that nothing is missing or misspelled. The moment of truth arrives when the book goes on press, and final press sheets are checked by the designer and production manager. A sigh of relief can usually be heard when the first press sheet is OK'd, and the press is activated to print the thousands of copies that will make up the edition.

But the book still must be bound, and the designer is involved in specifying cover materials for the binding, colors for the endpapers, and typographic styling for the title on the spine and front cover if warranted. After the final specs are delivered, all involved eagerly await the exciting moment when bound copies of the book arrive. The designer examines the object of his or her labors and usually experiences a combination of pride and regret—how beautiful the title page looks, but if only the folios were handled differently! Fortunately, the publishing process, unlike life, offers in the second edition a chance to correct serious errors, although usually of an editorial nature.

Much has been written recently concerning the possible demise of the book as we know it, with the CD-ROM and electronic book relegating ink on paper to the archival corner now occupied by the medieval manuscript. Without question, the new technology is influencing all facets of the book design and production process, and this will change forever the way that books are made. There is certainly room for both the traditional and electronic book forms to coexist comfortably, each one borrowing stylistically from the other. Indeed all books—in whatever form—will need to be designed. And any designer still doubting the ultimate survival of the book has only to refer to that most ancient of books—the Bible—to contemplate the wise and reassuring proverb in Ecclesiastes, "of making many books there is no end." ❧ CAROL GOLDENBERG

DE TREVIÑO, ELIZABETH BORTON

AMERICAN AUTHOR, B. 1904. Elizabeth Borton de Treviño's childhood interest in the Spanish language and culture led the author to spend most of her life in Mexico and to write several books with Spanish and Mexican settings. Born and educated in Bakersfield, California, de Treviño also developed an early interest in writing and was encouraged by instructors in high school and at Stanford University, where she earned a degree in Latin American history. After studying violin at the Boston Conservatory of Music, she worked as a newspaper editor, ran the advertising department at a publishing house, and was a music reviewer and general reporter for the *Boston Herald.* De Treviño was commissioned to write her first book, *Pollyanna in Hollywood* (1931), after Eleanor Porter, the originator of the "Pollyanna" series, died. Although she wrote several more books for established series, de Treviño did not publish an original children's book until 1955, many years after settling in her adopted country of Mexico, where she lived with her husband and family. *A Carpet of Flowers* (1955) concerns a blind, orphaned Mexican boy who makes a pilgrimage to the Basilica of Our Lady of Guadalupe to help create a carpet of flowers in the image of the Virgin Mary. When Chema brings flowers for the Virgin's eyes, his own eyesight is miraculously restored. This sentimental yet moving story has a limited audience because of its religious content; the Roman Catholic church plays a role in much of the author's work, but is most evident in this early novel.

Many of de Treviño's books were inspired by historical events. *Nacar, the White Deer* (1963) tells the story of an albino deer given to the king of Spain during the seventeenth century. As in the previous book, the author is most concerned with the transforming power of love and employs a similar plot device in making her protagonist a mute who only regains his speech at the end of the novel. Other historical novels include *Casilda of the Rising Moon* (1967), the story of an eleventh-century Moorish princess; *Turi's Poppa* (1968), which concerns a European violin maker and his son in post–World War II Europe; and *El Güero* (1989), which is based on the childhood of de Treviño's father-in-law. The author won the Newbery Medal for *I, Juan de Pareja* (1965), a novel about the black slave who served seventeenth-century Spanish painter Velázquez and became a gifted artist in his own right. Although it is refreshing to see issues of race relations and slavery played out in a sphere other than the United States, Juan's first-person narration is somewhat stilted and overwritten. With little dialogue or action and a protagonist who grows into adulthood after the first few chapters, the slow-paced book has almost no child appeal, despite some good characterizations and beautiful descriptive passages. Sadly, *I, Juan de Pareja* falls into the category of Newbery winners that are rarely read by children.

In addition to her novels for young people, de Treviño has written an informational book for children, *Here Is Mexico* (1970), and a number of novels and nonfiction works for adults that often explore the same themes and settings as her children's books. Although de Treviño writes about Spanish cultures with great integrity, her audience is limited by the topics she selects and the sometimes remote quality of her prose. ❧ P.D.S.

DICKINSON, PETER

ENGLISH AUTHOR, B. 1927. Sometimes referred to as a fantasy or science fiction writer, Peter Dickinson is a difficult author to characterize. Amazingly prolific and versatile, he has published over twenty books for children, with settings ranging from contemporary England to the Byzantine Empire. Although his subject matter varies considerably, critics and young readers alike appreciate the consistently high quality of his writing and his unerring ability to tell exciting stories rich with detail. Born in Zambia, Peter Dickinson was educated at Eton and Cambridge, where he received his B.A. in English literature. He worked for seventeen years on the editorial staff of *Punch,* the British humor magazine, and didn't begin writing until he was in his forties. He has been writing steadily ever since, alternating books for children with adult thrillers.

His first novel for children, *The Weathermonger* (1968), eventually became part of The Changes trilogy, which explores the time of The Changes, when the people of

England have been possessed by a mysterious aversion to machines. The Changes trilogy received critical acclaim, and both *Heartsease* (1969) and *The Devil's Children* (1970) were nominated for awards. Although Dickinson's full power as a young adult novelist isn't fully realized in these first books, his gifts as a writer are apparent. His mastery of the English language sets him apart from many other children's book authors. His flawless prose can be heartstoppingly beautiful, with an unusual attention to landscape. Dickinson's characters are unusual, fascinating and, despite their eccentricity, utterly believable and lovable.

Dickinson has said that "the intricate exploration and development of character plays no great part in my stories." Yet it is the remarkable people one finds between the covers of his books which make them unforgettable. His protagonists tend to be quiet, self-contained personalities whose inner strengths are drawn out by the remarkable situations they find themselves in. In *Emma Tupper's Diary* (1971) Emma finds herself on vacation at a remote Scottish loch with four flamboyant cousins. When her cousins dream up a scheme to fake the appearance of a Loch Ness–type monster, sensible Emma plays along with them. But when the young people find real prehistoric creatures living in the loch, Emma reveals her deeply passionate nature in her efforts to protect the secret of the animals' existence. *The Dancing Bear* (1972), a historical novel set in the Byzantine Empire, follows the adventures of the young slave Sylvester. When Sylvester's beloved mistress and childhood friend is captured by invading Huns, Sylvester sets out to rescue her, accompanied by Holy John, a decrepit prophet, and Bubba, a dancing bear.

Many of Dickinson's characters are intensely spiritual or possessed of paranormal abilities. Set in an imaginary world, *The Blue Hawk,* which won the Guardian Award in 1977, tells the story of a young priest whose true religious calling leads him to defy the priesthood which holds his country in an iron grip of servitude and stagnation. In *Tulku,* which won the Carnegie Medal and the Whitbread Award in 1979, the devoutly Christian son of an American missionary killed in the Boxer Rebellion is befriended by an unconventional British botanist and her Chinese lover and travels with them to Tibet, where they eventually find themselves virtually imprisoned in a Buddhist monastery, awaiting the birth of Mrs. Jones' child, believed to be the next Tulku. Dickinson's work resonates with affection and pity for the human condition, with its startling capacity for both cruelty and compassion, stupidity and intelligence. His books are infectiously joyful in their celebration of humanity and love for all living creatures. ❧ K.T.

Dillon, Leo
Dillon, Diane

LEO: AMERICAN ILLUSTRATOR, B. 1933; DIANE: AMERICAN ILLUSTRATOR, B. 1933. The lives of Leo and Diane Dillon have been blended into one for more than three decades. Only eleven days separate their births, but many miles and worlds initially separated their lives. Born in Brooklyn, New York, Leo was a loner who turned to art for pleasure and self-expression. His parents encouraged his talent, yet planned a future for him in law or medicine. In school, and later in the navy, Leo used his artistic talent as a means of coping with racial discrimination. Upon leaving the navy, he worked briefly for the family business and then enrolled in Parsons School of Design.

Diane, born in Glendale, California, moved with her family thirteen times within Southern California while growing up. She knew at an early age that she wanted to be an artist and found, during her childhood, that her family and her art were the only constants in her life. Her parents encouraged her talent but did not value it, expecting her to get married and become a housewife. She worked to put herself through two years of school at Los Angeles College and later attended Skidmore College for one semester before moving to Parsons. Diane and Leo became rivals at Parsons, and even after they fell in love, their rivalry continued. Upon marrying, and after holding individual jobs in advertising, they decided to collaborate on freelance work to avoid the rivalry and competition of their college days. This work included collaboration on album covers, advertisements, magazine artwork, movie posters, and book covers for paperbacks.

When they began illustrating children's books, however, the Dillons found freedom. Not all of their children's book illustrations have been in picture books. Many of their earlier illustrations appeared in novels and short stories written for juvenile readers, most of which were legends or folktales. For all of their work they spend much time researching the stories, time periods, cultures, settings, and artwork of these eras, incorporating their findings in their illustrations. Their early work used woodcuts, which the Dillons found to be a nearly universal art form, used by many cultures and during many time periods, and a style conducive to collaboration. From the mid-1970s their work has been noted for its diversity. Their illustrations for *Whirlwind Is a Ghost Dancing* (1974), an ALA Notable Book by Natalie Belting, brought them to the attention of the children's book establishment through the felicitous

Illustration by Leo and Diane Dillon for "Doc Rabbit, Bruh Fox, and Tar Baby" from *The People Could Fly* (1985), by VIRGINIA HAMILTON.

combination of art and folklore and fantasy themes and the inclusion of decorative motifs from the traditions of various Indian nations. They followed *Whirlwind* with wood-cuts in *Songs of the Boat* (1975) and the bleaching of dark brown watercolors in *The Hundred Penny Box* (1975).

In the same year, the Dillons won the Caldecott Medal for their illustrations for Verna Aardema's *Why Mosquitoes Buzz in People's Ears.* Acting on their philosophy that the role of the illustrator is not simply to duplicate the text but to enlarge on it, to restate the words in their own graphic terms, they used the African style of batik to create the lively fragmented forms. Their next book, *Ashanti to Zulu* (1976), by Margaret W. Musgrove, became their second Caldecott Medal winner and made them the first illustrators to win this award in consecutive years. Their research skills helped them to create accurate, authentic depictions of the twenty-six different African tribes introduced in the book, including distinctively representative artifacts, animals, dwellings, and a costumed person for each group. They also illustrated Leontyne Price's retelling of *Aïda* (1990), in which their son Lee collaborated in producing borders with the appearance of carved gold frames. Among the varied devices in the Dillons' work are marbleized paper, electrifying colors, and bas-relief decorations.

Leo and Diane Dillon have progressed from being two distinct artists who work separately, passing artwork between them, to becoming a "third artist," with thoughts and styles so blended that the resulting art could not have been produced by either working alone.

C.H.S.

DIME NOVEL, THE

The dime novel first appeared in America in the mid-1800s. The product of technological advances that allowed for cheap mass printing, the dime novel was wildly popular with a public in search of entertaining reading. In a country with a population under fifty million, some dime novels sold over 400,000 copies each. A single major publisher, Beadle & Adams, produced over three thousand separate dime novels at its four-story New York book factory. The physical format of the dime novel varied from publisher to publisher, but was typically four inches by six inches—easy to stick in a pocket—and about one hundred pages in length. An illustration usually graced the cover. Dime novels were sometimes called *yellowbacks* because of the yellow paper covers given the books published by Beadle & Adams. Other major dime novel publishers included Street & Smith, Robert Bonner, Norman Munro, and Frank Tousey.

Mass production of dime novels meant that a writer's speed and the quantity of words produced counted for more than style or substance. Writers worked from well-worn formulas that emphasized action and required frequent resort to crimes, rescues, and violence, all liberally mixed with doses of heroism and nationalistic sentiment. While the dime novel produced a few star writers, such as Ned Buntline, Bertha M. Clay, and Prentis Ingraham, most writers of dime novels were unknowns. In fact the names of the more popular authors were treated as company trademarks, and the books published under these famous names were often actually written by company hacks.

Western stories dominated throughout the dime-novel era. The pseudobiographical Westerns that came out under the name of Ned Buntline were extremely popular, as were books in the "Buffalo Bill" series. Indians figured as villains in many stories, and at least two dime novels took the Battle of the Little Bighorn as their subject. Besides Westerns, there were also dime novel romances, mysteries, sea tales, war stories, and tales of urban working girls and boys.

Though the audience for the dime novel was large, the exact make-up of that audience is not known. Boys were probably the largest consumers, but the books were also popular with girls, Civil War soldiers, working-class men and women, immigrants—just about everyone except the middle- and upper-class consumers of respectable literature. These readers frequently criticized dime novels as immoral trash, a criticism which no doubt enhanced the pleasure these books gave young readers. Despite their disreputable image, dime novels were rather tame. Their violence was not explicit, and sex was never part of their formula. About the worst that can be said about them is that they sometimes featured outlaw anti-heroes—Deadwood Dick, the James Boys, the Dalton Gang—who gallantly operated outside the law for the betterment of the common folk.

As popular as it was during the nineteenth century, the dime novel was dead by 1920. Changes in printing technology gave rise to the pulp magazine, the dime novel's immediate descendant and ultimate replacement. Because the dime novels were ephemeral publications that readers readily discarded, and because the acid paper on which they were printed deteriorated quickly, examples of this once-popular genre survive today only in the hands of collectors and in a few libraries. ❧ D.A.B.

Disney, Walt

AMERICAN FILMMAKER, 1901–1966. Nearly three decades after Walt Disney's death his impact on American popular culture is undeniable—and inescapable. In 1992 *Aladdin* was the thirty-first animated feature to bear his name. The Disney Channel is a cable television staple, and a thriving collection of Disney home videos usually dominates each week's list of top video sellers. Add to that the perpetual parade of products spawned by the Disney oeuvre, not to mention the two most successful theme parks in the history of the world, and you have a seemingly immortal industry.

The story of the mortal man who created it is an archetypically American one. Walter Elias Disney was born into a midwestern childhood of hard work, little money, and even less encouragement. By his early twenties he had turned a flair for cartooning into a small business making animated ads that ran between silent features in Kansas City, Missouri, movie houses. Disney left the Midwest for Hollywood in 1923, and just five years later Mickey Mouse debuted in *Steamboat Willie.* In 1932 Mickey won for Disney his first Oscar, and by the mid-thirties the mouse was an international celebrity as well. Even the queen of England was selecting Mickey chinaware as gifts for British children.

From the beginning Disney's career was built not on his own artistic talent but on his gift for visionary master plans and his ability to corral others into seeing them through. After 1926 he rarely drew a line of any of his animated characters—even Mickey himself was animated by Ub Iwerks, an early Disney collaborator. Disney's genius lay, instead, in a passion for new technology, an assured sense of story, and the skill to be the controlling hand in both.

When *The Jazz Singer* heralded the birth of talkies in late 1927, two silent Mickey cartoons were ready to go. Characteristically, Disney shelved them to explore what the budding technology had to offer. Rather than slapping sound onto what the studio had already created, he searched instead for a way to do something totally new. *Steamboat Willie* became the first cartoon with a fully synchronized soundtrack, a cartoon in which sound is so indelibly woven with story that without it the film would be meaningless. As it often would in his career, Disney's astute grasp of a technological innovation put him on the cutting edge.

This instinct for innovation was always at the core of Disney's best work. The film industry of the thirties took as gospel that the "cartoon antics" of animation could never sustain a feature-length film. With 1937's *Snow White and the Seven Dwarfs,* Disney, whose entire reputation was built on films no longer than eight minutes, proved them spectacularly shortsighted. By the time of his death from lung cancer nearly thirty years later, Disney was the master of the animated feature, leaving behind what has become a roster of film classics.

In 1965 Dr. Max Rafferty, then California's superintendent of public instruction, extolled Disney as "the greatest educator of this century," a claim that drew the ire of many who felt that Disney had mauled and mishandled not only folk and fairy tales but also children's literature classics. Frances Clarke Sayers, something of a legend in her own right as the onetime director of children's services for the New York Public Library, challenged Rafferty, taking Disney to task for what she saw as his corruption of children's literature by saying he had "scant respect for the integrity of the original creations . . . manipulating and vulgarizing everything for his own ends." She went on to insist that "the acerbity of *Mary Poppins* [1964], unpredictable, full of wonder and mystery, becomes . . . one great marshmallow-covered cream puff," adding, "He . . . transformed *Pinocchio* into a slapstick sadistic revel."

Disney did indeed tread on dangerous ground when he sought to adapt the classics, and he wasn't always successful. His animated *Alice in Wonderland* (1951) and *Peter Pan* (1953), for example, have their endearing moments, but their eccentric originality, so based in language, eluded Disney. The little-remembered *The Sword in the Stone* (1963) turned the Merlin of legend into a bumbling codger. And *Sleeping Beauty* (1958) showed what could happen when Disney's mind was elsewhere—in this case on the creation of Disneyland. But with *Pinocchio,* Disney created what is now acknowledged as a masterwork of animated film. Released in 1940, it was the first film to make full use of another technological innovation, the multiplane camera. With it Disney animators achieved a depth of scene extraordinary for the time. The film's opening shot, panning in over the rooftops of Geppetto's village and then down through the streets to a sleepy, shabbily clad cricket named Jiminy, cost over $45,000, an unheard-of figure at the time.

Though not absolutely faithful to the original text, no less a fan than author/illustrator MAURICE SENDAK, writing in his 1988 collection of essays, *Caldecott & Co.,* votes for Disney's version of the tale. "Collodi's book is of interest today," Sendak writes, "chiefly as evidence of the superiority of Disney's screenplay."

It should come as no surprise that how one feels about the legacy of Walt Disney is like the old adage—where you stand depends on where you sit. Disney can certainly be faulted for creating more than his fair share of too cute animals, and the charge of "Disneyfication"—the smoothing of those powerful edges so essential to any good story—is often warranted. But even though Disney's films may have outsold their original works, they've never supplanted them. The books easily survive the commercial success Disney avidly sought for his films and took great pride in achieving.

Ultimately Disney's film classics attest not only to his professional mastery in his chosen field, but to his artistry as a magician who left an indelible spell on twentieth-century popular culture. Nearly three decades after his death, "Disney" is no longer a name, but a conjuring word, summoning collective memories of poisoned apples, pumpkined carriages, and raucous blue genies. And still winningly grinning above it all is that immortal three-fingered, white-gloved mouse.

TERRI PAYNE BUTLER

DIXON, FRANKLIN W.

See HARDY BOYS SERIES; STRATEMEYER LITERARY SYNDICATE.

DR. SEUSS

See SEUSS, DR.

DODGE, MARY MAPES

AMERICAN AUTHOR, 1831–1905. Editor of the premiere children's magazine of its era, Mary Mapes Dodge is also noted for writing a novel generally regarded as a classic of juvenile literature. Born in New York City and educated by her father, Dodge published several articles while still a teenager. As a young widow, she began to support her family by writing for magazines such as *Century* and *Atlantic Monthly.* Her first book, *Irvington Stories* (1864), contains tales she originally told to her sons.

Although she published several minor volumes of stories and verse for children, the author is best known for the 1865 novel *Hans Brinker, or the Silver Skates*, which presents a vivid and appealing picture of nineteenth-century Holland. Although somewhat melodramatic, the story of fifteen-year-old Hans and his sister, Gretel, remains compelling, as the siblings struggle to help their father recover from an accident, then participate in an exciting skating contest. Unfortunately, the lengthy novel is slowed down by a subplot in which several secondary characters travel through Holland on skates. Their adventures are somewhat entertaining but predominantly didactic, as they visit numerous tourist sites and exchange historical anecdotes; Hans and Gretel are forgotten for nearly half the volume. Many later editions of the book are abridged to remedy this flaw.

In addition to her writing, Dodge served as the first editor of *St. Nicholas* magazine and continued as editor until her death. Founded in 1873, this periodical published the work of LOUISA MAY ALCOTT, RUDYARD KIPLING, ROBERT LOUIS STEVENSON, MARK TWAIN, and many other notable authors of the time. *St. Nicholas* continued to be published through 1940, and Dodge's most famous novel continues to be read today. P.D.S.

DODGSON, CHARLES LUTWIDGE

See CARROLL, LEWIS.

Doherty, Berlie

British author, b. 1943. A two-time winner of the British Library Association's Carnegie Medal, Berlie Doherty's interest in writing was inspired by her father, a railway clerk who wrote poetry and recited a new bedtime story each evening. Doherty decided at age five that she, too, would become a writer. The Liverpool-born author attended a convent school, where an encouraging teacher introduced her to drama and poetry. She received an English degree from the University of Durham and postgraduate certificates in social science and education. A social-work career was interrupted by marriage and motherhood, but her later work as a schoolteacher motivated Doherty to write for young people. Her first two short-story collections, *How Green You Are!* (1982) and *The Making of Fingers Finnigan* (1983), concern the everyday lives of English teenagers and contain autobiographical elements.

Doherty left teaching to work as a broadcaster in schools for the British Broadcasting Corporation. Many of her published books had their origins as radio plays, including *White Peak Farm* (1984), a series of interrelated stories narrated by teenage Jeannie Tanner, who lives in rural Derbyshire. The first story, "Gran," is a nearly perfect work of fiction about growing old, self-deception, bravery, and saying good-bye. Although the other stories are not as stunning in their impact, each is beautifully crafted and contains strong characterizations of a family growing apart yet bound together by their shared past and a familial love they do not always understand.

The Carnegie-winning *Granny Was a Buffer Girl* (1986) was Doherty's first book published in the United States. On the night before Jess leaves home to study abroad, her family gathers to share stories of the past. Sometimes humorous, often sad, the early stories about Jess's grandparents and parents are related in the third person. Particularly touching is "The Buffer Girl," an anti-Cinderella story in which Granny Dorothy, when she was a young factory worker, attends a ball and is pursued by the boss's son yet eventually marries a neighborhood boy. The later stories are told by Jess and include an account of her older brother's death and her own ill-fated first romance. Doherty writes of ordinary people with great emotional complexity, and the interrelated stories form a novel-length mosaic of one family's history.

Doherty creates a more focused, sustained work of fiction with her second Carnegie winner, *Dear Nobody* (1991), the story of a teenage pregnancy that is narrated alternately by each of the expectant parents. Eighteen-year-old Chris relates his love for Helen, his concern and confusion about the pregnancy, and his ambivalent feelings toward the mother who abandoned him as a child and whom he now wishes to meet. Helen's story is presented in a series of letters written to her unborn child. The novel is realistic in its depiction of an unplanned pregnancy, but ignores more practical aspects of having a baby, including the financial responsibilities of the father. Nevertheless, the characterizations are superb, the emotions are accurate, and the writing style is excellent.

Doherty has also written a number of plays for stage and television, the adult novel *Requiem* (1991), and the picture books *Snowy* (1992), about a horse who pulls a barge, and *Paddiwak and Cosy* (1989), a story of two cats, noted for its rhythmic writing. A beautiful writing style and memorable characterizations distinguish Doherty as one of today's finest authors. ❧ P.D.S.

Domanska, Janina

American author and illustrator of children's books, 1912–1995. Born in Warsaw, Poland, Janina Domanska immigrated to the United States in 1952. Throughout her career, Domanska was known for telling simple fables and folktales and for adorning the pages of her books with decorative art .

Domanska began her artistic career as a child in Warsaw. Though imprisoned in a concentration camp during World War II, she continued to paint. Upon seeing her artistic capabilities, a prominent visiting physician arranged her release. Indeed, Domanska has claimed, "My talent for drawing proved my salvation." After studying art in Rome, Domanska came to the United States. Proficient in artistic techniques ranging from watercolor to pen-and-ink to woodcut and fluent in four languages but unable to speak English, she found work as a textile designer. Over the next few years, Domanska's English skills improved and she sought work as an illustrator. Based on the illustrations of animals she had in her portfolio, an editor at *Harper's* magazine encouraged her to pursue work as a children's book illustrator.

Domanska's personal history is apparent throughout her work. Geometric patterns, flat picture planes, elaborate, highly textured backgrounds, and earthy green, brown, red, and blue tones in early work such as *Palmiero and the Ogre* (1967), *Look, There Is a Turtle Flying* (1968), and *Marilka* (1970) hail directly from the Slavic tradition. In *What Do You See?* (1974), *What Happens Next?* (1983)—both simple picture books for the very young—and *The First Noel* (1986), the layering of line, overlapping textures, repetitive patterns, and bright colors reveal the influence of her years as a textile designer. The illustrations in *Why So Much Noise?* (1964) have a lithographic quality, and coarse and fine crayon marks decorate the abstract shapes of the landscape.

In more recent work, the strong, linear, geometric images of the early years soften and Domanska's palette brightens as the colors become more vivid and bold. In *The Best of the Bargain* (1977), *The Bremen Town Musicians* (1980), *Marek, the Little Fool* (1982), and *Busy Monday Morning* (1985), splotches of royal blue, teal, bright orange, purple, pink, and aquamarine predominate, overlapping to create a collagelike effect. The childlike folk-art quality and humor in her drawings perfectly match these tales of beast outsmarting fellow beasts and beast outwitting man. In *The Coconut Thieves* (1964), a folktale set in the jungles of Africa, muted greens, ochers, reds, and black enforce the mood and setting. Though the animals depicted have fantastic spots and shapes decorating their hides, the patterned trees and thatched huts provide an African flavor to the tale. For *The Dragon Liked Smoked Fish* (1967), a folktale set in China, Domanska's watercolor technique and loose, expressive brush strokes evoke traditional Chinese brush paintings. Domanska simplified her artistic approach in the illustrations for folktale collections such as the *Harper Book of Princes* (1964), *More Tales of Faraway Folk* (1964), and the children's poetry collection *The Fifth Day* (1978). These books showcase Domanska's strong, linear drawing style in crisp, clean, black-and-white line illustrations.

Throughout her career, Janina Domanska's books received much critical acclaim, including citation in 1972 of *If All the Seas Were One Sea* (1971) as a Caldecott Honor Book. The most enduring quality of Domanska's work for children remains the fresh, humorous tales she told and the playful and fantastic pictures she created ❦

J.A.S.

Donovan, John

AMERICAN AUTHOR, 1928–1992. John Donovan, born in Massachusetts, received a law degree from the University of Virginia in 1957 and worked as a copyright lawyer at the Library of Congress before moving to the publishing concern of St. Martin's Press. In 1967 he became the executive director of the Children's Book Council; subsequently, his title was that of president. An ardent champion of children and their right to read, Donovan was a moving spirit in advocating and practicing cooperation among national and international organizations concerned with children and children's books.

Although Donovan wrote for a wide age range (he wrote some picture books and a play for adults), most of the books that received wide critical acclaim and are still in print were addressed to an adolescent audience. Keenly aware of the problems common to those often painful years, he wrote fiction that was relevant to those tribulations, and his work is distinguished by percipient insight, a compassion that never descends to sentimentality, and a wit that leavens the seriousness of the issues involved.

Most readers consider *I'll Get There. It Better Be Worth the Trip* (1969) his major book. It is certainly one of his best and, although published more than twenty-five years ago, has a timeless quality, an ineradicable relevance. Thirteen years old when his grandmother dies, David leaves the small town where they had lived to go to Manhattan. His divorced mother is irritated by Davy and by his beloved dog. His father just isn't interested. Depressed by his parents' indifference, Davy longs—as does everyone—for love and acceptance. It is within this framework that he and another boy find themselves, unexpectedly, sexually aroused by each other. The inclusion of this taboo-breaking incident impressed many critics, demonstrating the courage of the author and of his editor, Ursula Nordstrom, and impressing readers by the dignity with which Donovan treated the encounter; it was an introduction of an aspect of life and love that had, at that time, been absent from books for young adult readers.

Donovan was perceptively aware of the sense of isolation felt by so many adolescents. Like Davy, John, the protagonist of *Wild in the World* (1971), is alone; like Davy, John finds companionship and comfort in his dog. The writing in this stripped-down, powerful story is direct and deceptively simple; while the first book has a pathetic tenderness, *Wild in the World* has a tragic grandeur. In *Remove Protective Coating a Little at a Time* (1973) the appealing hero is a boy whose parents fail to communicate with him and who turns to an elderly woman; when Harry meets Amelia he knows she is an undependable vagrant, but he responds happily to the warmth of her interest in him. In *Family* (1976), the narrator is Sasha, one of the apes in an experimental laboratory. The novel is a tour de force, successfully blending a dry wit with a plot and mood that have the monolithic inevitability of a Greek tragedy.

Just as each book is carefully conceived, so is each character—yet each of them reminds us, at some point or in some way, of ourselves. Donovan's children and animals are memorable, forcefully depicted and set off by a stylistic simplicity that provides contrast rather than competition for the reader's attention. There is wit and sympathy in every book, but it is in fact a playwright's eye and ear that have produced the careful pruning of dialogue and exposition that makes John Donovan's writing so effective. z.s.

Voices of the Creators

Michael Dorris

I listened to stories before I read them, read them before I learned to write down what I tried to make up, and that linkage—hearing and seeing and speaking—is never far from my intention or my method as an author. Every published word, in sequence, is doubly tested: how does it play on the page? How does it sound to the ear? Does its precise meaning, its roll of syllables and vowels, fit the rhythmic cadence of the total piece, or does it jar, unintentionally call attention to itself, remind an audience of a lag between imagination and artifice? My object as a writer is to disappear into the voice of the story, to *become* that voice.

This act of submergence can't be counted on or summoned at will. Days pass, weeks, in which I stand outside trial sentences, dangled like bait, even while knowing that none of them will probably survive into print. "Try speaking this one," I coax illusory characters. "I'll bet you could say something like this." But usually, no matter how desperately I implore, those fictional men and women remain mute and stubborn, their lips sealed, unwilling to reveal themselves by an authentic utterance. As in any other intimate association, we must get to know each other before too much trust is extended.

Finally, if I'm lucky, a string of words will catch, tap into possibility. An arbitrary situation will be suggested that piques a character's interest and, like Star Boy, who can't stand it when Morning Girl claims credit for *his* mistake, a narrator will stop pretending to be a rock and turn human out of pure irritation with my fumbling efforts. "That's *not* the way I'd put it," I seem to hear inside my head. "Any fool could tell it should be like *this*."

An Inuit hunter is trained to endure bad weather and endless boredom while standing motionless beside a hole in the ice, optimistically forecasting that dinner will need to come up for a single breath of air. When nothing happens for an interminable stretch of time, doubts are sure to arise. The whole enterprise comes to seem irrational, impossible. And then, in a flash, there's a snatch of color, a flash of movement. The hunter must be ever vigilant, or the opportunity is past—and may never come again.

I wait, too, sitting at my desk in early mornings, dawdling in a restaurant until my order arrives, driving a familiar highway, shopping for groceries. My lance is a pencil or a ball-point pen, poised to write on any available scrap of paper when that flicker of unmistakable revelation bubbles into my consciousness. I recognized Morning Girl as herself and nobody else the second she said, "If the day starts before you do, you never catch up. You spend all your time running after what you should have already done, and no matter how much you hurry, you never finish the race in a tie. The day wins."

Gotcha, I recall thinking as I reached for my yellow pad. Now, tell me more.

The funny and fortunate thing is, as hard as characters might try to elude detection, once lured out in the open they often can't shut up. They dictate like a CEO impatient to finish a stack of important correspondence in one late-afternoon session. The minute hand on the clock, which previously dragged, suddenly accelerates. When at last one of these newly released personalities pauses for breath, I'm amazed to see that hours have flown by unnoticed, that the sun has gone down (or come up), that I've missed a meal.

Writing a story this way is very similar to listening. When characters are finally real, they inhabit so unique a confluence of specific traits that in any given context or encounter there is but one plausible way for them to behave—any variation from that proper course and a TILT sign illuminates in bright neon. Driven by the dictates of their own imagined history, the accumulation of incidents that happened only to them, the quirky details that differentiate their looks or choices of clothing style or favorite foods, they chart their own course through invented episodes. In short, if a writer has done the job well, the characters inevitably surprise, shock, entertain, disappoint, or make proud. An author, like a listener, like a reader, is, after all, just another kind of interactive audience, witness to the unpredictable and fascinating drama of human beings set in motion.

Dorris, Michael

American author, b. 1945. While it is tempting to categorize Michael Dorris's writing as purely Native American fiction, this classification tends to marginalize his diverse characters and ignore the originality of his stories. Dorris's books should be considered as contributions to both Native American literature and American literature, so intertwined are the two in Dorris's world.

Of Irish and French descent, Dorris, a member of the Modoc tribe, grew up in Kentucky and Montana. He is a graduate of Georgetown and Yale universities. Trained as an anthropologist, Dorris founded the Native American Studies program at Dartmouth College and is the author of *A Guide to Research in Native American Studies* (1984). In 1985 he received the Indian Achievement Award for his work in education. Dorris's first novel, *A Yellow Raft in Blue Water* (1987), straddles the genres of adult and young adult fiction; although placed on the adult shelves in most libraries, the novel is quite accessible to the teenage reader. A work that spans forty years and journeys from the Pacific Northwest to an isolated Montana Indian reservation, it is the story of three generations of Indian women torn apart by angry secrets and bound together by the bonds of kinship. Each of the three sections—narrated by one of the heroines, beginning with fifteen-year-old Rayona and moving backward in time to her mother, Christine, and her grandmother, Ida—is written with seductive and suspenseful prose.

In 1977 Dorris became one of the first unmarried men in the United States to legally adopt a child, a Sioux Indian boy he named Adam. Unknown to Dorris, Adam's mother had died of alcohol poisoning, and Adam himself suffered from fetal alcohol syndrome, a relatively unknown condition with no known cure. *The Broken Cord* (1989) tells the inspiring story of how Dorris, his wife, Louise Erdrich (the critically acclaimed novelist and poet), and their children dealt with FAS. The book was awarded the 1989 National Book Critics Circle Award for nonfiction, the Heartland Prize, and the Christopher Award.

In their first fiction collaboration, Dorris and Erdrich wrote *The Crown of Columbus* (1991), which chronicles the quest of a pair of mismatched lovers for the truth about Christopher Columbus and themselves. Vivian Twostar, anthropologist and single mother, and Roger Williams, distinguished scholar and poet, find themselves drawn into a journey to the Caribbean in an attempt to answer the questions posed in Columbus's recently discovered diary.

While all of Dorris's adult novels have been received positively by readers and critics, his first children's book, *Morning Girl* (1992), winner of the 1993 Scott O'Dell Award for New World historical fiction, astonished the public. Told in alternating chapters by Morning Girl and her brother Star Boy—two children as different as day and night—the book tells of a Taino family living on a Bahamian island. While both narrators speak simply and clearly, their lives are complicated—the siblings face and survive the grief of their mother's miscarriage and a tropical storm that almost blows Star Boy away. Morning Girl questions who she is: "But what *is* me? . . . I wouldn't recognize myself unless I was sitting on the bottom of a quiet pool, looking up at me looking down." Star Boy begins to understand the responsibilities that accompany adulthood: "At night you must be your own friend." The days and nights flow together in harmony until the morning that Morning Girl spots a large canoe filled with strangers. She welcomes them to her home; she has learned that one must always treat guests with respect, "even when they are as brainless as gulls." A two-page epilogue—a diary entry dated October 11, 1492—places the story in historical context as the reader realizes that the men in the canoe are Christopher Columbus and the crew of the *Niña*. Dorris has imagined a fictional family—generous, witty, considerate, and loving—and brought them realistically and lovingly to life; the story is one neither children nor adults should miss. M.I.A.

Dowden, Anne Ophelia

American author and illustrator, b. 1907. Anne Ophelia Todd Dowden's botanical illustrations and books provide scientific information and at the same time reveal the beauty of plant life. Dowden was fascinated with the natural world from an early age, and she spent countless hours collecting and drawing specimens from around her home in Colorado. She was particularly curious about insects, an interest that is reflected in her work. *The Clover and the Bee: A Book of Pollination* (1990) includes drawings of insects that are as graceful and detailed as the drawings of blossoms. After receiving a degree in art from the Carnegie Institute of Technology, she headed to New York City in hopes of securing a position as a book illustrator. Instead, she found a job as a drawing instructor at Pratt Institute, and after several years went on to become the head of the art department at Manhattanville College, where she worked for over twenty years. A sabbatical from Manhattanville College gave her time to return to botanical illustration. With renewed love for the subject and publishing success, she left the college to pursue illustration full-time.

Dowden's botanical illustrations, as well as her paintings and textiles, have been exhibited in many museums and galleries. Her artistry is most evident in her meticulous full-color illustrations. She works primarily in watercolor, and her colors are rich and precise. Accuracy is paramount, so she tries to present the illustrations consistently to scale; for example, making all of the illustrations in one book two-thirds of natural size. Even more significantly, she does all of her studies from living plants, growing many herself and gathering others from friends, botanical gardens—wherever she can find the specimens she needs. This requirement for living plants has sometimes necessitated masterful coordination. To complete the illustrations for John and KATHERINE PATERSON's *Consider the Lilies* (1986), which explores the symbolism of plants referred to in the Bible, she needed not only blossoming and fruit-bearing pomegranates but also frankincense, myrrh, and a host of other plants.

In the same way that her illustrations convey precise information about plant and insect life, so does the text of her books. Her writing is direct and positive without being sentimental. She respects—and assumes—her reader's intelligence. Her first book, *Look at a Flower* (1963), starts right off with a clear explanation of scientific classification. The book is suitable for a student of botany, but also for an artist or a reader who simply wants to know more about what is growing by the side of the road. Her interest in plants goes beyond their biology to include their role in the life of human beings. *State Flowers* (1978) tells the story behind the selection of each of the fifty states' emblematic flowers. Similarly, *This Noble Harvest: A Chronicle of Herbs* (1979) explains how herbs have been used throughout history—as medicines and for improving the smell of sixteenth-century castles as well as for cooking. Anne Ophelia Dowden's work quietly asserts the importance of combining the scientist's accuracy with the artist's personal passion. ❦ A.E.Q.

DOYLE, SIR ARTHUR CONAN

See SHERLOCK HOLMES BOOKS.

DOYLE, BRIAN

CANADIAN AUTHOR, B. 1935. Brian Doyle is one of Canada's most well-known, critically respected, and widely read fiction writers for children. Readers of his books tend to be evangelical about them, buttonholing their friends to read their favorite Doyle passages aloud. Yet his books are difficult to describe and classify. Critics and reviewers, trying to convey Doyle's unique voice and vision, have compared him to writers as diverse as Kurt Vonnegut, Charles Dickens, and J. D. SALINGER.

Doyle has explored the past, displaying obvious affection for its artifacts. Tommy in *Up to Low* (1982) and *Angel Square* (1987) and Hubbo in *Easy Avenue* (1988) and *Covered Bridge* (1990) live in 1940s Ottawa and the Gatineau hills north of that city, the landscapes of Doyle's own childhood. But the books are not memoirs; the lives of his first-person narrators are too immediate. Whether his characters are contemplating the fragile possibility of love, torn between two loyalties, incensed and impotent in the face of social injustice, or just plain confused at the chaotic richness of the world, Doyle respects the largeness and seriousness of their concerns.

Doyle's books, especially the more recent ones, feature young adult characters and young adult preoccupations—love, money, identity, rebellion against adult authority. And Doyle, as a father of two and a high school teacher of thirty years, certainly knows this territory. But his books have an entirely different flavor from the standard young adult novel. Doyle's characters describe their world with a wry, eye-rolling awareness of its hypocrisies and real evils, but they are never cynical, bitter, or solipsistic. The enclosing narrative voice of the books is warm and tolerant, emotionally vulnerable.

And while Doyle's stories certainly deal with problems—anti-Semitism in *Angel Square,* homelessness in *Easy Avenue,* environmental crime in *Spud Sweetgrass* (1992)—they are a far cry from "problem novels." His style goes under and beyond and above realism. He includes recipes, songs, lurid headlines, advertising jingles, and an unsurpassed use of the three-word paragraph. His worlds are at once the low comedy of outhouse jokes and slapstick, the magic realism of madmen and dreamers, a set of linked poetic images, and a good yarn told by somebody's uncle. Combining gossip, news, anecdote, admonition, and tall tale, Brian Doyle takes the novel back to its origins in story-telling—and forward to his own finely controlled mingling of comedy, romance, and epic. ❦ S.E.

DRESCHER, HENRIK

DANISH-BORN AMERICAN AUTHOR AND ILLUSTRATOR, B. 1955. When Henrik Drescher decided to become an illustrator at the age of fifteen, he did not

Illustration by Henrik Drescher from his book *Simon's Book* (1983).

choose to follow the route of formal art training. Instead, he traveled the world equipped with a drawing book, pen and ink, and an open mind. When he came to the United States in 1977, his drawing quality and freshness of vision landed him jobs as a political illustrator, and he contributed to *Rolling Stone* and the *New York Times Book Review.*

In 1982 Drescher published his first work for children, *The Strange Appearance of Howard Cranebill, Jr.* (selected as a New York Times Best Illustrated Book), an amusing allegory of a childless couple who discover an odd-looking child on their doorstep. Though this work shares with all of Drescher's later books a visual richness of design elements, such as a frenetic, energetic quality of line, a playful use of intricate, decorative borders, and splotches of color, and a lively combination of fantasy and humor, a distinct progression can be noted from this book to his later books. Offbeat and unique in story and presentation, *The Strange Appearance of Howard Cranebill, Jr.,* is visually more subtle than his later work. The softer, more muted pastel colors and subdued action that remains within borders surrounded by white space provide a constrained feeling.

In 1983 the book that defines Drescher's style was published. *Simon's Book* (a New York Times Best Illustrated Book, a "Reading Rainbow" selection, and Parents' Choice Award winner) tells a great tale involving a boy, a beast, a drawing pad, and three unlikely heroes—two pens and a bottle of ink! Only an illustrator could spin this tale, as only an illustrator would think of his pens and ink as heroic. In this adventure the drawings take over and almost leap off the page as they mirror the written action of the tale. Colorful backgrounds pulsing with rich color, borders that move and shift with colors and shapes, and unusual characters that jump from one page to the next enhance the high-speed pacing of this fantastic romp.

Though all of Drescher's books are filled with adventure and drama, their great humor prevents them from being threatening to his young readership. For instance, when the beast chasing Simon leaps forward, he plants a wet sloppy kiss rather than a painful blow on the boy's cheek. The adventures *Looking for Santa Claus* (1984) and *Look-alikes* (1985) may have less interesting plots, but visually the adventures equal the sophistication and imagination of *Simon's Book,* and all seem to draw from

Drescher's travel experiences. Maggie, the heroine in *Looking for Santa Claus,* travels around the world with Blossom the cow in search of Santa. *Look-alikes* tells of a boy and his pet monkey as they retreat to their playhouse to follow the antics of dolls that look like themselves. Both books make playful use of every element of the book, from the jacket flaps to the endpapers. In *Look-alikes,* Drescher uses trompe l'oeil techniques borrowed from M. C. Escher and Salvador Dali. Stairs travel up and down simultaneously while a waterfall falls nowhere at all. A solid bird's egg in one picture turns into a hole in the ground in the next.

Drescher's unique body of work includes two books of nonfiction, *Whose Scaly Tail? African Animals You'd Like to Meet* (1987) and *Whose Furry Nose? Australian Animals You'd Like to Meet* (1987). Not quite scientific references, the books provide a fun introduction to a variety of animals and include an informative double-page spread on the important habits of each animal. Drescher's work includes a wordless two-color adventure, *The Yellow Umbrella* (1987), the highly acclaimed *Poems of A. Nonny Mouse* (1989), selected by Jack Prelutsky, and *No Plain Pets!* (1991).

Inventive in both writing and depicting his stories, Drescher continually explores the boundaries of storytelling and the picture-book format. ❧ J.A.S.

DU BOIS, WILLIAM PÈNE

AMERICAN AUTHOR AND ILLUSTRATOR, 1916–1993. For more than fifty years, the works of William Pène du Bois have delighted audiences and critics with their original, fantastic stories and illustrations. Born in Nutley, New Jersey, du Bois moved with his family to France at the age of eight. Du Bois credits the French schools he attended with instilling in him a sense of order and meticulousness, which he applied in his work. Du Bois moved back to the United States at age fourteen and won a scholarship to Carnegie Technical School of Architecture, but he soon sold his first book, *Elisabeth the Cow Ghost* (1936), and never returned to school.

As a child, du Bois, whose family included many artists, was fascinated with JULES VERNE and pored over the illustrations of mechanical devices. He also loved the circus, and claims to have visited the circus an average of thirty times a year. His passions for France, the circus, and Jules Verne are all evident in du Bois's work for children. *The Twenty-One Balloons* (1947), winner of the 1948 Newbery Medal, recounts the fascinating story of Professor Sherman's unexpected visit to the Pacific island of Krakatoa, where the sophisticated islanders, with unlimited resources of diamonds, have invented complex work-saving and entertainment devices. The inventions, which recall those predicted by Verne, are rendered clear to readers through the precise text and beautiful, detailed illustrations.

Story and illustrations, perfectly integrated, are equally important to the reader's understanding and enjoyment of the story. *Lion* (1956), named a Caldecott Honor Book in 1957, also reflects du Bois's interest in invention. In it an angel invents the king of beasts, trying feathers, stripes, and fish scales before discovering just the right combination of attributes for a lion: a charming, accessible metaphor for the process through which artists create a thing of beauty. In keeping with its theme, *Lion* was handsomely produced; its design, type style, color, and the delicate line of the art all contribute to a visually striking, emotionally satisfying whole.

In all of his books, du Bois's stories and pictures combine humor, fantasy, and adventure with elegant simplicity. He begins with the familiar and takes the reader

Illustration by William Pène du Bois from his book *The Twenty-One Balloons* (1947).

from there to the absurd. *The Giant* (1954) explores the chaos that develops when a baby grows to enormous size, and the isolation and loneliness of a child outside of the norm. Along with eccentricity, du Bois writes about morality. *The Twenty-One Balloons* explores human greed, and *Lazy Tommy Pumpkinhead* (1966), one of du Bois's series of books about the seven deadly sins, examines the ramifications of sloth.

Du Bois has received critical acclaim for both his writing and his handsome, delicate artwork. Each illustration, painstakingly created in pencil, is traced with ink, a process that lends his art a draftsmanlike quality that suits his clear and direct writing style. Du Bois also illustrated works by other writers, including CHARLOTTE ZOLOTOW's *William's Doll* (1972) and CLAIRE HUCHET BISHOP's *Twenty and Ten* (1952). In each book, his style is unmistakable but tailored to suit the individual story. William Pène du Bois's enormous talent and consistent inventiveness have earned him an important place on children's bookshelves. ❧ M.V.K.

DUNCAN, LOIS

AMERICAN AUTHOR, B. 1934. Born in Philadelphia, Lois Duncan sold her first story at age thirteen and wrote her first book, *Chapters: My Growth as a Writer,* at age fifteen. Before graduating from Duke University, she was a three-time winner of *Seventeen*'s annual short story contest. She later taught journalism at the University of New Mexico. Duncan has written over forty books for children and young adults, from historical fiction such as *Peggy* (1970) to lullabies such as *Songs from Dreamland* (1989). About this diversity, she says, "As an adult I have tried my hand at many different kinds of writing—adult slick fiction, confessions, murder mysteries, books for small children, in-betweeners, and teenagers, but it is this last field to which I always seem to return. The teen years are such exciting ones, and it is a challenge to provide books that this age will find meaningful and interesting enough to compete with outside activities."

It is these books—the young adult suspense novels—for which Duncan has earned her success and fame. Duncan's first suspense novel, a tale of spies and Communist intrigue, *Game of Danger* (1962), established the general formula she would employ for the next three decades. Told in the first person by a female teenager, the story is exciting and fast-paced, with good characterization and a touch of boy-girl romance. Her next suspense novel, *Ransom* (1966), was nominated for the Edgar Allan Poe Award for mystery writing. With *A Gift of Magic* (1971), a recurring theme in Duncan's stories is first seen—characters who possess a supernatural personality trait, be it extrasensory perception, witchcraft, or astral projection. *Down a Dark Hall* (1974), *Summer of Fear* (1976), *Stranger with My Face* (1981), *The Third Eye* (1984), and *Locked in Time* (1985) all combine paranormal elements and realistic backgrounds so masterfully that the supernatural presence seems normal and believable and, therefore, more menacing. *Summer of Fear* was the winner of both the Dorothy Canfield Fisher Award and the California Young Reader Medal.

Considered a taboo-breaking book, *Killing Mr. Griffin* (1978) details the murder of a high school English teacher by five of his disgruntled students. Led by a psychopathic teen, the students become overwhelmed by the violent chain of events. The protagonist in *Don't Look Behind You* (1989), April Corrigan, was modeled on Duncan's eighteen-year-old daughter Kaitlyn. In the novel, April and her family, members of the Witness Protection Program, are chased across the country by a Camaro-driving hitman. Soon after publication of the book, Kaitlyn was murdered by a passenger in a Camaro. Frustrated by the lack of police cooperation in investigating the murder, Duncan began her own investigation, which included talking to parapsychologists and psychics. Her findings, published in *Who Killed My Daughter?* (1992), point to Kaitlyn's unknowing involvement with Vietnamese drug smugglers.

Duncan was awarded the Margaret A. Edwards Award for lifetime achievement in 1991. While not considered a literary stylist, she writes page-turning thrillers that simultaneously frighten and fascinate readers. ❧ M.I.A.

DUVOISIN, ROGER

SWISS-BORN AMERICAN AUTHOR AND ILLUSTRATOR, 1904–1980. The internationally popular books by Roger Antoine Duvoisin are praised for the author's skillful art and writing and his sure sense of what delights children. A prolific children's book creator, Duvoisin created over forty of his own books and illustrated more than one hundred forty written by others. He was one of the few who understood and mastered the unity found only in the finest children's literature.

As a child, Roger Duvoisin loved to draw, laboring to make his images lifelike. He was encouraged by his father, an architect, and his godmother, a well-known painter of enamels. After art school he began to paint murals and stage scenery, to make posters and illustrations. He became manager of an old French pottery plant, then turned to textile design, the occupation that brought him to the United States. When the textile firm folded, during the Depression, Duvoisin decided to remain in the United States, turning his diverse skills to children's books and magazine illustration.

Duvoisin's books all have a compelling graphic quality. The hallmarks are fine craftsmanship, a strong sense of composition and design, and humor. Of the books he illustrated for other writers, he is probably best known for the popular "Happy Lion" series, written by his wife, Louise Fatio. Equally notable is his 1948 Caldecott Medal–winning art in *White Snow, Bright Snow,* by ALVIN TRESSELT, part of a series about weather. Every book provided new challenges, which Duvoisin eagerly embraced.

In addition to his artistic mastery, Duvoisin was a skilled writer. He is respected for his translation and illustration of medieval European folktales, such as *The Crocodile in the Tree* (1973), and for his alphabet book, *A for Ark* (1952). But it is his homely animal tales that established him as a premier bookmaker. His delightfully original characters—personable animals such as Petunia the goose, Veronica the hippo, and Donkey-Donkey—are drawn with an economical humorous line and graced with understated color. Their escapades, the way they strut, poke, and race across the page, create drama and capture the sympathy of the reader. And Duvoisin's text is part of the book's unity, reinforcing the rhythm and pacing of the page. It is this consummate professional bookmaking, from sketch to text, from layout to jacket design, that sets him apart from many other children's book creators. Duvoisin believed, "A beautiful book is a beautiful object which the child may learn to love."

More recent illustrated books use fewer pages and employ tighter plots, so Duvoisin's stories can seem both overly long and repetitious. And, unfortunately, Duvoisin felt it important to do more than "merely entertain." He valued "that little sneaking desire to teach and to moralize, to pass on to children what we think of our world," a trait now dismissed as didactic. Still, Roger Duvoisin's art remains fresh, and his work has lasting appeal, largely because of his affection and respect for his audience. Children still respond to his sense of freedom, friendly humor, and playfulness, and his characters remain some of the best loved of all time. ❦ S.A.B.

E

Eager, Edward

American author, 1911–1964. Good old-fashioned magic and the adventures it brings never go out of style, especially in Edward Eager's books. Although the last was written more than three decades ago, Eager's stories are still full of humor and excitement as he interweaves the commonplace with the extraordinary. Ordinary children in cities like Toledo, Ohio (where Eager grew up), and Baltimore, Maryland, hungry for adventures like those they read about in books and see in movies, unexpectedly find themselves with magical powers. The magic doesn't always work the way they want it to, however, and that's when the adventures really begin.

A playwright and lyricist with several Broadway productions to his credit, Eager began writing children's books to entertain his young son, Fritz. Both father and son loved magical adventures, especially those by British author E. Nesbit, and Eager borrowed many conventions from these tales and acknowledged Nesbit's books in his own. Besides being full of wordplay and literary allusions, Eager's books are continually surprising; the reader and the characters never know where or when the magic will turn up next. What looks like a coin on the sidewalk turns out to be a talisman in Eager's first and most popular book, *Half Magic* (1954). Figuring out the true nature of the coin and trying to master its powers before its magic wears off save a family from an otherwise boring summer. The same family encounters a magical turtle that turns an ordinary lakeside vacation into a time-traveling extravaganza in *Magic by the Lake* (1957).

A strange toadlike creature rules over a magic thyme garden in *The Time Garden* (1958). A wishing well grants children's wishes—or are the fantastic happenings mere coincidence?—in *Magic or Not?* (1959) and *The Well-Wishers* (1960). A mysterious library book on a week's loan provides magic each day in *Seven-Day Magic* (1962). *Knight's Castle* (1956) brings the time and characters of *Ivanhoe* to life, with a time-traveling group of children meddling in the story's development. Eager's magic books empower the young protagonists; once they discover the magic, they are responsible for learning how to control it. In most cases, the assorted children must cooperate so they can all have turns before the magic runs out, and they must right any mistakes they've made along the way. The episodic chapters are perfect for reading aloud, and the books have the appeal of a series, as characters reappear in a variety of ways. The two children appearing in *Half Magic* and *Magic by the Lake* are the parents of the children featured in *Knight's Castle*, and with all this time travel, adventures eventually overlap and characters from different books literally bump into each other while adventuring.

Time has treated these books well; the pacing and plot easily keep young readers entertained and intrigued. There are a few unfortunate racial references that reinforce stereotypes and slightly date the books: The Arab the children meet in the desert in *Half Magic* is described as "crafty," "unpleasant," and "unattractive" and the children address him in mock Chinese; the dark-skinned natives in *Magic by the Lake* are illiterate cannibals speaking Pidgin English. Otherwise, the adventures in these books are still fresh and will spark plenty of imaginative trips in young readers' minds. § A.M.D.

Easy Readers

Forty years ago books for the child just learning to read tended to be dull—lacking excitement and originality. Written to reinforce existing reading skills, they failed to introduce reading as a pleasurable experience. At the point when it is essential to maintain a child's interest in reading, these books deadened it.

Then in 1957 two wonderfully unexpected books appeared. Although intended for the child with limited reading skills, they were far from simply utilitarian; they were well written and imaginative, offering stories and illustrations attractive not only to their intended audience of beginning readers but also to children not yet able to read. DR. SEUSS's *Cat in the Hat* (1957) offered children a zany story, inspired wordplay, and a glimpse of a fantasy world outside adult control. Seuss showed children just how much fun language and reading could be. The same year saw publication of *Little Bear* (1957), a collaboration between ELSE HOLMELUND MINARIK and illustrator MAURICE SENDAK, consisting of a series of comforting stories about a childlike bear cub and his family and friends. Although the story lines and vocabulary were clear and appealing enough to be read aloud to younger children, beginning readers knew that *Little Bear* was not a "baby book"—it had chapters. *Cat in the Hat* and *Little Bear* not only set the standard for quality publishing for early readers, they marked the beginning of two highly successful publishing series for children: Random House's "Beginner Books" and Harper's "I Can Read." Writers, illustrators, and publishers produced a number of fine books that have already been made classics by their devoted readers: Dr. Seuss's *Green Eggs and Ham* (1960), PEGGY PARISH's *Amelia Bedelia* (1963), ARNOLD LOBEL's *Frog and Toad Are Friends* (1970), and STAN and JAN BERENSTAIN's *The Bike Lesson* (1964). The timeless quality of these books speaks to conflicts and joys shared by most six- to eight-year-olds, generation after generation.

Thanks to the success of these groundbreaking books, children beginning to read today have a panorama of enticing books: books on the sciences; a wide selection of poetry; histories and historical fiction; books with simple science experiments, recipes, and arts and crafts projects; and stories from all the genres that their older siblings enjoy, including sports, mystery, adventure, and science fiction. In fact, there are so many books that the wise adult learns to turn to a knowledgeable children's librarian, teacher, or children's bookstore clerk for guidance in selecting the books that will most appeal to a particular beginning reader.

The challenge to today's writers, illustrators, and editors is to produce appealing, well-written, and factual books, often only thirty-two pages long, on a level easily read by the beginning reader. Confined to a brief text and simple language, an author's talents, strengths, and weaknesses are obvious. Because a child is not yet an accomplished reader and may be new to books, illustrations are essential: They must not only be accomplished, creative, and have child appeal, they must offer clues to the text—and not stray from it. When writers, illustrators, and editors successfully collaborate to create fine easy readers, children respond. Further, with the emergence of the "whole language" classroom in the 1980s and its demand for quality trade books to supplement or replace textbooks, libraries have seen a tremendous increase in the demand for books in all areas—including math, science, history, and poetry—for beginning readers.

Humor books are among the most popular easy readers. Illustrated collections of riddles and jokes such as *Bennett Cerf's Book of Riddles* (1960) and JOSEPH LOW's *A Mad Wet Hen and Other Riddles* (1977) are rarely on the shelf in public libraries. A seven-year-old delights in the same jokes that mom and dad or grandma and grandpa told when they were the same age, and they delight even more in finding them in books they can read themselves.

One of the funniest and most popular series of stories is that about Peggy Parish's Amelia Bedelia. When the good-natured but literal-minded maid carefully follows instructions to "draw the drapes" by getting out a pencil and paper, children not only have something to laugh about but they are also gaining familiarity with English language idioms.

Among the many Seuss favorites, children especially relish two: *Wacky Wednesday* (1974) (written under the pseudonym LeSieg) uses Seuss's zany rhyming to challenge children to find mistakes in the illustrations as they follow the hero from scene to scene; *Fox in Socks* (1969) pits Mr. Knox against Fox as poor Mr. Knox is almost overwhelmed by Fox's barrage of tongue twisters. No lover of humor should miss the hilarious books of author and illustrator JAMES MARSHALL. In his comic stories about Fox, *Fox and His Friends* (1982), *Fox on Wheels* (1983), *Fox on the Job* (1990), and so on, the lazy and conniving, yet basically decent, character all too often falls victim to his own schemes.

Although humor is the genre most popular with young readers, mysteries intrigue these children as much as they do their older siblings and parents. MARJORIE SHARMAT's perennially popular books about Nate the Great, boy detective, and his bedraggled, woebegone dog, Sludge, are a great introduction to mysteries. Each story about Nate and his friends involves children—and adults—in a good time, reading aloud in Joe Friday *Dragnet*-style voices as they try to solve Nate's latest case. The characters in the series live in a diverse urban area, a plus for families and schools trying to reinforce ethnic and racial understanding. Included among the popular titles in the series are *Nate the Great and the Stolen Base* (1992), *Nate the Great Goes Down in the Dumps* (1989), and *Nate the Great and the Sticky Case* (1981). Also in the mystery genre, Kin Platt's *Big Max* (1992) tells of a diminutive detective who travels by umbrella—not always the best means of transportation but definitely one of the silliest.

Children beginning to read often enjoy suspenseful,

slightly spooky stories. Few are able to resist ALVIN SCHWARTZ's ghostly folklore collections, especially *In a Dark, Dark Room and Other Stories* (1984). The stories are perfect for reading aloud or retelling at Halloween or summer camp-outs, and the illustrations offer a humorous touch that is reassuring to the ready-to-believe child reader.

Stories from the folklore of many nations of the world are also represented in books for this age group. JOANNA COLE's *Bony Legs* (1983) is a retelling of a Russian Baba Yaga story. It is just scary enough for a first- or second-grader. An almost-scary American folktale, MOLLY BANG's *Wiley and the Hairy Man* (1976), transports readers and listeners to Alabama's Tombigbee River and its swamp. There they meet young African American Wiley and cheer him on as he three times bests the hairy man, a comical yet slightly frightening conjurer.

Some of today's best writers and illustrators create books of fantasy and fairy tales specifically for the beginning reader. JANE YOLEN's fractured fairy tale *Sleeping Ugly* (1981) pits the beautiful but nasty Princess Miserella against poor but nice Plain Jane. In *Commander Toad in Space* (1980), Yolen has fun parodying the *Star Trek* television series. The characters and adventures of the amphibian crew of *Star Warts* are made even more humorous and vivid by the illustrations of Bruce Degen. SYD HOFF's *Stanley* (1992), set in a definitely imaginary time of cavemen and dinosaurs, is a good example of fantasy. The story humorously demonstrates how one nonconformist can make a tremendous difference to his society. An appealing addition to the books of original fantasy or fairy-tale stories is the "Dragon" series by Dav Pilkey. Generous, kind, comical, and not always patient, the little blue dragon is chronicled in brightly illustrated stories that begin with *A Friend for Dragon: Dragon's First Tale* (1991).

To children, family and friends are not just important parts of their lives but two of their favorite subjects for stories. Whether humorous or serious, books about families and friends offer young readers opportunities for affirmation, growth, or escape into a safer and more secure world. Frog and Toad appear in four books by Arnold Lobel, starting with *Frog and Toad Are Friends,* each containing several gently comical stories about the best friends and their adventures. Lobel's fine writing and illustrations earned his books both Newbery and Caldecott Honor Awards as well as a multitude of fans.

Mandy and Mimi, who debuted in Pat Ross's *M and M and the Big Bag* (1981), are best friends who manage to get each other into trouble—and out of it. The two little girls are curious, adventurous, often silly, and very real. In Joan Robins's *Addie Meets Max* (1985), fear of a new neighbor's dog nearly stops a friendship from developing. Addie, like so many children, has mixed feelings about her new neighbor. With her mother's help, Addie not only makes a new friend but overcomes her fear of Max's dog.

Family stories vary as much as families do. The protagonist of BARBARA PORTE's series is a young boy who lives with his widowed dentist father. Harry is shy, worries too much, and wants the same things other children want: acceptance, love, a pet, and to be good at sports. Porte and illustrator Yossi Abolafia have created a realistic and very appealing series that offers a positive portrayal of a single-parent family.

Jean Van Leeuwen's *Amanda Pig and Her Big Brother Oliver* (1982) is one of a series of books about a model "pig" family: a stay-at-home mother, loving father, adoring grandmother and brother and sister who usually get along. Though there are occasional rivalries between the brother and sister, problems at school, or misunderstandings of one kind or another, family love keeps them secure. Another kind of idealized family can be found in CYNTHIA RYLANT's *Henry and Mudge: The First Book* (1987). The boy and his big mastiff dog are the stars, but Henry's easygoing, loving parents unobtrusively watch over things, helping the little boy through difficult moments.

Since the late 1960s, exciting historical fiction has been a staple in publishing for children learning to read. Aware of the careful research and fine writing of authors such as NATHANIEL BENCHLEY and F. N. MONJO, teachers and librarians have enjoyed recommending these books to children. In Barbara Brenner's *Wagon Wheels,* the Muldie boys and their father head west to Kansas territory to get a homestead of their own. Based on a true story, the book shows the courage and resourcefulness of this real African American family of pioneers. A little girl and an amazing wild horse are the heroes of another pioneer story, *The White Stallion* (1982) by Elizabeth Shub. Set in Texas in 1845, the book tells how little Gretchen, separated from her family's wagon train, is miraculously rescued by the leader of a herd of wild horses. Based on historical accounts, the seemingly fantastic story is quite believable.

Another pioneer story, set in California during the gold rush, tells of Chang, a Chinese immigrant child, who spends his days working and occasionally dreaming of having a pony of his own. *Chang's Paper Pony* (1988) by Eleanor Coerr gives children an idea of the prejudice Chinese encountered, as well as the rare moments of kindness.

Nonfiction is another popular easy-reader category. Excellent, well-written, and enticing books have been published about math, dinosaurs, astronomy, human biology, and much more. Today's young readers are curious about many of the same subjects as are older children and adults. Fortunately, there are usually carefully written, well-illustrated easy readers available to satisfy that curiosity. Among the more prolific authors are Paul Showers and FRANKLYN M. BRANLEY. Showers most often writes about aspects of human biology; two of his titles are *The Listening Walk* (1991) and *A Drop of Blood* (1989). Branley has written many books on earth science and astronomy, including *The Planets in Our Solar System* (1987) and *Tornado Alert* (1988). Both authors present information clearly and provide opportunities for children to try simple experiments testing scientific concepts.

Other areas of nonfiction are also popular with young children. Two Old Testament stories, *Noah and the Flood* (1992) by Barbara Brenner and *David and the Giant* (1987) by Emily Little, offer children just honing their reading skills the opportunity to read on their own about these biblical heroes. For children curious about magic, Rose Wyler and Gerald Ames offer simple but fascinating instructions for fooling friends or for putting on a magic show in their two books *Magic Secrets* (1990) and *Spooky Tricks* (1968). Young sports fans can find books about their heroes and instructions for improving their playing in books such as Chuck Solomon's *Our Little League* (1988) and *Our Soccer League* (1988).

Among the several good poetry collections available are LEE BENNETT HOPKINS's *Surprises* (1984) and *More Surprises* (1987), which contain an assortment of poems, some thoughtful, some funny, and all accessible to the young reader. KARLA KUSKIN's *Soap Soup* flows from one poem to another, each about a child's world and the child himself. Kuskin's deceptively simple poems are sure to inspire children to try writing their own poetry. A well-known and popular poet for older children, JACK PRELUTSKY has also published poetry for beginning readers. His collections describe the seasons, holidays, and all the disappointments that the title *Rainy, Rainy Saturday* (1980) implies.

Libraries today are busier than ever, and in any children's department, books for beginning readers continue to be popular and in demand. Despite concern about the negative impact of television on reading habits, children in the primary grades seem as excited as ever about the first word and the first book they read. Most important, these children are constantly being offered not just the wonderful classic titles such as *Little Bear, The Cat in the Hat,* and *Amelia Bedelia,* but they are being encouraged to remain readers by new works of fiction and nonfiction written, illustrated, and produced with the care and sensitivity that young minds deserve. The response of today's children to these wonderful books bodes well for their future as readers in a literate world. ❧ BARBARA M. BARSTOW

ECKERT, ALLAN

AMERICAN NOVELIST AND NONFICTION AUTHOR, B. 1931. Allan Eckert was born in Buffalo, New York, and attended the University of Dayton and Ohio State University. His résumé is long and varied. By the time he was twenty-five, he had worked as a postman, private detective, fireman, plastics technician, cook, trapper, commercial artist, draftsman, and police reporter. In 1960 he decided to become a full-time writer; four Pulitzer Prize nominations indicate that his final choice proved the most successful.

Eckert's eclectic background helps explain his highly individualized writing style: his merging of fact with fiction. Writing about his two major preoccupations, American history and natural history, he combines thorough research and technical details with literary techniques—stream-of-consciousness and narrative devices—to create his own literary genre: "documentary fiction." His ability to write popular narratives from subject matter usually reserved for scholarly texts—the decline of the great auk (*The Great Auk,* 1963), the westward movement of the pioneers (*The Frontiersmen,* 1967)—places him in the often uncomfortable middle ground between academic and popular writers, criticized for using novelistic techniques to relay facts.

Eckert's writing is easily recognizable by his use of a technique he calls "hidden dialogue." He puts quotation marks around material that was not initially recorded as dialogue but reported as having been said, heard, or thought after an event. This technique is quite controversial and has been severely criticized by professional historians. Nevertheless, Eckert's hidden dialogue, almost identical to the speech of the era, proves that history doesn't need to be dull or inaccessible.

Unlike many authors who write for both adults and children, Eckert does not believe that there is a marked difference in his writing styles. He says, "There is no 'writing down' to a certain age level. I strongly believe that young readers can handle almost anything, providing it is interestingly presented."One of his adult books, *Incident at Hawk's Hill* (1971), is also his most critically acclaimed children's book, having won three major juvenile literature awards: Newbery Honor Book, George C. Stone Award of Merit for Children's Literature, and Austrian Juvenile Book of the Year Award. Based on an actual episode from Canadian history, the book chronicles the story of six-year-old Ben, a little boy with an uncanny, almost eerie kinship with animals. Ben wanders away from home and is eventually given up for lost. He is alive, however, having been adopted by a female badger and taken to live in her underground hideaway. When, weeks later, his older brother finds Ben, he must fight off the maternal badger to bring Ben back to his family. *Incident at Hawk's Hill* is a curious example of a book that received mixed reviews amidst much critical acclaim. In addition to being called old-fashioned and unbelievable, it was specifically criticized for its depiction of gratuitous, explicit violence in the natural world, but it is, in reality, a fascinating description of life in the wild and the magical relationship between Ben and the badger.

Eckert remains at his strongest when he concentrates on the nonfiction subjects he knows so well. *Savage Journey* (1979) tells the story of Sarah, a young girl who finds herself alone in the wilds of a South American rain forest. The vivid, often graphic descriptions of the army ants, boa constrictors, and foliage take center stage during Sarah's ordeal. *Blue Jacket: War Chief of the Shawnees* (1969) relates the true story of a boy who traded in his white identity to become a member of the Shawnee tribe. Eckert's story is terse and dramatic in its revelation of the white man's greed.

Eckert has established a reputation as a writer who makes his subject, scientific or historical, interesting and entertaining to his readers. § M.I.A.

EDMONDS, WALTER D.

AMERICAN WRITER, B. 1903. Walter Edmonds was born in Boonville, New York, a small town in the Mohawk Valley. He spent winters in New York City but considered his real home the family dairy farm in Boonville, where he spent summers. Edmonds was educated at St. Paul's and Choate schools and graduated from Harvard University in 1926. As a junior he took an advanced composition course and was persuaded to send a short story to *Scribner's Magazine.* It was accepted for publication, and Edmonds was on his way to a writing career.

Edmonds claims he has never written a book specifically for children: "The criterion of any child's book should be whether it has enough stuff, humor, reality, wisdom, excitement to be interesting to an adult mind." He writes about unusual topics, such as the plight of a young Confederate aeronaut in the Civil War story *Cadmus Henry* (1949), and he can tell a tall tale with humor and wit, as shown in *Uncle Ben's Whale* (1955). More often than not, however, Edmonds returns to his roots: the history of the Mohawk Valley region. Edmonds feels strongly about the continuity and relevance of American history and delves deeply into the history and the lives of the people who lived, worked, and struggled to survive on the frontier. A sense of possibility and adventure permeates these tales of quietly determined individuals who persevere against insurmountable odds. In his Newbery Award–winning book, *The Matchlock Gun* (1941), young Edward defends his mother and small sister against a savage Indian attack with an antique, unwieldy gun. Based on an actual incident, this story reflects Edmonds's preference for conducting research using original sources rather than formal history and immersing himself in the period about which he writes.

Two Logs Crossing (1943) relates the story of John Haskell, the son of a recently deceased ne'er-do-well father, who proves himself by supporting his family and repaying his father's debts through two hard winters of fur trapping. Edmonds's most accomplished work is *Bert Breen's Barn,* winner of the 1976 National Book Award. This lyrical ode to perseverance spans several years of young Tom Dolan's life, from the time he sets the goal of acquiring the barn through earning the money to buy it to its eventual erection and consequent impact on his family. Like John in *Two Logs Crossing,* Tom lives with the legacy of a lazy, shiftless father, but through diligence and hard work, both boys elevate their family's social and economic stature. Edmonds's considerable skills come together in *Bert Breen's Barn.* It has fine characterization, spare, eloquent prose, and a compelling plot with elements of mystery and adventure. In all of his books, Edmonds illuminates history with colorful characters and dynamic, accurately drawn historic episodes.

Edmonds has also written many books for adults, including *The South African Quirt* (1985), *The Night Raider and Other Stories* (1980), and *Drums Along the Mohawk* (1936). § M.O'D.H.

EGIELSKI, RICHARD

AMERICAN ILLUSTRATOR, B. 1952. At one time a student of MAURICE SENDAK at the Parsons School of Design, Egielski shares his teacher's devotion to idiosyncratic and highly personal picture books. In collaboration with Arthur Yorinks, as well as with other writers, he has created some of the most quirky and original children's books of recent decades.

Born in New York City, Egielski was an artistically inclined boy, but it was his desire to escape from parochial schools and not his interest in making a career of art that encouraged him to apply to the city's High School of Art and Design. Once there, however, his talent found root, and he later studied art at the Pratt Institute and Parsons. Upon graduating, he showed his portfolio to children's book publishers who, as he recalled, decided his work was a bit too strange and "sophisticated" for a young audience. Sendak thought otherwise and introduced him to another young man starting out, writer ARTHUR YORINKS.

Together, Egielski and Yorinks forged an unusually intimate collaboration, each critiquing the other's work and going through many phases of design before presenting a project to a publisher. In their first notable success together, *Louis the Fish* (1980), Egielski's illustrations capture the long shadows and dingy hues of his native city as well as the edgy tension that marks all true New Yorkers. His Louis, the butcher who loves fish, has a constantly bewildered air about him. His customers, even when they are pictured as fish, maintain a harried, belligerent posture.

A later Egielski and Yorinks collaboration, *Hey, Al,* won Egielski the 1987 Caldecott Medal. Here the depressingly claustrophobic apartment of Eddie, a janitor who lives alone with his dog, Al, is mostly rendered in shades of brown. Details that break out of the pictures' frames—a newspaper dropped outside the front door, a suitcase half in and half out of the bathroom—emphasize just how cramped a place it is. When Eddie and Al take flight to a seeming paradise in the sky, the art explodes with lush, tropical colors. Once again, details break through the frame, but the effect now suggests expansiveness and the island's amazing fecundity. When paradise sours, Al and Eddie struggle back to their old home, but in the last picture, gentle and triumphant, they find a more agreeable way to add color to their lives.

Egielski insists that provocative and wry texts interest him most as an illustrator, an assertion that has been borne out by his work with writers other than Yorinks. *The Tub People* (1989) and *The Tub Grandfather* (1993), both by PAM CONRAD, tell the story of a family of wooden tub toys who manage to stay together despite perilous trials. Egielski's illustrations endow these stiff toys with subtly powerful personalities, so much so that in *The Tub Grandfather* there is one double-spread picture of the Grandmother dancing with her newly found husband that is almost heartachingly tender. This astonishing picture, like all of Egielski's best work, reflects the singular vision, emotional urgency, and technical mastery of an artist at the top of his form. A.Q.

EHLERT, LOIS

AMERICAN AUTHOR AND ILLUSTRATOR, B. 1934. Lois Ehlert's background as a designer and graphic artist is apparent in her many acclaimed PICTURE BOOKS.

The Wisconsin native was encouraged by her parents to pursue the arts at a very young age, and they provided her with a private work space, scraps of cloth, and pieces of wood for her creations. After attending the Layton School of Art and the University of Wisconsin, where she received a B.F.A., Ehlert worked in the graphic arts as a production assistant, designer, and freelance illustrator. She began to illustrate children's books but was disappointed with the final production quality and stopped working on books to focus on other graphic design work. After several years she returned to children's book illustration because she felt that publishers were paying more attention to details of design and production.

Ehlert's illustrations for *Limericks by Lear* (1965) reflect her interest in design. Each illustration is created as a black print with overlays of shapes of color. The effect is bold and whimsical, suited to Lear's humorous limericks.

Ehlert turned to writing and illustrating her own books with *Growing Vegetable Soup* (1987) and *Planting a Rainbow* (1988). These books use flat shapes and bright colors combined with a simple text about gardening to convey both information and a story. Ehlert's success with these books led her to experiment further with color and form. *Color Zoo* (1989), a Caldecott Honor Book, was much lauded for the skill of the design. Each page is a different bold color and a shape is cut out of the middle. The combination of shapes and colors created by several pages overlaying the others reveals an animal's head. For example, a circle, a square, and a triangle form a tiger. The reader uncovers a new animal with the turn of each page. The book ends with a review of all the animals introduced earlier. *Color Zoo* is about concepts—shapes, colors, and animals—but also about looking at the world in a new and creative way.

Each of Ehlert's successive books explores the effects of shape, color, and form within her subject matter. Her books convey information to the youngest readers,

Voices of the Creators

Lois Ehlert

Although I've been a graphic designer and illustrator for many years, it was in 1984 that I first began to experiment, joining my own text and art in children's books. I think of these books as little love notes to children, records of things I care about, ideas and feelings I want to pass on to the next generation. I don't think of myself as doing things in a particularly conventional way, and none of my books has been very easy, simple, or just fallen into place. If a book ever just fell into place for me, that would probably mean that I was repeating myself. I'm interested in the book as a whole, not just the illustrations. I choose the size for the book, select the type style and size, and integrate all elements on the page. That's the graphic designer part of me at work.

I feel comfortable with multiple subjects for my books, both fiction and nonfiction, sometimes blending the two. I try to extend the age range of my readers by adding extra things, such as small labels, a glossary, or information so that the older reader can choose part or all of the book, while the younger child may just "read" the art. Depending on his reading ability, the child may notice something new tucked into a composition that he missed at the first reading. I always liked those books best myself, when I was learning to read—the ones with the little surprises to test my reading and observation skills.

Getting ideas for my books comes about in a variety of ways. Children always ask me where my ideas come from. I cannot fully understand it myself; I usually don't even know how an idea will work until I do a little bit of it. I've been known to do three or four dummies for one idea and usually change the text a dozen times, or more. Even the size and shape of the book continue to change as I move along. The beginning of an idea may come in the writing (sometimes only a title); other times it starts with the art style or subject matter.

Once I get one little glimmer of the book, I begin a dummy. If I can get one page right, it seems that things open up more easily from that point on. I go back and forth between the text and picture. If I say something in the picture, I can eliminate it in the text.

It's like a play, with stage directions—once the performance begins, the directions aren't needed anymore. I write the text in longhand, then type it, and begin to read it aloud to find the rhythm and music of the language. With a sparse text, each word has to work hard.

Once the idea for the book is decided upon, I begin research. I love doing the research for a book. I get to go to interesting places: museums, nature centers, aquariums, anywhere I can get the information or inspiration I need. I talk to experts in the field about details, such as the formulation of a vegetable soup recipe, what one calls a young sugar maple tree sprout, the origins of a Chinese fruit, or the many uses of a squirrel's tail.

I try to maintain a feeling of freshness in my work, and usually roughly sketch out the concept of what I want to do in pencil, including the type. I then collect or observe the objects I want to paint (I do as much as I can from real models). Then I begin to work with gay abandon. My art looks impressionistic rather than realistic. I work in collage, cutting paper and pasting, which allows me to be very spontaneous. I use a variety of papers (some of which I paint), watercolors, ink, and real objects and start to cut and paste. I have been an art teacher over the years and use some of the same materials the children use. I glue all of these pieces together on bond paper to form the illustrations, and then begin to move the art around on the page, adding to it or deleting a part, until I find the right composition. I try not to censor myself at this point, nor limit myself because of some preconceived idea. That's the beauty of collage. The "un-fun" part of it is painting all those cut edges so they won't show when the art is photographed for reproduction.

If there is a single thread that weaves its way through all of my books, it is a colored thread. I love color. When I'm painting in color, I'm in my most heavenly mood. I always hope that time will go on forever, although I know it won't and can't. There is an unearthly quality about this part of the creative process, impossible to describe. It commands my total being. It's as if I had stepped into the book and walked around in it.

I like to think that if I create a book properly, the hand of the designer does not show. If I do my work successfully, it will look very simple. With paper and glue, and my trusty scissors, I express the simple things of life—the homely, ordinary subjects that I love.

allowing them to explore a subject through dramatic visual presentation. *Eating the Alphabet* (1989) introduces the reader to fruits and vegetables beginning with each letter of the alphabet, and the glossary gives additional information about the foods, which include the Ugli fruit and the jicama. *Feathers for Lunch* (1990) is the story of a cat who is unable to catch a bird for lunch, and each page introduces the reader to a different life-size bird in a garden setting. Ehlert labels each bird and plant, using the typography as part of the overall design. Ehlert plays with color and size of typography in all her books, which have been well received by critics and lauded by teachers and parents for their educational value. Many of her books conclude with a glossary or a chart summarizing the information therein.

Ehlert's books are visually exciting and bold. Each is an experiment with form and a discovery for the reader. ❧ M.V.K.

Ehrlich, Amy

AMERICAN AUTHOR, B. 1942. Like many authors, Amy Ehrlich wanted to write from a very early age. Part of this desire stemmed from her love of books and reading, but she was also influenced by her father, Max Ehrlich, a television writer and suspense novelist. Born in New York, Amy Ehrlich grew up there and in Connecticut. One of her early short stories won a prize in ninth grade, an event that had a strong impact on the writer's development. She spent two years at a Quaker boarding school in upstate New York, then attended Bennington College in Vermont. Ehrlich never finished her degree, as she got caught up in the tumultuous 1960s. During that decade she lived in communes, spent time in Jamaica, and held a number of brief jobs, including hospital receptionist, fabric colorist, day-care worker, and proofreader. She also found employment in the publishing industry as a part-time copywriter and editorial assistant. One of her colleagues at a publishing company encouraged Ehrlich to try writing a children's book, but she suffered from writer's block and was unable to complete a manuscript until some friends had a baby they named Zeke Silvermoon. Inspired by the real-life child, Ehrlich wrote her first children's book in just one weekend. Published in 1972, *Zeek Silver Moon* details the everyday life young Zeek shares with his loving parents. The picture book received excellent reviews and appeared on many lists of the year's best books. The warm, episodic story still retains some appeal, although the seventies life-style Ehrlich depicts now seems extremely dated.

Ehrlich continued writing children's books while living in Brooklyn and working as an editor at several publishing houses. She wrote a number of picture stories, two easy-to-read books about classmates Leo, Zack, and Emmie and produced several adaptations of well-known fairy tales. It was not until Ehrlich moved to Vermont and married that she was able to devote more time to writing, and there she produced two important young adult books. *Where It Stops, Nobody Knows* (1988) is a suspenseful novel about teenage Nina, whose over-protective mother is constantly on the move. As Nina and her mother move from Vermont to Utah to California to New York, the teenager begins to realize her mother is running away from something. The conclusion is startling and thought-provoking, leaving readers with many questions to consider long after the book is closed. *The Dark Card* (1991) is equally disturbing. Seventeen-year-old Laura is spending the summer after her mother's death alone in Ventnor, New Jersey, where she becomes involved in the enticing world of gambling in nearby Atlantic City. Rich in metaphor, psychologically insightful, and filled with jolting surprises, the novel offers a glimpse of a dark and dangerous world. Some readers may be angered by the unsympathetic lead character or the novel's unresolved conclusion, but few will question its power.

Although Ehrlich's works for younger readers have been well received, her young adult novels have enhanced her reputation as a unique and multifaceted author. ❧ P.D.S.

Eichenberg, Fritz

AMERICAN WRITER AND ILLUSTRATOR, 1901–1990. Fritz Eichenberg was born in Cologne, Germany, in a historical period that frowned on creativity. All learning was done by rote, history centered on Germany, and introduction to the classics of literature was nonexistent. This life of grayness was lit by two things. One was Eichenberg's family, especially his mother, who filled the house with classical music, took the children to plays when finances allowed, and introduced them to whatever literary luminaries were available. His other saving grace was many trips to the zoo. Eichenberg remembers: "This means not only good company but good training for any future illustrator of children's books. Never to be without a sketch pad at the zoo or the circus proved more profitable to me than years of study at art school."

World War I ended in 1918 just as Eichenberg was finishing school. He reveled in the new freedom and embarked on an intoxicating tour of the literature that he had missed while living under the authoritarian rule of Kaiser Wilhelm. He began to identify with the writers who portrayed the serious problems of the world. He recalls: "I wanted to see these problems with the eye of an artist, an image maker, and to interpret them in my own way." First he was apprenticed to a lithographer, and then he was enrolled at the Academy of Leipzig to study under Professor Steiner-Prag, where he learned the art of illustration, lithography, and wood engraving. He became a successful social and political cartoonist, but began irritating a young politician on the rise: Adolf Hitler. Because Eichenberg did not like the direction that Germany was taking, he accepted a roving commission from a European publisher and was sent to Central America. A serious illness took him to New York, and while he was there he made the decision to immigrate with his young family to America.

Much of the severity of Eichenberg's early life, his resulting passion for the classics, and the early influence of the works of Goya and Daumier ultimately affected his art and technique. He has produced some sixty books, both illustrated classics and original books for children. Eichenberg is probably best known for his engravings, particularly wood engraving. Many of his projects have involved illustrating the classics that were of special significance in his life. Some of the illustrations, like that of Heathcliff on the cover of *Wuthering Heights,* have become the standard image for generations of readers. His artistic technique is also deeply imbued with his strong social and political beliefs.

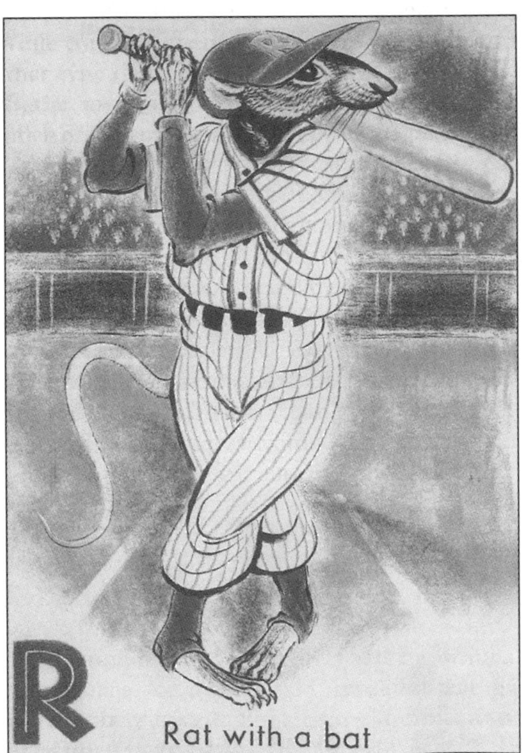

Illustration by Fritz Eichenberg from his book *Ape in a Cape* (1952).

Eichenberg is not, fortunately, without a light side. The two books he illustrated especially for young children were inspired by the birth of his son—*Ape in a Cape: An Alphabet of Odd Animals* (a Caldecott Honor Book in 1952) and *Dancing in the Moon: Counting Rhymes* (1955)—exhibit his artistry, his humor, and his lifelong love and respect for animals. ♠ A.I.

Ellis, Sarah

Canadian author, b. 1952. Sarah Ellis received attention and acclaim for her first novel, *The Family Project* (1988), and all her novels since have been well received by readers and critics.

Ellis, born in Vancouver, British Columbia, works as a children's librarian, storyteller, and critic as well as a writer. She claims to have developed her storytelling talents to gain attention as the youngest child in her family. Her fiction is marked by detail and honest, believable characters and situations.

The Family Project concerns an eleven-year-old girl's acceptance of her mother's pregnancy. Jessica is at once afraid of the unavoidable changes to come and excited at the prospect of a baby. Once the baby is born, Jessica is thrilled with the addition to the family. When the baby dies of sudden infant death syndrome, Jessica and her family struggle to re-create a family and accept Lucie's death. Each character in the tragic story is memorable and multifaceted, from a shopping mall manager who appears in one brief scene to Jessica herself.

Ellis's second novel, *Next-Door Neighbors* (1990), is about the friendship between a shy preacher's daughter and an outcast immigrant boy who wears odd clothing and cannot fit in with his peers. The two develop a grudging friendship with the help of a Chinese gardener and learn much about the costs of prejudice and the importance of personal strength. Like Jessica, Peggy develops an awareness of herself and her surroundings through gradual awakenings and recognition of the tragedies in human life.

Pick-Up Sticks (1991) is a third novel about a young girl struggling to make sense of family and her place in the world. Polly is being raised by a strong, independent mother who chose to have and raise a child on her own. When they must find another apartment, Polly decides to stay with relatives living a more traditional life until the ordeal is over. Away from home, she discovers that her own family, unusual as it is, is warmer and stronger than the sterile, uncommunicative household of her cousins.

All of Ellis's heroines are supported through their youth by understanding parents. The young girls discover the strengths of their own family and learn acceptance. The stories concern serious subjects but are never maudlin. Ellis skillfully inserts humor throughout her stories in characters and absurd situations. Polly and her mother interview at several cooperative houses and meet a cast of outlandish but entirely believable people. Jessica, while struggling with the addition of a baby to her household, reads the hilarious, overwritten parenting articles that her mother leaves lying around. Peggy, unhappy at school, pores over a self-help book, reading chapters such as "Ten Ways to a More Fulfilling Marriage." Each of Ellis's stories is memorable and written with a delicate, human touch. ❧ M.V.K.

Emberley, Edward

American author and illustrator, b. 1931. Edward Emberley, award-winning author and illustrator of lively, colorful picture books, was born in Malden, Massachusetts, and graduated from Massachusetts College of Art. Emberley was interested in art early on, when he was encouraged to draw primarily by "lack of discouragement" from his parents. Barbara Emberley, his wife and frequent collaborator, says he was a "serious" student of art during their undergraduate days. After a stint spent painting signs for the army, Emberley worked as a commercial artist specializing in cartoons before becoming interested in children's book illustration in the late 1950s. Fortunately for his many fans, Emberley is far from serious in his illustrations. The joy of his work lies in its humor and lightheartedness. He has a strong sense of design as well as a thorough knowledge of the production and printing processes that produce a finished book. As one critic noted, he has a grasp of the "cold practicalities of bookmaking," but always maintains a clear vision of the finished work. In fact, Emberley has said that "the necessity to be both dreamer and realist is what fascinates me most about picture book making."

Emberley dislikes reusing a technique he has already mastered, which may account for the wide variety of his work and his constant experimentation with different media, ranging from pen and ink and pencil to the woodcuts that brought him acclaim in *Drummer Hoff,* awarded the Caldecott Medal in 1968, and *One Wide River to Cross,* the sole Caldecott Honor Book in 1967. Both books were collaborations with his wife as author; her literary style is simple and straightforward, a perfect complement to Emberley's stylized art. The text of *Drummer Hoff* was adapted from a Mother Goose rhyme and concerns a boisterous group effort to build and fire off a cannon with a loud "KAHBAHBLOOM!" The story builds cumulatively in art and text to its explosive conclusion. The Emberleys changed the characters from ordinary men to military figures in part because military uniforms lent themselves so well to the richly intricate woodcuts, which are overlaid with brilliant color. As in *One Wide River,* an adaptation of the Noah's ark story, Emberley chose to create a unified, consistently striking work, rather than a few dazzling pages.

Emberley is perhaps best known for his drawing-book series that began in 1970 with *Ed Emberley's Drawing Book of Animals* and has continued through nearly every color of the rainbow, and from birds to farms to trains to weirdoes and more. These books illustrate simple, step-by-step suggestions and instructions for drawing fanciful creations. *Ed Emberley's Drawing Book of Faces* (1975) presents an intriguing cast of characters, while *Ed Emberley's Great Thumbprint Drawing Book* (1977) is an ingenious, extraordinarily simple means of producing art.

Other works of note include *Klippity Klop* (1974), a humorous tale of a prince and his horse, rendered in simple line drawings and hand-lettered type, and *A Birthday Wish* (1977), a zany, wordless picture book that proves that with Emberley's work words are not always necessary. Both books are characteristic of Emberley's style in that they appear simple on the surface but are so richly detailed and visually abundant that they invite numerous readings in which the reader can always find something new. ❧ M.O'D.H.

Engdahl, Sylvia

American author, b. 1933. Sylvia Louise Engdahl brought her deeply felt beliefs regarding space exploration to the field of young adult literature and produced several science fiction novels that have won critical praise and awards.

Engdahl was born and raised in Los Angeles, where

she considered herself an outsider and observer. She first became fascinated with space travel during a ninth-grade science class, but made no plans to pursue that interest. Instead, she attended several West Coast colleges, graduated from the University of California at Santa Barbara, taught fourth grade in Portland, Oregon, then quickly realized she was ill-suited for teaching. She developed programs for air defense computers, working in many parts of the country over the next ten years. Engdahl began to consider a writing career when she discovered how much she enjoyed the technical writing her job entailed; at the same time, her mother, Mildred Allen Butler, was beginning to experience success as a writer for young adults. Determined to share her theory that space travel is necessary for the survival of the human race, Engdahl quit her job in 1967 in order to begin a writing career of her own.

Engdahl's first futuristic novel, *Journey between Worlds* (1970), concerns a teenage girl who reluctantly accompanies her father to their new home on Mars. Engdahl's goal was to attract readers who had never given much thought to space travel. The book could not find a publisher until after Engdahl's second novel, *Enchantress from the Stars* (1970), was accepted for publication. An ambitious book, *Enchantress from the Stars* presents three civilizations at different stages of development. Its heroine, Elana, a member of the most advanced group, is trying to prevent space visitors from destroying a planet whose culture could be compared with that of Europe's medieval era. The story is presented in several writing styles—from Elana's first-person narration to the almost fairy-tale quality of the omniscient narrator of the medieval segments. Profound questions are raised in this exceptional novel, named a Newbery Honor Book in 1971. Engdahl wrote another powerful Elana story, *The Far Side of Evil* (1971), and a trilogy—*This Star Shall Abide* (1972), *Beyond the Tomorrow Mountains* (1973), and *The Doors of the Universe* (1981)—about a young man who questions his planet's social order, then must face serious issues involving religion, metaphysics, and genetics.

Engdahl's novels are labeled science fiction, but cannot be slotted with the traditional robot and ray-gun genre. Instead, they are vehicles for Engdahl's philosophical theorizing. Some readers are put off by the lack of action in these densely written, complex tales, yet the books are extremely rewarding for some readers. In addition to her novels, she has written a picture book, *Our World Is Earth* (1979), and several nonfiction books dealing with scientific issues, including *The Planet-Girded Suns* (1974), a historical survey of humanity's changing views of outer space. ❧ P.D.S.

Enright, Elizabeth

American author and illustrator, 1909–1968. Since Elizabeth Enright's mother was an illustrator and her father a political cartoonist, it was perhaps inevitable that Enright would follow in her parents' footsteps and become an artist. But after illustrating several books, Enright discovered she had an even greater talent for writing, and she produced a number of memorable children's books.

Although born in Oak Park, Illinois, the daughter of Walter J. Enright and Maginel Wright Barney, Enright was raised in New York. Her parents divorced when she was eleven, and Enright spent her teenage years attending boarding school in Connecticut and studying dance with Martha Graham. She trained at the Art Students League in New York and later spent a year at the Parsons School of Design in Paris. When she returned to the United States, she married, started a family, and began illustrating children's books. One day while doodling, Enright sketched a series of pictures with an African motif. She later wrote a text to accompany the drawings, and *Kintu: A Congo Adventure* was published in 1935. This least-known of the author's works is well designed but has an inconsequential story and caricatured illustrations of African children, which modern readers might deem offensive. Yet it is an important book in the author's career because it awakened Enright's latent talent for writing. In fact, many of the book's reviewers mentioned that the text was stronger than the illustrations. From then on, Enright included fewer and fewer illustrations in her work, to the point where her later books were illustrated by other artists. Enright wrote her second book while spending the summer on a Wisconsin farm owned by her uncle, the famous architect Frank Lloyd Wright. *Thimble Summer* recounts the experiences of nine-year-old farm girl Garnet Linden as she helps with harvesting, visits a fair, and gets locked in the town library, among other adventures. The book won the Newbery Medal in 1939, making Enright one of the youngest winners in Newbery history. Although Enright's gifts for description and character are evident in this fine book, her later work is even more impressive.

Perhaps her best-known books are those concerning the Melendy children—Rush, Mona, Randy, and Oliver—who live in a New York brownstone with their writer father and much-loved housekeeper, Cuffy. These cosmopolitan children are intelligent, artistic, affectionate, and, most of all, interesting. In their first book, *The Saturdays* (1941), the Melendys pool their weekly allowances so that each of them can spend one Saturday a month having an adventure. Later volumes, *The Four-*

Story Mistake (1942) and *Then There Were Five* (1944), move the Melendys to the country and add an adopted son to the family. The last book in the series, *Spiderweb for Two* (1951), disappoints only because the older Melendy children have left home, though the writing has the usual Enright percipience and charm.

Gone-Away Lake (1957), the story of two siblings and their cousin spending the summer in the country, where they discover an abandoned resort, may be Enright's finest achievement. Her descriptive powers and unique ability to observe the world through the eyes of a child were never stronger than in this unusual novel. Other notable Enright books include a sequel, *Return to Gone-Away* (1961), a pair of fairy tales, *Tatsinda* (1963) and *Zeee* (1965), and several volumes of adult short stories that also contain keen observation in their evocative prose. Although these adult works are largely forgotten, Enright's children's books are still enjoyed for their vibrant characterizations and fine writing. P.D.S.

Estes, Eleanor

AMERICAN AUTHOR, 1906–1988. With her rare gift for depicting everyday experiences from the fresh perspective of childhood, Eleanor Estes based many of her stories on memories of growing up in a poor but loving family in West Haven, Connecticut. Following high school graduation, the author worked at the New Haven Public Library, then won a scholarship to the Pratt Institute Library School in Brooklyn, where she met her husband. She worked as a children's librarian at the New York Public Library until her first book was published.

The Moffats (1941) is a charming, humorous story about a fatherless family in Cranbury, Connecticut. Older siblings Sylvie and Joey are well-defined characters, but the book usually focuses on the most original-thinking members of the family, eight-year-old Janey and five-year-old Rufus. In a series of loosely related episodes, the children attend dance school, frighten a school bully, and worry about moving to a new house. Although the events are commonplace, Estes perfectly captures children's observations, logic, and speech patterns in prose notable for its immediacy and insight. *The Middle Moffat* (1942) and *Rufus M.* (1943) are equally percipient and even stronger in portraying the World War I period. The latter book closes as the war ends, and the Moffats dream about the future—a comforting scene for World War II–era readers and a beautiful conclusion to a wonderful trilogy.

Nearly forty years later, Estes surprised everyone by writing another volume about the Moffats. *The Moffat Museum* (1983) includes such episodes as Sylvie's wedding and Joey's first job; the writing style proves the author's ear was still well tuned to the language and thoughts of children. Although the Moffat books celebrate a happy family, there is a realistic note of sadness behind many of the scenes, as when poverty forces the family to move and Joey to quit school. Much sadder in tone is *The Hundred Dresses* (1944), the haunting story of a poor girl teased by two classmates. Childhood cruelty has seldom been as effectively explored, yet the overriding theme is one of forgiveness and understanding, demonstrated by the final, kind gesture of the victimized girl. Like *The Middle Moffat* and *Rufus M.*, the story was named a Newbery Honor Book. Estes won the Newbery Medal for *Ginger Pye* (1951), which concerns Jerry and Rachel Pye's six-month search for their missing puppy. The sensitive depiction of the children's conversations, memories, and emotions adds to the novel's warm appeal.

Estes's books were usually illustrated by such fine artists as LOUIS SLOBODKIN and EDWARD ARDIZZONE. For *Ginger Pye*, Estes illustrated her own story in a primitive, amusing style. Among the author's other books are a sequel, *Pinky Pye* (1958); literary fairy tales such as *The Sleeping Giant and Other Stories* (1948); and *The Witch Family* (1960), an artful blend of fantasy and reality best appreciated by older readers, who unfortunately may not be interested in reading about six-year-old protagonists. Some of the same characters appear in Estes's last book, *The Curious Adventures of Jimmy McGee* (1987). The author also wrote *The Alley* (1964), which concerns the children of a small New York neighborhood, and its sequel, *The Tunnel of Hugsy Goode* (1972).

Illustration by Eleanor Estes from her book *Ginger Pye* (1951).

The author's clear-eyed, original view of childhood shines through all of her work, particularly her classic books about the Moffat family. ❧ P.D.S.

Ets, Marie Hall

AMERICAN AUTHOR AND ILLUSTRATOR, 1893–1984. Born in a small Wisconsin town that became part of Milwaukee, Marie Hall Ets loved to explore the woods and forests of her native state, and they appear in many of the pictures in her books. Her life as an artist and a social worker took her to such diverse settings as San Francisco, Los Angeles, Chicago, Czechoslovakia, and New York.

Her first picture book, *Mister Penny* (1935), like all her books to follow, was praised for its blend of rhythmic prose, action, humor, pathos, charm, and fantasy. *In the Forest* (1944) and *Mr. T. W. Anthony Woo* (1951) perfectly exhibit her bold batiks and simple story lines. "I had a new horn and a paper hat/And I went to work in the forest," runs *In the Forest*, her most popular text, and before the adventure has come to an end elephants, bears, rabbits, and a stork have joined a parade through the dense, black, and entirely magical forest. *The Story of a Baby* (1939) presents in vivid detail the development of a human fetus at a time when such material was often censored and banned for children. So sensitive was her handling of the subject that her book was accepted with acclaim. Ets's hallmark was her bold and expressive black-and-white artwork, but she won the Caldecott Medal in 1960 for one of her few books in color, *Nine Days to Christmas.*

Although most of her books have gone out of print, Ets was one of the handful of American artists creating PICTURE BOOKS in the 1930s and 1940s who helped to set the standards for the classic American picture book and thus to define the genre for future generations. ❧

A.S.

F

Fairy Tales

See Asbjörnsen, Peter, and Moe, Jörgen; *Cinderella;* Grimm, Jacob and Wilhelm.

Falls, C. B.

American illustrator, 1874–1960. When Charles Buckles Falls created his well-known *ABC Book* (1923), he was already a noted poster artist, having designed posters for the theater and for the government during World War I. In fact, illustration of books for children and adults represents only one aspect of Falls's career as a freelance artist. He produced magazine illustrations; murals; prints; paintings; furniture, carpet, and fabric designs; advertising art; and scene and costume designs for the theater. Falls taught himself his craft and continued his education on the job. In the February 1962 issue of *American Artist,* Norman Kent describes how Falls's early employment influenced his style. He suggests, for instance, that the year Falls spent working for an architect fostered an awareness of "form, volume, and space." Later, performing the role of today's news photographer, Falls worked as a sketch artist for the *Chicago Tribune,* a job that required quick draftsmanship and a flair for capturing the essence of the incident he was reporting.

In the *ABC Book* the large woodcuts, with their flat color, display the attention to positive and negative space praised by Kent. Each page depicts an animal, one for each letter of the alphabet, along with a boldly lettered sentence: "A is for antelope," "B is for bear," and so forth. While earlier books by British artist William Nicholson may have influenced Falls, Falls's *ABC Book* was welcomed as a landmark in American picture book production.

Falls published *Mother Goose* in 1924 and *The Modern ABC Book* in 1930. His second alphabet book features contemporary lettering and up-to-date elements such as "E is for electric engine" and "S is for skyscraper." Many of the images are more complex but not as striking as the woodcuts in the first book.

Falls also worked on books for older children. He created numerous black-and-white drawings for nonfiction titles, many on historical subjects. Examples include Mary Seymour Lucas's *Vast Horizons* (1943), about Portuguese exploration; Katherine B. Shippen's *New Found World* (1945), a Newbery Honor Book about the history of Latin America; and Elizabeth Baity's *Americans before Columbus* (1951), another Newbery Honor Book. Falls supplied illustrations for fiction as well, including Robert Louis Stevenson's *Treasure Island* (1946) and *Kidnapped* (1947) and Ann Weil's Newbery Honor Book *Red Sails to Capri* (1952). He both wrote and illustrated his last book, *The First 3000 Years: Ancient Civilization of the Tigris, Euphrates, and Nile River Valleys and the Mediterranean Sea* (1960).

Falls's artwork varies a great deal, from his line drawings to the patterns and stylized figures of Esther Singleton's *The Wild Flower Fairy Book* (1905) to the scratchy lines and muted colors of Jessie B. White's play *Snow White and the Seven Dwarfs* (1912). His *ABC Book,* which remained in print for many years, becomes even more noteworthy when considered in the context of his lifelong career as a designer and graphic artist. ❧ M.F.S.

Family Stories

"Happy families are all alike," Tolstoy tells us, but "every unhappy family is unhappy in its own way." A century and a half of family stories in the United States bear him out, to a great degree. From Louisa May Alcott's March sisters of 1867 to Betsy Byars's Blossom family of the 1980s and 1990s, the strength children draw from loving parents, siblings, and other relatives and the guiding principles set forth by elders for youngsters to follow remain constant, however different the principles or the family structure may have become. The things that cause unhappiness, pain, confusion, and angst, however, vary greatly, reflecting changes in the composition of the family and in society.

Only a handful of Alcott's immediate successors are still read, and their readership diminishes with each new wave of electronic competition. *Little Women* (1867), *The Peterkin Papers* (Lucretia P. Hale, 1880), *Five Little Peppers and How They Grew* (MARGARET SIDNEY, 1881), *Rebecca of Sunnybrook Farm* (KATE DOUGLAS WIGGIN, 1903), and DOROTHY CANFIELD FISHER's *Understood Betsy* (1917) are among the few pre-1930s survivors. While many later stories are set in times past, their writers speak a language that is closer by decades to our own—a language understood by children whose world turns at an increasingly rapid pace.

Beginning in the 1930s, American writers began to show rather than to tell children about their country's past, putting history in terms not of great men and dates, but of the ordinary people, and especially the children, who lived through it. LAURA INGALLS WILDER's *Little House in the Big Woods* (1932) and its sequels and CAROL RYRIE BRINK's *Caddie Woodlawn* (1935) vividly describe family life on the frontier—not the life of the solitary trapper or trailblazer, but that of the family making a home at the edge of civilization and bringing to it values from "back home," mingled with the venturesome spirit that carved paths through the wilderness. Both are still widely read. DORIS GATES's Janey Larkin, in *Blue Willow* (1940), is an only child who struggles, with her migrant parents, to find a way to make a home amid reduced circumstances. ALICE DALGLIESH introduces, in *The Courage of Sarah Noble* (1954), a protagonist strong enough to accompany her father into the wilderness to build a new cabin for their family and to remain there alone when Father goes back for the rest of the family. Whatever its composition, the family circle supports the child's growth and discovery.

Beginning in the late 1930s and early 1940s, a variety of stories focused on the individual among siblings. The wise parent of Alcott's day remains in the background, ready when support is needed. (Like the Marches' Marmee, some of these are single parents, in effect if not in actuality.) ELIZABETH ENRIGHT introduces Garnet in *Thimble Summer* (1938), set amid rural farm life of the Depression-era Midwest, and the four Melendys in *The Saturdays* (1941), who live in New York with their father and a housekeeper. ELEANOR ESTES adds *The Moffats* (1941) of Cranbury, Connecticut, a quartet of independent spirits who tumble into adventures within sight of home, never too far from the watchful eye of their indomitable mother. The Moffats and the Melendys are followed by a flood of characters whose friends and fellow adventurers are their siblings: The Pyes (*Ginger Pye*, 1951, and *Pinky Pye*, 1958, by Eleanor Estes); the four sisters of SYDNEY TAYLOR's *All-of-a-Kind Family* (1951); EDWARD EAGER's Jane, Mark, Katharine, and Martha of *Half Magic* (1954); and Portia and Julian of Elizabeth Enright's *Gone-Away Lake* (1957). In Jennie Lindquist's *Golden Name Day* (1955) it is cousins, rather than siblings, who become fast friends. John Fitzgerald, in *The Great Brain* (1972) and its numerous sequels, rings the changes on an intense sibling relationship in which an older brother skillfully manipulates situations so that his little brother gets the blame for most of his pranks.

Despite the number of parents who are absent in these stories—due to war, illness, or death—tragedy is seldom in the foreground. Little by little, however, the darker side of life begins to appear as a realistic element in the stories of the 1950s and 1960s. In MEINDERT DEJONG's *House of Sixty Fathers* (1956) the young protagonist is separated from his family by the vicissitudes of war. Virginia Sorensen's *Miracles on Maple Hill* (1956) portrays a family struggling to put their lives back together after the Second World War, as does MARGOT BENARY-ISBERT's work *The Ark* (1953). In MADELEINE L'ENGLE's *Meet the Austins* (1960) the rhythms of a happy family must be adjusted to make room for a child orphaned when her father is killed in an airplane crash, while Julie in IRENE HUNT's *Up a Road Slowly* (1966) must learn to live without her mother, who dies, or her father, who cannot cope alone and sends Julie and her brother to live with their aunt. Dave, EMILY CHENEY NEVILLE's protagonist in *It's Like This, Cat* (1963), expresses typical adolescent angst in his rejection of his father's advice. Harriet, in LOUISE FITZHUGH's *Harriet the Spy* (1964), identifies and interacts more closely with her nanny, Ole Golly, than with her busy socialite parents. Sara, in Betsy Byars's *Summer of the Swans* (1970), is responsible for her younger brother, who is mentally disabled, and suffers great guilt and anxiety when he becomes lost.

As the more realistic, less romanticized aspects of family life became more common in children's fiction, a parallel development was the increasing presence of stories reflecting America's ethnic diversity, often from firsthand experience. Among the early voices whose resonance has lasted are VIRGINIA HAMILTON, first heard in *Zeely* (1967), in which the young protagonist leaves her family in the North to spend a summer of self-discovery with relatives in the South; YOSHIKO UCHIDA, whose semi-autobiographical novel of a Japanese American family interned after Pearl Harbor (*Journey to Topaz*, 1971) was followed by her trilogy about a Depression-era Japanese American family in California (*Jar of Dreams*, 1981; *The Best Bad Things*, 1983; *The Happiest Ending*, 1985); LAURENCE YEP, whose *Dragonwings* (1975) and *Child of the Owl* (1977) explored the experience of Chinese Americans; and MILDRED TAYLOR, whose Newbery Award–winning *Roll of Thunder, Hear My Cry* (1976) follows the fortunes of an African American family determined to hold on to their land during the Depression. Both Taylor, in her Logan family saga and in *The Gold Cadillac* (1987), and Yep, in *The Star Fisher* (1991), explore the pain of segregation and the struggles of families to survive its cruelty. Hamilton, in *Cousins* (1990), probes the conflicts within families: the pain caused by differences of financial status, the struggle of a single parent to steer a family through rocky waters, and the fierce love between grandparent and grandchild that overcomes fear, guilt, and sorrow.

In 1968 BEVERLY CLEARY's *Ramona the Pest* appeared, and for twenty-five years Ramona and her family have been well known and loved by children everywhere. Readers have lived with the Quimby family through Ramona's entry into school, Mr. Quimby's loss of his job, and Ramona's determined efforts to help him quit smoking. Young readers can readily identify with Ramona's life or yearn to trade places with her. She has sympathetic parents with realistic human shortcomings; a sibling who alternates between caring and aloofness, rivalry and frustration; and a family circle in which the bonds are firmly knit with love and concern for one another and for others. Ramona has close kin in Peter and Fudge (*Tales of a Fourth Grade Nothing*, 1972), brothers whose creator, JUDY BLUME, has an unerring ear for the nuances of children's conversation and for their concerns of the moment; JOHANNA HURWITZ's Aldo (*Much Ado about Aldo*, 1978), whose busy mother juggles work and parenting with skill and care; and *Anastasia Krupnik*, LOIS LOWRY's 1978 creation, whose comfortable only-child status is upset by the impending arrival of a much younger brother but whose family circle widens easily to admit Sam. Each of these authors, in her own way, creates a family rich in traditional values, if not so rich in material things. Ann Cameron, in *The Stories Julian Tells* (1981), introduces a father whose fearsomeness in his sons' eyes takes on mythic proportions, but who is reliably loving and forgiving despite his forbidding sense of humor.

Side by side with these secure middle-class family circles, an extensive literature sprang up reflecting the less than secure lives of many other American families. In *The Pinballs* (1977), Betsy Byars introduced a group of foster children whose lives had been damaged either by parental abuse or neglect or by other circumstances beyond their control. The warm, wise foster parents manage, against considerable odds, to create a stable environment that helps these shaken youngsters to begin to trust in life again and to consider themselves part of a "family," albeit not a biological one. Byars, who understands the importance in a child's life of adult support that is wise and strong without being authoritarian, went on to create the Blossom family (*The Not Just Anybody Family*, 1986, and sequels), whose frequently absent mother is replaced, on a day-to-day basis, by Pap, a grandfather whose easygoing philosophy has plenty of backbone. The Blossoms live on the edge of poverty, a fact seldom stated but implicit in their surroundings; but there is nothing poor about their caring for one another, despite frequent rivalries among the siblings.

Close cousin to the "Pinballs" is KATHERINE PATERSON's Gilly in *The Great Gilly Hopkins* (1978), a foster child whose mother, a would-be movie star, is off "finding herself" while her daughter grows up with only a series of foster families for support. In nearly all of Paterson's work the links and supports of family are important, though they are perhaps most evident in *Jacob Have I Loved* (1980), focused on sibling rivalry and misunderstanding, and *Park's Quest* (1988), a son's search for information about his father, killed in Vietnam, and his family history, hidden by the mother who can't bear to explore her pain.

CYNTHIA VOIGT created one of the most memorable family sagas in *The Homecoming* (1981) and its sequels. The Tillerman family consists of four children, abandoned by their mother at a suburban shopping mall in New England, whose long journey in search of their grandmother becomes an odyssey of almost mythic proportions. Once they are reunited with their crusty but caring grandmother, the strength of Dicey, the take-charge sister, and of the family bond slowly heal the children's wounds. Voigt explores deep anger and distrust, guilt and denial, but she roots the Tillermans firmly to the home they find with their grandmother, and all of them, children and grandmother alike, grow as they are nourished by their relationship.

Like Byars, Paterson, and Voigt, PATRICIA MACLACHLAN explores a wide range of family relationships. From the very simple story lines of *Seven Kisses in a Row* (1983), in which loving parents leave their children with an uncle and aunt while on vacation, to the bittersweet pioneer story of motherless children whose father advertises for a new wife from back East in *Sarah, Plain and Tall* (1985), MacLachlan shows an understanding of the child's feelings in a world where all is not right. In *Arthur, for the Very First Time* (1980), a boy spending the summer with relatives while his parents await the birth of another child gradually develops the courage to explore his own fears—of losing his mother, of being displaced by the baby, of change—helped by the wise aunt and uncle who have become his "temporary" family. *Journey* (1991) explores the complex relationships among two children and their grandparents, surrogate parents for the mother who, like Gilly Hopkins's mother, has left them to "find herself." Journey's grandfather helps the boy to discover not only who his family is, but that parents are not necessarily the perfect creatures children would like them to be. In *Baby* (1993), Sophie's mother takes the risk of leaving her year-old daughter on the doorstep of a family she has watched, judging by their closeness that they will care for her child while she weathers a crisis. In the process, Sophie's presence helps her adoptive family come to terms with the death of their own second child, a loss they have not been able even to discuss.

PAULA FOX, in *Monkey Island* (1991), tells the story of a family that simply disintegrates in the face of poverty and insurmountable challenges, leaving the son to survive on the streets of New York. Like Virginia Hamilton's Buddy in *The Planet of Junior Brown* (1971) and the eponymous hero of JERRY SPINELLI's *Maniac Magee* (1990), this boy finds a "family" to help him survive, taking shelter with others on the street who respond to his need and teach him how to survive on his own. EVE BUNTING, in *Fly Away Home* (1991), uses the PICTURE BOOK format to tell the brief but powerful story of a boy and his father who live in an airport, carefully disguising their comings and goings so that they appear to be travelers, but hoping each day for a change of fortune that will allow them to find a home to go to, as the others who pass through the airport do.

Lois Lowry, whose families are generally strong and supportive, paints a grim picture in *The Giver* (1993) of a future in which families are carefully composed by community rules. Jonas, the twelve-year-old protagonist, is assigned the role of Receiver of Memory at the community's coming-of-age ceremony. In his year of tutelage with the elder who gives him, for the first time, knowledge of the world outside, where not all hills have been smoothed out nor wars eliminated, where disease and death await, he is horrified to learn the truth about his "perfect" family and the world in which he has grown up. It is his response to the concept of love, and his concern for Gabriel, an infant foster child whom his family has been nurturing, that gives him the courage to run away with Gabriel in search of another life—and a true family.

Families disintegrating and re-forming are part of life for today's children, and the candor with which authors address painful issues such as death, divorce, intolerance, abuse, and neglect in the late twentieth century reflects an awareness that children feel the pain of such changes as deeply as adults do. Yet for children, family is still a crucial factor in survival. The bonds of affection and concern; the warmth and shelter of home and its inhabitants, be they many or few; the depth of love and the tenacity that holds families together through hard times; and the thread that ties one generation to the next—these are themes that resonate through much of our best fiction and that keep stories alive from one generation to the next. ❧ DUDLEY B. CARLSON

FAMILY STORIES, ALTERNATIVE

Inscribing ownership in his geography book, Stephen Dedalus places himself firmly within his world:

Stephen Dedalus
Class of Elements
Clongowes Wood College
Sallins
County Kildare
Ireland
Europe
The World
The Universe.

James Joyce's *Portrait of the Artist as a Young Man* (1916) traces Stephen's journey toward self-identification through these ever-expanding circles of inclusion. Like all young adults, Stephen places himself at the center, believing his world revolves around him. Instead, it shapes him. Parents, aunts, friends, school, and the larger social and political universes all prove formative environments in which Stephen acts, reacts, and tests himself. Yet Stephen does not mention home, perhaps because home underpins and infiltrates all other spheres.

Home and family constitute the first developmental arena for children and young adults. Here, children learn who they are as connected to others and as apart from others. As does Stephen Dedalus, the young adult learns to stand alone and together in the family. The ideal family offers a place for self-measurement; it affords the generosity of love despite disappointment, of nurturing without qualification. In the family, one witnesses models of mature adult love and learns modes of communication, negotiation, and respect. The initial site of interpersonal relationships, family remains the most lasting influence on the adolescent's future social interactions and associations, for good or ill.

The great variations possible in these modes emerge both in adolescents' experience and in the literature directed to them, with the fictional reality of books either affirming or contradicting the reader's experience. GARY PAULSEN's *Sentries* (1986), for example, vividly expresses the varied and often isolated experiences of young adults. Of the four characters whose stories are interwoven in the novel, only one lives within a traditional, two-parent family. The 1991 Newbery Award winner, *Maniac Magee* by JERRY SPINELLI (1990), and the 1991 honor book, *The True Confessions of Charlotte Doyle* by AVI (1990), disturb the profile of the nuclear family with portraits of a contemporary, legendary orphaned boy who elects homelessness rather than endure the pain of family relationships and of a mid-nineteenth-century, newly empowered heroine who rejects the binds of her restrained Victorian family. CYNTHIA RYLANT's *Missing May* (1992), the 1993 winner, shows the family disrupted by death but mustering tremendous emotional and psychological support to reconstruct itself. This family is not traditional and not nuclear, but it builds relational bonds that tie.

The traditional nuclear family varies in size yet holds true in formation. What does a nontraditional family look like? It seems as protean as the ever-changing social exigencies that produce it. Alternative family stories include those about single parents and children of divorce; those focused on the biological family with one or both parents absent; books in which one parent or primary caretaker is homosexual; and novels about orphaned or homeless children. Adoptive families are conspicuously absent from this list because adopting a child represents a societally approved way of creating a nuclear family structure.

Portrayals of divorced families form the preponderance of alternative family stories. Rather than considering divorce a breakdown of the American family and social system, these books simply recognize the large number of divorces involving children and young adults. This category has seen tremendous growth, from books published primarily for their bibliotherapeutic potential and self-help perspective to books of exceptional literary merit. In these novels, divorce is not a problem to be conquered but a change in the essence of daily life and operations of the family.

Imported from New Zealand and embraced by American critics and readers, MARGARET MAHY's *Changeover: A Supernatural Romance* (1984) traces the unusual course of Laura Chant's maturation against the background of the sometimes distasteful changes resulting from her parents' divorce: she accepts her change-over to being a witch and she accepts the mysterious Sorensen Carlisle's romantic interest in her. Laura learns to appreciate the complexities of her mother, Kate, a frantic yet loving single parent. Laura's own sexual awakening helps her to become more sensitive to her mother's maternal selflessness even as she realizes Kate's need to express her own sexuality.

LOIS LOWRY in the well-loved Anastasia Krupnik books and BEVERLY CLEARY in the chronicles of Ramona describe the traditional family for young readers. Yet, Lowry in *Rabble Starkey* (1987) and Cleary in *Dear Mr. Henshaw* (1983) turn to a less idealized yet equally constructive family headed by a single mother. *Rabble Starkey* depicts a convincing relationship between a divorced mother, Sweet Hosanna, and her daughter, Parable (called Rabble) Starkey. In *Dear Mr. Henshaw*, a boy learns to deal with the pain of his parents' divorce through his correspondence with a favorite author. Lowry and Cleary celebrate with characteristic humor, resonant storytelling, and transcendent perspicacity the sustaining qualities of these nondysfunctional—yet nontraditional—families.

BRUCE BROOKS offers a more disturbing view of a divorced family in his first novel, *The Moves Make the Man* (1984). Jerome and Bix form a friendship that can heal only modestly the wound created by the absence of Bix's mother. Brooks juxtaposes Jerome's healthy nuclear family with Bix's shaky one with wisdom, insight, and fictional success. In Brooks's *Midnight Hour Encores* (1986), Taxi's divorce from Sibilance T. Spooner's flower-child mother proves fundamentally liberating for all. Brooks traces Sib's journey toward her mother with a sonorous, musical prose appropriate to his musical prodigy protagonist. In *What Hearts* (1992), Brooks demonstrates that talent cannot alleviate suffering for the children of divorced parents. Asa, intellectually gifted, endures his mother's divorce and remarriage with silence. While Asa measures his own happiness, he never condemns his alcoholic mother; he mourns her entrenched vision of herself as a failure. Through Asa's continual adjustment and readjustment, Brooks supports the adolescent's fluid acceptance of shifting family constellations.

BERLIE DOHERTY spotlights a family in transition in *Dear Nobody* (1992). When Helen decides to keep the child she and Chris accidentally conceive, they must decide if they have a stable, caring relationship out of which to mold a family for this child. Meanwhile, Helen's parents give her a home even as they face the uncomfortable changes in sight.

BROCK COLE gives voice to the young adult's perspective in *Celine* (1989). Ironic, quirky, animated, self-aware, and struggling to paint a self-portrait, Celine narrates her attempt to "show a little maturity" during her stay with her stepmother. Through counseling her young friend Jake, Celine speaks brutal truths about being the child of a divorce. Yet, she proves herself a triumphant survivor and her relationship with Jake confirms her capacity for maintaining firm emotional bonds.

Celine, like the title character in *Weetzie Bat* (1989) by Francesca Lia Block, refuses to dwell in a "broken Home" and instead creates her own nontraditional family. Weetzie Bat first befriends the gay Dirk who loves Duck. She then meets My Secret Agent Lover Man, and all four live together in Los Angeles, with a love strong enough to conceive a multi-fathered child, insistent enough to yearn for and eventually to define a family. This family may challenge conservative values, but at its heart lies Weetzie's conclusion about the essence of family: "I don't know about happily ever after, but I know about happily."

Willie Ramsey pursues the elusive happiness of understanding in *Unlived Affections* (1989) by GEORGE SHANNON. His grandmother has recently been buried, and Willie initially feels freedom from the constraints of family. Packing up the ancestral home, Willie discovers his father's love letters to his mother. Slowly, painfully, he deciphers both the protecting lies perpetuated within the family and the liberating truths about his parents. Shannon infuses Willie's knowledge of his father's homosexuality with realistic ambivalence and concern. Ultimately Willie, like Weetzie Bat, embraces the family he has, regardless of its seeming "alternateness."

Weetzie and Willie create new structures for their families. Without parental guideposts, they establish nontraditional families in which to ground and define themselves. CYNTHIA VOIGT's Tillerman children assume the same challenge. Abandoned first by their father, then by their ill mother, Dicey leads her two brothers and one sister on a peripatetic quest for family. She finds their grandmother, who resists this new family out of fear for her independence and of the emotional risk and financial burden the children pose. Through *Homecoming* (1980), *Dicey's Song* (1982), *Sons from Afar* (1987), and *Seventeen Against the Dealer* (1989), Dicey and her grandmother craft a responsible, nurturing family for the parentless children.

Jonny Dart, of Margaret Mahy's *Memory* (1988), acts as if he hasn't any parents. In his late teens, Jonny traverses the darkened city haunted by the ghost of his twin sister, Janine, pursued by the phantasm of guilt at her death. Jonny seeks forgetfulness; he finds release from his torturous memories with Sophie, an elderly victim of Alzheimer's disease. Sophie mistakes Jonny for a long-absent relative, and he moves into position as her caretaker. Together, they create a family that welcomes interdependence and provides a forgiving haven.

In *Somewhere in the Darkness* (1992) by WALTER DEAN MYERS, it is Jimmy's father, Crab, who arrives unexpectedly and pulls Jimmy on a trip toward forgiveness and understanding. While his father was in prison, Jimmy established a family with Mama Jean, which substituted to an extent for the nuclear families in which his peers live. Jimmy resists Crab's uprooting him from this family and returns to it after Crab's death, having gained poignant insight into his own abilities, desires, and intentions as a father. Like Weetzie and Dicey, Jimmy's experiences in this family give him the determination to form a solid, coherent family in his future.

Somewhere in the Darkness presents Jimmy facing challenges common to adolescents, those particular to an African American, and those individual to his personality and history. Like Myers, young adult author CHRIS CRUTCHER portrays without restraint the harsh realities some young adults face. In novels such as *The Crazy Horse Electric Game* (1987), *Stotan!* (1986), and *Chinese Handcuffs* (1989), and in the short story collection *Athletic Shorts* (1989), Crutcher places his adolescent characters in a variety of family structures. Nortie eventually leaves an abusive nuclear family; orphaned Lion lives alone; siblings die, endure sexual abuse, or commit suicide. Normalcy resists definition in Crutcher's fiction, which highlights friendship as the significant bond beyond family.

Similar to Crutcher's characters, Buddy, in VIRGINIA HAMILTON's visionary novel *The Planet of Junior Brown* (1971), turns to his friends. The homeless adolescent Buddy can rely on only two adults for assistance in crisis. Hamilton contrasts the lonely resilience of Buddy with Junior Brown's privileged dysfunction to reveal the power of human connectedness. Even without a social framework, without a recognizable family, Buddy survives and creates satellites of caretaking. It is his construction and support of these alternative families that eventually save Junior Brown.

The Planet of Junior Brown eerily forecast the 1990s phenomenon of homeless children living on the street, a phenomenon treated in many of the decade's children's books. The title characters of SYLVIA CASSEDY's *Lucie Babbidge's House* (1989) and Dennis Covington's *Lizard* (1991) live as state wards. The pupils and teachers at the Norwood School for Girls lack the ability to fashion a positive community to replace the family Lucie has lost.

Alone, homeless in spirit and heart, Lucie fantasizes about a family and a friend to sustain her. While Lucie escapes through her imagination, Lizard actually escapes the home for the mentally retarded where he has been mistakenly placed because of his physical deformity. As it did for Lucie, the hopeful promise of family pulls him out of the school; yet, it renders him truly homeless. His attachment to a group of traveling performers introduces him to other homeless children and ultimately returns him to the school once more.

Also abandoned by his mother and neglected by social service agencies, Clay, in *Monkey Island* (1991) by Paula Fox, has no choice but to live on the street. Clay maintains watch for his mother more out of habit than expectation. Luck brings him to two homeless men, Buddy and Calvin, who assume responsibility for him and act as a family of sorts. They protect and care for Clay; they offer him advice and hard-won wisdom. Clay, like Maniac Magee, yearns for family even though he has found it to be an inherently disappointing human relationship. Both characters conclude that the best family—traditional or alternative—is that in which one is truly wanted.

Yet amid the social reality and the literary depictions of the nontraditional, stories about nuclear families dominate literature for young adults. Lois Lowry returns to that familiar familial constellation in her riveting futuristic novel *The Giver* (1993). Jonas has two professional parents and one precocious younger sister. His peers all share exactly the same home structure, and the community functions smoothly. The society monitors its even growth and tenaciously holds constant its population. A wonder of social and human engineering, this environment slowly comes to distress Jonas and the reader with its astonishing lack of human feeling. The absence of emotion and color and the routine monotony of all communication create a vision of deadness. The community's Giver holds and transmits to Jonas the memory of a family as a connection to warmth and happiness, but this revelation contradicts Jonas's experience. As if he were homeless, Jonas must search for identity outside his family; though traditional, its hollow insistence on replication threatens the freedom of individuality that Jonas requires. *The Giver* sounds a piercing alarm against holding and prizing the familiar and traditional solely on those grounds. Through it, young adult readers (along with parents, educators, and critics) learn to appreciate, even celebrate, the exuberant, emancipating possibilities in stories about difference, about nontraditional lifestyles, about alternative families. ♠ CATHRYN M. MERCIER

FANTASY

Fantasy is the ultimate literature of the imagination. Since humans acquired the capacity to reason and imagine, fantastic tales have been told. Transcending the here and now, such tales relate larger-than-life deeds set in a moral landscape that both evokes and transforms the known world.

Engagement with a work of fantasy requires of the reader a willing suspension of disbelief: The reader must be willing to accept the premise of the fantasy. The secondary, altered world of the successful fantasy, according to J. R. R. TOLKIEN, is one "into which both designer and spectator can enter, to the satisfaction of their senses while they are inside." This requires of the writer extraordinary skill, in that the story must be so seamlessly written, the imaginary world so real, that the reader cannot help but accept it. The story cannot "clank," jarring the reader back to reality. As the children's fantasy writer SUSAN COOPER has said, "Fantasy, like the butterfly, flies without knowing how."

Although the origins of fantasy as a genre can be traced to the nineteenth-century revival of interest in traditional folk- and fairy-tale material, fantasies are distinguished by being manifestly the work of an individual sensibility. *Alice's Adventures in Wonderland* (1865) by LEWIS CARROLL, for example, noted for its playfulness with words and logic, displays its author's quirky personality, perspective, and preoccupations. Seizing on the popularity of the form, many works followed that used genre to gently point a moral lesson; rather than proving didactic bores, however, some of these works—including GEORGE MACDONALD's *At the Back of the North Wind* (1871) and C. S. LEWIS's Chronicles of Narnia (seven volumes, 1950–1956)—went on to become great CLASSICS. Perhaps influenced by *Alice*, a distinct strain of humorous fantasy also emerged, with such distinguished exemplars as L. FRANK BAUM's *Wizard of Oz* (1900), E. NESBIT's *Five Children and It* (1902), HUGH LOFTING's *Story of Doctor Dolittle* (1920), and P. L. TRAVERS's *Mary Poppins* (1934).

Given their origins in the oral tradition—from folktales to Homer—it is not surprising that many successful fantasies make overt use of traditional material. Legends of King Arthur and his court and the tales of the Welsh Mabinogion, in particular, have engendered a wealth of creative and captivating fantasies. Susan Cooper uses elements of both in her Dark Is Rising Quintet, in which her storytelling prowess engages readers through episodes of suspense, even terror, before light triumphs over dark. *Over Sea, Under Stone* (1965) introduces Merriman—who just might be Merlin. *The Dark*

Is Rising (1973), the most powerful of the books, brings Merriman together with Will, the seventh son of a seventh son just turned eleven, in an effort to defeat evil. *Greenwich* (1974); *The Grey King* (1975), which won the Newbery Medal; and *Silver on the Tree* (1977) followed, with King Arthur himself appearing at last. Also drawing on Arthurian legend, JANE YOLEN sparks the imagination with her tale *The Dragon's Boy* (1990). Artos, an orphan raised by Sir Ector, gains wisdom from Old Linn, and, subtly, the reader is led to understand that this is a story of Arthur and Merlin. LLOYD ALEXANDER's classic Chronicles of Prydain were inspired by Welsh myth. Taran, an assistant pig-keeper, appears in *The Book of Three* (1964), beginning a quest that will lead him to combat evil in *The Black Cauldron* (1965) and *The Castle of Llyr* (1966), on a search for self in *Taran Wanderer* (1967), and finally to triumph in both defeating evil and knowing and accepting himself in *The High King* (1968), which won the Newbery Medal.

The most developed secondary worlds appear in works termed *high fantasy*. Moved by their commitment to the themes and concepts that inspired them, the authors of these often multivolume works may create not only dramatic plots and fully developed characters, but geographies, languages, mythologies, histories, and traditions that may bear only an indirect relation to their stories but that immeasurably deepen their meaning, impact, and appeal. Other characteristics of high fantasy include an "Everyman" protagonist, female or male, who comes from humble beginnings to achieve great ends. The protagonist typically pursues a quest, often with the direct or indirect goal of searching for his or her own true nature. The struggle between good and evil pervades these tales, and events are tied to universal human values and ideals.

J. R. R. Tolkien's *The Hobbit* (1938), a favorite since its publication, is an outstanding example of high fantasy. Bilbo Baggins, the endearing main character, undertakes a dramatic quest for adventure and treasure and attains generous amounts of both, as well as a deepened appreciation of himself and his quiet life in the Shire. Although deeply steeped in the myths and legends of Northern Europe, *The Hobbit* bears its author's preoccupations lightly. Lewis's Chronicles of Narnia are weighted with the author's search for and desire to represent in allegory the deepest meaning of the Christian faith. His inventiveness; his skill with character, language, and plot; and his compelling theme of the conflict between love and hate have ensured the series many devoted readers. *The Lion, the Witch, and the Wardrobe* (1950), the first of the series, remains the most popular. URSULA K. LE GUIN's Earthsea Trilogy (*A Wizard of Earthsea*, 1968; *The Tombs of Atuan*, 1971; and *The Farthest Shore*, 1972) focuses on Ged, who in the course of the three novels metamorphoses from callow boy to Archmage, a position accorded the highest respect in his world. A much later Earthsea book, *Tehanu* (1990), returns to Tenar, the young high priestess of the Nameless Ones in *The Tombs of Atuan*, and follows her to her own maturity as a simple village woman with the power to redeem others through her belief in life and love.

The 1980s saw the emergence of strong female protagonists in fantasies as full of adventure as those with male protagonists. Exploring similar themes of coming of age, apprenticeship, and the nature of courage, these books, not surprisingly, deal forthrightly with the issues of gender bias and expectation. In *The Blue Sword* (1982) and *The Hero and the Crown* (1985), the Newbery Medal–winning ROBIN MCKINLEY presents two rousing tales of the land of Damar, replete with myth and magic. MEREDITH PIERCE's Darkangel Trilogy introduces Ariel, who in the first book, *The Darkangel* (1982), confronts a vampyre to rescue her mistress and ends up saving him from his evil past. As *A Gathering of Gargoyles* (1984) and *The Pearl of the Soul of the World* (1990) unfold, Ariel continues to vanquish the many evils threatening her land and becomes its acknowledged savior. The protagonist of *Alanna* (1983), by Tamora Pierce, is a young girl who wishes to become a knight. Hiding her gender, she trades places with her brother, who wants to be a sorcerer. How each attains her or his wish is entertainingly told in a series of five books. The supernatural intrudes into a realistic contemporary setting in MARGARET MAHY's *Changeover* (1984), in which fourteen-year-old Laura wrestles with both evil and her own nature in this quintessential—if unusual—coming-of-age novel.

Time, an obvious source of fascination to the young, has provided a theme for several major fantasies, beginning with E. Nesbit. An outstanding example from more recent years, *Tuck Everlasting* (1975) by NATALIE BABBITT, links the exploration of elusive time and the balance between life and death with provocative results. PHILIPPA PEARCE refines the thematic use of elusive time travel in *Tom's Midnight Garden* (1958), examining the transience of experience and the persistence of memory through this story of a boy who, when the hall clock strikes thirteen, joins a child of the past in a secret garden. L. M. BOSTON's Green Knowe books use the catalyst of an ancient, unchanging house to bring together its child residents of past and present in confrontation with equally enduring evils and human dilemmas. Anne Knowles, in *The Halcyon Island* (1980), explores similar themes in this story about Ken, who is deathly afraid of water and learns to overcome his fear with the help of Giles, a friend whom he meets along the river; only at the very end does the reader learn that Giles drowned several years earlier and has returned to help another child in need.

A major category of fantasy is the animal fantasy. With origins in AESOP, animal fantasies have taken divergent turns, from the somber elaboration of *Watership Down* (1972) by RICHARD ADAMS to the elegiac familiarity of *The Wind in the Willows* (1908) by KENNETH GRAHAME, to the gentle celebration of life in *Charlotte's Web* (1952) by E. B. WHITE. Related to animal fantasies are stories—owing much to such HANS CHRISTIAN ANDERSEN tales as "The Steadfast Tin Soldier"—that personify toys and machines. Among the classics in this subgenre are domestic tales, such as A. A. MILNE's *Winnie the Pooh* (1926) and Margery Williams's *Velveteen Rabbit* (1922), and more satiric near-epics, such as *The Mouse and His Child* (1967), by RUSSELL HOBAN. A more contemporary tale is Elizabeth Winthrop's *Castle in the Attic* (1985), in which a boy enters a medieval world through the device of a lead knight.

Fantasy allows authors to create extraordinary worlds and to people them with characters who challenge and expand our sense of the norm. Yet writers of fantasy use their imagined worlds to explore the basic truths of this world: good fantasy puts readers more closely in touch with reality. Ursula Le Guin has said that fantasy is truth—not factual, but true. "Fantasy's truth challenges, even threatens, all that is false, all that is phony, unnecessary, and trivial in life." Fantasy expresses reality through the universal language of the inner self. ⸙

M. JEAN GREENLAW

FARJEON, ELEANOR

ENGLISH POET AND AUTHOR, 1881–1965. The phrase *joie de vivre* describes Eleanor Farjeon's writings as it does her personality. Her sunny disposition is reflected in the many poems and stories she wrote for children. Her father did not believe in formal education, but his library was a treasure for a reader like young Eleanor. In her lively foreword to *The Little Bookroom* (1955) she describes her childhood house as itself a "bookroom." Books "lined the dining-room walls, and overflowed into my mother's sitting-room, and up into the bedrooms. It would have been more natural to live without clothes than without books. . . . [They] opened magic casements for me through which I looked out on other worlds and times than those I lived in." She shared her education and happy childhood with three brothers, and constantly referred to the four of them as her family, even into her eighties.

Illustration by E. H. SHEPARD from *The Glass Slipper* (1946), by Eleanor Farjeon.

Eleanor Farjeon wrote a number of histories. *Ten Saints* (1936) and *Mighty Men* (1926), along with her histories of English royalty, were standard titles in home and public libraries when in print. The witty accounts were excellent for families to share together.

Her novel *The Glass Slipper* (1946) began as a play written with her brother. It and *The Silver Curlew* (1953) are based on the tales of Cinderella and of Rapunzel, respectively. Adult royal figures in the two novels are portrayed as children with nannies, a comfortable idea for the child readers of that era. Now, however, the characters and setting seem old-fashioned rather than timeless, with an innocence that is refreshing, but dated.

Farjeon's stories in *Martin Pippin in the Apple Orchard* (1921) were originally written for adults, but they were quickly taken over by children. They are romantic stories tied together by one of the most romantic stories of all. Martin Pippin tells stories to seven young maids, one of whom he claims as his own sweetheart. The companion work *Martin Pippin in the Daisy Field* (1937) is full of humor, fairies, pigs, and mermaids. "Elsie Piddock Skips in Her Sleep" stands out as a favorite for many storytellers even today, and its theme of preserving nature is timely.

Farjeon enjoyed using a central theme to tie her

collections together and was successful in developing clever characters such as Martin Pippin. The old nurse in *The Old Nurse's Stocking-Basket* (1931) fits the story to the darning she is doing, a short story for a short darn and a longer story for a long one. Her witty stories are full of lovely descriptions of nature, whether field or sea, flower or season. Her poetry reflects her joy in words and rhythm. Often, the verse is so lilting it seems to be a nursery rhyme. WALTER DE LA MARE was a great friend of Farjeon's, and she is recognized along with him as a distinguished children's poet of the twentieth century. Her poetry sings with the joy of nature and the foibles of childhood. "The result of my gleanings from my nursery-garden is so largely lyrical that it seems to me I have always versified with a tune in my ear. I can hardly remember the time when it did not seem *easier* to me to write in running rhyme than in plodding prose," she writes in her foreword to *Poems for Children* (1951). Her childhood celebrations in verse (particularly of Christmas) are often found in collections for young children today. One of her verses is a well-known hymn, "Morning Has Broken."

One of her last pieces of writing was an introduction to Edward Thomas's poems in *The Green Roads*, published in 1965, just before her eighty-fourth birthday. It closed a distinguished career that spanned more than half a century.

Farjeon was the first recipient of two prestigious awards for children's literature. In 1956 she received the International Hans Christian Andersen Award for *The Little Bookroom*, and in 1959 she received the Regina Medal of the Catholic Library Association. ❧ J.B.

FARLEY, WALTER

AMERICAN AUTHOR, B. 1920. Whether fans are introduced to Walter Farley's Black Stallion in the original novel form, as it was abridged for a younger audience, or on the screen in the highly successful film version, they are meeting one of the most enduring and popular animal characters ever created. Farley has become one of the most respected authors of books for young readers because he consistently provides his audience with stories that maintain their sense of adventure while remaining true to the development of characters introduced over the course of many books.

Farley was born in Syracuse, New York. As a city boy he was interested in sports and horses, and the racetracks at Aqueduct and Belmont, as well as Central Park, gave him the opportunity to watch and be around the animals. Farley also enjoyed writing and even as a teenager felt there weren't enough good horse books for children. While still attending Erasmus Hall High School, Farley began to write the story that would become *The Black Stallion*. The novel was published in 1941 while Farley was a student at Columbia University and over the years was joined by many sequels.

It has thus been more than fifty years since the Black Stallion and Alec Ramsey first appeared together on board the tramp steamer *Drake*, Alec bound for his New York home after a summer visit with his uncle in India. The dramatic storm at sea, the sinking of the *Drake*, and Alec's desperate battle for survival on the tiny deserted island with only the Black for company are all familiar elements to Black Stallion fans—it is this time together on the island that allows Alec and the mighty stallion to forge the bond that will keep them together throughout Farley's series of novels.

Farley varies his pattern. He introduces another equine character, the equally imposing stallion Flame, in *The Black Stallion and Flame* (1960), and even introduces a female character in *The Black Stallion and the Girl* (1971), in memory of his teenage daughter, who died in an accident. But part of Farley's appeal comes from the fact that he is a series author. For young readers with an interest in a subject, there is reassurance in knowing that after the first book, there are twenty or more waiting to be devoured! Farley's particular skill lies in the fact that his stories in no way feel churned out as do so many contemporary series—although his books are linked by character and story, each can stand alone as a fine adventure tale. Alec and the Black Stallion and their counterparts Steve Duncan and Flame in the "Island Stallion" adventures remain interesting, vital characters in each book.

Farley has also produced some fine books for younger readers, especially those featuring the Little Black Pony. In Little Black's first adventure, *Little Black, a Pony* (1961), the young narrator's special relationship with the little black pony is threatened when the stallion Big Red proves to be more enticing. Little Black, understandably jealous of the attention his master gives to Big Red, tries valiantly to compete, but always falls short, until the climactic scene in which his small size enables him to save his young friend from an icy mishap. In other stories Little Black races (and naturally wins) and performs in a circus. Farley's readers immediately come to love this small star; this is especially noteworthy considering the beginning-to-read format with which Farley works and communicates his love of horses to a much younger audience.

Middle-grade readers can enjoy such titles as *The Horse That Swam Away* (1965) and *The Great Dane, Thor*

(1966). It is the Black Stallion, however, that remains Farley's greatest creation, and devoted horse fans will continue to cheer as the Black and Alec thunder down the homestretch for many years to come. ❧ E.H.

Farmer, Penelope

British author, b. 1939. Born in Westerham, Kent, England, just before the outbreak of World War II, Penelope Farmer was the second of twin daughters, a condition that she says she resented all during her childhood. She reports that she and her twin sister were extremely competitive and that growing up was a painful process for her, made more so by a prolonged childhood illness. She became an avid reader and began to write stories when she was very young; she wrote her first published book when she was fifteen. After boarding school, Farmer studied history at St. Anne's College, Oxford, and did graduate work at Bedford College, of the University of London.

Farmer's reputation in the United States rests mainly on her books about Charlotte and Emma Makepeace. The first of these, *The Summer Birds* (1962), had characteristics that were to become hallmarks of her fiction: lucid, poetic imagery, well-defined characters, sibling rivalry, and haunting settings. A birdlike boy, invisible to most adults, teaches first Charlotte and Emma, then all their schoolmates, to fly during their summer holiday. A Peter Pan figure, he is never clearly defined, but he remains a mysterious focus of their longings.

Emma in Winter (1966) continues the flying theme, but takes place after Charlotte has gone to boarding school, leaving Emma alone in the dreary Victorian house with her uncle and his housekeeper. She has strange dreams of flying over the downs with a fat, unpopular boy from school. Gradually, Emma realizes that he is having the same dreams, and their mysterious experiences draw them closer together until they can openly become friends.

Charlotte Sometimes (1969) is a carefully plotted time-travel FANTASY that begins when Charlotte falls asleep on her first night at boarding school and awakes to find herself in 1918, having switched places with a girl named Clare. The two girls swap their lives every night for several weeks, creating extreme confusion in Charlotte's mind about her identity. The problems inherent in two characters assuming each other's identity without arousing suspicion among their teachers are not resolved for Charlotte or the reader, thereby establishing a recurring theme in these books: the inexplicability of the adult world.

Farmer describes in minute detail the feelings of her characters, giving them as much weight as the plot or action of her stories. In *A Castle of Bone* (1972), Hugh is a painter whose vivid sensory experiences of his real and dream worlds form a compelling counterpoint to the story of a cupboard that changes anything or any person put inside it. She also writes with acute perception of the nuances of sibling relationships that alternate between love and rivalry, patient humor and irritable volubility.

Her latest book, *Thicker Than Water* (1993), is a ghost story told in alternating chapters by Becky and Will, two cousins who are the children of estranged twin sisters. When Will's mother dies and he comes to live with Becky's family, his grief is compounded by the presence of the ghost of a boy who died in a nearby mine a hundred years before.

Farmer's intriguing, supernatural plots and well-developed characters have secured for her a small but distinctive place in children's literature. ❧ J.S.

Feelings, Tom

American illustrator, b. 1933. In his life and work, Tom Feelings has tried to expose the reality of life for African Americans while depicting the beauty and warmth of black culture. In his autobiography for children, *Black Pilgrimage* (1972), he speaks of his struggles growing up in Brooklyn, New York, his years and growth in Africa, his return to the United States, and his success as an artist. As a student studying cartooning, Feelings was warned that the comic strip must not include the personal emotions of its creator. Unable to relinquish self-expression, he stopped working in that form. In the fifties, however, his first printed work, "Tommy Traveler in the World of Negro History," was carried by the *New York Age*. Through this comic strip Feelings shared his childhood quest to learn African American history, and he found an outlet for both his artistic interests and his sensibilities.

In the early 1960s, while on assignment for *Look* magazine, Feelings was struck by the uninhibited warmth and dignity of the children of the South as compared to the withdrawn attitudes and negative self-images of the children of the North. His discouragement over the situation of the northern children led him to Africa. There he found himself surrounded by physical and human beauty, and he worked on producing books with the Ghanaian government. Through his illustrations he tried to show what he saw in the faces of the people, what he describes as "a glow that came from within, from a knowledge of self, a trust in life, or maybe from a feeling of being part of a majority in your own world. I had seen this same glow in the faces of very young Black children in America, the ones who hadn't yet found out that they were considered 'ugly.'" This environment encouraged him to alter his black-and-white illustrations to include bright, vivid colors to represent the inner light that radiated from the faces of the Ghanaians.

When he lost his job in Ghana, he returned to the United States and continued to illustrate in the manner he had developed. He sought black writers with whom to collaborate, and the result was *To Be a Slave* (1968), recipient of a Newbery Honor citation, and *Black Folktales* (1969), both by JULIUS LESTER. The theme of African life and the beauty of its people continued to present itself in his work in *Tales of Temba: Traditional African Stories* (1969) by Kathleen Arnot and *African Crafts* (1970) by Jane Kerina. From 1970 until 1974, he collaborated with his wife, Muriel Feelings, to create picture books about their experiences in Africa, *Zamani Goes to Market* (1970) and the two Caldecott Honor Books, *Moja Means One: Swahili Counting Book* (1971) and *Jambo Means Hello: Swahili Alphabet Book* (1974). Following this Feelings worked for years on *The Middle Passage* (1995), the story of the African slave trade.

Today Feelings's work is widely embraced for its beauty and authenticity. He has accomplished what he set out to do: to portray positive images of black people and to convince black children of their worth. ❧ C.H.S.

FIELD, RACHEL

AMERICAN AUTHOR, ILLUSTRATOR, POET, AND PLAYWRIGHT, 1894–1942. Rachel Field became the first woman to receive the Newbery Medal when her novel *Hitty, Her First Hundred Years* (1929) was named the winner in 1930. Hitty, a lively but proper wooden doll carved in the early nineteenth century, writes her memoirs while sitting in an antique shop. She has led an exciting life, traveling on a whaling vessel, surviving a shipwreck, and exploring India and the United States. However, more than Hitty's adventures, it is Field's ability to develop the character of both the doll and her various owners that has endeared the book to generations of young readers.

Growing up in western Massachusetts, Field began writing before she could read, and her ability as a writer later earned her recognition and entrance to Radcliffe as a special student at age twenty. After college she moved to New York and worked as an editor. Although her first adult novel was rejected, several editors liked the beginning, the main character's childhood, and encouraged her to write for children. Her first published book was a volume of poetry, *The Pointed People: Verses and Silhouettes* (1924), illustrated with her black paper cutouts. In the next ten years she wrote four more books of poetry, three books of plays, three major novels, and some ten shorter stories, many of which she also illustrated. In addition, she edited two collections of folktales. However, after her marriage in 1935, Field wrote primarily for adults.

Field's poetry usually deals with simple, everyday subjects. The urban and nature settings reflect her love of both New York City and the island in Maine where she summered. Her eye for detail and her ability to remain in touch with her own child self enabled her to create quiet yet joyful bits of life. *Poems* (1957), compiled some years after her death, brings together some of her best work. More recently, two of her poems have been revived and turned into appealing PICTURE BOOKS. In 1988 both NANCY WINSLOW PARKER and Giles Laroche chose *General Store* to illustrate, and two years later Laroche illustrated *A Road Might Lead to Anywhere* (1990).

However, Field is best remembered for *Hitty, Her First Hundred Years.* She and Dorothy P. Lathrop, who illustrated the book, discovered a tiny wooden doll in a New York antique shop. Immediately, they began to imagine what her life had been like, and the book took shape. Field's next novel, *Calico Bush* (1931), set in the early eighteenth century on the remote Maine coast, was a Newbery Honor Book. The Sargent family take in thirteen-year-old, French-born Marguerite as a "bound-out" girl, or indentured servant. Once again, Field creates strongly drawn, interesting characters and a highly believable, fast-paced plot in a realistic setting. The book is marred only by Field's representation of American Indians, clearly a reflection of the time in which she was writing. Both in this book and in *Hitty,* she refers to indigenous peoples as "childlike." Nevertheless, Field has contributed colorful characters and rich stories and poems to the field of children's literature. ❧ P.R.

FINE, ANNE

BRITISH AUTHOR, B. 1947. Anne Fine explores the complexities of human relationships with dark humor and keen perception in her award-winning novels for young readers. Born in Leicester, England, Fine entered elementary school early, when her family's size suddenly increased with the arrival of triplets. She attended the University of Warwick, taught school, worked for a famine relief organization, married, and spent time living in Canada and the United States before attempting her first novel. *The Summer-House Loon* (1978), the story of a teenager involved in the romantic entanglements of her adult friends, was followed by a sequel, *The Other, Darker Ned* (1979). Fine has since written a wide range of fiction, from PICTURE BOOKS to adult novels.

Two of her books for a younger audience show a special interest in social problems. *Bill's New Frock* (1989), a comic examination of sexism, is one of Fine's most popular titles in Great Britain. *The Chicken Gave It to Me* (1992) is a humorous story of little green men who arrive on Earth with a taste for human beings; a chicken saves the day in a book that promotes free-range grazing for farm stock. Fine also uses humor and social concerns in her well-received young adult novels. In *The Granny Project* (1983), four children band together to prevent their grandmother from entering a nursing home. Some readers may be put off by the book's unflinching realism, indelicate humor, and cold adult characters.

Adults play a central role in several of the author's books, including the 1987 farce *Madame Doubtfire* (published as *Alias Madame Doubtfire* in the United States), which concerns an actor who, disguised as a woman, gets a housekeeping job in his ex-wife's home so he can spend time with his children. The novel was made into a popular 1993 film, *Mrs. Doubtfire,* starring Robin Williams. Children of divorce are also the focus of *Goggle Eyes* (1989), which was published in the U.S. as *My War with Goggle Eyes.* The novel, which won both the Carnegie Medal and the *Guardian* Award, presents Kitty's first-person account of the anger she feels toward her mother's new boyfriend, a conservative businessman with old-fashioned ideas about child-rearing. The theme of war also permeates *The Book of the Banshee* (1991), in which Will Flowers relates how his sister's tumultuous adolescence has thrown the family into an uproar. Human dynamics are well portrayed in both novels; every moment of humor, anger, and reconciliation rings true.

The young people in Fine's novels are unusually intelligent, with interests in reading, theater, school projects, and social issues. But the characters in *Flour Babies* (1992) are very different. These mildly delinquent, unmotivated students are unwilling participants in a science fair project that involves caring for sacks of flour as if they were babies, in order to learn parenting skills. The topic has been fictionalized in other children's books, most notably Eve Bunting's *Our Sixth-Grade Sugar Babies* (1990), but never with the depth of sympathetic insight that Fine demonstrates in her second Carnegie-winning novel. Her hulking teenage protagonist, Simon Martin, reaches new levels of self-awareness and is perhaps the most appealing character to be found in any of the author's books.

Fine's books are popular with young readers in both Great Britain and the United States. As her funny, contemporary novels have grown in depth and percipience, her characterizations have become warmer, displaying a generosity of spirit that makes the books richly rewarding. P.D.S.

Fischer, Hans

SWISS ARTIST, 1909–1958. While another artist might arduously belabor the details of a painting in an attempt to impersonate life, in just a swift stroke of a pencil Hans Fischer could capture a living, breathing character on the page. As a child he spent hours outdoors studying animals and plants, trees and birds. He brought a pencil and made sketches and studies of all he saw. He went to art school in Zurich and continued his studies at the Ecole des Beaux Arts in Geneva, where he studied under Paul Klee, who influenced both Fischer's design and his philosophy. As Klee had done, Fischer reduced a figure to its essential lines. Klee said, "It is not my task to reproduce appearances . . . for that there is the photographic plate. I want to reach the heart." With Klee, Fischer also gained insight into color.

In *The Traveling Musicians* (1944), the familiar story of four castoff animals who form a band, Fischer first outlined the donkey, dog, cat, and cock in simple pen and ink, then brushed on bits of brilliant primary colors. Most of the page remains white, so the bold, undiluted colors have even more of a magnetic effect on the eye. Although the donkey and cat are gray and the dog is brown, they each carry a ribbon or a collar or a drum of bright color, and the cock is resplendent in red, yellow, blue, and green. The focus on simple colors lends the book a folk-art quality, appropriate for this GRIMM folktale.

Fischer's treatment of a lesser-known Grimm tale, *The Good for Nothings* (1945), is done in the more muted colors common to the four-color overlay printing process. The yellow is a dull gold, the green mossy, the red a snapping orange, and the blue pale. Unlike the artwork in *The Traveling Musicians*, Fischer did not brush on these colors; rather, he used them as the lines themselves. The texture of the line is rough, and Fischer added only a few touches of black in pen and ink: an irritated eye, a sharp pin, feelers on a grasshopper, a caterpillar's legs. *The Good for Nothings* tells a scatterbrained story about a rooster and hen, Chanticleer and Partlet, who arrogantly take advantage of everyone they meet. The story is lively and childlike, and the illustrations keep the pace quick.

Fischer played a leading role in introducing American children to the European picture book. When editor Margaret McElderry saw his book *Pitschi* (1948) in a New York bookstore, she was so excited she went right back to her office and arranged to buy the rights to it. The story is about a rooster and a kitten who long to be something else; the pictures sparkle with child appeal. McElderry went on to publish Fischer's other books, including *The Birthday* (1954), in which the animals organize a surprise party for their beloved Lisette, an old lady in the tradition of Babar's friend. All these titles were immensely popular. No wonder, for what child can resist the lively stories with drawings whose lines and colors seem to ring with laughter? ❧ J.A.J.

Fisher, Aileen

AMERICAN POET, AUTHOR, AND PLAYWRIGHT, B. 1906. The best words to describe Aileen Fisher's writing are "prolific" and "varied." Her published works total over one hundred and include poems, prose, both fiction and nonfiction, and plays.

Raised on a farm in Michigan, Fisher attended the University of Chicago and the University of Missouri. In 1932, after working in Chicago at the Women's National Journalistic Register and the Labor Bureau, Fisher moved to a two-hundred-acre ranch in Colorado. The following year she published her first volume of poetry, *The Coffee-Pot Face* (1933), which dealt with such commonplace subjects as ladybugs, icicles, and tummy aches.

Although Fisher has written and compiled collections of plays, a number of biographies—the straightforward *Jeanne D'Arc* (1970), for instance, traces the path of the eleven-year-old Joan as she fulfills her destiny with grace and gentleness—and some nonfiction books, few have received critical acclaim. The exception is *Valley of the Smallest: The Life Story of a Shrew* (1966), which received the Western Writers of America Award for juvenile nonfiction and was named a Hans Christian Andersen Honor Book. Fisher describes the ecology of a Colorado Rockies valley near her home, focusing on the tiny shrew but widening the scope by introducing other animals through the shrew's relationships and survival skills. Combining her talent for observation with her poetic imagination, Fisher narrates the story with strength and beauty but does not lapse into sentimentality.

"My first and chief love in writing is writing children's verse," says Fisher, and when she combines this love with her other passion—nature—her poetry comes to life. *In the Middle of the Night* (1965) tells the story of a little girl who receives a nocturnal walk for her birthday. As she walks through the still night with her father, she is enthralled by the sky, the woods, and the silent world of night animals. The tone of the text, loosely poetic, matches the restrained awe of the girl's emotions. *Best Little House* (1966) tells of another type of country walk. This time it is a little boy who is sad at leaving his own house to move to the country. His mother takes him on a nature walk and shows him all types of houses: the ant's sand house, the wasp's mud hut, the butterfly's spun cocoon. Fisher's appreciation of the beauty of nature is matched by her understanding of children's fears and feelings.

Fisher's collections of verse and poetic stories are enhanced by the art that accompanies them. ERIC CARLE's linoleum animal cuts mirror the warm, affectionate, but not sugary text of *Feathered Ones and Furry* (1971); Marie Angel's watercolors capture the mischievous manner of cats in *My Cat Has Eyes of Sapphire Blue* (1975). The luminous watercolors of BLAIR LENT perfectly match the wonder and delight of the little girl exploring the origin of the world in *I Stood upon a Mountain* (1979). As the girl wanders through the seasons, she questions how the world came into being and receives a different explanation from each person she meets. At the end of her journey she is "filled with a wonder/that needs no answer,/no answer at all" and realizes that her experiences are more important than answers. While one critic called the book a "wishy-washy paean to the wonderful American world," it can be seen as serving to promote an appreciation for natural beauty and a spirit of tolerance toward different theoretical approaches to creation.

Fisher has defined poetry as a "rhythmical piece of writing that leaves the reader feeling that life is a little richer than before, a little more full of wonder, beauty, or delight." She received the National Council of Teachers of English Award for children's poetry in 1978. In her simple, quiet style Fisher has produced volumes of writing guaranteed to bring wonder and beauty into the lives of her readers. ❧ M.I.A.

Fisher, Dorothy Canfield

American author, 1879–1958. *Understood Betsy* (1917) was Dorothy Canfield Fisher's first book for children, and it remains her best known. The author was born in Lawrence, Kansas, and raised in a family that valued education. She attended Ohio State University, the Sorbonne in Paris, and received her doctorate in romance languages from Columbia University. Much of her life was dedicated to humanitarian causes. During World War I, she spent three years as a relief worker in France. She later served on the board of education in Vermont, where she lived with her husband and children.

Vermont is the setting for *Understood Betsy*, the story of a coddled nine-year-old girl sent to live with relatives on a farm. Through her experiences with this loving, no-nonsense family, Betsy discovers her own abilities and learns to reach out to others. The novel contains insightful characterizations and a finely detailed New England atmosphere. Fisher occasionally interrupts the narrative to make first-person observations about Betsy, but her remarks merely add an old-fashioned charm to a story that is quite modern in its themes of self-reliance, personal growth, and understanding.

Fisher also published short fiction for children, including *Made-to-Order Stories* (1925), a volume of unusual tales, each told within the framework of a little boy asking his mother for a special story; the stories were, in fact, written for the author's ten-year-old son. *Something Old, Something New: Stories of the People Who Are America* (1949) contains several historical tales.

Fisher died in 1958, shortly after the publication of Elizabeth Yates's biography, *Pebbles in a Pool: The Widening Circle of Dorothy Canfield Fisher's Life*. Although most of her books are no longer popular, *Understood Betsy* continues to be read and enjoyed. ❧ P.D.S.

Fisher, Leonard Everett

American illustrator and author, b. 1924. Leonard Everett Fisher, born in the Bronx, New York, entered the children's book field as an illustrator, then extended his talents to writing picture books, novels, and nonfiction. Fisher's artistic talent was discovered early and nurtured by his family. His draftsman father was a frustrated artist, and when two-year-old Leonard picked up a paintbrush and scrawled on one of his father's pictures, a closet was immediately converted to a studio for the budding young artist. Growing up in the Bronx and Brooklyn, Fisher attended special art classes, learned art appreciation via a radio program, and was exposed to culture through trips to museums, the theater, and the library. In school, he won awards for his artwork, including a float design competition sponsored by Macy's Thanksgiving Day Parade. Fisher's education at Brooklyn College was interrupted for military service during World War II, but he later received bachelor's and master's degrees from Yale University, where he was a graduate teaching fellow. He served as dean of the Whitney School of Art in New Haven, Connecticut, but continued painting and having his work exhibited.

He began illustrating children's books with Geoffrey Household's *The Exploits of Xenophon* (1955). The meticulously researched illustrations of ancient Greece established Fisher's reputation as a book illustrator and led to more such work, including over one thousand illustrations for all eight volumes of *The Reading Laboratories* (1956–1962). He produced artwork for new editions of works by Nathaniel Hawthorne, George Bernard Shaw, and Washington Irving and has illustrated books by contemporary authors such as Milton Meltzer, Madeleine L'Engle, Isaac Bashevis Singer, and Myra Cohn Livingston, as well as two picture books written by his wife, Margery M. Fisher.

Pumpers, Boilers, Hooks and Ladders: A Book of Fire Engines (1961) was the first book Leonard Fisher wrote and illustrated and is most distinctive for its bright-red double-page spreads of fire-fighting equipment. He created further picture books in various styles of illustration, from the cartoonish *A Head Full of Hats* (1962) to the darkly monochrome *Storm at the Jetty* (1981) to the bright acrylics of *Boxes! Boxes!* (1984).

As Fisher gained more confidence in his writing ability, he began publishing fiction for older readers. Titles such as *Death of "Evening Star": The Diary of a Young New England Whaler* (1972) and *The Warlock of Westfull* (1974) are skillfully written and atmospheric, but lack emotion and are sometimes bogged down by extraneous characters and details. Nevertheless, with their excellent illustrations and book design, they are handsome volumes.

The illustrated informational book seems to be Fisher's forte, and he has explored a gamut of topics, including art history, the Statue of Liberty, the Alamo, and the American flag. His greatest achievement is the nineteen-volume "Colonial Americans" series, which began with *The Glassmakers* in 1964 and concluded with *The Blacksmiths* in 1976. The books provide detailed accounts of various crafts and trades in American history and are accompanied by wonderful scratchboard illustrations. The "Nineteenth-Century America" series examines social history in *The Factories* (1979), *The Hospitals* (1980), *The Schools* (1983), and four other volumes. A deep appreciation for American history and culture shines through both outstanding series.

Fisher writes across several different genres, and his artwork encompasses a wide variety of styles, making him one of the most multifaceted creators in the field of children's literature. ❧ P.D.S.

Fitzgerald, John D.

American author, 1907–1988. John D. Fitzgerald is best known for his loosely autobiographical series of books that chronicle the adventures of Tom D. Fitzgerald, known to friends and family as "The Great Brain." Tom, modeled after the author's older brother, enjoys a well-earned reputation for swindling and conning other children in Adenville, Utah, during the early part of the twentieth century. The seven novels in the series are narrated by his younger brother John, Tom's regular victim and cohort.

These humorous, lively stories continue to appeal to a wide range of readers because they are family stories full of exaggerated humor, outlandish adventure, and insight. They are stories about the dynamics of a family of three unruly but sympathetic boys who compete for status and attention. Tom and his brothers describe growing up Catholic in an overwhelmingly Mormon town, when the tug of war during the annual town picnic is a contest between the Mormons and the Gentiles. In Fitzgerald's stories an indoor water closet is unheard-of and worth the attention of an entire town and a girl who dons a pair of dungarees is scorned by children and adults alike. The stories are also solid adventures, filled with excitement and tension. Tom is bold enough to try to fool the Jesuit priests at his strict boarding school, and John is foolish enough to face an armed outlaw with just a lariat. Fitzgerald tells a sensational tale grounded in enough truth and details of everyday life to be convincing. The novels are filled with facts from his own childhood, and readers recognize the authenticity.

Illustration by Mercer Mayer from *The Great Brain* (1967), by John D. Fitzgerald.

Fitzgerald, a journalist, wrote for adults for many years before his wife suggested he write down some of the stories from his childhood, which he told so well. His series of stories about the Great Brain, which began with *The Great Brain* in 1967, continue to be read and loved. ❧ M.V.K.

Fitzhugh, Louise

American author and illustrator, 1928–1974. Although she published only a few works, Louise Fitzhugh left a permanent mark on children's literature. Or perhaps Harriet M. Welsch, Fitzhugh's greatest literary creation, left the permanent mark, for *Harriet the Spy* (1964) is acknowledged as one of the most original and groundbreaking books published during the 1960s. Harriet is a privileged, upper-class eleven-year-old who lives in a New York brownstone with her somewhat distant parents and an eccentric nursemaid, Ole Golly. An aspiring writer, Harriet goes on a daily spy route and records her devastatingly honest observations in an ever-present notebook. Harriet is saddened when Ole Golly leaves to get married, but faces her greatest challenge when she is ostracized after her classmates read the caustic comments she has written about them in her secret notebook. Harriet M. Welsch represented a new kind of protagonist for children's literature. She is spoiled, self-absorbed, and often rude. She curses and throws tantrums, but is also vulnerable and touching.

This refreshing, fully realized character is very much a New York native, but Fitzhugh was born in Memphis, Tennessee, where she spent an unhappy youth. She was the only child of a wealthy family; her parents divorced early and custody was granted to her father. Fitzhugh was educated in private schools and attended several colleges before dropping out a few credits short of graduation. She then moved to New York, where she lived off a trust fund and trained as a painter.

Fitzhugh illustrated two picture books, *Suzuki Beane* (1961) and *Bang, Bang, You're Dead* (1969), both cowritten with Sandra Scoppettone. But it was the publication of *Harriet the Spy* that made her famous. Early reviews were mixed; some critics praised the book, but many others denounced it. Children, however, recognized its honesty and made it a bestseller. *Harriet the Spy* is now considered a landmark novel, which many believe signaled the true beginning of modern realistic fiction for children. Harriet M. Welsch also plays a role in Fitzhugh's follow-up novel, *The Long Secret* (1965), but the focus of this book is on Harriet's friend Beth Ellen Hansen. Many children enjoy this novel, and reviewers have praised its frank discussion of sexual development, but from a critical perspective it is not as successful as *Harriet the Spy.* Because she behaves so passively throughout most of the book, Beth Ellen is not a strong enough character to be the center of an entire novel. The biting satire about her jet-set family seems directed toward an adult audience rather than children, and some of the humor is too broad, resulting in caricatures, rather than characterizations.

Fitzhugh did not live to see her next novel published; she died unexpectedly of a brain aneurysm just a week before the release of *Nobody's Family Is Going to Change* (1974). This book is a humorous but angry story about two black children who do not conform to the upper-class lifestyle of their parents. Nonconformity is a theme that runs throughout Fitzhugh's writings and seems to be a trait she values, despite the costs; another theme in the books is the almost palpable sense of loneliness in her young people. Several of Fitzhugh's picture-book manuscripts have been published posthumously, as well as a farcical novel, *Sport* (1979), about Harriet's friend Simon Rocque. *Nobody's Family Is Going to Change* was adapted as a mediocre after-school television special; in another incarnation, it was a thoroughly enjoyable Tony Award–winning Broadway musical, *The Tap Dance Kid.* Reportedly, Fitzhugh left behind other manuscripts that may eventually find their way into print, but she will be best remembered as the creator of the inimitable *Harriet the Spy.* ❧ P.D.S.

FLACK, MARJORIE

AMERICAN AUTHOR AND ILLUSTRATOR, 1897–1958. "Once upon a time there was a beautiful young duck named Ping." With these words familiar to generations of American children, Marjorie Flack began *The Story about Ping,* a book continuously in print since its publication in 1933. Flack had a gift for creating books for the very young child. Born in Greenport, Long Island, she considered storytelling an intrinsic part of her personality. "As far back as I can remember, pictures were always an important part of my life. I can remember drawing pictures in the sand, pictures on the walls (and being punished for it), and pictures on every piece of paper I could find. For every picture there would be a story, even before I could write." At the age of eighteen, she enrolled at the Art Students League in New York City, where she met artist Karl Larsson. They married in 1919, and the following year their daughter, Hilma, was born.

Flack's first book, *Tak Tuk, an Arctic Boy* (1928), was written in collaboration with Helen Loman, who had lived most of her life in Alaska. Flack wrote and illustrated a story based on Loman's factual accounts of the lives of Eskimo children. *All around the Town* (1929) came next, the story of a boy enjoying the sights and sounds of New York, inspired by the author's own experiences exploring the city with her young daughter. In 1930, Flack wrote and illustrated *Angus and the Ducks.* The first of five books in a series about "a very young little dog" who is "curious about many places and many things," the book is a "true story about a real dog and some real ducks," Flack noted. "The other Angus books are also built around real incidents. The cat was Hilma's cat, and she really did hide on the roof. Wag-Tail Bess was our own Airedale." Although a highly competent writer and illustrator, Flack's true genius lay in her overall storytelling ability and in the graphic pacing of words and images, and nowhere is that talent more fully realized than in her Angus books. Like ROBERT LAWSON and JAMES DAUGHERTY, she uses word and image repetition, type layout, and page design to control timing and add drama. Preschoolers are drawn to her use of bright colors, forthright drawing style, and clear rhythmic prose. They also identify with the inquisitive Angus, who ventures out into unknown territories but always returns to the security of his own home.

Flack had the remarkable ability of instilling personality into her animal characters without denying their outward natural behaviors. While writing *Angus and the Ducks,* Flack became so interested in Peking ducks that she began a thorough investigation of the species, discovering that their ancestors lived in China on the Yangtze River. This fascination led her to write *The Story about Ping,* which Flack asked artist Kurt Wiese to illustrate because he had lived and worked in China. His rich zinc lithographs became as integral to the story as Flack's own lyrical prose, and their successful collaboration created one of the most beloved PICTURE BOOKS in all of children's literature. Flack collaborated with many talented authors and illustrators, including her second husband, Pulitzer Prize–winning poet William Rose Benét, but it is the story about Ping and his home, the beautiful wise-eyed boat on the Yangtze River, which remains her greatest contribution to children's literature. ❧ M.B.B.

FLEISCHMAN, PAUL

AMERICAN AUTHOR AND POET, B. 1952. Since the publication of *The Birthday Tree* (1979), a fanciful picture book in which a boy shares an uncanny relationship with a tree planted to celebrate his birth, Paul Fleischman has established himself as a writer of extraordinary originality and versatility. Fleischman's picture books, novels, short stories, and poetry are written with consummate skill, and his stylistic range is as varied as is his choice of format. The awards and honors Fleischman's books have garnered testify to his literary accomplishments. Many have been designated Notable Children's Books by the American Library Association, Best Books by *School Library Journal,* or Notable Trade Books for the Language Arts by the National Council of Teachers of English. Awards include the Newbery Medal and Newbery Honor, the Boston Globe–Horn Book Award, and the Golden Kite Award.

Paul Fleischman was born in Monterey, California, the son of SID FLEISCHMAN, a well-known children's book author. Fleischman credits his father as a literary influence; while growing up he served his story apprenticeship listening to his father read rollicking tall tales and adventure stories aloud. Since music has also been a strong force in Fleischman's life, it comes as no surprise that an astute attention to the power of sound and the musicality of words permeates his work. The harmonious melding of word and sound finds resonance in *Rondo in C* (1988), a mellifluous PICTURE BOOK in which a young girl's piano recital stirs a personal response in each member of the audience. Fleischman's colorful stories, often set in the past, reflect a keen interest in American history, and many are rooted in actual historical events. *Bull Run* (1993) weaves together the voices of sixteen individual characters, each of whom has a unique reason for participating in the Battle of Bull Run. Set during the Philadelphia yellow fever epidemic of 1793, *Path of the Pale Horse* (1983) makes evident the limitations of medicine and explores the relationships among science, religion, and superstition. *Saturnalia* (1990) presents a vivid, multifaceted picture of life in colonial New England for a Narragansett Indian captive-turned-printer's-apprentice. In these books, and in all of Fleischman's fiction, characters grapple with moral and psychological issues, but wry humor and unexpected plot turnings temper sobriety. Rich in figurative language, two short-story collections, *Graven Images* (1982), a Newbery Honor Book, and *Coming-and-Going Men* (1985), have been compared to the masterly tales of Hawthorne and Poe for their suspense, macabre tone, and ironic twists of plot.

Fleischman's work contains myriad images of bird and insect life. *Townsend's Warbler* (1992), the lyric chronicle of naturalist JOHN ROWE TOWNSEND's discovery of a new specimen of bird, draws directly on Fleischman's enthusiasm for natural history, as do the companion volumes of poetry *I Am Phoenix* (1985) and *Joyful Noise* (1988). Sound and word again dovetail to create poems "to be read aloud by two readers at once," the two parts "meshing as in a musical duet." *I Am Phoenix* features birds, from the passenger pigeon to the cormorant; *Joyful Noise,* the 1989 Newbery Medal winner, celebrates the "booming/boisterous/joyful noise" of the insect world. Keen observation and skilled imagery ensure that the birds and insects retain their true nature, providing a fascinating and participatory glimpse into the natural world. These inventive books of verse take their rightful place as some of this wordsmith's most remarkable work. ❧ C.S.

FLEISCHMAN, SID

AMERICAN AUTHOR, B. 1920. When humorist Albert Sidney Fleischman wrote *The Whipping Boy* (1986), he deviated from his usual American tall-tale humor, a hallmark of many of his novels, and created a broadly comic tale, with an Old World flavor, set in an undefined time and place. It won the 1987 Newbery Medal. A whipping boy was "a young boy kept by royal households, educated with a prince, and punished in his stead." In the tale, a bored Prince Brat forces Jemmy, his whipping boy, to escape the castle confines with him. They immediately fall into the hands of the villainous Hold-Your-Nose Billy, "who smells like a ton of garlic," and his sidekick. While the boys are catapulted through adventures and hairbreadth escapes—all richly spiced with comedy—they become friends. As in much of Fleischman's writing, beneath the surface of the rapid-

Voices of the Creators

Sid Fleischman

Novels are written in the dark. At least, mine are. Unlike more sensible authors, I start Chapter One with rarely a notion of the story that's about to unfold. It's like wandering into a pitch-black theater and groping around for the lights. One by one, the spots and footlights come on, catching a character or two against a painted backdrop. I sit back and enjoy the show. When the final curtain falls a year or two later, the stage is ablaze with lights, and I have a new novel.

One has to be balmy to work in this chancy and improvisational way—I agree. The textbooks tell us in bold letters to make a detailed outline in advance and even to prepare a dossier on each character. I have never done either. If I knew everything in advance, I'd find it tedious to sit at my desk for hours each day scratching out the story. Instead, I'm at my desk fifteen minutes after I get out of bed in the morning; I can't wait to find out what's going to happen next in the novel. I am audience as well as author.

I am not alone in these bungee jumps into the unknown. Both Jill Paton Walsh and the late Ellen Raskin told me they work the same way. Among others: Henry James, Tennessee Williams, and Neil Simon.

My working eccentricities do not stop there. I do not write the traditional rough draft. I tried that once almost fifty years ago, with my first novel, a hard-boiled detective story. I wrote a slapdash rough draft in three weeks, skipping along without pausing to find the right word or to look up information I lacked. The next several months of cleaning up and heavily rewriting almost 250 pages of manuscript were an agony. I said, "Never again."

I began a process of rewriting each page as it comes out of the typewriter, and of not moving on until that page is (in my view, at least) ready for the printer. It is not uncommon for me to redo pages ten or fifteen times. But once the novel is on paper, the job is done! Oh, it might require a change here and a chiropractic adjustment there, but within a week I'll have it out of the house and on to my editor.

While I recommend these working methods to no one, I'm certain they profoundly affect my scenes and plots. I know I could not have worked out in advance the story twists, comic surprises, and intricacies of such novels as *Humbug Mountain* and *Jim Ugly.* Only because I was not immobilized by an outline was I able to run with the sudden thoughts, accidentals, and inspirations of the moment. It was only a light-bulb idea that the one-man dog, Jim Ugly, might not be found grieving at the grave of his dead master. Why not? Hmmm. What if the grave were empty? The plot leaped up before me.

I started *Humbug Mountain* with nothing more in mind than the title. I certainly didn't know that I would shift the course of the Missouri River for a three-ring finish. With one exception, I've never known my endings in advance. Early in the writing of *The Ghost in the Noonday Sun,* I saw a sea battle looming ahead between the pirate ship and a whaler, with its harpoons and flensing knives. I think it would have made a great final curtain; I never wrote it. Just before the pirates set sail, a scene popped up out of nowhere, and I knew my story was complete. The sea battle would have been an anticlimax.

I don't know how one could write comedies, as I do, without the high wire of improvisation. Comedy is jack-in-the-box surprise. At the end of *The Whipping Boy,* when the two ghastly villains unknowingly stow away aboard a ship bound for a convict island, I was as surprised as anyone. In the broader tall-tale comedies of *McBroom's Wonderful One-Acre Farm,* I wrote that Josh McBroom would rather break a leg than tell a fib. I hadn't a notion that at the end the wind was going to drop a post hole on his farm. And that he'd step in it.

I've been asked more than once if I have apprehensions that I won't be able to tie up an ending for a novel underway. None at all. In writing that first, impromptu detective novel, I had no idea who was committing all the crimes. But as the pages stacked up on my desk, I realized the time had come to find my villain. And I made an interesting discovery. I could have created a rationale for *any* of my surviving characters to be the murderer! That gave me confidence. While I have abandoned a couple of novels in the very early stages, I have never had to shelve one because I couldn't figure out an ending.

My next novel? Oh, it's about a . . . well, let me sit down at the computer and find out.

Jacket illustration by Eric von Schmidt for *Humbug Mountain* (1978), by Sid Fleischman.

fire entertainment, the story resonates with the importance of such universal themes as trust, friendship, courage, justice, and—above all—humor in the face of disaster.

Few contemporary writers have infused comedy into children's books as successfully as Fleischman. He taps into the deep, rich vein of American frontier humor, adding his own brand of engaging, convoluted plots, peppery language, and a cast of picturesque characters dubbed with outrageous names. One of the finest examples of the genre he so facilely creates is *Humbug Mountain* (1978), winner of the 1979 Boston Globe–Horn Book Award. The hilarious story features a family down on their luck roaming the West looking for Grandpa. While searching, they find a ghost-haunted river boat, inadvertently start a gold rush, discover a petrified man, and straighten out the villains who plague them. Fleischman, a skillful writer, handily combines history with adventure, serious statements with fast-paced plots, and laces his tales with delightful doses of wild humor, as in *Chancy and the Grand Rascal* (1966) and *Jim Ugly* (1992). Although Fleischman's novels are exactly right for middle school readers, his "McBroom" series ranks as high humor with early elementary children. During his thirty years as a writer, Fleischman has seen "the status of humor in children's novels change immensely. In my first story, *Mr. Mysterious and Company* (1962), about a family of traveling magicians, I was asked to take out some of the humor, because editors were afraid reviewers would dismiss the book as a joke. Today, humor is enjoyed and no longer regarded as literary brummagem."

Fleischman grew up in California, where, before becoming an author, he was a professional magician. Prestidigitators often find their way into his books. *The Midnight Horse* (1990) is a story about an orphan, a blacksmith, a thief, and the ghost of the Great Chaffalo, a once-celebrated magician. Fleischman's son, Paul Fleischman, himself a children's book author, paid an appropriate tribute to his father's books when he wrote, "When [my father] gave up being a magician, he became a prestidigitator of words, palming plot elements, making villains vanish, producing solutions out of thin air. He knows how to keep an audience guessing, how to create suspense, how to keep readers reading." This is why new generations continue to discover and delight in the surprises found in Sid Fleischman's books. ❧ S.L.

Folklore

See American Folklore.

Forbes, Esther

American historical novelist, 1891–1967. Esther Forbes, an important historical novelist, secured a permanent place in children's literature with the publication of *Johnny Tremain* (1943), winner of the Newbery Medal. Praised by the *New York Times* as a "novelist who wrote like a historian and a historian who wrote like a novelist" and noted for her understanding of human nature, Forbes presents the events behind the American Revolution through the eyes of a young boy. The story spans two years in the life of Johnny Tremain, a young orphan and arrogant silversmith's apprentice. While casting the handle of a sugar basin for John Hancock, he burns his right hand as a result of the actions of the despicable young Dove and must give up his beloved craft. Crippled and bitter, Johnny endures difficult days before finding work as a horse-boy riding for the patriotic newspaper the Boston *Observer* and as a messenger for the Sons of Liberty. His new work brings him in touch with Rab, an aloof and intriguing young printer who becomes his closest friend. The historical figures Sam Adams, James Otis, Dr. Joseph Warren, and General Thomas Gage are important to the plot and are brought engagingly alive in Forbes's treatment.

Though she was not a professional historian, Forbes won a Pulitzer Prize in history in 1942 for the adult book *Paul Revere and the World He Lived In.* As a result of her research, she became interested in the lives of the apprentices in and about the shops and wharves of Boston during the eighteenth century. As she explains, "It was a horse-boy who brought word to Paul Revere that the British intended to march out of Boston on the night of April in '75. This little incident teased my mind." In her Newbery Medal acceptance speech in 1944, Forbes drew parallels between the Revolutionary War and Pearl Harbor: "In peace times countries are apt to look upon their boys under twenty as mere children and (for better or worse) to treat them as such. When war comes, these boys are suddenly asked to play their part as men. I knew I wanted to show the boys and girls of today how difficult were those other children's lives by modern standards. They were not allowed to be children for very long."

Forbes's vision of the Revolution is clearly reflected in her young protagonist's vision. In presenting some of the economic motivations behind the war, the author asks, "Weren't the Americans after all human beings?" Johnny, however, discovers with James Otis that revolution is "for something more than our pocketbooks." Johnny discovers a dying Rab and later reflects, "True, Rab had died. Hundreds would die, but not the thing they died for." Johnny's stance on the war is not based on the rhetoric that surrounds him. Although he is a patriot who believes in the cause, he also recognizes the personal sacrifices and loss involved, and Forbes indeed evokes with sympathy for both sides the common heritage of the British and the Americans.

What is remarkable about this vividly drawn work are the details that make the characters and the drama of the Revolution so real. Woven throughout the historical aspects of the historical tale is Johnny's own odyssey. In the beginning Johnny's talent and status in a household of less skilled and duller boys have made him arrogant and disdainful. His plunge into humiliation and an uncertain future ultimately changes the course of his development and destiny. In the end Johnny never receives the great fortune or success he hopes for. When Dr. Warren offers to operate on his hand, it is so the boy can hold a musket and fight among the ranks of young men serving their country and their beliefs, not to achieve the high honor and distinction accorded the famous patriots who appear in the novel. Yet Johnny become a hero, an emblem of sacrifice and spirit, both inspiring and real to generations of young readers. ❧ C.L.

Foster, Genevieve Stump

American author and illustrator, 1893–1979. Growing up, Genevieve Foster found nothing too hard to learn or remember—except history: "History confused me . . . the more I learned in high school and college, the more confused I became," she recalled. Consequently, she made it her mission to discover what she had always wanted to know about history and to bring it alive for children and readers of all ages.

Her prolific career as both an author and illustrator spanned six decades and resulted in the publication of nineteen nonfiction historical children's novels plus innumerable illustrations.

In the literary world of the 1940s, Foster was in the forefront of the trend that sought to illuminate history through a close focus on an individual seen within her or his milieu. Her first book, *George Washington's World* (1941), and all her subsequent works demonstrated her mastery of this genre. She was best known for her technique of choosing one significant historical figure and weaving a story around his perceptions of and reactions to everyday occurrences in his life.

All of her novels take a horizontal approach to history and address many facets of period life, including politics, culture, scientific discoveries, art, literature, and medicine. The style represented a drastic change from previous written history, which was presented sequentially with little correlation with events elsewhere in the world. The stories are full of questions about every conceivable aspect of the period, thus widening horizons on many different levels, and the books are vividly illustrated with carefully researched maps and charts that capture the imaginations of young readers.

During her career Foster has been the recipient of three Newbery Honor Book Awards. Her books have been translated into fifteen languages, including Urdu, Hindi, Bengali, Chinese, Korean, and Vietnamese. Her published works include: (self-illustrated) *Abraham Lincoln's World* (1944); (self-illustrated) *Augustus Caesar's World* (1947); *George Washington* (1949); *Abraham Lincoln* (1950); *Andrew Jackson* (1951); *Birthdays of Freedom* Vol. I (1952), Vol. II (1957), one-volume edition (1973); *Theodore Roosevelt* (1954); *When and Where in*

Italy (1955); *World of Captain John Smith* (1960); *World of Columbus and Sons* (1965); *Year of the Pilgrims, 1620* (1969); *Year of Lincoln, 1861* (1970); *Year of Independence, 1776* (1970); (self-illustrated) *The World of William Penn* (1973); (self-illustrated) *The Year of the Horseless Carriage, 1801* (1975); and (self-illustrated) *The Year of the Flying Machine, 1903* (1977).

Foster's writing style is clear, concise, and fluid and her story lines very easy to follow. Her great strength as a storyteller is her ability to bring her readers right into the minds and times of her characters. ❧ S.M.M.

Fox, Mem

AUSTRALIAN WRITER, B. 1946. Teacher, writer, and storyteller, Mem Fox was born in Melbourne, Australia, but spent only six months there before her missionary parents whisked her away to Rhodesia (now Zimbabwe). There she grew up happily, riding donkeys, climbing trees, writing stories, and reading voraciously. She had every intention of becoming a writer until the age of about thirteen, when the bright lights of the stage caught her eye. In 1965 she set off for drama school in London. She spent three years "learning how to act, being forced to learn how to teach and accidentally learning how to write." Although the experience eventually cured her of her interest in acting, it also, she claims, bestowed on her an "important and lasting gift . . . the gift of language." When she did finally return to Australia in 1970, her English husband accompanied her, and they settled in Adelaide, where their daughter was born. Teaching—"my real occupation, about which I'm passionate and about which I never throw tantrums"—began in Adelaide, where she taught drama in secondary schools and where she eventually became a senior lecturer in drama and language at Sturt College.

But in 1975 Fox also enrolled as a student at Flinders University. There she began studying children's literature. In its most embryonic stages, *Possum Magic* (1983), Fox's first book, went by the title of *Hush, the Invisible Mouse* and was written as an assignment for a children's literature course. The intrepid student/author then wrote to illustrator JULIE VIVAS, asking her to illustrate the hefty 1,400-word manuscript. Nine publishers rejected the result. Then, on the condition that it be rewritten and re-illustrated, with the mice changed to possums, the setting altered to Australia, and the text cut by two-thirds, the small, independent publisher Omnibus Books accepted and published *Possum Magic.* Since this magical "bush" story was first published, it has sold hundreds of thousands of copies in various forms—a phenomenon in Australian publishing. Mem Fox has proceeded to create a number of effervescent picture-book texts, including *Hattie and the Fox* (1986), illustrated by PATRICIA MULLINS; *Night Noises* (1989), illustrated by Terry Denton; and the well-loved *Wilfrid Gordon McDonald Partridge* (1985). In this book, illustrated by Julie Vivas, a little boy comes to appreciate the meaning of memory through his visits to an old people's home.

Illustration by JULIE VIVAS from *Wilfrid Gordon McDonald Partridge* (1985), by Mem Fox.

In addition to her children's books, Mem Fox is also the author of such works as a guide to teaching drama to children and an autobiography that fizzes and sparkles with her enthusiastic personality. She has endeared herself to readers worldwide. But her wonderful storytelling abilities, her legendary teaching style, and her writing have made her a truly extraordinary figure in her native country. As a salute to her remarkable contributions, she received the 1990 Dromkeen Medal, Australia's prestigious award for an overall contribution to children's literature. ❧ K.J.

Fox, Paula

AMERICAN AUTHOR, B. 1923. Paula Fox, born in New York City, was educated at schools in Cuba and Canada as well as in the United States. She has been a student at the Juilliard School, a teacher, a journalist, and a writer for television as well as an author. She is married to Martin Greenberg and has two sons by a previous marriage. Among her many honors are a Guggenheim Fellowship and a National Institute of Arts and Letters Award in 1972, the Newbery Medal in 1974, and—in the same year—an award from the National Endowment for the Arts. In 1978 she won the most prestigious of awards in the field of children's literature, the Hans Christian Andersen Medal, given for the author's body of work.

Paula Fox is a writer of distinction, producing four adult novels and many children's books, from such early stories for younger readers as *Maurice's Room* (1966), her first book, to more intricate and equally moving novels for older children. She attracted from the start devoted readers and appreciative reviews. When, in *Maurice's Room,* Maurice withstands parental wiles and continues to amass "things," young readers recognize a kindred spirit. His room is a collector's joy and a mother's despair. As is often the case in Fox's books, Maurice is an only child, a fact that focuses the story on adult-child relationships.

Also without siblings, Lewis in *A Likely Place* (1967) has been left in the care of delightfully peculiar Miss Fitchlow when his loving parents go off on a brief trip. Lewis is tired of being directed by adults, however loving, who want to help him improve, so his meeting in the park with elderly Mr. Madruga brings instant rapport. Like Lewis, the older man craves independence, and he asks the boy to write to his children, who have forced him into a life of ease. Both of these books have a quiet humor; both are written with fine-honed simplicity.

Of all the early books, it was perhaps *How Many Miles to Babylon?* (1967) that drew the most attention. This was due in part to the drama and suspense of the story line and in part to the fact that the central character is a child who—unlike Maurice and Lewis—is coping with disruption and loss. James is ten, living with three aunts because his disturbed mother is in custodial care. Imaginative and lonely, the small, shy African American boy encounters a gang that is stealing dogs; the gang members force James to go with them to Coney Island as their prisoner. Both his escape and his reunion with his mother are believable, a satisfying conclusion to the reader's suspense.

In *The Stone-Faced Boy* (1968), Gus, who is shy and withdrawn, takes refuge from his boisterous family by maintaining an impassive façade. Only one elderly relative sees the sensitivity behind the stoic mask. The same empathic relationship between a child and someone out of his habitual environment is used in a book for older readers, *Portrait of Ivan* (1969). Here there is a special understanding between motherless Ivan and the man who is painting his portrait, and both of them have confidence in an elderly woman companion. Through the strength gained from their support, Ivan finds the courage to approach his busy, remote father.

The insight and compassion that illuminate Ivan's story are equally apparent in *Blowfish Live in the Sea* (1970) and *One-Eyed Cat* (1984). In the former, the bonds of family love are exemplified in a young girl's acceptance of her half-brother's frailties. Carrie goes with Ben to meet his father, an irresponsible man, weak but lovable, whose absence and garrulous mendacity have embittered his son. Ben, nevertheless, decides to stay with his father. Astutely—and effectively—the author does not *tell* the reader but lets Ben's love and acceptance *show* in his words and deeds. The fact that the story is told by Carrie produces a convincing picture of the several relationships and of the maturation that leads to tolerance.

One-Eyed Cat is outstanding for the depth of its insight, the nuance of its writing style, and the many-layered development of its characters. Although Ned has been told not to use an air rifle, he sneaks out one night to try it, then fears he has shot something that moved. He is racked by remorse and guilt. His shame and regret are the core of a sensitive story that develops smoothly and powerfully.

In *The Moonlight Man* (1986), Fox shows the anguished ambivalence of a child's love for an alcoholic father. Like Ben in *Blowfish,* Catherine grows in understanding through the love and patience that enable her to see past her father's manipulative behavior to his pain. A child also deals with the effects of alcoholism in a family member, albeit more obliquely than does Catherine, in *The Village by the Sea* (1988). Because her father is having heart surgery and her mother is staying with him, Emma has been sent to her aunt's home. Aunt Bea, who has a history of alcoholism, is an unhappy, angry woman whose pervasive hostility includes her niece; she demolishes the miniature village Emma and a friend have painstakingly constructed of found objects on the seashore. The characterization has depth and consistency, and both motivation and relationships have an intricacy that never impinges on the clarity and focus of the story.

In *Monkey Island* (1991) Fox created one of the most touching and trenchant stories of homeless people that has been written for young readers. Clay is eleven; his father has decamped and now Clay's pregnant mother

Voices of the Creators

Paula Fox

Great stories give us metaphors which flash upon the mind the way lightning flashes upon the earth, illuminating for an instant an entire landscape.

Stories are always, in some sense, metaphors, and through them we are able to see more clearly what we have experienced. Carol Bly, in an essay on the uses of story, writes: "The human mind recognizes a feeling only when it has words for it—which means someone else has conversed about it. When Conrad Aiken, in his story 'Silent Snow, Secret Snow,' tells us how much the boy loves his beautiful, imagined inner life—the snow—we recognize the same love in our own inner life. If we hadn't had his story, and others like it, we might never recognize how dear we hold our private perceptions of the universe."

But can writers evoke, no matter how great their powers of imagination, the essence of our deepest experiences? Not, I believe, directly.

Yet vital language that seeks through imagination to grasp truth intimates what is unspoken, what can never be rendered into words—all that roiling mass of feeling and sensing which, like breathing, is fundamental to our humanity.

The language of great poets and writers alludes to all we cannot speak; it deepens our consciousness; it enables us to question the surface of life.

I have found writing to be hard and unremitting labor. In that labor, I can feel the weight and energy of my own life. That is writing's nettlesome reward.

It is not easy to persuade people who take writing courses just how much unremitting labor is required of a writer. After all—our mouths are full of words; we need only put them down on paper. Writing can't be really difficult, like learning the physics of a star, or how to play an oboe!

None of us, I think, is partial to slow, ruthless, wearying effort. But there comes a time when you know that ruthless effort is what you must exert. There is no other way. On that way, you will discover such limitations as to make you gasp with the knowledge of them. Still, you work on. If you have done that for a long time, something will happen to you. You will succeed in becoming dogged. You will have become resolute about one thing—you go to your work table day after day. You give up the hope that you can come to a conclusion about yourself as a writer.

Finally, you give up conclusions.

The stories that come out of a writer's hard labor are efforts to understand what has happened. They engage us, our deep interest, because we are always trying to understand what has happened to us; we are always trying to see ourselves. The task is nearly impossible. Max Planck, the founder of the quantum theory of physics, strongly suggests the nature of this problem in a different context when he writes about nature: "Science cannot solve the ultimate mystery of nature. And it is because in the last analysis we ourselves are part of the mystery we are trying to solve."

Stories, in my view, are *not* ideas. But when children write to me, the question they ask most frequently is: Where do you get your ideas?

Getting ideas, *as* an idea, seems to suit our times—it is a practical, consumer sort of endeavor. Find the place where they are sold, buy one, bring it home, and set it to work.

I answer these letters by saying that my stories begin with a person, grow out of my interest in that person's nature or character. I tell them, too, that there are an endless number of things to write about—subjects—and that for each writer there are certain subjects which wake up his or her imagination. But I cannot explain imagination to them. It remains a mystery, a thing we can recognize yet not analyze.

When children ask if a story is "real," I think of E. B. White's answer to that question: "Real life is only one kind of life—there is also the life of the imagination."

I write to the children that I did, for example, imagine the crew of the ship *Moonlight* in *The Slave Dancer.* But did it *really* happen, they ask. Did all those African men and women and children suffer so? I've said, yes, it did happen, that my story was an effort to bear witness to these terrible events, and that all stories spring from real life because that is all we know.

has abandoned him in their dingy hotel. Clay takes refuge with an odd couple of street people—an elderly alcoholic man and a young African American man become Clay's family. There is a reunion, at the end, between mother and son, but the message is that all love is sustaining.

The Slave Dancer (1973) is Fox's only work of historical fiction; in her acceptance speech for the Newbery

Medal, she spoke of slaves as "pioneers of the human condition in inhuman circumstances." Fourteen-year-old Jessie is horrified to discover that he's been impressed into service as a "slave dancer," playing his fife to keep slave-ship captives active and more salable. The book is a powerful indictment of the horrors of the slave trade as well as a somber, moving story.

In all her writing Paula Fox addresses the resilience of the human spirit; her special gift is that she sees the child's viewpoint while feeling the sympathy of an adult and the detachment of an observer. Her children move us because they are so true. One of the finest stylists writing for children today, Fox has the rare ability to create worlds that involve her readers, yet she never comes between the book and the reader. ❧

ZENA SUTHERLAND

François, André

FRENCH ARTIST, CARTOONIST, ILLUSTRATOR, AND AUTHOR, B. 1915. A talented and versatile artist, André François has received recognition not only as a children's book illustrator but also as a commercial artist, cartoonist, painter, sculptor, and set designer. His illustrations are dominated by vigorous, scratchy pen lines and a strong sense of humor.

Born André Farkas in what is now Romania, François studied drawing at the Ecole des Beaux-Arts in Budapest for two years. Then he went to Paris and studied with Cassandre, a poster artist. After becoming a French citizen in the mid-1930s, he changed his name to François. He began his career in advertising, but during the Second World War he turned to cartooning. His cartoons had a biting edge and were initially more popular in England than in France. But his humor and his sketchy, expressive drawings soon attracted attention in both France and America, and he was offered numerous commissions from magazines such as *Look*, *Holiday*, and *The New Yorker*.

At the time they were published, François's children's book illustrations were favorably received. A number of illustrators, including MAURICE SENDAK and MARCIA BROWN, praised his work, and five of his books were named New York Times Best Illustrated Books of the Year: *The Magic Currant Bun* by John Symonds (1952), his own *Crocodile Tears* (1955), *Roland* by Nelly Stephane (1958), *The Adventures of Ulysses* by Jacques LeMarch and (1960), and his own *You Are Ri-di-cu-lous* (1970).

Currently, however, most of his books are very hard to find. Some of François's illustrations have a harsh, discordant quality. For example, in *Travelers Three* (1953) by John Symonds, François uses many heavy, angular lines in the bare tree branches, blades of grass, and animals' whiskers, which give the book a mildly disturbing feel.

At the same time, much of his work possesses a delightful childlike view of the world. In *The Magic Currant Bun* François shows a street running horizontally across the page. Young Pierre, on the far side, gazes longingly into a bakery window, while the buildings on the near side, using child logic, are drawn upside down so that their fronts also face the street. His illustrations for *Little Boy Brown* (1949) by Isobel Harris capture a city boy's excitement at spending the day in the country. François's placement of figures, his use of line, which is softer in this book, and the textures of the buildings and backgrounds help create the sense of Little Boy Brown's joy.

François also wrote several of his own stories. *Crocodile Tears*, published in seventeen countries, is a whimsical explanation of crocodile tears. It reflects François's humor, which is both childlike and sophisticated. He uses an innovative design: The book is three inches high by ten inches long, emphasizing the long, low form of a crocodile. The front cover has no title, only the crocodile's body. Its head wraps around to the back cover, and its tail continues onto the inside of the front cover.

Whether he creates his own books or illustrates the work of others, including the traditional fairy tale *Jack and the Beanstalk* (1983), François's lively line and strong sense of humor permeate all his work. ❧ P.R.

Frasconi, Antonio

LATIN AMERICAN–U.S. ARTIST, ILLUSTRATOR, AND AUTHOR, B. 1919. Frasconi was already an internationally recognized fine woodcut artist when the curator of the New York Public Library Print Collection, Karl Küp, suggested to children's book editor Margaret McElderry that she have a look at Frasconi's artwork. Küp wrote enthusiastically of Frasconi: "He hews into the wood like a sculptor into stone . . . with energy-laden ebullience." McElderry, impressed by the subtle relationship of the strong color values and the textures in his large prints, asked Frasconi if he would like to do a children's book. He accepted the invitation and wrote his first children's book, *See and Say* (1955), consisting of definitions in four languages (English, Spanish, Italian, and French). Because he had had such trouble learning English, he wanted his young son, Pablo, to know that there were many ways of speaking. The *New York Times Book Review* Committee voted *See and Say* the best children's book of that year.

Frasconi was a natural for multilingual books because of his family background. Born in Argentina of Italian parents, he grew up in Montevideo, Uruguay, and entered the United States in 1945 on a student visa to study art at the Art Students League in New York City. Frasconi continued to write multilingual books: *The House That Jack Built* (1958) was written in French and English; *The Snow and the Sun* (1961) was a South American folk rhyme in Spanish and English; and *See Again, Say Again* (1964) was a picture book in four languages. These books, striking visually and textually, appeared well ahead of the 1980s proliferation of bilingual PICTURE BOOKS.

Frasconi's technique of printing his woodcuts by hand and rubbing a spoon over a paper laid on an inked block achieved subtle variations of tone. His fine artwork has continued to evolve, and in recent years he has used lithography and overlaid his woodcuts with a variety of other media to achieve more delicate effects and more dramatic color in such works as ISAAC BASHEVIS SINGER's *Elijah the Slave* (1970), MYRA COHN LIVINGSTON's *Monkey Puzzle and Other Poems* (1984), and *If the Owl Calls Again, A Collection of Owl Poems* (1990), and VALERIE WORTH's *At Christmastime* (1991). His remarkable sense of color is a feature of his work, which sensitively celebrates the earth, sea, and sky.

Frasconi lives in South Norwalk, Connecticut, with his wife, Leona, also an artist, in a house they built on a hillside overlooking Long Island Sound. He has influenced many young artists, including NONNY HOGROGIAN, and has taught at a number of institutions, including SUNY at Purchase, New York, where he was recently elected outstanding teacher of the year. He has received many international awards and honors and is recognized as the United States' foremost woodcut artist. In 1989, Frasconi was honored by the Library of Congress for his original contributions to children's book illustration. He has adhered all his life to his beliefs in justice and honesty, and feels strongly that an artist has to "stand up and be counted." This commitment to justice was instrumental in his creation of a stunning series of prints on the *Disporu*, the missing peoples of South America. ❧ B.J.B.

FREEDMAN, RUSSELL

AMERICAN NONFICTION AUTHOR, B. 1929. Born in San Francisco and educated at the University of California, Berkeley, Freedman is best described by the term Renaissance man. His résumé is long and varied: newsman at the Associated Press, television publicity writer, editor, and instructor at the New School for Social Research. But it is when he wears his hat as nonfiction writer of over thirty-five young adult books that he truly embodies the concept.

Freedman's books can be divided into two general areas: science and social studies, specifically American history. In each book, regardless of its topic, he carefully combines text and black-and-white photographs to create a medium in which the words reveal something hidden in the pictures and the pictures illuminate the unspoken words. The actions, behaviors, and peculiarities of the animal kingdom serve as the focus for the majority of Freedman's science books. From his first animal book, *How Animals Learn* (1969), to his twenty-third, *Sharks* (1985), Freedman has continued to present facts in a straightforward fashion. Not merely an encyclopedic catalog, his books also possess a writing style that conveys a subtle sense of drama that intrigues as well as instructs. Two of his books have received national awards; *Hanging On: How Animals Carry Their Own* (1977) was honored by the New York Academy of Science, and *Animal Superstars* (1984), by the National Science Teachers Association.

In order to immerse himself fully in the history of his social studies subject, he often goes on location with a book, traveling across the country searching for archival photographs to complement the text. A number of Freedman's books focus on the nineteenth-century American West. *Children of the Wild West* (1983), winner of the National Cowboy Hall of Fame's Western Heritage Award and a Boston Globe–Horn Book Honor Book, recounts the experiences of children traveling in covered wagons across the country and the American Indian children they meet along the way. *Cowboys of the Wild West* (1985) looks at the men who inspired the legends without belittling the real place the cowboy has in history and fiction. *Indian Chiefs* (1987) tells the story of six Indian chiefs who served during a critical point in their tribe's history; the tone, while always nonjudgmental, betrays an underlying sympathy for the American Indians' resistance. *Buffalo Hunt* (1988) follows as a logical extension of the three previous works, chronicling American Indian lore and hunting practices. *An Indian Winter* (1992), based on the journal of German prince Maximilian, describes the winter of 1833–34, when the prince and his party lived with American Indian tribes in North Dakota.

Of all his books, it is his biographies—which include bibliographies and lists of places to visit—for which

Voices of the Creators

Russell Freedman

My father was a great storyteller. The problem was, we never knew for sure whether the stories he told were fiction or nonfiction. He was also a dedicated bookman. In fact, my parents met in a San Francisco bookshop. She was a sales clerk, and he was a sales representative for a big publishing house. They held their first conversation over a stack of bestsellers, and before they knew it, they were married. I had the good fortune to grow up in a house filled with books and book talk.

As a young man, I worked as a journalist and later as a television publicity writer before discovering my true vocation. One day I happened to read a newspaper article about a sixteen-year-old boy who was blind; he had invented a Braille typewriter. That seemed remarkable, but as I read on, I learned something even more amazing: the Braille system itself was invented by another sixteen-year-old boy who was blind, Louis Braille. That newspaper article inspired my first book, a collection of biographies called *Teenagers Who Made History* (1961).

I hadn't expected to become a writer of nonfiction books for children. I had wandered into the field by chance and immediately felt right at home. I couldn't wait to get started on my next book. It was as if I had found myself—even though I hadn't really known that I had been lost.

The term *nonfiction* has always seemed unfortunate to me, because it is so negative. Fiction implies art, imagination, creativity. We take it for granted that good fiction will be a pleasure to read. Nonfiction is supposed to be utilitarian. It's expected to do its duty—to inform, instruct, enlighten. And yet a hard-working, nose-to-the-grindstone nonfiction book should be just as absorbing as any imaginary story, because it is, in fact, a story, too.

After all, there's a story to almost everything. The task of the nonfiction writer is to find the story—the narrative line—that exists in nearly every subject, be it the life of a person or the life of a cell.

Writers of nonfiction have traditionally been storytellers. The word *history,* remember, is made up mostly of the word *story;* it derives from the Greek *historein,* "to inquire"; a *histōr* was a learned man. Going all the way back to Homer and beyond, historians have been storytellers sitting around the fire inside the cave, holding their audience spellbound on a winter's night.

When I begin a new book, that's the tradition I like to remember. I think of myself first of all as a storyteller, and I do my best to give dramatic shape to my subject, whatever it is. I always feel that I have a story to tell that is worth telling, and I want to tell it as clearly, as simply, and as forcefully as I can.

By storytelling, I do not mean making things up, of course. I don't mean invented scenes or manufactured dialogue or imaginary characters. As a writer of nonfiction, I have a pact with the reader to stick to the facts, to be as factually accurate as human frailty will allow. What I write is based on research. And yet there are many storytelling techniques that I can use without straying from the straight and narrow path of factual accuracy. Facts in a literal sense do not rule out art, imagination, or creativity.

When I speak of nonfiction storytelling, I'm using the word *story* in the sense of igniting the reader's imagination, evoking pictures and scenes in the reader's mind. Storytelling means creating vivid and believable people, places, and events—creating a convincing, meaningful, and memorable world. It means pulling the reader into that world. And it means using a narrative framework, a storytelling voice, that will keep the reader turning those pages.

As I work on a book, I'm hoping to change the landscape of the reader's mind—to leave the reader with a thought, a perception, an insight that he or she did not have before. If I write about sharks or rattlesnakes, I want the reader to come away from my book with a greater appreciation of these remarkable living creatures and their place in nature. If I write about frontier children, or Abraham Lincoln, or the Wright brothers, I want to leave the reader with a deeper understanding of our nation's history and a feeling of kinship with people of another era. But most of all, I want to write a book that will be read from beginning to end with a mounting sense of anticipation and discovery—read willingly, with a feeling of genuine pleasure.

Freedman has become best known. Winner of the 1988 Newbery Medal, *Lincoln* is a chronological examination of the times and the life, personal characteristics, and career of Abraham Lincoln, with an emphasis on the politics of slavery and the Civil War. There have been more books written about Lincoln than any other American. Freedman's portrait, however, does not just repeat the myths that surround the Lincoln persona;

rather, his Lincoln is a man of integrity, deeply troubled by the evils of slavery and by the overwhelming human loss of the Civil War. *Franklin Delano Roosevelt* (1990), winner of the Orbis Pictus Award for outstanding nonfiction books, traces the personal and public events in the life of Roosevelt and tells the story of the era in which he was president; *Eleanor Roosevelt: A Life of Discovery* (1993) was named a Newbery Honor Book. *The Wright Brothers: How They Invented the Airplane* (1991), a Boston Globe–Horn Book Honor Book and a 1992 Newbery Honor Book, tells both the story of Orville and Wilbur Wright and the history of flight. Freedman won the 1992 Washington Post/Children's Book Guild Award for the body of his work. His personal hope that his books "will be read willingly, read from beginning to end with a sense of discovery and, with a feeling of genuine pleasure" is being fulfilled. ❧ M.I.A.

FREEMAN, DON

AMERICAN ILLUSTRATOR AND AUTHOR, 1908–1978. Born in San Diego, California, Don Freeman relocated to New York City in the late 1920s to make a living as a musician. A talented amateur artist, Freeman also studied at the Art Students League. Ironically, his permanent career in illustration began by accident. Traveling home one evening, he was so engrossed in sketching his fellow passengers that he left his trumpet lying on the seat as the train sped away. Freeman eventually found work as a freelance graphic artist covering the New York theater scene, contributing to the *New York Times*, the New York *Herald Tribune*, and numerous theater publications.

Then he discovered an outlet for his flair for the dramatic in writing and illustrating original PICTURE BOOKS for children. *Pet of the Met* (1953), a collaboration with his wife, Lydia, tells the story of a mouse maestro named Petrini who works as a page turner at the Metropolitan Opera. His nemesis, Mefisto the cat, lives in the basement, detesting mice and music with equal measure. The commotion that results when cat meets mouse is illustrated in wild, colorful chase scenes that culminate in a glorious finale as Mefisto falls under the spell of the music and is transformed.

Norman the Doorman (1959) relates the tale of Norman, a basement doorman in a large city museum who gives guided tours of the treasure-filled basement and dabbles in art and sculpture in his free time. After Norman's mousetrap masterpiece wins a prize in the museum's contest, Norman's talent is unveiled, and he receives a long-awaited tour of the museum upstairs. In *Bearymore* (1976) Freeman turns to the circus, where a performing bear must cope with both hibernation *and* developing a new act before spring. Using simple yellow-wash and pencil drawings, Freeman captures the animation of the circus and the sleepy activity of hibernation.

Freeman's work is extremely popular among very young children, to whom his basic texts and gentle messages are highly appealing. Both *Mop Top* (1955), the tale of an ornery redhead who refuses to get his hair cut, and *Dandelion* (1964), the story of a lion who remodels himself to the extent that nobody recognizes him, offer mild cautions against pretentiousness and stubbornness within deceptively simple, humorous tales. The most enduring of his books, *Corduroy* (1968), is the tale of a plain department store bear badly in need of a home. In order to present his best appearance, Corduroy searches the store after hours to replace a missing button on his overalls. Children responded so well to this unpretentious story that Freeman was persuaded to revive the bear in *A Pocket for Corduroy* (1978), his last work. There is a cosmopolitan aspect to Freeman's books that comes from years of observation. *Inspector Peckit* (1972), for example, a Parisian pigeon private eye, bears an uncanny resemblance to another famous French detective, and Freeman's subtle illustrations take anthropomorphic expression to amusing heights.

Despite the subtle humor of some of his allusions, Freeman never lost sight of the childlike. His understated artwork and his creative treatments of his themes led to charming books that feature an unmistakable sincerity. ❧ M.O'D.H.

FRITZ, JEAN

AMERICAN AUTHOR, B. 1915. The publication of the refreshing and unconventional biographical vignettes *And Then What Happened, Paul Revere?* (1973), *Why Don't You Get a Horse, Sam Adams?* (1974), *Will You Sign Here, John Hancock?* (1976), and *What's the Big Idea, Ben Franklin?* (1976), in the 1970s clearly established Jean Fritz at the forefront of a handful of authors who have mastered the art of writing biographies for children. Her distinctive style continues to enliven history and make the complicated lives and events of the past accessible to younger readers.

Fritz has been writing historical fiction for children since 1958, when *The Cabin Faced West*, a pioneer story about her great-great-grandmother, was published. Her earlier books, although not biographies, are firmly grounded in historical events. *Brady* (1960), for example, is set just before the Civil War and tells a runaway slave's story; its depth and drama are the result of vivid characterization and an honest depiction of the moral issues surrounding the abolitionist movement. In *I, Adam* (1963) and *Early Thunder* (1967), both set in New England, strong protagonists come of age against the background of turbulent periods in American history.

When Fritz began writing her "question biographies" (so named because the titles ask questions) for young readers, her irrepressible sense of humor and unique talent for "turning history inside out" was a breath of fresh air for younger minds who, upon reading the short biographies, discovered that learning about history could be fun. Fritz explains her purpose for writing these stories about several leaders in the American Revolution: "My objective was modest. I simply wanted to persuade children that these men were once truly alive, that history is made of the same stuff as our own lives. I hoped children would understand people and their paradoxes, without passing judgment or dividing them up into good and bad."

For thirty years her books have earned awards and honors and are always on best-books lists for young readers. Her autobiography, *Homesick: My Own Story,* was a Newbery Honor Book, and in 1983 *The Double Life of Pocahontas* won the Boston Globe–Horn Book Award for nonfiction. In 1986 Fritz was honored with the Laura Ingalls Wilder Award, which is presented to an author whose books have made an enduring contribution to children's literature.

Jean Fritz's reputation for bringing history to life rests on her ability to combine humorous and humanizing details with factual material. There are many humorous touches about the famous patriot from old Boston in *And Then What Happened, Paul Revere?* Children will delight in the fact that Revere was not only a secret agent and express rider for the American Revolutionary forces, but he also made false teeth. And they will discover he was in such a hurry to make his famous ride that he forgot his spurs and sent the dog home with a note so his wife could attach the spurs to the dog's collar. Mistrusting reverence and emphasizing the human side of heroism, Fritz reveals in *Where Do You Think You're Going, Christopher Columbus?* (1980) that the explorer was a hot-tempered, stubborn man, who died thoroughly convinced he had discovered the Indies and China.

Her books have lasting popularity because she writes with directness and integrity while speaking un-patronizingly to young people. Commenting on her unconventional, often humorous approach toward writing, Fritz says: "I realized when I started doing research for my first book that history wasn't what I'd been taught in school. History is full of gossip; it's real people and emotion. I kept being surprised by the real people I met in the past. They all had their foibles and idiosyncrasies."

Though humor often peppers her stories, in books for older readers, Fritz does not sidestep exploring serious issues or exposing the darker side of characters and events. The highly acclaimed *Traitor: The Case of Benedict Arnold* (1981) is a gripping historical thriller that reveals examples of Arnold's twisted personality from his childhood through his betrayal of the Revolutionary forces. Nor will readers find a typical history-book account of Chief Powhatan's daughter in *The Double Life of Pocahontas.* The thought-provoking story clearly shows the young girl as a pawn of history, trapped in the terrible dilemma of living between two cultures.

Fritz does not go looking for ideas. "A character in history will suddenly step right out of the past and demand a book. Once my character and I reach an understanding," she explains, "then I begin the detective work." Accuracy and meticulous research are hallmarks of her writing. "I want to get inside my characters and to do this I have to, first of all, get into their times." She reads old books, letters, and newspapers and visits places where her subjects lived.

Fritz attributes her preoccupation with research and

Illustration by MARGOT TOMES from *And Then What Happened, Paul Revere?* (1973), by Jean Fritz.

Voices of the Creators

Jean Fritz

If I arrange the books I've written chronologically on a shelf according to where they fit into American history, I am surprised at how much time they cover—from Columbus to Teddy Roosevelt. I didn't do this deliberately. I have just dropped in on people where and when I've found them—people whose lives seemed to fall into a story shape and whose stories I felt an urgency to tell.

There are over twenty books of nonfiction dealing with American history on my shelf, and, as I look at it, I think—well, that's where I've always wanted to be, right in the middle of what's happening. It is not that I am sentimental about the past, but ever since childhood I've wanted to be where it's *at.* The heroine of my first historical book, *The Cabin Faced West* (1958)—which happened to be fiction—expressed my feeling. She complained that she was stuck in an out-of-the-way place where, as she said, "nothing ever happens." Although in reality there are few places where nothing ever happens, I longed to be at the center—not of textbook history, but of *real* history.

I would be pleased if this shelf of books turned out to be useful to teachers, but I am not thinking in curriculum terms. I feel more like a journalist covering my beat. I am in no position to penetrate current history with the same depth as I can the past, where the record has come in, where the story can be examined as a whole. My beat may lie in another time, but my approach is that of a reporter, trying for a scoop, looking for clues, connecting facts, digging under the surface.

Most important, I am tracking down people. As far as I am concerned, there can be no understanding history without coming to terms with the makers and shakers, the oppressed and the oppressors, and seeing how they have been shaped by their times and in turn have shaped them. Enough of their personal record must be available so that I can attempt to figure out why they became who they were. In most instances, their childhood has been of primary importance to me. I could never have understood Stonewall Jackson, for instance, or Benedict Arnold or Teddy Roosevelt or, more recently, Harriet Beecher Stowe without meeting them first as children. In each case the central problem they struggled with their entire lives was the one they were dealt in childhood. It is at the heart of the interplay between their personal and public lives.

I like to think of a historian or a biographer as an artist who has made a compact with the past to be true to it. As an artist, the historian has to use his or her imagination to penetrate the record, to dig deep down into the past to the place where life emerges. At its best, the imaginative process is an electrical experience: the writer comes to the place where sparks fly, and, if all goes well, the excitement is passed on to the reader. The kind of imagination that is required is one that shakes up the twentieth-century mindset, transports the reader and writer alike into another world of place and time and rules and habits. The purpose and reward both of reading and writing biography, it seems to me, is to gain insight into the human condition. It is invigorating to step out of the limitations of one's own self and time and to experience life as someone else.

I've been asked if I always *like* my characters. It goes deeper than that. I have to *understand* them. There may be something of a love-hate relationship, but at the very least I have to feel compassion. I expect there is a certain amount of chemistry at work as I take on a character. Moreover, the chemistry has to work both ways. I feel that the character steps up to speak to me. When James Madison spoke (in a whisper, of course, as he always spoke), I thought he'd got me wrong. I didn't see his story possibilities, but he was insistent, and he was right. He was such a committed man that his story and the country's ran on the same path, with the same emotional ups and downs. I ended up admiring him more than anyone I've written about.

In my books for younger children, I've tried to catch my characters quickly, on the fly. The books are shorter; the style is brisker and, wherever possible, humorous. Indeed, throughout my work, when there is a hint of humor in the material, I pounce on it.

It is not surprising that biography should lead to autobiography. *Homesick: My Own Story* (1982) does not fit on my American history shelf, yet it belongs near it. The story of my childhood in China establishes, I think, why I am so preoccupied with America.

writing about American history to her own personal search for roots. As a child of missionary parents, she lived in China for the first thirteen years of her life, where, she admits, she spent a great deal of time "wondering what it was like to be an American."

For many years, she wanted to write about life in China, but not until her father's death did she feel an urgency to record her childhood. In 1982 *Homesick: My Own Story,* which combines her early personal search for her imagined homeland with a child's view of the poverty and political turbulence in China in the 1920s, was published.

"I needed to write *Homesick* before I returned to China," Fritz comments, "so I wouldn't mix up the present with memories." Fifty-five years after she left China she returned to see what Mao Tse-tung and the Cultural Revolution had wrought. In 1985 she wrote *China Homecoming,* which was followed by *China's Long March* (1988), an excellent introductory volume about Mao's legendary march through China and the beginning of the Cultural Revolution.

Whether she is writing for younger children or for young adults, Fritz's tactics for revealing her characters are always brilliantly conceived; her knack for effectively highlighting each character's personal eccentricities successfully hooks even reluctant readers.

The difficulty for the biographer is not only to develop an accurate picture of the subject at hand but an accurate sense and representation of historical facts, all set within a lively text that does not appear to teach or preach. Many biographers falter. Narratives that successfully mix humor, humanism, and history are rare. But Jean Fritz has found the appropriate blend, and her remarkable style enables her to extract the essence of her protagonists' accomplishments and characters and to place them firmly within the context of their times. STEPHANIE LOER

Frost, Arthur Burdett

AMERICAN COMIC ARTIST AND ILLUSTRATOR, 1851–1928. In the golden age of American illustration (1880–1915), Arthur Burdett Frost was one of the stars of a distinguished company and, like his fellow luminary and close friend HOWARD PYLE, equally an adults' and a children's illustrator. In Frost's case, there was hardly a distinction. Children and adults alike "doubled up" (in the words of an English admirer) at the sight of "Our Cat Eats Rat Poison" and other devilish comic sequences that first appeared in the back pages of *Harper's* magazine and subsequently in the albums *Stuff and Nonsense* (1884) and *The Bull Calf and Other Tales* (1892). All ages responded to his acutely observed, empathic illustrations, whether for stories in *Harper's, Century,* and other magazines or for such widely read books as FRANK STOCKTON's *Rudder Grange* (1885) or Thomas Bailey Aldrich's *Story of a Bad Boy* (1895). In the economically expressive use of line he had no master.

His great subject—when other artists were satirizing the rich or glorifying the past—was contemporary American rural life, its characters and crotchets. He caught the interplay between farmer and hired man, between humans and animals; atypically for his time, his rustics were not rubes and his animals were not figures of fun. In a few pen strokes he also captured the look and lay of the land, the aspect of a particular locale.

Altogether Frost was not only well suited to illustrate JOEL CHANDLER HARRIS's Uncle Remus tales, but in their breadth and abundance of nuance, their combination of humor and gravity, the doings of Brer Rabbit, Brer Fox, Brer B'ar, and the other creatures were a match for Frost's gifts. Not that Frost was the inevitable choice. The first collection of tales, *Uncle Remus: His Songs and Sayings* (1881), was illustrated jointly by Frederick S. Church, who drew the animal episodes, and James H. Moser, who drew the plantation scenes. Harris was not happy with the work of either. In 1884 *Century* magazine commissioned Frost to illustrate a notable Harris short story, "Free Joe and the Rest of the World." The author glowed: Instead of stereotypes, here was "character," Southern American character, and "individuality."

On a sketching trip south Frost called on Harris in Atlanta, and the two men—both diffident redheads, both modest and strong-minded—traveled companionably together into the Georgia countryside. The outcome was a lively, longtime correspondence and a fruitful partnership. Harris's one complaint about Frost's illustrations in their first collaboration, *Uncle Remus and His Friends* (1892), was that there were not enough of them, a deficiency Frost remedied in the remake of *Uncle Remus: His Songs and His Sayings* (1895). This classic edition, which Harris famously dedicated to Frost ("The book was mine, but you have made it yours, sap and pith"), boasts 112 small drawings spotted tellingly through the text. Ignoring some ambiguous secondary characters, Frost focuses to good effect on Uncle Remus and the animals. Physically, his Uncle Remus is modeled on Moser's Georgia prototype, but he is also a personage, a figure of grave, dark-skinned dignity.

Brer Rabbit had a more distant model, SIR JOHN

TENNIEL's White Rabbit in *Alice in Wonderland*, a depiction Frost knew, and knew well, as the vexed illustrator of later LEWIS CARROLL works. But where Tenniel's White Rabbit is an English dandy, Frost's Brer Rabbit is a rumpled Southerner. Like the other denizens of Wonderland, the White Rabbit is a fancy, an artifice, while Brer Rabbit, as conceived in black folklore, recorded by Harris, and interpreted by Frost, is the most human of humanized animals. Turn a corner and there he might be, matching wits with Brer Fox or gulling Brer B'ar.

The success of the Harris/Frost *His Songs and His Sayings*, in itself and in renewing interest in the Uncle Remus tales, gave rise both to new collections and to a variety of new editions. To this day, Frost's work is fresh and undated. Early in his career, he could be called a caricaturist; in the aftermath, he exemplifies the illustrator as participant-observer. B.B.

G

Gág, Wanda

American author and illustrator, 1893–1946. Ernestine Evans, editor for a new publisher, was determined to make children's books using the best fine-art artists in America. She knew the art of Wanda Gág—Gág's pictures, she recollects, were "beautiful, and very simple, and full of the wonder of common things." So Evans made an appointment to meet her at the Weyhe Gallery in New York, where Gág was having a one-woman show. Out of that meeting came the classic favorite: *Millions of Cats* (1928). Evans says, "When we had in the office the marvelous manuscript of *Millions of Cats*, I hugged myself, as children all over the country have been doing ever since."

The simple story, with its roots grounded in folklore, tells of a lonely old man and a lonely old woman who just want a kitten to love. So the old man trudges over hills and valleys until "he came to a hill which was quite covered with cats." And with this, Gág introduces the silly, lyrical lines that have delighted children for more than sixty years: "Cats here, cats there, Cats and kittens everywhere. Hundreds of cats, Thousands of cats, Millions and billions and trillions of cats." Of course, when the old man tries to choose among them, he ends up liking them all, for each one is as pretty as the next. When he brings these hundreds of cats back home, he and the old woman have to choose just one. The cats fight over who is the prettiest, and when they are done, only one very ugly kitten is left. The ending, as the kitten turns into the most beautiful cat in the world through loving care, is shown primarily through Gág's soft, round illustrations, lively with humor. The entire book is done in black-and-white—"small, sturdy peasant drawings," Gág called them, and the hand-lettered text, done by her brother, is as solid and round as the pictures.

The strength of *Millions of Cats* is that it has its roots in a compelling childhood. Wanda Gág was the eldest of seven children in a German family in New Ulm, Minnesota. Both her parents were artists; her father, in particular, had talent that was frustrated by the needs of providing for a large family. When he died of tuberculosis, his last coherent words were whispered to his fifteen-year-old daughter: "Was der Papa nicht thun konnt', muß die Wanda halt fertig machen."—"What your Papa could not do, Wanda will have to finish." This directive enflamed the girl's passion for art. She studied, all expenses paid, at the St. Paul Art School, and in 1926 her first major show opened in New York. After this exhibit, Gág focused on printmaking, an art that lent itself to the bookmaking she was one day to do.

The year after *Millions of Cats*, Gág came out with *The Funny Thing* (1929), artistically distinguished but with a disappointing story, and two years later *Snippy and Snappy* (1931), the story of two young mice. She used the same technique for refining the story line in all three books: She told it again and again to all the children she knew until the words sang with rhythm and internal rhyme.

Gág worked in lithograph for *The ABC Bunny* (1933), a technique of wax crayon on zinc plates that allowed for no mistakes. The medium provided her with a rich gray scale, and she played this off brilliant red capital letters. The book is a simple story of a bunny, set outdoors. The location gave Gág a framework to work out the artistic principles with which she was grappling. Especially on the page "V for View/Valley too," Gág created the rolling hills with a series of tightly formed contour lines, similar to Van Gogh's. She wrote: "Just now I'm wrangling with hills. One would never guess [they] could be composed of such a disturbing collection of planes. The trouble is each integral part insists on living a perspective life all its own." Far from the disturbing emotional quality Van Gogh projects, Gág's drawings fill the page with a sense of safe wonder.

As a children's book artist, Gág became interested in the old German *Märchen*, the folk and fairy tales of her childhood. She studied the Grimm stories in the original German and read them in English translation. Often they felt flat, affected, and artificial to her, lacking the lively vigor of a storyteller's voice. So Gág decided to retranslate the stories, a "free" translation that would be

Illustration by Wanda Gág from her book *Millions of Cats* (1928).

truer to their native spirit. She found most of her childhood favorites among the Grimms' collection, but one of the funniest was missing. Gág retold from memory the story that became *Gone Is Gone; or, The Story of a Man Who Wanted to Do Housework* (1935). A few years later she did a similar single-story volume of *Snow White and the Seven Dwarfs* (1938) to coincide with the release of the first WALT DISNEY movie, which she and many others felt had trivialized, sterilized, and sentimentalized the potent old story. In her first collection, *Tales from Grimm* (1936), Gág created a mesmerizing mood by using straightforward Anglo-Saxon words in rounded, repetitive lines: "A fiery dragon came flying along and lay down in the field, coiling himself in and out among the rye-stalks."

At last, by 1945, Gág felt that her life was in order: Her younger brothers and sisters were all well situated; her career was blooming with awards—she had won two Newbery Honor Awards for *Millions of Cats* and for *ABC Bunny* and two Caldecott Medals for *Snow White* and for *Nothing at All* (1941), a story about an invisible dog. She was ready to do her final volume of Grimm tales when she went to visit the doctor. Her husband, Earle Humphreys, hid the news from her: She had lung cancer and had only three months to live. They went to Florida for the warm air, and she continued working on the books from her bed. Defying all predictions, Gág lived another seventeen months, returned to her beloved home All Creation, in the Musconetcong Mountain region of New Jersey, and very nearly completed the final volume of Grimms' tales. She left clear notes and instructions for her editor, and except for a few unfinished drawings, *More Tales from Grimm* (1947) was published, in the form she had planned for it, after her death.

The works that Wanda Gág created in the first half of the century are still cherished today, for in her strong, homey pictures and singing text she produced classic books that children will return to time and time again. ❧ J. ALISON JAMES

GALDONE, PAUL

AMERICAN ILLUSTRATOR AND AUTHOR/RETELLER, 1914–1986. Hungarian-born Paul Galdone's career as an illustrator has few rivals in its length, variety, and prolificness. As a freelance artist in the 1950s, he illustrated numerous works by other writers, including Ellen MacGregor's popular *Miss Pickerell Goes to Mars* (1951) and its sequels; the Caldecott Honor books by Eve Titus,

Anatole (1956) and *Anatole and the Cat* (1957); and a series of short novels by Titus, starting with *Basil of Baker Street* (1958), that features a mouse detective who "studied at the feet of Mr. Holmes himself."

Galdone is best remembered today for his comical cartoon-style editions of individual NURSERY RHYMES—such as *Old Mother Hubbard and Her Dog* (1960) and *The House that Jack Built* (1961)—and for his illustrated retellings of both familiar and unfamiliar folktales. Most of his books have a comfortable, recognizable look and are set in the same folktale world. Indeed, his rotund men, corkscrew-curled women, and expressive animals could easily travel from one story to another. With their simple, repetitive language, bright, uncluttered illustrations, and memorable images, it is no wonder that Galdone's versions of popular folktales such as *The Three Little Pigs* (1970), *The Three Bears* (1972), *The Three Billy Goats Gruff* (1973), *The Little Red Hen* (1973), *The Gingerbread Boy* (1975), and *Puss in Boots* (1976) are still popular. Similarly, Galdone's scary stories—particularly *The Tailypo* (1977), retold by his daughter, Joanna Galdone, and *King of the Cats* (1980)—are often a child's first exposure to spine-tingling tales. While lacking some of the wit and sophistication characterizing more recent illustrators, Galdone's folktales have aged well and remain the old reliables of folk literature. ❧

P.O.B.

GAMMELL, STEPHEN

AMERICAN ILLUSTRATOR, B. 1943. Every line in Stephen Gammell's distinctive illustrations is imbued with emotion. Every color and change of value creates mood. Child and adult alike will find themselves shivering, chilled by his illustrations in ALVIN SCHWARTZ's *Scary Stories to Tell in the Dark* (1981). His colored-pencil drawings in the Caldecott-winning *Song and Dance Man* (1988) emanate warmth and joy. Together with Karen Ackerman's prose, they set one's feet tapping. In the Caldecott Honor Book *Where the Buffaloes Begin* (1981), one feels the vastness of the Western plains, the earth shuddering underneath the heavy hooves of the buffaloes. Gammell's illustrations capture the emotional impact of a story. "The first time I read a manuscript I can immediately tell whether I want to illustrate it. I may not know how the illustrations will look, but I get a certain feeling for the text. I respond to the words, and, if I can respond to a story, I can illustrate it."

Stephen Gammell was reared in Des Moines, Iowa. His father, an art editor for consumer magazines, brought home a variety of periodicals, and Gammell remembers being impressed with the illustrations, cutting them up to make scrapbooks. His father also gave him pencils and stacks of paper, which Gammell says were better than any toys. "My father was very encouraging. He would help me draw, supply the paper and pencils, but he would never coach me or tell me how to work. I picked up the interest on my own; my parents never pushed me. It got me through elementary school. If you could draw, the big kids were more hesitant about beating you up. I tried to make this work for me."

Gammell continued drawing on his own while attending high school and college in Iowa. In the late sixties, in Minneapolis, he began drawing small ads for friends' neighborhood businesses. While his commercial freelance work expanded, he became interested in children's book illustration. His first book illustration contract was for *A Nutty Business* (1973) by Ida Chittum. Gammell does research for stories only if absolutely necessary, preferring to draw directly from his own imagination. He believes that trusting his own feelings and imagination results in more expressive drawings. "I am inspired by a text which gives me freedom to interpret. I don't like being tied to a specific historical time period, style of architecture or costume. I enjoy elements of fantasy in a story and turn down anything that is too literal." In the rollicking *The Relatives Came* (1985), written by CYNTHIA RYLANT, Gammell's free interpretation communicates both the exuberance and exhaustion of a family reunion.

Gammell and his wife, Linda, make their home in St. Paul, Minnesota, where he enjoys solitude and works in his studio every day. Although he has authored several of his own stories, he finds writing terribly difficult. "I think of myself as an artist—admittedly a basic term that can mean almost anything. One of the forms my art takes is book illustrations. . . . In a deep sense, I am my work—what you see on the page is really me." ❧ M.B.B.

GANNETT, RUTH CHRISMAN
GANNETT, RUTH STILES

RUTH CHRISMAN: AMERICAN ILLUSTRATOR, 1896–1979; RUTH STILES: AMERICAN AUTHOR, B. 1923. Ruth Chrisman Gannett and her stepdaughter Ruth Stiles Gannett are best known for their collaboration as illustrator and author of the children's book trilogy about nine-year-old Elmer Elevator and a baby dragon.

Ruth Chrisman was born in Santa Ana, California, and began drawing at an early age. She received bachelor's

Illustration by Ruth Chrisman Gannett from *My Father's Dragon* (1948), by Ruth Stiles Gannett.

and master's degrees from the University of California at Berkeley and also attended the Art Students League. She taught art in California public schools, then moved to New York, where she worked for *Vanity Fair* magazine and did freelance artwork. Among the art books she illustrated were *Sweet Land* (1934), which was written by Lewis Stiles Gannett, who became her second husband, and the Modern Library edition of John Steinbeck's *Tortilla Flat* (1937). She received a Caldecott Honor for illustrating Rebecca Reyher's *My Mother Is the Most Beautiful Woman in the World* (1945), and her finely detailed illustrations perfectly complement the text of the Newbery Award–winning *Miss Hickory* (1946) by CAROLINE BAILEY. The artist was especially good at drawing animals that are realistic, yet reflect the individual personality described within the text. This talent was particularly important in drawing the cats, lions, canaries, and other animals included in the books of Ruth Stiles Gannett who, like her stepmother, began practicing her craft at an early age.

Ruth Stiles was born and raised in New York and attended City and Country School, where creative writing was encouraged. She continued her education at a Pennsylvania boarding school and received a bachelor's degree in chemistry from Vassar College. She worked as a medical technician, waited tables, and was employed at a ski lodge. Between jobs, she spent two weeks writing a children's story, which relatives urged her to publish. *My Father's Dragon* (1948) is the entertaining tale of Elmer Elevator, who travels to a distant island to free a baby dragon enslaved by a group of wild animals. Using his wits and the contents of his knapsack—which includes chewing gum, lollipops, and hair ribbons—Elmer outwits the dragon's captors in a series of humorous episodes. Although this talking animal story reads as a whimsical fairy tale, the young hero follows his quest bravely and soberly. Gannett uses the interesting technique of referring to nine-year-old Elmer as "my father" throughout, which gives the story an added dimension and also makes it a perfect choice for reading aloud. This popular title was named a Newbery Honor Book.

Ruth Stiles Gannett continued the story with *Elmer and the Dragon* (1950), which follows boy and baby dragon on their flight from the island, and *The Dragons of Blueland* (1951), which tells how Elmer helped save the dragon and his family from a new set of captors. Though these two books lack the unfettered creativity and mythic structure of the first volume, both are thoroughly enjoyable. All three are profusely illustrated by Ruth Chrisman Gannett, whose charming and funny pictures perfectly capture the tone of the writing. The author also wrote two minor children's books, *The Wonderful House-Boat-Train* (1949) and *Katie and the Sad Noise* (1961), but will be best remembered for writing the whimsical trilogy that her stepmother illustrated. P.D.S.

GARDAM, JANE

ENGLISH AUTHOR, B. 1928. With the near-simultaneous publication of *A Few Fair Days* and *A Long Way from Verona* (both 1971), Jane Gardam established herself as one of England's best chroniclers of the female adolescent experience. *A Few Fair Days,* a series of vignettes sketching the pre–World War II childhood of a young girl named Lucy, reflects many of the motifs present in Gardam's later work: vivid evocation of place, brilliant and original character conception, a fine comic touch, and lucid, economical prose.

Born in Coatham, Yorkshire, Gardam read few books as a child, although she was raised in an educated home. She attended Bedford College, where she completed undergraduate and postgraduate studies in English literature, and worked as a Red Cross librarian and a magazine editor before her career as a children's writer began with *A Few Fair Days.* Jessica Vye—the gifted, articulate thirteen-year-old who narrates her passage from intense self-absorption to tentative self-awareness in *A Long Way from Verona*—stands as Gardam's richest and most memorable character. Jessica's story is one of oppositions—humor and pathos, maturity and childishness—as she struggles to bring sense to a world made senseless by the grim realities of World War II. A feeling of loss permeates the book, but it is tempered by Gardam's characteristic comic dialogue and witty social commentary, reminiscent of Jane Austen.

Gardam states that she writes "mostly about the tragicomedy of being young," a theme again resonant in the Boston Globe–Horn Book Award book *The Summer after the Funeral* (1973), in which vulnerable sixteen-year-old Athene Price, left to fend for herself after the death of her clergyman-father, spends the summer in pursuit of undying romance, and in *Bilgewater* (1976), the poignant story of eighteen-year-old Marigold Green's coming-of-age. Designated an ALA Notable Book, *The Hollow Land* (1981) consists of nine linked stories in which the Cumbrian landscape is so sensitively evoked that it becomes both setting and character. A series of books for a younger audience includes *Bridget and William* (1981), *Horse* (1982), and *Kit* (1984), and *Through the Doll's House Door* (1987), an uneven story of a dollhouse, its inhabitants, and the families who own them, which marks Gardam's first essay into fantasy. While Gardam's work has met wide critical acclaim, perhaps the highest achievement of this distinguished writer has been to craft books about children in a way not exclusive of an adult readership. ❧ C.S.

Gardiner, John Reynolds

AMERICAN AUTHOR, B. 1944. Best known for *Stone Fox* (1980), one of the most popular and acclaimed adventure stories in recent decades, John Reynolds Gardiner is, in many ways, unlike most contemporary children's writers. He doesn't publish very much: *Stone Fox* is the first of only three books he has written. He doesn't have the traditional educational background of a writer: His degree is in engineering, and he has spent much of his adult life in Southern California working on such projects as the space shuttle. He did, however, take writing classes at night and worked for a while adapting children's stories for television. He also invented a plastic necktie filled with water and guppies, although that sideline proved to be less enduring than his writing.

Stone Fox is, by far, Gardiner's most successful book. Inspired by a Rocky Mountain legend the author once heard when he was visiting Idaho, this short novel chronicles a young boy's determination to win five hundred dollars in the National Dogsled Race. Set in some indeterminate time in the Old West, the story in outline is pure melodrama: Plucky little orphan Willy needs the prize money to save the farm of his ailing grandfather from the grasping hands of the tax collector; in order to win the race, he and his little dog, Searchlight, have to beat the great Stone Fox, a giant and silent Indian, who has five massive Samoyeds pulling his sled. Somehow, however, in the simple prose and relentlessly compelling plot, characters that could be merely clichés are drawn instead as archetypes, not perfectly defined like real people, but still satisfying and emotionally rich all the same. This is, in the end, a morality play in which good and bad, joy and sorrow all have their spotlighted solos on stage. Yet it is so moving and so thrillingly paced that readers of every age—no matter how jaded or cynical or tired of being preached to they may be—feel their hearts stopping when the story comes to its climax.

Gardiner's subsequent novels are *Top Secret* (1984) and *General Butterfingers* (1986). In *Top Secret,* a nine-year-old whiz succeeds in turning sunlight into food for humans, but nobody listens to him—until he catches the ear of the president. *General Butterfingers* tracks a little boy's efforts to keep three grizzled World War I veterans from being thrown out of a home that is rightfully theirs. Though both of these books are genial and high-minded entertainment, neither is as accomplished or as appealing as *Stone Fox.* ❧ A.Q.

Garfield, Leon

BRITISH WRITER, B. 1921. Born in Brighton, England, Leon Garfield left his career as a biochemist to begin writing full-time in 1966. His work covers a wide range, from PICTURE BOOKS to novels for children—many of them illustrated—to books for young adults and adults. Recalling how he came to write for children, Garfield said, "I drifted to the sort of writing I like—which can have wildly exciting adventures *and* something of character and morality." His remark highlights two major characteristics of his work: storytelling skill and a concern with moral issues. In addition, he tells his stories in a rich, distinctive style that has been compared to that of Charles Dickens.

Garfield recognizes the potential for story in a variety of sources. *The God Beneath the Sea* (1970), a Carnegie Medal winner, and *The Golden Shadow* (1973), both written with Edward Blishen, weave Greek myths into

Voices of the Creators

Leon Garfield

Nothing is more uplifting to the spirit than to discover that one has something in common with a great man. "I always do the first line well," wrote Molière, "but I have trouble doing the others." And so it is with me.

The above observation, I must confess, comes not from my own wide and cultured reading, but from a book of quotations. I have not read Molière. Indeed, there is a vast number of great books that I have not read. I have bought them; I have them on my shelves; I contemplate them with satisfaction and pride; *but I have not read them.* I have, in fact, read very few books; but those that I have read, I have read many times over.

I offer this both as a confession and an explanation of how I learned the craft of writing. In the writing of my own stories, I have pillaged wholesale from the works of my favorite authors. Indeed, they are treasure troves of stolen property, and I am always amazed that no one ever seems to notice. My very first published novel, *Jack Holborn,* owes more than I can ever repay to Stevenson's *Master of Ballantrae.* I remember, when the book came out, trembling with ghastly anticipation of being publicly castigated for plagiarism. But no one noticed. Instead, I was compared with Marryat, who was not even on my shelves. Some time later, I heard a talk on the radio, in which one of Stevenson's letters was read. He mentioned *The Master of Ballantrae* and confessed that he got the whole idea from Marryat! It seemed that I got Marryat by proxy.

There is a great storm in *Jack Holborn;* the ship survives it but goes down in the calm that succeeds it. This comes, with suitable trimming and minor embellishments, from *The Laughing Man* by Victor Hugo. But nobody noticed.

At first, like any beginner thief, I felt uncomfortable and guilty; but then, as my crimes went undetected, I gained in confidence and pilfered with ease. Let me say, in my own defense, that, although the gems were stolen, the cutting and setting were all my own.

But one crime leads to another. From stealing from the dead, I progressed to stealing from the living. Once I had acquired the knack of it, it became regrettably easy. Chiefly, I stole from my family. I stole parts of my father and put them into *Devil-in-the-Fog* and *John Diamond.* I stole an uncle, almost complete, and put him into *The Strange Affair of Adelaide Harris.* I stole another and put him into *The Empty Sleeve.* I grew bolder. I stole a house belonging to an aunt and put it into *The Ghost Downstairs.* I stole a gentleman I heartily disliked, put him into *Mister Corbett's Ghost,* and then murdered him.

But he was a later, rarer crime. Most of my thefts have been from childhood, where the pickings have always seemed richer. It's a curious thing, but I've found little of value in the happy times. It is the times of loneliness and anger, the times of misery, guilt, and injustice, seasoned with a little humor, that have always seemed the most productive. The hugely shouting uncle with his smugly virtuous wife, who, when I stayed with them in their camphorated tomb of a house, made my life hell, are now the very stuff of fairy-tale ogres, in hairy suits and shiny black.

I had a large and various family, and I can say without exaggeration that I stole from every single one of them, with the possible exception of an aunt who lived in Manchester, and whom I only saw once. And nobody has ever noticed!

The craft of storytelling, so far as I am concerned, would seem to be the craft of stealing without being detected; but the art of it is another matter. The art would seem to reside in throwing a new light on a character or circumstance, by finding the connection between unlikely parts, and seasoning the dish with something of your own. "A new light," I say? What a hope! It's all been done before. "But not by me!" whispers a voice, so on I go. "There is nothing new under the sun," said Solomon, and he probably got that from someone else. But it's important to remember that whenever the sun comes up, someone sees it for the first time.

book-length tales. Garfield has also created stories based on Shakespeare, the Bible, the memoir of a British seaman, and even the National Portrait Gallery, which he used as the framework for a narrative tour of eighteenth-century English culture. The eighteenth century serves as the setting for many of Garfield's short stories and novels. Examples for older readers include the short-story collection *The Apprentices* (1978) and *The*

Confidence Man (1978), a novel about Germans seeking to emigrate to America.

The love of a good story informs all of Garfield's work. He has confessed to "a passion for secrets and mystery"; certainly many of the plot twists in his book depend on things not being as they seem. In *Devil-in-the-Fog* (1966), George leaves his erstwhile family to join Sir John Dexter, who claims him as his son; however, when Sir John nearly murders him, George discovers who his real family and friends are. Likewise, the inexperienced boys in *The Drummer Boy* (1969) and *Footsteps* (1980) get into trouble by mistaking enemies for friends. In this uncertain world, Garfield's protagonists—boys, as a rule—must also struggle with problems of right and wrong. Both Peter in *The Empty Sleeve* (1988) and the penniless boy in *Smith* (1967) are tempted to "sell their souls" for a chance to change their lives.

Along with some despicable villains, Garfield describes numerous acts of heroism. However, for Garfield there is no satisfaction in unbending devotion to principle; justice should be tempered with tolerance. In *The December Rose* (1986), a tale of intrigue featuring an indigent chimney sweep, the man who adopts the sweep follows "the law of the heart, not of the State." At the end of *Young Nick and Jubilee* (1989), when the thief masquerading as Nick and Jubilee's father acts valiantly on their behalf, his accuser drops his complaint. Humor often tempers the presentation of moral issues; while humor figures in all of Garfield's work, it is preeminent in his two comic novels *The Strange Affair of Adelaide Harris* (1971) and *The Night of the Comet* (1979), both based on the escapades of the two boys Bostock and Harris.

Garfield occasionally plays on stereotypes common to the time periods of his books, but throughout his writing, amid the adventures couched in his vivid style, readers will detect a strong element of compassion and humanity. § M.F.S.

Garner, Alan

English author, b. 1934. Alan Garner, author of enigmatic works of fantasy for young adults, was born in Cheshire, England. His affinity for the land and the legends of this region is apparent, as its topography figures prominently in all his books. The first in his family to receive a formal education, Garner felt a sense of detachment from other family members, yet at the same time, by studying native myths, he felt more closely allied with the land on which he had been raised. This dichotomy is a theme that frequently emerges in his books.

Garner captures the essence of storytelling in his collections of folktales, among them *Fairy Tales of Gold* (1979) and *The Lad of the Gad* (1980). Garner begins to explore the ways in which the past intrudes upon and parallels the present in his first books for children, *The Weirdstone of Brisingamen* (1960) and *The Moon of Gomrath* (1963), in which he draws heavily upon Celtic mythology, particularly *The Mabinogion*, a collection of traditional Welsh tales. In his early books there is a sense that, as one critic points out, "the old myths embody some permanent truths about human nature . . . but those who would find them must travel far." The two books form a series wherein two children stumble upon the eternal struggle between the forces of the dark and the old magic. Drawn into the conflict by phenomena beyond their control, the two encounter trolls, elves, and all manner of evil beings in their attempts to forestall the sinister dark. Although characterization is weak and the plots somewhat cluttered, the books are fast paced and exciting. *Elidor* (1965), a quest story set in urban Manchester, continues to explore the theme of a time continuum yet moves closer to the sophistication of Garner's later work. *The Owl Service* (1967), recipient of the Carnegie Medal, involves the ancient legend of Blodeuwedd and its effect on the lives of three modern teenagers. The past and present merge as the tale is inevitably and tragically reenacted in the close confines of a Welsh valley. The otherworldliness is less tangible, more abstract in this book than in the others, but it is more palpable. *Red Shift* (1973) is an elusive, often disturbing, work that spans centuries, from the Roman conquests to Britain's Civil Wars to modern England. The link lies in a particular mound of earth whose history is interwoven with that of the people who traverse it. In this spare and innovative book, well-honed dialogue reveals all; there is little narrative description. Garner digs deeper into his native soil in the Stone Book quartet—*The Stone Book* (1976), *Tom Fobble's Day* (1977), *Granny Reardun* (1977), and *The Aimer Gate* (1978)—which eloquently connects the lives of one family through artistry in stone, wood, and metal. The craft that defines the artisan's position in his time also carries his legacy on to future generations.

Like his claim that he writes "onions," revealing meaning bit by bit, Garner's work is experienced on different levels. The early fantasies are accessible to a youthful audience, while the later books, by virtue of their experimental, abstract nature, are not really accessible to children. "Originality means the personal coloring of existing themes," Garner feels. His interpretation, while not always appropriate for children, is always intensely individual and original. § M.O'D.H.

Gates, Doris

American author, 1901–1987. Although Doris Gates didn't learn to read until she began attending school at age eight, she had already grown to love stories because her mother read aloud to the family every evening.

Gates was born in a small California town called Mountain View, where she experienced the San Francisco earthquake of 1906. Shortly afterward, her family moved to a prune ranch in the Santa Clara Valley, where Gates grew up. After high school, she worked for several years before entering Fresno State College as a twenty-two-year-old freshman. She later received advanced degrees from the Los Angeles Library School and Case Western Reserve University in Cleveland. She began her library career as an assistant at the Fresno County Free Library, then served as director of the children's department for nearly ten years. She lectured extensively and broadcast a storytelling program on a local radio station. When the Depression caused a cutback in library hours, Gates decided to use her extra day off and her storytelling skills to write books for children.

Her first published novel, *Sarah's Idea* (1938), is based on her childhood experiences on the prune farm. While Gates was working as a librarian, she had the opportunity to visit California migrant schools and meet children uprooted by the Depression and the Midwestern dust bowl. *Blue Willow* (1940) is the story of ten-year-old Janey Larkin who, since leaving her Texas home, has traveled five years with her father and stepmother as they search for work. Temporarily living in a small shack in Fresno, Janey's most cherished possession is a china plate with a blue willow pattern that symbolizes her desire for a permanent home. Gates makes excellent use of this symbol in a story filled with vivid characterizations, honest emotions, and a well-defined setting. The novel employs an omniscient narration that allows readers to understand the inner thoughts and feelings of a number of minor characters in addition to Janey. This popular novel was named a Newbery Honor Book and is considered a significant contribution to children's literature because of its realistic treatment of a contemporary social problem.

Gates also dealt with social issues in subsequent novels. *My Brother Mike* (1948) concerns an ex-convict returning to his family. *Little Vic* (1951) is the story of Pony Rivers, an orphaned African American boy, and his love for a racehorse. Black protagonists were rare in children's fiction of the 1950s, so Gates's book was a welcome addition to the field.

The author taught at several California universities and served as editor for a series of textbooks while continuing to write children's fiction, which included Westerns; an orphan story, *Sensible Kate* (1943); and the autobiographical novel *The Elderberry Bush* (1967). Gates also retold Greek mythology in six volumes, each centering around a different god or goddess, including Zeus, Athena, and Apollo. The author published books until she was in her eighties. Her last two novels deal with a horse-loving California girl; though they are far from Gates's best, they will appeal to fans of animal books.

By the end of her life, Gates had the satisfaction of knowing that she had produced a body of successful and popular work and of seeing the children's room of the Fresno County Library named "The Doris Gates Room." ❧ P.D.S.

Geisel, Theodor Seuss

See Seuss, Dr.

Geisert, Arthur

American illustrator, b. 1941. From the top floor of the house that Arthur Geisert and his wife, Bonnie, built in a deserted rock quarry, they can see for miles. The lovely pastoral landscape includes the town of Galena, Illinois, and the Mississippi River Valley stretching from Dubuque to Bellevue, Iowa. The massive stone walls of the first floor of the house shelter the 2,500-pound etching press that Geisert uses to make his prints. Clipped to lines overhead are prints of the copper-plate etchings for his latest book. The tools that Geisert uses daily are the same ones that etchers have used since the sixteenth century: copper plates coated with a waxy compound, Dutch mordant (an acid that eats away unprotected areas of the plate), and a variety of burins, or incising tools. Although Geisert is working in the same classical etching style as Canaletto and Piranesi, his subject matter reflects his own dry humor, his passion for building, and the pig-plentiful rural landscape around him. Many of Geisert's picture books feature the busy activities of pig families, and his finely detailed scenes depict the charm of their domestic arrangements as well as the intricate gears and pulleys needed for their building projects.

Born in Dallas, Texas, Geisert took degrees from Concordia College, Nebraska, and the University of California at Davis. He studied at the Chouinard Art Institute,

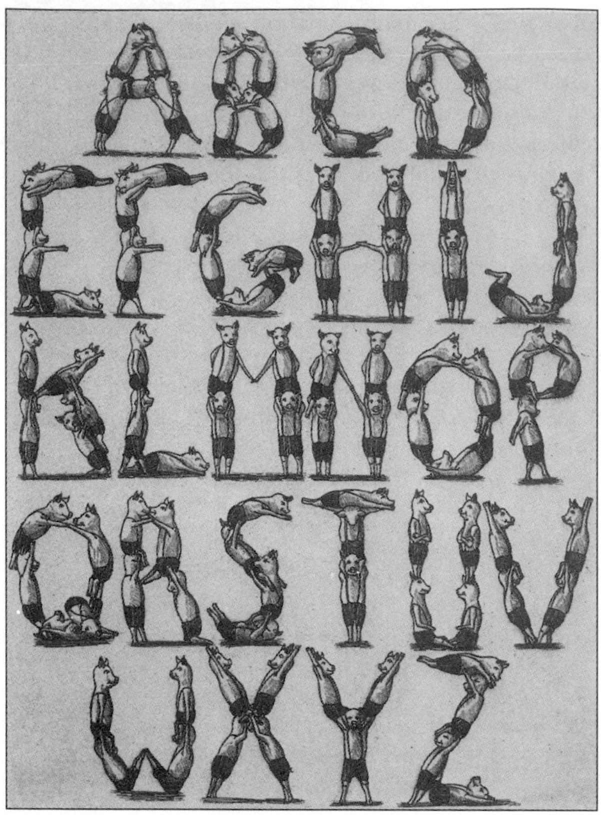

Illustration by Arthur Geisert from his book *Pigs from A to Z* (1986).

the Otis Art Institute, and the Art Institute of Chicago. A full-time artist, he was awarded a 1978 Purchase Award by the Seventh International Print Biennale in Kraków, Poland. He has participated in many group and one-man shows, and his work is represented in university and museum collections. Geisert has long been fascinated with the structure and beauty of arks, and it was his intricate ark prints, especially in cross section, that built his early reputation. In his third picture book, *The Ark* (1988), he carefully detailed the complex geometric interior of the ark, then filled all the spaces with the "organic chaos" necessary to the care and feeding of assorted animals.

This farm life is a part of the daily fabric of life around Galena, and Geisert even conducts life drawing classes of animals at various farms. It is rather unusual to see black-and-white picture books for children, but Geisert's work is very appealing to young readers, partly because children, like Geisert, are builders. They can enjoy the wonderful tree house in *Pigs from A to Z* (1986) and the suspension bridge in *Pigs from 1 to 10* (1992). Then, too, there is the game of finding the hidden letters and numerals that Geisert has cleverly concealed on each page. Geisert's pigs have immense charm: no roly-poly cherubs, these pigs are long-legged, lean, and canny, and endowed with vision and initiative. The strong storytelling quality of Geisert's pictures makes words seem almost superfluous. In *Oink* (1991) Geisert's mother pig expresses a wide range of emotions including panic, indignation, anger, and reassuring love with just one word—*oink*—when her piglets slip away to go exploring by themselves. In 1991 Geisert teamed up with scholar Barbara Bader to create *Aesop & Company: With Scenes from His Legendary Life.* In this handsomely designed book, the animal fables are all set in and around Galena, and the views are the ones Geisert sees every day.

Geisert's books have been recognized in many ways. He received a *New York Times* Best Illustrated Book of the Year Award for *Pigs from A to Z,* and he has heard howls of laughter when *Oink* is read aloud. His readers—both adults and children—are always entertained by the droll humor Geisert combines with his beautiful classic etching style. P.H.

George, Jean Craighead

American author, b. 1919. More than any other author, Jean Craighead George has brought to American children an awareness of the rich diversity of nature and the complex relationship that humans have with it.

The daughter of a naturalist and a sister to the Craighead brothers, known for their research on grizzly bears, George grew up in a family in which exploring the natural world, raising orphaned wild creatures, and learning about the behavior of animals were everyday activities. In her autobiography, *Journey Inward* (1982), George wrote, "For years I would be encountering wild birds and beasts, living with them, seeing myself in them, and all the while trying to understand what the experience meant to me."

George's earliest works were articles written for magazines and short nonfiction books about animals. In 1959 she published her first novel for children, *My Side of the Mountain,* about a young boy's experiences living alone in the woods, which was named a Newbery Honor Book and has been so popular with children that George finally produced a sequel to it, *On the Far Side of the Mountain* (1990).

George's novels are set in a variety of regions and generally focus on human interactions with animals and the natural environment. *Julie of the Wolves,* recipient of the Newbery Medal in 1973, is set in Alaska and

Voices of the Creators

Jean Craighead George

Last summer I built a pond with a waterfall on the dry wooded hillside at the back of my house. The very next day a northern tree frog leaped into the water and swam across the pond. An American toad croaked near the shallows to say he had found his niche. A few days later there were caddis fly larvae on the submerged stones and water striders on the surface. I put aside the biological supply catalogue from which I was ordering frogs, toads, and dragonflies and sat by the pond taking notes. I had created an environment, and through some mysterious grapevine, the wildlife had learned about it. They were arriving and taking their places in the scheme of pond life. Where had they come from? How did they know a pond existed today when only yesterday there had been dry land?

These are the mysteries that draw me out into nature and then back to my computer to write. From such holistic events come books: books about the poetic creatures that dwell in ponds, mountains, deserts, and oceans and about the children who venture among them.

I was lured into natural history by my father, an entomologist for the U.S. Forest Service. He took my brothers and me into what was once wilderness outside Washington, D.C., and taught us the names of the plants and animals. Once we knew what we were looking at, he presented us with brain teasers. Why, he asked one day, are there eight hawks circling the field we are in? When we ran out of guesses, he walked through the tall grass kicking up literally hundreds of voles that the hawks fed on. Then he asked why so many voles. We looked deeper and realized that the farmer had moved away, and the field had not been mowed for years. The grasses had grown dense and had borne millions of seeds. The voles had come to feed on the seeds and had multiplied profusely. Finally the hawks had come to eat the voles and were circling above the field in numbers indicating a vole population explosion.

To my father's natural history tutelage I added knowledge from college professors, scientists, and from my wild pets. Then, as chance often has it, I changed course. I became a newspaper reporter in Washington, D.C., covering Capitol Hill and occasionally the White House. I enjoyed the work, but my background kept pulling at me. At twenty-four I wrote a book about a fox and discovered I was a children's book writer. I love animals and the mysteries of nature; children love animals and the mysteries of nature. With a few exceptions, I've been writing ever since for readers who are excited by a frog that finds a pond and by hawks that know where there are dense grasses voles abound in.

The themes for my books came from three sources: my childhood, my research in books and in the field, and the wild creatures I raised or traveled to see in the wilds with my children. *My Side of the Mountain* is from my childhood living off the land with my father and brothers in the Potomac River wilderness. *Julie of the Wolves* evolved from a trip to the Arctic to meet wolves and wolf scientists. *The Cry of the Crow* is about our wonderful pet crow, Crowbar.

I have discovered I cannot dream up characters as incredible as the ones I meet in the wilderness. Take the three-toed sloth. It is the creation of the rain forest, a domain of greenery. The sloth eats leaves, and leaves grow on twigs, so the sloth developed light bones to keep from breaking the twigs that produce its food. Since leaves are everywhere in the rain forest, the sloth does not have to move very far to satisfy its hunger. Consequently, it hangs in one spot most of the time, using special hooks on its feet. Anything that does not move very much almost invariably becomes an ecosystem for tiny plants and animals out in nature, and the sloth is no exception. It harbors almost one hundred species. Now, who could dream up such an other-worldly character as that? Not me—so I write about reality.

In recent years I have added to my list one more source for ideas—my children and grandchildren. Twig once asked me what animals did in the month of May (*The Moon of the Monarch Butterflies*). Granddaughter Rebecca knew winter had come, but asked me what it was (*Dear Rebecca, Winter Is Here*). Craig, my son who lives in the Eskimo town of Barrow, Alaska, invited me to go whaling with him, the Eskimos, and whale scientists (*Water Sky*).

Each day is filled with excitement. I watch a pond or a tree or a rain forest, talk to scientists, observe my parrot, and listen to my children and grandchildren. After that the writing comes easy.

I love the audience I found when I was twenty-four, but I can tell you they are hard to hold. If I am disingenuous or inaccurate, they will politely slip away and listen to somebody else.

Illustration by Jean Craighead George from her book *My Side of the Mountain* (1959).

describes a young Eskimo girl's efforts to survive on the frozen tundra by learning about the behavior of a pack of wolves and becoming one of them. In *Water Sky* (1987) George contrasts the concerns of environmentalists with those of the Eskimo people, who rely on whale hunting for their living. *The Talking Earth* (1983), set in Florida, tells of a young Seminole girl who spends time alone with the wildlife of the Everglades as she learns to listen to the earth. In addition to these and other novels, George has written three "ecological mysteries," *Who Really Killed Cock Robin?* (1971), *The Missing 'Gator of Gumbo Limbo* (1992), and *The Fire Bug Connection* (1993).

As with her novels, George's nonfiction books for children reveal her love of the creatures and places she describes. The "Thirteen Moons" series was originally published from 1967 to 1969 and was rereleased in 1991 with new illustrations. In each of the thirteen volumes in this series, she focuses on the life of an animal in a different region. The "One Day" series includes books such as *One Day in the Alpine Tundra* (1984), set on a mountain in Wyoming. These books are brief studies of ecological niches in which the interactions of geology, weather, animals, birds, and humans on a given day are portrayed. Others of George's nonfiction books explore specific aspects of nature. Her *Wild, Wild Cookbook* (1982) introduces children to native plants and ways they are used. *How to Talk to Your Animals* (1985) shows how pets communicate through body language, behavior, and sounds.

George carefully researches her subjects through natural observations and reading. The data she collects often appears in several formats. Her research on wolves, for example, led not only to *Julie of the Wolves* but also to a picture book, *The Wounded Wolf* (1972), and *The Moon of the Grey Wolves* (1969, 1991), a volume in the "Thirteen Moons" series. Material about the Everglades appears in *The Talking Earth* (1983) and *The Moon of the Alligators* (1969, 1991), a "Thirteen Moons" title, as well as in *The Missing 'Gator of Gumbo Limbo*.

George is an eloquent advocate for the environment. Although she lovingly describes nature, she shares some harder truths about it with young readers: that creatures die or need to be wild, that creatures must be true to their natures as hunters or as prey, and that humans sometimes do more harm than good when they interfere in their lives. She also rewards readers with true stories of behaviors that endear animals to us, stories in which animals act in ways that seem loving or compassionate, loyal or courageous. George uses these stories to help us see ourselves in the creatures with whom we share the world. ❧ B.A.C.

Gibbons, Gail

American illustrator, b. 1944. Gail Gibbons was born in Oak Park, Illinois. Her father was a tool-and-die designer, from whom one can easily imagine she inherited her design ability and her interest in machines and processes. Awarded the Washington Post/Children's Book Guild Award for her overall contribution to children's nonfiction, Gibbons is widely known and admired among the "how do things work?" set—and by their nonplussed teachers and parents. From boats to clocks, from gas stations to recycling, Gibbons takes a common object or process and breaks it down to easily digestible pieces, using bright, flat color and innovative design.

After earning her B.F.A. at the University of Illinois, Gibbons began her professional career as a commercial artist for television stations and ad agencies. But it was while she was still in college that her interest in children's books was sparked. "I had an illustrating instructor who took a particular interest in the writing and illustrating of children's books. I believe he was the individual who opened up my interest in the area of children's books." Books, however, were placed on a back burner while Gibbons pursued a career in another medium, television. She moved to New York and was hired as a staff artist for WNBC. She did graphics for the local news programs and began illustrating for an audience of children when she was assigned to do the graphics for an NBC network children's program "Take a Giant Step." This baptism in the graphic arts world strongly influenced her book-illustration technique, with its heavy reliance on the visual presentation of information.

After the sudden, accidental death of her husband in 1972, Gibbons turned her attention from her television work to her teacher-inspired interest in children's book illustration. A friend in the children's book world encouraged her to try both writing and illustrating and suggested that she try her hand at a book about basic set theory—thus *Willy and His Wheel Wagon* (1975) was born. While it is quite obviously a first book, and today is noteworthy for the way it demonstrates how Gibbons has grown as both an artist and a writer, it nevertheless excited positive attention when it was first published and proved to be the starting point for a prolific career. *Willy* is the story of a boy who loves wheels and helps his friends when they need new wheels for their bikes, wagons, and go-carts; and in this helpful process, the book teaches children about sets. This sort of fictionalized informational story was Gibbons's chosen vehicle for her first few books, most of which were received rather lukewarmly by the critics.

Gibbons began to create "make and do" books, such as *Things to Make and Do for Columbus Day* (1977), which critics found cluttered and aimless. However, in 1979 she published *Clocks* and hit her stride with "how things work" concept books. *Clocks* was selected by *School Library Journal* as a Best Book of 1979, and it was quickly followed by such award winners as *Locks and Keys* (1980), named an NCTE Outstanding Science Trade Book. Books examining and explaining such things as dairy farms, fire fighting, skyscrapers, new roads,

Whales live in oceans. They are not fish. They are air-breathing, warmblooded mammals.

Illustration by Gail Gibbons from her book *Whales* (1991).

trucks, and the post office demonstrate her own wide-ranging interests and her feel for what puzzles and intrigues children. Her books are always externally driven: They are not "stories that demand to be told," arising from inside the artist; rather, Gibbons finds her inspiration in a process or an object that demands investigation and explanation. So her work proceeds from the outside, inward to a book.

As reproduction and printing technologies have improved, and as Gibbons's own awareness of and respect for her audience have deepened, her books have grown dramatically in scope and impact. From the highly simplified explanations of clocks and tools, Gibbons's latest works examine larger, more complicated topics, such as recycling and life on a New England fishing island. Her writing has strengthened, and her books have become much more visually complex, while she has retained her keen sense of design and organization. As each year brings several new books by this inexhaustible artist, one can only look forward to what will next pique her interest and satisfy the endless curiosity of her readers. ❧ S.G.K.

Giblin, James Cross

AMERICAN AUTHOR, B. 1933. Born in Cleveland, Ohio, James Cross Giblin was an only child. His father, a lawyer, also wrote poetry, and his mother, a former teacher, studied but did not practice law. Growing up in the company of adults, with few children in the neighborhood, Giblin says he enjoyed the conversations he heard among his parents and their friends.

Giblin wrote articles for the student newspaper in high school and college and acted in school plays in both places. He majored in English and dramatic arts, graduating from Case Western Reserve University in Cleveland with a B.A. degree in 1954. Because of his affinity for theater, he wrote a one-act play, *My Bus Is Always Late* (1954), which was his first published work. He studied playwriting at Columbia University, receiving an M.F.A. degree in 1955.

At age twenty-four, he began a career in book publishing at the British Book Centre. In 1962, after deciding to work with books for children, he joined Lothrop, Lee & Shepard Books as an associate editor; in 1967, he became editor in chief of a juvenile list at Seabury Press, which became Clarion Books. He still enjoyed writing, so he became a contributor to publications such as *The Horn Book Magazine* and *Cricket,* a magazine for children. An article for *Cricket* grew into *The Skyscraper Book* (1981), a photo-essay for which he wrote the text.

Giblin's forte is nonfiction books about unusual, mostly historical, subjects that capture his fancy. For example, in *From Hand to Mouth: Or, How We Invented Knives, Forks, Spoons, and Chopsticks and the Table Manners to Go with Them* (1987), Giblin begins with a description of a Stone Age man using a flint knife to spear a piece of meat from the cooking fire. He then describes utensils and customs through the centuries and throughout the world, generously illustrating the text with photographs of museum pieces, reproductions of illustrations of dining scenes throughout history, and drawings. The book's design is inviting, which is typical of Giblin's works, and, as is also typical, it garnered its share of awards and honors. A joint committee of the Children's Book Council and the National Council on Social Studies named it a Notable Children's Trade Book in the Field of Social Studies, and more of Giblin's books received that honor, including *The Skyscraper Book, Chimney Sweeps: Yesterday and Today* (1982), and *The Truth about Santa Claus* (1985). The latter was named a nonfiction honor book in the 1986 Boston Globe–Horn Book Awards. *Santa Claus* is a factual account of the original Saint Nicholas and of how he became a patron saint of sailors, maidens, and children. The evolution of the saint from a gift-giving person to the figure of our present-day Santa Claus legend is explained in Giblin's usual thorough and entertaining manner and illustrated by the fruits of his extensive research. The American Library Association has named many of Giblin's books Notable Books. Giblin has also written *Milk: The Fight for Purity* (1986), *Let There Be Light: A Book about Windows* (1988), and a book for adults, *Writing Books for Young People* (1990). ❧ S.H.H.

Gilson, Jamie

AMERICAN AUTHOR, B. 1933. The effervescent Jamie Gilson translates the everyday situations facing grade-school children to the written page with humor and vitality. Packed with fast-paced action and wisecracking argument and laughter, Gilson's stories feature characters growing together as they experience the ups and downs of childhood. Independent readers enjoy the snappy dialogue and identify with Gilson's characters, as is evidenced by the numerous child-voted state awards and lists on which her books have appeared. Her adept storytelling stems from her experience writing for radio, film, and television after she graduated from Northwestern University, where she studied radio and television education. Gilson's experiences growing up in

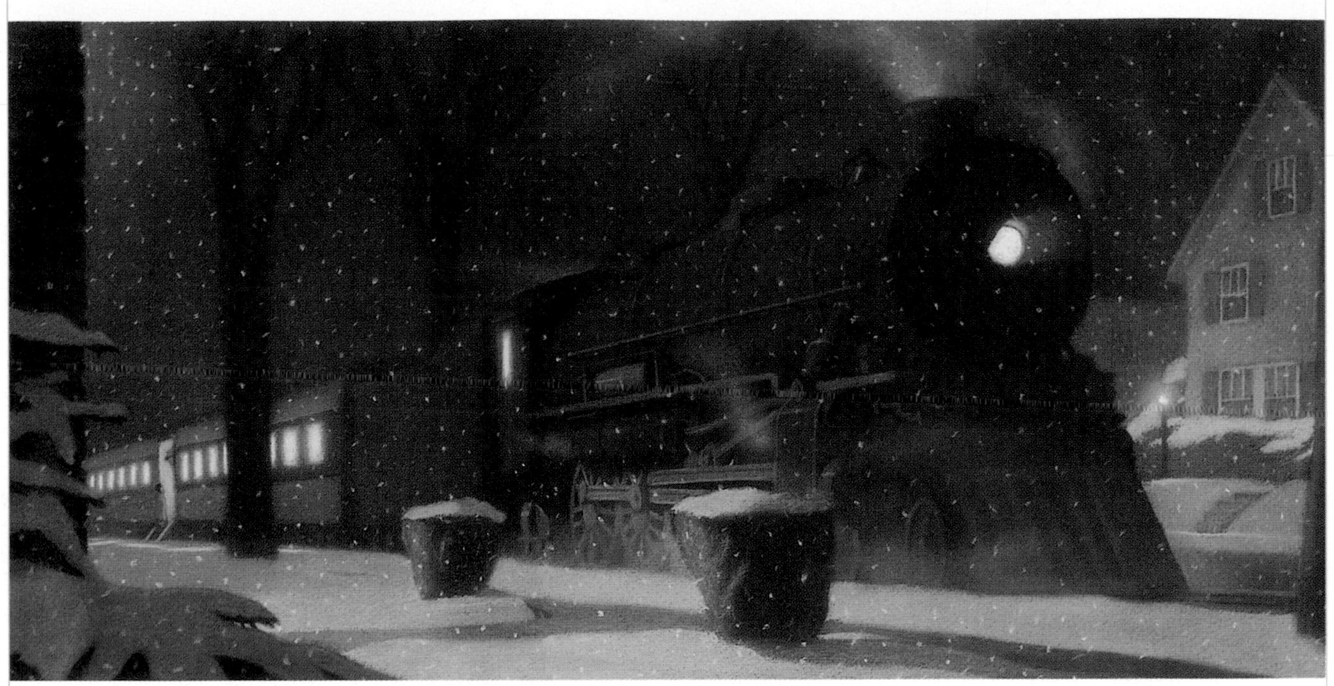

Illustration by Chris Van Allsburg from his book *The Polar Express* (1985).

Illustration by Edward Ardizzone from his book *Little Tim and the Brave Sea Captain* (1936).

Illustration by Ludwig Bemelmans from his book *Madeline* (1939).

Illustration by Jean de Brunhoff from his book *The Travels of Babar* (1934).

Illustration by John Burningham from his book *Mr. Gumpy's Motor Car* (1973).

Illustration by ERIC CARLE from his book *The Very Hungry Caterpillar* (1969).

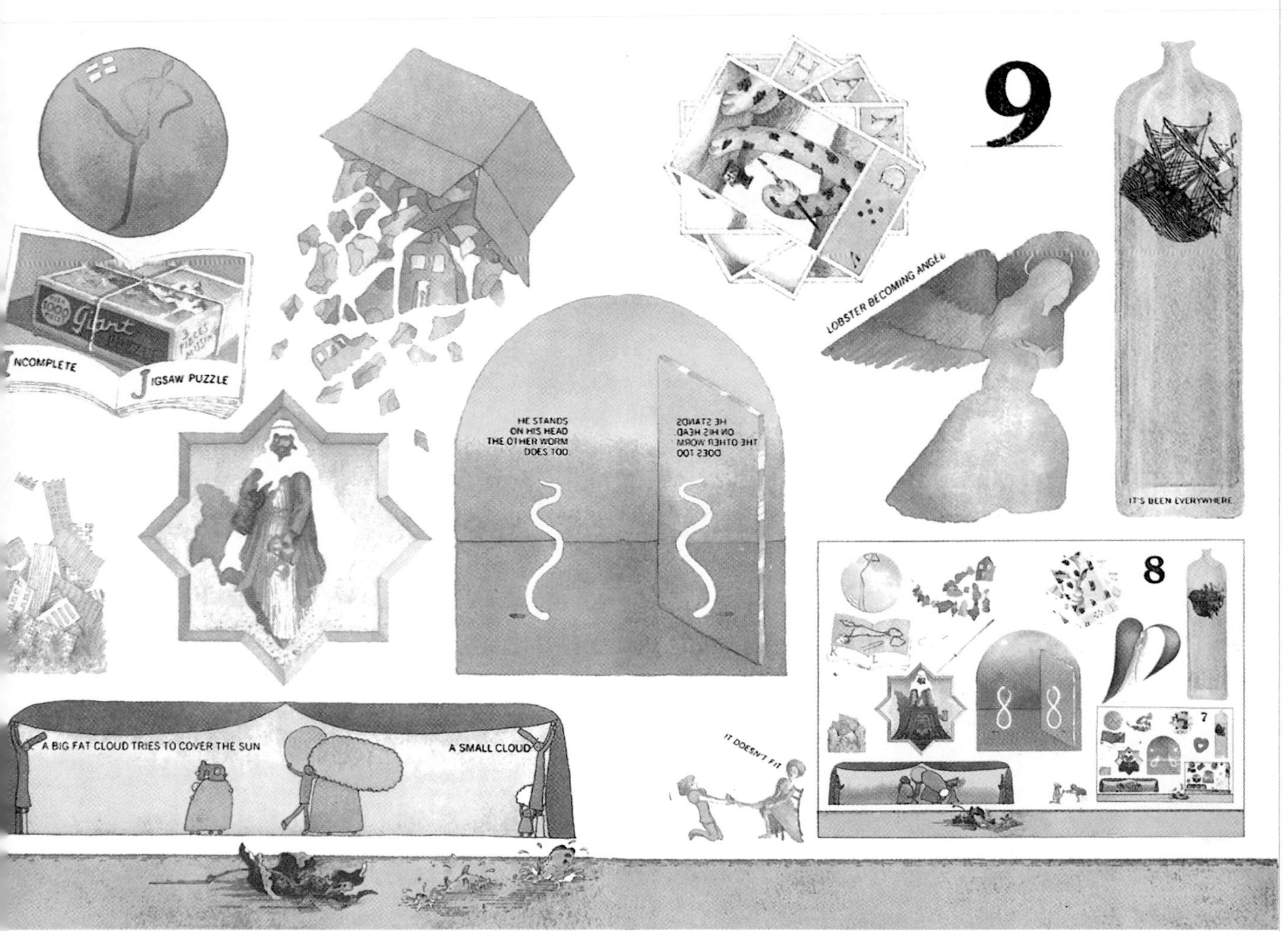

Illustration by Remy Charlip and Jerry Joyner from their book *Thirteen* (1975).

Illustration by Barbara Cooney from her book *Miss Rumphius* (1982).

Illustration by CLEMENT HURD from *Goodnight Moon* (1947), by Margaret Wise Brown.

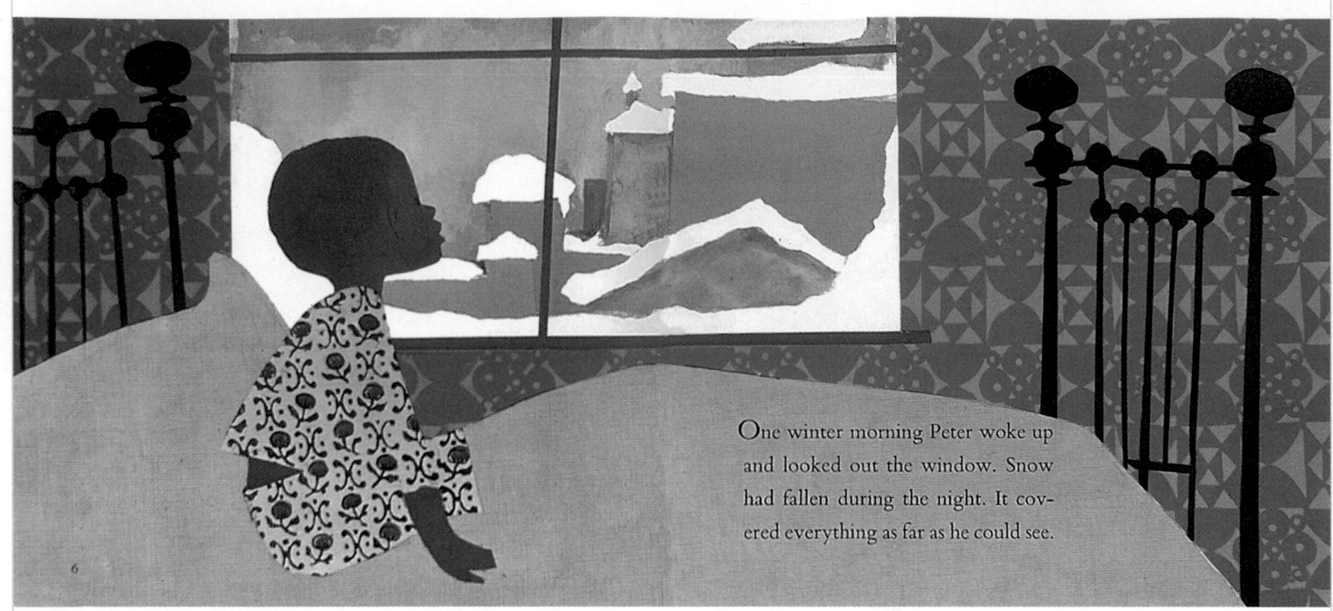

One winter morning Peter woke up and looked out the window. Snow had fallen during the night. It covered everything as far as he could see.
6

Illustration by Ezra Jack Keats from his book *The Snowy Day* (1962).

Illustration by Arnold Lobel from his book *Frog and Toad Are Friends* (1970).

the Midwest and her careful observations of neighborhood kids and her own children provide her with plenty of material for her books.

Although she has written several other books, Jamie Gilson is best known for her popular series featuring Hobie Hanson, his best friend, Nick Rossi, his arch nemesis, Molly Bosco, and their classmates. Hobie's world is filled with familiar elements of childhood: Big Wheels, pesky little brothers, PTA school fairs, disgusting school lunches, and feeling average. Readers first meet Hobie in *Thirteen Ways to Sink a Sub* (1982), a favorite among schoolchildren but certainly not among their teachers. When Hobie Hanson's fourth-grade class has a substitute teacher, Miss Ivanovitch, a boys-against-the-girls contest brings the teacher to tears. Miss Ivanovitch becomes their permanent teacher and joins the class on their overnight camp-out in *4-B Goes Wild* (1983), as they all discover the frights and delights of being out in the woods. Summer vacation without his best friend is Hobie's dilemma in *Hobie Hanson, You're Weird*. In *Hobie Hanson, Greatest Hero of the Mall* (1989), Hobie and his friends attend school at the local mall when their school is flooded and all the classes must be relocated to any available space until renovations can be completed. An empty store is graciously donated, and Hobie's class is set up in the purses and accessories department, a plot inspired by an actual event. By visiting schools as an observer, lecturer, and teacher, Jamie Gilson stays sensitive to the concerns and needs of contemporary children. ❧ A.M.D.

GINSBURG, MIRRA

RUSSIAN-BORN AMERICAN AUTHOR, EDITOR, AND TRANSLATOR, B. 1919? In the hundred years since children's PICTURE BOOKS became a distinct species of creation, and not simply old tales set to pictures, only a handful of persons have gained a name solely for writing them. Mirra Ginsburg is one of these rare exceptions, and it is not entirely accidental that she has also been a conduit between America, her adopted home, and her native Russia, where writing for small children became an art early in the Soviet era.

As an émigré linguist in lifelong love with "words, language, poetry, literature," she gladly took up TRANSLATION. A predilection for the fantastic, the satirical, the absurd, drew her to the work of the great Mikhail Bulgakov and other 1920s satirists of the topsy-turvy new world. She edited and translated three anthologies of science fiction, a subversive genre in the Soviet Union.

Meanwhile, she crossed the fine line into the young adult field. Two of the stellar works from a post-thaw spurt of Western publication, the true-life, Anne Frankish *Diary of Nina Kosterina* (1968) and Chingiz Aitmatov's visionary Kirghiz novel *The White Ship* (1972), owe not a little to her fine-tuned translations, her command in each case of the vernacular.

In the juvenile fold she produced three meaty collections of tales from the Russian borderlands, *The Master of the Winds and Other Tales from Siberia* (1970), *The Kaha Bird: Tales from the Steppes of Central Asia* (1971), and *How Wilka Went to Sea and Other Tales from West of the Urals* (1975). Is the very sound of Siberian folklore off-putting? daunting? Meet, then, the Selkup woman who puts out her fire in a rage and sees every other fire in the small encampment sputter and die at her approach; the Nivkh lad who brashly boasts of his fearlessness, and twice proves it; the three foolish Yugakirs who run away in circles from the stars. As Ginsburg writes in a useful introduction, the tales are part and parcel of the lives of their makers.

Translating folktales took Ginsburg into the realm of picture books, first as translator, then as adapter, eventually as cocreator "inspired by..." Folklore was not her only source, however. She also had on hand, from the 1920s interest in writing for young children, the prophetic example and nonsense verse of Kornei Chukovsky, reinforced by fellow advocate and children's poet SAMUEL MARSHAK and the playful, experimental absurdist poetry of Daniil Kharms and other members of the Oberiu group. This was the rich legacy of the 1920s, suppressed in the Stalinist years and revived in the 1960s, on which Ginsburg based two decades of effective to captivating picture books. The most characteristic, and the most distinctive, are very simple. They are also satisfyingly predictable, at least a little surprising, and susceptible of being illustrated in a variety of styles. They are the natural habitat, in many cases, of chicks and other fledglings. *Good Morning, Chick* (1980), an adaptation from Chukovsky, is told only half in words: "There was a little house, white and smooth... One morning, tap tap and crack!" The egg splits open and out comes a chick, "like this," ready to learn the ways of the farmyard from the few graphic, echoing words and BYRON BARTON's bright, slyly plain pictures.

Where Does the Sun Go at Night? (1980) and *The Sun's Asleep Behind the Hill* (1982), both based on Armenian lullabies, both built on repetitive patterns, are nonetheless—or all the more so—a study in contrasts. In the first, one question leads gaily to another, the whole pictured with cloud-borne abandon by JOSÉ ARUEGO and Ariane Dewey. In the second, a mood of hushed lyricism—"The sun shone in the sky all day/The sun grew tired and went away"—is reinforced by PAUL ZELINSKY's dusky landscapes.

Two spare, suggestive narratives, both "inspired by" still more terse Daniil Kharms verses, both pictured in large forms on large pages by NANCY TAFURI, take the questing child into unknown waters. *Four Brave Sailors* (1987) tells of four intrepid mice with a single, homely fear; *Across the Stream* (1982) describes how a hen and three chicks put a bad dream behind them.

Chukovsky, an unsparing critic of translation who publicly chastised the American translator of *From Two to Five,* his classic text on writing for the very young, wrote encouragingly to Ginsburg early in their correspondence: "So you turn out to be a master of folk verse as well." She has also shown herself to be endowed with a wise, empathic imagination. B.B.

GIOVANNI, NIKKI

AMERICAN AUTHOR, B. 1943. Racial pride informs the work of Nikki Giovanni, best known for writing poems that explore her African American heritage. Although primarily recognized for her adult books, the author has published several volumes of POETRY for young readers, including *Knoxville, Tennessee* (1994), which draws on summertime memories of her hometown.

Born Yolande Cornelia Giovanni, Jr., she entered Fisk University in Nashville at age sixteen and later attended the University of Pennsylvania and the Columbia University School of the Arts. Professionally, she has been a college professor, an editor, and a respected author of essays and fiction. Her first book for adults, *Black Feeling, Black Talk* (1968), is a collection of angry, somewhat militant poems addressing racial problems of the era. Some of these poems are included in her children's book *Ego-Tripping and Other Poems for Young People* (1973), a volume occasionally bogged down by rhetoric but highlighted by such poems as the title piece, which draws on black history to instill racial pride.

Giovanni's books for children illuminate the African American experience even when addressing more generic topics. *Spin a Soft Black Song* (1971) includes poems about basketball, friendship, mothers, and springtime written from an African American perspective. The unrhymed poems contain evocative images and fairly accessible themes, although the book is perhaps too broad in scope, focusing on children of all ages, including infants. *Vacation Time* (1980) includes more traditional rhyming verse. The selections are rhythmic and appealing, even though some of the rhymes are forced.

Giovanni's work is notable for providing an authentic African American voice for modern children's poetry. P.D.S.

GIPSON, FRED

AMERICAN AUTHOR, 1908–1973. Drawing on his own background, Fred Gipson brought the authentic flavor of rural Texas to his writing. Born in Mason, Texas, the author grew up on a farm, where he worked the fields and listened to his father spin tales. Gipson attended the University of Texas at Austin, worked as a ranch hand and newspaper reporter, wrote magazine fiction, and published several adult books, including *Hound-Dog Man* (1949), before entering the children's field with a tall tale, *The Trail-Driving Rooster* (1955). His best-known novel, *Old Yeller* (1956), concerns fourteen-year-old Travis Coates, who is trying to take care of his family in his father's absence. A stray dog called Old Yeller joins the household and eventually saves Travis, his younger brother, and their mother from a series of animal attacks. The growing relationship between boy and dog is related in Travis's fresh, appealing narration and played out against a grittily observed background of 1860s Texas farm life. The novel culminates in a heart-wrenching scene in which Travis must shoot his own rabid dog. Beloved by millions of readers, *Old Yeller* was named a Newbery Honor Book and is considered a modern classic. Gipson wrote the screenplay for a fine WALT DISNEY movie adaptation.

Savage Sam (1962) is a strong story about Old Yeller's son, who helps Travis, his brother, and their friend when they are captured by Indians. A posthumous book, *Little Arliss* (1978), develops the character of Travis's younger brother.

Gipson wrote many memorable novels about life on the Texas frontier, and created one of the most outstanding boy and dog stories of the twentieth century. P.D.S.

GLEESON, LIBBY

AUSTRALIAN WRITER, B. 1950. Because Elizabeth Gleeson's father, a teacher, taught at several different schools, her large family moved several times during her childhood, always from one New South Wales country town to another, environments that were later to influence strongly her first book, *Eleanor Elizabeth* (1984). As a child, Libby Gleeson read voraciously and always vowed to become a writer. But then, as she explains, she "went off and did lots of other things." Travel and teaching, both in Australia and abroad, including the United States, Europe, and Southeast Asia, intervened, and it was during a stay in London that she first seriously put pen to paper. Because she had observed that many children's books published in Australia "contained rigid gender stereotypes, saccharine families, and were written in an unreal language," she was determined to create fiction with understandable language, realistic situations, and strong, believable protagonists, particularly girls. She worked hard at her writing for a couple of years, reaping the benefits of a writers' group. The result was *Eleanor Elizabeth,* a novel concerning a young girl coming to terms with changes in her own life by reading her grandmother's diary. In addition to being a runner-up for the 1985 Children's Book of the Year Award in Australia, the novel achieved instant popularity with young readers. It also set Gleeson off on a successful writing path, with fellowships from the Literature Board of the Australia Council that enabled her to write full-time and produce her second novel for young people, *I Am Susannah* (1987), which also received critical and popular acclaim. Again, Gleeson writes effectively about an adolescent girl coping with upheaval, this time in an urban environment.

Since then Gleeson has written *Dodger* (1990), a novel about a boy with complex emotions and relationships but very much entrenched in the business of real life—a book clearly influenced by her teaching experiences. She is also the author of several picture books, illustrated by a variety of artists. Even her work for very young readers vibrates with the sounds of real relationships, although a bit of imaginative fantasy creeps in now and then. *Where's Mum?* (1992), illustrated by Craig Smith and set amid the familiar entropy of a family home, features an imaginative subplot involving a number of nursery and storybook characters. The successful combination of fantasy and realism earned the book a place on the short list for the 1993 Children's Book of the Year Awards. *Where's Mum?* and *Mum Goes to Work* (both 1992), concerning the professions or activities of various mothers while their assortment of children are at daycare, appeared during Gleeson's "mum period," when her three daughters were very young. Although she has never written biography or autobiography, she readily admits that each of her picture books and novels has its roots in "real people" she knows or in actual experiences people have related to her. She feels strongly about the importance of showing, rather than telling, and letting the reader come to his or her own often poignant conclusions about the situations she creates. As the books themselves demonstrate, Gleeson succeeds admirably: Her characters linger on in readers' minds well after their stories have been told. K.J.

Goble, Paul

English-born American author and illustrator, b. 1933. Paul Goble's fascination with the Indians of the Great Plains began when his mother read aloud the complete works of Grey Owl and Ernest Thompson Seton during his youth in Surrey, England. After graduation from London's Central School of Arts and Crafts, he acted on his passion by traveling to the United States to visit some Indian reservations and was adopted by the Sioux and Yakima tribes. Goble returned to England, where he taught and practiced industrial design, but after establishing his picture-book career, he moved to the Black Hills of South Dakota. Sioux, Cheyenne, and Blackfoot beliefs provide the core of all his stories.

In order to tell the Indian side of the Battle of the Little Bighorn, Goble and his first wife, Dorothy, created *Red Hawk's Account of Custer's Last Battle* (1969). In a seamless text, they alternate a fictitious Indian boy's view with historical commentary in an eye-opening tale. The pictures dramatically chronicle the events in a stiff, stylized manner taken from narrative drawings on tipis, buffalo robes, and the ledger-book drawings made while the Indians were held prisoner. The watercolor figures with ink outlines appear in profile on a white background, their featureless faces allowing the viewer to imagine their expressions. Here, as in his whole body of work, Goble's thorough research provides the foundation for his stories, and he almost always includes extensive references and notes.

After publishing two more accounts of historical fiction with Dorothy, Goble retold and illustrated *The Friendly Wolf* (1974), thus beginning a succession of myths and legends that are his most recognized work. In tales like *Buffalo Woman* (1984), in which the Buffalo Nation sends a wife to a kindhearted hunter, Goble strengthens his artistic vision, fusing his strong design and technique with Indian symbols and artistic traditions. The pages are filled with bold, flat watercolors amid prodigious amounts of white space, producing striking compositions full of motion despite the deliberately stiff, stylized figures. The animals, plants, clothing, and tipis are highly detailed records of the Great Plains environment and Indian folk art. Sometimes white space instead of ink line appears as outline to re-create the clear Plains air or the sparkling beadwork, as in *Her Seven Brothers* (1988), a legend about a young woman who decorates clothing with porcupine-quill beadwork for her new family.

In recent years, Goble has retold four tales of the spider trickster Iktomi. These hilarious stories, often pourquoi tales explaining why an animal looks a certain way, teach lessons in living. In *Iktomi and the Boulder* (1988), the clever but egotistical trickster insults a boulder that chases him and pins him down. Iktomi's utterances flow cartoon-style from his lips, and the text interjects leading comments in italicized asides. Goble's retellings are contemporary in picture and word: Iktomi wears athletic socks beneath his ceremonial garb and on one title page says, "There goes that white guy, Paul Goble, telling another story about me." Yet Goble still remains solidly in the Plains Indian tradition, for though the storytellers never vary from a story's theme, they freely adapt the details to suit their listeners.

Goble's understated, formal sentence construction and plain wording also reflects Indian storytelling. Often included are songs or chants, adding further cultural richness. Goble has won numerous awards, including a Caldecott Medal for *The Girl Who Loved Wild Horses* (1978). And, although he creates books with his Indian friends in mind, perhaps the greatest value of his work is making available to everyone these Plains Indian stories, with their focus on the interconnection of all living things. ❦ S.S.

Godden, Rumer

British novelist and poet, b. 1907. Margaret Rumer Godden wrote her first children's book, *The Dolls' House,* in 1947. Fascinated with miniatures and dolls since her childhood, Godden had wondered if a strong story could be developed within the confines of a doll's house. She proved that it could: The emotion and poignancy of human relationships are dramatically mirrored in the personalities and actions of her dolls. One of the most common types of personification for children is found in doll stories; younger readers easily identify with inanimate doll characters that possess human qualities and provide a child's-eye view of the adult world. Godden's doll books, unique in language, charm, and plot, share one thing—the dolls are originally mistreated or misunderstood. *Impunity Jane* (1954), a doll considered too small and insignificant to play with, is stuffed away for years until a young boy finds her and her life begins. All Godden's doll stories—*The Fairy Doll* (1956), *The Story of Holly and Ivy* (1958), and *Candy Floss* (1961)—reflect the complexities and differences in real family life, but the protagonists never lose their doll-like characteristics. *Miss Happiness and Miss Flower* (1961) is a fantasy about two Japanese dolls who help a timid, homesick English girl to develop her self-confidence. The story's secondary theme—friendship—leads to another doll adventure, *Little Plum* (1963).

Among contemporary authors, Godden stands out, as only a handful write eloquently and facilely for both adults and children. According to Godden, "One cannot learn to be a children's writer; one must be a born storyteller." However, her success is also due to her attitudes and opinions about the genre. "Writing children's stories are exercises for myself. I rank writing books for children next to poetry in difficulty. In each discipline every word must do its task. Getting sidetracked with wordy chunks of thought or description is confusing to children. A children's book is not necessarily more simple than a novel, it must be more clear. The story must move in a direct line, from beginning to end. When writing books for children you can't bend down to them—you must get down to a child's horizon, become a child."

Godden's ability to assume a child's perspective is evident in the language she uses in works such as *The Mousewife* (1951) to make the story believable to children. *The Diddakoi* (1972), a tale about a half-gypsy child, is one of her finest books. It features a spunky heroine, is peppered with engaging characters, develops universal themes—courage, acceptance, love—and is topped with a satisfying ending. Many of Godden's books reflect her childhood in India where, although her "life did evoke a princess quality," she was forced to discover resilience and self-reliance. The author's lifelong passion for horses and ballet, often subjects of her adult books, makes for appealing story lines in *Mr. McFadden's Hallowe'en* (1975), a solid horse story laced with dollops of humor, and *Listen to the Nightingale* (1992), a touching book about a girl, her dog, and ballet. *Great Grandfather's House* (1993) takes place in modern-day Japan and is based on the sensible bit of philosophy that Godden states early in the book: "Manners are like oil put into engines to make the wheels go round without trouble, otherwise they jar and grind, grrh, grrh, grrh"—a most appropriate comment for contemporary children of all cultures. ❦ S.L.

Goffstein, M. B.

American author and illustrator, b. 1940. Like a small white pebble gleaming on the beach, the books of Marilyn Brooke Goffstein enrich our lives with their simple beauty. Pared down to the essentials in line and word, her illustrations and stories speak directly to the heart. "A book is meant to communicate the best that's in you. You have to be honest, be yourself, be unselfconscious, say what you want to say and do it justice. There is no other reason to write or illustrate a book." From her parents, Albert, an electrical engineer, and Esther Goffstein, she learned the importance of meaningful work. "I grew up in St. Paul, Minnesota, feeling that work was the only real dignity, the only real happiness, and that people were nothing if their lives were not dedicated. My choice was art—a talent that shows up early." She attended Bennington College in Vermont, and by graduation in 1962, she had developed her skills in creative writing, art, and printmaking.

Goffstein moved to New York and worked in the children's department of two bookstores, all the while showing her portfolio to every major New York publisher. Editors liked her work but had no suitable manuscripts for her style, so she began to write. *The Gats*, her first book, was published in 1966, soon after her marriage to Peter Schaaf, a concert pianist. It was quickly followed by *Sleepy People* (1966), *Brookie and Her Little Lamb* (1967), and *Across the Sea* (1968). Goffstein's creative style involves understanding and visualizing her story and characters thoroughly before a word or line takes actual form on paper. She then writes her story out in longhand, taking a long time to select and refine her words. Conversely, her illustrations evolve quickly. "A lot of artists sketch and then watch what their hand is doing. They're thinking on paper. I do most of my work in my head and have few, if any, sketches."

After working alone for twenty years, Goffstein began teaching children's book illustration at the Parsons School of Design. Inspired by her students, she started working in pastels. Early in her career, simple, closed lines defined her illustrations. Now, shapes in colored chalk, resembling miniature Mark Rothko paintings, create an atmosphere, softly illuminating her stories. Her first two books using pastels, *School of Names* and *Our Snowman,* were published in 1986, the same year she married David Allender. Though she writes in different genres, her picture books, young adult novels, and nonfiction books are tied together by universal themes of love and truth. In *Brookie and Her Little Lamb,* Brookie tries to teach her beloved lamb to read and sing, but he can only say "Baaa." It doesn't matter: "She loved him any-how." Goldie of *Goldie the Dollmaker* carves popular wooden dolls. She is often lonely, but eventually realizes that through her love of and commitment to her art, she has created friends she may never meet and has unselfconsciously given the best of herself to them. *Fish for Supper,* the story of a grandmother's daily ritualistic fishing trips, is spare in words and linear imagery, but rich in the reassurance of closure. It won a Caldecott Honor Award in 1977. Although a quick glance at Goffstein's work may disarm the reader with its beguiling simplicity, a thoughtful perusal will reveal a core of inner emotional strength. § M.B.B.

Goodall, John S.

British artist and illustrator of wordless picture books, b. 1908. John Strickland Goodall's distinctive style is easily recognizable. In 1968 he introduced the technique of using alternating half pages between double-page spreads in a small-book format to advance the action in *The Adventures of Paddy Pork,* a tale of a brave and bold pig. While this harlequinade format had been previously used in the eighteenth century, Goodall's approach was fresh and humorous. He used no words but created wonderful stories of a marvelous, humorous hero in pen-and-ink line drawings. This was followed by *Shrewbettina's Birthday* (1971), in which he added watercolor to his precise pencil line drawings to create an exquisite, tiny, anthropomorphic, civilized world in which mice dress up, drink tea, play cards, and sleep in four-poster beds. He created beauty and humor in his first books and continues to combine these attributes in his more recent ones.

Goodall's pixyish sense of humor is evident in his choice of heroes and heroines, such as the mouse in *Naughty Nancy* (1975), who is a terror, but also quick-witted, as she shows in *Naughty Nancy Goes to School* (1985). Other characters, including Paddy Pork, who stars in ten of his own books, have many humorous misadventures but ingeniously romp through these wordless action-packed dramas with a certain élan.

In his later books, Goodall has become more "painterly" while continuing the fine draftsmanship that has been the hallmark of all his work. He demonstrates a deep understanding of British life and is praised as a social historian, as he does meticulous research of the customs, architecture, costume, daily life, and critical moments of the various periods of English history. This is very apparent in *The Story of a Castle* (1986), which details the building of a Norman castle and the subsequent changes made up to and including the 1970s. *Great Days of a Country House* (1992) shows five centuries of social history centered on the occupants, grounds, and interiors of an English country house. These titles and others, such as *The Story of the Seashore* (1990), blend humor with facts and have created an American interest in British life.

Goodall won the Boston Globe–Horn Book Award for illustration in 1969 for *The Adventures of Paddy Pork* and the New York Times Best Illustrated Children's Book of the Year for *The Surprise Picnic* (1977). He is recognized for his superb draftsmanship, precise line drawing, panoramic representational watercolors, strong composition, subtle shading, and the inclusion of fascinating and accurate detail.

Goodall, a widower, lives in the country near Tisbury, a little village similar to the one in *The Story of an English Village* (1978), about a half hour from Salisbury, in Wiltshire, England. He has created an enchanting home, Lawn Cottage, by connecting two small cottages. The present cottage is almost a small museum, filled with exquisite collections and paintings. The gardens, with great mounds of fragrant flowers that bloom in late spring and early summer, are lovely.

Even into his eighties, the prolific Goodall continues to be one of the best-known English watercolorists. He paints as he travels and has an exhibit every year of his seascapes and landscapes. He is a member of the Royal Institute of Water Colour Painters, the Royal Society of British Artists, and the National Society of British Artists. He continues to publish about one book a year for appreciative British, French, and American audiences. B.J.B.

Gorey, Edward

American author and illustrator, b. 1925. As an illustrator of books for adults, Edward Gorey has a distinctive, instantly recognizable style: intricately detailed pen-and-ink drawings capture characters, fur-coated, turtle-necked, or dressed in 1920s or Edwardian garb, frozen in moments of stoicism. Somewhat Gothic and ostensibly grim, these images are usually accompanied by macabre stories of death, dread, and gore or by humorous verses detailing situations of horror. Gorey's unique character is most pervasive in the works of which he is both author and illustrator. Though largely out of print, many of his books have been made available in the collections *Amphigorey* (1972), *Amphigorey, Too* (1975), and *Amphigorey Also* (1983).

Born in Chicago, Gorey attended the Art Institute of Chicago, served a short time in the U.S. Army, and received a B.A. in French from Harvard. After working in Boston at various jobs, including bookstore clerk and book jacket designer, he moved to New York in 1953 to become a staff artist at Doubleday. That same year, his first book, *The Unstrung Harp,* was published. It was followed by a succession of books, many of which were published under a variety of humorously anagrammatic pseudonyms such as Mrs. Regera Dowdy, Ogdred Weary, and Dreary Wodge.

Illustration by Edward Gorey from *The Shrinking of Treehorn* (1971), by Florence Parry Heide.

Though critics and fans are apt to analyze the dark humor in his work, Gorey maintains that his stories are simply entertainments in the nonsense tradition of Lewis Carroll and Edward Lear. His attraction to this genre is perhaps more evident in his work for children. In addition to illustrating a few of Edward Lear's poems, including *The Dong with the Luminous Nose* (1969), Gorey wrote and illustrated *The Wuggly Ump* (1963), a story in verse about a group of carefree children who end up in the belly of an obscure dragon-like creature. Gorey's ability to bring visual humor to a text has made him the appropriate illustrator of several collections of poetry, such as *The Monster Den* (1966) and *You Read to Me, I'll Read to You* (1962), by John Ciardi. His intuitive illustrations and graphic design added a narrative dimension to the witty text of Florence Parry Heide to create the award-winning *The Shrinking of Treehorn* (1971). With expressive visual detail, Gorey's line drawings add further dimension to parallel the story of an endearing, if slightly odd, only child who independently and rather ably copes with his mysterious condition of shrinking while his emotionally aloof parents carry on their trivial tasks with devout attention, ignorant of his diminishing stature. In a more traditional vein, Gorey produced illustrations for two versions of classic fairy tales: *Red Riding Hood* (1972), retold in verse by BEATRICE SCHENK DE REGNIERS, and *Rumpelstiltskin* (1974), retold by Edith Tarcov.

Reaching a wide audience through passions from PICTURE BOOKS and book jackets to the theater—one of the passions that he cites as among his main influences—Edward Gorey's work appeals to a mainstream audience as well as to devotees by bringing a lighthearted quality to dark humor. ❧ E.K.E.

GRAHAM, LORENZ

AMERICAN AUTHOR, 1902–1989. A pioneer African American writer for children, Lorenz Graham explored both the African and the black American experience in several trailblazing books. The son of a minister, he was born in New Orleans and spent his childhood in a succession of parsonages throughout the country. While still in college at the University of California at Los Angeles, he went to Liberia to teach. That experience, which showed him the wide disparity between the American idea of the "Dark Continent" and the reality of what he observed there, sealed his lifelong dedication to writing books that honestly portrayed African life.

Despite his conviction that books were needed, his early writing career was filled with disappointment. Publishers of the 1920s, he felt, were only interested in stories about African savages, and he put aside his writing ambitions to concentrate on a career in social work, doing graduate work at the New York School for Social Work and at New York University. In time, he and his wife settled in California, where they raised their family while he worked as a social worker and probation officer.

It wasn't until 1946 that his first book, *How God Fix Jonah,* was published. A collection of Bible stories written in the cadences of authentic African oral tradition, it featured an introduction by the legendary black activist W. E. B. Du Bois, who later became Graham's brother-in-law. Several African tales followed, among them *Song of the Boat* (1975), illustrated by Caldecott medalists LEO AND DIANE DILLON. The story of a father and son's search for the perfect tree from which to carve a canoe, it was written in the English that villagers in West Africa often used. Vividly poetic, the prose captures the strong rhythms of the region's folk speech.

His best-known novels form a series that follows David Williams, a young African American, from adolescence through adulthood: *South Town* (1958), *North Town* (1965), *Whose Town?* (1969), and *Return to South Town* (1976). Simply written and deeply felt, *South Town* tracks the ordinary and finally grotesque insults that an ambitious young man and his hardworking family endure in a small Southern town at midcentury. A portrait of ordinary people, not heroes, the book and its sequels were inspired by the kind of people Graham said he knew best, people, he once explained, who "feel pain but do not stop to complain, who want to make life better but hesitate to act for fear they will make things worse." Infused by hope and tempered by sorrow, *South Town* and the other novels in the series have lost little of their power even after three decades of profound social change. They ring true now as both a stirring affirmation of human kindness and a clear-eyed reckoning of the cost of racial bigotry. ❧ A.Q.

GRAHAM, MARGARET BLOY

CANADIAN-AMERICAN AUTHOR AND ILLUSTRATOR, B. 1920. Margaret Bloy Graham began her career as a children's book artist with considerable success. Her very first book, *All Falling Down* (1951), written by her then husband, GENE ZION, was a Caldecott Honor Book. The following year, *The Storm Book* (1952), by CHARLOTTE ZOLOTOW, was also selected as a Caldecott Honor Book.

Each book is illustrated in a quite different style. In *All Falling Down,* a satisfying survey of things that fall down (leaves, petals, rain) and things that don't (children caught in their father's arms), the double-page spreads are softly hued. There is a sweetness, arguably a bit too much, in each of the scenes. In contrast, and in keeping with its subject, *The Storm Book* generally has a darker palette, mostly grays and black. The sky looms large, crackling with energy and fury. The text and art never share a page, allowing sweeping pictures of the storm to dominate the double-page spreads unchallenged.

Graham's subsequent work went in another, more humorous direction. In 1956 *Harry the Dirty Dog* made its debut. It was the first in an enduringly popular series that also includes *No Roses for Harry!* (1958), *Harry and the Lady Next Door* (1960), and *Harry by the Sea* (1965). Written by Gene Zion, the Harry stories follow the escapades of an endearingly crafty dog who knows what he likes (his independence) and what he doesn't (washes, sweaters with roses, bad singers). Filled with oranges and greens, the art is loose and spaciously composed. The characters are rounded and simply drawn, wonderfully genial in appearance and attitude. There is a droll, seemingly effortless union of art and text in the Harry stories, a delicious mastery of everyday foolishness.

Born and brought up in Toronto, Graham spent most of her childhood summers in either England or the United States. She came to New York in the 1940s to establish her career as a commercial artist and worked for a time for the Condé Nast magazine empire, where Zion was also employed. They married in 1948, and she and editor Ursula Nordstrom of Harper and Brothers persuaded him to try writing for children. Their collaboration flourished for years, ending with their divorce in 1968.

On her own, Graham illustrated several more books, including some she wrote herself. *Be Nice to Spiders* (1967) dramatizes the value of staying on the good side of arachnids. She also created Benjy the dog, who starred in *Benjy and the Barking Bird* (1971) and *Benjy's Dog House* (1973). Like Harry, Benjy lives an agreeable suburban life and has a strong will. His antics are gently amusing but somehow lack the frisky wit of his canine predecessor. ❧ A.Q.

Grahame, Kenneth

British novelist, 1859–1932. A. A. Milne, author of the Winnie the Pooh stories, once called Kenneth Grahame's *Wind in the Willows* a "household book." And so it has become, with over a hundred editions and countless numbers in print, treasured by their owners and passed on to the upcoming generation as a children's classic.

Its creator was an unlikely candidate for this elevated status in the world of children's literature. Born in Edinburgh, Scotland, Grahame was taken to England to live with his grandmother after his mother's death. His father, unable to deal with the grief of loss, disappeared onto the Continent. While Granny Ingles provided all the necessary physical comforts, there was not much warmth and affection shown toward the Grahame children. Grahame, however, was captivated by the Berkshire Downs where they lived and eventually made them the backdrop for his beloved story of Rat, Mole, Toad, and Mr. Badger.

Grahame attended St. Edwards School in Oxford, where he began dabbling in writing but was forced by family pressure to apply for a clerkship at the Bank of England. Much of his early writing expressed resentment toward the ethic that revered the "real work" of a bank clerkship over the work of an artist. In 1879, at age thirty-nine, Grahame became one of the youngest secretaries in the history of the Bank of England. He was, however, ever rebellious as he pursued his social life in the various restaurants of Soho populated with the literary stars of the times. It was here that he fortuitously met with the great literary scholar F. J. Furnwall and the poet W. E. Henly. During this period he was introduced to neopaganism, the literary cult of Pan, which reinforced his own views on organized religion and pastoral escape. His first gathering of essays, *Pagan Papers,* was published in 1894. In 1895, *The Golden Age,* written in nostalgic praise of childhood, became the bible for children's writers and eventually an important source for the ideas in *The Wind in the Willows.*

In 1899, Grahame married. Although the marriage was not a happy one, the Grahames' son, Alastair, was the inspiration for the wonderful stories told at bedtime or, when he and his father were apart, in letters. In 1907, these stories were first published as *First Whisper of the Wind in the Willows.* Grahame then wrote out the stories as a novel, adding the two mystical chapters, "Pipers at the Gates of Dawn" and "Wayfarers All." Much of Grahame's own life can be seen in *The Wind in the Willows.* Some say that Mole was Grahame trying to relocate the child within himself. *Willows* reflects the townsman's nostalgic view of country life. The adventures of Mr. Toad, the part written especially for the adventure-hungry Alastair, serve as the main plot device. Mole is allowed his philosophical musings when Mr. Toad is flying off to follow yet another scheme. Each character is always anxious to return to his home, but Rat's home seems to be the most appealing, a reflection of Grahame's own propensity toward the peace and tranquillity of river life. He himself, like Rat, was especially happy just "messing about in boats."

Early in the 1930s Ernest Shepard (illustrator also for all of Milne's writings about Christopher Robin and Winnie the Pooh) visited Grahame to discuss Shepard's ideas for illustrations for the book. He was urged by an elderly Grahame: "I love these little people, be kind to them." Since Grahame's death in 1932, numerous editions have appeared, illustrated by artists including E. H. Shepard, Arthur Rackham, Tasha Tudor, and Michael Hague.

Even though *The Wind in the Willows* has been criticized for its old-boys'-club atmosphere, the writing is rich and the sense of place genuine, as is the expression of fondness for each of the characters, their sense of friendship, and the exaltation of nature. It is truly one of the classic read-aloud books that should not be missed by any family. ❧ A.I.

Gramatky, Hardie

American author and illustrator, 1907–1979. Best known for his first book, the classic *Little Toot* (1939), Hardie Gramatky uncovered the childlike in the mechanical—a tugboat, a plane, a caboose. These workhorses of the industrial age took on all the attributes of fun-loving, strong-willed children in his fanciful tales.

One can easily see in his books the hallmark of his first employer, the Walt Disney studio, where he worked as an animator from 1930 to 1936. Gramatky's stories are filled with fast action, endearing creatures, and exaggerated predicaments. In *Little Toot* the title character is the "cutest, silliest tugboat you ever saw," the son of the mightiest tugboat on the river and the grandson of a crusty old veteran of river commerce. But unlike his proud predecessors, Little Toot far preferred play to work. Then one day, ashamed of frivolousness, he resolves to try harder. In a heroic display of both courage and cleverness, he helps save an enormous ocean liner caught in a fierce storm. The genial moral goes down easy: Industry is more satisfying than idleness; small is sometimes better than big. The tone is unflaggingly upbeat and reassuring—if Little Toot can save the day, real-life children can, too.

With *Little Toot*, Gramatky began what became his lifelong exploration into the technical requirements of picture-book illustration. Printing limitations of the time made it uneconomical to reproduce his original illustrations, which were full-color watercolor paintings. So he began to experiment with a variety of color-separation techniques, striving, he once wrote, "for rich, harmonious colors. These are difficult to achieve with the color separation process, but when successful, the results are rewarding." To readers accustomed to today's full-color printing techniques, Gramatky's colors seem muted and sometimes muddy, but the effect is also engagingly cozy and comfortable. *Little Toot* is by no means a perfect book—the text leans toward cliché, the pictures can be almost gratingly cute—but it is an especially kindhearted one, told with genuine enthusiasm and respect for young children.

In Gramatky's subsequent books he returns to the theme of the small triumphing over the large. In *Loopy* (1941) a little airplane proves that he doesn't need a pilot, especially not a showoff, to become the most famous skywriter of them all. Similarly, in *Homer and the Circus Train* (1957), a little caboose demonstrates his mettle on a treacherous slide down a narrow mountain train track. *Nikos and the Sea God* (1963), inspired by a trip Gramatky took to Greece, chronicles the adventure of a little boy whose trust in Poseidon, the Sea God, helps him to save his ailing aunt.

Old-fashioned in their appearance and unabashedly sentimental in their tone, Gramatky's books are amiable entertainments, gently counseling children that hard work and a splash of spunk can get you far in this world. ❧ A.Q.

Gray, Elizabeth Janet

American author, b. 1902. The youngest child of a Scottish father and an American Quaker mother, Elizabeth Janet Gray drew from both sides of her family background to write historical books for young readers.

The author was born and raised in Philadelphia, where she attended a Friends school. Gray always hoped to become a writer, and she sold her first story to a religious publication while she was still a teenager. After graduating from Bryn Mawr, she spent a year teaching high school while writing her first novel, *Meredith's Ann* (1929), the story of a girl growing up in New Hampshire. Gray wrote about her mother's New Jersey childhood in *Tilly-Tod* (1929), the first of many books with a Quaker theme. After receiving a degree in library science from Drexel Institute, Gray worked at the University of North Carolina Library, where she did the historical research that resulted in her first Newbery Honor Book, *Meggy MacIntosh* (1930). This story of an eighteenth-century Scottish girl who immigrates to the Carolina Colony was the first book to demonstrate Gray's rare ability to combine fiction with history. Meggy is an engaging, well-realized character in an interesting plot that includes historical figures such as Jacobite heroine Flora Macdonald.

Research trips to Great Britain resulted in a pair of biographies honoring both sides of Gray's family heritage. Though written in a somewhat dated fictional style, *Young Walter Scott* (1935) remains an enjoyable book. The life of the Quaker leader, *Penn* (1938), is an even stronger effort because it follows a more conventional biographical style. Both titles were named Newbery Honor Books.

In 1943 Gray won the Newbery Medal for *Adam of the Road*, the story of an eleven-year-old minstrel traveling alone through England, looking for his missing father and stolen dog. Some readers may find the length and leisurely pace of the novel difficult, but those who persevere will be charmed by the characterizations and fine descriptive writing. Gray brings thirteenth-century England to life, skillfully blending historical fact with fiction. The volume is given added appeal by its beautiful design and Robert Lawson's illustrations. A later novel, *I Will Adventure* (1962), is an equally colorful view of England during Shakespeare's time. Although *The Fair Adventure* (1940) and *Sandy* (1945) were contemporary when published, references to World War II refugees and long-forgotten movie stars now make the books seem as historical as Gray's other novels.

Gray's work with the American Friends Service Committee during World War II led to an extraordinary career opportunity when she was chosen as the tutor for the crown prince of Japan after the war. *Windows for the Crown Prince* (1952) records Gray's experiences during the four years she held this position.

The widowed author occasionally used her married name, Elizabeth Gray Vining, on some of her later publications, which include adult novels, biographies, and autobiographical works such as *Return to Japan* (1961). Gray has faded in popularity over the years, but those who seek out her books will discover good characterizations, fine writing, and a sure sense of history that never overwhelms the story. P.D.S.

Green, Roger Lancelyn

ENGLISH AUTHOR, COMPILER, AND RETELLER, 1918–1987. It seems fitting for the heir to an ancestral home, occupied by his family for over nine hundred years, to become a reteller of ancient tales. Roger Gilbert Lancelyn Green inherited title to such an estate in Cheshire, England, the site claimed by his Norman forebears in 1066. As a child Green was often ill, but such times provided him with the opportunity to read widely. His favorite childhood author was ANDREW LANG, whose many-colored fairy-tale volumes left an indelible mark on Green's lively imagination. Green was later to select Lang as the subject of his college thesis, which in turn developed into an adult biography. Green wrote a number of biographies on literary figures for both children and adults, but his position as an important contributor to children's literature rests on his ability to retell myths and legends and his skill in compiling anthologies of classic tales.

A graduate of Merton College, Oxford, Green worked at various times as an antiquarian bookseller, an actor (he was a pirate in a touring company of *Peter Pan*, an experience which later resulted in his writing *Fifty Years of Peter Pan* [1954]), a librarian, an educator, an editor, and a writer. The few original stories Green wrote for children are not well known, but his anthologies of stories and his retold tales remain ever popular. After visiting Greece as a boy, Green developed a lifelong fascination with its history and lore, which became a source of inspiration for many of his books, such as *Old Greek Fairy Tales* (1958), *Heroes of Greece and Troy* (1961), and *Jason and the Golden Fleece* (1968). Although Green also acquired a thorough knowledge of the ancient world, going on to recount myths of Egypt, Sumer, and other early cultures, Greece remained his primary interest. His translated versions of Sophocles and Euripides are a testament to his erudition.

Despite his brilliance, Green never condescended in his writing for young people. He wrote simply, directly, and with authority. His aim was to tell a good story while remaining faithful to original sources. For example, in retelling *The Story of King Arthur and His Knights of the Round Table* (1953), a subject also dear to him, Green did not follow the usual dictum of relying on Sir Thomas Malory alone. Ever the scholar, he consulted many Middle English authorities, as well as the writings of the German Minnesinger Wolfram von Eschenbach. Green's aim was to provide readers with the authentic spirit of the times, a goal he achieved with laudable success. His extensive knowledge of myths and legends from around the world was an invaluable asset in compiling such books as *A Cavalcade of Dragons* (1970) and *A Cavalcade of Magicians* (1973). His selections were intelligent, wide-ranging, and often amusing. Green's introductions to his anthologies are models to be emulated. He addresses readers almost conspiratorially, setting both stage and mood by providing background information needed to embark on the adventures contained within.

Such is Green's literary legacy: He has bequeathed to young people the opportunity to experience unparalleled adventures, join in heroic deeds, follow challenging quests, trick fate, visit far-off lands, and share in the wondrous storytelling tapestry that has held humankind spellbound from the earliest edges of time. P.S.

Greenaway, Kate

ENGLISH ILLUSTRATOR AND AUTHOR, 1846–1901. Born Catherine Greenaway, Kate Greenaway became one of the most important and influential illustrators for children of the late nineteenth century, despite her shyness and avoidance of publicity. Indeed, a whole industry, which included china, fabrics, wallpaper, children's clothing, and dolls, grew up around her books, such as *Under the Window* (1879), *The Language of Flowers* (1884), and *A Day in a Child's Life* (1881). The fascination with the innocent childhood world she pictured continues to this day.

Illustration by Kate Greenaway for "A Romp" from *A Day in a Child's Life* (1881), with music by Myles B. Foster.

Greenaway's father, a wood engraver, had worked as an apprentice with Edmund Evans, the man who would have such an influence on children's book publishing in the late nineteenth century. Like Kate, John Greenaway was a gentle soul who loved children but who was not financially astute. When the family finances suffered, Kate's mother, Elizabeth, responded by opening a children's clothing shop stocked with designs she made and sewed herself. The loose-fitting, flowing garments she created were meant as an antidote to the tightly fitting fashions of the day, and Elizabeth's ideas about dress were reflected in the clothing Kate would make famous through her illustrations.

As a child, Kate loved to work beside her father, and in view of his profession in publishing and Kate's love for drawing, the family encouraged her to consider art as a career. At that time, with the periodicals market increasing, there was a need for trained engravers' assistants, and this was considered a suitable job for women. Kate began formal art training at the age of twelve and eventually studied at the Finsbury School, where artists were trained in such crafts as ceramics and textiles as well as in painting. While she attended school, she prepared for art exhibits, and her work began to be published in magazines. She came to be more widely known both in Britain and in America for her greeting card designs, in which her attention to detail of costume stemming from her work as a clothing designer and seamstress was highly valued. Eventually, John Greenaway introduced Kate to Edmund Evans, who by then had achieved success in color printing and was working with WALTER CRANE and RANDOLPH CALDECOTT. Evans was struck by Kate's sense of color and line as well as her detail of costume and setting, and he persuaded George Routledge to publish *Under the Window* in 1879. This was followed by many other books of rhymes, songs, and stories, which firmly established her reputation around the world.

Greenaway's children, with their heart-shaped faces, their large eyes, and their rather somber expressions, represented life in an idealized world where the countryside was always lovely, the weather fine, and the children clean and well fed. Her delicate lines and soft watercolor washes, her careful page design and layout, and her eye for every detail of costume and setting conveyed an almost mystical reverence for the world of children. Perhaps this was meant as an antidote to the gloomy and somber settings of the Gothic-revival period her books followed. More likely, however, the world she pictured was the world Kate remembered so lovingly from her own childhood. She frankly admitted that she didn't want to grow up and leave that happy time, and it was her artistic skill combined with her memory and imagination that appealed to her contemporaries as well as to the many generations since who have loved her books. ❧ B.K.

Greene, Bette

AMERICAN AUTHOR, B. 1934. A Southern writer known for the emotional intensity of her novels, Bette Greene was born in Memphis, Tennessee, but grew up in the small Arkansas town of Parkin, where her parents ran a country store. A Jewish child in a predominantly Protestant community, Greene always felt like an outcast. She began to write at an early age and earned her first byline in the local newspaper by the time she was nine years old. Although she attended several colleges, including Columbia, Harvard, and the University of Alabama, she never received a degree. She was employed as a newspaper reporter and an information officer for the American Red Cross, and she worked in a psychiatric hospital. After her marriage, she settled in Massachusetts with her neurologist husband, raised two children, and wrote *Summer of My German Soldier* (1973).

Greene's stunning first novel was rejected by eighteen publishers before finding its way into print. This World War II story concerns twelve-year-old Patty Bergen, a Jewish girl in Arkansas who helps hide a German prisoner after he escapes from a nearby POW camp. Patty pays dearly for her actions, but through her friendship with the escaped soldier and a supportive housekeeper, the lonely girl ultimately gains a sense of self-worth. The characterizations of Patty and her abusive family are painfully real, and the writing is so intense that most readers assume the novel is autobiographical. Greene is cagey about specifics but admits there is an autobiographical component to the story. Certainly, Patty's feelings of isolation and low self-esteem mirror the author's published comments about her own outsider status in Parkin. Several years after publication, *Summer of My German Soldier* was made into an Emmy Award–winning television movie.

Greene later wrote a sequel, *Morning Is a Long Time Coming* (1978), which follows Patty to Europe after her high school graduation. Greene again drew on personal experiences in writing this novel. Although it doesn't have the focus or intensity of Greene's first book, *Morning Is a Long Time Coming* is of great interest to readers of the first novel, who wonder what happens to Patty. Greene also wrote the Newbery Honor Book *Philip Hall Likes Me, I Reckon Maybe* (1974) and its companion volume, *Get On Out of Here, Philip Hall!* (1981). Both books concern Beth Lambert, a plucky and intelligent African American girl growing up in rural Arkansas, having boy problems, and learning about life. These charming and popular books are a surprising departure from the author's other work.

Them That Glitter and Them That Don't (1981) is notable for its characterizations of a teenage girl and her mother in the modern-day South. A story about homophobia in a small Southern town, *The Drowning of Stephan Jones* (1991) is a commendable effort, but this overwritten, wildly emotional novel fails on many counts. The omniscient narrative, with its self-referential comments about *Summer of My German Soldier*, distances the reader. Greene's greatest successes have been first-person stories in which emotional content is equally strong but much more controlled. ❧ P.D.S.

Greene, Constance C.

AMERICAN AUTHOR, B. 1924. Constance C. Greene is a popular author of MIDDLE-GRADE FICTION and YOUNG ADULT NOVELS, noted for her contemporary, breezy writing style. The author was born in Manhattan but grew up in Brooklyn. Both of her parents had written for the *New York Daily News*, and her mother published magazine articles and short stories while Greene was growing up. Not surprisingly, she became interested in writing at a very young age. An apathetic student, Greene took advantage of the World War II worker shortage to leave Skidmore College and find employment with the Associated Press, beginning in the mailroom and eventually working as a reporter. The postwar years were filled with the responsibilities of raising a large family; it was not until her youngest child entered kindergarten that Greene joined a writer's workshop and attempted her first book.

A Girl Called Al (1969) concerns a seventh-grade nonconformist who lives with her divorced mother in a New York City apartment. Narrated by Al's nameless best friend, the episodic story depicts the developing friendship between the two girls. The first in a series of novels that includes *I Know You, Al* (1975), *Just Plain Al* (1986), and *Al's Blind Date* (1989), the book has witty dialogue, salient characterizations, and an urban tone. The series touches on everyday situations, school problems, romances, and social concerns such as divorce and the problems of the elderly. Although Greene is quite adept at creating short, tightly written scenes, her overall plots are usually shapeless, and include extraneous episodes that develop characterization but fail to move the story forward. A second series of books, beginning with *Isabelle the Itch* (1973) and followed by *Isabelle Shows Her Stuff* (1984) and *Isabelle and Little Orphan Frannie* (1988), concerns a mischievous ten-year-old. Isabelle is an overactive, occasionally irritating character, but the stories are amusing for many young readers.

Greene often uses her gift for humorous dialogue and characterizations to deal with more serious issues. Beneath the glib, funny conversations of the two sisters in *Nora: Maybe a Ghost Story* (1993) is the aching grief they feel over the loss of their deceased mother. The author's best-known work, *Beat the Turtle Drum* (1976), also contains many humorous moments, as thirteen-year-old Kate relates how her younger sister, Joss, rents a horse for her eleventh birthday. The story turns into a tragedy when Joss falls from a tree and dies. The novel is disturbing yet realistic in its portrait of a young girl haunted by nightmares and imaginary playmates, its presentation of a family's grief, and its striking, unresolved conclusion. An adaptation, "Very Good Friends," was broadcast on television in 1976.

Greene has written one novel for adults, *Other Plans* (1985), as well as fiction for young adults. *The Love Letters of J. Timothy Owen* (1986) provides a refreshing portrayal of a lovestruck adolescent male. *Monday I Love You* (1988), the story of a fifteen-year-old girl who considers herself unattractive, contains some wrenching scenes of teenage cruelty but is flawed by an unlikely subplot involving an escaped criminal. Greene's forays into young adult writing are interesting, but she remains best known for her middle-grade books. Although often short on plot, they are witty, fast-paced, and modern. § P.D.S.

Greenfield, Eloise

AMERICAN POET AND WRITER, B. 1929. Eloise Greenfield has contributed significantly to the body of African American children's literature since the early 1970s. Her work includes numerous award-winning picture books, biographies, fiction, and poetry. Greenfield integrates a strong commitment to the minority experience with an impassioned love of words to create a wide range of fiction and nonfiction.

During the 1970s, while she was involved in the D.C. Black Writers' Workshop, Greenfield discovered the paucity of quality biographies about black historical figures. In response, she wrote three easy-to-read biographies: *Rosa Parks* (1973), *Paul Robeson* (1975), and *Mary McLeod Bethune* (1977). Greenfield said, "I want to give children a true knowledge of black heritage, including both the African and the American experiences." Greenfield pays further tribute to her cultural heritage with her collaborative autobiographical book, *Childtimes: A Three-Generation Memoir* (1971), in which she and her mother, Lessie Jones Little, combine their own reminiscences with material from the memoirs of Greenfield's grandmother, Pattie Ridley Jones. The three resulting first-person narratives include vignettes and anecdotes that reflect everyday family life from post–Civil War North Carolina to mid-twentieth-century urban Washington, D.C.

Greenfield's fiction addresses realistic childhood issues such as loneliness, anger, evolving independence, financial pressures, divorce, and death. Her characters rely on family support, and Greenfield often focuses on intergenerational companionship and guidance. She writes, "I want to present to children alternative methods for coping with the negative aspects of their lives and to inspire them to seek new ways of solving problems." Janell, an only child in Greenfield's picture book *Me and Neesie* (1975), plays with a mischievous imaginary friend until she begins school and makes "real" friends. In *Talk about a Family* (1978), an intermediate-level novel, Genny believes her older brother will reconcile her parents' disintegrating marriage when he returns from the army. Greenfield's poetry, however, remains her strongest contribution to children's literature. She brilliantly combines rhythm and free verse in *Nathaniel Talking*, winner of the 1990 Coretta Scott King Award, and *Night on Neighborhood Street* (1991), two volumes that contain her affectionate, realistic poems. Illustrator Jan Spivey Gilchrist's expressive pictures complement Greenfield's poetic view of the contemporary African American experience. When read aloud, her lyrical words almost dance, each stanza expressing a powerful sense of setting and character. Through her poignant images of family, friends, and neighborhood, Greenfield reveals a child's emotional reality without sentiment or nostalgia. Eloise Greenfield writes, "I want to be one of those who can choose and order words that children will want to celebrate. I want to make them shout and laugh and blink back tears and care about themselves." § S.M.G.

Greenwald, Sheila

American author and illustrator, b. 1934. "I started drawing too far back to remember and I did it all the time, as a habit, as a way to amuse myself," explains the author and illustrator of the "Rosy Cole" stories and other books for children. Born and raised in New York, Greenwald attended Sarah Lawrence College, where she majored in English. Though she enjoyed a creative writing course, she did not feel she had much to write about and drew doodles in the margins of her notebooks. The doodles were eventually gathered into a portfolio and presented to magazine and book editors. For fourteen years Greenwald created art for magazine articles and dozens of books. Though her focus was children's books, her art was also featured in a few cookbooks and humor anthologies.

When her two sons, Samuel and Benjamin, began school, Greenwald began to write for children. "It was exhilarating to both write and illustrate," she has said. "By then there were plenty of things to write about." Greenwald's protagonists are eminently real people who grapple with believable obstacles in their lives. In *Give Us a Great Big Smile, Rosy Cole* (1981), the humorous heroine must prove that she is not a violin prodigy. The unfolding of Rosy's story is entertaining, but it also gently touches on the experience of having to cope with expectations that can't be met.

In *Will the Real Gertrude Hollings Please Stand Up* (1983), Greenwald explores the perspective of a "learning disabled" youngster who must battle comparisons between herself and her perfect cousin. Gertrude's wry observations of life and her astute assessment of her cousin provide a subtle message about measuring success and self-worth. Rosy and Gertrude share with most of Greenwald's characters a vulnerable side that is sometimes disguised under layers of snappy comebacks and bold, elaborate schemes to get out of the muddles that befall them.

Most of Greenwald's writing is aimed at a middle school audience. The popularity of Rosy Cole has led to a series of books, including *Rosy Cole Discovers America!* (1992), that center around Rosy, a consistently imaginative and resourceful type, who has a difficult time avoiding trouble. In one book, for example, Rosy starts a club to persuade her more affluent classmates to "donate" their belongings to the less fortunate in school, who include Rosy herself.

Greenwald's illustrations are loosely drawn black-and-white sketches that capture in a few strokes her characters' essence with a quiet quality that fits in well with her novels' subtle nature. ❧ C.L.L.

Grimm, Jacob Ludwig Carl
Grimm, Wilhelm Carl

Jacob: German author, 1785–1863; Wilhelm: German author, 1786–1859. The brothers Jacob and Wilhelm Grimm, German scholars, philologists, collectors, and editors, are best remembered for *Kinder- und Hausmärchen,* translated under the titles *Nursery and Household Tales* or *German Popular Stories* and commonly known in English as *Grimm's Fairy Tales.* Originally, these stories were not published for children; the Grimms began collecting them as part of a scholarly study on the history of the German language and oral traditions. The first volume (1812) was not illustrated and included numerous scholarly notes; in the six editions that followed, tales were added and revised. Not until the Grimms saw the first English translation (1823), with its famous illustrations by George Cruikshank, did they design an edition for younger readers. Their second volume (1814) represents a collection of over two hundred stories and legends. In these editions are such favorites as "The Frog Prince," "Hansel and Gretel," "Rapunzel," "The Musicians of Bremen," "Snow White and the Seven Dwarfs," "Rumpelstilskin," and "The Twelve Dancing Princesses." The publication of *Kinder- und Hausmärchen* caused no particular stir in literary circles. In fact, several critics labeled the stories boorish and declared them an insignificant pursuit for serious scholars. In spite of such criticism, the tales were enthusiastically received in Germany and abroad.

A unique relationship existed between the Brothers Grimm, who remained remarkably close throughout their lives. Although their personal temperaments and intellectual pursuits differed, they worked together their entire lives, collecting stories for their book of fairy tales. Born near Frankfurt, they attended the same gymnasium and university, and both taught at Göttingen University. Jacob studied language, but Wilhelm was more interested in collecting folktales. Sources for these tales were often close to home. Wilhelm's wife and sisters were fluent storytellers; "Hansel and Gretel" was among the stories they contributed. A family nurse recounted the tale of "Little Red-Cap," a version of "Little Red Riding-Hood," and "Little Briar-Rose," an analogue of "The Sleeping Beauty." Wilhelm's research included letters to friends asking about folktales, songs, and legends in the oral tradition. The Grimms' tales have all the elements of popular literature: The characters are universally appealing, and plots are recounted with spellbinding quality. The children in the stories, though often dispossessed, fend for themselves and eventually find love and happiness. In these stories, foolhardy souls and humbled heroes accomplish impossible tasks while retaining—or regaining—humility, moral standards, and tenderness. A unique combination of fantasy and reality, the stories have stood the tests of taste and time; not only do they entertain, but they activate imagination, offer solutions to problems, promote confidence, and generally enrich their readers' lives.

Numerous versions of the fairy tales exist, but several are exceptional. *The Juniper Tree and Other Tales from Grimm* (1973), edited by LORE SEGAL and translated by Segal and RANDALL JARRELL, is illustrated with some of MAURICE SENDAK's finest work. European and American artists have illustrated individual stories: NANCY EKHOLM BURKERT's *Snow White and the Seven Dwarfs* (1972) and Gennady Spirin's *Snow White and Rose Red* (1992) are mesmerizing in mood, meticulous in detail, and vibrant in color. ❧ S.L.

GRIPE, MARIA

SWEDISH AUTHOR, B. 1923. When Maria Gripe was young, she handed her father a piece of her writing. She was proud and trembling with nervousness. He looked down on her from his six-foot-seven height and said sadly, "My dear, this is terrible. In order to write you need to (a) have something to write about and (b) know how to write; while waiting for (a) learn (b)." This judgment successfully stopped young Maria from writing until her daughter, Camilla, was born. Then the life that her father determined not substantial enough to write about became the source material for her twenty or more novels for children.

It is Gripe's very clear connection to her own childhood that gives her work such a convincing voice. *The Night Daddy* (1968, trans. 1971) and *Julia's House* (1971, trans. 1975) tell of an unusual relationship between a young writer and the young girl, Julia, for whom he is hired to baby-sit every night. Julia's mother is a nurse, on the night shift, and markedly absent from these books, which are, after all, a celebration of this new friendship. The two main characters write alternating chapters, making observations about the experiences they share as they get to know each other. The "night daddy," as Julia calls him, becomes a very real substitute for the father she doesn't have, and she is determined to convince the girls at school that he is not a figment of her imagination.

Elvis, a solitary little boy who appears outside Julia's window in *Julia's House*, has his own two books. Reviewers felt these were too difficult for children, who would not be interested in the observations of an unusual and precocious six-year-old. A more successful series is her earlier *Josephine* (1961, trans. 1970), *Hugo and Josephine* (1962, trans. 1969), and *Hugo* (1966, trans. 1970). In these books, Gripe captures a wild and stubborn little girl who looks deceptively like an angel and Hugo, the child of the woods who finds more to learn in watching water spiders for three weeks than in attending school. These three little books are satisfyingly similar to BEVERLY CLEARY's "Ramona" books. Even though Gripe's sharp criticisms of adults are filtered a little pedantically through a child's voice, the stories with their trials and delights ring true.

Some of Gripe's other books turn a sharp corner into the genre of fantasy, the most remarkable of these being *The Glassblower's Children* (1964, trans. 1974). Clearly influenced by HANS CHRISTIAN ANDERSEN—who was, according to Gripe's father, the only "person worthy of being called an author"—this book is particularly reminiscent of "The Snow Queen." Two children are spirited away from the marketplace and taken over by his Lordship. Gradually, they lose their identities and even their reflections in the mirror, becoming like puppets. It is only the love of their parents that saves them. *Agnes Cecilia* (1981, trans. 1990) joins the two sides of Gripe's writing, as she explores the mind of a lonely sixteen-year-old who is haunted by the ghost of an ancestor. The mystery is too loose to be very suspenseful, but, as always, Gripe is a master at seeing her character's point of view. In this book Gripe has given the adults more complex and compelling personalities. In 1974 she received the Hans Christian Andersen Medal for her body of work. With just her books that are available in translation, there is enough Gripe to keep children delighted from an early read-aloud age through their own teen years. ❧ J.A.J.

GUY, ROSA

AMERICAN AUTHOR, B. 1928. Rosa Cuthbert Guy—whose name rhymes with *me*—is best known for her stories of young people growing up in the inner city and struggling against great adversity for their very survival. The beautifully delineated characters in her best-known books are African Americans and West-Indian Americans. Rosa Guy draws directly on her own past for the settings she describes. She was born in Trinidad and was brought to New York City at the age of seven. Her mother died in 1934, and her father in 1937. As a child, she felt that she was an outsider, and she once wrote that the whole experience of "always being on the outside looking in" formed her perspective. Other important influences on Guy's work are her interests in theater, in politics, and in the Harlem community where she grew up. After attending New York University, she studied with the American Negro Theatre. She was cofounder of the Harlem Writers Guild, which she served as president from 1967 to 1978. Guy is the author of a one-act play, *Venetian Blinds*, which was produced by the American Negro Theatre in 1954. Her first novel, *Bird at My Window*, written for adults, was published in 1966. Her next work was an anthology of writing by black writers, called *Children of Longing* (1970).

The Friends (1973) was Guy's next novel. The theme of developing and nourishing a friendship is crucial to the novel. The first in a trilogy, it told the story of teenage sisters who travel from the West Indies to join their parents in Harlem. Phyllisia, the younger sister, is an outcast at school, taunted for her accent. One classmate, Edith Jackson, does offer her friendship, which Phyllisia accepts reluctantly because of Edith's bedraggled appearance. Edith is orphaned and desperately struggles against poverty and sickness to keep her and her sisters together. Phyllisia's mother is dying of cancer, and in a painful episode her father goes into a rage when Edith visits, because she is so obviously a street person. The sequel, *Ruby* (1976), follows the experiences of Phyllisia and her sister, Ruby, as they are raised by their father after their mother's death. Phyllisia escapes the stress created by their strict, overbearing father through reading, while her eighteen-year-old sister begins a lesbian love affair with a classmate. The last book in the trilogy, *Edith Jackson* (1978), follows Edith's fate as she and her three younger sisters go to live with a foster mother in upstate New York. The arrangement is a resounding failure; the children are scattered as the older girls become involved with men and the two youngest girls are adopted. The American Library Association named each book in the trilogy a Best Book of the Year.

A second trilogy for young adult readers followed; it begins with *The Disappearance* (1979) and has as its protagonist a sixteen-year-old Brooklyn boy who is on probation for a crime, but who has hopes for the future and works to move beyond mere survival to succeed. *New Guys around the Block* (1983) and *A Measure of Time* (1983) completed the trilogy. Among Guy's other books are a picture-book text translated and adapted from Birago Diop's *Mother Crocodile—Maman-Caiman* (1981), which won a Coretta Scott King Award in 1982 for JOHN STEPTOE's illustrations. She also has written for younger readers; in *Paris, Pee Wee, and Big Dog* (1985) she continues her theme of a child's life in the inner city by following the experiences of a nine-year-old boy who must learn to avoid the influence of a reckless boy who endangers his safety. Guy's loving attention to dialect and language is not surprising, as her dedication to them has led her to travel to Africa, Haiti, and Trinidad to study "the ways, customs, and languages retained over the years from Africa." She speaks French and Creole and does research in African languages for relaxation. § S.H.H.

H

Hader, Berta
Hader, Elmer

Berta: American author and illustrator, 1890–1976; Elmer: American author and illustrator, 1889–1973. Although each of the Haders had independent artistic careers, following their 1919 marriage they worked together in the production of their books. Elmer Hader grew up in San Francisco, where he studied at the Institute of Art. He later was a student at the Académie Julien in Paris, where he absorbed the techniques of the French impressionist and postimpressionist artists of the era. When he returned to San Francisco in 1914, he devoted himself to easel painting. His exhibitions of San Francisco scenes won both praise and criticism for their cubist style and their subject matter, realistic portrayals of the humble surroundings of the city's immigrants and working classes. Following service in World War I, Hader married Berta Hoerner. Her childhood interest in art and writing led her to study journalism at the University of Washington. Later, she

Illustration by Berta and Elmer Hader from their book *The Big Snow* (1948).

chose to focus on art as a career. Berta Hoerner's earliest work included fashion art and the painting of miniature portraits.

After their marriage, the Haders began the collaboration that characterized their career as creators of children's books. Initially, they produced artwork for special children's sections in magazines such as *McCalls, Good Housekeeping,* and the *Christian Science Monitor.* They did a series of drawings illustrating MOTHER GOOSE rhymes, which led to seven small PICTURE BOOKS called, collectively, "The Happy Hours." The Haders' art started appearing regularly in books by other authors, and, starting in 1928, the couple wrote as well as illustrated their own works. In their collaboration on over one hundred books, the Haders maintained a certain secrecy regarding the actual division of duties in development of the text, watercolor paintings, and their trademark soft charcoal illustrations. They did admit to mutual contribution to all matters of their books' creation and constant testing of each other's ideas. Some of their production secrets were shared in a promotional booklet produced for the Macmillan Company entitled *Working Together: The Inside Story of the Hader Books* (1937).

The building of the Haders' studio-home in a rural setting near Nyack, New York, suggested the subject of *The Little Stone House: A Story of Building a House in the Country* (1944). The Haders' shared interests in nature, the environment, and animal life is evident in such titles as *Lions and Tigers and Elephants Too* (1930), *Under the Pig-Nut Tree* (1930), *Spunky* (1933), *Cricket: The Story of a Little Circus Pony* (1938), *The Cat and the Kitten* (1940), *The Runaways: A Tale of the Woodlands* (1956), and *Quack Quack: The Story of a Little Wild Duck* (1961). Heavy snowfall in 1947 suggested the Haders' story of animal survival during the winter months in *The Big Snow* (1948). The book featured both Haders as characters, and in 1949 it was awarded the Caldecott Medal.

Throughout their prolific career, the Haders demonstrated the value and rewards of collaborative labor in the making of children's books. ❧ W.A.

HAGUE, MICHAEL

AMERICAN ILLUSTRATOR, B. 1948. Influenced by turn-of-the-century illustrators ARTHUR RACKHAM, N. C. WYETH, and HOWARD PYLE as well as by DISNEY comic books, Michael Hague has created his own distinctive illustrations of many classic works of children's literature. Among his titles are *Mother Goose: A Collection of Classic Nursery Rhymes* (1984), *Peter Pan* (1987), and *The Fairy Tales of Oscar Wilde* (1993).

Hague was born in Los Angeles and showed an early talent for drawing, encouraged by his mother, who had attended art school in England. Hague remembers making illustrations for his favorite King Arthur books and doing portraits of his favorite baseball players. Baseball was a serious interest of Hague's all through high school, but he returned to his early interest in art when he entered college. Both Hague and his wife, Kathleen, graduated from the Los Angeles Art Center College of Design and were married while they were students. After graduation, Hague worked for Hallmark Cards in Kansas City, and then for Current, Inc., in Colorado Springs, where he still lives.

While illustrating cards and calendars, he was invited to illustrate JANE YOLEN's *Dream Weaver* (1979), a book chosen for the American Institute of Graphic Arts Book Show. Five books illustrated by Hague were published in 1980, including *The Wind in the Willows* by KENNETH GRAHAME, and it was this book that earned Hague widespread attention. It is always intimidating to tackle the reillustration of a revered classic, but Hague felt a particularly strong bond with this riverbank tale of four animal friends. As Hague said, he did not intend to create a new look, but wanted to "infuse [his] illustrations with the same spirit that Kenneth Grahame's magic words convey." He succeeds admirably and with fond detail defines the personality of each character. The opening illustration captures the hubris of Mr. Toad as he stands in the splendor of his drawing room surrounded by likenesses of himself. The busy industry of Mole at work with his bucket of whitewash, the sumptuous bounty of Ratty's picnic repast, and the cozy security of Badger's warm and well-supplied home in the Wild Wood—all of these scenes prepare the reader to enjoy this classic tale of friendship and adventure.

Hague went on to illustrate *Michael Hague's Favorite Hans Christian Andersen Fairy Tales* (1981), L. FRANK BAUM's *The Wizard of Oz* (1982), and Nancy Luenn's *The Dragon Kite* (1982). With Kathleen he published *The Man Who Kept House* (1981) and *Alphabears: An ABC Book* (1984).

Hague is particularly adept at creating believable worlds for his characters to inhabit, from the very English setting of *The Wind in the Willows* to the fantasy world of J. R. R. TOLKIEN's *The Hobbit* (1984). The terrifying red dragon, the gigantic poisonous spiders, the spooky Mirkwood—all are rendered darkly ominous.

More comfortable than challenging, Hague's most successful illustrations are found in his versions of the well-loved classics of children's literature. ❧ P.H.

Haley, Gail E.

American author and illustrator, b. 1939. Gail Haley, born in Charlotte, North Carolina, and raised nearby in a small, rural town, remembers a childhood in which "fantasy and reality were interchangeable." She roamed the woods and fields near her home, developing a kinship with the woodland inhabitants that later found its way into her books for children. Haley attended the Richmond Professional Institute and the University of Virginia and has lived and traveled in many countries, fueling her innate curiosity about different cultures. Widely praised for her ability to combine the rich traditions of storytelling with diverse, innovative artwork, Haley's books present fresh versions of well-known as well as unfamiliar provincial folktales.

Haley spent a year living in the Caribbean, where the rich cultural tradition of the islands inspired her Caldecott Award book, *A Story, a Story* (1970), a retelling of a "spider story" from African legend in which a seemingly defenseless creature outwits a powerful foe against insurmountable odds. In this version, Ananse, the "spider man," must capture a fearsome leopard, a wily fairy, and ferocious hornets so the Sky God will release the stories he hoards in his kingdom. Haley captures the lilting cadence of the African storyteller with characteristic repetition of words and phrases throughout the tale. Illustrated with colorful, intricate woodcuts of characters, figures, and symbols, *A Story, a Story* is a visual and auditory delight. It was also the first children's book to present a black God.

Go Away, Stay Away! (1977) is the spirited tale of winter imps who are specially designed for individual pranks. Kicklebucket, Bunshee, and the cleat-shod Hobble Goblins are among the spirits driven away by masked villagers in a festive parade. An afterword explains that this "spring cleaning of the soul" is common in Central European and Slavic countries and in different forms in other cultures. Haley's black-lined block prints of the villagers form a vivid contrast to the ethereal, white-lined imps.

In books that often offer a moral viewpoint, Haley expresses her belief in presenting truth *and* hope when telling stories for children. *Noah's Ark* (1971) offers an environmental cautionary tale of a modern-day Noah who fights against animals' extinction at the hands of humanity. An original antiquing technique renders luminous illustrations painted on wood, and double-page murals reinforce the immensity of Noah's task. *Birdsong* (1984) spins a tale of greed and deception as an old crone befriends a beautiful, talented orphan whose captivating music lures birds to the crone's lair for devious purposes. The lyrical text is perfectly complemented by vivid artwork that mimics medieval illuminated manuscripts. Colorful plumage is interwoven with the orphan's hair and clothing in intricately detailed brush strokes.

Haley's experimentation with varied illustrative techniques reaffirms her commitment to the tradition of storytelling as an art form in constant motion, with the ability to adapt to its audience. Advocates for the importance of childhood, Haley and her husband, David Considine, work to promote media and visual literacy in the American curriculum and maintain the Gail Haley Collection of the Culture of Childhood, which was established at Appalachian State University in Boone, North Carolina, in 1984. ❦ M.O'D.H.

Hall, Donald

American poet, author, and anthologist, b. 1928. Born in Connecticut, Hall began writing poetry at age fourteen in order "to be loved by women." His opinion of poetry was altered slightly over the years; now he hopes that his listeners, both male and female, will "take [the poem] into [their] ears and be moved by it."

Hall attended Harvard University, where he was editor of *The Harvard Advocate Anthology* (1950), and Oxford University, where he was awarded the Newdigate Prize for his poem "Exile" (1952). During the 1950s, Hall served as poetry editor of the *Paris Review*, editing numerous anthologies that highlighted the younger contemporary poets. He taught at the University of Michigan for almost twenty years before quitting in 1975 in order to devote his time to writing at his family's farm in New Hampshire. Hall made use of his early editing experience when he edited *The Oxford Book of Children's Verse in America* (1985). The anthology presents poetry in chronological order according to the birth date of the poet; the material ranges from indigenous tribal songs and didactic Puritan poems to the lighter verse of more current nursery rhymes. Hall's preface, a minihistory of American children's poetry, speaks of the long relationship children and poetry have had and explores even some earlier poems for which the texts have been lost. An underlying theme running through Hall's poetry and prose is the exploration and celebration of the continuity between generations. Living in the same house that his great-grandfather first occupied in 1865, Hall cannot help but be influenced by the memories that house inspired. *String Too Short to Be Saved: Childhood Reminiscences* (1961) is a collection of prose narratives inspired by Hall's childhood summers; *Kicking the*

Leaves (1978) is a collection of poems that reflects his feelings on returning to the farm.

The spirit of the farm and the land is best seen in *Ox-Cart Man* (1979), the illustrations for which earned BARBARA COONEY the Caldecott Medal. The book is based on a family tale: "I heard the story from my cousin, who had heard it when he was a boy from an old man, who told him that he had heard it when he was a boy, from an old man. I was thrilled with it, thinking of man's past life described in cyclical fashion." The story is deceptively simple. In October a farmer journeys from his home to Portsmouth Market, where he sells wool, potatoes, maple sugar, and his ox and cart and carries home a kettle, needle, knife, and two pounds of wintergreen peppermint candies to his hardworking family for use and pleasure during the winter. The cycle of this rural nineteenth-century New England family never changes; it is calm, methodical, and precise. We watch them spend their winter and spring preparing their goods to sell once more in the fall, and we are led to believe that this process will continue each year without change. By using the poetic devices of alliteration and repetition to draw in the reader, Hall's prose becomes poetry: "He packed a bag of wool / he sheared from the sheep in April. / He packed a shawl his wife wove on a loom / from yarn spun at the spinning wheel / from sheep sheared in April. / He packed five pairs of mittens / his daughter knit / from yarn spun at the spinning wheel / from sheep sheared in April." The dignity of the words is matched by the eloquence of Cooney's illustrations, which capture the seasonal landscapes—the lush fall foliage, the crisp, clean winter snow, the pink and white springtime blossoms—and the hustle and bustle of Portsmouth Market. *Ox-Cart Man*, like many of Hall's poems and stories, is characterized by a nostalgic yearning for lost values and a strong respect for the cyclic nature of life. ❧ M.I.A.

HALL, LYNN

AMERICAN AUTHOR, B. 1937. A prolific author with an unadorned writing style, Lynn Hall has published books for many different age groups. Youngsters who begin by reading Hall's primary-grade animal stories may grow up with her work, progressing to her middle-grade novels and ultimately to her strong young adult books. Lynn Hall was born in Chicago, but grew up in Des Moines, Iowa. Animals have always been the most important thing in Hall's life, and, as a child, she read as many dog and horse stories as she could find. An independent spirit, she dreamed of someday living on her own, with only animals for companionship. The day after high school graduation, Hall left home, and for the next several years lived in Colorado, Texas, Kentucky, and Wisconsin, working as a telephone operator and veterinarian's assistant, among other jobs.

Eventually Hall returned to Des Moines, where she one day passed a bookstore displaying copies of a children's book about horses. She immediately knew that writing animal stories for children would be the perfect career for her. At the time, Hall was raising chinchillas for profit; she sold the herd in order to afford six months of writing time. She read and studied dozens of animal books from the library and completed two manuscripts before the chinchilla money ran out. Shortly after that, her first animal story, *The Shy Ones* (1967), was accepted for publication. From that point on, Hall has produced children's books with amazing frequency. Two of her early works were challenging young adult books. *Too Near the Sun* (1970) was a historical novel about an Iowa religious community; *Sticks and Stones* (1972) was one of the first young adult novels to deal with the subject of homosexuality. But Hall's main emphasis was on the middle-grade animal story. Early books such as *A Horse Called Dragon* (1971) and *Riff, Remember* (1973) are notable for their realistic, unsentimental portrayal of animals. In addition, Hall has written many minor books for younger children—mostly mysteries with an animal theme. As the number of her books multiplied, the author began to experiment with a variety of genres. She has written a problem novel about child sexual abuse; a series of humorous books about young Zelda Hammersmith, including *In Trouble Again, Zelda Hammersmith?* (1987), *Zelda Strikes Again!* (1988), and *Here Comes Zelda Claus* (1989); a comic mystery for teens, *Murder in a Pig's Eye* (1990); and endless variations on the animal story.

From a critical perspective, Hall's greatest success has been in the field of young adult literature. *The Leaving* won the Boston Globe–Horn Book Award for fiction in 1981. This brief and sensitive novel explores family dynamics as Roxanne Armstrong leaves the family farm after graduation. More than most young adult authors, Hall shows the world beyond high school, and often writes about characters who have already graduated. One book, *Where Have All the Tigers Gone?* (1989), is even written from the viewpoint of a middle-aged woman looking back on her high school years. Two of her best young adult novels are *The Giver* (1985) and *The Solitary* (1986), perceptively drawn character studies that, like most of Hall's novels, feature small casts of characters and are written in the lean, plainspoken style that is her hallmark. ❧ P.D.S.

Hamilton, Virginia

American author, b. 1936. Born in Yellow Springs, Ohio, Virginia Hamilton studied at Antioch College, Ohio State University, and the New School for Social Research in New York. She and her husband, Arnold Adoff, poet and anthologist, have two children. Among the awards Ms. Hamilton has received are The Mystery Writers of America Edgar Allan Poe Award in 1969 for *The House of Dies Drear;* the National Book Award in 1975 for *M.C. Higgins, The Great,* which also won the Newbery Medal; the Regina Medal in 1990; and—in a ceremony in Germany in 1992—the Hans Christian Andersen Medal, given by the International Board on Books for Young People for the body of an author's or an illustrator's work.

Hamilton's first two books—*Zeely,* the story of a young black girl's crush on a tall, regal black woman, and *The House of Dies Drear*—were published in 1967 and 1968. *Zeely* was touching but not wholly convincing; but the author's second book gave evidence of increasing control of narrative and a remarkable handling of mood and setting. It is the story of an African American family's frightening experiences when they move into a house which, a century earlier, had been a station on the Underground Railroad. Different as they were, both of the first two books presaged Hamilton's later statement that "Time, place and family are at the heart of the fictions I create."

It was not until her third book, *The Time-Ago Tales of Jahdu* (1969), that the fluency and inventiveness of this author's style and the distinctive way in which she uses and—occasionally—invents words, became apparent. Here she uses as narrator a storyteller, Mama Luka, who tells a story each day to a young boy, Lee Edward. The stories came "from a fine good place called Harlem," and "she told them slow and she told them easy." "Woogily!" says the hero Jahdu. The book is an example of, and a tribute to, the power of folk literature, and it is a moving presentation of a folk hero who is a role model for a black child. The same lyric quality emanates from the sequels and from the new tales added to the older ones in a fourth volume, *The All Jahdu Storybook* (1991).

Although many of Virginia Hamilton's books have memorable characters and settings, few have had a greater impact than *The Planet of Junior Brown* (1971). It was one of the first books about homeless children, and there is a chiaroscuro quality about the contrast between the bleak reality of Buddy's protective nurturing of a group of younger boys and the almost-fantasy of the mock solar system he and another eighth-grader, Junior, create in the school basement. What has been created here is a family: Buddy says, "We are together because we have to learn to live for each other."

Equally trenchant, *M.C. Higgins, The Great* (1974) is as quintessentially rural as *Planet* is urban. Thirteen-year-old M.C. sits atop his forty-foot pole to survey the mountain his family owns, pondering the encroachment of detritus from strip-mining and worrying about whether his mother will leave the mountain. The vivid creation of setting and the establishment of mood are remarkable. Hamilton's style is both graceful and intricate, with nuances that may be appreciated by mature readers but that will not come between other readers and the story.

The eponymous protagonist of *Arilla Sun Down* (1976) is twelve, daughter of an African American mother and a father who has both black and Native American origins; overshadowed by a brilliant and articulate brother, Arilla is slow to gain confidence. She is the narrator and, in incorporating flashbacks to her early childhood, Arilla uses language in an odd way: "Can't seeing his face, brown shade." Hamilton is, however, so deft with words that the reader, once accustomed to the pattern and cadence of this device, hears its singing quality. The recurrent theme of strong family bonds appears also in *A Little Love* (1984), in which Sheema and her lover go hunting for the father she has never known and finds that it is her grandparents who sustain and comfort her. In this book, too, Hamilton uses dialect like poetry. It is a grandfather also in *Junius Over Far* (1985) who is the catalyst for family love; Grandfather has returned to the Caribbean island of his youth, and his confused letters worry his grandson Junius so much that the boy and his father go to the island to see what is happening. The story alternates between the boy's and the old man's viewpoints, and the writing, while deliberate in pace, is clear and is richly rewarding for its subtlety and warmth.

There is an impressive variety in other realistic stories, which range from the sober *Sweet Whispers, Brother Rush* (1982) to the lively and often humorous *Willie Bea and the Time the Martians Landed* (1983), an amused and affectionate look at the response of an extended African American family to the news, taken at frightened face value by so many in 1938, that the Orson Welles broadcast of disaster was genuine. Hamilton has written such diverse stories as *A White Romance* (1987), which deals with four people from broken homes and their participation in the drug culture, and *Drylongso* (1992), the taut story of a family whose drought-threatened crops are saved by an itinerant stranger. The family is even more the focus in *The Bells of Christmas* (1989), a warm, nostalgic look at the Christmas reunion of an

Voices of the Creators

Virginia Hamilton

I call myself a storyteller, and I work alone. I spend large amounts of time in my study, which has expansive glass areas or "lights" which allow me to look out on a hundred-year-old hedgerow (my west property line) and cornfields beyond. The row of twisted osage orange trees are bare and black against the cold blue Ohio sky. The land, the last part of my family's farm, has been in my family for generations. The fields have the corn stubble showing, washed in pale winter sunlight. Those same fields have not changed their size and produce in more than a century.

In my tiny bailiwick of an Ohio village, I, of course, have aged, but life for me here is as it's always been. I was born here; I have lived most of my life here. Everybody knows who I am, and they leave me alone to do my work. Within, I have not changed much. I am still my mother's youngest daughter, still Dad's Baby, which is what he called me for far too long. Time inside my study, however, passes, changing quickly. My working and book process has literally exploded, as has multiculturalism across the American hopescape.

Working alone has to do with insights and outsights and my process of writing. A writer must not only have insight—that is, awareness through intuition—but she must also have the ability to see and understand externals, what we call outsight. Readers, too, are part of this process. Without readers, adults and children, I feel I am blind-sided. Writing without an audience is thus inconceivable, since I write for readers to read and to have them know my process for making fiction and nonfiction. I believe deeply that I have something original to say.

My approach to creating narrative has to do with memories from my childhood which fit within a creative process. This is my way of solving problems of experience and memory. It is the way I retain some essence of my past, perhaps for future generations. My fiction and most of my nonfiction writing have some basis in reality of a large or small experience, although they are rarely autobiographical. For instance, the making of *Many Thousand Gone: African Americans from Slavery to Freedom* grew out of personal family history. The fact that my own grandfather was a fugitive from slavery gave me the impetus to research two centuries of slave narratives and recast thirty of them for the collection.

Storytelling is my way of sharing in community. It is the method my own parents used to define the boundaries of their living. My mother and father were fine storytellers; they drew me close by their stories. When I was a child, the story lady at the library read stories to us children as we sat around her on what came to mean to me a magic carpet. Somewhere along the way I realized that peoples use story as a means to keep their cultural heritage safe, to save the very language in which heritage is made symbolic through story.

I write my stories down, just as did those authors whose story books my story lady read to us. In *The People Could Fly,* there is the old story called "A Wolf and Little Daughter," a black variation on "Little Red Riding Hood." In my version these words are sung by Little Daughter: "Traybla, traybla, cum qua, kimo." The wolf asks his would-be victim to sing that "sweetest, goodest song again." To escape the wolf, Little Daughter sings again, and she is saved. In the plantation era, African words in stories almost always were meant to empower the teller while saving some aspect of the mother language. Thus, the sung words of Little Daughter are magic and have the power to *save* her—that is, to save the African heritage.

I see my books and the language I use in them as empowering me to give utterance to the dreams, the wishes, of African Americans. I see the imaginative use of language and ideas as a way to illuminate a human condition. All of my work, as a novelist, biographer, creator, and compiler of stories, has been to portray the essence of a people who are a parallel-culture society in America. I've attempted to mark the history and traditions of African Americans, a parallel culture people, through my writing, while bringing readers strong stories and memorable characters living nearly the best they know how. I want readers, both adults and children, to care about who the characters are. I want readers to feel, to understand, and to empathize. I want the books to make a world in which characters are real.

There is an essential agreement between us, the writer and reader. We are not without the other. Our bond is our common language, books, schools, teachers, students, libraries, children, reading and writing, and our experiences as Americans. Ours is a multicultural nation of the world village, where in community we enter into the bond of learning together.

extended family that gathers on an Ohio farm, and in *Cousins* (1990), an intricate and subtle exploration of family relationships that focuses on girl cousins who carry on the hostility that exists between their mothers.

As one might expect of so proficient a fiction writer, Hamilton adds a compelling narrative flow to the meticulous research she has done for her several biographies. In *W. E. B. Du Bois* (1972) Hamilton concentrates on DuBois's career as a writer, teacher, and activist, and shows clearly in this study, as she does in her work *Paul Robeson: The Life and Times of a Free Black Man* (1974), the importance of both figures in African American political and cultural history. *Anthony Burns: The Defeat and Triumph of a Fugitive Slave* (1988) is both fictional and factual, offering a trenchant depiction of slavery and of those who struggled to escape or abolish it.

Equally adept at writing realistic and fantastic fiction, Virginia Hamilton has been both originator and adapter of the latter. As she did with the Jahdu stories, she continued the auspicious start made in *Justice and Her Brothers* (1978) by adding *Dustland* (1980) and *The Gathering* (1981). It is a stunning science fiction trilogy in which four time travelers combine their psychic forces to defeat, in classic high fantasy tradition, the forces of evil. This is potent stuff: the improbable made credible, the dramatic seamlessly fused with the mystical. *The Magical Adventures of Pretty Pearl* (1983), an inventive blend of history, fantasy, and American and African folklore, posits the arrival of a young African god, Pretty Pearl, and her brother John de Conquer to the United States during the Reconstruction era—and when they cross the river into Ohio, they take the name of the author's ancestors, Perry.

Retelling or adapting folk material, Hamilton has produced three fine collections: *In the Beginning: Creation Stories from around the World* (1988); *The People Could Fly: American Black Folk Tales* (1985); and *The Dark Way: Stories from the Spirit World* (1990). All are impressive for their range of material and for the effectiveness with which they are told.

In her Andersen Award acceptance speech, Virginia Hamilton spoke of her desire to mark the history and traditions of African Americans; she has done this with integrity and distinction. She has given all children a gift for all time. ❧ ZENA SUTHERLAND

Handford, Martin

See Waldo Books.

Hardy Boys Series

The crime-fighting team of brothers, Frank and Joe Hardy, was first introduced to the public in three books: *The Tower Treasure, The House on the Hill,* and *The Secret of the Old Mill* (all published in 1927). Edward Stratemeyer, founder of the Stratemeyer Literary Syndicate, developed the Hardy Boys series after noting the popular success during the 1920s of adult detective fiction stories; he correctly assumed that boys' detective fiction would prove just as successful. Using Stratemeyer's outlines, Leslie McFarlane wrote the first eleven books under the pseudonym Franklin W. Dixon. After McFarlane left the syndicate in 1946, the books were ghostwritten by numerous other authors, including Stratemeyer's daughter, Harriet Stratemeyer Adams.

In their original incarnation, it was almost impossible to tell Frank and Joe apart—they were depicted as two sides of the same coin, an inseparable pair who never experienced sibling rivalry. When the syndicate revised the first thirty-eight books (between 1959 and 1972), the characters of Frank and Joe changed dramatically. Eighteen-year-old Frank is rational and careful; he weighs all the options before taking action. He is the high-tech Hardy, an electronics specialist. Seventeen-year-old Joe is impulsive and passionate, never pausing to consider consequences. He is the athletic Hardy, adept at everything from gymnastics to boxing, and he is constantly falling in love.

Plots were also revised to reflect changing times—jewel thieves and buried treasure were replaced by egomaniacal dictators, nerve gas, and evil disk jockeys. Violence is prevalent in the series—bombs are detonated, knives are wielded, punches are thrown. Except for rare occasions, however, neither Frank nor Joe carries or uses a weapon; strength for each is found in brotherhood, not bullets. An adventure with Frank and Joe is seen by some readers as a fantasy come true—days filled with intriguing mysteries and pulse-pounding excitement take precedence over the more mundane aspects of teenage life, such as attending school. Frank and Joe Hardy—stars of the most popular boys' series in juvenile publishing history—are all-American boys next door. Almost every boy wishes he could be a Hardy. ❧ M.I.A.

Harris, Joel Chandler

American author and journalist, 1848–1908. Best remembered for his Uncle Remus tales about Brer

Rabbit, Brer Fox, and other animals, Joel Chandler Harris was a prolific writer of folktales, short stories, novels, and essays. Although he is seldom read today, at the time of his death he was one of America's most popular authors.

Harris was born near Eatonton, Georgia, and was raised by his unmarried mother; his father had deserted the family shortly after his son's birth. Harris attributed his desire to become a writer to his mother's reading of Oliver Goldsmith's *Vicar of Wakefield* to him as a young child. Although Harris was small and extremely shy, a trait he never outgrew, he was admired by his friends for his practical jokes. He left school at age thirteen to become an apprentice at a weekly newspaper, where he learned the printer's trade and editing skills and had a number of his own short pieces published. Harris lived at the Turnwold Plantation, where the newspaper was published, and his employer urged him to use his well-stocked library. Harris consequently read everything from Chaucer to Shakespeare to Dickens. In addition, he spent many of his free evenings listening to the slaves tell stories.

After the Civil War, the newspaper folded. Harris worked for a number of other papers, eventually ending up at the *Constitution* in Atlanta. It was here, in 1876, that Harris invented Uncle Remus, initially as a rural "philosopher." Later, he refined him into a storyteller. He published Uncle Remus pieces regularly in the *Constitution,* and they were extremely popular. In 1880 he collected them into his first book, *Uncle Remus: His Songs and His Sayings.* Eventually, seven more Uncle Remus volumes followed, and from 1907 to 1908 Harris edited the *Uncle Remus Magazine,* cofounded with his son Julian. Harris also wrote six other books for children as well as material for adults, although the Uncle Remus tales were by far the most popular.

Uncle Remus tells a young boy folk stories about Brer Rabbit and his friends. Brer Rabbit is a traditional trickster character, who usually outsmarts bigger and stronger animals such as Brer Fox, Brer Wolf, and Brer Bear, and the tales show a remarkable similarity to other trickster stories from around the world. Although Harris created Uncle Remus as a composite of three elderly slaves he had known, the stories themselves were his retellings of old African American tales. He rigorously researched his material, often collecting several versions of the same story until he felt he had the most authentic one. Realizing that the language of the African Americans who told the stories was an important ingredient in their flavor, Harris wrote in the dialect that was prevalent among former slaves in Middle Georgia.

Harris was considered progressive in the late nineteenth century, but, by today's standards, his use of dialect makes these stories extremely difficult to read and demeaning to African Americans. Furthermore, the stories Harris had heard originally were never meant to be told for the benefit of a white child; rather they were an integral part of the slave culture out of which they grew. Nevertheless, Harris made an important contribution by carefully and accurately preserving these stories. Recently, modern authors have taken his material and, by eliminating the character of Uncle Remus and using a modified form of black English, created wonderful books about Brer Rabbit. ❧ P.R.

Harrison, Ted

Canadian illustrator and author, b. 1926. For Ted Harrison, the term "Great White North" is clearly a misnomer. The British-born artist, who relocated to Canada's Yukon, has gained international fame portraying *his* North—a world of pink ice, purple trees, blue dogs, and orange rivers. Like a modern-day Gauguin, Harrison searched for and found his paradise, which he has translated for the world in a way that is uniquely his.

Harrison was born in the mining village of Wingate, County Durham, England. He received a classical art education at Hartlepool College of Art in Britain. After working and traveling around the world, Harrison, his wife, Nicky, and their son, Charles, settled in the Yukon in the late 1960s.

Having found his Shangri-la, Harrison now attempted to paint it. He has written, "I set up the easel and prepared to paint the vast panorama before me. The result was total defeat." The academically trained Harrison was forced to develop a whole new artistic vocabulary to capture the vast northern landscape. His response was to create a surrealistic representation of his surroundings in which he isolated color and form with a stark black line.

Harrison's interpretation of his northern surroundings was a smashing success; he has established a significant career as a fine artist with his Yukon work (his paintings have been purchased by *Reader's Digest,* Canadian Airlines, and Canadian Liberal politician Jean Chrétien, among many others). It is through his picture books, however, that his art has reached its widest audience. These include *Children of the Yukon* (1977), *A Northern Alphabet* (1982), and *The Blue Raven* (1989).

It was the successful marriage of Harrison's art to the famous verse of Robert W. Service that gained his books widespread international attention. Harrison's interpretation of Service's famous 1907 "gold rush" poem, *The Cremation of Sam McGee* (1986), was an American Library Association Notable Book and a New York Times Best Book selection. This was followed by the equally well received *Shooting of Dan McGrew* (1987). Both books are eagerly purchased by grandparents and parents alike, perhaps more for themselves than for the children in their lives.

In 1992, in honor of Canada's one hundred and twenty-fifth birthday, Harrison produced a tribute to his adopted country. Designed in a format similar to the Service books, *O Canada!* reproduces Canada's national anthem along with Harrison's artistic interpretations of every province and territory as viewed through his remarkable artistic filter. This book was short-listed for the Canadian Elizabeth Mrazik-Cleaver Picture Book Award.

What is it about Harrison's work that captivates readers of all ages? Perhaps it is that the viewer's surprise at the artist's palette is followed by a flash of recognition—for Harrison's unique mix incorporates many elements of the familiar. His work has been said to be reminiscent of stained-glass windows. Others have compared him to Matisse. And there appear to be elements of pop art in some of his illustrations.

By reinventing himself as an artist when he moved to Canada, Harrison has reinvented that country for the rest of the world. Refreshing in its audacity, reassuring in its subtle use of precedents, Harrison's picture-book art is a force to be reckoned with *and* enjoyed. M.B.

Haskins, Jim

American author of informational books, b. 1941. With 110 titles for adults and children to his credit, Jim Haskins is one of the most prolific authors of nonfiction in America. A professor of English at the University of Florida in Gainesville since 1977, he also resides in New York City. As a youngster in the segregated town of Demopolis, Alabama, he was not permitted to use the public library, but his mother's volume-a-week purchase of an encyclopedia from the local supermarket fed his intellectual curiosity. By age fourteen he had read the entire set.

Encouraged by his elementary school teachers, Haskins kept a diary. From this ongoing habit came his first book, *Diary of a Harlem Schoolteacher* (1969), based on his experiences as a special education teacher in a New York City public school. Inquiries from various publishers as well as his desire to encourage reading led him to consider writing for young people. Concentrating primarily on the African American experience, the author explores a wide range of topics. Haskins describes himself as "eclectic," and the accuracy of this appellation is clear in the diversity of his subjects and personal interests. As a music lover and trumpeter, he enjoys listening to jazz and the classics, and several of his titles are devoted to musical themes. He has written factual accounts on topics and events as varied as religion, politics, Vietnam, dance, gangs, sports, the Underground Railroad, and the occult. *India under Indira and Rajiv Gandhi* (1989) is an example of his interest in other cultures. This concern is also revealed in his "Count Your Way" series.

It is difficult for Haskins to single out an author he admires most, but he does recall how much he was influenced by the structure and clear graphic style of William Shirer's *Rise and Fall of the Third Reich* (1960), as well as by the works in his vast library on black history and culture. Often selecting persons whose lives have been neglected in books he portrays the struggles and major contributions of talented people, such as James Van Der Zee, Harlem photographer; Guion Bluford, astronaut; Corazon Aquino, former president of the Philippines; and Katherine Dunham, choreographer. Haskins has won many awards, including the Coretta Scott King Award twice, in 1976 for *The Story of Stevie Wonder* (1976) and in 1991 for *Black Dance in America* (1990). *Scott Joplin: The Man Who Made Ragtime* (1978), which he coauthored with Kathleen Benson, won the ASCAP Deems Taylor Award in 1980. His works have received citations from such institutions as the American Library Association, Child Study Association, and National Council for Social Studies. *The Cotton Club* (1977), a book for adults about the heyday of Harlem nightlife, inspired Francis Ford Coppola's motion picture of the same name. This multifaceted writer, teacher, and lecturer clearly explores the African American experience with enthusiasm. L.F.A.

Haugaard, Erik Christian

Danish author, b. 1923. The publication of *Hakon of Rogen's Saga* (1963), a powerful, epiclike tale set in Viking times, immediately established Erik Haugaard's reputation as an author who could command the respect of critics and readers alike. The book was Haugaard's first critical success, but each subsequent novel, all written in English, has also garnered widespread praise and recognition. Haugaard has received many prestigious awards, including the Boston Globe–Horn Book Award and the Jane Addams Children's Book Award for *The Little Fishes* (1967), the moving account of twelve-year-old Guido's harrowing experiences trying to survive in Nazi-occupied Naples. Haugaard has proved himself a master storyteller capable of recounting an affecting tale whatever the setting. The action may take place in ancient Israel, as in *A Rider and His Horse* (1968), a story based on the writings of Josephus in which a youthful David grapples with adult issues that culminate in the battle at Masada; or in sixteenth-century Japan, the setting for *A Samurai's Tale,* which relates Taro's adventures as he rises, against all odds, from kitchen help to warrior. Haugaard's assiduously researched background information firmly anchors each adventure in its proper time and place.

Although the stories may be set in widely differing periods and locales, they share a common theme: a world in which, despite unrelenting adversity, it is nonetheless possible to make moral choices. His books often focus on the horrors and pointlessness of war and the powerlessness of its victims. But Haugaard provides his protagonists with the opportunity to make decisions that may not change the world but will at least make a difference in their personal lives. In each book Haugaard adapts his writing style to conform to the period, capturing the flavor, even the cadence and sound, appropriate to the setting. His choice of words clearly conveys his meaning, and he shapes each phrase with the subtlety and grace of a poet. It is not surprising, therefore, to learn that Haugaard is a poet in his own right and playwright and translator as well. One of Haugaard's major accomplishments is his highly regarded translation, *The Complete Fairy Tales and Stories of Hans Andersen* (1974), an enormous undertaking that reveals Haugaard's skill in transmitting the intent of Andersen's stories while retaining his own distinctive writing style.

Haugaard was born in Denmark but can be considered a citizen of the world. He escaped from his homeland just before the Nazi invasion, served in the Royal Canadian Air Force, worked in Wyoming as a sheepherder and in Denmark as a farm worker, engaged in historical research in Japan, and makes his home in Ireland. He attended Black Mountain College in North Carolina and the New School for Social Research in New York, but his formal education has been augmented by personal experience.

Haugaard's books suggest that although he may be skeptical about adult values he maintains an enduring faith in youth. His stories derive vitality and credibility from his unique ability to observe the world from a young person's point of view. While his heroes are vulnerable, faced with grave problems, Haugaard achieves an evenhanded balance by providing them with comfort derived from friendship and love. Having stated that "no one . . . has been bored into wisdom," Haugaard makes sure that his novels are exciting adventures that provide an honest perspective on life irrespective of time and place. P.S.

Hautzig, Esther

Polish-born American author, b. 1930. Esther Hautzig is best known for *The Endless Steppe: Growing Up in Siberia* (1968), the affecting personal narrative of her life between the ages of ten and fifteen, which she spent as a deportee in a barren, impoverished Siberian village.

Nothing in her early childhood, however, prepared Hautzig for the harrowing experiences she endured and chronicled in her book. She was born into a family of wealth and prestige in Vilna, Poland. As a young girl, her governess instilled in her a love of books and learning, and Hautzig once said, "What I always wanted and loved to do was write." In 1941 her idyllic childhood ended when her family, accused of being capitalists, was arrested by Russian soldiers and shipped by cattle car to Rubtsovsk, Siberia.

Hautzig credits Adlai Stevenson for inspiring her to write *The Endless Steppe.* After going to Russia in 1959, Stevenson wrote a series of articles, including one on Rubtsovsk, about his trip for the *New York Times.* When Hautzig wrote him a letter about her experiences there, he encouraged her to write about those years. Nine years later, her autobiography was published, and it has remained in print ever since. The story of her family's survival, despite a multitude of hardships that included near starvation, hard physical labor, cramped living conditions in barracks and dung huts, arctic winters and scorching summers, and disease, pays tribute to the resilience of the human spirit in the face of overwhelming odds. While she vividly relates her particular privations, the tale Hautzig tells remains essentially a universal coming-of-age story. She grows from childhood to adolescence under daunting circumstances but approaches her experiences with the buoyancy and optimism of youth. Ultimately she recognizes and celebrates the positive aspects of her time in Siberia, noting the kindness she found in unexpected places, her development of a passion for the great Russian literature, an appreciation for the desolate beauty of the steppes, and, most important, the sustaining love of her family. After five long years in exile, Hautzig finally returned to Poland only to discover that Siberia truly had become her home. Among its many honors, *The Endless Steppe* was nominated for a National Book Award, won the Lewis Carroll Shelf Award as a book "worthy enough to sit on the shelf with *Alice in Wonderland*," and was named a Boston Globe–Horn Book Honor Book.

Hautzig also authored a number of books on crafts and cooking such as *Let's Cook Without Cooking* (1955), *Let's Make Presents* (1962), and *Make It Special* (1986). *A Gift for Mama* (1981) draws on memories of Hautzig's childhood to tell the warm, and gentle story of a girl who takes on mending to earn money to buy her mother a gift; in *Riches* (1992) an old Eastern European couple follow a rabbi's sage advice to discover the joy in giving of themselves to help others. Works for younger readers describe a child's day at home, in school, and at a park. All contain text in English, Spanish, French, and Russian.

While all of Hautzig's books have been well received, *The Endless Steppe* remains a rare and powerful reading experience, as popular today as when it debuted. C.S.

Hawthorne, Nathaniel

American author, 1804–1864. Appreciated today chiefly for *The Scarlet Letter* and *The House of the Seven Gables*, short stories, and two retellings of Greek myths for children, Nathaniel Hawthorne was born in Salem, Massachusetts, a descendant of an old New England family. His father, a sea captain, died when Hawthorne was four years old. He attended Bowdoin College, where he was a classmate of Henry Wadsworth Longfellow and a friend of future U. S. president Franklin K. Pierce, graduating in 1825 with the ambition to be a man of letters. His first novel, *Fanshawe* (1828), which he had published at his own expense, was a failure; however, it did bring him to the attention of the dynamic Samuel Goodrich, creator of the "Peter Parley" books and publisher of the literary annual *The Token*, in which a number of Hawthorne's short stories were to appear anonymously. Hawthorne became a hack writer for Goodrich, for whom with his sister, Elizabeth, he compiled *Peter Parley's Universal History* (1837). Compensation was poor. Nonetheless, the exercise aroused his interest in writing history for children.

Hawthorne married Sophia Peabody in 1842. Prior to this he had been appointed measurer of salt and coal in the Boston Custom House, a post he left to move to Brook Farm, not because he was a Transcendentalist but because he was looking for an inexpensive home for Sophia. The experiment was not successful, though he became friends with Thoreau and Emerson. He and Sophia then went to live in the Old Manse in Concord. The lack of money dogged him. He got a job as surveyor of the Salem Customs House, a political appointment with a regular salary, but a change of administration cost him the job. He returned to writing, completing *The Scarlet Letter* in 1850 and *The House of the Seven Gables* in 1851.

In 1852 he published *A Wonder Book for Girls and Boys*, the first retelling of Greek myths for children, predating Charles Kingsley's *The Heroes* (1856), a work Kingsley undertook out of disgust at Hawthorne's retellings. The stories retold here, and those in *Tanglewood Tales for Girls and Boys, Being a Second Wonder Book* (1853), were freely reshaped, losing their classical aspect to the romantic and the Gothic, as the author's fancy dictated. Hawthorne claimed the right to do this, for the stories, he said, have been around for so long that they are "legitimate subjects for every age to clothe with its own garniture of manners and sentiment, and to imbue with its own morality." He used the character Eustace Bright, a college student, to frame the retellings, having Eustace tell the stories to a "merry party" of children given such playful names as Cowslip and Primrose. The tone is avuncular, conversational. The stories are readable, although lacking the power of the originals.

"The Golden Touch," the story of King Midas in *The Wonder Book*, is one of the best loved of the stories. Hawthorne gave the king a little daughter, Marygold, who is turned into a golden statue by her father's kiss. Hawthorne created many memorable scenes throughout these two collections. In "The Minotaur," in *Tanglewood Tales*, there is the incident in which Theseus at last manages to lift the moss-covered stone that has concealed the sword and golden sandals his father had left for him to find; also vivid is the journey to Crete and the slaying of the Minotaur. Hawthorne's desire to remove "impurities," however, leads him to ignore the seduction and abandonment of Ariadne and instead have her stay behind to be with her father. These stories are more somber than those in *The Wonder Book*, but the author notes in the introduction that Eustace's claim that the objectionable elements in the originals were but a "parasitical growth" and would fall away made the adaptations acceptable.

Hawthorne also brought out *The Blithedale Romance* and *The Life of Franklin Pierce* in 1852. This last brought him the assignment from 1853 to 1857 of United States consul at Liverpool; following that stint, he lived in

Rome and Florence for a number of years. He died in 1864 in Plymouth, New Hampshire.

The Wonder Book and *Tanglewood Tales* have outlived Hawthorne's histories and short stories for children, such as "Little Annie's Ramble" (1837) and "Little Daffydowndilly" (1851), for the legends, despite their adaptations, have strong plots, memorable incidents, and action. Although watered down, as in "The Pomegranate Seeds," they are not overwhelmingly didactic and sentimental. Well-known artists who have illustrated them include WALTER CRANE, MAXFIELD PARRISH, ARTHUR RACKHAM, and FRITZ EICHENBERG. ❧

M.N.C.

HAYWOOD, CAROLYN

AMERICAN AUTHOR AND ILLUSTRATOR, 1898–1990. Since 1939 Carolyn Haywood's books have graced the shelves of children's libraries throughout America. In the more than fifty years that followed, this eminently successful author wrote over fifty children's books, most of which she also illustrated. Endearing millions of younger readers between the ages of seven and ten, Haywood created story after story filled with true-to-life characters who were happily and wholesomely engaged in everyday school and home activities. Best known for her "Betsy" and "Little Eddie" series, Haywood ranks significantly among those first American authors whose bodies of writing describe realistic yet humorous stories about children and their neighborhoods.

Born in Philadelphia, Haywood occupied much of her childhood spare time drawing and painting to fulfill her ambition of becoming an artist. She later attended the Pennsylvania Academy of Fine Arts, where she studied portrait painting with Jessie Willcox Smith. Haywood's writing career, however, began fortuitously, as she initially hoped to become a children's book illustrator. With aspirations of creating a picture book, Haywood showed some of her illustrations to Elizabeth Hamilton, editor of children's books at Harcourt, Brace and World, who suggested that she write about children in American neighborhoods and the everyday things they liked to do. *"B" Is for Betsy* (1939), Haywood's first and most recognized book, resulted from that timely prompting.

Illustration by Carolyn Haywood from her book *Eddie the Dog Holder* (1966).

This story tells of six-year-old Betsy in her first year of school—the kind of school one might have found in any small town in America—and relates the daily events of Betsy's life in a style both funny and exciting. Haywood attracted legions of young readers with this title and held them steadfast with numerous other titles about Betsy, Betsy's family, and Betsy's neighborhood friends. One such friend on Betsy's block was Eddie Wilson, an affable, enterprising, typical American boy, who loved to collect what he called "valuable property" (and what his mother called "junk") and stray animals of sundry shapes, sizes, and species. After the first Eddie book, *Little Eddie* (1947), Haywood went on to write more than two dozen books that chronicled the lives of these two beloved protagonists. The stories' appeal to newly independent readers embarking on chapter books lies in their structured, episodic chapters with flat yet consistently drawn characters engaged in activities and experiences familiar to those readers.

During her lengthy career, Haywood created other noteworthy books, many of which focused on holidays. Three other books are about red-headed Penny, an adopted boy; and in another book she compiled a selection of Bible verses for children. Completed just before her death, *Eddie's Friend Boodles* (1991) was Haywood's final story. Boodles Carey, known before as Eddie Wilson's sidekick, stars in his own book about a harebrained scheme to become a circus clown. Like Betsy and Eddie, Boodles proves once again Haywood's gift for creating ordinary, believable characters simply having fun at home and school. Haywood once explained her concerns: "I write for children because I feel that they need to know what is going on in their world and they can best understand it through stories about their world." Her memorable characters happily ensconced in typical childhood adventures embody her feelings and account for the trademarks of Haywood's notable and prolific writing career. ❧ S.L.S.

Hedderwick, Mairi

Scottish illustrator and author, b. 1939. Best known for her Katie Morag stories, which portray the quality of small island life, Mairi Hedderwick has been sketching and painting the place she knows best, Scotland, since childhood.

Born in Gourock, Renfrewshire, Scotland, she was raised an only child in a formal Scottish Calvinist home. Her missionary grandfather painted, her father was an architect who painted landscapes, and her inherent artistic talent was encouraged. Her formal art training led to a Diploma of Art from the Edinburgh College of Art, followed by an art teaching certificate from Jordan Hill College of Education in Glasgow in 1963. She was drawn into the children's book field when a vacationing book editor discovered her on the Island of Coll, where she and her husband were farmers. In order to support a growing family, they had set up the Malin Workshop, which in the beginning operated without electricity, producing hand-printed stationery and island-map postcards for tourists.

Although she had no book experience, she was invited to submit artwork for Rumer Godden's *The Old Woman Who Lived in a Vinegar Bottle* (1972) because Godden wanted to give unknown artists the opportunity to illustrate her children's books. Hedderwick was selected, and this success brought her the opportunity to illustrate Scottish writer Jane Duncan's three children's stories, *Herself and Janet Reachfar,* also published as *Brave Janet Reachfar* (1975), *Janet Reachfar and the Kelpie* (1976), and *Janet Reachfar and Chickabird* (1978). Hedderwick's impressionistic watercolors bring to life the Highlands farm setting of these warm family stories featuring a spunky young girl surrounded by adults. With a few lines, Hedderwick creates facial expressions and body language that convey both emotion and story action.

When Jane Duncan died in 1976, Hedderwick was encouraged by her editor to develop her own character, which several years later led to the birth of the fictional Katie Morag. Making good use of the endpapers, Hedderwick maps out the imaginary island community from full daytime activity to at-home after-dark quiet. Readers first meet the lively redhead in *Katie Morag Delivers the Mail* (1984), which was followed by *Katie Morag and the Two Grandmothers* (1985), *Katie Morag and the Tiresome Ted* (1986), and *Katie Morag and the Big Boy Cousins* (1987). Hedderwick's familiarity with childhood development, her intimate knowledge of island life, and her fluid artistic style help give these stories strong child appeal. Katie Morag is realistically mischievous, but she comes to terms with her own behavior and feelings, often with the firm yet gentle hand of Grannie Island. In Hedderwick's books traditional roles are abandoned. Mrs. McColl is postmaster, Mr. McColl wins a prize at "Show Day" for his baking, and Grannie Island, clad in overalls and boots, farms alone, operating her own tractor. Hedderwick's paintings provide many additional details.

Hedderwick's own adventuresome and independent spirit shows throughout her picture books and also forms the basis of two recent books for adults, *An Eye on the Hebrides* (1989) and *Highland Journey: A Sketching Tour of Scotland* (1992).

Throughout her career, Hedderwick has given children a vivid, unassuming, and rare glimpse of life in rural Scotland. ♠ G.W.R.

Heide, Florence Parry

American author, b. 1919. Florence Parry Heide, with over eighty books to her credit, is a prolific and versatile writer. From picture books to young adult novels, from humorous to serious, Heide writes in numerous genres. "There are so many ideas waiting out there, so many unwritten stories," she says. "What an adventure!" Yet a common theme runs through her books: Young people take control of their lives in some way. Heide recalls as a child making a conscious decision to face cheerfully what life had to offer. Her father died when she was three, and Heide and her brother lived with their grandmother until their mother was able to support the family.

Heide grew up in Pittsburgh, and after graduating from the University of California, Los Angeles, she returned to the East and worked for several years in advertising. Then she married, moved to Wisconsin, and raised five children. Once her children were in school, Heide wanted something more in her life. She and her friend Sylvia W. Van Clief tried to start a hot fudge sauce company, but, since neither liked cooking, they quickly abandoned the project. Instead, they wrote, collaborating on songbooks, picture books, and mysteries. After Van Clief's death in the early 1970s, Heide worked with her own daughter Roxanne on the Spotlight Club Mystery series, which she had started with Van Clief.

Of her humorous books, perhaps the best known are those about Treehorn, *The Shrinking of Treehorn* (1971), *Treehorn's Treasure* (1981), both American Library Association Notable Books, and *Treehorn's Wish* (1984), all of which are illustrated by EDWARD GOREY. Treehorn lives in a world in which the adults are wrapped up in their own concerns and interact with him only superficially. When he begins shrinking, for example, his teacher says, "We don't shrink in this class." With deadpan humor, Heide pokes fun at the serious adult world and creates a young boy who admirably takes care of himself. Gorey's line drawings complement the text delightfully. In *Tales for the Perfect Child* (1985), the children get what they want by perfecting skills such as whining and stalling. Again, Heide uses understated humor to create wonderful and wacky situations.

Heide also writes in a more serious vein. Primarily for young adults, these novels provide portraits of young adolescent girls coming to terms with themselves and making choices about their lives. Sara, in *When the Sad One Comes to Stay* (1975), must choose between the friendship of a run-down, warm, older woman and her mother's cold, calculating plan for social success. Though her mother is a somewhat one-dimensional character, Sara's dilemma is real and painful.

When writing the picture books *The Day of Ahmed's Secret* (1990) and *Sami and the Time of the Troubles* (1992), both illustrated by TED LEWIN, Heide teamed up with another daughter, Roxanne's twin, Judith Heide Gilliland, who spent five years in the Middle East prior to working on these books. Ahmed lives in Cairo, and his book is filled with the sounds and sights of this modern yet ancient city. Sami lives in war-torn Beirut and must cope with the daily terrors of war while he hopes for a brighter future. Whether Heide's characters, like Ahmed and Sami, populate highly realistic books, or, like Treehorn, inhabit fanciful stories, they are all strong, believable, and engaging. ❧ P.R.

HEINE, HELME

GERMAN AUTHOR AND ILLUSTRATOR, B. 1941. Giving character to everything from a pig on a bicycle to a crustacean on the tree of life, Helme Heine creates a watercolor world full of childlike simplicity. His paintings use thin, clear colors and take full advantage of the white paper. Like many great artists for children, Heine does not think about his audience as he works but about the child who still laughs and plays within himself. This outlook lends a truthfulness to his work; the humor rings with idiosyncratic charm, and new details materialize with each reading. *The Most Wonderful Egg in the World* (1983, trans. 1987) is a tale about three chickens who compete to produce the most extraordinary egg. Showing each chicken's unique vision, one egg is perfect, white, flawless. The second is huge and glorious. The third is not an egg but a cube, and each side is painted with primary colors. On the back jacket of the book, there is a vignette showing the three chicks who emerged from these eggs: one tiny and spotted, one huge, and a third a little multicolored cube with a beak and a comb. The value and beauty of each egg is obvious.

Heine excels with animal characters, such as Porker Pig and Curlytail in *The Pigs' Wedding* (1978, trans. 1979) and Harry Nibbler in *Superhare* (1979). But personification becomes personal in *Mr. Miller and the Dog* (1979, trans. 1980). The night watchman and his dog envy each others' lives until one day when they decide to change places. The Kafkaesque metamorphosis is subtly and delightfully worked.

Heine tries to write stories that have a moral substance beneath the light-hearted illustrations. Although his popular book *Friends* won the Boston Globe–Horn Book Award in 1983, his books are occasionally criticized by reviewers who bring their own interpretations to the meanings of his work. *The Pearl* (1984, trans. 1985) is a dream tale about Beaver, who finds a mussel and knows it contains a pearl. But in his dream, the wealth he has acquired undermines his friendships, and when he awakes, he throws away the mussel. One review suggested that this book is "one of those don't-dare-to-be-different stories that reinforces the worst aspects of peer pressure." His text is sometimes criticized as flat, dull, or stiff, but it could as easily be judged as subtly simple, matching the understatement that is so obvious in his paintings. His Tree of Life on the jacket of *One Day in Paradise* (1986, trans. 1986) is a giant daisy blossom, with members of the animal kingdom balancing on her fragile petals, while God, disguised as Claude Monet, liberally waters her roots. Inside, children are fascinated by God's studio, where in six days, He creates the universe. The illustrations show sketches of spider webs, the movement of the solar system and of electrons on the same design sheet, and a pictorial query of which came first, the chicken or the egg. Heine's use of two children for Adam and Eve allows the reader to view paradise through their wonder-filled eyes. Dinosaurs and polar bears drink at the same watering hole, and when the children are exhausted, they curl up against the huge brown back of a woolly mammoth and are rocked to sleep.

Whether Heine is working with whimsy or satire, his clear colors and playful lines are a delight to children around the world. ❧ J.A.J.

Henkes, Kevin

AMERICAN AUTHOR AND ILLUSTRATOR, B. 1960. Kevin Henkes is best known for his warm, lively, humorous PICTURE BOOKS, distinguished for their remarkable understanding of the true world of young children. Peopled, for the most part, with expressively drawn mouse characters who are completely human in their feelings and relationships, these picture books sound almost as if the author has been eavesdropping on children at play, so realistic and believable are they. Henkes is also the author of MIDDLE-GRADE FICTION—including the innovative (one chapter is told entirely in pictures), easy-to-read *Margaret and*

Voices of the Creators

Kevin Henkes

I think of my life as an ordinary one—and I sense that my books reflect this. I've also come to believe that by careful and loving observation, the ordinary reveals its complex nature. Take a simple life, a common experience, and render it precisely with words and images—build it with details—and if you're lucky you have an interesting story. A story that is rich enough to say something about the human condition.

I've written and illustrated books about things I know: sibling rivalry, making a new friend, getting lost, the arrival of a new baby. And whether I've chosen to use a picture-book format or a chapter-book format, whether I've chosen to render my characters as animals or humans, all my stories and protagonists are linked very closely to the life I led as a child.

I don't always remember specific events from my childhood, but I often remember the feeling, and I often remember certain tiny, tiny details very closely—what I wore on the first day of kindergarten, for example. I was very introspective, which I think helps intensify what I do remember.

As a child, my love of art defined me. And although I've had other interests at various times in my life, it was always art that I came back to. And I also loved to read.

My family made regular trips to the local public library. I remember stepping up onto the big wooden stool so I could watch the librarian check out my books. I remember wanting to carry my books all by myself, no matter how many I had chosen. And I remember how much I loved the way books from the library smelled. I'm certain that all those visits to the library had something to do with my becoming an author and illustrator.

More often than not, I chose books because I was drawn to particular illustrations. My favorite book as a child was *Is This You?* by Ruth Krauss, illustrated by Crockett Johnson. Interestingly enough, it is essentially a guide for making a book of your own. I was lucky enough to own that book, and I still have it. It is as important to me now as it was to me when I was a child. Other favorite books of mine included *The Carrot Seed,* also by Ruth Krauss and Crockett Johnson, and *Rain Makes Applesauce* by Julian Scheer, illustrated by Marvin Bileck. As I grew up, and the books I read grew longer, I was still inclined to choose books because of their illustrations. I admired Garth Williams's art and often looked for novels that he had illustrated.

When I was young, I often drew at the kitchen table. I am one of five children, so there was often a lot of activity going on around me while I worked. But it didn't seem to bother me. Now, I work in a spare bedroom in my own house. Sometimes it feels odd to have an entire room to myself for drawing and writing. And there isn't very much noise in the house while I'm working. Sometimes I turn the radio on.

I hope that my books convey a sense of joy and delight. I hope that they are thickly textured. I hope that there is something about my books that connects with children, and something that connects with the adult reader. Even if something traumatic happens to one of my characters, I like to have my stories end on a hopeful note. That's my gift to the reader.

I can still remember coming home from school after something awful had happened. I can still remember how simply stepping inside the back door lifted the weight of my emotions. I was home, and it smelled good, and it felt good. I'd put on my play clothes, and everything would be okay. Which doesn't mean that when I walked out the door the next morning—or ten minutes later—something else wouldn't go wrong. I know that this sense of comfort doesn't exist for every child, but I write about what I know. And I want to share this sense of hope through my books.

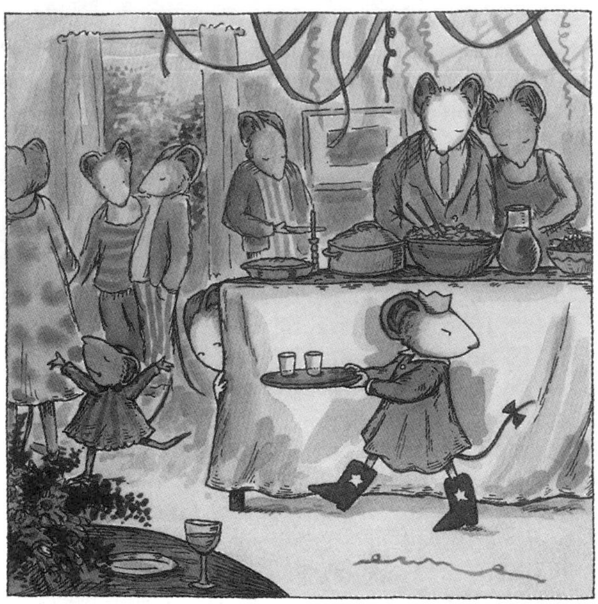

Illustration by Kevin Henkes from his book *Julius, the Baby of the World* (1990).

Taylor (1983), *Return to Sender* (1984), and *Words of Stone* (1992)—that focuses on the strength of family and children's struggles with emotional issues.

Henkes was born in Racine, Wisconsin, one of five children, and much of his work reflects his secure childhood and Midwestern upbringing. From an early age, he knew that he wanted to be an artist and was greatly influenced by the picture books of his childhood, books illustrated by such greats as CROCKETT JOHNSON and GARTH WILLIAMS. He never outgrew his love and appreciation for picture books, and with encouragement from his family to pursue his drawing and from a high school English teacher to continue to develop his writing, he put those two skills together and became a creator of picture books himself.

Henkes finished a draft of what became his first published picture book before the end of his senior year in high school. *All Alone*, an introspective mood piece in which a little boy thinks about all the things he can do when he is alone, was published in 1981; it was followed by *Clean Enough* (1982), an intimate, quiet portrait of an imaginative boy's bathtime; both featured human protagonists, rendered realistically.

A Weekend with Wendell (1986) was the first picture book in which Henkes's now familiar mouse characters—with their marvelously expressive ears and tails—appeared. Executed in pen-and-ink and watercolor, *A Weekend with Wendell* also introduced one of Henkes's favorite themes: friendships between bold, bossy children and meeker, quieter ones. Sophie's weekend guest is having all the fun—when they play hospital, Wendell is the doctor, the nurse, *and* the patient and Sophie is the desk clerk. But when Wendell plays one too many tricks on Sophie, she instigates a game of firefighter in which she is the fire chief and Wendell is the burning building—and soon they are having so much fun that they are both sorry when it's time for Wendell to go home. In *Sheila Rae, the Brave* (1987), boastful, good-at-everything Sheila Rae finds herself lost one day, only to be rescued by her timid little sister, Louise, who consequently discovers some of her own strengths.

Chester's Way (1988), an American Library Association Notable Book, introduced Henkes's favorite character, the spunky, extroverted, original-minded Lilly. Cautious, routine-loving best friends Chester and Wilson find their lives turned upside down when Lilly moves into the neighborhood with her crown ("I am Lilly! I am the Queen! I like everything!"), her red cowboy boots, and her jaunty red tail ribbon. Lilly also stars in *Julius, the Baby of the World* (1990), a hilariously funny, realistic portrayal of sibling jealousy. Henkes received his first major award—a Caldecott Honor Award—for *Owen* (1993), in which a little boy foils a nosy neighbor's attempts to make him give up his beloved fuzzy yellow blanket.

Henkes is the creator of true picture books—in which text and illustrations work together to make a seamless whole—that exhibit an innate understanding of children and always contain a strong element of security and comfort. M.V.P.

HENRY, MARGUERITE

AMERICAN AUTHOR, B. 1902. Marguerite Henry is one of the twentieth century's finest writers of horse stories. Her books depict the close bonds between horse and human, exciting races, and many other standard elements of the genre, but what sets Henry's work apart is the historical authenticity of her plots and the vigor of her writing.

Readers may be surprised to learn that the author grew up in a home without any pets. Born in Milwaukee, Wisconsin, Henry discovered early that her interest in books and writing could be profitable. She sold a magazine story at age eight and shortly thereafter found employment mending books in the local library. She attended the University of Wisconsin at Milwaukee, married at age twenty-one, and pursued her dreams of a writing career and owning lots of pets. She sold a few articles to magazines such as the *Saturday Evening Post* and wrote a number of very minor stories and INFORMATION BOOKS for children, including the sixteen-volume "Pictured Geographies" series, published between 1941 and 1946.

Henry's breakthrough book, *Justin Morgan Had a Horse* (1945), tells the true story of an eighteenth-century Vermont colt noted for his power and speed who fathered a new breed of American horse, the Morgan. Rich in drama and vivid historical detail, the prose of this Newbery Honor Book is perfectly complemented by the artwork of Wesley Dennis, whose beautiful drawings and watercolor illustrations add great appeal to most of the author's works.

Henry received a second Newbery Honor designation for *Misty of Chincoteague* (1947), the story of two children living on an island off the Virginia coast who long to own one of the wild horses from nearby Assateague Island. Every year some of the horses are captured and brought to Chincoteague, where they are sold to raise funds for the fire department. Paul and Maureen save money to buy the horse and colt that Paul captured on Pony Penning Day. Although the older horse becomes tame enough to win a race, she eventually escapes to her home island, leaving the children with their much-loved colt, Misty. Steeped in salty East Coast atmosphere, Henry's best-known book is a particularly vivid re-creation of real people and events on Chincoteague Island during the 1940s. Misty was an actual Assateague horse and came to live with the Henrys for several years. The author continued writing about Chincoteague in *Sea Star: Orphan of Chincoteague* (1949), *Stormy, Misty's Foal* (1963), and *Misty's Twilight* (1992).

Henry won the Newbery Medal for *King of the Wind* (1948), the story of a Moroccan colt cared for by a mute stableboy. Presented to the young king of France, the horse is rejected by the royal court and forced to perform hard labor before achieving fame as the sire of the Thoroughbred line. The book is compelling for its historical setting and almost mythical portrait of a great creature brought low before rising in triumph.

In addition to her excellent horse stories, Henry wrote an acclaimed story of a burro, *Brighty of the Grand Canyon* (1953), and a nonfiction guide to horse breeds, *Album of Horses* (1951). Several generations of young animal lovers have thrilled to Henry's well-written stories about some very memorable horses. § P.D.S.

HENTOFF, NAT

AMERICAN AUTHOR, B. 1925. *Passion* is no ordinary word, and Nat Hentoff's books for young adults prove that point. Hentoff's well-documented passions for jazz music and social causes have made their way into his young adult fiction. *Jazz Country* (1965), marketed as a juvenile novel, was a forerunner of modern young adult literature as it dealt earnestly and honestly with such subjects as race relations. His next young adult novel, *I'm Really Dragged But Nothing Gets Me Down* (1968), rode the crest of the realistic fiction wave, inspired by S. E. HINTON. Not as successful as *Jazz Country*, and now somewhat dated, the novel demonstrated that Hentoff, unlike other writers for teens, cared not just about social realism but social reform, as his protagonist wrestles with the draft issue. Hentoff's next two young adult novels, *This School Is Driving Me Crazy* (1975) and its sequel, *Does this School Have Capital Punishment?* (1981), involve a young man (Sam Davidson) enrolled in a private school where his father is headmaster. Sam comes out fine on his own in the first novel, but in the second it takes an adult, a jazz musician, to help him out of his dilemma. In both novels Hentoff's social concern about teenagers' legal rights and his ability to capture the nuances of teen dialogue are at their peak.

Two more books, *The First Freedom: The Tumultuous History of Free Speech in America* (1980) and the young adult novel *The Day They Came to Arrest the Book* (1982), were written at a time when book banning and censorship were on the rise. *The First Freedom* is a nonfiction work documenting the history of free speech and challenges to it, while *The Day* puts the subject in a fictional context and concerns an attempt to ban MARK TWAIN's *The Adventures of Huckleberry Finn* from a school. *American Heroes: In and Out of School* (1987) is a nonfiction work about teenagers fighting for their legal rights. While Hentoff has never achieved the popularity among teens or the critical acclaim that authors such as S. E. Hinton have, his contribution is considerable. His books are not polemics, but they have a political edge to them which is missing in most teen fiction. Hentoff is also a dedicated advocate for the rights of teenagers—all of his books in one way or another explore the freedoms allowed and disallowed teens. Finally, Hentoff is a writer with many credits to his name and has chosen, on occasion, to bring his passionate and liberal voice directly to teens. § P.J.

HERGÉ

BELGIAN AUTHOR AND ARTIST, 1907–1983. Translated into over thirty languages, Hergé's adventure stories about the brave and resourceful young reporter Tintin are popular with both children and adults throughout the world. In twenty-four book-length comic strips, Tintin and his faithful fox terrier, Snowy, embark on a series of thrilling global adventures set in remarkably detailed, meticulously researched landscapes.

Hergé, whose real name is Georges Rémi (he devised his pen name by inverting his initials to R.G.), published the first Tintin adventure in *Le Petit Vingtième*, the children's supplement to *Le Vingtième Siècle*, in 1929. Published in book form in 1930 as *Tintin in the Land of the Soviets*, this primitive work is the only one of the series that was not later translated into color, with the exception of *Tintin and the Alpha-Art*, a work unfinished when Hergé died and left in sketch form at his request. The second adventure, *Tintin in the Congo* (1931), reflects a contemporary European view of Africa based on ignorance and portrays the African people as gullible and naive. Neither *Congo* nor the fanatically anti-Communist *Soviets* has yet been published in the United States.

In *Tintin in America* (1932), Tintin takes on Chicago mobster Al Capone, and Hergé's sociopolitical satire becomes more sophisticated as he depicts the National Guard driving the Blackfoot Indians away from their ancestral lands. But it is probably *The Blue Lotus* (1936) that marks Hergé's refinement of detail and concern for accuracy. After befriending a young Chinese student who urged him to avoid common stereotypes, Hergé began to delve further into research of the physical and cultural landscape. The story is a clear protest of Japanese expansionism on the Chinese mainland and of the treatment of the Chinese people by many Westerners. Hergé's friend appears as young Chang in *The Blue Lotus* and later in *Tintin in Tibet* (1960), a story of true friendship Hergé claims as his favorite.

Ostensibly a journalist, Tintin is seen reporting to his editor only once in the series and follows his sense of adventure and justice rather than any particular assignment. In the course of his adventures he encounters a colorful cast of characters who become his cohorts: The bumbling, ineffectual detectives Thompson and Thomson, the rough old sea dog Captain Haddock with his legendary penchant for drinking whiskey and hurling passionate but innocent insults, and the absent-minded but ingenious Professor Cuthbert Calculus provide both help and hindrance throughout Tintin's travels.

All of these characters find their way aboard the first manned rocket bound for the moon in *Destination Moon* (1953) and *Explorers on the Moon* (1954), in which Tintin, Snowy, Captain Haddock, and Thompson and Thomson set foot on the moon fifteen years before Neil Armstrong landed in Apollo 11. Hergé constructed a detailed scale model of a German U2 rocket to create the drawings, and his extensive scientific research gives the books remarkable accuracy and foresight. While most of the Tintin stories are noticeably devoid of women, opera singer Bianca Castafiore takes center stage as a strong female character in *The Castafiore Emerald* (1963).

Charles de Gaulle once remarked, "My only international rival is Tintin." Intelligent, courageous, and kindhearted, Tintin is a seemingly invincible but human hero who has blazed a trail around the world. ❧ L.A.

Herriot, James

Scottish author, 1916–1995. In 1972, *All Creatures Great and Small*, a book written by a Scottish veterinarian living in Yorkshire, England, became a number-one best-seller in the United States. Although his real name is James Alfred Wight, he is known to the world as James Herriot, and his many books about veterinary life in the Yorkshire dales have captivated readers of all ages. Because it is considered improper for veterinarians in England to advertise in any way, Wight disguised the names of his partner and the market town where he lived as well as his own name. A great sports fan, he chose his nom de plume while typing and watching a football match on television: Herriot was the goalkeeper's name. Herriot began writing his autobiographical series after the age of fifty out of a "compulsion to ... record ... a fascinating era in veterinary practice ... in the days before penicillin." His stories begin in the 1930s in what he called "those old black magic days with their exotic, largely useless medicines reeking of witchcraft." He was intrigued by the stolid farmers, fascinated by their dogged determination to eke a living from the often grudging land, and charmed by the gracious but silent hospitality with which they treated him. A veterinarian's life is not for the squeamish, yet Herriot, with his innate storyteller's skill, regaled his readers with touching, heartbreaking, and downright funny stories.

Herriot was born in Scotland to parents who were musicians. When he graduated from Glasgow Veterinary College, his intention was to practice small-animal medicine, but veterinary's assistant positions were scarce in the late 1930s, and Herriot received only one reply to his job queries. This interview serendipitously placed him, not in Scotland, but in a small market town in Yorkshire. "Darrowby," with its surrounding dales, fells, and moors, held an enchantment Herriot had never anticipated. Such was its hold that he continued to live there and practice with "Siegfried Farnon," his original employer and partner, for the rest of his life.

Herriot's love of animals and his work as a veterinary surgeon, his keen insight into the lives of the people he meets, and his delight in being fortunate enough to live in Yorkshire shine through in his books. Five of them, all best-sellers—*All Creatures Great and Small* (1972), *All Things Bright and Beautiful* (1974), *All Things Wise and Wonderful* (1977), *The Lord God Made Them All* (1982), and *Every Living Thing* (1992)—chronicle his life from the first day he met and was employed by "Siegfried," through his courtship, marriage, and partnership, his experience in the Royal Air Force during World War II, and his postwar return to his practice, wife, and children. On a slightly different tack, *James Herriot's Yorkshire* (1979) and *The Best of James Herriot* (1982) are large, hardcover collectors' editions replete with historical information and breathtaking pictures of Yorkshire.

In 1984 the first picture book for children containing a Herriot story was published. Now *Moses the Kitten* (1984), *Only One Woof* (1985), *The Christmas Day Kitten* (1986), *Bonny's Big Day* (1987), *Blossom Comes Home* (1988), *The Market Square Dog* (1989), *Oscar, Cat-About-Town* (1990), *Smudge, The Little Lost Lamb* (1991), and *James Herriot's Treasury for Children* (1992) introduce a new generation of readers to Herriot's heartwarming stories. ❧ S.R.

Highwater, Jamake

American author, b. 1942. According to Jamake (pronounced "Ja-*mah*-ka") Highwater, he was born in Montana in the early forties and because his natural parents—Jamie and Amanda Highwater—were too poor and unstable to care for him, they placed him in an orphanage. Somewhere between the ages of six and ten he claims to have been adopted by Alexander and Marcia Marks, an Anglo couple from California. "I have no original birth certificate," Highwater maintains. "It is often difficult to know the difference between what I personally remember and what I was told."

As an emerging author, he felt he was part of both the Indian and Anglo cultures. The Indian takeover of Alcatraz island in 1969 stirred in him what he refers to as "a sense of visibility and courage as an Indian person." It was then that he began working on his first book to bear the name Jamake Highwater—*Fodor's Indian America: A Cultural and Travel Guide*, published in 1975. Earlier works, written under the name of J. Marks or J. Marks-Highwater include *Rock and Other Four Letter Words: Music of the Electric Generation, Europe Under Twenty-Five: A Young People's Guide,* and *Mick Jagger: The Singer, Not the Song.* Since changing his name to Jamake Highwater, however, Indian concepts have been the focus of much of his writing. Legends figure prominently in his first work of fiction, *Anpao: An American Indian Odyssey* (1977). A rite-of-passage novel, *Anpao* won the Newbery Honor Award, the Boston Globe–Horn Book Award, and Best Book for Young Adults Award in 1978.

The 1980s were a very productive period for Highwater, as he wrote nonfiction, novels, a book of poems entitled *Moonsong Lullaby* (1981), and television scripts for the Public Broadcasting Service. He also began the "Ghost Horse" Quartet award-winning young adult novels that trace the lives of three generations of a Northern Plains Indian family: *Legend Days* (1984), *The Ceremony of Innocence* (1984), and *I Wear the Morning Star* (1986). Sitko, a character who initially appears in *The Ceremony of Innocence* and is the narrator of *I Wear the Morning Star,* has a mother of French and Indian ancestry who is married to a rodeo clown and movie stuntman. After being placed in a foster home, the boy straddles two worlds until his ability to capture his lost heritage through his talent as a painter enables him to find his true identity.

Highwater has been praised for his "strong, incantatory prose," meaningful metaphors, and "awe-inspiring" imagery. His essay "The Americas in 1492," one of several articles by children's book writers comprising *The World in 1492* (1992), reveals the influence of the Incas, the Aztecs, the Mound Builders, and the Plains Indians in the New World. In it, he re-creates the people and their varied ways of life. Highwater says of his storytelling, "I have always preferred the night and the shadow side of existence, because I believe that the unknown is knowable and that the real effort of the artist is to describe the fragile place where the inner and outer worlds meet." His insight into the consciousness of Native Americans evokes both the pain of their great loss and a sense of future hope. ❧ C.K.S.

Hill, Eric

British author and illustrator, b. 1927. Eric Hill is the ingenious creator of the most popular puppy in children's books, the tawny-colored dog named Spot. Spot made his debut in the best-selling *Where's Spot?* (1980), a lift-the-flap book that shows mother dog Sally searching for her son. As Sally and the reader look under the bed, in the closet, and even in the grand piano, they find a different animal behind each flap. Finally, mischievous Spot is discovered hiding in a basket and is sent off to eat his dinner. The inspiration for the book came when Hill, working as a freelance artist and designer, noticed that his two-year-old son was amused by the flaps and hidden pictures on an advertising novelty. He combined the flap idea with his love for dogs and created a book for his son. On publication, the title was an immediate success, and Hill gave up his graphic work to pursue a career in children's books.

Like a child, Spot progresses from playing close to home to venturing farther away. He steps outside on his own, briefly but eagerly, in *Spot's First Walk* (1981), and in *Spot's Birthday Party* (1982) he plays hide-and-seek with his new friends. He finds that school is "great!" in *Spot Goes to School* (1984) and learns about siblings in *Spot's Baby Sister* (1989). In other books he visits the beach, the circus, and stays overnight with his friend Steve Monkey. The lovable pup is also featured in the "Little Spot" BOARD BOOKS, a series geared toward children too young for lifting flaps; titles such as *Spot's Toy Box* (1991) are plotless, naming objects and actions that are easy for toddlers to recognize. Another board-book series created by Hill—the "Baby Bear Storybook" series—features a friendly brown bear who shows readers a collection of familiar items in titles such as *At Home* (1983) and *The Park* (1983).

Where's Spot? and the many books that followed it are favorites with children and adults for a variety of reasons. The flaps, in the form of different objects, have the appeal of pop-ups but are sturdier and less complicated in design and therefore easier for small hands to manipulate. Integral to the story rather than mere gimmicks, the flaps allow children to help tell the tale, making storytime more interactive. The simple texts are brief, and Spot's small adventures are fun and familiar to children. The well-designed ink-and-watercolor illustrations and the bold type are uncluttered, both standing out clearly against the white backgrounds. This art style is a result of the only art training Hill ever received; leaving school at age fifteen, he was hired as a messenger for a commercial art studio, where a newspaper cartoonist encouraged him and taught him how to draw in the cartoon style.

Cover illustration by Eric Hill for his book *Spot Goes to the Beach* (1985).

Though some of the books following *Where's Spot?* have been criticized as having harsher colors, a less precise style, and a more anthropomorphic Spot, the books are still praised as gentle, imaginative stories with universal appeal for young children. World renowned, the "Spot" books have been translated into fifty languages in one hundred countries. J.M.B.

HINTON, S. E.

AMERICAN AUTHOR, B. 1950. Young adult author Susan Eloise Hinton's career is one of firsts: from writing what is widely recognized as the first important contemporary YOUNG ADULT NOVEL, *The Outsiders*, in 1967, to being honored twenty years later with the first Margaret A. Edwards Lifetime Achievement Award by the American Library Association's Young Adult Services Division and *School Library Journal*. The award seems fitting because Hinton's adult lifetime has been spent writing young adult literature, a field she helped create. *The Outsiders*, her first novel, was written while she was a junior in high school and published two years later. It created a sensation, controversy, and a new realism in fiction for teenagers.

It is difficult to imagine a better young adult novel than *The Outsiders*. Everything works: the characters are real, the plot intriguing, the themes engaging, and the writing simple yet powerful. As the title reveals, *The Outsiders* is a book about feeling left out and seeking desperately to be accepted. In Hinton's world, the gang provides the missing family and an opportunity to establish identity. From the minute Pony Boy steps onto the page, the novel becomes his search to find a place in the world: to both grow up and to remain innocent, or as the book says, to "stay gold." A marketing decision was made to put "S. E. Hinton" as the author to disguise the fact that the writer of a book with primarily male characters and a lot of violence was, in fact, a young woman. The book received rave reviews. Shortly after, Hinton wrote an article for the *New York Times Book*

Review called "Teen-Agers Are For Real," and her place in literary history was assured before she had even graduated from college.

Three years later, *That Was Then, This Is Now* was published. A more complex work, the book received favorable reviews as Hinton continued to write about boys and violence. *That Was Then* moves away from the gang setting to tell a tale of friendship and betrayal. *Rumble Fish* (1975) and *Tex* (1977) followed, mining the same territory: an Oklahoma setting, tough talk, missing or ineffectual adults, and the hard choices with often violent outcomes made by a young, sensitive male protagonist. All four books are told in the first person with Hinton's voice being among the purest in capturing teenage dialogue, inflection, and attitudes. None of these books could be mistaken for those of any other author.

The second phase of Hinton's career found her involved in translating her novels into film. Oscar-winning director Francis Ford Coppola made two Hinton films, *The Outsiders* and *Rumble Fish,* both released in 1983. *Tex* was a WALT DISNEY production in 1982 and *That Was Then, This Is Now* was released in 1985. Hinton was not involved with *That Was Then,* and it proved to be the weakest of the four films. Hinton made cameo appearances in *The Outsiders* and *Tex,* increasing the films' realism. The translation of Hinton's novels to film was natural, as her writing has a cinematic quality: it is loaded with strong characters, plenty of conflict, lots of action meshed with stinging dialogue, and the struggle between reality and idealism.

The third phase of Hinton's career began in 1988 with the publication of *Taming the Star Runner.* Although the landscape and characters are similar to those in her earlier novels, important changes had occurred. The first-person voice is gone, yet the novel is more autobiographical than her others in its story of a young man writing and publishing a novel while still a teenager. After a nine-year hiatus from publishing, Hinton proved in *Taming the Star Runner* that she had lost none of the power in her writing or in her ability to provide insight into the lives of adolescents. ❧ P.J.

Historical Fiction for Children

Historical fiction as a genre sometimes appears to be self-consciously searching for definition as well as justification and approval. It is a hybrid and a shape-shifter: it combines history with fiction; it has been adapted to a number of forms, from PICTURE BOOKS to novels. It is a field that has attracted many of the finest writers for young people, including K. M. PEYTON, ROSEMARY SUTCLIFF, and JILL PATON WALSH in England and SCOTT O'DELL, KATHERINE PATERSON, and ELIZABETH GEORGE SPEARE in the United States. Given the number of awards garnered by historical novels, the genre impresses critics, as the following selective sampling of Newbery Medal winners indicates: *Caddie Woodlawn* by CAROL RYRIE BRINK (1935), *Adam of the Road* by ELIZABETH JANET GRAY (1942), *Johnny Tremain* by ESTHER FORBES (1943), *Island of the Blue Dolphins* by Scott O'Dell (1960), *The Slave Dancer* by PAULA FOX (1973), *Roll of Thunder, Hear My Cry* by MILDRED TAYLOR (1976). Yet, popular opinion holds that, despite the appeal of individual titles, as a genre it does not excite the majority of young readers. Debates continue not only over presentation but also over content, plot, and setting. For example: Just when does the past become historical? It seems as if historical fiction poses as many problems as history itself.

One problem is definition. It seems to be a common assumption that the term "historical fiction" refers to the "historical novel," the classic conventions for which were established by Sir Walter Scott early in the nineteenth century. As adapted from the commentary on the historical novel in Thrall and Hibbard's *Handbook to Literature* (revised and enlarged by C. Hugh Holman, 1960), these conventions include setting the story in a time when differing cultures are in conflict, placing fictional characters in situations in which they encounter actual historical figures, and using these fictional characters to demonstrate the effects that opposing views had upon those then living. Many of these conventions have been modified. Not all contemporary historical fiction, for example, features encounters between fictional and historical characters. Nor is the blending of fact and fiction confined to longer works, particularly in books for children. All of which explains why the term "historical fiction," a more inclusive designation than "historical novel," seems preferable for use in general discussion. But it is surprising how frequently one traditional requirement—that the story be set in a time when differing cultures are in conflict—appears in works by noted writers for children; for example, the late Rosemary Sutcliff set many of her major works in Britain during the last years of the Roman occupation.

Regardless of modifications in the classic conventions, serious historical fiction is more than a story set in the past. Setting must be integral to the plot, otherwise the tale is simply a "costume romance" that exploits rather than explores history. Yet, at its best, most critics agree, historical fiction can illuminate the past so that history becomes vital and exciting, experienced rather than studied. There is also general agreement that a book that deliberately re-creates an earlier time is different from one written in that time. LOUISA MAY ALCOTT's *Little Women* (1868–1869), despite its references to the Civil War, is not historical fiction, in contrast to IRENE HUNT's *Across Five Aprils* (1964).

Whether a picture book, a book for beginning readers, or a novel, the historical story is composed of two elements. To be taken seriously, it must fulfill the requirements for both good history and good literature. To be truly successful, it must become more than merely the sum of its parts. Ideally, it must be honest, balanced, and enticing, the product of serious scholarship, a distinctive style, and fervent interest in the subject. Unfortunately, old attitudes and stereotypes can be overtly or covertly persistent. Historian Allan Nevins commented: "The facts of the past do not change, but our view of them does." Consequently, reevaluating history as presented in books for children has become a significant aspect of critical analysis—particularly with regard to portrayals of minorities and Native Americans. And writers such as VIRGINIA HAMILTON, Mildred Taylor, and LAURENCE YEP, who write from minority perspectives, have become important contributors to a fuller understanding of times past.

Writers of historical fiction, like conscientious historians, must work within certain restrictions: accuracy (what is fact as opposed to speculation); consistency (establishing and maintaining a thesis and point of view); and selectivity (eliminating the relatively unimportant from the essential, otherwise defined as solving the problem of too little versus too much). Emphasis on scholarship, however, should not eliminate laughter. The past, like the present, could be ridiculous and amusing as well as grim or noble as demonstrated in British writer LEON GARFIELD's period piece *The Strange Affair of Adelaide Harris* (1971), a comedy of errors set in eighteenth-century Brighton, England, where a certain Dr. Bunnion has established his Academy for the Sons of Gentlefolks and Merchants.

Given the origin of the genre with Sir Walter Scott and the popularity of SURVIVAL STORIES such as Defoe's *Robinson Crusoe* (1719), it is not surprising that classic examples of historical fiction written for children during the Victorian period tended to emphasize adventure, although the best of them, like ROBERT LOUIS STEVENSON's *Kidnapped* (1886), also evoked political and social concerns. While adventure stories set in the past, as exemplified by AVI's *True Confessions of Charlotte Doyle* (1990) with its strong female central character, are still a significant subgenre of historical fiction, domestic dramas such as PATRICIA MACLACHLAN's *Sarah, Plain and Tall* (1985)—the poignant tale of a mail-order bride and her new family—are firmly established not only as a continuing theme in American literature for children but also as one of its more enduring contributions. Like the "Little House" books (1932–1943) crafted by LAURA INGALLS WILDER, ELIZABETH COATSWORTH's *Away Goes Sally* (1934), and ALICE DALGLIESH's *Courage of Sarah Noble* (1954), they draw significance from the lives of ordinary people. Similarly, the plight of Native Americans, overlooked and misunderstood, has made considerable impact on works such as Scott O'Dell's *Sing Down the Moon* (1970), the story of the tragic displacement of the Navajos in 1864, and MICHAEL DORRIS's *Morning Girl* (1992), a touching, ironic depiction of the first encounter between the Tainos and Columbus.

Recent historical fiction has a broader scope than that of its nineteenth- and even twentieth-century antecedents. But whether a novel, a book for beginning readers, or a picture book, certain criteria are equally applicable: a sense of history, a sense of story, a sense of audience. These three phrases not only provide common ground for evaluation but also indicate the directions toward which contemporary historical fiction has moved.

First: a sense of history. Many of today's outstanding writers of historical fiction not only possess a sense of the past, they are also aware, as Allan Nevins remarked, that each era tends—and perhaps needs—to reevaluate history in the light of its own experience. One significant example is *My Brother Sam Is Dead* (1974) by JAMES and CHRISTOPHER COLLIER. In an article written for *The Horn Book Magazine*, Christopher Collier observes that *Sam* presents a view of the American Revolution more attuned to twentieth-century historiography than Esther Forbes's classic *Johnny Tremain* (1943). Implicit in the Colliers' work, written during the Vietnam era, is the idea that war may not be the solution to political problems, that issues underlying the American Revolution—or any major historical event—are never simple. In contrast, *Johnny Tremain*, written at the time of World War II, deplores loss and suffering but subordinates that idea to the sacrifices demanded by such glorious causes. This is not to say that the latter is inaccurate in detail, but rather that it examines the past through a different lens.

Prominent writers emphasize the necessity of research in order to create the sense of place that informs their plot and their characters. Explanatory prologues of appended notes, such as those addressed to young audiences by the late PATRICIA BEATTY, draw the audience

Illustration by LYND WARD from *Johnny Tremain* (1943), by ESTHER FORBES.

into the historian's worldview. Today's historical story may also include a bibliography of sources or suggestions for further reading.

But scholarship is not a substitute for a good tale well told. *History*, after all, is rooted in the French word *histoire*, which means "story." Therefore, the second criterion, a sense of story, requires that the books withstand analysis according to literary standards.

Although thinly disguised textbooks have not entirely disappeared, there is now a considerable body of historical fiction that is as compelling as it is illuminating, whether it is drawn from family reminiscences, as in Mildred Taylor's *The Friendship* (1987), a dramatic novella of the black experience in 1930s Mississippi, or from research, as in Jill Paton Walsh's elegantly crafted *Grace* (1992), based on the story of the British heroine who, in 1838, assisted her father in rescuing the survivors of a shipwreck. It can employ elements of fantasy, as in NANCY BOND's *Another Shore* (1988), in which a contemporary young woman is transported back into the Nova Scotia of 1744, or in ELIZABETH MARIE POPE's *Perilous Gard* (1974), which blends a scholar's knowledge of Tudor England with a believable variation on the old ballad of Tam Lin. Or, as in PAUL FLEISCHMAN's *Bull Run* (1993), it can introduce the many facets of one historic event through a series of dramatic monologues.

Whatever the era or source of inspiration, the author must create a palpable setting with believable characters whose diction suggests the time in which they live. In contrast to adults who, it seems, buy books by the pound, today's youthful audiences generally prefer their encounters with the past to be of shorter duration than did their nineteenth-century counterparts. Consequently, writers have little opportunity for digressions that interrupt the primary narrative flow. Only the most skilled can evoke significant issues while observing the limits imposed by a young audience—the third sense which the writer of historical fiction must develop.

Nowhere is this skill more in demand than in the writing of a picture-book text or a book for beginning readers. Consequently, those working in these genres must narrow their focus, restricting the size of the canvas but not the intensity of emotion, a balance successfully struck in GEORGE ELLA LYON's *Cecil's Story* (1991). Illustrated by PETER CATALANOTTO, the book explores a child's universally recognizable fears during wartime, and only through the pictures is the Civil War setting revealed. Picture-book versions of history require illustrations that are as accurate as the text, for there is a symbiotic relationship between them. BARBARA COONEY, for example, deserves acclaim for the research that informs her illustrations in books such as *Ox-Cart Man* by DONALD HALL (1979), set in the New Hampshire landscape of 1832.

The more successful historical stories for beginning readers offer vignettes of events or figures as perceived by a child. Exemplified by F. N. MONJO's *One Bad Thing About Father* (1970), a fictionalized view of Theodore Roosevelt's presidency as narrated by his son, this approach demythologizes history without diminishing it. Heroes become approachable; the past becomes comprehensible in human terms.

Influenced by the social upheavals of the 1960s and awareness that today's young readers, conditioned by a media-dominated environment, are less easily shocked than those of previous generations, contemporary historical fiction has changed not only in selection of subject and theme but also in the language and details through which these are conveyed. Although very different in style, novels such as WALTER DEAN MYERS's *Fallen Angels* (1988), a devastating look at the Vietnam conflict, and Katherine Paterson's *Lyddie* (1991), the story of a Vermont girl's efforts to gain independence by working in the mills of Lowell, Massachusetts, during the 1840s, are woven from tougher fiber than books written before 1960. Advances in technology have encouraged the production of lavish picture books. But whether designed as a chapter book for beginning readers or a novel for adolescents, it is desirable that the perspective be compatible with the experience of the intended audience, which perhaps explains the proliferation of first-person narratives.

No artificial boundaries should be set in searching for "the right book for the right reader," as the old maxim states. Many books speak to all ages, like Patricia MacLachlan's *Sarah Plain and Tall*; others, because of vocabulary or length, may be restricted to an older audience. Some, like Christophe Gallaz and ROBERTO INNOCENTI's *Rose Blanche* (1985), a grim story of the Holocaust in picture-book format, have engendered lively debates about appropriate readership. More such controversies will undoubtedly occur.

If written with passionate attention to story, scholarship, and audience, tales of times past can awaken in many children the idea that they are part of history. They will have experienced it as lively, significant, and engrossing, for, as ERIK HAUGAARD, the author of many fine historical novels, observed in an article written for *The Horn Book Magazine*, "No one as yet, that I have heard of, has been bored into wisdom."

MARY MEHLMAN BURNS

HOBAN, LILLIAN

AMERICAN AUTHOR AND ILLUSTRATOR, B. 1925. Lillian Hoban studied art at the Philadelphia Museum School of Art and worked as a dancer and dance instructor before beginning her career in children's literature. In 1961 she illustrated *Herman the Loser* (1961) for her husband, author RUSSELL HOBAN. After several years as an illustrator, she began writing her own books while continuing to illustrate the work of others.

Hoban's many PICTURE BOOKS and beginning readers have been praised by critics and the public. With a few pencil lines, she gives her people and animals a wide range of expressions and emotions, and her work is characterized by realism, even when she writes or illustrates stories about animals who live like humans. Especially well known are Hoban's illustrations for the several stories written by Russell Hoban about Frances, the cheerful, childlike badger, who overcomes familiar childhood traumas—including the addition of a new baby sister—with humor and poetry. Lillian Hoban gives Frances the same honest, childlike attributes and expressions that she gives to all her animal characters: Frances is more child than badger when she takes a school bus or pulls a wagon down the sidewalk with her friends. Both adults and children sympathize with the universal dilemmas presented in the Frances stories and recognize themselves in the cozy relationships of the badger family. In the delightful critical and popular success *Bread and Jam for Frances* (1964), for example, Frances insists on eating only bread and jam. But guided gently by her parents, she decides for herself that she would rather eat a variety of foods.

Equally popular have been Hoban's Arthur books, which she both writes and illustrates. In each, Arthur, a young monkey, encounters a very real childhood dilemma. In *Arthur's Honey Bear* (1974), Arthur has a yard sale to get rid of the toys he has outgrown, but he is not yet ready to sell his Honey Bear, the only toy his younger sister wants to buy. The tension is resolved through compromise, however, and Arthur becomes Honey Bear's uncle. As in the Frances books, Arthur and his sister behave entirely like humans. Readers recognize themselves in Hoban's animals but are able to laugh at Arthur's foibles because he is, after all, a monkey. Hoban often uses wash and pencil for her illustrations, although she has illustrated her later books with watercolor. In each, the soft colors are well suited to the story's tone and subject.

Hoban again exhibits her interest in the ordinary events in children's lives in her artwork of chubby, cheerful children for Miriam Cohen's books about an elementary school class. Each book in the series focuses on an everyday event or turning point for young children. *Will I Have a Friend?* (1967) concerns Jim's first day of school, and the later books cover themes of fear, friendship, and growing independence. Hoban's children, like her animals, are fully realized characters, although defined by very few lines.

Hoban's cheerful style and her attention to the emotions of young children give life to the books she writes and illustrates. Her books appeal to adults because they present a world in which adults nurture and instruct children, and at the same time, children recognize and respond to her sympathy with the common experiences of childhood. M.V.K.

HOBAN, RUSSELL

AMERICAN AUTHOR, B. 1925. Whether he is writing of humble domestic childhood dilemmas or spinning fantasy tales of courageous survival, Russell Hoban instills his work with pathos and humor so that both children and adults find his stories equally absorbing.

Illustration by Lillian Hoban from *Bread and Jam for Frances* (1964), by Russell Hoban.

His rhythmic prose paints such colorful descriptions of both characters and settings that it is not surprising to learn that he began his creative career as an illustrator. In Lansdale, Pennsylvania, he was the only son and youngest of the three children born to Abram and Jeanette Hoban. His father, an advertising manager for the *Jewish Daily Forward,* rewarded his children with nickels for clever remarks and exceptional drawings. "As a child I drew very well and was expected to be a great artist when I grew up," Hoban recalls.

Fulfilling parental expectations and the predicament children often find themselves in when those expectations and their own needs conflict are recurring themes in Hoban's life and work. His father died when he was eleven, and after graduation from high school at sixteen, Hoban turned down a scholarship offered by Temple University and enrolled at the Philadelphia Museum School of Industrial Art. He served overseas in the armed forces and in 1944 married fellow illustrator LILLIAN HOBAN. Fulfilling his father's expectations, he became a successful freelance illustrator, and his work appeared in such noted publications as *Time, Sports Illustrated,* and the *Saturday Evening Post.* Although he wrote and illustrated his first book for children, *What Does It Do and How Does It Work?* (1959), others illustrated his work after 1960. Lillian Hoban notes, "Russ and I have completely different feelings about illustration. It was always a heavy thing for him—he used to sit at the easel groaning and yawning, and he was glad to give it up when he did."

Bedtime for Frances (1960), the first of several Frances stories, evolved from Hoban's observations of his own four children. In *Bread and Jam for Frances* (1964), Frances, a small badger, sings soliloquies expressing her fondness for bread and jam and her disdain for all foods which are not bread and jam, most especially soft, runny boiled eggs. She refuses to eat anything but jam sandwiches, which her parents then give her on every occasion—morning, noon, and night. Frances soon yearns for spaghetti and meatballs, acknowledging that variety is indeed the spice of life. The Frances books are delightful to read aloud. Hoban's words skip across the pages, and the characters and the situations in which they find themselves are so simply truthful that any family would maintain that the author had been secretly observing the goings-on in its own household.

The Hobans collaborated on many projects, including *The Little Brute Family* (1966), *Charlie the Tramp* (1967), and *Emmet Otter's Jug-Band Christmas* (1971). In 1967 Hoban published *The Mouse and His Child,* his first children's novel. Illustrated by Lillian, it was acclaimed in England, but American critics were not markedly impressed. Children rarely, if ever, read literary critics, however, and they soon discovered *The Mouse and His Child.* Among preteens and adolescents it has become a cult classic. In this many-layered novel, two clockwork toy mice—father and son—are bought and taken from the warm comfort of their toy store. Years later a tramp finds them broken and discarded in a trash heap. He does his best to repair them, then winds them up and lets them go. "Be tramps," the tramp declares, and he walks away. The mouse and child begin their journey, and Hoban does not hesitate to portray cutthroat survival in an evil world in which the villainous Manny Rat plots to enslave the toys. Hoban also, willingly and winningly, shows the great love which exists between the mouse, his child, and the true friends they discover on their journey. Readers admire the courage of the mouse child who yearns for home and family, love and self-determination. English critic John Rowe Townsend writes, "There's hope as well as pain in this pilgrimage; and, significantly, it's the child who hopes, the child who perseveres when the father would give up. This is a book which can be returned to at many times, at many ages, and there will always be something new to be found in it."

After divorce and remarriage, Hoban moved to England and began writing adult novels, most notably *Riddley Walker* (1980). His work continues to reflect his own deeply felt personal experiences: "Life is a continuous presentation of sensation and event. Faced with that presentation and faced with himself facing it, the artist represents it. Why? He can't help it . . . Art, like babies, is one of the things life makes us make." ♘ M.B.B.

Hoban, Tana

AMERICAN PHOTOGRAPHER AND AUTHOR/ILLUSTRATOR, B. ? Tana Hoban presents children with brilliant photography in beautifully designed PICTURE BOOKS. Critics praise her energetic, graphic skill and her ability to fuse photography and objects with the child in mind.

Hoban's photographs, by presenting difficult concepts through familiar objects and surroundings, allow children to look at their world with fresh eyes. The minimal texts keep readers focused on the pictures. Her strong, deceptively simple images usually portray shapes, sizes, or other concepts in subtle ways. Hoban's first concept book, *Shapes and Things* (1970), for example, presents simple black-and-white photograms without captions. The forms, though familiar to young children, are made to appear abstract through the photogram technique. No other photographer extends a child's world or expands imagination through everyday experiences as does Hoban. Her works are often recommended for a variety of ages and for bilingual children.

Hoban's photographs speak for themselves. Lively and spontaneous, they often provide emotion along with concepts—a child in a silly hat, adult and child hand in hand. Most of her work portrays urban settings, and since moving to Paris in the mid-1980s, her pictures have displayed a subtle combination of Parisian and American city life.

Impressive camera work provides unexpected viewpoints, but Hoban's artistic content remains within the realm of the child's familiar landscape. Her titles often stand as the only books available to children on that subject. *I Read Signs* (1983), *I Read Symbols* (1983), and *I Walk and Read* (1984) provide parent and child with a leisurely look at signs encountered on a walk. Through these books, children can study everyday settings that in reality receive only a quick look. Hoban's titles appeal not only to sight. Her book *Is It Rough? Is It Smooth? Is It Shiny?* (1984) provides photographs that appeal to the sense of touch.

Design is an important aspect of Hoban's success. *Look Again!* (1971), *Take Another Look* (1981), and *Look! Look! Look!* (1988) are original concept books. First, objects are presented through a cutout allowing a partial view; then, by turning the page, the entire object can be seen. The object in its environment appears on the following page. The books are delightful guessing games and invite close examination. Hoban's *26 Letters and 99 Cents* (1987) is a clever two-in-one book. One half of the book presents the alphabet in glistening, brilliantly colored upper-and-lower-case letters with photographs of one object for each letter. The other half depicts coins arranged to make up sums from one to ninety-nine cents. Each sum is photographed as if for "making change"—for example, ten cents is presented as one dime, as a nickel and five pennies, and as ten pennies—allowing small fingers to count the change coin by coin. By separating the concepts on each page through four lined blocks of color, Hoban achieves a cohesive design.

Hoban attributes her ideas for successful picture books to an experiment at the Bank Street School in Manhattan in which teachers provided children with cameras. The children found new perspectives and fresh ways of looking at their world through the camera lens. The experiment made a lasting impression on Hoban, and she began to look at her urban landscape with new eyes. Hoban says of her photographs, "I try to say, 'Look! There are shapes here and everywhere, things to count, colors to see and always, surprises.'"

Hoban's work includes filmmaking, and her photographs have appeared in numerous national magazines and are part of the permanent collection of the Museum of Modern Art. ♘ J.B.

Hoberman, Mary Ann

AMERICAN POET, B. 1930. Mary Ann Hoberman remembers swinging in her backyard as a child and making up songs to sing to herself. This love of matching words to rhythm has been a constant in Hoberman's life. She is a poet who writes for both adults and children, and her work has appeared in *Harper's* and the *Southern Poetry Review* as well as poetry anthologies.

Hoberman was born in Stamford, Connecticut, and graduated from Smith College, where she studied history. She married Norman Hoberman, an architect who also illustrated some of her books of children's poetry, including *All My Shoes Come in Two's* (1957) and *Hello and Good-by* (1959). Hoberman's professional life has included work as a newspaper reporter, an editor in the children's book department of a publishing house, a poetry consultant, and a visiting poet to schools. She is also the founder of a children's theater in Connecticut.

Hoberman's poetry celebrates the everyday lives of children and uses poetic technique to enhance a child's natural interests. In *A Little Book of Little Beasts* (1973), illustrated by PETER PARNALL, Hoberman writes about worms, snakes, mice, frogs, and other common creatures, while *Bugs: Poems* (1976), illustrated by VICTORIA CHESS, draws attention to the particular characteristics that distinguish one insect from another. Not only can the reader almost hear the snap in "Clickbeetle," the lines of the poem on the paper form an almost beetlelike shape. In "Praying Mantis," Hoberman reminds the reader that "preying (with an 'e')" is really what you see.

Hoberman is equally adept at describing children's emotions, perhaps because she has such a clear memory of her own childhood feelings and reactions. The buzzing, patter-style rhythm of "Brother," a humorous poem about a little brother who is a bother, is as pesky as a tag along sibling. This poem is from a collection called *Yellow Butter Purple Jelly Red Jam Black Bread* (1981), illustrated by Chaya Burstein.

Hoberman is at her best when representing interesting concepts to children in unforgettable poetic form. Her book-length poem, *A House Is a House for Me* (1978), illustrated by Betty Fraser, is a small masterpiece of metaphor that moves a child beyond the obvious image of "a hole is a house for a mole or a mouse" and on to the intriguing "a throat is a house for a hum." Once started with the wonderful examples in this poem, children readily invent interesting house ideas of their own. Of all Hoberman's work, *A House Is a House for Me* most clearly supports the idea that poetry is the natural language of children. Memorable, playful, and intriguing, it has the qualities of enduring oral literature.

P.H.

HODGES, MARGARET

AMERICAN AUTHOR, B. 1911. Margaret Moore Hodges has written more than thirty books for children—including novels, PICTURE BOOKS, HISTORICAL FICTION, INFORMATION BOOKS, and retellings of folktales and legends. The range and depth of her interests are quite remarkable. Her first book, *One Little Drum* (1958), told the story of a boy earning money to buy a new drum after the one he received for Christmas broke. Like other early fiction by Hodges, it was based on events in the lives of her three growing sons—as well as on memories from her own childhood. *The Making of Joshua Cobb* is one of three books about a young boy gaining independence and a sense of identity when he leaves home to attend boarding school. Filled with gentle humor and quiet insights, it dramatizes many of the everyday challenges one encounters during adolescence and was named a New York Times Outstanding Book of 1971.

Hodges's interests broadened to include history and BIOGRAPHY, and she wrote about subjects as diverse as Queen Anne of England (*Lady Queen Anne*, 1969), a boy living in ancient Greece (*The Avenger*, 1982), and the relatively contemporary Sherwood family of Cornwall, New York (*Making a Difference*, 1989). Hodges brings each historical period to life through the careful development of character and setting; she is known for her painstaking research and close readings of primary sources, and she often travels to the places she writes about. In her wonderful biography, *Lady Queen Anne*, Hodges writes with compassion and insight, probing the psychological makeup of a shy, retiring young woman who was thrust into a position of power during a time of great political turmoil. In *Making a Difference*, Hodges explores the dynamics of a strong American family of the early twentieth century and also reveals a great deal about what it was like to be a woman striving to make a place in the world at that time.

Another great love is myth and legend—an outgrowth of Hodges's years as a storyteller in libraries and on radio and television. She has retold many tales, some of which were anthologized and others of which were illustrated as picture books. *The Wave*, a Japanese legend about an old man's sacrifice during a tidal wave, was illustrated by BLAIR LENT and named a Caldecott Honor Book in 1965. The battle between a young knight and a dragon was another story Hodges believed would appeal to small children; *Saint George and the Dragon* was illustrated by TRINA SCHART HYMAN and won the Caldecott Medal in 1975. Hodges also collaborated on a revision of the 1937 edition of *The History of Children's Literature* by Elva Smith, a scholarly volume spanning Anglo-Saxon times through the nineteenth century.

Hodges has been consistently praised for her books' thoroughness, accuracy, pacing, and solid character development. Among her enduring themes are personal integrity, taking responsibility for one's actions, achieving independence, and reconciling differences with friends and enemies.

Hodges graduated from Vassar with honors in 1932

and received her masters in library science in 1958 from the Carnegie Library School, where she later taught and became a full professor; a scholarship for library students has now been established in her name. Hodges says she always found it "bliss" to be in a library. Her deep love of storytelling and for bringing alive historical events through setting and character has informed a life of ongoing research and a passion for sharing books and literature with children. ❧ K.M.K.

Hoff, Syd

American cartoonist, author, and illustrator, b. 1912. Noted for his books for children just learning to read, Syd Hoff has written and illustrated more than fifty beginning-readers as well as several picture books and a children's novel. He creates uncomplicated, humorous stories and illustrates them with cartoon drawings.

Hoff began his career as a cartoonist. After dropping out of high school, he attended the National Academy of Design in New York City. He entered as a fine arts student but received little encouragement from his instructors because of the humorous quality of his work. He turned to cartooning, sold his first cartoon to *The New Yorker* at age eighteen, and became a regular contributor to that and other magazines. Later, he created his own syndicated comic strips: "Tuffy," which ran from 1939 to 1949, and "Laugh It Off," running from 1958 to 1977. Hoff's career took a major turn in the mid-1950s, however, when his daughter was ill and he made a series of drawings to take her mind off her treatment. These drawings evolved into *Danny and the Dinosaur* (1958), perhaps his most popular book for beginning readers. When Danny goes to the museum, a dinosaur miraculously comes to life, and he and the boy set out on a day's adventures. Although they engage in simple and predictable activities, Hoff's humor comes through making the events funny and appealing. For example, the dinosaur plays hide-and-seek with the children but finds nothing large enough to hide behind. When he gets discouraged, the children pretend they can't see him so he won't feel bad. Hoff's illustrations are classic Hoff: simple cartoons with a minimum of background and details. While a number of his books are about animal characters who leave their natural habitat and enter the world of humans, such as *Sammy, the Seal* (1959) and *Chester* (1961), a carousel horse, others feature children facing common situations.

Hoff has said that the best humor springs from the familiar. Drawing on his own experience with relatives, Hoff wrote *My Aunt Rosie* (1972), which is about an overbearing aunt who praises Sherman indiscriminately and greatly embarrasses him. When she gets sick and Sherman doesn't see her for a while, he realizes he misses Aunt Rosie and her "baloney." In *The Horse in Harry's Room* (1970), Hoff deals with the importance of a child's imagination. Although no one else can see it, Harry keeps a horse in his bedroom. To discourage his fantasy, his parents take him to the country to see real horses. But the plan backfires when Harry, realizing that horses need freedom, offers to let his horse go. The horse, however, stays, and Harry knows he can keep him as long as he wants.

Hoff has tackled historical themes in some of his more recent books. He introduces children to Thomas Nast's cartoons and the role they played in bringing Boss William Marcy Tweed to justice in nineteenth-century New York City in *Boss Tweed and the Man Who Drew Him* (1978). Although the beginning-reader format demands that much of the information is greatly simplified, Hoff includes Nast's cartoons to add to the book's authenticity. Although Hoff's plots are not complicated and his characters are not highly developed, his simplicity and his humor are great achievements. ❧ P.R.

Hoffman, Felix

Swiss artist, 1911–1975. Considered one of the finest illustrators of the century, Felix Hoffman refused to leave his wooden studio on a Swiss hillside for big-city fame. The land was a gift to him from the village of Aarau, where he grew up, in recognition of the service he had done for the community.

Best known in this country for his fairy-tale picture books, Hoffman had many genres. His stained-glass windows spread illuminated grandeur through churches across Europe, and his meticulous wood-and-stone engraving techniques were relieved by work on vast murals and frescoes.

The series of Grimms's fairy tales eventually won him the Hans Christian Andersen Award in 1972, the highest European children's book honor, for his lifetime work. Most of these books are done in a five-color lithographic process on either stone or acetate. Because he did his own separations and had an intimate understanding of the printing process, he had exacting control over the shading produced by the overlay of colors. The opening of *Rapunzel* (1960, trans. 1961) has strong horizontal lines of a sickly olive green that is reflected in the husband's face and the back of the mother's hand, covering her womb. Hoffman illustrated an elegant retelling of

The Story of Christmas (1975), and the rich colors and delicacy of the illustrations have been compared to those in medieval illuminated manuscripts. Hoffman's classic modeling of figures and drapery gives a wild holiness to his angels, while his spare, simple figure of Mary reflects her virgin purity. With watercolors only, Hoffman is able to re-create the effect of gilded paint, playing intense reds, blues, and greens off the white of the page and setting a glowing yellow inside midnight blue so that it seems to shine forth.

Hoffman's sense of color is brilliant, and he is a superb draftsman, but what sets his books apart is his ability to create moving, living characters that seem to have just this moment walked onto the page. He liked to spend his evenings at the theater, where, he said, "the play presents me with living illustrations," and he would strive to capture the "single pregnant moment" that illuminates "one's whole understanding of the play." It was such a moment when he showed the devil begrudgingly cutting the hair from the title character in *The Bearskinner* (1978), who had lived out the seven years of a bargain, not taking a bath or cutting his hair or his nails. It was such a moment when he showed Rapunzel with her Prince, through the window, with birds winging on the breeze, both of them oblivious of anything but a discovery of themselves.

Hoffman created these masterpieces of children's books not to be published, but as gifts for his own daughters. When one was sick, he feverishly worked on illustrations so she would have a new picture each night. For another, it was a celebration of something she'd done. But the gifts he gave his children struck a universal chord and now are loved by children around the world. ❧ J.A.J.

Hogrogian, Nonny

AMERICAN ARTIST AND WRITER, B. 1932. Nonny Hogrogian is a two-time winner of the Caldecott Medal. The first award was for her illustrations in SORCHE NIC LEODHAS's *Always Room for One More* (1965), a rollicking Scottish folksong, and the second was for *One Fine Day* (1971), an Armenian folktale she learned from her family. Comparing the two books reveals the range of Hogrogian's versatility as an artist. In *Always Room for One More,* the figures are drawn in pen-and-ink line and crosshatch and the background combines a gray wash with lavender and green pastels. In *One Fine Day,* she uses oils in bold, simple compositions of vigorous, warm colors.

Hogrogian has a remarkable ability to vary the medium or technique in her illustrations to reflect the text's mood. Her exquisite and nuanced sense of design can be broken down into geometry and shape. Her illustrations spill across the page, often regardless of margins: they may have borders, not have borders, or go through the borders.

Hogrogian illustrated her first children's book, *King of the Kerry Fair* (1960), with woodblocks. She led the way in putting expression on the faces of animals and bringing heart and emotion to her animal characters, as in *Carrot Cake* (1977). In her Caldecott Honor Book *The Contest* (1976), she overlays her rich texture and controlled color with skeletal pencil studies of two rogues. Her work is childlike in its creation of wonderful, joyful, playful characters who always have depth, and it is recognizable by its richly colored folk illustrations, depth of heart, and humor. Her illustrations for RUMER GODDEN's *Candy Floss* (1991) are grand and have a romantic sense of color. When she uses pastels she creates rich texture and color, but she has used water-colors for her most recent illustrations, such as those in *Feathers and Tails: Animal Fables from Around the World* (1992), one of several books written by her husband DAVID KHERDIAN for which she has supplied the art.

Hogrogian is a native New Yorker of Armenian heritage who majored in art at Hunter College, then studied the art of the woodcut with Antonio Frasconi at the New School for Social Research in New York City. Her first job in children's book publishing was as a book designer and art buyer, an experience that has contributed to the deft design of her own books. She takes each manuscript and, after careful research, creates the entire design for the book, including cover, end papers, and typography.

Hogrogian led the way in children's book illustration with innovative design, the use of mixed media, and the introduction of folk characters with Mediterranean features rather than the more commonplace northern European countenance so familiar in earlier illustrated folktales. Her influence on children's literature has been significant and has been recognized by two Caldecott Medals. ❧ B.J.B.

Holland, Isabelle

AMERICAN AUTHOR, B. 1920. Isabelle Holland was born in Switzerland and lived in many countries throughout her father's foreign service career. During World War II, she settled in New York City and found a career working in publicity for a number of publishers before turning to writing full-time in 1967. Holland considers herself a storyteller first, attributing this gift to her mother, who kept her daughter occupied with stories derived from the Bible, mythology, and history. Holland writes of children struggling to survive in the modern world with its moral, emotional, and social complexities. She explains, "'Character is plot' . . . I write about what interests me the most: the development of character, its growth of understanding of self, and its relationships to others."

Indeed, believable characterization and subtle humor sustain Holland's novels. In *Dinah and the Green Fat Kingdom* (1978), Dinah is an overweight preteen who creates a sylvan fantasy world where fat is beautiful. Amanda, in *Amanda's Choice* (1970), is an emotionally starved child who learns to choose cooperation over aberrant behavior so that she can accept the love of her father and stepmother. Individual choice and accepting responsibility for one's own actions are themes that Holland feels very strongly about, and they permeate all her books. This "conservative" philosophy has prompted some to accuse Holland of being manipulative to illustrate her point. *The House in the Woods* (1991) *is* a bit contrived, but it is redeemed by Holland's well-honed skill. *Alan and the Animal Kingdom* (1977) concerns a child fighting to keep his "kingdom" of animals together after the death of his last living relative. Alan has been called "as vulnerable and lonesome a child as has been portrayed in recent children's fiction." Yet despite the obstacles the characters face in these and other books, they show a resourcefulness and a determination to triumph that is the nature of the human spirit. Regardless of the bleakness of a character's situation, Holland chooses to impart a strong sense of hope for that child's ultimate survival.

Many consider *Of Love and Death and Other Journeys* (1975) Holland's masterpiece. In this novel about an unconventional family, Holland deals with adult themes in a noncondescending manner. When Mopsy's free-spirited mother is stricken with cancer, her illness and death are portrayed in an honest, straightforward manner. The rather cosmopolitan characters engage in sophisticated conversation and offer witty commentary on humanity. Respecting her audience, Holland refrains from explaining every reference. Like many of Holland's books, *Of Love* has been heralded as a refreshing change from standard young adult stories. Holland's most controversial work is *The Man Without a Face* (1972), the story of a boy, emotionally isolated within the predominantly female influences of his home, who befriends a disfigured man. A vaguely defined homosexual incident provided the basis for vigorous discussion of this book, yet "I didn't set out to write about homosexuality," Holland says, "only the idea of a fatherless boy who experiences with a man some of the forms of companionship and love that have been nonexistent in his life." Unlike many books in this genre, the problem aspect in Holland's books is secondary to the process by which a character resolves a situation and develops a sense of self-worth that is essential to his happiness. ❧ M.O'D.H.

Holling, Holling C.

AMERICAN AUTHOR AND ILLUSTRATOR, 1900–1973. In 1941 Holling C. Holling won instant acclaim and made a lasting impression with *Paddle-to-the-Sea*, a big handsome geo-history of a hybrid sort not seen before. *Tree in the Trail* (1942) and three other, somewhat lesser successors demonstrated that *Paddle* was not a one-shot phenomenon. In fact Holling and his collaborator and wife Lucille Holling had been working on children's books of one kind and another, mostly to do with Indian life and lore, since the mid-1920s, and two of those books were distinctive in ways of their own.

The open spaces of the passing frontier were Holling's native landscape as a Michigan farm boy, a sailor on the Great Lakes, an anthropological researcher in New Mexico, a zoological observer in the Rockies, and a muralist in Montana—roles in which he had been securely trained at Chicago's Art Institute and Field Museum of Natural History and in private study with anthropologist Ralph Linton. Among the first products of these exploratory years, when the Hollings also camped on Indian reservations and attended tribal ceremonies, was a story of early conflict between the Chippewa (or Ojibway) and the Sioux, *Claws of the Thunderbird* (1928). The mid-1930s, in turn, yielded an immensely popular mass-market pair, *The Book of Indians* (1935) and *The Book of Cowboys* (1936), which convey a great deal of information via detailed illustrations, large and small, and semifictional narratives about, for example, in *The Book of Indians*, Otter-Tail, a Woodland Indian, and Buffalo-Calf, an Indian of the Plains. Shortly after its appearance, the education division of the U.S. Indian Service hailed *The Book of Indians* as "one of the few books for children about Indians which we can wholeheartedly recommend," adding that it was "almost unique [in] having no misstatements, either in the text or in the pictures." Some fifty years later a prominent anthropologist, passing over hundreds of books from the intervening years, singled out for praise *Claws of the Thunderbird* and *The Book of Indians*, along with *Paddle-to-the-Sea*. *Claws* is an exciting, even hair-raising story about two young Indians, an evenly matched boy

Illustration by Holling C. Holling from his book *Minn of the Mississippi* (1951).

and girl, who together are crucially involved in tribal conflict—not conventional pap about prototypical Indians, a description that fits adult as well as juvenile fiction published at that date.

In *Paddle-to-the-Sea* the story-line is also a travel route as a tiny carved Indian-in-a-canoe, launched by an Indian boy in the melting snows north of Lake Superior and bearing the words "Please put me back in the water," makes its way through the Great Lakes and down the St. Lawrence River to the Atlantic, cheered on by the intent reader (and assisted by an occasional human hand) past the perils of sawmill and fishing net, of fire and ice and Niagara Falls. Marginal line drawings, a Lucille Holling specialty (though she is not publicly credited in every volume), demonstrate exactly what happens and precisely how; full-color paintings on every facing page make the setting and the drama vividly present. In the illustration as well as the narrative, fact and fiction balance out—the book cannot be said to be more one or the other. Younger children naturally respond more to the story and to the corresponding paintings; at an older age the factual details in text and pictures tend to hold greater interest.

Tree in the Trail features a lone cottonwood on the Great Plains where the Santa Fe Trail eventually goes through—a tree that, dying, sends its "best part" traveling westward as an ox yoke to the end of the Trail. The narrative is something of an artificial construct, the paintings are smooth and slick in the period-manner of popular magazines, but the intermesh of time and place, of people and natural forces, again captures the imagination. "It opened my eyes at age eight to social and ecological history," a Harvard professor of landscape architecture attests, nominating *Tree* as the most influential book of his childhood.

Holling's books have a way of passionately engaging their readers. Unlike *Paddle-to-the-Sea,* which taps into the historic romance of America's inland waterways, and *Tree on the Trail,* which evokes legendary markers on the wagon trails, *Seabird* (1948), *Minn of the Mississippi* (1951), and *Pagoo* (1957), pegged respectively on the life story and geographic range of a seagull, a snapping turtle, and a hermit crab, are informational make-believe with pictures of varying effectiveness; *Minn* is the beauty and the encyclopedic treasure of the three. Both *Seabird* and *Minn* were Newbery Honor Books. But all had their articulate fans.

As for *Paddle-to-the-Sea,* it continues to inspire American fathers and sons to launch wooden replicas. Like many juvenile authors and some illustrators, Holling made the kind of books he had found lacking as a child—in his case, books that would tell him what he wanted to know about Indians. He achieved his aim with fidelity and imagination and, at least once, a transcending vision. ❧ B.B.

Holman, Felice

American author, b. 1919. Using a poetic writing style, Felice Holman has published a diverse body of work for young people that includes fanciful tales of talking animals and grimly realistic novels of urban life.

Holman was born in New York City and grew up on Long Island in a family that encouraged creativity. She began writing poetry at an early age and had her first poems published in anthologies while still studying at Syracuse University. Graduating with a degree in journalism, Holman soon realized that she lacked the bold personality required of a reporter so instead spent several years writing advertising copy before marrying and raising a daughter. She continued freelance writing and entered the children's book field with *Elisabeth, the Bird Watcher* (1963), the story of a little girl who helps her father build a bird feeder, then worries when a squirrel begins stealing the seeds. This slight, pleasant volume contains so much factual information about birds that some libraries classify it as nonfiction. A second volume, *Elisabeth, the Treasure Hunter* (1964), conveys facts about seashore life, as Elisabeth and her father hunt for a buried treasure. The same characters are also featured in *Elisabeth and the Marsh Mystery* (1966).

Some of the author's finest writing is included in her volumes of poetry for children, *At the Top of My Voice and Other Poems* (1970), *I Hear You Smiling, and Other Poems* (1973), and *The Song in My Head* (1985). In both rhymed and free verse, Holman uses evocative imagery to explore nature and empathetically writes about children visiting the supermarket, walking on tiptoe, and sulking. Poetic writing also suffuses the author's fantasies, including *The Future of Hooper Toote* (1972), which concerns a boy who has the ability to float in the air, and a book composed of two Christmas stories, *The Holiday Rat and the Utmost Mouse* (1969). Her best-known fantasy, *The Cricket Winter* (1967), tells of a nine-year-old boy who learns to communicate with a cricket using Morse code. Although the lyrical prose occasionally seems overwritten and portentous, these charming, inventive fantasies appeal to many younger readers.

Holman's novels for older readers concern social issues and have a much darker tone. *Slake's Limbo* (1974), the story of a disturbed and isolated boy who seeks refuge in a cave beneath Grand Central Station, anticipated the problem of New York's homeless children by several years. This grim, introspective novel realistically details the four months that thirteen-year-old Aremis Slake spends living on his own. Homelessness is also addressed in *Secret City, U.S.A.* (1990), which concerns a group of boys restoring an abandoned home for themselves, and *The Wild Children* (1983), a story of homeless children in 1920s Russia, after the Bolshevik Revolution. Another story of the past, *The Murderer* (1978), relates the experiences of a young Jewish boy in a Pennsylvania mining town during the 1930s. Although their experiences are unpleasant and sobering, the boys in Holman's novels emerge as survivors; the conclusion of each book is hopeful, yet realistic.

A rich, poetic style of writing distinguishes both the author's light fantasies and her dark works of realism. ♘ P.D.S.

Holocaust Literature for Children

> Among the myriad slaughtered were the Jews. Six million of them. Two out of every three in Europe. One third of the world's Jews. Statistics. But each was a man, a woman, or a child. Each had a name. Each suffered his or her own death.—Milton Meltzer, *Never to Forget: The Jews of the Holocaust*

The trauma of World War II that resonated throughout the country was deepened by the knowledge of what came to be known as the "Holocaust." For twelve years from 1933 to 1945, the Nazi regime in Germany was bent on making their world *Judenrein*—free of Jews. Other victims were caught up in that net of hatred, but the death of approximately six million Jews defines the experience of the Holocaust.

How do you explain that phenomenon to children? How do you convey the reality of such horror? The stories come in many forms—biography, fiction, personal testaments, and photo-essays. The writers who engage with the topic struggle to explain to children what happened and why. When the "why" remains inexplicable, the authors seem to shake their heads and return to the "what" and "where."

The following books for children about the Holocaust published from 1950 to 1992 include many stories and memoirs told by people who either were part of the experience or were entrusted with another person's story. A basic knowledge of the history of the period provides a helpful context. Some excellent overviews of the Holocaust for older children that are useful for any reader include *Never to Forget* by MILTON MELTZER (1976), *Smoke and Ashes* by Barbara Rogasky (1988), and *A Nightmare in History* by Miriam Chaiken (1987).

Successful attempts to deal with the subject in books for children ages six to nine have been few. Two books—written forty years apart—do introduce the subject in a way that younger children can comprehend and accept. *Twenty and Ten* by CLAIRE HUCHET BISHOP (1952) was told to the author by Janet Joly, who serves as the narrator. In the French countryside, twenty fifth-graders, who have been evacuated with their teacher, hide ten Jewish children from the Nazis. The tension and sense of adventure convey the threat, which is real without overwhelming seven-, eight-, and nine-year-old readers.

Children from six to nine will understand *The Lily Cupboard* by Shulamith Levey Oppenheim (1992), set in Holland. Miriam, young and alone, has been sent to the country to be hidden by a non-Jewish family who make her welcome and explain that when soldiers come she must hide in a secret cupboard. The soft watercolor and gouache illustrations are idyllic, but the plot is very real indeed. In both books the emphasis on how it feels to be uprooted from one's family can stimulate discussion and empathy.

Two powerful books, packaged in picture-book format but clearly more appropriate for older children, revolve around children's experiences in and near concentration camps. Although the tone of the text and the use of illustrations are in sharp contrast, both books can break your heart.

Rose Blanche by Christophe Gallaz and ROBERTO INNOCENTI (1984) is a disturbing book. For Rose Blanche, war enters her German town on tanks manned by soldiers who wink at her. She describes following a truck into the country, where she finds hungry people imprisoned behind barbed wire. At that point the narration abruptly switches to third person, and the reader knows Rose Blanche will not survive this war. The large, detailed illustrations are dominated by browns and grays with only cautious touches of red.

The illustrations in *Let the Celebrations Begin!* by MARGARET WILD (1991) are alive with colors on open white space that begin in pastel, but deepen as the preparations for the celebration and the expected liberation of the concentration camp grow nearer. The story was inspired by a quotation from *Antique Toys and Their Background* by Gwen White describing a collection of stuffed toys made by women in Belsen for a party for the children held after the liberation.

Books for older readers in the more traditional format are set mostly in the European countries directly affected by the war. With few exceptions plot dominates the novels of the 1950s and 1960s. The tension of a survival story is, of course, present in the later novels and memoirs, but the impact of the books of the 1970s, 1980s, and 1990s comes from the emphasis on individual tragedies and triumphs. These books share a picture of the gradual deterioration of daily life for Jewish children and their families and a reluctance on the part of the adults to accept the reality of what was happening. Trapped by disbelief that leaving their home and country is necessary for survival, they wait too long. Many do not survive.

The best of the books not only relive the horror, but also bring to life the humanity. They are somber in tone with little, if any, "comic relief," but they do create memorable characters. Anne Frank best summarizes the mood and emotions of these books in her poignant declaration, "It's really a wonder that I haven't dropped all my ideals, because they seem so absurd and impossible to carry out. Yet I keep them, because in spite of everything I still believe that people are really good at heart." *Anne Frank: The Diary of a Young Girl* (1952) is one of the earliest and certainly the best known of all the memoirs. Written during the years 1942 to 1944 while she and her family were in hiding in Amsterdam, the diary's lively style, compelling story, and tragic end have captured readers of all ages. From the *Diary* has grown a body of literature that includes an award-winning play, *Anne Frank's Tales from the Secret Annex,* numerous biographies, and even a critical edition of several versions of *The Diary.*

Written in the 1960s, James Forman's unhurried narratives make for somber reading. *My Enemy My Brother* (1969) focuses on three young people who are deported from the Warsaw Ghetto, escape from a concentration camp, survive a harrowing trip, and end up fighting for survival again in the newly formed state of Israel. In *The Traitors* (1968) thirteen-year-old Paul is pulled in several directions trying to protect his best friend, who is Jewish, and to understand his brother, a passionate follower of Hitler. Forman has also explored the period from other perspectives including fictionalized retellings of the lives of Adolf Hitler and the young resisters Sophie and Hans Scholl. In *The Endless Steppe* (1968) ESTHER HAUTZIG recounts the story of how she and her family were exiled from their home in Vilna to the harsh steppes of Siberia, a turn of fortune that probably saved their lives.

Other books of interest from the 1960s include *Miriam* by Aimee Sommerfelt (1965), an uneven but tightly plotted book that chronicles the experience of a young Norwegian living in a house taken from a Jewish family, who learns how pervasive anti-Semitism is in her country. In Jane Whitbread Levin's *Star of Danger* (1966) the drama is in the chase as the reader follows the dangerous journey of two Jewish boys from Germany to temporary safety in Denmark and finally a haven in neutral Sweden.

It was not until the 1970s that a number of significant books were published in the United States chronicling experiences in Austria, France, Holland, Poland, the Ukraine, the United States, and, of course, Germany, the scene of the darkest of these novels and memoirs. In two powerful novels, *Friedrich* (1970) and *I Was There* (1972), Hans Richter bears witness to what he knew and experienced as a youth in Nazi Germany. In contrast to Forman's and Richter's more leisurely style, Yuri Suhl's crisp dialogue and fast-paced plotting put his message across. *On the Other Side of the Gate* (1975) combines suspenseful action and fully realized characterizations in the story of a young doctor and his wife who use their wits to make connections outside the Warsaw Ghetto and send their infant son to safety. Suhl's *Uncle Micha's Partisans* (1973) quickly engages the reader as the protagonist, twelve-year-old Motele, becomes involved with Jewish partisans in the Ukraine in an exciting, but extremely dangerous, mission.

Three distinguished and distinctive memoirs were published in the 1970s. JOHANNA REISS's *The Upstairs Room* (1972), named a 1973 Newbery Honor Book, is set in Holland. Annie and her sisters are literally farmed out to be hidden for the duration of the war. Among the many memorable characters are the Oosterveld family, with whom they live for most of the war. A sequel, *Journey Back* (1976), deals with the family's postwar adjustments. Judith Kerr's family, who had the foresight to leave Germany, suffered a kinder fate, but the toll on parents and children was high, as told in *When Hitler Stole Pink Rabbit* (1971). That a stuffed pink rabbit is not the only thing that Hitler's Germany extracted from the family is clear from the sequels *The Other Way Round* (1975) and *A Small Person Far Away* (1978). The third memoir is written by a *Michling Second Degree* (1977), a term designating a person with one Jewish grandparent. How Ilse Koehn balanced her allegiances and survived makes dramatic reading.

In MARILYN SACHS's novel *Pocketful of Seeds* (1973), set in France, eight-year-old Nicole comes home from school one day to find her family gone. For the duration of the war she is hidden in a Catholic school, and at thirteen must face the fact that she will probably never see her family again. Survival means more than just living, as Myron Levoy's novel *Alan and Naomi* (1977), set in New York City, vividly describes. Twelve-year-old Alan is asked to help Naomi, a refugee who watched her father die and whose emotional stability is understandably precarious. Alan finds no "happily ever after" but learns enough about friendship and commitment to sustain him for a lifetime. Friendship is also the key to survival for thirteen-year-old Inge and her family in the novel by DORIS ORGEL. Although Inge's best friend's father represents *The Devil in Vienna* (1978), the two friends' loyalty to each other allows both of them to retain their humanity.

The flow of books about the Holocaust continued in the 1980s. The decade was launched by ERIK CHRISTIAN HAUGAARD, whose clearly autobiographical novel, *Chase Me, Catch Nobody!* (1980), tells how Danish schoolboys on a visit to Germany help a young Jewish girl escape. It ended with LOIS LOWRY's Newbery Medal winner, *Number the Stars* (1989), which tells the story of how a young girl's best friend escapes from occupied Denmark to safety in Sweden. Other significant novels of the decade include Uri Orlev's grim, but ultimately triumphant, novel *The Island on Bird Street* (1984), in which a young boy holes up out of the reach of death in the Warsaw Ghetto. Orlev followed up with an equally strong story, *The Man from the Other Side* (1991), about a man who chooses to return to the Warsaw Ghetto to fight with the resisters. *Lisa's War* (1987) is fought in the Danish resistance until she and her brother must leave to seek a haven in Sweden. Author Carol Matas's sequel focuses on their non-Jewish friend who becomes *Code Name "Kris"* (1992).

Using time travel, JANE YOLEN crafted a memorable story of a contemporary child who finds herself in the midst of the horror of a Nazi concentration camp. *The Devil's Arithmetic* (1988) is calculated in powerful human terms. Although classified as fiction, *Touch Wood: A Girlhood in Occupied France* (1988) by Renee Roth-Hano is an autobiographical story of separation, fear, and ultimately an uneasy but relieved reconciliation. Aranka Siegal uses evocative language and unforgettable images in her memoirs *Upon the Head of the Goat: A Childhood in Hungary, 1939–1944* (1981). An indomitable mother and a wise grandmother make the difference between life and death. Siegal also wrote about her postwar experiences in the touching *Grace in the Wilderness* (1985).

The early 1990s have already yielded a number of titles about experiences told from different perspectives. For example, it was only when she was an adult that Olga Levy Drucker learned that she was one of ten thousand children who were rescued and sent to England. How she dealt with the separation from her family, her language, and her world is conveyed through feelings with which a child can identify in *Kindertransport* (1992). In a sparely written memoir that nine- and ten-year-olds could read, Isabella Leitner with Irving Leitner tells how *The Big Lie: A True Story* (1992) came to Hungary and devastated her family. An important character in JAN SLEPIAN's *Risk n' Roses* (1990), set in the Brooklyn streets, is a death camp survivor whom a girl hungry for friendship betrays—so that he becomes a victim again. In a French village a father is *Waiting for Anya* (1991) in Michael Morpurgo's novel, which chronicles how a whole village works together to spirit a group of Jewish children over the border to safety in Spain.

From the number of books published in the early 1990s, it is clear that new books about the Holocaust will continue to find their way into print. Survivors, who were children and young people in the years 1939 to 1945, and children of survivors feel the need to testify about their experiences. New books for children and young people need to be evaluated on the basis of literary merit, fidelity to the times, honest emotions, and reportage that avoids sensationalism. When such an unforgettable voice is heard through the printed page, the reader will not forget. § AMY KELLMAN

HOOVER, H. M.

AMERICAN AUTHOR OF SCIENCE FICTION FOR YOUNG ADULTS, B. 1935. Seeing mutated snails and gulls on a beach near a dumping site in New York prompted H. M. Hoover, a native of rural Ohio who grew up appreciating nature, to write her first book, *Children of Morrow* (1973). This science fiction adventure posits that pollution has led to the ecological devastation of the Earth and that only two very different societies, unbeknownst to each other, have survived. One primitive and militaristic, the other technologically advanced and adept at communicating telepathically, the societies have something in common: Tia and Rabbit, two children born and raised on the primitive Base, but descended from the more advanced Morrow and therefore able to communicate with the benevolent Morrowan leaders through their dreams.

Hoover has imagined many possible worlds since. *The Delikon* (1977) proposes a future in which humans have been subjugated by beings from the stars. *This Time of Darkness* (1980) gives a horrifying picture of an indoor underground community, tricked by authorities into believing the cramped, cockroach-ridden habitat is the best available. Many of the societies she portrays have progressed to a certain stage and then regressed. Earthlings in *The Shepherd Moon* (1984), for example, once built and populated four extra moons, but by the forty-eighth century, they have forgotten how the moons came to exist—forgotten even how to travel through space.

All of Hoover's books combine drama and suspense with food for thought. Whatever century or setting she envisions, she frequently writes of the complications that arise when two worlds—be they planets or social classes—meet. Tia and Rabbit finally escape to Morrow's more nurturing culture in the sequel, *Treasures of Morrow* (1976), and have difficulty adjusting to a foreign way of life. They have the unsettling experience of viewing their old life from the outside when they return to the Base with a Morrowan observation expedition.

One of Hoover's most provocative and gracefully achieved explorations of gaps between cultures is *Another Heaven, Another Earth* (1981). In it, a research crew from Earth arriving on the presumably uninhabited planet Xilan discovers a lost colony, abandoned hundreds of years ago by its founders and regressed to a primitive agrarian existence. Female biochemist Lee Hamilton, though one of the more sensitive of the research crew, cannot truly understand how the colonists accept their dirty, tenuous existence dominated by manual labor. Gareth, the colony's intelligent doctor, warily befriends the researchers when they invade her community to assist with a pneumonia epidemic, but she bristles at their contempt and pities their sterile world in which machines take most of the work—and, she believes, most of the satisfaction—from their lives. Without holding one culture over the other, Hoover sets forth differences that only tolerance and kindness can attempt to bridge.

Twice Hoover has imagined worlds of the past: nineteenth-century Russia in *The Lion's Cub* (1974), based on the true story of Jemal-Edin, son of a warring Dagestanian tribal leader, who is taken hostage to live with Czar Nicholas I; and ancient Greece in her young adult novel *The Dawn Palace: The Story of Medea* (1988). Through these compelling stories Hoover once again explores aspects of the outsider. ❧ C.M.H.

Hopkins, Lee Bennett

AMERICAN AUTHOR AND ANTHOLOGIST, B. 1938. When asked to speak, Lee Bennett Hopkins is far more comfortable talking about his mission than his books, which number more than seventy. His mission, which he speaks of with passion, is to recognize quality children's poetry, bring such work to the attention of teachers and librarians, and nurture conversation and dialogue among children about poetry.

Hopkins was born and spent the first ten years of his childhood in Scranton, Pennsylvania. He recalls, "I was Dick straight out of *Dick and Jane*, the basals that taught me to read." Life changed dramatically in 1948 when his family moved to Newark, New Jersey. Turmoil struck again when Hopkins was fourteen and his parents' marriage collapsed. Money was tight and life uncertain. Officially, Hopkins was enrolled at the South Eighth Street School, although by his own admission he spent more time out of than in school: "I hated school and everything associated with it," he recalls, "including books and reading." Luckily, a teacher introduced him to the magic of books and the theater. Hopkins graduated from high school and went on to college and graduate school.

Hopkins's first book, *Let Them Be Themselves: Language Arts Enrichment for Disadvantaged Children in Elementary School* (1969), was reissued in its third edition in 1992. Other books include young adult fiction, anthologies, and nonfiction for adults. *Mama* (1979) and *Mama and Her Boys* (1981) are semiautobiographical remembrances of life in the Hopkins home. His anthologies represent a number of influences. *Surprises* (1984), *Best Friends* (1986), *More Surprises* (1987), *Good Books, Good Times* (1990), and *Questions* (1992) celebrate the exuberance of youth. The world surrounding children is the subject of several collections, including *On the Farm* (1991), *Still a Star: Nighttime Poems* (1990), and *To the Zoo* (1992). As an anthologist, Hopkins collects poetry he admires. On two occasions, this admiration resulted in anthologies devoted solely to one poet, *Rainbows Are Made: Poems by Carl Sandburg* (1982) and *Voyages: Poems by Walt Whitman* (1988). "Good poetry," he notes, "is by a master craftsman who knows the rules of his craft. He/She gets the maximum impact from a minimum number of words."

Over the course of two decades, Hopkins has also been the voice of social warning. *Wonder Wheels* (1980) was one of the first young adult novels about teen suicide. *Pass the Poetry, Please!* (1972) exposed elementary classrooms for the dreary places they were in the late eighties—rooms of potentially creative youngsters lacking rhyme. Now in its second edition, the book continues to challenge educators. *Through Our Eyes* (1992) also contains a plea of sorts. In sixteen short poems, Hopkins presents the hopes, fears, and observations of today's youth. The anthology is honest, hard-hitting, and revealing.

Hopkins closes the third edition of *Let Them Be Themselves* with the hope that we—the collective society responsible for children—begin to value their words. If we do this, then perhaps "they will begin to think more about thinking." B.A.M.

Horror Stories

Children have always been fascinated with horror: Dracula and Frankenstein remain popular heroes of the genre today. But the trend toward teen thriller fiction was probably accelerated, if not spawned, by the spate of horror movies that enticed a young group of viewers to box offices in the early 1980s and by the tendency of children's books to parallel current adult reading interests. When Stephen King and similar authors of adult books began giving mystery stories a supernatural twist peppered with violence and horror, the trend was bound to be reflected in some form in children's publishing.

Children's book editors publishing horror fiction took their cue from these movies and from the representation of society's fascination with violence in adult mass-market books. Publishers began looking for writers who could take an ordinary teenage situation and give it a horror slant. In the late 1980s, legions of youngsters in the fourth through seventh grades became hooked on paperback horror stories starring teenage protagonists. According to booksellers, this phenomenon in children's literature is not just a marketing ploy by publishers. Young people are the promoters: The marketing is done by them—by word of mouth.

Controversy surrounds the books. Parents are concerned that the stories might lead to psychological or behavior problems. However, the opinions of several child psychiatrists seem to indicate that if the books do not imitate the lascivious, sensational violence in the movies and on television, they will probably not promote violent behavior. Although some parents are troubled about the books' adverse effect upon their children, most are amazed and annoyed that preteens are reading such pap. Within the entire context of children's literature, critics see teen horror fiction as a minor, nonliterary fad. Generally, the consensus is that these books are not good literature, but they are not harmful. Enticing, recreational reading, they can be a hook to get reluctant readers into libraries where they will find books of more substance.

How horrific is the horror? In most cases it means a threatened or actual murder. Suspense is created, but readers are spared bloody details, explicit violence, or any sort of twisted sexual element. If boyfriend-girlfriend relationships exist within the story line, kissing is about as far as these novels go.

Plots are predictable. A teenager, featured as the main character, usually finds a murder victim or discovers a plan to commit murder. The protagonists, and often their friends, are stalked; suspense builds as friends suspect each other; sometimes a romance angle develops; and either a surprise bit of realistic detective work or a supernatural event exposes the perpetrator of the crime. The final chapters proceed at a rapid pace, often including a catastrophic ending. Not surprisingly, the characters are usually one-dimensional, and the stories often tend to be tiresomely repetitious.

Editors who publish suspense thrillers agree that these stories could never really happen; they are sheer escapist reading. The books appeal because kids are the victims, kids solve the crime, and adults are only peripheral characters. Children aren't reading them for grisly violence; they simply love to be scared. The books offer horror with a beginning, middle, and end—children read them and then put them down. They can control the fear, as the children in the stories have the power to resolve their situations.

Although protagonists in the novels are fifteen- and sixteen-year-olds, the readership is approximately ages eight through fourteen. Children, no matter what books they read, generally like to read about older characters. Editors recognize this tendency to read "up" and consider it foolhardy not to have responsible standards for content. In the long run, bizarre, gratuitous, and offensive violence would end the trend's popularity, due to objections from parents, librarians, and critics.

Christopher Pike was the first to enter the field

with *Slumber Party* (1985), *Weekend* (1986), and *Chain Letter* (1986); he began to hit his stride in the "Final Friends" series. R. L. Stine's "Fear Street" series is also popular. Two women making a niche in horror with a supernatural ambiance are Richie Tankersley Cusick, who wrote *The Mall* (1992) and *Silent Stalker* (1993), and Caroline B. Cooney, author of *Vampire's Promise* (1993). These authors are popular because they were the first to create the spine-tingling tales and got a jump on the market. Newcomers to the field are John Peel and Bruce Coville.

One publisher approaches the trend from a different angle. The firm's juvenile department takes young adult literature originally popular in hardcover, applies a frightening cover, then markets it in paperback. Most of the authors thus published are fine writers—PETER DICKINSON, ROBERT CORMIER, JOAN AIKEN, LEON GARFIELD—who are addressing more complex issues while using the suspense-mystery form to sustain dramatic action. The same publishing house also uses seasoned mystery writers who write for young adults, such as LOIS DUNCAN and JOAN LOWERY NIXON, authors well known for depth in plot and character, to produce mystery thrillers with solid quality.

Numbers substantiate the strength of the current preteen/teen reading fad; The two foremost paperback publishers in the field acknowledged they "shipped over 10 million teen suspense novels to buyers from 1989 to 1992." Another indicator of the books' popular appeal is that teen horror titles are consistently showing up on the young adult bestsellers' list of *Publishers Weekly.* The periodical reported in 1993 that the popular Babysitters Club was being "edged out by horror books. YA horror author, Christopher Pike . . . is on a goosebumpy ride to the top of the charts."

Though publishers claim there is no end in sight for middle-grade horror paperbacks, the current glut of these books on the market might indicate otherwise. The sameness of plot and stereotypical characters may eventually cause them to lose appeal and give way to another new twist in the combination of mystery, horror, and the supernatural. One thing, however, will remain the same. There will always be a new audience of children coming along, and scary stories inevitably will cast their spell on the younger set. STEPHANIE LOER

HOUSTON, JAMES

CANADIAN AUTHOR AND ILLUSTRATOR, B. 1921. In 1948, having made it to the northeast coast of Hudson Bay, James A. Houston decided to forgo his return flight and stay at an Eskimo settlement with only his sleeping bag, sketch materials, and a can of peaches. Fourteen years later, after working as civil administrator of West Baffin, Northwest Territories, where he introduced printmaking to the Inuit and established the West Baffin Eskimo Co-operative to help them market carvings and prints, Houston left the Arctic for New York City and a job as associate director of design for Steuben glass. He still works for Steuben, as master designer, but now he and his wife, Alice, divide their time between homes in Connecticut and the Queen Charlotte Islands.

"Tlingit Helmet" from *Songs of the Dream People: Chants and Images from the Indians and Eskimos of North America* (1972), edited and illustrated by James Houston.

The North, which he visits regularly, continues to serve as inspiration for Houston's books and much of his art. Almost five decades after first setting foot in the Arctic, he introduces readers of all ages to a way of life most will never experience themselves. Some of those books—beginning with *Nuki* (1953), illustrated by Houston and written by his first wife, Alma—have been labeled children's literature, although, as Houston points out, "the Inuit made no difference between children's stories and adult stories; children stayed around and were aware of everything at all times."

The Toronto-born author admits he was relatively clueless when first in the Arctic—he managed to fall through the sea ice five times the first year he was there—but the Inuit shared their knowledge and their stories, which he in turn shares with his readers. The first book he both wrote and illustrated was *Tikta'liktak: An Eskimo Legend* (1965), which won the Canadian

Library Association's Book of the Year for Children Award. He also won the prize for two other volumes: *The White Archer: An Eskimo Legend* (1967) and *River Runners: A Tale of Hardship and Bravery* (1979).

In all his books, whether they are Inuit or Native American stories, Houston is at his best when recounting tales of traditional nomadic life. *Drifting Snow* (1992), for example, about a girl who returns to the North in search of family she lost when she was sent south for tuberculosis treatment as a toddler, is most riveting when it involves the girl's experiences camping on an island with an Inuit family but stalls when dealing with contemporary issues. Houston himself seems to breathe easier when his characters are away from civilization; it is there that his writing is most evocative. In books like *Akavak: An Eskimo Journey* (1968), *Wolf Run: A Caribou Eskimo Tale* (1971), *Frozen Fire: A Tale of Courage* (1977), and *The Falcon Bow: An Arctic Legend* (1986), he makes readers feel bone-numbing cold, mind-altering hunger, the joy of a successful hunt, and gratitude for that first hot meal. The author tells us how to build an igloo, how to stave off frostbite, how to help and rely on others. He describes a life among people of great generosity, respect, and ingenuity.

Houston's tales of adventure are as captivating in short form—*Long Claws: An Arctic Adventure* (1981) at thirty-two pages is hardly a tome, but tells a thrilling story about children who save their family from starvation—as are his full-length novels such as *Whiteout* (1988), the story of a rebellious teenager sent north for a year of community service. The author, meanwhile, has carved himself a solid niche in the history of Canada's Arctic. At a time when cultural appropriation has become a hotly debated subject, Houston's books about the Inuit stand as testimony to the fact that cultures *can* be bridged—and that stories from an oral tradition can be respectfully retold in print. ❧ B.G.

HOWE, JAMES

AMERICAN AUTHOR, B. 1946. If there are any common defining features of James Howe's MYSTERIES and PICTURE BOOKS, novels and INFORMATION BOOKS, they are the author's respect for and understanding of children and childhood. He remembers well what it is like to be small and powerless, and his books all strive, in different ways, to connect with his readers through those feelings. One of his most successful and effective devices is humor, which he feels is "the most precious gift I can give my reader."

Although Howe grew up telling stories, writing plays, and editing *The Gory Gazette,* the official newspaper of his Vampire Club, his first desire was to be an actor. After graduating from Boston University in 1968 with a degree in theater, Howe moved to New York City to pursue his acting career. In 1981, after the success of his first three children's books, he left his job as a literary and theatrical agent and turned to writing full-time. Howe and his late wife, Deborah, had no idea, however, when they began writing their first book, *Bunnicula* (1979), just for fun, that it would be as popular as it was or that it would launch his career as a children's book author. But their mystery was embraced by middle-grade readers and won over twenty state awards. *Bunnicula* and its sequels, which Howe wrote after Deborah's death, are all infused with generous doses of humor and wordplay. Having trained as an actor and a director, Howe understands how to build suspense, and he has a fine sense of dramatic timing.

Bunnicula is a little black-and-white rabbit who, in the first book, comes to live with the Monroe family. The human members of the household don't notice anything strange about their new pet, but Chester, the family cat, who has a vivid imagination, is convinced that Bunnicula is a vampire. The story of Chester's hilarious attempts to warn the Monroes of this evil in their midst is told by Harold, the family dog. In *Howliday Inn* (1982), Harold and Chester are boarded at Chateau Bow-Wow when the Monroes go on vacation. They soon find themselves caught up in a suspicious chain of events that Chester believes involves murder. Bunnicula returns in *The Celery Stalks at Midnight* (1983), which introduces the newest Monroe pet, Howie, the dachshund puppy. Howe feels that his series of picture books featuring the popular Bunnicula characters are a suitable introduction to mysteries for younger children. This particular genre speaks directly to children because, Howe has written, in addition to being fun to read, "mysteries allow us mastery and control." To children, this desire for control is fundamental. "Through reading," Howe says, children "gain some measure of control. They are able to see something through to a neat resolution; and perhaps through the children in the story, gain a sense of themselves as human beings who are valid and powerful."

Howe's concern for his readers' empowerment is evident in his other books as well. *The Hospital Book* (1981), a sensitively written nonfiction photo essay, helps children anticipate what a hospital stay is like—from the staff, to the equipment, to the feelings with which they may have to cope. Howe's series for beginning readers featuring best friends Pinky and Rex celebrates childhood friendships. As with all of Howe's characters, Pinky and Rex appeal to children because they know the challenges and rewards of being best friends. With them children learn something about what it means to be a friend while maintaining individuality. Howe's stories are funny, but they are also about the joy and pain of being human. K.F.

Howker, Janni

English author, b. 1957. In the mid-1980s, Janni Howker emerged as the most formidable new British author of young adult fiction, turning out three critically acclaimed books in three years. Reviewers praised the skillful craftsmanship of her debut, a collection of five stories entitled *Badger on the Barge* (1984), which seemed the mark of a veteran, not a twenty-seven-year-old fresh from writing school. Yet they also noted, as they would for her two novels to come, the commendably jagged edges of her polished stories.

Her writing's sticking power no doubt derives largely from her affinity for her perennial focus: the working classes of northern England, where she makes her home. Her characteristic use of that region's vernacular combined with resonating imagery never fails to evoke a strong sense of place. And whether in the economically depressed Lancashire mill town that is the setting for *The Nature of the Beast* (1985) or the temporally but not spatially more distant turn-of-the-century horse farm of *Isaac Campion* (1986), discerning readers can recognize not only the harshness but the profundity in the lives of her characters. While individually distinct and multifaceted, all of Howker's plots involve an adolescent protagonist struggling to confront harsh realities at this already vulnerable stage of life. In each of the stories in *Badger on the Barge,* a relationship with an elderly loner facilitates that confrontation. Some face the reality of death, as Helen does in the title story when she gains the strength from feisty Mrs. Brady and her badger Bad Bill to break the circle of guilt and denial her family has trod since her brother's death. Others come up against social injustice. After hearing old Sally the gardener's life story, Liz in "The Topiary Garden" comes to see the long-standing oppression of women as keeping them—herself included—distorted like topiary bushes, unable to express their true forms. Howker portrays more fearsomely the menace of injustice in *The Nature of the Beast,* significantly coupling a period of massive unemployment in a northern English town with savage attacks on the town's livestock by a beast that inhabits the shadows. But no matter how bleak the circumstances, Howker's protagonists remain survivors. *Isaac Campion* shows this most plainly, as ninety-six-year-old Isaac looks back unsentimentally on a childhood during which he witnessed the accidental death of his older brother and came to mix a degree of pity and understanding with the fear, suppressed rage, and desperate loyalty he felt for his hot-tempered, apparently cold-hearted father. Awards Howker has received for her work include the International Reading Association's Children's Book Award in 1985 for *Badger on the Barge* and the 1985 Whitbread Book of the Year, children's novel section, for *The Nature of the Beast.* C.H.

Hughes, Langston

American poet and author, 1902–1967. Primarily known for his poetry, James Langston Hughes also wrote fiction, drama, autobiography, and information books. Born in Joplin, Missouri, he spent his formative years in Kansas and Cleveland. His childhood was not easy. An only child, Langston began to read books to escape his deep loneliness. In his first autobiography, *The Big Sea* (1940), he refers to his second-grade year: "Then it was that books began to happen to me, and I began to believe in nothing but books and the wonderful world in books." Among the books he enjoyed were the *Bible,* and the works of W. E. B. Du Bois, Mark Twain, and Paul Laurence Dunbar; he also avidly read news articles about race relations. His eighth-grade class in Lincoln, Illinois, elected him class poet, and during his sophomore year at Central High School in Cleveland, his first poems appeared in print. In his senior year, he wrote the appealing commentary on black beauty, "When Sue Wears Red." Two rarely cited poems for children—"Winter Sweetness" and "Fairies"—were published in *The Brownies' Book* in 1921, and in the same year *The Crisis* published one of his most popular poems, "The Negro Speaks of Rivers."

Travel, adventure, and a move to Harlem influenced the style and content of his work. Simple and informal, his poems were composed in free verse and rhyme. His works flourished during the Harlem Renaissance in the 1920s. Hughes drew his inspiration from urban black life, managing to capture its essence and at the same time express in language the rhythm of the jazz and blues music that meant so much to him. The ability to write about ordinary people and the accessibility of his lyricism contributed to the popularity of his poetry with children. A literary descendant of Dunbar, Hughes sometimes wrote in dialect. Despite his despair about racial injustice in America, he was able to imbue much of his creative output with a sense of humor, an affirming spirit, a love for the natural world, and optimism. Although many of his poems were not specifically intended for young people, he published his collection *The Dream Keeper and Other Poems* (1932) especially for them. Many of his poems appeared in anthologies, and in 1967 LEE BENNETT HOPKINS compiled for children *Don't You Turn Back,* a selection published in 1969 after the poet's death. A poet of the people, Hughes was properly dubbed the poet laureate of Harlem.

Hughes explored several genres, including autobiography, novels, short stories, drama, and nonfiction. For children, he coauthored with ARNA BONTEMPS a story about poor people in Haiti titled *Popo and Fifina* (1932). Among his books that introduced young readers to various topics are *The First Book of Rhythms* (1954), an engaging look at rhythm around us, and *The First Book of Jazz* (1955). Through his collective biographies *Famous American Negroes* (1954) and *Famous Negro Heroes of America* (1958), young readers were introduced to outstanding persons. These short informative books highlighted the lives of black achievers at a time when few sources on black history were available. In 1956 Hughes published, with MILTON MELTZER, an enlightening overview, *A Pictorial History of the Negro in America.* His last work was a book of aphorisms for children, *Black Misery* (1969), published after his death.

Hughes had great pride in his race. His poems continue to inspire readers seeking a voice against injustice. ❧ L.F.A.

HUGHES, MONICA

ENGLISH-BORN CANADIAN AUTHOR, B. 1925. Monica Hughes easily claims celebrity as one of Canada's most distinguished authors of juvenile literature. While she has written realistic and historical stories, she is particularly renowned for her science fiction. Hughes's themes are often uniquely Canadian, but they transcend their rootedness to become concerns with global dimensions.

Born in Liverpool, England, and raised in Egypt until the age of six, Hughes received her education at private schools in England and Scotland. As a girl she read voraciously, but her discovery of JULES VERNE sparked a lifelong love of science fiction. Widely traveled, Hughes lived in Zimbabwe for two years before settling in Canada in 1952 and becoming a naturalized citizen. While she had begun to struggle with writing before coming to Canada, it was the early 1970s before she decided to spend a year attempting to write professionally. After her first publication, a commissioned historical novella called *Gold-Fever Trail: A Klondike Adventure* (1974), Hughes shifted her focus to sophisticated works of science fiction. The near future is generally Hughes's setting of choice, her protagonists most often adolescents struggling on a path toward responsible adulthood. Hughes has said that she uses science fiction as a medium through which to deal with the myriad problems young people face in today's society. Resonant with philosophical underpinnings characteristic of the best science fiction, Hughes's multivalent works thoughtfully explore social and moral issues: isolation, the preservation of heritage, the exploitation of natural resources, adaptation to hostile environments, communication across distances and between individuals.

Beyond the Dark River (1979) limns the clash of two disparate cultures, the Hutterites and the Cree Indians, in postapocalypse Canada. Disparity between cultural groups also provides the tension for *Ring-Rise, Ring-Set* (1982), in which the solution that inhabitants of an artificial underground world devise to prevent an imminent Ice Age destroys a native people's environment. *Devil on My Back* (1984) addresses issues of power and freedom as it details a totalitarian, computer-driven society in which status is predicated on knowledge. Set in the year 2011, *The Crystal Drop* (1992) reveals the devastating consequences of environmental neglect and human greed in the face of diminishing resources. *Hunter in the Dark* (1982), one of the author's few works of realistic fiction, plumbs the depths of isolation and identity as a sixteen-year-old comes to terms with his approaching death from leukemia.

Critics judge Hughes's richest achievement to be the Isis Trilogy—*The Keeper of the Isis Light* (1980), *The Guardian of Isis* (1981), and *The Isis Pedlar* (1982). This series focuses on the development and near-disintegration across a three-generation span of a colony on the planet Isis and introduces Olwen Pendennis, one of Hughes's most complex and fully realized characters. *The Keeper of the Isis Light* received a Certificate of Honor from the International Board on Books for Young People, and *The Guardian of Isis* won the Canada Council Children's Literature Prize. ❧ C.S.

HUGHES, SHIRLEY

ENGLISH AUTHOR AND ILLUSTRATOR, B. 1927. Sit down with a pile of Shirley Hughes books and come away certain that this woman loves children. Invite her to tea, and there is no reason to send the dog to the cellar and the kids off to play; she will revel in whatever comes. Her characters are dressed to play; she has elevated scruffiness to an art form. And if her children do not look steamed and pressed, they do look well loved.

Hughes has illustrated more than two hundred books and written more than a dozen of her own, several of

Voices of the Creators

Shirley Hughes

Alfie made his first appearance as a felt-pen sketch. He was running up the street ahead of his mum, who was trundling behind with the shopping and his baby sister in the buggy. A lot had happened, mostly in my head, before I got him to this stage, but it was something of a turning point to see him there on the page.

Picture book ideas, like movies, are unthinkable without the visual element. The illustrations are not added to the words as a mere afterthought. An idea usually floats about like an iceberg, largely below the surface, for some time before something triggers it urgently into focus. As I am an illustrator, I reach for a pencil to get some roughs down at an early stage. Having a good narrative in mind stimulates the desire to draw. In this case I wanted to tell a simple tale turning on an event which is common enough in everyday life but nevertheless of dramatic and memorable importance to a four-year-old—like slamming the door and getting stuck inside. When I was making that first drawing, I was concentrating hard on Alfie's concentration—that mighty, breathless, all-out effort which children of this age give to the matter in hand. And the consternation which sometimes ensues when things go wrong. Alfie's character crystallized the moment I drew him and developed from there.

Characterization is at the root of storytelling. Even very young readers can form a strong loyalty to fictional characters once they have taken them to heart. It is up to us creators to invent characters who inspire this kind of loyalty—though it's not all that easy. To rely on merely repeating a formula is the kiss of death. Writing for this age, one is aware that the words of the story line are a thread—a vital one—but that the fleshing out of the characters, the setting, much of the humor and drama of the plot is going to be discovered in the pictures. Comments and observations are made; a delightful dialogue emerges. This is an unforgettable shared experience, a first introduction to fiction.

Getting the words right is a demanding business. Sometimes, as with *Dogger* (1988), they seem to write themselves. But often they can take more time and trouble than a much longer piece. The aim is to achieve a rhythmic quality that bears reading over and over again, a satisfying onionlike whole, lucidly simple but containing many layers within.

The rough dummy is the essence of the book. You work out the pattern by disposing the blocks of text and pictures so they work in conjunction. I use smooth drawing paper which I can just see through, so that I can place one idea for a spread over another and compare them. At this stage I draw in pencil and go over it with a felt pen, which gives a good clear photocopy. Unfettered by the tensions which are imposed when you are doing the finished artwork—an altogether slower and more meticulous process—you are drawing very unselfconsciously, concentrating entirely on the story line and characters. The resulting sketches, not surprisingly, have a vitality and economy of gesture which is quite hard to reproduce when it comes to the finished artwork.

This stage comes later, sometimes six months or a year. Whether I'm using color or black-and-white line, I work tonally—that is to say, to try to create a three-dimensional quality of depth, to open up the page so that the reader can enter the scene, perhaps fantasize about what is not shown. The color washes go on in layers, solidifying toward the foreground (I use gouache, which is similar to watercolor but with a bit more body). The underlying pencil drawing disappears under these layers but is brought back again at the final stage with very fine brushwork. It is all too easy to overwork the process at any stage and so lose the freshness and spontaneity.

When I am working on a book, I am running on two tracks, controlling the technique (or trying to) and at the same time inhabiting my characters. It is important to build on detail, to beguile the reader with reassuring familiarity but at the same time tell him or her something new with each story, to reveal just a little more about this imaginary but very "real" world. All this is underpinned by making careful observations from life, keeping sketchbooks, cultivating an eye for a telling gesture, a figure in motion, the way people (especially children) group together when absorbed in a game or conversation. But in the end you go home and make it all up.

There seems to be no limit to the possibilities offered by the pages of a picture book. It's an adventure without end.

Initial sketch by Shirley Hughes for *Alfie's Feet* (*above*) and an illustration from the book (*right*).

them about one of her outstanding characters, a mischievous little guy named Alfie. In *Alfie Gets in First* (1981), Alfie squeezes through a window when the family's locked out; in *Alfie Gives a Hand* (1983), he takes his blanket to a birthday party; in *An Evening at Alfie's* (1984), he comforts baby sister Annie Rose when the pipes spring a leak. The first book Hughes illustrated was Doris Rust's *Story a Day* in 1954. Since then, she has illustrated dozens of others, including LOUISA MAY ALCOTT's *Little Women* in 1960 and books by MARGARET MAHY, NINA BAWDEN, HELEN CRESSWELL, and Alison Uttley.

Her own first book was *Lucy and Tom's Day,* the first in the "Lucy and Tom" series, in 1960. *Dogger* (1977), which she also both wrote and illustrated, won for her the Kate Greenaway Medal, Great Britain's highest picture-book honor.

Born in Holylake, England, near Liverpool, Hughes is married to an architect, and they have three grown children. She had a childhood full of acting out plays with her older sisters and of writing. Plenty of books were always around, so she got to know the work of illustrators such as ARTHUR RACKHAM and Edmund Dulac. After attending the Liverpool Art School and Ruskin School of Drawing and Fine Arts in Oxford, she taught at Oxford.

Hughes compares PICTURE BOOKS to a small theater production, in which the illustrator is the stage manager, lighting specialist, playwright, and costume designer. She did, in fact, take classes in costume design, thinking she might go into that field, but her devotion to writing and illustration turned her toward children's books. Another push toward children's books as a career choice was Hughes's family life itself, her observation and participation in the day-to-day chaos. She knew, too, from her own children how a book needs to be strong enough to withstand the test of repeated readings. In all her books Hughes's generous spirit shines through, providing a warm place from which all small readers can explore their world. ❧ A.C.

HUGHES, TED

ENGLISH POET, PLAYWRIGHT, AND FICTION AUTHOR, B. 1930. The poet laureate of England since 1985, Ted Hughes is among the most honored English-language poets of our era. He is, arguably, equally well known for his failed early marriage to Sylvia Plath, the American poet, novelist, and children's book writer (*The Bed Book*).

Though his POETRY for adults has brought him his greatest critical acclaim, he has written many volumes of poetry, plays, and prose for children, the best known of which are *The Iron Giant: A Children's Story in Five Nights* (1968). Acclaimed by the English newspaper the *Observer* as "one of the greatest of modern fairy tales," it is fairly described by its subtitle. This is a book to be read aloud, and it is perfectly in pitch with the mysteries of the night. The five chapters are short, satisfying on their own, yet build to a resounding conclusion.

The story begins enigmatically with the appearance of the Iron Man—no one knows why and no one knows from where—on the top of a cliff. He tumbles over it, is torn asunder by the fall, and then reconstructs himself (minus one ear) with the unwitting help of sea gulls. He then travels to a village, terrifying its inhabitants until a quick-witted young boy named Hogarth finds a way to make peace. Calm reigns until a new, vastly more dangerous creature appears, and Hogarth and the Iron Man join forces in a spectacular rescue mission that not only saves the whole planet but improves the night sky.

While *The Iron Giant* is rich with allegories—the conflict between the industrial and the pastoral, paranoia versus peace, trust versus fear, good versus evil, to name just a few—the book does not have to be read on any deeper level to be appreciated. It works beautifully all on its own. Despite Hughes's daunting reputation as a serious poet (along with its nearly unshakable corollary, "more praised than read"), at its core this is a rip-roaring story, filled with adventure, infused with kindness, and told with a rhythmic, precise, and simple voice that is a joy to read and to hear.

Other children's books by Hughes are likely to have a more specialized appeal. His picture book, *Nessie, the Merciless Monster* (1964), is a rollicking poem about the Loch Ness monster's improbable and ultimately triumphant visit with the Queen. English to its core, both in allusion and in vocabulary, it is unlikely that this rather long verse would engage many American children. Similarly, the arch tone of his *Tales of the Early World* (1991), a collection of creation tales for older children, probably requires a sophisticated literary sensibility to be enjoyed. ❦ A.Q.

Hunt, Irene

American author, b. 1907. When she wrote her first book, *Across Five Aprils* (1964), Irene Hunt crafted one of the most critically acclaimed historical novels published in American children's literature. After receiving a 1965 Newbery Honor Book award for that title, she further established herself in the critics' circles with her second book, *Up a Road Slowly* (1966), which garnered the 1967 Newbery Medal. Brilliant characterization, a telling sense of story, an uncanny ability to balance fact and fiction, and compassionate, graceful writing mark Hunt's small but distinguished body of work.

Born in Illinois, Hunt was just seven when her father died; she and her mother then moved to her grandparents' farm, where Hunt lived a lonely childhood. Her grandfather, a talented storyteller, filled Hunt, an eager listener, with tales of his youth during the Civil War. After obtaining degrees from the University of Illinois and the University of Minnesota, Hunt began a teaching career in 1930 that spanned thirty-five years. As an educator, Hunt observed that her students learned history more effectively through literature than through textbooks; remembering her grandfather's boyhood stories, Hunt used them as grist for *Across Five Aprils.*

Hunt's protagonist, Jethro Creighton, age nine in April 1861, grows quickly to manhood during the tragic years of America's Civil War. The naive Illinois farm boy enviously watches an older brother and a cousin enlist in the Northern army, while his favorite brother, Bill, joins the Southern troops. Letters from Jethro's relatives sustain the action and direct the powerful narrative to different places and differing opinions regarding the war. In the fifth April, at the war's end, Jethro somberly realizes the calamitous cost the war has exacted from his family and the entire nation.

Like Jethro Creighton, Hunt's grandfather was a nine-year-old Illinois farm boy at the outbreak of the Civil War. For historical accuracy and authenticity, Hunt relied heavily on her own family letters and records to research her book. Recalling her grandfather's vivid stories allowed her to write intimately about the ravaging impact of war on one family; with *Across Five Aprils,* Hunt succeeds extraordinarily in humanizing history.

Remembering her own father's death provided the inspiration for *Up a Road Slowly.* Shortly after her mother dies, seven-year-old protagonist Julie Trelling reluctantly goes to live on a Midwestern farm with her spinster aunt. Staying with her mother's older sister for ten years during the 1930s, Julie grows up, maturing into a high school graduate who quotes Edna St. Vincent Millay and Sara Teasdale. Hunt renders this first-person, coming-of-age narrative in the past tense without becoming mawkish; her major and minor characters are convincing and credible; and she handles issues of alcoholism, mental illness, and stepparents honestly yet graciously.

Hunt wrote six other books, mostly historical novels that bear her trademark style but are less well known than her first two works. She once said, "The wish to write pages full of words, to make them tell the stories that I dreamed about, haunted me from childhood on." Hunt's masterful writing reflects that close affinity with her own childhood. She offers young readers unforgettable stories about genuine characters; her children's books uphold fine literary standards and bring history alive. ❦ S.L.S.

Voices of the Creators

Mollie Hunter

Some people—myself included—seem fated to miss the obvious.

I've always loved words, and I'm a natural-born storyteller. I also love children; and yet, it was still only because my own young sons clamored for me to "make a book" out of stories I had invented for them that I turned from other forms of writing to writing for children.

These stories, as it happens, had derived from what has now been a lifelong study of folklore. But it is still the Celtic folklore of my native Scotland that has particular interest for me; and mainly so because of its language form—bone-smooth in its simplicity, shot through with symbolism emerging in sudden flashes of high, poetic imagery. And yet, even though the cadences of this come easily to me in speech, to convey the same effect in written form presented its own peculiar difficulties.

The book was written, nevertheless; the children were delighted with it, and, since it quickly also delighted a publisher, it proved eventually to be only a beginning to the long line of my books classed as fantasies. As I've since been amused to note, too, these fantasies have been described as being for readers "from nine to ninety—provided the older ones have strong enough nerves." And that may well be the case. But even so, my equally long line of historical adventure novels is definitely for those with reading skills not reached until around the age of twelve.

Their narrative style, for a start, follows the conventions of literature in general, and cannot therefore be so easily assimilated as that of the fantasies—all of which derive as much as did that first one from folklore, and are similarly designed to give the impression of being "told" tales. In keeping with this, therefore, the plot line of each has to be of the simple kind in which events run sequentially.

The "historicals," on the other hand, must project a story much more sophisticated, not only in the style of its telling, but also in its content. And so the challenge here is that of creating characters powerful enough to carry a strong story line tightly plotted and of achieving enough interplay between the two to infuse the whole with plenty of well-paced action.

Just as the fantasies have given me joy through the color and music of language, then, so the "historicals" have given me a different kind of joy in trying always to rise to their specific challenge. Besides which, they have enabled me to exploit yet another lifelong study—that of Scottish history; and out of the treasure trove of tales gathered from this, to create the kind of book that appeals to the distinctly dramatic side of my temperament.

It could be said, of course, that writing derived so much from a native culture is inevitably exclusive. But far from this being so—as I'm glad to note the critics agree—I have managed always to make my work open and accessible to readers all over the world. That circumstance applies also to my "realistic" novels for young adults, in which I have explored yet another form of writing—this time by drawing solely on personal life experience.

In all these novels, also, I have further changed tack by creating a female protagonist, thus giving myself an opportunity previously denied me in the characterization needed for other types of story—that of expressing myself specifically from the female point of view.

When one has grandchildren, finally, it is wonderful to be once again in demand as the family storyteller. At the time I wrote that first book for my own children, however, they were well past the picture storybook stage—and this is not so with the grandchildren! For each one that has arrived, therefore, I have written his or her own picture storybook—and have indeed just delighted the latest of these by publishing what he proudly calls "my *own* book."

It's taken more than thirty years to come full circle like this. But there have been nearly as many books in the course of that time; and my only regret out of it all is that I just don't have enough lifetime left to write as many more.

Hunter, Mollie

Scottish author, b. 1922. In her book of autobiographical essays on writing for children, *Talent Is Not Enough*, Mollie Hunter writes, "The child that was myself was born with little talent, and I have worked hard, hard to shape it. Yet even this could not have made me a writer, for there is no book can tell anything worth saying unless life itself has first said it to the person who conceived that book. A philosophy has to be hammered out, a mind shaped, a spirit tempered. . . . There must be a person behind that book." Behind Hunter's work we find a strength and independence of soul, love, integrity, high-spirited imagination, a person who feels deeply for history.

Maureen McIlwraith, who writes under her great-grandmother's name of Hunter, was born in Longniddry, East Lothian, Scotland. While she was growing up in a small village of Lowland Scotland, her great-grandmother talked and sang to her of their past, and she knew early her own real place in living history. The family could afford no more than the legal minimum of schooling, so Hunter turned to books and to the original sources of history—state papers, diaries, letters, and legal records—drawing her own conclusions and building her knowledge. In 1940 she married Thomas McIlwraith, and they had two sons, Quentin Wright and Brian George.

Out of her instinctive love of the past and ongoing research came her historical novels: *Hi Johnny* (1963), *The Spanish Letters* (1964), and, many titles later, *The Thirteenth Member* (1971) and *The Stronghold*, which won the Carnegie Medal in 1974. In these, and in her folklore, Hunter creates a powerful sense of place, a tangible atmosphere, and characters with whom readers identify deeply. Hunter gets behind the eyes of her characters, allowing her readers to be present in the story and, seeing themselves in another, to face significant moral decisions. Her vivid character development provides a unique anchor in her work, especially in folklore such as *The Kelpie's Pearls* (1964) and *The Walking Stones* (1970), in which the central characters have supernatural powers. Because they are created fully, the reader experiences events with them and more easily accepts the supernatural elements. The reader's identification with a book's protagonist is possibly deepest and the writing most vigorous and insightful in Hunter's autobiographical novel, *A Sound of Chariots* (1972), in which she tells the story of her childhood and of how she came to terms with the death of her father.

Much of Hunter's work employs the theme of the narrow, limited nature of modern technological and scientific thought when confronted with life's spiritual dimension. Against the blind willfulness of technology, Hunter pits the values of sensitivity and compassion, the love of our fellow creatures, and the harmony of and human oneness with nature. Above all, she shows us the importance of seeing beneath the appearance of things, of thinking deeply and for oneself. In both *The Kelpie's Pearls* and *The Walking Stones*, young protagonists face the decision to ally themselves with the past and with goodness, as embodied in individuals, despite fear of their supernatural powers. These decisions arise from the soul: "He looked up and saw her standing calm and still in the center of the storm . . . the light came from Morag herself, and it seemed to him that it was the reflection of some great goodness that shone out of her that no storm or night could darken" (*The Kelpie's Pearls*). This "great goodness" we discover in Hunter herself, shining through the full substance and quality of her work. ❧ L.L.H.

Hurd, Clement

AMERICAN ILLUSTRATOR AND AUTHOR/ILLUSTRATOR, 1908–1988. Clement Hurd's career lasted from 1939 to 1980, during which time he illustrated over seventy books, five of which he also wrote. He is best known for *Goodnight Moon* (1947), written by MARGARET WISE BROWN, a frequent collaborator. He also illustrated nearly fifty books written by his wife, EDITH THACHER HURD.

Hurd was born in New York City and spent his childhood in New York and Locust, New Jersey. He started drawing in boarding school at age thirteen. After graduating from Yale University, he spent one year at the Yale School of Architecture before traveling to Paris, where he studied painting under Fernand Léger for two years, developing his style of bold, well-defined shapes and clean, flat colors. Returning to the United States, he found work painting murals and doing small design jobs. In the late 1930s, Hurd joined the Writer's Laboratory at the Bank Street College of Education, the program that so influenced Margaret Wise Brown's successful method of writing for small children. Edith Thacher was also a member of this group, and in 1939 they married, beginning their prolific professional collaboration. Nineteen thirty-nine also brought Hurd's first published illustrations: two wordless books for William R. Scott, *Town* and *Country*, and Gertrude Stein's *The World Is Round*. Hurd died of pneumonia in 1988, and now his son, Thacher Hurd, continues the family's creative tradition, writing and illustrating children's books.

Goodnight Moon has become a picture-book classic that continues to mesmerize the very young. Of his collaboration with Brown, Hurd said, "Maybe collaboration on a creative level is always difficult, and maybe the more creative a person is, the more difficult he or she is to work with; but I do feel that all Margaret's main illustrators did their best work on her books. . . . [W]orking with Margaret was difficult but at the same time stimulating and satisfying." The collaboration of text and art is integral to *Goodnight Moon*'s success, with the minimal, carefully chosen list of objects and nearly the same picture on each color spread. Like the mouse hidden on each spread, the child experiencing the story is allowed to explore both the familiar and the unknown, saying, "Goodnight nobody," "Goodnight air," and finally to set aside fears by facing them, saying, "Goodnight noises everywhere." Hurd's increasingly darkened room with dark green walls, red balloon, and cozy yellow lights in the doll's house has become a symbol of comfort and safety for thousands of children.

Illustration by Clement Hurd from *The Runaway Bunny* (1942), by MARGARET WISE BROWN.

Hurd's style of flat, bold colors that bleed off the page, as in *Goodnight Moon, The Runaway Bunny* (1942), and *The Little Brass Band* (1955), all written by Brown, was well suited to the color separations he used at the beginning of his career. But he enjoyed experimenting with a variety of media, particularly creating hand-pressed prints combining wood grains, plants, and linoleum cuts, which he printed on a variety of papers. Some of his favorite books use these methods, including *Christmas Eve* (1962) and *The So-So Cat* (1965), both by Edith Thacher Hurd. In the three-color "Johnny Lion" books and other "I Can Read" books his wife wrote, the loose, expressive line drawings take center stage. The other two colors are added simply, using a texture or visible brush strokes when appropriate, liveliness prevailing over accuracy.

Perhaps Hurd's most remarkable accomplishment is his use of bright colors in vibrant combinations that nonetheless convey a sense of comfort through sympathetic characterizations, carefree lines, and page designs that show both playfulness and order. ❧ L.R.

HURD, EDITH THACHER

AMERICAN AUTHOR, B. 1910. Edith Thacher Hurd's straightforward prose for children's books was refreshing and unique when she began her career in the late 1930s. A practical person, Hurd's texts for PICTURE BOOKS describe everyday happenings in the life of a small child. She collaborated with MARGARET WISE BROWN on several books published under their own names. These are "tough old . . . stories . . . the stuff that a six year old boy's imaginative play is made of," says Hurd. But they are also filled with good humor and excellent rhythms, strong texts that complement the robust art of the early illustrators. Brown and Hurd also collaborated under the pseudonym Juniper Sage, a name Brown invented with Juniper standing for Brown and Sage for Thacher.

Hurd became a member of the Writer's Laboratory at Bank Street after her graduation from Radcliffe. Lucy Sprague Mitchell, the school's founder, became interested in children's literature and began the Writer's Laboratory to encourage students to write. "Posy" (as Hurd was affectionately called) contributed to Mitchell's book *Another Here and Now Story Book* (1937). It was at the Writer's Laboratory that Thacher met Margaret Wise Brown. It was here, too, that she met her future husband, CLEMENT HURD. They began working together on children's books before they married and eventually collaborated on more than seventy-five books over the years. Her gentle texts are a perfect complement to his drawings. *Johnny Lion's Book* (1965), *The Day the Sun Danced* (1966), and *Stop, Stop* (1961) are titles still enjoyed by children today.

When Harper launched the innovative "I Can Read" books in the early 1960s, Hurd produced several titles, among them *Last One Home Is a Green Pig* (1959) and *Come and Have Fun* (1962). The simple story lines and funny situations are exactly suited to youngsters just learning to read. *Hurry, Hurry,* originally published by Scott in 1938, was reissued by Harper in 1960 as an "I Can Read" book.

Hurd wrote a series of titles depicting the life cycle of animals that were handsomely illustrated by her husband. *Starfish* (1962), *The Mother Beaver* (1971), and *The Mother Owl* (1974) were part of Harper's "Let's Read and Find Out" series. Her texts for these titles are simple but well crafted and show a respect for the animal and the surroundings in which it lives.

Many of Hurd's books still grace children's library shelves, though many are out of print. The information is accurate, the prose borders on the poetic, and Clement Hurd's strong, handsome drawings help produce works that speak to children. ❧ J.B.

Hurd, Thacher

American author and illustrator, b. 1949. Thacher Hurd's books are filled with exuberant energy and vibrant color. Remembering what delighted him as a child, he tries to make his stories alive and funny.

Hurd grew up in a household where the creation of children's books was commonplace; his mother, Edith, was a writer and his father, Clement, an illustrator. As a young child living in Vermont and later in California, he often spent time in his father's studio, where he was given paints and encouraged to experiment. It was not until he was in college, however, that he began to study art formally. He then transferred to California College of Arts and Crafts and earned a B.F.A. In addition to developing a career in writing and illustrating, Hurd, with his wife, founded Peaceable Kingdom Press, a publisher of children's posters.

His early books, gentle mood pieces, were influenced by his parents' style. In *The Quiet Evening* (1978), Hurd describes how a household settles down for the night, with alternating scenes of activities at home and those far away. His illustrations reflect the hushed and peaceful text, using appropriately dark colors.

Gradually, however, Hurd found his own voice and colors, and his stories became more exuberant. The settings shifted from home to the larger world, and he began using animals for characters. For example, rats populate *Mystery on the Docks* (1983). After his favorite opera singer has been kidnapped, Ralph, who runs the diner on Pier 46, helps rescue him. The colors are bolder and the cartoonlike pictures are in keeping with the fast-paced story.

Hurd describes himself as a frustrated musician and says that music often creeps into his books. At the end of *Axle the Freeway Cat* (1981), for instance, Axle and his newfound friend watch the sunset and play a duet for harmonica and auto horn. Music has also been the direct inspiration for several other stories. While listening to a jazz program on the radio, Hurd heard an unusual song, "Mama Don't Allow." Suddenly he had images of a swamp, alligators, and a band. But it took several years before he finally worked out how to put all the parts together. The resulting book, *Mama Don't Allow* (1984), received the Boston Globe–Horn Book Award for picture books. When the town sends Miles and his loud band to the swamp, the alligators invite them to play for their Saturday-night ball. Hurd's spirited story line, his loose style, his strong colors, rich greens and blues, and the occasional use of balloons for dialogue all give the book its boisterous energy. Both *Mama Don't Allow* and *Mystery on the Docks* have been adapted for television.

The *Pea Patch Jig* (1986) was also inspired by music, this time by an old fiddle tune. While her family prepares for a party, Baby Mouse wanders off and gets into all sorts of trouble. Baby Mouse is a delightful character, and Hurd creates a wonderful sense of orderly chaos as she romps through her adventures in this and the other two books about her: *Blackberry Ramble* (1989) and *Tomato Soup* (1991).

Mice continue to appeal to Hurd. Little Mouse, the star of another series, worries that his friends have forgotten his birthday and goes off skiing in *Little Mouse's Birthday Cake* (1992). Using a more controlled composition and quieter colors in these snow-filled pictures, Hurd explores Little Mouse's emotions.

Although Hurd continues to develop as both storyteller and artist, his books consistently reflect his energy and humor. ♠ P.R.

Hurwitz, Johanna

American author, b. 1937. Johanna Hurwitz determined at an early age that she would someday work in a library and become a writer. She achieved both goals as a children's librarian who writes humorous, realistic books for young readers. Born and raised in the Bronx, New York, Hurwitz began working at the New York Public Library as a teenager. She attended Queen's College and received a master's degree in library science from Columbia University.

Hurwitz's first book, *Busybody Nora* (1976), was inspired by events in the Manhattan apartment where she lived with her husband and two children. This story of a six-year-old girl who wants to meet all the residents of her apartment building inaugurated the career of an author with a talent for depicting everyday incidents in the lives of urban children. Hurwitz has written series about many of her best-loved characters. Nora's family and friends appear in several books, including *Superduper Teddy* (1980) and *Rip-Roaring Russell* (1983). *The Adventures of Ali Baba Bernstein* (1985) introduces a lively third-grader, and *Much Ado About Aldo* (1978) is the first in a series about the Sossi family. Although usually slight in content, these books contain humor and warmth and are accessible to early readers.

Hurwitz has also published fiction involving more serious themes. Two of her best are *The Law of Gravity* (1978), which describes Margot's attempts to help her agoraphobic mother and is notable for its childlike perspective and realistic conclusion, and *The Rabbi's Girls* (1982), a family story set in the 1920s that includes such issues as death and anti-Semitism. However, the author has achieved her greatest popularity by writing simple, amusing stories about contemporary children for a somewhat younger audience. ♦ P.D.S.

Hutchins, Pat

British author and illustrator, b. 1942. With the publication of *Rosie's Walk* in 1968, Pat Hutchins became established as a gifted creator of picture books for young children. The clean, white background of the pages and large type size made the book open and inviting; textured patterns used for fox and chicken and flowers and trees had the wonderfully appealing symmetry of patterns found in nature. But the look of the book was not its only strength; a great joke unfolds in the pictures as a fox tries fruitlessly to pounce on Rosie the hen—a joke never mentioned in the minimal text but one that even very young readers appreciate enormously. In Hutchins's first book lie the qualities and strengths that characterize much of her work: a great sense of humor, a brilliant graphic design, and a simple, logical story line. Hutchins went on to create many other books with animal characters, including *The Surprise Party* (1969), *Good-Night Owl!* (1972), and *What Games Shall We Play?* (1990), to name a few.

Hutchins credits her early years as one of seven children with giving her the time and freedom to roam the woods and fields surrounding her home in northern England, where she developed a love of woodland creatures. Her books are always childlike in their worldview, taking seriously the things that matter to children. In *Happy Birthday, Sam* (1978) she shows how only a gift from Grandpa allows Sam to reach the things he *thought* he'd be tall enough for on his birthday. *The Very Worst Monster* (1985) and *Where's the Baby?* (1988) are about sibling rivalry in a monster family. *Changes, Changes* (1971) is another groundbreaking title, with Hutchins's trademark balance of bright, bold colors, clean line, and lots of white space. Here, two wooden figures arrange and rearrange colorful blocks to make all sorts of shapes: a house, a fire truck, a boat, and more. There is not a word of text, but a delightful story emerges from the pictures. The Weston Woods film studio did a filmstrip adaptation of *Changes, Changes*—using all wooden instruments in the sound track—as well as of *Rosie's Walk* and other Hutchins picture books.

Hutchins clearly intended some of her books to teach, but they are never dull or preachy. *One Hunter* (1982) is an ingenious counting book in which the hunter can't find any of the animals, although readers see them on every page. Hutchins has written longer books as well—beginning novels full of tongue-in-cheek humor, fast-moving action, hilarious characters, and outlandish situations. Most of them, including *The House That Sailed Away* (1975), *The Mona Lisa Mystery* (1981), and *The Curse of the Egyptian Mummy* (1983) were illustrated by her husband, film director Laurence Hutchins. Overall, she has written more than twenty picture books as well as several novels, demonstrating a great breadth of talent.

Hutchins began drawing at an early age and earned a scholarship to art school at sixteen. After graduating, she worked for an advertising agency in London, where she met her husband. They lived in New York for a brief time, and there she showed her work to American publishers. An editor's suggestion that she write her own text resulted in *Rosie's Walk*. Her work has been widely praised by critics on both sides of the Atlantic, not only for illustration and story but for the buoyant warmth and gaiety that emerge from every page. Many titles have been named American Library Association Notables and have received illustration honors. *The Wind Blew* (1974), a humorous, rhyming picture book about people chasing after possessions that have been whipped away by the wind, was the 1974 winner of the Kate Greenaway Medal. ♦ K.M.K.

Hutton, Warwick

British illustrator and reteller, 1939–1994. Warwick Hutton, best known for his award-winning picture books based on Bible stories, was born in England. He studied at the Colchester Art School, graduating in 1961, and was a visiting lecturer at Cambridge College of Art and Technology and at Morley College. A full-time artist and a member of the Cambridge Society of Painters and Sculptors, he considered himself to be primarily a painter.

Hutton's first children's book, *Noah and the Great Flood*, appeared in the United States in 1977, illustrated with line drawings and delicate watercolor washes. His paintings typically show vast expanses of sky and land in glowing pastel colors. The figures are drawn oversized and sketchy, with little detail in form or features, but posed in graceful attitudes. Composition is used to enhance mood and atmosphere, and with each book, the angles become more varied and interesting.

Jonah and the Great Fish won the 1984 Boston Globe–Horn Book Award for illustration. In an acceptance speech presented to the New England Library Association, Hutton described how the book began: Working in cramped quarters, he placed his watercolor materials in his lap and started to paint scenes from both the Noah's ark story and the story of Jonah. He had never been satisfied with versions of the stories that he had seen; he discovered while working, for example, that the Bible describes a great fish, not a whale. After *Noah's Ark* was published, Hutton set *Jonah* aside for some time so he would not be labeled as only a religious author-illustrator. But he later illustrated *Adam and Eve: The Bible Story* (1987) and *Moses in the Bulrushes* (1986), which was named a Notable Book of 1986 by the American Library Association (ALA).

Hutton also turned his luminous style of illustration to folktales. *The Nose Tree* (1981) introduces more humor than is usual in his narrative, with the improbable figure of a man whose nose grows to reach the ground. It was named Best Illustrated Book of 1981 by the *New York Times*. *Jonah* won the same honor in 1984. A later book, *Beauty and the Beast* (1985), employs particularly theatrical settings, using light and shadow as if in a stage production, to tell the familiar story. Hutton also illustrated *The Sleeping Beauty* (1979) and *The Tinderbox* (1988), a HANS CHRISTIAN ANDERSEN tale. Hutton illustrated Greek myth in *Theseus and the Minotaur* (1989) and adapted Homer in *The Trojan Horse* (1992), which treats the theme of the horror of war as well as the heroic story. Hutton illustrated the works of others, including SUSAN COOPER's *The Silver Cow: A Welsh Tale* (1983), which was also named an ALA Notable Book.

In addition to his illustrating career, Hutton executed glass engravings for churches, homes, and civic buildings, using a large-scale technique that his artist father invented. He also wrote a book for adults, *Making Woodcuts*, published in 1974. ❧ S.H.H.

HYMAN, TRINA SCHART

AMERICAN ILLUSTRATOR, B. 1939. Trina Schart Hyman has been hailed as one of the great romantic illustrators of our time, and her gloriously illustrated fairy tales—the best known of her many works—are a true testament to this high praise. The gifted creator of many of the most beautiful princesses, gallant knights, gruesome monsters, and frightful hags ever to grace the pages of a PICTURE BOOK, Hyman has brought brush to paper and captured the essence of fantasy.

Born in Philadelphia, Hyman studied art in Philadelphia, Boston, and Stockholm and served as art director of *Cricket* magazine for seven years. Her first publication, the Swedish tale *Toffe och den lilla bilen* (1961), which translates into "Toffe and the little car," took longer to decipher than to illustrate, but it nonetheless launched a highly successful career. Since then she has illustrated over 130 books, many of which she wrote herself. Hyman recalls being disappointed with her picture books as a child; the beautiful princesses were simply not beautiful enough. Indeed, while very precise and technically skilled, her illustrations are remarkable primarily for their great beauty. Hyman won the Caldecott Medal in 1985 for her work on MARGARET HODGES's retelling of *Saint George and the Dragon*, an excellent example of her technique. Using an elaborate series of borders that enclose one page of text and one page of illustration per double spread, Hyman creates the illusion that each scene is being viewed through a window. Every text page is enclosed by a different border of flowers indigenous to the story's setting; illustration pages, however, are framed simply so as not to interfere with the depicted scene. The child observer is therefore given a special glimpse through the window of history, turning a book with a universal message into a very personal experience. In less structured books, Hyman's work is notable for other design features, including accommodation of text. Rather than create a painting into which words must be placed, she designs her pages to flow

Illustration by Trina Schart Hyman from *King Stork* (1973), by HOWARD PYLE.

Voices of the Creators

Trina Schart Hyman

I began my life as an artist with the hope of someday illustrating editions of folklore and myths, because I have always felt most comfortable with the old stories linking human drama with the mysteries of nature. I like the idea that magic can be hidden under the surface of everyday life.

As a child, I was raised with Grimms' and Andersen's fairy tales. I was encouraged to believe that supernatural beings hover just outside the periphery of our vision. The romantic and the fantastic—always in simple, unsophisticated forms—were common elements of my childhood. I believe I've carried this over into my illustration work, along with other purely personal and autobiographical points of view.

Nevertheless, my main point of departure for every job of illustration is the story itself. I try to gear the color, mood, energy of line, and atmosphere of my pictures to the feeling and intent of the text. If there is a particular historical, geographical, or cultural framework to the story, I take great pains to research the period or place as thoroughly as I can, to give the illustrations as much authority and integrity as possible. These researches are used as a kind of ground work for me to build on with my own imagination, to get "inside the skin" of time, place, and character. What I want to be able to do is to take the reader by the hand, visually, and say, "Look: this is what I think it must have been like."

I am primarily a draftsman. My illustrations are always based on black-and-white line drawing, which I do with pencil, brush, and ink. The style is flowing and conventionally representational. The effect is romantic, emotional, somewhat theatrical, and archaically idealized.

The color is usually laid on with acrylics (although lately I have taken to mixed media) and is generally based on earth tones, with occasional bright touches of transparent red, green, or blue. The effect is dark, complex, and sometimes somber, although I try to suit my palette to the mood of the story and have often used color in a more direct and light-handed way. I enjoy using pattern and folk motifs; both have appeared in decorative borders as design elements when appropriate to the story.

The focus of my illustrations—largely because of the kinds of stories I choose to illustrate—is almost always on human beings. People—and this includes monsters and other fantastic creatures—are endlessly fascinating to me as subject matter. Facial expressions, body language, gestures of both action and repose can express a wealth of information about what is happening in addition to what the text is already saying. The story within the story can nearly always be found in my illustrations.

I don't use models or photographs for my work. The drawing comes entirely from my memory, from a lifetime of close observation. I also love to use landscape in its various moods and weathers (especially trees and skies), animals of all kinds, and still lifes and interiors. Architectural detail does sometimes give me trouble, though, because I don't have a good "feel" for inanimate structure.

The only thing I won't do is put clothes on animals. Anthropomorphism can be amusing, but I don't believe in it. I have a sense of humor, however, and I like to put little jokes in my pictures when I can. This has sometimes landed me in more trouble than the joke was worth. Children's book people don't like jokes.

When I do illustrations for a book, the work is more to me than just a charming way to earn my living (although it is that, too, of course). It is a way of trying to communicate what I feel, what I have learned, what I am thinking, and what I see. With the text of the story as an honored guide and vehicle, I am trying to share my observations and feelings about life and the world we live in, albeit in what has to be necessarily an oblique and restricted way. It has never bothered me that my audience is supposed to be children and young people. I communicate best with children and other domestic animals anyway, and it seems right that my work should be directed toward them.

It has never been easy for me to do this work; I was not blessed with a particularly great talent, and facility (especially of the technical sort) has never been my strength. I was never sophisticated or self-confident or shrewd enough to settle on a "style" and stay with it. I struggle to learn, and my work changes slowly as a result of this struggle. I know that my illustrations are often criticized for being overblown, over the top, too sensuous, too prettified, too scary, too old-fashioned, too emotional, too obvious, too subjective, and otherwise excessive and immoderate. And I think that's absolutely right.

around the story, forming a visually dynamic and unified whole. Striving for the perfect integration of text and artwork, she is an illustrator in the classic Caldecott mode.

While Hyman is best known for her fairy tales, she has illustrated many other important books as well, including a rendition of *Swan Lake* (1989) retold by Margot Fonteyn; the Caldecott Honor Book *Hershel and the Hanukkah Goblins* (1989), with text by ERIC KIMMEL; LLOYD ALEXANDER's original folktale *The Fortune-Tellers* (1992), set in the exotic country of Cameroon; *King Stork* (1973), by HOWARD PYLE, a Boston Globe–Horn Book Award winner; and a picture-book autobiography, *Self-Portrait: Trina Schart Hyman* (1981).

Hyman is as proficient with pen and ink as with the richly hued colors of her most recent illustrations and considers her work for Norma Farber's *How Does It Feel to Be Old* (1979) to be her best. In this quiet glimpse into the lives of a thoughtful girl and her grandmother, Hyman's softly rendered sketches capture the reflective mood and broaden the themes of love and loss to create a book that is genuine in its emotion and message. Regardless of subject matter or medium, Hyman's illustrations have a special impact on children, who respond positively to their sensitivity and beauty. ❧ C.C.B.

I

ILLUSTRATING FOR CHILDREN

If the children's book writer was once publishing's stepchild, the illustrator was, until the 1980s, its orphan. But because of solid sales, quality reproduction, and recognition of artistic merit, new respectability has been heaped upon the PICTURE BOOK and its creators.

Although the results may appear naive and spontaneous, the artist's task is neither simple nor easy. MOLLY BANG's search to understand what happens on the page, what "picture structure" means and how it works, led her through a variety of activities with simple shapes and limited colors. In *Picture This: Perception and Composition* (1991), Bang reconstructs these explorations, identifying the emotional responses to an image or series of images and asking what elements have prompted the emotions. The resulting "Principles," with "Some Remarks about Space," set the stage for a series of exercises children and adults will find insightful.

At the very least, illustrators need strong artistic skills and the ability to depict consistently animals or children in a sequence of activities. In addition, as Barbara Bader observes in *American Picturebooks from Noah's Ark to the Beast Within* (1976), "[the picture book] hinges on the interdependence of pictures and words, on the simultaneous display of two facing pages, and on the drama of the turning of the page."

URI SHULEVITZ explores these more elusive demands in *Writing with Pictures: How to Write and Illustrate Children's Books* (1985). After publishing many children's picture books, Shulevitz realized his visual approach—seeing the book before writing it—is valid for all book creators. *Writing with Pictures,* a highly visual and lively book, is based upon ten years of conducting workshops and classes with this approach. He concludes, "Only by understanding the [children's] book's structure—including its mechanical structure—and how it functions can you make a good book."

Howard Greenfeld takes the requirements a step further. In his revised and updated *Books: From Writer to Reader* (1989), he asserts that an illustrator's special training includes technique and craftsmanship, expert knowledge of drawing and of the various artistic media, and "a thorough familiarity with printing." Artists coming to children's books without a knowledge of publishing will benefit from Greenfeld's demystifying of the process by which a manuscript becomes a book. Just as helpful is the way he delineates the professional duties of, among others, the editor, designer, compositor, and printer.

But what of those who aren't even sure they want to enter the field? Nancy Hands's *Illustrating Children's Books: A Guide to Drawing, Printing, and Publishing* (1986) is intended for the parent or teacher with little artistic training, as well as the schooled artist unfamiliar with children's book conventions, as it introduces "the areas of knowledge the illustrator must know well in order to succeed." Every highly illustrated chapter contains either exercises or activities to take the novice from sketch to dummy, from portfolio to contract.

Those illustrators who also write their own text increase their control over a book and double their royalties. Treld Pelkey Bicknell and Felicity Trotman, editors of *How to Write and Illustrate Children's Books* (1988), have compiled a lively, abundantly illustrated collection of essays that provide an introduction for the illustrator who also wants to write. Essays cover a variety of topics, such as "The Art of the Storyteller," "The Basics of Writing for Children," and "Illustration—Building a Career in Children's Books." The authors and illustrators cited are mostly British professionals, but the ideas are highly accessible.

A more comprehensive and technical book is Frieda Gates's *How to Write, Illustrate, and Design Children's Books* (1986). In addition to exploring the diversity of "Markets, Categories, and Trends," Gates details the strengths and weaknesses of the many artistic techniques available to illustrators and spells out all the production considerations. The glossary and bibliography are particularly comprehensive, making the book a fine reference text.

For illustrators simply interested in developing writing skills, Ellen E. M. Roberts's *The Children's Picture-book: How to Write It, How to Sell It* (1981) is the book of choice. Roberts addresses adults who haven't given in to logic, experience, and good sense—those who still possess the "special insight" of a child. For them she sets forth an overview of the picture-book field; the principles of plotting, character development, and setting that produce effective texts; and a "Practical Guide to Publication," including a discussion of agents, promotion, and contacts. The glossary is helpful, and the bibliography is full of picture-book examples for study.

To get work, illustrators must make the rounds of art directors and editors, presenting their portfolio and leaving samples of their work. But finding the appropriate publishers requires homework. *Artist's Market* and *Writer's Market,* two standard, annual professional references, have joined forces to offer the specialized annual volume *Children's Writer's and Illustrator's Market,* edited by Lisa Carpenter. Essays on developing a portfolio and on a variety of business considerations precede the detailed entries about book and magazine publishers who accept the work of freelance writers and illustrators. The extensive resources provided include a glossary and listings of workshops and professional organizations.

The primary organization to serve the needs of children's book creators is the Society of Children's Book Writers and Illustrators (22736 Vanowen Street, Suite 106, West Hills, CA 91307), founded by writers in 1968. The increasing membership of illustrators necessitated an expansion of services and, by 1992, a change of name. Now, with an international combined membership of over nine thousand, SCBWI offers members grants and awards, conferences, a bimonthly "Bulletin" with professional articles and marketing information, and a series of specialty publications.

Success in the children's book field, as in many others, is largely a matter of luck—being the right person in the right place at the right time. But illustrators can increase their chances of success by being highly skilled, persistent, and flexible. They can build credentials by illustrating for magazines and textbooks and can build editorial relationships through a willingness to undertake cover art. Most beginners must remember not to become discouraged by rejections and to remain open to suggestions for growth.

Bicknell and Trotman observe, "When you write and illustrate for children there are two kinds of success: one is getting published and sold; the other is knowing that your book *really works* for children." Hands adds, "Every book offers the chance to create images that can enrich children's lives and remain in their minds throughout adulthood." ❧ SUSAN A. BURGESS

Information Books

Fictional classics, such as *Charlotte's Web* (1952) and *A Wrinkle in Time* (1962), have no nonfiction counterparts. Books that enticed yesterday's youngsters with real wonders—dinosaurs, disasters, deep space, and the like—will hold little interest for today's children. *Sesame Street*–MTV–Nintendo familiars will find them unattractive at best and possibly inaccurate.

A generation or so ago, writers described Brontosauruses with short snouts and a two-mooned Neptune; a Titanic that rested somewhere at unreachable depths and a dormant Mt. St. Helens; and, if the words appeared at all, *recycling* referred to a process in petroleum technology and AIDS was an inadvertently capitalized and misspelled synonym for helpers.

Today, children read that Brontosaurus is really Apatosaurus whose long, flat head was accidentally switched with another dinosaur's round head during reconstruction (*The Great Dinosaur Atlas,* William Lindsay, 1991); photographs taken by *Voyager 2* revealed eight moons orbiting Neptune (*Neptune,* FRANKLYN M. BRANLEY, 1992); Robert Ballard reached the *Titanic* (*Exploring the Titanic,* Robert Ballard, 1988); Mt. St. Helens blew its top (*Volcano,* PATRICIA LAUBER, 1986); and *recycling* and AIDS have acquired new meanings of international significance.

A generation or so ago, illustrations were almost always black and white; pages of photographs were assembled in sections far from the words they pictured; and design and layout were pedestrian. Today, nonfiction is radiant with color and eye-catching design.

Contemporary, beautifully illustrated, and imaginatively designed nonfiction abounds on just about any subject, from Richard Merryman's *Andrew Wyeth* (1992) to Bernard Most's *Zoodles* (1993). The challenge is to select the very best.

There is only one *Charlotte's Web:* E. B. WHITE's. But there are scores of books about spiders, pigs, farms—or any animal, vegetable, or mineral. How does one select the best book from the armful available?

One doesn't. There are as many "best" ways of telling a nonfiction story as there are styles of writing, angles of approach, methods of presentation, breadths and depths of scope, orders of sequence, and types and styles of illustration.

And that is as it should be. Every child brings to a subject a level of awareness, interest, set of questions, and learning style and ability that no one book can satisfy.

Take dinosaurs, for example: A balanced selection of today's best would include (1) a dictionary of dinosaurs (*The New Illustrated Dinosaur Dictionary,* HELEN

RONEY SATTLER, 1990); (2) overviews of the saurian world (*The Dinosaur Question and Answer Book,* Sylvia Funston, 1992); (3) introductions to dinosaur behavior (*Dinosaurs and How They Lived,* Steve Parker, 1991); (4) a peek behind the scenes at dinosaur exhibits (*Barosaurus,* William Lindsay, 1992) and the people who create them (*Dinosaurs All Around,* Caroline Arnold, 1993); (5) a look at how scientists form dinosaur theories (*Discover Dinosaurs,* Chris McGowan, 1992); (6) dinosaur facts with a touch of humor (*Where to Look for a Dinosaur,* Bernard Most, 1993); (7) instructions on how to draw dinosaurs (*Dinosaurs!* Michael Emberley, 1985); (8) dinosaur pop-ups (*Dinosaur Skeletons,* Keith Moseley, 1992); (9) dinosaur jokes (*Why Didn't the Dinosaur Cross the Road?* Joanne E. Bernstein and Paul Cohen, 1990); and, of course, dinosaur poems (*Dinosaurs,* LEE BENNETT HOPKINS, 1987).

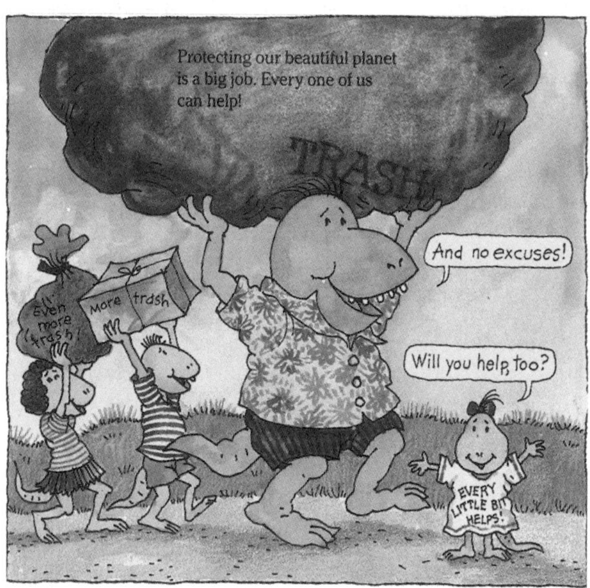

Illustration by MARC BROWN from *Dinosaurs to the Rescue* (1992), by Laurene Krasny Brown and Marc Brown.

With photographs and illustrations for perusers of all ages, the assortment has something for beginning to fluent readers, from casual browsers to dinosaur devotees.

Although there is no classic nonfiction, the qualities that make good nonfiction books are classic. First, does the story grab the reader? Masterful storytellers, whether of things real or imagined, evoke a sense of place and time, vivify the subjects, and so engage the reader that "the end" brings simultaneous satisfaction and hunger for more. Such authors are plentiful in children's nonfiction. Among them are BRUCE BROOKS, whose *Predator* (1991) and *Nature by Design* (1991) contain refreshing perspectives on the food chain and animal architecture; KATHRYN LASKY, who salted *Surtsey: The Newest Place on Earth* (1992) with the seemingly prescient prose of a 700-year-old Icelandic epic; Jim Murphy, with his eloquently antiwar *Boys' War* (1990) about the youngest Civil War soldiers; RUSSELL FREEDMAN, whose *The Wright Brothers* (1991) traces the trauma and triumph behind the airplane's invention; JAMES CROSS GIBLIN, who commemorates the creativity behind the commonplace, as in *From Hand to Mouth: Or, How We Invented Knives, Forks, Spoons, and Chopsticks and the Table Manners to Go with Them* (1987); Judith St. George, as she writes of the men, women, and circumstances behind such monumental constructions as *The Panama Canal* (1989); and MILTON MELTZER, whose autobiography *Starting from Home* (1988) tells of the experiences and events that shape his choice of subject matter.

Children will likely pore over the pictures before they read the words in any book. In the best nonfiction, illustrations and page design are relevant and uncluttered, size relationships are clear, and charts are neatly drawn and easy to understand. A text can't be left unread when enhanced by eye-catching illustrations that satisfy and pique curiosity at first glance.

Here, with one representative title each, are some artists who entice readers and enrich authors' words with their illustrations: Martha Weston (*Take a Hike,* 1990); Linda Allison (*The Stethoscope Book,* 1991); True Kelley (*How Many Teeth,* 1991); Joyce Powzyk (*Animal Camouflage,* 1990); and Barbara Bash (*Shadows of Night,* 1993).

Among artist-authors are JIM ARNOSKY (*Every Autumn Comes the Bear,* 1993); GAIL GIBBONS (*Beacons of Light,* 1990); Piero Ventura (*Clothing,* 1993); Ruth Heller (*Many Luscious Lollipops,* 1989); LOIS EHLERT (*Eating the Alphabet,* 1989); Jennifer Owings Dewey (*A Night and Day in the Desert,* 1991); and Carol Lerner (*Cactus,* 1992).

Children assume that what they see, *is*—especially when what they see is a photograph in a nonfiction book. Yet photographs are as susceptible to creative manipulation as any images.

In some nonfiction books photographs clarify information—as in the spectacularly color-enhanced images of SEYMOUR SIMON's *Our Solar System* (1992) and color-enhanced x-rays, electron micrographs, and sonograms of Sandra Markle's *Outside and Inside You* (1991). The pseudo- or false colors make visible what the naked eye cannot see.

Photographs are often arranged to support the narrative, as in *A Guide Dog Puppy Grows Up* (1991). Caroline

Arnold describes Honey as she grows from puppy to professional, but to illustrate the book, Richard Hewett photographed many golden retrievers during different stages of training.

Photographs are also used as discrete design elements to provide otherwise impossible juxtapositions, as in the *Visual Dictionary of Animals* (1991). Artfully displayed on a two-page spread aptly entitled "Animal heads," for example, are seven heads of species ranging in size from beetle to elephant. The individual images have been enlarged or reduced to produce heads of approximately the same size.

All illustrations, whether photographic or hand drawn, are but artists' interpretations. Children should be taught to understand and appreciate them for the art that they are.

Among the author-photographers who illustrate their own works are George Ancona (*Man and Mustang,* 1992); Bianca Lavies (*Secretive Timber Rattlesnake,* 1990); Margaret Miller (*Where Does It Go?* 1992); Gloria Skurzynski (*Here Comes the Mail,* 1992); Catherine Paladino (*Our Vanishing Farm Animals,* 1992); Rosmarie Hausherr (*The Wind Warrior,* 1992); BRUCE MCMILLAN (*Mouse Views,* 1993); and Hanna Machotka (*Breathtaking Noses,* 1992).

Some author and photographer collaborators are Dorothy Hinshaw Patent and William Muñoz (*A Family Goes Hunting,* 1991); Diane Hoyt-Goldsmith and Lawrence Migdale (*Cherokee Summer,* 1993); BRENT ASHABRANNER and Jennifer Ashabranner (*Always to Remember,* 1990); and Ron Hirschi and Thomas Mangleson (*Summer,* 1991).

Although accuracy in information books is crucial, there is no practical way for the average reader (or reviewer) to be certain that what she or he reads is true. Children given one information book may look no further, yet that single edition might contain errors of omission or typographical errors or have been based on assumptions or beliefs refuted or reinterpreted after the manuscript was finished. Handed many books, children compare information and discover that, often, the writers have offered mere approximations, educated guesses, unsettled controversies, or compromises.

One can deduce the relative reliability of a writer's words, however, from the prefatory or appended sections. These frequently reveal evidence of the depth and breadth of an author's experience, research, professional guidance, and knowledge of pertinent literature. In Helen Roney Sattler's acknowledgments for *The New Illustrated Dinosaur Dictionary,* for example, you will find a who's who in paleontology; Jan Reynold's "about this book" sections leave little doubt that she knows her material when she writes about families in the *Himalaya* (1991), *Down Under* (1992), and other places in her "Vanishing Cultures" series; RHODA BLUMBERG's addenda to *The Remarkable Voyages of Captain Cook* (1991) attest to her thorough scholarship.

Readers must also check copyright dates. A new book isn't necessarily a *new* book. The information in a hot-off-the-press volume may be a year old, since it can take that long or longer for a manuscript to become a published book.

When a book has two copyright dates, an ever-increasing phenomenon, it might be the latest printing of an old book, for instance, a paperback version of a hardback, or the old text with new illustrations, such as the abridged edition of Leonora and Arthur Hornblow's *Prehistoric Monsters Did the Strangest Things,* in which a 1974 text was updated with 1990 illustrations. In ALIKI's *Digging Up Dinosaurs* (1981, 1988), a revised text is accompanied by new full-color illustrations that now show a woman paleontologist on the cover instead of a man, a long-nosed Apatosaurus instead of a short-snouted Brontosaurus, and a museum-goer in a wheelchair. Two copyright dates can also indicate the American printing of a book originally published elsewhere, such as Reijo Karkonen's *Grandchildren of the Incas,* published in Finland in 1974, and in America in 1991.

Finally, nonfiction need not be nonfunny. The humorous Ms. Frizzle, JOANNA COLE's intrepid teacher nonpareil, started her *Magic School Bus at the Waterworks* in 1986, and has since led captivated readers on field trips inside the earth, through the human body, across the solar system, and onto the ocean floor. ALEXANDRA DAY's entrepreneurial bear and elephant, *Frank and Ernest* (1988), introduce children to the colorfully idiosyncratic lingo of the short-order cook. The animated archosaurs of Laurene Krasny Brown and MARC BROWN gently explain such diverse topics as changing families (*Dinosaurs Divorce,* 1988) and recycling (*Dinosaurs to the Rescue,* 1992). Henry Wilson, the youngster in Robin and Sally Hirst's *My Place in Space* (1990), knows *exactly* where in the universe he lives. Joan Richards Wright cleverly alternates corny riddles with the facts about *Bugs* (1987) and *Frogs, Toads, Lizards and Salamanders* (1990). NANCY WINSLOW PARKER's *Working Frog* (1992) is an insider at the Bronx Zoo's amphibian display. In *Eight Ate* (1982) and *In a Pickle* (1984), Marvin Terban highlights the humor inherent in language.

Unless nostalgia is the aim, nonfiction handed children must be up-to-date, because without a doubt, *they* are. Choose from the best of the newest, from authors and illustrators who radiate enthusiasm, excitement, and expertise, such as those noted above. The search for the rest of the best in nonfiction will reward both adults and children. ❧ BEVERLY KOBRIN

Ingpen, Robert

AUSTRALIAN AUTHOR AND ILLUSTRATOR, B. 1936. Many of the books Robert Ingpen illustrates are set in his native Australia, and his passion for the land is evident in such books as *Australian Gnomes* (1979) and *The Voyage of the Poppy Kettle* (1980), in which he wrote and illustrated narratives about the supernatural inhabitants of his country. But in his prolific career, he has also illustrated books that reach beyond continental borders; the *Encyclopedia of Things that Never Were* (1987), a massive volume, explores mythological and folkloric elements from the entire human experience.

Ingpen grew up and still lives in Geelong, Victoria. After attending Geelong College, he received training in scientific illustration at the Royal Melbourne Institute of Technology. He has received the Hans Christian Andersen Award and the Dromkeen Medal, as well as awards for individual titles. Though he uses a variety of techniques and presentations, his style is distinct. He has a sure sense of perspective and composition and often emphasizes the effects of light and shadow. His paintings are authentic both in setting and historical detail, and the integrity of his vision reveals the emotional truth of the stories, while avoiding sentimentality.

Ingpen's technical training as a scientific illustrator helped develop his talent as a book illustrator. The strongest element of his work is the melding of his imaginative vision with his "representationist" approach to art, that is, the realistic style reminiscent of the art of N. C. WYETH. In *The Great Deeds of Superheroes* (1989) and *The Great Deeds of Heroic Women* (1990), for example, the characters' bodies often extend off the pages and the reader seems to look up at them, as the vague backgrounds set the focus solidly on the figures. They are thus portrayed as larger than life, yet their face and body expressions are vibrantly real, making them simultaneously heroic and human. By conveying personality instead of action, Ingpen encourages the reader to spend time with the picture, imagining the person's thoughts, feelings, and circumstances. Even when Ingpen paints animals and plants or landscapes, his pictures focus on the psychological or historical truths of the narratives instead of the action. In *Lifetimes* (1983; originally *Beginnings and Endings with Lifetimes in Between*), a picture book about living and dying, and in *Peace Begins with You* (1990; originally *Peacetimes*, 1989), a picture book about working toward individual and world peace, Ingpen employs concrete images of everyday life to convey the complex ideas of the narratives. By capturing specific subjects at a point in time, a boy having a splinter removed, for instance, these focused pictures reveal much about the philosophical texts.

Ingpen's paintings have a highly textural appearance that gives immediacy to his characters and a sensual quality to his objects. Using watercolors, pencils, and pastels, he deftly portrays each hair and wrinkle. Ingpen is at his peak depicting a colorful character like Long John Silver in *Treasure Island* (1992), but he can also paint ethereally transcendent figures, often appropriate in supernatural tales. Most of Ingpen's work is done with earth tones, with one hue sometimes pervading an entire picture from colored paper background to the central subject. At times the ochres, browns, and greens are bleak and humorless, like the texts they so aptly illuminate. In books with happier themes, the same shades, by their lack of color, enliven the grand colors of the reader's imagination. And that is Ingpen's ultimate goal: to engage young people's imaginations both with his art and with the stories he chooses to illustrate. ❧ S.S.

Innocenti, Roberto

ITALIAN AUTHOR AND ILLUSTRATOR, B. 1940. Roberto Innocenti's classical, painterly style bespeaks a scrupulous devotion to realism, a meticulous eye for detail, and a sophisticated mastery of palette and perspective, qualities one might not expect to find so finely honed in an artist with no formal training.

Born in a small town near Florence, Innocenti was forced by the straits of Italy's postwar economy to go to work in a steel foundry at age thirteen. Five years later he moved to Rome to work in an animation studio, where his artistic career began to take root. He soon returned to Florence, where he designed books and illustrated posters for film and theater, and where, in 1970, he met the American artist John Alcorn, who encouraged him to try book illustration. After illustrating a number of Italian and English texts, Innocenti was asked to interpret CHARLES PERRAULT's *Cinderella* (1983) as part of a twenty-title series of fairy tales. As it happened, this was but the first of several classic stories to which he would turn his hand. He took the unconventional step of locating the tale in an English village during the Roaring Twenties in order, he said, to avoid graphic clichés and "make [Cinderella] come out of her time" as a universal figure.

Although *Cinderella* was positively received, it was the book that followed that made Innocenti's name. *Rose Blanche* (1985), a picture book for older children written with Christophe Gallaz, is the haunting story of a German child who brings scraps of food to the children in a nearby concentration camp, only to be shot by a soldier as the war draws to a close. Its deceptively simple text deftly depicts war through a child's eyes, capturing the peculiar naiveté of a young girl who witnesses horrors she does not comprehend. But the story's emotional impact comes largely through its illustrations: somber, ultrarealistic paintings that with merciless detail delineate the ominous features of war, from the soldiers' uniforms and weapons to the townspeople's fearful, furtive demeanors. *Rose Blanche* was inspired by Innocenti's own childhood recollections of the Second World War, especially of two German deserters his family harbored and of awkwardly truncated conversations with his normally straightforward father concerning missing Jewish friends. Reviewers praised the book for its hard-hitting message and avoidance of sentimentality and cliché. *Rose Blanche* received extensive media coverage in Europe, especially during President Reagan's visit to Bitburg Cemetery, and won the Bratislava Golden Apple Award. In the United States it was named an American Library Association Notable Book and a Boston Globe–Horn Book Honor Book and won the Batchelder Award.

Innocenti's remarkable ability to create drama and story through visually eloquent yet unsentimental paintings remains in full evidence in subsequent works: an exquisitely detailed but unprettified version of CARLO COLLODI's *The Adventures of Pinocchio* (1988; originally published in Italy in 1927) and an interpretation of *A Christmas Carol* (1990; originally published in 1843) that renders both the vigor and squalor of Dickens's London. The illustrations in Innocenti's books have gained notice in fine arts journals as well as in the field of children's literature. ❧ A.J.M.

IRVING, WASHINGTON

AMERICAN AUTHOR, 1783–1859. Washington Irving was born in New York City, the youngest son of a Scottish immigrant and successful businessman. He studied law and on the side wrote entertaining pieces for various journals and periodicals. After an illness, he was sent by his older brothers on a two-year grand tour of Europe to regain his strength.

When he returned to the United States, he resumed his study of law and with his brother William and James Kirke Paulding started the *Salmagundi* papers, a semimonthly periodical, to which he contributed under the pseudonym "Jonathan Oldstyle, Gent." He completed his satirical *History of New York* "by Diedrich Knickerbocker" in 1809. His great success came in 1819–1820 with the publication in four installments of *The Sketch Book of Geoffrey Crayon*, a delightful compendium of sketches of English life and European traditional lore. Two quintessential American classics, "Rip Van Winkle" and "The Legend of Sleepy Hollow," here made their first appearance. "Rip Van Winkle," based on a German legend, is set in the Catskill Mountains. Irving takes the motif of a hero caught in a magic sleep and reshapes it to tell of a lazy, ne'er-do-well Dutch farmer in colonial times who goes into the mountains one day to escape from his termagant of a wife, not to return for twenty years.

Also based on European folklore is "The Legend of Sleepy Hollow," or "Headless Horseman," which describes Ichabod Crane, a self-important, superstitious, scrawny schoolmaster who might easily be mistaken "for some scarecrow eloped from a cornfield"; his courtship of the fair Katrina Van Tassel, only child of a prosperous Dutch farmer; and his rout at the sight of what he believes to be a specter horse with a headless rider. Evocative language, exquisite delineations of characters, and sensuous descriptions of food and the countryside add to the pleasures of the story, although they slow its pace for young readers. Recent editions of this tale have been somewhat abridged for them.

In the late 1820s, Irving served in the diplomatic corps in Madrid and London. The romantic history and landscape of Spain cast such a spell over him that he produced *The Alhambra* (1832), a miscellany of sketches of Spanish life, archaeology, and tradition in the vein of his earlier *Sketch Book*. He returned to the United States in 1832 and bought Sunnyside, an old Dutch farm in Tarrytown, New York. In 1842 he was appointed American ambassador to Spain, where he served, in Madrid, until 1846. His last major work, *The Life of George Washington*, was published in five installments from 1855 to 1859. He died at Sunnyside in 1859.

Irving never wrote for children, although his natural ebullience, enthusiasm, and ability to tell a good story made many of his stories appealing and accessible to them. Compilations of these stories include *Tales from the Alhambra*, adapted by Josephine V. Brower (1910); *The Alhambra: Palace of Mystery and Splendor*, selected and rearranged by Mabel Williams, illustrated by Warwick Goble (1926), and reissued in 1953 with illustrations by LOUIS SLOBODKIN; *The Bold Dragoon and Other Ghostly Tales* (1930), selected and edited by Anne Carroll Moore and illustrated by JAMES DAUGHERTY. In these adaptations, Moore and others who issued these stories for children attempted to leave the drama in them untouched while editing out those sentences and paragraphs that might impede the narratives' progress.

Irving was a man of letters, a brilliant essayist who was one of the first Americans to be recognized abroad for his writings. He was perhaps America's first master of the short story. His most popular stories are still "Rip Van Winkle" and "The Legend of Sleepy Hollow." They have attracted the attention of artists in the United States and in England from the nineteenth century's F. O. Darley, Frank Merrill, Gordon Browne, and ARTHUR RACKHAM to today's Thomas Locker and BARRY MOSER. The stories have been made into plays, operas, and operettas. They evoke a golden America, a youthful, optimistic America with faith in her destiny—no mean legacy for today's young. M.N.C.

ISADORA, RACHEL

AMERICAN AUTHOR AND ILLUSTRATOR, B. C. 1953. Rachel Isadora's life has had an enormous impact on her art. Born in New York City, she grew up wanting to be a ballerina and began dancing professionally at age eleven. When an injury forced her to give up dancing, she turning to writing and illustrating. Not surprisingly, many of her books are about dance.

Her first book, *Max* (1976), about a boy who uses ballet exercises to warm up for his baseball games, was named an American Library Association Notable Book. In *My Ballet Class* (1980), a young girl explains the essence of ballet lessons, and the illustrations, soft black-and-white line drawings with just a hint of color, demonstrate the various ballet steps and capture the intensity of the young dancers. As is typical in her books, this class is well integrated and includes African Americans, Asian Americans, and a few boys. Isadora's early illustrations are predominately in black-and-white. But her rich use of patterns, created by composition and by shading and crosshatching, make lush pages that don't need color. Nowhere is this more evident than in *Ben's Trumpet* (1979), a Caldecott Honor Book. Ben dreams of playing a trumpet like the musician at the local jazz club and practices on an imaginary horn. The book's design is striking. Starting with the endpapers, Isadora uses a zigzag line to represent Ben's music. As he delights in his melodies, this line grows to create more and more elaborate patterns until they fill an entire page. When other children ridicule Ben, the line suddenly goes flat. Isadora does not describe Ben's feelings; the picture and design tell the viewer everything.

In the mid-1980s Isadora added full color to her books. She created two series for toddlers: *I See, I Hear,* and *I Touch* (all published in 1985) and *Babies* and *Friends* (both published in 1990). Using bright simple pictures and minimal text, she portrays the everyday activities of a young child, capturing natural body postures and delightful facial expressions, thus making real little people to whom the youngest reader can relate. Spending time in South Africa with her second husband, Isadora was struck by the beauty of the landscape and the plight of the blacks. *At the Crossroads* (1991) and *Over the Green Hills* (1992) are simple yet moving stories. In the first, children wait at the crossroads for their fathers to come home for the first time in ten months, while the other describes a family's long walk to visit their grandmother in a country where blacks have few conveniences. Isadora's vibrant watercolors capture the energy and joy of the people as well as the results of apartheid.

In general, Isadora uses simple language to create uncomplicated plots and straightforward characters. But she enriches and brings them to life with her illustrations. Using gesture, expression, composition, and now color, she creates delightful and vigorous stories and people. P.R.

ISH-KISHOR, SULAMITH

AMERICAN AUTHOR, 1896–1977. Sulamith Ish-Kishor illuminated the Jewish experience for young readers in both fiction and nonfiction. One of nine children, the author was born in London, began writing at age five, and was publishing poetry in literary magazines by the time she was ten. In 1909 Ish-Kishor immigrated to the United States with her family. They settled in New York, where she attended Hunter College, studying history and languages. She wrote articles and fiction for religious periodicals as well as secular magazines like *The New Yorker* and *The Saturday Review of Literature.*

Ish-Kishor first became known for her nonfiction books of Jewish history, including the three-volume *Children's History of Israel from the Creation to the Present Time* (1933) and *American Promise: A History of Jews in the New World* (1947). Many of her early works were published by smaller publishers, and though they may have found their way into synagogues and Jewish bookstores, often they were not available in public and school libraries, so the author's audience was limited. It was only at the end of Ish-Kishor's career that her books began to be published by larger, mainstream publishers and receive a wide readership. This change was partially due to a greater demand in the 1960s for multiculturalism in children's books, but it was also the result of Ish-Kishor's switching her focus to writing novels. Her highly acclaimed *A Boy of Old Prague* (1963) tells the story of a sixteenth-century Christian boy and his involvement with a Jewish family. Ish-Kishor also received praise for two retellings of Hebrew legends: *The Carpet of Solomon* (1966) relates King Solomon's dream of a magic carpet ride, and *The Master of the Miracle* (1971) tells of an orphan who is charged with guarding the Golem of Prague.

Ish-Kishor's best-known work is the realistic novel *Our Eddie,* which was named a Newbery Honor Book in 1970. This story of a Jewish family focuses on the troubled relationship between the English youth Eddie and his stern, schoolteacher father. Narrated by Eddie's sister Sybil and by their American friend Hal, the novel takes place in the early twentieth century and follows the family from their impoverished existence in London to an equally difficult life as immigrants in New York City. Although the surface elements may suggest the novel is autobiographical, Ish-Kishor took great pains to state that *Our Eddie* was a work of fiction, yet the characters are as vivid and three-dimensional as anyone the reader may know in real life. The depiction of Mr. Raphael, who sees his Old World traditions slipping away as his children grow up, is masterful. Eddie is headstrong and impetuous, but, as the oldest son, he must take on overwhelming responsibilities when his father immigrates to America before the rest of the family. Even when Eddie becomes involved in criminal activity, the reader can understand the circumstances and never loses affection for him. Other characters are equally well defined, and Ish-Kishor's use of voice in the dual narration of Hal and Sybil is particularly effective. The most accessible and mainstream of Ish-Kishor's writings, this intense and emotional novel may lead readers to discover her lesser-known works. P.D.S.

J

Jacobs, Joseph

English folklorist, 1854–1916. Joseph Jacobs was one of a number of folklorists who collected folk and fairy tales in the late nineteenth century and retold them especially for children. Thanks to the popularity of his collections such as *English Fairy Tales* (1890), *Celtic Fairy Tales* in two volumes (1892, 1894), and *Indian Fairy Tales* (1892), children have come to know such tales as "The Three Bears," "Henny Penny," "The Old Woman and Her Pig," and "Jack and the Beanstalk." Like his contemporary Andrew Lang, who produced the "color" fairy books in the 1890s, Jacobs wanted to capture the vibrant life of tales from the oral tradition.

Jacobs was trained as a scholar. He was a well-known folklorist who edited the British journal *Folk-Lore* for several years. He is considered to be among the great Jewish historians of the Victorian age and taught at universities in England and the United States. What sets Jacobs's collections apart from those of earlier folklorists such as the Grimm Brothers is that he collected tales not for folklore collections and archives but for children. Jacobs's daughter has written movingly about her father's love for children, describing him as a born tease and storyteller who loved nonsense. As a result of this awareness of his audience, Jacobs was less concerned with the absolute purity of a tale than he was with its "tellability." He tended to use written versions of tales rather than collecting them directly from tellers, and he always searched for what he considered to be the best version of each tale he included.

Unlike other folklorists, Jacobs believed in altering tales to fit his young audiences, omitting incidents he felt were too violent or coarse, changing episodes to make them more interesting, and altering language when he felt it was too complex or dialect-laden. He was careful, however, to acknowledge his written sources and to include notes and references at the back of each book that tell adults about the changes he has made and his reasons for making them.

Among the tales Jacobs collected are the British versions of well-known tales that children may know best from German or French traditions. His "Tattercoats," for example, is a version of the Cinderella story in which a young girl is able to free herself from an unloving father, marry a prince, and live happily ever after. Margot Tomes illustrated a picture-book edition of this tale in 1989. His "Tom Tit Tot" is funnier than the better-known "Rumpelstiltskin" and has a catchy refrain, "Nimmy, nimmy, not, my name's Tom Tit Tot," which adds to oral retellings. Evaline Ness created an illustrated version of this tale in 1965.

The continuing popularity of Jacobs's work is indicated by the number of picture-book versions of his tales that continue to be released. American illustrator Paul Galdone is especially fond of Jacobs's tales, having created illustrated versions of *Henny Penny* (1968), *The Three Bears* (1972), *King of the Cats* (1980), and *The Three Sillies* (1981), among others. Other well-known illustrators of the tales include Margot Zemach, Marcia Brown, Lorinda Bryan Cauley, and Errol Le Cain. Edward Ardizzone was illustrating his favorite twenty-five tales from Jacobs's collections at the time of his death. The twelve tales he had illustrated were published as *English Fairy Tales* in 1980.

Even though Jacobs simplified the language and eliminated the dialect from many tales, they still prove to be somewhat difficult reading for younger children. Virginia Haviland has retold six tales, simplifying the language but remaining faithful to Jacobs's stories, in *Favorite Fairy Tales Told in England* (1959). Anne Rockwell and Helen Oxenbury have also included simplified versions in their books of folktales for young children. Older children and storytellers, however, can still feel the power of Jacobs's language and laugh at his humorous insights into human nature as they read or listen to his classic stories. ❧ B.A.C.

Jacques, Brian

British author, b. 1939. A series of fantasy novels about the animals that live in and around Redwall

Abbey has propelled author Brian Jacques to international success with readers of all ages.

Born in Liverpool, England, Jacques attended local Catholic schools until he became a sailor at age fifteen. He also worked as a longshoreman, truck driver, radio broadcaster, and professional comedian. His first book was written to entertain the students at a school for the blind. *Redwall* (1986) concerns a community of field animals that join together to fight off an invading army of rats. The plot contains many standard fantasy elements, including the quest for a legendary sword, an awkward young hero who discovers the secret of his heritage, and the omnipresent war between good and evil. The second book in the series, *Mossflower* (1988), goes back in time to tell the story of Martin the Warrior, the original mouse hero of Redwall Abbey. *Mattimeo* (1989), *Mariel of Redwall* (1991), *Salamandaston* (1993), and *Martin the Warrior* (1994) record the history of preceding and succeeding generations. Some readers may find the novels overlong and the prose overwritten, but fantasy fans enjoy every page of the often thrilling adventures, which include detailed descriptions of battles and sumptuous feasts.

Jacques has also written an acclaimed collection of scary stories, *Seven Strange and Ghostly Tales* (1991), but he remains best known for his impressive, multivolume cycle of fantasy that continues to win legions of admirers with each new volume. P.D.S.

James, Will

AMERICAN AUTHOR AND ILLUSTRATOR, 1892–1942. When the rodeo paraded down Fifth Avenue in New York City, it always made a special stop at the Scribner Building so William Roderick James could wave to his friends inside. James was a cowboy and rodeo performer, but he was also a well-known author and illustrator.

Born in Great Falls, Montana, James was orphaned at age four. He received no formal education, but discovered early a talent for drawing. He worked as a cowhand, served in the army, and performed as an extra in Western films. James began selling horse illustrations to magazines while recuperating from an accident, but he never considered writing until a friend suggested that James create stories to accompany his artwork. His best-known work, *Smoky the Cowhorse* (1926), is the minutely observed story of a colt tamed by a cowboy, then stolen. Smoky performs on the rodeo circuit before being reunited with the cowboy. Enlivened by James's realistic illustrations, the novel was a surprising choice for the Newbery Medal because it was originally published for adults. Although many thought the ungrammatical, colloquial prose was inappropriate for young people, the book soon became quite popular with children. Fans of horse stories find the book thoroughly satisfying; other readers may consider it slow and overly detailed. All of the author's novels, including *Sand* (1929) and *Big Enough* (1931), concern horses and cowboys and are written in the Western vernacular. James also published an account of his early life, *My First Horse* (1940), and a full autobiography, *Lone Cowboy* (1930).

A love of horses and the West is evident in every volume written and illustrated by this genuine American cowboy. P.D.S.

Janeczko, Paul

AMERICAN POET, ANTHOLOGIST, AND AUTHOR, B. 1945. Since the publication of his first anthology, *The Crystal Image* (1977), Paul B. Janeczko has been more responsible than any other individual for putting poetry into the hands of young adult readers. Dissatisfied with the poetry collections available to him as a high school English teacher, Janeczko collected, mimeographed, and shared with his students contemporary poetry that spoke directly to them. From those mimeographed pages came the first of nearly a dozen anthologies that have captured the imaginations of young readers and gratified their teachers. Several of the collections—including *Don't Forget to Fly: A Cycle of Modern Poems* (1981), *Poetspeak: In Their Work, about Their Work* (1983), *Strings: A Gathering of Family Poems* (1984), *Pocket Poems: Selected for a Journey* (1985), and *The Place My Words Are Looking For* (1990)—have been named to the American Library Association's annual list of Best Books for Young Adults. Janeczko's second anthology, *Postcard Poems* (1979), set a standard for the compilations that followed, a thematic collection of carefully selected poems, distinctive for their vivid imagery and economy of language, diverse in style and tone, skillfully organized, and representing both acknowledged masters of the craft and fresh new voices.

Janeczko's particular skill is in selecting poems with themes that touch and move young adults, then deftly ordering them so that each poem lures the reader on to read one more. With each anthology Janeczko takes a unique and fresh approach. *Pocket Poems* reflects life's journey as well as actual departures and returns and can be carried comfortably in a back pocket—the very image chosen for the book's cover art. For *Poetspeak* and *The Place My Words Are Looking For,* Janeczko asked poets to share not only their poems but their thoughts and feelings about poetry, their sources of inspiration, and their own writing processes. Several of Janeczko's articles, original poems, and stories have appeared in magazines. Only occasionally does he include one of his own poems in the anthologies.

A work of nonfiction, *Loads of Codes and Secret Ciphers* (1981), teaches readers how to write and decode secret languages. His first novel, *Bridges to Cross* (1986), portrays the pivotal summer between eighth grade and high school for a boy and his closest friend. In his first book of original poetry, *Brickyard Summer* (1989), Janeczko revisits the themes, setting, and some significant events from *Bridges to Cross.* Both books are colored by the author's childhood experiences in a small mill town and his strict Catholic education. The poems evoke the essence of a New England mill town and its inhabitants with poignancy, sensitivity, and narrative unity. After twenty-two years of teaching, Paul Janeczko left the classroom in 1990 to devote more time to his own writing and to the compilation of yet another poetry anthology. Ever committed to sharing his enthusiasm for poetry, he frequently conducts workshops for teachers, visits classrooms, and serves as poetry editor for *English Journal.* ❧ D.M.L.

Jansson, Tove

FINNISH ARTIST, AUTHOR, AND ILLUSTRATOR, B. 1914. All across the world, children have treasured the Moomin Valley peopled by Misabel and Little My, the Snork Maiden, and the Moomintrolls themselves. Using words and detailed pen-and-ink drawings, Tove Jansson has created a cast of lovable eccentrics. The Moomins are small and rounded, with noses like those of a hippopotamus. Using a line or two, Jansson depicts the wide eyes and wild hair that emphasize the innocence and curiosity of the characters. There are nine books in all that have been translated from the Swedish. Jansson is also an accomplished fine artist and has other books to her name, but it is for the immense universe that these small adventure sagas create that she is best known and loved. For these she has received all the major Scandinavian awards, as well as the international Hans Christian Andersen Award.

Jansson grew up in a wild and unpredictable household; her father was a sculptor and her mother a book designer. In the summers they went to an island far out in the Finnish archipelago, where they went sailing whenever the weather was bad enough. Jansson writes, "Far out from the coast there's an uninhabited island which I used to think was more dangerous than the other islands. Every time my father took us out to sea, I hoped he would sail there. And every time we got there, the wind increased or there was a thunderstorm, and Father said, looking very pleased, 'Now we must stay the night.'" When they were curled up under the sail of their boat and Jansson heard scurryings and rustlings, she knew there were trolls outside. She asked her mother how big and angry trolls were, and her mother said, "They're small . . . small and nice. They like gales, just as we do."

When the Moomins are stranded on an island by a violent storm in *The Finn Family Moomintroll* (1949, trans. 1950), it is not nice trolls who disturb their sleep but hundreds of tiny milk-white Hattifatteners who are after their stolen barometer. The Moomins live on the edge of danger; Jansson says she tries to keep "the balance between the excitement of the commonplace and the safety of the fantastic." In keeping with the haphazard, playful nature of Moomin Valley, Jansson's texts are fairly thin structurally, and she has been criticized for her lack of characterization and inattention to plot. It is this very scattered vision, though, that makes Moomin Valley so wonderful. As Tootick says in *Moominland Midwinter* (1957, trans. 1958), "Everything is so uncertain, and that is what I find so reassuring." But there is no contesting that Jansson's language is delicious: In *Finn Family,* the friends had climbed to the top of a mountain on the first day of spring, where "the March wind gambolled around them, and the blue distance lay at their feet." And when Snuffkin the wanderer watches his little boats float off, Moomintroll asks him where they are going. "'To places where I'm not,' Snuffkin answered as, one after another, the little boats swirled away round the bend of the river and disappeared. 'Loaded with cinnamon, sharks' teeth and emeralds,' said Moomintroll." Snuffkin tells Moomintroll that he too must be going, and Moomintroll is filled with sadness. Delicately Jansson probes the most poignant of human emotions, fear and loss, joyful abandonment, loneliness, and being recognized as yourself. For as Moominmamma says, "'You see, I shall always know you whatever happens.'" ❧ J.A.J.

Japanese-American Children's Books

Since the groundbreaking folktales and fiction of YOSHIKO UCHIDA began to appear in the 1950s, many children's books about Japan and Americans of Japanese descent have been published. Seeking to both inform and entertain young readers, the authors and illustrators of these books present the distinct, intriguing culture and people of Japan and of Japanese Americans through folktales, HISTORICAL FICTION and nonfiction, and contemporary fiction.

Editions of folktales dominate the field of Japanese-American children's books, providing children with a good introduction to—though an incomplete picture of—the land and culture of Japan. Some of the many noteworthy picture-book editions of Japanese folktales, produced by those inside and outside the culture, include Japanese woodcut artist Tejima's *Ho-limlim: A Rabbit Tale from Japan* (1990); Sheila Hamanaka's *Screen of Frogs: An Old Tale* (1993); Dianne Snyder's *The Boy of the Three-Year Nap* (1988), illustrated by ALLEN SAY; and *The Tale of the Mandarin Ducks* (1990), retold by KATHERINE PATERSON, who spent four years in Japan studying the language, and illustrated by LEO and DIANE DILLON, who modeled the art on *ukiyo-e*, a style of Japanese woodblock prints. Authoritative folktale collections include *Tales from the Bamboo Grove* (1992) collected by Japanese-American author Yoko Kawashima Watkins and *The Shining Princess and Other Japanese Legends* (1989) collected by Eric Quayle.

Historical fiction set in Japan helps create the context for appreciating books on the Japanese-American experience. Most historical fiction set in Japan offers tales of action and intrigue that tell exciting stories while informing readers about Japan's history. One of LENSEY NAMIOKA's mystery-adventure novels set in feudal Japan, *The Coming of the Bear* (1992), focuses on two cultures that learn to coexist despite their differences. Katherine Paterson's well-researched novels of feudal twelfth-century Japan are highly acclaimed, as is her National Book Award winner *The Master Puppeteer* (1975), which takes place in eighteenth-century Japan. ERIK CHRISTIAN HAUGAARD immersed himself in Japanese life, history, and culture before writing his novels set in sixteenth-century Japan, which include the picaresque epic *The Boy and the Samurai* (1991).

Several books about Japan's modern history tell true stories about the tragedy of war. In Yukio Tsuchiya's picture book *Faithful Elephants: A True Story of Animals, People and War* (1988), Tokyo zookeepers mourn the death by starvation of three elephants that were among the many animals killed during World War II to prevent their escaping and endangering people if the zoo was bombed. Toshi Maruki's *Hiroshima no Pika* (1980) and Junko Morimoto's *My Hiroshima* (1990) are personal, wrenching, picture-book accounts of the day the bomb was dropped on Hiroshima. Two brief novels on the use of the atomic bomb are Eleanor Coerr's *Mieko and the Fifth Treasure* (1993), about a girl injured during the bombing of Nagasaki who overcomes her bitterness, and *Sadako and the Thousand Paper Cranes* (1977), the true story of a girl who died of leukemia as a result of radiation from the atom bomb. Coerr's *Sadako* (1993), a picture-book version of the novel, features illustrations selected from ED YOUNG's artwork for the film of the book. Yoko Kawashima Watkins's autobiographical novel *So Far from the Bamboo Grove* (1986) is a moving account of the Japanese author's childhood escape from war-torn northern Korea to Japan.

Historical fiction about Japanese Americans instills in children of Japanese descent a sense of pride in their identity and teaches all children about American history. Yoshiko Uchida's *Samurai of Gold Hill* (1972) tells about the first Japanese immigrants to California in 1859, while her novels *A Jar of Dreams* (1981), *The Best Bad Thing* (1983), and *The Happiest Ending* (1985) focus on eleven-year-old Rinko, a Japanese-American girl growing up during the Depression. Picture books on the 1942 imprisonment of Japanese Americans are Uchida's *The Bracelet* (1993), in which a seven-year-old girl is strengthened by the power of her memories, and Ken Mochizuki's *Baseball Saved Us* (1993), about a boy whose father organizes baseball games to help fellow prisoners deal with their feelings of anger and boredom. Uchida's *Journey to Topaz: A Story of the Japanese-American Evacuation* (1971) and its sequel *Journey Home* (1978) are novels based on the author's family's experiences during and after their internment in the prisons; a memoir of her childhood and her time in the camps is told in *The Invisible Thread* (1992). Sheila Hamanaka's *The Journey: Japanese Americans, Racism, and Renewal* (1990) is a picture book for older readers that depicts the entire history of Japanese Americans, focusing in particular on the so-called relocation centers. The book was inspired by a mural the artist, a third-generation Japanese American, painted "to open the past, hoping to help chase away the demons of prejudice and injustice."

Contemporary stories about Japan allow readers to explore the differences and similarities between Japanese and American culture. Picture books set in twentieth-century Japan include Takaaki Nomura's *Grandpa's Town* (1991), featuring a bilingual text about a boy's day with his grandfather, and Allen Say's *Tree of Cranes* (1991), in which a boy is introduced to the Christmas holiday celebrations his mother enjoyed in her American childhood. A beautifully crafted young adult novel set in modern-day Japan is Kyoko Mori's *Shizuko's Daughter* (1993), about a girl's long journey toward hope and acceptance following her mother's suicide. Allen Say's autobiographical novel *The Ink-Keeper's Apprentice* (1979) relates his experiences as a young apprentice to a Japanese cartoonist, and his picture book *Grandfather's Journey,* winner of the 1994 Caldecott Medal, depicts the love for two lands—the United States and Japan—felt by his grandfather and himself.

Books set in the contemporary United States and featuring Americans of Japanese descent are few in number. Taro Yashima's picture book *Umbrella* (1958) tells a story featuring Momo, his Japanese-American daughter, who was born in New York and whose name means "peach" in Japanese. Ina R. Friedman's picture book *How My Parents Learned to Eat* (1984), illustrated by Allen Say, is narrated by a biracial girl whose parents met when her American father was stationed in Japan. In Hadley Irwin's novel *Kim/Kimi* (1987), a half Japanese, half Caucasian adolescent's search for information about the Japanese father she never knew leads her to the site of an American concentration camp.

Almost nonexistent prior to the 1950s, Japanese-American children's books are now available in a variety of genres. Although some of this literature aims at pure entertainment, many of these books seek to pass on important historical lessons about war and racism, impressing upon readers of all backgrounds the necessity for mutual respect among peoples of different cultures. Closer understanding between Japanese Americans and American children of other ethnic backgrounds continues to be enhanced by publication of these works. ❧

JENNIFER M. BRABANDER

JARRELL, RANDALL

AMERICAN POET AND AUTHOR, 1914–1965. Randall Jarrell came to the creation of children's books late in his writing career. By the time he published his first work for children in 1964, he was already a novelist, a well-known critic, and an award-winning poet for adult audiences. Yet these same poetic gifts led him into writing for children. He had been asked by Michael di Capua, the noted editor, to translate a GRIMM brothers' fairy tale for a collection of new versions of the stories that di Capua was planning to publish. Jarrell's retelling had such stylistic grace and evocative power that di Capua urged him to try writing his own original works for children.

The result of that first effort, *The Gingerbread Rabbit,* with illustrations by GARTH WILLIAMS, was a revision of the traditional story "The Gingerbread Man." The familiar character made from cookie dough has a happy fate in Jarrell's version; rather than being devoured by the foxes of the world, he is adopted into a family of real rabbits, where he at last finds a home and safety from the threats of death that have kept him running throughout the book.

A similar quest for a loving community provided the emotional foundation for Jarrell's second children's book, *The Bat-Poet* (1964), illustrated by MAURICE SENDAK. In this story about a young bat who cannot sleep during the day and follows his own individual and isolating creative lights, Jarrell offered his young readers what many consider to be one of the best statements about the plight of the artist in his search for creative independence on the one hand and his longing for acceptance on the other.

In *The Animal Family* (1965), which is generally regarded as one of the CLASSICS of children's literature, Jarrell once again found an unusual subject and succeeded in transforming it into a work of breathtaking imaginative and emotional beauty. His narrative brings together a lonely hunter, a mermaid, a shipwrecked boy, a lynx, and a bear into an unlikely family that takes up loving, harmonious, timeless residence in the hunter's cabin, "where the forest runs down to the ocean."

Jarrell's last children's book, *Fly by Night,* published posthumously in 1976 with Sendak's haunting illustrations, again expressed one of Jarrell's abiding interests: the mysterious overlapping of the worlds of dream and walking. David, the young hero of the story, floats through the house and around the countryside, observing the dreams of those he encounters in his own dream state—his parents, the dog, the sheep, and an owl family, whose tale of loss and rescue, of isolation and loving adoption, sound themes that lie at the heart of this and all Jarrell stories.

Though his writing for children spanned only a few years and a handful of works before his untimely death in 1965, Jarrell left classic works for children that are distinguished by their numinous poetry, their imaginative energy, and their transcendent vision. One wishes there had been dozens more such books, but because they are so few and so unique, they are all the more rare. ❧ J.O.C.

JEFFERS, SUSAN

AMERICAN ILLUSTRATOR, B. 1942. Starting with *Three Jovial Huntsmen* (1973), her first book to receive wide attention, Susan Jeffers's art has gone on to enchant and

Voices of the Creators

Susan Jeffers

It may have been Balanchine who said to his dancers, "You must wait for the music. Everything depends on the music!" For me the story is the music, and I am the dancer.

When I consider my artwork, I realize that for a picture book, I must first have a heart-gripping story or poem, or I might as well not begin. Over the years I have been invited to draw pictures for popular topics, like unicorns. An easy subject—a horse with a long pointed horn on its forehead. How difficult could that be? And such a book certainly would be a good income producer. But I have learned to be wary of these motives—my pictures suffer, because I have no interest in unicorns.

As I am not a writer, I have to sift through a great amount of material to find something to illustrate. Good writing, not to say great writing, is dreadfully difficult to find. It is no accident that writers like Hans Christian Andersen, Jane Austen, Leon Uris, Josephine Tey—to mention a disparate group—are read all over the world. What they all have in common is the ability to tell a moving story.

Great literature, including great children's literature, concerns itself with questions of being human. It helps children and other readers to come to grips with their fears, angers, and jealousies. Sometimes it uses the voice of a beautiful, gentle animal, such as Black Beauty, who calls upon us to care for and be generous toward creatures who are at our mercy. Hansel and Gretel wrestle with the problem of growing up without the help of dependable adults. They know love and loyalty, and they find the courage to stand up to evil and push it into an oven. Gerda in "The Snow Queen" followed her heart across a sometimes kind, sometimes cruel world to save her friend Kai from an icy fate, with only the power of her innocent love to help her.

I was horrified recently to see Hans Christian Andersen's "Little Mermaid" gutted in the latest movie version. In the original, the Little Mermaid does not marry the prince. Her sacrifice in leaving her family and giving up her beautiful voice is useless. She is offered a chance to save herself from death by killing the prince, but she refuses. In so doing she dies, yet she wins her eternal spirit. Children dwell with heroes in this story. They are involved in the experiences of life, and they identify with the courage and despair of the characters. They should not be deprived of the author's intent with a vapid adaptation.

My book with Rosemary Wells, *Waiting for the Evening Star,* is an evocation of a time in United States history just before World War I. The book is about a boy named Berty and his family's Vermont farm. He had a childhood when family and neighbors worked together, and enough was plenty. People lived closer to the natural circle of the seasons then. I am a generation away from this time, but my parents passed on their deep love of the wild places to me. This story calls it forth. When I read it—again and again, as an illustrator must—a lump rises in my throat and tears well in my eyes. The odd thing is that I don't know why. Perhaps this is as it should be. Rosemary Wells, with her acute observation, supplies an inner vision of this life, combined with the warmest sympathy, and conveys it by suggestion, leaving me the space to contribute the pictures that the story needs to become a picture book.

I take literature and the art of children's books very seriously—even humorous ones, for they are a very high art form. My pictures follow and support the text—I revere the words. I cannot create a collection of pretty pictures, for that is a calendar, not a picture book.

inspire countless children and adults. After graduating from Pratt Institute in Brooklyn, New York, Jeffers worked "behind the scenes" in children's book publishing in the art departments of several publishers. As she worked on other artists' children's books, she says, she "began to feel again the love I had for them as a child . . . and I became more and more eager to do my own." She quit the security of her publishing day job and plunged into the life of a full-time artist, sharing studio space with Rosemary Wells, who also went on to great success in children's books. Jeffers occasionally refers in her own work to this early partnership, as in the picture of a Wells character hung in the room of the little boy who is afraid of the dark in *Midnight Farm* by Reeve Lindbergh (1987). She published her first book, *Buried Moon,* an English folktale by Joseph Jacobs, in 1969. Her first version of *Three Jovial Huntsmen,* a traditional poem, she submitted soon thereafter, but it turned out to be so unsatisfactory for both Jeffers and her publisher that it was abandoned before going to print. She revised it, resubmitted it, and in 1974 it was named a Caldecott Honor Book.

Jeffers's interest in and knowledge of the natural world shows in her finely detailed drawings of animals and forests, skies, meadows, and farms. Her eloquent illustrations for Robert Frost's *Stopping by Woods on a Snowy Evening* (1978) demonstrate this aspect of her work quite well. Often unabashedly sentimental, Jeffers's work is tempered by a sly humor, which peeks through in the hidden images she often employs and in the visual commentary she makes on the texts, as in the three jovial huntsmen's bumbling unawareness of the teeming animal life around them or the harried father's attempts to put his energetic son to bed in *Close Your Eyes* by Jean Marzollo (1976). In addition to skillfully rendering animals in their natural habitat, Jeffers often integrates fantastic imagery in her work, merging the natural world with a dream world that she indicates exists just outside the perception of our senses. It is this spiritual aspect of nature that Jeffers has most fully realized in *Brother Eagle, Sister Sky* (1991), a heartfelt elegy to modern man's lost sense of kinship with the earth. While criticized by some for an overly romanticized, factually inaccurate portrayal of American Indian culture, *Brother Eagle* and *Hiawatha* (1983)—Jeffers's illustration of a portion of HENRY WADSWORTH LONGFELLOW's poem—can be viewed as highly personal meditations on the American Indian legacy in modern American culture. *Brother Eagle, Sister Sky,* with Jeffers's own adaptation of the words attributed to Chief Seattle, spent time on the *New York Times* best-seller list, one of the few children's books ever to do so, a testament to the eloquence and timeliness of both the words and the pictures.

Jeffers's pictures usually start with a precise pencil drawing that she then renders in ink, before she adds dyes and washes for color. This technique gives her work a sense of clarity that grounds it in reality and a glowing color that transcends the everyday. Her use of perspective, as she fills the foreground of her pictures with large, bold images, gives her readers a feeling of immediacy—of being surrounded and enveloped by her world. ❧ S.G.K.

JENNINGS, PAUL

AUSTRALIAN AUTHOR, B. 1943. In 1992, when Paul Jennings's book sales soared past the 1 million–copy mark, no one in Australia was flabbergasted. This author had been almost an instant sensation as soon as he put pen seriously to paper, as young readers devoured his short-story collections almost as soon as they came off the press.

Born in Middlesex, England, at the age of five Jennings packed up with his family and sailed to Australia, where they settled in Melbourne. Although Jennings's father struggled to find employment and both his parents suffered terribly from homesickness, they vowed to stay in Australia "for the children," believing the country could offer them opportunities unavailable in England. And stay they did, much to the eventual delight of their son, who later wrote, "There is nowhere that I would rather be." He did, unfortunately, get his first rejection slip at the tender age of sixteen and was so discouraged that he didn't write again until he reached his forties. In the meantime, however, he stepped into the classroom, where he held various positions as a teacher of disabled and socially deprived children, a speech pathologist, and a lecturer in special education and language and literature. Then, in the mid-1980s, he again began writing, mainly because he had become concerned about the plight of the reluctant reader. This was the child, he said, "for whom adults have not been able to find a good enough book." And when Jennings could not find a book good enough for his own son, he decided to create one. He spent six months researching accessible speech patterns and came up with strategies related to syntax, story structure, and predictability. But overall he wanted to create tales packed with interest. The resulting collection of short stories, *Unreal!* (1985), immediately set him on the road to popularity and success. Other collections of humorous, quirky stories, including *Unbelievable!* (1986), *Unmentionable!* (1991), and *Round the Twist* (1990), have followed, winning the writer a number of children's choice awards. Packed with surprising twists and turns, his prose generally consists of relatively short, almost staccato sentences, with few compound sentences and even fewer complex ones. Although his main readership lies in the nine- to twelve-year-old age range, precocious readers as young as six or seven and others as old as fourteen are fervent fans. They are held spellbound by his tales, spooky or humorous, which are often intentionally revolting, as well. Jennings knows that readers like to recognize and laugh at their own embarrassing moments.

While short stories have been the author's forte, he has also written picture-book texts, television scripts of his stories, and a collaboration with Ted Greenwood and Terry Denton called *Spooner or Later* (1992), a rollicking game book on spoonerisms. One of his stories became the text for a hauntingly illustrated picture book called *Grandad's Gifts* (1992), a short-listed title in the 1993 Australian Children's Book of the Year Awards.

Fortunately for young readers, Jennings shows no sign of relinquishing his talented hold on the pen. ❧ K.J.

Johnson, Crockett

American author and illustrator, 1906–1975. Best known as the creator of Harold and the "Purple Crayon Books" and as illustrator of Ruth Krauss's *The Carrot Seed,* Crockett Johnson was a cartoonist whose simplest, sparest, and boldest outlines produced unforgettable, gently humorous, and always endearing caricatures in the world of American children's picture books. Johnson's natural gift for drawing and writing from a young child's viewpoint enabled him to craft more than twenty juvenile books, two of which have entertained children for more than four decades.

Johnson, whose real name was David Johnson Leisk, was born in New York City and studied art at Cooper Union and New York University. He worked as an art editor of several periodicals, in advertising and design, and as a cartoonist. First recognized in 1942 for his syndicated newspaper comic strip, "Barnaby," Johnson gained national acclaim when the strip's characters, five-year-old Barnaby Baxter and his imaginary Fairy Godfather, Mr. O'Malley, appeared in the tabloid *PM.* Four years later, "Barnaby" appeared in more than fifty newspapers with a total circulation of over five million. Two cartoon books that contained selected episodes, *Barnaby* (1943) and *Barnaby and Mr. O'Malley* (1944), were among Johnson's first books published; though not intended for children, "Barnaby" and his books delighted young and old alike.

Johnson made his picture-book debut in 1945 when he illustrated *The Carrot Seed,* written by his wife, Ruth Krauss, a respected author of children's books for the very young. Johnson's simple cartoon drawings seamlessly match Krauss's poetic, imagistic text of a young boy whose green thumb and self-confidence triumph over his naysaying family. The boy plants the tiniest of carrot seeds and lovingly nurtures it, while his parents and older brother insist that nothing will grow from it. Throughout the entire book, organic browns and tans of the paper, illustrations, and typeface amplify the story's warmth and lend a rich earthiness to the boy's expectant patience. Then, to convey the boy's feat of faith and the tremendous flurry of the ground's activity, Johnson adds a dash of luxuriant green for the towering carrot top and an even bolder splash of bright red-orange for the colossal carrot. Still in print, *The Carrot Seed* continues to entertain young audiences.

Johnson alone wrote and illustrated the enormously successful *Harold and the Purple Crayon* (1955), a small book about a little boy's nighttime jaunt that he, with the aid of his purple crayon, draws for himself. Together, Harold and his purple crayon trek through woods, encounter a ferocious dragon, sail the high seas, and conquer mountaintops; together, they wend their way home, with Harold finally safe, sound, and comfortable in bed. With the fewest of lines, Johnson depicts Harold as a toddler clad in sleepers, his chubby hand gripping a fat plum-colored crayon. From page to page, the thick, firm, purple mark delineates Harold's actions against the stark white background so effectively and ingeniously that the crayon is as much a character as Harold. The same economy that informs Johnson's art permeates his text; he writes so concisely of Harold's moonlight stroll that his style perfectly echoes the clarity of his boldly outlined cartoon illustrations. Johnson created five other "Purple Crayon Books" that take Harold to such places as a castle, outer space, the North Pole, the circus, and on a clever trip through the alphabet; an additional book, *A Picture for Harold's Room* (1960), is an early reader. But none succeeds as well as Johnson's never-out-of-print *Harold and the Purple Crayon.*

Two other notable books, *Ellen's Lion* (1959) and *The Lion's Own Story* (1963), further establish Johnson's talent for writing from a child's point of view. Both titles feature brief, witty stories and gloriously pure and simple cartoon illustrations about a charming duo: Ellen, a garrulous, egocentric preschooler, and her sagacious, realist, stuffed lion, with whom she has conversations. Ellen and the lion, her alter ego, cavort through escapades exclusively reserved for the world of very young children, a world that few picture-book author-illustrators have captured as superbly as Johnson. ❧ S.L.S.

Jonas, Ann

American illustrator and author, b. 1932. A keen graphic eye and dramatic sense of design give Ann Jonas a perspective that is not bound by traditional picture-book formats or viewpoints. From the simple curiosity of toddlers in *Holes and Peeks* (1984) to the fascinating presentation of endangered animals in *Aardvarks, Disembark!* (1990), Jonas uses a preciseness of line, a uniquely appropriate style, and subtlety of image to convey visual treats.

Growing up in suburban, semirural Long Island, Jonas and her brother spent a lot of time outdoors. Her family attached great importance in knowing how to do as many things as possible, from car repairs to cabinet building. While everyone worked on numerous projects, drawing was considered to be an incidental skill, only necessary for the planning phase. Jonas's enjoyment in designing and making objects carried over into adulthood. She didn't seriously consider college after high school, but after working a few years in a department store's advertising department, she felt the need to build an art career. While studying at Cooper Union, she met her husband, DONALD CREWS. Following his military stint in Germany, they returned to the States and started a freelance design business. Years later, when Crews had illustrated a number of children's books, his publisher urged Jonas to try her hand at one. The result was a charming preschool book, *When You Were a Baby* (1982).

Her background as a designer enables Jonas to approach each book individually, using different styles and techniques. Almost all involve some visual activity or game with a storyline carefully designed into the experience. It was the publication of her third book, *Round Trip* (1983), that generated awards for its stunning graphic design; the black-and-white book can be read forward and then turned upside-down and in reverse as a day trip to the city becomes a return trip to the country. The next visual game was *The Quilt* (1984), which effectively evoked the transitions in the patterns of a young girl's quilt into a dream sequence. Jonas's love for the hidden picture puzzles in children's magazines led to *The Trek* (1985). On her way to school a girl sees a myriad of zoo animals camouflaged in the scenery. In *Aardvarks, Disembark!* Jonas changes the format to fit the topic; hundreds of endangered animals leave the ark, descending down the pages in Z to A order. A magnifying glass on the cover invites the reader to pick up *The 13th Clue* (1992) to follow the heroine on a merry chase from the attic through the woods to a surprise ending.

Each of Jonas's books explores new ways to stretch children's imaginations and encourages them to look at familiar things in different ways. The clue to her creativity is her designer's eye, her love for graphic challenges, and her ability to shape and illustrate the experience of discovery for children. J.C.

JONES, DIANA WYNNE

BRITISH AUTHOR, B. 1934. Diana Wynne Jones recalls that she chose to write FANTASY "because I was not able to believe in most people's version of normal life." Jones grew up in Britain during the disruptions of World War II, and her parents' devotion to their work as educators often left her and her sisters to fend for themselves. As an adult, she discovered that her children enjoyed the same sort of books she had missed having as a child, and she continues to try to create such stories, "full of humour and fantasy, but firmly referred to real life." Writing for children and young adults, she has produced novels, short stories, plays, and a picture book called *Yes, Dear* (1992). In her "Dalemark" novels—*Cart and Cwidder* (1975), *Drowned Ammet* (1977), and *The Spellcoats* (1979)—Jones explores the connections between magic, folklore, and real life for the citizens of Dalemark, a land she invented.

She frequently invokes a broader version of reality, one that extends beyond the boundaries humans normally perceive. In *The Homeward Bounders* (1981), beings known only as "They" play a vast game with a whole range of worlds. *A Tale of Time City* (1987) describes a city "that exists outside time and history" from which residents can influence events on Earth. For her "Chrestomanci" books—*Charmed Life* (1977), a Guardian Award winner; *The Magicians of Caprona* (1980); *Witch Week* (1982); and *The Lives of Christopher Chant* (1988)—Jones envisions a universe of parallel worlds. From one of them, the Chrestomanci, a magician with nine lives, strives to regulate the use of magic.

The Chrestomanci novels and a number of her other books feature gifted but as yet unrecognized protagonists who finally come into their own. While humor is prevalent, true disaster often threatens. In *Archer's Goon* (1984), young Howard realizes that he is actually a wizard, just in time to prevent his siblings from attempting to conquer the world. *Aunt Maria* (1991) takes place in the village of Cranbury, where traditional divisions between men and women, carried to extremes, have resulted in a serious imbalance of magical powers. *Dogsbody* (1975) tells how the "luminary" inhabiting Sirius the Dog Star, unjustly banished into a dog's body on Earth, must remember his identity and find the mysterious Zoi before someone else misuses its power. Frequently Jones's characters must not only recognize their gifts but also learn to control them. The Wizard Howl in *Howl's Moving Castle* (1986) almost comes to grief because he has overexploited his talents by trading his own heart in a magical bargain.

Well known for her ingenuity, Jones may begin with elements from folklore or mythology, such as the tales of Tam Lin and Thomas the Rhymer for *Fire and Hemlock* (1984) or the Norse gods who appear in the contemporary world of *Eight Days of Luke* (1975), but in the end her stories, with their unusual twists, are all her own. Following those twists may occasionally present a challenge, but readers who choose to share her vision will have an uncommon imaginative experience. ❧ M.F.S.

Jones, Elizabeth Orton

American author and illustrator, b. 1910. Religious themes dominate the artwork of Elizabeth Orton Jones, who illustrated several volumes of Bible verses and won the Caldecott Medal for the picture book *Prayer for a Child* (1944).

Jones was born and raised in Highland Park, Illinois, and began to write and draw as a child. She majored in art at the University of Chicago, then studied painting in France. After returning to the United States, Jones began drawing scenes of Paris and found herself including children in the pictures. She then wrote a text to accompany her artwork, which resulted in her first children's book. *Ragman of Paris and His Ragamuffins* (1937) concerns two brothers, Mich and Tobie, who are adopted by a Parisian ragman. This loose collection of vignettes has an uneven tone, veering from scenes of realism to a fantasy involving a talking cat and including intrusive tales told by various minor characters. Although the book provides an evocative picture of Paris, there is a saccharine element in both the illustrations and the text. An overtly sweet writing style also impairs *Maminka's Children* (1940), the story of a Bohemian family living in the United States. Family relationships and holiday celebrations are depicted with warmth, but the prose is filled with coy conversations and cloying endearments. There is great charm and energy, however, in the numerous color illustrations.

Although Jones wrote several other books, including *Twig* (1942), a fantasy about a little girl who meets an elf, she is no longer remembered for her writing but is best known today for illustrating the works of other authors. Beginning with the Bible story *David* in 1937, Jones provided artwork for a number of religious books. *Small Rain: Verses from the Bible* (1943) was compiled by Jessie Orton Jones, the illustrator's mother; there is a purity and simplicity in the black-and-white, occasionally pastel, illustrations of cherubic children enjoying nature and friendship in this Caldecott Honor Book. Jessie Orton Jones also selected the Bible verses for *A Little Child* (1946), which presents the Christmas story through pictures of modern children performing a nativity pageant. The black-and-gray illustrations are given depth and power by the addition of a vivid red. In an unusual choice for that era, Jones included multiethnic children in her illustrations for both books and in Rachel Field's *Prayer for a Child*, which is luminously illustrated in soft pastels that are perfectly suited to the mood of this simple good-night prayer. *A Prayer for Little Things* (1946) by Eleanor Farjeon is also nicely illustrated, but the book seems derivative of the successful *Prayer for a Child.*

Jones ceased writing and illustrating children's books in the mid-1950s. Although her prose style now seems dated, her artwork remains enjoyable in several memorable picture books. ❧ P.D.S.

Jordan, June

American author and poet, b. 1936. June Jordan has explored the beauty and struggle of the black experience in the United States through poetry, essays, plays, novels, and short stories, which range in audience from juvenile to adult. She has been influenced by the settings and experiences of Harlem, New York, where she was born, and Bedford-Stuyvesant, New York, where she was raised. Through her childhood and religious training, she was taught that the word is the truth, and the power and importance of words began to interest her. Her recognition of the beauty and vulnerability of children prompted her to focus her writing so that it would be accessible to them, and her initiative in also writing for adults was done as a means of providing a better world for the children.

Prior to 1969, June Jordan contributed poems and stories to magazines under the name June Meyer. Her transition to the various forms of literature began when the Academy of American Poets asked her to complete a project begun by Milton Meltzer and the late Langston Hughes. From that project was created *Who Look at Me* (1969), a collection of paintings that portray a historical account of blacks in America accompanied by an interwoven poem, whose text is written in the black dialect for which her work has become known and whose themes are the beauty and pain of being black in America. *Who Look At Me* received the American Library Association's Notable Book Award in 1969. The diversity of Jordan's writings became further evident in 1971, when she penned poetry in *Some Changes,* wrote *The Voice of the Children,* a reader edited by Terri Bush, and wrote her first young adult novel, *His Own Where—,* which she refers to as "a latter day revision of Romeo and Juliet." She received a Nancy Bloch Award and a Coretta Scott King Honor for *The Voice of the Children,* and *His Own Where—* (1971) was a finalist for the National Book Award and one of the year's outstanding novels, as selected by the *New York Times.* In 1972 Jordan approached historical writing for juveniles with biography in *Fannie Lou Hamer* and with fiction in *Dry Victories.* Through the voices of the characters in *Dry Victories,* the author expresses her connected writing for children and adults as Kenny and Jerome hope that "parents and them other folk" will act upon the changes necessary to make the world a better place. Her later writing includes a collection of essays and articles in *Civil Wars,* whose themes extend from the black experience to feminism, children, and education.

Jordan views her writings as words that promote "positive, and radical, and loving, social change." The response to her work acknowledges that she is accomplishing her goal. ❧ C.H.S.

JOSLIN, SESYLE

AMERICAN AUTHOR, B. 1929. *What Do You Say, Dear?* (1958) launched Sesyle Joslin's career as a popular and perceptive children's author. This refreshingly funny book about manners originated from games Joslin devised to teach her three daughters the basic niceties of "please and thank yous." She set up playful and unexpected situations requiring simple, polite responses. With MAURICE SENDAK's engaging artistic interpretations of Joslin's fanciful predicaments, this became a 1959 Caldecott Honor Book. Because *What Do You Say, Dear?* was so successful, the editors of *Highlights for Children* magazine commissioned Joslin and Sendak to collaborate on the equally delightful counterpart on proper behavior, *What Do You Do, Dear?* (1960). In a similar format, *Dear Dragon* (1962) helps children develop correspondence skills, while *Please Share That Peanut!* (1965) introduces children to "the pleasurable practice of sharing."

Joslin's works can be divided into her manners and etiquette books, the "Baby Elephant" series, language and pronunciation guides, and her longer children's novels like *The Spy Lady and the Muffin Man* (1971). The "Baby Elephant" series portrays a little elephant's experiences in learning independence. In *Brave Baby Elephant* (1960) the young pachyderm prepares himself for an evening's adventure. The reader is kept in complete suspense until the very end, when Baby Elephant takes himself up to bed alone for the first time. Unconditional love and acceptance fill this warm and wonderful series. Although Joslin introduces some French, Spanish, and Chinese into the "Baby Elephant" books, *There's a Dragon under My Bed* (1961), *Spaghetti for Breakfast* (1965), and *There's a Bull on My Balcony* (1966), respectively, are specifically formatted as introductory phrase books for French, Italian, and Spanish. Each illustrates the hilarious romps of two young travelers and tells them when to use a particular phrase. In her writing Joslin realistically and humorously captures a child's miraculous ability to transform ordinary situations into fantasy as well as a young child's absurdly logical way of interpreting words and phrases literally. Illustrations by Maurice Sendak, Leonard Weisgard, Irene Haas, and Katharine Barry, who depict children playing at being adults, perfectly complement Joslin's texts.

Regarding her own childhood, Joslin says she was taught to read and write in "a winter's sun-beamed attic playroom." Having "become the young mistress of these skills [I] never let go of them for a moment after but began at once to fashion small stories . . . to write and read became my work, my treasure." She says her first full-length novel, *The Night They Stole the Alphabet* (1968), "perhaps in some way . . . reflects that long-ago child learning her letters in the attic." After attending college, Joslin worked as an editorial assistant, an assistant editor, a book columnist, a freelance writer, and a movie production assistant. In 1950 she married the novelist Al Hine. Collaborative works with him under the pen name G. B. Kirtland include a clever trio of adventures in which the reader becomes the protagonist experiencing life in historical settings, *One Day in Ancient Rome* (1961), *One Day in Elizabethan England* (1962), and *One Day in Aztec Mexico* (1963), and *Is There a Mouse in the House?* (1965), which they wrote under the pseudonym Josephine Gibson. ❧ S.R.

JOYCE, WILLIAM

AMERICAN AUTHOR AND ILLUSTRATOR, B. 1959. J. R. R. Tolkien spoke of the "cauldron of story." If ever there were a "cauldron of illustration," William Joyce would be its master chef.

Joyce, who resides in Louisiana, was educated at Southern Methodist University and sold paintings through galleries before discovering that children's book illustration provided the ideal mode of expression for the ideas simmering in his imagination. His creations are a subtle blend of a lifetime of accrued American interests and influences, and each offers something for nearly everyone's tastes.

Every art aficionado will savor the rich, Edward Hopper–like paintings of *Dinosaur Bob* (1988). The minimalist text and expressive illustrations recount the

Voices of the Creators

William Joyce

It used to puzzle me, but grown-ups tend to like my books as much as kids do. I've never made much of an effort to appeal to any set age group. I do my books for myself as much as anyone. Today's families seem so hazed by MTV, Nintendo, and other techno-cherry bombs that I thought maybe my books were a soothing alternative. I do blissful, high adventures where everyone is kind, good, witty, brave, and frightfully well dressed and where everything works out for the best.

Much of the blame for this esthetic can be placed squarely on the influence of television. As a child my brain might as well have been welded to the solid-state circuitry of our RCA Viewmaster black-and-white television set. The endless tales this electronic Scheherazade told each day and night set my mind on fire. Men of steel, flawlessly heroic dogs, invaders from outer space, sword-fighting Spaniards, incredible shrinking men, monsters galore, cartoons of the gods: no generation ever had such a cascade of pop splendors spilled upon it, and I took in every drop.

The other major influence on my fiction was my family. I was raised by a collection of congenial, southern screwballs. My house was like the household in *You Can't Take It with You,* only with more humidity, and false teeth. Everyone over fifty had dentures, which were always being misplaced and mixed up. We sometimes played shuffle board with them. My grandfather had the added bonus of a glass eye which he swore to me could see even when outside his head. I had an uncle who convinced me that he was from another planet. All of them were fiercely independent. We had artists, bongo players, photographers, opera singers, actors, and geologists among our ranks. And we had a demented number of pets: mice, fish, dogs, ducks, geese, a horse, something we called a "horn toad," and at the beginning of every spring an aquarium full of tadpoles which became by summer's end a house full of frogs.

With the facts of my upbringing as interesting as any fiction, writing and illustrating stories came to me early. When I was five years old, I was watching on television *The Adventures of Robin Hood,* with Errol Flynn. It had just ended, and I was in a swashbuckling frenzy, completely taken away by the perfection of Errol's heroism and the music and pageantry. Then *King Kong* came on. Something in me identified with that hapless giant. I loved King Kong like a brother. But then the planes came and mighty Kong was felled. My heart was broken; I was inconsolable. My parents tried to explain to me that Kong was made up. He hadn't really died. It was all a story. The truth began to sink in. If it's all a story, what about monsters? What about Oz? What about the Jolly Fat Man at the North Pole?

"Who makes this stuff up?" I asked. "Grown-ups," sneered the kid down the street. I felt bitter and betrayed. But fate played its hand well. A few days later there was a new book at the library called *Where the Wild Things Are.* Some grown-up had drawn these great, scary, funny pictures. I liked to draw scary, funny things so I kept doing it, but now with a little more purpose. Making up my own epics helped fill the void. My first full-fledged book, entitled *Billy's Booger,* got me sent to the principal's office. But my work became less excremental, and by the end of college I was published.

All my works come from those beloved cinema and familial escapades. *George Shrinks* is King Kong in reverse. And mighty Kong makes a guest appearance in the background of almost every book. *Nicholas Cricket* is *Casablanca* with bugs. In *Dinosaur Bob* I have a dinosaur who visits New York, but doesn't die. In *Bently & Egg* I have a tree frog who's as dashing and heroic as Robin Hood. In *A Day with Wilbur Robinson* I chronicled my unusual family: false teeth, frogs, and all. In *Santa Calls* I mix them all together. There are bits of my own family dynamics fused with elements of the Wizard of Oz, Robin Hood, Davy Crockett, the Lone Ranger, Rin-Tin-Tin, Little Orphan Annie, Jules Verne, the Warner Brothers cartoons, Sci-Fi, and all the other stuff I thought was cool when I was a kid.

I try in my books to create that heady buzz I felt when I was young and the movies gave me worlds populated with stalwart heroes, beloved monsters, and adventures too good to be true. In my books high spirits are always shared, good humor is appreciated, and eccentricity is not only tolerated, but encouraged. My characters are willing to fight for their right to act odd and suave. Kids like to believe in these things, and grown-ups still try to. Which is why, I suppose, adults like my books as much as kids do. They're trying to hold on to something they thought they had lost.

story of the family Lazardo and Bob, the dinosaur they befriend and bring home to New York from their safari in Africa. Add a few futuristic elements to the nostalgia of *Dinosaur Bob* and you have *A Day with Wilbur Robinson* (1990), in which a spaceship is parked on a lawn that, judging by the garb sported by those gracefully relaxing on it, one would think belonged to Gatsby. Wilbur's eccentric extended family is a surrealist's cup of fur: an uncle who blasts himself from a cannon, a robot, a cousin who floats with the aid of an antigravity device, and some yodeling frogs. The pokerfaced text relies on the visual punch lines to complete this story, in which Wilbur's visiting friend joins in the family search for Grandfather's missing teeth. After they are found—in a frog's mouth—everyone celebrates with a pillow fight.

Joyce, a fan of cartoons, television, and movies (from science fiction and horror to classic), maintains that a career goal is to see one of his stories produced as a feature-length film. His enthusiasm for this medium is evident in *Santa Calls* (1993), which is the closest thing on paper to an animated film production and is the movie buff or fantasy lover's dream. Spiced with moments of Wild West adventure and bravado, the story includes a trip to the North Pole by Art Atchinson Aimesworth; his little sister, Esther; and his best friend Spaulding, a young Comanche. Unbeknownst to Art and Spaulding, the adventure has been arranged by Santa in an effort to meet Esther's only Christmas request: her brother's friendship. The wish is fulfilled when Art rescues Esther from the terrible Dark Queen.

Another book of movie influence is Joyce's first book as both author and illustrator, *George Shrinks* (1985), which Joyce refers to as "King Kong in reverse." A young boy, George, awakes to find himself about the size of a mouse. On his night table is a list of chores left for him by his parents that he manages to complete with comic ingenuity.

Joyce has even concocted something for the sentimentalist. *Bently and Egg* (1992), rendered in gentle pastels, contains a playful use of language. The affectionate story of Bently, who is asked to egg-sit for his friend, Kack Kack the duck, turns to adventure when the egg, beautifully painted by Bently, is mistaken for an Easter egg and heisted. Bently, however, successfully tracks it down and saves the day, not to mention the egg.

Joyce's interests and influences blend so creatively in his work that, though detectable, they subconsciously meld to produce a completely original flavor. The results, the books that are "vintage Joyce," are presentations of a talent that pleases a great variety of tastes and satiates even the most finicky connoisseur. ❧ E.K.E.

Juster, Norton

AMERICAN AUTHOR, B. 1929. Norton Juster's *Dot and the Line* (1963), a small, allegorical book detailing the precarious romance of a straight line and a round dot who learn to accept their differences and adapt their ways in order to get along, has always been popular with adults and children. *Alberic the Wise and Other Journeys* (1965) contains three brief FANTASY stories about searching for fulfillment in life. Norton is best known, however, for his first book, *The Phantom Tollbooth* (1961), which is a favorite fantasy among children.

When young Milo, bored with life and its possibilities, drives his small electric car past the toy tollbooth that has mysteriously appeared in his room, he enters a world ruled by words and numbers. An architect by trade, Juster displays considerable skill in building with words; by depicting common sayings, phrases, and clichés literally, he throws a spotlight on the idiosyncrasies of human behavior and creates a believable, though absurd, secondary world. Populated by an unforgettable cast of characters, including Tock the Watchdog, whose body is an alarm clock; Kakofonous A. Dischord, Doctor of Dissonance, and his assistant, the awful DYNNE; and two unique, oversized insects called Humbug and the Spelling Bee, the Kingdom of Wisdom has problems so outrageous that Milo becomes determined to help. His journey to rescue Rhyme and Reason, twin sisters banished by their feuding brothers, King Azaz of Dictionopolis and the Mathemagician, ruler of Digitopolis, takes him from one fantastic region of the land to another. The broad humor and magnificent wordplay carry the reader swiftly through a text that possesses a strong thematic base. Although perhaps too directly stated at times, the stress on communication and cooperation—the elements obviously lacking in the fantasy world—and on the importance of continually seeking knowledge for its own sake will always be pertinent. Highlighting the pitfalls into which individuals so easily fall, the fabulous farce ultimately reaffirms creativity, inquisitiveness, and optimism. ❧ A.E.D.

K

Kalman, Maira

American picture-book author and illustrator, b. 1949. Maira Kalman, born in Tel Aviv and raised in Riverdale, New York, studied music at the High School of Music and Art and turned to illustration after majoring in English at New York University. Her work is a harmonious blending of her talents and education. With music as her educational foundation, it is appropriate that her first book, *Stay Up Late* (1987), was a collaboration with David Byrne, of the rock group Talking Heads, to illustrate his song of the same title.

In subsequent books Kalman provides illustrations for her own lyrical texts, which are often enhanced by typography that rhythmically follows suit. Stanzas of text blocks form an Eiffel Tower or fill a swimming pool or a zigzagging sidewalk. Tiny staccato words crescendo into larger, louder letters, guiding a reader's speech as they convey the lively adventures of Max, the Bohemian beagle poet who authors a book in *Max Makes a Million* (1990), finds love in Paris in *Ooh-la-la (Max in Love)* (1991), and attempts to direct a movie in *Max in Hollywood, Baby* (1992). Though some of Kalman's literary and artistic asides are undoubtedly beyond the very young reader's comprehension, the cadence of her verse is more than aurally palatable and makes for melodious, poetical reading aloud. While in Paris, Max meets eccentric characters with such names as Peach Melba and Crepes Suzette and stays in a little hotel run by the aromatic Madame Camembert of whom he says, "I adore her and she adores me. It's not always that simple in this town of Paree."

Of all Kalman's work, *Sayonara, Mrs. Kackleman* (1989) speaks most directly to children. The story is told from the perspective of siblings Lulu and Alexander, who journey to Japan, escaping Lulu's piano lesson with the dreaded Mrs. Kackleman. Alexander creates the brutally childlike poem "Hey Hiroko, / are you loco? / Would you like / a cup of cocoa?" and eats at a restaurant where they are served "oodles and poodles of noodles."

Kalman's stories are often of fantastical journeys narrated in stream of consciousness. Her energetic illustrations visually parallel the text, providing a fluid, dreamlike quality. Predominantly void of perspective and reminiscent of Chagall, Matisse, and Picasso, the impressionistic paintings are visual fantasies full of crazy, colorful details that either fascinate or overwhelm the young reader. Although young readers are unlikely to pick up on all of Kalman's ever-present visual and verbal punnery, such as an exhibit of amazing hairdos at the Pompadour Museum, this sometimes criticized technique creates the very quality that garners such enthusiastic devotees of varying ages. In wild and whirling words and images, Kalman melds her talents with unique synergy to successfully entertain at many levels. ❧ E.K.E.

Kästner, Erich

German author, 1899–1974. Born at the turn of the century, Erich Kästner spent a lifetime challenging old ways of looking at things. He grew up in Dresden, with a mild father and an exceptional mother. Her whole life was centered around little Erich, an only child, and she was determined to educate him well. They would stand in line for hours just to get standing-room tickets to the theater, and the boy would be riveted by the performances, even through a three-hour opera. In return for her devotion, Kästner always strived to do his best, for with a mother like that, he could do no less.

These childhood influences come through clearly in Kästner's characters, especially in *Emil and the Detectives* (1929, trans. 1931). The first chapter vividly describes how hard Emil's mother must work to give Emil what all the other children have. She scrapes aside any spare change into a jar, so when she entrusts 140 marks into Emil's care, he is terrified of losing it. With this background, it is all the more devastating when the money is stolen, setting off the rollicking plot. In Kästner's world, children have power, even enough to capture a dangerous criminal. *Lisa and Lottie* (1949, trans. 1951), perhaps the most controversial of his books, deals with divorce, one of the first children's books to do so. Meeting each other as young teens, Lisa and Lottie realize they are twin sisters and concoct a complicated plot to reunite their parents. This book is perhaps now better known from the 1961 DISNEY film version, *The Parent Trap*. In a children's book, unrealistic though it might be, Kästner thought that the children should be successful.

Kästner's own successes earned him numerous awards, including the Hans Christian Andersen Award in 1960 and the Lewis Carroll Shelf Award in 1961, which was for his autobiography, *When I Was a Little Boy* (1956, trans. 1959). Through a child's eyes, he is an acute observer of the climate of Dresden just before the First World War, though he says, "Not everything that children experience is suitable for other children to read about." *The Little Man* (1963, trans. by James Kirkup, 1966) received the Batchelder Award in 1968 for its translation. Maxie is, literally, a little boy. He is two inches tall and goes around in the pocket of Professor Hocus Pocus, Magician. Critics have found fault with this book and its sequel, *The Little Man and the Big Thief* (1967, trans. 1969), for overelaborate plots with too much sentiment. But if the prose is uneven, they are still lively, fast-paced books for children.

Kästner was not only a writer for children. He was a novelist, poet, and playwright whose works were so piercingly insightful that they were banned and burned during the Hitler regime. His painful experiences give human ballast to his work. Knowing his past, a statement that from another might sound sentimental, from him is profound: "Childhood is the quiet, pure light that shines consolingly out of the past into the present and the future. Truly to hold childhood in the memory means to know again, suddenly and without long contemplation, what is genuine and what false, what is good and what bad." J.A.J.

KEATS, EZRA JACK

AMERICAN AUTHOR AND ILLUSTRATOR, 1916–1983. Whether Ezra Jack Keats used Matisse-colored collages or expressionistic blends of dark acrylic paints, he successfully illustrated the emotive landscape of an urban child's life, reflecting both its exuberance and squalor. Boldly stylistic, Keats's early work was marked by strong graphics and vibrant colors and his later work by intense and dramatic contrasts of lights and darks. His picture-book portrayal of the city moved it beyond mere setting into the realm of characterization so that it, too, grew and changed along with his stock company of characters.

Born in Brooklyn, Keats, the son of Polish immigrants, was himself a child of the city. He began drawing at the age of five and remembered covering the enamel-topped table in his mother's kitchen with doodles and drawings. He expected his mother to react in anger, but instead she exclaimed with obvious delight. Keats remembered, "She got out the tablecloth which we used only on Friday nights, and she covered the whole little mural, and every time a neighbor would come in, she'd unveil it to show what I had done." His father, Benjamin, warned his son, "Never be an artist; you'll be a bum, you'll starve, you'll have a terrible life." Despite his father's criticism and ridicule from the neighborhood toughs, Keats taught himself to paint. Upon graduation from public high school, he won three scholarships to art schools. After serving in the Air Force in World War II, he worked as an illustrator, receiving his first assignment from *Collier's* magazine. He spent a year in Paris, came home, and began illustrating adult and children's book jackets, which quickly led to a career in children's PICTURE BOOKS.

Keats illustrated nearly a dozen books before writing his first, *The Snowy Day*, which won the 1963 Caldecott Medal. A celebration of color, texture, design, and childhood wonder, *The Snowy Day* is significant in that it was one of the first picture books in which a minority child is seen as Everychild. Years before, Keats had come across photos of a young boy, and he recalled that "his expressive face, his body attitudes, the very way he wore his clothes, totally captivated me." This boy was to become Peter, who, in his red snowsuit, discovers the joys of dragging sticks and making tracks in the snow. After its publication, Keats found out that the photos had come from a 1940 *Life* magazine—he had retained the images for over twenty years.

With solid and patterned paper as wedges of color, Keats used collage to create endearing characters and energetic cityscapes, not only in *The Snowy Day* (1962) but in *Whistle for Willie* (1964) and *Peter's Chair* (1967). In *Whistle for Willie*, Keats takes the act of learning to whistle and, with his superb designing ability, creates a book that delights the eye and engages the senses. In his later books, *Goggles!* (1969), *Hi, Cat!* (1970), *Pet Show!* (1972), and *Dreams* (1974), Keats allows Peter and his friend Archie to grow up and explore the city. Keats's palette grows darker as his characters' experiences broaden, and his use of patterned papers become accents in illustrations thick with paint. *Apt. 3* (1971), with its somber and unflinching view of urban apartment life, prompted some critics to ask, "For whom do we create children's picture books and why?"

For Keats, honesty was the priority; reality was beautiful. His philosophy remains with us: "If we all could see each other exactly as the other is, this would be a different world. But first I think we have to begin to see each other." ❧ M.B.B.

Keene, Carolyn

See Nancy Drew Series; Stratemeyer Literary Syndicate.

Keeping, Charles

English author and illustrator, 1924–1988. Charles William James Keeping started illustrating at the age of five or six, when he drew pictures for his sister's stories about their colorful London neighborhood, and he never stopped. After serving as a printer's apprentice and a wireless operator in the British navy, he attended the Polytechnic School of Art in London. To pay his way he worked as a gas meter man in a slum area—"marvellous for a potential illustrator, it's a crumby, seedy part of London with a wealth of stories and characters." He married artist Renate Meyer, with whom he had four children, and over the years he taught at several art schools. His first attempt at children's book illustration received positive critical attention, and he eventually garnered many prizes, including Kate Greenaway Medals for *Charley, Charlotte and the Golden Canary* (1967) and for Alfred Noyes's tragic ballad *The Highwayman* (1981).

Keeping was known for pushing the limits of illustration technique and format, for which he was highly praised and soundly criticized. Even in his first children's book, Rosemary Sutcliff's novel *The Silver Branch* (1957), he challenged conventional illustration placement by using margin drawings and double-page spreads. In the 1960s he experimented with brilliant colors, bold patterns, and symbolism. And with even more daring, he made picture books for older readers, such as *The Wedding Ghost* (1985) by Leon Garfield, in which the story moves forward through both text and copious illustrations.

Keeping's style depends heavily on his magnificent draftsmanship: contour ink drawings provide the basis for most of his illustrations, which may include black wash or color in gouache, tempera, and watercolor. He masterfully conveys a gamut of images, from a horse in full stride to a crazed young man to a tangle of tree branches covering an empty road. His line has an energetic, sketchy quality but also shows a surety that denies frivolity of expression.

Keeping often illustrated macabre stories, and one of his trademarks is the use of vertical lines to represent flowing blood. After Beowulf tears off the monster Grendel's arm in Kevin Crossley-Holland's retelling of the ancient story of *Beowulf* (1982), Keeping depicts Grendel's shoulder as black nothingness with black lines dripping straight down from it. The blood moves down the page with a forceful, terrifying, symbolic regularity, yet the lines swell and curve in places, giving the soft, tangible, organic sense of real drips. This dichotomy—the tension-filled balance Keeping mastered by including contradictory images—is seen in various ways throughout his work: as cold, dark lines tempered by soft shading, or hate-filled eyes housed in a sensuous body, or ferocious movement balanced by a symmetrically stable form.

Keeping strove most for emotion in his illustration, even to the exclusion of plot. "I don't like my drawings to illustrate a particular incident, but more to set a mood throughout the whole book." Even his picture books hang more on a series of tableaux than plot. In *Through the Window* (1970), a child watches an incident in the street from his window. The reader empathizes with the child's shifting emotions, conveyed through the effects of predominating color, changing from page to page, and of the moving curtain that frames and emphasizes the events.

Keeping is praised as one of Britain's most original children's book illustrators. Also prolific in illustrating adult books, he believed that nearly any book could benefit by appropriate illustration. By focusing on mood and emotion, he maintained his distinguished reputation through the publication of more than two hundred books. ❧ S.S.

Keller, Holly

American author and illustrator, b. 1942. Born in New York, Holly Keller received an undergraduate degree from Sarah Lawrence College and a master of arts from Columbia University. She took art classes at Manhattanville College and the Parsons School of Design. All of Keller's characters—and sometimes they are human beings—are rendered in a cartoonlike style; bright and round, they are drawn in black ink and filled in with watercolor.

Childhood is full of painful incidents, and Keller has touched on many of them. Being the new kid in school, getting the short end of sibling relationships, being the butt of bullies' vengeance, turning a security blanket into something that is more socially acceptable are all subjects of her PICTURE BOOKS. In *Goodbye Max* (1987), an empty dog bed reveals the poignant message that a very sick pet has died. In *The New Boy* (1991), Milton tries to fit in but never makes his way in the class until Stanley arrives and takes over the new-boy slot. And in *Lizzie's Invitation* (1987), Lizzie suffers in agony as she watches while everyone else in school gets an invitation, and she is left out. Keller somehow always finds the right place to end up, somewhere real but still reassuring.

Of all her characters, Horace is the most endearing. *Horace* (1991) appeals to any child who has ever felt the least bit on the outside of things. Horace, a leopard adopted by tigers, a spotted child who doesn't match his striped family, cannot hear his parents' reassuring message until it has been repeated over and over: "We chose you when you were a tiny baby because you had lost your first family and needed a new one. We liked your spots, and we wanted you to be our child." Keller's books always tell a good story, but each also imparts a strong message, whether it is about survival after rejection or reaching out to someone in need. A.C.

Illustration by Steven Kellogg from *How Much Is a Million?* (1985), by David M. Schwartz.

KELLOGG, STEVEN

AMERICAN ILLUSTRATOR AND AUTHOR, B. 1941. Steven Kellogg has loved "telling stories on paper" his whole life. As a boy growing up in Darien, Connecticut, he used that phrase to describe a favorite activity: He entertained his younger sisters by telling them stories and drawing illustrations to accompany them. He has said that he would happily continue to make up these tales "until my sisters were too restless to sit there any longer or until they were buried under pieces of paper." This is an apt image for this prolific artist, who was awarded the Catholic Library Association's 1989 Regina Medal for the body of his work.

His early years greatly influenced his future work as a picture-book illustrator. Young Steven loved any kind of animal story and spent much of his free time drawing animals and birds. In addition to the childhood interests that inspired his adult work, a year in Italy studying the work of Florentine Renaissance artists was an important influence. But it was his honors fellowship from the Rhode Island School of Design that inspired him to pursue seriously his desire to become a professional artist. He graduated from RISD in 1963 with a major in illustration, and in 1967 he illustrated his first book, *Gwot! Horribly Funny Hair-ticklers*, by George Mendoza.

Kellogg's early fascination with animals was good preparation for his series of "Pinkerton" books, based on his experiences with his rambunctious but lovable Great Dane puppy. The first book in this series was *Pinkerton, Behave* (1979). Pinkerton and the chaotic situations he inadvertently creates are the perfect vehicles for Kellogg's unrestrained and humorous style of illustration. In *A Rose for Pinkerton* (1981), the combination of the energetic Great Dane and Rose, an ornery cat, leads to a typical Kellogg scenario—the characters become embroiled in a commotion of such hysterical proportions that, like an exploding pressure cooker, they invariably end up in an out-of-control mass of animals and people.

Kellogg has used a variety of techniques in his full-color artwork; in his later books he usually employs a combination of colored inks, watercolor, and acrylics. Not all of Kellogg's books have a design line; especially

Voices of the Creators

Steven Kellogg

In Robert Frost's poem "The Tuft of Flowers," a worker sends a message in thought to an absent colleague: "'Men work together,' I told him from the heart, / 'Whether they work together or apart.'" I believe that all those who work with children—teachers, parents, librarians, booksellers—collaborate this way with authors and illustrators. We are colleagues and co-conspirators who put our energies separately, and yet together, into the important work of bringing books to life for young readers.

Part of the power of the picture book as an educational tool and as an art form is derived from the fact that it communicates in two voices—visual and verbal. In the most successful examples of the picture-book genre, these components do not rehash the same material but rather reinforce and enhance each other like two dissimilar but related melodies in a duet eloquently sung by different instruments. Each distinctive voice provides its own information and insights, but if the two are orchestrated within the format of the turning pages so that they intermingle and merge with harmony, vitality, tension, and excitement, the new entity they create will soar powerfully and magically above the sum of its parts, and the result will be a feast for the eye, the ear, and the spirit.

When I create both text and art, I have to work out both these voices. But when a book's author and artist are not the same person, the two usually work separately. The illustrator receives the manuscript from the editor at the publishing house to which the author submitted it, and, as the visual life of the book develops, the editor keeps the author apprised of the artist's progress. The way in which the editor oversees the collaboration is akin to the spirit in which a conductor coordinates the instruments in different areas of the orchestra, the difference being, of course, that the editor-conductor is presiding over the creation of an entirely new piece. Inspiration, collaboration, and trust are important ingredients in the creation of a picture book. I am very grateful to the authors whose stories I have been asked to illustrate, and also to the editors, art directors, designers, and printers with whom I've been privileged to collaborate over the years. The successful completion of a picture book depends on the contributions of many talents.

However, when the books are printed and bound, the creative role passes to the people who are closest to the children, and we depend upon them to share the books with care, enthusiasm, and love. Until a picture book is looked at and read, it remains a darkened theater. That theater is illuminated when an adult opens the book with a child, and, as the pages turn, the curtain rises on successive acts and scenes. Through the reading and sharing, the words pulsate with life, and the illustrations move and glow with action, feeling, and vitality. Of course, each book must stand on its own merit and earn applause and approval from whomever experiences it. But if a teacher, librarian, or parent brings the child and the book together with a sensitive understanding of that individual child and with an enthusiasm for that particular book, it makes an enormous difference in the quality of the book's reception. When caring adults recommend and share and read the book aloud as if they were part of its creative life—as if they were presenting it as a treasured gift—then that book has a much greater chance of being special to the child with whom it is shared, and the adult reader will be remembered as being part of that book, and part of that gift, as surely as if his or her name was engraved on the jacket and the title page—as a colleague, a coconspirator, a creative partner.

with his early books; publishers didn't always use his work to the best advantage. Of Kellogg's more than eighty picture books, the retellings of tall tales and folktales achieve the best match of story and illustration. In *Pecos Bill* (1986), his energetic style is perfect for depicting this larger-than-life hero whose exploits embody the raw American pioneering spirit. The art crackles with vitality, and the characters almost whirl off the pages. *Paul Bunyan* (1984), *Johnny Appleseed* (1988), and *Mike Fink* (1992) also perfectly blend dramatic retellings and vibrant illustrations. Quiet, incidental pictures would not do for these lively tales about the frontier days.

Kellogg says he approaches the picture book as a child's introduction to art and literature and believes the text is as important as the art. He made *Chicken Little* (1985) and *Jack and the Beanstalk* (1991) fresh for readers by adding humorous twists to the texts that complement his illustrations. Steven Kellogg's artwork captures the true spirit of childhood, in all its limitless energy and zest for life. K.F.

Kemble, Edward

American illustrator, 1861–1933. Edward Windsor Kemble, an entirely self-taught artist of the pen-and-ink school, was already an established cartoonist with the *Daily Graphic* when Mark Twain offered him the substantial sum of $2,000 to illustrate the forthcoming subscription book *The Adventures of Huckleberry Finn.* One story has it that Kemble was offered the job because Twain had been amused by a Kemble cartoon depicting a homeowner fending off a subscription-book salesman. The fact that the Sacramento-born Kemble was the son of the founder of the *Alta California,* the newspaper that helped launch Twain's career, also may have had something to do with Twain's choice. In either case, Kemble accepted Twain's offer and so took his place as the first of dozens of artists who would illustrate Twain's masterpiece.

The tone of Kemble's 174 black-and-white illustrations for *Huckleberry Finn* is comic, emphasizing the lighter side of what is at times a profoundly dark novel. Most of Kemble's illustrations add to Twain's humor as they help tell the story; a handful edge over into the dramatic or sentimental, but none are dark or graphic. Kemble, well aware that in his day the text could get away with a great deal more explicitness than could the illustrations, goes out of his way to underplay the novel's often violent and earthy reality of slavery, feuds, and deceptions. Twain himself was even more circumspect, censoring Kemble's illustration of the lecherous King kissing a young girl.

Overall, Twain was not pleased with Kemble's work on *Huckleberry Finn.* Though he declared some of Kemble's drawings "most rattling good," he later stated his aversion to the artist's "black board outlines and charcoal sketches." In dismissing Kemble's illustrations, Twain overlooked the appropriateness of Kemble's style to his own text, which, narrated by Huck, seems crude at first glance but turns out to be brilliantly crafted. In the same way, Kemble's illustrations seem crude at first glance but turn out to be quite sophisticated. Like the text, the illustrations *almost* seem as if they could be the work of an unrefined boy, though of course they are not.

Kemble illustrated some sixty books, including *Pudd'nhead Wilson, Uncle Tom's Cabin,* Knickerbocker's *History of New York,* and *Mark Twain's Library of Humor.* He earned a reputation as an illustrator of African Americans and Southern life and consequently was chosen to illustrate the work of Joel Chandler Harris and African American poet Paul Laurence Dunbar. Similarly prolific as an illustrator of periodicals, Kemble published an estimated twelve thousand illustrations in magazines, including *St. Nicholas.* Perhaps his biggest popular success as a children's illustrator was his coloring book featuring the African American Gold Dust Twins, the advertising symbols of Fairbank's Washing Powder. Illustrations of black caricatures like the Gold Dust Twins, as well as the artist's publication of books with titles like *Kemble's Coons,* have left him with a reputation for racism that his strong, if distorted, sympathy for African Americans cannot erase. However well deserved Kemble's racist reputation may be, his illustrations for *Huckleberry Finn* are unmatched in so many ways that he remains, after more than a century, the premier illustrator of what might be the most frequently illustrated novel in publishing history. ❧ D.A.B.

Kendall, Carol

American author, b. 1917. Best known for her fantasy novels, Carol Kendall has also demonstrated a sure hand in writing realistic fiction for children. Born in Bucyrus, Ohio, the author attempted her first novel in fourth grade. Although this early effort was disparaged by a teacher, Kendall continued writing for newspapers in high school and at Ohio University, where she met her husband, an English professor who shared his wife's literary interests. Her first book resulted from a love of mystery novels and her belief that she could write a better story than some she had read. *The Black Seven* (1946) was published for adults, but it features a twelve-year-old detective who solves a second mystery in *The Baby-Snatcher* (1952).

Writing about children was so appealing that Kendall decided to create a story especially for them. *The Other Side of the Tunnel* (1957) is a mystery about four children who discover a diary written in secret code. They crack the code, then tunnel to a nearby mansion, where they find a new friend. Although it takes place in the United States, the story has a vaguely British atmosphere—perhaps because the book was first published in that country. The novel contains sparkling dialogue and strongly individualized characters, some of whom appear in *The Big Splash* (1960), a sequel in which a group of young friends build a parade float for a local charity contest. Long out of print, this comic adventure is fresh, exciting, and delightful from start to finish; it deserves to be rediscovered by a new generation of readers.

Kendall's Newbery Honor Book, *The Gammage Cup* (1959), continues to be read and enjoyed by children, many of whom develop a deeply personal attachment to this intriguing fantasy about the Minnipins, a group of little people who live in a series of villages in the Land Between the Mountains. When a contest is held to determine the finest village, the residents turn against a small band of villagers who do not live in typical Minnipin fashion. These nonconformists have never married, do not wear the usual village apparel, and refuse to paint their front doors a uniform green. Banished from the village, they travel to the wilderness to create a new home, only to become heroes when they rally the villagers to fight off an invading army. The theme of nonconformity is beautifully woven into the story, particularly with the character of Muggles, who moves from distant admiration for the local eccentrics to become a full-fledged nonconformist with a strong sense of her own worth. The book is also memorable for providing an interesting historical background for the Minnipins, for its enjoyable wordplay, and for including female characters among its heroes. A sequel, *The Whisper of Glocken* (1965), examines the origins and nature of heroism and is written in an equally winning style. Both Minnipin stories were adapted for television. Kendall has also written *The Firelings* (1982), an ambitious fantasy about a civilization living on the edge of a volcano; *Sweet and Sour: Tales from China* (1978), a collection of retold stories from various historical eras; and *The Wedding of the Rat Family* (1988), another Chinese folktale.

Ancient China, contemporary America, and fantasy worlds filled with little people are all brought vividly to life in Kendall's deeply satisfying works. ❧ P.D.S.

KENNEDY, RICHARD

AMERICAN NOVELIST, B. 1932. Richard Kennedy once shared the secret for his steady literary output: "Write a page each day and in a year's time you'll have 365 pages." In fact, Kennedy has not been merely prolific. He also has one of the keenest ears for the lilt of the language, a sharp sense of humor, and an extraordinary knack for clear, fast plot. "Once upon a time at the edge of town lived a harsh man with a timid daughter who had grown pale and dreamy from too much obedience," Kennedy begins his picture-book story, *The Porcelain Man* (1976), in what must count as one of the most engaging openings in contemporary literature. And that opening, folkloristic in its devices and its tone, is typical of the majority of his nineteen books to date.

With little fanfare, Kennedy came onto the children's book scene in 1974 with *The Parrot and the Thief,* a transformed folktale of a parrot trickster, a story classic in its balance of structure and its variations on the old theme of the powerless outwitting the mighty. Continuing with almost two books a year, Kennedy successfully employed folklore elements of incremental repetition of events, formulaic devices for attaining magical results, and a sharp colloquial dialogue that begs to be read aloud. Among the books best displaying these characteristics are *The Blue Stone* (1976), a series of rambunctious tall tales of magic and transformation, and *Crazy in Love* (1980), a tale of love lost and magically found again. Somewhat different from these is *The Song of the Horse* (1981), a lyrical and ecstatic monologue, a hymn of praise for a young girl with a passion for her horse. When Kennedy first submitted the manuscript, his publishers expressed nervousness about what a reviewer later called its "submerged eroticism." Kennedy thereupon wrote his illustrator, MARCIA SEWALL, that the publisher's suggested changes wouldn't affect her work, "except that the horse is now a goat, there are three children and a dog who ride it, and it's set in Lapland, and at the end they all run off a cliff into the sea. But otherwise it's much the same."

Kennedy's major work, *Amy's Eyes* (1985), a panoramic sea story infused with the author's wide reading in *The Arabian Nights,* the Bible, the works of ROBERT LOUIS STEVENSON and Jonathan Swift, and the MOTHER GOOSE nursery rhymes, echoes the rhythms of three hundred years of English prose. This novel, mythopoeic in tone, apocalyptic in its conclusion, is both odd and ambitious. The "Captain" doll protagonist becomes human, and the little girl heroine becomes a doll. The supporting cast of characters, one of whom is a set of long underwear, also come alive, demonstrating an extravagant inventiveness that has puzzled some delicate critics but clearly impressed the Germans, who bestowed on the book the Rattenfänger ("Pied Piper") Prize for the best foreign book translated in 1988.

If one were to look for a unifying theme in Kennedy's work, it would be his repeated rendering of the misadventure in the quest for "true love" and the redemptive powers of that love when found, a theme not irrelevant to Kennedy's retelling of HANS CHRISTIAN ANDERSEN's "The Snow Queen," set to music by Mark Lambert. One may most easily sample Kennedy's wit, iconoclasm, wild exuberance, narrative skill, and poetical prose in *Collected Stories* (1987). ❧ P.F.N.

KENNEDY, X. J.

AMERICAN POET AND ANTHOLOGIST, B. 1929. X. J. Kennedy, poet, teacher, anthologist, textbook author, and humorist, claims to be "one of an endangered species: people who still write in meter and rime." Kennedy has written or compiled more than forty books for young people and adults. He began to write POETRY for children because, he says, he "has a tremendous respect for children's intelligence" and finds that adults often underrate a child's ability to understand and enjoy poetry. The anthology *Talking Like the Rain: A First Book of Poems* (1992), for which Kennedy and his wife, Dorothy, selected more than a hundred entries, is his most popular juvenile anthology. It includes contemporary and traditional selections for preschoolers as well as poems for older, more sophisticated readers. The verbal feast served up by the Kennedys is brilliantly enhanced by delicate and expressive watercolor illustrations by artist Jane Dyer. The book design is outstanding, as it invites readers to enjoy this unique partnership of words and pictures as they work together to portray universal events and experiences in the life of a child.

Kennedy, a native of New Jersey, wrote his first book of poems for adults, *Nude Descending a Staircase*, in 1961. Kennedy's first volume published for children, *One Winter Night in August and Other Nonsense Jingles* (1975), successfully blends contemporary subject material with traditional verse form to produce some hilarious absurdities. In this book, Kennedy's juxtaposition of humor and seriousness, reality and fantasy sets the tone for subsequent books he has written for young people. When it comes to children and their penchant for nonsense verse, Kennedy is right on target. His original poetry recalls the dexterous rhythms, sparkling imagery, and unexpected rhymes of such masters of nonsense as EDWARD LEAR and LEWIS CARROLL. Particularly representative of this style are the "Brats" books: *Brats* (1986), *Fresh Brats* (1990), and *Drat These Brats* (1993). Children love Kennedy's outrageous characters and the zany, sometimes slightly blood-curdling verses these books feature. Characteristic of the fare is this poem, titled "Gosnold," from *Brats*: "Gosnold! Watch out with that match / Or the dynamite might catch! / There goes Gosnold: living proof / That a kid can raise the roof." These quirky rhymes, with their unexpected twists and bizarre protagonists, are bouncy and eminently recitable.

In *The Forgetful Wishing-Well: Poems for Young People* (1985), some verses are funny, but here the poet balances humor with experiences that are serious and poignant. Adding further depth to the content of this particular collection are different verse forms, varied rhyme schemes, and infectious rhythms. Distinguished by fresh, colorful imagery, Kennedy's poems for children stimulate the mind, delight the ear, and echo the natural playfulness and imagination of the young. Not surprisingly, they are popular features in anthologies. ❧ S.L.

KEPES, JULIET

AMERICAN AUTHOR AND ILLUSTRATOR, B. 1919. Juliet Kepes's animals spring, scamper, and cavort across the pages of her books. "As far back as I can remember I was always drawing, and as far back as I can remember I was always fascinated by living, moving, and acting things," she recalls. Her fascination with, and knowledge of animals, is readily apparent in all her PICTURE BOOKS. Combining a highly gestural drawing style and a strong sense of design and color, Kepes infuses her animals with an abundance of energy, animation, and character such that no realistic portrayal could possibly project.

Kepes was born in London, England, the daughter of a ship chandler. She attended the Brighton School of Art, and in 1937 moved to the United States. That same year she entered the Chicago School of Design and married Gyorgy Kepes, a Hungarian painter and author who would later become a professor of visual design at the Massachusetts Institute of Technology.

Kepes is at her best as a storyteller in her first book, *Five Little Monkeys*, which she began working on in 1944 and which was published in 1952. *Five Little Monkeys* was innovative in its expressive brushwork, overall graphic book design, and color usage at a time when illustrators had to master the sometimes tedious technical task of color separation. Kepes's monkeys, Buzzo, Binki, Bulu, Bibi, and Bali, are gleeful imps, brought to life with a few simple brushed strokes of ink from Kepes's deft hand. The five monkeys' mischievous antics and pranks cause universal consternation among their fellow animals in the jungle but universally delight Kepes's young readers. Apparently, Kepes brought pleasure to a number of adult readers as well, for *Five Little Monkeys* was named a Caldecott Honor Book in 1953.

Kepes illustrated William Smith's *Laughing Time* (1953), and then, in 1954, Emilie McLeod's *The Seven Remarkable Bears*, the story of a terribly underfed but clever polar bear who convinces his stingy zookeeper that he needs more fish in his cage. In a successful collaboration the sum is always stronger than any one individual's contribution, and such is the case with *The Seven Remarkable Bears*. As Barbara Bader wrote in *American Picturebooks from Noah's Ark to the Beast Within*: "Horace Mann proposed to found a school with a teacher and a student on a bench; with three McLeod sentences and a Kepes bear (and a designer in the bushes), one might start a book." A number of Kepes's books have been named among the Ten Best Books by the *New York Times*, including *Beasts from a Brush* (1955), a book of imaginative animal drawings which recall both Picasso's lithographs of "The Bull" and the evocative brushwork of thirteenth-century Chinese scroll painters.

Juliet Kepes's illustrations, pared down to their linear emotive essence, continue to intrigue and delight children. § M.B.B.

Kerr, M. E.

AMERICAN AUTHOR, B. 1927. With the publication of *Dinky Hocker Shoots Smack!* in 1972, M. E. Kerr moved to the forefront of the field of the YOUNG ADULT NOVEL and has remained there for more than two decades.

Voices of the Creators

M. E. Kerr

Writing has been the only constant in my life. The wish to be a writer has been there since I was a child; there was no other dream that took precedence.

I was a typical small-town American kid from upstate New York. My father was a zealous reader. The one comfortable armchair in our living room was his, and most of the time that he spent at home, he sat there reading—everything. Newspapers, magazines, books. I still see him with the visor on his head, the pipe in his mouth, oblivious to the ringing phone, romping dog, and children rushing in and out as he read quietly in a corner. On Sundays, when my brother and I were not allowed to go to the movies because it was "the Lord's Day," he read aloud to us. Dickens was his favorite for those occasions.

Then my mother: a world-class gossip. I would come home from school each afternoon and be regaled with all the latest news about our neighbors; on those days when she had gone to the beauty parlor, there would be insider information straight from her hairdresser concerning all the local celebrities, as well as Hollywood and radio stars. My mother's favorite way to begin these reports was "Wait till you hear this!"

From these two I learned most of what I know about storytelling.

My viewpoint was molded by them, too. My father was the fair and cautious one, "politically correct" ahead of his time, sensitive to ethnic slurs and callous judgments of outsiders and misfits. He was slightly eccentric himself, pedaling to work (he was president of Ivanhoe Foods, Inc.—mayonnaise manufacturing) wearing a beret, a souvenir from his days in the French army in World War I. My mother stood corrected by him, but not changed, and her gossip was unadulterated, enthusiastic, heartless. She knew *everything* that was going on *everywhere.* Her curiosity about people had no limits.

In college, I set aside hours for myself to write my stories. Even then I was aware of the market, of the need to bridle self-indulgence and think of how to shape my stories so they would interest editors—and I had the rejection slips to prove it. I always had something in the mail.

My first sale was a year after I graduated from the University of Missouri. It was a paperback novel about sorority life. Then I switched my focus to suspense, largely because I knew that mystery and suspense books were reviewed by the *New York Times,* in Anthony Boucher's column. He was a supportive critic of Vin Packer, the name I chose for that venture. (I have always loved pseudonyms—disguises for the various voices I had, and still have.)

I came to children's literature late in life, after some twenty-two novels. Of all my writing, I enjoy writing for kids the most. I think it is because I feel I have an audience which is more receptive to wonder, speculation, and change. I like to provoke questioning about what is right and what isn't. Crime writing does that, too, but more often it makes the judgment and delivers the punishment. I like to try and leave some questioning in the reader's mind, so that the reader does not distance himself from evil to the point where he never sees himself as a possible party to it.

I like to write about the underdog, the outsider, the person who is different. I've seldom met a kid who didn't feel he was different in one way or another. Kids are so vulnerable, so sure they're alone in whatever it is they're struggling with. I like to tell them they're not alone.

When I write for children, I write for *them,* not for the adults who teach them, or the critics who review the books. I try hard to make my stories immediately accessible, because I know that, unlike other kids in history, they have so many seductive options luring them from books. Television, music, computers—how hard it is for a kid to sit down somewhere quiet and read! I see it as my job to help them enjoy reading, and to give them substance at the same time. §

The story of Dinky—the wisecracking overweight daughter of a Brooklyn Heights do-gooder, her emotionally damaged cousin Natalia, and their friend Tucker is written in a style that combines laugh-out-loud humor with moments of wrenching poignancy. Critics marveled that a first-time novelist could produce such an accomplished work. Few knew that M. E. Kerr was the pen name of Marijane Meaker, who had been writing adult books for over twenty years under a variety of pseudonyms.

Meaker was born in Auburn, New York, and educated at a Virginia boarding school. She later shared autobiographical vignettes from her early years in *Me, Me, Me, Me, Me: Not a Novel* (1983). After obtaining a degree in journalism from the University of Missouri, Meaker moved to New York, where she had a succession of clerical jobs before beginning her career as a professional writer, using the name Ann Aldrich for paperback nonfiction, and Vin Packer for suspense novels. Unwittingly, she was already preparing for her career as a young adult author since many of the Packer novels touched on issues and themes that would subsequently find their way into the M. E. Kerr books. The author's ability to write about teenagers was already evident in her suspense titles *The Evil Friendship* (1958) and *The Twisted Ones* (1959).

Meaker had two primary reasons for entering the young adult field. One was the encouragement of her friend LOUISE FITZHUGH, author of *Harriet the Spy;* the other was her admiration for PAUL ZINDEL's novel *The Pigman.* At the time, Meaker was a visiting writer at a New York high school, where she met a student who inspired the character of Dinky Hocker. These three factors led to the creation of her first young adult work. Since then, her novels have won critical acclaim and a legion of readers; many have been designated Best Books for Young Adults by the American Library Association. They are distinctive for their breezy, economical writing style; razor-sharp dialogue; humor that ranges from subtle to wild, yet is never mean-spirited; and a keen understanding of the human heart. Major and minor characters are brilliantly conceived, and there is a special empathy for loners and outsiders. While many young adult novels falter under the weight of important issues, Kerr's best books often deal with serious topics, such as the revelation that a beloved grandfather was once a Nazi in *Gentlehands* (1978) and the boarding school story *Is That You, Miss Blue?* (1975) in which a teenage girl gains empathy and maturity through her relationships with a number of offbeat characters, including a mentally unbalanced teacher. *Night Kites* (1986) was the first young adult novel to deal with AIDS and remains one of the best. The books that take place in the fictional community of Seaville, New York, based on Meaker's home in East Hampton, provocatively explore the issue of class differences. She has also focused on one of her most interesting characters, John Fell, in a series of teenage suspense novels and has written books for the middle-grade audience under the name Mary James, including *Shoebag* (1990), the story of a cockroach who is transformed into a human boy. Although the Mary James books are fantasies, they, too, contain the trademark Kerr wit and style. P.D.S.

KHALSA, DAYAL KAUR

CANADIAN AUTHOR AND ILLUSTRATOR, 1943–1989. When Dayal Kaur Khalsa was a little girl growing up in Queens, New York City, she had two ambitions. She wished to be a writer and a cowboy. The first ambition she achieved in fact, growing up to become the author and illustrator of the eight exuberant, pawky picture books on which her reputation is based. The second ambition she also achieved—in fantasy. In her penultimate book, *Cowboy Dreams* (1990), written just before her death from cancer, Khalsa puts her heroine and alter ego, the sturdy and resilient May, into the world of buffalo and lariats in a final exploration of the ephemeral joys of childhood.

Born Marcia Schoenfeld, Khalsa moved to Canada in 1970 and changed her name on joining a Sikh ashram there in the mid-1970s. Her publishing career was tragically short, but she left the legacy of a unique vision. Khalsa's early works, a set of board books and the fable-like story *The Snow Cat* (1993), published posthumously, showcase her talent for clear rhythmical prose and her use of bright, blocky color. But Khalsa's best-known works feature the domestic adventures of her russet-haired protagonist May, depicted in a more detailed style. Khalsa puts an original spin on the stuff of childhood—family, friends, pets. As a child she had been cared for by her grandmother, and she celebrates this relationship in *Tales of a Gambling Grandmother* (1986), an extravagant, almost-tall-tale of love, sadness, and poker. May faces parental opposition in her desire for a dog in *I Want a Dog* (1987), but her determination and imagination save the day. A very young May observes how others doze off but stoutly maintains "I never sleep" in *Sleepers* (1988). A trip to Florida provides a background to shifting family dynamics in *My Family Vacation* (1988), and in *How Pizza Came to Queens* (1989) the kindness of May and her friends to a lonely old woman results in the glorious introduction of pizza into their lives. A grown-up May in *Julian* (1989) tells the familiar yet fresh story of an overly excitable dog.

In her pictures Khalsa gives her stories a highly specific setting, re-creating the artifacts of the forties and fifties—saddle shoes, minigolf emporiums, and Tinkertoys. She embeds subplots and jokes in the pictures, parodies of famous paintings, and bookshelves featuring her own complete works, but she never loses sight of her strong, well-shaped, broadly appealing stories and her pleasure in remaking her own past. ❧ S.E.

KHERDIAN, DAVID

AMERICAN AUTHOR AND POET, B. 1931. David Kherdian's passions for his family heritage, nature, and fishing provide inspiration for much of his writing. His most notable book, *The Road from Home: The Story of an Armenian Girl* (1979), tells of his mother's survival during the Turkish massacres of the Armenian people, and many of his novels for middle-grade readers use fishing as a central event.

Kherdian grew up in a close-knit Armenian community in Racine, Wisconsin. Unmotivated and discriminated against in school for his ethnic background, he left high school without finishing. Eventually, he earned his high school equivalency and a B.S. in philosophy from the University of Wisconsin. He began his writing career as a poet for adults and in 1971 married his second wife, children's book author and illustrator NONNY HOGROGIAN.

After working in the New Hampshire school system as a poet in residence, Kherdian edited several volumes of POETRY for young people. The poems he chose were not necessarily written for children but were ones he felt had strong child appeal. In *The Dog Writes on the Window with His Nose and Other Poems* (1977), illustrated by Hogrogian, he includes short poems by such modern poets as Jack Kerouac, William Stafford, and William Carlos Williams. In a collection of his own poems, *Country, Cat City, Cat* (1978), Kherdian presents brief, expressive images of nature, while Hogrogian's simple woodcuts of cats tie them together.

Kherdian's mother had often urged him to tell her story, and the resulting book, *The Road from Home*, is a powerful tale of young Veron's courage and determination to survive despite deportation, brutality, and the cholera that wiped out her family. Writing in the first person, Kherdian creates an intimate and poignant fictionalized autobiography. The book received numerous awards, including Newbery Honor Book, the Boston Globe–Horn Book Award for nonfiction, and the Jane Addams Award. Kherdian continued his mother's story in *Finding Home* (1981). Here, Veron, now sixteen and living in Greece, agrees to be a mail-order bride to a man twice her age in order to come to America. Although this book lacks the emotional impact of *The Road from Home*, it chronicles the hardships of a new immigrant to the United States in the 1920s. His family trilogy concludes with *Root River Run* (1984), a series of vignettes about his own childhood. Many of these events show up in slightly altered forms in his novels. For example, his beloved Uncle Jack is the model for Uncle Harry in *A Song for Uncle Harry* (1989), and *It Started with Old Man Bean* (1980), a story set in the 1940s about a fishing trip two boys take, draws heavily on his own fishing experiences.

Kherdian has also written a number of PICTURE BOOKS, all illustrated by Hogrogian. His cat provided the inspiration for *The Cat's Midsummer Jamboree* (1990), in which a cat who loves to sing joins other animals who play various instruments in a joyous jamboree. In *Feathers and Tails: Animal Fables from Around the World* (1992), Kherdian retells a delightful collection of stories from diverse cultures.

As a reteller, anthologist, poet, and novelist, Kherdian has made his mark on children's literature. ❧ P.R.

KIMMEL, ERIC

AMERICAN STORYTELLER, B. 1946. Born in Brooklyn, New York, Eric Kimmel is the product of a culturally diverse neighborhood. "Puerto Rican, Hispanic, Yiddish kids were running around together all on the same block," he recalls. For fifteen cents, he could take the subway to Rockridge or Greenwich Village, wherever his endless curiosity led him. An avid reader as a child, Kimmel grew up with his parents, a younger brother, Jonathan, and his Yiddish grandmother, from whom he acquired his storytelling knack.

"Nana," Kimmel says, "always told us stories. Ghost stories, Bible stories, stories of mysterious trickery." His favorite was the "bitza" story, about a bear that tried to eat the grandchildren in Grandma's house when she was out, but Granny always managed to fool the shaggy creature. As an adult on a trip to Montreal, Kimmel learned that there was an original Yiddish version of that story, which, translated, means "Grandma and Her Grandchildren." "Many of my books," says the author, "began as stories which I told to audiences for years before writing them down." Now, in addition to preserving the oral tradition, this professor of education at Portland State University in Oregon is penning his stories for posterity. "It's the rhythm of the language that makes a good book," he says. "If a story reads aloud well, there's a good chance it'll be a winner." In *Nanny Goat and the Seven Little Kids* (1990), he combined the bitza story with a classic from the Brothers GRIMM, "The Wolf and the Seven Kids," sometimes called "The Wolf and the Seven Goats." A frequent contributor to *Cricket* magazine, Kimmel also takes readers to distant places through his books. Journey to the Caribbean with *Anansi and the Moss-Covered Rock* (1988), to Russia in *Bearhead* (1991) and *Baba Yaga* (1991), to Japan via *The Greatest of All* (1991), to Norway through *Boots and His Brothers* (1992), and, in order to witness a traveler rid a village synagogue of goblins by outwitting them, to Eastern Europe with *Hershel and the Hanukkah Goblins* (1989), named a 1990 Caldecott Honor Book for TRINA SCHART HYMAN's illustrations.

In 1989 the Oregon Reading Association presented this storyteller with the Ulrich H. Hardt Award for his contributions to reading and literacy throughout the state. But Kimmel does not believe that awards are enough to entice children to read. Frequent visits to classrooms in the Portland area have taught him that what young audiences often want from a book is "a vacation from civilization." That's one of the reasons he enjoys the folktale genre: It allows characters to do things ordinary people could never accomplish. "And, in the end, they make a point," he says.

Kimmel is constantly searching for good stories that will expand young imaginations, improve children's reading skills, and open new worlds of enjoyment for them. He generally portrays the underdog overcoming enormous odds, often through cleverness or trickery, and gets a positive message across with a generous dose of wit. ❧ C.K.S.

KINGSLEY, CHARLES

BRITISH AUTHOR AND POET, 1819–1875. A contemporary of LEWIS CARROLL and GEORGE MACDONALD, Charles Kingsley was a cleric as well as a writer. His book *The Water-Babies* (1863) just preceded Carroll's *Alice's Adventures in Wonderland* and MacDonald's *The Light Princess.* Kingsley is often faulted for his didacticism, but his writings contain a consistent expression of his faith. His "muscular Christianity" demanded social action, and sometimes his outspokenness brought public argument. He welcomed the ideas of Charles Darwin, seeing no division between religion and science, and delighted in the knowledge of and reverence for nature.

Three books by Kingsley still hold a place in many twentieth-century collections. They are *Westward Ho!* (1855), *The Heroes, or Greek Fairy Tales for My Children* (1856), and *The Water-Babies.* Some critics, who acknowledge the continuing value of the poetic lines and compelling adventures of *The Heroes,* who "dared do more than other men," are quick to dismiss *Westward Ho!* and *The Water-Babies,* complaining that one is blatantly biased against Roman Catholicism and the other hopelessly didactic. There is disagreement, however, by some who were introduced as children to the swashbuckling action and romance of unsettled Elizabethan times and the delightful fantasy image of four-inch water babies frolicking in clear streams. For this audience, all three books still live. The Reissued Classics Edition of *Westward Ho!* (1992), with full-color illustrations by N. C. WYETH, still actively circulates in public libraries. Though originally written for adults, its greatest appeal has been for adolescent males, and it still appears on some school reading lists.

British critic and writer JOHN ROWE TOWNSEND claimed that in spite of the "splendid" beginning, *The Water-Babies* contained "a good deal of dross" and that Kathleen Lines's edited version was preferable to the original. It is true that the avuncular voice intrudes occasionally, and the author does preach educational reform, but he does it with some humor. Kingsley wrote, "I have tried in all sorts of queer ways to make children and grown up folk understand that there is a quite miraculous and divine element underlying all physical nature, and if I have wrapped up my parable in seeming Tom-fooleries, it is because only so could I get the pill swallowed." The stark realism of Tom's plight as a chimney sweep contrasted with his adventures as a water baby—his eventual reunion with his Ellie and the inclusion of some of Kingsley's best-known verse—make *The Water-Babies* a book that children can still enjoy.

There is no disagreement about the continuing value of *The Heroes.* Kingsley's graceful, poetic retellings of the stories of Perseus, the Argonauts, and Theseus were sparked by his low opinion of NATHANIEL HAWTHORNE's "distressingly vulgar" versions in *The Wonder Book* and *Tanglewood Tales.* Kingsley wrote out of a deep understanding and affection for authentic Greek culture, and *The Heroes* remains a continuing classic.

Though some fault Kingsley for his "aggressive patriotism" and "violent Protestantism," others have described him as a kindly, humorous man who always gave highest priority to his parishioners and their needs. He provided his four children with a childhood of "perpetual laughter" and was always accessible to them. He achieved high position, serving successively as Chaplain to the Queen, Tutor to the Prince of Wales, and Canon of Westminster. Now, more than a century later, Charles Kingsley is remembered primarily as the creator of Tom, the little chimney sweep, and his fantasy adventures in *The Water-Babies.* ❧ E.C.H.

King-Smith, Dick

English author, b. 1922. Dick King-Smith draws on his twenty years as a farmer and experience as a primary school teacher in England to write his popular, humorous, outrageous farmyard adventures, which combine elements of FANTASY with concrete details of farm life as they follow the adventures of remarkable animals who try to overcome natural obstacles.

Pigs Might Fly (1982) is the story of the young pig Daggie Dogfoot, the runt of a litter, who escapes from the farm each day and turns his disability—poorly formed front feet—into an advantage. He learns to swim and his skill saves the farm from a terrible flood. Daggie is followed by Babe and Ace, King-Smith's other heroic pigs, who each find fame by developing unusual talents and firmly establish the author's belief in pigs' intelligence. Babe, the only pig on a sheep farm, is sure to end up on the breakfast table, but the hero of *Babe the Gallant Pig* (1985) unwittingly controls his destiny and makes himself indispensable by learning to herd sheep. The novel, published as *The Sheep Pig* (1983) in England, won the Guardian Award and was a Boston Globe–Horn Book.

Each of King-Smith's carefully crafted fantasies is well grounded in reality, using the physical details of the rural surroundings to create a credible base. The farm scenes are authentic and detailed and the animals behave characteristically, so the reader is required to accept little on faith. Babe lives in a barnyard and eats slop, so the reader must only accept that he can communicate with other animals to believe the story of his triumph at the Sheep Dog Trials. *Pretty Polly* (1992) begins with the premise that many of the peeps young chickens make are remarkably similar to human speech. It is a short step, therefore, to teaching one talented chicken, Polly,

Voices of the Creators

Dick King-Smith

I came late to writing for children. In fact, when my first book was published, my eldest grandchild was already nine years old. Apart from having always taken pleasure in writing verse of various kinds, I had no early intention of becoming an author.

As a young man and, at first, perforce, a soldier, I ended my war on the receiving end of a British hand-grenade thrown at me by a German paratrooper in an Italian wood. Then, by choice, I farmed for twenty years and achieved the modest record of losing money in each one of them. The farming at an end, I was for a short time a not very successful salesman; then for three years an unremarkable worker in a shoe factory; finally, at the age of forty-nine, I went to a teacher training college, took a degree at fifty-three, and taught for seven years in a village primary school. I wrote my first book at fifty-four and had it published at fifty-six. This shows you how long it took my first editor to knock the thing into shape.

That first novel, *The Fox Busters*—its theme a confrontation between foxes and chickens—was, like several of the stories that were to follow, a tale of courage in the face of adversity and of terrible odds to overcome. But the chief element, I hope, in my stories is not drama or suspense or pathos—but humor. After all, I'm writing to amuse myself.

Though I do write books whose central characters are children, most of my stories are about animals, with which, either as pets or as farm livestock, I have been concerned all my life and in which I have always been interested. Because of the conventions that fantasy allows me, I enjoy putting words into their mouths. As well as conferring on my protagonists the gift of articulated speech, I also allow them to be brave or cowardly, wise or foolish, loyal or treacherous, nice or nasty—just like humans.

But I never dress them up as people. Not for me the elephant in a pin-striped suit and bow tie or the mini-skirted mouse. My animals appear *au naturel*, and each acts in the manner of its species—so that you will find no carthorses smoking pipes or billy goats riding bicycles. My pigs, for example, are pigs, pure and simple, except that they talk. What fun it is to think of dialogue for them.

I still write comic verse, usually about animals, and I have done a number of short picture-book texts. But what I enjoy doing most is to write—or try to write—a story that is tridentate in aim: one that will please the competent child reader; is suitable for reading aloud to a younger, less able child; and is acceptable to that reader-aloud, the parent or teacher.

Since the publication of my first book, the tally of grandchildren has risen to ten, and I've rather lost count of the number of stories I've written. It's somewhere around seventy, approximately my age; I hope that there will be time for plenty more.

Illustration by MARY RAYNER from *Babe the Gallant Pig* (1983), by Dick King-Smith.

to say "Eat Wheaties." From there, it is another small step to believing that Polly learns other human words. The reader knows that parrots can learn to talk, so why not chickens if they receive the same attention? *The Fox Busters* (1978) chronicles the successful efforts of three chickens who, due to the ineffectual methods of their farmer, must protect themselves from clever foxes. The traditional farmyard battle between foxes and chickens is elevated to riotous levels when the Fox Busters prepare a dangerous new weapon—hard-boiled eggs. Once again, King-Smith asserts that the underdog is able to succeed with cunning and perseverance, and that the silliest animal is more clever than a human.

King-Smith uses humor to tell his stories and create memorable characters. His dialogue is full of wit and humor and broad slapstick pervades his plots. His well-developed human characters are as funny and unusual as his farm animals, but the novels remain centered around the animals, and, inevitably, the animals are the ones to solve the problems that arise. King-Smith's novels combine elements of fantasy and humor with themes of survival and achievement, and his protagonists accomplish great things with their skills. King-Smith incorporates these universal themes into rollicking adventure stories with sympathetic, memorable characters to create novels that are popular with readers and critics. ❧ M.V.K.

KIPLING, RUDYARD

ENGLISH SHORT-STORY WRITER, POET, AND NOVELIST, 1865–1936. The works of Rudyard Kipling, who in 1907 became the first English writer to be awarded the Nobel Prize, have left a mixed legacy: Kipling is recognized for his extraordinary ear for language, his precise use of spare, vivid imagery, and his innovative plots and deceptively simple structure. He has also been accused of vulgarity, sentimentality, and copiousness and has been identified with imperialism, jingoism, fascism, and racism. Critics and proponents alike, however, tend to agree that Kipling's most uncontroversial achievements are his children's stories.

Born in India of English parents, Joseph Rudyard Kipling spent the first years of his life speaking Hindustani and living in a bungalow. At age six, he was taken to England to board with an unsympathetic foster family, a miserable experience he later wrote about in "Baa, Baa, Black Sheep," one of the short stories in *Wee Willie Winkie* (1888). In 1878 he entered an inferior boarding school and later fictionalized his schoolboy days in *Stalky and Co.* (1899). By the time Kipling was twenty-five, he had traveled back and forth from England to India and had over seventy short stories, poems, and novels in print. Marriage to an American woman brought Kipling to Brattleboro, Vermont, where he wrote some of his best children's stories.

The Jungle Book (1894) and its sequel *The Second Jungle Book* (1895) chronicle, in both narrative and verse, the adventures of a human boy, Mowgli, who is raised by wolves and instructed in the legend and lore of the Jungle by Baloo the bear and Bagheera the panther. The Jungle Books are replete with adventure and excitement—Mowgli swings from the treetops with the *Bandar-log* (monkeys), he wrestles with Kaa the giant python, he discovers jewels guarded by the White Cobra. There is also conflict and a strict sense of law and order in Kipling's jungle: "Now this is the Law of the Jungle—as old and as true as the sky; And the Wolf that shall keep it may prosper, but the Wolf that shall break it must die." The lessons Mowgli learns from the Jungle-people serve him when he is exiled to the superstitious world of man. The outsider Mowgli served as a prototype for Kipling's most famous hero, Kim, in the novel *Kim* (1901): Kimball O'Hara, an Irish orphan, is raised in India and "adopted" by a *lama* (holy man) from Tibet who is on a quest for the mystic River of Arrows. Kim's intimate knowledge of India makes him a valuable asset to the English Secret Service, and he soon distinguishes himself by capturing the papers of Russian spies. While *Kim* has been criticized for the young protagonist's lack of introspection, the book presents a vivid portrait of India, its teeming populations, and it superstitions, and it is generally considered Kipling's masterpiece.

In 1896 Kipling returned to England, where he wrote

Just So Stories (1902). The stories gave humorous accounts of the development of certain animals' physical characteristics: "How the Camel Got His Hump" tells of a camel who hawed and humphed so often that his *humph* was transformed into a *hump;* "The Elephant's Child" explains how a baby elephant stretched his nose into a trunk while trying to free himself from the mouth of a crocodile. *Puck of Pook's Hill* (1906) and *Rewards and Fairies* (1910), collections of tales inspired by his house in the English countryside, followed. After this last book, Kipling stopped writing specifically for children—the death of his daughter, Josephine, may have been a factor in this decision with the exception of *A History of England* (1911), in which he wrote the verse to punctuate C. R. L. Fletcher's narrative.

Much of the controversy that surrounds Kipling stems from his conviction that it was the responsibility and right of the English to civilize the world's heathen. The imperialistic phrase "the white man's burden" was taken from Kipling's poem of the same name (1899), in which he wrote, "Take up the White Man's Burden—Send forth the best ye breed—Go bind your sons to exile—To serve your captives' need." These paradoxes, Kipling's jingoism, and his ability to understand the role of the outsider, as seen in Mowgli and Kim, leave biographers and critics puzzled. Nevertheless, the concerns of critics are not those of the children who read or listen to Kipling's stories. That children today listen as eagerly to hear the adventures of Kim, the songs and wisdom of Baloo, and the hilarious myths of the animal kingdom as they did when these books were first published serves as a testimony to Rudyard Kipling's power as a storyteller. ❦ M.I.A.

Klein, Norma

American author, 1938–1989. Norma Klein was born and grew up in New York City. When a graduate student in Slavic languages at Columbia University, she intended to become a college professor or a painter but chose writing as a full-time career at age twenty-five. She had about sixty short stories for adults published by the time she was thirty, several of which were collected in anthologies, and a story collection for adults, *Love and Other Euphemisms,* published in 1972.

As a child, Klein read books about "cheerleaders or football stars" but could not find the kind of books she would be interested in—about people she knew in New York City, which she loved, and about people who were "bright, thoughtful, idealistic." Klein, along with contemporaries in the fledgling field of young adult literature, began to write realistic fiction about contemporary teenagers with unusual family situations or problems. Her best-known work remains *Mom, the Wolf Man, and Me* (1972). A groundbreaking work in contemporary American literature for young adults, the book describes eleven-year-old Brett, who thrives on living with her artistic single mother, a photographer who, in contrast to her friends' parents, runs their household in a free and unstructured way. Their close relationship is threatened, however, by the mother's involvement with a new boyfriend; the book won critical praise for the way it sensitively and honestly described Brett's situation. It was followed by other realistic contemporary novels that reflected evolving American familial arrangements. In *Taking Sides* (1974), a girl and her brother live with their father and see their mother only on weekends. In *What It's All About* (1975), eleven-year-old Bernie, a New Yorker who lives with her mother and stepfather, gets a sister when her family adopts a four-year-old Vietnamese child. In *Hiding* (1976), a seventeen-year-old who is in London to study ballet has her first sexual love affair. In *Breaking Up* (1980), a fifteen-year-old girl whose parents are divorced must decide to live with either her remarried father or her gay mother. All of Klein's books are not equal critical successes, and she has been criticized for writing more about the problems in some of her books than about the characters who have the problems.

Klein alternated between writing for children and young adults and writing for adults. She came to prefer writing for adults, which she found to be less subject to censorship. Klein wrote the novelization, nevertheless widely read by teenagers, for a popular film, *Sunshine* (1975) and its sequel, *The Sunshine Years* (1975). One of Klein's books for younger readers is *Girls Can Be Anything,* a picture book illustrated by Roy Doty. It was published in 1973, when feminism was beginning to have some influence on children's books published in America, and it was named a Junior Literary Guild selection. Klein once described herself as an "ardent feminist." She considered equal rights for women as the most important issue of the modern world, and her work reflects that view. ❦ S.H.H.

Klein, Robin

Australian writer, b. 1936. Awards and prizes galore have showered down on Robin Klein's many children's books over the years. Even though she came to writing fairly late, she quickly skyrocketed to enormous popularity and continues to collect new readers, with each book she publishes.

Klein grew up on an isolated farm in Kempsey, New South Wales, Australia, with eight brothers and sisters. Because of their isolation and because the family didn't have much money, the children entertained themselves by writing a family newspaper, performing plays, and inventing games. Although her family remained poor throughout her childhood, her mother wrote short stories for the Australian *Women's Journal,* and Klein maintains that she "grew up knowing that one could escape the restrictions poverty brings by having a private, creative world of one's own." She herself started writing stories and poems at age five. By the time she turned sixteen, her parents could no longer afford her education costs, so she left home, intending to see Australia on a working holiday but getting no farther than Melbourne, where she settled. During that time she had a string of jobs—library assistant, nurse, photographer, teacher, telephone operator—that occasionally popped up later in her fiction. After marrying in 1956, she spent twenty years raising four children. Not until 1982, when she and her husband were divorced and she needed to support herself, did she seriously take pen in hand. Her initial stories, poetry, and plays appeared in the New South Wales and Victoria *School Magazines* and were broadcast on ABC's children's programs. But soon she was publishing books as well. In 1983 her third title, *Thing,* won the Children's Book Council Junior Book of the Year Award. Ever since the Literature Board of the Australia Council awarded her a senior writing fellowship in 1984, she has been writing full-time in a cottage in the hills near Melbourne.

Klein produces an incredible array of writing, ranging from poetry and stories for younger readers to sophisticated young adult novels. *Came Back to Show You I Could Fly* (1989) concerns the friendship of an eleven-year-old with a drug-troubled eighteen-year-old, and it received the CBC Book of the Year Award for older readers. Her character Penny Pollard, star of *Penny Pollard's Diary* (1983) and other titles, has acquired a Ramona Quimby type of status for Australian readers, so familiar and well loved is she. *Hating Alison Ashley* (1984), another popular title for middle readers, has been adapted as a play and consequently has become even more widely known.

Categorizing Klein's work is difficult because of the range she covers. Readers seem to respond well to her humor and unconventional characters. She admits to being an eavesdropper, and her books have wonderfully realistic dialogue. Above all, perhaps, is their accessibility, which has helped them win so many young readers' hearts. ❧ K.J.

KNIGHT, ERIC

BRITISH-BORN AMERICAN AUTHOR, 1897–1943. *Lassie Come-Home* (1940) is perhaps the best-known dog story of the twentieth century. This tale of a collie journeying through Great Britain drew on the author's memories of his native country.

Eric Knight was born in Menston, Yorkshire, England. He and his brothers were separated and sent to live with relatives after their widowed mother found employment as a governess to the Russian royal family. While still a child, the author worked in a steel mill, a cotton mill, and several factories. In 1912, the Knight family reunited in Philadelphia; the author attended the Boston Museum of Fine Arts School, among other American schools. He attempted a career in art, wrote for several newspapers, worked as a screenwriter, and published a number of adult novels, including a bestseller, *This Above All* (1941).

An incident involving Knight's own missing dog inspired *Lassie Come-Home,* a realistic account of a collie living in Yorkshire with young Joe Carraclough and his family. When Joe's unemployed father, Sam, sells Lassie, the collie makes an arduous four-hundred-mile trek from Scotland to Yorkshire to be with Joe. Lassie's journey is harrowing, but also picaresque in its encounters with colorful characters; Knight skillfully includes information about English social classes and the hard lives of coal miners. The book was adapted for a 1943 motion picture starring Roddy McDowall and Elizabeth Taylor, which was followed by several film sequels. A television version, featuring Lassie as the pet of an American farm boy, ran for nearly twenty years.

Knight died in an airplane crash while serving in World War II, but his novel depicting the love between a dog and her boy continues to be popular with modern readers. ❧ P.D.S.

KOERTGE, RON

AMERICAN AUTHOR, B. 1940. Between 1973 and 1986, Ronald Koertge (pronounced KUR-chee) published fifteen books, mostly of POETRY. In 1986 he entered the field of children's literature with the highly successful YOUNG ADULT NOVEL, *Where the Kissing Never Stops.* This was followed by *The Arizona Kid* (1988), *The Boy in the Moon* (1990), *Mariposa Blues* (1991), and *The Harmony Arms* (1992), all of which have been equally well received. Koertge's stories are set in areas with which he is familiar: the fictitious Bradleyville, Missouri, based on Koertge's hometown; Tucson, Arizona; and

Los Angeles, California. Raised in Colinsville, Illinois, near the Missouri border, he studied English, first at the University of Illinois, earning a B.A., and later at the University of Arizona, where he earned his M.A. Koertge now teaches English at City College in Pasadena.

Events in Koertge's stories usually take place during summer vacation. His protagonists are not handsome hunks, they are ordinary teenage males who stand on the precipitous edge of sexual awakening. They are boys who are unsure of themselves, who are easily embarrassed, whose skin breaks out, whose voices crack. They are too short, thin, heavy, or just too average to be noticed. They have no siblings. Koertge always keeps the safety net of love and support in place for his protagonists, even though parents may be sorting out problems of their own. He delves into the sensitivity and self-centeredness the average teenager experiences. Shyness, moodiness, concern about appearance, establishing self-confidence and self-identity, and the need for friendship are all part of the tumult of growing up that his characters must sort through. "Who am I?"—the question he has Mr. Evars in *The Boy in the Moon* assign the class as their end-of-semester essay—is the thematic question he asks with wit and empathy in all his novels. His format may seem pat since themes of sexuality and self-identity are integral to many young adult novels, but Koertge puts spin on his stories by intertwining quirky subplots and using an eclectic supporting cast of characters, few of whom are what they seem. This cast serves to evoke an underlying theme of encouraging tolerance or acceptance of people whose appearances, lifestyles, and backgrounds are unlike the norm. Although never heavy-handed or didactic, Koertge is clear and candid when addressing sexual issues like AIDS and the use of condoms. His openness about the average teenage boy's sexual arousal and confusion puts Koertge's writing on the cutting edge, which some adults may find objectionable. Yet sex is not gratuitous in his books; it is a natural part of life to be discussed and dealt with openly.

Ron Koertge's warm and witty honesty and understanding in addressing all aspects of the teen experience make his books refreshing and popular. S.R.

KONIGSBURG, E. L.

AMERICAN AUTHOR AND ILLUSTRATOR, B. 1930. Elaine Loeb Konigsburg's entry into the field of children's literature was a dramatic one. In 1968 she won the Newbery Medal for her second novel, *From the Mixed-Up Files of Mrs. Basil E. Frankweiler* (1967), and that same year her first novel, *Jennifer, Hecate, Macbeth, William McKinley, and Me, Elizabeth* (1967), was named a Newbery Honor Book. Both novels are remarkable for their inventive plots and strong characters. Both are urban stories, and both are concerned with the lives of intelligent, nonconformist children.

Konigsburg is herself a creative, original writer. Born in New York City, she grew up in a small town in Pennsylvania and studied chemistry and taught science before leaving work to have three children of her own. While her children were young, she became interested in writing and art. In her writing Konigsburg finds herself drawn to the urban experience, and many of her books are set in and around New York. She illustrates her own novels in ink and has published several picture books, which she has written and illustrated.

Konigsburg's novels, short stories, and picture books are imaginative, unpredictable, and peopled with individuals. Elizabeth, the heroine of *Jennifer, Hecate,* allies herself with Jennifer, the newcomer and only African American child in her class. The two loners find friendship through a complex relationship, which shifts from inequality to balance. Jennifer teaches Elizabeth to be independent and a strong nonconformist. Konigsburg develops this theme of independence in all her novels. Claudia, the heroine of *From the Mixed-Up Files,* learns to rely on herself and to celebrate her strengths when she and her brother run away from their family and live in the Metropolitan Museum of Art. During their stay at the museum, they discover the secret of a new acquisition and meet the eccentric Mrs. Basil E. Frankweiler. The novel succeeds because it is filled with unusual details, strong characters, adventure, and mystery. The Met is a perfect fantasy setting, in which the children wash in the fountain and sleep in luxurious antique beds. The museum setting fosters the intellectual and personal explorations of the characters and reflects Konigsburg's own interest in fine art. This fascination with artistic creativity appears again in the historical novel *The Second Mrs. Giaconda* (1975), in which Konigsburg uses an artist's apprentice to tell the story of the life and motivations of Leonardo da Vinci. After writing many novels and short stories, Konigsburg published her first picture book, *Samuel Todd's Book of Great Colors* (1990). Samuel Todd, like Konigsburg's other characters, is a gifted child able to see possibilities in the world around him.

Throughout her writing, Konigsburg emphasizes the importance of taking risks, and her own writing is a tribute to that philosophy. She experiments with writing style, point of view, and structure, taking chances and achieving varying success. Her inventiveness is her greatest strength but makes the quality of her books unpredictable. In *(George)* (1970), for example, Konigsburg explores the schizophrenic behavior of a young boy who believes himself to have a concentric twin, but the voice of the narrator is not clear or direct and the plot is more contrived than it is in others of Konigsburg's works. Although her writing is not uniformly excellent, Konigsburg exhibits a playful love of words, and her best writing is some of the finest available for children. ❧ M.V.K.

Krasilovsky, Phyllis

American author, b. 1926. Many of Phyllis Krasilovsky's stories for children revolve around personal, albeit small, journeys that take place at or near home. Following the formula of her first children's book, *The Man Who Didn't Wash His Dishes,* published in 1950, she has written *The Man Who Tried to Save Time* (1979), *The Man Who Entered a Contest* (1980), *The Man Who Cooked for Himself* (1982), and *The Man Who Was Too Lazy to Fix Things* (1992). Although these titles may sound simplistic, the protagonist in each story is forced to save himself from chaos. Each story begins, "There once was a man who lived with his cat in a little house on the edge of [a] wood/town. He didn't have a wife or children so . . ." Each man lives a routine existence until one day a kernel of discontent sets in. This serves as the call to adventure, if only in a limited sphere.

These picture books follow a heroic cycle of adventure while hilariously pushing absurdity to its limit: The hero leaves home when he departs from his normal routine, crosses the threshold into adventure, finds himself in peril—the chaos his discontent has created—either saves himself through his own inner resources or receives unexpected help, and returns to an orderly state. In Krasilovsky's stories, the boon with which the hero returns is a clearer understanding of his own needs. For example, the man who refused to wash his dishes realizes that he has so many dirty dishes, he cannot find his sink. As it begins to rain, he piles all his dishes into the back of his truck and the rain washes them. With order restored, the little man is content to resume his life, knowing that order is important to him.

Krasilovsky has traveled all over the world. One of her journeys took her to Holland, and this trip resulted in two children's books. In the first, *The Cow Who Fell in the Canal* (1957), Hendrika, the cow who produces thick, creamy milk from which Mr. Hofstra makes cheese, is unhappy. When Pieter, Mr. Hofstra's horse, tells her about the wonderful town and marketplace, with its cheese sellers who wear straw hats with ribbons, Hendrika longs to go there—and longs for a straw hat. Her fall into the canal results in an adventurous trip to the marketplace. She returns home, content with her happy memories—and her straw hat with streamers. The second story, *The First Tulips in Holland,* illustrated by S. D. Schindler, won the 1982 Parents' Choice Award

Illustration by Peter Spier from *The Cow Who Fell in the Canal* (1972), by Phyllis Krasilovsky.

for illustration. In it, Krasilovsky uses the historical facts that tulips originated in Turkey and were first brought to Holland by a Dutch merchant to create a love story and a legend.

Krasilovsky has written many other children's stories, among them *The Very Little Girl* (1953), *The Very Little Boy* (1962), *The Very Tall Little Girl* (1969), and *The Shy Little Girl* (1970). Each gives a child's-eye-view of the frustrations children experience as they grow and mature, of the small dreams that are of great importance to the dreamer.

Krasilovsky knows that dreams can come true, and she is no stranger to hard work. After high school, she worked full-time while studying English literature, evenings, at Brooklyn College. She continued to take courses at Cornell University, where her husband attended law school. She has taught children's literature and creative writing, as well as lectured and written travel, magazine, and newspaper articles. Krasilovsky's forte in writing for children is her ability to advance her protagonists, gently and humorously, along life's growth spiral. She uses discontent and experimentation as the vehicles that bring her small heroes and heroines to a happier, wiser level of self-awareness, thereby showing change as a normal, necessary life experience. ❦ S.R.

Kraus, Robert

American author and illustrator, b. 1925. Unlike his beloved character Leo, Herman Robert Kraus bloomed at an early age, and he still continues to delight his young fans. He was born in Milwaukee, where he pursued his love of drawing by following suggestions he found in books about cartooning. By age ten he had sold one of his cartoons to a local barbershop, and after this early success his first published cartoon appeared on the children's page of the *Milwaukee Journal.* During high school Kraus drew for *Esquire,* the *Saturday Evening Post,* and other magazines, and after graduating he headed for New York and the Art Students' League. During this time Kraus began his association with the *New Yorker,* contracting for fifty cartoons a year. He also began to write and illustrate children's books, and his first, *Junior the Spoiled Cat,* appeared in 1955.

Kraus founded his own publishing house, Windmill Books, in 1965, and began writing stories illustrated by his friends at the *New Yorker,* including Charles Addams and William Steig. Windmill earned "an enviable reputation," according to *Publishers Weekly,* for its variety of children's books, including some award-winners. Unfortunately, financial and distribution problems forced Kraus to sign over the company to Simon and Schuster in the early 1980s. At various times Kraus has also written under the pseudonyms Eugene H. Hippopotamus, E. S. Silly, and I. M. Tubby, the last as author of the "Tubby Books." The "Tubby Books," with their vinyl "pages" and ability to float, have been many a toddler's first bathtub toy.

Kraus's animal characters are sure to bring a smile of recognition to parents of young children, and titles such as *Leo the Late Bloomer* (1971), *Owliver* (1974), and *Herman the Helper* (1974) deserve space on any parenting shelf, along with Spock, Leach, and Brazelton, for their on-target insight into toddler behavior. With gentle humor, Kraus pokes sly fun at Leo's worried father: "A watched bloomer doesn't bloom." Leo's reassuring "I made it!" at the end delights young listeners who may also have been scrutinized for early blooming by well-intentioned moms and dads. Owliver must overcome his dad's wishes that he become a doctor or a lawyer, and his wise mom recognizes Owliver's theatrical talent and insists he be allowed to follow his dream. Kraus surprises his readers with a gently humorous ending, as Owliver fulfills every young boy's fantasy and grows up to become a fireman!

Many of Kraus's successful picture books have resulted from a collaboration with illustrators José Aruego and Ariane Dewey. With simple lines and bold, vibrant colors, the pictures perfectly complement the text. With such simple statements as "Herman liked to help. He helped his mother. He helped his father" and brief questions and answers such as "Whose mouse are you? Nobody's mouse. Where is your mother? Inside the cat," Kraus evokes universal childhood experiences. In *Where Are You Going, Little Mouse?* (1986), his young protagonist feels unloved by his family and goes off in search of new parents and siblings. Any toddler who has ever had a predawn adventure will sympathize with the title character in *Milton the Early Riser* (1972), although not many would share Milton's sense of responsibility as he cleans up the mess he's made. Nonetheless, Kraus always places his characters in a reassuring family scene, and this sense of family pervades his work. Many of these toddler favorites are accessible to beginning readers, who can appreciate on their own these stories told with limited vocabulary and appealing illustrations. ❦ E.H.

Krauss, Ruth

American poet and author, 1901–1993. Inspired by the experimental atmosphere in child development circles during the 1940s and 1950s, Ruth Krauss created simple stories and POETRY for young children. Best known for her classic PICTURE BOOK, *The Carrot Seed* (1944), illustrated by her husband, CROCKETT JOHNSON, Krauss went on to publish more than thirty books over the next four decades. Among them were eight picture book collaborations with illustrator MAURICE SENDAK. Their fortuitous beginning resulted in the publication of *A Hole Is to Dig: A First Book of First Definitions* (1952), the small innovative picture book that established Sendak as a formidable figure in children's book illustration.

During the early 1940s, Krauss was a member of the experimental Writers' Laboratory at the Bank Street School in New York City, a program that fostered the talents of other great picture-book writers, such as MARGARET WISE BROWN. Krauss incorporated the "here and now" philosophy originated by educator and author Lucy Sprague Mitchell, founder of the Bank Street School, who maintained that "young children live in the 'here and now' world around them, which they use as a laboratory for their explorations." Krauss furthered Mitchell's ideas by incorporating psychologist/pediatrician Arnold Gesell's theories on the acquisition of language to create her own playful perspective on a young child's reality. She adopted Mitchell's concept of "direct observation" and went to the children themselves to glean her text for *A Hole Is to Dig*. She queried the young students to determine their meanings for words and in doing so created one of the first concept books for young children. Definitions like "Dogs are to kiss people" or "A lap is so you don't get crumbs on the floor" reflect a child's pragmatic approach to language.

Illustration by CROCKETT JOHNSON from *The Carrot Seed* (1945), by Ruth Krauss.

In her books Krauss often used a child's natural word forms and expressions, most notably in *A Very Special House*, the Caldecott Honor Book in 1954, in which the young narrator pontificates in an unselfconscious, child-centered stream of thought. Krauss's imaginative and humorous use of language in the form of invented words and nonsensical rhymes inspired the first books for young children reflecting the child's inner life. Widely acclaimed as "the little book with the big idea," *The Carrot Seed*, which masterfully builds tension by using repetition in its short, 101-word text, has remained in print since 1945. Unflappable and confident, a little boy weeds and waters his precious carrot seed even though his parents and brother believe "it won't come up." With the simplest word *and*, Krauss paces the story while Johnson intensifies the climax by introducing bold color and oversized scale to picture the boy's huge red carrot topped with bushy green fronds—a carrot so big the boy needs a wheelbarrow to hold it. In *The Happy Day*, selected as a Caldecott Honor Book in 1950, Krauss's word patterns create rhythm in the simple text. Following a linear progression, several woodland animals sleep, sniff, and run to discover a bright yellow flower growing in the snow. Repetition and rhythm allow Krauss to seamlessly introduce five different species to the youngest listeners and readers.

Ruth Krauss's intuitive ability as a writer to capture the free-spirited thought processes and language of young children ensures her books' widespread acceptance and timeless appeal. ❧ S.M.G.

KREMENTZ, JILL

AMERICAN PHOTOGRAPHER AND AUTHOR, B. 1940. Jill Krementz, who has dozens of children's books to her credit, demonstrates in each that her photographic talent is complemented by her sensitivity in tackling tough topics. She asks children hard questions, listens for the answers, and reports with warmth and skill.

Krementz grew up in Morristown, New Jersey, and attended Drew University for a year before moving to New York City. After working as a secretary at *Harper's Bazaar* and *Glamour*, she took a trip around the world, stopping off in India to work in public relations for a few months. She became interested in photography and was hired at age twenty-four as the first woman photographer at the *New York Herald-Tribune.* She photographed the noncombat side of the Vietnam war and collaborated with Dean Brelis on *The Face of South Vietnam* (1968). The following year she wrote and photographed her first children's book, *Sweet Pea: A Black Girl Growing Up in the Rural South* (1969). Her distinguished portraits of writers include a classic study of E. B. WHITE.

In 1976 Krementz wrote and did the photography for the first book in what was to become a series, *A Very Young Dancer* (1976), which has remained the most popular of a successful line. Following the same format, she created books about a rider, a skater, a skier, a gymnast, and an actress. Each looks at the whole child, including life at home and on the road, the hard work, and some playful moments. To capture the lives of her subjects fully, Krementz went to dozens of rehearsals, got up early, and traveled to Europe to go to competitions. In *A Very Young Actress* (1991), Krementz takes readers backstage to observe the exciting but sometimes uncomfortable life of the star of *Annie.*

A Visit to Washington, D.C. (1987) shows children what a diverse adventure a trip to the nation's capital can be, as parents take two lively boys on a tour of their hometown—climbing into a cherry tree in full bloom, shaking hands with an Arlington National Cemetery bugler, and feeding the ducks at the Reflecting Pool.

Observing a child at a funeral inspired Krementz to begin the "How It Feels" series with *How It Feels When a Parent Dies* (1981), a book often recommended for children in that tremendously painful situation. *How It Feels to Be Adopted* (1982) and *How It Feels When Parents Divorce* (1984) followed, each with first-person narratives by young people of all ages and circumstances; points are given for honesty, even when it obviously hurts.

Jill Krementz married writer Kurt Vonnegut, a former photographic subject, in 1979, and they adopted a little girl, Lily, following the publication of Krementz's book on adoption. ❧ A.C.

KROEBER, THEODORA

AMERICAN AUTHOR, 1897–1979. Perhaps best known for her BIOGRAPHY of Ishi, the last surviving member of the Yahi tribe of Native Americans, Theodora Kroeber wrote for adults and children. For adults she collected folk tales from California Indians, coauthored a book of early photographs of Native Americans from extinct California tribes, and wrote a biography of her late husband and noted anthropologist, Alfred L. Kroeber.

Kroeber grew up in Telluride, Colorado, then moved to Berkeley, California, and attended the University of California, from which she received a bachelor's and a master's degree. She married A. L. Kroeber in 1926 and had four children, one of whom, URSULA K. LE GUIN, became an author of children's fantasy and science fiction. Kroeber was in her fifties when she began writing. She started with a novel, which was never published, but from it she learned the discipline of writing and developed a writing pattern that she followed nearly every day.

Illustration by Ruth Robbins from *Ishi, Last of His Tribe* (1964), by Theodora Kroeber.

In 1961 she published *Ishi in Two Worlds: A Biography of the Last Wild Indian in North America.* This eloquent biography for adults, an ALA Notable Book, was followed three years later by *Ishi, Last of His Tribe,* a fictionalized account for young people. In 1911 Ishi wandered out of the foothills of Mount Lassen in northern California, the sole survivor of a Native American tribe that had lived in the region for thousands of years. A. L. Kroeber and fellow anthropologist T. T. Waterman, both professors at the University of California, took him to the Museum of Anthropology in San Francisco, which became his home until his death in 1916. Ishi was very cooperative in telling Kroeber and Waterman about the Yahi culture and about his life during the long period of concealment from the whites who were determined to exterminate all the Indians in the area. Many aspects of this time, however, were too painful for him to talk about. For example, it was taboo to use the name of a dead relative or friend. Thus, it was difficult to ascertain exactly how many people had survived with

Ishi, their names, or their relationships to each other. Even "Ishi" was not his given name; it is a generic word meaning "man." Despite these problems, Theodora Kroeber created a poignant story of Ishi's life based on the vast quantities of information gathered by her husband, Waterman, and Ishi's other friends. She included not only information about how Ishi and his family lived but also many of their cultural beliefs and their myths. *Ishi, Last of His Tribe* was named an ALA Notable Book.

Later, Kroeber wrote a picture book, *A Green Christmas* (1967), based on her own first Christmas in California. Written in the form of a prose poem, it describes two young children who move to California from Colorado and face a warm and snowless holiday. In *Carrousel* (1977), a fantasy novella, the Keeper of the carrousel fails to close the door tight one night—who's to say if he did or did not see that it was open? The carrousel animals come out and frolic on the grass. With poetic charm, Kroeber describes the desire of Pegason, the winged horse, to fly free and the concern and sadness of Keeper and the village children when they find him gone. Although *Carrousel* has a mythical, lyrical quality, *Ishi* remains Kroeber's most powerful work. ❧ P.R.

Krumgold, Joseph

American author, 1908–1980. As the first two-time winner of the Newbery Medal, Joseph Krumgold holds a unique place in children's literature, an especially surprising accomplishment considering he produced only four children's books during his career.

Krumgold was born and raised in Jersey City, New Jersey, where his father ran movie theaters. Joseph shared his father's interest in film and, after graduating from New York University, moved to Hollywood. Working as a press agent, producer, and screenwriter, Krumgold wrote over a dozen film scripts, as well as two adult novels. After spending World War II with the Office of War Information, he married and had a son, began filming documentaries, and lived in Israel for four years. Returning to the United States, he produced a documentary about New Mexican sheep farmers for the State Department. Since the film focused on a Mexican American boy, a publisher suggested Krumgold adapt it into a children's book. *...And Now Miguel* (1953) was highly praised for its evocative southwestern setting and multidimensional portrait of a boy who hopes to join his father and brothers on their annual sheep drive to the mountains. The book's most impressive quality is the first-person narration, which, in its rhythm, formality, and occasional awkward phrasing, perfectly captures Miguel's heritage, intelligence, and wit. This wise and poetic novel won the Newbery Medal in 1954.

Six years later, Krumgold won the medal for his second children's book, *Onion John* (1959), which concerns twelve-year-old Andy's friendship with an eccentric immigrant called Onion John. Led by Andy's father, the townspeople build a home for Onion John, but their good intentions ultimately cause him to leave town. *Onion John* is a strong, thoughtful novel, although its young protagonist often functions as an observer, rather than a full-fledged participant in the events. Krumgold again uses the first person to narrate the story, but the awkward phrasing, employed so artfully in *...And Now Miguel,* seems out of place in the second novel. This is also true in *Henry 3* (1967), the dated story of Henry Lovering and his family's adjustment to suburban life. The book presents an interesting picture of a complex friendship, but the plotting is shaky and many of the characters are not fully realized. Although Krumgold later wrote one slight book for younger readers, *The Most Terrible Turk* (1969), he is best known for the trio of novels about adolescent boys. One unusual aspect of the books is that they concern boys who don't rebel or crave independence but prefer to follow conventional community behavior. Miguel wants to be a sheep farmer like his ancestors. Andy, despite his father's protests, hopes to join the family hardware business. Henry hides his high IQ so he can fit in with his classmates.

Krumgold has been criticized for his treatment of female characters. Women barely figure in the first two novels and are caricatured in *Henry 3,* a work that also contains a surprisingly harsh indictment of woman's role in modern society. Nevertheless, there is much to recommend in the books. Krumgold writes with intelligence about boys moving from childhood to maturity. Whether Miguel is telling how to catch a fish with his bare hands, or Andy is describing his Halloween activities, or Henry is creating a game involving an imaginary road trip, the author remains true to the inner thoughts and feelings of a boy's life. ❧ P.D.S.

Krüss, James

German author, b. 1926. If his semiautobiographical novels speak the truth, James Krüss has been "rhyming" for much of his life. Unfortunately, Krüss's lively writing style makes translation a difficult job at best. Some of Krüss's best novels are actually a series of stories and verses, lightly strung together by a narrative commentary. Krüss spent his boyhood on the North Sea island of Helgoland, where storytelling was a way of life. As an uncle in *My Great-Grandfather, the Heroes and I* (1973) said, "On a small island where there are few places of amusement, one has to pass the time. So people learn to tell stories." Krüss's rhymes and tales have a message of peace, freedom, and courage that give ballast to his lighthearted verse. When he was still a teenager, he had to serve in the German Air Force, and he is poignantly articulate years later about questioning authority and the madness of war. His memoir, *Coming Home from the War* (1970), details his journey back to the island from Bohemia, where he was released. As he traveled, the hard shell of Hitler's dogma peeled away and left him vulnerable but free. It is a physical journey but a spiritual odyssey.

Krüss stayed only a short time on the island after the war before moving to Hamburg for a job as a newspaper editor. One day, short of money, he tried to peddle a few children's poems to a radio station and a newspaper. To his delighted surprise, both accepted them, and his career as a children's book writer was started. Over the years, he has written more than seventy books and a number of stage and radio plays. For some of these, he collaborated with the creator of *Emil,* ERICH KÄSTNER, with whom he shared a penchant for zany, fast-paced storytelling.

In 1960 Krüss's *My Great-Grandfather and I* (trans. 1964) won the German Children's Book Prize, and soon thereafter he was honored with the Hans Christian Andersen Medal for his body of work. Both this book and its sequel, *My Great-Grandfather, the Heroes and I,* tell of a young teen, modeled after Krüss himself, who holes up with his great-grandfather and spends a week rhyming and storytelling. In the first book, they decide to write poems and stories about words themselves—about the sounds and meanings and ambiguities of language. Far from being dull as the boy fears, the stories are lively and full of wordplay. The second book is more serious. Great-grandfather has a legacy to pass along to his favorite descendant, and that is to clarify the truth about heroes. The layers of insight are powerful. Each day the stories delve more deeply into the nature of heroes and false heroes, from a tale of a lobster who sacrifices himself to a saga of a soldier in Cortes's war in Mexico. Krüss is writing about his childhood, a time when Hitler was coming into power, when the only safe way his great-grandfather could warn the boy was through allegory.

Krüss clarifies his philosophy at the end of *The Lighthouse of the Lobster Cliffs* (1969): "Now we no longer need to ask whether a story is true because we know that if a story is beautiful, it must also be true." ❧ J.A.J.

Kurelek, William

CANADIAN ARTIST, ILLUSTRATOR, AND AUTHOR, 1927–1977. William Kurelek is a highly respected artist whose work is represented in the collections of the Museum of Modern Art in New York, of Queen Elizabeth II of England, and of the Montreal Museum of Fine Arts. He is also noted for the great charm of his children's books, which depict rural life on the Canadian prairie in the 1930s. The beautiful scenes in *A Prairie Boy's Winter* (1973), *Lumberjack* (1974), and *A Prairie Boy's Summer* (1975) give barely a glimmer of the difficult and unhappy childhood the artist experienced.

Kurelek was raised in the Ukrainian farming communities of Alberta and Manitoba. His immigrant father was a morose and unsuccessful man, and, as the weakest of his three sons, Kurelek experienced a childhood of fear, bullying, and abuse. By the time he entered high school, Kurelek felt estranged from his family and often retreated behind a wall of silence; drawing was the sole area in which he experienced the admiration of his peers. Kurelek's feelings of worthlessness and loneliness continued during his years at the University of Manitoba, but it was there that he discovered James Joyce's *Portrait of the Artist as a Young Man* and felt a strong bond of sympathy with the author and the character he had created. Kurelek decided that he, too, would devote his life to art, but his depressions continued, and in his mid-twenties he went to England to commit himself to psychiatric care. While he was hospitalized, Kurelek continued to paint, creating horrific paintings such as *The Maze,* a representation of his state of mind. Kurelek credited his eventual recovery to shock therapy, an important friendship with his Catholic occupational therapist, and, primarily, his wholehearted conversion to Roman Catholicism.

Back in Toronto, Kurelek looked for work as a picture framer, carrying his canvases with him as a demonstration of his framing skill. One gallery owner recognized his ability and offered him a show. The pictures sold, and Kurelek had his first evidence that the public recognized him as an artist. Grateful for his recovery, Kurelek embarked on a major project—150 paintings that represented the St. Matthew Passion. The completed series is housed at the Niagara Falls Gallery and Art Museum. Kurelek painted quickly and even obsessively and alternated paintings of moral message with landscapes and scenes of rural activities from his childhood. These were the scenes that filled his children's books.

Kurelek's vigorous style is perfect for the worlds he knew, including the almost mythic world of the logging camp. His book *Lumberjack* is a wonderful album of the skills and strengths needed to bring the logs out of the isolated forests. *Prairie Boy's Summer* depicts a time before agriculture was industrialized when draft horses were used and the simple beauty of farm machinery was apparent. Kurelek creates a joyful sense of community at the swimming hole and in celebration of harvest. His naive style creates a magical landscape out of the flat, gold expanses of wheat and the vast blue sky. ❧ P.H.

Kuskin, Karla

American poet, author, and illustrator, b. 1932. Karla Kuskin's long, varied, and acclaimed career was presaged by the immediate success of her first book for children, published before she was twenty-five. *Roar and More* (1956), which Kuskin wrote, illustrated, designed, typeset, printed, and bound as part of her academic course work at Yale University, was instantly hailed for its original use of typography to represent an array of animal sounds. She revisited this technique in *All Sizes of Noises* (1962), in which the size, shape, and placement of letters convey the multitude of sounds—"HONNNNNNK," "THUDthudTHUDthud," "Hurryuphurryhurryup"—a child encounters in the course of a day. This book, with its urban focus, reflects the many years its creator spent in her native New York City as a child, wife, and mother.

Kuskin is a prolific author and illustrator who has created the text or artwork or both for more than thirty-five books. She is most often cited for her ability to craft nimble verses whose musical lilt and graceful internal and end rhymes all but demand they be read aloud. She demonstrates, as well, an intuitive feeling for a child's perspective, whether she is addressing children's concerns about their size (*Herbert Hated Being Small,* 1979), their unshakable attachment to favored possessions (*A Boy Had a Mother Who Bought Him a Hat,* 1976), or, as in so many of her poems, their love of whimsy and gift for imaginative projection. Her child's-eye view of the world can also be seen in her characteristically small, precisely drawn illustrations, with their clean, uncluttered design and close attention to detail. In two books, *Near the Window Tree* (1975) and *Dogs & Dragons, Trees & Dreams* (1980), Kuskin pairs her poems with autobiographical notes detailing the inspiration for each one in an effort to inspire children's own poetic undertakings.

Kuskin has won many honors over the years, including several citations from the American Institute of Graphic Arts. In 1979 the National Council of Teachers of English recognized her with their Award for Excellence in Poetry for Children, given for her body of work. Soon thereafter she garnered new accolades for the brilliantly simple, meticulously executed *The Philharmonic Gets Dressed* (1982), which brings a symphony orchestra to life by recounting the preparations, from showering to setting-up onstage, undertaken by its 105 musicians in anticipation of an evening's performance. Illustrated by Marc Simont, this work was named a Notable Children's Book by the American Library Association and the *New York Times* and was designated a Library of Congress Children's Book. In addition, it was nominated for an American Book Award, a rare honor for a children's book and one that testifies to the breadth and endurance of Kuskin's appeal. ❧ A.J.M.

Illustration by Marc Simont from *The Philharmonic Gets Dressed* (1982), by Karla Kuskin.

L

La Fontaine, Jean de

French author, 1621–1695. Jean de La Fontaine dedicated his first volume of fables to the dauphin of France, and since that time they have been enjoyed by generations of other young readers.

La Fontaine was born and raised in Château-Thierry, where his father was a forest ranger. He entered a seminary to study theology, left to pursue a law career, then became interested in poetry. With encouragement from his friends, the writers Molière and Racine, La Fontaine wrote his first comedy for the stage in 1651, *L'Eunuque*. He continued to write plays, poetry, novels, and short stories, including the controversial *Contes et Nouvelles* (1665), a collection of ribald tales.

His best-known works are the *Fables*, published in twelve volumes between 1668 and 1694. Written in verse and using animals to illustrate universal truths about human behavior, the fables were often suggested by the works of Aesop, including "The Grasshopper and the Ant" and "The Fox and the Grapes." Some of La Fontaine's original fables, such as "The League of Rats" and "Husband, Wife, and Robber," are based on historical events of the seventeenth century. Because the fables were written in accessible rhyme, they have become a staple of French children's literature. English editions include *The Fables of La Fontaine* (1954), which was translated by Marianne Moore, and three volumes by Edward Marsh, *Forty-two Fables* (1924), *More Fables* (1925), and *Collected Fables* (1930).

Although few American children read La Fontaine's work in either the original French or in English translation, the author played a major role in the historical development of the fable form, and his influence can still be found in many modern retellings of these well-known stories. § P.D.S.

Lagerlöf, Selma

Swedish author, 1858–1940. At the beginning of the new century, members of the Swedish National Teachers' Association wanted to provide children with the finest materials possible, so it commissioned Sweden's best-known writer to create a geography primer for middle-grade students. Selma Lagerlöf researched her native land for three years but still had no idea how she would write this book. But then she visited Mårbacka, the farm in southern Sweden where she had spent her childhood. She wrote about this visit, how she rescued a small boy named Nils from an owl and how, in return, Nils told her all about his adventures: "'What luck to run across one who has travelled all over Sweden on the back of a goose!' thought she. 'Just this which he is relating I shall write down in my book.'" The book became *The Wonderful Adventures of Nils* (two volumes, 1906–1907), and it has risen above the geography textbook it was supposed to be to take its place with the classics.

Nils Holgersson is a wicked boy who cares for no one and is cruel to animals. When he catches an elf one Sunday morning and tries to play a trick on him, the elf turns Nils into an elf-sized boy. With the change comes the ability to understand animal speech, but, unfortunately, the animals still recognize him. He escapes the fury of the barnyard animals and jumps on the back of their gander, who flies up to be with the wild geese returning north to Lapland. The leader of the wild geese, Akka of Kebnekaise, is a classic wise-woman figure, translated beautifully into an old gray goose: "Her entire feather outfit was ice-gray, without any dark streaks. The head was larger, the legs coarser, and the feet were more worn than any of the others. The feathers were stiff; the shoulders knotty; the neck thin. All this was due to age. It was only upon the eyes that time had had no effect. They shone brighter—as if they were younger—than any of the others!" Traveling with this extraordinary goose and her flock, Nils, due to his unusual size and ingenuity, is able to help many different animals. He has adventure after adventure, building his reputation as he subtly shapes his character. Each event occurs in a different town or part of the country, drawing on Sweden's geography as vivid background for the drama. Partly due to the wonderful success of Nils Holgersson, as well as her famous novel *Gösta Berlings saga* (1891), Lagerlöf was awarded the Nobel Prize for Literature in 1909, the first woman ever to receive that honor. Five years after that she was admitted as the first woman to the Swedish Academy, the highest recognition her country could offer her. Since 1950, a Swedish children's author has been chosen annually to receive the Nils Holgersson Award. Where other lands decorate their money with kings, queens, and presidents, in Sweden, Nils, flying on the back of his goose, and, on the other side, Selma Lagerlöf herself, grace the Swedish twenty-krona note. ❧ J.A.J.

Lampman, Evelyn Sibley

American author, 1907–1980. Without fanfare Evelyn Sibley Lampman produced a body of responsible fiction about the Indians of Oregon that is unparalleled in its historical span, from white conquest to Indian resurgence, and in its close, detailed regional focus. The great-granddaughter of Willamette Valley pioneers, Lampman was steeped in tales of early life in and around the small town of Dallas, and many of the characters and incidents turn up in her books—some more than once, from both a white and an Indian perspective.

Pioneers and Indians were not the only subjects of Lampman's fifty juveniles. Apart from a number of negligible books written under the pseudonym Lynn Bronson, she contributed two popular tales to the 1950s dinosaur whimsy spree, *The Shy Stegosaurus of Cricket Creek* (1955) and *The Shy Stegosaurus at Indian Springs* (1962), cast a boy and girl as captives of an ant colony in *The City Under the Back Steps* (1960), and looked into the lives of other cultural minorities, notably the Chinese of Portland around 1900 in *Elder Brother* (1951). She had previously honed her skills as the writer-producer of an educational radio program for children that was also designed to be entertaining, and that dual commitment shaped her writing.

What Lampman knew best—communal life in western Oregon, reaching back into the precontact experiences of Indians and whites—was like family history in her hands, something she could relive and rearrange almost kaleidoscopically. In thirty years, however, the books exhibit no consistent or sustained development—either as fiction, in choice of subject matter, or, most surprising, in the handling of their themes.

The greater the number of white fictional characters, the less consequential the book. Still, as a story of early town life in the Willamette Valley, *The Bounces of Cynthiann'* (1950)—about a passel of orphans named Bounce who, literally, work themselves into the hearts of the local citizenry—is engaging in a sunny, weepy, folksy way that once made it quite popular. *Tree Wagon* (1953) traces the overland journey, hazardously overloaded with growing stock, of the West Coast's first, famous orchardist and his family; *Bargain Bride* (1977) is a Cinderella story hinged securely on land-claim law.

Of the many Indian stories, the strongest are *not* about the internal conflicts of biracial boys or Indian youths of divided allegiance—situations common to juvenile fiction that tend to result, with Lampman, in typecast whites and flat-out messages. Where she scores, rather, is where other authors cannot readily go: into the differences among Indians as well as the varied concerns of Indians (or part Indians) secure in their identity.

Of particular interest as cultural history is *Treasure Mountain* (1949), a story that also carries an emotional charge. Irene and Hoxie Chubfish, students at the up-to-date Chemawa Indian School, come to stay with Great-aunt Della, an "old blanket Indian" who lives in squalor, speaks no English, and, far from wishing to change her lot, brooks no interference—to the horror and revulsion of Irene and the discomfort of Hoxie, the elder. Aunt Della is *theirs*, Hoxie reminds Irene in a strikingly blunt exchange. Do they want to behave like bigoted whites?

In *Treasure Mountain*, written sometime before the Indian resurgence, Irene and Hoxie make peace with the surviving past of their people by recognizing hunter-gatherer ways as viable and satisfying alternatives to money. *The Potlatch Family* (1976), written more than twenty-five years later, calls for a more sophisticated form of adaptive reuse. A group of assimilated Indians are suddenly called upon by a young Vietnam veteran to revive Indian customs and publicly affirm their Indian identity—and, most disconcerting of all, to sell tickets and peddle crafts. Why not show pride *and* turn a profit? The abrupt, flagrantly manipulated death of the mysteriously wounded vet is unworthy of the trenchant, funny, down-to-earth proceedings.

Only two of Lampman's fictional works deal with prominent historical matters. Both are so keenly imagined and effectively constructed, however, that it is a pity she did not write others or produce more than one work of nonfiction. The too-little-known nonfiction *Once Upon the Little Big Horn* (1971) reconstructs the Sitting Bull–Custer conflict in alternate, interwoven sequences. *Cayuse Courage* (1970), about the 1847 slaying of missionary-doctor Marcus Whitman, his wife, and twelve other whites by aggrieved Cayuse tribesmen, rests largely upon Lampman's ability to make the Indians' behavior both plausible and understandable—and her ability to portray the historical Marcus and Narcissa Whitman, who were less than saintly or selfless, as not wholly obnoxious. The one fictional character, a Cayuse youth, throws light on both sides.

White Captives (1975), a more delicate undertaking, is also well executed. The question is why try: from the narrative of Olive Oatman, written by a minister after her release from five years of captivity by the Apaches and Mohaves (1851–56), Lampman has devised a scenario to account for what Olive and her younger sister (who died) perceived only as abuse. The result, invoking both known cultural differences and possible fictional elements, is a small tour de force—*if* one is willing, like Lampman, to assume the veracity of one of many "vehicles of Indian-hatred," to quote a historian of captivity narratives. In this instance Lampman was perhaps blind-sided by her skill at role-playing. But usually her insights and her talents worked in tandem, to the benefit of Indian-white understanding. BARBARA BADER

Lang, Andrew

BRITISH MAN OF LETTERS, EDITOR, AND RETELLER OF TRADITIONAL TALES, 1844-1912. At the brink of the twentieth century, *The Blue Fairy Book* (1889) appeared, the first of twelve fairy-tale books designated by color (blue, red, green, yellow, pink, gray, violet, crimson, brown, orange, olive, lilac) and edited by Andrew Lang. Publication of *The Blue Fairy Book* marked a return to respectability for the imaginative traditional tale, which had been largely rejected in Victorian England in favor of realistic, didactic children's stories. In *The Green Fairy Book* (1892), Lang explains respectfully to his child audience that though some adults believe fairy tales are harmful to children, Lang himself has faith that his readers "know very well how much is true and how much is only make-believe." Lang clearly aligns himself with those who support children's literature for delight rather than for instruction.

Immersed in NURSERY RHYMES and folktales as a young child, Lang took lifelong pleasure in this literature, a pleasure which took an academic turn when he discovered Homer and later studied classics at Oxford; his subsequent scholarly work in anthropology, particularly mythology, further developed the groundwork for his fairy-book series. *The Blue Fairy Book* brings together thirty-seven well-known tales, carefully chosen by Lang from the best of collectors such as the Brothers GRIMM from Germany and CHARLES PERRAULT from France.

Initially Lang had no intention of establishing a series, but the immense popularity of each volume seemed to demand another. Lang felt that his careful assembly of tales in *The Blue Fairy Book* was superior to subsequent volumes, but the harder-to-locate tales from around the world make the later books even more appealing to some. It is important to note, however, that Lang heavily edited tales from cultures outside of Western Europe to remove elements he believed offensive or boring to his young readers. Interspersed throughout the Lang volumes are tales with active heroines, possibly reflecting the influence of Lang's wife, Leonora Blanche Alleyne Lang, whom he credits with much of the translation and revision of the stories.

Illustration by H. J. Ford for "The Magician's Horse" from *The Grey Fairy Book* (1900), edited by Andrew Lang.

The irony of Lang's life and work is that although he wrote for a profession—literary criticism; fiction; poems; books and articles on anthropology, mythology, history, and travel; original stories for children, including *The World's Desire* (1890), a continuation of Homer's *Odyssey*—he is best recognized for the books he did *not* write. Although many people mistake Lang for an original recorder of tales, like the Grimm Brothers, his great contribution was, instead, overseeing the gathering of others' collected tales and providing for their wide dissemination. In *The Lilac Fairy Book* (1910), the last in the series, Lang laments that "in the nurseries of Europe and the United States of America" he is regarded "as having written the tales."

Children through the years have continued to delight in the original editions of Lang's fairy books, illustrated by H. J. Ford, as well as in other editions. Lang's collection *The Nursery Rhyme Book* (1897), illustrated by L. LESLIE BROOKE, and his literate retellings of the *Arabian Nights* (1898) and *Tales of Greece and Troy* (1907) also remain childhood favorites. Lang further enriched children's literature by discovering and encouraging other authors, including E. NESBIT, ROBERT LOUIS STEVENSON, RUDYARD KIPLING, and Arthur Conan Doyle. ❧

E.T.D.

LANGONE, JOHN

AMERICAN AUTHOR, B. 1929. John Langone writes about a variety of issues that are of interest to young adults, such as aging, death, mental illness, sexuality, AIDS, and the environment because he feels strongly that adolescents need information on these critical, too often neglected subjects. His journalistic background strongly influences his writing, instilling a desire for accuracy and clarity. His concise, direct style and objective presentation enable readers to look at complex problems and make their own judgments.

Langone grew up in Cambridge, Massachusetts, and although he spent time as a teenager working with family members in their science laboratories at Harvard University, he always knew he wanted to be a journalist, not a scientist. After receiving a B.S. from Boston University, he began his career first as a reporter and later as a medical editor. He was a Kennedy Fellow in medical ethics at Harvard University and then became a senior editor for the science magazine *Discover.* In addition, he has written more than fifteen nonfiction books for both adults and young adults.

From Langone's experience as a medical journalist came many books dealing with health-related subjects. Early on, he wrote about death (*Death Is a Noun: A View of the End of Life*, 1972) and mental illness (*Goodbye to Bedlam: Understanding Mental Illness and Retardation*, 1974), topics that were taboo at the time. In them Langone clearly defines and explores the material in an even-handed, unemotional manner. He covers controversial issues, including such topics as euthanasia and abortion, by rationally presenting the arguments on all sides of the subject.

In *Bombed, Buzzed, Smashed or . . . Sober: A Book about Alcohol* (1976), Langone presents a realistic and objective view of drinking. In addition to information about alcohol and its effects, he includes personal history about his alcoholic father and about his warm memories of his grandfather's wine cellar, which taken together helped him to draw a balanced conclusion about drinking.

Langone is well aware that he writes in an area of fast-breaking developments. He explains in his preface to *AIDS: The Facts* (1988) that "AIDS is a topic of motion," notwithstanding that writing under a deadline for publication seems to stop the subject and freeze it in time. Yet the book, an American Library Association Best Book for Young Adults, offers succinct, useful information about how the AIDS virus works, how AIDS is spread, and how it can be prevented and treated.

In addition to writing about medical issues, Langone has written about Antarctica, ethics, prejudice, and the environment. In *Our Endangered Earth: What We Can Do to Save It* (1992), Langone discusses a variety of problems plaguing the planet and follows each discussion with possible solutions. He presents each problem as a multifaceted challenge and the solutions as having both positive and negative ramifications.

In all his well-researched books, Langone works hard to present a balanced picture and to encourage his readers to think about the issues and ultimately to draw their own conclusions. ❧ P.R.

LANGSTAFF, JOHN

AMERICAN AUTHOR, B. 1920. It is small wonder that John Meredith Langstaff has devoted his life to song. Born on Christmas Eve, the night his parents led a procession of carolers through their Brooklyn Heights neighborhood each year, he grew up immersed in music, singing at home and as a choirboy at his church.

Langstaff has spent much of his career bringing music into the lives of children through teaching and writing. Though a classically trained singer who has soloed with symphonies around the world, most of the songs he shares in his books have communal significance. Appalachian folk songs, Scottish ballads, African American spirituals: These and other traditional forms of music delight him with their rich, sometimes ambiguous origins and ever-changing natures. He encourages children to compose their own verses to their favorite songs, as his three-year-old daughter did when she decided a "worm" going out to "squirm" belonged in the carol "On Christmas Day in the Morning." Such active participation, he believes, keeps a song alive and lively.

The introduction to his picture-book adaptation of *Frog Went A-Courtin'*, the 1956 Caldecott Medal winner, tells how this ballad changed as it was passed along—

"sometimes the grownups might forget the words, and the children would make up words they liked better"—so that it "belongs to all of us today." Langstaff has successfully transformed numerous songs into picture books, including the whimsical *Oh, A-Hunting We Will Go* (1974)—in which his hunters go after the likes of an armadillo and a brontosaurus—and the rousing *Ol' Dan Tucker* (1963).

In deciding which tunes and musical arrangements to use, Langstaff most often goes with the simplest. If guitar chords become a struggle, he suggests singing a capella because, as he notes in the introduction to *Jim Along, Josie* (1970), a folk-song collection he compiled with his wife, Nancy, not only were folk songs originally sung this way, but "above all, music should be fun." Visiting playgrounds across the United States with his daughter Carol to collect material for *Shimmy Shimmy Coke-Ca-Pop! A Collection of City Children's Street Games and Rhymes* (1973), he realized that while communal song and celebration play an ever smaller part in modern society, children still harbor their own vital folk culture.

Recognizing a need for communities to come together in celebration more often, Langstaff organized the "Christmas Revels" in 1957, a combination of singing, dancing, play-acting, and general merrymaking that harkens back to ancient festivals marking the solstice. Since then the Revels productions—one in winter, one in spring—have become much anticipated events in several East Coast cities. Like his songbooks—*The Christmas Revels Songbook* appeared in 1985—these productions draw from a wide variety of cultures and eras. And, characteristically, Langstaff doesn't expect his audiences to sit politely and listen. He expects them to sing. ❧ C.M.H.

Langton, Jane

American novelist, b. 1922. Jane Langton has been an inspired and inspiring author for three decades. Having immersed herself in the "layers of history" bordering her home near Walden Pond, she likes to write about contemporary children in real settings "littered with the past." Her fascination with Henry David Thoreau and the nineteenth-century transcendental movement provides the backdrop for such fantasies as *The Diamond in the Window* (1962), *The Astonishing Stereoscope* (1971), *The Fledgling* (1980), a Newbery Honor Book, and *The Fragile Flag* (1984).

Born in Boston, Massachusetts, Langton was intrigued by the colors of her crayons and paints at an early age. She vividly recalls the children's room of the library in Wilmington, Delaware, where her family moved in 1930. It was there that she plucked from the shelves works by Arthur Ransome, E. Nesbit, A. A. Milne, and Kenneth Grahame. Not only can she still quote passages from these authors, she credits them with fortuitously having taught her how to form sentences and dialogue, how to create characters and plot. Her interest in art, combined with a best-seller she had read about Marie Curie, determined her totally diverse choice of courses in astronomy and art history at Wellesley College. After her sophomore year, she transferred to the University of Michigan, where she met and married Bill Langton. Reading picture books to the first two of their three sons stirred up memories of her childhood crayons and paints, and Langton began to think about writing and illustrating a book of her own.

Langton's earliest attempts were "under the spell of those remembered English stories of gardens and kings and castles," but it was Eleanor Estes's Moffat stories that set her on the right path. "Reading about the Moffats," Langton has said, "I understood that children's books didn't have to be about princesses in imaginary countries. They could be about ordinary people here and now." This realization launched her first book, *The Majesty of Grace* (later retitled *Her Majesty, Grace Jones*), in 1961. After that she turned her attention primarily to writing for both children and adults, and she has been creating memorable American protagonists ever since. Langton's characters often find themselves in the midst of mysterious situations that transport them to other places and times. In *The Diamond in the Window,* Eleanor and Eddy Hall enter a frightening dream world to search for relatives who had disappeared and a lost treasure. With the help of a Canada goose in *The Fledgling,* Georgie Hall fulfills her longing to fly. And by carrying "the fragile flag" from Concord, Massachusetts, to Washington, D.C., Georgie tries to stop the president from launching his "peace" missile.

Good versus evil, right versus wrong, justice versus injustice—these values permeate Langton's books. Like the transcendentalists, her characters are willing to risk personal well-being in their pursuit of more idealistic goals. ❧ C.K.S.

Larrick, Nancy

American author and anthologist, b. 1910. Nancy Larrick has enjoyed an influential career focusing on children and education. Born in Winchester, Virginia, she attended Goucher College and received a master's degree from Columbia University and a doctorate in education from New York University. She began her career as a teacher in her hometown, then became educational director with the U.S. Treasury Department at the War Bond Division. Later, she was named editor of the weekly newsmagazines *Young America Readers* and education director for children's books at Random House. In addition, Larrick has held teaching and lecturing positions at numerous colleges and universities throughout the country. From 1956 to 1957 she served as president of the International Reading Association, of which she was a founder.

Larrick has been a frequent contributor to periodicals such as *Publishers Weekly, Saturday Review,* and *Parents' Magazine* and was editor of the *Reading Teacher* for two years. One of the most important of her scholarly works is *A Parent's Guide to Children's Reading,* originally published in 1958; its fifth edition, updated with feedback from readers and new titles, was published in 1982. Subtitled "How to Introduce Your Children to Books and the Joys of Reading," the book answers questions and addresses concerns relevant to today's youth and their varied interests and includes an extensive list of "Books They Like" as well as a final chapter guiding parents in selecting books for their children.

Larrick also edited more than twenty-two anthologies of POETRY for children and young people. *The Night of the Whippoorwill: Poems Selected by Nancy Larrick* (1992), illustrated by David Ray, was inspired by a memorable evening in which Larrick experienced the elusive song of the whippoorwill. Larrick's choices "celebrate the night," and readers find themselves pondering its mysteries, captured by Ray in dreamy, twilit illustrations. The images of night are expressed in dreams and pre-scientific personifications of natural elements; centuries-old fables are recounted in Larrick's own brief poems. Night was also Larrick's subject in the earlier volume, *When the Dark Comes Dancing: A Bedtime Poetry Book* (1983), illustrated by John Wallner. *Mice Are Nice: Poems Compiled by Nancy Larrick* (1990) is a lighthearted look at one of the smaller inhabitants of our world, often celebrated in children's books. Larrick compiled the "choicest poems about mice," and ED YOUNG's charcoal and pastel illustrations beautifully complement her selections. From country mouse to city mouse, naughty mouse to industrious mouse, all are represented in this captivating marriage of fine art and skillful text. A similar volume about another household creature, *Cats Are Cats* (1988), was also illustrated by Young. ❦ M.O'D.H.

LARSSON, CARL

SWEDISH ARTIST, 1853–1919. It is difficult to believe that the Swedish artist whose paintings are the embodiment of delightful family life could have grown up in the squalor of the slums of Stockholm. He wrote, "If I say that the people who lived in these houses were swine I am doing those animals an injustice. Misery, filth and vice . . . seethed and smoldered cozily." Larsson went to a "poor school," where, when he was thirteen, a teacher recognized his talent and encouraged him to attend Stockholm's Royal Academy of Fine Arts. When he was twenty-two, one of his paintings won the Royal Medal. Two years later, he moved to France; there he fell in love with another painter, whom he had met earlier in Stockholm. Within a few days Karin Bergöö and Larsson were engaged. Feeling holed up in his studio, Larsson switched from painting in oils to watercolors; he then joined the movement of "open air" painters. "I looked at Nature for the first time," he said. "I chucked the bizarre into the trash-heap . . . I have now given Nature a wide embrace, no matter how simple it may be. The pregnant, lusty earth is going to be the theme of my painting."

Larsson and Bergöö married in 1883, and his painting of her as a bride was the first in his lifelong series of family portraits. Carl Larsson had been in and out of France for the better part of eight years when it occurred to him: "Why in the name of all that's blue-green not paint Swedish nature in Sweden itself!" Then Karin's father left them a cottage—Little Hyttnäs—and at last they had a place to call home in Sweden. Scraping together what money they could, they took the tumbledown shack on a pile of slag and added a room here and there, built some furniture, and of course painted everywhere, creating a monument to everyday beauty.

This home at Sundborn is celebrated in Larsson's own book *Ett Hem* (1899). Lennart Rudström has written a biography for children based on Larsson's book: *A Home* (1968, trans. 1974) was a New York Times Best Illustrated Children's Book. Rudström's series continued with *A Farm* (1966, trans. 1967) and *A Family* (1979, trans. 1980). The books are all illustrated by Larsson's paintings of rooms in his home, the fields of the farm, the river, and the island. But most of all they are filled with his seven children.

"The first picture in the whole series is the one [of] Pontus, who . . . had been impertinent at the dinner table and been ordered out of the room." Larsson found the boy sulking in a corner and "noticed how the rebellious lad stood out sharply against the plain background." Most often the paintings are of happy, cherished children, in daily life or ritual festivals, articulated

Illustration by Carl Larsson from his book *Ett Hem (A Home)* (1899).

by Larsson's characteristic curling lines. It was as if by creating the home for them to live in, and then painting his children in this idyllic setting, he was banishing all the ghosts of his miserable childhood. And in doing so, he has given people the world over enduring images of home. ❧ J.A.J.

Lasky, Kathryn

American author, b. 1944. Kathryn Lasky is a prolific writer with a widely varied range of interests. Born in Indianapolis, Indiana, her gift as a "compulsive story maker" surfaced in private at an early age. It was only after sharing her work with her parents years later, and sensing their support, that she considered writing a reputable career. Since then her contributions to the literary world have included numerous books for children and adults.

Lasky is probably best known for her young adult novels and her juvenile nonfiction works, many of which are about traditional crafts and have been illustrated with photographs by her husband, Christopher Knight. In *The Weaver's Gift* (1981), for which she won a Boston Globe–Horn Book Award, the pair combine their talents to show how wool is sheared from sheep and made into a child's blanket and other products. *Dollmaker: The Eyelight and the Shadow* (1981) and *Puppeteer* (1986) similarly reveal the intricacies of these skills as well as the professional and artistic concerns of the craftspeople involved. Lasky and Knight themselves participated in the process of turning sap into maple syrup and recorded their experiences in *Sugaring Time* (1983), which was a Newbery Honor Book; the book was later adapted to a filmstrip. In order to gather research for *Dinosaur Dig* (1990), the entire Knight family—including children Maxwell and Meribah—left the comfort of their home in Cambridge, Massachusetts, to go on a fossil hunt in Montana. Lasky's capacity to draw readers into their journey stems from her eloquent storytelling knack. Along with Lasky and her family, readers stumble down rocky slopes, feel the blistering heat of the sun, and share the excitement of unearthing ancient bones.

History plays a major role in many of Lasky's novels. *The Night Journey* (1981) moves back and forth in time, between Nana Sashie's stirring tale of her Jewish family's perilous flight from czarist Russia and Rachel's comparatively commonplace life in present-day America. *Pageant* (1986), which begins on the eve of the 1960 presidential election, is the humorous-yet-poignant story about a Jewish teenager at an exclusive Christian school for girls. In *The Bone Wars* (1988), an orphan hired as a Harvard scout encounters adventure while on a search for fossils in the Badlands of Montana in the late 1800s. In each case, ethnic or societal challenges provide character conflict, and underlying all of these fictional accounts is fact. But Lasky wrote in *The Horn Book,* "I really do not care if readers remember a single fact. What I do hope is that they come away with a sense of joy—indeed celebration—about something they have sensed of the world in which they live." Conflict for her stalwart protagonists is ultimately resolved by their discovery of the importance of continuity in life. Recognition of the link between past and present is, in the end, the most essential element in finding contentment.

C.K.S.

Latham, Jean Lee

American author, b. 1902. Historical figures come vividly alive in Jean Lee Latham's biographical writing. The author was born and raised in Buckhannon, West Virginia, where she told her first stories to her brothers as they washed the dishes each evening. Latham began writing plays in high school and continued writing while attending West Virginia Wesleyan College, New York's Ithaca College, and Cornell University, where she earned a master's degree. She taught English and drama at the high-school and college levels before becoming editor-in-chief at the Dramatic Publishing Company. Weekends were spent writing stage and radio dramas, including many children's plays published under the name Julian Lee. During World War II, she worked for the U.S. Signal Corps, where she wrote and supervised a training course for radio inspectors.

Latham returned to freelance writing in 1945 and, following her brother's suggestion, concentrated on BIOGRAPHIES for children. *The Story of Eli Whitney* (1953) presents this historical figure in a tightly focused, clearly written story that is factual in content but fictional in style. This technique results in what might best be termed a biographical novel, in which basic historical facts are combined with invented dialogue and fabricated scenes. All of Latham's biographical works are written in this style, including the well-known *Carry On, Mr. Bowditch* (1955), which concerns an early nineteenth-century seaman and mathematical genius who made major advances in the science of navigation. Nathaniel Bowditch is not a widely known figure in the modern era, but Latham re-creates his life with such integrity and immediacy that readers become deeply engaged in the story of this self-educated man. Major and minor characters are equally well drawn, and Latham's dialogue is so realistic that one may forget that it was completely imagined by the author. Most impressively, a great deal of technical information about navigation and ocean travel is effortlessly blended into the novel, making challenging concepts accessible to the general reader without slowing down the plot.

After winning the Newbery Medal for this fine work, Latham published several more biographical novels with nautical themes, including *Drake, the Man They Called a Pirate* (1960), *Anchors Away: The Story of David Glasgow Farragut* (1968), and *Far Voyager: The Story of James Cook* (1970). In these books, as in *Retreat to Glory: The Story of Sam Houston* (1965) and *On Stage, Mr. Jefferson!* (1958), which concerns the nineteenth-century actor and dramatist Joseph Jefferson, the author presents involving, complex portraits of real-life figures. Unfortunately, her biographical stories for primary-grade readers, such as *Rachel Carson: Who Loved the Sea* (1973) and *Elizabeth Blackwell: Pioneer Woman Doctor* (1975), present their subjects in an idealized, simplistic manner, and are written in a lifeless, nearly monosyllabic style. Latham's other works for very young readers include retellings such as *Hop-o'-My-Thumb* and *Nutcracker* (both 1961), as well as a series of original tales, including *The Man Who Never Snoozed* (1961), which was also published in a Spanish edition that the author translated herself. Although Latham's purely fictional works are competently written, they lack the vigor of the novels in which she mixed historical fact with imagined dialogue and created superior works of biographical fiction. P.D.S.

Latino Children's Books

The current renaissance in books for and about Latino children is a source of joy and satisfaction to those who serve the reading needs of Latino young readers. In contrast to the situation just a few years ago, Latino/Hispanic/Spanish-speaking young readers can now select from an increasing number of insightful, well-written books—in English and Spanish—that will entertain them, inform them, and enrich their lives in numerous ways.

Perhaps this wonderful state of affairs is a result of the recent realization by publishers worldwide of the potentially vast market of Latinos and Spanish speakers in the United States and abroad. The statistics are difficult to ignore: The U.S. Hispanic-origin population is approaching 25 million—an almost 60 percent increase from the

1980 census. The U.S. Department of Education estimates that Hispanic children make up 73 percent of the two million children in the United States who have limited proficiency in English. In addition, it is important to note that Spanish is now the second language in the Western world—352 million Spanish speakers worldwide. These numbers, coupled with the fact that the field of children's literature in many Spanish-speaking countries is barely developing, may be the catalyst for the constantly improving selection in the quality and quantity of books for and about Latino children.

But numerous problems still persist. Foremost among these is the controversy surrounding bilingualism in the United States. On one hand are those who believe that the United States should be an English-only country. English-only supporters believe that Spanish (or other languages) may be spoken at home but that educating children in languages other than English results in cultural and linguistic barriers. On the other hand are numerous researchers and educators who believe that developing literacy in the first language can make a substantial contribution to literacy development in the second language. Moreover, supporters of bilingualism (and multilingualism) believe that free speech in the United States should not be limited to speakers of English.

Despite the controversy, the good news is the increasing number of books about Latinos now being published for young readers in English in the United States. The best of these possess all the qualities of well-written fiction—honesty, integrity, and imagination.

Foremost among these are the delightful stories, novels, and poems by two Latino authors, GARY SOTO and NICHOLASA MOHR. The trials and tribulations of growing up are beautifully depicted in Gary Soto's ever-popular collections of short stories, *Baseball in April and Other Stories* (1990) and *Local News* (1993). Mexican American neighborhoods come alive in Soto's heartfelt poems included in *A Fire in My Hands: A Book of Poems* (1990) and *Neighborhood Odes* (1992).

Family squabbles and misunderstandings with a strong Puerto Rican flavor are honestly portrayed in Nicholasa Mohr's sensitive novel *Going Home* (1986). Mohr's depictions of strong, lovable characters, beautiful warm personalities, and happy Puerto Rican families will be enjoyed by younger readers in *Felita* (1979). And adolescents will be moved by Mohr's collections of poignant short stories, *El Bronx Remembered: A Novella and Stories* (1975) and *In Nueva York* (1977), which reflect the sad, depressing, and difficult lives of many Puerto Ricans in New York City.

Selectors also will note the increasing number of nonfiction books that will satisfy young readers' curiosity about Latino people and cultures. The exemplary ones can answer questions on particular aspects of the Latino experience or can satisfy the reader's desire for broader knowledge.

The bad news is that many recently published books continue to provide a very limited, one-sided, or even incorrect view of Latinos. They either foster the stereotypes of fiestas, piñatas, and other "artsy-craftsy" views of Latino people or abound in sensationalistic information that distorts specific aspects of Latino cultures—for instance, the Aztec civilization is depicted as if the Aztecs were barbarians involved in gory practices of human sacrifice, disregarding their many wonderful achievements.

Another important issue that selectors should note about books in Spanish published in the United States is the inferior quality of the texts of many of the translations from English into Spanish as well as of works originally published in Spanish: incorrect lexical constructions, unclear phrases, and numerous grammatical, spelling, and typographical mistakes. Some U.S. publishers are indeed starting to pay attention to their Spanish publications; others, however, show a complete disregard for the Spanish language.

The most important feature regarding recently published books in Spanish for young readers is the increasing number of distinguished books that have a high potential for reader involvement or interest. These books—published either in the United States or abroad— can appeal to a wide variety of young readers' interests, backgrounds, and ages. Many are truly outstanding books that provide Spanish-speaking children and adolescents with a sense of wonder and satisfaction that is enjoyed by readers everywhere.

Some noteworthy authors from the Spanish-speaking world are the Argentine María Elena Walsh, whose delightful rhymes and amusing stories provide children with endless joy as they read about their treasure collections in *El reino del revés* (The upside down kingdom, 1989) or the King of the Compass who searches for his round flower in *El país de la geometría* (Geometryland) which is included in *El diablo inglés y otros cuentos* (The English devil and other stories, 1969). *El diablo inglés* tells about the English devils that appeared in Argentina in 1806.

Maribel Suárez and Laura Fernández, two young Mexican authors and illustrators, truly understand children's sensitivities and interests. *Miguel y el pastel* (Miguel and the cake, 1992) by Suárez shows how Miguel's baking experiences can result in a joyous, unexpected treat, and *Luis y su genio* (Luis and his genie,

1986) by Fernández is a delightfully honest story about a boy's real dilemma—should Luis do his math homework or enjoy a day with his genie?

The Venezuela author Daniel Bardot depicts children's fears about losing their first tooth in the amusing story *Un diente se mueve* (A loose tooth, 1990-1991), and Rosaura, a hen, enjoys a bicycle as a special birthday gift in *Rosaura en bicicleta* (A bicycle for Rosaura, 1990).

Children of all ages enjoy Violeta Denou's amusing, colorful illustrations of small children in contemporary Spanish settings. Her numerous, profusely illustrated stories thrive with the activities common to young children, such as *Teo en un día de fiesta* (Teo during a holiday, 1987), *La familia de Teo* (Teo's family, 1991), and *Vamos al zoo, Teo* (Let's go to the zoo, Teo, 1991).

There is no question that Latino young readers will benefit from the efforts of teachers, librarians, publishers, parents, and others who wish to entice them into the world of reading through insightful books that they can read and understand. The challenge, however, is to ignore long-standing myths that have discouraged Latino young readers from the pleasure of books and to concentrate on books—in English and Spanish—that appeal to the universal likes, wishes, dreams, and aspirations of children everywhere. ❧ ISABEL SCHON

Lattimore, Eleanor

American author and illustrator, 1904–1986. Eleanor Frances Lattimore spent most of her first sixteen years in Chinese villages, where she was taught at home by her college-professor father. She and her brother (the diplomat and China scholar Owen Lattimore) and three sisters were brought up in a ruling-class household and, according to Owen's memoirs, were not allowed to learn Chinese because their father felt that in conversing with the servants they would develop a servant's mentality. On a British ship to Europe, one of the younger girls was shocked to see "white men doing work." But Eleanor was artistic, and through drawing her surroundings she gained an intimate appreciation for Chinese village life. What she had observed in China made a lasting impression on her and was recorded in 1931 in her first book, *Little Pear: The Story of a Little Chinese Boy,* and in some of her other children's books.

After her family returned to the United States in 1920, she attended art schools for several years to become an illustrator. "But it is hard for a beginner to get stories to illustrate," she explained, "so I started writing in order to have something to illustrate." As it turned out, she was a talented writer as well as a strong illustrator, effortlessly writing *Little Pear* in a week. "I've never forgotten what it felt like to be a child," said Lattimore, and she was able to convey how it feels to be a child through her writing and art. Little Pear is described as "mischievous" by the author and "naughty" by his sisters and father. "But his mother said, 'He is very little; when he gets bigger he will be good; you wait and see. It doesn't matter if he is naughty now, sometimes!' And they all loved Little Pear very much." It is easy for a child of any time or place to identify with this boy, whose curiosity and five-year-old's logic lead him into trouble. He is the kind of child who needs to find out for himself that "green peaches are not good for children, after all." As he grows a little older in Lattimore's four books about him, he learns many lessons the hard way; for example, it is not a good idea to trade your baby brother for another baby brother.

Despite the inherent difficulties in accurately portraying another culture, especially with a background that could be called elitist, Lattimore respectfully shared extensive information about a life very alien to most of her readers at the same time revealing the commonality of child consciousness. She wrote at least fifty-seven books for children, most of which, with the exception of the "Little Pear" series, have faded into oblivion. All but one of her books—*Felicia* (1964), about a cat who becomes human—are realistic, simple stories with a similar format and main characters who are about six years old. On almost every page a detailed pen-and-ink drawing enhances the text. These episodic stories are suitable for a child who has been reading for a year or so and can also be successfully read to younger children. ❧ D.C.

Lauber, Patricia

American author, b. 1924. Patricia Lauber's nonfiction books provide a tour of the universe in time and space, making the wide natural world as real and immediate as opening one's eyes. Through her descriptions, readers see small organisms growing in the aftermath of a forest fire; bits and pieces of fossilized bone that reveal the nature of long-dead mammals; geologic formations on the moon and distant planets; and the drama of flowers living and dying in an ordinary backyard. In Lauber's skillful prose, earthquakes form the Rocky Mountains, dinosaurs prowl the forests, and seeds begin their journey of the cycle of life. Her powerful words spark the imagination to accept the reality found through a microscope or a telescope, and even the titles of her books suggest an awaiting ringside seat on the action.

Lauber's *Journey to the Planets* (1990) alerts readers to an orbit alteration that makes Neptune the farthermost planet until 1999. Seen from space, Earth, she writes, resembles a big blue marble, unusual in the amount of water available and the atmosphere retained by the planet's gravity. The fossilized records she describes in *Dinosaurs Walked Here* (1987) show the passage of huge creatures who left an earthly diary marked with questions for scientists to explain. Lauber herself answers some questions by describing life 75 million years ago in *Living with Dinosaurs* (1991), placing her readers in a world where Montana exists on the banks of an ocean, seabirds squabble in the dim light, earthquakes rock the ground, and the Great Plains rest at the bottom of an inland sea. She describes another world in *From Flower to Flower* (1987), in which industrious honeybees, bumblebees, bats, birds, moths, and butterflies contribute to growth by pollinating trees, flowers, and grasses. And further adventures take place in *Seeds: Pop, Stick, Glide* (1981), as tiny packages of life move through oceans (like the coconut), on an animal's fur (like burdock burrs), or on a fickle wind (like the dandelion) and so propagate their species. Even natural disaster takes on a new light when Lauber describes the 1988 Yellowstone National Park conflagration in *A Summer of Fire* (1988). Following the disaster, animal and plant life grew and rejuvenated. The thousands of acres blackened by summer fires produced lush green meadows in the fall and riotous colors and remarkable diversity in the spring.

Throughout her work, Lauber describes nature's eminently sensible way of maintaining order and promoting prosperity—a natural direction she has followed in her writing. Encouraged to express herself in words even as a child—"Being born wanting to write," she says—she began reading and later experimented with putting words on paper. Since 1945, her writing and editing have evolved into fiction and nonfiction books, essays, and short stories on topics ranging from natural history to humor, from cowboys to the forest, from outer space to backyard gardens. For myriad subjects, Lauber retains a childlike excitement about the world. "I like to stand and stare at things," she says, "to talk with people, and to read a lot." Along the way, this well-respected researcher and author travels, having fun and "doing research" for her next book. For over sixty books and almost fifty years, she has expressed her enjoyment of the world around her in ways that gently force thousands to experience the great and small, the distant and personal, the beauty and reality, of the world around us. ❧ B.C.

Lawson, Robert

American author and illustrator, 1892–1957. One of the most prolific and notable figures in American children's literature during the first half of the twentieth century, Robert Lawson achieved distinction both as an illustrator and as an author, winning the Caldecott Medal in 1941 for *They Were Strong and Good*, a picture-book tribute to his forebears, and the Newbery Medal in 1945 for *Rabbit Hill*, the story of an animal community and its relationship to the New Folks who come to the neighborhood. This feat, which no one has as yet duplicated, makes his work particularly significant in the context of American culture as well as in the history of publishing. Lawson's contributions ranged from endpapers for T. H. White's *Sword in the Stone* (1939) to illustrations for Ginn's *Mathematics for Success* (1952). By 1957, when the *Great Wheel* was published posthumously, he had written and illustrated twenty books and illustrated forty-six for other authors, in addition to the considerable number of drawings and etchings published before his success as a writer and illustrator for children.

Illustration by Robert Lawson from his book *Ben and Me* (1939).

Born in New York, Lawson grew up in New Jersey, graduated from art school in 1914 at the beginning of World War I, and worked as a freelance artist for several popular magazines, including *Harper's Weekly* and, after the war, *Delineator* and *Designer*. In 1917–18 he served in France with the 40th Engineers, Camouflage Section. In 1922, he married artist Marie Abrams, and in 1923, they moved to Westport, Connecticut, where they designed Christmas cards—one a day for three years—to pay off the mortgage. Like Dr. Seuss, Lawson worked extensively as a commercial artist. Then his collaboration with Munro Leaf for *The Story of Ferdinand* (1936), although not his first venture into children's books, brought him national and ultimately international recognition. In 1939, with *Ben and Me*, the story of Benjamin Franklin as told by the irreverent mouse Amos, he became a writer as well as an illustrator. Three more similarly iconoclastic historical fantasies followed, each featuring a talkative pet who presented an insider's view of its famous owner: *I Discover Columbus* (1941), *Mr. Revere and I* (1953), and *Captain Kidd's Cat* (1956). Of these three, *Revere*, closest in comic tone to *Ben and Me*, is probably the most successful, with the fewest unfortunate stereotypes.

As a writer, Lawson was essentially a raconteur, creating characters through dialogue rather than description. As an illustrator, he was, as critics have remarked, a traditionalist in composition and style. The demands of commercial art and his prize-winning work as an etcher made him a master of line—fluid and expressive—emphasizing his talent for visual storytelling characteristic of American art and attuned to American aesthetic sensibilities. He was so clearly of his times that he captured both its strengths and its weaknesses. His love of his country and its heroes is contagious, but his depictions of women and minorities are clichés. But then, most of his human characters were singularly one-dimensional, in contrast to such unforgettable animal creations as Ferdinand, perhaps the first flower child, and the varied denizens of Rabbit Hill, where there was indeed "enough for all." M.M.B.

Leaf, Munro

American author and illustrator, 1905–1976. During his forty-year career in children's literature, Munro Leaf wrote and illustrated nearly forty books. He is best known as the creator of *The Story of Ferdinand* (1936), a modern juvenile classic that has charmed children worldwide for more than half a century. Unforgettably paired with Robert Lawson's black-and-white etchings, Leaf's beloved tale of a peaceful Spanish bull ranks significantly in the field of American children's literature as the first picture book to be labeled subversive, as well as an exemplary, seamless union of text and art.

Born in Maryland, Leaf obtained degrees from the University of Maryland and Harvard University. He taught secondary school, then worked as editor and director for Frederick A. Stokes Company, a publishing firm in New York. His first children's book, *Grammar Can Be Fun* (1934), came about because he overheard a mother lecturing her young son about the inappropriateness of saying "ain't." Using stick figures, Leaf illustrated the didactic yet humorous text, which is meant to entertain as well as edify. *Grammar Can Be Fun* earned critics' acclaim; it also launched Leaf's "Can Be Fun" series, in which he wrote and illustrated nine equally successful titles whose topics range from health, safety, and manners to classroom subjects such as arithmetic, history, and science.

Leaf garnered universal fame when he wrote *The Story of Ferdinand*, his most successful and finest work. He penned the brief text on a yellow legal pad in less than an hour for Lawson, his illustrator friend. Viking's gifted juveniles editor, May Massee, immediately accepted the collaboration and, in the fall of 1936, published the story of gentle Ferdinand, a young bull in rural Spain who prefers solitude and smelling flowers to the company of his fellow ruffian bulls. When stung by a bee, Ferdinand's antics are misinterpreted by scouts as belligerent behavior, and they quickly transport him to Madrid for a bullfight. In the arena, sanguinary spectators watch a phalanx of banderilleros, picadors, and the chivalrous matador readying for battle. But once in the ring, Ferdinand sees only the floral decorations adorning the ladies' hair and tranquilly succumbs to his favorite pastime: smelling flowers. Taken home to his pasture, Ferdinand returns to the quietude and contentment that his special cork tree and flowers offer him.

Ferdinand created a global controversy overnight. *The Story of Ferdinand* was denigrated and banned in civil war–torn Spain, scorned and burned as propaganda by Hitler, and labeled in America as promoting fascism, anarchism, and communism. Others heralded the innocent bovine as an international emblem of pacifism. Leaf rebutted the attacks, stating that he wrote the story simply to amuse young children. With more than sixty foreign-language translations, the never-out-of-print title still enjoys widespread popularity. Leaf's ability to establish a strong character and comic situation with so few words is extraordinary; so, too, is Lawson's gift at interpreting Leaf's understated humor with spirited images that accurately reflect the emotions portrayed in the text. Both talents combine inseparably to craft a perfect picture book.

Leaf and Lawson's second collaboration, *Wee Gillis* (1938), also received wide critical acclaim. A small, orphaned lad who lived neither in the Highlands of Scotland nor in the Lowlands, but halfway between, Wee Gillis warms children's hearts just as humorously as Ferdinand does. Lawson's black-and-white etchings won the critics' hearts, too, and they named *Wee Gillis* as a 1939 Caldecott Honor Book. The third of Leaf's notable collaborations—this time with illustrator LUDWIG BEMELMANS—produced *Noodle* (1937), a happy, moral tale about a dachshund who, even after a visit from a magical wish-granting dog-fairy, judiciously chooses to remain exactly the same size and shape he is.

Leaf once said, "Early on in my writing career I realized that if one found some truths worth telling they should be told to the young in terms that were understandable to them." Few, if any, characters in American children's picture books are better understood or more loved by multitudes around the world than Ferdinand, Leaf's reluctant hero who likes "to sit just quietly and smell the flowers." ❧ S.L.S.

LEAR, EDWARD

ENGLISH WRITER OF NONSENSE, 1812–1888. Born the twentieth child of twenty children, Edward Lear experienced an early life of hardship, loss, and sadness. Even though Lear never had any formal artistic training, by the age of twenty his drawings of animals and birds were well enough known that he was invited by Lord Stanley to make drawings of the animals that were kept on his estate. It was here that Edward Lear first began writing his ingenious limericks to amuse the children of the household. Lear actually viewed himself as a landscape artist, and at the age of twenty-five set off on travels to pursue his artistic career. He described himself as a "Nartist who drew pigchers and vorx of hart."

Lear spent a good part of his early artistic career attempting to become established as a landscape artist and traveled extensively, returning to England to facilitate the publication of his verse, which in turn supported his travels. But success came from the publication of his nonsense verses and sketches, not his work as a landscape artist. *The Book of Nonsense* was published in 1845 under the pseudonym Derry Down Derry. It was a critical and commercial success and is commonly regarded as a pivotal work in children's literature. The continuing popularity of this first edition convinced him to publish under his own name in a 1861 reissue, followed by *Nonsense Songs* (1871), *More Nonsense* (1872), and *Book of Limericks* (1888). There have been numerous books containing individual story poems published since then, both with Lear's illustrations and those of other artists, including *The Owl and the Pussycat, Quangle Wangle's Hat, The Scroobious Pip, The Nonsense Alphabet,* and *The Jumblies.*

Illustration by Edward Lear for "The Dong with a Luminous Nose" from his book *Laughable Lyrics* (1877).

Edward Lear appeals as much to the children of the late twentieth century as he did to the children of his own day. Because of his unhappy childhood, Lear was determined to bring joy and amusement into children's lives. He saw nonsense as a means of escape from life's harsh realities. His poems avoided the strong didactic strain then common in books for children. Lear never moralized; his only purpose was entertainment. Some adults, however, objected to Lear's approach and to his use of misspellings and incorrect grammar as well, fearing his influence.

Lear applied his peculiar blend of artistic and poetic talent and playfulness to create a narrative as well as a visual form for his nonsense. His ingenuity in the invention of new words and sounds created an audible feast.

E was once a little eel
Eely
Weely
Peely
Eely
Twirly, Tweely
Little Eel.

Lear's alliteration and rhythmic patterns are flawless, and he was at his best when writing verse that combined invented words with conventional poetic meter. But to fully enjoy Lear's poems, one must see and appreciate the illustrations with which he accompanied them. Their humor enhanced by their spontaneity, many were apparently done as Lear recited his limericks to a roomful of children. The inventive yet spare ink drawings, rendered with just a few lines, make no attempt at realism in their depictions of fantastic beasts and birdlike humans.

Lear reveled in upsetting the expected social patterns, maintained that anything is possible, and advocated that all experience should be peppered with humor. MYRA COHN LIVINGSTON wrote of Lear: "And you laugh, and through that laughter grow and recognize that the nonsenses abiding in the real world can be overcome by your belief in yourself and your imagination." Lear's delightful humor, inventiveness, alliteration, and illustrations continue to entertain and tickle the imagination—just as Lear desired. ❧ A.I.

Lee, Dennis

CANADIAN POET, B. 1939. Dennis Lee is the author of children's POETRY books that are irreverent, contemporary, and thoroughly Canadian. Lee received both his B.A. and his M.A. in English from the University of Toronto and taught at the college level. He also co-founded the House of Anansi Press, Toronto. A successful poet for adult readers, Lee won the 1973 Governor-General's Award for poetry with his volume *Civil Elegies.*

When Lee's children were young, he entertained them with Mother Goose NURSERY RHYMES and noticed that while the children loved the rhymes, the way of life they described was archaic and unfamiliar. As a poet, it was very natural for Lee to experiment with bringing Mother Goose into the land of laundromats and hockey sticks. He started with short, bouncy rhymes for babies and with nonsense verse and was soon adding the wonderful place names of Canada. "Someday I'll go to Winnipeg to win a peg-leg pig" begins "Tongue Twister," and in "Rattlesnake Skipping Song," "Mississauga rattlesnakes eat brown bread. / Mississauga rattlesnakes fall down dead." Both of these poems appear in *Alligator Pie* (Toronto, 1974; Boston, 1975), illustrated by Frank Newfeld, which won the Canadian Library Association's Book of the Year Medal and was on the Hans Christian Andersen Honor List. Lee is a firm believer in the value of poetry that children create themselves, and in a postlude to *Alligator Pie* he suggests that the place-name poems are especially amenable to substitution and extension by children.

Nicholas Knock and Other People (Toronto, 1974; Boston, 1976) and *Garbage Delight* (Toronto, 1977; Boston, 1978) continued the Lee-Newfeld partnership. *Garbage Delight* is very appropriate for children beginning school: "Being Five" and "Half Way Dressed" are celebrations of everyday life, while the title poem and others such as "Bloody Bill" appeal to a child's pleasure in the outrageous. Lee's poetry is so playful and has such a strong rhythm that it is easy to chant and might easily be music. In fact, Lee has been a songwriter for the "Fraggle Rock" television program. ❧ P.H.

Lee, Mildred

AMERICAN AUTHOR, B. 1908. Mildred Lee was born in Blockton, Alabama, the daughter of a Baptist minister. She traveled throughout the South during her childhood, living in various small towns but always in close proximity to rural life. Lee attended Bessie Tift College, Troy Normal School, Columbia University, New York University, and the University of New Hampshire. Her earliest experience with the creative process came when she was stricken with scarlet fever at age seven. Quarantined in her father's care for the length of her recovery, Lee and her father created stories based on the paintings hanging in his study. Like many of her characters, Lee was deft at making up stories to entertain her younger siblings and for the pure pleasure of words.

Lee was thirty years old when her short stories were first published in *Redbook.* Lee's best writing depicts the South of her childhood. In an evocative style, she captures the slow, sultry quality of Southern life. Drawing heavily on impressions gathered as a child, Lee creates characters who are victims of adversity, often faced with poverty and isolation amid the grueling manual labor that makes up their lives. The struggle between accepting one's fate and trying to change it is epitomized in *The Rock and the Willow* (1963), a moving story that spans four years of Eenie Singleton's life, culminating in her graduation from high school. Eenie stubbornly holds fast to her dream of leaving Tired Creek for college and the wide world beyond. Despite seemingly insurmountable obstacles, namely, her father's disapproval and pressing family obligations after her mother's death, Eenie achieves her dream. In *The Skating Rink* (1969), Tuck's father, embittered by tragedy and business failures, resigns himself to a dismal future. Tuck seems similarly doomed, both by the firsthand memory of his mother's death and his consequent speech problems. Yet he works doggedly to break free of the specter of the past that forms his life. By achieving success as a skater, Tuck is empowered to make something of himself and change his fate. Although circumstances have hardened the father characters in both books, Lee evokes sympathy for these men by writing with a genuine warmth and sincerity.

All of Lee's books are characterized by a vivid sense of place, sensitively drawn. Lee has a keen ear for the rhythm of Southern speech; her dialogue is accurate and never falls into caricature. Less memorable, yet small gems in their own right, are *Honor Sands* (1966) and *Sycamore Year* (1974). Typically, characters in conflict drive the plots in Lee's novels. When the situations presented are less desperate and the characters are faced with little real adversity, Lee's narratives lose focus. In *Honor Sands,* the problem that affects average, well-adjusted Honor is self-imposed guilt about her resentment of her mother's overprotectiveness. *Sycamore Year* deals with teenage pregnancy, but the story does not supply sufficient dramatic tension to make the reader really care about Anna's plight. Despite the flaw in this novel, Lee consistently creates books that remain outstanding examples of writing for young adults.

M.O'D.H.

Le Guin, Ursula K.

AMERICAN WRITER, B. 1929. Ursula Kroeber Le Guin, daughter of the anthropologist Alfred L. Kroeber and the writer Theodora Kroeber, was born in Berkeley, California. After attending Radcliffe College and Columbia University, she spent a year as a Fulbright scholar in Paris, where she met and married the historian Charles A. Le Guin. She began publishing SCIENCE FICTION stories in the early 1960s and has since written numerous novels, short stories, plays, poems, and essays. Widely known for her innovative, award-winning science fiction for adults, Le Guin also wrote the intimate yet epic children's FANTASY, the Earthsea cycle, consisting of the original trilogy—*A Wizard of Earthsea* (1968), *The Tombs of Atuan* (1971), and *The Farthest Shore* (1972)—and a later volume, *Tehanu* (1990).

Earthsea—a collection of archipelagoes amid a constantly changing sea—is as fully developed a fantasy world as J. R. R. TOLKIEN's Middle Earth, with which it is often compared. Le Guin creates a setting both familiar and dreamlike, a pervasive metaphor for life as a perilous yet rewarding journey. Again like Tolkien, Le Guin strengthens readers' belief in and commitment to her created world by interweaving her plot with references to Earthsea's geography, languages, flora and fauna, histories, mythologies, traditions, and superstitions.

A Wizard of Earthsea tells the story of Ged's apprenticeship as a wizard. While still a boy on Gont, Ged reveals a gift for magery when his spell saves his village from Karg invaders, and, as a consequence, Ogion, the local mage, teaches him to read and write in the Old Speech, the language of magic and dragons. Ogion also tries to teach him the observant patience of mages, but Ged, restless and proud, wants more knowledge, faster. His training accelerates at the School of Wizards on Roke, where he learns such skills as shape-changing, summoning, and naming, but, still proud, Ged takes a dare and rends the fabric of being, unleashing an unknown beast from the realm of the dead to which his fate is thenceforth tied. Chastened and driven to conquer the protean, elusive beast, Ged earns his staff and leaves Roke. His subsequent journeys and adventures—including confrontations with a zombielike creature, a beguiling witch, and an ancient dragon—satisfyingly complete this bildungsroman, written with a wry nod toward the process of a legend in the making.

The Tombs of Atuan depicts Ged as a mature man, with clear goals and full control of his powers. The story focuses not on Ged, however, but on Tenar, a priestess of the Nameless Ones, powers ostensibly worshipped by the rulers of the warlike Kargs, but in reality the focus of an ancient cult in which few believe but which none dare to deny. Consecrated to the Nameless Ones from early childhood, Tenar has been stripped of her name, her past, and any future. She is Arha, the Eaten One, the ever-reincarnated priestess of the Tombs, living only for the endless repetition of the cult's dark, arid rites, which she has killed to uphold. Ged interrupts this sentence of death in life. Searching for the lost fragment of the ring of Erreth-Akbe, a talisman of peace that if made whole would presage the return of a King to Earthsea, Ged finds his way into the forbidden labyrinths of the Nameless Ones. Trapped by Arha, Ged breaks through her indoctrination and, using his genius for discovering true names, returns Tenar to Arha. Only then, acting together, can they then fulfill his quest.

The Farthest Shore takes Ged beyond the limits of his powers. The springs of magery are running dry, and a seductive, cruel decadence is spreading from the islands of the outer reaches toward the heart of Earthsea. Ged, now Archmage of Roke, undertakes a final journey to discover and eliminate the source of the contagion. He takes with him a young man, Arren, Prince of Enlad, of the lineage of the old kings, and together through many trials of body and spirit they achieve a greater end than they had hoped: Earthsea is restored to wholeness and peace, and a king is restored to the long-empty throne.

The trilogy thus forms an elastic cycle, combining epic deeds and human qualities. In it we see a young hero grow to manhood as perhaps the greatest of Earthsea's many great mages; we see unfolded the most significant achievement of his prime; and we see him complete his life's work, both as a man and as a mage. Further, each volume describes Ged's exploration of a distinct realm of being and knowledge: the personal in *A Wizard of Earthsea;* the social in *The Tombs of Atuan;* and the spiritual in *The Farthest Shore.* Le Guin has described the three themes as coming of age, sexuality, and death, further underscoring the completeness of the whole. Successfully combining Jungian concepts, such as the shadow, and concepts from Eastern philosophy, such as equilibrium of opposing forces, with the Western tradition of the hero-tale, Le Guin creates a fantasy epic with contemporary yet enduring resonance.

This self-containment makes all the more surprising the author's decision to return to Earthsea in *Tehanu.* Set contemporaneously with the events in *The Farthest Shore, Tehanu* provides a closer look at the nature and consequences of the dissolution of civilizing bonds chronicled there. Many years after the events in *The Tombs of Atuan,* Tenar is a widow living alone on a farm on Gont. Accepted and yet always a Karg stranger, she is immediately drawn to a severely abused and abandoned young girl and takes her into her home. Thus embroiled in the ebb and flow of power and evil that mark a lawless time, Tenar struggles to protect and nurture first her damaged young charge, Tehanu; later, the weary and emptied Ged who has returned to find oblivion on Gont; and ultimately, herself. The book's focus on sexuality, cruelty, and violence; the closely paced plot; and the use of Tenar's thoughts to establish point of view, all clearly differentiate it from the three earlier, more sweeping and traditional fantasy volumes. *Tehanu* tells a fascinating story, built on the compelling theme of differences between men's and women's ways of being and knowing and the possibility of somehow, someday synthesizing these, but it is a story with more appeal and meaning for adults than for children. *Tehanu* disturbs rather than completes the reader's understanding—and enjoyment—of the Earthsea cycle.

Le Guin's other books for children include a realistic novel for young adults, *Very Far Away from Anywhere Else* (1976), and, for younger readers, two brief, dreamlike tales, *Catwings* (1988) and *Catwings Return* (1989). In *A Ride on the Red Mare's Back* (1992) an Andersen-like fairy tale, a brave and resourceful young girl rescues her brother from trolls, with the help of a magical red mare lovingly carved and painted for her by her father. Simple objects—bread, knitting needles, woolen scarf, each made by her for others or by others for her—and the homely virtues of perseverance and kindness also help her in her quest. Through this skillful union of the fruits of simple domestic labor with the strength of family love, Le Guin creates a story from the magic of making and doing for the benefit of others, a story she told first and most satisfyingly in the Earthsea cycle. ❧ SUSAN BOULANGER

LEMIEUX, MICHÈLE

CANADIAN ILLUSTRATOR AND AUTHOR, B. 1955. In one of Michèle Lemieux's earliest PICTURE BOOKS—*What's That Noise?* (1984)—she tells the story of a bear who discovers that the mysterious sound he keeps hearing is his own heart. The subject is a fitting one for Lemieux, as she is an artist who searches for—and finds—the heart of every book she creates.

Lemieux was born in Quebec City and was educated there and in Montreal, where she studied graphic design and fine arts. Upon graduation, she secured a contract with a Quebec publisher to illustrate three picture books. In 1978 she moved to Germany, where three picture books with her illustrations were published.

In 1982 Lemieux returned to Quebec, where, on the strength of her European credentials, composer Gian Carlo Menotti asked her to illustrate a picture-book version of his opera *Amahl and the Night Visitors* (1986). Lemieux's glowing watercolors, successfully evoking the atmosphere of Palestine at the time of Christ's birth, attracted the favorable attention of reviewers across North America and was an American Library Association Notable Book. The success of *Amahl* led to the publication in English of two of Lemieux's German books, *What's That Noise?,* which she also wrote, and *Winter Magic* (1984), written by Eveline Hasler.

In 1988, Lemieux published an illustrated collection of German songs; in 1990, these illustrations were adapted to a collection of English-language children's poems: *Voices on the Wind: Poems for All Seasons,* selected by David Booth. Painted in acrylics, *Voices on the Wind,* a Canadian Library Association Notable Book, is filled with playful vignettes that mix everyday realism with a magical dream world.

In a trio of books created in the late 1980s and early 1990s, Lemieux has continued to reveal her dimensions as an artist. For *A Gift from Saint Francis* (1989), written by JOANNA COLE, Lemieux faithfully emulated Italian art from the late Medieval and early Renaissance periods in oil paintings featuring warm, rich hues. She has said, "I really learned a lot from that book—painting, organizing space and composition in an artwork, and this helped me . . . for *Peter and the Wolf,* which is for me one step nearer to what I'm going to."

Indeed, *Peter and the Wolf* (1991), inspired by Sergei Prokofiev's classical work, was another breakthrough for Lemieux. Here she looked to Russian folk art for inspiration, shifting her palette from warm Mediterranean colors to cooler hues. Juxtaposing complementary colors, Lemieux created a new tension in her work; at the same time, she further experimented with space, utilizing aerial views and oblique angles to arrest the viewer's gaze.

In the *Pied Piper of Hamelin* (1993), Lemieux charted yet another course. For this thirteenth-century German tale, her choices of peppermint greens, salmon pinks, and lemon yellows are at first surprising, as are her streamlined buildings, which have an almost modular, modern look. Yet these illustrations, like those in *St. Francis,* have solid foundations in later Medieval and early Renaissance paintings.

Lemieux is an artist who has chosen picture books as her medium. For her fans—and they come in all ages—watching her move step by step toward "what I'm going to" is both challenging and exciting. M.B.

L'Engle, Madeleine

American author, b. 1918. Madeleine L'Engle's life is as interesting and inspiring as her books—if not more so. From the high points of winning the Newbery Medal for *A Wrinkle in Time* (1962), garnering a Newbery Honor mention for *A Ring of Endless Light* (1980), and obtaining her current position as writer in residence at the Cathedral of St. John the Divine (Episcopal) in New York City through the lows of her "dry decade," when nothing she wrote was accepted for publication, and the wrenching agony of watching her beloved husband of forty years die from cancer, L'Engle has struggled with her often conflicting roles of wife, mother, artist, and Christian. She has also struggled to place herself in time, both in Kronos—eternal time, in which God moves—and Chairos, "clock time," in which man lives. It is from these struggles that her work derives, and it has been a fruitful struggle: nearly twenty books for children and nineteen for adults, including essays, poetry, fiction, and two plays.

L'Engle began the struggle early, writing her first story at age six. "All about a little 'grul,'" she says, "who lived in a cloud," something that could be said of many of her time-traveling, space-bending, star-talking protagonists in the books she would write as an adult. L'Engle led an isolated, if somewhat romantic, existence as the only child of sophisticated, older parents. Her father had been gassed during a stint as a war correspondent during the First World War and subsequently "spent eighteen years coughing his life away." Her mother spent most of L'Engle's childhood caring for her failing father. L'Engle says she felt very loved by her parents but completely apart from their world. She created her own world as an escape and a solace, which was especially important during a series of painful school experiences—first at a "really repulsive New York–type school," where she was labeled "the unpopular one," then at a boarding school in England, where she was sent after her father's ill health forced the family to relocate to the Swiss Alps. "It was absolutely splendidly horrible," she writes. "I still get books out of it." Indeed, her awkward, intense, oddly brilliant heroines are not unlike the author's descriptions of herself. Faith and family are two important themes in her work, as they are in her life: "My own lonely childhood is very likely the reason why family is so important to me—my own present family of children and grandchildren and the families in my stories."

Her first book to be published to wide acclaim was *Meet the Austins* (1960), a family story in the classic mold: The large, noisy, happy Austin family teaches unhappy orphan Maggie the meaning of life and love. This book drew heavily on L'Engle's own life at Crosswicks, the Connecticut country home where she and her husband, actor Hugh Franklin, and their three children retreated in the 1950s, the period the author terms her dry decade. After modest initial success as a young author fresh out of Smith College—three books and one play published—she was unable to get one piece published for nearly ten years: "The only thing I was selling during this decade was stuff from the store," the store being the general store she and her husband bought, renovated, and ran to support their young family. The publication of *Meet the Austins* ended the drought and established two of her three most important themes: a distinctly spiritual element in the lives of her protagonists, explicitly Christian in most of her books, and a strong belief in the healing power of love, most significantly the love between family members.

The third element in L'Engle's thematic trinity, the world of scientists and scientific exploration, makes its appearance in L'Engle's next work, *A Wrinkle in Time,* in which a physicist's large, cozy family battles Evil in order to save their father and their world. Myopic, coltish Meg Murry and her precocious little brother Charles Wallace join forces with three delightful entities—Mrs. Whatsit, Mrs. Who, and Mrs. Which—to save their scientist-father from the clutches of IT, a giant pulsating brain that wishes to control all thought and action. At once a science-fiction story, a philosophical meditation on the nature of Evil and Love, and a coming-of-age novel, *Wrinkle* broke new ground in what was considered appropriate for young readers. Rejected by several publishers for being too complex, this title has amply proven L'Engle's belief that "children are excited by new ideas" and has been credited with bringing SCIENCE FICTION into the mainstream of children's literature. This is L'Engle's best work, with deft, appealing characterizations and a well-crafted plot balancing the strongly stated thematic elements that often overwhelm her later work. *Wrinkle* has received the highest critical acclaim in a career that has been liberally rewarded with praise and condemnation. In the "Time Fantasy" series L'Engle follows the Murry family, most notably in *A Wind in the Door* (1973) and *A Swiftly Tilting Planet* (1978), which won the American Book Award. All of the Murry family books have elements of FANTASY and science fiction to link them, as well as an apocalyptic struggle between Good and Evil. The Austin family saga, on the other hand, which the author has continued in books such as *The Moon by Night* (1963) and *The Young Unicorns* (1968), are reality-based, coming-of-age novels in which the adolescent protagonist is tempted by the seductive wiles of cynicism and despair—often personified by a love interest—but is ultimately won over to the side of good by the warmth and decency the Austins exhibit.

It is L'Engle's thematic concerns that are her forte, as well as the aspect of her work that has brought on the most controversy. Her ability to give face and voice to such abstract ideas as Love, Good, Despair, and Evil and to make the struggle among them believable in her characters' lives are what make her work timeless and important to generations of readers. L'Engle understands that it is of these things that adolescent angst is made, not simply immediate concerns such as pregnancy, AIDS, and gang violence. L'Engle places her characters and her readers in a larger context, one in which individual actions have universal implications, or what the author calls "the butterfly effect": the death of a butterfly has an effect in a galaxy light-years away. But it is this dominating thematic element in her work that has caused some critics to term her books didactic and the religious implications of her themes that have caused some schools to remove her books from library shelves for their "anti-Christian" message. For while some may find her overt Christianity an artistic detriment, fundamentalist Christian groups have found it "contrary to Biblical teaching." For the author, who has several books of essays published by Christian presses, this sort of thing is nonsensical: "People are reading with a list of words, they're not reading for content." Well into her fourth decade of writing, L'Engle is still going strong, continuing to "listen to her work" and write about what she most strongly believes in: a universe of randomness and chance but one in which everything is completely interdependent. "To hurt a butterfly," she says, "is to shake the universe." ❧ SARAH GUILLE KVILHAUG

LENSKI, LOIS

AMERICAN AUTHOR AND ILLUSTRATOR, 1893–1974. One of the most prominent and prolific writers for children in the twentieth century, Lois Lenski is highly acclaimed for her authentic, perceptive interpretations of American childhood. Lenski was born in Springfield, Ohio, and grew up in nearby Anna, a small farming community. She received a degree in education at Ohio State University but decided to follow her dream of becoming an artist. After studies at New York's Art Students League and London's Westminster School of Art, she began working as an illustrator. In addition to illustrating all of her own work, she has illustrated books by KENNETH GRAHAME, CORNELIA MEIGS, Watty Piper, MAUD HART LOVELACE, and CLYDE ROBERT BULLA.

Skipping Village (1927) and *A Little Girl of Nineteen Hundred* (1928), the first books Lenski both wrote and illustrated, drew on her childhood experiences but met with little critical success. Lenski's son Stephen was the inspiration for the popular and enduring series of picture books about Mr. Small. In *The Little Auto* (1934), Mr. Small oils his car, pumps the tires, and drives with careful attention to the traffic rules. The matter-of-fact presentation of information and the simple two-color washed line drawings provide the young child with the reassuring familiarity of everyday experiences. Accessible, accurate explanation of vehicles, as in *The Little Train* (1940), or occupations, as in *Policeman Small* (1962), characterize all the Mr. Small stories. Eventually, Lenski began to view herself more as an author who illustrated her own books than as an artist or painter. Although she produced books for the preschool through early teenage audience, historical and regional fiction aimed at the upper-middle grades comprise the bulk of her writing. Both genres share the plain narrative style and authenticity of the Newbery Honor recipient *Indian Captive: The Story of Mary Jemison* (1941), a book that explores the conflict between the Indians' and the settlers' way of life.

The regional stories, however, are Lenski's most distinguished contribution to children's literature. In these, she often focused on disadvantaged and working-class families. Believing that firsthand experience was necessary to write serious regional fiction, she traveled around the country, living, working with, and sketching those about whom she wrote. In the foreword to *Strawberry Girl* (1945), a story about Crackers in the Florida backwoods and a Newbery Medal winner, Lenski wrote, "I am trying to present vivid, sympathetic pictures of the real life of different localities . . . we need . . . to know and understand people different from ourselves." *Blue Ridge Billy* (1946) concerns the Appalachian people of North Carolina, Arkansas sharecroppers are depicted in *Cotton in My Sack* (1949), and *Prairie School* (1951) details life's trials on a snowbound South Dakota prairie.

While many of the stories are episodic and predictable, both text and plentiful soft-pencil sketches convey the distinctive flavor and dialect of a locale. Unwaveringly honest, these realistic stories are steeped in respect for cultural differences and present to children a richly diverse picture of America.

Lenski received the Regina Medal and the University of Southern Mississippi Medallion for her work, but fewer than fifteen of her more than one hundred books remain in print. ❧ C.L.S.

Lent, Blair

Author and illustrator, b. 1930. Self-described as "fat and clumsy at sports," Blair Lent, an only child in a family of limited means, grew up in an affluent suburb of Boston. He felt himself an outsider in a town where, he has stated, "money, appearance, and athletic prowess were considered one's most important attributes." Lent's father, an engineering student, shared his love of literature and books with his young son, and this love of story provided Lent with a healthy escape from the peer rejection he experienced. Lent was soon writing and illustrating his own stories.

"When I look back on my childhood," Lent wrote for an autobiographical sketch, "I realize that although I was unhappy growing up in that atmosphere, it was partly the reaction against it that gave me the determination to stick with what I really wanted to do. And without this determination, I might not be writing and illustrating today." Upon graduation from high school, Lent briefly studied economics, then worked at odd jobs, which included a stint as a short-order cook. He decided to act on his dreams and enrolled in the Boston Museum School, where he studied graphics and design. Graduating with honors in 1953, he received a traveling scholarship for additional study in Europe. When he returned to Boston, Lent took a position as a window-dresser in a department store after an unsuccessful search for a job as a graphic designer. He eventually landed a job as a creative designer in a major Boston advertising firm. His day job increased his knowledge of design and provided him with the money to support his real passion, writing and illustrating picture books. His hard work and dedication paid off, for in 1964, *Pistachio,* a book he wrote and illustrated, and *The Wave,* a Japanese folktale adapted by Margaret Hodges, which he illustrated, were published. Pistachio is an unusually talented green cow who wants nothing more than the taste of fresh country hay, while her beloved friend, Waldo, yearns for the excitement of a circus life. Overcoming rejection, both eventually get their wishes. *The Wave* is a powerful story in words and pictures. Lent used a limited palette of rich siennas, warm ochers, and cool blacks and grays to illustrate the tale of an old farmer who burns his rice fields to warn his village of an oncoming tidal wave. The illustrations were made from prints from cardboard cuts; Lent studied them and then he selected the best sections from numerous prints to cut and piece together for his finished artwork. Lent feels cardboard is a perfect medium for the illustrator because it creates unusual textures, and since the cardboard is less resistant than wood or linoleum, ideas can be realized much sooner. He also enjoys working with cardboard because, as a child, it was the material he used most often to create his own toys.

Lent went on to produce a number of picture books, including *Tikki Tikki Tembo* (1968), a Chinese folktale retold by Arlene Mosel. Lent's page design, his use of white space, and choice of viewpoint and type placement are as important to the pacing of the story as Mosel's crisp prose. When younger brother, Chang, runs for help to save his older brother from drowning in

Illustration by Blair Lent from his book *Pistachio* (1964).

a well, Lent's illustrations of the distances Chang travels are the visual equivalent of the older brother's dangerously long name.

Always taking creative risks, he produced illustrations that became less graphic and more drawn, as he experimented with various mediums from pen-and-ink to wash drawings and full-color paintings. His Caldecott Medal–winning book, *The Funny Little Woman* (1972) by Arlene Mosel, was produced after many years of such experimenting. Lent has said about his work, "Books were important to me as a child, and it is for that little boy that I am working. I can never know other children's innermost thoughts as well as I can remember my own." ❧ M.B.B.

Leodhas, Sorche Nic

See Nic Leodhas, Sorche.

Lester, Julius

American author, b. 1939. Julius Lester honors the rich, varied, sometimes sad history of African Americans in his prose for children. His award-winning books include nonfiction, story collections, and volumes of folktales that reflect the traditions of the author's heritage. Although he later embraced the Judaic religion, as related in his memoir, *Lovesong: Becoming a Jew* (1988), the author was the son of a Methodist minister. Born in St. Louis, Missouri, he was raised in Kansas City, Kansas, and Nashville, Tennessee, where he attended Fisk University. In addition to writing, Lester has worked as a musician, an editor, a college professor, and a radio and television host. His earliest adult books, including *Look Out, Whitey! Black Power's Gon' Get Your Mama!* (1968), reflect the more radical aspects of the civil rights movement, although the author never considered himself a militant figure.

Lester's editor suggested that he try writing for children, and his first major effort, *To Be a Slave* (1968), was selected as a Newbery Honor Book and remains a towering achievement in children's literature. Composed mostly of first-person narratives by former slaves that were collected by the Federal Writers' Project, the volume provides a multifaceted, painful overview of the slavery experience and includes recollections of the journey from Africa to America, life on the plantations, slave insurrections, and the United States after emancipation. Lester's accompanying text provides continuity and places the material in historical perspective.

Although he has written one adult novel, *Do Lord Remember Me* (1985), Lester utilizes the short-story format in writing fiction for young readers. His stories are based on actual incidents and characters from the slavery era, but he does not write about widely known historical figures, preferring to tell the stories of ordinary people who have done great things. *Long Journey Home: Stories from Black History* (1972) contains six fictional tales suggested by interviews and previously published accounts. "Satan on My Track" is the story of a rambling blues musician who observes how slaves are kept in servitude even after emancipation; "The Man Who Was a Horse" relates the feelings of an ex-slave cowboy as he captures a herd of wild mustangs. The title story is a monologue concerning dozens of slaves who walk into the ocean hoping they will be carried home by their gods, a powerful incident diluted by the negativity of the narrator. A later volume of stories, *This Strange New Feeling* (1982), concerns three eighteenth-century African American couples who fall in love; the book works well as both historical and romantic fiction.

Lester has also received acclaim for retelling African American folktales, including *The Knee-High Man and Other Tales* (1972) and *How Many Spots Does a Leopard Have and Other Tales* (1989), which also contains some Jewish legends. His volumes about Brer Rabbit, the well-known trickster from African American folklore, *The Tales of Uncle Remus: The Adventures of Brer Rabbit* (1987), *More Tales of Uncle Remus: Further Adventures of Brer Rabbit, His Friends, Enemies, and Others* (1988), and *Further Tales of Uncle Remus: The Misadventures of Brer Rabbit, Brer Fox, Brer Wolf, the Doodang, and Other Creatures* (1990) are notable for their humor, breezy storytelling, and distinctive use of language and are especially enjoyable when read aloud. In these folktales, as in all his works, Lester records and celebrates African American history for today's young readers. ❧ P.D.S.

Lewin, Ted

American artist, b. 1935. Ted Lewin was born in Buffalo, New York, and received a bachelor of fine arts degree from the Pratt Institute of Art, where he was awarded the Dean's Medal at his graduation in 1956. A freelance illustrator since then, he supplemented his income by wrestling professionally until 1965. He has illustrated more than seventy books by other authors and has written and illustrated three books for the series

"World within a World" entitled *Everglades* (1976), *Baja* (1978), and *Pribilofs* (1980).

Lewin describes himself as an "artist-illustrator" and notes that his writing grew as a result of his interest in the natural world. He is an ardent environmentalist and conservationist who travels "around the world for graphic and literary material." In 1978 Lewin presented a one-man exhibit at the Laboratory of Ornithology at Cornell University. Lewin's regard for birds is demonstrated in *Listen to the Crows* (1976) by LAURENCE PRINGLE, an informative book about the language of crows, and *Bermuda Petrel: The Bird That Would Not Die* (1981) by Francine Jacobs, the fascinating story of an ancient bird's near extinction. Both are enhanced by Lewin's sympathetic black-and-white drawings. In a different genre, Lewin's meticulously drawn watercolors amplify and enrich JANE YOLEN's collection of poetry, *Bird Watch* (1990).

Many of the books Lewin has illustrated fall into the middle reader or young adult categories, and his illustrations are used to punctuate important events in the story. *Grandma Didn't Wave Back* (1972) by Rose Blue is a moving story about advancing senility. In black-and-white drawings that have a density reminiscent of watercolors, Lewin conveys emotion through the expressive faces detailed on Blue's characters. Similarly, Lewin's subtle gradations of black-and-white complement Rita Micklish's novel about an interracial friendship, *Sugar Bee* (1972), and Brenda Seabrooke's *Judy Scuppernong* (1990), a series of poetic narratives highlighted by Lewin's quirky illustrations from various points of view. LEON GARFIELD's *Young Nick and Jubilee* (1989) allows Lewin to experiment with historical illustration. His accurate, finely detailed costumes are in perfect harmony with this Dickensian adventure story.

Two books, both coauthored by FLORENCE PARRY HEIDE and Judith Heide Gilliland, spotlight the strength and beauty of Lewin's talent. *The Day of Ahmed's Secret* (1990) takes place in the busy streets of Cairo, which Lewin captures in all their movement and color with intense blues, tones of white, and his renderings of colorful mosaics. *Sami and the Time of the Troubles* (1992) is a story set in modern Beirut. Lewin juxtaposes larger-than-life, vibrant watercolors portraying the colorful carpets, flowers, and lush bounty of prewar Beirut with the devastation, crumbling buildings, and twisted metal wrought by repeated bombings. These foreign streets come alive in Lewin's capable hands, yet the reader perceives a stillness, a tranquillity in the face of much commotion that captures the essence of both cultures.

Lewin is a talented artist, fortunate in his ability to create luminous works of art that form a perfect complement to an author's text, regardless of format, subject, or medium. ♠ M.O'D.H.

LEWIS, C. S.

BRITISH AUTHOR OF CHILDREN'S FANTASY NOVELS, 1898–1963. A scholar and teacher at Oxford and Cambridge in England, Clive Staples Lewis wrote fiction, science fiction, poetry, literary criticism, and books of Christian apologia. It was his seven FANTASY books for children, however, that made him one of the most successful and well-loved writers of the twentieth century. Widely read, the Chronicles of Narnia are considered CLASSICS of children's literature.

Growing up in Northern Ireland, Lewis and his brother were surrounded by books and even wrote and illustrated their own stories about invented lands. The citizens of Animal-Land, Lewis's imaginary world, were chivalrous animals—forerunners of his Narnian Talking Beasts. In the autobiography *Surprised by Joy* (1955), which describes his conversion to Christianity, Lewis talks about influential books from his early life, and it is the authors GEORGE MACDONALD and E. NESBIT whose impact is most clearly seen in his children's books.

In the first book in the "Narnia" series, *The Lion, the Witch and the Wardrobe* (1950), four siblings find their way into another world through a magic wardrobe. Peter, Susan, Edmund, and Lucy meet Aslan, the lion who has come to free the land of Narnia from the evil spell of the White Witch. Aslan sacrifices his life to save Edmund after the boy is lured into treachery by the Witch, but the noble lion comes back to life again through an older magic; after the Witch is defeated, the four children are crowned kings and queens of Narnia. When they return to England after many Narnian years, they find that only minutes have passed in their own time. The book received the Lewis Carroll Shelf Award in 1962.

Prince Caspian (1951) relates the foursome's adventures on their second visit to Narnia, where they learn that hundreds of years have gone by since they were last there. Prince Caspian has used a magic horn to call the long-ago rulers to help him take Narnia back from the Telmarines and restore it to the Old Narnians—the Fauns, Centaurs, Talking Beasts, and others. With Aslan's help, Caspian's evil uncle, King Miraz, is defeated, and the children again return home.

Edmund and Lucy, along with their spoiled cousin Eustace, return to Narnia and find themselves on board a ship with Caspian in *The Voyage of the "Dawn Treader"* (1952). They help King Caspian search for the seven lords whom his evil uncle had sent away, sharing several adventures before going home, including one involving a dragon that changes Eustace forever.

In *The Silver Chair* (1953), Eustace, along with his classmate Jill, is whisked away to Narnia, called by Aslan to help the aging King Caspian find his missing son. Guided by a pessimistic but likable creature known as a Marsh-wiggle, Jill and Eustace brave giants and the cold Northern winter to free Prince Rilian and hundreds of gnomes enchanted by the evil Emerald Witch. Aslan then returns the children to their school in a dramatic, satisfying ending.

The story told in *The Horse and His Boy* (1954) takes place during the long reign of Peter, Susan, Edmund, and Lucy, beloved Narnian rulers. In the land of Calormen, a boy named Shasta meets Bree, a Talking Horse originally from Narnia, and together they decide to run away to that land. Joined by Hwin, another Talking Horse, and a girl named Aravis, the group reaches its destination—with Aslan's help—in time to warn the Narnians of an impending attack, after which Shasta learns he is of Narnian royal blood.

The creation of Narnia is described in *The Magician's Nephew* (1955). Two children, Digory and Polly, are sent out of their world by Digory's magician uncle and then return to London with an evil queen, Jadis. Attempting to take Jadis back, the children stumble into an empty world where Aslan is about to create Narnia. Digory and Polly triumph over temptation and doubt when Aslan sends them on a quest to right the wrong they committed by allowing evil to enter Narnia.

The Last Battle (1956) takes place during Narnia's final days. Jill and Eustace come to help good King Tirian after an Ape named Shift disguises his poor donkey friend Puzzle as Aslan. The resulting chaos signals the end of Narnia but the beginning of something even better; soon Jill and Eustace are joined by all the friends of Narnia—Peter, Edmund, Lucy, Digory, and Polly. The unusual book provides an intense and joyful depiction of life after death. *The Last Battle* was awarded the Carnegie Medal in 1957.

The stories are unforgettable not only for the excitement and suspense of the adventures but also for the strong emotions they describe so well, especially the deep despair and fear caused by death and the unspeakable joy when death is conquered. Aslan is killed by the witch, but deeper magic brings him back to life; Narnia is taken by the Telmarines, then Aslan returns to claim it back; Digory's mother is dying, but Aslan gives him a magic apple that will heal her; and in *The Last Battle*, the children discover that death is merely a door to another, more beautiful world.

The imaginative and emotive stories are further enriched by Lewis's skillful use of language. Much is expressed in names: Cair Paravel and Aslan are regal, beautiful names; humorous names fit the characters of Puddleglum and Dufflepuds; and Jadis, Shift, and Miraz have harsh-sounding names that reflect their evil natures. Lewis's inventive characters also add appeal to the books. Among the many memorable Narnians are tender-hearted Tumnus the faun, the kindly Mr. and Mrs. Beaver, Reepicheep the valiant mouse, Puddleglum the pessimistic Marsh-wiggle, and the loyal dwarf Trumpkin.

Though most readers go through the books in the order in which they were published, Lewis agreed with an American child's preference—written in a letter to the author—for reading them in chronological order according to Narnian time: *The Magician's Nephew; The Lion, the Witch and the Wardrobe; The Horse and His Boy; Prince Caspian; The Voyage of the "Dawn Treader"; The Silver Chair;* and *The Last Battle.*

Though some adults dislike the heavy Christian allegory contained in the books, children—even those aware of the symbolism—enjoy the books because they are good stories first and allegory second. If the symbolism took precedence over the stories, the books would never have had such a large audience: Millions of copies have been sold. Lewis, who claimed he wrote stories he would have liked to read as a child, said that the Narnia Chronicles began with pictures he had in his mind. It is the magic and wonder of these images that readers remember years after encountering the books. ❧

JENNIFER M. BRABANDER

LINDGREN, ASTRID

SWEDISH AUTHOR, B. 1907. Best known for her books about the irrepressible heroine Pippi Longstocking, internationally acclaimed author Astrid Lindgren was born in Vimmerby, Sweden, and grew up on a farm just outside of the village. She was one of four children and describes her own childhood as being much like those depicted in her Noisy Village books. She and her siblings were allowed many freedoms and spent a great deal of time at play, although they were also expected to help with work on the farm. Lindgren read a great deal as a child but declared, when a teacher suggested she might become a writer when she grew up, that she would never write books.

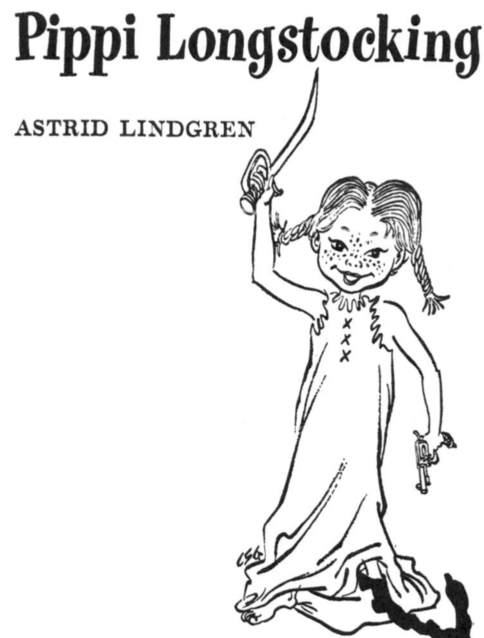

Title page illustration by Louis S. Glanzman for *Pippi Longstocking* (1950), by Astrid Lindgren.

After finishing school, Lindgren worked as a secretary and had children of her own. *Pippi Longstocking* (1950) came out of the stories she told her own daughter. She decided to write down the stories as a gift to her daughter and sent the completed manuscript to a publisher. The story was rejected, but the following year Lindgren submitted *Pippi Longstocking* to a contest at another Swedish publishing house and won first prize. *Pippi* became an international success and led to Lindgren's long and prolific career writing well over one hundred books for children, more than half of which have been translated into English. Astrid Lindgren won the Hans Christian Andersen Medal in 1958, presented by the International Board on Books for Young People (IBBY) for her outstanding contribution to the field of children's literature.

Lindgren's many books include MYSTERIES, FANTASIES, adventures, and realistic stories of family life in Sweden. She writes both PICTURE BOOKS and novels, and her work appeals to children from preschool through elementary school. Pippi, the heroine of *Pippi Longstocking, Pippi Goes on Board* (1957), and *Pippi in the South Seas* (1959), lives without parents in the middle of a small town in Sweden. Pippi is amazingly strong, able to pick up her own horse, and leads the life she chooses. She refuses to go to school until she hears about vacations and "pluttification" but quickly decides that the rules and structure are not for her. She is an outrageous heroine, anarchic and clever, continually inventing ways to amuse her more traditional friends Tommy and Annika. *Pippi Longstocking* is a perfect fantasy, a way for readers to revel in the possibilities of life without parents but with an endless supply of time and gold coins. Lindgren firmly grounds her story in reality through the characters Tommy and Annika, children who, like her readers, must go to school and observe strict bedtimes but who can also enjoy the larks invented by their neighbor Pippi.

Lindgren wrote many books based on her own childhood in a safe, warm Swedish village. *The Children of Noisy Village* (1962) and *The Children on Troublemaker Street* (1964) are two such novels. Each consists of episodic chapters that tell of the small adventures in the lives of children nurtured by close families and communities. Her characters go on picnics, invent games, and celebrate traditional Swedish holidays. Unlike the larger-than-life Pippi stories, these are tales of the excitement that everyday life can hold for children.

Bill Bergson, Master Detective (1952) and the subsequent adventures of Bill Bergson bridge the distance between Lindgren's impossible fantasies and her concrete family stories. Bill and his friends live in a typical Swedish village and play games much like their counterparts in Noisy Village, but Bill hopes to be a detective and finds himself solving crimes and becoming involved with bandits and thieves. The satisfying mysteries appeal to the reader's sense of adventure while remaining firmly planted in reality. *Rasmus and the Vagabond* (1960) is another mystery complete with thieves, stolen jewels, and a chase through an abandoned town, but it is also the story of an orphan, Rasmus, who runs away from an orphanage to find himself a family. Rasmus discovers a gentle, loving vagabond, and the two tramp through the summer countryside singing and working for sandwiches. Again Lindgren convinces her readers that a child who goes looking for parents will certainly find them. Lindgren recognizes the central, yet conflicting longings of childhood—to have the security of a loving family but also a measure of adventure and excitement. In *Brothers Lionheart* (1973), two brothers die young but continue to have heroic adventures together in Nangilyala, an imaginary country invented by the author. Lindgren hopes that, while the book may disturb some adults, it will comfort young children wondering about death.

Astrid Lindgren recognizes and writes about the needs, dreams, and fantasies of children. Her characters, always strong and well defined, are remembered long after readers finish each book. Her range is tremendous, from the quiet, mysterious picture book *The Tomten* (1961) to the hilarious, exaggerated adventures of Emil in *Emil in the Soup Tureen* (1963). Lindgren's vivid writing and imaginative stories achieve a timeless quality that will ensure them an appreciative audience for many years to come. ♧ MAEVE VISSER KNOTH

Lionni, Leo

AMERICAN AUTHOR AND ILLUSTRATOR, B. 1910. In Leo Lionni's *Frederick* (1967), a shy, poetic fieldmouse refuses to help harvest food for the approaching winter because he is busily gathering the warmth of the sun, the colors of the summer, and words to describe the seasons. Late in the winter, when it is dark and the mice are cold and hungry, Frederick's words spark the imagination of his fellow mice so that they can see colors and feel the sun's warmth. In *Frederick,* as in his other picture books, Lionni uses evocative words and expressive art to kindle the imagination so that the reader, too, can dream.

Illustration by Leo Lionni from his book *Alexander and the Wind-Up Mouse* (1969).

Although he has written more than thirty books for young children, Lionni did not start writing until he was a grandfather. The inspiration for his first book came during a train ride, when he was trying to entertain his grandchildren by telling them a story with pieces of paper that he had torn from a magazine. From this experience came *Little Blue and Little Yellow* (1959), the story of two small circles of color who are best friends and one day hug each other until they turn green. The strong design and marvelous color in Lionni's work reflect his lifelong career as an artist and graphic designer.

Born in Amsterdam, Lionni spent his childhood living and traveling throughout Europe. Although he earned a Ph.D. in economics, he pursued a career in graphic arts instead and worked as a freelance designer before coming to the United States in 1939. In the States he worked for several corporations as an art director and was also the head of the Graphics Design Department of the Parsons School of Design. His contributions to the field of graphic design resulted in his receiving an American Institute of Graphic Arts Gold Medal in 1984. Given such a distinguished career, Lionni's contribution to the world in his books for children is even more remarkable. Filled with small animal characters, these picture books unapologetically champion individuality and quietly celebrate the beauty of the natural world. Quite simple, the storylines assume the form of fables, and they almost always have more than one level of meaning. Most often he uses collage—although he sometimes relies on other media—to create a rich, lively, and textured art. These bold colors and designs make his books particularly suitable for reading aloud to a group. Lionni is one of the few artists to have four books designated as Caldecott Honor Books—*Frederick, Inch by Inch* (1960), *Swimmy* (1963), and *Alexander and the Wind-Up Mouse* (1969). His stories often treat serious subjects—war, friendship, and honesty—although generally the tone is playful. In *Swimmy,* a tiny fish encourages the other small fish to form collectively a giant fish so the larger fish won't eat them. The tale works as a simple story, although most adults see an underlying message in this book as well as in his others. Probably the only criticism of his work comes from those who find his messages and morals a bit too pointed. But what emerges most clearly is his consistent invitation for the reader to imagine, to experiment, and most of all to feel good about being an individual. ♧ A.Q.

Lipsyte, Robert

AMERICAN AUTHOR, B. 1938. As a child, Robert Lipsyte, a confirmed book junkie and "voracious, addicted word snorter," never considered himself a sports fan and hardly ever read SPORTS STORIES. Ironically, his first job upon graduating from the Columbia School of Journalism was as a copy boy for the sports section of the *New York Times.* He quickly advanced to become a prize-winning sports columnist and host of a PBS late-night talk show, "The Eleventh Hour," for which he won an Emmy. During a discussion with boxing manager Cus D'Amato, Lipsyte learned about the narrow, dark,

Voices of the Creators

Robert Lipsyte

I was lucky as a kid, although I didn't think so at the time. I was too fat for basketball or making out. Since I wasn't a real boy in those days, I was free to read.

Boys aren't encouraged to read in this society—not good books, anyway, about relationships or feelings or how to treat girls. Boys are allowed to read books about conquering the world or gluing balsa plane models or scoring from second on a single, but nothing that might really help them or the planet in later life. Boys don't read as much as we would like them to, and they don't read *what* we would like them to, because most current books do not deal with the real problems and fears of individual boys. There is the tendency to treat boys as a group—pack, team, gang, or board of directors—which is where males are always at their worst, instead of as individuals who need to be led into reading secretly and one at a time.

Boys are afraid. They are afraid of being humiliated, of being hurt, both emotionally and physically. You can translate that into being hit by the ball and then laughed at. Boys are afraid of being made to look dumb or inadequate in front of other boys and in front of girls, on the field or in the classroom. Boys are afraid of each other, and they are afraid of girls—especially athletic boys and the boys groomed for corporate success who are taught that female is "the other" who will bring them down unless kept in place and used properly. And many boys are afraid of homosexuality because so much of boys' behavior, from sports to gang rape, is confusingly homoerotic.

My adolescent luck held; by fourteen I was no longer fat. I looked as though I was ready to play basketball or make out. (It was too late for basketball.) And I had long since decided to be a writer as a shield against all those people who had never been fat. It was accidental that I became a newspaper boxing writer or that my first novel, naturally about boxing, was marketed as a young adult novel, a fairly new genre in 1967. Although I kept writing journalism, "old adult" novels, and films, I kept coming back to YA over the years because it was interactive writing—these readers were young enough to change. I could make a difference.

While my mail tells me my audience is at least half female, in my mind I am writing for boys like me—boys who need reassurance that their fears of violence and humiliation and competition are shared fears, and that these fears can be channeled into growth. To be able to read a book, really read a book, you have to be able to sink into a scene, to absorb characters, to care, to empathize. You have to be willing to make yourself vulnerable to a book as surely as you need to make yourself vulnerable to a person to have a real relationship. This is still not easy for a male in this society, particularly an adolescent male who may be unsure of his own identity, his sexuality, his future. From my own children and their friends, I sense that kids only *look* more confident than they did when I was young.

So, we need to change society before boys will read good books. True. But in this circle of change, if we can get a few boys to read some good books, we will have begun the transformation. A revolution, page by page.

Boys have to learn what girls already know—that a book is something you can make into a cave, and that you can crawl into that cave, roll around in it, explore it, find out what's in it and what's in you. Someday, there will be more books that boys really need, about how they can be friends with other boys by sharing emotions rather than scuffling, and how they can be friends, even friendly lovers, with girls. There will be books that assure boys they are not alone.

A good book should be a secret place in which you can find your own secret places, where no one can see you laughing or crying until you're ready to come out . . . at least to play basketball.

twisting flights of stairs that led to D'Amato's Manhattan gym. Lipsyte was fascinated by the type of boy who would climb the stairs, alone and afraid. This image, along with a request by a publishing house for Lipsyte to write a novel using the boxing ring as its milieu, led to Lipsyte's first novel, *The Contender* (1967). Winner of the Child Study Association Best Children's Novel, *The Contender* tells the story of Alfred Brooks, a high school dropout from Harlem who is struggling to become "somebody," to become a "contender." As the discipline he learns from training crosses over into other parts of his life, Alfred's metamorphosis begins. He decides to start night school, rescues his best friend James from descending into drug-induced oblivion, and recognizes his potential outside of the boxing ring. The book was a commercial and critical success but left most readers with questions and a strong desire to journey further with Alfred.

Thinking that he was meant for something other than just being a young adult author, Lipsyte waited ten years before he picked up his pen to write another young adult book, this one based on his own experiences of growing up fat in the fifties. *One Fat Summer* (1977), recognized by the *New York Times* as an Outstanding Children's Book, chronicles one summer in the life of overweight fourteen-year-old Bobby Marks. It is a turning-point summer in which he learns to stand up for himself, gaining self-esteem as he loses pounds in a realistic transformation. The response to Bobby Marks was so overwhelming that Lipsyte continued Bobby's story in *Summer Rules* (1981). Losing weight had not solved all of Bobby's problems. At age sixteen he has to deal with an unwanted camp counselor job, his first loves, and the repercussions of his decision to remain loyal to old friends. The trilogy concludes with *The Summerboy* (1982). Spending his last summer before college working at the local laundry brings Bobby unrequited love and confronts him with prejudice; rallying the workers to demand better conditions, he learns the importance of standing up firmly for principles. "Boys are afraid of being humiliated, of being hurt, both emotionally and physically," says Lipsyte. Bobby Marks, the scared, obese boy who grows into a responsible, mature young man, shows that a hero isn't always strong, that a hero can have fears. Bobby's humanity has led some critics to call Lipsyte the adolescent male's answer to Judy Blume.

Again Lipsyte took a ten-year break from the world of young adult novels to pursue his career as a television journalist. Nevertheless, the questions about Alfred Brooks's future kept coming; a generation of readers wanted his story to continue. A midnight discussion with a Native American boy who felt trapped on the reservation enticed Lipsyte to confront the dark stairs once more. *The Brave* (1991) follows the journey of Sonny Bear, half Indian, half white, from his upstate New York reservation to the seedy, drug-infested underworld of Manhattan. Unable to control his rage and feelings of alienation, Sonny finds himself in jail. He is rescued by Officer Alfred Brooks, who befriends him, recognizing Sonny's hunger to become "somebody." The protagonist in *The Chemo Kid* (1992), Fred Bauer, is an ordinary, unremarkable high school student who often questions his own existence. Fred's life dramatically changes when he develops a cancerous lump on his neck. His chemotherapy drugs appear to give him unexpected surges of superhuman strength, allowing him not only to rid the town of its toxic waste and its drug dealers but also to change his own image from wimp to warrior.

Generally, books that feature male protagonists and center on a sporting activity tend to attract an overwhelmingly male and sports-oriented audience, but Lipsyte's characters—Alfred, Bobby, Sonny, and Fred—speak to all readers, regardless of sex or race. Lipsyte successfully transcends the genre, smashing sexist myths of manhood, while losing none of the excitement and vivid imagery of a sports book. M.I.A.

Lisle, Janet Taylor

AMERICAN AUTHOR, B. 1947. Janet Lisle grew up in Connecticut, the oldest of five children and the only girl. She went to Smith College, graduating in 1969. After college, she was a Vista volunteer, living and working in Atlanta to set up food co-ops. She went to journalism school at the University of Georgia and worked for local newspapers for ten years. But she wanted to expand her writing scope to books and began to write fiction.

Lisle's books are uniformly delightful. Her first was *The Dancing Cats of Applesap* (1984), about cats who spring into action when everyone goes to bed. Her second, which takes place during World War II, was a spy MYSTERY called *Sirens and Spies* (1985). In this book, Elsie thinks she knows about her music teacher's involvement with the Germans, but she finds that people's motivation and morality are sometimes more complicated than she imagined. Her teacher, Miss Fitch, has her own story.

Lisle continues to write books with widely diverse topics; if she has a trademark, it is her versatility. All her books are complexly plotted and ultimately satisfying. *The Great Dimpole Oak* (1987), Lisle's best-known FANTASY, is the story of an old oak tree that is significant to the townspeople for its powers to bring people together under its branches. *Afternoon of the Elves* (1989) is about a miniature, magical culture just in the next backyard, and touched not just on fantasy but on families. *Sirens and Spies* was selected by the American Library Association as one of the Best Books for Young Adults in 1985, as was *The Great Dimpole Oak* two years later. *Afternoon of the Elves* was named a Newbery Honor Book. With later books, *The Lampfish of Twill* (1991) and *Forest* (1993), Lisle moves even more firmly in the direction of fantasy with stories that enchant readers with their lyrical settings and characters. A.C.

LITTLE, JEAN

CANADIAN AUTHOR, B. 1932. Although Jean Little was born with scarred corneas that severely impair her vision, she has always loved to read and to write stories and poetry. She had a book of her poetry published when she was seventeen, and she received a B.A. in English and literature from the University of Toronto in 1955. After college Little worked as a camp counselor for disabled children, and for several years following this, she

VOICES OF THE CREATORS

JEAN LITTLE

"How do you know how to do it?" a child asked me. It sounded like a simple, straightforward question. When I tried to answer it, however, I found that it was so profound that I had no idea of what to say. I believe it is the one question no good writer can answer. I have some inkling of how I do it, but how I know how remains mysterious. But I have a few pointers I have picked up from my reading of other people's books and my own experiences creating novels.

The single most important thing that I have done to help myself become an able writer is to read. Good books are my first and best teachers. This may seem self-evident, but not everyone seems to grasp how crucial it is for any writer to be on friendly terms with words. I do not mean that I need to sit down and analyze, searching out theme, symbols, and structure as though I were writing an essay for English class. When you want to get to know a person, you do not start by doing an autopsy. That way, you end up with a corpse instead of a friend. I try to read with loving attention, taking myself into the rhythms, the quirkiness, the enticing, exciting possibilities in our language.

For me, a book that needs to be written almost always comes in the form of a child—and a question. What if a child realized, after his father's death, that his mother's Christmas stocking holds nothing but an orange and a candy cane, because his parents had always filled each other's stockings? Wondering what he would do led me to write *Mama's Going to Buy You a Mockingbird?*

But I cannot even begin writing until I get to know the people. I have to hear them talking, follow them around awhile. As I write my opening pages, I know that I will be rewriting them many times before a book is done. When I wrote *Kate*, I revised the first chapter twenty-five times.

I love writing beginnings. I start the story at a point of tension or change. I never start with the main character cozily waking up to another sunny morning. He or she is usually puzzled, afraid, irritated, or sad. The first sentence should pull the reader right into the thick of things. It should leave the reader wondering, what next?

The second sentence is as important as the first. I try to make the opening chapter lively and full of feelings children instantly recognize. I do not introduce the whole cast of characters in one long descriptive paragraph. The information might be useful, but it is not emotionally engaging. Once in a while, a major character is physically absent early in the book for some reason. In that case, I pique the reader's curiosity by circulating rumors about this soon-to-be important person.

I try to reveal the thoughts and emotions of my characters through what they say and do, their silences, their shrugs. When you are watching television, nobody stops the story to say, "Laura is feeling unhappy." You see her misery in the droop of her shoulders and hear it in her glum speech. It is hard not to explain everything, but I always assume my reader is perceptive. Even babies read body language accurately. I try not to tell too much—but to show enough.

When I believe, from the first page to the last, that I have written a masterpiece, I haven't. If, on the other hand, I am sunk in gloom, convinced that every word I have written or ever will write is worthless, I try to remind myself to be of good cheer. That is normal; all writers have felt this way. Sometimes I try this test. I pitch the whole manuscript in the wastebasket. Can I walk away and leave it there? If I find myself sneaking that hated manuscript out of the basket, I usually discover a spark somewhere in all those ashes, a character crying out to be given a chance at life. So I go to the rescue—start working. Writing is hard work. Joyous, absorbing, frustrating, exciting, soul-satisfying, lovely hard work. Worth doing well.

This essay is adapted from a piece in *Writers on Writing*, edited by David Booth, published by Overlea House (Ontario, Canada), distributed by Grolier Limited, 1989.

taught in a special school for motor-disabled children. While teaching, Little discovered that when she read classics such as *The Secret Garden* and *Little Women* to her students, they were puzzled by the plight of the disabled characters, who either died or were miraculously cured. None of these characters ever remained physically handicapped and they grew into self-sufficient, happy individuals who loved life and took on its challenges. This insight inspired Little to write about Sally, a little girl with cerebral palsy. Sally, who had attended a special needs school, came home to live with her family and enter into the mainstream of regular school. Little's story is insightfully written, never sentimental, and depicts Sally with all the same basic fears and insecurities that the other students in her class have. She needs to learn how to manage everyday routines by herself, she needs family support, she needs friends, and she needs to learn how to reach out to help others.

In 1961 Little entered this story in a Canadian writing contest sponsored by the publisher Little, Brown. She won the competition, $1,000, and the guarantee that her book, *Mine for Keeps* (1962), would be published the following June. Elated by this success, she persevered to make her dream to write full-time come true. Among her books are several stories about children with various handicaps, including cerebral palsy (*Mine for Keeps*), visual impairment (*From Anna*, 1972, and *Listen for the Singing*, 1977), and mental retardation (*Take Wing*, 1968). In these, she gives voice and recognition to children who live with physical and mental challenges. Because she writes from personal experience, she can tackle these once delicate issues honestly with compassion and humor.

Little is also well known for her Kate books about friendship and self-discovery—*Look Through My Window* (1971), *Kate* (1971), and *Hey World, Here I Am!* (1984)—as well as her Anna books (*From Anna* and *Listen for the Singing*), which have been cited as two of the few Canadian books that give a perspective on World War II.

Other themes she explores include conquering fears (*Different Dragons*, 1986, and *Stand in the Wind*, 1975), the death of a sibling or parent (*Home from Far*, 1965, and *Mama's Going to Buy You a Mockingbird*, 1984), and lying (*One to Grow On*, 1969). In all her books, strong parental and family support, plus friendship and love of life, prevail.

Little writes with a voice-activated computer, SAM, and travels widely with her Seeing Eye dog, Zephyr. She has written fifteen books for middle-school-age children, a book of poetry, a picture book, and a two-part autobiography. ❧ S.R.

Lively, Penelope

ENGLISH AUTHOR, B. 1933. In Penelope Lively's ghost story *The Revenge of Samuel Stokes* (1981), Grandpa disapproves of people who "think in straight lines," and he speaks for Lively herself when he insists that "you've got to think flexibly." Lively sees layers where others might see straight lines, and flexible thinking is a hallmark of her work, which includes short stories and novels, a number of them illustrated. She has also written several brief illustrated books set in the past, among them *Boy without a Name* (1975) and *Fanny's Sister* (1976), the first in a series about a Victorian girl. Lively, who writes for adults as well as for children, has said, "one of the things we can do for children, in books, is...expand the child's vision of a world that is too often rooted both in place and in time."

Born in Cairo, Egypt, Lively moved to England in 1945, where her interest in place and time led her to study history at St. Anne's College, Oxford. Lively's readers are well acquainted with these interests; she regularly weaves them into her writing. At her most successful, she creates an intriguing juxtaposition of old and new, which is sometimes humorous and sometimes poignant. In early fantasies like *The Whispering Knights* (1971) and *The Wild Hunt of Hagworthy* (1971), Lively describes ancient universal forces that resurface at different times throughout history. Later, she concentrates more on the way individual characters experience time and place. In *The Ghost of Thomas Kempe*, the 1973 Carnegie Medal winner, protagonist James realizes that the passage of time adds layer upon layer to everyone's personality. His encounter with an irritable, centuries-old ghost leaves him with a sense of his own position in the flow of time, of his position between the past and the future. Likewise, *The Revenge of Samuel Stokes* introduces characters who must deal with a ghost from the past who meddles in present-day affairs. In *A Stitch in Time* (1976), by rediscovering snatches of another girl's long-ago childhood, Maria comes to terms with the passage of time and begins to resolve her contradictory feelings about growing up. In much of Lively's work, strong emotions reverberate throughout time, causing a memory, a place, or a human personality to acquire a separate vitality. The Victorian house in *The House in Norham Gardens* (1974) is not just a simple structure; it contains echoes from the lives of all its occupants, past and present. In *Going Back* (1975), a woman ponders the nature of her memories of growing up during World War II.

If flexible thinking provides Lively with a broad view of history, it also allows her to find stories in the narrowest places. The humorous short stories in *A House Inside Out* (1987) describe events in the lives of the nonhuman inhabitants of a house, including even the pill bugs living in the bathtub drain. Lively also takes the animals' point of view in *The Voyage of QV 66* (1978), which chronicles the adventures of a group of animals traveling through England after a disastrous flood has forced the evacuation of the human population. As she notes, "writing about animals is one of the most satisfactory ways I know of writing satirically or otherwise about people." In addition to exploring the human condition, Lively's work extends the borders of what she calls "the child-reader's . . . imaginative landscape." ♠

M.F.S.

Livingston, Myra Cohn

American poet and anthologist, b. 1926. Early in her career, Myra Cohn Livingston was faced with a major decision: whether to pursue a career as a musician or as a poet and writer. There is no question that whatever her choice, she would have become eminently successful. It must have been with some trepidation, however, that she abandoned her career as a professional French horn player (sufficiently gifted to have studied with Darius Milhaud) to follow a writing career.

Born in Omaha, Nebraska, Livingston grew up in California. She returned to California after graduating from Sarah Lawrence College in New York and worked as a personal secretary for several notable Hollywood personalities and for the illustrious violinist Jascha Heifetz. She wrote *Whispers and Other Poems* while she was a college student, but it was not until 1958 that she made an effort to have it published. Since that time she has written and compiled well over fifty books of poetry that have set new standards of distinction. There is little doubt that Livingston's musical ability influences her poetic skill, for she has an ear attuned to rhythm, lyricism, and the interplay of sounds, all of which demand that her works be read aloud. She applies the same rigorous criteria in selecting poems for her anthologies that she uses in creating her own poetry. *What a Wonderful Bird the Frog Are; An Assortment of Humorous Poetry and Verse* (1973) shines as a bright and sprightly collection of arch verse for older children. Not to be rivaled is her brilliant tour de force *Speak Roughly to Your Little Boy: A Collection of Parodies and Burlesques, Together with the Original Poems, Chosen and Annotated for Young People* (1971). This anthology, for all its fun, is instructive, in that it teaches children that pompousness and didacticism lay themselves open to ridicule.

Livingston has created a series of books, illustrated by Leonard Everett Fisher, that demonstrate her talent as an exemplary poet. *A Circle of Seasons* (1982), *Sky Songs* (1984), and *Celebrations* (1985) are all prime examples of lyrical imagery that transforms the everyday world into one of unlimited wonder. Fisher has captured the same spirit, rendering paintings that are profound yet completely accessible. The two have achieved a remarkable blending of talents. Other outstanding artists such as Trina Schart Hyman, Margot Tomes, Erik Blegvad, and Antonio Frasconi have also added to the enjoyment of Livingston's books.

In addition to writing and compiling her poetry books and anthologies, Livingston coedited the authoritative text *The Scott Foresman Anthology of Children's Literature* (1984) with Zena Sutherland, and she teaches about and lectures on poetry. Her books have received numerous citations, including many American Library Association Notable Book Awards, the Parents' Choice Award, the National Jewish Book Award, and the National Council of Teachers of English Excellence in Poetry Award. The music world may be poorer without Livingston's talents, but there is no question regarding the positive impact she has had on the world of children's literature. ♠ P.S.

Lobel, Anita

American author and illustrator, b. 1934. The folk tradition and designs of Poland and Sweden, where she grew up, have provided inspiration for Anita Lobel's art and writing, which is often either a retelling of old tales or an original story clearly influenced by folklore. Lobel feels particularly drawn to folktales because the main character usually ends up living happily ever after, while the villain gets his just deserts. For example, in *A Birthday for the Princess* (1973), the young princess longs for personal attention from her parents, the King and Queen, but they are too busy to attend to her. After befriending an organ-grinder and his monkey, she saves them from prison and they escape together. She loves her new life, but the final picture shows her parents looking miserable without her.

Lobel was born in Cracow, Poland, and during the Second World War she and her brother were hidden with a Catholic family. In 1944 the Germans captured them and sent them to a concentration camp in Germany. After the war, they were rescued by the Swedish Red Cross and went to Stockholm, where they were eventually reunited with their parents. In 1952 she and her

Illustration by Anita Lobel from *On Market Street* (1981), by Arnold Lobel.

family immigrated to the United States. While attending Pratt Institute in Brooklyn, New York, she met ARNOLD LOBEL, whom she married when she finished school. Initially, she worked as a textile designer, while her husband wrote and illustrated children's books. Then his editor encouraged her to try a book herself, and she created *Sven's Bride,* which was named one of the New York Times Best Illustrated Books of the Year for 1965.

Lobel is also an actress, and her love of theater is reflected in her picture books. As she starts working on a book, she often thinks of it as staging a play: Each page is a scene. In some cases this can be seen directly. In her husband's *How the Rooster Saved the Day* (1977), her pages are bordered by curtains and the rooster and a robber are clearly performing on a stage. The title page of her own *The Seamstress of Salzburg* (1970) is also a stage with the curtain closed. As the story begins, we see the curtain opening on a young woman sewing an elegant gown. In the end, after the seamstress marries the prince, all the members of the cast appear for a final bow and the curtain is closed. In other cases the theatrical device is more subtle. There are no curtains in her *The Troll Music* (1966), but the pages have the feel of stage sets. The simplified backgrounds are reminiscent of stage scenery, and each detail has been carefully placed on the set.

Lobel often collaborated with her late husband, illustrating his texts. For their joint venture, *On Market Street,* a Caldecott Honor Book in 1982, Lobel was inspired by seventeenth-century French engravings for her illustrations of a young boy's shopping spree. With a wonderful sense of humor, she creates each merchant the boy visits out of the items he or she sells—from apples to zippers. In another alphabet book, *Alison's Zinnia* (1989), which she wrote and illustrated, Lobel concentrates on flowers. For each letter of the alphabet, a girl picks a flower starting with that letter for a friend whose name starts with the next letter. Lobel uses a more painterly style for these illustrations, moving away from her earlier reliance on pen and ink. As Lobel's work evolves it still retains a freshness and a strong appeal for children. ☙ P.R.

LOBEL, ARNOLD

AMERICAN AUTHOR AND ILLUSTRATOR, 1933–1987. Arnold Lobel's creation of a kinder, gentler world, where laughter, happy endings, and the return to a snug home are the norm, have become his signature in the I-Can-Read, EASY READER, and PICTURE-BOOK annals of children's literature. Lobel wrote and polished his stories before illustrating them. In his art, he established mood by setting cartoon animals in pastoral and Victorian surroundings. Dressing his animals in formal Victorian attire allowed Lobel to incorporate "amiable incongruities," as critic George Shannon noted, thereby pushing human foibles humorously and inoffensively to their extremes. While this playful sense of the ridiculous abounds in Lobel's work, his stories and pictures examine the human condition with warmth and compassion. Lobel unified text and art in his I-Can-Read books by limiting the use of color. Other books, however, displayed a full palette. Pen-and-ink detailing added depth and dimension to his watercolors, fleshing out characters and background.

Although he wrote and illustrated twenty-eight of his own books and illustrated over seventy for other authors, Lobel is probably best remembered for his four award-winning touchstone I-Can-Read stories: *Frog and Toad Are Friends* (1970), *Frog and Toad Together* (1972), *Frog and Toad All Year* (1976), and *Days with Frog and Toad* (1979). They are considered CLASSICS because they exemplify friendship, acceptance, and reliability in a timeless setting. They take place in an idyllic world, free from outside intrusion and adult supervision. Frog and Toad's world is self-contained and secure: a child's paradise. Frog and Toad are complementary personalities: Frog, more adult, practical, and self-directed, is sometimes bossy, but, with his energetic optimism, he always knows how to cheer up Toad. Toad, more passive and pessimistic, is truer to his hibernating nature. He likes his bed and his naps. He needs guidelines, like his list of things he must do daily; he is very cautious; he needs encouragement and assurance, especially the assurance that Frog is, and will always be, his friend.

In other books—such as *Gregory Griggs and Other Nursery Rhyme People* (1987); *Fables,* the 1981 Caldecott Medal winner; *The Book of Pigericks* (1983); and *Whiskers and Rhymes* (1985)—Lobel, an admirer of EDWARD LEAR, incorporated nonsense verse, used Victorian settings and clothing, and pushed the improbable to its limit, humorously exposing the pretentious absurdities of societal and self-imposed values with which people shackle themselves. Delightful examples of Lobel's collaborative work with his wife, ANITA LOBEL, are the two folktales he wrote for her to illustrate: *How the Rooster Saved the Day* (1977) and *A Treeful of Pigs* (1979).

Lobel's fascination with books and illustration began at an early age. When he was six months old, his parents divorced, and he was raised by his grandparents. Ill health caused him to miss a year of school and, when he returned to third grade, he felt excluded. Telling and illustrating stories for his classmates eased this isolation. His fascination with children's stories and illustrations continued throughout high school. Lobel attended Pratt Institute, majored in illustration, and graduated with a B.F.A. in 1955. While at Pratt, he met Anita Kempler, whom he married after graduation. Lobel illustrated more than twenty books for other authors during the 1960s. His own career as a children's picture-book author/illustrator began in 1962 with *A Zoo for Mister Muster* and its sequel, *A Holiday for Mister Muster* (1963). During his career, Lobel received numerous awards, culminating with two citations for his body of work: the University of Southern Mississippi School of Library Science Silver Medallion in 1985 for "Distinguished Service to Children's Literature" and the Laura Ingalls Wilder Medal nomination in 1986 for "Distinguished, Enduring Contribution to Children's Literature." S.R.

Illustration by Arnold Lobel from his book *Whiskers & Rhymes* (1985).

LOFTING, HUGH

BRITISH AUTHOR AND ILLUSTRATOR, 1886–1947. Hugh Lofting is best known for creating Doctor Dolittle, one of the most enduring characters in children's literature.

Lofting was born in Maidenhead, Berkshire, England, and attended a Jesuit boarding school. Although he was interested in books and writing as a child, Lofting studied civil engineering and architecture in college. He attended Massachusetts Institute of Technology, but finished his degree at London Polytechnic. Lofting traveled to Canada as a surveyor and prospector, then worked for railroad companies in West Africa and Cuba before settling in New York, where he wrote humor stories and journalism pieces. During World War I, he joined the British army. While serving in Flanders and France, Lofting began to write and illustrate stories about a kindly animal doctor, which he mailed to his children in the United States. On his voyage home from Europe, Lofting met a novelist who suggested he publish these children's stories as a book.

The Story of Doctor Dolittle (1920) was an instant success. Nineteenth-century English physician John Dolittle lives in Puddleby-on-the-Marsh. When Doctor Dolittle's many pets drive away his human patients, he becomes an animal doctor and naturalist. With the help of Polynesia, an abrasively humorous parrot, the doctor masters a variety of animal languages, then travels to Africa to fight a mysterious illness that is killing off the monkey population. The episodic book is memorable for its entertaining adventures, whimsical animal dialogue, and, above all, the unflappable and humane title character.

Lofting's second book, *The Voyages of Doctor Dolittle* (1922), is narrated by Tommy Stubbins, a ten-year-old aspiring naturalist who becomes the doctor's assistant on a lengthy ocean voyage. Awarded the 1923 Newbery Medal, it remains one of Lofting's finest books due to its sustained humor and imagination. The author continued to publish Dolittle books in rapid succession, with Stubbins returning as narrator several times. The quality of the series is uneven, but critics have cited some of the later titles, including *Doctor Dolittle in the Moon* (1928), as among the author's best, owing to their inventiveness and thought-provoking philosophical content.

Lofting's other writings include picture books that are similar to the Dolittle stories in their anthropomorphic treatment of animals; *The Twilight of Magic* (1930), a serious, traditional fantasy; and his only adult work, *Victory for the Slain* (1942), a book-length war poem.

Lofting's greatest achievement, however, is the Doctor Dolittle series, which also inspired a 1967 movie musical. The books remain popular, although their relative length can be daunting to younger readers. The most serious charge leveled against the stories is that they contain racist writing and illustrations. Polynesia uses a number of racial epithets in speaking of Africans, while Lofting's illustrations of black characters are grotesque caricatures. Several episodes, including one in which an African prince wishes he were white, are also deemed offensive. Certain scenes in Lofting's books have been rewritten, and the offending epithets and illustrations have been removed from later editions. Literary purists may disagree with this tampering, but others argue that the books would not otherwise be purchased by libraries or sold in bookstores. Young readers of the edited volumes continue to find the stories appealing, and Doctor Dolittle remains a delightful character. ♘ P.D.S.

London, Jack

AMERICAN AUTHOR, 1876–1916. Jack London's life was filled with contradictions. He grew up with little money or education, but became a wealthy writer. He was a confirmed Socialist, but owned an expensive yacht and lavished money on a dream home. He wrote tales of survival, but committed suicide at age forty. And though he always claimed his adventure stories were potboilers, they remain his best-known works.

London was born in San Francisco to an unconventional family. His father held a variety of unsteady jobs, and his mother was an astrologer. The author, who lived on a ranch during his early years, became a voracious reader, though his formal education was haphazard. Much of his youth was spent earning money by delivering newspapers and working at bowling alleys and factories. He left home at age fifteen to become a sailor and fisherman. Two years later, a seal-hunting voyage to Japan resulted in his first published work. The essay, like most of the author's subsequent writing, drew on personal experiences.

Similarly, London's adventures in the Klondike during the Alaskan gold rush provided background material for *The Call of the Wild* (1903), his most famous novel, which concerns Buck, a large, domesticated dog stolen from his California home and shipped to Alaska. Buck is harnessed, beaten, and forced to work as a sled dog in this wild, uncivilized environment. Relying on instinct, he slowly adapts to a savage new life of beatings, violent dogfights, and survival of the fittest. By the novel's conclusion, Buck's association with humans has ended and he joins a pack of wild wolves. This compelling SURVIVAL STORY has the raw power of a myth and can be read as an allegory. The book continues to enjoy great popularity in schools, although some readers may find the narrative overstated and occasionally slow. Another London novel that continues to be read is *White Fang* (1906), which reverses the plot of *The Call of the Wild* by following a wolf dog from his wild existence in Alaska to life as a tamed pet in California. Both books contain strong scenes of adventure as animals fight nature and adapt to new surroundings.

A third survival story focuses on a human character facing a harrowing environment and is based on London's experiences on a seal-hunting vessel. *The Sea Wolf* (1904) is the first-person story of Humphrey Van Weyden, who, despite his aristocratic background, is forced to become a cabin boy on *The Ghost*, a schooner that rescues him after a shipwreck. Humphrey must adapt to the brutal atmosphere of the ship, which is captained by the hated, domineering Wolf Larsen. Both men are strongly defined characters in this vivid, very readable novel.

London remains best known to young readers for these three novels of adventure, although he also wrote acclaimed short stories, plays, nonfiction, and novels that espoused his political convictions. The author published over fifty books in a brief life that he ended early due to ill health, financial woes, and personal problems. Nevertheless, his legacy of stirring survival stories continues to entertain and inspire young readers. ♘ P.D.S.

Longfellow, Henry Wadsworth

AMERICAN POET, 1807–1882. Henry Wadsworth Longfellow was born in Portland, Maine, the son of a socially prominent mother and a Harvard-educated father. Longfellow graduated in the same Bowdoin College class as NATHANIEL HAWTHORNE and for a time served as college librarian. In 1836 he became Smith Professor of Modern Languages at Harvard University, where he made friends with such important figures as Charles Sumner, Louis Agassiz, and James Russell Lowell. Longfellow's first collection of verse, *Voices of the Night* (1839), which included the popular "A Psalm of Life," sold 43,000 copies and helped to establish Longfellow as America's favorite poet. Later collections of his poems were similarly successful, and most would contain individual poems of such popularity that they entered America's national consciousness and mythology. The preeminent example of such mythmaking poetry is "Paul Revere's Ride" (1863), a poem that appeals to children through its rousing pace and dramatic plot.

As his poetic stature grew, Longfellow began to produce long narrative poems on American themes. *Evangeline* (1847) is the story of two Acadian lovers displaced by the misfortunes of war. *The Song of Hiawatha* (1855) renders in English verse the story of an American Indian hero. *The Courtship of Miles Standish* (1858) is a verse tale of love among the Pilgrims that includes as a central character John Alden, one of Longfellow's ancestors. While all of these poems have passages that appeal to children, their overall length is forbidding for most young readers.

Although Longfellow's long narrative poems tell American stories, the poet was more interested in a romanticized "antiquity" than in America, or any other country, and so his poems often seem more in touch with a foggy, unlocalized past than with any particular place. During Longfellow's life his poetry was accepted (and purchased) by readers of all ages, and it drew critical praise from such diverse sources as John Greenleaf Whittier and Walt Whitman. Perhaps no other poet has ever received the unconditional acceptance Longfellow enjoyed in his lifetime, or suffered such a reversal of reputation afterward. In the twentieth century Longfellow came to be dismissed as a stereotype of Victorian-American respectability and a crafter of prosaic plots, linguistic nonsense, and orthodox rhythms. *Hiawatha,* with its overtly archetypal plot, sprinkling of preposterous-sounding Indian words, and persistent tom-tom rhythm, remains the great example of Longfellow's poetic excesses.

Longfellow never wrote specifically for young readers, but the prevalence of his poetry in nineteenth- and early-twentieth-century schoolrooms has linked him to the young. Longfellow's portrait was once a fixture in many schoolhouses, and schools all across the United States observed his seventy-fifth birthday. Memorizing and reciting "The Village Blacksmith" (1839) or a passage from *Hiawatha* was a rite of passage for millions of American schoolchildren. Today Longfellow has vanished from the classroom. Perhaps someday the best of his work will be rediscovered and reintroduced so that children will again know the pleasure of getting caught up in the rhythm and adventure of one of Longfellow's compelling verse narratives. ❧ D.A.B.

Lord, Bette Bao

AMERICAN AUTHOR, B. 1938. Born in Shanghai, Bette Bao Lord left China as a child to start a new life in the United States. This experience would later serve as the basis for her only children's book to date, *In the Year of the Boar and Jackie Robinson* (1984).

Lord graduated from Tufts University from which she would later receive an honorary degree. At the Fletcher School of Law and Diplomacy she completed the master's program and also met her future husband.

Eighth Moon (1964) was Lord's first venture into print. This factual account describing the difficult years experienced by Bette Bao Lord's sister, who had remained in China, met with widespread acclaim and is still featured on many adolescent reading lists. Lord's first novel, *Spring Moon* (1981), which chronicles the saga of a Chinese family during recent decades of political upheaval, received an American Book Award nomination and became a national best-seller.

In the Year of the Boar and Jackie Robinson also garnered its share of praise; it was selected as an American Library Association Notable Book in 1984, included in the Child Study Association Children's Books of the Year in 1987, and won the 1985 Virginia Library Association's Jefferson Cup. The story describes Shirley Temple Wong's transition from a pampered child growing up in an affluent, traditional Chinese household to that of a plucky youngster attempting to cope with a wholly unfamiliar culture. Shirley proves herself equal to the task, but not without some bumps along the way. It should be noted that the portrayal of Mabel, an African American classmate, is perceived by some critics as an unflattering stereotype; nonetheless, no other book has so successfully depicted the amalgamation of a foreign-born child into the American mainstream. Popular with both boys and girls, it remains an endearing and enduring favorite. ❧ P.S.

Lovelace, Maud Hart

AMERICAN AUTHOR, 1892–1980. The fact that Maud Hart was born in Mankato, Minnesota, was important to her writing. After graduation in 1910 from Mankato High School, she attended the University of Minnesota, traveled in Europe, and in 1917 married Delos W. Lovelace, another writer. In *Black Angels*, her first novel, published in 1926, Lovelace wrote of a Minnesota family of traveling theater folk in the 1800s. She wrote other historical novels set in Minnesota, the best known of which is *Early Candlelight* (1929), about the early days of Fort Snelling. With Delos she wrote other historical novels, including *Gentlemen from England* (1937), again set in Minnesota. Although these novels were for adults, they are interesting reading for adolescents a well.

It is her children's books for which Lovelace is best known and remembered, however. After telling her daughter stories about the fun she had growing up, she began what are known as the "Betsy-Tacy" stories. The setting, Deep Valley, Minnesota, is Mankato, and many of the characters and events are drawn from Lovelace's life and from the people she knew. The first four books take Betsy and Tacy and their friend Tib from age five to age twelve and have the naiveté of childhood at the turn of the century. In the six later books in the series, the characters are in high school or older. The focus in all of the stories is on the fun of being children and young adults. Betsy, patterned after Lovelace herself, sometimes seems almost silly, from an adult's perspective, in what she worries about, but that is typical of and appealing to many young people.

Despite the focus on fun, each book deals with serious issues. In the first, *Betsy-Tacy* (1940), Tacy's baby brother dies and Lovelace portrays well the way in which five-year-olds try to cope with this loss. In later books, Lovelace tackles problems of prejudice, dealing with the community's views about Little Syria, an area outside of town settled by Syrian immigrants. In *Over the Big Hill* (1942), Betsy, Tacy, and Tib make friends in Little Syria, and in another Deep Valley story, *Emily of Deep Valley* (1950), concern about the Syrians and pleasure in their culture are part of the plot. Three books about other Deep Valley characters and another five books for children were published between 1942 and 1966.

The first of the ten "Betsy-Tacy" books appeared in 1940, more than a half century ago. The books were enjoyed by children, mostly girls, throughout the country. Today there is a wave of nostalgia for the books, evidenced by the formation of a national and several local Betsy-Tacy societies in the early 1990s. After some years of being out of print, several of the books have been reissued. Although dated in some ways, such as in the use of certain racial or cultural terms, and set back almost a century in time, the characters and the events are still of interest to many of today's young readers.

Lovelace won few prizes during her lifetime, but now the Minnesota Young Readers Award is named for her, the societies to study and admire her work have come into being, and it is likely that her work will continue to be read and enjoyed well into the next century. ❧ B.J.P.

Low, Joseph

AMERICAN ILLUSTRATOR AND AUTHOR, B. 1911. Joseph Low was born in Coraopolis, Pennsylvania, and spent much of his childhood there before moving to Oak Park, Illinois. He attended the University of Illinois from 1930 to 1932 where he fell under the spell of the medieval woodcut form and was inspired to teach himself typesetting and printing. He studied drawing at the Art Students League in New York in 1935, and he continued his self-education at museums and libraries.

From 1942 to 1945 he was an instructor in design and graphic art at Indiana University. Wendell Wright, dean of the School of Education, had compiled a dictionary for preschoolers, and Low accepted the commission to illustrate it. *The Rainbow Dictionary* (1947) was published successfully and enabled Low to move to New York, set up a handpress, and announce his readiness to do design, illustration, and drawings. Art directors found his line crisp, clear, and sharp, as well as original, and he was soon dividing his time between advertising, magazine work, and book publishing. He then established Eden Hill Press to publish his own art. He illustrated editor Milton Allan Rugoff's *Harvest of World Folk Tales* (1949) in black-and-white and went on to illustrate, with his wife, Ruth, a colorful *Mother Goose Riddle Rhymes* (1953), chosen by the *New York Times* as one of the Best Illustrated Books of the Year.

Departing from his work on fiction, Low illustrated Helene Jamieson Jordan's *How a Seed Grows* (1960), one of the first of the Crowell "Let's-Read-and-Find-Out Science Book" series. He went on to illustrate several other titles in this series, and the clarity of his style contributed much to these informational books for young children.

Although Low's free and spontaneous line makes an immediate impression on the reader, his use of color is also distinctive. In Henry Wadsworth Longfellow's *Paul Revere's Ride* (1973), he uses a wide variety of almost neutral grays, greens, and ochers to express the feeling of a river fog on a dark night; his watercolor work is brushy and never intended to be confined within his inked lines. In *A Learical Lexicon* (1985), selected by MYRA COHN LIVINGSTON, Low's witty drawings are accented simply by various gray washes.

Low is the author of several of his illustrated books for children, including *Adam's Book of Odd Creatures* (1962) and *A Mad Wet Hen and Other Riddles* (1977). Low's work is represented in the permanent collections of many museums and libraries, and he has received numerous awards from such groups as the American Institute of Graphic Arts and the Society of Illustrators.

Although his body of work is small, each of Low's books demonstrates his sensitivity toward the bookmaking arts. His use of space, choice of style, and appreciation of the printing process result in fine illustration in the most classic sense. P.H.

LOWRY, LOIS

AMERICAN AUTHOR, B. 1937. Lois Lowry is well known as the author of the books about Anastasia Krupnik and her precocious younger brother, Sam. Always getting herself in trouble, Lowry's irrepressible heroine has a good-natured sense of humor that has made popular such titles as *Anastasia at Your Service* (1984), detailing her first job, and *Anastasia's Chosen Career* (1987), tracing her search for a profession. The first book about Anastasia's brother, *All about Sam* (1988), tells his life story from Sam's own comical point of view, beginning with his first impressions of the world as a newborn. Also popular with middle-grade readers are the amusing books about siblings Caroline and J. P. Tate. In *Switcharound* (1985), Caroline and J. P. make separate plans for revenge to get back at their father and his wife, who invited them for the summer only to stick them with some heavy responsibilities. The normally feuding siblings join forces when they realize at the last minute that they must help each other undo their awful plans.

Lowry is equally adroit at telling stories in a more serious vein, as evidenced by *A Summer to Die* (1977), which marked her debut as a children's book writer. In this novel, winner of the International Reading Association's Children's Book Award, thirteen-year-old Meg's friendship with an elderly but lively and active neighbor gives her strength through the summer during which her older sister suffers a serious illness and eventually dies. The sensitive and moving account also portrays the hope and joy of a new life when Meg witnesses the birth of a neighbor's baby.

In *Autumn Street* (1980), Lowry's finest piece of writing, the narrator looks back on the year she was six, when her father left to fight in World War II. The story begins with the carefree innocence of Elizabeth's close friendship with Charles, an African American boy, and ends with the violence and shock of his murder. When Elizabeth's father is injured and subsequently returns home, he and his young daughter make an "impossible promise" to each other that their separate fears and hurts will go away, knowing that sometimes hope is more important than truth. The flawlessly crafted prose is only one of the reasons the story lingers in the reader's mind long after the book has been closed.

In *Rabble Starkey* (1987), twelve-year-old Rabble Starkey's mother serves as housekeeper and baby sitter for the family of a woman eventually hospitalized for mental illness. When Mrs. Bigelow recovers and returns home, Rabble and her mother move on, saying goodbye to people who have become their friends and family. The first-person narrative is written in an authentic-sounding down-home voice, and the characters, learning the joys and sorrows of loving and of leaving, are especially well drawn.

Number the Stars (1989), winner of the 1990 Newbery Medal, tells about ten-year-old Annemarie Johansen, who lives in Denmark in 1943. When her family helps

Illustration by Jenni Oliver from *A Summer to Die* (1977), by Lois Lowry.

Voices of the Creators

Lois Lowry

My grandson, James, nine years old when he visited me in Boston in the summer of 1992, had really outgrown the traditional swanboat ride that he had enjoyed as a wide-eyed toddler. We went anyway, for nostalgia's sake; and we watched idly as gleeful children tossed chunks of bread to the ducks that swam beside the boat.

"Have you ever noticed," James asked me casually, "that when people think they are manipulating ducks, actually ducks are manipulating people?"

It is not often, if ever, that a casual remark haunts me and that I can, later, connect it to the origin of a book. But my grandson's perceptive and somewhat cynical words that summer coincided with my awareness of a rapidly changing world. A presidential election was looming and was much on my mind. The Berlin Wall, which I had rejoiced to see topple not long before, now appeared to have been the perching point for all the Humpty Dumpties of Eastern Europe, and it was frightening to realize that they might not ever be put back together again.

Maybe it was simply that my parents, both in their mid-eighties, were dying that summer. They were, in essence, turning over the world to my generation; it was a world I didn't understand, and suddenly time seemed to be passing so quickly. I was beginning to feel responsible for what I would eventually turn over to kids like James, who at nine could already see through so much sham. I began then to write *The Giver* (1993). It would be my twenty-first novel for young people.

Looking back seventeen years to the writing of my first, *A Summer to Die* (1977), I can see that I began with the smallest and most personal of themes. Critics would not agree with that, pointing out rightly that the life-death continuum which is central to that book is hardly a "small" theme. But for me, writing it then, it was no more than a retelling of a personal experience: the gathering together of the details and fragments that accompanied a time of saying goodbye in the lives of two sisters.

My succeeding books, for some years, followed the same pattern, I think. As a former photographer, I have sometimes likened writing to a choice of lenses and apertures. The writer, after all, utilizes focus in the same way that a photographer does. I can come in close on the details, open up to get it good and sharp, and blur the background into oblivion. I did that in my first book: focused sharply on those sisters, on that family, and that house. And I blurred the greater world that lay behind and around them. The reader does not know, or need to know, exactly where or when *A Summer to Die* takes place.

Gradually, often without any awareness of it myself, I have changed my lenses. A book called *Rabble Starkey* (1987) stepped back a bit. Now there was not only a house but a town and a state. Now there were social issues: still seen through a personal and subjective eye, but social issues nonetheless.

Number the Stars (1989) went much further. Although intermittently, still, I was writing books that gently examined family life, *Number the Stars* was the first of all my books to expand from that domestic scene out into the much greater scope of world concerns.

Finally, in writing *The Giver,* I looked through a panoramic lens with the f-stop all the way down. It was frightening to do that, as a writer: to try to scrutinize everything that was there, to give it meaning and depth. I was dealing with an entire *world,* after all; it was a long distance from the cozy country house, purposely isolated, which I had created seventeen years before when I wrote my first book.

And now? I will go back, inevitably, to re-create the close-focused glimpses of family life which I love. Children will always need those as part of their literature. But having now created a world, I will revisit and re-examine it, as well. My grandson and his friends are getting older, and the world will be theirs before we know it. I think all of us should be responsible for helping them see it—people and ducks; ducks and people—crystal clear, with its sparkles and its flaws.

smuggle their Jewish neighbors, including the young protagonist's best friend, into Sweden, something goes wrong and Annemarie must exhibit a kind of bravery she never knew she had. The suspenseful, unforgettable novel is geared toward a young audience but does not oversimplify the story of the multitude of people forced to flee their homeland.

Lowry won a second Newbery in 1994 for her innovative novel *The Giver* (1993). Set in a futuristic world that seems to have solved all of humanity's problems—

poverty, unemployment, inequality, the loneliness and insecurity of the aged—the story recounts the coming of age of twelve-year-old Jonas. Jonas's gifts of clear sight and empathy earn him the apprenticeship to the Giver, the community's reclusive keeper of all that it has given up—the good and the bad—to achieve its stable placidity. Jonas, in seeing both sides, learns to question the bargain struck, and his responses to his discoveries make *The Giver* a provocative, moving, haunting work.

Lowry, who as a child moved from Hawaii to Pennsylvania, then to Japan, is an author who writes from experience. The act of leaving is repeated several times in her books as characters pull up roots and move away, end painful relationships, or lose loved ones to death or distance. The author's experience as a journalist and photographer has provided her with an eye for detail, a skill manifested in her clear, vivid descriptions of place and time. Called the new Judy Blume, Lowry has lived up to that description with her tremendous popularity among middle-grade readers. ❧ J.M.B.

Lunn, Janet

CANADIAN AUTHOR, B. 1928. Janet Lunn's pioneering contributions to the Canadian children's book scene extend well beyond her novels, PICTURE BOOKS, and NONFICTION. An influential children's book critic, first with the Kingston (Ontario) *Whig-Standard* and later with the Toronto *Globe and Mail,* she was for many years the only children's reviewer in Canada addressing the general public. As the first Canadian children's author to be a writer in residence (at Regina Public Library, Saskatchewan) and as chairperson of the Writers' Union of Canada, Lunn helped establish the high profile at home and abroad that Canadian children's writing currently enjoys. She has also been on the board of the Canadian Children's Book Centre, worked as an editor, taught children's literature, and told stories. She often tells children she has a head like an attic: "It's full of memories that come charging out to astonish me and make new books."

Born Janet Louise Swoboda in Dallas, Texas, Lunn grew up in Vermont, New York, and New Jersey, moving to Ottawa, Ontario, in 1946, where she finished high school. She then attended Queen's University at Kingston, where she met and married Richard Lunn, with whom she raised a family of five. Lunn became a Canadian citizen in 1963 and began a body of work rooted in Canadian history. In *Double Spell* (1968), her first novel for children (published in the United States in 1969 as *Twin Spell*), modern-day twins encounter a ghost from 1840s Toronto. *The Root Cellar* (1981) is a time-shift novel about Rose, an unhappy girl befriended by young people embroiled in the American Civil War. The old house in the novel is based on the nineteenth-century farmhouse in Hillier, Ontario, where Lunn lives and works. *The Root Cellar* won the Canadian Library Association Book of the Year for Children Award, was an IBBY Honor Book, and made several Best Book lists in the United States. An ambitious novel for older children, *Shadow in Hawthorn Bay* (1986) is historical fiction with Celtic underpinnings and a supernatural twist that swept the major Canadian children's book awards in 1987. As a child, Lunn was greatly moved by FRANCES HODGSON BURNETT's *The Secret Garden,* so it is no surprise that the search for identity and self-acceptance runs throughout her fiction, as does the redemptive power of love and forgiveness.

Lunn's books for younger children also have been well received. Two playful picture-book collaborations with illustrator Kim LaFave—*Amos's Sweater* (1988) and *Duck Cakes for Sale* (1989)—have a rural setting, while Lunn's retelling of *The Twelve Dancing Princesses* (1979) is set firmly in the land of Faerie. *One Hundred Shining Candles* (1990) is a Christmastime pioneer story; *Larger than Life: True Stories of Canadian Heroes* (1979) is easy nonfiction. Lunn's lifelong passion for history and storytelling is evident in *The Story of Canada* (1992), cowritten with historian Christopher Moore and illustrated by Alan Daniel. The first illustrated general history of Canada for young people, it was the Canadian children's publishing event of the year and a highlight in a distinguished career. ❧ A.G.

Lyon, George Ella

AMERICAN AUTHOR, B. 1949. In George Ella Lyon's work, which includes many fine PICTURE BOOKS and novels for older children, the reader can sense the importance of family and the mountain heritage on which Lyon frequently draws. Born in Harlan, Kentucky, Lyon's successful first work was *Mountain* (1983), a poetry chapbook, which was followed by plays and poetry for adults.

Lyon's background as a poet is evident in many of her works for children, as her texts feature a rhythmic, lyric cadence. Lyon says, "Being a poet was a great help to me in learning about picture books. As NANCY WILLARD pointed out in a talk I heard . . . poems are the closest genre to picture books, with their use of sound, rhythm, economy of language, and surprise." Lyon also draws on her own children's questions in her work for young readers, attempting to provide answers in books such as *Together* (1989) and *The Outside Inn* (1991).

Lyon began writing for children in 1984, when her letter to poet PAUL JANECZKO led his editor to approach Lyon about writing for children. *Father Time and the Day Boxes* (1985) resulted, as well as a short story that later became the novel *Borrowed Children* (1988). *Father Time* excites a young child's imagination: "Now I expect you've been wondering how the days go by and all that." In *Together* the delightful rhythm of lines such as "You cut the timber and I'll build the house. You bring the cheese and I'll fetch the mouse" lead to the reassuring refrain "Let's put our heads together and dream the same dream." The interconnectedness of family is clearly portrayed in works such as *Who Came Down That Road?* (1992), the result of a young child's question about the history of a nearby mountain path, and *Come a Tide* (1990), in which the grandmother's experience of the floods of Spring gives the young narrator a sense of being involved in the cyclical effects of the weather.

In her two novels for older readers, Lyon's belief in the importance of family pervades the text. In *Borrowed Children,* Amanda Perritt questions her role in the family during her mother's difficult recovery from childbirth. Sumi in *Red Rover Red Rover* (1989) also has a strong sense of her place in the family, but events such as the death of her beloved grandfather and her older brother's departure for boarding school challenge her understanding of that world. Both novels sensitively explore the transition from child to young woman. It is easy for the reader to become involved in these stories. As Lyon has said, "Books are a collaborative enterprise, not just between author, editor, and illustrator but between those folks and the reader." Readers willing to experience this collaboration should come to Lyon's work expecting to be amply rewarded. ❧ E.H.

M

Macaulay, David

American author and illustrator, b. 1946. Born in Burton-on-Trent, England, David Macaulay, like many young boys, found himself fascinated with technology. But unlike most youngsters, he would later take that interest and create the kind of books that he would have loved as a boy. Macaulay has credited his parents with his interest in making things; everyone in the family fashioned items and used their hands—from sewing to wood carving. Eleven when his parents left England to move to Bloomfield, New Jersey, Macaulay continued drawing and enrolled in the Rhode Island School of Design. After receiving his bachelor's degree in architecture, he spent a fifth year studying in Rome, an experience that would eventually be used in his book *City* (1974), in which he explores the development of a Roman city.

After a short stint as a junior high school teacher, Macaulay began instructing art students at the Rhode Island School of Design, and he has continued to teach at various institutions throughout his career as a book-maker. While teaching, he became intrigued with the process of creating his own books. His first book idea undoubtedly was not his most inspired; this picture book depicted a gargoyle beauty pageant. Fortunately, the book never saw the light of day. What it did do was land on the desk of an editor who was impressed by a picture depicting a gargoyle against the backdrop of Notre Dame. After talking over his enthusiasm for cathedrals in general, Macaulay was inspired to create a book of information that focused on the building of a cathedral. One of the freshest, most innovative information books to appear in decades, *Cathedral* (1973) was to completely alter the face of American information books for children.

If one looks back over the past fifty years, one can see that there are certainly those who created information books with the skill and artistry that David Macaulay brought to them—Edwin Tunis and Holling C. Holling being two fine examples. But in *Cathedral* Macaulay crafted a visually stunning information book that worked equally effectively with adults and children. Easily shared and enjoyed on many levels, it is truly a book for all ages. Since both words and pictures are integral to the information shared, *Cathedral* is as interesting to look at as it is to read—and that combination had rarely before been applied to the field of children's nonfiction.

Many of the titles to follow *Cathedral* would employ the same oversized format Macaulay chose for his first book; executed in black and white, they showed the structures of various edifices and the human communities that worked around them. For the books are not only testaments to the ways things were built, they also provide a vision of a whole society; social hierarchies, rituals, and life styles play as active a role in the books as do tools, materials, and techniques. *City* demonstrated the construction of a Roman city; the building of the monuments to the pharaohs was explored in *Pyramid* (1975); the evolution of a nineteenth-century New England mill was featured in *Mill* (1983); the life that goes on underneath the surface of modern city streets forms the theme of *Underground* (1976). In *Unbuilding* (1980), Macaulay hypothetically demonstrates how the Empire State Building would be demolished. As critic Barbara Bader has noted, Macaulay in his books combines "a rare historical imagination, a keen eye, a gift for topographical structural delineation, and a deep sense of the human condition."

Macaulay's sly sense of humor also led him to craft some light and farcical books—*Great Moments in Architecture* (1978), *Motel of the Mysteries* (1979), and *Why the Chicken Crossed the Road* (1987)—all of which exhibit Macaulay's freewheeling sense of humor. His Caldecott Medal book, *Black and White* (1990), part of this whimsical series of titles, explores cause and effect. A continuation of the theme explored in *Why the Chicken Crossed the Road*, *Black and White* contains four stories that can be read in four different ways; in them Macaulay plays with the concept of time, simultaneity of events, and one story impinging on another. In this

Voices of the Creators

David Macaulay

I am frequently asked where I get my ideas. I always answer by saying "from everywhere"—or "by keeping my eyes and ears open." Although vague, both responses have always seemed to serve the needs of the moment. But it is a good question. Where *do* I get my ideas?

First of all, what are ideas? I think of them as living, breathing critters. Offspring if you will, created by and in people's minds from all sorts of fragments and sensations which are everywhere all the time. You go for a walk or a bike ride and bam, you've picked up at least half a dozen just by keeping your eyes and ears open. Once aboard and often even before the journey is over, these seemingly disconnected bits and pieces have begun to organize themselves through some sort of internal dating service developed by, and unique to each of us, into ideas. These ideas then grow into all shapes and sizes. And, like their owners, they begin to show a variety of distinct characteristics ranging from whimsical, intriguing, and even inspiring to demanding, stubborn, and insidious. Not surprisingly, some of what turn out to be the best ideas are more heavily imbued with the latter characteristics. They have no choice if they are to reach adulthood. There is only so much available cerebral real estate, so competition can get fierce.

It is not always easy to recognize a potentially good idea in its early stages because it rarely looks anything like the idea into which it might eventually develop. Some ideas are fairly modest, satisfied to gently nudge their unwitting host from time to time but otherwise quite willing to hang around and wait their turn. Other ideas stomp around day and night just looking for attention, desperate to see themselves in print. Regardless of their personalities, though, once aboard, ideas have a tendency to stay. The reclusive ones often remain locked up for years, while their gregarious counterparts hang out the windows shouting back and forth across the folds of the cortex as they put out their wash.

At least one good idea, and preferably one only partially formed, is necessary if creative thinking is to be undertaken. Without it, the would-be creator is on very thin ice. *Castle* was an easy book to make but a very difficult one to stay with because the idea behind it was already a *fait accomplis,* having been developed in *Cathedral* and thoroughly tested in *City* and *Pyramid.* There was no new ground to break. The most important result of that often-frustrating undertaking was that it forced me onto another track. *Great Moments in Architecture* was a collection of little ideas, some of which, farther along that same track, became the basis of *Motel of the Mysteries.* Ideas beget ideas. You just never know which will blossom and which will wither on the vine.

Shortly after completing *Unbuilding* I began to entertain the notion of a book about a journey. I wanted to use a journey as subject matter. All books are journeys, although not all are interesting journeys. The best books take us to places we've never been, be they distant lands or uncharted internal realms. Many others can accurately be described as dead ends. Over the next ten years, I found myself on this path often, although it never seemed to lead anywhere. I have several sketchbooks filled with what look like twisted triptychs from some demonic travel agent. While I could never complete a journey, I also couldn't get off the road. I would return to my sketchbooks between each published effort and look again for ways of identifying and hopefully satisfying my quest. With each visit, the path grew increasingly convoluted until finally there emerged *Why the Chicken Crossed the Road,* a simple cause-and-effect tale of a chicken and an accidental hero named Hooper. After working on the relentless *Way Things Work* for almost four years, I returned with considerable relief to those old ideas and set off on another journey. *Black and White* emerged comparatively quickly—after a mere ten years of aborted liftoffs—as four distinct journeys juxtaposed to create a fifth. *Ship* was finally launched after only three years of false starts. It is also a journey book: first, that of the historian attempting to understand the design and construction of a sixteenth-century caravel from its scattered remains; second, the story of the ship itself, a product of the historian's scholarship, common sense, and informed imagination.

No matter how aggravating or impossible some ideas may seem, no matter how reluctant or uncooperative they are, you can't throw them away carelessly—not that they'd leave even if you tried. Ideas are a necessary fact of my life; and, while sometimes I can barely live with them, I could certainly never live without them. Perhaps the answer to the question "where do I get my ideas?" should be "I don't." They get me.

Illustration by David Macaulay from his book *Pyramid* (1975).

free-spirited book, Macaulay also plays with the form of a book itself and what can be done in designing one.

By far Macaulay's most comprehensive, most ambitious, and most creative use of the book form came in *The Way Things Work* (1989); in it he demystifies a veritable smorgasbord of mechanical and electrical machines. He is equally at ease explaining simple principles—such as the inclined plane—and intricate processes, such as nuclear fission and fusion. From the zipper to the atom bomb, from the plow to the microcomputer, Macaulay focuses, distills, organizes, and explains hundreds of items. That he manages to do so and to remain funny at the same time is an unparalleled accomplishment.

Macaulay has garnered an impressive number of awards: the Caldecott Medal and Honor Awards, Boston Globe–Horn Book Award, Christopher Award, an American Institute of Architects Medal, Washington Children's Book Guild Nonfiction Award, nominee for the Hans Christian Andersen Award, Deutscher Jugendliteraturpreis, a Dutch Silver Slate Pencil Award, and the Bradford Washburn Award, presented by the Museum of Science in Boston for an outstanding contributor to science.

Time magazine once wrote of David Macaulay, "What he draws he draws better than any other pen and ink illustrator in the world." A superb craftsman, a dedicated bookmaker, Macaulay has no contemporary equals in the art of the information book. He knows how to clarify, to make the difficult simple, to communicate, and to make the process of learning enjoyable. It is in the latter that he particularly succeeds. When it comes to nonfiction, no one can equal David Macaulay in his ability to keep readers turning the pages, eager for more. ❧ ANITA SILVEY

MacDonald, Betty

AMERICAN AUTHOR, 1908–1958. Betty MacDonald's published works all had their origins in real life. Her adult books are autobiographical; her children's stories were derived from original bedtime tales she told relatives. Born Anne Elizabeth Bard in Boulder, Colorado, MacDonald spent her early years traveling to various western cities with her mining engineer father. After his death, the family settled in Seattle. Betty's childhood in this large, fun-loving family is described in several of her books. At age sixteen, she enrolled in the University of Washington but left two years later when she married. Her story of married life on a chicken farm is recounted in the best-selling *The Egg and I* (1945). Subsequent books relate MacDonald's experiences as a divorced mother looking for work during the Depression, her confinement in a tuberculosis sanatorium, and the years she spent on a Puget Sound island with her second husband and family. These genuinely funny books are filled with pithy characterizations and earthy good humor. The writing is so accomplished that it is hard to believe MacDonald had no literary aspirations before her sister suddenly suggested she try writing a book. Over the years, MacDonald's adult works have faded in popularity, but they remain ripe for rediscovery.

Today, MacDonald is best known for her stories about Mrs. Piggle-Wiggle, which are still read and loved. Mrs. Piggle-Wiggle, a charming, elderly widow who lives in a small town, is described as loving children and having an upside-down house that is always overflowing with young visitors. Beginning with *Mrs. Piggle-Wiggle* in 1947 and followed by *Mrs. Piggle-Wiggle's Magic* (1949), *Mrs. Piggle-Wiggle's Farm* (1954), and *Hello, Mrs. Piggle-Wiggle* (1957), the books present a variety of children with unmanageable behavior problems. Each chapter is an individual, unlinked story about a problem child who has been cured with the assistance of Mrs. Piggle-Wiggle. The stories are didactic yet enjoyable to young readers, who delight in the exaggerated bad behavior of children who tattle, interrupt, answer back, and show off. Mrs. Piggle-Wiggle deals with these situations using various remedies, and therein lies the dichotomy of the books. While many of the stories are grounded in reality, as Mrs. Piggle-Wiggle manipulates natural circumstances to provoke a cure, others veer into fantasy, as she dispenses magic potions, such as the Crybaby Tonic that causes the user literally to cry a river of tears. While both types of stories are entertaining, those involving magic are less satisfying. Consequently, *Mrs. Piggle-Wiggle's Farm* is the finest book in the series because all its episodes involve children who use their own resources to solve their problems. Also, Mrs. Piggle-Wiggle is a stronger presence in this work. Surprisingly, she is rarely shown interacting with children in the other volumes, frequently dealing only with their parents—and that by phone. The books are dated by their lack of ethnic divergency and by the fact that all the children come from two-parent, sex-stereotyped families. Also, the idea of parents covertly medicating their children with a variety of pills and potions may make modern-day readers uneasy. Despite these flaws, the books are humorous and appeal not only to children but also to adults who appreciate their satirical tone.

MacDonald's other foray into children's books, *Nancy and Plum* (1952), is a tale about ophans. Although MacDonald died at an early age, she left children an endearing and enduring character in Mrs. Piggle-Wiggle. ❦ P.D.S.

MacDonald, George

Scottish author, 1824–1905. Experts in children's literature consider George MacDonald's fantasies both enlightening and entertaining. Children often think they are just plain fun. Fantasy writers have often turned to his books for inspiration. Whatever the audience, one thing is certain: The author's stories contain highly adventurous plots, carefully constructed characterizations, and plausible fantastic elements that are accessible to a wide range of readers.

In *The Princess and the Goblin* (1872), MacDonald used the typical bipolar fairy-tale structure of opposite lands inhabited by very different characters, one human and one fantastic. The subterranean fantasy world is occupied by goblins who earlier rejected the human king's rule and have established a continual battle with the people on earth. Aboveground, the king's daughter, Princess Irene, meets a commoner, the youthful miner Curdie. Throughout the story Curdie and Princess Irene travel and strive together in an effort to defeat the evil goblins.

MacDonald employed common FANTASY motifs found in earlier myth and folklore, among them the deviousness and mean-spiritedness of the goblins; the innocence and purity of the princess; and the courage and resourcefulness of Curdie. The plot follows the traditional fairy-tale structure: A princess, entering a secret passage, finds her mysterious great-great-grandmother. Initially, she cannot return to her grandmother's tower because she does not believe in her own earlier experiences. The goblins hope to capture the princess and marry her off to their son so they can rule both the earth and the underworld. A poor boy saves the kingdom from disaster and gains the king's blessing. In the second "Princess" book, *The Princess and Curdie* (1883), the action centers more on Curdie's acceptance of the great-

great-grandmother as "real." In the end, Curdie once again helps save the king and he and Princess Irene are married.

While in many ways the stories resemble fairy tales, MacDonald created unusual fantasies that were lighthearted and entertaining. MacDonald's trusting youths could enter a fantasy world and survive only when they believed that earthly logic must give way to innocent faith. MacDonald depicted a world in which children become heroes because they believe in the mythic, supernatural, righteous spirits they encounter. MacDonald sent these heroes (and their readers) on a journey through fantasy lands in order to promote his own beliefs in religious spiritualism. MacDonald wanted to entertain and to educate children at the same time. He sought to develop a style that placed children as "believers" within a context of religious allusions.

In addition to the "Princess" series, MacDonald's audiences continue to read and enjoy his earlier mystical story, *At the Back of the North Wind* (1871). *North Wind* contains the familiar home/away/home journey of the folkloric hero, but in this tale the hero returns to the mystical country, an ending more fitting to religious parables. Thus, the story is both a tale of the hero's welcome return in his own society and his acceptance of the ways of a new world.

MacDonald has been called the father of modern children's fantasy. His literary patterns were imitated by later fantasy writers. J. R. R. TOLKIEN read MacDonald and credited him as a mentor. C. S. LEWIS also read MacDonald and admired his talent. In his anthology of MacDonald's work, Lewis wrote, "I have never concealed the fact that I regarded him as my master; indeed I fancy I have never written a book in which I did not quote from him." J.P.M.

MACLACHLAN, PATRICIA

AMERICAN AUTHOR, B. 1938. Born in Cheyenne, Wyoming, Patricia MacLachlan graduated from the University of Connecticut and taught English and creative writing. Married and the mother of three children, MacLachlan reveals herself in her MIDDLE-GRADE FICTION and PICTURE BOOKS to be a keen observer of the complexity of familial relations. The family, in its various forms and moods, is at the center of all her stories. MacLachlan is best known for her Newbery Medal–winning book, *Sarah, Plain and Tall* (1985), considered by many critics to be the great American children's novel of the 1980s. Written in simple, understated prose, the brief novel tells the story of a young brother and sister who fear that their father's newly arrived mail-order bride will decide to leave them and their prairie home and return to her beloved Maine coast. Their fears melt away in a heartwarming but decidedly unsentimental conclusion.

Jacket illustration by MARCIA SEWALL for *Sarah, Plain and Tall* (1985), by Patricia MacLachlan.

Children in MacLachlan's books often face a major change in their lives, and from fear and worry at the outset they move toward courage and acceptance. The eleven-year-old boy in *Journey* (1991) struggles to understand his mother's desertion and is helped to reach a slow acceptance of it by his sister and loving grandparents.

Seeing through another's eyes is also a common theme in MacLachlan's books. In *Arthur, for the Very First Time* (1980), ten-year-old Arthur Rasby spends the summer with his eccentric great-aunt and great-uncle and their pet chicken. Arthur worries about the baby his mother is expecting but learns to see a point of view other than his own and comes to believe, as he writes in a letter home, that "things will work out." Many of MacLachlan's characters are artists: musicians, painters, writers, and photographers. In *The Facts and Fictions of Minna Pratt* (1988), Minna is a promising young cellist

Voices of the Creators

Patricia MacLachlan

I was not born a writer. I didn't actually put words on paper until the age of thirty-five. "Pretty old," one of my children commented. I made a conscious and fervent decision at the age of eight not to become a writer because I read all the books I could find, many of them over and over, and I believed that writers had all the answers. Since I did not have the energy, inclination, or expertise to go out into the world and find the answers, I decided to become an actress or a symphony conductor.

The only story I remember writing in school was part of a school assignment. "Write a story for tomorrow," said my teacher. "It must have a beginning, a middle, and an end, and it must be about your pets." I wrote a story on a three-by-five card: "My cats have names and seem happy. Often they play. The end." My teacher was not impressed. I was discouraged, and I wrote in my diary: "I shall try not to be a writer." I was very fond of *shall* at age eight. I find the word *try* interesting. It did not occur to me then that everything in my diary was fiction, carefully orchestrated and embroidered tales of an exciting life—an unreal life. Or was it? The question of what was real and what was not fascinated me, and I spent lots of time asking people, becoming a general annoyance.

Like my character Cassie in *Cassie Binegar*, I spent hours in hidden places, listening to conversations I was not meant to hear and often did not understand, yet found fascinating. Sometimes I sat under the dining room table out of sight, viewing and listening to the world—the same thing that Cassie does in the book. I never realized how close this book was to me, to my life, until I sent my mother the manuscript to read. Several days later a package arrived for me in the mail. It contained a huge tablecloth, rather worn, that I'd forgotten. It was white with windy swirls of green—exactly like the one I had described in the book, in a work of fiction.

I now believe that writing is for me like tending a garden. There are plants that come up every year, perennial plots and themes and characters. There are the seeds you plant that never flourish, that become bits and pieces of people or places you set aside for later. Then there are what my father has always referred to as volunteers, which come from somewhere unknown, from someone else's garden: "Look, right there in the compost heap. A volunteer!" And we would smile.

Sarah of *Sarah, Plain and Tall* was from a volunteer from long ago. The facts of it haunted me. There once was a woman—an "unclaimed treasure," as my mother called older, unmarried women—who lived by the same sea where I spent my summers. She traveled to the prairie where I was born. My mother loved her.

So the idea of *Sarah* was one I had had for many years. My need to complete it, however, became personal and urgent. My mother, we learned, had Alzheimer's disease. Her recent memory began to fade, although her great humor remained. Soon, I knew, she would have only past memory, then none. In the book I wanted to write the story of a woman who left her roots and the story of children who needed her to preserve theirs. It is now clear that I also needed to preserve this piece of my mother's past for her, for me, and for my children.

Years ago, when I first began to write, wondering all the while whatever I could write about, something happened that made it clear. At the age of five my daughter Emily complained that she could not sleep at night because in her closet there lived a giant shadow that came out only at night to threaten her. My husband went upstairs, and engaged in a dialogue with the shadow. A few weeks later when I lay in bed with Emily, trying hard not to fall asleep before she did, I asked her about the shadow. "Oh," she said happily, "I named that shadow. He's Henry, and he visits at night when the moon is out. See?" And I did see. For now, as in the past, I can only write about the questions and the issues that confront me, that trouble me—the ones that whisper in my ear or, like Emily's shadow, threaten me. It is my way, whether by fact or fiction, of naming my own shadows.

whose struggle with her music parallels her struggle with her family, particularly with her mother. MacLachlan's protagonists often come to a new understanding and a deeper acceptance of themselves and their families. They are suddenly made aware of the love that exists in their family and the strength and courage that the power of that love grants them. The protagonist in *Cassie Binegar* (1982) envies her friend's calm, conventional parents and their clean, uncluttered house and resents her own loud and loving family, with their messy home and casual ways. With help from a visiting writer and her Gran, Cassie discovers how deeply she loves her raucous family. Willa, in *Unclaimed Treasures* (1984), believes that life is for doing extraordinary things and insists that her mother, who is about to have a baby, is doing a very ordinary thing. An emergency helps bring Willa to a realization of the love that lies within her truly extraordinary family.

MacLachlan's works are peopled with the young and the old, and her stories delineate the affinity that exists between these two groups. Animals, too, find themselves an accepted part of the family, from cats and dogs to pigs and chickens. The humor in MacLachlan's books is gentle, a perfect match for the true tenderness in her entertaining and highly accessible stories. ✥ J.M.B.

Magazines for Children

When the twentieth century began, the field of children's magazines was just emerging from an extremely successful era. The concept of magazines for young readers was still relatively new, but it had already proven fruitful.

The first American magazine edited specifically for children, *The Children's Magazine: Calculated for the Use of Families and Schools,* appeared in Hartford, Connecticut, in 1789, almost fifty years after Benjamin Franklin and Andrew Bradford brought out the first periodicals for adults in Philadelphia, Pennsylvania. Like Franklin's *The General Magazine, and Historical Chronicle, for All the British Plantations in America,* and Bradford's *American Magazine, or A Monthly View of the Political State of the British Colonies, The Children's Magazine* was a short-lived effort, folding in just four months; but it introduced Americans to a new type of magazine that was soon to thrive.

During the nineteenth century, children's magazines flourished, both in number and in quality. In his guide *Children's Periodicals of the United States,* the American historian R. Gordon Kelly lists 279 magazines that started up between 1802 and 1899, and his bibliography is not comprehensive. This list of publications designed to educate and entertain young readers includes religious magazines, literary miscellanies, and general interest and regional periodicals. It also includes the two best-known and best-loved children's magazines ever published in America: *The Youth's Companion,* from Boston, and *St. Nicholas,* from New York City.

In 1900 *The Youth's Companion* was seventy-three years old and still a vital magazine. A weekly for most of its life, this publication, originally called *Youth's Companion,* was launched in 1827 with high aspirations. "Our children are born to higher destinies than their fathers," wrote founder Nathaniel Willis in the magazine's prospectus; "they will be actors in a far advanced period of the world. Let their minds be formed, their hearts prepared, and their characters moulded for the scenes and the duties of a brighter day."

With ambitions for the role *The Youth's Companion* would play in this education of the nation's young, Willis began a magazine that would continue to publish for just over a hundred years, more than forty of them under the astute editorial guidance of Daniel S. Ford. During its lifetime, *The Youth's Companion* achieved an extraordinarily large circulation for its day—approximately 500,000 in the 1890s—partly because of its annual premium scheme offering gifts to subscribers who recruited new subscribers and partly because of the broad appeal of its family-oriented material, contributed by such famous authors as Harriet Beecher Stowe, Oliver Wendell Holmes, Jr., and JACK LONDON.

In 1900 *St. Nicholas,* which is widely considered to be the best children's magazine ever published in this country, was also still strong. Originally conceived by Roswell Smith, one of the founders of the well-respected *Scribner's Monthly, St. Nicholas* was launched by Scribner & Co. in 1873 and "conducted" for its first thirty-two years by MARY MAPES DODGE, who had not only high aspirations for her publication but also a clear vision of what she considered "the ideal child's magazine." In *Scribner's Monthly* in July 1873, Dodge wrote her well-known lines asserting that "the child's magazine needs to be stronger, truer, bolder, more uncompromising" than a magazine for grown-ups. "Its cheer must be the cheer of the bird-song, not of condescending editorial babble," she said. "If it *mean* freshness and heartiness, and life and joy, and its words are simply, directly, and musically put together, it will trill its own way."

Setting the highest standards for the fiction, nonfiction, and illustrations that would appear in *St. Nicholas,* Dodge drew the best children's artists and authors to the magazine, including LOUISA MAY ALCOTT, RUDYARD KIPLING, FRANCES HODGSON BURNETT, and HOWARD PYLE. In the "St. Nicholas League," one of the departments the shrewd editor created to involve readers in the magazine, *St. Nicholas* published the work of such young subscribers as William Faulkner and Edna St. Vincent Millay. With its outstanding editorial contributions, beautiful illustrations, and distinctive, charming ambiance, *St. Nicholas* won a devoted following whose loyalty, observes Theodore Peterson in *Magazines in the Twentieth Century* (1964), seems to have bordered on "fanaticism."

But while both these magazines were still strong as they entered the twentieth century, that strength did not endure very long. *The Youth's Companion* declined in circulation and, in 1929, folded. *St. Nicholas* survived until 1943, but after Dodge's death in 1905, it never again achieved the quality of its best years. Not only did these two ambitious and successful publications fail to thrive in the twentieth century, but, more important, they could not serve as models for further progress. Comparable magazines did not arise to replace them.

In fact, as children's magazines entered the twentieth century, they began an era characterized largely by struggle. Throughout the century, these publications have fought to hold their ground as new media have encroached upon their terrain. Radio and comics, movies, television, and electronic games have absorbed a sizable portion of the hours children might once have spent with a magazine. An expanding book-publishing industry has provided reading matter that might diminish a child's desire for magazines, literary magazines in particular. The competition has taken its toll on the importance of children's magazines, on their survival rate, and on their quality, as publishers, courting readers, have emphasized lightweight matter over substance.

In their struggle against an increasing array of new media, children's magazines have played out the general pattern of media in the twentieth century: Radio, newspapers, movies, television have all in their time been forced to confront new media that cut into their audience and sources of advertising. Like these other media, children's magazines, after a period of upset, have managed to survive and even thrive by adapting to change.

By mid-century, the field of children's periodicals had begun to regain momentum, and by the eighties, it had experienced tremendous growth. In *Magazines for Young People* (1991), Bill Katz and Linda Sternberg Katz, basing their statistics on *Ulrich's International Periodicals Directory,* estimate that the number of children's magazines has increased more than ninefold since 1940.

But these twentieth-century magazines for the most part have borne little resemblance to their nineteenth-century literary predecessors. In the early 1990s, the only primarily literary magazine that has gained wide recognition, apart from such publications as *Stone Soup* or *Merlyn's Pen,* which are comprised entirely of children's own work, is *Cricket,* which was started in 1973 specifically to "attempt to bridge the gap existing in children's magazine publishing since *St. Nicholas* ceased publication." Devoted to bringing high-quality stories, poems, and artwork to young readers, the magazine is published by Open Court Publishing Company, in La Salle, Illinois, which also started *Ladybug* in 1990 and *Babybug* in 1995 to bring a comparable magazine to younger readers.

In contrast, most publications of this era have been primarily nonfiction. Some have been general-interest magazines, such as the widely circulated *Highlights for Children,* founded in the forties, and *National Geographic World,* launched by the National Geographic Society in the eighties. But many children's magazines, like their adult counterparts since the fall of the great general-interest publications such as the *Saturday Evening Post* and *Life,* have developed more specialized niches.

As R. Gordon Kelly observes, the tendency toward more specialized children's magazines began as early as the turn of the century. He notes in particular that these publications, which had formerly addressed both boys and girls, began more frequently to affiliate themselves with a single gender. In the early 1900s, a slew of single-sex magazines emerged, including, in 1911, *Boys' Life,* which became the official magazine of the Boy Scouts of America and which continues to publish more than eighty years later.

In the late twentieth century, fewer children's magazines have tended to distinguish their identity by gender, but many have sought to establish other specialized niches for much the same reasons: to target a particular audience in order to capture readers and, in some cases, advertisers. *Boys' Life,* by affiliating with the Boy Scouts of America, secured a large circulation. Scholastic, Inc., developed another excellent special-audience technique by gearing its magazines to classroom use and marketing them to schools. Launching its first magazine in 1920—the *Western Pennsylvania Scholastic,* which would later become *Senior Scholastic*—the company has continued to add numerous titles to its stable.

Most twentieth-century children's magazines that have specialized have done so by subject, with themes ranging widely, from sports in *Sports Illustrated for Kids,* the younger sibling of *Sports Illustrated,* also published by Time Inc., to science and astronomy in *Odyssey.* This emphasis on specialized nonfiction is not surprising in a century that has placed much emphasis on specialized information. Nor is it surprising that many weaker children's magazines have overvalued facts, providing little more than numerous bits of data. But the best of these modern specialized magazines have provided a broad cultural, ethical, or intellectual context that makes their factual information meaningful.

In the area of the natural world, for example, a subject popular in children's magazines because it lends itself to youngsters' natural curiosity and to beautiful illustrations, the best American publications have emphasized an awareness of environmental issues. The National Wildlife Federation's two publications, *Your Big Backyard* and, for slightly older readers, *Ranger Rick*, both help children understand, enjoy, and respect the natural world. *Dolphin Log*, which revolves around the world of the sea, informs young readers about "the interconnectedness of living organisms, including people," as does *Zoobooks*, which devotes each issue to a specific animal or group of animals, describing their particular ecological niche and their relations with other animals and human beings.

In the realm of the social sciences, *Cobblestone Magazine*, a periodical devoted to American history launched by Cobblestone Publishing, Inc., in 1980, brings youngsters a broad interpretation of history by including such topics as music, medicine, and clothing in its purview, while *Faces*, an anthropological magazine from the same publisher, by exploring customs in other societies alerts children to the many differences in cultures throughout the world. One of the few magazines to specialize in the subject of daily life, *Zillions*, a children's version of *Consumer Reports*, also published by Consumer Union, helps youngsters become intelligent shoppers, involving them in the process of evaluating both products and the advertising that sells them.

Children's magazines have developed various ways of carving out audiences for themselves. Recognition of ethnic diversity in the 1970s and 1980s gave rise to such publications as *Daybreak Star*, a Native American magazine, and *Skipping Stones: A Multiethnic Children's Forum*, devoted to encouraging an appreciation of cultural differences. Numerous religious magazines have started up throughout the century, some dating far back, such as *Young Judaean*, begun in 1910, and others launched more recently, such as *The Friend*, a magazine of the Church of Jesus Christ of Latter-Day Saints, begun in 1971, and *Brilliant Star*, a magazine of the Baha'i faith, begun in 1983.

One kind of magazine that carries particularly contemporary overtones is the publication linked to other areas of the mass-entertainment world, such as television and popular toys. *Sesame Street*, associated with the long-lived television show, makes good use of this affiliation, offering young readers the comfort of a familiar environment and recognizable characters and adapting the television program's entertaining modes of education for a print medium. But in such magazines as the Welsh Publishing Group's *Barbie*, associated with the popular doll, the line between a magazine and a marketing tool grows thin.

As the twentieth century draws to a close, children's magazines, in decline at the start, have emerged as a busy industry. From a commercial viewpoint, publishers and advertisers have seen in these publications the possibility of reaching young consumers who represent a multibillion-dollar market. From an editorial viewpoint, publishers have seen a rich field that can support a wide range of interesting publications. No magazine born in this century has equaled *St. Nicholas* in quality; none has commanded its loyal following. Nor has any, upon folding, been missed as it is said *The Youth's Companion* was missed when it died. Children's magazines, for all their activity, have played a lesser role in this century than they did in the last, when they had more of a youngster's world to themselves. But on this smaller stage, many have performed with admirable skill.

GAIL POOL

MAGORIAN, MICHELLE

BRITISH NOVELIST, B. 1947. Because of her abiding interest in children's literature, Michelle Magorian decided to write a book of her own based on the two main characters of a short story she had read. The result—*Good Night, Mr. Tom* (1981)—won the International Reading Association Children's Book Award, which is given to a promising new writer for an exemplary first or second book. Although *Back Home* (1984) and *Not a Swan* (1991) do not have the emotional intensity of Magorian's first book, with its horrifying scenes of child abuse, the three novels are linked by a similarity of style, theme, and subject matter. Magorian displays her strong interest in and knowledge of the period surrounding World War II, when the children of London were evacuated to the countryside or to the safety of other countries.

In *Good Night, Mr. Tom*, a frail, frightened, abused boy named William Beech thrives and learns how to trust and what it means to be loved and cared for when he lives for six months with Tom Oakley, an elderly man who has been reclusive since the death of his beloved wife and infant son forty years earlier. Caring for Will softens Mr. Tom's heart, and when Will does not write to him after he has been reclaimed by his religiously fanatic, mentally unstable mother, Mr. Tom travels to London and rescues the boy he now considers his son. Filled with heart-wrenching scenes, authentic dialogue, and masterful characterization, the novel touched the hearts of critics and readers.

When Rusty Dickinson returns from America to

England at the end of World War II in *Back Home*, she must adjust to living once again with her mother, who expects her to be the quiet six-year-old she sent away; the little brother she has never seen; her stiff and proper father, whom she does not remember; and her old-fashioned, uptight grandmother. Miserable in boarding school and at home, Rusty struggles to retain her identity in a conformist world that has vastly different expectations and boundaries from what she experienced living in the United States. As in her depiction of the relationship between Will and Mr. Tom, Magorian stresses the positive impact that children can have on the lives of their parents by allowing the reader insight into Rusty's mother's thoughts, dreams, and disappointments.

Not a Swan twists that theme a bit by concentrating on the problems and joys of illegitimate birth from the perspective of seventeen-year-old Rose, who befriends an unwed, pregnant woman; a young man who has never known the details of his parentage; and, through letters and diaries, a deceased woman whose family not only forced her to give up her son but locked her away in a mental institution. An evacuee, Rose discovers more about her talents and dreams, as well as love and sexuality, when her mother, chaperone, and sisters join the war effort one by one, leaving her to revel in her newfound independence. Although somewhat overlong, the novel explores issues of interest to many young adults and brings readers to an awareness of the ways of life in England during that era.

Magorian, an actress and dancer who studied at Marcel Marceau's school of mime, invests in her characters an artistic drive that is nurtured by an older character in each book: Will has tremendous artistic and theatrical talent; Rusty loves interior decorating, particularly stenciling and woodworking; and Rose is a budding author. ❦ A.E.D.

MAHY, MARGARET

NEW ZEALAND AUTHOR, B. 1936. A masterful storyteller who captivates audiences young and old, former children's librarian Margaret Mahy successfully writes YOUNG ADULT NOVELS, MIDDLE-GRADE FICTION, and PICTURE BOOKS. Her characters are memorable; she is adept at combining humor, suspense, and imagination; and underlying all her work is an obvious and abiding love of language, which manifests itself in a distinct and dexterous style. The first of Mahy's picture books was published in 1969. One that exemplifies her unique brand of humor is *The Great White Man-Eating Shark: A Cautionary Tale* (1990), in which a young lad's greedy plan to keep a lovely cove to himself backfires when a female shark finds him irresistible in his clever—and convincing—shark disguise. Mahy's first middle-grade novel, *The Haunting* (1982), which received the Carnegie Medal, showcases her talent for weaving tales of suspense that remain grounded in the realities of contemporary family issues. Eight-year-old Barney Palmer's mother died at his birth, and his concerns about his stepmother's pregnancy are compounded by his fear that he may possess powerful psychic abilities. Mahy's gift for nonsense writing is revealed in all its glory in the middle-grade novel *The Blood-and-Thunder Adventure on Hurricane Peak* (1989). The complex plot involves two children, a sorcerer, a variety of zany characters, and a school with the motto "Always Expect the Unexpected."

Mahy's storytelling ability is also apparent in her books for young adults, as is her perceptive understanding of adolescent minds and emotions. In *Memory* (1988), a nineteen-year-old struggling with the vivid but incomplete memories of her sister's accidental death meets up with an elderly woman also wrestling with memory—the almost complete loss of her own. *The Catalogue of the Universe* (1986), another realistic novel, is an intelligent story of young love. Short and brainy Tycho has always loved his childhood friend, the beautiful and popular Angela. The feeling is mutual between the unlikely pair, though it takes a crisis for Angela to find that she loves Tycho, who is her main source of comfort in a mixed-up world.

Mahy's greatest skill is her ability to enrich a story rooted in realism by adding an element of the supernatural. Her novels are given verity by the detailed descriptions of the New Zealand surroundings and her clearly delineated characters; thus, when the supernatural world begins to impinge on the natural one, the reader, and protagonist, astonished by these strange events, find they have no choice but to accept them as real. In *The Changeover: A Supernatural Romance* (1984), fourteen-year-old Laura Chant is preoccupied with her mother's dating life until a more dangerous threat poses itself. She seeks help from a strange young man when a demon, disguised in human form, begins draining the life from her three-year-old brother, Jacko. Not at all the tale of horror it may seem, the novel is a touching coming-of-age story in which Laura undergoes a moving, and irreversible, transformation. In *The Tricksters* (1987), another enchanting blend of realism and fantasy, seventeen-year-old Ariadne, called Harry, seems to have conjured three strange visitors out of thin air, for the young men bear a strong resemblance to characters in

Voices of the Creators

Margaret Mahy

When I was about three, a successful hunter gave my parents a cock pheasant, still in its feathers. I vividly remember standing in a doorway staring up at this heraldic bird hanging by its feet over our washing tubs. The house seemed transformed by its presence, and I felt transformed too. When it was taken down and plucked, my distress was intense. I knew it was dead but somehow imagined it could still feel, and I hated to see such a beautiful object vanishing through a process of reduction. I screamed with horror and had to be taken away and comforted. (I was not so sensitive, however, as to refuse to eat any of it when, later in the day, it appeared, further transformed, as dinner.) For years after this I made up stories about two pheasants who were my friends. I was trying to remake a fearsome event through fiction, and I gave myself a magical function as a person whom pheasants loved. Fantasies such as these became part of the way I explored and reorganized my immediate world.

I was born in 1936 in Whakatane, a country town in New Zealand, and was almost immediately entranced by the stories that were read to me, entertained (I now think), not only by intimations of adventure and mysteriousness, but by the humor and drama inherent in words themselves. In the beginning, before I could write, I made up small rhymes which I learned by heart, and acted out stories, vaguely based on events in my own life but filled with the fascinations of another sort of existence. For as far back as I can remember, I wanted to write a book.

I had to wait until 1969 when *A Lion in the Meadow* was first published in the United States. I had already seen it in print, for it had been originally published in the *New Zealand School Journal*. However, as I held my story—bound, covered, and transformed by illustration and print—it suddenly seemed to me that, though I had written it, it was no longer mine. The story had indeed become a book, and the book belongs to a reader.

On the blurb of one of my books it was once stated that I had been educated at the University of Whakatane. To anyone in New Zealand, the idea that Whakatane might have a university was a funny mistake, but to me there was something essentially true about the error. I still think, in my heart of hearts, that I was educated at the University of Whakatane and that I finally graduated. A more official graduation took place in the city of Christchurch, where, in due course, I completed a bachelor of arts degree. I then qualified as a librarian by doing the diploma course of the New Zealand Library School. I became a librarian because I had to do something to earn a living, but—as I tried to order and manipulate the wild, sprawling, disorderly, and contradictory fields of human knowledge—the library came to seem like a major point of collision between anarchy and order, a constantly changing tension, serious yet funny too, incapable of final release.

By now I have published over one hundred stories—many of them, including the very short stories which are used in reading programs, for young children and some for young adults. Initially all these stories at an emergent, primitive stage are for my own listening self, though at a later stage of writing I do consciously think of children who might some day read these stories. I redirect the stories toward those children, by simplifying the language a little or perhaps by adapting the original story-line. I like stories, even those which are too long to be read aloud, to *sound* a certain way, for, even when reading silently from the page, we all have some idea of the story's voice. We invent it as we go along. This is one of the creative elements in reading. As I write, I receive a similar pleasure to my pleasure in reading, though it is a more hesitant and uncertain pleasure.

I live just outside of Christchurch in the South Island of New Zealand in a house with a straggling garden, four cats, and a dog. One of my daughters, her husband, and her little daughter live next door. I visit a lot of schools and attend many conferences, but when I am at home I spend a lot of time writing, ordering the cats and dog around (though without much conviction or success), and fussing over my granddaughter. It is an ordinary life, but like many ordinary lives it is astonishing and mysterious to the person actually living it.

the romantic fantasy she has been writing. Incredibly complex, *The Tricksters* is a demanding novel that, in turn, rewards readers willing to fall under the spell of its intricate and richly layered narrative. A prolific writer, Mahy has contributed significantly to children's literature with her exquisitely crafted and compelling stories that continuously prompt readers to "Always Expect the Unexpected." J.M.B.

Marino, Jan

American author, b. 1936. Jan Marino has written newspaper columns and short stories for adults, but she says she derives the most satisfaction from writing in the voice of a child—the clearest voice of all, in her opinion.

Her clear and honest voice spoke to young readers for the first time in *Eighty-Eight Steps to September* (1989), which addresses through the character of eleven-year-old Amy a long-taboo subject in children's literature, a sibling's death. Few authors, fledgling or established, can create a consistently believable first-person child narrator; with Amy Marino accomplishes this feat poignantly. A typical sister and brother, Amy and Robbie fight. They can't even agree about the gender of their new puppy, christened Samantha by Amy but more aptly named Samuel. Marino carries Amy's stubbornness through to her denial that Robbie will never come home from the hospital, and when Amy can no longer turn away from the facts, her stubbornness becomes her kernel of strength. The author knows intimately the confusion and grief her character experiences: Marino's own brother died when she was a child. Setting the novel in the past, 1948, she reaches back into her own life to depict Amy's struggle.

For her next novel, *The Day That Elvis Came to Town* (1991), Marino moves forward to 1963, when the family of protagonist Wanda Dohr takes in a new boarder, a glamorous and warm-hearted jazz singer named Mercedes Washington. Different problems confront Wanda. Her father's on-again, off-again drinking renders home life emotionally and financially rocky. Her friend and idol Mercedes, Wanda eventually discovers, must constantly endure discrimination for being half-black. But just as Amy can't wish on an eyelash to bring her brother back, Wanda discovers she can't make the world as bright and glittery as one of Mercedes' dresses simply by believing it so. Not a writer of mere problem novels, Marino offers Wanda no quick fixes or easy outs. Instead, she promotes meeting injustices as Mercedes does: with courage born of belief in oneself.

Ted Bradford in *Like Some Kind of Hero* (1992) plainly has this lesson to learn, although once again Marino constructs a complex situation, not presenting one obviously right or wrong path. Ted excels at playing classical guitar, a talent respected by his musically inclined family and friends. But he wants to excel at a sport, to be admired by cool girls, "not girls who carry violin cases with the bow strapped to the side." When he goes for lifeguard training, spurred on by visions of bikini-clad beauties fawning under his chair, he discovers he has a real shot at the job. Then he must tackle the even more difficult job of deciding what matters most to him in life. For Ted—and for Jan Marino, it seems—the answer turns out to be real relationships over appearances, self-respect over praise from the crowd. ❦ C.M.H.

Mark, Jan

British author, b. 1943. Echoing the title of her short-story collection *Nothing to Be Afraid Of* (1980), Mark wrote an article called "Something to Be Afraid Of" for the British education journal *English in Education*. The article's title highlights a recurring theme in her work: there is indeed something to be afraid of, particularly for the sensitive, isolated, or unusual child who must come to terms with the rest of the world. In the Carnegie Medal winning *Handles* (1983), Erica longs to become a motorcycle mechanic, an ambition that spells trouble for a girl. When Mr. Angel comes to work next door, his boisterous, aggressive family threatens to overwhelm Matthew in *Under the Autumn Garden* (1977). Another Carnegie Medal winner, *Thunder and Lightnings* (1976), introduces Victor, the bright airplane aficionado who cannot learn in the accepted way. For him and for others school becomes a hazard; if they do not exactly fear it, they often distrust it. Here Mark draws on her own experiences as student and educator; she earned a National Diploma in Design, spent six years as an English and art teacher in a secondary school, and also worked with education students.

In Mark's novels for this age group—upper-elementary and middle-school students—relationships with other people, though not easily found or maintained, help children in their struggle with their difficulties. In *Trouble Halfway* (1985), for example, Amy's stepfather shows her that she need not be immobilized by fear of life's very real dangers. In Mark's FANTASY and SCIENCE FICTION novels for older readers—*The Ennead* (1978), *Divide and Rule* (1979), and *Aquarius* (1982)—the characters are generally not so fortunate. They have reason to fear not only their own faults but also the inexorable pressures of religion and society. While Mark's other books often have the distinctive regional flavor of Norfolk in eastern England, these stories take place in imaginary worlds. As she says, "In novels for older readers I prefer to place a character in an unfamiliar environment and watch him struggle . . . in the best traditions of tragedy, through his own shortcomings." Strand by strand, Mark builds a complicated web, until her protagonists find themselves completely caught. Nevertheless, she favors acts of defiance, even when they cannot lead to a happy ending. A the end of *The Ennead*, Isaac helps an embattled sculptor run away from the authorities, even though the fugitives will probably not escape for long.

Such self-assertive gestures are also one source of the multifaceted humor that enriches Mark's other writing. In "Chutzpah," a story in *Nothing to Be Afraid Of*, a girl claiming to be a new student wreaks havoc in a school that seems to deserve it; she finally reveals herself as a bored visitor on holiday from another school. In addition to short stories and novels, Mark has also written picture books, such as *Fur* (1986), *Fun* (1987), and *Silly Tails* (1993). Her work offers a worthwhile experience to readers who like stories with a bite—either a comic twist or a tragic one. ❧ M.F.S.

MARSHAK, SAMUEL

SOVIET POET AND TRANSLATOR, 1887–1964. The leading Soviet children's poet of his generation, Samuel Yakolevich Marshak is also well known for his classic Russian TRANSLATIONS of English literature, including Shakespeare's sonnets and the works of many of the English Romantics. After studying at London University from 1913 to 1914, Marshak returned to Russia and became active in children's relief work and the development of educational programs. A protégé of Maxim Gorky's, Marshak was invited to report on the state of children's literature at the First All-Union Conference of Soviet Writers in 1934, and by organizing the first state publishing house for children, he was instrumental in shaping Soviet literature for the very young.

Marshak's own writing for children was largely influenced by English and Russian folklore and by the poetry of Aleksandr Pushkin. Marshak's play *Twelve Months* (published in the United States in 1946 in Alexander Bakshy's collection *Soviet Scene: Six Plays of Russian Life*), for which he won the Stalin Prize in 1946, is based on a Czechoslovakian tale and is the only one of his innumerable works for children written in prose. A picture-book adaptation of the play, *The Month Brothers* (1983), translated by Thomas P. Whitney and illustrated by DIANE STANLEY, tells the story of a young girl who is helped and comforted by the twelve months of the year—personified as brothers—when she is forced out into a January blizzard by her cruel stepmother.

Marshak's admiration for Pushkin is demonstrated in his lively, direct, and action-oriented style of POETRY, which is also characterized by his own unique charm, humor, and vigorous rhythm. "The Ice-Cream Man," which describes a fat man who eats so much ice cream that he turns into a snowman, was published in the United States in *The Ice-Cream Man and Other Stories* in 1943, but little of Marshak's poetry has been published in this country since.

Two of his poems, however, have been given glorious new life in collaborations by translator Richard Pevear and illustrator Vladimir Radunsky. *The Pup Grew Up!* (1989) is a comic verse about a lady who checks into a train station with a tiny Pekingese but is presented at the end of her trip with a Great Dane. The ludicrous text in brisk rhythm is extended by the spirited line and oddball characters of the expressive illustrations. Pevear and Radunsky team up again for *Hail to Mail* (1990), a translation of Marshak's famous poem about a certified letter that follows its addressee all around the world through the postal system. With large expanses of bold color and intriguingly shifting perspectives, the illustrations depict the letter's travels "by water, air, and land / To Idaho, to Switzerland." Both of these exuberant productions provide well-deserved recognition for the beloved Russian poet. ❧ L.A.

MARSHALL, JAMES

AMERICAN AUTHOR AND ILLUSTRATOR, 1942–1992. Born in San Antonio, Texas, James Marshall never planned to become a children's book author and illustrator. He studied at the New England Conservatory of Music and played the viola. But a physical accident ended his career, and he then studied French and history, receiving a master's degree at Trinity College.

For a time Marshall supported himself by teaching French and Spanish in a Boston school. Although he himself would eventually teach students at Parsons School of Design in New York City, he was an untrained artist. Meanwhile he doodled, placing eyes and lines to create characters. Eventually those doodles reached an editor, who gave Marshall his first illustrating assignment, *Plink, Plink, Plink* (1971) by BYRD BAYLOR, probably Marshall's only uninspired book. His next book, which came out the following year, was to demonstrate to adults and children the potential that Marshall possessed; *George and Martha*, a collection of five vignettes about two hippopotamuses who have a unique friendship, was a critical success and enthusiastically received by children. As Marshall was later to say, he knew with this book that he had found his life's work.

That life's work was to last for twenty years and bring about the creation of dozens of PICTURE BOOKS and novels, including six more "George and Martha" books, Harry Allard's *Miss Nelson Is Missing!* (1977), and OGDEN NASH's *Adventures of Isabel* (1991), as well as his own *The Stupids Die* (1981), *Fox and His Friends* (1982), and *The Cut-Ups* (1984).

Marshall's talent was wide-ranging; he had an intuitive grasp of how to reduce a visual object to its most basic elements, the type of genius found in the sculptures of Alexander Calder. Marshall's most famous characters, George and Martha, were created with two dots for eyes, a nose, and a mouth. Marshall's compositions depended on his line rather than his color; he began publishing books when artists were still required to create color separations, and even in his later books he always retained his strong black line, which was filled with verve.

From Marshall's notebooks, available among other places at the De Grummond Collection at Hattiesburg, Mississippi, it is immediately apparent that he drew with great spontaneity and energy. But unlike many artists who lose this spontaneity in the books themselves, Marshall kept it in abundance. His sketches in his books maintain a vitality rare in contemporary children's picture books; his final drawings were not studied or finished but still feel like exuberant sketches.

Marshall's greatest contribution to the children's book field was his ability to develop character. He captured the foibles and idiosyncrasies of his characters; his humor was always gentle; the lessons about life were present, but never heavy-handed, as when George pours his split-pea soup into his shoes so as not to hurt Martha's feelings. The Marshall canon of characters is legendary: Viola Swamp, George, Martha, the Stupids, Emily Pig, Fox, the Cut-Ups. After reading books about a Marshall character, children believe he or she truly exists as an individual.

Marshall was equally brilliant as a writer. Even in those books that bear other authors' names, Marshall worked and reworked text to have that perfect combination of text and art. His own writings, *A Summer in the South* (1977) and *Rats on the Roof and Other Stories* (1991), demonstrate his abilities as a storyteller and what he could accomplish with words alone.

As brilliant as Marshall's work was, as devoted a readership as he found, he won few major awards in his lifetime. The University of Mississippi presented him with its Silver Medallion in 1992, and he was given the Caldecott Honor Medal for *Goldilocks* (1988). His greatest number of awards were those children voted him.

In the latter part of the twentieth century, there have been many fine practitioners of the art of the picture book, but Marshall was one of the finest. His books were classics that have and will endure. A.S.

MARTIN, ANN M.

AMERICAN AUTHOR, B. 1955. Baby-sitting has proven to be a fun and profitable business for Ann Martin, author of the incredibly successful "Baby-Sitters Club" SERIES. A children's book editor, Martin had already written some children's novels when the concept for the series was suggested to her. Like series character Kristy Thomas's idea for a baby-sitting club, the idea for the series was "simple but brilliant." The first books about a group of girls who form a child-care cooperative were so popular that the original plans for a four-part series were quickly forgotten. The series, begun in 1986, has 100 million books in print, has been translated into nineteen languages, and boasts a fan club of more than sixty thousand members. "Super Special" editions feature the series characters away from home on trips, mystery books have been added to the series, and younger readers have their own series, "Baby-Sitters Little Sister."

Martin bases the characters and events on her childhood friends and experiences. Memories of her own phase of lifeguard-watching created *Boy Crazy Stacey* (1987), and *Claudia and the Sad Good-bye* (1989) contains feelings about her own grandmother's death. The stories, each told from the point of view of a different club member, involve problems such as divorce, deceased or strict parents or stepparents, and occasional fights between club members—interspersed with frequent trips to the mall. But Martin has cleverly latched on to very specific interests of girls ages eight to twelve. Most obvious is the obsession with hairstyles and clothing: readers are provided with lengthy, detailed descriptions of what each character, adult or child, is wearing, from socks to earrings. Stories about baby-sitting are tailor-made for the fascination preteen girls have with large families, especially those that include twins and triplets. Martin has combined the appeal of the impeccably dressed NANCY DREW with that of the multiply cute BOBBSEY TWINS and added to these the attractive ideas of clubs and earning money. The main ingredient that hooks readers, however, is the empowering stories of girls calmly solving problems on the job and at home. At work they handle a variety of baby-sitting difficulties, including emergencies, and back home they learn to act maturely, bargaining instead of arguing with Mom and Dad.

Growing up in Princeton, New Jersey, Martin loved to baby-sit and to read, passions she passes on to her fans. Though adults may wish preteens were reading something other than formulaic series books, most are grateful that their children are reading at all. The books have also created an interest in business, and girls nationwide are starting their own baby-sitting clubs, a far more practical venture than that of earlier generations of series-crazed girls who lurked about looking for clues and crooks.

Martin is also the author of several MIDDLE-GRADE and YOUNG-ADULT NOVELS, including *Me and Katie (the Pest)* (1985), *With You and without You* (1986), and *Ten Kids, No Pets* (1988). Martin's entertaining novels about family life are praised for the gentle humor and fast pace of the light, upbeat, easy-to-read stories. ❧

J.M.B.

Martin, Bill, Jr.

AMERICAN PICTURE-BOOK AUTHOR AND EDUCATOR, B. 1916. Bill Martin, Jr., purposefully writes books to be read aloud, paying attention to, as he says, the "rhythms, melodies, and sounds of language" to create stories that delight both the ear and the tongue of young children, who ask to hear them over and over again.

Perhaps part of his insistence on read-alouds goes back to his own early reading days. As a child growing up in Kansas, he was basically a nonreader. What saved him was a storytelling grandmother and a fifth-grade teacher who read aloud to his class twice a day. From them, he learned to savor the rich and varied quality of language. In spite of his reading problems, he graduated from Kansas State Teachers College (now Emporia State University) and taught high school. In 1945 Martin wrote *The Little Squeegy Bug,* illustrated by his brother, Bernard, which he published himself. When Eleanor Roosevelt mentioned it on her radio program, his writing career was launched. Bill and Bernard continued to collaborate until 1953, publishing a total of seventeen books. After receiving his Ph.D. from Northwestern University in 1961, Martin became an editor at Holt, Rinehart & Winston, creating numerous educational reading programs. He originally wrote *Brown Bear, Brown Bear, What Do You See?* (1967) for one of these, and after several incarnations, it was reissued as a trade book in 1983. Enhanced by ERIC CARLE's illustrations, its simple but melodious repetitions delight children and encourage them to participate. Using a similar formula, *Polar Bear, Polar Bear, What Do You Hear?* (1991), also illustrated by Carle, plays with animal sounds in patterned repetitions. Although Martin introduces words that may be unfamiliar to preschoolers, such as "fluting" flamingos and "braying" zebras, the words themselves are appealing and fun to say.

Martin maintains it is not essential that children understand every word "so long as they . . . assimilate the sounds, the music, the poet's vision." Teaming up with John Archambault, a poet, journalist, and storyteller, Martin has written nine other books, most of which are illustrated by Ted Rand. Using a combination of rhyme and narrative, *The Ghost-Eye Tree* (1985) describes a scary evening's walk past a haunted tree. Again, the sound of language draws the reader into the story, but in this book the characters of the young boy and girl hold one's attention. The sibling rivalry and affection create a nice counterpoint to the delicious fear they experience on their trip. In *Barn Dance!* (1986) Martin and Archambault use the rhythm of a square dance to recount the adventures of the "skinny kid" when he goes to a midnight hoedown in the barn. *Knots on a Counting Rope* (educational series edition, 1966; trade edition, 1987) tells of an American Indian boy's courageous efforts to overcome his blindness. Martin and Archambault use two voices, a dialogue between the boy and his grandfather, to recount the child's growing ability to negotiate his dark world. The result is poetic and moving. In *Chicka Chicka Boom Boom* (1989), illustrated by LOIS EHLERT with bright, bold graphic shapes, Martin and Archambault create a delightful alphabet chant in which the letters become characters participating in a rambunctious romp up a coconut tree. Rhythm and rhyme once again encourage the reader to join in, snapping fingers and celebrating the joy of playing with and appreciating language. ❧ P.R.

Martin, Patricia Miles

AMERICAN AUTHOR, 1899–1986. Most notable among the more than eighty children's books that Patricia Martin wrote (often using the pseudonyms Miska Miles or Jerry Lane) are her novels for younger readers and her PICTURE BOOKS. The straightforward story lines of these books focus on individual children or animals and reflect Martin's deep understanding of young people and her respect for the natural world.

Her connection to the natural world began early. She was born in Cherokee, Kansas, and grew up in Oklahoma, Missouri, and Colorado, returning every summer to her grandparents' Kansas farm. The language in her best work is spare and evocative, deftly illuminating scenes with its poetic phrasing. The books Martin has written under the pseudonym Miska Miles have received the most recognition. Among these, she is best known for *Annie and the Old One* (1971), a Newbery Honor Book and winner of a Christopher Award, which reflects her lifelong interest in American Indians. Annie is a Navajo girl whose grandmother says one day, "When the new rug is taken from the loom, I will go to Mother Earth." Annie tries everything she can to prevent the rug's completion so that her grandmother will not die. This powerful book sets Annie's fierce determination to stop time against her grandmother's calm acceptance of the cycle of life and death. Here, as in her other books that feature children from various cultures, Martin makes the culture an element in the story but not its point. This is particularly true in her short novels for young readers, which feature children in a variety of settings, frequently focusing on those who are trying to make sense of feelings in a world quite beyond their control. That world may include earthquakes, blizzards, or severe poverty, but these hardships never dominate; instead the focus remains on the children as they cope—with piercing honesty and often humor. In *Hoagie's Rifle-Gun* (1970), Hoagie sets out to shoot something for dinner rather than face a meal of boiled potatoes—again. He finds only an elusive bobcat, a target for his anguished frustration but a winner, finally, of his respect.

Martin has written a number of picture books about animals, the most striking of which are her collaborations with illustrator John Schoenherr. In these books the animals remain wild animals; they do not become vehicles for human emotions. The tension in these stories is most often caused by the animals' interaction with humans. In *Otter in the Cove* (1974), a young girl is delighted to discover a small herd of otters swimming in a nearby cove. Her father, however, an abalone fisherman, decides he must kill the otters in order to protect his livelihood. The girl begs him to let them live, and finally, painfully, he decides to do so. But here, as in many of Martin's books, the ending is not tidy. The book finishes with a picture of a playful otter happily eating abalone in the cove. This honest portrayal of life is a common element in Martin's books. She combines it effectively with her warm voice and appealing array of characters to produce books that are uncomplicated but deeply affecting. ❧ A.Q.

Mathers, Petra

American artist and author, b. 1945. Petra Mathers's deceptively simple stories offer characters whose comical pathos and quiet courage strike a chord of recognition in her readers. Her work is fresh and original and, best of all, straight from the heart.

Mathers was born in the Black Forest and grew up in postwar Germany. Before beginning her career in children's books, Mathers built on her childhood love of books with an apprenticeship in a bookstore. With her then husband and her child, Mathers emigrated to America, living in Portland, Oregon, where she painted in her spare time, exhibiting her work in several gallery shows while helping to support her family with a series of waitressing jobs. In 1980 Mathers left the United States for a time to dive for treasure in the South China Sea.

Her first children's book, *How Yossi Beat the Evil Urge* (1983) by Miriam Chaikin, featured black-and-white illustrations. Though her buoyant artwork has graced several picture books, including *The Block Book* (1990), *Frannie's Fruits* (1989), and *Molly's New Washing Machine* (1986), Mathers is best known for her own books, which are marked with her distinctively elegant style and wit. Her debut with *Maria Theresa* (1985), about a hen who literally flies her otherwise happy coop in Manhattan to find fulfillment as a member of a circus act in the country, surprises readers with an ending that is laced with a little romance and the notion of finding one's rightful place in the world, themes that recur in Mathers's other work.

Mathers's gentle endings remind us that not everything is a perfect fit at first, although with a little courage and openness people can find their right match. This idea is cleverly pursued in *Theodor and Mr. Balbini* (1980), in which Mr. Balbini wants only a simple canine companion. Instead, he finds himself saddled with a cantankerous and talkative dog with a taste for French and a litany of complaints. It is with the help of Theodor's French tutor, a woman whose own dog eschews all forms of sophistication, that a solution is found with resulting new friendships for all concerned.

In *Sophie and Lou* (1991), recipient of the Boston Globe–Horn Book Award, readers meet Sophie, a mouse so shy that she can only shop during the slow hours, who becomes entranced by a dance studio that opens across the street. Sophie is pulled into the world of tangos and rumbas, which she practices alone in her living room until one day she is asked to dance by Lou, a debonair mouse who has been shadowing her all along. Mathers is also the author and illustrator of *Aunt Elaine Does the Dance from Spain* (1992) and *Victor and Christabel* (1993).

The charm of Mathers's work lies in her bold fresh pictures with their flat perspective and clean, spare lines. Mathers's unerring eye for detail, whether it is a plumber's car sporting a leaky faucet as a hood ornament or Sophie's winged alarm clock, have a warmth and subtle humor. Mathers's simple watercolors combine tenderness and humor. Of her creations, the author comments, "The characters I invented now live their own lives. They are quietly minding their own business—none of them will set the world on fire. But they are decent, a little comical, and open to love." ❧ C.L.L.

Mathis, Sharon Bell

American author, b. 1937. Sharon Bell Mathis entered the field of children's books in the 1970s, a decade that introduced a number of fine African American authors. Although her best-known books were all published within five years, the author made a significant contribution to children's literature with realistic stories about urban African Americans confronting societal and family problems.

Born in Atlantic City, New Jersey, Mathis grew up in Brooklyn, New York, where she began writing poetry and stories with the encouragement of her family and teachers. She attended Morgan State College in Baltimore and, over the next fifteen years, taught school while raising three daughters. During this time, she continued writing and discovered that her best work usually involved young characters.

Her first book, *Brooklyn Story* (1970), concerns a teenage brother and sister whose long-absent mother reappears the same week that Martin Luther King is killed. *Sidewalk Story* (1971), an intermediate-grade book about a girl who tries to stop her best friend's family from being evicted, won a contest sponsored by the Council on Interracial Books for Children. Both books are notable for their authentic dialogue and contemporary view of African American life. Occasional sudden shifts in perspective reflect the author's inexperience, but her subsequent books are more sure-handed and controlled.

Perhaps her best-known work is *The Hundred Penny Box* (1975), which was named a Newbery Honor Book. This touching story for younger readers examines the special bonds between children and the elderly, as young Michael is the only person in his family to truly understand the importance of his great-great-aunt's box full of pennies, one for each year of her life. Mathis realistically depicts Aunt Dew's occasional confusion and beautifully hints at the wealth of memories each coin represents.

Two young adult novels are equally memorable. *Teacup Full of Roses* (1972) explores the despair of an inner-city family as seventeen-year-old Joe deals with an addicted older brother and a gifted, but unappreciated younger brother. The characterizations are particularly good in this vivid novel, which, like all of the author's books, is presented within a time frame of less than a week. Although this brevity provides immediacy and tension, the story occasionally has a rushed feeling. *Listen for the Fig Tree* (1974) takes place in the week before Christmas, as a sixteen-year-old blind girl prepares for Kwanza and worries about her widowed mother's heavy drinking. The characters of Muffin and her mother are exceptionally well defined in this accomplished and moving novel.

At the time of publication, Mathis's works were highly acclaimed. Although their dialogue may now seem somewhat dated, the books present interesting portraits of African American life in the 1970s. That decade also brought many changes in the author's personal life. She received a master's degree in library science from Catholic University and began working as a school librarian, her marriage ended in divorce, and she suffered a lengthy bout of writer's block. Mathis returned to children's books with *Red Dog Blue Fly: Football Poems* (1991), a short collection of poems about a youth football team. Although a modest effort, the long-awaited volume was welcomed by readers who continue to look forward to future works by this gifted author. ❧ P.D.S.

Mayer, Mercer

American author and illustrator, b. 1943. Mercer Mayer's enduring popularity comes from his creative versatility, wide-ranging artistic skill, and the humor he infuses in all of his work for children. His roles include author, illustrator, and author/illustrator of more than one hundred children's books, and his collaborators include Marianna Mayer, Steven Kellogg, Jane Yolen, and Jan Wahl.

Mayer began his career in 1967 with the publication of an original series of wordless, one-color minibooks featuring the adventures of the title characters in *A Boy, A Dog and A Frog*, perfect for preschoolers. His work continued in many directions. Tackling such quintessential childhood fears as nightmares and hidden monsters, *There's a Nightmare in My Closet* (1968) (a "Reading Rainbow" book), *There's an Alligator Under My Bed* (1987), and *There's Something in My Attic* (1988) became enormously popular with the kindergarten set. Mayer's young protagonists always show strength, ingenuity, and resourcefulness in overcoming their anxieties.

Moving to a full-color palette and a lavish, romantic,

painterly style, Mayer retold and illustrated classic folktales, including *East of the Sun, West of the Moon* (1980), *The Sleeping Beauty* (1984), and *The Pied Piper of Hamelin* (1987). Mayer's written work includes such books of nonsense fiction as *Terrible Troll* (1968), *Appelard and Liverwurst* (1978), and *Liverwurst Is Missing* (1982), the last two illustrated by Steven Kellogg, and the "Professor Wormbog" books, which Mayer both wrote and illustrated.

As author and illustrator, Mayer created three series of books for young children featuring the cartoonlike creatures "Little Monster" and "Little Critter" and "Tink! Tonk! Tales." Older readers enjoy Mayer's humorous pen-and-ink drawings in JOHN D. FITZGERALD's "Great Brain" series and JOHN BELLAIRS's *Figure in the Shadows* (1975). In 1977 *Everyone Knows What a Dragon Looks Like,* written by JAY WILLIAMS, received the Irma Simonton Black Award and a Best Illustrated Children's Books of the Year citation from the *New York Times,* and *Liza Lou and the Great Yeller Belly Swamp* (1976), which Mayer wrote and illustrated, received the 1983 California Young Reader Medal. ❧ J.A.S.

MAYNE, WILLIAM

ENGLISH AUTHOR, B. 1928. At the age of fourteen, William Mayne decided he wanted to become a writer, and he has single-mindedly achieved this goal at a steady, sometimes furious, pace for the past forty years. Working for most of this time from a cottage on the edge of a moor in Yorkshire, the county where he was born, he has written or edited more than eighty books for children in a variety of genres from the picture book to the short story. Novels, however, represent the bulk of his output—novels that have led many to question whether he truly writes *for* children.

Although his work received critical acclaim virtually from the beginning, it has never been popular among its intended audience. *A Grass Rope,* winner of Britain's Carnegie Medal in 1957, combines elements children would typically love: a mystery involving the long-ago disappearance of a pack of hunting dogs, a possible hidden treasure, an elusive unicorn, and a youngest child who finally finds the key to it all. But while other writers recognize his achievement as a stylist, even intelligent, eager young readers find it challenging, at best, to follow his stories. "If we had to understand everything we heard, we'd be a long time learning a little," says Billy, the stonemason to Debby and Lesley, the young heroines of Mayne's *The Battlefield* (1967), who are eager to separate fact from legend regarding the mysterious piece of land near their home. The author apparently agrees with his character. Like the treasure hunts many of his plots involve, Mayne's books don't come with handy maps. His tendency for beginning in the middle and doubling back later to explain has helped further his reputation as a keen observer, able to capture the esoteric nature of interaction among children and family members. It has also at times hindered readers from penetrating the surface of his characters. An ability to render the commonplace uncommon, often through aptly poetic yet sophisticated use of language, has both earned him fans and turned away those who demand more straightforward action. Yet within a complex framework, Mayne habitually reveals a childlike fascination with the natural and the supernatural, with science and with what science seemingly can't explain. In his first fantasy, *Earthfasts* (1966), the line between the two grows increasingly fine as two boys realize they must rely less on geology and more on local legend to account for the strange phenomena in their midst. Conversely, he gives a nod to science in the fantastic *Antar and the Eagles* (1990), lending credence to a boy's capture by eagles by addressing the realities of eagle life to which a human in such a situation would need to adapt in order to survive. In *A Game of Dark* (1971), Mayne presents a grim battle for psychological survival as fifteen-year-old Donald periodically escapes the guilty animosity he harbors for his critically ill father by entering a medieval world. But even there he faces a terrifying dragon.

While Mayne's stories have taken place on several continents, for the most part he has kept them close to home, unfolding upon the Yorkshire dales. For four of his earliest books, beginning with the highly commended *A Swarm in May* (1955), he drew upon his own childhood experiences in a Yorkshire choir school. Some of his characters have traveled no further than their own front doors to encounter mystery. A delightful, accessible series of four picture books, all published in 1984 and illustrated by Patrick Benson, records the "Hob stories," which feature a little man who lives under the stairs and ventures out at night to protect his host family from anything from mumps to bad temper. The adults of the family consider Hob "nonsense." As in much of Mayne's writing, the children know otherwise. ❧ C.M.H.

MAZER, NORMA FOX

AMERICAN AUTHOR, B. 1931. One of three sisters, Norma Fox Mazer grew up in Glens Falls, New York, a small town near the Adirondack Mountains. Her father drove a bread truck, and her mother was a saleswoman. Her grandparents were all from Europe, and Mazer has said that for her the "whole weight of the past" was of immigrants who struggled and were poor. As a child Mazer was imaginative and intelligent and aspired to be a teacher or social worker. Married at eighteen, after a short time at Antioch College in Ohio, she began to raise the first of four children and started to fit writing into her daily life. She began with descriptions, letters, and short stories. Her husband, Harry Mazer, also wanted to be a writer, so the two set early-morning hours and began years of intense, disciplined work, writing for magazines in order to break into the field. Mazer still writes every day and still begins in the early hours of the morning.

Though most of Mazer's more than twenty books are YOUNG ADULT NOVELS, her first, *I, Trissy* (1971), was for a younger audience. Its protagonist, like most of Mazer's, is a strong girl coming to terms with the real problems in her life and facing them with courage. The novel was an experiment with literary devices such as epistolary fiction, an early example of Mazer's interest in varying her style. Mazer wrote two collections of short stories, *Dear Bill, Remember Me?* (1976) and *Summer Girls, Love Boys* (1982). These two books contain fine examples of a genre that is rarely as successful when attempted by most young adult writers.

Mazer has the feeling of being an outsider, which she says may be from being Jewish but may be from being bright and female as she grew up. "It just wasn't the thing to be," she states. The themes of being an outsider and of having a working-class background are often apparent in her fiction. In *Mrs. Fish, Ape, and Me, the Dump Queen* (1980), the protagonist's father runs the town dump, and the two of them live in a trailer. Mazer also writes about current issues that intrigue her. In *When We First Met* (1982), a Romeo and Juliet story, a child is killed by a drunk driver. *Up in Seth's Room* (1979) is a thoughtful treatment of the quandary of whether a girl should sleep with her boyfriend. Mazer has also written FANTASY; *Saturday, the Twelfth of October* (1975), one of her own favorites, is a time-travel fantasy in which Mazer creates a matriarchal society, including its religion, folklore, speech, and rituals. A suspense novel, *Taking Terri Mueller* (1981), won the Edgar Allan Poe Award for the Best Juvenile Mystery. She has also written a series of lighthearted novels, starting with *A, My Name Is Ami* (1986), and has collaborated with her husband on two books. Many of Mazer's books have been named Best Books for Young Adults by the American Library Association. *After the Rain* (1987) is the story of a teenage girl who learns that her unpleasant, overcritical grandfather has only a few months to live. A better relationship slowly develops between them as she gives up her free time to help care for him until his death. The ALA named this novel a 1988 Newbery Honor Book. ❧ S.H.H.

McCaffrey, Anne

IRISH AUTHOR OF SCIENCE FICTION, B. 1926. As a child, Anne McCaffrey was determined that one day she would be a famous author; the large number of her books that have become best-sellers is a testimony to her success in achieving that goal. Born in Cambridge, Massachusetts, McCaffrey resides in Ireland in a home she calls Dragonhold. Her SCIENCE FICTION has received numerous prizes, including the Hugo and Nebula awards, and is widely read by adults and adolescents.

Best known are her novels set on Pern, a planet colonized by and later isolated from Earth. With genetic engineering, the inhabitants of Pern adapted a beast native to the planet to fight with fire the invasive, sporelike Thread that jumps from the Red Star to Pern during certain periods of its orbit. Each of these massive, sentient creatures, called dragons because of their similarity to the mythical Earth creatures, forms at hatching a lifelong, telepathic attachment, called Impressing, to one human, who becomes its dragonrider. Upon this complex, but fully developed premise, more than a dozen tales have been founded. Three—*Dragonsong* (1976), *Dragonsinger* (1977), and *Dragondrums* (1979), together known as the "Harper Hall of Pern" series—were written specifically for young readers. Although the dragons are featured as an integral part of Pernese life, the trilogy focuses more closely on the role of the harper in Pern society.

McCaffrey, who studied voice for nine years and for a time was involved in the theater, brings her love of music to her fiction by exploring its importance to culture, not only as entertainment, but as a way of transmitting knowledge and history from generation to generation. In *Dragonsong*, Menolly, an extremely gifted musician, runs away from her native fishing community because her father believes girls have no right to compose or play music in public. Accidentally, Menolly Impresses nine fire lizards, miniature cousins of the dragons, when she seeks refuge in a cave sheltering the eggs from which they hatch. Unbeknownst to her, the Master Harper of Pern has been seeking her after hearing two songs she wrote, and *Dragonsinger* relates her adjustment to being apprenticed to him at Harper Hall, where she learns about the demands, difficulties, and joys of life as a harper. *Dragondrums* features the adventures of Piemur, a young friend of Menolly's, as he succeeds Menolly as Master Harper Robinton's special apprentice and finagles his way into Impressing his own fire lizard.

Because of McCaffrey's in-depth exploration of character in her works and her smooth integration of the necessary technical information into the backdrop of her stories, some people term her writing "science fantasy" rather than "science fiction." Certainly, her stories have wide appeal among many who eschew the high-technology focus of most science fiction, but McCaffrey never neglects the careful research that backs up the scientific aspects of the novels. By creating well-rounded characters who must overcome numerous setbacks and challenge the restrictions of tradition to achieve their goals, McCaffrey develops an atmosphere in which those who are thought to be weak prove themselves strong and in which female characters, in particular, find fulfillment.

In her adult works, McCaffrey has sculpted many other scenarios that push back the boundaries of the known universe and open the reader to new possibilities, but her books about the dragons and people of Pern have found an overwhelming number of fans. Dragons hold great appeal for many fantasy lovers; in the series, McCaffrey redefines the beast and therefore adds depth to any understanding of the mythical creatures. Her work draws in readers of fantasy and science fiction, as well as those who simply love adventurous stories with strong, determined characters. A.E.D.

McCloskey, Robert

AMERICAN AUTHOR AND ILLUSTRATOR, B. 1914. Probably best known for his PICTURE BOOKS, including two Caldecott winners, *Make Way for Ducklings* (1941) and *Time of Wonder* (1958), Robert McCloskey is also loved for his contemporary tall tales for older

Illustration by Robert McCloskey from his book *Make Way for Ducklings* (1941).

children, including *Homer Price* (1943), and for his illustrations for KEITH ROBERTSON's "Henry Reed" books.

McCloskey was born in Hamilton, Ohio, where he spent his youth in a town very much like the ones he later described in *Lentil* (1940) and *Homer Price.* As a boy, his interests included drawing, music (harmonica and oboe), and inventing gadgets. After high school, he won a scholarship to the Vesper George School of Art in Boston and continued his studies at the National Academy of Design in New York City. His first book, *Lentil,* was published in 1940, the same year he married Margaret Durand, the daughter of children's author RUTH SAWYER. Though he had been awarded the Prix de Rome in 1939, World War II prevented his study abroad until 1949. He spent the war in the United States, putting his inventing skills to use making visual aids. With characteristic humor and modesty, he says, "My greatest contribution to the war effort was inventing a machine to enable short second lieutenants to flip over large training charts in a high breeze." In 1946, after the birth of their daughter, Sally, the McCloskeys moved to an island on the Maine coast, which provided inspiration for most of his subsequent books. These include *Blueberries for Sal* (1948), about a bear cub and its mother looking for blueberries on the same hill as Sal and her mother; *One Morning in Maine* (1952), in which Sal spends the morning with her father and loses her first tooth; and *Time of Wonder,* with its misty watercolors and evocative text, which shows both the beauty of Maine and the variety of activities undertaken there.

McCloskey has described how he creates his stories. "The book starts with an idea/ideas inside my head. I imagine a lot of pictures. I almost have the book planned before I first put pencil to paper . . . It usually takes about two years from the first time I write the story until it ends up being a completed book. The first drawing has changed but the text reads almost exactly as it did in my first draft." Each of his books is a gem, and each accomplishes a different goal, though they are alike in their innocent, homey humor and the best kind of patriotism. *Blueberries for Sal,* printed with blue ink, is sweet and cozy. *Journey Cake, Ho!* (1953) by Ruth Sawyer is appropriately bombastic with its red-brown brush line and blue-green litho crayon showing bold areas of pattern and white space. *Time of Wonder* describes a summer in Maine, using paintings with a gentle and joyful color sense and with people depicted in a sketchy yet realistic way that is always kind. And *Burt Dow, Deep-Water Man* (1963) is brighter and more caricatured, with pinks, greens, reds, blues, and daring white space.

While he was working on the illustrations for *Make Way for Ducklings,* in which a family of mallard ducks walks through Boston's streets to the Public Garden, McCloskey realized he needed live models. He bought four mallard chicks at a market and brought them home to his New York City apartment. When he went to Boston to sketch backgrounds, he brought back six more ducks. "All this sounds like a three-ring circus," he says, "but it shows that no effort is too great to find out as much as possible about the things you are drawing. It's a good feeling to be able to put down a line and know that it is right."

In his career, McCloskey wrote and illustrated eight books and provided illustrations for ten more. Though he chose to stop illustrating in 1970, his combined skills as humorous storyteller and illustrator ensure the longevity of his books. ❧ L.R.

McCord, David

AMERICAN POET, ESSAYIST, EDITOR, AND TEACHER, B. 1897. Among twentieth-century writers for children, David McCord undoubtedly has one of the more extensive and distinguished résumés. Sampling his honors demonstrates not only remarkable achievement but also the breadth of experience distilled in his POETRY for young readers. Ranging from numerous honorary degrees to appointment as Benjamin Franklin Fellow of the Royal Society of Arts, from exhibitions of his watercolors to service on the usage panel of the *American Heritage Dictionary,* his achievements indicate understanding of disciplines as varied as history, literature, art, education, and medicine. In 1977, the year in which he read his "Sestina to the Queen" at ceremonies marking the state visit of Elizabeth II to Boston, he received the first award for excellence in poetry for children given by the National Council of Teachers of English.

Born in New York City, David Thompson Watson McCord spent his early years on Long Island and in New Jersey and his adolescence on a ranch in Oregon near the Rogue River. After graduating from Lincoln High School in Portland, Oregon, he came east to Cambridge, Massachusetts, receiving his A.B. (1921) and A.M. (1922) from Harvard University. Except for service as second lieutenant in the U.S. Army (1918), almost his entire life was intertwined with the university, primarily as the executive director of the Harvard Fund Council. He was already known as a poet, essayist, and editor when, in 1952, *Far and Few,* his first collection of verses selected for children, was published. Ten more would follow.

An only child, afflicted with recurring attacks of malaria, he was solitary but, as he remembers, never lonely. Solitude permitted time for reading, experimenting, observing, listening—and for developing the sense of wonder that infuses his poetry. Sensitivity to the sounds and rhythm of language, appreciation of nature, and knowledge of writers such as William Blake, EDWARD LEAR, and LEWIS CARROLL in-formed his mind and influenced his theories of what poetry for children should be. McCord has acknowledged and written perceptively about the contributions of these and other poets to his development. Among those he has cited are Blake for emphasizing the child's need for joy and laughter; Lear and Carroll for introducing nonsense and word play; ROBERT LOUIS STEVENSON for recognizing the significance of ordinary experiences; and Elizabeth Madox Roberts for capturing the authentic voice of the child. As MYRA COHN LIVINGSTON commented, McCord could "remember, extract, and discern the best of the past, reshape and apply it to the present, and in the process offer others a generous share of his unique celebration of life."

John Rowe Townsend, in citing McCord's work for the "light, dry humor and a good deal of technical virtuosity" typical of contemporary American poetry for children, singles out his instructions for composing varied verse forms using the forms themselves. And yet, while these are dexterous examples of his genius, children are probably better acquainted with his onomatopoeic "Pickety Fence," with its infectiously rhythmic instructions:

Give it a lick
Give it a lick
Give it a lick
With a rickety stick
Pickety
Pickety
Pickety
Pick

Equally remarkable is the subtlety that frequently transforms his verses into epiphanies for all ages, as in the last stanza of "Runover Rhyme":

Even the leaves hang listless,
Lasting through days we lose,
Empty of what is wanted,
Haunted by what we choose.

❧ M.M.B.

MCCULLY, EMILY ARNOLD

AMERICAN ILLUSTRATOR AND AUTHOR, B. 1939. Emily Arnold McCully illustrated her first book for children—*Sea Beach Express* by George Panetta—in 1966. In this book young readers were introduced to the first of hundreds of distinctively "McCully" children. Drawn in a sketchlike style with lots of line to create small faces, halos of hair, and childish movements, McCully's illustrations have a spontaneous quality that brings to life the characters in books of realistic fiction. From her first book to the present, McCully has been a prolific illustrator, providing pictures for several books a year for authors of novels, picture books, poetry, and nonfiction. Her illustrations for novels such as MEINDERT DEJONG's *Journey from Peppermint Street* (1968) and Barbara Williams's *Mitzi and the Terrible Tyrannosaurus Rex* (1982) are done in pen-and-ink. In her earlier picture books, such as BETSY BYARS's *Go and Hush the Baby* (1971), she uses pen-and-ink with a wash of a single color. An exception is Mildred Kantrowitz's *Maxie* (1970), in which McCully's dark, subdued colors and striking textures capture the tone of this story about a lonely old woman.

McCully's more recent picture books feature the same lively pen-and-ink characters as her earlier books but are enhanced with watercolor washes reflecting the mood and setting of each story. For KATHRYN LASKY's *My Island Grandma* (1979), for example, McCully's pictures use the pale blues and greens of its seaside setting. For *Dinah's Mad, Bad Wishes* (1989) by Barbara M. Joosse, she uses bright aqua, chartreuse, and pink to evoke the strong anger felt by the mother and daughter.

In 1984, McCully published *Picnic*, the first picture book in which she created both the story and the pictures. This book introduced children to a new and delightful set of McCully characters. A wordless book, *Picnic* recounts through pictures the story of a little mouse who falls from the back of the family truck on the way to a picnic, becomes lost, and is then reunited with its family. Grandpa mouse with his glasses, cap, and cane, Mama with her distinctive kerchief, and the small lost mouse with its own stuffed pink mouse—not to mention a small mouse with a very large watch—all become familiar to children in further volumes in this "mouse" series. These include *First Snow* (1985), *School* (1987), *New Baby* (1988), and *Christmas Gift* (1988), a delightful Christmas story about the warm relationship between the grandfather mouse and the youngest mouse.

In 1988 McCully wrote and illustrated her first "I Can Read" book. Called *The Grandma Mixup*, it featured realistic human characters, two grandmas of very different styles and temperament. *Grandmas at the Lake* (1990) and *Grandmas at Bat* (1993) have followed the grandmas through several more adventures. McCully has also produced a trilogy of picture books about a theatrical family of bears with longer texts and bright illustrations. *Zaza's Big Break* (1989) and *The Evil Spell* (1990) were followed by *Speak Up, Blanche!* (1991), in which a winsome, shy sheep comes to work at the Farm Theatre with the bears. McCully's use of tiny print for Blanche's shy dialogue strikes young readers as hilarious.

For *Mirette on the High Wire* (1992), McCully returned to human characters, but she took on a new setting and a vivid new style. In this Caldecott Medal winner, she uses lush paintings filled with the details of life in turn-of-the-century France as she tells the story of a young girl who heartens a faltering man, an aerialist who has lost his courage, with her ambition to be a high-wire performer. McCully, in her Caldecott speech, acknowledged Mirette as a highly personal metaphor for the risks that one takes as an illustrator and writer for children. After nearly thirty years of work in this field, McCully continues to take chances and to show her versatility as she shares her thoughts and images with children. ❧ B.A.C.

McDermott, Gerald

AMERICAN ILLUSTRATOR AND AUTHOR, B. 1941. Gerald McDermott's bold graphic designs interpret folktales in a dramatic style. But his unique approach of balancing modern art and traditional folk design did not occur by happenstance but came via his work in another visual form—film.

At age four, McDermott began taking classes at the Detroit Institute of Art. In high school, his focus on art continued as he received formal training in Bauhaus principles. His silk-screen prints and watercolors gained him a National Scholastic Scholarship to Pratt Institute. Once in New York, he pursued a dual interest in graphics and filmmaking; he also toured Europe and exchanged ideas with filmmakers. Returning to Pratt, McDermott began to produce and direct a series of animated films on mythology. Meeting Jungian scholar Joseph Campbell was a milestone in McDermott's career. Campbell consulted on McDermott's films, making the artist aware of the psychological depths of mythology and the potential for integrating cultural symbols into his art. McDermott's first book, *Anansi the Spider* (1972), was written and adapted from his own animated film. The transition from film to print form was not easy, as he ended up rendering all new art for the picture book to "retain the bold, graphic feeling of the film and carry over its visual rhythm to the printed page." *Anansi* was a Caldecott Honor Book in 1973. Two years later, McDermott's second book, *Arrow to the Sun* (1974), was awarded the Caldecott Medal, establishing him as a contemporary children's book creator. McDermott continued exploring myths and traditional tales and retelling them with dramatic flair and strong strokes. *Sun Flight* (1980), *Daughter of Earth* (1984), and *The Voyage of Osiris* (1977) are boldly drawn and glowingly colored. His only black-and-white rendition is *The Knight of the Lion* (1978), the twelfth-century Arthurian legend, which was appropriately foreboding in tone.

Changing his pace from the archetypal mythology of Egypt, Greece, and Rome, McDermott chose a pair of sprightly Irish stories. In *Tim O'Toole and the Wee Folk* (1990) and *Daniel O'Rourke: An Irish Tale* (1986), he playfully depicts his characters with a befitting lilt and bounce, a departure from his previously assertive lines.

McDermott's fascination with the trickster motif in folklore led him to the West African story of *Zomo the Rabbit* (1992) and the Pacific Northwest tale of *Raven* (1993). Inspired by the traditional designs of both areas, his artwork combines textile patterns and totems with vivid colors and vigorous lines. McDermott assimilates the patterns and designs of various cultures to shape his representation of the story. In his Caldecott acceptance speech, he said, "The role of the artist is that of the shaman, penetrating surface reality to perceive a universal truth, drawing out the essence of an idea." His visual expressions of modern telling of myths and trickster tales have successfully achieved that role. With his stylized perspective, his vibrant colors, and his rhythmic energy, he has become an original interpreter of multicultural tales. ❧ J.C.

McKillip, Patricia A.

AMERICAN AUTHOR, B. 1948. Born in Salem, Oregon, Patricia McKillip grew up both in America and overseas. She began writing in high school, and her first book, *The House on Parchment Street* (1973), was published the same year she received a master's degree from San Jose State University. A contemporary ghost story set in England, this novel was followed by a series of FANTASIES set in imaginary worlds. In *The Forgotten Beasts of Eld* (1974), a powerful wizard woman controls a collection of mythic animals, but shuns the warlike world of men until a king almost kills her, and she yearns for revenge. Sybel's pride in her wizardry almost destroys her, but she is saved by her love for the young nephew left in her care and for the lord who brings her the infant. Winner of the World Fantasy Award, the novel was named an American Library Association Notable Children's Book. A powerful female is also featured in *The Changeling Sea* (1988), though fifteen-year-old Peri has yet to discover her magical gifts. When she hexes the sea for taking away her fisherman father, she is visited by a sea-dragon, and with the help of Lyo, a magician, Peri unravels the mysterious connection between the animal and the king's son.

McKillip's best-known works are the lengthy, complex books featuring a young prince named Morgon. *The Riddle-Master of Hed* (1976), *Heir of Sea and Fire* (1977), and *Harpist in the Wind* (1979) compose a highly philosophical and often dreamlike trilogy. The first book introduces Morgon, who, despite his skills as a riddle-master, wishes only to lead an unassuming life on the small island he rules. But when strange creatures threaten his life—apparently in response to the three stars on his forehead—he is forced to undertake a dangerous journey in search of an answer to the riddle of the stars. In the second volume, Morgon's betrothed, a magically gifted, strong-minded woman named Raederle, sets out to find the prince, who is believed to be dead. Accompanied by Morgon's sister and a warrior-princess, Raederle's search is long and perilous but ultimately successful. In the third book, which received the Balrog Award and a nomination for the Hugo Award, Morgon and Raederle together find the answers to many riddles, and Morgon accepts his destiny as inheritor of power over all the lands. The suspenseful endings of the first two volumes lure readers on, as do the appealing characters of Morgon, the peace-loving, reluctant hero, and Raederle, whose intelligence and courage match her beauty. McKillip's dialogue is natural and humorous, and her descriptions provide a clear view of Morgon's world, although some readers find the many strange names of people and places difficult to remember.

McKillip's fantasy worlds are given a sense of history and culture through the inclusion of the ancient, universal art of riddles. Music also adds dimension to her stories, which feature harpists as treasured, highly honored artists; and the songlike, emotive qualities of certain passages attest to the musicianship of the author, who almost chose a career as a concert pianist. The main attraction to McKillip's books, however, remains the irresistible and timeless combination of adventure, magic, and romance. ❧ J.M.B.

McKinley, Robin

AMERICAN FANTASY WRITER, B. 1952. Robin McKinley first received recognition as an important writer of FANTASY fiction for young adults with the publication of her first novel, *Beauty,* in 1978. A retelling of "Beauty and the Beast," *Beauty* brings a tremendous vibrancy to the original fairy tale. Beauty's relationships with her friends and family, her heroic determination to do what is honorable in spite of her fear, and, most important, the love that develops between her and the mysterious beast are all explored with sensitivity and depth. McKinley's astute "reading between the lines" of this classic brings the story to unforgettable life.

Born in Warren, Ohio, McKinley grew up traveling around the world with her parents since her father was a naval officer. She has frequently said she keeps track of her life by what books she was reading at a given time. An avid reader since her earliest childhood, she has a perception of the world that was heavily influenced by classic fantasy literature for children: L. FRANK BAUM's Oz books, ANDREW LANG's collections of fairy tales, J. R. R. TOLKIEN, and RUDYARD KIPLING. These influences are apparent in her writing and in her ability to create worlds of wonder and magic resonant with the elements of a child's imagination, yet McKinley has managed to use the traditional format to create stories wholly her own.

Although *Beauty* was critically acclaimed and extraordinarily popular with young readers and adult fantasy buffs alike, writing it was simply a diversion from the project nearest to McKinley's heart, the writing of the Damar stories. McKinley first introduced her readers to Damar, an imaginary desert kingdom, with *The Blue Sword* (1982), a Newbery Honor Book, and *The Hero and the Crown,* a prequel to *The Blue Sword,* which won the Newbery Medal in 1985. The Damar books combine adventure and romance with elements of mythological symbolism to weave two epic tales of the timeless struggle between good and evil. Their special significance is that they explore this struggle from a feminine perspective. In *The Blue Sword,* Hari, a young "outlander" woman, comes to the kingdom of Damar in its time of greatest need and leads the Hill Folk to victory in their battle against the dark forces from the North. *The Hero and the Crown* is the story of Aerin the Dragon Slayer, the original wielder of the Blue Sword, and her struggle to wrest the hero's crown from a wicked enchanter. With the creation of Hari and Aerin, McKinley has added to the ranks of literary heroes two remarkable young women more than able to hold their own with their male counterparts.

The trademark McKinley characters—strong, competent young women who distinguish themselves through courageous acts of leadership—are also found in *The Outlaws of Sherwood* (1988). In this distinctively contemporary version of the Robin Hood legend, female characters aren't neglected, and Maid Marian and the surprising Lady Cecily take on roles as glamorous and challenging as the rest of Robin's Merry Men.

In addition to her full-length novels, McKinley has also published *The Door in the Hedge* (1981), a book of short stories, including several retellings of fairy tales, which highlights her profoundly personal connection to the fantasy genre, and she has edited an elegant collection of original stories by prominent fantasy writers, *Imaginary Lands* (1987), which received a World Fantasy Award in 1986. With her beautiful adaptations of *Jungle Book Tales* (1985), *Black Beauty* (1986), and *The Light Princess* (1988), McKinley passes on to a new generation of young readers the priceless gift of classic children's literature. ❧ K.T.

McKissack, Patricia

AMERICAN AUTHOR, B. 1944. Patricia McKissack feels strongly that all young people need good literature by and about African Americans. An African American writer, McKissack is committed to producing strong, accurate, and appealing stories. Alone and with her husband, Frederick (b. 1939), she has written more than fifty books, including picture books, beginning readers, information books, and biographies.

McKissack grew up in a storytelling family in Tennessee. Her picture books draw on this rich heritage and continue the tradition. *Flossie and the Fox* (1986), illustrated by RACHEL ISADORA, derives from a story her grandfather told her, and an old photograph of her great-grandparents inspired *Mirandy and Brother Wind* (1988), a Caldecott Honor Book and winner of the Coretta Scott King Award for Jerry Pinkney's illustrations. The settings are the rural South, and the tales are told in an easily readable Southern dialect. McKissack frequently picks strong heroines who outsmart their adversaries, but in *A Million Fish . . . More or Less* (1992), illustrated by Dena Schutzer, she writes of a young boy who learns the art of telling tall tales. All her picture books demonstrate her sense of humor and joy in sharing a tale.

After McKissack graduated from what is now Tennessee State University, she moved to St. Louis, Missouri, with her husband and taught English to junior high school and college students. Her teaching experience gave her a genuine appreciation of the needs of young people, inspiring both her books for beginning readers and her information books. She has written biographies about important African Americans, such as Frederick Douglass, W. E. B. Du Bois, Mary McLeod Bethune, Martin Luther King, Jr., Michael Jackson, and Jesse Jackson, for a variety of grade levels from the newly independent reader to middle-school students. She has coauthored many nonfiction and a few fiction books with her husband. Frederick was originally a civil engineer; now, he says, he "builds bridges with books."

McKissack tries to present an evenhanded picture of her biography subjects, including both positive and negative details. For example, in *Jesse Jackson: A Biography* (1989), she discusses many of the criticisms leveled at Jackson after Martin Luther King's assassination.

Together the McKissacks have also written histories of the African American experience. They feel that to put the civil rights movement of the 1960s in perspective, one must go back and understand the events that followed the Civil War. *The Civil Rights Movement in America from 1865 to the Present* (1987) covers these events, focusing on African Americans, but it also touches on the experiences of other minorities. In *A Long Hard Journey: The Story of the Pullman Porter* (1990), which received the Coretta Scott King Award and the Jane Addams Peace Award, the McKissacks present a fascinating account of the Pullman porter, his struggles with racism, and the rise of the first all-black union. As usual, they have researched their subject well, drawing on primary sources, including personal interviews, to make this a very readable history.

Patricia McKissack has stated a dual goal of improving the self-image of African American children and of encouraging an open attitude in all children toward cultures different from their own. By telling engaging stories, both fiction and nonfiction, her books clearly move us in this direction. ❧ P.R.

McMillan, Bruce

AMERICAN PHOTOGRAPHER AND AUTHOR, B. 1947. Bruce McMillan's enthusiasm is contagious. Neither the children nor the adults who pore over the photographs in his stunning books for the very young can help but share his obvious enjoyment of his subject and his medium. A school visit from this energetic writer and photographer sparks excitement as he shares with students and teachers his process of creating a book and his unique way of seeing. With no formal training in photography, McMillan produces images that are technically superb, outstanding for their clarity, vivid color, and consistently interesting composition.

Born in Boston but a resident of Maine for most of his life, McMillan drew upon his experience, with his wife and young son, as caretaker of a small island to produce his first book, *FinestKind O'Day: Lobstering in Maine* (1977). Another early work, *The Remarkable Riderless Runaway Tricycle* (1978), was inspired by his rescue of an old tricycle from the Kennebunkport dump. The book, illustrated with black and white photographs, remains popular today and has been adapted into a highly acclaimed film. Two books of visual puns published for an adult audience reflect McMillan's quick sense of humor and foreshadowed the wit and wordplay that appear in his later full-color picture books for children: *One Sun* (1990) and *Play Day* (1991), collections of images illustrating pairs of rhyming words ("wet pet") that the author terms "terse verse." McMillan is perhaps best known and most highly regarded for his photographic concept books such as *Counting Wildflowers* (1986), *Dry or Wet?* (1988), and *Time to . . .* (1989), in which events in the small child's daily routine—waking up, eating breakfast, going to school—are used to illustrate both the passage of time and the measurement of time in hours by the clock.

Particular strengths of McMillan's books are the various methods he uses to reinforce the concept presented in the illustrations or to extend the book's appeal and usefulness for older readers. *Eating Fractions* (1991), for example, shows two winsome children preparing and eating food they have divided into halves, thirds, and fourths. Recipes for four of their appetizing creations appear at the end of the book. *Super, Super, Superwords* (1989) demonstrates the grammatical concept of comparison: positive, comparative, and superlative. Colorful images of energetic kindergartners illustrate such concepts as "small, smaller, smallest" and "loud, louder, loudest." McMillan uses every element of the book's design to reinforce the concept—the graduated size of the images, the size and darkness of the printed text, the intensity of hue. Gorgeous photographs of baby kittens, cubs, and lambs in *The Baby Zoo* (1992) will charm the smallest child. In addition, each of the animals selected represents a rare or endangered species, and McMillan provides detailed information and habitat maps for older readers. The simplicity of McMillan's picture books belies the meticulous attention he pays to the smallest detail and the painstaking care he gives to the composition of each picture. The resulting images convey an air of exuberance and spontaneity.

The prolific McMillan continues to sustain freshness and high quality while producing as many as three to four new titles each year, earning high praise from reviewers, teachers, and librarians. McMillan's conviction that photography was underutilized in books for children launched a career in which he has ably demonstrated the creative power and charm of photography for children's picture books. ❧ D.M.L.

McPhail, David

American illustrator, b. 1940. David McPhail was raised in Newburyport, Massachusetts, surrounded by a large extended family. He attended Vesper George University on a scholarship but left after a year to pursue a musical career. After several lean years, he decided to return to his studies at the Boston Museum of Fine Arts School, where he studied graphics yet felt his calling was illustration. He wished to "escape the edict that illustration was not 'art'" and felt convinced that his paintings "told stories." Indeed, his editor, Emilie McLeod, later pointed out that he often told two stories, one in the text and one in the illustrations. In his first book, *In the Summer I Go Fishing* (1971), the text relates the simple tale of a young boy who creates a lemonade potion. The illustrations reveal the effects of the potion on his customers and their interactions create an auxiliary story line. Even in McPhail's debut, a distinctive style is emerging: The illustrations contain an energy and inventiveness that remain a trademark of his work.

As a child, McPhail often played in the woods and fields near his home, fueling his interest in animals, which frequently appear as characters in his books. McPhail finds character development is easier with animals: "Animal characters can be genderless . . . I can even endow them with bad qualities without reflecting on a particular kind of person." Some of the most de-lightful examples of McPhail's work occur when he integrates animals and human beings. The humans blithely coexist with an oversized bear family in *Emma's Vacation* (1987) and witness the zany antics of a very large bear as he learns to ride a bicycle in *The Bear's Bicycle* (1975), written by Emilie McLeod. In *First Flight* (1987), a nervous, unruly bear demonstrates how not to behave on an airplane. McPhail concludes that his best efforts come as a result of working in a "free and easy way," and the exuberance of his watercolor drawings for *Captain Toad and the Motorbike* (1978) and *Great Cat* (1982) are testimony to this freewheeling method. Both books contain large, full-page spreads depicting the huge great cat and the larger-than-life hopping hero of *Captain Toad.*

Believing that the creation of each book brings a renewed sense of discovery in his craft, McPhail works in a variety of media. He is especially gifted in pen-and-ink, deftly using crosshatching and simple strokes to portray both vivid expression and fine detail. The sensitivity of his drawings is exhibited in one of McPhail's favorite books, *Henry Bear's Park* (1976), a quaint little book with frames and borders surrounding the illustrations. Both *The Train* (1977) and *The Dream Child* (1985), for which his daughter provided the inspiration, reveal the power of a few swift strokes to create a mood of dreamy nighttime adventure. Yet another technique is exhibited in the very popular "Pig Pig" series, a lively group of books about an adventurous pig. In these books, McPhail uses simple line drawings washed with luminous color.

McPhail has been the recipient of numerous honors for his books, among them the Boston Globe–Horn Book Award. ❧ M.O'D.H.

Means, Florence Crannell

AMERICAN AUTHOR, 1891–1980. During the first half of the twentieth century, publishers of children's books made an effort to provide stories about foreign lands but often ignored the various cultures found within the borders of the United States. Therefore, young readers were more likely to find books about African children than African American children. There were stories set in Spain but very few with Spanish American protagonists. Florence Crannell Means was one of the earliest children's authors to write consistently about the lives of American minorities.

The daughter of a Baptist minister, Means was born in Baldwinsville, New York, and raised in a family that appreciated ethnic diversity. She grew up in a number of states, including Colorado and Kansas, where her father was president of the Kansas City Baptist Theological Seminary. After high school, the author attended art school and continued taking extension college courses for much of her life. Means did not publish her first book until long after she married and began raising a daughter. *Rafael and Consuelo* (1929), written with Harriet Fullen, concerns Mexicans living in the United States. Her first solo effort was *A Candle in the Mist* (1931), a story about a nineteenth-century teenage girl with teaching and writing aspirations who travels with her family from Wisconsin to Minnesota. This still readable pioneer novel contains interesting period detail and empathic characterizations.

Means brings this same empathy to numerous novels concerning minorities, which she researched by visiting ethnic communities. *Shuttered Windows* (1938) concerns an African American high school senior whose move from Minneapolis to South Carolina prompts her to try to improve living conditions for her race. George Washington Carver makes a brief appearance in *Great Day in the Morning* (1946), the story of twenty-year-old Lilybelle, who attends Tuskegee Institute. Both books are dated, and may be offensive in their use of dialect, but the characterizations of strong-willed young women are impressive. Means wrote about Spanish Americans in *Alicia* (1953), migrant workers in *Knock at the Door, Emmy* (1956), and American Indians in such novels as *The Rains Will Come* (1954) and *Our Cup Is Broken* (1969), in which the literary realism of the 1960s allowed her to portray a twenty-year-old Hopi Indian who is raped, gives birth to a blind illegitimate daughter, marries, and has a stillborn child.

Perhaps the author's most important work is her Newbery Honor Book, *The Moved-Outers* (1945). Means introduces a "typical" California family in the days before the Pearl Harbor bombing, not revealing that they are of Japanese descent until the end of the second chapter. The story of their subsequent internment in government relocation camps is powerful and extremely moving, as the family submits to bureaucracy yet never loses faith in the United States. Bravely published while the war was still being fought, the novel delivers a gentle, yet stinging rebuke against then current government policy.

Means also wrote intelligent biographies, including *Carvers' George: A Biography of George Washington Carver* (1952), but is best known for fiction that combines social themes with well-rounded characters, often in their late teens or early twenties. While some of the books are dated, and the prose is occasionally more purposeful than inspired, the author's convictions give the novels an enduring power. Means can be credited with bringing an early social conscience to children's literature. ❧ P.D.S.

Meddaugh, Susan

AMERICAN AUTHOR AND ILLUSTRATOR, B. 1944. By happy accident, Susan Meddaugh, creator of the widely acclaimed *Martha Speaks* (1992), the hilarious picture book about a painfully honest talking dog, is now doing professionally what she first began doing as a ten-year-old in Montclair, New Jersey—telling herself stories with pictures. And they are highly original, humorous stories, illustrated with a confident and spontaneous line that is as personal as handwriting.

In the years between childhood desire and adult accomplishment, Meddaugh was a student of fine arts at Wheaton College in Massachusetts, where she painted in a representational style. Upon graduating, she worked briefly for an advertising agency in New York City and then moved to Boston, where she worked for ten years with a major publishing company, first as a designer of children's books and later as art director for children's books. During this time, Meddaugh rediscovered *Curious George* by H. A. REY and had the powerful experience of seeing the art again as she had for the first time as a child. Her response to this revelation was a conviction that art that is meaningful to a child cannot be judged in the same way as art for adults. Meddaugh's philosophy and her enjoyment of the whole process of bookmaking soon encouraged her to write and illustrate her own books. Her distinctive color and dramatic use of shadow and light create tension in *Beast* (1981). At this time Meddaugh also began designing jackets for young adult novels and was the designer and main artist for the *New Boston Review*. When illustrating the work of other authors, Meddaugh looks for "humor, an unusual story, a story worth doing." She has illustrated several of EVE BUNTING's stories, including *In the Haunted House* (1990) and *A Perfect Father's Day* (1991), as well as a poetry collection, *The Way I Feel . . . Sometimes* (1988) by BEATRICE SCHENK DE REGNIERS, and books by Verna Aardema and Jean Marzollo.

Meddaugh is a very visual storyteller whose books can often be summed up by just one of the images. For example, in *Martha Speaks*, the significant illustration shows the alphabet soup going up to Martha's brain rather than down to her stomach, an idea suggested by Meddaugh's young son, Niko. Suddenly Martha can talk, and her proud owners can ask the questions dog owners have always wanted to ask. They ask, "Why don't you come when we call?" And Martha answers, "You people are always so bossy. COME! SIT! STAY! You never say please." But Martha is as honest as a child, and when her candid opinions cause trouble she quietly sulks until her owners appreciate her volubility once more.

Meddaugh's texts can be admirably economical because so much of the story is carried in her very expressive artwork. Her readers will find more humor the closer they look. In *Witches' Supermarket* (1991), the grocery shelves are filled with everything from "Shake 'n Bake Snake" to "Apples with Worms" (more expensive than without). The dog in *Witches' Supermarket* is the same dog who subsequently starred in her own book, *Martha Speaks*. Martha captivated readers and reviewers alike, and the book was named one of the New York Times Best Illustrated Books of 1992 as well as an ALA Notable Book. Martha, a stray adopted by the family and "so drawable with her big chest," has taken her fame in stride. Once again Meddaugh has created a book with illustrations that appeal directly to children and humor that is irresistible to all. Readers will demand more stories about Martha. ❧ P.H.

MEDIA ADAPTATIONS FROM BOOKS

Book lovers often await book-based films with trepidation, knowing from experience that much loved characters or favorite scenes can emerge from the adaptation process hardly recognizable. Endings change; three characters become one; weeks become days. A heroine envisioned as willowy and ethereal turns out to be Bette Midler, or fresh-faced Tom Cruise takes on a character every reader imagined as Clint Eastwood.

But there are times when the magic works, when a film transcends its print-bound roots, grows into something marvelously new and takes on a life of its own. Far from displacing the book, it stands alongside as an equally authentic expression of the same story in another medium. And if it is an especially successful film, it may stand tall enough to cast a shadow that changes our sense of the book forever.

A consummate example is *Gone with the Wind*. Whatever Margaret Mitchell had in mind, it is images from the film—Clark Gable at the foot of Tara's staircase, Vivien Leigh with a fistful of red Georgia clay—that remain not just in moviegoers' but in readers' minds long after the covers close. Released in 1939, *Gone with the Wind* went home with the Oscar for Best Picture that year, edging out one of the greatest fantasies—and one of the most successful book-based films of all time—*The Wizard of Oz*.

The Wizard of Oz was an immediate hit when published in 1900, selling out its first edition in two weeks. Children today are still avidly reading—and being read to—from the forty books in the Oz series. And half a century after its first release, the film proved enduring as well, selling 850,000 copies when it appeared on video in 1988.

But any reader—or film fan—knows that *The Wizard of Oz* on screen and *The Wizard of Oz* on the page are two very different things indeed. Seeking to write a uniquely American fairy tale, L. FRANK BAUM introduced *Oz* as a book in which "the wonderment and joy are retained and the heart-aches and nightmare are left out."

Thus Dorothy's trip to Oz, far from the country of the Brothers Grimm, is a series of escapades filled with exotic creatures like the bodies-of-bears, heads-of-tigers Kalidahs. Dorothy's central quest—to find the Wizard and get back to Kansas—is so eclipsed by her mildly threatening adventures that the reader is likely to hope she doesn't get there too soon. Home is not where Baum's heart is—he wastes no more than five pages on it before whisking Dorothy away to Oz.

By contrast, it's Dorothy's longing for home that propels the film. *Oz*'s screenwriters sliced a no-nonsense trajectory through the story, excising anything that deviated from the yellow brick road and dumping less worthy adversaries in favor of a sole menace—the Wicked Witch of the West. Baum's paltry witch, desperately afraid of water and the dark, gave way to one more classically malevolent and so terrifying that even though she's on screen for only twelve minutes, her cackle is as memorable as the film's forty minutes of unforgettable songs.

Songs were just one element MGM used to transform Baum's flatly written adventures into a musical with such staying power that its characters and dialogue have long since passed into cultural metaphor. The new magic of Technicolor was used to set Oz ablaze, and the vaudeville roots of Bert Lahr and Ray Bolger gave the Lion and the Scarecrow the animated talents of song and dance men. One hundred twenty-four elaborately dressed midgets made the Munchkins real. And not the least of the film's enchantments was the extraordinary voice of seventeen-year-old Judy Garland.

No book could compete with such riches, but the point is more that competition is beside the point. Neither medium detracts from the other. Baum's Oz is a real place brimming with adventures the reader can't find in the film. Indeed, Oz is so much more real than dreary Kansas that in later books Baum moved Dorothy there permanently, bringing along Aunt Em and Uncle Henry as well.

On screen Oz is a dream, somewhere over the rainbow. Its lavish charms never turn Dorothy aside from her and the film's one certain truth—"There's no place like home." By the time she clicks her slippers three times—they're ruby in the film, silver in the book—we too yearn for Dorothy's return to the plain and simple people who love her best. Readers and moviegoers should not feel compelled to favor one medium's truth over the other, but be free to accept the authenticity of both.

Though neither the book nor its film adaptation have had the impact of *The Wizard of Oz*, another work to make a successful journey from page to screen is Walter Farley's *The Black Stallion* (1941). In language sometimes as rough and choppy as the sea which nearly swallows them, Farley weaves the tale of a shipwrecked stallion and the boy who saves him.

Illustration by W. W. Denslow from *The Wizard of Oz* (1900), by L. Frank Baum.

Followed by over twenty sequels before Farley's death in 1989, the story of Alec Ramsay and the Black is a book much loved by several generations of children. *New Yorker* film critic Pauline Kael remarked about the 1980 film version, "It was a hushed, attentive audience. . . . *The Black Stallion* on a Saturday afternoon . . . was proof that even children who have grown up with television and may never have been exposed to a good movie can respond to the real thing when they see it."

The filmmakers took some liberties with the book, adding a drowned father, deleting a side trip to Rio, placing a venomous cobra a few inches from Alec's sleeping face rather than leaving it curled under a nearby boulder. But ultimately the story of the Black Stallion was only enriched by the camera, especially in its centerpiece—a long, wordless sequence of Alec and the Black on a breathtaking island as their friendship turns to love and undying loyalty.

Like *The Wizard of Oz, The Black Stallion* transcends its literary birth to emerge newly realized on film. But the essence of the story—the overpowering love of a boy for a horse—remains. Nothing is lost that is crucial to that central narrative. And as with any good book-based film, the movie leads children back to Farley's original stories, where new adventures and undiscovered delights await them.

With rare exception, it's difficult to find an intact piece of dialogue from *The Wizard of Oz* or *The Black Stallion* alive and well in the subsequent films. Such is not the case with Kevin Sullivan's 1985 film of *Anne of Green Gables.*

A four-hour television adaptation of L. M. MONTGOMERY's 1908 novel, the film stays true to the things readers remember about "Anne-with-an-E Shirley"—her language, spirit, and irrepressible character. Sullivan's adept screenwriting neglects not a heartbeat of Anne's passion for life, and a distinguished cast headed by Megan Follows as Anne and Colleen Dewhurst as Marilla makes the film an acclaimed classic in its own right.

A close comparison of the film with the book, however, reveals it is not the carbon copy it first appears. Some episodes are omitted. Dialogue spoken by one character comes out of the mouth of another. Gentle Matthew collapses not at home, as in the novel, but in the fields, with Anne as his last companion. What makes the film echo so faithfully a reader's experience of the book is an unwavering allegiance to the relationships at its heart's core.

Sullivan himself says that when he first decided to film *Anne* his strong memories of the book came from having it read aloud by his fifth-grade teacher. "We knew it as a Canadian classic," he says. "We found it amusing and there were moments that affected the whole class deeply." It was not until much later that he read it for himself. "My first reaction was, 'Oh no, this is not what I remember at all. This is a book for twelve-year-old girls!'"

But subsequent readings underscored the universality of the story of an orphan girl whose radiance bestows unexpected blessings on those around her. Sullivan saw his task as the creation of a new work loyal to the story's essence, built from the most memorable incidents and best moments of dialogue. The resulting film made more than one viewer exclaim, "It's so much the way I remember the book." Unfettered by the novel's turn-of-the-century narrative conventions, the film went on to reach not only the book's original fans, but audiences who otherwise might never have known Anne Shirley and her Green Gables.

Sarah, Plain and Tall is one of the acknowledged masterpieces of more recently written children's literature. This elegantly simple story of a Maine spinster who answers a newspaper ad and journeys to the Great Plains to try out life with the widowed Jacob and his two young children has a spacious power beyond its sixty-four pages. *Sarah, Plain and Tall* won the Newbery Medal in 1986, and five years later the film version was the highest-rated television movie of the 1990–91 season.

Yet some readers expressed disappointment at seeing on screen a story that differed in crucial ways from the book. *Sarah* the film and *Sarah* the book begin and end with the same dialogue, and in between the story unfolds much the same way, but the film takes a very different perspective. PATRICIA MACLACHLAN, author of the book and cowriter of the screenplay, has said, "If it were a retelling of the same story, I would not want to do it. But there was more for me to learn [about this story and these characters]."

At the core of *Sarah, Plain and Tall*—the book—is the narrative voice of Anna, a little girl with a great big hole in the middle of her life where her mother used to be. Through her eyes we watch as Sarah's zest for life and gentle wisdom slowly weave a new family out of the tattered one. Sarah, Anna, younger brother Caleb, and Papa sing together. Anna and Caleb tensely watch for signs that Sarah will stay. Papa smiles. The healing power of love finally binds them all together.

On film it is a long time before Papa smiles. Beneath the simplicity of Anna's story lie not only her own sorrow and grief but her father's as well. The film explores what the book could not—the painful struggle of Sarah and Jacob to find their way through loss to each other.

That Jacob is so near center stage is a primary change from the book. MacLachlan has said that Jacob was the character she knew least. "He whispered to me, 'You didn't give me many lines to say in the book.' There was more to learn about him." And it is Jacob, haunted by guilt never expressed on the page, who is for some viewers the troubling aspect of the translation of *Sarah, Plain and Tall* to the screen. Not so for MacLachlan.

"There are different ways of telling a story," she says. "My words are like guideposts. I whisper in [the actors'] ears. It's more like writing a picture book and it comes back illustrated. A screenwriter's job is to let go."

It is difficult for readers to let go of expectations—good or bad—about an adaptation of a treasured work. There is always a secret hope, most often dashed, that a film will duplicate the cherished experience of reading a favorite book. But if they don't let go—as Patricia MacLachlan says that even an author must—they're likely to miss among the filmic mistakes the potential for an equally moving experience with a different but just as authentic version of a much loved story.

Filmmaker Tom Davenport, who successfully dresses ancient folk and fairy tales in contemporary clothing, expresses well a reader's sometimes too-quick aversion to an adaptation on film: "It's like someone gives you red candy and you expect it to taste like cherry. If it tastes like grape, you spit it out." In a world too often flavored with bitterness and indifference, it's important not to spit out a good one even if it tastes different than we thought it would. TERRI PAYNE BUTLER

Media for Children

Television and other forms of video are omnipresent facts in the American household. Because of the lack of any significant regulation of this powerful medium as it affects children, most American youngsters are exposed to an average of thirty hours per week, most of it in the form of commercially-driven programs, much of it not, strictly speaking, intended for children at all. As a result, little of the adult world remains inaccessible to the curious eyes of children during those hours after school and before bedtime when they can be reasonably expected to be awake and, with remote control in hand, often busily sampling a wide range of products from the video supermarket.

Yet all of these choices do not necessarily mean more or better television programming for children. The economics of competition for an ever-shrinking share of the adult viewing market has led to even fewer new programs for children and families in the "prime time" hours after dinner. (Much of what is aired on the Disney Channel relies on reusing material that has already been released as movies or cartoons.) To date, because federal and state governments have been unwilling to assume the leadership to persuade commercial networks to make the effort to provide such programming, the networks have concentrated on more lucrative markets. Only one cable TV channel, Nickelodeon, is devoted almost entirely to children's programs. However, because it is not as generally available as the national networks and does not have their financial resources, it cannot consistently produce the same number and quality of programs with which it must often compete.

The national, noncommercial channel, PBS, has provided the support for a number of extremely successful and critically-acclaimed television shows—"Sesame Street," "The Electric Company," "Mister Rogers' Neighborhood," "Reading Rainbow," "Wonderworks," "Long Ago and Far Away," and "Where in the World Is Carmen Sandiego?"—that have become the hallmarks in innovative educational and quality entertainment programming. Despite the wide recognition they have received, these programs, too, are not always as accessible as the standard fare of the commercial networks, which, with the demise of "Captain Kangaroo," currently do not sponsor a single daily children's show. As Joan Ganz Cooney, the president of the Children's Television Workshop, which has produced a number of PBS's best children's shows, has pointed out, commercial television as a whole has failed to realize that children's television is "a readily available means of meeting the country's need of high quality, low cost supplemental education" and thus to use it "to enrich the learning process" for future generations of Americans.

Television, both in the United States and globally, has been further shaped by the presence of the video cassette recorder (VCR), which is now a component of media technology in nearly seventy percent of American households. The commercial explosion of this medium has led to another avalanche of video possibilities that might never reach a given family's television in any other way—from anthologies of classic 1930s short cartoons to an operatic version of MAURICE SENDAK's *Where the Wild Things Are*, from instructional tapes that explain, for instance, how children can ensure their safety at home while their parents are at work to five different versions of *The Velveteen Rabbit*, the sentimental fantasy about how toys become real. This plethora of material makes it clear that our children's options for exploration of this media are limited only by a store's inventory, a child's viewing time, and a family's budget.

But what also becomes apparent when one looks at the quickly expanding field of children's media is how little discussion of it actually takes place between the children for whom it is intended and the adults who are bringing it into classrooms, homes, and school and public libraries. Despite our long-standing awareness of the power of the media to mold opinions, shape tastes, and affect the emotions, we are reluctant to develop for our children a discourse about the media that can be critical of its intentions and methods. The leading citizens' action group for better, more child-sensitive television, Action for Children's Television (ACT), has been urging for the past two decades that parents should not simply abandon their children to television's agenda but must, instead, take responsibility for monitoring the programs that enter their homes and help their children to interpret the positions and values that these programs, however slickly and seductively packaged, may be advancing.

Happily, one can set aside such reservations when viewing any of the dozens of films produced by Morton Schindel and his Weston Woods Studios. Since the 1950s, when he founded Weston Woods, Schindel has been one of the strongest defenders of the rights of children to quality media. In the dozens of films he has made, Schindel has remained intensely interested in preserving the original children's books upon which his films have been based—thus, ultimately, encouraging children to return from movie or video screens to books. Schindel has adapted the work of many of the best-known authors and illustrators creating for children today—among them, MARGARET MAHY, JAMES MARSHALL, Maurice Sendak, WILLIAM STEIG, and ROSEMARY WELLS. Many of Schindel's award-winning films were the mainstays of early television shows like "Captain Kangaroo," and Schindel's dedicated focus on and celebration of exceptional children's books is at least in part responsible for inspiring the PBS program "Reading Rainbow." They are also responsible for influencing a generation of young filmmakers and fledgling production companies that have busily begun over the past decade to follow Schindel's lead of translating children's books into other media.

One of the pioneering recyclers of children's literature has been the actress Shelly Duvall. Her retellings of fairy tales have employed the talents of her internationally famous friends, celebrities like Mick Jagger, Bernadette Peters, Christopher Reeve, and Mary Steenburgen. Duvall's basic idea has led to an explosion of other similar projects and variations, such as the combination of classic children's stories and newly commissioned artwork with "star" readers (Jack Nicholson intoning KIPLING's "The Elephant's Child"; Robin Williams soaring through the Pecos Bill tales to the accompaniment of Ry Cooder's folk-rocking soundtrack), the whole repackaged as an audio- and/or videotape with a book.

But the most skilled of all commercial translations of the traditional tale into video was a short-lived television series, "The Storyteller," produced by the late Jim Henson. Henson managed to capture both the mystery and the playful vitality of the original stories without sacrificing their dark resonances or failing to respect the viewer's intelligence. Indeed, these programs represented some of the most satisfying, innovative commercial viewing for children in the 1980s.

Of course, the storyteller is the most ancient creator of media events, serving as she or he did as the intermediary between the world of the imagination and the reality of the audience. But in the United States, the art of the storyteller has all but vanished from the public eye in favor of more active and more complexly produced media. In the hope of rescuing this dying art form the National Association for the Preservation and Perpetuation of Storytelling (NAPPS) was founded in the mid-1970s. NAPPS sponsored storytelling festivals and workshops and served as the distributor for audio recordings and videotapes of the stories told by its members. One of the bright, lasting moments of the revolution in children's media of the past decades has been to make readily available performances by some of our best storytellers (like Jay O'Callahan, Laura Sims, and Rafe Martin) at most local video stores and public libraries. These unadorned moments, involving simply the voice, facial expressions, and physical gestures of the tale-teller are oases of peace and uncompromised skill in what can often be the extremely noisy world of video. By their quiet directness, they manage to communicate, in the simplest, truest terms, the power of a story and the generosity of its bringer, who was, as Walter Benjamin put it, the one "who could let the wick of his life be consumed by the gentle flame of his story."

One of the other success stories in children's media has been the proliferation of audio works for children, whether in the form of the many tapes of traditional and classic literature mentioned earlier or in the burgeoning field of children's music. The 1980s drew enthusiastic public attention to this musical genre and launched the careers of a number of dedicated, innovative performers, such as RAFFI; Barry Louis Polisar; Bill Harley; David Holt; and Sharon, Lois and Bram. By the mid-1990s, it has become a highly sophisticated and richly varied field of musical production. Its offerings include, for example, dozens of recordings of lullaby music (in a culturally diverse spectrum of languages); nursery versions of works by Bach, Mozart, and Beethoven (in the "Classical Kids" series); reworkings for toddlers of rock 'n' roll songs by, say, the Beatles ("Baby Road"); and, most recently, rap revisionings of traditional rhymes ("Mother Goose on the Loose").

Unfortunately, the same kind of dramatic expansion has not taken place in children's theater in the last several decades, despite a general acknowledgment of the importance of such enriching cultural experiences. Because of the rising costs of most theatrical productions, it has been difficult for many communities to sustain local theater for children, let alone to import such spectacular new efforts at bringing serious, professional theater to young audiences as Maurice Sendak's Night

Kitchen Theater. Though there are major centers of children's theater in such urban areas as Washington, D.C., St. Louis, Minneapolis, and Atlanta, most theater still reaches children in the form of amateur productions mounted by schools or small, struggling community theaters.

The history of American children's media is full of contrasts and tensions between commercial interests, on the one hand, and a commitment to serving the best interests of children, on the other. Though one waits for more signs from network television to indicate that it is at last ready to accept the imaginative responsibility and ethical resolve to restore the wasteland it has made of children's programming, there is some reason to hope that the video and cable revolutions will integrate the lessons to be learned from the high standards of public television and the active, creative voices of those who have been working hard for decades to bring refreshing new (and revitalized) ideas to American children's media. It may be that by the turn of the millennium, with the help of the choices provided by an ever more enlivening media (and the larger, more generous spirit that must be summoned to sustain such cultural changes), the controlling metaphor for our children's daily condition may be shifted from one of beleaguered survival "home alone" to one of positive possibilities within a welcoming, astonishingly imaginative community. JOHN CECH

Meigs, Cornelia

AMERICAN AUTHOR, 1884–1973. One of the most honored authors of her era, Cornelia Meigs is now best remembered for her award-winning BIOGRAPHY of LOUISA MAY ALCOTT, *Invincible Louisa* (1933). Born in Rock Island, Illinois, she was raised in Keokuk, Iowa, where she grew to love storytelling as she learned family tales of seagoing and pioneering ancestors. Meigs attended Bryn Mawr College, then returned to Iowa, where she taught school. She later worked for the War Department and taught writing and American literature at Bryn Mawr. Her first book, *The Kingdom of the Winding Road* (1915), originated with the stories she told students during her first year of teaching. This collection of literary fairy tales is dated in style and fairly standard in content.

Meigs turned to realistic, HISTORICAL FICTION with her next book and continued writing in this genre for most of her career. *Master Simon's Garden* (1916) is the story of a seventeenth-century Massachusetts family persecuted for growing a colorful garden and befriending people outside their narrow Puritan society; one hundred years later, Master Simon's descendants use the garden to assist George Washington during the Revolutionary War. Acclaimed for its perceptive examination of intolerance, the novel established Meigs as an important author. Her subsequent work continued to receive praise and awards, including the Drama League Prize for her children's play *The Steadfast Princess* (1916) and the Beacon Hill Bookshelf Prize for her eighteenth-century nautical adventure, *The Trade Wind* (1927). Three of the author's novels were selected as Newbery Honor Books. *The Windy Hill* (1921) concerns two teenagers involved in a family land dispute; *Clearing Weather* (1928) is the story of an eighteenth-century teenager who designs a ship and sails it to China; *Swift Rivers* (1932) tells of a Minnesota boy who works transporting timber down a river. Meigs's novels, somewhat dated in their treatment of ethnic groups and containing somewhat ponderous prose and occasionally contrived plots, remain rich in atmosphere and contain affecting scenes.

Meigs received the 1934 Newbery Award for *Invincible Louisa*. In writing the book, Meigs interviewed some of Louisa May Alcott's family and friends, which gives an added measure of authenticity to this literary portrait. Alcott comes alive as an independent, creative spirit in a biography that vividly re-creates the social history of the mid-nineteenth century. Meigs avoided the then fashionable fictional approach to juvenile biographies, which relied on invented scenes and dialogue. Instead, the book observes Alcott from an objective distance and presents an accurate characterization that even today remains fresh and appealing. Meigs later published other works about the author, including *Louisa May Alcott and the American Family Story* (1970).

Among her other books, the author wrote adult nonfiction, such as *The Violent Men: A Study of Human Relations in the First American Congress* (1949), and four minor novels for young readers published under the pseudonym Adair Aldon. Meigs, also a noted critic of children's books, edited *A Critical History of Children's Literature* (1953), for many years considered a classic in the field.

Although her dated novels are no longer popular, Meigs's biography of Louisa May Alcott, a landmark book that set a high standard for subsequent children's biographies, is still read and enjoyed. P.D.S.

Meltzer, Milton

AMERICAN HISTORIAN AND BIOGRAPHER, B. 1915. Milton Meltzer is one of the preeminent historians writing for young people. His first book, *A Pictorial History of the Negro in America* (1956; reprinted in 1983 as *A Pictorial History of Black Americans*), which he coauthored with LANGSTON HUGHES, was published for adults, but he felt compelled to write for a younger audience after surveying the lifeless, textbook synopses of history they were usually fed. Over seventy books followed, most dealing with Americans and their history and all informed by Meltzer's conviction that children will find the past meaningful only if they see it as a human drama and not a litany of dates and battle names. Whenever possible Meltzer lets excerpts from letters, diaries, newspapers, speeches, and other original documents tell the story. His readers hear voices they may have never heard before, voices of ethnic minorities, women, and the poor.

In *The Black Americans: A History in Their Own Words, 1619–1983* (1984), both famous and "ordinary" black Americans, from ex-slaves to modern civil rights leaders, chronicle their struggle against oppression. Books on the Great Depression, the American labor movement from 1865 to 1915, the American Revolution, and the Civil War tell about these events from the perspective of those who lived through them. Meltzer always connects the different voices with his own remarks, believing the historian must provide context for the moments in the past he or she reveals.

Growing up in Worcester, Massachusetts, the son of Austrian-Jewish immigrants who suppressed their heritage in an effort to Americanize, Meltzer thought little about the context of his own life. As he says in *Starting from Home* (1988), an autobiography of his childhood and adolescence, "[My parents] never talked about life in the old country and I never asked them about it. . . . Now I think how stupid I was, how self-centered, not to be curious about the origins of my own family." Later in life he made up for his lack of curiosity not only by researching his family history but by delving into the history of the Jewish people in several books. The winner of numerous awards and honors, *Never to Forget: The Jews of the Holocaust* (1976) combines Jews' eyewitness accounts of the atrocities committed against them by the Nazis with Meltzer's tracing of the origins of anti-Semitism and bureaucratization that made these atrocities possible. A companion book, *Rescue: The Story of How Gentiles Saved Jews in the Holocaust* (1988), recognizes the individuals who staked their lives against institutionalized evil.

From high school, when his favorite English teacher introduced him to Thoreau and antislavery poets and his history teacher encouraged him to find out about Worcester abolitionists, Meltzer has admired activists. He has written biographies of such pioneers of human rights as feminist Betty Friedan, abolitionist Thaddeus Stevens, and nineteenth-century author and reformer Lydia Maria Child. His biographies of historical icons such as George Washington, Thomas Jefferson, Benjamin Franklin, and Christopher Columbus seek to reveal the human beings behind the myths and monuments. As he does with all his subjects, Meltzer puts the life of each man or woman into context, trying to explain their considerable strengths and weaknesses in light of the world that helped shape them. C.M.H.

MERRIAM, EVE

AMERICAN POET, AUTHOR, AND PLAYWRIGHT, 1916–1992. Eve Merriam, a writer of many talents, was a poet of adult verse, an author of influential feminist works, an Obie Award–winning playwright, and one of the most anthologized writers of children's poetry in the country. Whether with light verse, wordplay, or satire, her mastery of and dexterity with words and language was astounding.

Born and raised in Philadelphia, Pennsylvania, Eva Moskovitz enjoyed the works of Gilbert and Sullivan and reading poetry, fairy tales, and myths from various cultures. Books and reading were enthusiastically advocated in her Russian-born parents' household; to young Eva, puns and rhymes were as much fun as games like hopscotch and tag. After she graduated from the University of Pennsylvania in 1937, she did some graduate work but soon began to work under her pen name, Eve Merriam, as a copywriter, radio scriptwriter, and a fashion editor at *Glamour.* Although she began to write when she was young, it wasn't until 1946, when she won the prestigious Yale Younger Poets Prize for *Family Circle,* a collection of adult poems, that she turned her attentions to writing full-time. Her first book for children was *The Real Book about Franklin D. Roosevelt* (1952), and after her sons were born she began to write picture books such as *A Gaggle of Geese* (1960) and *Mommies at Work* (1961), which discussed changing traditional gender roles, as well as poetry for young children. Perhaps one of her best-known works, however, is a book of poetry originally written for adults. The poems in *The Inner City Mother Goose* (1969) focus on the problems of urban areas. The issues—crime, welfare, social injustice—were ones that inner-city children could understand and appreciate, and they made the book their own. Some people felt the book's subject matter was not suitable for young readers, and there were calls for it to be banned across the country. Merriam felt the book was misunderstood by those who criticized it. Despite the controversy, the book obviously struck a chord with urban children, for whom inner-city problems are harsh realities. Merriam's poems gave voice to their frustrations and anger and also, perhaps, let these children feel that their situation was not forgotten and unnoticed. Merriam wrote the lyrics for a musical based on the book, which opened on Broadway in 1971.

Her children's poems are incredibly varied, from nonsense rhymes showing the fun one can have with sounds and language to poems dealing with sexism, social and humanitarian concerns, and first love. In her poems for young children, she uses lively, bouncy rhythms and repetitions that capture the exuberance of that age group. How could one resist the infectious beat of the verses from *You Be Good & I'll Be Night* (1988): "Hello, hello, / who's calling please? / Mr. Macaroni / and a piece of cheese." In this and her other books for the young, such as *Blackberry Ink* (1985) and *A Poem for a Pickle* (1989), the poems are a joy to read aloud and a celebration of sound. Merriam has said that she not only strived to develop an appreciation of language in children but also in their teachers. In 1981, the National Council of Teachers of English awarded her the NCTE Award for Excellence in Poetry for Children.

One theme that runs through many of Merriam's poems is the nature of poetry itself and the reader's relationship to the poem. She once said: "Poetry is different from playwriting and prose because there is no middle person. When there aren't any characters, you're dealing directly with emotions." Yet she was also aware that to some readers poetry seems like a code, impossible to decipher, so many of her poems attempt to demystify poetry in enjoyable lessons. Merriam's poems also deal with complex contemporary issues, as she felt that today's problems—pollution, technology, racism, and war—affect children as much as adults. Merriam's poems give voice to her readers' hopes, concerns, fears, and joys, as she encourages readers to test the limits of their imaginations and use language to express their experiences, real and fanciful. K.F.

Merrill, Jean

American author, b. 1923. Jean Merrill has written a number of unusual books for children, including *The Pushcart War* (1964), considered by many to be a modern classic. Born in Rochester, New York, the author grew up on an apple and dairy farm in nearby Webster, where she developed a love for nature as well as for books and reading. She studied English and theater at Allegheny College, received a master's degree from Wellesley College, and later studied Indian folklore as a Fulbright scholar at the University of Madras. During much of her writing career, Merrill worked as an editor for *Scholastic* magazine and *Literary Cavalcade*. Her published work is amazing in its diversity and includes picture books, poetry, plays, adaptations of folktales, and novels for readers in the intermediate grades.

One of Merrill's finest picture books is *Blue's Broken Heart* (1960), the moving story of a dog grieving over the death of his best friend. The kindness of an understanding veterinarian helps Blue recover from sadness. Writing a picture book about death and grieving was an unusual, daring choice for that era, but Merrill's books have often been ahead of their time in terms of content, style, and characterization. Even an otherwise slight and inconsequential title, *The Bumper Sticker Book* (1973), is noteworthy for containing early references to feminism, recycling, animal rights, and race relations. Merrill also helped widen the scope of children's books by including multicultural characters in her intermediate novels. *Maria's House* (1974) is the story of a talented young artist attending Saturday art classes at a museum; an assignment to paint her house leads Maria to share her lower-class, immigrant background with her teacher and classmates. *The Toothpaste Millionaire* (1972) features twelve-year-old Rufus Mayflower, who invents an amazingly successful new toothpaste. Rufus's African American heritage is incidental in this entertaining novel, which also includes subtle lessons on economics as Rufus and his friends do mathematical equations to learn about production, marketing, and sales in the business world. This humorous and popular novel was adapted for television.

The Pushcart War may be Merrill's most unconventional book. Written as a mock historical document and including footnotes, inside jokes, diary excerpts, and transcribed conversations, the narrative tells of a war between pushcart peddlers and truckers on the streets of New York. At one point in the steadily mounting campaign, the pushcart owners flatten the tires of thousands of trucks by blowing tacks through peashooters. Part allegory, part farce, the novel is unusual in that almost everyone in the large, multicultural cast of characters is an adult. The absence of children in the story has not limited its readership; *The Pushcart War* is a favorite novel among many young readers.

Merrill has also adapted several Asian folktales for children, including *The Superlative Horse* (1961), *High,*

Wide and Handsome and Their Three Tall Tales (1964), and *The Girl Who Loved Caterpillars: A Twelfth-Century Tale from Japan* (1992). *Mary, Come Running* (1970) is an adaptation of a Spanish Christmas carol; *A Song for Gar* (1957), a brief story about a rural boy and his pet raccoon, features traditional and original folk songs. These adaptations are enjoyable, but the author's best books are those in which she gives full play to her originality and willingness to break down barriers. ❖ P.D.S.

Middle-Grade Fiction

While children's varying development makes it difficult to define exactly the term *middle-grade fiction,* the genre is intended for pre- and early adolescents, roughly speaking those in the upper elementary and middle school grades. Works of literature for these young people assist them in understanding themselves, empathizing with others, learning about the complexities of human relationships, and finding their own special voice. Novels can be viewed as cultural artifacts that simultaneously reflect and create society's values and concerns. Changes in society influence children's books and are mirrored in them. As young adolescents have grown in sophistication with exposure to a media-dominated world, they have voiced their awareness of current social problems. Authors and publishers have responded with books that instead of presenting ideal images of children and families mirror the sometimes rough realities of the contemporary scene—dealing with blacks, women, various kinds of abuse, ecology, pollution, alcoholism, the elderly, and death. These honest images are tempered with hope, thereby empowering children to find solutions to their own concerns.

Realistic fiction has shown more change over the past several decades than any other kind of children's book. This change manifests itself not only in the subject matter but in the style in which it is handled. One need only compare the nearly ideal families of novels written in the 1940s and '50s with the diminishing appearances of the image of the perfect parent and the nuclear family in later novels for middle-level readers. ELEANOR ESTES's Moffats in *The Moffats* (1941), its two sequels, and other books and ELIZABETH ENRIGHT's series on the Melendy children, which began with *The Saturdays* (1941), portray children playing in safe, loving environments. The four Moffat children and their mama represent the noble poor; they live a fun-filled and satisfying life even in the face of, or perhaps especially because of, their poverty.

The works of BEVERLY CLEARY serve as a microcosm of the change in subject matter and tone of novels for middle-level readers. The early Cleary works are pure, nostalgic Americana, all barbecues and supermarkets. *Henry Huggins* (1950) is the story of a typically mischievous small boy who, much like ROBERT MCCLOSKEY's midwestern child in *Homer Price* (1943), finds himself in humorous predicaments at home and at school. Cleary's title character in *Ellen Tebbits* (1951) is a third-grader concerned with braces and ballet lessons. Her biggest secret is her woolen underwear, and her greatest satisfaction derives from her realization that her new friend is similarly adorned. Cleary's books about Ramona begin with five-year-old Ramona being a trial to her older sister in *Beezus and Ramona* (1955). In the ensuing years, to 1977, Ramona only reaches the age of seven; much else, however, changes in the books. In *Ramona and Her Father* (1977), Ramona's dad finds himself unemployed, does housework, and is a nurturing role model whose smoking habit worries Ramona. By the 1980s, Cleary's families look even less like the models of perfection of the fifties, a clear reflection of the families of her middle-reader audience. Ten-year-old Leigh Botts, the protagonist in Cleary's Newbery Award–winning *Dear Mr. Henshaw* (1983), writes letters to a favorite author to help him adjust to his parents' recent divorce and his father's absence.

The social upheaval of the 1960s had a dramatic impact on middle-level fiction. Long-standing taboos were broken in a trend toward more controversial themes handled with candor. Indeed, if one year can be isolated as singularly significant in heralding the arrival of the new realistic fiction, it would be 1964. This year was made important in the history of children's fiction in America by two significant books: *It's Like This, Cat* by EMILY NEVILLE won the Newbery that year, and *Harriet the Spy* by LOUISE FITZHUGH was published. Neville's book is about a white fourteen-year-old boy growing up in the New York City neighborhood of Gramercy Park. Not only is its urban setting a change from more rural ones, its fresh, honest exploration of the inner feelings of an adolescent is also unique. Dave's relationship with his parents, particularly his father—whose desire for him to be a "Real American Boy" Dave rebels against—is uneven at best, yet realistic in its very complexity.

Harriet the Spy is also a boundary-breaking story, candid and perceptive, about an unhappy yet irresistible female whose parents are too busy with their social life to notice their eleven-year-old. The novel's depiction of urban life and the power structure of the sixth grade from the perspective of the loner signaled a change in realistic fiction for middle-level readers. Its sequel, *The Long Secret* (1965), is remarkable for the discussions Harriet and her friends have about the long-taboo subjects of menstruation and developing breasts. Fitzhugh's 1974 novel *Nobody's Family Is Going to Change,* challenges assumptions of race, gender, and parental wisdom. In a middle-class black family, eleven-year-old Emma's aspiration to be a lawyer meets with parental disapproval as does her younger brother Willie's yearning to be a dancer.

Illustration by Louise Fitzhugh from her book *Harriet the Spy* (1964).

Harriet was the harbinger of one notable development in novels for young readers: lively, independent, strong female protagonists. In response to the feminist movement, and paralleling contemporary society, girls play more active roles in later novels. Certainly one of the strongest and most memorable heroines is Mary Call Luther in Vera and Bill Cleaver's *Where the Lilies Bloom* (1969). When her sharecropper father dies, the fourteen-year-old becomes the head of a household that includes a gentle, mentally challenged sister. Mary Call secretly buries her father and tenaciously fights to ensure the family's survival. Divorce is the theme of the Cleavers' first novel, *Ellen Grae* (1967), while *Grover* (1970) tells of a young boy's attempts to deal with his mother's suicide and *I Would Rather Be a Turnip* (1971) is the poignant story of an illegitimate child's attempts to find acceptance. Clearly there is a trend in young readers' novels written after the early 1960s toward confronting concerns with directness, creating potentially real rather than ideal images.

Judy Blume is astute in her choice of contemporary concerns and direct in her handling of them with humor, natural dialogue, and believable characters. Her *Are You There, God? It's Me, Margaret* (1970) is the story of a twelve-year-old girl, the child of a Jewish-Protestant marriage, and her emotional, physical, and spiritual ups and downs as she expresses her confusion about all sorts of things, ranging from religion to menstruation. Blume's *Then Again, Maybe I Won't* (1971) contains candid treatments of a boy's first sexual stirrings and teenage shoplifting.

Betsy Byars similarly acknowledges the variety of children and families and the concerns they share. Byars's quiet, understated humor and her compassion and understanding are evident in her 1971 Newbery Award–winning *The Summer of the Swans,* one of the early books about a mentally challenged child. Fourteen-year-old Sara is jolted out of her self-pity when her little brother, Charlie, disappears while trying to find some swans he had previously seen. *The Pinballs* (1977) is the story of three children, deeply scarred by parental neglect and abuse, who come together in a caring foster home. In *The Night Swimmers* (1980), Retta, whose mother is dead, tries to be both mother and sister to her two younger brothers while their father works at night. In 1985, in *Cracker Jackson,* Byars explores wife battering and child abuse through the eyes of young Jackson and his attempts to help his former, yet still much-loved, baby sitter.

Other authors similarly display an increased sensitivity to the variety of children, loved or neglected, bright or slow, rural or urban, homeless or wealthy, and representing many races, classes, and religions. The concerns that touch these young people, such as alcoholism, drug abuse, sexual abuse, death, divorce, handicaps, and abandonment are reflected in contemporary realistic fiction for middle-level readers. The best authors present these situations with dignity and honesty, creating characters that evoke readers' understanding.

The civil rights protests of the 1960s exposed the dearth of real rather than stereotypical blacks in children's books. Socially aware authors responded promptly. E. L. Konigsburg's 1968 Newbery Honor winner, *Jennifer, Hecate, Macbeth, William McKinley, and Me, Elizabeth,* is the story of an interracial friendship between two fifth-grade girls, one of whom is the first black child in a middle-income suburb. John Neufeld's *Edgar Allan* (1968) is a tersely told depiction of the reactions of a family and a community to a white family's adoption of a three-year-old black boy. Alice

CHILDRESS's novel *A Hero Ain't Nothin' but a Sandwich* (1973) uses Black English to describe the seesaw battle with drug addiction experienced by thirteen-year-old Benjie. *M.C. Higgins, the Great,* by VIRGINIA HAMILTON, is the story of a young black boy's dream of saving his family's home from an Ohio strip-mining slag heap. M.C. finds the answer to his dream by coming to terms with his heritage and his own identity. *M.C. Higgins* was the first book to win the Newbery Medal, the Boston Globe–Horn Book Award, and the National Book Award.

Death of a sibling or young friend is sensitively handled by several fine authors. CONSTANCE GREENE's *Beat the Turtle Drum* (1976) tells of eleven-year-old Joss's sudden death from a broken neck in a fall from an apple tree and the resulting trauma to his family. Kate, older by two years, is left to her own resources as their mother turns to tranquilizers and their father to alcohol to numb the pain. LOIS LOWRY's *A Summer to Die* (1977) recounts Meg's difficulty coping with her older sister Molly's degenerating illness and eventual death. *Bridge to Terabithia,* KATHERINE PATERSON's 1978 Newbery Award winner, tells of the sudden death of a ten-year-old boy's new friend as she tries to reach their secret hideaway in the midst of a storm. Paterson is also the author of *The Great Gilly Hopkins* (1978), a National Book Award winner about a tough foster child whose protective shield dissolves as she learns to give and receive love.

The impact of divorce on young people and the variety of the new family arrangements it engenders are the subjects of many novels for middle-grade readers. GARY PAULSEN's *Hatchet,* a 1988 Newbery Honor winner, tells not only of Brian's struggle to survive in the Canadian wilderness following an airplane crash but of his inner struggle to accept his parents' recent divorce and the crushing secret that a love outside the marriage precipitated the separation.

Marlene Fanta Shyer's *Welcome Home, Jellybean* (1978) conveys with convincingly painful honesty how difficult a young adolescent finds living with a profoundly mentally challenged sibling. *Do Bananas Chew Gum?* (1980), by JAMIE GILSON, realistically exposes the anguish, fear of discovery, and damaged self-esteem of a learning-disabled sixth-grader. The gifted student's difficulties with socialization are vividly described in ZILPHA KEATLEY SNYDER's *Libby on Wednesdays* (1990). The homeless and acts of violence against them are a theme in MARILYN SACHS's *At the Sound of the Beep* (1990). Sex abuse against children is Becky's concern in Laura Nathanson's *The Trouble with Wednesdays* (1986), as the girl dreads her weekly appointment with her orthodontist, who is becoming increasingly sexually aggressive.

Critics of the trend toward the realistic inclusion of adolescent concerns and societal ills in books of fiction for middle-level readers feel that this realism has gone so far in its quest for truth that it has drained children of their hopes and dreams. This clearly is not the case; in fact, the opposite is true. Truth is more cruel than fiction, for fiction can offer hope as well as honesty. Good novels have moved away from didacticism, and capable authors write books that empower children, from the protagonist's beginning steps, through his or her growing awareness of available options to some form of resolution. Parents are no longer portrayed as all-wise, and families are defined in a myriad of configurations. But the children featured in modern realistic fiction are young people of strength who, in the best of these books, grow, change, and take responsibility for their futures, regardless of gender, race, or class. What could be more reassuring and empowering to the abused, disabled, neglected, or ridiculed young child or to any child who is struggling with adolescent concerns of identity, independence, and maturation? In *The Fragile Flag* (1984), JANE LANGTON's protagonist is a nine-year-old girl who leads a march on Washington to protest a new missile capable of destroying the world. The very power of books is their ability to enlarge the reader's world, allowing deeply involved yet vicarious experiences. Readers can test their beliefs and their values without consequences, for good literature ultimately is about values, one's own and those of the story's characters.

Realistic fiction for middle readers continues its trend of reflecting society's concerns and changes and being sensitive to the variety of children. Books with multicultural themes demand a shift in our notion of the United States as a melting pot, an image that negates cultural uniqueness and works against a respect for and celebration of diversity. Furthermore, the continued trend to reflect contemporary society will produce more books dealing with homosexuality and AIDS. A danger is that the trend will produce something akin to "docu-novels," works that will diminish in the quality of writing precisely as the presentation of controversial materials increases. Yet good writers will continue to write with respect for their young readers. Their concerns will be contemporary, their style direct, their dialogue natural, and their characters believable. Finally, the increasing trend toward the child-protagonist's point of view will enhance the notion of voice, that readily discernible yet difficult-to-define quality that distinguishes the best writing. ❧ CONSTANCE BURNS

Mikolaycak, Charles

American illustrator and book and graphic designer, 1937–1993. Recognized for the authenticity of detail in his work and handsome book design and illustration, Charles Mikolaycak's creative style brought his subject matter to life. Though most of his books appeared in picture-book format, his sophisticated approach and the mature subject matter he often chose to illustrate resulted in books appropriate for young adults as well as young children. His prolific career included works ranging from biblical epics (*I am Joseph*, 1980; *He Is Risen*, 1985) to Greek mythology (*The Gorgon's Head*, 1972; *Orpheus*, 1992) to historical events (*The Tall Man from Boston*, 1975) to European (*Grimms' Golden Goose*, 1969), Russian (*Babushka: An Old Russian Folktale*, 1984), Ukrainian (*The Rumor of Pavel and Paali*, 1988), Hawaiian (*The Surprising Things Maui Did*, 1979), and African (*Tiger Hunt*, 1982; *Juma and the Magic Jinn*, 1986) folktales.

All of his books share similar design elements, including an exacting truth in detail from costumes to architectural details, patterns, textures, and colors to flora and fauna. To create the settings and artistic frameworks for each story, Mikolaycak spent much time researching his tales. Whether drawn in pencil or rendered in paints and colored pencil, he used perspective, overlapping line, and form and realistic, often sensuous, figurative renderings that created a moment in time, a specific place, and fully realized characters. In *Peter and the Wolf* (1982), the double-page spread of Peter perched high above the wolf as he sets a trap allows the reader to witness the dramatic scene from Peter's precarious perspective, looking down as the earth drops away into a white void.

Mikolaycak's use of negative spaces heightened the dramatic effect in his illustrations. In many of his books, he left a distinct edge around his illustrations, abruptly ending the background details to emphasize a figure or shape. This effect accentuates the somber mood in *The Tall Man from Boston*, a grim retelling with black-and-white illustrations of the true story of a man accused of witchcraft in Salem Village in 1692. The negative spaces visually isolate one character from another, enhancing the plight of the accused.

As a teenager, Mikolaycak drew inspiration from film, often illustrating the sequential events of a movie or capturing the story in a poster format. This overlapping action in double- or multiple-page spreads that create a cinematic effect appeared in many of his books, particularly those in black-and-white, such as *Three Wanderers from Wapping* (1978), the true story of three men fleeing from the horrors of the black plague in 1665. Many of Mikolaycak's artistic techniques joined together in *Babushka: An Old Russian Folktale*, chosen as Best Illustrated Children's Book of 1984 by the *New York Times Book Review*. His rich palette accentuated the elements of the Russian setting from the dress, scarf, and architectural details to the decorative ceramic tiles in Babushka's kitchen as the action plays out in overlapping illustrations depicting sequences of events.

Mikolaycak designed many of the books he illustrated, often including notes about the typeface, paper, and artistic techniques he used to create the book. When appropriate, Mikolaycak included annotations to aid a young reader's understanding of the story. These annotations included historical notes, and, in *Orpheus*, popular interpretations of the myth and musical references. His work received critical acclaim that included recognition by the American Institute for Graphic Arts and the Society of Book Illustrators and inclusion on the American Library Association's Notable Books list. Mikolaycak's collaborators included many of the best children's storytellers writing today: Jan Wahl, Eve Bunting, Bernard Evslin, Jane Yolen, Mirra Ginsburg, Edwin Fadiman, Jr., and his own wife, Carole Kismaric. ❧ J.A.S.

Milne, A. A.

British writer, poet, and playwright, 1882–1956. One would have to search far and wide to find fictional characters as beloved to so many readers as Winnie-the-Pooh, Piglet, Christopher Robin, and their many animal friends. Although Alan Alexander Milne wrote novels, short stories, poetry, and many plays for adults, in addition to his work as assistant editor of *Punch* from 1906 to 1914, it is his writings for children that have captured the hearts of millions of people worldwide and granted Milne everlasting fame.

Published in 1926 and 1928 respectively, *Winnie-the-Pooh* and *The House at Pooh Corner* introduced the stuffed-animal friends of Christopher Robin, Milne's small son. Dorothy Milne, Christopher Robin's mother, had given each toy a voice, and Christopher Robin engaged in active, imaginative play with them. According to Christopher Milne's account of his life with his father, A. A. Milne's role in his son's life was as an observer and a chronicler more than as a participant, and, as he grew older and began school, the boy came to resent the world's perception of him as merely a storybook character. Although it caused his son some grief,

Illustration by E. H. SHEPARD from *Winnie-the-Pooh* (1926), by A. A. Milne.

Milne's depiction of the sweet child who acts as a kind of parent to the animals of the Hundred Acre Wood while maintaining a childlike artlessness has created a lasting tribute to the dignity and joy of childhood.

Milne's lighthearted prose, periodically interspersed with simple verses composed by Pooh, is a joy to read and displays Milne's mastery of the English language. The reader responds not only to the story but to the words themselves; Milne capitalizes various words and phrases to stress their importance to the characters, which provides the narrative with a distinctive charm and emphasizes the characters' näiveté. Stylistically, the books shine. The animals of the Hundred Acre Wood possess endearing traits that allow them to be quickly described, but they are far from simple caricatures. At various moments, readers can identify with fearful Piglet, bossy Rabbit, single-minded Kanga, glum and underappreciated Eeyore, the irrepressible, energetic Tigger, or Winnie-the-Pooh himself, a lovable, "hummy" sort of bear, who, more than anything, loves "a little something" at eleven o'clock. Whether building a trap for Heffalump; planning an Expotition to the North Pole; staging the kidnapping of baby Roo in order to scare his newcomer mother, Kanga, into moving out of the Wood; or playing Poohsticks on the bridge over the river, Pooh Bear and his friends make their adventures memorable with their silly observations, calculations, and deductions.

Milne frames *Winnie-the-Pooh* with scenes showing Christopher Robin, faithful teddy bear in hand, requesting and listening to his father's stories about Pooh, which sets the stage for the other tales by making clear that they are—however completely fleshed out and believable—mainly stories. Although *The House at Pooh Corner* contains similar charming tales about the "Bear of Very Little Brain" and his companions, Milne carefully depicts Christopher Robin's gradual separation from his toys and his attraction to school and the opportunity to learn. Indeed, Owl and Rabbit consider themselves more educated than the other inhabitants of the forest, but their unintentional silliness and innocent ignorance, as well as Owl's secret insecurity about his own wisdom, allow the young reader to feel comparatively knowledgeable. Simultaneously, they highlight Christopher Robin's need to step away from the security and authority of his childhood world in order to embark on the adventures involved in growing up. Even as Milne celebrates childhood, he subtly prepares both characters and readers for the inevitable need to forge ahead.

ERNEST H. SHEPARD's illustrations, modeled after the actual toys, show character and movement in simple line vignettes, which add so much to the books that most people consider them to be inseparable from the texts. Shepard's artwork also graces *When We Were Very Young* (1924) and *Now We Are Six* (1927), which contain poems that are, regardless of their simplicity, flawless in rhyme scheme, meter, and general composition. Many feature or are spoken by Christopher Robin; all reveal Milne's superior understanding of the world as viewed through a child's eyes. Verses about toys, Nanny, friendships, ridiculous scenarios, and ordinary aspects of daily life represent the concerns of Christopher Robin's boyhood. Despite the fact that the poetry depicts what is, in modern eyes, an overly idealized childhood and that some critics have suggested they are sentimental, the verses remain extremely popular with children and adults alike.

Publishers and producers have capitalized on the enduring success and appeal of the four books by making widely available countless cartoons, pop-up books, and condensed and colorized versions of the stories. Unfortunately, many of these efforts involve tampering with or completely changing the artwork and text to something incalculably inferior to the inimitable collaboration of Milne and Shepard; at best, these versions lead at least some children back to the classic editions.

Milne's contributions to the world of children's literature include a fantasy entitled *Once on a Time* (1917 in England, 1922 in the United States) and *Toad of Toad Hall*, a play based on *The Wind in the Willows* by KENNETH GRAHAME. But best loved are those books, set in the Hundred Acre Wood, that touch a chord in the hearts of readers of all ages. Expert characterization, a carefree pastoral setting, and Milne's precision of language and style put *Winnie-the-Pooh* and *The House at Pooh Corner* in a class of their own. Winnie-the-Pooh's adventures are not only arguably the greatest toy fantasies ever written for children, they are also, simply and undeniably, great literature. ANNE DEIFENDEIFER

MINARIK, ELSE HOLMELUND

AMERICAN AUTHOR, B. 1920. When she first arrived in the United States from Denmark at the age of four, Else Holmelund Minarik hated the English language. Since that time, however, she has not only learned English but grown to love it, and she has translated that love into warm and entertaining books for young readers, much to the delight of two generations of children.

After getting degrees in education and in psychology, Minarik taught first grade for many years. An avid gardener, she often found inspiration for her books as she worked in the garden. She wrote for beginning readers to answer the needs of not only her students, who were just learning to read, but also her young daughter, who started reading very early. In the mid-1950s there were few easy-to-read books. Ursula Nordstrom, her editor at Harper and Row, was so delighted with her first book, *Little Bear* (1957), that she used it to launch the highly successful "I Can Read" series. Although the language in *Little Bear* is simple and the sentences are short, Minarik created a truly lovable character. Little Bear's escapades are filled with humor and the right mix of fantasy and realism. But the emotional tone of the book, which speaks to the universal needs for love, acceptance, and independence, is particularly captivating. The relationship between Little Bear and his mother is especially respectful, warm, and playful. In one story, Little Bear decides to fly to the moon. After jumping off a little tree on a little hill, he imagines himself on the moon and marvels at its similarities to Earth. Mother Bear plays along with Little Bear's fantasy, and, pretending not to recognize him, invites him in for lunch. When Little Bear tires of the game, he tells his mother, "You are my Mother Bear and I am your Little Bear and we are on Earth, and you know it." Mother Bear gathers him into her arms and reassures him that he is indeed her little bear and "I know it." What Minarik does not put into words, illustrator MAURICE SENDAK more than ably adds in the illustrations.

Four more books about Little Bear followed over the next eleven years. *Little Bear's Visit* was named a Caldecott Honor Book in 1962 for Sendak's illustrations, and *Father Bear Comes Home* and *A Kiss for Little Bear* were both on the *New York Times* list of Best Illustrated Books of the Year in 1959 and 1968.

Although Minarik's language is easily accessible to beginning readers, her humor and character development keep the books from becoming dull or monotonous. She likes the device of a story within a story. She uses it not only in *Little Bear's Visit,* in which Little Bear's grandmother tells him about his mother as a child, but also in *No Fighting, No Biting!* (1958). Two children want to sit beside their older cousin Joan as she is reading. They squeeze and push to be next to her. To calm them down, Joan finally tells them a story about two young alligators who always fight and bite. More recently, Minarik has turned her skills to picture books. In *It's Spring!* (1989) two kittens vie to see who can imagine jumping the highest as they celebrate spring. Here, as in her other books, humor is an important ingredient. But what comes through most strongly in all of Minarik's work is her skill in using simple but expressive language to create delightful and memorable characters. P.R.

Illustration by MAURICE SENDAK from *Little Bear* (1957), by Else Holmelund Minarik.

Mohr, Nicholasa

American author and illustrator, b. 1935. Nicholasa Mohr draws from her experiences as a Puerto Rican growing up in New York City to create her honest, powerful novels and short stories. Mohr attended a trade school in New York City at the encouragement of a high school counselor who believed that Puerto Ricans were naturally good seamstresses. She studied fashion illustration and later art and printmaking at the Pratt Center for Contemporary Art. She became a writer when her art agent and one of her collectors, the head of a publishing company, insisted that she write about her own life.

Mohr's first novel, *Nilda* (1973), based on her childhood, begins as the ten-year-old Nilda is sent from the sweltering heat of New York's El Barrio to a Catholic camp for girls, where children are given doses of prayer and laxatives to "be clean and pure" for God. Nilda escapes the humiliations imposed on her by poverty and racism by developing her talent as an artist and escaping reality. Her mother encourages her daughter's art and before she dies tells her, "A little piece inside has to remain yours always." This theme, survival by maintaining a sense of self, is carried through Mohr's writing for children and young adults. Each of her characters struggles with the physical realities of living in poverty and isolation within mainstream America, but each maintains a saving personal identity. *El Bronx Remembered* (1975) is a collection of short stories that together create a powerful portrait of lives punctuated by poverty, religion, and memories of the green island of Puerto Rico. Mohr is best known for *Felita* (1979), a novel more powerful and direct than her earlier works. Felita and her family choose to move from their close-knit Puerto Rican community in New York to a more expensive neighborhood so Felita can attend a better school. She hopes to make friends with her new neighbors, but the other children's parents insult her family and call them "spicks." Finally, after suffering many humiliations, Felita and her family move back to their old neighborhood, where they are accepted. Felita is a spunky, resilient character who reappears in *Going Home* (1986), a novel about her experience traveling to Puerto Rico to stay with relatives. She and her family dream of this trip home, but they find that Felita is an outsider among the Puerto Ricans. The children tease her because she has an accent and comes from New York, but Felita, a good artist, earns their respect by directing the painting of the sets for a play to be performed at the church youth center. As in *Felita,* she goes home to her neighborhood in New York with a new sense of self and a greater understanding of human nature.

Because Mohr was herself an artist before she was a writer, art plays a role in many of her characters' lives and in several of her books. She illustrated her first novel with graffitilike collections of words and images. Each of Mohr's powerful works creates a vivid portrait of the difficult and sometimes tragic realities minority groups face and the small details of the daily life of Puerto Rican Americans. Mohr's works have been well received by the public and by reviewers, particularly for their authentic rendering of her culture and for the high literary quality of her honest and skillful writing. ❧ M.V.K.

Monjo, F. N.

American editor and writer, 1924–1978. Ferdinand Nicolas Monjo grew up in Stamford, Connecticut, attended Stamford High School, and graduated from Columbia University in New York City. History was one of Monjo's great passions; music was the other. He had grown up hearing stories of his father's fur-trading ancestors and of his Southern great-grandmother, who as a young woman single-handedly managed an all but deserted plantation during the Civil War. As a children's book editor, he became aware that most history books for the young were stiff, sanitized, and devoid of the intriguing details that impart life to a person or period, and he determined to write—and publish—easy-to-read HISTORICAL FICTION for seven- to nine-year-olds.

Indian Summer (1968), Monjo's first book, a suspenseful story about a pioneer woman whose quick wit enabled her to save herself and her four children from an Indian attack, was initially well received, but was later criticized for its depiction of the Indians. Monjo courageously defended his right as author to choose the point of view from which he would tell a story.

His most popular books include *The Drinking Gourd* (1970), a genial blend of historical fact and fiction about the Underground Railroad and a minister's son who helped a family of escaped slaves on their way to freedom; *The One Bad Thing about Father* (1970), a delightful, easy-to-read story about Theodore Roosevelt as seen through the eyes of Quentin, Roosevelt's youngest child; *Poor Richard in France* (1973), seven-year-old Benny Franklin's unsentimental, somewhat irreverent account of his grandfather's activities in Paris as he worked to secure French help for the revolutionaries back home; and *Me and Willie and Pa: The Story of Abraham Lincoln and His Son Tad* (1973). Here he chronicles without sentimentality the events and tragedies of Lincoln's White

House years as Tad, Lincoln's youngest son, might have experienced them.

Perhaps Monjo's most remarkable accomplishment is *Letters to Horseface: Being the Story of Wolfgang Amadeus Mozart's Journey to Italy, 1769–1770, When He Was a Boy of Fourteen* (1975). He managed to get inside the mind of the intelligent, gifted fourteen-year-old so well that a reader or Mozart student might well think the letters genuine. His intimate knowledge of the period, of the music scene, of life in the great cities enabled him to reconstruct the journey with its strains on a boy forced to perform as well as to create.

F. N. Monjo was a gifted writer and editor whose appealing historical fiction is, with the possible exception of the biographies by JEAN FRITZ, his colleague and friend, unequaled. ❧ M.N.C.

MONTGOMERY, LUCY MAUD

CANADIAN AUTHOR, 1874–1942. Born with what she called "an itch for writing," Montgomery began her literary apprenticeship at a young age. Eleven when she started submitting manuscripts to magazines, she was fifteen when her first poem appeared in a small Canadian newspaper. By age twenty-one she was earning her living in the thriving periodical market of turn-of-the-century North America. International acclaim came in 1908 with the publication of her first novel, *Anne of Green Gables,* which instantly became—and remains—a best seller. By the end of her life, Montgomery had produced twenty-three books of fiction, a short autobiography, and an estimated five hundred poems and five hundred stories written for popular magazines. Selections from her ten volumes (more than five thousand pages, including photographs) of personal diaries, chronicling in compelling detail her life from 1889 to 1942, have also been edited and published.

Writing served several purposes in Montgomery's life. She was raised in the small Prince Edward Island town of Cavendish by dour Scots-Presbyterian grandparents. They were ill equipped to handle a high-strung child, and as a young girl she channeled repressed energies into creating stories and poems. She lived most vividly in the book worlds of Bunyan, Bulwer-Lytton, Scott, Tennyson, Austen, and the Brontë sisters, writers whose influence is evident in her work. As an adult woman living with her widowed grandmother and, later, as the frustrated wife of a depressive Presbyterian minister, she again turned to writing as an outlet for pent-up emotion. A restorative process itself, writing also earned Montgomery accolades from a world literary community that too seldom honored its female members. In 1923, she became the first Canadian woman to be appointed a member of the Royal Society of Great Britain; in 1935, she was made an officer of the Order of the British Empire and was selected for the Literary and Artistic Institute of France.

No less important to Montgomery were the financial rewards of being a successful writer. She savored the social standing and legitimacy that money brought with it. Unwilling to jeopardize her status as a best-selling author, she produced what the market demanded: romantic stories with "happy endings" that were, perhaps simply because they were popular, often dismissed by the arbiters of literary taste as shallow formula fiction.

Were that an adequate assessment of Montgomery's work, it would be difficult to explain her enduring popularity. Even more difficult to account for would be the profound, lasting effect her writing has had on readers of all ages, from countries as diverse as Canada and Japan, Poland and Sweden. For example, one of Canada's most celebrated writers, Alice Munro, speaks of the empowering model for female authorship she found in Montgomery's autobiographical Emily of New Moon trilogy of novels. Interesting thematic comparisons have been drawn between Montgomery's writings and those of Canadian Margaret Atwood. And Sweden's ASTRID LINDGREN—whose own redheaded heroine, Pippi Longstocking, is beloved by readers worldwide—cites Montgomery as a powerful literary influence.

In part, what Montgomery's readers respond to so deeply and with such emotion are the same things that elevate her writing above the sentimental fiction of other popular writers of her day: lively storytelling seasoned with equal parts realism, folklore, and Celtic mythology; a tart sense of humor and a deft comedic touch; and a richly detailed evocation of setting. All but two of her novels are set on Prince Edward Island, and the tiny Canadian province today counts Montgomery-inspired tourism among its major industries. The exceptions are *The Blue Castle* (1926) and *Jane of Lantern Hill* (1937), both set at least partly in Ontario, where Montgomery lived from 1911 until her death.

But there is energy of another type that animates Montgomery's books, which retain a strong hold on adult readers. It is the energy of social critique, and it operates just below the surface of many of her novels. Anne and Emily, her two best-known and best-developed heroines, may fulfill their womanly duty by marrying the saccharine-sweet boy next door, but not before each voices loud and angry criticisms of the way in which girls, orphans, and other disempowered members of society are ignored and trivialized. In the later of the nine "Anne" books, the popular redhead capitulates to social convention and becomes the matronly, submissive Mrs. Gilbert Blythe. Out of the mouths of secondary, marginalized characters like Leslie Moore in *Anne's House of Dreams* (1917), however, come caustic comments that subtly undercut the artificially blissful Blythe household.

Of course, not everything Montgomery published in her long, prolific career was entirely successful. Many of her short stories do not reward repeated readings, and her ear-pleasing poetry is little more than that. But recent critical reevaluation of Montgomery's literary output, prompted largely by the publication of her journals, has reversed some earlier assessments of her work. For example, *Rilla of Ingleside* (1920), once considered a lesser light in the Montgomery canon, is now recognized as a valuable fictional account of the Canadian experience on the World War I homefront, one of very few such records.

Much of the historical detail in *Rilla of Ingleside* is drawn from Montgomery's long, anguished diary entries during the tumultuous war years. The impassioned tone of these entries is typical of the journals, which combine to form a lively and riveting narrative of a remarkable woman's life. Uniquely valuable documents of social history, they provide crucial insight into the conditions of women's lives during an era of radical social change. In writing and recording her own life, L.M. Montgomery created a character as engaging and memorable as Canada's most famous fictional heroine, Anne of Green Gables. ❧ MARIE C. CAMPBELL

MONTRESOR, BENI

ITALIAN AUTHOR AND ILLUSTRATOR, B. 1926. Born in Bussolengo, Italy, "with a pencil in my hand," Beni Montresor spent much of his childhood in Verona. "I first saw Verona when I was six years old. I remember driving past the vineyards and down from the Lessini hills. As we crossed the Adige River the warm colors of Verona rose up to greet me: soft yellows, pinks, terra cottas." These same colors, this warm to vibrantly hot palette, permeate Montresor's work. They cast a brilliant glow over his set and costume designs for the ballet and opera and act as a shimmering contrast to the fractured black-and-white line drawings in his other narrative art form, the picture book.

Montresor never aspired to a career as a children's illustrator or writer. He grew up in the cold and hunger of a country at war and never saw a picture book, much less owned one. In Italy, the Catholic Church was the hub on which family life revolved, and it was the churches, their walls and brilliant stained-glass windows, that gave Montresor his first and most formative experiences with visual storytelling: "I grew up looking at church and palace walls covered with medieval frescoes. They were all visual stories done for people that didn't know how to read, telling about heroes and their adventures and saints and their miracles. Those walls were my picture books. I spent hours and hours looking at them, living with them, intrigued by everything I saw. I make my books thinking of those walls of my childhood." Montresor studied at the Verona Art School and the Academy of Fine Arts in Venice, and in 1950 he won a two-year scholarship to study film design at the Centro Sperimentale di Cinematografia in Rome, edging out over two hundred other aspirants. Upon graduation, he began working as a set and costume designer for such noted film directors as Fellini, De Sica, and Rossellini before coming to the United States in 1960. He continued his career, designing sets and costumes for the Metropolitan Opera and the New York City Ballet, and when asked at a party shortly after his arrival in the United States if he would like to illustrate children's picture books, he impulsively answered "Yes!" although he had still never seen one. He literally became an overnight success in children's books, illustrating four books in 1961, including MARY STOLZ's Newbery Honor Book, *Belling the Tiger.* In 1962 *House of Flowers, House of Stars,* which he wrote and illustrated, was published, and that same year *The Princesses: Sixteen Stories about Princesses* was named one of the New York Times Best Illustrated Books of the Year. His illustrations for BEATRICE SCHENK DE REGNIERS's book *May I Bring a Friend?* won the Caldecott Medal in 1965.

Montresor's work is quite graphic, and at times his viewpoint is distanced so that a child views the characters and scenes in his books as he or she would see actors on a stage. Over the years, his illustrations have become less decorative and more narrative. In his stories and book concepts he remains true to his own inner vision, although some adults have found *Bedtime* (1978) and *Little Red Riding Hood* (1991) disturbing in their visual content. Montresor's depiction of bedtime involves use of religious imagery in both dreamlike and nightmarish scenarios, and the wolf in *Little Red Riding Hood* is actually seen devouring the protagonist.

Montresor lives in New York and maintains a home in Italy. His work is his life. "My approach to life and my work is very sensual and very emotional. I prefer to put my emotions and fantasies into my work. That's my reality, my true identity, my real life!" ❧ M.B.B.

Moore, Clement Clarke

American author, 1779–1863. On the night before Christmas, families all around the world read the poem "A Visit from St. Nicholas." This classic verse was written by a New York–born minister's son who received advanced degrees from Columbia University and taught Interpretation of Scripture, as well as Oriental and Greek literature, at New York's Diocesan Seminary, later known as the General Theological Seminary. As a writer, Clement Clarke Moore published political tracts, a Hebraic dictionary, and poetry.

Moore first recited "A Visit from St. Nicholas" at an 1822 Christmas Eve celebration as a present for his ailing daughter. The poem paints an early picture of today's Santa Claus figure, whom Moore based in spirit on a fifth-century saint from Asia Minor and in appearance on a local handyman who wore a red parka and frequently dispensed sugarplums to children. Many modern Christmas motifs have their origins in this work, including Santa's use of chimneys and reindeer, although the names of the reindeer were borrowed from Washington Irving's *Knickerbocker Tales.* Moore's niece anonymously submitted the poem to the *Troy Sentinel,* where it was published in 1823; more than twenty years passed before Moore acknowledged authorship of the verse. Now part of the public domain, "A Visit from St. Nicholas" has been presented in song and on film, has been satirized and parodied, and is available in countless printed editions illustrated by artists as diverse as Tasha Tudor, James Marshall, Tomie dePaola, and Grandma Moses.

This perennial favorite continues to be shared each holiday season, as children eagerly memorize Moore's poem and recite the unforgettable closing line, "Happy Christmas to all, and to all a goodnight." P.D.S.

Moore, Lilian

American author and poet, b. 1909. Born and raised in New York City, Lilian Moore attended Hunter College and Columbia University. Books were an important part of Moore's childhood—"I still can't walk into a children's library without a rush of love," she recalls—as were the summers she spent in the knee-high grass and clover fields of the more rural parts of early-twentieth-century Manhattan. Moore's first job was as an elementary school teacher; she later became a reading specialist after discovering her aptitude for teaching children to read. Moore was one of the founding members of the Council on Interracial Books for Children. After the birth of her son, she left teaching, entered the world of publishing, becoming the first editor at *Scholastic*'s Arrow Book Club. She calls this experience "one of the most satisfying things I ever did, helping to launch the first quality paperback book program. It was a job that brought together my experience as a teacher, my interest in children's books, and my downright pleasure in the endearing middle-grader."

While editing early-reader books, she began to write her own stories. She wrote eleven "Wonder Books"—easy readers whose goal was to show children the excitement of reading—under the pseudonym Sara Asheron and *The Magic Spectacles and Other Easy-to-Read Stories* (1966) under her own name. The latter collection contains seven stories encompassing a wide range of genres—suspense, humor, realism, fantasy, and adventure—and features a number of animal protagonists. Moore uses animals in many of her stories, but they are not meant to be surrogates for children. It is important that "the character of the animal must be animal-like, but the emotional content reflects a child's development," she points out. *Little Raccoon and the Thing in the Pool* (1963) tells the story of Little Raccoon's surprise at seeing his reflection in the water. Moore's educational background is apparent in her repetition of phrases to help slower readers. The succeeding two "Little Raccoon" books, *Little Raccoon and the Outside World* (1965) and *Little Raccoon and No Trouble at All* (1972), follow the earlier pattern. The animal characters are appealing, and the repetition invites reading aloud.

Moore may have begun her career as an author of easy-to-read fiction, but it is her poetry that best combines her understanding of the child's mind and her ability to find beauty in familiar and unexpected places. *I Feel the Same Way* (1967) is a collection of short and simply written poems that speak with the voice of Moore's own childhood memories, which look at the commonplace—the rain, the ocean, the wind, the fog—but see the extraordinary. Moore's innovative choice of words and her vivid imagery—"a sea breathes in and out upon the shore," "that wind/could wrinkle water so"—appeal to the reader's imagination.

The poems in *I Thought I Heard the City* (1969) deal primarily with urban experiences—construction sites, rooftops, window shopping—but avoid the seamier side of city life. Rather, Moore highlights the quiet beauty of the city after a snowfall and the bare trees in the winter: "You really do not see / a tree / until you see / its bones." By contrast, *Sam's Place: Poems from the Country* (1973), a collection of twenty nature poems, has its origin on the Upstate New York farm of Moore's husband, Sam. Moore says she always "wanted to make things grow and live with the light of the sky," and she expresses this impulse clearly and powerfully with words and images: a sunset, a chestnut tree, a winter cardinal. There is a crispness and a graceful cleanness to Moore's poetry—no clichés or forced metaphors cloud the images. Moore received the National Council of Teachers of English Award for excellence in poetry for children in 1985.

Moore says, "What I would love to see happen with poetry for children is to have it become a part of their lives." With her insight and sensitivity into the mind of the child, her ability to express her thoughts concisely and creatively, and her evocative imagery, Moore's poems provide an ideal introduction to the universal nature of poetry. ❧ M.I.A.

Morey, Walter

AMERICAN AUTHOR, 1907–1992. Compelling adventure stories, a love of the wilderness of Alaska and the Pacific Northwest, and an optimistic outlook characterize Walt Morey's writing. Morey pits adolescent boys against ordeals such as the death of a parent, a cruel person who mistreats animals, or a town's mistrust of a boy's pet. In many of his stories, the hero, bolstered by his love for a wild or partially wild animal, matures as he copes with adversity. And always, Morey presents the Alaskan or Northwest wilderness as a wondrous and challenging place. Although it is fiction, Morey's writing is rooted in reality. The saloon with an altar hanging from the ceiling described in *Gloomy Gus* (1970) actually existed in an Alaskan ghost town Morey had visited nearly twenty years earlier, and Morey himself once repaired a salmon trap after it had been damaged by a whale just as he has Joe do in *Deep Trouble* (1971).

Morey was born in the state of Washington, and his family moved frequently around the Northwest following his father's construction jobs. Functionally illiterate until the age of fourteen, Morey never went to college. After high school he worked at a variety of jobs, including a stint as a projectionist in a movie theater. While watching the films over and over, he studied them closely to see what made a good story. He sold his first adult short story to a pulp magazine and continued to write regularly for the pulps during the 1930s and 1940s. With the advent of television, however, the pulp market disappeared and Morey, who was running a filbert farm in Oregon with his wife, stopped writing for nearly ten years. Then his wife, a teacher, urged him to try writing for children. To prove to her that he couldn't do it, he wrote *Gentle Ben.* He found writing for children, with its requirement for tighter plots and totally believable characters, far more challenging and demanding than writing for adults. Nevertheless, the book was named an ALA Notable Book in 1966, made into a movie, and became the basis for a television series. With *Gentle Ben,* the story of Mark, a quiet boy who befriends a mistreated captive brown bear, Morey established his reputation as a children's author, and he went on to write fourteen more books. Although most of his books center on a boy's love for an animal, *Kävik the Wolf Dog* (1968) is the story of a dog's love for a boy. This love drives him to make a two-thousand-mile trek from Seattle to Alaska to return to Andy, who had rescued and befriended him earlier. Morey does not anthropomorphize the dog as he describes his journey north, maintaining Kävik's character and dignity. *Year of the Black Pony* (1976) tells of Chris's longing for a pony while trying to survive on a small ranch in Oregon at the turn of the century. Morey draws on his personal experience for the flavor of homesteading and for the final climactic scene. His last book, *Death Walk* (1991), is the survival tale of Joe, lost in the Alaskan wilderness, who not only must face harsh elements and outlaws but his own fears as well.

Morey's main characters and their mentors are usually multidimensional people who grow as they overcome obstacles. His villains, however, tend to be stereotyped and one-sided. Nevertheless, his fast-paced adventure stories are enjoyable and entertaining. ❧ P.R.

Morrison, Lillian

AMERICAN POET AND POETRY ANTHOLOGIST, B. 1917. Born in Jersey City, New Jersey, Lillian Morrison received her graduate degree in library science from Columbia University. She began working at the New York Public Library in 1942—"I was surrounded by books . . . I knew I was in heaven!" she remembers—and became the coordinator of young adult services in 1968. Working in one of the branches of the public library, Morrison was often asked by her young patrons to sign their autograph books.

Morrison says, "I became curious as to what others had written. I began to collect the comments for fun, realizing that the simple messages were actually a form of folklore." She compiled these collections of verse—sentimental, mocking, nostalgic, and silly—into *Yours till Niagara Falls* (1950), *Remember Me When This You*

See (1961), and *Best Wishes, Amen* (1974). The last title also includes a group of Spanish rhymes and their English translations. These collections, like all folklore, reflect current concerns—pollution and women's liberation—and touch upon the basic subjects of children's thoughts—school, success, personality, love, and marriage. As Morrison says in her introduction to *Best Wishes, Amen,* the entries "are true Americana, expressing the rhythm, wit, warmth, originality, and irrepressible vitality of the young."

In 1965 Morrison completed a project that she had been working on for ten years: *Sprints and Distances: Sports in Poetry and the Poetry in Sport.* This anthology, including works ranging from Pindar and Virgil to Yeats and Wallace Stevens, highlights the wide range of athletes' moods and emotions. By linking poetry and sports, Morrison combined two elements that were constantly connected in her own mind. As she says, "I love rhythms, the body movement implicit in poetry, explicit in sports. And there are emotions connected with sports, a transcendence and beauty one wants to catch. One turns naturally to poetry to express these things."

With the publication of *The Sidewalk Racer and Other Poems of Sports and Motion* (1977), Morrison continued her exploration on the theme of sports and poetry with a significant difference. Morrison wrote these poems herself. The verse deals with a wide range of sports—biking, boxing, basketball, stickball, figure skating—speaking sometimes from the viewpoint of the participant and sometimes that of the spectator. Morrison's spare style matches the pulses of excitement and relaxation in sports, and her rhythms match the natural fluidity and gracefulness of the athletes. The collection includes a number of poems in which women and girls are described as athletes, and the photographs show both boys and girls in action.

In another collection of original poems, *Overheard in a Bubble Chamber and Other Sciencepoems* (1981), Morrison chooses to use scientific terminology as a metaphor for human emotions and experiences; the poetry is tight and precise, reflecting the concise, exacting nature of science. The thirty-eight poems are divided under five headings—Natural Histories, Mathematical Measures, Physical Properties, Heavenly Bodies, and In Search of Verities—but these categories are not concrete, and the sophisticated scientific language masks simpler ideas and concerns, as evidenced by "The Flow, the Void," where Morrison writes, "Yes, we are bits of energy/but we have names."

Morrison is also drawn to dancers, drummers, and jazz musicians—the beat of their instruments and voices echoes the beats she hears in poetry. Accordingly, her collection *Rhythm Road: Poems to Move To* (1988) reflects the sounds of instruments and the cadence of the dance floor. Morrison has compiled poems from more than seventy poets—ranging from Edgar Allan Poe to John Updike—and arranged them by topic: music, dance, movement, and Motion of the Mind. The richly worded poems sing and capture the imagination with clear images and patterns of sound that reverberate in the mind.

Morrison's original poems and her poetry anthologies help break down prejudices about poetry held by many young readers, as she proves that poetry can speak, jump, and dance. ❧ M.I.A.

MOSER, BARRY

AMERICAN ILLUSTRATOR AND DESIGNER, B. 1940. The first books Barry Moser illustrated were literary classics, mostly for adults, such as *Moby-Dick,* issued in a limited edition by a small press. Since the 1980s, he has also applied his artistry to the field of books for children.

Born in Chattanooga, Tennessee, Moser was raised in a loving environment and introduced to diverse cultural experiences such as Italian opera, musical comedy, and the music of Fats Waller. But he also recalls that he was "taught to be a racist, to be anti-Catholic, anti-Semitic, and xenophobic." He hated school, but had a talent for drawing, which was encouraged, and he benefited from the direction of an uncle who had a woodworking shop and worked with him there, giving him a drawing table. At age twelve, Moser was sent to military school; in 1958 he attended Auburn University and had his first instruction in drawing and design. He then attended and graduated from the University of Chattanooga as a painting major in 1962. He found a mentor there who led him to study the works of Cézanne, Braque, and Shahn, among others. After teaching in Tennessee, he and his family moved to Williston Academy in Easthampton, Massachusetts. For fifteen years, he taught himself the skills of making etchings and wood engravings, working with type, life drawing, art history, book design, and calligraphy.

In 1969 Moser met LEONARD BASKIN, who helped him improve his drawing and also made an introduction to a pressman who taught Moser how to improve his skills in printing wood engravings. He designed and printed his first book in 1969. Since then, Moser has illustrated more than 120 books, and his work is

Voices of the Creators

Barry Moser

I made my first book in 1969, a slender little presentation of an essay by the American painter James Abbott McNeill Whistler called *The Red Rag.* I made it by hand. I set the type. I ran the printing press. I folded and gathered the sheets. Since that modest beginning, I have in one way or another been involved in making around 150 books. There is a botanical treatise in the stacks called *The Flowering Plants of Massachusetts* and another called *The Adventurous Gardner.* There is Melville's *Moby-Dick* and Dante's *Divine Comedy.* Virgil's *Aeneid* and Homer's *Odyssey.*

If there is one thing I have learned from these books and the years it has taken me to do them, it is that illustrations by themselves do not make handsome books. Handsome books are the result of harmony—the arranging and combining of all the various graphic elements in pleasant and interesting ways that ultimately form a whole. The books I make for children, like the books I make for adults, are all done for the same purpose—to make a beautiful *book.*

I begin my work, of course, by reading the text. Several times. I am mindful not only of narrative content, place, and characters but also of the mood, scope, and timbre of the text. Mood, scope, and timbre tell me how big a book should be, how generous its margins should be, what typeface and leading it wants, where its folios should go, what kind of imagery is appropriate, and even how many pictures there should be. These are subjective choices to be sure, choices that are determined by the prejudices of taste. For example, I never use sans serif typefaces; I prefer wide margins so that hands and fingers never cover up type; I eschew all decoration except calligraphic embellishments; and for pictures I prefer simple compositions that focus on character, setting, or objects.

It might seem from what I have just said that I subordinate illustrations. I do not. Making pictures for books is important to me but only in that it contributes to the overall beauty of the book. I see illustration as equal to, not superior to, text, typography, and overall design.

As for my illustrations, or "pictures" as I prefer to call them, they are rarely based on fantasy or flights of imagination. I base my images on facts and on things observed. I find that nature and the world around me create and suggest things stranger and more wonderful than things my mind and eye invent.

To this end I have built an extensive library and a bulging scrap file from which I borrow and steal freely, being, as I am, unconcerned about originality. I think of myself, as Christopher Hogwood said about George Frideric Handel, as an artist who polishes other men's stones into jewels—a *bricoleur,* if you will, a user of discarded things.

Originality is a result, not a task. Originality cannot be sought. Seeking to be original is like staring at a star—it disappears just when you think you've got it. Further, history teaches us that all things have antecedents and that only time and history itself can fairly judge what has been original and what has not.

As for media, I prefer the demanding and unforgiving: wood engraving and transparent watercolor. *The Red Rag* was illustrated with a portrait of Whistler drawn on scratchboard and reproduced to look like a wood engraving. Wood engraving is a relief printmaking technique invented in the eighteenth century specifically for book illustration, and it took me years to master that which I could only at first slavishly imitate. Wood engraving is by its nature dark. It is demanding and unforgiving because errors cannot be repaired except through virtuoso games of hide-and-seek.

The influence of wood engraving on my watercolor painting is, to me, apparent. First, my watercolors employ a dark palette that is not typical of the medium; second, the paintings have specific and definite edges; and third, the paintings reflect my sense of chiaroscuro that was inculcated through printmaking.

If my work as an *artiste de livre* is successful, my books will not only have striking and provocative images but a sense of harmony, wholeness, and inevitability—a sense of "Of course, how could it be any other way?"

---

represented in many museums and collections, such as the Library of Congress, Harvard University, the London College of Printing, the British Museum, and Cambridge University.

His powerful watercolors for Dante's *The Divine Comedy* (1980) are typical of his style. In black-and-white wash, he delineates the gnarled roots of a tree and so mimics the tangled veins and blood vessels imposed on the bodies of tortured souls. His use of light and dark shading is dramatic and powerful, and his exquisite calligraphy is an instantly identifiable aspect of his books. In 1982 his illustrations for LEWIS CARROLL's *Alice's Adventures in Wonderland* were published. The book won an American Book Award for pictorial design. Moser illustrated classic JOEL CHANDLER HARRIS tales, adapted by Van Dyke Parks and Malcolm Jones, in *Jump!: The Adventures of Brer Rabbit* (1986). Another example of his fine work in books for children is *In the Beginning: Creation Stories from around the World* (1988), retold by VIRGINIA HAMILTON, which was named a Newbery Honor Book by the American Library Association. Because Moser has applied his distinctive style, coupled with his trademark calligraphy, to a great number of works of classic literature for adults and for children, he has distinguished himself as a major American book illustrator. S.H.H.

MOTHER GOOSE

Young children naturally love rhymes. The rhythm, repetition, action, and subject matter—ranging from nonsense and games to ballads—particularly suit them. As NURSERY RHYMES go, nothing has stood the tests of taste and time with small children as well as Mother Goose. Rhymes such as "Hey diddle diddle" and "Jack and Jill" have for centuries been the beloved possessions of the very young.

When it comes to the origins of this lady who figures so prominently in childhood literature, facts and legends become difficult to separate. The name Mother Goose was first associated with eight folktales—including "Cinderella," "Little Red Riding Hood," and "The Sleeping Beauty"—recorded by CHARLES PERRAULT in 1697. The frontispiece showed a woman telling tales to children; a plaque on the same page stated "Contes de Ma Mère L'Oye" (Tales of Mother Goose), a generic phrase of long-standing for a folk- or old wives' tale. The name today is not usually associated with folktales but rather has become inextricably connected to traditional, popular verses for very young children. The connection was originally forged through the rhymes in "Mother Goose's Melody or Sonnets for the Cradle," published in England between 1760 and 1765 and in the United States around 1785. Two more notable American editions followed, "Mother Goose's Quarto, or Melodies Complete" (about 1827) and "The Only True Mother Goose Melodies" (1833); both served as important sources for later collections.

American affection for Mother Goose rhymes is particularly strong and, in part, responsible for a popular legend. In 1860, John Fleet Elliot published a letter in the *Boston Transcript* declaring that Mother Goose had been a Boston woman, a forebear of his named Goose or Vergoose. When her daughter married Elliot's great-grandfather and had a child, Grandmother Goose kept the infant occupied by singing songs, chants, and ditties, which were collected and printed in 1719. This bit of invented history was taken as fact and printed in some editions of the rhymes. The story still surfaces today. And the fact that the epithet "the real Mother Goose" has been given to a Mary Goose, who died in 1690 and is buried in a Boston graveyard, lends it a charming though false sense of credibility. S.L.

MOWAT, FARLEY

CANADIAN WRITER, NATURALIST, SOCIAL CRITIC, B. 1921. Farley Mowat looms larger than life on the Canadian cultural scene. The social-critic-in-a-kilt has written dozens of books, is quoted frequently on environmental issues as well as other political matters, and is altogether thoughtful, provocative, outspoken, outrageous, and entertaining. His children's books, largely written in the earlier part of his career, are filled with humor, nostalgia, and adventure. There is a reverence for the environment and all living creatures and irreverence for the bureaucracy in human society.

Never Cry Wolf (1963), perhaps Mowat's best-known children's work due to the 1983 WALT DISNEY film, is based on Mowat's own experience and was conceived as a satire on the Canadian government's arbitrary and often destructive policies concerning the wildlife of the North. Instead, the book turned into a love story about a wolf family and a plea to respect the life of these animals instead of destroying it. Though its theme is serious, *Never Cry Wolf* is a very funny and engaging story about Mowat the biologist and his trial-and-error approach to learning about both the North and the wolves. It is Mowat's great sense of irony that saves the book from becoming a diatribe. The story is engrossing from beginning to end.

Owls in the Family (1961), read in hundreds of classrooms every year, is a Canadian classic. Based on Mowat's childhood in Saskatoon, Saskatchewan, it looks back nostalgically at his unorthodox family and his habit of adopting unusual pets, in this case the two owlets Wol and Weeps. The owls unrelentingly plague Mowat's faithful dog Mutt, the main character of his own story, *The Dog Who Wouldn't Be* (1957). Mowat lovingly depicts the animals in his life, especially Mutt. Who could not love a dog who suffered from nightmares and needed goggles when traveling in the family car? *The Dog Who Wouldn't Be* elevates the boy-and-his-dog story to great heights of hilarity and devotion. Meant initially for adult audiences, it was rightfully appropriated by children.

Mowat's adventure stories, *Lost in the Barrens* (1956) and its sequel, *The Curse of the Viking Grave* (1966), rely on the author's extensive first hand knowledge of Canada's North. His detailed descriptions of the barrens, for example, belie the name. These are not barren lands, but country where living things, even human life, sustain themselves. Though these "boys'" adventure stories suffer from the social conventions of the time in which they were written—the native, Inuit, and female characters are stereotyped—the books authentically and respectfully depict the place. Today's readers will be carried away by the adventure while being critical of the dated characterizations.

Mowat's great gift to children's literature is twofold: He brings his own love of nature to his stories, and he spices it up with his wry sense of humor. Today Mowat writes almost exclusively for an adult audience, most recently publishing the memoir *Born Naked* (1993), but such books as *A Whale for the Killing* (1972) and *Sea of Slaughter* (1984) are read by young adults as well. ❧ T.H.

Mullins, Patricia

Australian illustrator, b. 1952. Collage illustrations whose beauty makes their viewers almost gasp have become Patricia Mullins's hallmark, as she has established herself as one of Australia's most gifted artists.

Born in a Melbourne suburb in 1952, she grew up there and shared her childhood with a small menagerie of animals, along with her human family, including a supportive, artistically encouraging mother. Mullins has always been addicted to drawing, and with a vast assortment of pets around her, she naturally spent plenty of time drawing them. She also liked to make toy animals—unwitting preparation for her work in puppet making in conjunction with BBC Television. In the late 1960s and early 1970s she attended the Royal Melbourne Institute of Technology, taking a diploma course in graphic design, followed by a fellowship in illustration.

Mullins was then on her own, working initially as a package designer while illustrating her first books. In general, her artwork for these early books used the more conventional line drawings and colored pencils. But soon she began using natural materials—sand, grasses, feathers, wood, fur, leaves, even the tail of a cow—to make a collection of models of creatures from myth and legend. Out of these creatures emerged *Fabulous Beasts* (1976), a groundbreaking book in its time because of its approach and materials. At this point Mullins ventured overseas to make puppets and work with a puppet theater. Being involved in an activity that required such close attention to fabrics and texture turned out to be the perfect preparation and inspiration for the next illustration project: her artwork for Christobel Mattingly's *Rummage* (1981), in which she effectively combined ink and crayon with fabric, fur, and newspaper collages.

For the next few years Mullins worked in design and production in a publicity branch of the federal government. But, fortunately, her eye-dazzling contributions to children's literature continued. More and more she began using tissue-paper collage, and books such as *Hattie and the Fox* (1986) and *Shoes from Grandpa* (1989), both written by Mem Fox, were the highly successful result. She also produced *Dinosaur Encore* (1992), an innovative, visually striking nonfiction title for very young readers that explains the features of various dinosaurs. Her illustrations are always the result of plenty of observation, research, or both, and she often does much drawing and redrawing before she applies tissue paper. Although she spends hours and hours in meticulous assembly of her artwork, the resulting collages, with their glowing colors, still manage a feeling of freedom and freshness. When she illustrates someone else's prose, her artwork is always the perfect partner, extending wonderfully but never dominating.

Currently working as a freelance artist, Mullins lives with her husband and son in a Melbourne suburb. Behind their cottage is a small garden inhabited by many of the creatures and objects familiar to viewers of her artwork. From the studio behind that garden emerge the marvelous contributions that are Mullins's gift to children's literature. ❧ K.J.

Munro, Roxie

American illustrator and author, b. 1945. Looking at a picture book illustrated by Roxie Munro is a challenge to visual perception of place and space. Perspective is the one single word that immediately comes to mind when attempting to describe her "inside-outside" approach to cities. Traditional lines of linear perspective, relative position, and aerial viewpoint do not hold true in her representations of buildings, monuments, and views. The reason they do not is her "active way of seeing" and her placement of the viewer emotionally within the space that is being seen.

Schooled in fine art at the University of Hawaii and the Maryland Institute College of Art in Baltimore, Munro came to children's books via a path that started with dress designing and manufacturing for small boutiques after college. Next came her work as a courtroom artist for television and newspapers. Her first trial was Watergate in 1976 in Washington, D.C. During that time she continued her oil painting and exhibited in prestigious group and one-woman shows. In 1981 she sold her first cover painting to the *New Yorker* and immediately moved to New York City. A rejected *New Yorker* cover led her to a children's book editor; the result was *The Inside-Outside Book of New York City,* which was named one of the *New York Times* Best Illustrated Books in 1985.

Since then, Munro has created nonfiction picture books that utilize a spatial perspective: *Blimps* (1989), *Christmastime in New York City* (1987), *The Inside-Outside Book of London* (1989), *The Inside-Outside Book of Washington, D.C.* (1987), and *The Inside-Outside Book of Paris* (1992). Munro's pictures combine a view of the space the person is in and the space the person is looking at.

In *The Inside-Outside Book of New York City,* the reader sees a panoramic view as if standing inside the top of the Statue of Liberty. Working in ink and colored dyes, she uses details, patterns, color, and interior space as her design elements and composition. While the views look real, almost photographic, they are in fact manipulated to convey their emotional impact to the reader. For example, in *The Inside-Outside Book of Washington, D.C.,* the Supreme Court Building tilts away, as if the person standing in front of it is looking upward at this imposing, awe-inspiring bastion of justice. In contrast, a bicycle rider jockeying amidst the truck traffic driving down Park Avenue in New York City feels the tall buildings looming over him from his perch on the lowly bicycle seat.

The research Munro has done is evident in the amount of detail in each illustration. By creating pattern from the real thing and by breaking up the symmetry, Munro enlivens the space. Both adults and children who discover her books discover new places, new views, and new ways of seeing them. J.C.

MUNSINGER, LYNN

AMERICAN ILLUSTRATOR, B. 1951. There is no mistaking Lynn Munsinger's interest in creating visually memorable characters. Smug llamas, disgruntled porcupines, and bemused kangaroos fill the pages of her books. A close observer of the emotions that play over the human face and figure, Munsinger applies these same expressions to animals with extremely effective and often humorous results.

Munsinger was born in Greenfield, Massachusetts, graduated from Tufts University, studied illustration at the Rhode Island School of Design, and continued her study of art in London. Munsinger began her career using black-and-white line illustration. One of her first book assignments was *An Arkful of Animals* (1978), a collection of poetry selected by WILLIAM COLE. Munsinger's whimsical drawings of animals were a perfect complement to the poems and made her natural choice to illustrate *Hugh Pine* (1980), a short novel by Janwillem van de Wetering. Her scratchy, prickly, black-and-white line work was admirably suited to the illustration of Hugh Pine, a scratchy, prickly porcupine. Hugh dresses like his human friend, Mr. McTosh, in order to avoid the hazards of the highway, which too frequently result in flattened porcupines. Yet even when there is little to be seen of Hugh between his pulled-down hat and turned-up overcoat, his posture can be clearly read as dejected, cunning, or self-satisfied in Munsinger's drawings.

Munsinger has illustrated books by Pat Lowery Col-

Illustration by Lynn Munsinger from *A Zooful of Animals* (1992), by WILLIAM COLE.

lins, Ann Tompert, and Sandol Stoddard, and while she is adept at working from the inspiration of each author's text, she has also worked very effectively as a collaborator. Helen Lester as author and Munsinger as illustrator have worked as a team to create books that are great favorites with young children. Their first book, *The Wizard, the Fairy and the Magic Chicken* (1983), is full of the droll expressions Munsinger uses to establish character and is enhanced with soft watercolor. Six other books followed, each marked with the duo's mischievous, joke-filled humor. *Tacky the Penguin* (1988) is particularly popular and has won the California Young Reader Medal (1991), the Colorado Children's Book Award (1990), and the Nebraska Library Association's Golden Sower Award (1991).

More than ten years after *An Arkful of Animals,* William Cole chose a new selection of witty and wise animal poems for illustration. *A Zooful of Animals* (1992) stands as tribute to Munsinger's development as an artist, for this volume is a lavishly produced showcase of her work. The large trim size gives her plenty of room for a toe-dancing, ballerina giraffe to stretch overhead and for a quizzical, gift-wrapped elephant to fill a spread. Munsinger has added to the book's appeal by using a variety of presentations. Some of the art is enclosed in charming borders, while some exuberantly runs off the page. A nice rhythm is established by the llamas moving down, across, and up the mountain crags that surround their poem. The changes in scale, the placement of spot art, and the effective use of soft background color keep the reader's eye moving from poem to poem. Munsinger's watercolor is clean and fresh, and ample white space sets off her ever-expressive line. From her smartly sleek seals to her lonely platypus, Munsinger has matched and extended the poetic animals in Cole's collection. ❧ P.H.

Myers, Walter Dean

American author of fiction and nonfiction, b. 1937. Walter Dean Myers recalls that when he submitted what would become his winning entry, *Where Does the Day Go?* (1969), to a picture-book competition sponsored by the Council on Interracial Books for Children, "it was more because I wanted to write *anything* than because I wanted to write a picture book." Myers did, however, publish several PICTURE BOOKS, as well as two works of nonfiction, before he began to focus on YOUNG ADULTS NOVELS, beginning with *Fast Sam, Cool Clyde, and Stuff* (1975), which chronicles the adventures of a group of friends in Harlem and reflects, as Myers says, "the positive side" of his childhood in New York City. Other books written in a similar vein include *Mojo and the Russians* (1977), *The Young Landlords* (1979), and *Won't Know Till I Get There* (1982). *Me, Mop, and the Moondance Kid* (1988) and *Mop, Moondance, and the Nagasaki Knights* (1992) follow the fortunes of two adopted brothers, a white girl named Mop, and their Little League ball team. While these novels have their serious moments, they display an engaging sense of humor that also surfaces in Myers's Wild West tale, *The Righteous Revenge of Artemis Bonner* (1992), with its exaggerated, flowery language, and in *The Mouse Rap* (1990), with its clever wordplay.

In addition to lighter novels, Myers has written some powerful, hard-hitting books about contemporary young African Americans, usually boys. In *Motown and Didi: A Love Story* (1984), Motown has made surviving on the street into an art, while Didi longs to escape the city and go to school elsewhere. *Scorpions* (1988) tells how Jamal, plagued by feelings of helplessness at school and at home, becomes entangled in an inner-city gang and finds himself in possession of a gun. The young soldiers in *Fallen Angels* (1988), a gripping novel about the Vietnam War, must fight to preserve their humanity as well as their lives. *Somewhere in the Darkness* (1992) skillfully explores a troubled father-son relationship, a recurrent motif in Myers's work. Lonnie's seriously ill father, Crab, escapes from prison and seeks out his son after years of absence. On a trip back to Crab's native Arkansas, father and son confront the nature of the link between them, which is not what either of them had hoped it would be.

An advocate of looking back to the past in order to progress into the future, Myers has recently turned his attention to writing history and biography. He published *Now Is Your Time!: The African-American Struggle for Freedom* in 1991 and *Malcolm X: By Any Means Necessary* in 1993. *Now Is Your Time!* offers an intriguing combination of historical survey, biography, storytelling, and family history. *Brown Angels: An Album of Pictures and Verse* (1993) uses a different format to celebrate black history. In this attractive book, Myers's poetry accompanies turn-of-the-century photographs of African American children, most of them collected by the writer himself. Over the years, the prolific Myers has continued to improve his craft, garnering a number of honors for his work. The poetry in *Brown Angels* offers further evidence not only of his commitment to children but also of his willingness to broaden his scope as a writer. ❧ M.F.S.

Voices of the Creators

Walter Dean Myers

When I was a kid in Harlem, I used to imagine that there were two kinds of life, one the life that we kids had, and the other the life of adults. The street life of kids was, to me, especially wonderful. All we needed was an old ball, a piece of chalk, or a tin can, and we would have a game going. We usually played in front of the church, running into the church offices to get a cool drink or a band-aid. Away from the streets I would still spend time daydreaming about being a cowboy, or a great ballplayer. Sometimes my imaginary wanderings would be inspired by my grandfather's Bible-based stories or by the scary stories of my stepfather.

Somewhere along the line I discovered that books could be part of a child's world, and by the time I was nine I found myself spending long hours reading in my room. The books began to shape new bouts of imagination. Now I was one of "The Three Musketeers" (always the one in the middle), or participating in the adventures of Jo's boys. John R. Tunis brought me back to sports, and I remember throwing a pink ball against the wall for hours as I struggled through baseball games that existed only in the rich arena of invention.

As a teenager I quickly realized that the world of imagination had its limitations. I wanted a *real* girlfriend, and I wanted more of a social life. Yet I seemed drawn to the life of the mind, and to books. After leaving school and a stint in the army, I bounced around in a series of jobs, none very satisfying, until I finally reached a point where I was writing full time. I was writing fiction primarily, putting my world on paper, exploring the real and imagined lives that comprise my existence. I had found that my real life, the life in which I found my truest self, was the life of the mind. And this life is the one I would use to write my books.

Sometimes, as in *The Revenge of Artemis Bonner,* my imagination has free rein, and I allow it to go where it will, enjoying the journey, delighting in the characters I meet along the way. It is both creation and discovery. The creative process seems to be a synthesis of present thought and the memory of those thoughts and feelings long past. A book like *Somewhere in the Darkness* deals more with imagined feelings and encounters that might have been. Although I did meet my real father, I had never had an intimate moment with him, had never seen him in that wholeness of being with which we get to know people.

Oddly enough, it is my imagination, my novelist's freedom to create characters and situations, that fuels my nonfiction as well. To write *Malcolm X: By Any Means Necessary,* a biography of the fiery black leader, I played his taped voice constantly, surrounded myself with pictures of him as a boy and as a young man, walked down the same Harlem streets that he walked down, and tried to put myself in his classroom when a teacher said that it wasn't practical for him to be an attorney because of his race. In seeing what Malcolm saw, in allowing his voice to fill my imagination, by touching upon those instances of racism that touched my life and mirrored his, I recreated Malcolm as surely as I have created fictional characters. As I wrote, I felt him looking over my shoulder, and so I could write with a sureness of voice, with an authority that went beyond the factual material.

When my son comes home from college, he finds it amusing to walk into a room to discover me in conversation with imaginary companions, or to see in my face the reflection of some inner dialogue, some adventure of the mind. He has forgotten that the world of the mind has always been my landscape. The stories I told him as a child are the ones that eventually ended up in books and magazines. The broccoli space people that he still remembers have always been important to me, even if they grow less so to him.

What I do with my books is to create windows to my world that all may peer into. I share the images, the feelings and thoughts, and, I hope, the delight.

Mysteries

Suspicious strangers, strange occurrences, secret codes, stashed treasures—few armchair sleuths can resist the challenge of matching their wits alongside those of the protagonists of mysteries for young readers. This strong involvement of readers certainly contributes to the widespread appeal of the genre. Furthermore, mysteries allow young people to experience, vicariously, pulse-quickening elements such as danger, intrigue, and suspense. And mysteries usually place the child investigator, like Donald Sobol's Encyclopedia Brown, in a position of power by solving crimes that may baffle adults.

The emergence of the mystery genre for young people is a relatively modern phenomenon of the first part of the twentieth century. It owes its existence more to the writings of Wilkie Collins and Agatha Christie than to a traditional juvenile literature. One of the first mysteries written specifically for children, *Emil and the Detectives* by ERICH KÄSTNER, came from Germany in 1930. In the tradition of the youthful detectives who would later emulate him, Emil and his band of friends use their determination and ingenuity to catch a thief, to the great admiration of the Berlin police force. In the last thirty years, the preoccupation of television and other media with mystery and crime detection has resulted in an outpouring of junior whodunits.

Aspects of mysteries cut across the boundaries of many types of juvenile fiction. For example, mysteries occur regularly in LLOYD ALEXANDER's fantasies, such as *The Illyrian Adventure* (1986), and ELEANOR CAMERON weaves a mystery into her contemporary novel *The Court of the Stone Children* (1973). Even those books categorized specifically as mysteries vary greatly in flavor, from the detective novel to stories of the supernatural to the historical tale. The range of mysteries now available for young people is rich and varied enough to suit every taste. These types include the formulaic or plot-driven mystery, which is usually strong on action and suspense; clever and sophisticated puzzles; tests of deduction and problem-solving; and multi-layered novels in which an element of mystery may simply be a catalyst motivating other themes.

While most children's mysteries are written for the eight- to twelve-year-old group, more and more are being published each year for picture-book readers or those who are just beginning to read. Standard mystery conventions such as clues, sidekicks, setbacks, and solutions can all be found, but the plots tend to center on one strand, are not very frightening, and fit understandably into the world of the four- to seven-year-old. Many also have a humorous or witty side. For example, *Piggins* (1987), by JANE YOLEN, illustrated by Jane Dyer, introduces the upstairs/downstairs world of the very proper Reynard family. When Mrs. Reynard loses her diamond lavaliere at an elegant dinner party, it is Piggins, the portly and imperturbable butler, who saves the day with his clever deductions. Elegant and detailed, the illustrations do their part not only to describe the Edwardian milieu but to give sharp-eyed readers pertinent visual clues.

Aimed at beginning readers, *Nate the Great* (1972), by MARJORIE WEINMAN SHARMAT, illustrated by MARC SIMONT, features a self-styled detective, who, along with his faithful dog, Sludge, has built a reputation among his peers for finding lost objects. Dressed in the garb of Sherlock Holmes, Nate delivers his pithy observations in the deadpan voice of a young Sam Spade. This terse style works well with the simple vocabulary.

Female detectives, full of ingenuity and spirit, are well represented in mysteries for the youngest. *Something Queer at the Library* (1977) is one of a series of lively mysteries by Elizabeth Levy, illustrated by Mordicai Gerstein, featuring two exuberant girl sleuths, Gwen and Jill. The zesty style of the story is complemented by humorous line drawings that make the most of every situation. In *Jane Martin, Dog Detective* (1984) by EVE BUNTING, illustrated by AMY SCHWARTZ, the young female sleuth finds two missing dogs and clears the name of a third whose reputation has been wrongfully sullied. Jane charges twenty-five cents a day to do her sleuthing, while her mother tails the suspects at night. But true to the junior mystery convention, it is Jane who always solves her case. *Encyclopedia Brown, Boy Detective* (1963) and the many other books in the series by Donald Sobol have long been a staple for new independent readers who wish to match their wits with the genius with an encyclopedic memory. With the publication of David Adler's *Cam Jansen and the Mystery of the Dinosaur Bones* (1981) readers were introduced to Encyclopedia Brown's counterpart, a female sleuth, who with a photographic memory remembers facts as if she had taken pictures of them.

For those who enjoy observation and deduction, Sherlock Holmes still lives in a number of juvenile spinoffs. Robert Newman's *The Case of the Baker Street Irregulars* (1978) is the first in a series featuring a group of poor London neighborhood children who do special errands for Holmes. Using techniques modeled after the feats of reasoning found in Conan Doyle's original stories, the plot combines a group of sinister characters to be outwitted and a series of seemingly disparate strands that keep the suspense high until Holmes ties it all together. Also, in a humorous parody of Holmes for younger children, Eve Titus developed a series featuring Basil, the English mouse detective, who studied at the feet of Holmes. In *Basil of Baker Street* (1958), his friend and associate Dr. Dawson tells how Basil solves a baffling kidnapping case, restores the children to their parents, and brings the dangerous kidnappers to justice.

Animal characters such as Basil can be marvelous detectives. Acting like humans, they are part of a familiar tradition within children's literature that borders as much on animal fantasy as on mystery. With the publication of *Bunnicula, A Rabbit Tale of Mystery* (1979), Deborah and JAMES HOWE achieved new levels of sophisticated wit in their combination mystery/animal fantasy. When the household vegetables are drained of their juices and turn white overnight, Chester (the family's bookish cat who sits up nights reading Edgar Allan Poe) is convinced that the family's new pet rabbit, which popped up in the local theater one night, is actually a vampire bunny. Chester enlists the help of the dog, Harold, in getting to the bottom of the mystery. With an abundant dose of puns, slapstick humor, and wild chases, the mysterious adventures of Harold and Chester are continued in *The Howliday Inn* (1982) and *Nightly Nightmare* (1987).

JAMES MARSHALL is another writer who has a grand time placing animal characters in mysterious situations. In his first novel, *A Summer in the South* (1977), a hilarious spoof set at a resort, a ghostly figure tries to frighten the tender actress Marietta Chicken. Readers will discover that it is one of the hotel guests, the renowned detective Eleanor Owl (a Miss Marple lookalike), who exposes the culprit with the aid of the hotel's assortment of zany guests.

Humor can serve as both a tension reliever and a source of entertainment, and when authors such as Marshall and the Howes combine humor and mystery, they create a winning combination of the two most sought-after subjects by children. Newbery Award winner PHYLLIS REYNOLDS NAYLOR also uses humor to provide comic relief in *The Bodies in the Bessledorf Hotel* (1986). As Bernie Magruder saves his father's job as hotel manager by nabbing the person who has been planting dead bodies throughout the hotel, Naylor uses standard mystery conventions such as cliff-hanging chapter endings and a number of red herrings to keep the well-constructed story moving. Another Newbery–award winning author, SID FLEISCHMAN, dabbles in lighthearted, easy-to-read fare in a series created for the Children's Television Workshop featuring the Bloodhound Gang. In *The Case of the Cackling Ghost* (1981) the gang is hired by rich Mrs. Fairbanks to sort out the curse of the Darjeeling Necklace. Ranging in ages from ten to sixteen, the gang acts believably in a professional manner, entirely without the benefit of adults (payment for the services is never mentioned), and Fleischman, himself a professional magician, adds a touch of hocus-pocus to the solution.

There is humor too in EVE RICE's *The Remarkable Return of Winston Potter Crisply* (1978), but it is the setting that distinguishes this mystery romp through Manhattan. When Becky and Max discover that their older brother is not at Harvard but is skulking about the Big Apple in a black cape, they trail him. Based on pieces of evidence, they suspect he is the central figure in a CIA case, but after many twists and turns of the plot, they discover a far different truth.

Setting not only provides a rich backdrop but is crucial to the plot of *The December Rose* (1987), a historical mystery by the British novelist LEON GARFIELD set in Victorian London. Barnacle, a chimney sweep, mistakenly falls down the wrong flue, tumbling headfirst into a skullduggerous plot involving international intrigue. The authentic British dialect gives flavor to the period, and the memorable images, unusually well drawn characters, and hair-raising escapades make this picturesque novel both a page-turner and a literary delight. Another historical mystery with an equally strong sense of place is AVI's complex novel *The Man Who Was Poe* (1989). Drawing upon historical facts known about the time Edgar Allan Poe spent in Providence, Rhode Island, the author spins the story of young Edmund, who in 1848 finds himself alone after both his aunt and sister mysteriously vanish. Seeing a possible story in Edmund's predicament, Poe promises to help the boy. Cryptic clues and Poe's brilliant, if at times irrational, behavior sustain the high suspense in this engrossing novel.

While set in present-day Ohio, VIRGINIA HAMILTON's modern classic *The House of Dies Drear* (1968) adroitly blends history, mystery, and lost treasure in a beautifully taut story. Moving into the Drear house has had a profound effect on Thomas Small and his family. It is a former station on the Underground Railroad, filled with a labyrinth of tunnels, concealed closets, springs and locks, and the ghosts of former slaves. Hamilton's absorbing story is filled with delicious tension as well as meaningful personal relationships, and the dramatic denouement is highly satisfying. Almost twenty years later, Hamilton concluded the "Dies Drear" chronicle with *The Mystery of Drear House* (1987). Another mystery that makes important historical connections to a present-day black community is Eleanora E. Tate's *The Secret of Gumbo Grove* (1987). Twelve-year-old Raisin Stackhouse is full of gumption and community spirit, so it is not surprising that Miss Ellie (the aging church secretary out to save the cemetery) selects Raisin to help her make the black community recognize their history. The portrait of the town characters and several subplots involving sibling and family relationships serve to make this more than just a mystery.

Like the writers of historical mysteries who use facts for the foundation of their tales, writers of informational mysteries draw upon pertinent research to authenticate their novels. At the height of the fight to ban DDT, naturalist JEAN CRAIGHEAD GEORGE wrote a unique ecology mystery titled *Who Really Killed Cock Robin?* (1971, reissued with a new introduction in 1991). When the town's prized robin dies on the mayor's front lawn, environmental detective Tony Isidoro, assisted by his sidekick, Mary Alice Lamberty, uses scientific methods and determination to describe and trace the ecological imbalances that caused the bird's death. George, who "sees all of nature as a mystery," works a good deal of sound ecological information into her novel and humorously delivers it in the manner of a hard-boiled detective. Another mystery laced with ecology information for younger readers is *Elisabeth and the Marsh Mystery* (1966) by FELICE HOLMAN. Elisabeth, her father, Mr. Threw from the wildlife museum, and Elisabeth's friend Stewart search for the source of spooky sounds coming from the marsh. Through their humorous efforts they find that the culprit is a sandhill crane that has become lost while migrating.

Some juvenile mysteries border on novels of the occult and the supernatural. JOHN BELLAIRS, for one, is particularly skillful at blending mystery, sorcery, and the macabre, while adding a touch of humor to the cauldron. In the first novel featuring the orphan Lewis, *The House with a Clock in Its Walls* (1973), Lewis discovers that his Uncle Jonathan is a wizard, that the next-door neighbor is a witch, and that there is a magic clock hidden in the walls of his uncle's mansion ticking away the hours to doomsday. Here the time element is used as an effective device in maintaining suspense. Betty Ren Wright's novels also contain satisfying touches of the supernatural. In *The Dollhouse Murders* (1984), Wright gives an added dimension to the spooky story by melding twelve-year-old Emily's family concerns with the solution to a mysterious murder that happened long ago.

Wright, like many mystery writers for the young, conveniently relegates her murders to the past. While crimes such as shoplifting, kidnapping, dope smuggling, and terrorism do occur in juvenile novels, violence is kept at a minimum and murder is usually avoided or committed "off-stage." A novel that broke with this tradition is *The View from the Cherry Tree* (1975) by Willo Davis Roberts. Here eleven-year-old Rob witnesses the murder of the old lady next door, and, because no adult will pay attention to his story, he narrowly misses becoming the killer's next victim. There are some implausible plot elements, but it is still a chilling tale with real suspense and danger.

Readers are told that a murder has been committed in ELLEN RASKIN's unparalleled mystery puzzle, *The Westing Game* (1978), but the crime here is more cerebral, for all is not what it appears to be in this Newbery Award–winning novel. Offering the ultimate challenge for those who love to reason through a highly intricate plot, Raskin assembles an unconventional group of sixteen characters who are possible heirs to Samuel Westing's fortune. In the Christie tradition, the heirs are isolated, then paired off and given clues to a puzzle they must solve, but "some are not who they say they are, and some are not who they seem to be." Admitting her "strong aversion to the obvious," Raskin indulges in developing shifting identities, enigmatic clues, and a surprisingly sympathetic set of eccentric characters in this complex tour de force.

While Raskin's novels represent the height of sophisticated mental games, few books intertwine mystery and imaginative play with as much originality as ZILPHA KEATLEY SNYDER's *The Egypt Game* (1967). Fascinated with Egypt, an ethnically diverse group of neighborhood children re-create the ancient world in a deserted storage yard, a world complete with hieroglyphics, oracles, evil gods, and ceremonies. But a murderer is terrorizing the neighborhood and, in a frightening climax, it is the Egypt game that leads to his capture. But beyond the mystery, the importance of the make-believe world is evident. "It had been a place to get away to—a private lair—a secret seclusion meant to be shared with best friends only." It was a game "full of excitement and way out imagining" that greatly affects the lives of the children.

Many juvenile novels contain imaginative writing with mystery as the underpinning, providing a rewarding literary experience for readers. *The Way to Sattin Shore* (1983) by the distinguished British writer PHILLIPPA PEARCE is a beautifully crafted family story with rare emotional depth; the element of mystery simply propels the plot. Kate Tranter, the youngest in her family, discovers some incongruities about her father's death and sets out to learn the truth. The elegant prose and the understated pace of the unfolding events belie the mounting tension as Kate slowly uncovers each piece of her family's hidden secret.

Another skilled stylist, the American writer NATALIE BABBITT, places mysterious elements in many of her highly regarded novels. But in *Goody Hall* (1971), the mystery is unabashedly full-blown. This witty Gothic mystery involves ten-year-old Willett Goody and his tutor, the erstwhile actor, Hercules Feltwright, in an Odyssey-like search for the whereabouts of Willett's father. Impersonation, robbery, stolen jewels, empty coffins, gypsy seances, and a cast of characters with names like Alfresco Rom keep the unpredictable plot boiling. The climax is dramatic and satisfying, with all the loose ends tied together and a moral on human behavior thrown in for good measure.

Like *Goody Hall,* VIVIEN ALCOCK's novel *The Mysterious Mr. Ross* (1987) is often described as a Gothic mystery, but it has an unusual twist, for here the mystery is never solved. Twelve-year-old Felicity, who is clumsy, insecure, and can never manage to get things right, becomes a heroine overnight when she rescues a young man from a dangerous tide near her English seaside home. Cleverly, Alcock never reveals the man's identity but allows his presence to irrevocably change the lives of Felicity and her family. Alcock has a knack of imbuing commonplace situations with mysterious touches, and her characters, even the minor ones, are fully realized.

The popularity of the mystery genre continues unabated, and many are published each year for children. The majority tend to fall into the comforting familiarity of a series format or to rely heavily on action-filled plots. Few match the inventive game playing of Ellen Raskin. Occasionally an author comes along, like Annette Curtis Klause, with a totally fresh approach to the mystery genre. Klause's novel *Alien Secrets* (1993) playfully integrates a mystery and a ghost story into a science-fiction setting. It is novels like this that satisfy the necessary thrills of the mystery genre, while providing originality of narrative, fully developed characters, and a stylistic wit and grace that places them alongside the finest novels written for young people. ❧ CAROLINE WARD

N

Namioka, Lensey

Chinese-American author, b. 1929. When Lensey Namioka began writing fiction in the 1970s, she didn't realize she was writing for children. She just wrote what she liked to read: adventure stories filled with action, mystery, and suspense. As a child she found such stories in her mother's collection of Chinese pulp novels, and she and her sisters made up their own tales of valiant sword-fighting outlaws to amuse one another after the family's move to the United States during World War II.

Later, after she had been a freelance writer and translator for a number of years, her Japanese father-in-law introduced her to Japanese adventure stories about *ronin*, unemployed samurai, who wandered the country getting into scrapes. He also told her the ghostly legends surrounding the castle in his hometown of Himeji. Both provided the inspiration for *White Serpent Castle* (1976), the first of Namioka's samurai books, which take place in feudal Japan and feature Zenta and Matsuzo, a duo of *ronin* with a relationship not unlike that of Sherlock Holmes and Dr. Watson. Master swordsman Zenta can usually solve a mystery before anyone else has sorted out the clues. And Matsuzo, the more romantic of the two, remains loyal to his teacher even when he questions his actions. Besides fighting sinister villains such as the one murdering young girls in *Village of the Vampire Cat* (1981) or discovering the men behind the supposed monsters in *Island of Ogres* (1989), Zenta and Matsuzo teach readers by example about the honor code of the samurai.

Each of Namioka's samurai books acts as a window into ancient Japan, revealing the food, dress, customs, and life-style of the different social classes, from peasants to royalty. In *The Coming of the Bear* (1992) Zenta and Matsuzo come to accept if not wholly embrace a foreign culture when they are shipwrecked on the northern Japanese island of Hokkaido and rescued by the Ainus, hunter-gatherers who once inhabited all of Japan.

When Namioka's editor suggested that she try her hand at realistic fiction, she drew upon her own experience adapting to a foreign culture. Set in the 1950s, *Who's Hu?* (1981) recounts the sometimes humorous dilemmas of Emma Hu, a Chinese teenager trying to fit in at her high school in Massachusetts. As a girl who likes math, Emma gets hassled by the other students, who think she should spend less time working equations and more time preparing for the prom. Namioka received similar treatment in high school, but went on to major in math in college and to teach math at the college level before turning to writing. She believes her mathematics background lends a thriftiness to her writing, born of a desire not to waste a word or, in her mystery stories, a clue.

Yang the Youngest and His Terrible Ear (1992) continues the theme of tolerance. Although Yang's whole family is musical and his parents push him to continue his violin lessons, hoping that with practice he can carry a tune, Yang feels more at home on the baseball diamond than at a recital. Yang finally convinces his father to let him trade his violin for a bat in a prank gone comically awry, a scene consistent with Namioka's belief that the more important an author's message, the more fun her book should be. ❧ C.M.H.

Nancy Drew Series

The character of Nancy Drew, girl detective and reigning queen of the juvenile formula fiction world, was created in 1930 by Edward Stratemeyer, founder of the Stratemeyer Literary Syndicate. The first three Nancy Drew mysteries (*The Secret of the Old Clock, The Hidden Staircase,* and *The Bungalow Mystery,* all written in 1930, the year of the author's death) were written by Stratemeyer but were published under the pseudonym Carolyn Keene. After Stratemeyer's death, his daughter, Harriet Stratemeyer Adams, assumed Carolyn Keene's writing duties until her own death in 1982. Since then, numerous anonymous writers have continued writing the mysteries under Keene's name.

Nancy was first introduced as a sophisticated blond sixteen-year-old. She wore thirties-style hand-sewn dresses, felt hats, and gloves; she drove a blue roadster with running boards. This image was updated during the 1960s so that she resembled a Kennedy daughter rather than Carole Lombard. Nancy had aged—she was eighteen so that she could legally drive—and changed her hair color to titian red. With the addition of steady boyfriend Ned Nickerson, even Nancy's love life changed. The syndicate extensively revised the first thirty-four books of the series to remove any anachronisms and inconsistencies; racist and anti-Semitic characterizations were erased. The third incarnation of Nancy Drew was seen in the 1980s. Truly a teenager of the eighties and nineties, Nancy carries credit cards, watches music videos, and drives a flashy sports car. She spends her spring break in Fort Lauderdale and dances the evenings away at local discos. In this updating of her image, she has also become more sensitive to the pangs of uncertainty and self-doubt that plague the teenage years. But despite these alterations, the intrinsic Nancy Drew has never changed. She remains a wholesome, attractive, level-headed young woman—an expert dancer, swimmer, horseback rider, skier, golfer, tennis player, artist, botanist, and mechanic.

The Nancy Drew Mysteries have never been known for their high literary content and are often considered to be fluff reading. Despite such criticism, Nancy Drew remains in a class apart from the rest of the young adult heroines—*Ms.* magazine has called her a "role model for young feminists." She continually counters stereotypes of feminine weakness by demonstrating her ability to be both a young woman and a competent individual at the same time. By doing so, Nancy Drew remains as much a favorite today as she was more than sixty years ago, delighting grandmothers, mothers, and daughters alike. M.I.A.

NASH, OGDEN

AMERICAN AUTHOR, 1902–1971. Called "the leading American exponent of humorous verse," Ogden Nash wrote funny, insightful, whimsical pieces that speak to both the child in grown-ups and the adult in children.

Born of a father in the naval stores business and a mother from a scholarly Southern family, Nash spent his childhood swinging between summers in Rye, New York, where the headquarters of the family business were located, and winters in Savannah, Georgia, with his parents' families. His early education took place in different private schools as the family fortunes waxed and waned. He gained admittance to Harvard, but, deciding he didn't have the "gumption" to work his way through all four years, he quit after the first. He taught for a while at a private school in Rhode Island and eventually made his way to Wall Street, where he worked at a bond house. Nash had been jotting down verses since he was six or seven and tried to make a career as a serious poet, but he couldn't sell a single verse of his serious poetry. About this time, he wrote his first children's book, *Cricket of Carador* (1925), with his roommate, Joseph Alger. The young men decided that "the easiest book to do would be a juvenile," and they finished and sold it quickly. Nash continued to sell advertising verses, but nothing else, until he decided to make fun of his more serious poetry attempts with a parody, which he sold to the *New Yorker*. He continued to write and sell his bits of light verse to the magazine, and when a pub-

The Mules
In the world of mules
There are no rules.

Illustration for "The Mules" from *Custard and Company: Poems by Ogden Nash* (1980), selected and illustrated by QUENTIN BLAKE.

lisher approached him about a collection of his verses the result was *I'm a Stranger Here Myself* (1927). Nash was on his way. His quirky humor and deft verse contributed greatly to the *New Yorker*'s tone in the thirties, and he spent a very brief time as its managing editor. He traveled to Hollywood in 1935, with disastrous results. He returned to New York two years later, much reduced in confidence and nerve, but a collaboration with S. J. Perelman and Kurt Weill on the musical *One Touch of Venus* left him the toast of the 1943 Broadway season.

In 1951 Nash published his second book for children, *Parents Keep Out: Elderly Poems for Youngerly Readers,* a collection of poems from the previous twenty-five years that he had written for his own two daughters and published in various magazines. In this volume and in his subsequent books for children—such as *The Christmas That Almost Wasn't* (1957) and *Custard, the Dragon* (1959)—Nash demonstrates his conviction to "absolutely avoid the tendency to write down." The puns, made-up words, and sentiment of the pieces are every bit as clever, amusing, and smart—sleekly economical in words—as those in his works for adults. Between 1951 and his death, Nash wrote nearly a dozen books for children. Some of them, like *The Moon Is Shining Bright as Day* (1953), are anthologies of poems by other writers, favorites of his that Nash wanted to share with children. Many of them, like the books about Custard the Dragon, are illustrated by his daughter, Linell Nash Smith. Recent editions of Nash's work, such as *The Adventures of Isabel* (1991), illustrated by JAMES MARSHALL, reveal that the author's sly wit is as amusing today as it was thirty years ago.

In all of his work, Nash blurs the line between childhood and adulthood. His awareness that things like "Dragons Are too Seldom" infuse his writings with a childlike wonder at the world that weary adults can remember and recapture with him. But when he explains "The Facts of Life," a cataloguing to his daughter of all the wondrous things he is not, he does so with a conspiratorial air that children find irresistible. ❧ S.G.K.

NAYLOR, PHYLLIS REYNOLDS

AMERICAN AUTHOR, B. 1933. Because she had always been an avid writer, Phyllis Reynolds Naylor was delighted when, as a teenager, some of her works were published in a church paper. Bolstered by this success, she submitted short stories to children's magazines, only to have them rejected. She quickly realized that writing was a demanding business. Naylor married when she was eighteen, received an associate degree from Indiana's Joliet Junior College in Illinois, and moved to Chicago, where her husband planned to pursue a master's degree. She worked as a clinical secretary, taught third grade, and wrote. When the onset of her husband's illness created the need for additional money to cover living expenses and the cost of his treatments, she accelerated her submissions to various magazines. After she and her husband divorced, she married Rex Naylor and returned to college to become a clinical psychologist. Although she received a B.A. in psychology from American University, she realized that writing full-time was her greatest desire.

Since the publication of her first children's book, *What the Gulls Were Singing* (1967), Naylor has produced one to two books annually, encompassing a broad range of topics. Acute sensitivity to childhood and teenage experiences has made her the successful author of over seventy books, both fiction and nonfiction. Naylor loves variety but admits to being partial to suspenseful tales. She spices her mysteries with numerous seasonings: the "Besseldorf" series, with humor; the "York" series, with fantasy, time travel, and the search for a cure for the hereditary Huntington's disease; and the compelling six books of the "Witch" series, with fantasy and the occult. Naylor's serious topics include coping with parental divorce (*The Solomon System,* 1983), crib death and loss of religious faith (*A String of Chances*), living with a mentally ill father, based on the ordeal of her first marriage (*The Keeper,* 1986), teenage rebellion (*No Easy Circle,* 1972), watching a mother die from cancer (*The Dark of the Tunnel,* 1985), and the anguish of being a middle child (*Maudie in the Middle,* 1988). On the lighter side, experiments in an annual school science contest, in *Beetles, Lightly Toasted* (1987), result in unusual lunches for unsuspecting classmates, and *Eddie, Incorporated* (1980) explores the trials and tribulations of an eleven-year-old's attempts to start his own business. The delightful "Alice" series focuses on a spunky preteen girl's search for a female role model.

Naylor's acute observations of human nature make her books touching, comical, and uplifting. While facing one's fears is the underlying theme in Naylor's narratives, family issues, getting along with others, and moral values are also strong elements. Naylor allows her characters to evolve intellectually, socially, and morally. She focuses on those first moments of awareness young people experience and also examines the parameters of right and wrong, placing her protagonists in situations where they must rely on their own judgments. Naylor portrays life as a series of compromises and offers her readers a view of life as a multifaceted, unfolding adventure, a growing experience, and a challenge. Naylor is the recipient of many awards, including the Edgar Allan Poe Award from the Mystery Writers of America for her children's thriller *Night Cry* in 1985, and a Creative Writing Fellowship Grant from the National Endowment for the Arts (1987). In 1991 she received the Newbery Medal for *Shiloh,* the compelling story of a boy's attempt to save an abused dog while discovering that life is not fair, no one is perfect, and compromise is a necessary art. ❧ S.R.

Nesbit, E.

British author, 1858–1924. One wonders if Edith Nesbit was at all aware of just how unconventional her children's novels were and that they would determine the direction for both realistic family stories and fantasy in the twentieth century. What set her books apart from those that preceded them was that Nesbit did away with the didacticism prevalent in Victorian children's books, which sought to "improve" young readers. Nesbit's narrators don't talk down to children; Nesbit speaks to her readers as respected and admired equals. Her characters—imaginative, intelligent, strong-willed individuals—are well intentioned if not always well behaved: They are real children with whom readers identify and empathize. Nesbit's fantasy novels combine her successful formula for the realistic family story with the added enticement of magic. Unlike fantasies of the past, her stories take place in the everyday world of Edwardian England, not in a make-believe fairyland. Nesbit did not sentimentalize children and childhood. She once wrote: "When I was a little child I used to pray fervently, tearfully, that when I should be grown up I might never forget what I thought, felt, and suffered then."

As a child, Nesbit was said to have been a rebellious tomboy with a great imagination and a passion for reading and writing. Her father, who ran a London agricultural college, died when she was three, and she was raised by her mother along with four older brothers and sisters. When she was fifteen years old, a newspaper published some of her verses, and she began to dream of becoming a poet. A few years later, soon after her marriage to businessman Hubert Bland, her comfortable Victorian life took a turn when Bland, seriously ill with smallpox, lost his money when his partner absconded with the business's funds. It fell to Nesbit to support her small family. For the next nineteen years, she poured out a stream of novels, essays, articles, poems, greeting-card verses, and short stories. Most of her work during that time was not memorable and today would be judged as highly sentimental.

Nesbit's first successful book for children was published in 1899, and nothing she had written before anticipated it. *The Story of the Treasure Seekers* essentially launched her career as a children's author. In this book, the motherless Bastable children decide to search for treasure to restore the family fortune after the failure of their father's business, and their attempts result in many humorous disasters. Two sequels, *The Wouldbegoods* (1901) and *The New Treasure Seekers* (1904), continued the comic misadventures of the Bastable children. Of the three, *The Wouldbegoods* is the best tribute to a theme in many of Nesbit's books: the power of literature and the imagination. The Bastables are well read and highly imaginative. Their delight in pretending and make-believe, as inspired by stories, is contagious. In *The Railway Children* (1906), reality, merely a device lending credibility in the Bastable stories, has a darker side. Bobbie, Phyllis, and Peter have to move with their mother to a smaller house in the country because not only has the family fallen into financial difficulties, but their father is in prison. It is through their adventures at a nearby railroad station that the children are able to amuse themselves and cope valiantly with their situation.

Five Children and It (1902) was the first of Nesbit's fantasy novels. Set in contemporary England, this book must have been enchanting fare for young readers who solemnly believed magic was all around them, if only they knew where to look. The children in the story discover not a beautiful fairy godmother, but an ill-tempered, odd-looking creature called a Psammead. The Psammead (often unwillingly) grants their wishes—not without short-lived, comic results—and the children learn that getting what one wishes for is not the key to happiness. In the sequels *The Phoenix and the Carpet* (1904) and *The Story of the Amulet* (1906), the fantasy and humor are more and more refined. *The Enchanted Castle* (1907) is in many ways the most sophisticated achievement of Nesbit's career. It shares the same elements of Nesbit's other successful fantasy novels, yet the magic in this book is more mysterious and, at times, terrifying. The children's wishes produce unexpected and often undesirable results, and their attempts to understand the rules of the magic are frustratingly in vain.

Nesbit continued writing until her death from a bronchial illness. While her children's stories brought her fame and wealth, ironically, her true ambition was to be a poet, and she always regretted that she had not spent more time on her poetry. Nevertheless, her influence on twentieth-century British and American children's literature has been widely acknowledged; perhaps it was the naïveté of her own genius that freed her to produce such lasting and beloved classics. ♠ K.F.

Ness, Evaline

AMERICAN ILLUSTRATOR AND AUTHOR, 1911–1986. Evaline Ness, author and illustrator of the 1967 Caldecott Medal–winning *Sam, Bangs, and Moonshine,* was a well-established studio artist and a highly paid commercial artist when she was first asked to illustrate a children's manuscript. She recalled, "[It was] so unlike the frantic hot-air environment of advertising production [that] I never went back to the 'rat-race' again." She found that every manuscript—like SORCHE NIC LEODHAS's *All in the Morning Early* (1963) and REBECCA CAUDILL's *A Pocketful of Cricket* (1964)—offered new challenges, new opportunities to strengthen existing skills and experiment with new techniques. But this outpouring of originality was a far cry from her youthful efforts in Pontiac, Michigan: "As soon as I was able to read and write, I copied down my favorite stories on the hundred-yard rolls of white paper that backs ribbons. . . . And with that same critical industry, I searched through magazines to find appropriate pictures to illustrate stories . . . [a] sister turned out daily. It never occurred to me to compete with ready-made words and pictures."

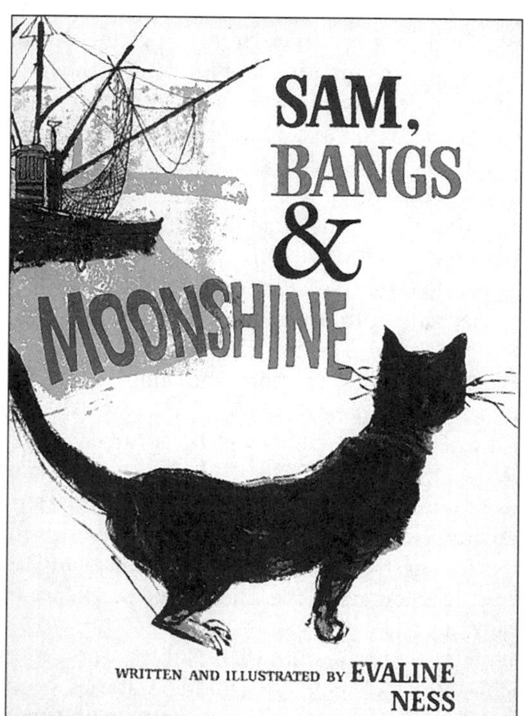

Jacket illustration by Evaline Ness for her book *Sam, Bangs & Moonshine* (1966).

It was only as a young woman that Ness decided, on a whim, to be a commercial artist. She took several wrong turns—most notably enrolling in the fine arts department of the Art Institute of Chicago instead of the commercial art department because she didn't know the difference—before beginning a limping artistic career. There followed years of apprenticeship, course work, and learning fundamentals, in Chicago, New York, and Washington, D.C., but as her skills grew, so did her ambition. Eventually the effort paid off: Ness got her break back in New York illustrating for *Seventeen* magazine and then fashion drawing for Saks Fifth Avenue department store. She became successful and her work was very well paid, but it was grueling. No wonder she found such relief in children's books.

Ness began writing when she created a text for some woodcuts set in Haiti: *Josefina February* (1963) is the simple tale of a girl's search for a lost burro. *Sam, Bangs, and Moonshine* began with some portfolio drawings, one of a "shabby misplaced child" and several of fishing boats. The story came from nowhere: the tale of a girl whose "reckless habit of lying" almost causes a tragedy. The daughter of a fisherman, motherless Samantha ("always called Sam") lives in a fantasy world with her talking cat Bangs. But her announcement that a pet kangaroo is visiting her mermaid-mother at Blue Rock almost causes the drowning of her gullible young friend, Thomas. The scare finally enables Sam to distinguish between reality and "moonshine." Some Ness texts, like the English folktale retellings *Mr. Miacca* (1967) and *The Girl and the Goatherd* (1970), are criticized for their weak plots, but she gets praise, especially with her original tales, for economical language, sprightly storytelling, and skillful interweaving of art and words. A Ness hallmark is the uncanny match between story and technique—whether in the woodcuts of *Josefina February,* set in the Caribbean; the ink and color wash of *Sam, Bangs, and Moonshine,* with its Mediterranean setting; or the contemporary world of LUCILLE CLIFTON's *Some of the Days of Everett Anderson* (1970). Ness's selection of medium is skillful whether she is working with her own text or the words of others. The child once content to play with copied words and pasted pictures became an artist admired for her range of skill and craftsmanship, her continual experimentation and growth, and her freshness and originality. ♠ S.A.B.

NEVILLE, EMILY CHENEY

AMERICAN AUTHOR, B. 1919. Readers of Emily Cheney Neville's fictionalized autobiography, *Traveler from a Small Kingdom* (1968), know about the Cheney place, a compound of over a dozen buildings in South Manchester, Connecticut, where members of the extended Cheney family lived while working for the family silk mills. This was where Emily, the last of nine children, was born and raised. She was educated with relatives at the Cheney Family School and did not have any outside friends until she began attending public school in the seventh grade. Neville went to Bryn Mawr College as a sixteen-year-old freshman. Graduating in 1940, she had no specific career goals but wanted to live in New York City. She found employment at the New York *Daily News,* then later worked for the New York *Daily Mirror,* first as a copygirl, then as a newspaper columnist. Although Neville had been published in her high school magazine, this was her first professional experience as a writer. It was not until many years later, after she had left journalism and was raising a family, that she began submitting book manuscripts to publishers.

Her first efforts were picture-book stories. None were ever published, but an editor who was interested in Neville's work encouraged the struggling author to expand one of her short stories, "Cat and I," into a full-length book. *It's Like This, Cat* (1963) concerns a fourteen-year-old boy growing up in New York City. Dave Mitchell relates the arguments he has with his father, the adventures he has with his cat, and his first, hesitant romance with Mary. At the time of its publication, Dave's breezy first-person narration blew into the children's book world like a breath of fresh air. *It's Like This, Cat* won the 1964 Newbery Medal and was considered startlingly contemporary and original. The book remains an enjoyable, loosely structured novel, but time has somewhat dimmed its appeal. The characters now seem to be types rather than fully developed creations. Dave is a likable but bland protagonist, his dad a stock "harried father." Other characters, such as Dave's sad mother and his older friend Tom, are intriguing, but two-dimensional. The real hero of the story seems to be New York City, which is lovingly presented in vivid detail.

Neville's second novel, *Berries Goodman* (1965), tackles such issues as anti-Semitism and a family's adjustment to suburbia. More tightly focused than *It's Like This, Cat,* the first-person narration shows Neville's artistic growth in both plotting and character development. Other books include *The Seventeenth-Street Gang* (1966), a pleasant story about a ten-year-old New York girl, and *Fogarty* (1969), which stretches the age limits of traditional young adult fiction by concentrating on a twenty-three-year-old law school dropout who attempts playwriting before becoming a teacher. Neville has also written a picture book, *The Bridge* (1988), and *The China Year* (1991), which features an American girl visiting China at the time of the demonstrations in Tiananmen Square. *Garden of Broken Glass* (1975) uses shifting viewpoints to examine a group of lower-class multicultural teenagers. Some readers may find Neville's use of dialect in the novel to be inauthentic, but it remains a thought-provoking, ambitious book.

After many years as a successful author, Neville attended law school and began dividing her time between her law practice and her writing projects. Neville's writing continues to fascinate readers. Her ability to place likable protagonists in little-explored settings from 1960s New York to modern-day China, has helped open new vistas to young people. ❧ P.D.S.

NEWBERRY, CLARE TURLAY

AMERICAN AUTHOR AND ILLUSTRATOR, 1903–1970. Clare Turlay Newberry always lived with and loved cats. As a child, she included them in all her drawings. Born and raised in Eugene, Oregon, Newberry attended the University of Oregon for one year, then pursued but never completed her academic studies in art, finding that she worked best alone. In 1930, on the eve of her departure to study in Paris, Newberry wrote a story about a little girl, Sally, who adamantly wanted and received a lion for her birthday. In order to earn return passage, Newberry illustrated the story. *Herbert the Lion* (1931), Newberry's first picture book for children, met with immediate popularity and acclaim. While living in New York City, Newberry's original plan to make her fortune in portraiture failed, but not her determination to make art her life's endeavor.

In 1934 she turned to the subject that had fascinated her all her life and that became her hallmark: cats. Her ownership, observation, and love of felines naturally led to her incorporating their antics and poses in her books: the tucked paws and pure contentment of a dozing cat; the irritable tail twitch of a harried one; the ornery, mischievous glare in a feisty cat's eyes; the frisky romping and tumbling of kittens. Her cats looked so alive they could have stepped out of her books. In 1936, *Mittens,* the first of many books in which Newberry relied on her own cats and children as models, introduced her as an artist-illustrator who knew how to appeal to both young children and the parents who read to them. Her subtle humor, straightforward dialogue, and simple plots were elemental to her success. Four of her works were named Caldecott Honor Books: *Barkis* (1938), about a sister's spiteful antics which endanger her brother's new puppy; *April's Kittens* (1940), about a family who must resolve how they will keep an extra kitten in a one-cat apartment; *Marshmallow* (1942), about a baby rabbit who endears himself to a confirmed bachelor cat; and *T-Bone the Baby-sitter* (1950), about a usually reliable cat who experiences spring fever. *Mittens*, Newberry's bestseller about a six-year-old boy whose ad for his lost kitten brings unexpected results, was chosen as one of the Fifty Books of the Year by the American Institute of Graphic Arts. While the body of Newberry's work involves cat protagonists, the puppy in *Barkis* and the baby rabbit in *Marshmallow* are equally unforgettable.

Although Newberry took her subjects from real life and customarily worked in watercolors, pencil, or Conté crayons, two of her books stylistically depart from this format. Both *Herbert the Lion* and *Lambert's Bargain* (1941), a wonderfully funny story about the problems that ensue when a brother is talked into accepting a hyena as a birthday gift for his little sister, are fantasies drawn in line figures. For Newberry, daily life with its ironic humor and challenges between parents and young children who want pets, provided inspirational grist for seventeen stories, most of which were about or included cats. In the field of children's literature, Clare Turlay Newberry and cats have become nearly synonymous. ❧ S.R.

Newell, Peter

American humorist and illustrator, 1862–1924. Peter Newell drew like no one else and created picture books like no others. A humorist famously sober of mien, he was a true original.

Two anecdotes are always told about Newell—stories that, poker-faced, he liked to tell about himself. As a young tyro in a small Illinois town, he sent a humorous drawing to the editor of *Harper's Bazaar* with a note asking if it showed talent. "No talent indicated," came the reply, but a check was enclosed. Sales to other magazines took him to New York and a few months' formal study before he decided to remain unschooled and unassimilated, or, to his way of thinking, himself.

He was, however, a thoroughgoing professional. Capitalizing on the new method of halftone reproduction, he introduced in America the technique of drawing in flat halftone washes developed by the French illustrator Maurice Boutet de Monvel, and, for maximum effect at minimum cost, he planned many of his illustrations to be printed in black-and-white with a single second color each, a practice that later became common. His plain-as-plain style, with its moon-faced, popeyed, goblinlike figures, looked decidedly spooky to some and like no style at all to many. But as the graphic arts connoisseur Philip Hofer points out, "He used simple means because he liked simple subjects. Probably he chose both because he was thinking of his audience: children, and grown-ups who retain their youth."

Much of Newell's work has that dual appeal. His first big success was an illustrated nonsense jingle, "Wild Flowers," which appeared in *Harper's* magazine in August 1893. A solicitous schoolmaster bends over a trembling little girl: "'Of what are you afraid, my child?' inquired / the kindly teacher. /'Oh, sir! the flowers, they are wild,' / replied the timid creature."

At the same time he illustrated books: nonsense for all and sundry by Guy Wetmore Carryl and Caroline Wells; the absurdist humor of John Kendrick Bangs's

Illustration by Peter Newell from his book *The Rocket Book* (1912).

Houseboat on the Styx (1896) and its sequel, *The Pursuit of the Houseboat* (1897); and, following LEWIS CARROLL's death in 1898 and the end of his control, *Alice's Adventures in Wonderland* (1901) and *Through the Looking Glass* (1902).

Newell's *Alice,* the most prominent of four new American editions issued between 1899 and 1904, was roundly denounced and just as firmly if less widely defended, with Newell himself taking the lead in favor of fresh interpretations. Today, after a century of *Alice in Wonderland* makeovers by artists of every bent, Newell's formalized compositions and histrionic airs look considerably less peculiar and often quite aptly comical.

His third major sphere of activity, the making of picture books, came about by chance, though given his inventiveness, hardly by accident. As the cherished Newell anecdote goes, he spotted one of his offspring looking at a picture book upside down and determined to produce a book that could be turned around. The result was *Topsys & Turvys* (1893), which is reversible page by page. Thus, "In sandy groves Adolphus swings when Summer zephyrs blow" reverses to become "And slides headforemost down the hill when Winter brings the snow." Acclaim was immediate, and a second series of *Topsys & Turvys* appeared the next year.

How *The Hole Book* (1908) came about we do not know, or need to. Of picture-book inventions, it comes close to sheer, ungimmicky inspiration; among novelties, it is one of the few with perennial appeal. The fun starts on the cover, as a procession of boys and girls approaches a tantalizing hole straight down into the interior; who, then, can resist the invitation to "OPEN THE BOOK AND FOLLOW THE HOLE." Inside a boy accidentally shoots off a gun and the bullet makes a flying entrance into scene after peaceful scene, cutting the rope of a backyard swing, shattering a goldfish bowl, sending a high silk hat a-sailing via a hole cut in each page. An instantaneous hit, so to speak, *The Hole Book* led Newell into other innovations in format. *The Slant Book* (1910), in the shape of a parallelogram with pictures and verses on the diagonal, has a runaway baby carriage spilling the contents of a pushcart, tumbling a painter from his ladder (with messy results for a passer-by), literally slicing through a watermelon patch—all to the intense delight of the infant passenger. *The Rocket Book* (1912) repeats the pattern of *The Hole Book* on the vertical, as a rocket set off by the janitor's son Fritz in the basement shoots up through the twenty-one stories of the apartment house, causing predictable and unpredictable havoc among the social types en route.

Philip Hofer, a Newell fan, saw in his work admirable, all-American slapstick. American-art historian Edgar Richardson discerned in Newell a forerunner of "the gentle humor of the absurd" later cultivated in *The New Yorker.* Both, of course, were right. B.B.

NICHOLSON, SIR WILLIAM

BRITISH ARTIST, ILLUSTRATOR, AND AUTHOR, 1872–1949. William Nicholson's relatively small body of work made a tremendous impact on the development of the picture book as a significant literary form. He wrote as well as illustrated only two of his own PICTURE BOOKS, *Clever Bill* (1926) and *The Pirate Twins* (1929). These works, published between the two world wars during a productive and creative period in children's literature, inspired such innovative illustrators as the American fine artist WANDA GÁG and renowned author-illustrator MAURICE SENDAK. Today, Nicholson is best known for his woodcut illustrations for Margery Williams's classic story *The Velveteen Rabbit* (1922).

At the end of the nineteenth century, Nicholson published his first book, *An Alphabet* (1898), using a genre known to serve aspiring artists and writers as a "peg to hang pictures and rhymes on." Two years later, he illustrated Arthur Waugh's rhyming text *The Square Book of Animals* (1900). Nicholson's bold, graphic style, no doubt influenced by his background in poster making, heralded a new look in children's books. In addition to book illustration, poster making, and portrait painting, Nicholson was involved with the theater. During the early twenties, he designed the costumes and sets for J. M. BARRIE's *Peter Pan.*

First published in England, *Clever Bill* served as a prototype for the modern American picture book. Published in the United States in 1927, the book featured an oblong format, rarely before seen in children's picture books, that enhanced the overall design while facilitating the quick pace of the story. Nicholson's spare text, hand-lettered in his own script and paired with the simply rendered but detailed woodcut illustrations, races along from the very first page. By using an incomplete sentence—"One day the Postman brought Mary a letter from her—" Nicholson lures the reader into turning the page, an innovative stylistic technique later employed by other great picture-book authors such as MARJORIE FLACK in her "Angus" books. Drama and tension build as Mary tries to pack her favorite belongings into her green suitcase. Of course, Clever Bill gets left behind, but not for long; he chases the train and surprises Mary with a welcoming salute at the train station in Dover. Nicholson's use of line adds levity and action to the pictures, enhancing the story's lively spirit of adventure. He unified art and text by using the same bold lines in both his drawings and the hand-lettered words that tell the story. Even the book cover and end papers are similarly decorated. Maurice Sendak, one among the many contemporary illustrators who have admired and learned from Nicholson's work, has written, "*Clever Bill,* I have long felt, is among the few perfect picture books ever created for children." ❧ S.M.G.

Nic Leodhas, Sorche

AMERICAN AUTHOR, 1898–1969. Leclaire Gowans Alger published much of her writing under the pseudonym Sorche Nic Leodhas, which means Claire, daughter of Louis, in Gaelic. This salute to her heritage seems fitting for an author best known for her books of Scottish folklore. Born in Youngstown, Ohio, to a family that had collected Gaelic legends and songs for generations, Leclaire learned to read at an early age and published her first story at twelve. Growing up in Pittsburgh, she was often too sickly to attend school and spent some years studying at home. She began working for the Carnegie Library of Pittsburgh as a page in 1915, then left to marry and have a child. After her husband's early death, she worked for the New York Public Library, then returned to Pittsburgh to attend Carnegie Library School. Although she had no college education, she was permitted to enter by special examination and graduated in 1929. For the next thirty-seven years, she worked in branches of the Carnegie Library, often as a children's librarian.

Alger began her writing career with three long-forgotten children's books, *Jan and the Wonderful Mouth Organ* (1939), *Dougal's Wish* (1942), and *The Golden Summer* (1942), which were published under her own name. Nearly twenty years passed before she assumed the name Sorche Nic Leodhas and wrote *Heather and Broom: Tales of the Scottish Highlands* (1961), a delightful collection of "seanichie" stories—tales originally told by wandering storytellers. Some of the stories are serious, others are humorous, and many incorporate supernatural themes. All are written in cadenced prose that emphasizes the stories' oral tradition. The tone of *Thistle and Thyme: Tales and Legends from Scotland* (1962), is even stronger in Scottish language, rhythms, and atmosphere.

In addition to seanachie stories, Nic Leodhas includes Lowland tales and oral narratives called "sgeulachdan," such as "The Laird's Lass and the Gobba's Son," which tells of a headstrong young woman who falls in love with a blacksmith. *Thistle and Thyme* was named a Newbery Honor Book and remains one of Nic Leodhas's best-known works. Other collections include *Gaelic Ghosts* (1963) and *Ghosts Go Hunting* (1965), which are filled with spooky and humorous stories; *Sea-Spell and Moor-Magic: Tales of the Western Isles* (1968), each of which comes from a different island in the Scottish Hebrides, including one from a mythical isle; and the densely written *Claymore and Kilt: Tales of Scottish Kings and Castles* (1967), which contains stories that date from A.D. 211 to the seventeenth century. These collections are important contributions to folklore because the stories all stem from the oral tradition. The author gathered stories from family, friends, and anyone she happened to meet who had a Scottish background; if a tale had been previously published, she did not include it in her books.

Nic Leodhas also wrote notable picture books based on Gaelic folk songs or poems. A cumulative poem about Sandy's trip to the mill forms the basis of *All in the Morning Early* (1963), which was named a Caldecott Honor Book for EVALINE NESS's illustrations. Nonny Hogrogian won the Caldecott Medal for *Always Room for One More* (1965), a poem about Lachie MacLachlan, who shares his home with all who pass.

In both her picture books and her volumes of folktales, Sorche Nic Leodhas shares the oral traditions of Scotland in fine written prose. ❧ P.D.S.

Nielsen, Kay

DANISH ILLUSTRATOR, 1886–1957. When Kay Nielsen died in California in 1957, he was virtually penniless and forgotten. From the height of his career as a celebrated illustrator of fairy tales, he had seemingly fallen into obscurity at the close of his life. But since his death, Nielsen's place in history has become universally acknowledged and his name is invariably invoked as one of the deities of the golden age of illustration, alongside such immortals as ARTHUR RACKHAM, WALTER CRANE, and Edmund Dulac.

Brought up in an artistic household, Nielsen felt it was inevitable that he should have a career in the arts. His father rose to become the managing director of the Dagmartheater in Copenhagen; his mother was an actress at the Court of the Royal Theater in the same city. Their home was a salon of sorts, and young Kay was on familiar terms with many of the great Scandinavian artists and intellectuals of the day. He was continually drawing as a child and youth, inspired by Chinese

Illustration by Kay Nielsen from *East of the Sun and West of the Moon: Old Tales from the North* (1914).

carvings and Japanese watercolors his mother's father had brought back from his many travels. As a mature artist, Nielsen's style shows the influence of many cultures and periods, from the Mideast to Art Deco, while maintaining a highly individual stamp. He might be viewed as an artistic Viking, bringing to his distinct Scandinavian landscape the spoils of many lands. After attending the Academie Julienne in Paris, Nielsen returned to Copenhagen and held his first exhibition in 1912, a series of black-and-white drawings. The British publisher Hodder and Stoughton felt that his style would be appropriate for a deluxe edition of fairy tales it was planning to publish. Nielsen's reputation as an artist rests largely on the strength of his illustrations for those four books of fairy tales. *In Powder and Crinoline* (1913), a collection of fairy tales retold by Sir Arthur Quiller-Couch, was the first of the series and *East of the Sun and West of the Moon* (1914), a collection of Norwegian folktales retold by the great folklorists PETER CHRISTIEN ASBJÖRNSEN AND JÖRGEN MOE, the second. Many think this book contains Nielsen's most characteristic, if not his greatest, work. The illustrations are pensive, filled with dramatic space and strong lines creating a terrific sense of movement. The deep Northern skies he depicts give his work a celestial scale that imparts a mythic impact to his heroes and heroines. The delicacy and elegance of the illustrations completely disregard the rough, folksy quality of the tales, leaving each to be enjoyed separately.

The onset of World War I brought a break in Nielsen's illustrating career, so he turned to the arena of his childhood and began designing for the stage. After the war, Nielsen illustrated *Fairy Tales by Hans Christian Andersen* (1922), in which the formality of the language, the fancy of ANDERSEN's images, and the poignancy of the stories complement the art brilliantly. This was followed by *Hansel and Gretel: Stories from the Brothers Grimm* (1925), which would prove to be his last great work. The pictures show a still-evolving artist; they are slightly less formal, demonstrating perhaps a folk-art influence, with greater use of color. Concentrating then on his theater work, Nielsen traveled to California in the late 1930s to design sets for a stage production, which led to work at the Walt Disney studios, where he designed the "Night on Bald Mountain" sequence for the film classic *Fantasia.* He never returned to Denmark, remaining in California until his death. Nielsen's work went unremarked until the 1970s, when a new appreciation of children's literature sparked renewed interest in and appreciation of his major contribution and ensured his place in the history of children's literature. S.G.K.

NIXON, JOAN LOWERY

AMERICAN AUTHOR, B. 1927. Whether it's the page-turning suspense of *A Deadly Game of Magic* (1983) or the broad comedy of *You Bet Your Britches, Claude* (1989), Joan Lowery Nixon's creative talent is evident in her more than eighty books for young readers. The prolific Nixon successfully offers something for all ages; one can begin with her PICTURE BOOKS of tall tales and EASY READERS and "graduate" to the wonderfully creepy suspense novels about teens in peril, among them *Secret, Silent Screams* (1988) and *Whispers from the Dead* (1989), for which she is justly celebrated.

Nixon spent her childhood in Los Angeles. During college, her journalism training at the University of Southern California gave her a solid background for creative writing; it was also at USC that Nixon met her future husband, geologist Hershell H. Nixon, with whom she has collaborated on several notable nonfiction titles, among them *Earthquakes: Nature in Motion* (1981) and *Land under the Sea* (1985). A brief teaching career in Los Angeles led her to a writers' conference, which inspired her to try writing for children. Drawing on her own children, Nixon began her writing career with *The Mystery of Hurricane Castle* (1964), which featured two of her daughters as the main characters. The "Claude" series (*If You Say So, Claude* (1980), *Beats Me, Claude* (1986), *Fat Chance, Claude* (1987), and *You Bet Your Britches, Claude,* starring those pioneer lovebirds, Claude and Shirley, features several tongue-in-cheek episodes with characters as broadly drawn as the flat Western landscapes against which these yarns are spun. Nixon provides older readers with a taste of historical fiction in her "Orphan Train" quartet (*A Family Apart,* 1987; *Caught in the Act,* 1988; *In the Face of Danger,* 1988; and *A Place to Belong,* 1989; each story introduces one or more of the six Kelly children, separated from their widowed mother and each other and sent west on the orphan trains of the nineteenth century. Nixon's accurate historical detail combines with excellent storytelling to make this series a favorite with middle-grade readers.

Nixon is best known for her young adult mystery novels, shown by the many awards she has received. The only three-time winner of the Edgar Allan Poe Award, given by the Mystery Writers of America, Nixon places ordinary teens in realistic, believable settings and then draws them into terrifying scenarios. Whether they are trapped in eerie, deserted houses during driving rainstorms, mistakenly accused of plotting their own kidnapping, or finding dead bodies in the most inconvenient places, Nixon always gives her characters a good dose of common sense and often humor. Her teen sleuths may find themselves in extraordinary circumstances, but they operate against a background drawn from reality. The audience may not have experienced a particular character's circumstance, but hairstyles, school, and teen romance can be universally appreciated by young adult fans.

In a recent picture book, *If You Were a Writer* (1988), Nixon shares some of her feelings about her craft: "If you were a writer, the stories you wrote might make people laugh, or shiver, or even cry. They'd be your stories. They'd belong to you because they'd be part of you." ❧ E.H.

Nonfiction

See Information Books.

Norton, André

American author, b. 1912. A prolific writer of science fiction and fantasy for children and adults, André Norton has more than a hundred books to her credit, many of them still in print. Her first, *The Prince Commands,* came out in 1934; a historical fantasy, it was the third novel she had written, and she was not yet twenty-one when it was published. Because female adventure/science fiction writers were not being published at the time, she legally changed her name from Alice Mary Norton to André Norton.

When she began writing it was taboo to use female protagonists, so she developed strong male characters with rough, dynamic personalities. When she ventured into the realm of women as main characters (a vanguard in sci-fi publishing), they were equally powerful, inventive, curious, and courageous. Indeed, in the best of her books, it is the characters and their internal, interpersonal, and intercultural conflicts that become the life force of the story, rather than the more technical scientific aspects that dominate much science fiction.

Norton is one of the first writers for young people who casually used characters of many nationalities and races in her stories. One fantasy novel for younger readers, *Lavender-Green Magic* (1974), is about a black family that is relocated from its integrated Boston neighborhood into an all-white suburb. Magic from the witches of the past helps Holly accept herself and allow people to accept her. Although the portrayal of racism is simplistic, it is admirable that Norton attempted it when she did. Norton did not set out to write books in a series, though many have continuous plots and characters, as in the "Witch World" books that began in 1963, a series of nearly twenty sword-and-sorcery fantasies, the most recent of which is *Flight of Vengeance* (1992). Most of the science fiction titles are, if not siblings, cousins. Norton uses the same language and the same assumptions about the universe, so when one enters a book, the territory is familiar. But the invented galactic logic is grounded by a rich base in Western mythology and history, and familiar stories are rewoven in stellar patterns. In her short book *Outside* (1974), the pattern is based on the tale of the Pied Piper, as a magical minstrel gathers up the children and leads them outside the enclosed city sphere. The air inside is becoming fouled, and the outside, which once was hazardous due to nuclear fallout, now has regenerated itself into a green and promising land.

Norton centers her stories on familiar, human themes. Her characters are often loners who, through the events of each book, reach a certain maturity. In *The Time Traders* (1958), one of several books in the "Time Travel" series, Ross Murdock is arrested and, instead of getting a jail sentence, is given over to an experimental process. Steeped in a cold war atmosphere, the book depicts brave men traveling through time into prehistory and discovering alien spaceships among Bronze Age peoples.

Norton's later novels became more sophisticated, crossing myth with history and a projected future. In *Forerunner Foray* (1973) Ziantha is a young woman trained in the sensitive arts of telepathy and psychometry. She discovers a rock that conceals a gem that has gathered power for centuries by being used as a focus point for energy. This stone takes her on an intergalactic journey and thrusts her back through time to encounter the women who were the stone's keepers, one a human sacrifice for a warlord's tomb, another a mermaid priestess.

Living alone with her cats, Norton creates characters who hearken to the universal longing: finding one's path through the stars. Among many other awards and honors, Norton received the Nebula Grand Master Award for her life's achievement in 1984. J.A.J.

NORTON, MARY

BRITISH AUTHOR OF FANTASY NOVELS, 1903–1992. An actress and one-time member of London's Old Vic Theatre Company, Mary Norton used her tremendous stagecraft and vivid imagination to create classic works of fantasy that continue to captivate young audiences. *The Magic Bed-Knob,* her first book, was published in the United States in 1943, and its sequel, *Bonfires and Broomsticks,* was published in England in 1947. A combined edition of the two, *Bed-Knob and Broomstick* (1957), was the inspiration for the 1971 DISNEY film *Bedknobs and Broomsticks,* starring Angela Lansbury. Norton's story tells of three siblings who, when they discover that a neighbor is secretly training to be a witch, offer to keep quiet in return for some magic. The children's subsequent adventures traveling by bed through space and time are exciting and memorable, though one episode is marred, by contemporary standards, by a racist depiction of "cannibals." The amusing portrayal of the ladylike Miss Price primly studying the dark arts and trying in earnest to be more wicked firmly established Norton as a master of comedy.

Norton is best known for the series that begins with *The Borrowers* (1953), a book that earned its author the Carnegie Medal and the Lewis Carroll Shelf Award. Equally popular are the books that followed: *The Borrowers Afield* (1955), *The Borrowers Afloat* (1959), and *The Borrowers Aloft* (1961). Scientists have yet to provide a better explanation than Norton's for the mysterious disappearance of small household objects such as safety pins, crochet hooks, pencils, stamps, and matchboxes. Norton posits that these items are "borrowed" by a race of small people who stay hidden away, living in old, quiet houses. The stories have the appeal of the cozy, miniature world of dollhouses, pixies, and talking mice, but without the magic and whimsy. There is nothing cute about the Victorian-era Clock family—Arrietty and her parents, Pod and Homily—who are very human in their thoughts, actions, and appearance and who struggle daily for their survival while being careful never to be "seen." Readers can easily sympathize with the young, high-spirited Arrietty, who longs to satisfy her intense curiosity about humans and the world outside. Both

Illustration by Beth and Joe Krush from *The Borrowers* (1953), by Mary Norton.

fairy fans and adventure lovers can appreciate the Borrowers' ingenious use of human scale objects and their execution of numerous escapes: through a drain in a soapbox lid, down a river aboard a cutlery tray, and out an attic in a homemade hot-air balloon. Readers care deeply about what happens to these characters, but the suspense is always tempered by humor and wit.

After a gap of ten years, Norton published *Poor Stainless: A New Story about the Borrowers* (1971). The brief tale is told to Arrietty by her mother and describes a young Borrower who disappears and spends a free-wheeling week in a village shop on his own. Next came a whimsical story, unrelated to the Borrowers, entitled *Are All the Giants Dead?* (1975), about a boy who travels to the land of fairy tales. In 1982 fans and critics were pleasantly surprised by the unexpected publication of a fifth Borrowers novel, *The Borrowers Avenged.* The acclaimed book features the illustrations of Beth and Joe Krush, whose depictions of the Clock family had added a further dimension to the previous books. Norton's well-loved stories continue to instill in audiences a sincere desire for a magic bed-knob or a glimpse, at least, of a Borrower. ❧ J.M.B.

Nöstlinger, Christine

Austrian author, b. 1936. "I began writing because I was not a good artist. I illustrated a picture book and wrote my own text for it. The book was published; the text won more approval than the pictures. As I was very keen on approval at the time, I took to writing," Christine Nöstlinger explains.

Nöstlinger's crisp writing and her saucy sense of humor have continued to gain her critical acclaim. Describing why the committee chose Nöstlinger for the 1984 Hans Christian Andersen Medal, Patricia Crampton says her books point to a clear moral: "No one should be made to suffer just because she is different; no one should believe that their position, as parent or teacher or official, gives them the right to wield undisputed authority over others, including and especially children." This is the firm foundation upon which Nöstlinger's books dance. Her first novel, *Fly Away Home* (1973, trans. 1975), was her way of processing her own wartime childhood. Writing in the first person, Christel describes Vienna, first as it is bombed, then as the Russian forces replace the Nazis. Even in this starkly realistic portrayal of the war, Nöstlinger manages to throw a humorous coverlet over the pain.

Nöstlinger has gone on to write over fifty books, nearly a dozen of which have been translated by Anthea Bell into English. Most of her books for younger readers have a fantasy element, while her stories for young adults are cutting commentaries on teenage concerns. *The Cucumber King* (1972, trans. 1985), which won the German Children's Literature Prize, tells in sensible twelve-year-old prose how the Cucumber King, exiled from his kingdom, comes into a family's kitchen asking for political asylum. The father respects the King and relates to his problems. But the rest of the family side with the oppressed subjects who had good reason for kicking out their King. *Konrad* (1975, trans. 1976) is an absurdly delightful tale about a woman who is so eccentrically independent, most people think her crazy. She gets a package containing a factory-made boy, but, unfortunately, he has been programmed to be perfect. He loves algebra, goes to bed on time, and throws a fit when he is forced to eat candy. In order to save him from going back to the factory, he has to be trained to be an ordinary, obnoxious boy. *Luke and Angela* (1978, trans. 1979), for older readers, is a multilayered story of friendships. Luke and Angela have been inseparable since they were in strollers together, and, at fourteen, Luke is questioning the friendship for the first time. He longs to have a personality and feels that having been guaranteed a friend in Angela all his life, he hasn't needed to develop one. Luke is exploring his first feelings of sexuality as well, and when he can't make Angela understand the magnetic attraction that should happen when they kiss, he is lured away by a twenty-two-year-old woman. All this is told through Angela's point of view. The characterization gives the book the classic Nöstlinger humor and makes the ending both delightful and poignant. As Anthea Bell says, Nöstlinger knows "the importance of not being earnest." ❧ J.A.J.

Nursery Rhymes

The infant gurgles and coos, smiles and wiggles; the adult reaches out, grabs the little hands, and brings them together, reciting "pat-a-cake, pat-a-cake, baker's man," as indulgent predecessors have been doing for centuries. The rhyme, stored unused by the adult for decades, springs unhesitatingly to the lips. Humpty Dumpty, Georgie Porgie, Little Miss Muffet, Old King Cole and company, dormant, unretrieved for years, can be called back just as effortlessly while other more newly acquired literary acquaintances have faded and disappeared.

Nursery rhymes, both in the culture and in individual consciousness, have been remarkably durable. Some verses were already aged when Shakespeare was a lad, a few finding a home in his plays. Even without so august a setting, the rhymes persisted, carried on initially through the oral tradition but now increasingly in written form. Although most are firmly within the province of the nursery—lullabies, counting rhymes, finger plays, and the like—many derive from adult sources: peddlers' cries, street chants, tavern songs, or ballads.

Whatever the source, students of language development have convincingly demonstrated the causal relationship between early familiarity with MOTHER GOOSE and subsequent linguistic competence. Internal and end rhymes, assonance, onomatopoeia, alliteration, and repetitions sensitize toddlers to the sounds and patterns of language and help them make those distinctions that they will later employ in correlating phonemes and letters. The best preparation infants can have for their later role as readers and spellers is to be immersed in nursery rhymes.

But such academic purposes are irrelevant to the young child, who finds in these rhymes only an enduring source of pleasure. The baby's first encounter with Mother Goose provides a visual and sensory feast. He sees the adult's approving, smiling face, hears the rhythmic sounds, and feels his arms or hands moved in synchronization. It is the best possible introduction to a lifelong involvement with books.

Although Mother Goose is sustained by the oral tradition, illustrators have found the challenge of interpreting these familiar verses irresistible. In the many, many editions of Mother Goose published, there is a virtually limitless choice of style, quantity, and selection. In fact, it is possible to chart the history of juvenile illustration in this century through an examination of editions of nursery rhymes alone.

In the first quarter of the twentieth century, British editions dominated the American nursery. KATE GREENAWAY's Victorian children, RANDOLPH CALDECOTT's lively and spirited characters, and Arthur Rackham's porcelain-faced youngsters and wittily rendered adults appear in books that show every indication of surviving into the next century. A persisting favorite is L. LESLIE BROOKE's *Ring O'Roses* (1922). His ability to give human expression to animals remains unsurpassed as seen in the poor befuddled pig going to market who is clearly on a mission beyond his limited abilities. Later editions chronicle the changes in children's book art: Byam Shaw's Pre-Raphaelite art; Jennie Harbour's art deco pictures; Mabel Attwell's evocations of images from 1930s advertising and movie cartoons; FEODOR ROJANKOVSKY's *The Tall Book of Mother Goose* (1942), with its benign realism and political allusion (Humpty Dumpty as Adolf Hitler); MARGUERITE DE ANGELI's *Book of Nursery and Mother Goose Rhymes* (1954), with its charming and serene drawings; and the exciting use of color in *Brian Wildsmith's Mother Goose* (1964).

Illustration by Randolph Caldecott from *The Diverting History of John Gilpin* (1878), by William Cowper.

Contemporary titles offer a cornucopia of choices of artistic styles, format, size, and individual rhymes. Everything from huge compendiums of use to scholars to profusely illustrated single-rhyme editions are available.

Styles range from sweet, serene, delicately colored pictures suitable for bedtime reading to raucous, witty drawings more appropriate for the fully energized toddler—as found in AMY SCHWARTZ's depictions of characters on the verge of catastrophe in *Mother Goose's Little Misfortunes* (1990). For those who cannot favor one artist over another, there are collections such as *The Glorious Mother Goose* by Cooper Eden (1988), which recapitulates nursery rhyme interpretations from 1870 to 1933, or *Tail Feathers from Mother Goose* (1988), which offers illustrations by sixty-two contemporary British artists.

At one end of the spectrum is *The Mother Goose Treasury* (1966) by RAYMOND BRIGGS, which offers slightly over four hundred verses, and ARNOLD LOBEL's superlative *Random House Book of Mother Goose* (1986) featuring over three hundred rhymes. At the other end are the single-rhyme picture books such as SUSAN JEFFERS's delicate, detailed *Three Jovial Huntsmen* and

PETER SPIER's *London Bridge Is Falling Down* (1967). Beyond the simple verse, Spier's illustrations depict a history of London Bridge from the first Roman span to its 1970s reconstruction.

For children who have outgrown the nursery, Kevin O'Malley's *Who Killed Cock Robin?* (1993) uses the familiar rhyme to provide a frame for a mystery replete with clues as to the deceptive and "fowl" practices of birds. MAURICE SENDAK has several credits in this genre, most notably *Hector Protector and As I Went Over the Water* (1965), *I Saw Esau* (1992), and *We Are All in the Dumps with Jack and Guy* (1993), in which his interpretation and illustrations comment on poverty and homelessness among children in America.

Mother Goose in this century has gone from innocence to experience: Initial images of a gentle, serene, bucolic world have been gradually supplemented by more worldly ones. There are still many volumes for the infant and toddler, but these have been joined by new titles for the more mature reader, offering varied choices and more opportunities for pleasurable exploration of this elastic genre. ❧ KAREN HARRIS

O

O'Brien, Robert C.

American author, 1918–1973. During his brief career as a novelist, Robert C. O'Brien earned great acclaim but remained an enigma. What little personal information he released to the public was often incomplete or confusing. At the time of his greatest professional triumph, O'Brien did not deliver his own Newbery Medal acceptance speech but asked that his editor speak in his place. Perhaps one reason behind these mysteries was that, under his real name, Robert Leslie Conly, he worked as an editor of *National Geographic,* a publication that discouraged any outside writing by its staff. Born in Brooklyn, the author was raised in Amityville, New York. After receiving a degree in English from the University of Rochester, he worked as a reporter for *Newsweek* and several other publications before joining *National Geographic* in Washington, D.C. O'Brien began writing fiction in the mid-1960s.

His first novel, *The Silver Crown* (1968), is a fantasy about a girl who finds a magic crown, loses her family, then undertakes an arduous journey. The writing style is promising, with an intense aura of danger and violence, but while the novel contains many exciting scenes, the pace occasionally lags. There are also a few loose ends in the plot. Some later editions include an alternate final chapter, which clears up a key plot question, but the reader may remain unsatisfied.

In *Mrs. Frisby and the Rats of NIMH* (1971), the author successfully combines an old-fashioned talking-animal story with futuristic scientific speculation. When a widowed field mouse named Mrs. Frisby learns that her home and family may be destroyed by a farmer's plow, she seeks assistance from a group of superintelligent laboratory rats. The core of the book is a lengthy first-person account in which Nicodemus relates how he and the other rats were captured by the NIMH labs, treated with steroids, and taught to read, before eventually escaping to form an advanced rat society. Structurally, this long story-within-a-story disrupts the narrative flow of Mrs. Frisby's tale, but the material is fascinating and raises many questions about what constitutes intelligence and civilization. With its interesting plot and fine blend of scientific and nature writing, this unique fantasy would surely have built a large audience eventually, but it was helped immeasurably by winning the Newbery Medal in 1972. The book continues to be extremely popular with young readers and was the basis for an animated feature, *The Secret of NIMH* (1982).

O'Brien published an adult novel in the early 1970s and was working on *Z for Zachariah* at the time of his death. Completed by his wife and one of his daughters and published in 1975, this young adult novel is a com-

Illustration by Zena Bernstein from *Mrs. Frisby and the Rats of NIMH* (1971), by Robert C. O'Brien.

pelling first-person account of a teenage girl surviving alone after a nuclear war and the ominous stranger she meets. All of O'Brien's novels concern characters trying to make the best of a terrible situation, with a threat of danger lurking in the background. In these intriguing, unusual books, the fantastic exists side by side with the mundane. The children in *The Silver Crown* deal with magic in twentieth-century suburban America. Mrs. Frisby receives assistance from intelligent rats in fighting a common garden plow. Masterfully written, Robert C. O'Brien's novels show a love of nature and raise thought-provoking questions. ❧ P.D.S.

O'Dell, Scott

AMERICAN AUTHOR, 1898–1989. Scott O'Dell wrote his first novel for young people at an age when many Americans consider retirement. Published in 1960, *Island of the Blue Dolphins* is based on the true story of an Indian girl who spent eighteen years living alone on an island off the California coast. Using the few facts known about this incident, O'Dell created a riveting survival story that speaks to the heart. Karana's tribe is permanently departing from the island when the girl realizes her young brother, Ramo, has been accidentally left behind. Since weather conditions will not permit their ship to turn around, Karana jumps overboard and swims back to join her brother. After Ramo is killed by a wild dog, the girl must survive alone on the island. Karana's haunting first-person narrative records her triumph over adversity and loneliness. She builds a home, survives an earthquake, and tames wild birds. Although she initially vows to kill the dog that murdered her brother, he eventually becomes her devoted companion. The beautifully cadenced prose sings with courage, dignity, and an appreciation for nature. This modern classic received the 1961 Newbery Medal.

Scott O'Dell spent part of his childhood living in a seaport town near the island where the real Karana once lived. The Los Angeles–born author attended a number of colleges, including Stanford, the University of Wisconsin, and the University of Rome, but never received a degree. He found work in the motion picture industry, wrote for magazines and newspapers, labored on a citrus ranch, and served as book editor for the Los Angeles *Daily News*. He also wrote several books for adults, including historical novels about California. But O'Dell found his greatest success writing for children. Three of his novels were named Newbery Honor Books. *The King's Fifth* (1966) concerns sixteenth-century Spanish adventurers seeking gold in the American Southwest; *The Black Pearl* (1967) is based on a California legend; *Sing Down the Moon* (1970) tells of Bright Morning, who joins her Navaho tribe on the U.S.-government-enforced three-hundred-mile Long Walk of 1864. All are first-rate historical novels, strong in character, plot, and incident.

O'Dell drew on events both famous and little known in his novels about the American Revolution, the Civil War, and a slave revolt in the West Indies. Francis of Assisi, Pocahontas, Sacagawea, and William Tyndale are among the historical figures featured in his books. *The Captive* (1979), *The Feathered Serpent* (1981), and *The Amethyst Ring* (1983) comprise a trilogy about sixteenth-century Central and South American cultures. *Zia* (1976), a sequel to *Island of the Blue Dolphins*, concerns Karana's niece. O'Dell occasionally made forays into contemporary fiction. Two of his best, *Child of Fire* (1974) and *Kathleen, Please Come Home* (1978), are arresting problem novels, despite the author's questionable use of adult narrators.

O'Dell's use of the first-person voice, however, has proven to be particularly apt for his historical narrators, whose distinctive language and speech patterns always reveal their culture and background. The author's novels are also notable for their strong female protagonists;

Jacket illustration by EVALINE NESS for *Island of the Blue Dolphins* (1960), by Scott O'Dell.

this unspoken yet impassioned statement about women's rights is particularly impressive coming from a male author.

Scott O'Dell received the international Hans Christian Andersen Medal in 1972 for the body of his work. He later established the Scott O'Dell Award for Historical Fiction, an annual prize that continues to reward outstanding works of historical fiction for young people. O'Dell's ability to bring the past alive through the words and experiences of his unforgettable protagonists establishes his work as a touchstone by which all children's historical fiction can be measured. P.D.S.

Voices of the Creators

Zibby Oneal

My grandfather used to like to read me adventure stories, hardly bothering to disguise the fact that reading them to me was his excuse to reread them. Wishing to be equally honest, I made no attempt to hide the fact that these stories of his bored me witless.

It is possible, of course, to love someone enormously while disagreeing with his taste in literature, and this was our situation. Fond as we were of one another, our tastes diverged. My grandfather was keenly interested in plot. I cared about characters. What happened in a story seemed far less interesting to me than the characters to whom it happened. A story that was mainly plot struck me as lacking meat on the bone.

Naturally enough then, when I began to write, it was the characters who absorbed me. I left the plot to take care of itself, or, rather, I left it up to the characters' devising. Never sure exactly what will *happen* in the book I am writing, I let the characters lead the way, their unfolding personalities guiding the direction the narrative takes. I trust them to know what needs to happen, and, by and large, they have not let me down.

So long as I let the story evolve in this way, it moves along fairly smoothly, characters and events in harmony. But, of course, I cannot always resist the urge to be a busybody. Once in a while I decide to exert my authority as author. I drag some cumbersome plot device banging and clanking into the midst of things. I decide to put on the brakes, make a U-turn, get us off the back roads. Ill-advised as I know these urges to be, I sometimes let them overwhelm me.

Partway into the writing of *The Language of Goldfish,* I began to see, with growing discomfort, the direction my character, Carrie, was heading. Though I had created this troubled girl and had set her on her course, though I had provided the bottle of pills waiting on the shelf in the linen closet, nevertheless as I approached the inevitable, I was unwilling to let the inevitable occur. A suicide attempt was, as it turned out, more than I was willing to deal with. And so I decided to remove the pills, thinking I could find some equally strong statement for Carrie to make.

Not surprisingly, Carrie turned stubborn. She let me see there was no statement she could make that was half so strong or, in this case, truer to the character I had created. For several weeks we argued this point, but in the end I agreed to return the pills.

I have tried to force compromises on other characters in other situations, shying away from the inevitable consequences of personality. But this is no more possible in fiction than it is in life. I wanted, for example, to effect a reconciliation between Kate and her father at the end of my novel *In Summer Light.* I arranged a sentimental fade-out from which the two emerged full of goodwill and mutual understanding. Writing the final chapters of *A Formal Feeling,* I became reluctant to let my character, Anne, recognize and acknowledge the depth of resentment she felt for her mother. Fortunately for both books, my editor was wise. I had created these characters, she told me, and it was far too late to alter their course.

This, ironically, is true. Once you have brought characters into being, complete with minds and emotions and histories, you are no longer free to push them around. Their personalities shape their destinies as surely as if they were living beings, and there is nothing an author can do to alter the outcome short of resorting to a species of dishonesty.

There are risks involved in letting characters lead the way. Often they head for murky terrain that seems suddenly too familiar. Out of the writer the characters come, and back into the writer they go from time to time, plumbing in unexpected ways for hidden or half-remembered shadows.

At such times a writer may grow wistful, fancying how pleasant it would feel to be in charge of plot. I imagine a straight and well-lit highway, clear signs at every exit, and myself, fully confident, at the wheel. I imagine, in other words, the impossible. This well-lit journey belongs to other writers. My own must be as I have described it—a zigzag trek that the characters choose once I have agreed to set them in motion.

Oneal, Zibby

American author, b. 1934. Zibby Oneal is a graduate of the University of Michigan, where she is now a lecturer in the English department. Oneal's most prominent contributions to children's literature to date have been her three coming-of-age novels and a brief, easy chapter book of historical fiction. Believable, with plenty of historical details, *A Long Way to Go* (1990) is both entertaining and informative. Ten-year-old Lila feels stifled by the restrictions placed on her as a young female in the early 1900s. Convinced by her grandmother's ardent support of the burgeoning women's suffragist movement, Lila must in turn reason with her father, who forbids her to march in an upcoming suffragist parade.

Oneal's three young adult novels feature three very different but equally intriguing female protagonists. Though her subjects include mental illness, death, first love, and family conflict, Oneal's books are much more than problem novels. Her subtle character development, skillful writing style, and use of art and literature as thematic imagery in her stories raise them far above the level of the problem novel. In *The Language of Goldfish* (1980), thirteen-year-old Carrie finds herself feeling increasingly uncomfortable in school and at home. Slowly it is revealed that the heart of Carrie's problem is her paralyzing fear of entering the adult world. What begins as a series of fainting spells escalates to a suicide attempt that lands her in the hospital and brings her to an initial meeting with an understanding and helpful doctor. Oneal's moving portrait presents an adolescent garnering courage to face the strange and awesome challenge of adulthood. Sixteen-year-old Anne, the protagonist in *A Formal Feeling* (1982), cannot believe her father has remarried so soon after her mother's death. As did Carrie in Oneal's first novel, Anne must learn that there are certain things over which a person has no control. In time, Anne comes to realize that her mother was not the perfect person she remembers. Fearing then that perhaps she never loved her mother, she eventually sees that, in their imperfect ways, they cared deeply for each other. *In Summer Light* (1985) chronicles the summer of Kate's seventeenth year. Home from boarding school, Kate struggles to write a paper on *The Tempest*. Nursing a silent conflict with her famous artist father, whom she sees as a modern-day Prospero, Kate finds solace in her friendship with Ian, a college student who has come to catalog her father's work. With Ian's encouragement, Kate confronts her grudging feelings toward her father, who she feels has dismissed as minor her own ability as an artist. In a wholly believable and satisfying ending, Kate and her father reach an almost unspoken understanding of each other.

Oneal's novels should be read carefully in order to savor the subtle repetition of images that resurface throughout the narratives, underscoring and linking together the evolving emotions the protagonists express. Her perceptive understanding of the journey taken by adolescents has culminated in honest and affecting young adult novels. ❧ J.M.B.

Opie, Peter
Opie, Iona

Peter: English author and folklorist, 1918–1982; Iona: English author and folklorist, b. 1923. An article in *Research Update* was headed: "Peter and Iona Opie: Patron Saints of Children's Literature," and their contribution has indeed been both prolific and unique. Both are British, although Peter was born in Egypt; both saw military service during World War II; they married in 1943, and their interest in NURSERY RHYMES and the folklore and games of children was sparked by a chance discovery that they remembered the same verse about "Ladybird" or "Ladybug."

Thus, because of their own passionate interest, the Opies began their long career of gathering, sorting, comparing, validating, analyzing, and interpreting. Neither had had formal training in folkloric theory or in research methodology; yet as all who have been the beneficiaries of their findings know, their knowledge of the body of folklore is vast, their research skills impeccable. Both have received an honorary degree of master of arts from Oxford University, and together they were awarded the Chicago Folklore Prize in 1970. In 1988 the American Folklore Society established the Peter and Iona Opie Prize in memory of Peter, who had died six years earlier.

Although the Opies had published a small and saucy selection of nursery rhymes in 1947, *I Saw Esau*, it was not until 1951 that their first major work appeared, *The Oxford Dictionary of Nursery Rhymes*. It is an exhaustive and scholarly study of the origins of nursery rhymes, of their earliest recordings, and of variations over the years. Other books of and about nursery rhymes are *The Oxford Nursery Rhyme Book* (1955), *A Family Book of Nursery Rhymes* (1964), and *Tailfeathers from Mother Goose* (1988). *A Nursery Companion* (1980) contains reproductions of early nineteenth-century booklets of folktales and nursery rhymes, with erudite commentary on their history and use.

The Lore and Language of Schoolchildren (1959) includes rhymes, riddles, childhood customs and beliefs and is rich in perceptive commentary; a series based on the book was broadcast by the BBC. *Children's Games in Street and Playground* (1969) is based on the Opies' observation of more than ten thousand children in England, Scotland, and Wales; it excludes party games, organized sports, and team games, focusing on what children of about ages six to twelve play "of their own accord when out of doors and usually out of sight." The book is voluminous, illuminating, and detailed. The last two books the Opies worked on together were *The Classic Fairy Tales* (1974) and *The Singing Game* (1985), which won several awards, including the Children's Literature Association Book Award.

A 1989 volume, *The Treasures of Childhood: Books, Toys, and Games from the Opie Collection*, catalogs the product of their years of collecting. In 1992 a new edition of *I Saw Esau* appeared, revised by Iona Opie and illustrated by MAURICE SENDAK. *The People in the Playground* (1993) shows how children change folk material and pass it on.

In 1986 a public appeal was made so that the Bodleian Library at Oxford could accept Iona Opie's generous offer to sell it the Opie book collection at half its value of one million pounds. In less than two years, the goal of the Opie appeal was met. This wealth of primary sources and the integrity of its collectors led a London newspaper to refer to the Opies as "the pioneer anthropologists of the previously uncharted world and lost tribes of childhood." ❧ Z.S.

ORGEL, DORIS

AMERICAN AUTHOR, B. 1929. In one of her best-known works, *The Devil in Vienna* (1978), Doris Orgel tells the story of an Austrian girl who leaves her homeland because of the encroaching threat of Nazism. This autobiographical novel describes Orgel's early life. Born in Vienna, she began writing at an early age, but life was soon interrupted by the political climate, which forced her family to flee the country. They escaped to Yugoslavia and later immigrated to the United States. The family spent a year in St. Louis before moving to New York, where Orgel has spent most of her life. She attended Radcliffe College, graduated from Barnard, and worked in publishing for several years before devoting her time to family responsibilities. Raising three children, Orgel discovered the world of children's literature and embarked upon a career as a writer and translator.

Her first publication was a 1960 translation of Wilhelm Hauff's *Dwarf-Long-Nose*. She then began retelling European tales for children, including *The Tale of Gockel, Hinkel, and Gackeliah* (1961) and the well-received *Long John* (1972), which was illustrated by ANITA LOBEL. Orgel's original work is notably diverse and includes POETRY, PICTURE BOOKS, MIDDLE-GRADE FICTION, and a frank YOUNG ADULT NOVEL. *Sarah's Room* (1963) concerns a preschooler who covets her older sister's room, which is filled with such treasures as a dollhouse and glass animals. The appealing rhymes capture a child's longings and are further enlivened by MAURICE SENDAK's amusing illustrations. Other picture books include *On the Sand Dune* (1968), the story of a girl too small to join her older friends as they play at the beach, and *Whose Turtle?* (1968), which concerns Rachel's new pet. Although not particularly inventive or memorable, the stories are convincingly childlike in emotion. Orgel's sensitivity to the emotional lives of children highlights such middle-grade novels as *The Mulberry Music* (1971), which details a sixth-grader's reactions to her grandmother's death, while a series of simply written, amusing books about eight-year-old Becky, including *My War with Mrs. Galloway* (1985), *Whiskers Once and Always* (1986), and *Midnight Soup and a Witch's Hat* (1987), provide a first-person perspective on being the only child of divorced parents.

Other novels are more serious but equally perceptive in revealing a child's inner life. Besides providing an accurate view of life in prewar Austria, *The Devil in Vienna* faithfully records in diary format the sometimes naïve thoughts of a Jewish girl whose Christian best friend moves to Munich and becomes involved in the Hitler Youth movement. A college student's psychotherapy is explored in *Risking Love* (1985), a book that may offend some readers with its casual drug use and fairly explicit scenes of unprotected sex. Although the insights into Dinah's therapy are intriguing, the book is flawed by overwritten dialogue. Also, the self-involved first-person writing style, which gives authenticity to many of the author's books for younger readers, grows tiresome in this young adult novel. In addition to her fiction, Orgel has written several volumes of poetry for children, including the humorous *The Good-byes of Magnus Marmalade* (1966).

Orgel has published a varied and interesting body of work. She accurately records the everyday emotions of young people in prose that is sometimes humorous, sometimes sober, often self-absorbed, but nearly always true to youthful experience and emotion. ❧ P.D.S.

Voices of the Creators

Jan Ormerod

Designing picture books for very young children, I am aware that such a book is almost always shared by the child and a caring adult. I find the challenge of communicating on two levels a demanding, intriguing, and rewarding task.

As someone who earns her living as an author and illustrator of books for and about children, I find it difficult to confess that I was not a very maternal young woman. We had decided definitely *not* to have children, and my first pregnancy was entirely unplanned. I think my books have been, in part, a way of savoring and expressing the positive elements of parenthood I had not anticipated—the fun, warmth, and love.

I trained, in Australia, as a designer, but all my options took me into the area of fine art—drawing, painting, printmaking, and sculpture. I was obsessed by the human figure, face, and gesture. I then trained as a teacher, and worked as an art teacher in secondary schools on an enrichment program for talented students, then in teachers' college, and, finally, at art school. My career in colleges of further education was dramatically changed by the birth of my first daughter, Sophie. For the first time since I was five years old, I left the school environment. I resigned, relaxed, and slowed down to infant pace. I reorganized my priorities and worked part-time, teaching design and drawing to art students, and for the first time began fully to understand the problem-solving function of design in relation to my own work.

My daughter and I discovered picture books together, seeing for the first time Arnold Lobel, Peter Spier, and Maurice Sendak. We found that Shirley Hughes tells good simple stories with clever design, clear informative drawing, and humorous detail. Brinton Turkle and Trina Schart Hyman use simple story, clear logical organization of material, and exquisite drawing and make small-scale domestic stories rich with all kinds of emotion. I was hooked. I knew I wanted to make picture books. I resigned my job, let the house, and set off for London and my career in picture books.

Most of my books for babies and young children are the result of close observation and recording of the day-to-day activities of children. For example, when my small daughter, Laura, was crawling, she was often accompanied by her young cat as they explored their environment. He seemed to be at about the same developmental stage as Laura. They would approach a saucepan in the same way. They would sniff it, taste it, hop inside it, sit on it—explore it in the same sensory fashion—*The Saucepan Game.* This process of observing and recording happened with *Kitten Day,* which was the result of watching Laura, age five, longingly waiting for the arrival of a new kitten, chosen by her some weeks before, when he was ready to leave the litter and become hers. She drew a heart on the calendar around the date of his arrival and wrote "kitten day" in crayon. As I watched his arrival and watched their relationship develop, I realized that I was observing something universal and important—the tender empathy of a young child for another small vulnerable creature, and the comfort of such companionship.

Every page of a picture book has many potential alternatives; each one is thought about and drawn about until a decision is made. My task as storyteller is to observe, record, and edit. Some images go straight from life into the book. Others need to be carefully sifted, reorganized, reinvented. Telling a story with pictures is a little like watching a movie, then selecting the evocative moment, like a still taken from a film. I need to capture the moment that has clarity and simplicity, invites empathy, and allows the reader to bring her own knowledge to that moment, to enrich it and develop it according to her own life experiences.

I design picture books for children and adults because I depend on an adult to create the right atmosphere and help children with my books. All young children need sometimes to be accompanied by an adult, even in books, and I believe that teachers, librarians, and parents can enjoy identifying with the adult in the book, while the children see the book from their perspective. When this happens, it is a time for physical closeness and comfort, a quiet time for sharing ideas and feelings, for laughing and learning together. Any adult who takes time to share books with small children will be rewarded, enriched, and revitalized by it every time.

This is what keeps me hooked on picture books.

Ormerod, Jan

Australian illustrator, b. 1946. Though Jan Ormerod's work celebrates the minutiae of domestic life, the acclaim her books have generated has been wide in scope. Her first book, *Sunshine* (1981), won praise and awards not only in her home country—where it was named Australian Picture Book of the Year—but across the seas, where it garnered a Kate Greenaway Medal commendation, a Mother Goose Award, and an American Library Association notable mention. Universally praised for her ability to bring humor, insight, and tenderness to the most ordinary domestic situations, Ormerod found that her own family life inspired her career in children's books.

After graduation from the Western Australian Institute of Technology, Ormerod earned her teacher's certificate and went on to teach art for many years, mostly at the college level. It was when her first child was born that she began to take an interest in the books her husband, a librarian, was bringing home for the baby. Ormerod began experimenting with her own ideas and, deciding that she could make a go of it as a full-time children's book illustrator, packed up her small family and made the great trek from the relative isolation of Australia to the hustle and bustle of London.

Sunshine and its companion, *Moonlight* (1982), established Ormerod's visual style and narrative realm. Both books wordlessly depict aspects of happy—though not tranquil—domesticity. In *Sunshine*, Ormerod shows the sleepy beginnings of a family's day; in *Moonlight*, the same family prepares for bed. Ormerod's attention to detail in both character and setting and her creative use of sequential slide-strip serial borders make a text not only unnecessary but superfluous. The evenhandedness with which she presents the adults' skills and foibles alongside the children's contributions and contradictions has made her work popular with both grown-ups and children.

Ormerod went on to explore the small things that loom so large in family life in books such as *101 Things to Do with a Baby* (1984), about the introduction of a new sibling, and *The Story of Chicken Licken* (1986), in which the traditional tale is presented as a grade-school play, with a secondary narrative concerning the antics of a very active toddler in the audience depicted in silhouette. Ormerod's skill at visual communication lends itself particularly well to the BOARD-BOOK format, and she has made her mark there also, with the "Jan Ormerod Baby Book" series.

She has also illustrated the work of others, in particular *Happy Christmas, Gemma* by Sarah Hayes (1986),

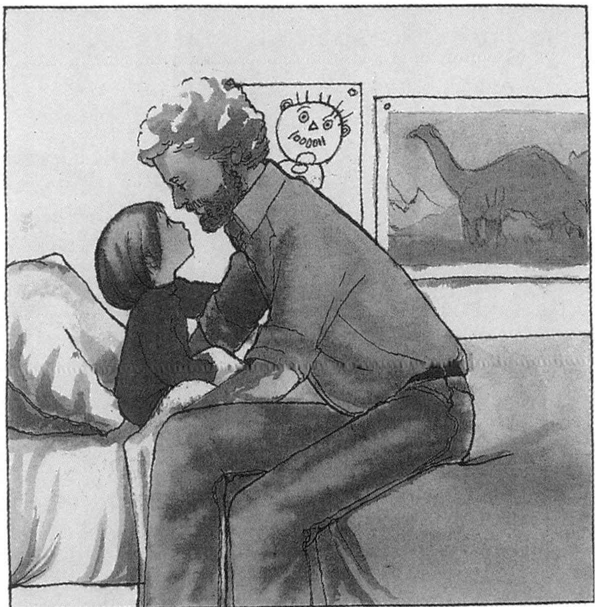

Illustration by Jan Ormerod from her book *Moonlight* (1982).

which was named an ALA Notable Book. She has occasionally expanded her line of sight beyond the home life of babies and toddlers. In *The Frog Prince* (1990), which she retold along with David Lloyd, she uses decorative borders and more traditional double-page spreads. Perhaps the best metaphor for Ormerod's charm is found in *When We Went to the Zoo* (1991). Here she takes her family out of the house and to the zoo, where her devotion to the domestic hearth is highlighted by the family's preference for some sparrows building a nest over the more exotic zoo animals.

Ormerod's sharp eye and gentle sense of humor have complemented each other in PICTURE BOOKS that have enabled countless families to remind themselves of the beauty in their own tumultuous lives. S.G.K.

Oxenbury, Helen

British illustrator and author, b. 1938. Nowhere have the ups and downs of baby and toddler life been more accurately depicted than in Helen Oxenbury's many books. A former set designer for theater, television, and film, Oxenbury began to illustrate books after the birth of her children and had her first book published, in England, in 1967. Though her husband, JOHN BURNINGHAM, was already a well-known author-illustrator, she made her own name as a keen

Voices of the Creators

Helen Oxenbury

When I read a manuscript, either it instantly appeals to me or it doesn't. I can't persuade myself to like a story. It's very difficult to put my finger on just what in a book attracts me. First, the story has to have a certain amount of humor. I don't like very sentimental stories. I like books that are down to earth, that portray things and people as they are. I have to be able to see the characters. I read a lot of manuscripts and have a chance to choose what I illustrate. But very few texts appeal to me. A book constitutes over nine months of work, a good chunk of my life, so I have to really love what I'm working on.

I was brought up in Suffolk by a river estuary, and the surrounding landscape was characterized by mud flats, high East Anglian skies, and crisp air. The quality of light is very particular, clearer and brighter than the south and west of England. But Suffolk can be freezing cold and very bleak—which doesn't put off a variety of wading birds, though a lot of people find it too austere in the winter months.

I've always drawn. My father used to send my drawings off to competitions, and they seemed to do well. Drawing was one of the few things I was good at in school. My father was an architect, so there was no opposition to my going to art school. I thoroughly enjoyed art school; imagine every day being allowed to do something you really enjoy.

My husband, John Burningham, has been a very strong influence on me. I learned the rather specialized process of creating picture books—as opposed to fine art—mostly from him. John and I don't work in the same place. We've never worked together. I can think of a lot of people who do actually create books together, but I'm not sure that it would work for us. We certainly ask each other, "What do you think about this drawing?" We consult each other about our work. I hope we help each other.

I met John at art school in London. I used to work in the theater during school holidays, painting scenery, and I thought it would be very nice to learn more about it, become more proficient. So I took a course in theater design at art school, and John was studying illustrations. The more I saw him working on books, the more I thought that I would love to try it myself. When I had my first child, working in the theater became impossible. So I illustrated a children's book, and a publisher accepted it.

Sebastian Walker of Walker Books was the one who first encouraged me in the idea of creating books for very young children. My youngest daughter was a baby at the time, and I found there was almost nothing for her age—except, of course, the excellent board books by Dick Bruna. So when I was looking for board books for Emily, I thought I could perhaps create them myself. Sebastian was very enthusiastic about the idea. I found that the actual process of working on a board book was the same as the process for any picture book. You just simply have to pare down the material for the age group, keep the concepts extremely simple, and make sure that very small children will recognize the objects and situations.

Seeing the finished product is not the best part of doing books. Absolutely not. I can't bear to look at the finished book, because I can't change anything at that point. The best part is when I think I know what I'm doing and I've completed a few drawings. In fact, when I get about a third of the way through, and I feel I'm on my way, then I'm happy. It's like reading a good book—you don't want it to end.

observer of the preschool-age experience. As a parent, Oxenbury noticed a lack of books created specifically for preschoolers and became one of the first author-illustrators to design BOARD BOOKS. These durable volumes—made to fit in little hands and to withstand serious teething—were a hit with toddlers and parents alike, as were the simple pictures with little or no text.

Small domestic events are the subjects of Oxenbury's beloved books and round-faced babies and sturdy toddlers the unassuming stars. The series of wordless books that include *Beach Day* and *Mother's Helper* (both 1982) trace a toddler's daily life, and *I Can, I Hear, I See,* and *I Touch* (all 1986) comprise a series highlighting the objects and actions of the toddler world. Small-sized books such as *The Checkup* and *The Dancing Class* (both 1983) are for children just past the board-book stage who are beginning to venture into the world outside the home.

Oxenbury's popular series about toddler Tom and his companion, a stuffed monkey named Pippo, are presented in a bigger, picture-book format. Titles such as *Tom and Pippo and the Washing Machine* (1988), *Tom and Pippo Go Shopping* (1989), and *Tom and Pippo at the Beach* (1993) follow the stalwart child as he and the monkey brave a number of miniadventures, narrated in the authentic-sounding voice of young Tom. Oxenbury's talent for subtle humor is revealed in the expressions on the toy monkey's face as ever-patient Pippo silently endures the capricious friendship of his preschooler pal.

An award-winning illustrator, Oxenbury garnered Kate Greenaway Medals for her art in EDWARD LEAR's *The Quangle Wangle's Hat* (1969) and MARGARET MAHY's *The Dragon of an Ordinary Family* (1969). *We're Going on a Bear Hunt* (1989), Michael Rosen's version of the well-loved song, is another of Oxenbury's highly acclaimed picture books. In it, her black-and-white sketches alternating with watercolor paintings capture the high spirits of the family setting out on a cross-country search for a bear. The illustrations offer readers a glimpse of the Suffolk countryside, where the artist spent her childhood, and a chance to admire Oxenbury's atmospheric use of landscapes, a skill not usually employed in board books. A picture book for older readers, *The Three Little Wolves and the Big Bad Pig* (1993) by Eugene Trivizas, reverses the roles established in the traditional tale; the amusing text is well matched with Oxenbury's art. One illustration depicts the wolves demurely playing croquet, and when the big bad pig approaches their brick house, the threesome are shown nervously trotting out the back, clutching their beloved china teapot.

Gentle humor and warmth are the hallmarks of this author-illustrator, whose down-to-earth stories provide young children with both amusement and comfort. ❦ J.M.B.

P

Parish, Peggy

American author, 1927–1988. When children first become independent readers, humor is an important ingredient for them, and Peggy Parish is one of the authors to whom they turn. Parish wrote close to fifty books, most of them for beginning readers. Best known for her "Amelia Bedelia" series, Parish also wrote a number of other easy readers, some nonfiction and craft books, and a mystery series for the middle grades.

Amelia Bedelia, that wacky, literal-minded housekeeper, constantly misinterprets instructions in the dozen or so books about her. She sketches the drapes when asked to draw them in *Amelia Bedelia* (1963); she shouts, "Roll. Hey, roll!" as she calls the roll in *Teach Us, Amelia Bedelia* (1977); she uses tea to make tea cakes in *Amelia Bedelia Helps Out* (1979); and when her employers suggest she invite everyone to a party in *Amelia Bedelia's Family Album* (1988), she does just that—she stands in the middle of the street and invites everyone. Parish seems to know exactly what will tickle children as she plays with the ambiguities of the English language.

Parish was born in South Carolina and after college began teaching third-graders, first in Kentucky, then in Oklahoma, and finally in New York City. Her teaching experience provided her with an appreciation of newly independent readers. She says, however, "I don't try to teach anything in my stories—I write just for fun." And most of her books can indeed be described as fun.

She frequently writes of the foibles of adults with childlike qualities. In addition to Amelia Bedelia, she created Granny Guntry, Miss Molly, and Aunt Emma. In the three "Granny Guntry" books, Granny, an independent pioneer woman with a gun that doesn't shoot, appears naïve and helpless. Yet in the end she manages to get just what she wants. Although the story lines are slight, the action and humor provide amusing tales for young readers. Miss Molly is terribly forgetful, so forgetful, in fact, that in *Be Ready at Eight* (1979) she forgets her own birthday. In *The Cats' Burglar* (1983) Aunt Emma's neighbors try to tell her what to do. They insist she has too many cats, but when the cats save her from a burglar, Aunt Emma feels justified in keeping them. Young readers easily identify with these characters and, at the same time, feel in charge as they laugh at the adults' mistakes.

Parish also wrote a mystery series for slightly older children. Jed, Liza, and Bill, the three sleuths, solve family-related mysteries. For example, in *The Key to the Treasure* (1966) Grandpa tells them of an unsolved puzzle left by his grandfather, who was killed in the Civil War. Clues are provided in the form of coded notes, and readers will enjoy matching wits with Jed, Liza, and Bill to figure out the codes. Although some of the situations in the six mysteries are improbable, the action is fast-paced and the three children have enough individual personality to hold the reader's interest.

Throughout her career, Parish felt a strong commitment to encouraging children to read, a commitment clearly reflected in her books. ❧ P.R.

Parker, Nancy Winslow

American illustrator and author, b. 1930. After twenty years of working in public relations for several large corporations, Nancy Winslow Parker left the business world to fulfill a lifelong ambition: In 1973 she began illustrating and writing children's books. *The Man with the Take-Apart Head*, her first book, was published the following year.

Although Parker had no formal artistic training until she attended Mills College in Oakland, California, as a child she felt that she would always be an artist. While her three basic biology books, *Bugs* (1987), *Frogs, Toads, Lizards and Salamanders* (1990), and *Working Frog* (1991), written with Joan R. Wright, are highly popular with elementary school children, they represent only a portion of her work in contemporary children's picture books. Parker's distinctive signature illustrations —bold, stylized, two-dimensional pictures—are often executed in watercolors, colored pencil, and black pen.

The artwork and narratives are infused with humor that, though usually subtle, can at times border on slapstick and is well suited to young readers. Just as humor is a characteristic of Parker's books, so is her meticulous attention to detail. For example, the illustrations of animal and insect specimens in the trio of science books are accurate and realistic, but she retains an inviting tongue-in-cheek humor throughout the texts.

Parker's research and attention to accuracy are also evident in two historical vignettes, *Paul Revere's Ride* (1985), based on HENRY WADSWORTH LONGFELLOW's poem, and *Barbara Frietchie* (1991), John Greenleaf Whittier's tribute to patriot Frietchie's dramatic stand with the Union flag during the Civil War. In these well-designed books, illustration is the unifying, visual background, against which Parker successfully integrates poetry, history, and factual information. These books, documenting science and history, are picture books for children old enough to relate facts to the context of their general knowledge.

Parker has also illustrated and written stories for younger readers. *Love from Uncle Clyde* (1977), *Love from Aunt Betty* (1983), and *The Christmas Camel* (1983) comprise a series of comical, imaginative picture-book fantasies that involve young Charlie, who receives a variety of unusual gifts—a hippopotamus, ingredients for an exploding birthday cake, and a camel—from his delightfully bizarre uncle and aunt.

Parker has illustrated a number of books for other authors, among them EVE RICE's winning story for preschoolers, *Peter's Pockets* (1989), in which a youngster, while on an outing with his uncle, discovers his new pants have no pockets, and so must use his uncle's pockets for the treasures he finds. When he returns home, his mother remedies the situation by sewing him a pocket for every item he has collected. Parker's illustrations comfortably complement the story, as they match the contents of each pocket with other items that appear in pictures throughout the story, providing an intriguing game for the author's youngest readers.

Parker's other titles include *General Store* (1988) by RACHEL FIELD, a cheerful rendering that captures the pleasures of an old-fashioned general store, and *Black Crow, Black Crow* (1990) by Ginger Foglesong Guy, which follows the activities of a mother crow tending her brood. ❧ S.L.

PARKER, ROBERT ANDREW

AMERICAN ILLUSTRATOR, B. 1927. Robert Andrew Parker lives in a Connecticut farmhouse, and the walls of his large barn studio are lined with his art of fifty years. Energetically working on several projects simultaneously, he makes clear that his many passions—travel and hiking, jazz, and family, as well as literature and art—spill over into his diverse creative work, including illustrations for dozens of children's books.

Parker, who was born in New Jersey and has lived in Seattle, St. Louis, and Chicago, began his travels early. Being part of a jazz-loving family, he became a proficient clarinet, sax, and drum player. While recuperating from a childhood illness in New Mexico, he started drawing, mostly Indian battles. His short experience in World War II and his exposure to the powerful war drawings of Otto Dix spurred him to draw more soldiers. Then he trained in art, in painting and printmaking at the Chicago Art Institute and, in New York, at Atelier 17. Influenced by the 1920s Stieglitz school, Charles Demuth, Max Beckmann, and Paul Klee, Parker went on to develop his own color-rich style. Parker was sent by *Fortune* magazine around the world to paint scenes such as Central American fruit plantations. He created art for the 1956 biographical film about Van Gogh, *Lust for Life,* opera sets, and album covers, including one for his favorite jazz musician, Thelonious Monk. He did drawings, lithographs, monoprints, and paintings. His art has been shown in several dozen one-man shows and hangs in many museums and private collections.

Parker still draws with the scribbly, energetic line he used at age ten, though his subject matter has expanded to include grim war scenes, voluptuous women in Vladimir Nabokov stories, portraits, and landscapes. His George Grosz–like distortion, his Emil Nolde–like vivid colors, often gouache or oil, show the influence of German expressionists whom he admired.

Parker has illustrated more than forty children's books, including *The Trees Stand Shining* (1971), a volume of North American Indian POETRY edited by Hettie Jones. He has sensitively illustrated two poetry collections by WILLIAM COLE. He produced accurately detailed ships and planes for *Battle in the Arctic Seas* (1976) by THEODORE TAYLOR. He has won prizes: *Pop Corn and Ma Goodness,* an imaginative story by Edna Mitchell Preston, was a 1970 Caldecott Honor Book; *Liam's Catch,* by Parker's first wife, Dorothy D. Parker, won an American Institute of Graphic Arts 1972 Book Show prize. It is the story of an Irish boy's opportunity to prove himself, watching from a lookout tower for the salmon to run. *The Whistling Skeleton,* Indian tales of the supernatural edited by JOHN BIERHORST, was a 1982 American Library Association Notable Book.

Parker skillfully modulates his style to suit the text.

Sometimes he chooses black-and-white watercolor, as he did for Richard Kennedy's touching tale of a widower sworn off fiddling, *Oliver Hyde's Dishcloth Concert* (1977). Other times he begins dark and moves to warm colors, as in Cynthia De Felice's *The Dancing Skeleton* (1989), in which the stiff, idiosyncratic figures give way to the warm red fiddler furiously playing the parts off the skeleton. In other books Parker's love of music and jazz translates into vibrant rhythms, with Native American braves dancing or swans flying. He has also illustrated with etchings, as in *The Magician's Visit* (1993), a Passover tale retold by Barbara Goldin.

Parker, still drumming, biking, hunting in Ireland, hiking in Nepal, teaching and lecturing, is also actively creating children's books. With his energetic interests and talents as a fine artist, he has produced an exciting body of work for young children. ❦ H.S.N.

Parnall, Peter

American author and illustrator, b. 1936. From the desert Southwest to the coastal Northeast, Peter Parnall's work explores the natural world. With stunning attention to detail, his more than eighty books survey the many complex relationships found in the wild.

Peter Parnall grew up in the Mojave Desert and the Big Bend country of Texas. This vast, open terrain and the wildlife he carefully observed influenced many works, especially those on which he and author Byrd Baylor have collaborated. They shared their talents in seven titles, three of which were Caldecott Honor Books: *The Desert Is Theirs* (1976), *Hawk, I'm Your Brother* (1976), and *The Way to Start a Day* (1978). Together, Parnall and Baylor look beyond the obvious to the quiet, simple beauty of the desert. Ten creatures, from the young jackrabbit to the old tortoise, speak to the reader in *Desert Voices* (1980). Black line drawings are shaded with only enough hints of color to capture the artist's focus. The result creates an interesting visual dichotomy, inviting readers to examine Parnall's chosen subject while reiterating the vastness of nature that often goes unnoticed. Such perspective also appears in the books written and illustrated solely by Parnall. In *Feet* (1988), for example, the youngest readers are invited on a "ground-up" tour of eighteen animals. Big feet, fast feet, thin, wet, and slow feet are the close-up illustrations set against a backdrop of subtle detail. If one looks closely, the rest of the animals to whom the feet belong can be found in Parnall's panoramas.

The influence of years spent on a farm along the rugged Maine coast is evident in a number of Parnall's books. In *Winter Barn* (1986) an ecosystem unto itself slowly evolves as the temperature drops below zero. Carefully, with great reverence and awe, Parnall peeks into every corner to reveal the creatures who have taken refuge. Some, like the horses and mice, are yearlong residents, while others, including a bobcat and porcupines, seek warmth only in winter. While *Winter Barn* provides shelter to a variety of creatures, *Cats from Away* (1989) introduces generations of felines who, at one time or another, lived on Parnall's farm. There is Burl, Ives, Tigger, Cud, Blackie, and Thumbs, to name a few. All come from a place the author refers to as "away," and most stay for a long time.

In addition to his picture books, Parnall is the author of several short-chapter novels, including *Water Pup* (1993). When not working on books for young readers, Parnall pursues a number of other interests—riding, painting, and tending sheep. ❦ B.A.M.

Parrish, Maxfield

American illustrator, 1870–1966. Though the height of Maxfield Parrish's career was nearly one hundred years ago, his celebrated illustrations, with their intense colors and languid surrealism, seem strikingly contemporary. Christened Frederick Parrish by his parents, Parrish took his paternal grandmother's maiden name as his middle name when he began painting professionally, and eventually dropped his given name altogether. Encouraged in his artistic inclinations by his father, whose own artistic leanings had been stifled by a strict Quaker upbringing, Parrish always observed the world around him with an artist's eye. His letters home from the requisite trip abroad are filled with his impressions not only of the great cities he visited but also of the artists working in them and their art. His impatience in those letters with the conservatism of the European art world is an indication of his independence of mind.

While Parrish is best remembered today for his illustrations for children's books, during his lifetime he was renowned as a commercial artist and magazine illustrator. His commissions for commercial goods, the most famous of which was for Crane's Chocolates, brought his name to the attention of the American public. These commissions paved the way for a steady, lucrative income from the sale of color reproductions, and his famous "blue paintings" of the 1920s became common

Illustration by Maxfield Parrish for "Humpty Dumpty" from *Mother Goose in Prose* (1897), by L. Frank Baum.

household items. The first children's book Parrish illustrated was L. Frank Baum's *Mother Goose in Prose* (1897). Its immediate success led to subsequent books, the most famous of which was Eugene Field's *Poems of Childhood* (1904). This is the first book in which Parrish's paintings were reproduced in full color, and it contains the famous illustration of "The Dinkey Bird," which depicts a nude youth on a swing, airborne against a deep blue mountain topped by a white-walled city, characteristic elements in Parrish's work. Prior to illustrating *Poems,* Parrish illustrated editions of *The Golden Age* (1900) and *Dream Days* (1902), nostalgic stories of childhood by Kenneth Grahame, and his pictures for these works have been praised for their ability to capture and refine the mood set by the author. After *Poems,* his next book for children, *The Arabian Nights* (1909), edited by Nora Smith and Kate Douglas Wiggin, incorporated the sweeping architectural elements—magnificent staircases, towering pillars, huge urns—that were to become identified with Parrish's name. *Greek Mythology* and *The Wonder Book* and *Tanglewood Tales* by Nathaniel Hawthorne (1910) contain illustrations Parrish had originally done for *Collier's* magazine. His final book for children was *The Knave of Hearts* (1925), a play by Louise Saunders. Glorious color and formal composition are the keynotes of this work.

In the 1930s, Parrish was able to leave all commissioned work behind him and concentrate on his first love, landscape painting. He did this until arthritis forced him to put down his paintbrush in 1962, at the age of ninety-one. While to the casual observer his illustrations for children's books seem to continue the romantic line of Howard Pyle, with whom he studied, and of N. C. Wyeth, a closer look reveals his witty and unique use of traditional romantic subjects. Parrish uses elements of heroic realism mythic themes, voluminous drapery, vast vistas—and by rendering them in photographic detail in vivid colors, using several different techniques in one picture, he creates a distinctly surrealistic, dreamlike quality. Parrish's style might well be called "heroic surrealism." Parrish referred to his paintings as evoking "realism of impression, realism of mood of the moment, yes, but not realism of things." S.G.K.

Paterson, Katherine

American author, b. 1932. Katherine Paterson's powerful novels unveil humanity's most humble and truthful themes of personal growth. Realistic characters, usually outsiders, gain self-acceptance and the courage to accept everyday existence and its limitations by confronting difficult situations and sacrificing grandiose ideas about their futures. Their newfound self-realizations allow them to continue with their lives in hopeful, if not fully optimistic, anticipation of the future. Readers become passionate about Paterson's characters, accepting them as role models and referring to them as prototypes of literary personalities.

Philosophy and place are important to Paterson's work, evidence of the influence of her own life experience. Born in China to missionary parents, Paterson moved frequently during her childhood. She became a missionary in Japan after teaching for several years and receiving a master's degree in the English Bible. Returning to the United States to accept a fellowship and receive another master's degree, at Union Theological Seminary in New York, she met and married John Paterson. She and her husband, a Presbyterian minister, became parents to four children, two of whom are adopted.

While it is not generally viewed as didactic or proselytizing, Paterson's Christian theology pervades her work: an occasional religious zealot adds flavor to over-

Voices of the Creators

Katherine Paterson

Why do I write for children? This is not an easy question to answer. I don't know why I became a writer at all. I never meant to be a writer. I was already a writer and well past my thirtieth birthday before I realized that a writer was indeed what I wanted to be when I grew up.

I wrote as a child, but I certainly didn't plan to be a writer. I loved books, and I read a great deal, but I never imagined that I might write them. Actually, when I was nine, I had a dual fantasy life in which on some days I was the leader of a group of commandos saving the world from Axis domination, and on others I was the benevolent queen of the United States of America. Of course, I indulged in these grandiose fantasies because I was finding the real world a tough place to inhabit.

I do still have lots of childhood goblins that need exorcising. And now that I have been a parent and a writer as well as a child, I seem always to be on the child's side. But I know that children are not fair. They do not see their teachers and their parents objectively. They only see from their own limited vision. When I write for children, I try not only to be true to a child's point of view but I try as well to give hints that the world is wider than it seems to a child, and that other people may be more complex and even more understanding and compassionate than the child character sees them to be.

For a writer to succeed in this attempt, however, demands the cooperation of a careful and perceptive reader. There are those who think that a writer for children should not ask for this level of wisdom from her readers. Maybe not. But I don't seem able to write in any other way, and I have been very fortunate in the readers who choose my books. A great number of them seem not only willing to dig below the surface, they seem eager to. "I didn't catch on the first time I read it, but when I read it again . . ." is a refrain I hear surprisingly often. And, I must say, it is music to a writer's ears.

Although I became a writer for children more or less accidentally, I soon learned that I had stumbled into what was for me the world's best job—perhaps, as I say to my husband, the only job I will ever be able to keep.

Any freelance writer has the opportunity of choosing her own subjects and her own work methods and schedules, but I, as a writer for children, have an even more enviable situation. I know when I spend a year, two years, or more on a book, that I will be sending it to people who value books. I know that the book I have written will be carefully, even lovingly, edited and copyedited. If a book is to have illustrations, I know that a lot of thought will be given to selecting an appropriate illustrator. Whether the book is illustrated or not, a designer will make sure that its look will be satisfying. I have had books where jacket illustration after jacket illustration was rejected because it didn't reflect what my editor felt was the heart of the story. My publishing houses have known that it takes time for a children's book to find its readers, and they are willing to keep a book in print long enough for that to happen. I have friends who write novels for adults who find their books on a remainder table within less than six months of their original publication.

It's interesting how often people say to me, "Well, of course, your books aren't really for children," and think, thereby, that they have complimented me. Actually, my books are for anyone who is kind enough to read them. The great majority of those readers are, have been, and I profoundly hope will continue to be under the age of fourteen.

I got a letter once from a troubled child who poured out her anguish over her parents' divorce and her own subsequent behavior. "When I read *Gilly Hopkins*," she said, "I realized that you were the only person in the world who could understand how I feel." Poor child, I thought, can anyone understand your pain?

As much as we adults wish to spare children pain and so try to pretend to ourselves that they cannot feel as deeply as we, they do hurt; they do fear; they do grieve. We who care for them must take these feelings seriously.

Why do I write for children? Because I'm practicing. Someday if I keep working at my craft, I may write a book worthy of a child—I may write a book worthy of the readers who have come to my books.

riding themes of compassion, self-acceptance, personal strength in the face of adversity, and unconditional love. And, though some of Paterson's settings are countries on the other side of the globe, she is familiar with most of her locations from firsthand experience. With respect and great care in research, she places her first three stories in eighteenth- and feudal twelfth-century Japan. Primarily noted for their suspense and the writer's craft, these works also contain characters as believable and fully realized as those in her contemporary settings.

The Master Puppeteer (1975), a National Book Award winner, is the most successful of these stories. The plot involves the intricacies of operating a Japanese puppet theater and a main character who discovers the reflection of life in art as he deals with a trying family situation amidst the chaos of civil strife. *The Sign of the Chrysanthemum* (1973) and *Of Nightingales That Weep* (1974), set in medieval Japan, have equally exciting stories. Another historical novel, *Lyddie* (1991), set in early nineteenth-century Lowell, Massachusetts, presents an independent and determined young female character and an eye-opening look at the labor conditions for mill workers, most of whom were women. While many readers enjoy these historical works, a greater number are drawn to Paterson's contemporary novels, which offer more immediately involving issues. Each of Paterson's characters experiences a different process of self-realization, but each story is equally powerful. *Bridge to Terabithia* (1977) recounts both the friendship between a country boy, Jess, and an uprooted city girl, Leslie, and the story of how Jess comes to terms with Leslie's accidental death. In developing their touching friendship, Jess and Leslie invent the special kingdom of Terabithia. When Leslie is killed trying to reach their magical hideaway during a torrential downpour, Jess is overcome with grief and guilt. A realistic portrayal of the healing process shows him eventually accepting this tragedy and moving on by welcoming his younger, sometimes bothersome sister into the private place he had previously shared only with Leslie.

Another character who learns to accept her life is the inimitable Gilly Hopkins. In *The Great Gilly Hopkins* (1978) Paterson provides moments of pure comedy through the manipulations and wisecracks of this sharp-tongued, precocious protagonist who willfully steers her own progression through a series of foster homes, keeping all intimate relationships at bay until the most unlikely character—the overweight, almost illiterate, "religious fanatic" foster mother, Maime Trotter—wins her love. For years, Gilly has fantasized about a reunion with her real mother, the "beautiful" Courtney; yet, when it finally happens, Gilly learns that the flower-child mother who abandoned her still has no intention of staying around. Through Trotter, Gilly begins to realize that life is tough and "all that stuff about happy endings is lies" as she gains the strength to face life with the grandmother she has just met and who has volunteered to be responsible for her.

Like Gilly, Louise Bradshaw in Paterson's Newbery Medal–winning *Jacob Have I Loved* (1980) struggles to find a happy ending. In a serious, sophisticated novel that gets its name from the biblical passage "Jacob have I loved, but Esau have I hated," the self-pitying Louise takes years to overcome feelings of jealousy toward her favored twin sister. In the closing chapter, Louise, in her twenties, serves as a midwife at the birth of twins. After finding herself paying more attention to the weaker, younger child, a reflective Louise comes to a greater understanding of herself, and, finally, her feelings of resentment begin to fade.

Though some readers and critics have questioned the endings of Paterson's books—Leslie's death; Gilly's estrangement from the foster mother she's come to love; the final chapter of Louise's adult reflection—Paterson maintains that she does everything in her power to make the story live for the reader. Speaking of an intended reader, she says, "She may not like how the story ends, but I want her to see that this ending is the inevitable one. I want her to want to keep reading, to wonder with a pounding heart how it will all come out; and then, when she comes to the final page, I want her to say: 'Of course! It had to be. No other ending was possible. Why didn't I realize it all along?'"

In addition to her masterly works of fiction, historical and contemporary, Paterson has written two collections of inspiring essays and speeches on writing books for children. Whatever the genre, Paterson makes all her stories live in the imaginations of her readers. And, laying bare the soul of her characters and revealing truths about the nature of humanity, she gently exacts emotion from even the most stoic reader.

EDEN EDWARDS

Paton Walsh, Jill

British novelist, b. 1937. From the dawn of civilization to the destruction of Earth, Jill Paton Walsh's novels span the course of time. *Toolmaker* (1973) takes place during the Stone Age; *Children of the Fox* (1978), a collection of three novellas, is set in classical Greece; the devastating plague in seventeenth-century England is the historical context for *A Parcel of Patterns* (1983); and *Fireweed* (1969) occurs during World War II. *The Green Book* (1981) explores the world of the future, and Paton Walsh uses contemporary settings for novels such as *Goldengrove* (1972) and its sequel *Unleaving* (1976).

Despite the diversity of settings, all of Paton Walsh's characters must come to grips with the complexities of their world. Whether she writes for middle-grade readers or young adults, her stories deal with complex themes. She says that "there is no such thing as a simple story." The main character of *The Emperor's Winding-Sheet* (1974), for example, a young English boy stranded in Constantinople during the fall of the Byzantine Empire, finds it is no easy task to define good or bad, hero or coward. In *A Chance Child* (1978) a severely abused twentieth-century child travels back in time to find a place for himself—and even peace—in the nineteenth century, despite the horrible conditions experienced by children during the Industrial Revolution. As James, in *Gaffer Samson's Luck* (1984), struggles to be accepted in a new school and town, he must decide whether to keep a good luck charm that seems to stave off death or to take his chances in the world.

The author of more than twenty books for children, Paton Walsh was born in London but spent the Second World War in Cornwall away from the bombing. Her memories of that area provide the setting for *Goldengrove*. She received a degree in English from St. Anne's College, Oxford, and met her husband while she was a student. She taught English at a girls' school until her children were born and then took up writing. Her books have received numerous awards, including the Boston Globe–Horn Book Award for *Unleaving*. Both *Fireweed* and *A Chance Child* were American Library Association Notable Books.

Although Paton Walsh deals with sophisticated themes, her stories are accessible. She says, "I like plot ... and I like simple methods of narration." But for Paton Walsh *simple* does not means *simplistic*. She has a tremendous respect for her readers, and her writing displays richness, sincerity, and warmth. In *Goldengrove*, the poignant coming-of-age story of a young girl, Madge and her brother each live with a different parent after a nasty divorce and see each other only once a year at their grandmother's. When they are together, they just have now, and Paton Walsh uses the present tense to tell their story, thus highlighting the intensity of their visit.

Paton Walsh's historical novels afford young people a look at an earlier time. They are well researched and accurate, but she is not writing to teach. By combining detailed, authentic settings with strong plots and memorable, engaging characters, she creates books that speak not only of a historic time but of the human condition as well. P.R.

Paulsen, Gary

AMERICAN AUTHOR, B. 1939. In Gary Paulsen, young readers craving fast-paced action, harrowing escapes, and near-death experiences have found their savior. But these swift stories, so compelling to hungry readers, only serve as gateways to a literature that extends far beyond the realm of the average adventure novel. Paulsen's rich and powerful prose evokes the sights, sounds, and feelings of a wilderness setting while gently nudging the special issues of adolescence with sensitivity, integrity, and compassion. It is no wonder that his many fans return to his books again and again.

Although his main occupation is writing, Paulsen has at various times been a teacher, field engineer, soldier, actor, director, farmer, rancher, truck driver, trapper, professional archer, migrant farm worker, singer, and sailor. Born in Minneapolis and raised by a grandmother and several aunts, he was shuffled from school to school and met his father for the first time at age seven. Paulsen enjoyed hunting and trapping, but after he tried dogsledding he found he could no longer kill another animal. Dogs taught him about the "ancient and ... beautiful bond" between humans and the natural world. This new passion for dogsledding soon found its way into several books, most notably the autobiographical *Woodsong* (1989). Like the most successful of his books, this documentation of Paulsen's experience running the famed Iditarod has at its core a genuine awe for humanity's dependence on and alliance with the forces of nature.

A tale of strength, courage, and intelligence, Paulsen's acclaimed novel *Hatchet* (1987) has rapidly become one of the most popular adventure stories of all time. Written with the spare, evocative prose that has become the author's signature style, this brief tale documents the struggle of a troubled city boy to survive for two months in the Canadian wilderness, with only a hatchet to aid him. Through his ordeal, Brian Robeson gains an enduring respect for the forces of nature and a greater understanding of himself and those who play important roles in his life. Like many of Paulsen's most successful books, *Hatchet* combines elementary language with a riveting plot to produce a book both comprehensible and enjoyable for those children who frequently equate reading with frustration.

Paulsen's young protagonists are often faced with difficult home environments in which parents are abusive or physically or emotionally absent. The ability of the young hero—usually a boy—to overcome his physical surroundings through some wilderness adventure correlates with a sense of self-development and the ability to understand, if not change, the emotional conflicts in his family. These honest and hopeful portrayals, combined with a low reading level, makes the books ideal for reaching children at risk.

In addition to his young adult novels, Paulsen is also known for his informational books on nature and sports. Using insight gained from experience, Paulsen's nature books often combine fact with personal anecdote to present a highly readable source of information, and they extend his novels' themes by addressing the survival skills of various animals such as moose, elk, buffalo, rabbits, and mice. His books on basketball, hockey, and even hot-air ballooning carefully cover the basics while also providing the little-known facts that are so appealing for children to master and share.

But it is in the fiction category that Paulsen's work has truly been hailed. Several of his novels have been named Newbery Honor books, among them *Dogsong* (1985), *Hatchet* (1987), and *The Winter Room* (1989). In addition to his numerous books for children, Paulsen has written voluminously for adults, and he ranks among the most prolific writers in the nation. ❧ C.C.B.

Pearce, Philippa

BRITISH AUTHOR, B. 1920. Recognized internationally for her complex, classic time FANTASY *Tom's Midnight Garden* (1958), which was awarded the British Library Association's prestigious Carnegie Medal, Philippa Pearce has written a number of novels and short stories that explore the ordinary experiences of memorable, solitary children who are often propelled by intense thoughts and secrets. The most compelling of her child characters is Tom Long from *Tom's Midnight Garden*, who has been sent to spend part of the summer with a distant aunt and uncle. Through two devices, a grandfather clock that strikes thirteen and an old woman's dreams of the past, Pearce connects two worlds: Tom's boring present and a Victorian-age garden. There Tom finds a friend in Hatty, another lonely child who is struggling to make a place for herself in an unsympathetic family following the death of her parents. Suspense builds as Tom nears the end of his summer stay, trying desperately to understand the complexities of time in two worlds.

In *Minnow on the Say* (1955), which was published in the United States as *The Minnow Leads to Treasure*, young David Moss finds a canoe that has floated downriver during a storm. Reluctantly setting out to return it, he meets its owner, Adam Codling, who is determined to recover a legendary family treasure and save an old family home for his elderly aunt. The two boys join forces in what becomes their secret quest. This, Pearce's first novel, won a Carnegie Commendation, as have two of her other books, *The Shadow-Cage and Other Tales of the Supernatural* (1977) and *The Battle of Bubble and Squeak* (1978).

In *A Dog So Small* (1962), Ben Blewitt, the middle child in a family of seven, doesn't receive the real dog that his grandfather promised him as a birthday present. Disappointed, Ben retreats into a fantasy world where "a dog so small you can only see it with your eyes shut" becomes his constant companion. His obsession with the imaginary dog reaches its climax when Ben is hit by a car as he crosses a busy street with his eyes closed. While there is little plot or action, Pearce engages the reader with ordinary family vignettes and recognizably real dialogue.

Protagonist Kate Tranter, in *The Way to Sattin Shore* (1983), cuts school and bicycles many miles alone to find out about her father, who she previously assumed had died on the day she was born. In her quest to unravel the full truth, Kate excludes her only friend and involves her immediate family just when necessary and never with their full understanding. In the end, only her paternal grandmother shares the knowledge of what really happened.

Pearce's rich and precise language was developed and polished during years as a storyteller, scriptwriter, radio producer, and children's book editor. The mill house, garden, and countryside settings along the Say River, so vividly described in her work, hearken back to Pearce's own childhood. In many of her novels, Pearce explores relationships between children and the elderly, often grandparents, and, through Hatty in *Tom's Midnight Garden*, she also explores the relationship between aging and the passage of time. Pearce does not provide readers with exact ages or physical descriptions of her fictional children, choosing rather to concentrate on the inner character of each.

Her short story collections, particularly *Lion at School and Other Stories* (1985), introduce other unique children and add to Pearce's reputation as one of the twentieth century's outstanding children's authors. ❧

G.W.R.

Pearson, Kit

Canadian author, b. 1947. Born and raised in Edmonton and in Vancouver, Kathleen Pearson always wanted to be a writer. She worked as a children's librarian until she attended graduate school in children's literature, where she took writing courses from Nancy Bond and Jane Langton. The experience persuaded her to take a part-time job and devote her energy to writing.

Her first novel, *The Daring Game* (1986), draws on her own experience at a Canadian boarding school. The story focuses on Eliza's adjustment to a new school, her life away from home, and her friendship with the brash, daring Helen. The tale is remarkable for the honesty of the characterization and an old-fashioned sense of story.

Her second novel, *A Handful of Time* (1987), was named Book of the Year for Children by the Canadian Library Association. As in her first novel, the central character is separated from her parents and must struggle with loneliness and find a place for herself away from home. Patricia is sent to stay with relatives for the summer while her parents work out the details of a divorce. She is miserable until she discovers a watch that allows her to travel back in time to the summer when her own mother was twelve years old. There she learns to accept her relatives as individuals and to see her mother as a fragile human being like herself. Time travel provides an exciting framework for the story of a sympathetic girl with very real problems.

The Sky Is Falling (1989) is the first of three novels about Norah and her younger brother, Gavin. In this novel, named Book of the Year for Children by the Canadian Library Association, two children are sent from England to Canada as war guests during World War II. Norah is unhappy, unpleasant, and prone to sulking. The wealthy Ogilvie women grudgingly accept Norah because they want to care for Gavin, delighting in having a little boy to dote on. Norah, bitter and feeling unloved, ignores her brother and causes as much trouble as she can. Like Mary in *The Secret Garden*, Norah, although not likable, wins readers' sympathies because she is trapped by circumstances outside her control. By the end of the novel she makes peace with herself and her host family when they all agree to try and make the best of the less than ideal situation. *Looking at the Moon* (1991) again centers on Norah, who is spending the summer with Ogilvie cousins. Becoming attached to a young man who is afraid to enlist, Norah deepens her understanding of the war. *The Lights Go on Again* (1993) focuses on Gavin, telling his story as the war comes to a close.

Although Pearson's characters are often separated from parents, they are usually surrounded by extended family. Pearson herself grew up with many relatives and writes about the sprawling family she experienced. Pearson's firm sense of place helps ground the reader in her books' real-life locations, such as Toronto. The Canadian cities and countryside are integral parts of her stories, and her characters are aware of their surroundings and gain strength from them.

Pearson's novels have received wide acclaim in Canada and the United States, and she has earned a devoted readership. Her goal was to write the kind of book she herself read as a child, and she has succeeded in writing thoughtful, rich novels, filled with adventure and powerful characters. ❧ M.V.K.

Peck, Richard

American author, b. 1934. Richard Peck is the renaissance man of contemporary young adult literature. Since he wrote *Don't Look and It Won't Hurt,* his first book, in 1972, Peck has been one of the most recognizable names, one of the most dependable writers, and one of the most passionate advocates for teenagers. He has written in almost every genre: *Voices After Midnight* (historical, 1989), *Ghosts I Have Been* (horror, 1977), *Dreamland Lake* (mystery, 1973), *Secrets of the Shopping Mall* (humor, 1979), and books that combine all these elements, such as *The Dreadful Future of Blossom Culp* (1983). Writing in the realistic genre, Peck has tackled some of the toughest problems that teenagers face: suicide, in *Remembering the Good Times* (1985); rape, in *Are You in the House Alone?* (1976); death, in *Close Enough to Touch* (1981); peer pressure, in *Princess Ashley* (1987); single parenting, in *Don't Look and It Won't Hurt* (1972); and family issues, in *Father Figure* (1978).

In addition, Peck has published essays, poetry, adult novels, and short stories. His books are often used in schools, and most have remained in print since they were first published. He is a much-sought-after speaker and logs many miles each year visiting schools and libraries to meet his fans. Peck has also been honored in just about every way possible. His books regularly receive strong reviews and appear on the Young Adult Library Services Association's Best Books for Young Adults list. He received the Margaret A. Edwards Lifetime Achievement Award from *School Library Journal* and the Young Adult Library Services Association of the American Library Association for his body of work; his life and work were detailed in *Presenting Richard Peck* (1989), by Donald Gallo, as part of Twayne's series on young adult authors.

Peck started writing late, not publishing his first novel until he was thirty-seven. Before that he was a teacher, and the influence shows heavily in his work. Peck's books often contain the central message of "think and act independently." In his poem "A Teenager's Prayer,"

Voices of the Creators

Richard Peck

Though it's perfectly possible to be a writer for the young without having been a teacher, it would not have been possible for me. It was as a teacher that I learned to ask the writer's first question, the question that has to be asked before putting pen to paper: "Who are the people who might be willing to read what I might be able to write?" I found those people in my roll book.

They were adolescents and the pubescent—high school and junior high students—the people I knew best and liked best. They had me outnumbered all day long. Their whims took precedence over my needs, and from our first hours together, I knew things about them their parents dare never know.

Entering teaching in 1958, as I did, was the moral equivalent of moving to Rome just ahead of the Visigoths. The world in which we taught, the world we tried to prepare our students for, had less than a decade to run. I was to teach through the greatest watershed in American history, that time when power in our country passed from adults to children. I saw it passing across the desk in my own classroom. The revolutionary young won all their real battles with adults, but not with each other.

A literature was born out of that late 1960s time to question the young about their new freedoms and their ominous options and, not least, about what they were doing to each other. These young adult books were the first that didn't trivialize and sentimentalize being young or coming of age. I quit teaching one afternoon in 1971 and went home to try to write one, after seventh period. But teaching turns out to be a job you never really quit. You just go on and on trying to turn Life into lesson plans.

All novels are about private life, and I found myself writing about young people already possessed of more private life than I have ever known and more time they couldn't structure. After nineteen novels that ask them questions about their choices, I find I'm still mining the material of teaching, returning to classrooms and drawing upon what I'd learned as the only adult in the room.

From teaching came the theme that informs all my books—that you never grow up until you declare your independence from your peers. As a teacher, I'd noticed that nobody ever grows up in a group. People grow up, if at all, one at a time in spite of their peers. More than any parent, I was awed by the unchecked power of the peer group, how the young accept treatment from friends they would label *abuse* if it came from adults. Novels traditionally celebrate the individual. Young adult novels, including mine, became direct encouragements to the individual.

Some of my novels are comedies. A recurring character—heroine—in four books is a spunky little outcast named Blossom Culp, who, being an utter social reject, lives the freest, most interesting life in town. More seriously, *Princess Ashley* is a realistic examination of the teenage peer-group leader in an era when peer groups set the tone for schools. It's harder to grow up now, and my books are homages to those among the young who still see adolescence as a preparation for adulthood and not as a celebration of power already consolidated.

Young adult books were born in response to the collapse of home and school authority. We developed a literature of fathers for the fatherless. One of mine is *Father Figure,* about a boy in the aftermath of divorce who believes he has to play the paternal role for his younger brother. Another is *Unfinished Portrait of Jessica,* about a girl who turns on her mother because her father has left. The letters I get from young readers who see their own situations in print, and alternatives to their own responses, spur me on to more books. Possibly the greatest role a book can play in the lives of young readers is to assure them that they aren't alone.

"It is an act of faith to be a writer in a post-literate world," says the novelist Rita Mae Brown. Maybe it's an irony that a literature for and about the young appeared at just that historic juncture when most of them couldn't read it. But I write in hope that I can encourage a lifelong reading habit among young people who can find themselves in my pages.

he writes: "Give me the understanding that nobody ever grows up in a group so I may find my own way." Although the plots of his novels vary widely, this theme informs every book. All his characters face the challenge of trying to grow up. With wit, compassion, an ear for true dialogue, an insight into the adolescent heart, and an easy-to-read writing style, Peck writes novels that help teenagers in that difficult task. ❧ P.J.

Peet, Bill

AMERICAN AUTHOR AND ILLUSTRATOR, B. 1915. Ask any child from age five to eight about his or her favorite authors, and it is very likely that Bill Peet will make the list—with good reason. The creator of whimsical fantasies featuring a bevy of lifelike and lovable creatures, Peet has consistently produced the rare combination of excellent storytelling with appealing, enduring illustrations for over thirty years.

Born in Grandview, Indiana, William Bartlett Peed (later changed to Peet) nurtured his childhood drawing talent and graduated from the John Herron Art Institute in Indianapolis. Left to find employment in the midst of the Depression, he worked briefly at a greeting-card company before heading west to California, where he was recruited by WALT DISNEY as a sketch artist and continuity illustrator. Although he considered the position temporary, Peet remained with Disney for twenty-seven years, eventually becoming a screenwriter. His work helped produce such beloved films as *Fantasia, Sleeping Beauty, Alice in Wonderland, Peter Pan,* and *101 Dalmations.* With this background and a great lack of recognition, it is no surprise that Peet went on to create his own stories for children. After several years of rejection, his first book, *Hubert's Hair-Raising Adventure,* was published in 1959. This tale of a haughty lion who accidentally loses his mane would be the first of a long chain of successful books combining sketchy, cartoon-like illustrations in full color, engaging animal characters, and fast-paced stories of fantastical adventures delivered with warmth and laugh-out-loud hilarity.

Illustration by Bill Peet from his book *The Wump World* (1970).

Often compared to DR. SEUSS for his whimsical creatures and fablelike tales, Peet is known for his concise writing style, clever verse, and individualistic illustrations of animals and anthropomorphic machines. Working primarily with pen-and-ink and crayon, he creates humorous and highly expressive characters with a down-home flavor. Wide eyes, furrowed brows, and open mouths on animals and humans capture moments of near catastrophe that evolve into the high-intensity adventure and sheer fun bursting from every colorful page. Although his tales are always humorous and usually nonsensical, Peet does not sacrifice integrity and warmth, and his characters' plights often involve some universal difficulty such as fear, loneliness, or self-doubt, which they are able to overcome in a satisfactory manner. Stories featuring endearing characters that are either logical (a lion with "cage" fright, as in *Randy's Dandy Lions* [1964]) or loony (a pig whose spots resemble a world map, as in *Chester the Worldly Pig* [1965]) cannot help but draw the reader's attention and hold it straight to the conclusion.

Peet is one of the few authors working today who can successfully address current world issues for young children, using humor to keep plots fresh and ease didacticism. In *Farewell to Shady Glade,* published in 1966 but still more than relevant today, he tackles the issue of urbanization from the point of view of a small band of meadow animals repeatedly uprooted by the great earthmoving machines that continue to pursue them. In contrast, *The Wump World* (1970) is an allegorical world of verdant pastures that is suddenly invaded by a band of intergalactic polluters who have destroyed their own planet and need a new one to ravage. These books, and others, are recommended by teachers and librarians as a means of introducing important, difficult concepts to young children.

Peet has thoroughly documented his life in his autobiography for children, *Bill Peet: An Autobiography.* Featuring an inviting, down-to-earth writing style and lavish black-and-white illustrations on every page, this

Voices of the Creators

Bill Peet

Looking back on those early days in Indianapolis, I realize that it was as good a place as any for a boy to spend his childhood. Until I was twelve we lived near the edge of the city, no more than a half-hour hike from the open countryside, with its small rivers and creeks that went winding through the rolling hills and wooded ravines. On Saturdays and all during the summer my two brothers and I along with the neighborhood boys would organize safaris to explore this region.

One of the most memorable experiences of early childhood was a trip to my grandfather's farm in southern Indiana. It was the first train trip for me and my two brothers, something of a treat in itself. Not that it was at all eventful. The old two-car train clickety-clacked along through a hilly landscape of barns and haystacks dotted with horses, cows, and pigs, past small towns, over rivers and creeks, and through forests. Since I was fond of the farm country, it was a great pleasure to see it all pass by in rapid review, and so conveniently. A fine show to the very last scene, which was the railway station in the historic town of Vincennes. There we were met by our grandfather in his dusty old touring car, and we were off again, bouncing along for the last thirty-five miles on rambling dirt roads that were forever doubling back and forth all over the county.

Drawing had been my main hobby from the time I was old enough to wield a crayon, and I drew just about anything that came to mind, all sorts of animals (including dragons), trains, fire engines, racing cars, airplanes, gladiators, pioneers fighting Indians, World War I battles, Revolutionary War battles, football games, and prizefights.

Then at some point during high school it occurred to me that drawing was something I couldn't possibly give up, and somehow it must be turned into a profession. And upon graduation, to clinch matters, I was awarded a scholarship to the John Herron Art Institute there in Indianapolis where I studied drawing, painting, and design for the next three years. Outside of school in my spare time and during vacations I continued to sketch and paint. The subject matter of these pictures was usually the farm, the circus, the slums and shantytowns along the railroad, zoo animals, and a variety of quaint old characters.

A number of these pictures received prizes, which was greatly encouraging, but after leaving school I realized I would have to do something else. I had met Margaret in art school, and we were planning to be married as soon as I could figure out a way to make a living. When I learned that Disney needed artists in the movie industry out in California, I headed west. There I became a sketch artist, laying out screen stories with a continuity of drawings, and as soon as the job began to show promise, Margaret and I were married.

When our two sons, Bill and Steve, were very young I would make up a bedtime story for them almost every night. With so much storytelling practice I began to think in terms of writing and as the years passed contributed more and more ideas to the motion picture stories. Finally I became a screenwriter, still illustrating the continuity. After all, I couldn't possibly give up the drawing habit. As a hobby I began to experiment with ideas for children's books. Once the first one was published it became more than a hobby; it grew into a second career. And just in time too. By then my bedtime-story audience had grown up. Now Margaret is my best audience, and her interest and encouragement have been most important to the books.

So my early ambition to illustrate animal stories was finally realized, and a little bit more, since I had never considered writing one. This way I can write about things I like to draw, which makes it more fun than work. And I still carry a small tablet around with me and sneak a drawing into it now and then.

volume has been sought after by fans of all ages since its publication in 1989 and serves as an excellent example of the caliber and style of his work as a whole. With humor, compassion, and an innate knowledge of just what details are important, Peet's life story is as fascinating as any fiction—a story that established him once and for all as not just the creator of characters, but a grand teller of tales. C.C.B.

Perkins, Lucy Fitch

American author, 1865–1937. In *The Eskimo Twins* (1922), Meni and Monnie, Eskimo twins out coasting in the spring snow with their dogs, are frightened by a bear, and their quick summoning of hunters wins them praise and a part in the village feast. This skillful, realistic tale full of information about seal hunting, building igloos, and daily life is one of a popular series of twin books by Lucy Fitch Perkins. Her pattern for this series, which sold more than two million copies, was established in *The Dutch Twins* in 1911. Here, the adventures of five-year-old Kit and Kat are lively and humorous, and the author includes information about canals, windmills, wooden shoes, and Dutch country customs. In each of Perkins's twenty-six books the protagonists are twins, boy/girl in all cases except the Spanish male twins. The style is fresh and playful, having been tested by a group of young critics whom Perkins called her "poison squad." The books, which take place in twenty different countries, range from encounters with a mischief-making Norwegian goblin to a kidnapping by Italian Gypsies.

Lucy Fitch was born in rural Indiana. With her four sisters, she was educated at home by her parents, both former teachers. In an atmosphere of hard work, thrift, and Puritan respect for learning, she excelled. She also loved drawing, so after her family moved back to their ancestral home outside Boston, she studied art at the Museum of Fine Arts. She went on to illustrate for the Prang Educational Company and then to teach at Brooklyn's Pratt Institute. Fitch married an architect, Dwight Heald Perkins, who respected her talent and built her a studio in the house, so that while raising their two children she could continue to illustrate. Her literary break came after a publisher friend who saw her Dutch drawings suggested she create her own book. She brought him sketches, and the series was launched.

Two experiences strongly motivated her work: a visit to Ellis Island, where she was moved by the number and diversity of the "oppressed and depressed" newcomers to the United States, and visits in the Chicago schools, where children of as many as twenty-seven different nationalities were being taught. Perkins became convinced that through her stories she could help children appreciate and respect how life is lived all over the world and that she could make interesting and graspable to children problems of injustice and suffering in the past.

Perkins published from the early 1900s, starting with illustrations for other authors, to 1937, when after her death her last book was completed by her daughter. Some of her work now seems old-fashioned, sometimes even offensive (for example, *The Pickaninny Twins*, 1931). Her information, gathered not from firsthand travel but from interviews and reading, tended toward clichés, but the soft pencil drawings are still expressive, and the stories are essentially lively. Though she wouldn't have considered herself a feminist, Perkins did have her girl twins share in most of the adventures and often voice frustration with the feminine role.

Through her stories, Perkins expressed her beliefs that big and important issues can be grasped by children, and in order to achieve world peace we must have mutual understanding and respect for the diversity of peoples. These messages are alive today, and many of Perkins's books are still in print. ❧ H.S.N.

Perrault, Charles

French author, 1628–1703. The fairy tales written by the French aristocrat Charles Perrault have become such a part of our cultural lexicon that to consider him the "author" of such tales as "The Sleeping Beauty," "Little Red Riding-Hood," or "Cinderella" would seem almost on a par with naming the "author" of the Old Testament. The tales, first published in 1697, are by now an integral part of our collective childhood. Nearly every adult brought up in Western Europe and the United States has heard of one or more of the eight tales; they are, in addition to the three above, "Tom Thumb" (or "Hop O' My Thumb"), "Bluebeard," "Puss in Boots," "The Fairies" (or "Diamonds and Toads"), and "Ricky of the Tuft."

Certainly, Perrault did not make up out of whole cloth the tales that bear his name. Prior to writing down the tales in *Histoires et contes du temps passé, avec des Moralités,* he had heard them from nurses, parents, and other storytellers or had read versions of the tales himself, perhaps in such works as the Italian Renaissance *Pentamerone* by Giambattista Basile. The book came to be known as *Les Contes de ma mère l'Oye,* in recognition of its sources in the traditional tales associated with Mother Goose, a personification of a village storyteller. The literary structure of the tales—the repetition, for instance, in "Little Red Riding-Hood" ("My, what big eyes you have, Grandmother!") or the gifts bestowed by the fairies on Sleeping Beauty, accomplishments prized by members of the court of Louis XIV—are all Perrault's own invention. It is in these embellishments that Perrault made the leap from collecting folklore to writing what has been termed the first "true literature for children." Prior to his collection of elegant fairy tales, most books written for children were intended solely to instruct, in keeping with the prevailing attitude that the primary value of children was as the adults they would become. The glorification of childhood for itself and the celebration of children for their innocence and proximity to nature and to God were ideas not fully realized until the Victorian era, a good hundred or so

Illustration by Gustave Doré for "Little Red Riding Hood" from *Perrault's Fairy Tales* (1921; originally *Les Contes de Perrault, dessins par Gustave Doré,* 1867), translated by A. E. Johnson.

years away. Perrault's voice was a unique and prophetic one in children's literature.

Surely he sought to inculcate his young audience with moral character; thus, his stories always see evil punished and virtue rewarded, and each tale is completed by a moral in verse. "Bluebeard," one of the best known, emphasizes the danger to young girls of succumbing to the blandishments of men. But any reader of the stories can see that Perrault's primary goal was to entertain. For example, the moral tacked on to "Puss in Boots"—that native cunning is better than inherited wealth—is completely irrelevant to the rollicking trickster humor of the tale. Perrault did write one tale, "The Princess," that carried heavy moral weight, but it is rarely retold. The true value of Perrault's contribution was not his moral instruction but his literary vision. S.G.K.

PETERSHAM, MAUD
PETERSHAM, MISKA

MAUD: AMERICAN AUTHOR AND ILLUSTRATOR, 1889–1971; MISKA: AMERICAN AUTHOR AND ILLUSTRATOR, 1888–1960. The Caldecott Award–winning husband-and-wife team of Maud and Miska Petersham left a tremendous legacy to children through their distinguished books, which influenced the development of illustrated books for children in America. For more than thirty years, from the 1920s to the 1950s, they produced colorful, lively, sometimes tender, sometimes humorous PICTURE BOOKS that have charmed, delighted, entertained, and instructed several generations of young readers.

Maud Sylvia Fuller, a minister's daughter, grew up nourished by Bible stories, a parsonage life, and visits to her Quaker grandfather. After graduating from Vassar, she spent a year at art school in New York, where she met her future husband and lifelong collaborator. Miska Petersham, born Petrezselyem Mikaly, had left his native Hungary after graduation from the Budapest Academy of Art, immigrated to the United States in 1912, and become a naturalized citizen in "a country that I had dreamed of but never thought could really exist." After their marriage Miska left commercial art, and the couple devoted themselves entirely to children's books.

The Petershams' attractive illustrations for children's reading texts made them leaders in that field during the twenties. At this time and throughout their career, they also illustrated trade books written by others. *Poppy Seed Cakes* (1924) by Margery Clark was a milestone for them and for children's books. A charming story for early readers with an Old World setting and flavor, it was illustrated in the colorful peasant style that came to be recognized as pure Petersham, and its decorative borders and endpapers showed their feeling for good book design.

Miki (1929) was the first book the Petershams both illustrated and wrote, the first big colored picture book printed in the United States, and the first of a tide of picture books set in a foreign land. It was written for their six-year-old son and portrayed an imaginary trip to the land of his forebears. The Petershams visited Hungary in preparation for the book, and their passion for travel and the portrayal of authentic detail also led them to Palestine for *The Christ Child* (1931), the story of the Nativity as told by Matthew and Luke, which was illustrated in glowing watercolors that were reproduced in Germany. The use of watercolors represented a break from their customary use of lithography and resulted in what has been called "one of the most beautiful books for children ever made." *The Christ Child* is still in print. *Get-a-Way and Hary Janos* (1933) was illustrated in bright colors alternating with the grayed tones and shading in which Miska excelled. In this original story with great child appeal, toys from the Petershams' own collection were used as models.

The lavishly colored, detailed illustrations for the Petershams' series of informational storybooks, written between 1933 and 1939, set a new standard in nonfiction for children. A group of Old Testament tales rounded out their group of Bible stories. In the forties and fifties the Petershams celebrated America's heritage in a number of books, including *An American ABC* (1941), a Caldecott Honor Book, and *The Rooster Crows: A Book of American Rhymes and Jingles*, which was awarded the Caldecott Medal in 1946 in the patriotic atmosphere prevalent during and after World War II.

The Petershams' weakness was in portraying the human face, whether it was strong-featured or doll-like. Two rhymes and their accompanying pictures of blacks were eliminated from the fourteenth printing of *The Rooster Crows* because they were considered offensive stereotypes. Two of their last books, *The Box with Red Wheels* (1949) and *The Circus Baby* (1950), continue to charm the youngest readers and listeners.

The Petershams' art and writing were infused with their backgrounds, their deep convictions and feelings, and their life together. Their joy, their sense of fun, their buoyant optimism, their respect for children and for all of life, and their response to beauty are reflected in all their work. As Maud Petersham herself said in an interview, "Anyone who knows our books knows us." ❧ S.L.R.

Peyton, K. M.

English author, b. 1929. Having written from the time she was "physically able to push a pen," Kathleen Wendy Herald Peyton (her nom de plume contains an "M" for her husband, Michael, with whom she collaborated on some of her earlier books) published her first book at age fifteen and has continued to delight young adult readers ever since. Drawing on her own experiences and interests, she has written about fishing and sailing in *Sea Fever* (1963; originally published as *Windfall*, 1962) and *The Maplin Bird* (1964), horses in *Fly-by-Night* (1968), *The Team* (1975), and the "Flambards" series, music in *The Beethoven Medal* (1971), and art in *A Pattern of Roses* (1972).

Peyton was born in Birmingham and attended art school before marrying and raising two children. She has skillfully illustrated some of her stories herself. An award-winning and prolific author, Peyton officially began her career in 1962 with the publication of *Windfall* (*Sea Fever*). She earned the Carnegie Medal in 1970 for *The Edge of the Cloud* and the Guardian Award for the Flambards Trilogy the same year. The dramatic "Flam-

Jacket illustration by K. M. Peyton for her book *Fly-By-Night* (1969).

bards" books later became a popular British television series. Peyton's superb writing has earned her a devoted audience. With each new title readers find the hallmarks of excellence that they have come to expect: a solid, involving story; fully realized characters who are sympathetic, yet complex; thoroughly believable plots and dialogue; an energetic narrative style that manages to capture both action and introspection; a wry sense of humor; historical accuracy; and striking descriptions that successfully evoke the setting of each story.

The reader who steps into Peyton's fictional world is warmly welcomed into a family of characters, events, and places. Many of her stories use relationships and characters from previous works, revealing new and interesting angles. For instance, Patrick Pennington, the handsome, long-haired rebel hero of *Pennington's Last Term* (1971; originally published as *Pennington's Seventeenth Summer,* 1970), meets and marries Ruth Hollis, the anxious but determined heroine of *Fly-by-Night,* in *The Beethoven Medal,* and both characters appear significantly in *Falling Angel* (1983; originally published as *Marion's Angels,* 1979). This skillful interweaving of characters creates a distinctive and cohesive body of work that offers a thoughtful and insightful commentary on love, devotion, work, art, and independence. Peyton's heroines are particularly notable—spirited, determined, brave, and strong. Her heroes are cut from similar cloth, although they tend to be rebels and outsiders, in one sense or another, struggling with the very definition of hero. Many of her main characters choose an unconventional or unexpected path—the surly Pennington, featured in a series of books, is drawn to classical music, Tim in *A Pattern of Roses* abandons his parents' bourgeois plans and takes up a humbler trade, Christina in *Flambards* (1967) defies social conventions. Peyton's historical fiction offers a wonderful opportunity to experience an earlier era. The "Flambards" series is set in a great manor house in 1901. *The Right-Hand Man* (1977) tells the tale of a dashing young eighteenth-century coachman, and *A Pattern of Roses,* considered by many one of Peyton's finest works, is a time-travel fantasy that contrasts modern and Edwardian England.

In these books, as well as in her contemporary stories, Peyton astutely conveys the social and class issues that are an integral part of British history and culture. Above all, Peyton's novels are passionate. She has an unerring ability to capture the inner workings of her characters, who resonate with emotion and conviction. Their adventures, combined with a stirring blend of romance and action, offer a memorable tour of English life, as invigorating as a strong cup of tea. ❦ C.J.

Phipson, Joan

Australian writer, b. 1912. Although Joan Phipson wrote her first few books to satisfy the child within her, most of her novels evolved from one particular theme that possessed her. It is, as she once described it, "man's relationship with the earth he lives on and with the universe about him." She would, she further stated, go on writing until that particular idea left her in peace. Since she wrote what she claimed to be her last novel, *Bianca,* in 1990, she must finally have been released from her bond. But quite a legacy resulted from that possession.

Phipson was born to English parents near Sydney, Australia, and had quite an active childhood, geographically at least. She was christened in England, started school in India, switched to an English one, and attended her third in Australia. This was typical of her entire childhood and young adult years. But these many years spent traveling in the company of adults provided solitude and plenty of time for reading. Finally, in about 1937, the shifting between England and Australia came to an end and she settled herself, more or less, in New South Wales. Before marrying Colin Fitzhardinge in 1944, she worked in an array of jobs, including librarian, secretary, radio copywriter, and even Women's Auxiliary Air Force telegraphist. After her son and daughter were born, she turned her hand to writing. And then she tried it only out of "sheer boredom." But when her first book, *Good Luck to the Rider,* published in 1953, won the Australian Children's Book Council Book of the Year Award, the success—and also her interest in the realistic fiction genre—gave her the impetus to continue. After that she wrote fairly prolifically, producing over twenty wide-ranging titles for children and young adults. While her first few titles seemed to establish her as a writer of realistic family stories set in the Australian outback, she also became known for books that contrasted, in one way or another, city and country. Her books generally create a strong sense of community and a feeling, too, for the individual's need for acceptance. *Peter and Butch* (1969), for instance, deals with manliness, and *The Grannie Season* (1985) addresses more questions of stereotyping, as Phipson relates the story of a boy and his cricket-playing grandmother. Her writing ranges from short, simple texts to longer, far more complex works that delve into psychological recesses. In *The Watcher in the Garden* (1982), Catherine and Terry's commitment to a garden helps them to move from anger to peace, while *The Way Home* (1973) concerns the mystical journey of a trio of children following a car accident. Phipson is also known for finely crafted tension, such as in the survival story *Keep Calm* (1976), in which Sydney is paralyzed, and in the suspenseful *Hit and Run* (1985), concerning a chase between a policeman and a boy running from an accident. Many of her books have been translated into other languages, and a number have received widespread critical acclaim. *The Family Conspiracy* was the winner of the 1963 Australian CBC Book of the Year Award, and *The Watcher in the Garden* earned Phipson a diploma from the International Board on Books for Young People in 1984. In all corners of the world her novels continue to introduce young readers to the Australian outback and its people. ❧ K.J.

Photography in Nonfiction for Children

The science of photography is one of several photographic trends enhancing informational literature for children in the late twentieth century. Two parallel developments have been the growth and refinement of documentary work by particular photographers specializing in the creation of children's books and greatly improved scholarship incorporating photographs as part of the historical record. The skills of both photographers and historians offer children abundant exposure to beauty and information through photographic images.

Many factors affect the integrity of photography as information and illustration in children's books. At the same time that beautifully designed books effectively integrating text and photographs have become much more abundant, other formats either make very cursory use of photographs or exploit the dramatic capabilities of pictures to command attention. Some books are little more than albums, each page featuring a photograph accompanied by text that is little more than caption. Books dominated by text may include a clutch or two of pictures gathered together somewhere in the book; here the photographs are not integral but only an accompaniment. A popular format choice has become the large slim volume with pages liberally scattered with assorted pictures, often photographic images without background or context. Depending on intelligent selection and format design, such books can be visually exciting or cluttered and confusing.

Distinctive photography in children's nonfiction began to flourish in the 1960s, and through the following decades many skilled photographers have developed a personal body of work either in collaboration with writers or in illustrating books they have also written. George Ancona, who has photographed a great variety of subjects, demonstrates mature skill in selecting and framing his subjects as well as in use of the camera in his striking volume *Pablo Remembers: The Fiesta of the Day of the Dead* (1993). Bianca Lavies, whose handsome photographs chronicle the behavior and life cycles of animals, concludes each of her books with a page describing her experience photographing the featured animal. In *A Gathering of Garter Snakes* (1993) Lavies is photographed lying at the entrance of limestone pits with numerous small snakes slithering over her—a view sure to intrigue children. The work of wildlife photographers is featured in Jim Brandenburg's *To the Top of the World: Adventures with Arctic Wolves* (1993), an autobiographical account of the adventure, logistics, and artistry of photographing wild animals in their natural habitat. Similarly, writer KATHRYN LASKY and photographer Christopher G. Knight document the work of Jack Swedbord through the seasons and in varied locations in *Think Like an Eagle: At Work with a Wildlife Photographer* (1992).

A trend toward deepened scholarship in books dealing with social phenomena and historical events has led authors to a more systematic and perceptive gathering of photographic material from archival sources. Such photographs are often integral to the information developed in these books. Russell Freedman, in *The Wright Brothers* (1991), offers a masterly melding of visual material and text, incorporating photographs made by Orville and Wilbur Wright as well as other fine photographs that recorded their experiments in flight. Many other writers make astute use of selected photographs to illuminate their subject matter, but Freedman's books have achieved a very high standard. A pair of books by journalists Edward Wakin and Daniel Wakin offer an interesting lesson in the role of photographs in affecting as well as recording history. The two volumes of *Photos That Made U.S. History* (1993) feature fourteen photographs, each accompanied by text describing the event, the picture, its effect, and the photographer. The selected pictures powerfully evoke awe and even horror as they present places and events "from the Civil War to the atomic age" and "from the cold war to the space age."

Early uses of photography in book illustration treated this medium as a valued art form. Photographs in children's books, however, have generally been viewed as documentary material and accorded less stature than the "artistic" forms of illustration. More recently, a small number of photographers have been recognized for the high degree of artistry they achieve through the creative use of film and camera. KEN ROBBINS hand-tints photographs to create softened images and evocative lighting in numerous slim volumes. *Bridges* (1991), for example, presents vaguely surrealistic views of particular structures; each bridge becomes timeless in appearance, a beautiful example of a principle in bridge building. The photographer's creative technique is unusually successful in establishing mood and in communicating essential qualities of the subject; these are truly expressive pictures.

Of all photographers illustrating children's books, TANA HOBAN is undoubtedly the most admired and emulated for her virtuosity in creating photographic images. She is exceptional both in her camera skill and in her imaginative presentation of pictures. Her early black-and-white volumes—*Look Again* (1971) and *Count and See* (1972), for example—challenge children to consider new views of familiar items. In turning to color photography Hoban became interested in isolating a central image from its background. Brightly colored objects stand out in purity against the white page in a wide variety of concept books, including small BOARD BOOKS for the very young. The images are at once bold and subtle, reflecting unusual skill and insight in the use of light. Objects gleam with their own light, cast the barest suggestion of shadow, or are highlighted in interesting ways. *Of Colors and Things* (1989) provides sumptuous examples of the technique.

Bold photographic techniques offer marvelous viewing opportunities in children's nonfiction science books of the 1990s. Imagine geysers of ice shooting up through the surface of Triton, the largest moon of the planet Neptune, three billion miles from Earth. In *Voyager to the Planets* (1991) astronomer Necia Apfel describes some of the photographic processes by which the probing of *Voyager 2* has expanded our understanding of the cosmic world. SEYMOUR SIMON's handsome books on planets—*Jupiter* (1985), *Uranus* (1987), and others—aptly demonstrate the magnificent views transmitted by planetary probes. In *Seeing Earth from Space* (1990) PATRICIA LAUBER explains how space technology creates revealing images of the geological and meteorological conditions on Earth. Weather patterns, fossil locations, pollution damage, and the effect of volcanic eruptions and earthquakes are among the many subjects captured for easy viewing in a wide variety of photographically illustrated science books.

As cameras, assisted by telescopes, rockets, computers, and other marvels of technology, have pictured the reaches of outer space, so have they joined with microscopes and lasers to journey inward to the very smallest recesses of life. Though the techniques were already well established at the time, the 1978 book *Small Worlds Close Up* by Lisa Grillone and Joseph Gennaro was fresh and creative in its dramatic views of familiar items. Continuing development of microscopy has greatly refined the imagery of photographs, and "close-up" views are now routinely incorporated in books on many scientific subjects. Cellular activity in plants and animals, insect metamorphosis, the structure of feathers, and many other objects and phenomena are seen in amazing detail. When time-lapse photography is used along with the microscope, it is possible to follow such processes as the growth of plants, the drying wings of a newly emerging butterfly, or the stages of embryonic growth of various creatures.

Added techniques such as x-ray and infrared photography and computer-assisted scans used in medicine allow fantastic explorations of that most fascinating subject, the human body. Lennart Nilsson's photographs in a number of books, including his own *How Was I Born?* (1975) and Sheila Kitzinger's *Being Born* (1986), never cease to amaze in their almost ethereal quality and their store of information about the human fetus. The beauty and clarity of these pictures, however, have given way in more recent books to quite different views of human anatomy. Sandra Markle presents many magnified and color-enhanced views in her book *Outside and Inside You* (1991). The magnified photographs usually have the appearance of living—if rather unrecognizable—tissue. The color-enhanced images have an unreal quality even when the organs are at least vaguely recognizable. The narrative in this well-crafted book illuminates the images, but other books move so far into the realm of computer enhancement that the alleged photographic images cease to be recognizable.

An increasing number of books attempt to explain photographic technology itself. VICKI COBB's *Fun & Games: Stories Science Photos Tell* (1991) explains the new understanding of sports and other recreational pastimes made possible through special photographic techniques. Multiple-exposure strobe photos follow the path of a gymnast's center of gravity; thermography reveals the heat buildup in different shoes; and an oscilloscope makes visible the sounds of two musical tones. The text fails to explain the images adequately, however, leaving the reader with questions about both the photographic and the scientific processes depicted. Such displays of photographic methods continue to have the aura of magic tricks, of technological sleight of hand.

Another book that more successfully uses an unusual technique and explains the photographic process is Barbara Embury's *The Dream Is Alive* (1990), in which photographs shot in 65-millimeter film as part of a movie to be shown in IMAX theaters depict the life of astronauts aboard a space shuttle. The well-worn topic of space travel here takes on an interesting new look. The images are not dramatically different from the multitude of pictures most readers have seen previously, but a subtle shift in perspective has occurred through the exceptional breadth and depth of the images captured by this method. The pictures, while not exactly three-dimensional, wrap around the interior of the space vehicle in a comprehensive way that offers the viewer a greater sense of immediacy and involvement in the scene. Embury incorporates an explanation of why the IMAX camera was aboard the shuttle and how the process works into the larger, well-developed presentation on current work in space exploration.

Though photographs have become by far the most prevalent mode of illustrating children's nonfiction, photography has received only cursory attention in the critical literature related to children's books. Despite the popularity of photography since its invention in the 1830s and the power of photographic images, photographic illustration has not earned its due recognition as a potent factor in conveying and shaping ideas and information. Yet a critical approach is necessary. Using the newer technologies, photographers assemble unfamiliar images that challenge the viewer's understanding. More conventional images may be exciting, manipulative, or poorly made. The growing number of books that explain photography and the work of photographers are particularly welcome as photographic material becomes an ever more varied, and in some respects dominant, component of nonfiction. ❧

MARGARET BUSH

Picture Books

In 1658, Comenius, a Moravian bishop and educator, produced what is considered the first picture book for children, *Orbis Sensualium Pictus* (Visible world). If today he could survey a well-stocked children's library, he would likely be bemused if not overwhelmed by the seemingly limitless choices available. Comenius's objective in adding illustrations to an informational text—for such was the *Orbis Pictus*—was "to stir up the attention . . . by sport, and a merry pastime." Today, nonfiction is only one of many genres formatted as picture books. These varied types can be loosely organized into at least five categories:

The "pure" or "true" picture book with little or no text: Most ALPHABET books, COUNTING books, or concept books fit into this category.

The wordless book with no text: These tell a story or impart information through a sequential arrangement of carefully designed illustrations.

The picture storybook and the picture INFORMATION BOOK: In these books the illustrations are as integral to the content as the text.

The illustrated book: This category includes most books for beginning readers; these may have more text than pictures, but the pictures offer important interpretations of characters and situations, or, in the case of information books, extend or explain the factual material presented in the text; sometimes, the pictures may be simply decorative.

Toy and movable books (pop-up, lift-the-flap, pull-tabs, and so on): Although usually designed for the very young, elements of these may be used, particularly in information books, for older readers. Their effectiveness depends on the quality of the paper engineering and the relationship between form and content.

Within each division are many variations. Some books with pictures span more than one category; that is, a concept book may also be a picture story; an alphabet book may provide information beyond letter and word identification; a folktale or poem may be designed in picture-story format; a movable or toy book may also be a story or information book.

Although there are remarkable achievements within these varied configurations, citations of the picture book as a unique art form usually refer to the exceptional combination of text and pictures found in the picture storybook. Alphabet, counting, or concept books may be acclaimed for graphic elegance, originality of execution, pedagogical applications—or all three—but in general, sequence and frequently even the text itself are predetermined. Spectacular results can be achieved despite the restrictions of these formats: Consider MITSUMASA ANNO's pyrotechnical display of seemingly three-dimensional shapes in *Anno's Alphabet* (1975) or TOM FEELINGS's sculptured African figures in *Moja Means One: Swahili Counting Book* (1971) by Muriel Feelings. They are not, however, picture storybooks. And when the text is substantial, as in Margaret Musgrove's *Ashanti to Zulu* (1976), illustrated by LEO and DIANE DILLON, the concept picture book moves toward the illustrated-book category.

The wordless story—such as RAYMOND BRIGGS's *Snowman* (1978), remarkable for an almost ethereal blending of reality and fantasy—can be a tour de force for the illustrator, but the text changes with the interpretation of each "reader." While the "storyline" may remain constant, the text does not. Toy and movable books may depend too heavily on kinesthetic effects, although a few author-illustrators, like ERIC CARLE in *The Very Hungry Caterpillar* (1969), have successfully made the manipulation of physical form into an integral story element.

Folktales and FANTASY, like the alphabet, are set pieces for interpretation. Consequently, they can sometimes pose problems when translated into the picture-book format. Most are illustrated stories in that the text can be read independently of the pictures. In many books, such as *Hansel and Gretel* (1984) retold by Rika Lesser and illustrated by PAUL ZELINSKY, the art adds new dimension to familiar materials. Sometimes, however, one wonders, particularly when yet another version of an old favorite appears, just how deep is that "cauldron of story" to which folklorists refer. Tales may be newly translated, as some are; they may be heavily edited, as some are; but the success of the folktale as picture-storybook text relies on the illustrator's and reteller's sense of pacing and editing so that the illustrations, like the voice of the true storyteller, offer a fresh, authentic interpretation rather than mere embellishment.

Original fantasy sets yet another trap. Adapting a text to the picture-storybook format may eradicate phrases that convey a distinct authorial tone; HANS CHRISTIAN ANDERSEN is particularly susceptible to such well-meaning but unfortunate efforts. Then there is MOTHER GOOSE, who has survived any number of attempts to adapt her unquenchable vivacity to showcase an illustrator's talents.

Despite its complex evolution, the history of the picture storybook is not very long. The idea of using pictures to complement instruction was devised by Comenius, but the concept of extending the meaning of the text beyond literal visualization belongs to the great nineteenth-century illustrator RANDOLPH CALDECOTT (1846–1886). Exemplified in his transformation of "Hey Diddle Diddle" (1882) into a story of star-crossed lovers, the interdependence of text and pictures is a fundamental element in the picture storybook. Marked by economy of line and a genuine sense of humor, Caldecott's illustrations are yardsticks against which others are measured. The printer Edmund Evans (1826–1905) also deserves mention for his pioneering work in the field of color printing, ensuring not only the beauty of Caldecott's work but also that of WALTER CRANE (1845–1915) and KATE GREENAWAY (1846–1901), both of whom had an enduring influence on children's book illustration. Crane envisioned text and illustrations as "an harmonious whole." Greenaway popularized the appealing view of childhood as quaint, charming, and unsullied. Later influential illustrators included LESLIE BROOKE (1862–1940) and the incomparable BEATRIX POTTER (1866–1943). Sized to fit children's small hands, Potter's books have texts so well composed that they could stand alone, but the accompanying meticulously executed illustrations drawn to the perspective of a small animal—or small child—add invaluable details that place the stories in particular seasons and locales. Like Caldecott, she set a high standard for the art of the picture storybook.

Until the late 1920s, the United States tended to celebrate the aesthetics of English or continental picture books as its standard. In addition to books by Brooke, Caldecott, Crane, Greenaway, and Potter, the work of French illustrator MAURICE BOUTET DE MONVEL (1851–1913), notably his *Jeanne d'Arc* (1896), beautifully printed and exquisitely composed, also exerted a strong influence on the formation of critical opinion.

Two other important English contributions to the art of the picture book were provided by WILLIAM NICHOLSON (1872–1949). Nicholson's use of strong graphic elements in the *Square Book of Animals* (1899), with a text by Arthur Waugh, was reflected in the design of C. B. FALLS's *ABC* (1923), acclaimed as a significant accomplishment in American publishing for children. Even more important, perhaps, was Nicholson's devising of the "running text" for *Clever Bill* (1926), which completed the transformation of the illustrated story into the picture storybook. An important element in the overall design of these books, the term "running text" describes the division of sentences or paragraphs into short, precise units, which, when placed with interpretive illustrations, create a sense of movement and anticipation. Innately dynamic, this technique impels the reader to turn the pages.

By 1930, the conventions of the picture storybook had evolved: interdependence of words and pictures, expansion of text in pictures, precise text placed not as captions but as an integral element, and the concept of the book as a total design from casing to endpapers. For approximately thirty-five years, most illustrators attempted to codify the form, exploring its possibilities even as they adapted the conventions to their individual styles.

Some of the artists who became popular in the decades between 1930 and 1960 had emigrated from Europe to the United States: LUDWIG BEMELMANS, ROGER DUVOISIN, FEODOR ROJANKOVSKY, and TOMI UNGERER. All brought new visions and styles to picture-book aesthetics, adding an international flair to American publishing. Others, like ROBERT MCCLOSKEY and GLEN ROUNDS, were more firmly grounded in American traditions. In contrast, WANDA GÁG, although born in the United States, drew upon the old-country customs of her immigrant family for inspiration. Still a classic, her *Millions of Cats* (1928) combined a memorable text with peasantlike illustrations in describing the adventures of the old man who, seeking a cat to keep himself and his wife company, encountered "Hundreds of cats, / Thousands of cats, / Millions and billions and trillions of cats." In black and white, not color, *Millions of Cats* has delighted millions of children. Its popularity confounds those who maintain that only a compelling palette guarantees success.

Similarly, ROBERT LAWSON's black-and-white illustrations for MUNRO LEAF's *Story of Ferdinand* (1936) —very different in style from Gág's—have also endured, despite efforts in the thirties to squelch the book for what was perceived to be subversive pacifism. Ten years later, in December 1946, Jella Lepman, founder of the International Board of Books for Young People, would distribute thousands of cheaply produced copies to the children of war-ravaged Berlin.

Ferdinand also represented the felicitous blending of two talents, writer Leaf and illustrator Lawson. While such collaborations are not uncommon, many classic American picture storybooks from the first half of the century were conceived and executed individually: just a few examples are *And to Think that I Saw It on Mulberry Street* (1937) by DR. SEUSS, *Andy and the Lion* (1938) by JAMES DAUGHERTY, *Mike Mulligan and His Steam Shovel* (1939) by VIRGINIA LEE BURTON, *Make Way for Ducklings* (1941) by ROBERT MCCLOSKEY, and *In the Forest* (1944) by MARIE HALL ETS. Of writers who worked with illustrators, MARGARET WISE BROWN, "the laureate of the nursery," was particularly fortunate in the varied talents of the artists with whom she worked, including LEONARD WEISGARD for *The Noisy Book* (1939) and JEAN CHARLOT for *A Child's Good Night Book* (1943). RUTH KRAUSS was similarly successful in her collaboration with, among others, CROCKETT JOHNSON for *The Carrot Seed* (1945) and MAURICE SENDAK for *A Hole Is to Dig* (1952).

As picture books became a significant part of American publishing for children in the pre-1960s era, trends were established that would be further developed in the post-1960s decades. The nursery books of Margaret Wise Brown would find reflection in the deceptively simple BOARD BOOKS of ROSEMARY WELLS, featuring the long-suffering but always triumphant rabbit hero Max, who made his debut in 1979. Photography as illustration, anticipated in the forties and fifties by Ylla, would find greater artistic expression in the work of TANA HOBAN. The wildly improbable cartoon visions of Dr. Seuss and the quirky talents of GENE ZION and MARGARET BLOY GRAHAM in *Dear Garbage Man* (1957) paved the way for such *New Yorker* artists as WILLIAM STEIG and JAMES STEVENSON. But, for the most part, the years from 1930 to the 1960s seem more continuum than revolution.

Then, in 1963, *Where the Wild Things Are* was published. In 1964, its creator, Maurice Sendak, received the Caldecott Medal. Perhaps it was content more than execution that made the book so much of a milestone and initially so controversial. The format is the cumulative expression of picture storybook conventions: pictures expanding text in the Caldecott tradition; the horizontal format and running text used by Nicholson; and quality of design and reproduction that would have pleased the nineteenth-century printer Evans. It is perhaps as close to the perfect picture storybook as an imperfect world allows. Then why the fuss? Perhaps because the vision of childhood presented is neither idealized nor nostalgic. When Max, the independent protagonist, tells his admonishing mother that he hates her, his imagination transforms his room into a wilderness and then populates it with monsterlike wild things over whom he comes to exert total command.

Whatever its magic, one fact is indisputable. With the publication of *Wild Things*, the modern era in children's books began. The picture storybook had received its ultimate codification. After 1963, coinciding with societal and technological change, would come a period of expansion, exploration, and sometimes exploitation, as seductively elaborate art would overwhelm story or distract readers from weak texts. A number of Sendak wannabes would produce variations on his theme or style.

As for Sendak, he continued to exemplify the trends of the late twentieth century in two additional picture storybooks that form a trilogy with *Wild Things*: *In the Night Kitchen* (1970) and *Outside Over There* (1981). While all explore children's psyches, each is different in style. *Wild Things*, with its use of cross-hatching, recalls nineteenth-century engraving; *Night Kitchen* employs images from twentieth-century popular culture—films and comics; *Outside Over There* is more painterly. Together they demonstrate three current approaches to children's book illustration: traditional draftsmanship, contemporary references, and fine art. Given technological advances, illustrators can now be less concerned with the strictures of the printing process. The result is a dazzling array of techniques: from the stylized graphics of GERALD MCDERMOTT to the intricate collages of JEANNIE BAKER; from the surrealistic perspectives of

CHRIS VAN ALLSBURG to the exquisitely rendered illustrations of BARBARA COONEY.

Should there be doubt that the picture storybook is a unique art form, one has only to examine such books as TOMIE DEPAOLA's *Charlie Needs a Cloak* (1974), a seamless blend of information and story, or *The Snowy Day* by EZRA JACK KEATS (1962), with its poetic simplicity, for reassurance. While no art form can remain blindly constant to conventions without becoming static, various critics have expressed concern about a tendency to celebrate showmanship over substance. Although many styles, techniques, and subjects are possible, the picture book works within a framework defined by form, function, and audience. In the last years of the twentieth century, we may be in danger of confusing gilt with gold when we should perhaps be asking whether or not the emperor is wearing clothes. ❧ MARY MEHLMAN BURNS

PIENKOWSKI, JAN

POLISH-BORN ENGLISH ILLUSTRATOR AND AUTHOR, B. 1936. From a childhood spent moving to different parts of Poland, then to Austria, Italy, and finally England, Jan Pienkowski remembers primarily visual images. The frost patterns on the windowpanes of his family's house in western Poland and the perversely beautiful fires set during the 1944 German assault on Warsaw: These memories manifest the designer's instinct in his many books for children.

An ambivalent classics major but avid poster maker at King's College, Cambridge, Pienkowski's pluck and artistic promise landed him a job in the art department of a London advertising agency upon graduation. A disdain for the structure of office jobs led him to work that much harder and succeed enormously as a freelance designer, which in turn led him to draw for the BBC children's program "Watch!" and team with Helen Nicoll, the show's director, to create the "Meg and Mog" series of picture books. Beginning with *Meg and Mog* in 1972, these stories about a scraggly witch and her cat — sometimes fat and sleepy, sometimes thin and supercharged—establish the Pienkowski illustrative trademarks. Electric colors provide the background and fill the interior of deceptively simple, bold line drawings. Meg the witch, like other Pienkowski figures, is a glorified doodle, with dot eyes, a line mouth, a ragged triangle dress, and chaotic lines of hair. The placement of text often corresponds visually with the activity at hand—the words descending the stairs along with Meg, for example—joining the illustrations to create a self-contained, whimsical world. Pienkowski's style of illustration has made him a natural success at concept books.

Numbers, Colors, Sizes, and *Shapes* (all published in 1973) and other titles entice and teach the very young with saturated colors and basic, clearly defined shapes. Another technique with which he has made a name for himself is the silhouette. He began working with silhouettes when he discovered they allowed him to universalize his characters—to let his readers, whatever their race, imagine themselves into the pictures. The products of this discovery won him the Kate Greenaway Medal in 1972 for *The Kingdom Under the Sea,* a collection of Eastern European fairy tales adapted by JOAN AIKEN, an author with whom he has collaborated on numerous books. Spidery and intricate, Pienkowski's fairyland scenes nevertheless exhibit his characteristic energy and sense of whimsy. In 1979 his energy ran wild to stupendous effect in his first pop-up book, *Haunted House.* This ghostly jamboree features not one but several spooky goings-on to a page, including the sound—generated by the opening and closing of the book—of someone or something sawing its way out of a crate. *Haunted House* won him another Kate Greenaway Medal, and successors like *Robot* (1981), a futuristic postcard from space, and *Dinnertime* (1981), less busy than the first two but just as flamboyant, solidified his reputation for revitalizing the pop-up genre, the accomplishment for which he is best known in America. ❧ C.M.H.

PIERCE, MEREDITH ANN

AMERICAN AUTHOR, B. 1958. Meredith Ann Pierce wrote her first novel at the age of twenty-three, inspired by Carl Jung's account of a patient's fantasy of life on the moon. *The Darkangel* (1982), a gothic tale of vampires and gargoyles with elements of "Beauty and the Beast" mixed in, drew rave reviews and several children's book awards. A tightly paced, highly original FANTASY, it is the first volume in The Darkangel Trilogy. The three books detail the efforts of the slave girl Ariel first to save the glacially beautiful Prince Irrylath from his vampire curse and ultimately to save her entire world. The themes of compassion and determination that thread through all of Pierce's work are seeded in *The Darkangel.* The book's heroine moves from fear of her vampire captor through pity for his cursed entrapment and finally to love for the man he was and could become again, if Ariel can complete her mythic tasks in time. Pierce's work, with its strong female hero and feminist themes, stands out in a genre that is traditionally macho and swashbuckling. Without being didactic or scholarly, Pierce manages in *Darkangel,* as well as in the succeeding books in the trilogy—*A Gathering of Gargoyles* (1984) and *The Pearl of the Soul of the World* (1990)—to weave ancient feminine myths into a dramatic and satisfying tale. The author herself says that what links her characters is their "refusal to subscribe to the philosophy of inevitability, of placidly accepting whatever fate sends. Instead, they maneuver within circumstances to face down the odds, determine their own fate."

These elements, as well as the central role of a strong female hero, appear again in Pierce's second fantasy series, The Firebringer Trilogy, a tale of a clan of horses in an anthropomorphic alternate world, which Pierce has begun with *Birth of the Firebringer* (1985) and *Darkmoon* (1991). In *The Woman Who Loved Reindeer* (1985), a single-volume story, Pierce explores her interest in man's essential kinship with animals in a tale of a warrior queen inspired partly, the author says, by a Native American figure named Woman Chief, who became a leader of the Crow tribe. In her only picture-book text, *Where the Wild Geese Go* (1988), Pierce does not have the scope she needs to develop her strengths, and this is her least satisfying work.

Prolific and inventive, Pierce has staked out her own territory in the young adult fantasy field. While the exact extent of her contribution remains to be seen, she has already made a name for herself with her fresh voice and inherently feminist point of view. ❧ S.G.K.

PINKNEY, JERRY

AMERICAN ILLUSTRATOR, B. 1939. Born in Philadelphia, Jerry Pinkney drew constantly and was recognized as a talented child in school. His parents encouraged him to pursue his talent. As a boy of about twelve, he sold newspapers at a stand, and because he was drawing between sales, he was noticed by a cartoonist, John Liney, who showed him some of the tools of his trade and became one of several mentors. The high school Pinkney attended had a commercial art program, and one of his teachers had a sign-painting business, so Pinkney was able to spend some after-school time gaining experience in several artistic skills. He won a scholarship to the Philadelphia Museum College of Art, where he studied for a number of years and where his technique was at odds with the abstract expressionism his teachers admired. He states that the artists who influenced him were Thomas Eakins, Charles White, ARTHUR RACKHAM, and Alan E. Cober.

A few years later, a designer led him to a job at a greeting-card company, where he pursued his interest in the use of typography with illustration. He then became an illustrator-designer for a design studio and illustrated his first book, *The Adventures of Spider: A West African Folk Tale,* which was published in 1964. Pinkney later described the sensation of opening that book for the first time and knowing then that creating books was what he wanted to do. In an extensive biographical article in *The Horn Book,* Pinkney has extolled the marriage of art and design, emphasizing that text and art should work together on a page. He says, "The book represents the ultimate in graphics." The pacing of narrative, the design, the drawing, and the typography are crucial elements.

He continued to illustrate a succession of folktales. When he illustrated *Kasho and the Twin Flutes* (1973), however, he states that he began to "deal with getting some kind of emotion and more action in my figures instead of the people just being part of the composition." He began to take photographs of models reacting to one another, in order to record the movement between them. He illustrated MILDRED TAYLOR's 1975 novel, *Song of the Trees,* the first in her well-known books about the Logan family, using his own family as models. As he built up a body of work that included many African and African American characters, he realized that he "had something to contribute, especially in portraying black people." His realistic drawings of Cassie Logan and her family are synonymous with segregation for a generation of young readers.

His illustrations for *The Patchwork Quilt* (1985), a warm story of the members of an extended family who construct a quilt together, won a 1986 Coretta Scott King Award. He won the award again the next year for *Half a Moon and One Whole Star* (1986). In 1987 he illustrated *The Tales of Uncle Remus,* in which JULIUS LESTER retold the JOEL CHANDLER HARRIS collection of folktales. Two more volumes of the highly acclaimed stories were published with his illustrations. *Mirandy and Brother Wind* (1988), a 1989 Caldecott Honor Book and a winner of the 1989 Coretta Scott King Award for illustration, celebrates African American culture in a picture book based on a cakewalk dance contest in the 1900s.

Pinkney says he likes to put a lot of information in his artwork. For this reason, research is important to him. In addition to his books for children, he has illustrated many limited-edition books of classic literature and has

Voices of the Creators

Jerry Pinkney

I grew up in a small house in Philadelphia. One of six children, with two older brothers and one older sister, I was the middle child. I started drawing as far back as I can remember, at the age of four or five. My brothers drew, and in a way I was mimicking them. I found I enjoyed the act of putting marks on paper. It also gave me a way of creating my own space and quiet time, a way of expressing myself.

I attended an all-black elementary school. Because of the difficulty African American teachers had finding employment, Hill Elementary School attracted the best. I left there prepared and with a sense of who I was.

In first grade I had the opportunity to draw a large picture of a fire engine on the blackboard. When the drawing was finished, I was complimented and encouraged to draw more. The attention felt good, and I wanted more. I was not a terrific reader or an adept speller in my growing-up years. Drawing helped me feel good about myself.

My mother and father both supported me. My mother had a sixth sense about me and encouraged me to pursue my dreams. My dad was apprehensive about my pursuing art, but he was responsible for finding and enrolling me in after-school art classes.

There were mentors throughout my life. At age twelve I had a newspaper stand and would take a drawing pad to work with me, sketching people as they waited for a bus or trolley. John Liney, at that time the cartoonist of "Little Henry," would pass the newsstand on his way to his studio. He took notice of my drawing and invited me to visit his studio. There I learned about the possibility of making a living creating pictures. What an eye opener! I visited John's studio often, and we became friends.

Roosevelt Junior High was an integrated school. I had many friends, white and black, at a time when there was little social mixing in school. At Roosevelt the spark for my curiosity about people was lit. This interest and fascination with people of different cultures appears throughout my work.

My formal art training started at Dobbins Vocational High School, where I majored in commercial art. There I met my first African American artist and educator, Sam Brown. Upon graduation I received a scholarship to the Philadelphia Museum College of Art, where I studied in advertising and design.

When I left school, I freelanced in typography and hand lettering. In 1960 I had the opportunity to go to Boston and work for Rust Craft Greeting Cards. Along with my wife, Gloria Jean, and our first child, I moved to Boston. Boston provided good opportunities for me, because it was a publishing center. I was there at a time during which publishers were reconstructing their ideas about textbooks. The late 1960s and early 1970s brought about an awareness of the need for African American writers. Publishers sought out African American illustrators for this work. And there I was.

From the very beginning of my career in illustrating books, research has been important. I do as much as possible on a given subject, whether it has anything directly to do with the project or not, so that I live the experience and have a vision of the people and the places. To capture a sense of realism for characters in my work, I use models that resemble as much as possible the people I want to portray. Gloria has been assisting me in finding the models. We keep a closet full of old clothes to dress up the models, and I have people act out the story. I take photos to aid me in better understanding body language and facial expressions. Once I have that photo as reference, I have freedom, because the more you know the more you can be inventive.

In illustrating stories about animals, as with people, research is important. I keep a large reference file and have over a hundred books on nature and animals. The first step in envisioning a creature is for me to pretend to be that particular animal. I think about its size and the sounds it makes, how it moves, where it lives. When the stories call for anthropomorphic animals, I've used Polaroid photographs of myself posing as the animal characters.

Recently, I have been concentrating on doing books about people of color. As an African American artist doing black subject matter, I try to portray a sense of celebration, of self-respect and resilience, and also a sense of dignity.

It still amazes me how much the projects I have illustrated have given back to me—the personal as well as the artistic satisfaction. They have given me the opportunity to use my imagination to draw, to paint, and to travel through the voices of the characters in the stories—and above all else, to touch children.

created commemorative stamps for the U.S. Postal Service. He has had many one-man shows and has been a speaker at colleges, universities, and museums. He is also associate professor of art at the University of Delaware and enjoys encouraging young artists. ❦ S.H.H.

Pinkwater, Daniel

AMERICAN AUTHOR AND ILLUSTRATOR, B. 1941. Daniel Manus Pinkwater has created numerous weird and whimsical stories that play upon the absurdity of reality. His books derive from an imagination that allows for such fantasies as a 266-pound chicken running loose and a blue moose helping in a kitchen. Yet children do not have to consider the logic of the story; they simply let go and follow "the fantastic Mr. Pinkwater," as he has been called.

Born in Memphis, Tennessee, Pinkwater grew up in Chicago and Los Angeles. At Bard College, he studied sculpture; later he moved to New York to pursue a career in fine arts. Currently, Pinkwater's humorous commentaries can be heard on National Public Radio's "All Things Considered."

It was only after a trip to Africa that Pinkwater decided to illustrate a story—and he hasn't stopped since. His books embrace the ridiculous and rollick in the pleasure of it. Pinkwater's simple, cartoonlike illustrations have often been described as resembling children's art, yet his energetic lines effectively complement the droll and quirky text. Critics of his books accuse Pinkwater of relying on the absurd instead of creating a coherent plot. Others just don't appreciate his humor and desperately search for logic. When the stories are at their best, however, these concerns drop away, and their jocularity carries them to ludicrous new heights. In *Blue Moose* (1975) Pinkwater shares a bizarre yet engaging tale of friendship between a chef and a moose. *The Hoboken Chicken Emergency* (1977) is a tall tale about Henrietta, a tall chicken, and Arthur, a little boy. Frightened by a dog, Henrietta runs loose in Hoboken; the loony adventure subsides with the affirmation of Arthur's love for his chicken. *Roger's Umbrella* (1982) explores the pure silliness of things as Pinkwater details the familiar foibles, illustrated by JAMES MARSHALL, of an untamed umbrella. In *Pickle Creature* (1979) a bumpy green being who savors raisins meets the tender Conrad in a supermarket and follows him home. This endearing tale wonderfully contrasts the apparently dull supermarket with the mysterious surprise within.

Two delightful insights into young boys' imaginations occur in *I Was a Second Grade Werewolf* (1983) and *Wempires* (1991). When Lawrence Talbot becomes a werewolf, he expects to see some changes in his life, but much to his dismay, nobody notices. Similar surprises occur when the young vampire discovers that real vampires, called "wempires," like to drink ginger ale instead of blood. *Guys from Space* (1989) relates the day's events as the young protagonists blast off to another planet. Like wempires, the guys from space enjoy such simple pleasures as root beer floats. The more realistic *Author's Day* (1993) presents the visit of a famous children's author to an enthusiastic classroom. Unfortunately, the excited children confuse Bramwell Wink-Porter with another author. Surely Pinkwater's fans would get it right, for he has captivated many with his straightforward text, odd sense of humor, and equally amusing illustrations.

Pinkwater's gang of offbeat characters and preposterous occurrences blend nicely with commonplace settings, forcing the reader to question reality—and then to laugh at it. ❦ C.H.

Poetry

The nonsense verse of the nineteenth century could be considered the beginnings of modern children's poetry. Prior to that, poetry written for children had been entirely religious, moralistic, or didactic in nature. Reacting to the hidebound conventions of the Victorian era, the zestful wordplay and subversive wit of writers like EDWARD LEAR and LEWIS CARROLL caught the attention of children, and the influence of these writers has carried over into the twentieth century. For much of the early part of the century, however, the poet whose work was most admired by critics was WALTER DE LA MARE. Although his poetry is not as widely known as it once was, it still has the power to move readers. *Peacock Pie,* first published in 1917, was reissued in 1989; his incomparable anthology, *Come Hither,* which contains more than five hundred traditional poems accompanied by his own insightful comments, was reissued in 1990.

The work of a handful of other children's poets from the first half of the century still appears in anthologies today. Harry Behn is chiefly remembered for his brief, deceptively simple verses that communicate his sense of wonder about the world. His contemporaries Aileen Fisher and Lilian Moore, who were also writing nature poems, continue to write verse. *Adam Mouse's Book of Poems* (1992) is a fine introduction for younger children

Illustration by JAMES MARSHALL from *Miss Nelson Is Missing!* (1977), by Harry Allard.

Illustration by Beatrix Potter from her book *The Tale of Squirrel Nutkin* (1903).

Illustration by ARTHUR RACKHAM from *Alice's Adventures in Wonderland* (1907), by Lewis Carroll.

Illustration by MAURICE SENDAK from his book *Where the Wild Things Are* (1963).

Illustration by MARC SIMONT from *Many Moons* (1943), by James Thurber.

Illustration by WILLIAM STEIG from his book *Doctor De Soto* (1982).

Illustration by Tomi Ungerer from his book *The Beast of Monsieur Racine* (1971).

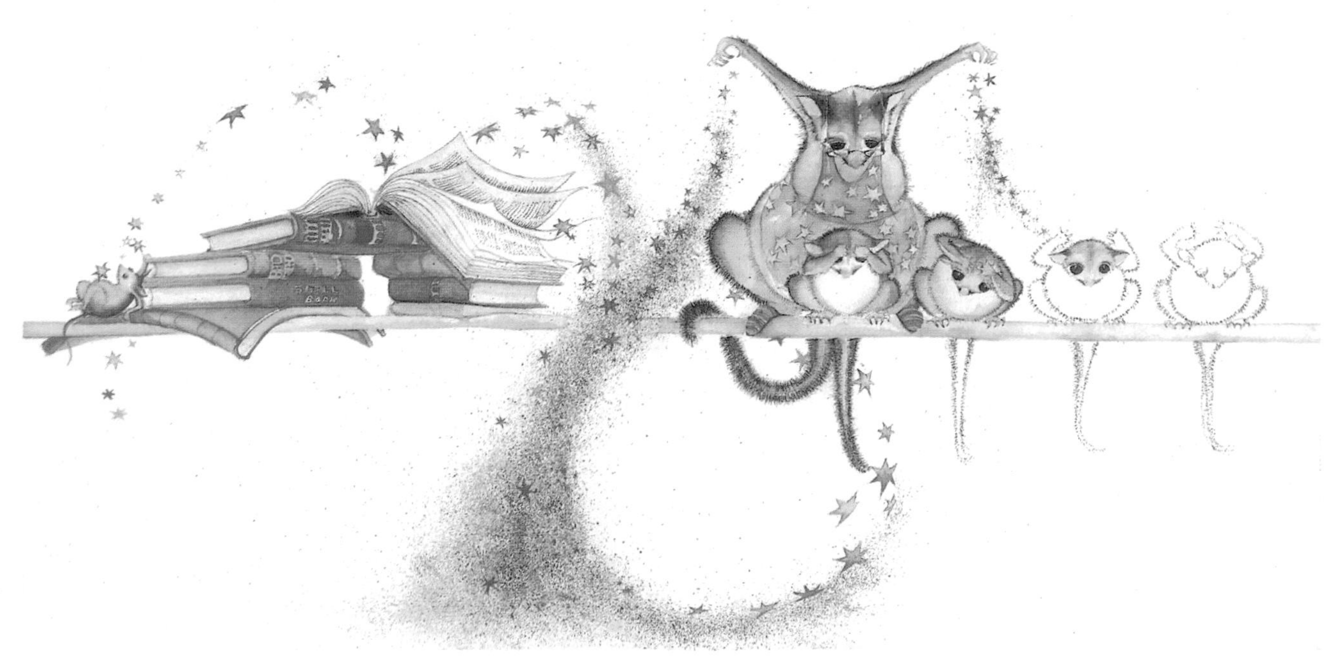

Illustration by Julie Vivas from *Possum Magic* (1983), by Mem Fox.

Illustration by N. C. WYETH from *Treasure Island* (1911), by Robert Louis Stevenson.

Illustration by MARGOT ZEMACH from *Duffy and the Devil* (1973), retold by Harve Zemach.

to Lilian Moore's perfectly tuned lyric lines, where "Fireflies / Flash / Their cold glow" ("Fireflies") and a cricket makes "music / far into the / middle / of the soft summer / night" ("Fiddler"). The mid-century children's poet whose body of work surpasses all others, however, is DAVID MCCORD. The playful spontaneity that permeates his writing keeps it fresh. "Pickety Fence," with its inventive rhythms and sound effects, is a favorite with children. A prolific writer, McCord has published hundreds of poems that vary widely in theme, subject matter, and emotional range. His first book of verse for children was *Far and Few* (1952). *All Small* (1986) is a collection made from the poet's previous books of appealing shorter poems.

During the sixties, American poets began to explore new subjects, ones they felt drew a more accurate picture of their own time. Issues of war and peace, social injustice and racial prejudice, technology and urban life were addressed in children's poetry for the first time. They also began experimenting with new forms, such as free verse, concrete poetry, and the use of dialect. In *Poems to Solve* (1966) and *More Poems to Solve* (1971), May Swenson constructed clever riddle poems, visual patterns, and word puzzles. A new edition, which includes many selections from her previous books, has recently been published under the title *The Complete Poems to Solve* (1993). Another poet who adroitly manipulates free verse forms is EVE MERRIAM. In *Finding a Poem* (1970) she comments wryly on modern technology and modern humanity. The concluding essay detailing the process of writing a poem offers some revealing insights into the creative process.

Also well regarded for his verbal craftsmanship, JOHN CIARDI has experimented with controlled vocabulary designed for beginning readers. *I Met a Man* (1961) and *You Read to Me, and I'll Read to You* (1962), with their humorous easy-to-read riddles, make deft use of internal rhymes and puns. Along with Ciardi, DENNIS LEE reintroduced some of the nonsense to poetry that had lost favor in the early part of the century. In *Alligator Pie* (1974) and *Garbage Delight* (1978) he adopts the speech patterns of children to create verses full of high-spirited energy, catchy rhymes, and repetitive phrasing. Another poet whose dancing rhythms and humorous twists and turns of phrase have attracted children is N. M. Bodecker. The playfulness of *Hurry, Hurry, Mary Dear! and Other Nonsense Poems* (1976) is reinforced by his black-and-white drawings. *Water Pennies and Other Poems* (1991), published posthumously and illustrated by ERIK BLEGVAD, is a whimsical reverie on insects and other small creatures and contains some of the poet's finest lyric verses.

As the subject matter of children's poetry expanded in the 1960s to include a wider world, a new awareness of the country's cultural diversity led to the publication of a greater number of African American poets. One of the first books of poetry to describe the experience of urban African American children was Gwendolyn Brooks's *Bronzeville Boys and Girls* (1956), which adhered to standard language and poetic forms as it described young children in an essentially middle-class environment. The distinctive patterns of idiomatic black speech expressing a wider range of experience and emotions were heard in *Don't You Turn Back* (1969), a collection of poems by LANGSTON HUGHES that are accessible to children. That same year saw the publication of *Hold Fast to Dreams*, an anthology compiled by ARNA BONTEMPS, a distinguished poet in his own right. ARNOLD ADOFF is another important anthologizer of poetry for and about African Americans. ELOISE GREENFIELD's *Honey, I Love and other Love Poems* (1978) reflects a child's love for her family and for life around her. Such poems as "Keepsake" and "Aunt Roberta" are profound in their unadorned emotional expression. In the later volumes *Nathaniel Talking* (1989) and *Night on Neighborhood Street* (1991), both illustrated by Jan Spivey Gilchrist, Greenfield again displays a wealth of emotions and scenes from African American life in poetry that is realistic yet full of the nurturing spirit of community.

Voices from other cultures are being heard in increasing numbers as well. GARY SOTO's writings reflect the Latino experience in California. An example of the poetic sensibility of American Indians is found in the collection of prayers, lullabies, chants, and songs gathered by Hettie Jones in a fine book, *The Trees Stand Shining*. First published in 1971, it was reissued in 1993. JAMES BERRY's poems ring with the mellifluous cadences of the Caribbean.

Another positive development that grew out of the freedom of the sixties was the flowering of lyric poetry in free verse form as poets searched for new and natural ways to express their thoughts and feelings. KARLA KUSKIN, intent on breaking down formalities, frequently illustrates her books with her own line drawings. In *Near the Window Tree* (1975), her brief, imaginative poems are accompanied by her own notes describing her sources of inspiration. Siv Cedering Fox has created vivid imagery around such bedtime themes as sleeping, dreaming, and night fears in *The Blue Horse and Other Night Poems* (1979), the images reinforced by DONALD CARRICK's dreamy, gray-toned washes. SYLVIA CASSEDY's *Roomrimes: Poems* (1987), an alphabet of poems about rooms and other spaces, is noteworthy for its clever, unforced rhythms within an original conceptual framework. "Just what *is* it / in the closet / that I positively / hear?" asks the young narrator in "Closet." The poems are brief and easily accessible to children. Barbara Esbensen's *Who Shrank My Grandmother's House* (1992) creates a new world of discovery in ordinary objects. Her poetry sparkles with crisp images and sounds. In "Sand Dollar" this marine animal is transformed into money "spilled / from the green silk / pocket / of the sea." Of all those writing brief, unrhymed lyric verse for children, perhaps the most consistent in excellence was VALERIE WORTH, with her series of poems that first appeared in 1972. Using simple language in surprising ways, she celebrated the minutiae of everyday life. Poems like "Mice" and "Rags" can be enjoyed by adults and children in equal measure.

An undeniable impetus behind the increased interest in children's poetry in the last few decades has been the phenomenal popularity of SHEL SILVERSTEIN's two volumes, *Where the Sidewalk Ends* (1974) and *The Light in the Attic* (1974). Both books make impudent sport of children's fascination with the messy and the ridiculous. Second only to Silverstein in popularity is JACK PRELUTSKY. *The New Kid on the Block* (1984) and its companion volume, *Something Big Has Been Here* (1990), are full of puns and nonsense in the strong, unvarying beat and childlike language that characterize his work. His unerring sense of a child's notion of fun is nowhere more apparent than in his selections for the brief anthology *Poems of A. Nonny Mouse* (1989), complemented by the surrealistically outlandish illustrations of HENRIK DRESCHER, and its sequel, *A. Nonny Mouse Writes Again!* (1993), with illustrations by Marjorie Priceman.

Literary honors bestowed on books of poetry have earned them new cachet with adult readers as well as with children. NANCY WILLARD's *A Visit to William Blake's Inn* (1981), with its fanciful and mystical references, was the first volume of poetry to receive the Newbery Medal. In 1988 the same honor was accorded *Joyful Noise: Poems for Two Voices*, PAUL FLEISCHMAN's lyrical paean to the insect world, meant to be read by two people simultaneously or in alternating voices. "Cicadas" and "Fireflies" are notable among these triumphs of sound and harmony.

The highly visual treatment of poetry in an attempt to integrate art and text is a current publishing phenomenon. Narrative poems, with their strong element of story, adapt easily to this single-poem picture-book format. Some recent examples include Ernest Thayer's classic "Casey at the Bat," which has been illustrated with droll wit by WALLACE TRIPP (1980) and by BARRY MOSER, whose more painterly style has produced a more elegant version (1988). The amusing possibilities inherent in OGDEN NASH's "The Adventures of Isabel" have been impishly detailed by illustrator JAMES MARSHALL (1991).

Children are drawn to the illustrations in these books, but critics have raised questions about whether such illustrated editions stifle the imagination by eliminating the text's challenge to readers to create their own mental images. Works in which the words of the poet and the illustrations are universally agreed to complement and not detract from each other are the collaborations between MYRA COHN LIVINGSTON and LEONARD EVERETT FISHER. *A Circle of Seasons* (1982), *Sky Songs* (1984), *Earth Songs* (1986), and *Space Songs* (1988) form a cycle of books celebrating the wonders of the world and the universe beyond. The artist's swirling abstract paintings evoke the spirit of the words with color and form rather than with concrete images. In like manner, ED YOUNG suggests rather than interprets the meaning of the lines in Robert Frost's narrative poem *Birches* (1988), with his muted impressionistic paintings. Barry Moser uses ink and transparent watercolors on glossy black pages to evoke the spooky, mysterious nuances of HENRY TREECE's *The Magic Wood* (1992), with its hints of creatures hidden in the night forest.

Large general anthologies typifying the trend toward the more concrete, visual interpretation of poetry include *The Random House Book of Poetry for Children* (1983), profusely illustrated with color and black-and-white drawings by ARNOLD LOBEL, and *Sing a Song of Popcorn* (1988), illustrated by nine Caldecott Medal artists. Most anthologies today, however, are leaner and concentrate on specific themes, genres, ethnic groups, or audiences. LILLIAN MORRISON, who began editing her series of thematic anthologies in the fifties, continues to create noteworthy titles. *Rhythm Road* (1988) is a joyous, wide-ranging collection, pulsing with sounds and visual action in its graphics. Of the several anthologies compiled by NANCY LARRICK, two outstanding titles were illustrated by Ed Young, *Cats Are Cats* (1988) and *Mice Are Nice* (1990). Editor WILLIAM COLE's collections frequently take a humorous turn. One of the most recent is *A Zooful of Animals* (1992) with its saucy illustrations by LYNN MUNSINGER reinforcing the absurdities in the verses. The collections compiled by LEE BENNETT HOPKINS appeal to a wide range of readers. *Surprises* (1984) contains short poems for beginning readers. *Side by Side: Poems to Read Together* (1988) is also a collection for younger children. LILIAN MOORE has edited *Sunflakes* (1992) for this same audience, illustrated by Jan Ormerod with beguiling children engaged in a variety of activities. X. J. Kennedy, another accomplished poet, has compiled *Knock at a Star: A Child's Introduction to Poetry* (1982), a unique contribution to the current spate of anthologies with more than one hundred fifty entries, most of them infrequently anthologized, and containing brief, conversational comments appealing to and easily understood by children.

The past decade has seen an increased interest in poetry for young adults. Preceding this trend, and foreshadowing it, was the appearance of *Reflections on a Gift of Watermelon Pickle* in 1966. Containing more than one hundred contemporary poems by writers such as William Jay Smith, Theodore Roethke, Donald Hall, and Maxine Kumin, among others, the collection reflects the interests and moods of adolescents with incisive clarity. Paul B. Janeczko continues the effort to bring many modern poets to the attention of young adults in his carefully crafted anthologies. In *Poetspeak* (1983) sixty-two poets share their works and their comments about the writing process. *The Place My Words Are Looking For* (1990) does much the same for a slightly younger audience.

Brickyard Summer (1989) is a collection of Janeczko's own poems about growing up in a New England mill town. In *Judy Scuppernong* (1990), Brenda Seabrooke has created a sensitive coming-of-age narrative in a series of poems revolving around one eventful summer in the lives of three girls growing up in Georgia. Another distinctly regional voice is heard in Jo Carson's *Stories I Ain't Told Nobody Yet* (1989), in which the poet speaks in the rough, eloquent voice of the people in her home mountains of Tennessee. These poems are as intimate and unconstrained as a conversation between old friends.

As the gradual shift of emphasis from print to the electronic media makes young people more accepting of the new, the spontaneous, and the informal, poetry like Carson's seems to bring the form closer to its roots in oral tradition. In *This Same Sky: A Collection of Poems from Around the World* (1992), a book that cuts across language and culture, editor Naomi Shihab Nye includes a folk poem from Mali, translated by Judith Gleason, that typifies this bridge between the old and the new:

The beginning of the beginning rhythm
Is speech of the crowned crane;
The crowned crane says, "I speak."
The word is beauty.

NANCY VASILAKIS

Polacco, Patricia

American author-illustrator, b. 1944. Patricia Polacco's artistic and storytelling abilities, reflected in eighteen highly praised books published within an eight-year span, brought her swiftly to the forefront of the picture book field. Her exceptional talents were clearly evident in her first book, *Meteor!* (1987), based on a childhood memory of a meteor landing in the yard of her grandparents' Michigan farm. Polacco's Michigan childhood and her Russian and Irish heritage have inspired many of her books. Her Russian grandmother is a dominant recurring character in her stories, but other family members and friends are also portrayed in *My Rotten Redheaded Older Brother* (1994), *The Bee Tree* (1993), *Picnic at Mudsock Meadow* (1992), *Some Birthday!* (1991), *Thunder Cake* (1990), *Casey at the Bat* (1988), and *Uncle Vova's Tree* (1988).

The autobiographical *The Keeping Quilt* (1988), with its story of how a family quilt is used as it is passed from generation to generation, further reflects Polacco's Russian-Jewish heritage. But not all of Polacco's books are autobiographical. The fanciful *Babushka Baba Yaga* (1994) offers a sympathetic view of the legendary Russian witch, and *Rechenka's Eggs* (1988) features Ukrainian Easter eggs. Although preferring to write within her heritage, Polacco effectively explored aspects of contemporary Amish life in *Just Plain Fancy* (1990).

Some of Polacco's most touching stories focus on cross-cultural friendships. In *Mrs. Katz and Tush* (1992), an African American boy befriends an elderly Jewish woman, and Polacco celebrates her childhood friendship with a black family in *Chicken Sunday* (1992). Polacco, who has lived most of her life in Oakland, California, paid homage in *Tikvah Means Hope* (1994) to how her diverse neighbors supported each other during Oakland's devastating 1991 firestorm. But perhaps her most poignant portrayal of a cross-cultural friendship is in *Pink and Say* (1994), a story passed down on Polacco's father's side of the family. It tells of how her Yankee great-great-grandfather was rescued during a Civil War battle by a young black soldier before they were both captured and sent to the Confederate Andersonville Prison.

Polacco's stories are perfectly complemented by her distinctive style of art. She uses pencil, color marking pens, pastels, and acrylic paints to create bright, intense paintings set against a white background. The characters in her Russian-influenced stories wear clothing with multiple patterns and prints, giving those books a folk art quality. Sometimes faces and hands are left white, with expressive details sketched in with pencil. The autobiographical quality of some of Polacco's stories is heightened by the incorporation in her illustrations of framed family photographs. She also incorporates reproductions of Russian icons in some of her books, reflecting not only her Russian heritage but her Ph.D. in art history.

Patricia Polacco may have begun her career as a children's author-illustrator rather late in life, but she shows no signs of slowing down. Her best work may yet be ahead of her. ❧ P.O.B.

Politi, Leo

AMERICAN AUTHOR AND ILLUSTRATOR, B. 1908. Leo Politi's stories and illustrations demonstrate a quiet respect for children. Writing at a time when few authors noticed the country's cultural diversity, Politi was delighted by the many different children who lived around him in Los Angeles. A deeply religious man, he was also intrigued by the variety of celebrations they observed, from a Mexican Christmas procession or a Sicilian blessing of the fishing fleet to the Chinese New Year. His books reflect this multicultural nature of his world. He often integrated foreign words and phrases into his text, and several of his books were published in English and Spanish editions.

Illustration by Leo Politi from his book *Song of the Swallows* (1949).

Politi was born in California to Italian immigrant parents, but returned to Italy with his family when he was seven. At fifteen, he received a scholarship to the National Art Institute of Monza, near Milan, where he studied art for the next six years. He returned to California in 1931 and settled on Olvera Street in a Mexican section of Los Angeles. Here he struggled to earn his living as an artist and spent long hours drawing and painting the local people and street scenes. He finally began to achieve success in the early 1940s when he illustrated a series of books about California. The first book he both wrote and illustrated, *Pedro, the Angel of Olvera Street* (1946), was named a Caldecott Honor Book, as was *Juanita*, which he wrote in 1948, and in 1950 he received the Caldecott Medal for *Song of the Swallows.*

Politi's books convey an innocence, a naiveté, in which bad things work out in a loving and positive way. Peppe's father, for example, in *A Boat for Peppe* (1960) gets caught in a storm and his fishing boat does not return with the rest of the fleet. Although the picture shows the raging storm, Politi's words are reassuring. The fishermen urge Peppe to "keep faith." Then a rainbow appears, and when the sea is calm, they quickly find his father. In part, this idealized view of childhood stems from the era in which Politi was writing: During the 1940s and 1950s difficulties were often minimized in children's books.

Politi says he feels a strong love for "people, animals, birds and flowers... for the simple, warm and earthy things." This is particularly evident in his illustrations, which are filled with images of nature. Flowers, insects, and birds form decorative elements on each page. He uses soft tones to create a gentle quality in his pictures. The dominant color themes in *Song of the Swallows* are muted greens and browns, highlighting the close relationship between the natural cycle of the swallows' arrival at the mission at Capistrano and the people. Yet the composition of his pictures creates a sense of vitality in spite of the quiet colors.

Later, he moved to a somewhat brighter palette. Piccolo, an organ grinder's monkey, escapes from his master and hides under a cable car in *Piccolo's Prank* (1965). The story is set in the center of Los Angeles, and the color scheme reflects the energy of the naughty monkey and of the city. Once again, Politi demonstrates his love for Los Angeles and its diverse neighborhoods and people, which have provided him with a lifelong source of inspiration. ❧ P.R.

Pope, Elizabeth Marie

AMERICAN AUTHOR, B. 1917. Although Elizabeth Marie Pope has written only a few novels, her Newbery Honor Book, *The Perilous Gard* (1974), stands as a significant accomplishment in children's literature. Blending elements from the fantasy, romance, and historical genres, Pope presents a fresh plot founded on the Scottish legend of Tam Lin, who was rescued from the Fairy Queen by his true love. Kate Sutton, banished to Elvenwood Hall from the court of Princess Elizabeth, unwittingly becomes deeply entangled with the pagan people who live under the hill near the castle. The attention to detail in *The Perilous Gard,* set in 1558, demonstrated Pope's knowledge of life during the Elizabethan era; a professor of English at Mills College in Oakland, California, for thirty-eight years, Pope examined the works of Milton and Shakespeare in her critical writing. In her fiction, she explores her interest in history and the way the past affects the present.

The Sherwood Ring (1956), more dated than *The Perilous Gard* but still an effective fantasy, consists of a similar blend of genres, although it takes place during the twentieth century and the Revolutionary War era. Orphaned Peggy finds companionship with the ghosts who linger in and about her ancestral home and relate to her incidents involving the war and their romantic entanglements. By surmising plausible explanations for the fantasy elements in her novels, Pope establishes a realistic tone but retains an aura of magic and mystery. The graceful, stoical Fairy Folk are not supernatural beings but humans who isolated themselves from the rest of humanity during the rise of Christianity, which forbade the open worship of pagan deities; and ghosts, according to a book Peggy finds, appear in order to provide comfort to their lonely female descendants. Pope's skillful characterization makes the stories memorable, particularly in *The Perilous Gard*: Taken prisoner by the Fairy Folk and made to toil for her captors deep beneath the earth, strong-willed Kate clings to her Christian faith and refuses the mind-altering drugs that would make her stay in the realm more bearable. Her relationship with Christopher Heron, marked by stimulating dialogue and an absence of sentimentality, is practical yet passionate. While they are imprisoned, Kate spends her nights talking to Christopher about ordinary things, feeding his hope and his strength and creating a bond that is ultimately strong enough to break the psychological hold the Fairy Folk have over him. The main characters in both novels possess intelligence and value it in others, which adds unique twists to the plots and to the developing romances.

The culture of the Fairy Folk and their subterranean world are remarkable creations, comparable to the secondary worlds found in novels in the high fantasy genre. Pope's outstanding descriptions of life underground and the occasional, unbearable sensation of the weight of the earth overhead pressing down on the inhabitants of the caverns bring the setting sharply into focus. Written for Pope's younger sister and her niece, the two historical fantasies hold lasting appeal for older children and young adults. ❧ A.E.D.

Porte, Barbara Ann

AMERICAN AUTHOR, B. 1943. Barbara Ann Porte was raised in New York City and graduated from Michigan State University and the Palmer Graduate Library School at Long Island University. She was a children's services specialist in the Nassau Library System in Uniondale, New York, for twelve years. Porte's father, a pharmacist, urged his three daughters to read and write something every day, "no matter what else you do with your lives." Mrs. Porte, a lawyer, was more pragmatic, cautioning her daughters against revealing too much information to others. Nonetheless, the girls invented stories and whispered them to each other. Following her father's advice, Porte read and wrote a good deal, and her stories and poems for adults have appeared in several publications. Inspired by her library work with children, Porte has written many books for young people. For young children, her popular "Harry" series includes *Harry's Dog* (1984), *Harry's Mom* (1985), and *Harry's Visit* (1983), all of which were named Notable Books by the American Library Association. These stories are a perfect choice for beginning readers. The travels and adventures of young Harry are presented in lighthearted, simple prose, highlighted by Yossi Abolafia's cheerful color illustrations.

Taxicab Tales (1992) and *Ruthann and Her Pig* (1989) expand Porte's range to include middle readers. *Taxicab Tales* is a series of amusing anecdotes about taxicab passengers related by a cabdriver to his two children. *Ruthann and Her Pig* is the humorous tale of a girl and her unusual pet—a pig named Henry Brown. Although Ruthann's parents try to persuade her to accept a "normal" pet, such as a dog or a cat, Ruthann is completely satisfied with her pig. After all, Ruthann's parents agree, Henry Brown is a vast improvement over the squash that was previously the object of their daughter's affections! When Ruthann's cousin Frankie visits and wants to borrow Henry Brown as a bodyguard, Ruthann must do some quick thinking to avoid sending her beloved pet to the dangerous city where Frankie lives.

Porte is a consummate storyteller whose books are marked by subtle humor and reveal a wry understanding of parent-child relationships. *Jesse's Ghost and Other Stories* (1983) is a collection of tales, some of which are adapted from folklore and some of which are Porte's own creation. The stories span a variety of topics, and each is prefaced by the wise storyteller. Some of the stories are magical, some are fables, some are pure nonsense, and some are no more than short jokes, but all benefit from the wealth of Porte's original and vast imagination. Porte's novel for older readers, *I Only Made Up the Roses* (1987), is an unusual, introspective book that takes on the quality of a series of photographic images. Indeed, photographs figure prominently in the vignettes of the Williams family's history that are related through seventeen-year-old Cydra's eyes. Through her parents' and relatives' reminiscences, Cydra comes to a unique understanding of her rich cultural heritage. The body of Porte's work reflects her desire to explore varied themes and reveals an author whose scope is not limited to one genre or age group. ❧ M.O'D.H.

Potter, Beatrix

English author and illustrator, 1866–1943. Beatrix Potter's legacy to children's literature includes twenty-three small books and one longer collection of stories. Strict integrity to the natures of her animal characters, an ear for striking, precise language, and an eye for detail have made her stories perennial favorites since the early 1900s. Potter insisted that her books, which address children intelligently and with humor, remain inexpensive and small enough to fit in a child's hands.

Potter grew up in a wealthy London family. Educated by governesses and isolated in a nursery much of the time, she kept a secret menagerie of pets. At various times these included rabbits named Benjamin and Peter, mice, newts, a frog, a tortoise, and a hedgehog named Mrs. Tiggy-winkle. She spent hours observing and painting her animals, immortalizing many of them later as characters in her books. Both Potter and her younger brother enjoyed drawing, although Potter did not care much for her art instructors and was mostly self-taught. Each summer, the family rented a large house or a castle in the Lake District or in Scotland where Potter sketched the country landscapes, many of which would become the settings for her books. Throughout her life, she had passionate interests to which she devoted her full concentration. With the benefit of her considerable intelligence and perfectionism, she excelled at each. In her twenties and early thirties, for example, she was fascinated by fossils and fungi, creating detailed paintings of the specimens she collected and conducting original research in mycology. It is during this period that she developed and refined her detailed dry-brush painting style.

With the success of *The Tale of Peter Rabbit* (1902), when she was thirty-six, Potter began concentrating on creating books, publishing two a year from 1902 to 1909. When the little books began to earn substantial royalties, she bought a farm in the Lake District, where she found excuses to spend more and more of her time, escaping from a stifling family situation. There, at the age of forty-seven, she married her solicitor, William Heelis. By then, her focus had begun to shift again, this time to land conservation, local antiques, and especially the breeding of Herdwick sheep, where she again achieved great success. Although she produced nine books between 1910 and 1930, her attention was divided, and the quality of those books is uneven. For the rest of her life, she was Mrs. Heelis—sheep breeder, farmer, and landlord—and preferred to ignore her past success as Beatrix Potter. When she died in 1943, she left four thousand acres to the National Trust, including fifteen farms.

The Tale of Peter Rabbit, in which a young rabbit named Peter disobeys his mother, loses his way—and nearly loses his life—in Mr. McGregor's garden, and finally returns to the safety of home, is one of the great success stories of children's literature. It was first written in 1893 as an illustrated letter to Noel Moore, the five-year-old son of Potter's friend and former governess, while he was sick. Noel, like Peter, had three sisters at that time. When Potter tried to have it published, she was rejected by at least seven firms, and eventually decided to print it in black-and-white at her own expense. It was not until the private edition was nearly complete that Frederick Warne & Co. reconsidered its initial rejection and agreed to publish the story, provided that Potter repaint the illustrations in full color. Published by Warne in 1902, the book was an immediate success, selling 50,000 copies by the end of 1903. *Peter Rabbit* continues to sell at least 75,000 copies a year and has been translated into thirty languages.

Just why has *Peter Rabbit* been so successful? It contains, first, one of the oldest, simplest, and most compelling plots: separation from home, adventure, escape, return to home. This plot, occurring in favorite stories from Daniel Defoe's *Robinson Crusoe* to Maurice Sendak's *Where the Wild Things Are,* embodies the wishes and fears of every child. Then there is Peter. As a rabbit and a child, he is adventurous and timid, clever and incompetent, sweet and naughty. Both text and pictures show that Peter is not a boy thinly disguised as a rabbit, but a real animal who goes "lippity-lippity" when he walks and has powerful kicking hind legs, young large ears, and sensitive whiskers. Potter's understanding of animal anatomy, combined with her observations of animals in motion and her understanding of each animal's nature, are channeled into her characters so that readers believe instantly in the honesty and authenticity of her portrayals.

The Tailor of Gloucester (1903), Potter's own favorite among her books, contains her only sympathetic human character. A Christmastime favorite for many families and for library story hours, it tells of a poor tailor who becomes ill before finishing the Lord Mayor's waistcoat. The mice in the tailor's shop take pity on him and finish all but the last buttonhole, despite the malicious meddling of the tailor's cat, Simpkin. Potter had heard this tale during a stay in Gloucester, though it was originally told as a fairy story. How much more appealing and sensible it becomes when the fairies are replaced by mice and a cat appears as their antagonist.

Some people have a mistaken impression of Beatrix Potter as the creator of cute animal characters in slightly sentimental stories. This could not be further from the truth. Some of her strongest characters are delightfully unsavory, like the foxy-whiskered gentleman in *The Tale of Jemima Puddleduck* (1908), Mr. Tod and Tommy Brock in *The Tale of Mr. Tod* (1912), and Samuel Whiskers, the rat, in *The Tale of Samuel Whiskers* (1908). The importance of the food chain is just below the surface of all her stories, and she always made it clear exactly what was most frightening to each animal. Surely any sentimentality is in the eye of the beholder.

She was also keenly aware of mischief and how much fun it can be, as in *The Tale of Two Bad Mice* (1904) and *The Tale of Samuel Whiskers*. These books give an occasional nod to proper behavior for the sake of the adults, but leave children with no doubt that they are really about the joys of destructive behavior. Potter, who had been of necessity a proper, well-behaved child, intuitively understood the delight of breaking and entering, smashing dishes, and hiding from adults. In *Samuel Whiskers*, as in *The Tale of Tom Kitten* (1907) and *The Tale of Pigling Bland* (1913), the parents are portrayed as foolish and sometimes cruel, and the children, while disobedient, are only displaying natural behavior. Her young animals frequently shed their clothes, being more active and less concerned with appearances than their elders.

All of Beatrix Potter's books have remained in print continuously, to the delight of generations of readers. Despite the occasional dated turn of phrase, these books seem to appeal to children of any time because they are true to the nature of both children and the animals they portray. Potter's respect for children's integrity and intelligence and her intuitive understanding of childhood fears and delights are timeless. ❧ LOLLY ROBINSON

Poulin, Stéphane

French Canadian illustrator and author, b. 1961. Stéphane Poulin was barely twenty-four and spoke little English when he achieved acclaim across Canada with *ah! belle cité!/a beautiful city* (1985), a bilingual ALPHABET BOOK based on his hometown, Montreal.

In the many volumes that Poulin has contributed to the field of children's books since then—which include French-language novels for young people that he illustrated—he has consistently used gentle themes of love, togetherness, and family life. But by also imbuing his work with a dry, mischievous sense of humor and by placing his characters in surroundings that are, for the most part, unblinkingly realistic, he has kept the books from becoming cloying and saccharine. Even in his fantasies—such as *My Mother's Loves* (*Les amours de ma mère*, 1990) and *Travels for Two* (*Un voyage pour deux*, 1991), both part of a series blatantly tagged "Stories and Lies from My Childhood" ("Contes et mensonges de mon enfance")—reality intrudes, in the form of too many people in too small a house or the untimely need to go to the bathroom while in transit.

Poulin's families tend to be of the single-parent variety. The series about Josephine the cat, which brought his work international recognition, involves a young boy living with his father. The "Stories and Lies" series features a family of nine children living with their mother, a situation that parallels Poulin's own background. In fact, the rambunctious children depicted in these two books are patterned on Poulin and his siblings. His father left when Stéphane was twelve years old; he himself left home at seventeen but continues to admire his mother and to credit her with having raised nine children on her own. *Have You Seen Josephine?* (*As-tu vu Joséphine?*, 1986), the first book in the three-volume "Josephine" series, is dedicated to her. The series owes much of its success to the fact that Poulin, in many of his detailed and colorful oil paintings, keeps Josephine partly hidden. Children enjoy finding the elusive feline; adults, reading the books to their preschoolers, are rewarded with Poulin's often subtle wit.

Poulin twice received the Governor General's Literary

Award for illustration of a book in French, the 1986 prize for *As-tu vu Joséphine?* and *Album de famille* (Family album, 1991) and the 1989 prize for *Benjamin et la saga des oreillers* (Benjamin and the pillow saga). He received the 1988 Elizabeth Mrazik-Cleaver Canadian Picture Book Award from IBBY-Canada for *Peux-tu attraper Joséphine?* (Can you catch Josephine?).

While he normally works in oils, Poulin is equally adept in pencil, as evidenced by the sketches that alternate with his paintings in the "Josephine" series (which ended in 1988 with *Could You Stop Josephine?/Pourrais-tu arrêter Joséphine?). The Outspoken Princess and the Gentle Knight: Timely Fairy Tales for Tumultuous Times* (1994), collected by Jack Zipes, is illustrated in black-and-white and shows how well Poulin can handle drama as well as humor: His images range from poignantly bleak to deliciously appealing.

Whether in oils or pencils, the artist has a distinctive style that combines naiveté of content (characters tend to be squat, round-faced children with honest, eager faces) and a sophistication of delivery (detailed backgrounds executed with great care, grace, and accuracy). There is a warmth in Poulin's work that brings out the best of human responses. ❧ B.G.

PRELUTSKY, JACK

AMERICAN POET, B. 1940. For poetic creativity, accuracy, and appeal, there is no match for Jack Prelutsky. With a keen sensitivity to children's fears, pleasures, and funny bones, this prolific and gifted poet delivers verses that are capable of converting the staunchest cries of "I hate poetry!" into a ceaseless clamoring for more. Possessing a restless spirit, Prelutsky tried a number of careers before settling on poetry. As a child in Brooklyn, New York, he was recognized as a gifted musician, a prodigy who was often paid to sing at various occasions and was even offered free lessons by the chorus master of New York's Metropolitan Opera, but he abandoned the idea of a singing career when he realized he might not become the best in the field. Success at other endeavors, including photography, pottery, folk singing, and drawing, was similarly forsaken. His talent for poetry was discovered by an editor at Macmillan to whom Prelutsky had submitted fanciful drawings with accompanying verse. The drawings were not accepted, but the verse was considered exceptional. Prelutsky was on his way. With over thirty volumes of poetry published since his debut in 1967, he has demonstrated a facility with words and images that has placed him among the best in his field.

Illustration by JAMES STEVENSON for *The New Kid on the Block* (1984) by Jack Prelutsky.

Prelutsky is known for his irreverent style, technical versatility, and awareness of juvenile preferences, and his nonsensical subjects and surprise endings merit his audience's instant approval. While most of his volumes are composed of a brief series of verses centering around one overarching theme, his two most successful books, *The New Kid on the Block* (1984) and *Something Big Has Been Here* (1990), are larger volumes that address a vast array of topics both real and ridiculous. Ranked alongside SHEL SILVERSTEIN's *Where the Sidewalk Ends* and *A Light in the Attic* in terms of popularity and style, *The New Kid on the Block* has rapidly become a classic in the field of children's poetry. Its 107 verses have found a devoted readership in primary grade children, who are unable to resist such unforgettable creatures as the Slyne, the Gloopy Gloppers, and Baloney Belly Billy. But amusement is not the only theme here; Prelutsky's poems lend expression to the difficulties and frustrations of children, who recognize a true advocate in the voice behind the verse.

On a smaller scale, children in search of ghost stories and other terrors find satisfaction in Prelutsky's several volumes of frightening poems, whose enticing covers and titles such as *Nightmares: Poems to Trouble Your Sleep* (1976) and *The Headless Horseman Rides Tonight* (1980) never fail to evoke a thrill. Similarly, several dozen marvelous monsters, with names like the Sneezy-Snoozer and the Nimpy-Numpy-Numpity, ooze, snarl, and otherwise cavort across the pages of *The Snopp on the Sidewalk* (1977) and *The Baby Uggs Are Hatching* (1982). Aside from creating such fanciful creatures, Prelutsky is also attuned to the basic subjects that children find most interesting, relevant, and fun. His subjects include dinosaurs, summer vacation, snow days, and the unpleasantness of going to bed, among many others, and he has also issued several holiday volumes for beginning readers.

In addition to his own writing, Prelutsky has translated several volumes of German and Swedish poetry into

English. He has been compared with OGDEN NASH, LEWIS CARROLL, and EDWARD LEAR, and critics have praised his rhythm, wit, and facility with words. Developing rhyming verse and standard metric schemes through carefully chosen onomatopoeic words and phrases, he achieves a near-perfect structure that is especially rewarding when read aloud. A great crusader for the teaching and appreciation of poetry, Prelutsky is hailed for writing verse that attracts young readers to this long-stigmatized genre. ❧ C.C.B.

PRESCHOOL BOOKS

Stories, rhymes, and lullabies have always been shared with young children. MOTHER GOOSE rhymes, fingerplays, and other ditties are standard in the nursery—and rightly so. The sound of language delights an infant. The rhythm and pattern of Mother Goose rhymes read or sung, for example, are magical for babies as they begin to absorb sounds and sights. The comfortable lap of a caring adult and a soothing voice add to the pleasure of sharing books. There is magic in books for young children.

Adults help children see, understand, and explore a spectrum of objects, activities, experiences, information, and ideas. Visual and verbal images combine in books for the young child to help them focus, empathize with others, vicariously experience emotions and activities, learn about their world, and perhaps most important, share all of this with a caring adult. As Dorothy Butler notes in *Babies Need Books* (1980), "It is not possible to gauge the width and depth of the increase in a child's grasp of the world that comes with books." It is possible, however, to make books available to all children—beginning with infants.

Adults who bring together children and their books must choose from a vast, sometimes overwhelming quantity. What books are likely to appeal to very young children? What makes a book appropriate for children? Children's book editor Louise Seaman Bechtel wrote in a 1941 *Horn Book* article that children need and enjoy books long before they reach five years, that they respond to the same age-old keys: "rhythm and laughter, the sense of climax, the magic of words."

Author-illustrator MARCIA BROWN writes in *Lotus Seeds: Children, Pictures & Books* (1986), "[It is] in their first books [that] children begin to form their taste for art and literature." Through early exposure to these books, children unconsciously develop an approach to their "visual world of order, rhythm, and interesting arrangements of color." Burton White, in *First Three Years of Life* (1990), contends that books with stiff pages "feed a baby's interest in hand-eye practice" and soon will "support the development of language, curiosity, and a healthy social life." Not only do books shared with young children stimulate intellectual development, but the pleasure of sharing these books is an early experience with other people—including authors and illustrators. The early work of psychologists such as Jean Piaget and Arnold Gesell continues to be refined, increasing our understanding of children's development and how they learn. However, it is still an elusive magic that we most seek in the growing pool of books for young children.

Publishers have responded to the demand for interesting but simple books for the youngest child. Since the early 1980s, books for the very young, often by well-known children's book illustrators and authors, have proliferated. About five thousand children's books were published in 1992.

Bright colors and clear shapes illustrate Max and Ruby's recognizable mini-adventures on sturdy board pages. *Max's Bath, Max's Birthday, Max's Bedtime,* and *Max's Breakfast* (all 1985), written and illustrated by ROSEMARY WELLS, were perhaps the first BOARD BOOKS with action and characterization as well as concepts understandable by the very young. These child-sized books remain appealing to children and to adults,

Illustration by ROSEMARY WELLS from her book *Max's Bedtime* (1985).

who will recognize the subtle humor and nuance of character. In addition, since these books are also a tactile experience, felt and tasted by children, their rounded corners and small size allow for safe, independent handling.

My Daddy and I, I Make Music, and *My Doll Keshia* (all 1991), board books written by ELOISE GREENFIELD and illustrated by JAN SPIVEY GILCHRIST, simply relate the everyday activities of an African American child within the family. Small in size, with rounded corners, the books are realistically illustrated in wash and line. Adults appear less often as a multiracial cast of children engage in familiar activities in HELEN OXENBURY's *Tickle Tickle, All Fall Down, Say Goodnight,* and *Clap Hands* (all 1987). Slightly larger in size, these board books provide ample white space to highlight engaging, well-defined watercolors that chronicle babies' joyful play.

Board books do not differ significantly from longer PICTURE BOOKS. Author-illustrator Helen Oxenbury has said about creating board books that she strives to "keep the concepts extremely simple—objects and situations that very small children will recognize." Adults selecting such books for young children must also consider the simplicity of the concept, presentation, and format. Pleasing language, clear illustrations, and familiar objects and activities, all contained within sturdy books with rounded edges, encourage the youngest children to explore with and focus on their books.

Toddlers rapidly gain language, begin to manipulate ideas and deal with abstractions, start to pretend, and although they remain the vertex of their world, become social creatures. Books that present easy concepts or simple stories with concrete action, identifiable experiences, and recognizable characters will be relished by toddlers. Not only are such books this developmentally appropriate, they can provoke memorable shared activity for both child and adult.

Most often, books that appeal to toddlers present familiar ideas and activities. Many adults still remember the cozy green bedroom created by MARGARET WISE BROWN in *Goodnight Moon* (1947). The simple, rhyming, evocative text is enriched and extended by CLEMENT HURD's uncluttered but satisfyingly detailed illustrations in striking, almost flat colors. *Goodnight Moon* is more than a bedtime story. It becomes a naming game as each object is examined again and again and as the familiar, such as the cow who jumped over the moon, is found and associations are made. The poetic, repetitive language of the simple text, when coupled with the dramatic flow of illustration, becomes unforgettable.

ANN JONAS chronicles a small boy's explorations in *Holes and Peeks* (1984) using minimal language and well-delineated, full-color illustrations. The child can see through peeks but not holes and remains frightened of the latter—until he gains a sense of control over them. Getting dressed can pose as many problems for young children as holes do. An awkward young bear cub, however, entertainingly overcomes the difficulties of appropriate attire in Shigeo Watanabe's *How Do I Put It On?* (1984). The softly lined and colored illustrations are childlike and appealing. Affection abounds in the families presented in VERA WILLIAMS's *"More More More," Said the Baby* (1990). Three families with young children live and play together, lovingly pictured in rich watercolors and a carefully crafted text.

These and other books that continue to appeal to young children are memorable because they demonstrate a respect for and understanding of the small child's world. They are remembered by adults, perhaps because the books help adults revisit, recall, and enjoy again earlier experiences. Through them, the everyday, creatively viewed, becomes magical.

Ideas or concepts, too, can create magic. Black-and-white photographs of objects common in a child's world effectively convey the notion of opposites in TANA HOBAN's *Push Pull Empty Full* (1972). A single word appears with a full-page photograph; its opposite appears on the facing page, thus clearly defining the concept in word and image. A child can count from one to ten in English and Swahili with *Moja Means One,* written by Muriel Feelings (1971). Though counting may be too abstract for younger children, the sounds are satisfying and the soft lines of TOM FEELINGS's monochromatic illustrations provide a respectful glimpse into another culture.

Many stories invite young children to participate in them and, like *Goodnight Moon,* incorporate patterns or objects to name. In *Spots, Feathers, and Curly Tails,* written and illustrated by NANCY TAFURI (1988), a partial picture (actually a very close-up view) accompanies a simple question such as, "What has spots?" The entire animal—"A cow has spots"—appears on the next double-page spread. Crisp, cleanly lined, full-color illustrations of farm animals accompany the minimal, predictable text. Children are immediately drawn in as they eagerly respond to the text's questions.

Tafuri's interesting use of perspective enhances *Have You Seen My Duckling?* (1984), enabling young children to find the errant duckling, even when its mother cannot. Clear, appealing and playful illustrations engage children in this satisfying, safe jaunt in which children (and the young duckling) are one step ahead of Mother.

Children look for the little black-and-white dog in *Where's Spot* (1980) and the numerous other Spot books by ERIC HILL, as they lift flaps covering small surprises until Spot is found. Children eat through a week with *The Very Hungry Caterpillar* (1981) by ERIC CARLE and feel the holes left by the caterpillar's munching spree. Brilliant color and stylized pictures bring the story to a satisfying conclusion when the caterpillar—no longer either hungry or small—emerges as a beautiful butterfly. In addition to their visual and verbal appeal, these books share an emotional appeal for young children. They are predictable though not contrived, and their texts and illustrations are satisfyingly complementary. The young child's world is rendered orderly and understandable through such books.

Many of the qualities of these books continue to appeal to the slightly older child, though the scope of books created specifically for them broadens in several important ways, reflecting their physical, mental, and emotional development and increasing experience. For example, as children grow more autonomous and their language becomes better developed, they enjoy dealing with increasingly abstract concepts in their explorations of their world. Children enjoy books of many kinds, but the qualities that render books exciting and give them the power to last are fairly consistent.

Books for very young children, including board books, are essentially picture books, books in which verbal and visual images work together to create a unified whole. And as Marcia Brown has recognized, "[a] picture book is somewhat related in its effects to that of a painting. The whole is greater than any of its parts, but all parts must relate directly to each other in harmony." To be fully savored, books for the very young, like paintings, must be shared. ❧ MARIA B. SALVADORE

PREUSSLER, OTFRIED

GERMAN AUTHOR, B. 1923. Preussler is one of the foremost authors of children's fantasy and has been honored three times with the German Children's Book Award. The three books that won are lighthearted stories with serious underlayers that give them more weight than the usual children's fantasy. One is *The Wise Men of Schilda* (trans. 1962), an elongated fool's tale in which the entire town is foolish. Some of the anecdotes are familiar, some are new, but they all play on the classic fool motif.

In *The Tale of the Unicorn* (1988; trans. 1989), illustrated by Gennady Spirin, Preussler again acknowledges his rich folktale heritage. Three brothers set off to hunt the mysterious unicorn, but the older two get waylaid—one by a lovely woman, one by wealth—so it is the youngest alone who finds the unicorn. But just as his finger is on the trigger, the unicorn enchants him with her eyes.

Satanic Mill (1971; trans. 1973), an American Library Association Notable Book, is also an allegory but on a symphonic scale. Young Krabat is called through his dreams to come to the desolate mill at Schwartzkollm, which is run by a diabolical master who teaches his journeymen the black arts in exchange for their binding servitude—the men are never free to leave. Dark secrets grind like gnashing teeth, and Krabat secretly decides to overthrow the master. This can be done only with true love, and the master does everything in his enormous power to make that impossible. In Preussler's masterpiece, the terror is real, the love sweet, and the suspense twisted tight. ❧ J.A.J.

PRINGLE, LAURENCE

AMERICAN AUTHOR, PHOTOGRAPHER, AND EDITOR, B. 1935. Exploring the human population's effect on the natural world is a recurring theme in naturalist Laurence P. Pringle's work. The author has written that he wants to "encourage readers to feel a kinship with other living things and a sense of membership in the earth ecosystem."

Pringle's interest in nature began when he was a youngster in rural New York, where he learned how to hunt, fish, and trap wild animals. He also became an avid observer and photographer of birds, flowers, wildlife, and natural settings. As a result of Pringle's upbringing, he studied wildlife biology and eventually wrote dozens of children's books focusing on science and nature.

Pringle strives to correct popular but incorrect theories about everything from dinosaurs to killer bees. A firm believer in challenging authority, he encourages young readers always to keep an open mind and never stop exploring new alternatives for old scenarios. His books can be counted on to provide clear, accurate, thoughtful perspectives on complex topics.

Three of his books, *Listen to the Crows* (1976), *Death Is Natural* (1977), and *Wild Foods: A Beginner's Guide to Identifying, Harvesting and Cooking Safe and Tasty Plants from the Outdoors* (1978), received Notable Book Awards from the American Library Association. In 1978 the National Wildlife Federation presented him with a

Special Award for his commitment to conservation. Over the years he has contributed articles to *Audubon, Ranger Rick, Highlights for Children,* and *Smithsonian,* sometimes under the pseudonym Sean Edmund. He has also illustrated many of his books with his own photographs.

Pringle is best noted for his ability to generate excitement in young readers to explore further the scientific and ecological themes in his work. ❖ S.M.M.

Provensen, Alice
Provensen, Martin

ALICE: AMERICAN AUTHOR AND ILLUSTRATOR, B. 1918; MARTIN: AMERICAN AUTHOR AND ILLUSTRATOR, 1916–1987. As Aaron Copland's musical compositions draw heavily from the American experience, the Provensens' illustrations, with their deceivingly simplistic primitive style, their often limited palette, and their remarkable visual continuity, have a distinctive American flavor.

Both were born in Chicago, and during the Great Depression their families moved across the country, from town to town, in search of economic security. Both won scholarships to the Art Institute of Chicago. Both transferred to the University of California, Alice in Los Angeles and Martin in Berkeley. Both served an apprenticeship in the animation industry. Alice worked in the animation department of the Walter Lantz Studios, and Martin created storyboards for Walt Disney, working on such films as *Fantasia* and *Dumbo.* "No matter where we moved or how often," said the Provensens, "the libraries were safe havens for us. In the course of growing up, our paths must have crossed many times—in Chicago, in Los Angeles, in schools, in museums—but we did not meet until we were both working in the same animation studio during the Second World War. Now we often wonder if we couldn't have been sitting across from one another at one of those library tables so long ago." They married in 1944, moved to New York in 1945, and there began their work as children's book illustrators, creating over five hundred illustrations for *Fireside Book of Folksongs* (1947). In the early 1950s they traveled extensively in Europe, collecting material for illustrations and filling sketchbook upon sketchbook with drawings that provided a creative foundation for many of their early books, including *The Golden Bible: The New Testament* (1953) and *The Iliad and the Odyssey* (1956). They also bought a farm near Staatsburg, New York, and converted its barn into a studio. Maple Hill Farm, with its many animals and pastoral setting, became the backdrop for

Illustration by Alice and Martin Provensen from their book *Our Animal Friends at Maple Hill Farm* (1974).

several of their books, including *The Year at Maple Hill Farm* (1978), *An Owl and Three Pussycats* (1981), and *Town and Country* (1985). The ornery goose, Evil Murdoch; cats Webster, Crook, and Fat Boy; Bashful the horse; and Goat Dear are among the many delightful characters cavorting across their well-designed pages. Drawing on their animation training, the Provensens used unique perspectives, color, creative hand lettering, and strong design to capture the reader and entice him or her to turn page after page. Children still delight in the escapades of the plucky Color Kittens from the Little Golden Book of the same name written by MARGARET WISE BROWN in 1949. In Caldecott Medal winner *The Glorious Flight* (1983), the Provensens illuminate, literally and figuratively, the tale of Louis Blériot's triumphant flight across the English Channel.

In 1987 Martin Provensen died of a heart attack. He and Alice had spent over forty years creating beautiful picture books for children. They maintained a happy collaboration, not unlike the medieval scribes and scriveners, passing sketches back and forth, critiquing, reworking "to find the right, the inevitable, pictures and words that say what we have to say." Alice Provensen persisted in their work. *The Buck Stops Here* (1990), her book of presidential history, continues the Provensen tradition of strong design and unique personal viewpoint. M.B.B.

PUBLISHING CHILDREN'S BOOKS

Until the early twentieth century, American book publishers, like those of many other countries, offered children's books as part of their general trade list. But then, with the economy markedly expanding, several companies decided that the juvenile market had become large enough to warrant special attention and so appointed an editor whose specific responsibility was to produce an independent list of children's books. This pioneering juvenile editor had to perform as a book designer, publicity director, and sales manager while carrying out the basic duties of manuscript acquisition and preparation. Gradually, however, as the market share of children's books increased within the company, publishers began to provide their juvenile editorial departments with these services. Now, after seventy-five years, the lone, self-sufficient children's book editor has matured into a broad-based manager with the title of publisher or editorial director, supported by separate departments of production, marketing, and sales.

In the course of this far-reaching change, an indigenous body of children's literature emerged; printing techniques were revitalized; and the art of illustration flowered. The story begins with three developments that occurred almost simultaneously on three different fronts in the aftermath of World War I. By that time, the trend toward separate children's rooms in public libraries, presided over by a specialist in library services for children, was well established, creating a demand for original books in addition to new editions of familiar classics. In 1919 the first Children's Book Week promotion was launched by Frederic G. Melcher, editor of *Publishers' Weekly,* and Franklin Mathiews, librarian of the Boy Scouts of America; Anne Carroll Moore of the New York Public Library started the first full year of her children's book review page in the *Bookman* magazine; and Louise Seaman (later Bechtel) became the first children's book editor at Macmillan Publishing. Although Macmillan was the only company with a separate juvenile department, in 1919 it saw the publication of 433 new children's books.

During the ten years that followed, other publishing companies set up juvenile departments, and the books that resulted more than justified their existence. In 1922 May Massee became the second children's book editor with her own list, at Doubleday Doran, and she quickly drew attention with the publication of such books as *The Poppy-Seed Cakes* by Margery Clark, illustrated by MAUD and MISKA PETERSHAM. At the same time, Melcher established the Newbery Medal for the best children's book of the preceding year, inaugurating it with the first winner, *The Story of Mankind* by HENDRIK VAN LOON, and establishing an award with both literary and commercial weight. Other influential editors starting their careers in this period included Virginia Kirkus at Harper Brothers in 1926 and Elisabeth Bevier (later Hamilton) at Harcourt, Brace in 1928. The new books that they produced were enthusiastically supported by children's librarians, so much so that *The Horn Book,* a preeminent journal of criticism, devoted its August 1928 issue to an appreciation of Seaman's editorship, giving fourteen editorial pages to a reproduction of her fall catalog. Truly, editors and librarians seemed to have entered into what some in retrospect call "a benign conspiracy."

The first setback to these years of steady growth came in 1932 with the onset of the Great Depression. As managements trimmed staff in response to hard times, Massee apparently was let go at Doubleday, relocating soon after at Viking, where she organized a new department. Kirkus also left Harper when it merged its juvenile department with the general trade department, ironically the year after she acquired *Little House in the Big Woods* (1932) by LAURA INGALLS WILDER, an all-time best-seller for the company. Even at Macmillan, where juvenile publishing had begun, Seaman lost her assistant, Eunice Blake, who then started up a children's department of her own at Oxford University Press. Nevertheless, fifteen children's book departments remained in place, and growth resumed shortly, with more companies deciding to compete in the juvenile market as trained personnel became available.

By 1938, output of new children's books had more than doubled since Louise Seaman's early days, reaching a total of 1,041 titles, and both reviewers and buyers were beginning to complain about overproduction. In the same year, Frederic Melcher instituted the Caldecott Medal for the best picture book of the preceding year, thus giving official recognition to the art of illustration and to the illustrator as a key member of the team creating the picture book. Because of the interest of Massee and other editors in the graphics of their books, a number of gifted artists arriving from Europe found an outlet for their work in American children's books and produced landmark titles. One of these artists was the prolific KURT WIESE, who is remembered for his visual interpretation of many enduring stories, including the classic *The Five Chinese Brothers* (1938) by CLAIRE HUCHET BISHOP, an immediate contemporary hit, published by Rose Dobbs at Coward, McCann. But home-grown talent was developing as well. The year before, in 1937, DR. SEUSS had burst on the scene with *And to Think that I Saw It on Mulberry Street* on the Vanguard list, selling the then large number of 31,600 copies in six years—and the picture book was never quite the same again. Another distinctively American artist to emerge was GLEN ROUNDS, whose 1936 debut title, *Ol' Paul, The Mighty Logger,* is credited by publisher Vernon Ives with single-handedly saving his year-old company, Holiday House, from an early demise.

Two schools of thought on the most appropriate content for children's books were taking shape during this period, and each was often highly critical of the other. Some dubbed this differing point of view the "milk bottles versus Grimm" controversy, as it seemed to pit proponents of everyday realistic material against those of the fantastical themes found in more traditional storytelling. Lucy Sprague Mitchell of the Bank Street College of Education, whose staff was working directly with children and reading in her Writers Laboratory, pressed hard for what she called the "here and now" in children's books. But Anne Carroll Moore, still a critical arbiter of great influence, found many of the stories coming out of this program prosaic and uninspiring, including MARGARET WISE BROWN's beloved *Goodnight Moon,* whose appeal for very young children was unrecognized by many at the time of its publication in 1947. Closely allied with these realistic stories were the informational books written in narrative style that had begun to appear, an early example being *The Earth for Sam* by W. Maxwell Reed, published in 1930 by Harcourt editor Bevier, a former school library supervisor, who was keenly aware of the need for lively, accurate juvenile nonfiction.

Again, however, children's book publishing encountered a slow period with the entrance of the country into World War II in 1941 and the diversion of national resources to the wartime effort. Especially difficult for publishers was the rationing of paper, now in short supply, and within three years new book production had dropped by a third, to a total of 645 titles. Nevertheless, more talented editors continued to join the business, and more successful companies continued to emerge. In 1941, Ursula Nordstrom took over the children's book department at Harper Brothers, expanding the staff from three to twenty-five and annual sales from a few hundred thousand to ten million over the next twenty-five years. Shortly after, in 1942, the innovative imprint of Golden Books made its debut, opening up an additional mass market by producing inexpensive books priced at only twenty-five cents and selling them through general retail outlets. Under the guidance of Georges Duplaix, Lucille Ogle, and Albert Rice Leventhal, a trio who worked together closely for many years, the experiment proved itself quickly, achieving annual sales of thirty-nine million in five years. Another influential children's editor starting her career at this time was Margaret K. McElderry, who succeeded Elisabeth Hamilton at Harcourt in 1946. With thirty or so editors now holding this position, the need for a professional organization was becoming apparent, and in 1945 the Children's Book Council was founded by publishers as a center for cooperative projects benefiting the whole industry.

As what some have called the boom decade of the 1950s started, 1,400 new children's books were being published annually, and juvenile publishing had achieved the status of "big business." With this success came keener competition and diversification as companies began to look for new writing and artistic talent to add to their lists and for new markets to cultivate. At Harper, two major finds came to widespread recognition with the publication in 1952 of *Charlotte's Web* by E. B. WHITE and RUTH KRAUSS's *A Hole Is to Dig* with illustrations by MAURICE SENDAK. At Random House, attention turned to innovative market strategy, which led to the launching in 1950 of its history and biography imprint known as Landmark Books and the opening up of sales outlets outside the traditional book market. In fact, the imprint's format proved to be so well suited to the expanding school market for trade books that some publishers, such as Franklin Watts with its "First Book" series, began to specialize in this kind of publishing exclusively.

When the Soviet Union became the first country to launch an unmanned satellite, the *Sputnik*, into space in 1957, the school market for children's books surged into the forefront of juvenile publishing. Convinced that American schools needed help if students were to be able to compete internationally, Congress passed the National Defense Education Act in 1958, making federal funds available to schools for the purchase of library books in the fields of science and mathematics. What followed was a vast outpouring of nonfiction, bringing overdue attention to creative nonfiction writers, but also sparking the publication of hasty work designed to share in the demand that seemed to materialize overnight. Still, out of this period emerged a number of pioneering authors, such as ISAAC ASIMOV, FRANKLYN BRANLEY, MILLICENT E. SELSAM, and HERBERT S. ZIM, who were able to interest young readers in subjects previously thought too complex for them.

During these years, the business of publishing books specifically designed to meet the interests and needs of children also began to diversify geographically. International recognition of its importance came in 1953 with the organization of the International Board of Books for Young People by Jella Lepman in Switzerland. Three years later the Hans Christian Andersen Medal was established to honor writers and illustrators from around the world for their body of work, and slowly American editors started to form links with their counterparts in other countries. One who became especially well known for her international projects was Harcourt's McElderry, who introduced such artists as the Swiss HANS FISCHER to the country. Domestically, too, the process of decentralization from east to west was taking place with such ventures as the founding in California of Parnassus Press by Herman Schein in 1957 for the purpose of providing a showcase for western talent.

During the early 1960s, steady growth continued, the annual output of new books reaching 2,300 titles in 1963. Then, in 1965, another federal government program sent the industry into a dizzying upward spiral. The Elementary and Secondary Education Act was passed, again making money available to schools for the purchase of library books, and publishers were caught unprepared for the buying frenzy that followed. Book inventories were sold out; new printings were delayed at overloaded printers; and some publishers reported as much as a third of their backlist temporarily out of stock. If a publisher did not have a children's book department, it tried to organize one quickly to share in what seemed an unlimited market. Unfortunately, by the time companies were finally able to gear up for this new level of business, the money to support the legislation had begun to dry up, and in the 1970s the boom of the Great Society turned into a bust.

Disillusioning and disruptive as the cycle was, however, in time it further broadened and diversified children's book publishing. Until now, librarians had been the dominant influence on editorial programs in hardcover if not mass-market houses, because they were the primary buyers; their approval could make or break a book. But as library budgets tightened and book purchases dropped, the public began to turn elsewhere for new titles, and the phenomenon of the children's specialty bookstore appeared. By 1985, these stores were numerous enough to form their own professional organization, the Association of Booksellers for Children, and in five years its membership grew from 40 to 800. Although many ABC members were former librarians and teachers, their buying patterns differed to some extent, weighted more toward picture books and younger readers, and in recent years a number of publishers have emphasized this portion of their lists accordingly. For some editors, the single most important change of the last fifteen years has been the expansion of the partnership between juvenile editor and children's librarian to include the children's bookseller.

Out of this expansion has come a second boom period of the 1980s, producing an annual output of what some sources estimate as over 5,000 new titles, wider public consumption, and business consolidation. In order to increase their market share of the industry as quickly as possible, corporations have acquired additional juvenile imprints and brought them together under joint management. Today Macmillan owns ten imprints managed by eight editors; Penguin follows with six; William Morrow with five; while Harcourt and Putnam each have four. Though smaller in number, the remaining children's book publishers are vastly bigger in terms of both book production and support staff. For American children's book publishing, the twentieth century has been a time marked by two seemingly contradictory trends: increasing specialization on the one hand and corporate consolidation on the other.

CONNIE C. EPSTEIN

Pullman, Philip

British novelist and playwright, b. 1946. With the publication of *The Ruby in the Smoke* in England in 1985 (1987 in the United States), Philip Pullman, a former schoolteacher raised in Rhodesia, Australia, London, and Wales, launched his career as a writer of young adult novels. Set in London during the Victorian era, the novel relates the adventures of Sally Lockhart, an inventive, courageous sixteen-year-old who finds herself caught in dangerous intrigue when she delves into the circumstances surrounding the death of the man she believed was her father. The setting is effectively realized in the engrossing tale, which begins a trilogy that continues with *The Shadow in the North* (1988), published in Great Britain in 1987 as *The Shadow in the Plate*, and *The Tiger in the Well* (1990). Sally's character develops as she grows older, falls in love, and becomes an unwed mother who runs her own financial consulting business. Over and over she displays her resourcefulness as she meets each new threat head-on.

Pullman's greatest strength is his ability to weave complex and riveting plots that wrap the reader in suspense. In *The Shadow in the North*, Sally investigates the failure of a shipping business she had recommended to one of her clients as a secure investment and uncovers not only fraud but murder and the invention of a devastating war weapon. The third book depicts Sally's desperate efforts to find her daughter, who has been kidnapped by a man she has never before met, but who legally claims to be the child's father. Pullman brings the trilogy to a close by reintroducing one of the most malevolent villains of the first book. Although the novels contain some adult sexual imagery and disturbing violence, they remain within the limits of good taste. Unfortunately, the same cannot be said of *The White Mercedes* (1992), in which a streetwise, sexually abused runaway is murdered due to an arbitrary string of coincidences that bring her into the path of a man attempting to kill someone else. Pullman's descriptions of the sex and violence are unnecessarily graphic. By shifting the point of view among three characters—Jenny, the runaway, Chris, the boy she becomes romantically involved with, and Chris's employer—Pullman forces a sense of irony on the reader by revealing the secrets each fatally hides from the others.

The critically acclaimed novel *The Broken Bridge* (1990 Great Britain, 1992 U.S.), which focuses more on character, represents not a departure from Pullman's previous style, but an expansion of his technique. Ginny, a biracial teenager raised by her white father in a predominantly white community in Wales, seeks out the truth about her past and her parents and, with difficulty, adjusts to living with the brother she never knew she had. Pullman's depiction of Ginny's sense of alienation and search for identity provides universality and draws the reader into her life, while the tightly constructed plot offers numerous surprises that ensure that readers of Pullman's historical fiction will not be disappointed with this modern novel. At their best, Pullman's novels, daring and inventive, are page turners that immediately hook readers into the story and often introduce them to the Victorian age. His credits as a playwright include adaptations of Mary Shelley's *Frankenstein* and of *The Three Musketeers* by Alexandre Dumas as well as original work. A.E.D.

Pyle, Howard

American illustrator and author, 1853–1911. Considered by many to be the father of children's book illustration in America, Howard Pyle was developing his talents in the United States at the same time that Walter Crane, Randolph Caldecott, and Kate Greenaway were becoming influential in England. Pyle did not have the advantage of working with printer Edmund Evans, and thus most of his work for children was in black-and-white rather than in color. Moreover, while his illustrations were beautifully composed and designed, his pictures were often single-page or partial-page illustrations that supplemented a long text rather than double-page drawings that interacted with the words in relatively brief passages as did Crane's, Caldecott's, and Greenaway's. Yet Pyle's work was known and admired by these three, particularly Walter Crane, and Pyle contributed ideas and methods to the field of children's book illustration that still have important influence today.

Pyle was born and grew up in the Brandywine Valley in Wilmington, Delaware, and he remembered his childhood as an idyllic time that was centered on the wonderful old stone house he and his family lived in and on its garden, filled with profuse blooms and hidden wonders. His mother, who loved books and art, was a great influence on him, and both parents encouraged his talent for art, finally agreeing that he should be trained at a small art school in Philadelphia rather than attend college.

Because of problems with his father's leather business, Pyle spent several years after completing this training helping out in the family business. But in 1876 his mother sent an essay and sketches he had done while on vacation on Chincoteague Island to *Scribner's Magazine*, and the editor accepted the article for publication, suggesting that Pyle come to New York to illustrate and write for periodicals. Once in New York Pyle sold his first painting to *Harper's Weekly*, a magazine that would continue to be an important venue for his work for many years. Indeed, the publisher of *Harper's Weekly* had assembled an exceptional group of professionals who were knowledgeable about illustration and trained in the newest methods of printing, and the House of Harper became an informal training ground for Pyle to learn every facet of the publishing process.

During his time in New York Pyle became more and more convinced that he wanted to write and illustrate books for children. He drew upon his vivid childhood memories to contribute stories to *St. Nicholas* magazine, and he read and studied many of the old folktales that he'd loved as a child, extending his reading to include less familiar tales from many nations. These folktales and the romances of his boyhood would become the central core of his work over his lifetime; although he is primarily remembered today for his contributions to illustration, he was a writer of some skill. Indeed, he has been compared to HANS CHRISTIAN ANDERSEN in the way his unique voice and imagination shaped his traditional folklore and fantasy material.

Illustration by Howard Pyle from his book *The Story of the Champions of the Round Table* (1905).

After three years in New York, where he established himself with a reading public and a professional circle of fellow artists, Pyle returned to Wilmington in 1879. He illustrated two short children's books, *Yankee Doodle* (1881) and *The Lady of Shallott* (1881), both done in color in an experiment that sought to emulate the success of Edmund Evans's work in England. American printers, however, did not have Evans's skills, and the books were disappointing. Pyle returned to black-and-white illustrations with *The Merry Adventures of Robin Hood*, which he wrote and designed himself. This book, published in 1883, is generally considered Pyle's first children's book. Although the careful attention to book design that he insisted upon raised the cost of the book, eventually it was a great success. Even while he continued to illustrate for magazines, Pyle's best love seems to have been writing and illustrating for children, and he went on to do thirteen more books for this audience. Among these were *Pepper and Salt* (1886) and *The Wonder Clock* (1887), collections of stories in the folktale tradition, and *Otto of the Silver Hand* (1888) and four volumes of the King Arthur legends, which were longer romances.

Influenced by the Arts and Crafts movement in England, Pyle's illustrations have the strong sense of line and composition that marked the work of many English artists of the same period, particularly Walter Crane. Yet Pyle became a master storyteller in pictures as well as words, and he never let his illustrations become fussy with decorative detail. His first works were wood engravings, but when halftone methods of printing were introduced, in which a continuous-tone image can be created by using a pattern of dots of varying sizes (as in newspaper photographs), he was able to achieve finer distinctions in tonal values. In all of these he exhibited a carefully restrained sense of drawing and composition. His lines had great strength as well as flowing movement, and he used the white spaces to create a balance in his pictures, just as he used lines to convey drama. His characters were real people with distinct personalities and emotions, and his illustrations lent important energy to the long printed text.

Pyle is notable not only for his contributions to children's literature but also for his dedicated teaching of illustration. He was dissatisfied with the formal methods of instruction then prevailing in most art schools, and he took a job teaching at Drexel Institute in Philadelphia, where he could expound upon his strong views about art and illustration. His courses were in great demand, and later he started a school in his backyard in Wilmington, where he taught promising students for free, charging only room and board. He believed that book illustration was the ground from which to produce painters, and his experience in publishing was invaluable to students like N. C. WYETH and JESSIE WILLCOX SMITH. Even more important, perhaps, were his ideas on illustration, which were at odds with many of the beliefs of the day. He felt that artists needed to get beyond the stiff figures of the studio life class and let their figures and scenes come from the imagination rather than from a frozen pose. Believing in the importance of the overall design of the book, he helped his students learn how to integrate their illustrations into a whole. Pyle taught that the illustrator's role was to extend the text in personal ways rather than simply to reproduce what the text described. Through his many books and his teaching, Pyle made a contribution to children's literature that is acknowledged by readers and artists to this day.

BARBARA KIEFER

Rackham, Arthur

English illustrator, 1867–1939. Of all those illustrators to follow in the footsteps of Randolph Caldecott, Walter Crane, and Kate Greenaway, perhaps none had a greater sense of mystery and magic than Arthur Rackham. Yet Rackham had a conventional middle-class childhood, growing up near London as one of twelve children and training as an insurance clerk. Like Caldecott, he loved drawing from a young age and knew that he wanted someday to be an artist. He therefore studied nights at Lambeth School of Art while working by day for the Westminster Fire Office. Unlike Caldecott, however, Rackham's approach to his work was painstaking and methodical rather than spontaneous. He was just as careful in planning his training and his life; his move from clerk to illustrator took more than eight years. Rackham sold his first drawings to illustrated papers in London in 1891 when he was twenty-four, but he didn't leave the insurance office until 1893, when he was hired to work full-time as an illustrator for the *Westminster Budget*, a London newspaper. Rackham found the work there hard and later declared this period the worst time of his life. The newspaper's rigid schedules demanded quick sketches rather than the careful work Rackham preferred. Rackham also believed that photography was going to supplant illustration in newspapers, giving him anxiety over the future of his livelihood. The sheer volume of work required by the newspaper, however, provided him with valuable practice.

At the age of twenty-seven Rackham was given a commission for a travel book on the United States called *To the Other Side*. The success of this book was followed by other commissions, and although he had not yet achieved his unique and distinctive style, his work was good and in enough demand that in 1896 he was finally able to resign his job on the *Westminster Budget*. By the end of the 1800s, as he entered his thirties, he had illustrated nine books, among them Mary and Charles Lamb's *Tales from Shakespeare* (1899).

It may be that love was the catalyst that released his full artistic talents, for it was only in 1900, after meeting his future wife, painter Edyth Starkie, that he felt encouraged to follow his natural inclination to draw worlds of fantasy and magic. That same year he illustrated *The Fairy Tales from the Brothers Grimm* (1900), tales he remembered fondly from his own childhood, with one full-color illustration and ninety-nine drawings in black and white. This book was an overwhelming success and was reprinted twice. It was so popular that in 1909 he illustrated it again, this time with forty colored pictures and fifty-five in black and white. Rackham approached each picture in a similar manner, carefully drawing his subject in pencil until he was satisfied with the result and then inking over the pencil lines in India ink. For his color pictures he used transparent watercolors and laid down wash upon delicate wash. This technique gave his pictures an ethereal, otherworldly quality and was especially suited to subjects of fantasy that he so loved.

During this time the process of photo separation and reproduction of original artwork had been refined, making it possible to print color illustrations much more easily, although each illustration had to be printed separately on special paper and pasted into the book. As a result, deluxe art book editions became highly prized in the years before the First World War. Because he worked mostly in single-page illustration rather than in fully illustrated books, Rackham's style lent itself to this method of reproduction, and he benefited both financially and artistically. In 1905 Rackham contributed fifty-one illustrations to Washington Irving's *Rip Van Winkle*. When the original art was exhibited in London, almost all the paintings were sold, and a signed, limited edition of 250 copies was sold out even before the exhibition ended. His illustrations for J. M. Barrie's *Peter Pan in Kensington Gardens* (1906) enjoyed similar success and brought Rackham international fame.

Despite his financial and professional success among collectors, Rackham never lost his quiet, unassuming manner, his love for magic, or his appeal to children. He firmly believed that children would benefit from the imaginative, the fantastic, and the playful in their art and in their books, and he showed the greatest respect for his child audience in all his works. In the thirty-three years that followed the publication of *Peter Pan in Kensington Gardens*, Rackham went on to illustrate other well-loved stories and enjoyed continued success. After World War I, however, the market for gift books declined, and the greatest demand for his books turned out to be in America rather than in England.

Throughout his career Rackham was not content to remain with a proven style but sought new artistic challenges, illustrating *Cinderella* (1919) and *The Sleeping Beauty* (1920) in silhouette and experimenting with line and color in *Irish Fairy Tales* (1920) and *The Tempest* (1926). He also had the courage to tackle works that were considered sacrosanct, illustrating *Alice in Wonderland* (1907) and *The Wind in the Willows* (1940). Rackham considered the opportunity to illustrate *The Wind in the Willows* a great gift, for he had been offered the original commission but had had to turn it down because of other commitments. He consulted with KENNETH GRAHAME's widow about the illustrations for the new edition and finally finished the book just weeks before his death. Like his other work, the book is a fine example of his unique vision and his singular way with line and color. ❧ BARBARA KIEFER

RAFFI

CANADIAN SONGWRITER AND AUTHOR, B. 1948. Raffi has used his immense popularity as a performer and recording artist as a springboard for publishing several appealing volumes of children's songs. Raffi Cavoukian was born in Cairo, Egypt, and immigrated to Canada with his family when he was ten. As a teenager, he began to play guitar and performed folk music in clubs and coffeehouses while attending the University of Toronto. When asked to perform for a nursery school class, Raffi learned children's songs from a kindergarten teacher whom he eventually married. His nursery school performance was so well received that he began to write and record almost exclusively for children. His first album, *Singable Songs for the Very Young*, was released in 1976 and became an immediate favorite with young people. He has performed on television and done countless live concerts; his records have sold millions of copies and been nominated for Grammy Awards. Raffi's music has been praised by critics for its interesting variety of styles, including jazz, country, folk, and ragtime. His friendly, wholesome songs often encourage movement and activity from the listener, are sometimes purposefully silly, and occasionally deal with more serious issues such as appreciation of friends and family and concern for the environment. One of his most notable songs, "Baby Beluga," is a paean to a young whale.

Raffi entered the field of children's books with *The Raffi Singable Songbook* (1987), a volume that includes the words and music to fifty-one songs performed on his early recordings. The book includes original Raffi songs about sharing, growing up, dinosaurs, and peanut butter sandwiches, as well as adaptations of traditional favorites such as "Swing Low, Sweet Chariot" and "Goodnight, Irene." Several more volumes followed, including *The Second Raffi Songbook* (1987), *The Raffi Christmas Treasury* (1988), and *The Raffi "Everything Grows" Songbook* (1989). Because the songbooks include music for piano accompaniment, as well as charts for guitar and ukelele, they represent a significant contribution to children's music books of the 1980s.

The volumes in the "Raffi Songs to Read" series are more problematic. Each picture book consists of one Raffi song presented in a picture-book format. With only one or two lines printed on each page, the songs are sometimes too slight to hold up as a text. The success of the picture books is usually dependent on how well the song adapts to illustration. The inspirational *One Light, One Sun* (1988) works because of Eugenie Fernandes' charming color artwork, and Nadine Bernard Westcott's illustrations contribute to the fun and silliness of *Down by the Bay* (1987). The text of *Five Little Ducks* (1989), however, does not lend itself to much variety, resulting in page after page of humdrum duck drawings by JOSÉ ARUEGO and Ariane Dewey.

Raffi took a sabbatical from performing in the early 1990s in order to concentrate on environmental concerns. He returned to the stage in 1993 and began to earn a new legion of youthful fans. Although he is best known for his recordings and concerts, Raffi's young audience may gain an early appreciation for reading as they follow along to the words of his familiar songs in book form. ❧ P.D.S.

RANSOME, ARTHUR

ENGLISH AUTHOR, 1884–1967. Arthur Ransome's childhood summer holidays in northern England's Lake District led him, much later in his life, to write *Swallows and Amazons* (1930), the first of his popular series, "Swallows and Amazons," of twelve books for children. His success was due at least in part to his vivid recollection of the ingredients of childhood happiness, but his own childhood was not all joyful. In school, he recalls, he was "extremely miserable." When he was thirteen, his father died and the family no longer vacationed at the lake, although in his twenties he spent some time there with a family who provided models for some of his fictional characters. Ransome's career as a journalist took him, among other places, to revolutionary Russia. There he met Trotsky's secretary, who later became his wife. The success of his first books enabled him to spend the rest of his life in the Lake District, where he continued the series, fulfilled at last.

"It seems to me," he wrote, "that in writing children's books I have the best of childhood over again and the best of being old as well." The best of childhood, he perceived, was the holidays, and in his books the characters are left alone to enjoy their holidays as they choose. Together they create their own adventures, on small sailboats, exploring an island, camping, seeking treasure, solving small mysteries. Group play is an important aspect of their adventures. The four older Walker children act out the roles of a traditional nuclear family, with patriarchal Captain John (ship's master) and maternal Susan (first mate) providing a secure environment in which their younger siblings, Able Seaman Titty and Ship's Boy Roger, can develop their own competence. Other children (and adults), such as the Blackett sisters, who are the Amazon pirates of the lake, and their fearsome/fun uncle, Captain Flint, sometimes take part in the group play, helping to shape the adventures. Like a father, Ransome is fond of all his characters. All have well-developed, individual personalities, and episodes are presented from their respective points of view. But he seems to have an especially strong attachment to dreamy, emotional Titty, who is not always able to distinguish between the real and the imagined and who draws the others into her fantasy world. Plausible experiences are amplified by the group imagination; once a fantasy has been developed (the little sailboat *Swallow* is a large sailing vessel, the *Amazon* is a pirate ship, there is a lost gold mine in the nearby hills, they are on an expedition to the North Pole), they all become serious about believing it. Occasionally, the children's adventures are exciting and even dangerous enough without the need for imaginative enhancement. For example, they are caught in a forest fire in *Pigeon Post* (1936), and they accidentally cross the English Channel in a fog while spending the night on an anchored sailboat in *We Didn't Mean to Go to Sea* (1937). Distinctive in Ransome's fiction is his attention to detail. He unobtrusively provides a wealth of practical information about activities such as sailing, camping, prospecting, and signaling.

At the time of their publication in the 1930s and '40s the books were immensely popular. Today they are as well loved by a fewer number of readers who are still inspired by Ransome's warm, resourceful, energetic characters. ❧ D.C.

Raskin, Ellen

AMERICAN AUTHOR AND ILLUSTRATOR, 1928–1984. Born in Milwaukee, Wisconsin, Ellen Raskin credits her inability to sing, dance, or play hopscotch to her love of reading: "Books were my escape; books were my friends."

Raskin graduated with a fine arts degree from the University of Wisconsin. She settled in New York City and began her career as a freelance commercial artist, designing and illustrating more than one thousand book jackets, for which she received fifteen major awards. Her entry into the world of children's literature began by illustrating the works of others. Her art can be seen in over a dozen books, whose subjects range from biography, in *We Dickinsons: The Life of Emily Dickinson as Seen Through the Eyes of Her Brother Austin* (1965) to Greek legends, in *The King of Men* (1966), from mathematics, in *Probability: The Science of Chance* (1967) to poetry, in *D. H. Lawrence: Poems Selected for Young People* (1967).

With her artist's eye and her perspective of the world—she felt her short stature allowed her to see as a child sees—she created books "consciously and proudly" for children. "I plan margins wide enough for hands to hold, typographic variations for eyes to rest, decorative breaks for minds to breathe. I want it to look like a wonderful place to be," said Raskin. The books that followed combined the same artistic vision, original stylized drawings, and offbeat, ironic sense of humor. The first book she both wrote and illustrated, *Nothing Ever Happens on My Block* (1966), was named Best Picture Book of the Year by the New York *Herald Tribune*. *Ghost in a Four-Room Apartment* (1969), chosen to represent the United States at the second Biennale of Illustrations in Czechoslovakia, provides a lesson in genealogy through cumulative, repetitive rhymes. *Franklin Stein* (1972) contrasts the blatant, yet consistent, red of the character Franklin with the everchanging and mutable blues, greens, and whites of his relatives. *Who, Said Sue, Said Whoo?* (1973) is illustrated with a Rousseau-like charm and filled with nonsense rhymes. *Moose, Goose and Little Nobody* (1974) blends repetitive text with acrobatic calligraphy in an elegant and witty way.

Raskin once asked herself, "Switching from commercial art to picture book is plausible, but what about from picture book to the novel?"

The question was satisfactorily answered with the publication of Raskin's first full-length story. *The Mysterious Disappearance of Leon (I Mean Noel)* (1972) is crammed with word puzzles, zany characters, slapstick, and ingenious pictures created from letters and words. *Figgs & Phantoms* (1974), a Newbery Honor Book, chronicles the story of the Figg family's search for "Capri," their own personal paradise. Cryptic references to Velázquez, Gauguin, Schubert, Gilbert and Sullivan, Milton, Joseph Conrad, and WILLIAM BLAKE provide Raskin with the opportunity to explore her own passions, but may not be understood or appreciated by younger readers. In *The Tattooed Potato and Other Clues* (1975) budding artist Dickory Dock finds herself entangled in the mysterious world of Greenwich Village painter/detective Garson. While Raskin entertains the reader with nonsensical wordplay and rhyme, her story is more concerned with the idea of reality and illusion. "What I can teach you," Garson explains, is "how to observe ... how to see through frills and facades ... how to see through disguises." This book received the Mystery Writers of America's Edgar Allan Poe Special Award.

Raskin's last novel, *The Westing Game* (1978), received both the Newbery Medal and the Boston Globe–Horn Book Award. The book—the seemingly simple tale of an eccentric millionaire's will that sends his heirs off on a search for his murderer—combines Raskin's flair for word games, disguises, multiple aliases, and subterfuges with her love for the stock market, the game of chess, and her hometown. On being awarded the Newbery Medal, Raskin rejoiced in the fact that all her "beloved characters are alive and well and forevermore will be playing The Westing Game." The continued popularity of *The Westing Game* has assured the long life of heroine and puzzle-solver Turtle Wexler and her fellow heirs.

Illustration by Ellen Raskin from her book *The Mysterious Disappearance of Leon (I Mean Noel)* (1971).

As Uncle Florence in *Figgs & Phantoms* said, "I dream of a gentle world, peopled with good people and filled with simple and good things.... From books I built my dreams; in books I found Capri." Through her picture books and novels, Raskin has allowed children and adults alike to find their own Capri. ❧ M.I.A.

RAWLINGS, MARJORIE KINNAN

AMERICAN AUTHOR, 1896–1953. Marjorie Kinnan Rawlings discovered her literary voice in Florida, where she produced several classic works of American fiction. Although her best writing concerned rural regions, the author was born and raised in Washington, D.C., where her father was a patent attorney. Rawlings developed an early interest in writing and had a story published in the *Washington Post* at age eleven. She attended the University of Wisconsin in Madison, where she edited the school literary magazine and met her first husband. The author's early work experiences include writing publicity for the YWCA, editing a magazine, reporting for the Louisville *Courier-Journal* in Kentucky and the Rochester *Journal* in New York, and writing poetry for a newspaper syndicate.

In 1928 Rawlings left her husband and used an inheritance to purchase a seventy-two-acre orange grove in Cross Creek, in rural Florida. Rawlings immersed herself in the backwoods atmosphere, exploring nature and spending time with country people, who told her stories and took her hunting. Inspired by the locale, she began writing stories of rural life, including the classics "Jacob's Ladder" and "Gal Young Un."

Her first novel, *South Moon Under* (1933), which concerns the life of a Florida moonshiner, was followed by her masterpiece, *The Yearling* (1938), the story of twelve-year-old Jody Baxter, who lives in the Florida scrub country with his pragmatic mother and kindly, storytelling father. Rawlings beautifully describes the natural setting and the poor, yet proud families who reside there. Jody adopts an orphaned fawn, which is named Flag by the tragic, mystical Fodder-wing, youngest son of the wild Forrester clan. During the course of one year, against a background that includes farming, hunting, a community feud, a weeklong rainstorm, Christmas, and many other events, Jody tames the fawn and the two grow to be close companions. But when Flag begins to trample and eat the family's crops, the yearling deer must be killed, and Jody runs away from his family. He soon returns home, with the newfound awareness that he is no longer a "yearling" himself; he has left childhood behind. Rawlings's evocative descriptions of rural Florida and its people make *The Yearling* regional fiction at its best, yet the novel is universal in its depiction of the human experience. The book was awarded the Pulitzer Prize and made into a 1946 motion picture starring Gregory Peck and Jane Wyman as Jody's parents. Although originally published for adults, it is now primarily read and enjoyed by children.

Rawlings wrote only one work expressly for children. Published posthumously, *The Secret River* (1955) is a timeless story about Calpurnia, an aspiring young poet who journeys from her Florida home to a secret river, where she catches some much-needed fish for her father to sell. Although the dialogue is occasionally sentimental, there is a magical quality to this gentle, allegorical tale, which was named a Newbery Honor Book. Among Rawlings's other works is the autobiographical *Cross Creek* (1942); actress Mary Steenburgen portrayed Rawlings in the 1983 film adaptation.

The last decade of the twentieth century marked a renewed interest in the life and writings of the author, suggesting that Rawlings's evocative stories of rural Florida will continue to be widely read and enjoyed in the twenty-first century. P.D.S.

Rawls, Wilson

AMERICAN AUTHOR, 1913–1984. Although he had little formal education, Woodrow Wilson Rawls wrote two novels that have achieved great popularity with young readers. Born in Scraper, Oklahoma, and raised on a farm, Rawls was taught at home by his mother. He decided to become a writer at age ten after reading Jack London's *Call of the Wild*. Rawls later attended school in Tahlequah, Oklahoma, but the economic Depression of the 1930s caused him to drop out in the eighth grade and seek work as a carpenter in Mexico, South America, Alaska, Canada, and throughout the United States. He constantly wrote, but didn't seek publication until he married and settled down in his mid-forties.

Where the Red Fern Grows (1961), based on his childhood experiences, appeared in the *Saturday Evening Post* before it was published as an adult novel. This first-person story of Billy Colman, an Ozark farmboy, and his hunting adventures with a pair of coon hounds is extraordinarily popular, possibly because it is often assigned in schools. The book is notable for its rural setting and emphasizes the strong bonds between humans and animals, but is flawed by an overly emotional writing style. Billy weeps so frequently that his tears have lost their impact long before the final, touching chapters. A film version was released in 1974. Rawls's second novel, *Summer of the Monkeys* (1976), is similar to his first in its early-twentieth-century Ozark setting, characterizations, and themes, and it even contains a nearly identical closing sentence. However, Jay Berry Lee's quest to capture some lost circus monkeys has a somewhat lighter tone. Both books are rich in rural atmosphere and feature adolescent boys single-mindedly pursuing a goal with tenacity and grit. P.D.S.

Rayner, Mary

BRITISH AUTHOR AND ILLUSTRATOR, B. 1933. Mary Rayner was born in Mandalay, Burma. Some of her earliest memories include watching elephants drag logs through the jungle, going on fireside camping trips, and journeying up and down the wide Irrawaddy and Chindwin rivers by paddle steamer. When the Japanese invaded Burma, eight-year-old Mary, her mother, and two siblings walked over the mountains into India. Her father, having joined the army in Burma, was killed. After spending the remainder of the war in India, her family returned to the United Kingdom. Educated at the University of St. Andrews in Scotland, Mary received a degree in English, then worked in various London publishing houses from 1956 to 1962. She married E. H. Rayner in 1960, and the couple had three children, all of whom earn their livings as writers.

Rayner's own career as a freelance book illustrator and writer began in 1972. Her first book for middle-grade children, *The Witch-Finder* (1976), was followed by two picture books, *Mr. and Mrs. Pig's Evening Out* (1976) and *Garth Pig and the IceCream Lady* (1977). "The pig stories," she has said, "began as stories invented for my children, and, although they have now grown beyond picture books, their comments and criticisms are a great help to me still." Both books received critical acclaim at the time of their publication. *Mr. and Mrs. Pig's Evening Out* is a clever tale about a family of anthropomorphic porkers in the midst of a crisis familiar to most human children: contending with a new baby sitter while Mom and Dad step out alone. Following their groans, the ten piglets ask the usual question, "What is her name?" The answer turns out to be especially portentous, for the baby sitter is just what her appellation—Mrs. Wolf—implies. Rayner's lively, whimsical blend of art and text culminates in a highly satisfying resolution. *Garth Pig and the IceCream Lady* represents another episode in which the young protagonists outwit the hungry wolf, disguised as the icecream vendor herself. Additions to the pig saga include *Mrs. Pig Gets Cross and Other Stories* (1986), a seven-tale volume for ages six to eight, and *Garth Pig Steals the Show* (1993), featuring the musical "Pigs Von Trapp." The wolf makes a comeback in both titles.

What distinguishes these books is the brilliantly concise elucidation that although they are small in stature and limited in terms of life experience, children can triumph over seemingly formidable odds. ❧ C.K.S.

Reid, Barbara

Canadian illustrator, b. 1957. *The New Baby Calf* (1984) launched Barbara Reid into international prominence in the children's book world. Her distinctive bas-relief Plasticine illustrations for Edith Chase's gentle farmyard tale exhibit Reid's trademarks: vibrant colors, aerial views, attention to detail, and sense of fun.

Reid grew up in Toronto, where she still lives. While studying at the Ontario College of Art, she had to reproduce Botticelli's *Birth of Venus* in a different medium. After several ill-fated attempts using tissue paper, she tried Plasticine, which was a great success. She still enjoys the challenge of artistic problem solving, which, she avers, is why she became an illustrator rather than a fine artist, and she continues to experiment. Her palette ranges from the warm earth tones of *The New Baby Calf* to the brilliant multicolored plumage of Joanne Oppenheim's *Have You Seen Birds?* (1987). This book so delighted readers that it won five major Canadian children's book awards in 1988, the same year Reid received the prestigious Ezra Jack Keats Award, given to a promising young illustrator of international stature.

Character development is the key to *Effie* (1990), Beverly Allinson's story of a loudmouthed ant—no easy task when the text requires that all the ants look alike. For *Zoe's Snowy Day, Zoe's Rainy Day, Zoe's Sunny Day,* and *Zoe's Windy Day* (all 1991), named for her young daughter, Reid had complete artistic control. The award-winning result is a set of utterly charming child-sized and child-centered wordless board books. At *Scholastic*'s suggestion, she wrote her first picture-book text: *Two by Two* (1992), her version of a traditional song about Noah's Ark, it is a virtuoso performance. It was reprinted several times within the year of its publication and made Reid the first two-time winner of the Elizabeth Mrazik-Cleaver Canadian Picture Book Award.

Reid also works in pencil, ink, and watercolor, with less noteworthy results. She has illustrated a number of nonfiction activity books this way, including her own *Playing with Plasticine* (1988), a generous response to the many children who wanted to know "how she did it." Reid begins by spreading the Plasticine background onto a piece of illustration board. She applies the rest of the picture in layers and adds the tiniest details last. She uses everything from her fingernails to fabric scraps to create texture, sometimes adding metallic paint and beads, she says, "for a bit of sparkle." The originals are approximately twice the size of the book illustrations. Her husband, photographer Ian Crysler, shoots the finished pieces under carefully arranged lighting. For the sharpest image, the photos are all printed from slides—Reid's exuberant creatures seem to leap off the page.

In taking a whimsical medium and making it her own, Reid has established herself as a unique and major children's illustrator, Canada's queen of Plasticine. ❧ A.G.

Reid Banks, Lynne

British author of fiction, plays, and history, b. 1929. Lynne Reid Banks was born in London. During the Second World War, she was evacuated to Saskatchewan. After returning to England, she studied acting, hoping to become an actress, like her mother. After graduation from the Royal Academy of Dramatic Art in London and five years of work, however, she found she could not support herself in that career. She then worked as a journalist, becoming the first woman reporter on British television, and she was also a teacher on a kibbutz in Israel before she eventually became a full-time writer.

Reid Banks is known as a fine storyteller. Among her first works for adults is *The L-Shaped Room,* which was published in 1960. The protagonist, unmarried and pregnant, is turned out of her home by her angry father. The girl lives by herself in a small rented room, where an odd collection of neighbors extend their friendship to her. The book is widely read by young adults.

Her most popular books for children are those in a series that began with *The Indian in the Cupboard* in 1981. In this fantasy, a magic cabinet, or cupboard, is used to bring to life a toy plastic figure of an American Indian. The tale is one of adventure, with life-and-death situations, spiced by the boys' fear of discovery as they enjoy the excitement of having such an important secret. The relationship drawn between friends—the arguments, the friendship—rings true and makes the fantasy element more believable. Although extremely popular, the book has been criticized for its stereotypical portrayal of American Indians. It has three sequels: *Return of the Indian* (1986), *The Secret of the Indian* (1989), and *The Mystery of the Cupboard* (1993). Her other works for children include *I, Houdini: The Autobiography of a Self-Educated Hamster* (1988), a story of a conceited hamster who loves to escape from his cage and wreak havoc in the house where he lives with a family that includes three boys. *Melusine: A Mystery* (1989), for young adults, is a novel based on a twelfth-century French legend in which a young woman is condemned to change into the form of a snake. The chilling tale has elements of incest and murder. One of her books written for the adult market, *Dark Quartet: The Story of the Brontës,* was named a Best Book for Young Adults in 1977 by the American Library Association. Reid Banks has also written books of history for adults and plays for stage, television, and radio. She sometimes acts in plays on the radio. Her flair for suspense and adventurous storytelling makes her stories compelling and popular. ♘ S.H.H.

Reiss, Johanna De Leeuw

AMERICAN AUTHOR, B. 1932. Johanna Reiss spent her childhood in her native country, Holland; and as the Second World War began, she and her Jewish family suffered under Hitler's rule. Reiss wrote two fictional books based upon her experiences, *The Upstairs Room* (1972) and *The Journey Back* (1976).

As recounted in *The Upstairs Room,* when she was ten years old Reiss and Sini, her sixteen-year-old sister, were hidden from the Nazis by a Christian couple, Johan and Dientje Oostervelds, in the farmhouse they shared with Johan's mother, Opoe. The Oostervelds risked death by their actions, and in the course of the book, others who were caught hiding Jews were revealed to be shot. The girls were confined to one upstairs room for two and a half years, where they had to stay away from the windows and avoid making noise that would alert the Nazis to their presence. They constantly risked discovery, but they also suffered from many other deprivations during their long confinement—especially, the absence of the rest of their family. The inability to go outdoors had serious consequences. Annie (Johanna) began to lose the ability to walk because of her inactivity. And Sini, as she grew into her late teens, despaired of growing up, of ever meeting someone to marry, and of living the life she had expected before the war. At one point, Nazis searched the house and the girls had to be concealed in a hidden compartment that Johan had wisely built into a closet.

The story of a girl who, like Anne Frank, was hidden from the Nazis, but who survived, would be remarkable merely for the events described. But the book is all the more remarkable for the way Reiss is able to recall and record the events she saw and experienced as a young child. While great dangers to her world and her survival loom, Annie portrays the concerns of the adults around her, but vividly recalls such details as her annoyance at being pushed away by her usually attentive father while he strains for radio reports of the impending war. The most powerful example of this child's perspective is the moment when ten-year-old Annie reads the underground newspaper Johan gives her and learns what is really happening to Jewish people and others the Nazis deem undesirable. Previously, she had had no real idea of what happened when Jewish people were taken away on trains; and she expresses her thoughts about these revelations in the language and perspective of a ten-year-old.

Both girls survived the war, and their father and another sister survived as well. In *The Journey Back,* Reiss describes how, after the war ended, those who survived were again free and how her country began to rebuild itself as she became reacquainted with her father and her older sister, Rachel.

The Upstairs Room was awarded the Buxtehuder Bulle, a German children's book award, in 1976. The American Library Association named it a Newbery Honor Book, and it won the Jane Addams Children's Book Award in 1973. It also received the National Jewish Book Award in 1972.

Reiss graduated from college in Holland and taught elementary school for several years. She immigrated to the United States, married, and had two children. Though she settled in New York City, Reiss frequently travels to Holland and has visited the Oostervelds many times since the war. ♘ S.H.H.

Rey, H. A.

AMERICAN AUTHOR AND ILLUSTRATOR, 1898–1977. Hans Augusto Rey combined an inquisitive mind and an extensive knowledge of natural sciences with a talent for expressive drawing and achieved an internationally recognized career as a creator and illustrator of picture books for children and adults. Through the character of Curious George, the adventurous tailless monkey, he projected his own lively curiosity in the world around him and at the same time kept his stories within the realm of children's activities and comprehension. His books are rooted in his keen empathy with children and with their efforts to discover and try new things. Although Curious George began in England as a character named Zozo and is known in France as Fifi, his mischievous exploits in such books as *Curious George* (1941), *Curious George Takes a Job* (1947), *Curious George Rides a Bike* (1952), and *Curious George Goes to the Hospital* (1966) are universal and have been translated into more than a dozen languages.

After laying out a rough dummy, Rey did the artwork for many of his books by making the color separations himself. His illustrations make vivid use of strong colors, often with an incisive black outline of objects and figures. They interplay on the page with the text and are full of action and humor. Rey gives his animals, such as George and Cecily G., the giraffe in *Cecily G. and the 9 Monkeys* (1942), individuality as characters, but their actions are informed by his precise knowledge of their anatomy.

During World War II when toys and paper were scarce, Rey anticipated the flap books children enjoy today with a series of small-sized books, *Is Anybody at Home?* (1939), *How Do You Get There?* (1941), and *Where's My Baby?* (1943), in which the answers were hidden under flaps. His scientific knowledge and interest in stargazing prompted him to write and illustrate *The Stars: A New Way to See Them* (1952), a picture book for adults. Here his ability as an artist to see spaces and forms led him to try various connecting lines between the stars of a constellation until he had a shape that made visual sense to the layperson. He followed this with *Find the Constellations* (1954).

After World War I, in which he spent two years as a soldier in the German army, Rey studied languages, philosophy, and natural sciences at universities in Munich and Hamburg, and worked as a lithographer and illustrator. In the 1920s he lived in Brazil. There he met and married his wife, Margret, an artist and writer who was a partner in his work, often cowriting the texts for their books, as well as creating stories of her own, such as *Pretzel* (1944) and *Spotty* (1945), for him to illustrate. He also used the pseudonym Uncle Gus. In 1936 the Reys moved to Paris, and several of his early picture books were published there. When the Nazis approached, the Reys fled on bicycles to Lisbon, eventually reaching New York via Rio de Janeiro in 1940. For many years they lived in Cambridge, Massachusetts, and summered in New Hampshire.

Illustration by H. A. Rey from his book *Curious George* (1941).

Since Rey's death in 1977, a series of books has appeared with the text by Margret Rey and artwork by another artist working in Rey's style and using the Curious George character, but the art lacks the quality of Rey's illustrations. Curious George remains, however, a recognized and beloved monkey who will continue to amuse and comfort children for years to come. L.K.

Rice, Eve

American author and illustrator, b. 1951. Starting with simple, everyday subjects such as buying shoes (*New Blue Shoes,* 1975) and an afternoon's walk (*What Sadie Sang,* 1976), Eve Rice combines a gentle sense of humor with a genuine feeling for preschoolers and toddlers. Her eye for details and her appreciation of the rhythm of language ground her stories in a child's world. She illustrates her books using line drawings, frequently with only one or two colors. The illustrations are uncomplicated but, at the same time, filled with details such as delightful facial expressions that make them appealing to very young readers.

As a child in Bedford, New York, Rice loved to draw and early on decided to be an artist when she grew up. Getting her to read was another matter; it was not until college that she learned to appreciate literature. After graduating from Yale University, Rice moved to New York City and worked full-time writing and illustrating children's books. In the mid-1980s Rice started medical school, graduating in 1989. Although she continued to write, she gave up illustrating while pursuing her studies.

Illustration by Eve Rice from her book *Goodnight, Goodnight* (1980).

In addition to her books for the very young, Rice has written several beginning readers and a novel for older children. She carries her love of details to a ridiculous extreme in her novel, *The Remarkable Return of Winston Potter Crisply* (1978). When Becky and her little brother see their oldest brother, Potter, who is supposed to be at Harvard, in Central Park, they realize something unusual is going on. Donning outlandish old clothes as disguises, they follow him to find out why he is in New York. Rice's two young detectives draw all the wrong conclusions from their observations of Potter and come up with an elaborate spy network.

Her books for beginning readers are also filled with humor. In *Mr. Brimble's Hobby and Other Stories* (1975), it ranges from slapstick when Mr. Brimble's hobby of collecting musical instruments forces his family to move out of the house to a more subtle play on words when Willy and Polly Brimble, having discovered a new word—*serendipity*—try to find the dictionary and serendipitously find their lost toys instead.

It is, however, the very youngest audience that most strongly appeals to Rice. In *Sam Who Never Forgets* (1977), it appears that Sam, the zookeeper, has forgotten the elephant's dinner. But Sam hasn't forgotten. Because he knows the elephant so well, Sam brings him a special wagon full of his favorite hay. The illustrations in this reassuring book are quite different from some of Rice's others; they consist of flat, simple color shapes that create interesting patterns on the page. Lewis, in *Oh, Lewis!* (1974), has to contend with his boots coming unbuckled, his hood coming untied, and his jacket coming unzipped, a familiar predicament for most children. After his mother wishes he would not come undone anymore, Lewis finds he can't undo anything when he gets home—until his mother suggests he try taking off his mittens first and then unbuckle and unzip his clothes.

Rice's celebration of the ordinary mixed with warmth and humor make her books very popular with preschoolers. ❧ P.R.

Richard, Adrienne

AMERICAN WRITER, B. 1921. Adrienne Richard was born in Evanston, Illinois, and graduated from the University of Chicago in 1943. She completed further study at the Writers Workshop at the University of Iowa and at Boston College.

Richard's first novel for young adults, *Pistol* (1969), was named a Horn Book Honor Book and an American Library Association Notable Book. *Pistol* began as a short story based on Richard's husband's experiences on a snowbound cattle drive in Montana. As Richard began to imagine the emotions of a young boy involved in such an adventure, the story grew into a compassionate account of a boy's struggle to find himself while his world crumbles. Richard explains, "I have tried to portray a maturing boy in a dying land." Set in the cattle country of Montana just prior to the Great Depression, *Pistol* is full of the life and vigor of the ranchers and cow punchers. When Billy signs on as a horse wrangler for the summer, he feels he has reached the pinnacle of happiness, as he experiences ranch life to its fullest potential and begins to imagine a permanent place for himself among the gruff ranch hands. When he returns home after his second summer, however, Billy is faced with the start of the Depression and his father's desertion. Richard's fondness for the land is evident in the wealth of rich and colorful detail she conveys.

Richard's other books for young people include *The Accomplice* (1973), a novel about growing up in war-torn Israel, *Wings* (1974), which chronicles life in the United States in the early part of this century, and *Into the Road* (1976), a young adult novel concerned with motorcycle touring. Fueled by a "need to know everything" about a particular time and place, Richard conducts extensive research for each of her books. By immersing herself in an era and combining her findings with her own experiences, Richard creates books that explore the moments in history that shape a society. ❧ M.O'D.H.

RICHARDS, LAURA E.

AMERICAN AUTHOR, 1850–1943. Laura E. Richards was the daughter of highly achieving, gifted parents. Her father, Samuel Gridley Howe, was director of the Perkins Institution and Massachusetts School for the Blind. Her mother was the poet Julia Ward Howe, best known for writing "The Battle Hymn of the Republic."

Born in Boston, the author grew up in a warm family environment that she describes in her autobiographical book for children, *When I Was Your Age* (1894). After she married in 1871 and became a mother, Richards began writing verses for children's magazines such as *St. Nicholas*. Her first book of POETRY, *Sketches and Scraps* (1881), contains "A Legend of Okeefinokee," the well-known humorous verse about a discontent frog and a joke-playing mockingbird. Richards published numerous volumes of children's verse, including the highly regarded *In My Nursery* (1890), which presents a fine variety of work, including poems about everyday activities such as walking in the rain, reverent religious verse about Easter, story-poems, a lofty paean to "The Flag in the Classroom," and much nonsense verse that relies on made-up words and silly situations.

Tirra Lirra: Rhymes Old and New (1932) is considered Richards's most lasting contribution to children's literature. Fun and good humor abound in this collection of poetry, much of which was previously published in books and periodicals. Especially memorable are "The Monkeys and the Crocodile," which concerns five simians who learn the dangers of teasing, and "Eletelephony," a tangled tale of an elephant on a telephone. Unfortunately, some of the verses, such as "An Indian Ballad" and "The Buffalo," propagate racial stereotypes; other poems contain comic scenes of beheadings, drownings, and hangings and may now be considered excessively violent. Yet most of Richards's poetry remains fresh and enjoyable for the modern reader.

The same cannot be said of her novels for children, which today seem sentimental and dated. The "Hildegarde" series, which includes *Queen Hildegarde* (1889) and *Hildegarde's Holiday* (1891), features an idealized teenage girl doing good deeds. *Captain January* (1890) concerns a girl rescued from a shipwreck and raised by an elderly lighthouse keeper; Shirley Temple starred in the 1936 film adaptation.

Richards also wrote a number of biographical works for young readers, including *Florence Nightingale, the Angel of the Crimea* (1909) and *Joan of Arc* (1919), which are weakened by a fictionalized writing style. The author's adult biographies are much more successful. *Julia Ward Howe, 1819–1910*, a two-volume work written with her sister, Maud Howe Elliott, was the first biography to win a Pulitzer Prize (1917).

Although most of Richards's prose is long forgotten, her poetry demonstrates a rare ability to tickle the ear and funnybone and continues to delight young readers. ❧ P.D.S.

RILEY, JAMES WHITCOMB

AMERICAN POET, 1849–1916. To the thousands of schoolchildren over the years who read, memorized, and recited his poetry, James Whitcomb Riley has been known as "the Hoosier Poet." Although his nickname implies a regional appeal, during his lifetime Riley was one of the most popular and critically acclaimed poets in the United States.

Riley's poetry is part of the regional literature of the Midwest, characterized by verse written in a folk dialect long since vanished. Riley once explained, "I talk of the dear old times when there were no social distinctions, of pioneer homes and towns, where there was a warm welcome for all." An exaggerated estimate of his abilities as a children's poet prevailed during his era because the rose-tinted "Currier and Ives" picture of childhood portrayed in his verse struck a tremendous popular nerve.

By today's more objective standards, Riley is not considered a great children's poet.

Some of his poems, however, so perfectly capture and express the myth of rural America that phrases such as "When the frost is on the punkin" and "the old swimmin'-hole" have become a permanent part of our cultural heritage. And it was Riley who supposedly inspired fellow Hoosier author Johnny Gruelle in naming Raggedy Ann, a hybrid of "The Raggedy Man" and "Little Orphan Annie."

His literary reputation stands on three enduring poems: "The Raggedy Man," "Nine Little Goblins" ("with green-glass eyes"), and "Little Orphan Annie," with its famous line, "An' the Gobble-uns'll git you/Ef you/Don't/Watch/Out!" These works are distinguished by a true child's view of the world. "Nine Little Goblins" is all about rhyming nonsense, while "Little Orphan Annie" has the shivery fascination of mock-macabre terror. "Ain't he a' awful good Raggedy Man?/Raggedy!/Raggedy!/Raggedy Man!" is a perfect example of Riley's skillful use of swinging rhythms and chiming refrains so appealing to the child's ear.

Few boys enjoyed a happier childhood than "Bud," who was born in a log cabin in Greenfield, Indiana. He loved nature, the fields and the streams and the farmers who worked the land. Memories of this pioneer past were a fertile landscape for Riley in later years. Applying his imagination and rhythmic skills to familiar rural speech, manners, and characters, he fashioned his trademark Hoosier dialect. In 1875 Riley received his first check for a poem from his hometown newspaper. Riley developed his talent for making a living quite by accident. Formal education played a minimal role in his development. He showed no inclination toward any sort of professional career, drifting through numerous occupations: selling Bibles door to door, writing jingles for newspapers, and traveling with a medicine show, Dr. McCrillus' Standard Remedies. Beginning in 1883, however, Riley shrewdly parlayed his talent for dramatic recitation and a gift for salesmanship into a successful career as a star poet/entertainer on the lecture circuit throughout the United States.

His creative cycle seemed to complete itself by the age of forty. Thereafter, he spent most of his time preparing manuscripts for publication. Riley's children's verse were originally collected in three volumes: *Rhymes of Childhood* (1891), *A Child-World* (1897), and *Book of Joyous Children* (1902).

In the city and state, where his memory is a living presence, stands the perfect tribute to the Hoosier Poet. At the front entrance of the Central Library are gates with a bronze tablet: "These gates are the gift of the children of Indianapolis in loving remembrance of their friend James Whitcomb Riley." ❧ M.W.

Robertson, Keith

AMERICAN AUTHOR, 1914–1991. Keith Robertson composed several of his children's books not with a pen or typewriter but by dictating the stories into a tape recorder. This may come as no surprise to readers who have found Robertson's writing style clear, conversational, and unpretentious. The Iowa-born author did not harbor lofty literary aspirations, but preferred to tell a rousing story filled with adventure, suspense, and humor.

Illustration by Robert McCloskey from *Henry Reed's Baby-Sitting Service* (1966), by Keith Robertson.

Robertson grew up in rural areas of Kansas, Missouri, Minnesota, Wisconsin, and Oklahoma. He was always interested in writing but had little success with the manuscripts he submitted to periodicals during his high school years. When finances made college seem an impossibility, Robertson enlisted in the navy, hoping it would provide entrance to the Naval Academy at Annapolis. After performing as a radioman on a battleship, he was accepted. Robertson left the service after his graduation but returned to duty during World War II, spending the next five years as an officer on navy destroyers.

After the war, Robertson's desire to write was reawakened, and he went to work as a publisher's representative. As he traveled the country selling children's books to bookstores, he began to read his wares and discovered they were the kind of writing he wanted to do. His first book, *Ticktock and Jim,* a suspenseful story about a boy and his horse, was published in 1948. Robertson and his family settled on a small New Jersey farm where the new author continued writing books for the middle-grade audience. Among his children's books are mysteries, animal stories, historical sea adventures—some taking place in the nineteenth century, others during World War II—and three nonfiction volumes. Under the name Carlton Keith, Robertson published six adult mysteries.

But the author achieved his greatest success writing for a younger audience. The "Carson Street Detective" stories, beginning with *Three Stuffed Owls* in 1954, revolve around boy detectives Swede and Neil and are filled with adventure and fun. Robertson's most popular books are the "Henry Reed" stories, which began with *Henry Reed, Inc.* in 1958. Henry Reed lives overseas because his father is in the diplomatic service, but he visits his Uncle Al and Aunt Mabel in Grover's Corner, New Jersey, each summer. With his friend and business partner, Midge Glass, Henry becomes involved in a number of moneymaking enterprises, including a baby-sitting service and a think tank. Robertson based the character of Henry on a female schoolteacher who seemed to be a lightning rod for unusual events. Henry is a similar character—wherever he goes, peculiar things happen. With a deadpan style, Henry records the wildly funny occurrences in Grover's Corner in his journal entries, often failing to see the humor in these experiences or notice how many of the events he himself has precipitated. Although Henry indulges in a little 1950s-style female bashing when he talks about his friend Midge, she is shown as a witty, competent person who eventually wins Henry's grudging respect. Both characters are marvelous creations, and the books are filled with good humor and hilarious minor characters. Robertson's gift for writing appealing and entertaining books is most evident in this still popular series.

P.D.S.

Robin Hood

"Will you come with me, sweet Reader? . . . Give me your hand." So begins Howard Pyle's classic version of *The Merry Adventures of Robin Hood* (1883). It's an invitation that few readers have refused. The legendary outlaw known as Robin Hood has been a favorite romantic character for centuries. Possessing the ideal heroic characteristics—good looks, a noble cause, and superior skill—Robin Hood has been adapted and adopted by generations eager for rousing adventure and the triumph of a free-spirited rebel.

Although many have tried to prove that Robin Hood was a real person, his actual identity remains unknown. There is an intriguing mention of a "Robertus Hood fugitivus" (a fugitive named Robin Hood) in an English legal document in 1230. Some believe Robin Hood was actually Roger Godberd, who developed a notorious reputation for robbing and killing travelers in Sherwood Forest in the 1260s. Joseph Ritson (1752–1803), who published what he declared to be the definitive book about the hero in 1795, insisted that Robin Hood was actually Robert Fitzooth, born in 1160 at Locksley in Nottinghamshire, and later made Earl of Huntingdon. Appearing first in early medieval English ballads and poems, Robin Hood continued to be a popular character in various songs, poems, broadsides, and chapbooks throughout the next three centuries; by the late eighteenth century Robin Hood could be found in operas and musicals, as well as the plays of William Shakespeare, Ben Jonson, and Anthony Munday. In addition to an appearance in Sir Walter Scott's *Ivanhoe* (1819), Robin Hood is also featured in many other works, including poems by Lord Tennyson and Alfred Noyes and two novels by Alexandre Dumas. Ritson's version was used as the basis for the first children's book (and thus many subsequent versions) about Robin Hood, published in 1840 by Pierce Egan the younger. Children found the short, episodic chapters easy and enthralling to read.

American audiences were particularly receptive to the handsome English robber, beginning in 1883 with Pyle's beautifully designed and illustrated edition. Although long and archaic in language, *The Merry Adventures of Robin Hood* inspired many others and still remains a standard. Well-known children's authors who have written about Robin Hood include Enid Blyton in *Tales of Robin Hood* (1930), Geoffrey Trease in *Bows Against the Barons* (1934), Rosemary Sutcliff in *The Chronicles of Robin Hood* (1950), Roger Lancelyn Green in *Adventures of Robin Hood* (1956), and Ian Serraillier in *Robin in the Greenwood* (1967) and *Robin and His Merry Men* (1969). Some notable recent versions are *Robin Hood, His Life and Legend* (1979) by Bernard Miles and *The Outlaws of Sherwood* (1988) by Robin McKinley. Among the many illustrators who have brought their talents to the tale are Walter Crane, Virginia Lee Burton, Louis Slobodkin,

N. C. WYETH, and Victor G. Ambrus. There have also been a host of Robin Hood films and television series, starring famous swashbucklers such as Douglas Fairbanks, Errol Flynn, Sean Connery, and Kevin Costner. Walt Disney Studios made an animated version in 1973, in which the characters are cast as animals (Robin is a fox).

Young readers today continue to relish the energy and excitement of the Robin Hood story, which features nonstop action, intrigue, romance, and daring rescues. In some ways Robin Hood is a quintessentially modern hero. Living freely in the forest with his communal band of "merry men," Robin derives his strength from his youth, defiance of authority, harmony with nature, and the use of clever guerrilla warfare tactics to outsmart and outwit the enemy. Set firmly in a particular place and time, the Robin Hood story has nevertheless managed to transcend its origins to become a timeless tale, as fresh and compelling as when it was first heard. C.J.

Robinson, Barbara

AMERICAN AUTHOR, B. 1927. Many readers are first introduced to Barbara Robinson during the holiday season, when her book *The Best Christmas Pageant Ever* (1972) is read aloud in classrooms and libraries. Although she has written several other titles, the author is best known for this perennial holiday favorite. Robinson was born in Portsmouth, Ohio, and began writing as a child. She studied theater at Allegheny College, then worked in a library until she married. As a freelance writer, Robinson has sold fiction to a number of women's magazines, including *Ladies' Home Journal, McCall's,* and *Good Housekeeping.* Her first book, *Across from Indian Shore* (1962), was inspired by her interest in American Indians. It is the story of a boy who is friends with an aged Wampanoag princess. Robinson followed this novel with another Indian adventure, *Trace through the Forest* (1965), and a rather didactic picture book, *The Fattest Bear in the First Grade* (1969).

The author's most popular book, *The Best Christmas Pageant Ever,* concerns the lying, stealing, cigar-smoking Herdman children, who are lured into church with the promise of treats and end up taking over the annual Christmas nativity program. This short, fast-paced novel contains laugh-out-loud humor that is slightly irreverent but never sacrilegious. The book's conclusion, in which the Herdmans come to appreciate Christmas, is moving but not saccharine. The nameless narrator represents the community's gradual, grudging respect for the Herdman family but plays no significant role in the story. Further, the six Herdman children are fairly interchangeable as characters. Nevertheless, the book is great fun and continues to be enjoyed by readers each holiday season. It has also been adapted for the stage and produced as a television special.

Illustration by Judith Gwyn Brown from *The Best Christmas Pageant Ever* (1972), by Barbara Robinson.

Robinson developed *The Best Christmas Pageant Ever* from a story she had originally published in a woman's magazine. She expanded another magazine story into *Temporary Times, Temporary Places* (1982), which tells of a teenage girl's first romance. This introspective, mature novel depicts fifteen-year-old Janet's crush on Eddie, then follows the relationship as they begin dating and eventually break up when Eddie starts seeing another girl. The conflicting emotions of young love are sensitively and honestly explored in this well-written novel. Robinson abandoned quiet introspection for broad comedy in *My Brother Louis Measures Worms and Other Louis Stories* (1988), a collection of interrelated stories about the Lawson family. Although narrator Mary Elizabeth Lawson is a rather indistinct character, her tales are filled with eccentric and colorful family members involved in zany situations, including her seven-year-old brother's experiences driving the family car.

Robinson's work demonstrates a talent for engaging the reader's emotions, whether she is poignantly writing about a first romance or provoking laughter with her humorous stories. ❧ P.D.S.

ROCKWELL, ANNE

AMERICAN AUTHOR AND ILLUSTRATOR, B. 1934. Anne Rockwell has written and illustrated more than seventy books and collaborated with her husband, HARLOW ROCKWELL, on over twenty more. Among them are PICTURE BOOKS, INFORMATION BOOKS for middle-grade readers, folktales, and folktale collections, including *The Three Bears and 15 Other Stories* (1975), a delightful collection of brightly illustrated tales. But her most significant contribution has been her informational books for preschoolers. Characterized by simple text and vibrant, clear illustrations, these works capture the perspectives and interest of the youngest children.

Rockwell was born in Memphis, Tennessee, and spent her childhood in various parts of the United States. She developed an early interest in drawing and went on to study art at the Sculpture Center in New York City and at the Pratt Institute in Brooklyn. After the first of her three children was born, she began writing and illustrating children's books; her first, *Paul and Arthur Search for the Egg*, was published in 1964. Her books about transportation, including boats, cars, planes, trains, and trucks, are among her most popular. In each, a clearly delineated vehicle is depicted in context with a peppy animal operator. Rockwell starts with the familiar: On the title page of *Boats* (1982), a young bear heads to the bath with his toy boat; on the next page the same boat—now piloted by a bear—is accompanied by the simple text "Boats float." She goes on to introduce less familiar concepts, but eventually returns to the boat of the first page.

Rockwell presents a number of other concepts with books that feature Bear Child. *First Comes Spring* (1985) discusses seasons and seasonal activity with a nicely patterned structure. Each season is introduced with a picture of the world right outside Bear Child's house and with what Bear Child is wearing. The subsequent two-page spread shows bears doing all kinds of seasonal activity, and, on the next two pages, each activity is depicted and labeled—everything from making mud pies to putting screens on the windows.

Things that Go (1986) and *Things to Play With* (1988) help children classify and arrange their world. Each two-page spread describes an overall concept, such as "things that go in the air," and is illustrated with a dozen familiar and less familiar examples. Each "thing" is operated by an animal—with a pleasing absence of sex-role stereotyping—and is shown in use. The pages have enough activity to be exciting without being overwhelming.

Among the books that Rockwell has written with her husband are those in the "My World" series, which help young children feel comfortable with new ideas, such as baby sitters and being sick. The books maintain a young child's perspective by using a first-person narrative and providing details important to children. In *When I Go Visiting* (1984), the narrator talks about visiting his grandparents in the city: "I bring my bear so he won't be lonesome." Notable among her works for older children are her books for beginning readers, which include simply colored illustrations and inventive, often funny, storylines.

Rockwell approaches her subjects with a deep understanding of early childhood and a light hand, helping children feel good about their growing mastery of the world around them. ❧ A.E.Q.

ROCKWELL, HARLOW

AMERICAN AUTHOR AND ILLUSTRATOR, 1910–1988. Harlow Rockwell devoted his creative life to the interesting world of preschoolers. Alone, he created six concept and craft books. With his wife, ANNE ROCKWELL, he collaborated on more than twenty others.

Largely self-taught, Rockwell gained experience working as a lettering man, advertising art director, freelance magazine illustrator, printmaker, and new products designer. Some informal education included course work at Albright-Knox Art Gallery in Buffalo and Pratt Institute in New York City.

Harlow and Anne Rockwell began working together in the early seventies. Several of their first joint ventures introduced youngsters to the wonders of tools and machines. In clear representational paintings and simple text, *The Toolbox* (1971) depicts the important components of a father's toolbox, right down to the sturdy wooden carrier with hand smudges from use. With energy and enthusiasm, *Machines* (1972) shows how things work. Included is an introduction to such simple machines as levers, wheels, and ball bearings. Rockwell went on to describe familiar and sometimes unfamiliar places for beginning readers: *My Doctor* (1973), *My Dentist* (1975), *My Kitchen* (1980), and *My Nursery School* (1984).

Apparent in Rockwell's work is his affirmation of the ability of even the very youngest readers to understand the scariest situations. A visit to the doctor or dentist is not nearly as frightening when one understands the tools used. *The Emergency Room* (1985) explains stretchers, needles, and X-ray machines.

In addition to his concept books, Rockwell authored two Ready-to-Read Handbooks: *I Did It* (1974) is a collection of simple stories that teach children how to make six craft projects; *Look At This* (1978) contains the exuberant voices of three children as they share simple projects made from easily attainable materials.

The tradition of creating thoughtful, boldly illustrated first readers established by Harlow and Anne Rockwell is being carried on by their children. *My Spring Robin* (1989), written by Anne Rockwell, was illustrated by Lizzy Rockwell after her father's death. Harlow Rockwell's books continue to entertain, educate, and comfort young children. B.A.M.

Rockwell, Thomas

AMERICAN AUTHOR, B. 1933. With his knack for creating humorous stories with strong child appeal, Thomas Rockwell has achieved great popularity and success. Born in New Rochelle, New York, the author is the son of illustrator Norman Rockwell, famous for his *Saturday Evening Post* covers. Thomas Rockwell was raised in rural Vermont, where he developed an early love of reading. After majoring in literature at Bard College, he worked for a gardening magazine, taught school, sold used books, and attempted writing for advertising and television. He also assisted his father in writing autobiographical material and compiling books of Rockwell illustrations. Reading aloud to his young son led the author to the field of children's books, resulting in the publication of *Rackety-Bang and Other Verses* (1969), which was illustrated by his wife, Gail. Reviews of this original poetry collection were widely mixed, so the discouraged author switched from writing verse to children's fiction with *Humpf!* (1971), the story of a hungry bear's search for honey.

Rockwell's breakthrough book was the middle-grade novel *How to Eat Fried Worms* (1973), which shows how Billy Forrester eats one worm a day for fifteen days in order to win a fifty-dollar bet. With its irresistible title and premise, the book enjoys huge popularity and has received numerous awards voted by young readers. Yet from a critical perspective, this poorly written story is almost a complete failure. Greed seems to be the prime motivation as Billy chokes down worm after worm to win the fifty dollars from his nemesis Alan; there is no depth or subtext to his dilemma. The characterizations are weak, the dialogue is very much overwritten, the plot is frantic, and the general tone of the novel is mean-spirited rather than truly humorous or witty. Rockwell adapted his story for the stage in *How to Eat Fried Worms and Other Plays* (1980) and has published two more books about Billy and his friends that are equally flawed, but also employ attention-grabbing plot devices. In *How to Fight a Girl* (1987), Alan tries to get even with Billy for winning the worm bet. *How to Get Fabulously Rich* (1990) is the unlikely story of Billy winning a fortune in the lottery.

In a novel for a slightly older audience, *Hey, Lover Boy* (1981), thirteen-year-old Paul plans to write a pornographic play for a school assignment. Paul plays strip poker and attempts visits to adult bookstores and massage parlors, but the overall effect is more prurient than insightful. As in other Rockwell novels, sophomoric humor involving dialects—this time Italian, Jewish, and Chinese—is sure to offend and alienate many readers. The author has also written equally slight novels about more serious issues, such as *Hiding Out* (1974), in which a boy runs away from home when his mother announces plans to remarry, and *Tin Cans* (1975), a strange and unsatisfying fantasy about children who use a magic tin can to retrieve material goods.

Rockwell is not a major talent in children's literature, but he is adroit at creating plots that garner attention from young readers. Whether he is writing about eating worms, sex, running away, or wish-fulfillment stories involving winning the lottery or using magic, he has a keen ability to focus on topics that children find interesting and appealing. P.D.S.

Rodgers, Mary

AMERICAN NOVELIST, B. 1931. The daughter of Richard and Dorothy Rodgers, Mary Rodgers was born in New York City. Following her education at Wellesley College in Massachusetts, she returned to New York where—like her composer father—she originated and wrote lyrics for several Broadway musicals, including *Once Upon a Mattress*. From 1957 to 1971, she worked as assistant producer of the New York Philharmonic's Young People's Concerts. Her musical scores for children include *Davy Jones' Locker* (1959) and *Pinocchio* (1973), both performed with the Bill Baird Marionettes, and *Young Mark Twain* (1964). She was also a contributing

Jacket illustration by Edward Gorey for *Freaky Friday* (1972), by MARY RODGERS.

editor to the best-selling book and record *Free to Be . . . You and Me.*

But Rodgers is probably best known for her breakthrough novel, *Freaky Friday* (1972). "Since I had nothing to do but take care of five children, a nine-room apartment, an eleven-room house in the country, and show up once a month at the Professional Children's School Board of Trustees meeting, once a month at the Dramatist Guild Council meeting, and eight times at the A&P," she has said with the same wry wit that infuses her writing, "I thought I'd be delighted to write a children's book because I had all this extra time on my hands. (Between the hours of two and five A.M., I just loll around the house wondering how to amuse myself.)" The result was *Freaky Friday,* which became an ALA Notable Book and winner of numerous awards. The novel is about a thirteen-year-old who, the morning after an argument with her mother, is astonished when she awakens to find herself transformed. "You are not going to believe me," begins Annabel Andrews, "nobody in their right minds could *possibly* believe me, but it's true, really it is! *When I woke up this morning, I found I'd turned into my mother.*" At first overjoyed with the independence she had been fighting for all along, Annabel soon discovers what a damper adult responsibilities can put on one's fun. She also gains insight into how others— namely, the younger brother she calls Ape Face ("His real name is Ben")—view her.

Freaky Friday gained instant recognition and remains a highly successful, timeless story. It was followed by a sequel, *A Billion for Boris* (1974), a comedy of misadventures centered around Annabel's boyfriend and the problems he faces with his eccentric mother. In a third book, *Summer Switch* (1982), a sequel to both *Freaky Friday* and *A Billion for Boris,* Annabel's younger brother literally trades places with his dad.

All three novels deal with family and social issues such as freedom, manners, tidiness, sibling and parent-child relationships, even bigotry. Through her spontaneous use of humor and offbeat, enduring plots, Rodgers captures children in the throes of trying to comprehend the adult world surrounding them. ❧ C.K.S.

ROJANKOVSKY, FEODOR

RUSSIAN ILLUSTRATOR, 1891–1970. During the 1940s, Feodor Rojankovsky was one of the first European artists whose creative talents infused the field of American children's picture-book illustration with a boldness of color and the vitality of fine, modern design. Often using crayon to create mood and texture, Rojankovsky imparted a childlike quality to much of his work, drawing simple, cheerful pictures of true-to-life animals and ordinary children.

About his youth, the Russian-born Rojankovsky remarked: "Two great events determined the course of my childhood. I was taken to the zoo and saw the most marvelous creatures on earth: bears, tigers, monkeys and reindeer; and, while my admiration was running high, I was given a set of color crayons." Passionate about nature and drawing, Rojankovsky honed skills and techniques that allowed him to matriculate at the Moscow Fine Arts Academy in 1912. His studies ended two years later with military service in World War I, followed by the Russian Revolution, in which he first began to illustrate Russian children's books.

After the war, Rojankovsky lived in Paris, where he worked for Domino Press, a small publishing firm owned by two American women. *Daniel Boone* (1931), Domino Press's first publication, was America's introduction to Rojankovsky's talent as an illustrator. Emblazoned with brilliant colors and an impeccable sense of design, *Daniel Boone* was hailed by Anne Carroll Moore as "a unique first book in American history." The spirited lithographs spoke of Rojankovsky's affinity for the American frontier, and critics lauded him as a fine colorist. With unusual color schemes that combined red, yellow, purple, and green, the illustrations in *Daniel Boone* conveyed a liveliness and a daring befitting their subject.

Rojankovsky emigrated to America in 1941, where he joined the Artists and Writers Guild, then headed by Georges Duplaix. One year later, Duplaix arranged with Ursula Nordstrom, the gifted Harper juveniles editor, to publish Rojankovsky's *Tall Book of Mother Goose* (1942). Its elongated size—approximately five by twelve inches—ideal for presenting a great number of rhymes individually, each with its own illustration, was a new shape for "MOTHER GOOSE" BOOKS. Also new was the look of Rojankovsky's goose. Late nineteenth-century collections often depicted a quaint, grandmotherly woman and her goose seated among dainty, well-behaved children, or a saccharine twosome in flight across the sky. Rojankovsky's goose, cheery and colorful, was without its human counterpart, and the children he pictured were just as natural and homely as the ones next door. His penchant for highly vibrant colors injected a gaiety into his remarkably unsentimental drawings.

Rojankovsky also illustrated some of the first Golden Books for Duplaix, founder of that imprint. In more than twenty Golden Books, Rojankovsky used color, realistic animals, and lively children; all three became his trademarks. *The Three Bears* (1948), a Little Golden Book Classic still in print, displays his trademarks with exceptional distinction: a peasant cottage filled with a riot of colors and a great deal of Russian folk art; three husky, auburn bears; and one knavish Goldilocks whose braids are more red than blonde.

Equally respected in the trade-book field, Rojankovsky's talent for observing and drawing nature enabled him to craft several other noteworthy titles; his illustrations for editor JOHN LANGSTAFF's *Frog Went A-Courtin'* earned him the Caldecott Medal in 1956. His choice of medium, crayon reinforced with pen-and-ink line, gave the drawings a rich grainy texture and conveyed a characteristic childlike quality that flawlessly matched the simplicity and the cheerfulness of the Scottish children's ballad.

When he died in 1970, Rojankovsky had illustrated more than one hundred children's books; his flair for color, his vision of design, and his love of nature have greatly enriched American picture books. S.L.S.

Illustration by Feodor Rojankovsky from his book *Animals in the Zoo* (1962).

ROSSETTI, CHRISTINA

BRITISH POET, 1830–1894. The youngest child in a family of scholars and writers, Christina Rossetti grew up in a literary household. Her father, Gabriele Rossetti, was a renowned Italian poet before he immigrated to London, England, for political reasons; her older brother Dante Gabriel, a poet and artist, helped form the Pre-Raphaelite Brotherhood; and her other siblings became scholars.

Very early in life, inspired by the visitors to her home, Christina began writing poetry, some of which she shared with her family in journals compiled by the Rossetti children, and at age seventeen a volume of her poetry was published by her grandfather on his private press. By her thirties, she had achieved public recognition for her work. During the Victorian age, when very few books were written especially for children, Rossetti published *Sing-Song: A Nursery Rhyme Book* (1872), *Speaking Likenesses* (1874), and *Maude: A Story for Girls* (1897), all directed toward a juvenile audience. Posthumously, selections of her POETRY have been collected in numerous anthologies of children's verse.

Raised a strict Anglican, Rossetti remained devoted

to exploring and expressing spiritual truth throughout her life, and much of her work—for children and adults—reflects on nature, faith, and death. Included in *Sing-Song* are many simple poems about death and, as in her description of the metamorphosis of a caterpillar into a butterfly, rebirth. "Goblin Market," published in *Goblin Market, and Other Poems* (1862) and later illustrated for children by ARTHUR RACKHAM, among others, relates a young girl's fall into temptation, decline into a deathlike state, and regeneration. In the narrative poem, when Lizzie becomes ill after eating the fruit offered her by goblin men, her sister, Laura, cares for her tenderly and finally seeks the goblins in order to purchase more fruit, for which Lizzie is pining. Virtuous Laura returns victorious, although not unscathed, to save her sister, who kisses the juice of the mashed fruit off Laura's face. Although Victorian children may have enjoyed the verse merely for its story line, enjoyable rhyme and rhythm, and the intriguing goblin men, who have animal-like features and characteristics, the imagery throughout the poem is distinctly sexual. Rossetti never married, but she had several serious romances, and her poetry reveals her intensity of thought and feeling about the nature of male-female relationships.

Although her two children's stories are out of print, Rossetti's poems still find an audience among young readers, and her contributions to children's literature during the nineteenth century set a precedent for the creation of high-quality literature for children. ❧ A.E.D.

ROUNDS, GLEN

AMERICAN AUTHOR AND ILLUSTRATOR, B. 1906. Born in the Badlands of South Dakota, Glen Rounds was brought up on a ranch in Montana, so it is no surprise that his collection of work for children resonates with the vitality characteristic of the Western frontier.

Before and after attending the Kansas City Art Institute, Rounds held a number of jobs, including sign painter, textile designer, baker, and cowboy. He arrived in New York in 1930 and attended night school at the Art Students League. In 1935, with drawings in hand, he appeared on publishers' doorsteps around lunchtime; although many of the editors thought his work too coarse and wanted something more in the prevailing "slick and mannered" style of the day, he usually managed to get a good lunch.

It was not until 1936 that he became a full-time author and illustrator of children's books. He began his career by sketching and later, at an editor's suggestion, wrote his first story, *Ol' Paul, the Mighty Logger* (1936), to accompany his illustrations. In this first attempt at juvenile fiction, Rounds tells the "true" account of Paul Bunyan. Testifying that he had previously worked for the giant logger, Rounds recounts ten tales about Bunyan, including how he built the Rockies. The rough black-and-white illustrations scattered throughout the chapters give a glimpse of the real West, the West that Bunyan created.

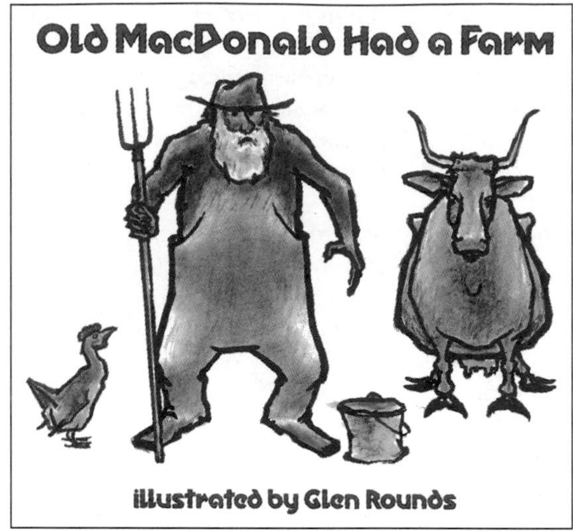

Jacket illustration by Glen Rounds for his book *Old MacDonald Had a Farm* (1989).

In *The Blind Colt* (1941) Rounds tells the heartwarming story of how a blind colt survives life in the Badlands. In chapter-book format, with straightforward text and simple black-ink sketches, Rounds captures the vitality of the young horse and illustrates how it manages to see by using its other senses.

Rounds is best known for his "Whitey" series, which stars the young cowboy, Whitey, and his cousin, Josie. With his humorous black-and-white illustrations, Rounds engages the characters and the reader in adventures on a ranch. Critics and children alike have acclaimed these books because of their realistic depiction of Western life. He won the Lewis Carroll Shelf Award twice for *Wild Horses of the Red Desert* (1969) and *Stolen Pony* (1969).

In his eighties, Rounds continues to create books and to engage his young audience with his scraggly line. He has retold favorite songs in *Old MacDonald Had a Farm* (1989), *I Know an Old Lady Who Swallowed a Fly* (1990), and *Three Little Pigs and the Big Bad Wolf* (1992).

Throughout his career, Rounds has employed a variety of tools—pens, brushes, a house painter's brush—

depending on the style he wanted to achieve. He has provided the world of children's literature with a vast collection of written and illustrated works—and an appealing array of heavily outlined, bowlegged characters. ♠ J.S.C.M.

Rubel, Nicole

American illustrator and author, b. 1953. Looking at the vivid colors and complex patterns that distinguish Nicole Rubel's watercolors, it's no surprise to learn that she was born and raised in the rich, tropical landscape of Florida. Her earliest childhood drawings were filled with the exotic forms of palm trees and the brightly colored shapes of the Chinese-style houses in her neighborhood. As a teen, Rubel explored three-dimensional art by making brilliantly colored papier-mâché monsters. She went on to work in ceramics and silk-screen and took a joint degree from the Museum of Fine Arts School in Boston and Tufts University.

When author Jack Gantos saw a series of Rubel's drawings, he offered to write a story for them; thus began a collaboration that resulted in many children's books, including *Rotten Ralph* (1976). Ralph, a very bad cat who resembled Rubel's huge white cat, Carew, is always forgiven by his patient mistress, no matter how scurrilous his misdeeds. *Rotten Ralph* was included in the Children's Book Showcase of 1976 for outstanding graphic design and became the first book in a series. Among the other titles are *Worse Than Rotten Ralph* (1978), *Rotten Ralph's Rotten Christmas* (1984), and *Rotten Ralph's Show and Tell* (1989), which won an International Reading Association Children's Choices Award.

After illustrating many children's books, Rubel was inspired to tell her own stories, including some that came from her childhood experiences with her twin sis-

Illustration by Nicole Rubel from *Rotten Ralph* (1976), by Jack Gantos.

ter, Bonnie. Substituting twin kittens for twin sisters, Rubel wrote adventures that include *Sam and Violet Go Camping* (1981) and *Sam and Violet's Bedtime Mystery* (1985). Rubel is also the author of *It Came from the Swamp* (1988), *Pete Apatosaurus* (1991), and *The Ghost Family Meets Its Match* (1992). Her bold, splashy art is perfectly suited to the fun and humor of her riddle books, *Batty Riddles* (1993) and *Funny Bunny Riddles* (1994).

Rubel surrounds herself with colorful and interesting objects—she collects vintage hats, china bunnies, and hundreds of plastic dinosaurs. Now living on the West Coast, she has brought the tropics with her in the shape of two large and vocal cockatoos. She continues to work in the plastic arts and has created fish tiles for her own fireplace, which look very much like those in *Not So Rotten Ralph* (1994).

With her use of flat planes of vibrant color and her offbeat sense of humor, Rubel contributes a unique artistic vision to the art of children's picture books. ♠

P.H.

Russo, Marisabina

AMERICAN AUTHOR AND ILLUSTRATOR, B. 1950. By focusing on routine situations and viewing them from a small child's perspective, Russo succinctly extracts the subliminal essence of childhood behavior. Fodder for her stories comes from her acute observations of her children's activities as well as her own experiences.

Russo's story lines are simple yet valid. For example, in her first book (winner of The International Reading Association Award for Best Picture Book), *The Line Up Book* (1986), Sam has just dumped out his blocks when his mother calls him for lunch. Russo taps into a child's logic to provide an amusingly satisfactory way for Sam to play with his blocks while wending his way from bedroom to kitchen. In *Why Do Grown-Ups Have All the Fun?* (1987), she creates a child's fantasies about how wonderful it would be to stay up late. *Only Six More Days* (1988) has Ben counting down the days to his birthday to the point where his sister becomes increasingly annoyed with him. Her gift shows a sibling's knack for gracious retaliation! In the beautifully circular story, *Waiting for Hannah* (1989), Hannah's mother tells her a parallel story about anticipating her birth and the blossoming of morning glory seeds. Hide and seek is the theme of *Where Is Ben?* (1990), while *A Visit to Oma* (1991) tells of Celeste's visits to her great-grandmother. Since Celeste cannot understand the foreign language she speaks, she conjures up her own story about the woman's life, relying on photographs she sees around the room. *Alex Is My Friend* (1992) investigates a special friendship between the author's son and a special needs child. In *Trade-in Mother* (1993), Max thinks he has the meanest mother in town and wants to trade her in for "a more cooperative model." Russo presents a tactful twist, causing Max to change his mind.

In her art as well as her stories, Russo attends to the comfortably familiar. Her distinctively colorful, two-dimensional, gouache illustrations are filled with details: a dinosaur poster, stuffed animals, a rabbit lamp in a child's room, a child's art on the refrigerator, family pictures on the walls, and, always, an individually detailed quilt on a child's bed. This knack for working with the familiar fills her books with a reassuring aura of love, understanding, and acceptance.

Russo always wanted to be an artist of some sort. She says, "As a child I drew pictures all the time. A lot of my drawings told stories about large families with lots of children, dogs, big yards: exactly the opposite of [mine]. In junior high I began writing short stories. I remember the thrill of having a story published in our school yearbook." Russo says that although she loved to draw, she never won any art awards in school. Because she was shy, drawing became a satisfying way to express herself. Russo graduated from Mount Holyoke with a degree in studio art, studied lithography at The Boston Museum School, and life drawing at the Art Students League in New York. She began her career as a freelance illustrator for *The New Yorker* magazine. She says her next phase was cookbooks; she illustrated four and won awards for two. However, she distinctly remembers that the turning point in her career came when a children's book editor "handed me a blank thirty-two-page dummy and said, 'Here. Go home and write a book.' It was the first time anyone had shown such utter certainty that I could do it."

Russo proved that the editor's faith was not misplaced and has been successfully producing appealing picture books for preschool through third-grade children yearly since 1986. ♠ S.R.

Rylant, Cynthia

AMERICAN AUTHOR AND POET, B. 1954. Through picture-book texts, poetry, short stories, and novels, Cynthia Rylant demonstrates an inimitable ability to evoke the strongest of emotions from the simplest of words. For much of her writing, she extracts experiences

VOICES OF THE CREATORS

CYNTHIA RYLANT

I came to children's books a bit later than most people. I was raised in a part of rural West Virginia where libraries were, at that time, nonexistent, and books were scarce. This was the 1960s, and I suppose I would have been one of those children targeted in the War on Poverty. I read now that Appalachia was considered at that time a disgrace to the country (given its destitution), and living on government commodities in a house without indoor plumbing I expect I would have been included in that disgrace. Thankfully no VISTA volunteers made it to Cool Ridge, West Virginia, and I was saved from realizing that I was poor. I was having a wonderful time growing up and loved everything about life. I was, in my small way, quite rich.

I see now some of the sources for my works as a writer: a charming performer of a father who longed to be an actor, a musician, a star. But like many with strong artistic streaks, he managed only to be a sad alcoholic whose wonderful imagination could not save him from the knowledge of his own failure, his unworthiness. He died young, broke, and ashamed. He left me his flair for storytelling, his magic. And I often feel that he protects me now, trying to earn some redemption. And perhaps still trying, stubbornly, to entertain.

My mother, still living, is eloquent on paper—a wonderful letter writer. Without a college degree, she has read more serious literature than anyone I know. She loves beautiful writing and perhaps, given a life lived anywhere except coal camps and hospitals, she might have found her own incomparable voice, and we could have been graced with another Harper Lee or Eudora Welty. She never had the faith, though, the confidence, to try. Somehow, she planted these things in me instead.

My grandmother blessed me with the sound of her beautiful wisdoms at the kitchen table of the house where she raised me for four years, until I was eight. My grandfather, a careful listener, chose his words just as carefully. He taught me discretion.

I was graced with silence in those mountains, and the smell of flowers and pines, and space. I was allowed to play, to walk, to think all I wanted. The days were steady, and there were hot biscuits every morning, real carrots pulled loose from the garden, wild squirrel meat to eat. There was church and the lovely repetitions of hymns and the sweeping cadences of sincere and desperate preachers. The rest of the world was reading *Charlotte's Web, Make Way for Ducklings, Wind in the Willows.* I did not know these, would not know them until I was twenty-four years old. But they were not missed when I was six, seven, eight. I had the world.

I ended up going to college, rather by mistake (I broke up with my boyfriend and was forced toward other options). In college I enrolled in the required freshman English course, and that was all it took. I began to find out what I was.

I finished college with a degree in English and waitressed for several months. Then, desperate for anything more stimulating, I applied for a minimum-wage position as a clerk in the public library. I was assigned to the children's department. The rest, as they say, is history. I began writing stories and mailing them to publishing houses in New York, and, when I was twenty-five, my first book was accepted.

That children like my books sometimes surprises me, though I know it shouldn't. Because they love reading comic books and tacky pulp series, watching inane TV sitcoms and listening to cheesy music, I sometimes forget that beneath all of this are human beings who are so much closer to God than I. I believe that in childhood we are not yet too far from the angels we used to be. I don't mean to imply that all children are angelic. Once earthbound and influenced by all that comes with being bound, tied into this earthly life, we become complex—and sometimes corrupt—human beings. But children, early here, have not been so long away from their wings. And being this, they understand my books *An Angel for Solomon Singer* or *Appalachia: The Voices of Sleeping Birds* or *Children of Christmas.* They understand the depth of these, and they also, I hope and believe, are comforted by them—and inspired.

I am a little timid in life—not a good traveler, not very bold. Nevertheless, I am brave in my work. I try picture books, then short stories, poetry, novels, easy readers. Now I am even trying illustration and have learned that there is some sort of visual artist in me. After that, I'll be looking for something else to try.

But I still want to be that really good writer. That E. B. White. That James Agee.

I am still hoping to be that good. Maybe my father, with wings and imagination, is listening.

from her Appalachian childhood. Born in Hopewell, Virginia, Rylant lived in a small town in West Virginia with her grandparents from the time she was four until she was eight while her mother attended nursing school. Though she says she has never taken a creative writing class, it is apparent in her work that what she did study, especially during the early period of her life, was the language of the people around her and their amazing inner strength, despite financial or cultural impoverishment. In her work she re-creates in her characters the unconditional love and acceptance she felt from family and those around her. Rylant has three degrees from three universities and has taught English at various universities in Ohio.

The impetus to write came from working at a library in the children's department, where she first discovered children's books, and from the birth of her son, Nathaniel. The images and reminiscences of her childhood begin to appear with her first book, *When I Was Young in the Mountains* (1982), a peaceful, warm reflection of her days in Appalachia. More PICTURE BOOKS followed, including *The Relatives Came* (1985), a visual and verbal depiction of a lovingly tumultuous visit from relatives, and *Appalachia: The Voices of Sleeping Birds* (1991), which has a text that flows like poetry and was subtitled after a passage by James Agee, one of Rylant's main influences. Both *When I Was Young in the Mountains* and *The Relatives Came* were Caldecott Honor Books.

In her short stories, Rylant takes advantage of added room to flex her writing muscle, creating powerful images, such as those in *A Couple of Kooks: And Other Stories about Love* (1990). Not your typical collection of young adult love stories, these pieces show how Rylant challenges herself as a writer by playing with perspective. The stories vary in points of view, ranging from that of a mentally challenged adult with a crush on a shopkeeper to a grandfather reflecting on love at his granddaughter's wedding. It is in the shorter form of picture books, poetry, and short stories that Rylant prefers to work, often perfecting in one sitting what becomes the published piece.

Though her novels may not come as easily, they do not falter in intensity but instead make her storytelling skill obvious. Her novels appear subdued on the surface, slow, almost silent, but their themes run deep, evoking emotions that much literature for children, or adults, does not dare stir. In *A Blue-eyed Daisy* (1985), we meet introverted Ellie, a girl on the verge of adolescence who lives with her family and alcoholic father in a small Appalachian coal-mining town; in *A Fine White Dust* (1986), a Newbery Honor Book, we are introduced to Pete, a young boy who becomes mesmerized by an itinerant preacher; and in *Missing May* (1992), we become involved in the search for the spirit of May by her husband, Ob, and her niece, Summer, who have grieved tremendously since her death.

In 1987 Rylant began "Henry and Mudge," a successful series of books in the EASY-READER genre about a charming character, Henry, and his big, affectionate dog, Mudge. The mild dramas of the domestic adventures of this dynamic duo emanate humor and warm emotion, and often leave the reader with a comforting, reassuring feeling of quietude. A strong sense of family underlies each story, while the action centers on episodes celebrating simple, everyday pleasures and experiences such as spring, Thanksgiving, snow, puddles, and grandmothers. Rylant's recognizable style brings an uncommonly poetic narrative to the easy-reader genre, making her texts resonate with the oral cadences of a storyteller and the natural rhythms of speech.

In her work, Rylant gives depth and dignity to a litany of quiet characters and sagaciously reflects on some of life's most confusing mysteries. E.K.E.

S

Sachs, Marilyn

American author, b. 1927. Growing up in the East Bronx in a family of storytellers, tremendously imaginative, and an avid reader, Marilyn Stickle knew from an early age that she would be a writer. When she was twelve her mother died, and at seventeen she left home after arguing vehemently with her father over her desire for a college education. She studied English at Hunter College and in 1947 married Morris Sachs, a sculptor. Certain she would be a writer, but not yet knowing what she would write, she took a job in the Brooklyn Public Library as a children's librarian. Here Sachs soon found her direction and wrote her first book, *Amy Moves In*. Considered too realistic for the times in that it dealt openly with family problems, it was ten years before the novel was published. By 1960 Sachs had had a young daughter, Anne, and a son, Paul. In 1961 the family moved to San Francisco, where Sachs continued working as a librarian.

The publication of *Amy Moves In* in 1964 led quickly to *Laura's Luck* (1965) and *Amy and Laura* (1966), all drawing deeply from her childhood in the Bronx with her strong family and overshadowing, protective big sister. In Amy we glimpse Marilyn as she describes herself as a child: imaginative, caught up in lying, and easily bullied. In these early titles we feel emerging Sachs's unique warmth and the themes that will grow stronger through her later work, especially the underlying themes of family unity and love, sympathy for "losers," and the power of the child's imagination to transform and sustain.

Out of the backdrop of *Amy and Laura* came the humorous *Veronica Ganz* (1968), the formidable Veronica a composite of all the bullies Sachs suffered as a child. *Peter and Veronica* (1969) followed soon after, drawn from a special longtime friendship Sachs had growing up. Here, as in all of Sachs's work, the writing is delightfully rich in detail, the child's perspective true, and the sheer energy and the joy and pain of childhood sharply felt. In her award-winning *The Bears' House* (1971), Sachs brings us a family falling apart—young Fran Ellen's father has disappeared, her mother has had a nervous breakdown, and the children are struggling to survive on welfare, concealing the truth of their situation, afraid they will be separated. Badly bullied at school and caught between siblings at home, Fran Ellen creates a vivid inner world of her own as she plays with a beautiful dolls' house with a family of bears in the classroom. Here Sachs best demonstrates the child's imagination and the refuge it offers, as well as its power to sustain one under the worst of circumstances. Sachs's writing is intensely compelling, the story moving in its exploration of the question of truth and lying that riddled her own childhood and in its understanding of people and the ambiguities of relationships. It closes unresolved, and fifteen years and many titles later Sachs resumes the family's story in *Fran Ellen's House* (1987), in which Fran Ellen and the other children are reunited with their mother and face new difficulties as they work to rebuild their lives. Here, even more than in *The Bears' House*, we feel a strong underlying reassurance, a warmth in spite of their adversity, and the theme of the powerful resource of family love that is felt throughout Sachs's work comes to full expression. L.L.H.

Saint-Exupéry, Antoine de

French author, 1900–1944. Published in 1943, Antoine de Saint-Exupéry's sole children's book, *Le Petit Prince*, has been issued in more than fifty languages, including an English translation, *The Little Prince*. Born in Lyons, France, the author attended the College de Fribourg in Switzerland and was employed as a mechanic and factory worker before his childhood interests in aeronautics and poetry were utilized in a career that combined flying with writing. As a commercial pilot, he carried mail between France and Africa, and he wrote a novel loosely based on his experiences, *Courrier Sud* (1929).

Saint-Exupéry spent the early years of World War II in New York City, where he wrote and illustrated an allegorical children's story about a downed pilot who meets an unusual boy in the Sahara Desert. The Little Prince has journeyed from his tiny home planet, met a number of unpleasant adults on neighboring asteroids, and arrived on Earth, where he learns lessons about love, responsibility, friendship, and beauty. This whimsical, sad fairy tale satirizes adult behavior and celebrates the purity and innocence of children. The fanciful writing and charming watercolor illustrations of the hardcover edition appeal to young readers, although the philosophical component of the story may elude them; the volume is most popular with adults who appreciate the Little Prince's aphorisms and the spiritual awakening of the narrator.

Illustration by Antoine de Saint-Exupéry from his book *The Little Prince* (1943).

After the book's publication, Saint-Exupéry joined the war effort as a pilot and was soon listed "missing in action." Produced for the stage and as a poorly received 1974 movie musical, *The Little Prince* continues to be enjoyed by readers of all ages, although adults and children often derive very different pleasures from this classic. ❧ P.D.S.

Salassi, Otto

American author, 1939–1993. "Everybody in Mississippi told stories," Otto Salassi once said. Born and raised in Vicksburg, Salassi is no exception to that rule. Educated in the South—at Memphis State University, Vanderbilt University, and the University of Arkansas—Salassi began his career as a mathematician with the air force but eventually returned to his storytelling roots, becoming first a librarian and then a writer. He was the author of a weekly sports column and contributed stories to *Boy's Life* and the *Southern Humanities Review.* Salassi recalled, "After years of semisuccessful storytelling, I decided that my stories ought to be preserved for future generations."

On the Ropes (1981), set in 1951 in Texas, is the ultimate tall tale. After the death of their mother, eleven-year-old Squint and his older sister, Julie, are forced to find and bring home their absent father, Claudius Gains, who deserted them five years earlier. Claudius, "a pool shark, a manager of a girls' softball team, a soldier in the war, the road manager for a circus, a farmer, a wrestling manager," turns the about-to-be-foreclosed family farm into a wrestling college in order to raise the money to save it. The real fun centers not on Squint but on the secondary players—Seymour, the retired circus bear; Herman, the four-hundred-and-fifty-pound hired man; Claw, the deranged dentist—whose good-natured eccentricities provide the perfect backdrop for Claudius's, and Salassi's, showmanship and imagination.

With an equally fantastic plot but more realistic characters, *And Nobody Knew They Were There* (1984) tells of the disappearance of a Marine troop from a Texas fairground in 1956. The police, military, and FBI are unable to locate the troop. Thirteen-year-old cousins Jakey Darby and Hogan McGhee, characters constructed from the Tom Sawyer/Huck Finn model of American boys who cannot keep out of trouble, are the unlikely pair of opposites who discover the Marines' plan. The interaction between clever city dweller Jakey and his country cousin Hogan lends sharp, ironic charm to the two boys' education about the realities of combat and the myth of the macho soldier. Salassi's narrative, sometimes straining credibility, shines with the added texture of snippets of small-town Americana, notably a hilarious Louisiana pie-eating contest.

In *Jimmy D., Sidewinder, and Me* (1987) Salassi returns to his earlier tall-tale storytelling format. A series of twenty-five letters from Dumas Monk to the judge who is due to sentence him for the murders of seven men provides the pretext for a journey through the Southwest of the 1930s and '40s. Fifteen-year-old

Dumas, orphaned son of a gambler, is befriended and abandoned by Jimmy D., a pool hustler, and "adopted" by Sidewinder, an old cardsharp. Despite his sordid adventures, Dumas remains an innocent who tells his life story with a down-home drawl and a naiveté that is refreshingly honest and wholly believable. The book ends with the conclusion of Dumas's last letter to Judge Francis, leaving the reader to guess the judge's verdict. One clue to Dumas's future lies in Salassi's own theory of life: "One of the things I learned was, if you could keep someone listening long enough, you could get away with murder."

Salassi's stories are full of action, crammed with colorful and memorable characters and hilarious depictions of the South of yesterday. Claudius Gains from *On the Ropes* promised to give his audience a "no-holds-barred good show." The same can be said of Salassi. M.I.A.

Salinger, J. D.

American author, b. 1919. Born in New York City, Jerome David Salinger had his first story published in *Story* when he was twenty-one and, by 1948, he was publishing almost exclusively for the *New Yorker.* Some of the stories included in the magazine, "Franny" (1955), "Raise High the Roof-Beam, Carpenters" (1955), "Zooey" (1957), and "Seymour" (1959), shared a similarity of character—sensitive and perceptive, bright yet naive young narrators who feel trapped by the hypocrisy surrounding them. Of the many "lost" adolescents who people the pages of Salinger's writings, none is as famous as Holden Caulfield.

"If you really want to hear about it, the first thing you'll probably want to know is where I was born, and what my lousy childhood was like . . . and all that David Copperfield kind of crap." So begins *The Catcher in the Rye* (1951), a book that has become both a classic in American literature and an object of heated debate and that made Salinger and his hero, Holden Caulfield, literary phenomena. Holden, a model of innocence and illusion, tells the story of his two-day adventure in New York City from inside a psychiatric hospital where he is recovering from a breakdown. On the surface, Holden appears to be an unlikable character—he alienates himself from his peers, is unable to tell the truth, and is being expelled from his third prep school—yet the reader is fascinated by him in his role as the "outcast." Just as Huckleberry Finn, the original adolescent outcast, struggles to find his place in a complex and changing world, Holden navigates his way through the traumatic and very real problems of adolescence. The link between Huckleberry and Holden is strengthened by their choice of language—the informal and colloquial speech of the American teenager. Holden peppers his speech with slang, four-letter words, and the often repeated *goddam.* It is this raw, honest, and authentic language that caused the book to be temporarily banned in South Africa, Australia, and numerous classrooms and libraries across America.

Salinger has become almost as notorious as Holden. Soon after the publication of *The Catcher in the Rye,* Salinger retreated to New Hampshire and, since 1965, has published nothing. Having created the voice of a generation, Salinger silenced his own, claiming that he found the attention he received to be "hectic and professionally and personally demoralizing." Unaffected by Salinger's reclusive behavior, *The Catcher in the Rye,* the story of a young man caught between childhood and maturity and unsure which way to go, captured—and continues to capture—the hearts and minds of young adults as no other book has. M.I.A.

Salten, Felix

Hungarian author, 1869–1945. Using the pseudonym Felix Salten, journalist Siegmund Salzmann wrote several anthropomorphic animal tales, including the novel *Bambi: Eine Lebensgeschichte aus dem Walde,* published in English as *Bambi: A Life in the Woods* in 1926. The author was born in Budapest, Hungary, but grew up in Vienna. He worked as a journalist and drama critic for many years before publishing his first book, *Der Hund von Florenz* (The hound of Florence) in 1923. The novel was later adapted for the 1959 Disney film *The Shaggy Dog.*

Disney's animated version of *Bambi* (1942) is so well known, and inspired so many poor-quality print adaptations, that the original novel is sometimes overlooked by readers. But this story of life in the forest is written with integrity, emotion, and great skill. As the seasons pass, Bambi evolves from a carefree fawn to a mature, solitary deer. The creatures of the forest converse in dialogue but always remain true to animal nature. In one of the most touching chapters, the author ascribes dialogue to a pair of dying autumn leaves. The novel contains beautifully descriptive scenes of nature but also realistically presents the bloodshed caused by hunters and wild animals. Salzmann wrote a sequel, published in English as *Bambi's Children* (1939), and several other

ANIMAL STORIES, including *Fifteen Rabbits* (1930) and *Perri: The Youth of a Squirrel* (1938), which was also adapted as a Disney film, *Perri*, in 1957.

After spending his life in Vienna, the author fled to Switzerland during World War II and died in exile. *Bambi* remains his best-known work, and it is a classic in the genre of animal stories. P.D.S.

Sandburg, Carl

AMERICAN AUTHOR, 1878–1967. Carl Sandburg is known for his celebration of the American spirit, and he embodied that spirit in his maverick approach to literature. His poetry did not fit the accepted forms and did not deal with accepted poetic subjects; his biographical work did not have the expected footnotes; and his children's stories, which some consider his best work, were like nothing ever written. Everything he wrote was both lauded and scorned, and consensus has yet to be reached on his literary stature.

The son of Swedish immigrants, Sandburg spent most of his life in the Midwest. After fighting in Puerto Rico in the Spanish-American War, he attended college but did not graduate, preferring to get his education on the road. As he traveled through the United States, he took careful note of the vernacular and music of the people he met. He settled in Chicago and wrote for newspapers, raising three daughters with his wife, Lillian (sister of photographer Edward Steichen). He always wrote prolifically and became well known for his "performances," during which he might lecture, read his poetry, tell stories, and sing folk songs. Eventually, he was able to devote himself entirely to his writing at his family farm, making occasional public appearances, including the first address by a private citizen to a joint session of the houses of Congress.

Sandburg's straightforward poetry is accessible to a wide and diverse audience that includes children, so it is frequently included in anthologies of children's literature. Likewise, his children's biography, *Abe Lincoln Grows Up* (1928), was not originally written for children but adapted from the first chapters of his monumental six-volume Lincoln biography, for which he won a Pulitzer Prize. Only the collections *Rootabaga Stories* (1922), *Rootabaga Pigeons* (1923), and *Potato Face* (1930) were written intentionally for children. He wrote these stories for his young daughters upon noticing that their scenery had little in common with that of traditional fairy tales. Sandburg's fairy tales take place not in ancient gnarly forests but in the "Rootabaga Country," which resembles the raw prairie, small towns, and farmland of Midwestern America in the early twentieth century. Instead of kings and woodcutters, his characters are whimsical exaggerations of Midwestern rural folks. And instead of fairy princesses and gossamer-winged sprites, corn fairies sew their overalls with corn silk and corn leaves between the cornrows and potato bugs wear frying-pan hats. Each story is complete, but they are connected through their characters and settings. Sandburg's use of language here is poetic and playful; he chooses his words and phrases for their sounds and their absurdity and makes use of repetition, rhythmic cadences, and startling juxtapositions.

Illustration by MAUD AND MISKA PETERSHAM for "How They Bring Back the Village of Cream Puffs When the Wind Blows It Away" from *Rootabaga Stories* (1922), by Carl Sandburg.

As a "nonsense" writer, he has been likened to English authors RUDYARD KIPLING (in his *Just So Stories*), LEWIS CARROLL, and EDWARD LEAR, but Sandburg's nonsense is clearly of the homespun American variety. His most enthusiastic fans have acknowledged that the *Rootabaga* stories, in their rollicking spontaneity, are uneven in quality, and some of the stories were probably better appreciated in their own time. Even so, many of them still hold enormous imaginative power and should not be lost to those readers of all ages who appreciate surrealism. ❧ D.C.

Sasek, Miroslav

European author and illustrator, 1916–1980. Colorful panoramas and precise architectural drawings are characteristic of Sasek's illustrated travel books for children. Sasek's distinctive style is not only informative but also entertaining and witty. It captures the ambiance of cities (Paris, London, Rome, New York, Edinburgh, Munich, Venice, San Francisco, and Washington, D.C.), countries (Israel, Greece, and Australia), and other places of interest (Cape Kennedy, Hong Kong, Texas, and historic Britain).

Sasek left his homeland for studies in Paris upon the Communist takeover of Czechoslovakia after World War II. For several years he traveled and studied throughout Europe and North Africa until he settled in Munich, where he worked for Radio Free Europe. Noticing that young tourists were ill prepared for sightseeing, Sasek wrote and illustrated his first book, *This Is Paris*, in 1959. This was quickly followed by volumes on London and Rome, which met with such success that the "This Is" series continued for thirteen additional titles.

Sasek's education in art and architecture merged effectively with his peripatetic nature. His renderings of historic buildings, soaring cathedrals, and other significant structures arrest the eye with their clarity of detail. Sasek intersperses these tourbook sites with glimpses of everyday life. He is careful to include scenes of interest to children: parks and zoos, shops, signs and vehicles, policemen, schoolchildren, and tourists like themselves. Sasek's picture-book format is deceptive, for his books demand an inquiring eye. Each one demonstrates Sasek's creative mind and attention to small, telling details. Native languages, stamps, currency, flags, ethnic foods, costumes, and customs are skillfully integrated into the plentiful illustrations. Sasek used several art techniques in his illustrations. Cityscapes and countrysides are impressionistic. Photographs authenticate statuary, postage, and postcards. The features of cartoon-style people are similar from culture to culture, but their expressions and dress are distinctive. White space is used effectively to frame an object or person and to focus attention. Bright colors of the present provide a lively contrast to the muted tones of the past. The oversize books are easily recognizable by their format. The bright, bold covers feature a native resident in uniform or in national costume. Coins, statuary, documents, and other derivative symbols decorate the frontispiece. The locale is also reinforced by the lettering and incidental drawings of the title page. Tongue-in-cheek sketches of the artist, portfolio under arm, begin and end each sojourn.

No longer in print, the Sasek books have been replaced by other series books with color photographs, maps, charts, and facts-at-a-glance. Only Roxie Munro's "Inside-Outside" books and Mitsumasa Anno's travel books offer the original and expressive approach that distinguished Sasek's series. Sasek's text is enlivened by his humor, his use of quotations, and his distinctive introductions, some of which provide historical notes or legends. The text offers a pattern of captionlike sentences combined with longer factual and descriptive sections. The books conclude with wit, wisdom or wistfulness, and a sense that there are other places to visit. ❧ J.E.G.

Sattler, Helen Roney

American author, b. 1921. Whether millions of years in the past or thousands of fathoms in the ocean, Helen Roney Sattler's books allow living beings to share an armchair with you. Sattler describes ancient creatures—such as humanity's ancestors who lived 4.5 million years ago and the dinosaurs that prowled the earth 60 million years ago—and modern ones—such as eagles, whales, and sharks—with a matter-of-fact sensibility and an appreciation for all forms of animal life and for the sciences that explain it. Her wide-ranging, well-researched books depict reality and never succumb to anthropomorphism.

Sattler's life fostered her connection with nature. Her Midwestern farm upbringing featured animals and outdoor adventures. As a child, she admits to being "a bit of a tomboy . . . adventuresome . . . [with] lots of self-confidence." An education at Southwest Missouri State College followed by several years of teaching in country schools, and a stint as a children's librarian continued these rural influences. While teaching in the Netherlands Antilles, she met her husband, Robert, with whom she later settled in Oklahoma.

Reflecting her own interests and a grandson's request, Sattler began writing about dinosaurs in a style that offers vivid descriptions and intimate details of life among creatures extinct for 65 million years. To give her readers perspective, she explains that they can reach 65 million by counting day and night for two years and that one dinosaur weighs as much as two fire trucks. Each tongue-twisting dinosaur name is followed by a phonetic spelling. On her tours of the Cretaceous, Jurassic, and Triassic periods of the Mesozoic era—in *Dinosaurs of North America* (1981), *Pterosaurs* (1985), *Stegosaurs* (1992), *Tyrannosaurus Rex and Its Kin* (1989), and *The New Illustrated Dinosaur Dictionary* (1990)—Sattler describes the creatures, what they ate, who ate them, how they survived, the possible reasons for their extinction, and the resemblance their descendants bear to them. Sidelights on plate tectonics and continental drift explain how dinosaurs were able to roam all over the world.

Another, more personal brush with the past occurs in *Hominids, A Look Back at Our Ancestors* (1988), in which Sattler describes the life and habits of *Australopithecines*, who lived 4.5 million years ago, the genus *Homo*, who replaced them, and the subsequent development of humankind about forty thousand years ago. We learn that each species possessed different sized brains and produced unique tools, ate different foods, and lived in different places in different types of shelters. With honesty and thoroughness, Sattler describes paleoanthropologists who try "to solve a mystery or put together a jigsaw puzzle with many pieces missing."

Sattler features contemporary creatures in *Whales, the Nomads of the Sea* (1987) and *The Book of Eagles* (1989), describing their habits and habitats and admitting that scientists know little about the natural world. Her simple questions combined with details about these creatures illustrate larger scientific issues of exploration, knowledge, and information gathering.

Sattler's more than thirty science books are informative, incisive, and thorough. She introduces interesting subjects and leads the way to more complex science literature without diluting the facts or overly sanitizing the natural world. § B.C.

SAWYER, RUTH

AMERICAN AUTHOR AND STORYTELLER, 1880–1970. Ruth Sawyer came under the spell of folklore and magic early in her life through tales told her by her Irish nurse, Johanna. Sawyer was magically transported to distant places, acquiring an affection for other cultures that is ever-present in her work.

Born in Boston and raised in New York, Sawyer studied storytelling and folklore in Boston and at Columbia University in New York and started the first storytelling program for children at the New York Public Library. Sawyer practiced her art with varied audiences at missions, asylums, schools, and libraries, yet she somehow felt she could not convey the magic—the living of the tale—that Johanna and others imparted so effortlessly. Given the opportunity to visit Ireland to write a series of articles on Irish folklore for the New York *Sun*, Sawyer leapt at the chance. There, among the Irish storytellers, the "seanchies," with Johanna's fairy music all around, Sawyer began to weave her own stories from the tales she heard. One of her favorite tales was "The Voyage of the Wee Red Cap," which she first published in *Outlook* magazine. This story, together with other folktales, was published in *This Way to Christmas* (1916), a wonderful, ageless collection of folktales bound together by the story of a lonely boy separated from his family at Christmas.

Sawyer was a prolific writer whose passion for folktales is evident in numerous books, including *The Long Christmas* (1941), *The Christmas Anna Angel* (1944), which was chosen a Caldecott Honor Book in 1945, the popular picture book *Journey Cake, Ho!*, illustrated by her son-in-law, ROBERT MCCLOSKEY, which was chosen a Caldecott Honor Book in 1954, *The Enchanted Schoolhouse* (1956), and *The Year of the Christmas Dragon* (1960). Sawyer had an affection for Christmas stories; her daughter wrote that "the name Ruth Sawyer is associated with Christmas." In 1942 (revised in 1962) Sawyer wrote *The Way of the Storyteller*, a handbook for storytellers. In this valuable guide, Sawyer does not dictate recipes for successful storytelling but urges "questing," searching for one's own inspirations and insights, for one's own stories to tell.

Sawyer's Newbery Award–winning *Roller Skates* (1936) is the tale of one Lucinda Wyman, aged ten, a plucky, determined young lady. Lucinda is allowed the privilege of a year separated from her family in New York City in the 1890s. Privilege, indeed, for Lucinda has been scheduled, regimented, and organized until her trapped soul longs for wings. Those wings come in the form of roller skates that transport Lucinda all over the city as she makes friends with nearly everyone who crosses her path, a wide range of appealing characters who reflect the ethnic diversity of that era.

Lucinda is autobiographical. Sawyer was "brought up on bells and whistles" and as a child began to develop a "never-diminishing sense of rebellion." Like Sawyer, Lucinda was, as Sawyer herself points out, "not well adjusted." The openness of childhood without adult-imposed ideas and the notion of the free child as happy child are central themes in Sawyer's work. Indeed, in her Newbery Award acceptance speech, Sawyer stated, "If there be any point to *Roller Skates*—which I very much doubt—it lies in the urge of freedom for a child."

When accepting the 1965 Laura Ingalls Wilder Medal for her enduring contribution to children's literature, Sawyer commented on the similarity of Wilder's and her own work: "It so happened that our books had grown from childhoods that held deep significance for us."

M.O'D.H.

Say, Allen

Japanese-American illustrator and author, b. 1939. Allen Say is widely hailed for his talent as both artist and author of books for children of many ages. Aside from showcasing an ever-developing illustrative technique that has garnered multiple awards, Say's work is noted for its gentle message of respect for the earth and for all peoples, its strong depiction of family, and its sensitivity to the similarities and differences between Eastern and Western cultures.

Born in 1937 in Yokohama, Japan, Say could not hide his love of drawing from his practical parents. At the age of twelve he apprenticed himself to the renowned Japanese cartoonist Noro Shinpei, who introduced him to both Eastern and Western drawing styles and impressed upon him the necessity of movement and fluidity in art. His tenure under Shinpei is documented in Say's critically acclaimed young adult novel, *The Ink-Keeper's Apprentice* (1979). Say came to the United States at the age of sixteen and attended several art schools and universities before settling into a career in commercial illustration and photography. His cross-cultural upbringing, coupled with his early training under Shinpei, are the greatest influences on his artistic style.

Say began publishing books for children in 1968. His early work, consisting mainly of pen-and-ink illustrations for Japanese folktales, was generally well received; however, true success came in 1982 with the publication of *The Bicycle Man*. Based on an incident in Say's life, the tale describes the appearance of two American soldiers at spring sports day in a post–World War II Japanese elementary school. The students and their families, at first alarmed by the appearance of the two men, are quickly charmed as one soldier demonstrates an uncanny ability to perform acrobatic stunts on a borrowed bicycle. The book is notable for the individuality of its characters, its subtlety and dramatic timing, and its thoughtful approach to emphasizing the similarities between two cultures. Say later returned to illustrating folktales with great success. *The Boy of the Three-Year Nap* (1988), written by Dianne Snyder, was selected as a 1989 Caldecott Honor Book and winner of the Boston Globe–Horn Book Award for best picture book. In this wry tale, a lazy boy concocts a plan to win the hand of a merchant's daughter and secure a life of leisure, only to have his clever and persistent mother manipulate events just enough that her son is compelled to work for his living. Say's illustrations, rendered in brush line and vibrant color, recall the work of traditional Japanese painters while incorporating humor through exaggerated gestures. They represented a significant break from the artist's early pen-and-ink style and won universal critical acclaim.

Since that time, Say's work has revolved around one or both of two distinct themes: the relationship between parent and child and the relationship between Asian and American peoples. A very successful combination of these themes appears in *Tree of Cranes* (1991), in which a young Japanese boy's American-born Japanese mother shares her reminiscences of Christmas by creating for him a special Christmas tree adorned with silver peace cranes. This beautifully crafted autobiographical story is also visually stunning; its soft, jewellike paintings are filled with the glowing warmth of holiday candles and represent a more personal style than the vivid caricatures of *The Boy of the Three-Year Nap.* The same style resonates throughout *Grandfather's Journey* (1993), another intimate autobiographical portrait. With these

Illustration by Allen Say from his book *Grandfather's Journey* (1993).

Voices of the Creators

Allen Say

The first time I heard about Billy Wong was in 1967, the year he became a matador called "El Chino." I was a hungry young artist then, and the story made a deep impression on me. In those days, Asian American boys were expected to become gardeners and laundrymen, chop suey cooks and storekeepers—maybe engineers and even doctors if they were really smart.

But here was a Chinese bullfighter! The world had never seen one before. How did he get such a dream? How did he pursue it? I was more than curious because I had a big dream of my own. Ever since I was a small boy, I wanted to be a famous artist, and I longed to see my dream in bright sunlight, as Billy did. I felt a kinship with him.

Billy Wong died in a car accident two years later. I went on chasing after my dream and soon thought no more about the Chinese matador. Then in 1989, when my daughter was in second grade, I went to her school party and met a woman named Janet Wong. Her husband, Dr. Art Wong, turned out to be the baby brother of El Chino! When I heard this, I was overcome with a powerful urge to write a story about Billy Wong. I had no idea how I was going to do it. Would any publisher buy such a story? After all, bullfighting was—and is—as popular as whaling or bashing baby seals. Still, I wanted to write about Billy. His dream was what interested me.

I interviewed Art Wong and two of Billy's sisters, Lily and Rose. I borrowed their family albums and scrapbooks and pored over them, but Billy Wong remained a stranger to me. I didn't know where his dream came from or what it meant. I couldn't start writing.

So I worked on the illustrations first, and a wonderful thing happened. I began to see through Billy's eyes. Not only that, I began to think with his mind and feel with his heart. As a great Chinese painter once said, "When you paint a tiger, you must become a bit of the tiger yourself."

The pictures took eleven months to complete. The story took two days to write. I simply told my own story, through Billy's mouth. When I was sixteen, I came to the United States. For a long time I felt both visible and invisible in this country. I was visible because I looked different; I was invisible because I didn't belong. So I understood exactly what Billy meant when he put on his bullfighting costume and said, "For the first time, people were taking notice of me, and that was magic."

When the book was finally published, Billy's younger sister, Florence, wrote to thank me. She said, "He [Billy] lives." That is the greatest compliment an artist can receive. That was *my* day in the sun.

two books, Say has taken the children of story, those of *The Bicycle Man, The Boy of the Three-Year Nap,* and the many folktales he has so successfully brought to Western readers, and made them real. His ability to thus successfully bridge two cultures is unparalleled. C.C.B.

Scarry, Richard

American illustrator and author-illustrator, 1919–1994. Since the mid-1960s, Richard Scarry's books have provided hours of entertainment for young children, who eagerly pore over his outsize volumes, gazing at the cheerful faces of such Busytown inhabitants as Huckle Cat and Lowly Worm, Mr. Frumble and Mr. Fix-It, Miss Honey and Bugdozer. The books attract preschoolers and young readers with their colorful pages jam-packed with busy activity and hundreds upon hundreds of labeled objects, while brief texts, almost lost in the chaos, tell simple stories that often exhort gentle readers to be kind, polite, helpful, and to brush their teeth and be good sports. The young recognize themselves in the ever-industrious characters, who enjoy going about the fascinating business of everyday life. And like children, Scarry's characters carry with them a clear sense of right and wrong—readers cheer along with Busytown whenever Sergeant Murphy catches Bananas Gorilla stealing his favorite yellow fruit from the grocer. International best sellers, Scarry's numerous books have been translated into twenty-eight languages.

Richard Scarry is not popular with everyone. Elitist attitudes about mass-market books have caused some to label Scarry's books as unimaginative carbon copies of each other, though a more accurate criticism might be that Scarry's brand of humor suits children more than it does adults. Slapstick appeals to the young, who find humor each day in their own slips, frequent bumps, spills, and goof-ups. Critics who have commented on the violence in his books—car wrecks, accidents, wild chases—fail to note that the only injuries are to someone's dignity. Scarry's deliberate use of anthropomorphic animals makes his books accessible to children of every color, but his lack of sensitivity regarding gender continues to be criticized. The early books depicted few females, and those that did appear were limited in their occupations and activities. Small improvements can be spotted in some of the later books: both mothers and fathers commute to work on the train; the term *firefighters* has replaced *firemen*; and boys learn to bake pies—though Mother Cat, sad to say, still can't change a tire.

Born in Boston, Massachusetts, Scarry attended the Boston Museum School from 1938 to 1941, completed a five-year stint in the army during World War II, and then moved to New York City to become a commercial artist. He began instead to illustrate children's books for Golden Press, and eleven years later started writing his own books. He found a successful formula with *Richard Scarry's Best Word Book Ever* (1963) and continued to reap the benefits of that discovery throughout his long career. Among the many titles that followed are such perennial favorites as *What Do People Do All Day?* (1968), *Richard Scarry's Best Mother Goose Ever* (1970), and *Richard Scarry's Busiest People Ever* (1976). ✤ J.M.B.

Illustration by John Schoenherr from *Rascal* (1963), by Sterling North.

SCHOENHERR, JOHN

AMERICAN ILLUSTRATOR, B. 1935. Known for his black-and-white illustrations of nature stories and picture books, John Schoenherr received new acclaim when his full-color paintings for *Owl Moon* by JANE YOLEN won the 1988 Caldecott Medal. This award caps a career that has produced numerous paintings on wildlife subjects, illustrations for hundreds of science fiction book covers and magazine articles, and pictures for over forty children's books.

Schoenherr discovered early in life that he loved painting and at thirteen started to take art classes at the Art Students League in New York City. At the same time his interest in the natural world began to emerge, and he regularly visited local museums and zoos, observed displays and live animals, and sketched continually. He seriously considered becoming a biologist, but a high school science lab convinced him that he would prefer drawing live animals to dissecting dead ones. Graduating from Pratt Institute with the intention of being a painter of wildlife, he made his living by illustrating children's books and science fiction.

After moving his family from New York City to an old farmhouse in rural New Jersey, he turned increasingly to wildlife illustration, stimulated by the surrounding fields and woods and by the animals and scenes he encountered in his extensive travels. His black-and-white pictures showing man and animals interacting with their environment grace the pages of such award-winning books as *Julie of the Wolves* by JEAN CRAIGHEAD GEORGE, which won the Newbery Medal in 1971, and the Newbery Honor Books *Rascal: A Memoir of a Better Era* (1963) by Sterling North, *The Fox and the Hound* (1967) by Daniel P. Mannix, and *Incident at Hawk's Hill* (1971) by ALLAN W. ECKERT. In the sixties and seventies, Schoenherr illustrated several picture books by Miska Miles, which also had strong nature themes. In the early eighties, feeling limited by the demands of book illustration, he decided to devote himself exclusively to creating the dramatic, large wildlife paintings that expressed his own ideas.

His seven-year interlude from illustration was ended by the arrival at his farm of an old friend, book editor Patricia Lee Gauch, who came bearing the spare poetic text of *Owl Moon,* a story about a girl and her dad who tramp through the snow on a moonlit night calling for a great horned owl. Here was the kind of adventure that Schoenherr had actually shared with his own children, and he readily agreed to illustrate this story. With powerful watercolors, he captured the expectancy and excitement of the special nocturnal outing.

In 1991 he wrote and illustrated his own full-color picture book, *Bear,* a realistic account in which the dangers of a bear's coming of age are enhanced by dramatic scenes of the northern landscape. Still an avid traveler, photographer, and outdoorsman, Schoenherr continues to express his love of nature through wildlife paintings and illustrations for children's books. ❧ H.G.N.

Schwartz, Alvin

American folklorist, 1927–1992. More than almost any other contemporary author, Alvin Schwartz has single-handedly dusted off American folklore archives and made this rich tradition come alive for young readers with his collections of wordplay, riddles, nonsense, scary stories, whoppers, tall tales, and folk poetry. A prolific author, Schwartz was able to appeal to a wide range of ages with his combination of extravagant humor and compelling material.

Born in Brooklyn, Schwartz grew up thinking he would become either an archaeologist or a journalist. Though his interest in writing ultimately led to a career as a newspaper reporter and an author, the fascination of "digging out and understanding the unknown," he once recalled, remained with him for life. While his earlier writing focused on social issues and American institutions, his real interest was folklore. "I first became interested in folklore when I was a child," Schwartz explained, "but I had no idea that the games, songs, rhymes, and jokes I used or the tales I learned, or the customs we practiced were folklore. I also did not know that this material often was very old or that it was created by ordinary people like me, or that it survived simply and remarkably because one person told another."

With the success of *A Twister of Tongues, A Tangler of Tongues: Tongue Twisters* (1972), Schwartz knew he was on the right track and pursued his passion. His reputation as a rigorous researcher and scholar was well earned. Schwartz combed library archives across the country and worked with leading folklorists to track down material. His favorite interview subjects included children and older people, and he routinely mined schoolyards, classrooms, camps, street corners, and country stores for sources. Frequently, his research took him across the country and sometimes involved translating material from other languages. It was not unusual for him to juggle several projects at once: "I overlap my work—sometimes I'm working on three things at once, and I do that for practical reasons. One of the reasons is that I 'block' or simply become very bored with what I am doing if I work with it too intensively."

His hard work and research translates into a high level of accuracy, careful source notations, and background information, but from his readers' point of view his books are just plain fun. The "Noodle Stories" are light and funny, and his wordplay and riddle books offer "the kind of jokes that break up wise guys of nine or ten." With his collection of *Scary Stories to Tell in the Dark* (1981), Schwartz had a phenomenal success. Schwartz's collection developed from his research into stories on the theme of the unknown. As he saw it, some of the stories' appeal was as "self-chosen dares," in which readers explore, at arm's length, subject matter that intrigues or frightens them, in particular the idea of death. The stories were not gruesome, and the documented sources left readers pondering how much truth lived in the tales. Though he was reluctant to become a "scary-story specialist," Schwartz went on to write two more collections of scary stories. *In a Dark, Dark Room and Other Scary Stories* (1984) and *Ghosts! Ghostly Tales from Folklore* (1991) provided a deft combination of spookiness and humor that were designed to appeal to younger readers.

Shortly before his death, Schwartz published a collection of folk poems he had been researching for years entitled *And the Green Grass Grew All Around* (1992). In keeping with his other collections, Schwartz continued to show his readers that authentic folklore has many forms. In this truly delightful collection, readers are treated to a selection of poems that are as amusing as they are diverse and original.

Schwartz left behind a huge legacy of folklore that might otherwise have never reached an audience of younger readers. ❧ C.L.

Schwartz, Amy

American author and illustrator, b. 1954. Amy Schwartz's illustrative trademarks, in her own stories, as well as those she creates for other authors, are characters with soft, rounded or elongated stuffed-doll shapes. All expression is contained in their eyes and mouths. Schwartz works in both pen and ink and watercolor washes, sometimes combining media. By texturing her backgrounds with crosshatching and dressing her two-dimensional people in uniquely patterned clothing, she infuses her illustrations with three-dimensional vitality.

In the picture books she creates, for five- to eight-year-olds, Schwartz uses inspiration founded on her family and ethnic background. Her first book was the whimsical fantasy *Bea and Mr. Jones* (1982). Bea is bored with kindergarten; her father is equally disenchanted with corporate life. Deciding to change places, each confidently strides forth to meet the day: Bea in her father's suit, Mr. Jones in plaid slacks and sweater. The change works so well that Bea remains a successful executive, creating innovative advertising proposals, while Mr. Jones charms and entertains both kindergartners and teacher. The germ for the story came from Schwartz's curiosity about where her father went dressed in his suit and tie each workday and about what those serious-looking businessmen in Manhattan did all day. Some of her other works include the tale of spunky *Annabelle Swift, Kindergartner* (1988), based on a story which Schwartz's sister wrote as a teenager. Annabelle, happily confident that she will be the smartest kindergartner because her sister has prompted her with all the "right" answers, ends up embarrassing herself in class, but Schwartz exonerates her with true empathy. In *Oma and Bobo* (1987), she retells the relationship between her dog and her grandmother. In this story, Oma overcomes her dislike of dogs in order to help Alice and Bobo win a blue ribbon at dog-obedience class. *Camper of the Week* (1991) asks how will Rosie, the Camper of the Week, reconcile her conscience when her friends are punished for putting worms in bully Bernice's bed and she, having secretly abetted them, goes unpunished? Two books, *Yossel Zissel and the Wisdom of Chelm* (1986), and *Mrs. Moskowitz and the Sabbath Candlesticks* (1983) stem from Schwartz's Jewish heritage. In the first, she adheres to Jewish folklore, creating an original tale about the simpletons of Chelm who are considered wise men. In the second, she shows how warm memories of the importance and comfort of Shabbat tradition motivate Mrs. Moskowitz to establish new memories in her new apartment. Humor abounds in Schwartz's adaptation of the Victorian "noodlehead" story, *The Lady Who Put Salt in Her Coffee* (1989), and in her *Mother Goose's Little Misfortunes* (1990), which she wrote with Leonard Marcus.

Schwartz admits to having been a voracious reader as a child. Her favorite pastime, next to reading, was drawing. She received a B.F.A. from the California College of Arts and Crafts in 1976 and has worked as a freelance illustrator, art teacher, and production assistant. She has received many awards for both stories and artwork. With warmth and gentle irony, Schwartz insightfully and delightfully focuses on creating individuals who surprise themselves when they win minor victories over everyday problems by tapping unsuspected inner resources. ❧ S.R.

Science Fiction

What if there were a nuclear holocaust? What if we discovered life on another planet? What if we were able to recover DNA from an insect encased in amber and re-create dinosaurs? Science fiction books explore these and many other equally provocative topics. Science fiction is an imaginative literature, but it depicts plausible events, events that *might* happen. These events might not happen in our time or on our planet, but they are logical extrapolations from known facts. Science fiction writers take that which is known and project into the future to explore that which is unknown. Science fiction thus reflects the time period in which it is written more than does any other literature.

Science fiction is a recently developed genre. As Isaac Asimov, the late noted scientist and author, stated, "In fact, it is the only kind of literature that fits this age and no other, for there is no way in which it could exist until modern times." Though individual books by H. G. Wells, Jules Verne, and a few others could be classified as science fiction, the term *science fiction* was not coined until 1926, when a sufficiently large body of this type of writing had accumulated, warranting examination as a distinct genre.

Hugo Gernsback, often considered the father of science fiction, founded the pulp magazine *Amazing Stories* in 1926. He coined the term *science fiction,* and kept his magazine going by reprinting stories by Wells and Verne in serial form. The Hugo Awards, given for science fiction writing, are named in his honor.

John Campbell Jr. founded the magazine that was known as *Astounding Science Fiction* in 1938. Campbell moved beyond reprints of Verne and Wells, demanding from his writers a level of sophistication in their work that went beyond what had been acceptable in earlier magazines. Early science fiction had focused predominantly on emerging technological developments and the wonders of science. Especially after the explosion of the atomic bomb in 1945, social science and the consideration of the moral dilemmas posed by science became a thematic mainstay. Campbell encouraged the writing of stories that explored the social impact of technology and the philosophy and value systems of society; he broadened science fiction to include social protest of politics, business, war, and religion. Campbell's writers influenced the course of the genre for the next fifty years. They included E. E. ("Doc") Smith, L. Sprague De Camp, Lester del Rey, Robert Heinlein, Theodore Sturgeon, and Isaac Asimov, among others. In the 1940s, many of these writers began to write for children as well as adults.

The emergence of science fiction for children or young adults can be traced to *The Angry Planet*, by British writer John Keir Cross, published in 1946. The first American children's science fiction was *Rocket Ship Galileo*, written by Robert Heinlein and published in 1947. Heinlein followed this book with twelve junior novels, publishing one each year thereafter. They are some of his finest writing. Heinlein dominated the late 1940s, exemplifying the three major themes of the period: In *Rocket Ship Galileo*, good triumphs over evil, with evil represented by Nazi forces. The struggle between science and values is emphasized in *Beyond This Horizon* (1948). *Red Planet* (1949) extols the need for individualism.

The shift to social concerns continued in the 1950s. When the threat of Communism pervaded the American psyche, science fiction writers reflected society's concern, weaving the struggle between good and evil into their story lines, with evil now personified by Communists and the "good guys" by the Americans. Among the best of these books were Arthur C. Clarke's *Childhood's End* (1953) and Lester del Rey's *Step to the Stars* (1954) and *Mission to the Moon* (1956). Another major theme of the 1950s was the need for racial tolerance and commentary on racial intolerance. Though in earlier books this took the form of tolerance toward "aliens," it began to be more direct during this decade. Both Asimov in *Pebble in the Sky* (1950) and Heinlein in *The Last Planet* (1953) examine this theme. Heinlein also wrote a very moving and powerful plea for individualism and the need for racial tolerance in *Methuselah's Children* (1958), the story of a "family" of people who inherit longevity through genetic planning and of the envy that develops in the rest of society.

Upheaval was the byword of the 1960s. Society was in turmoil, and writers were trying to make sense of it all. Many authors wrote of the need for individualism in a society that inhibits it. In *Orphans of the Sky* (1964) Heinlein's four main characters try to raise themselves above the primitive level of the culture existing in the remnants of a starship. When their efforts are thwarted and their lives threatened, they leave the ship in search of a new planet on which to begin again.

The book that gave science fiction respectability in the field of children's literature was MADELEINE L'ENGLE's *A Wrinkle in Time* (1962), which won the prestigious Newbery Award. Although rejected by many publishers, when finally published it caught the imagination of readers and remains a great favorite today. The strong characterization and intriguing plot make compelling reading. Focusing on the need to respect individual differences, L'Engle places her characters in a struggle to defeat a world where everything is controlled by a computer.

JOHN CHRISTOPHER, a British writer, wrote movingly of an alien invasion of Earth in which the Tripods have taken over and implant a Cap on every human at age fourteen, rendering the wearer helpless and little more than a robot. In his trilogy, *The White Mountains* (1967), *The City of Gold and Lead* (1967), and *The Pool of Fire* (1968), Christopher details the struggles of a few to escape Capping and to defeat the alien society. In 1988, in response to many readers' demands, Christopher returned to his story of the Tripods and provided a prequel, *When the Tripods Came*.

Another influential author of science fiction is ANDRE NORTON, who began publishing her works for children in 1952. She adopted her androgynous pseudonym to circumvent the 1950s prejudice that women could not write solid science fiction. Her works often broke barriers to discussing issues such as racial tolerance and the antiwar movement. Norton's book *Postmarked the Stars* (1969) was one of the first works of science fiction to recognize ecological concerns.

The 1970s were replete with *isms*, social unrest, and a concern for ecology. Alarmed at television's pernicious hold on families, science fiction writers began to emphasize the need for an active, thinking society. With so many areas for concern and contemplation and with the growing appreciation of science fiction for children, the number of books published as well as the number of authors who wrote successfully increased. An outstanding example of the period's thoughtful and thought-provoking offerings is ROBERT C. O'BRIEN's Newbery Award–winning *Mrs. Frisby and the Rats of NIMH* (1971), a highly popular exploration into the responsibilities attendant on intelligence and civilization.

The 1970s also saw the beginning of a continuing trend in which women writers began to be the most prolific and eminent in creating science fiction for youth. Among them were Kate Wilhelm, Vonda McIntyre, H. M. HOOVER, Louise Lawrence, Pamela Sargent, Pamela Service, Wilanne Belden, and ANNE MCCAFFREY.

Anne McCaffrey's books about the inhabitants of the planet Pern were wildly successful with adults. Persuaded by editor Jean Karl, a successful writer of science fiction herself, to write stories about Pern for younger readers, McCaffrey produced *Dragonsong* (1976) and *Dragonsinger* (1977), beautifully written character studies of a young woman finding her place in an unaccepting society. There is adventure aplenty, but the focus is on the universal coming-of-age theme.

H. M. Hoover writes poignantly of the need for social

harmony, for acceptance of cultural differences, and for concern about ecological matters. Her characters are strong. *The Delikon* (1977) has a unique beginning: "In the palace gardens were reflecting pools and an enclosure for tigers. Three children played in the garden; Alta was ten, Jason was twelve, and Varina was three hundred and seven." Varina is a Delikon, a member of an alien race that has conquered Earth, who has been transformed into human shape to serve as a teacher to humans. The book offers a fast-paced science fiction plot: Alien beings, spaceships and aircars, war, and a race against time all combine to keep the reader turning pages rapidly. But it also goes far beyond this to explore both love and the conflicts that arise from cultural clashes. *Only Child* (1992) continues these themes. A young boy who has only known life on a spaceship visits a colonized planet and discovers that its sentient inhabitants are being destroyed. Cody's fight to expose and end this evil is both daring and thought-provoking.

Cultural conflict continued as an important theme in the 1980s. Monica Hughes wrote two stimulating novels, *Devil on My Back* (1984) and *The Dream Catcher* (1987), that examine the inherent evil of a rigid class system and the power of a computer gone amok. In *Moon–Flash* (1984), Patricia McKillip tells of two youths who leave their primitive culture of Riverworld on a quest and discover a world that travels the stars. *The Moon and the Face* (1985) brings the two full circle, as they discover that even with their new technological knowledge, their roots remain in Riverworld.

The 1980s saw the publication of a number of somber books about nuclear holocaust and its frightening aftermath of genetic mutation, fight for survival. and nuclear winter, in the tradition of O'Brien's *Z for Zachariah* (1975). In Robert Swindell's *Brother in the Land* (1984), three children struggle to survive in the weeks following a nuclear holocaust. Louise Lawrence portrays the fates of three generations of one family following a nuclear war in *Children of Dust* (1985), which compares the loves of those who survived in a bunker living a constricted life with those who remained outside and mutated. The most intriguing novel of the period, Whitley Strieber's *Wolf of Shadows* (1985), is told from the viewpoint of a wolf that survives nuclear destruction and the ensuing nuclear winter.

Unfortunately, the early 1990s saw a decline in the quality and quantity of science fiction written for young readers. Two powerful books stand out as models for the future. In *Eva* (1988) by Peter Dickinson, the title character wakes up in a hospital and realizes immediately that something is very wrong; she can't move and there are no mirrors in which she can see herself. She gradually learns the appalling truth: Following a terrible accident, her brain has been transplanted into a chimpanzee's body. Dickinson's provocative and well-written story explores the social questions of overpopulation, the destruction of animal species, and the moral limits of science.

The second major work is *The Giver* (1993) by Lois Lowry, winner of the 1994 Newbery Medal. She presents a Utopia, free from pain and poverty, racism and riots. But at what price? With meticulous plotting, Lowry leads the reader on an inexorable march from comfort to horror, from Utopia to dystopia, revealing the ramifications of this "ideal" world through the eyes of one boy. Readers will be forced to confront their beliefs, and the implications will long echo in their minds.

In its short, dramatic history, science fiction has stimulated and provoked, satisfied and prodded. Those who write science fiction are on the cutting edge of knowledge and seek to share their vision of where that knowledge might lead. Science fiction has an important place in a well-rounded reader's library.

M. JEAN GREENLAW

Scieszka, Jon

American author, b. 1954. Jon Scieszka enters classic fairy tales, turns them upside down, and exits with a smirk. What remains is hilarious buffoonery within these energetic, yet sophisticated parodies.

Born in Flint, Michigan, and raised in a large family, Scieszka was educated at Albion College and received a master's degree from the writing program at Columbia University. As an elementary school teacher, Scieszka found inspiration for his lessons by rewriting fairy tales; the lessons, in turn, led him to write successful stories offering fresh perspectives on dusty old tales. Although publishers once thought them too sophisticated for children, Scieszka's stories now arouse endless laughter from an enchanted young audience.

His first book, *The True Story of the Three Little Pigs* (1989), is a delicious retelling of the famous tale. Narrator Alexander T. Wolf desperately defends his bad rap by arguing that he was framed. With prim spectacles and a proper bow tie, A. Wolf pleads that he was innocently borrowing a cup of sugar to bake a cake for dear granny, when he was suddenly seized by a case of the sneezes that left him huffing and puffing. Is he innocent? Perhaps not, yet this comic perspective sheds new light on the Big Bad Wolf. Scieszka challenges the Grimm brothers as *The Frog Prince, Continued* (1991) dares to ask what comes after "happily ever after." Plagued by the nagging princess, the Frog Prince can't help but wonder if he was happier as his original frog self, before the day of the fateful kiss. As the satire plays out, the Frog Prince confronts familiar witches from "Sleeping Beauty," "Snow White," and "Hansel and Gretel." The tale finishes with a twist, but once again the Frog Prince and the princess live "happily ever after."

Scieszka provides "cool" books for the often overlooked middle reader with his "Time Warp Trio" series: *Knights of the Kitchen Table* (1991), *The Not-So-Jolly Roger* (1991), *The Good, the Bad, and the Goofy* (1992), and *Your Mother Was a Neanderthal* (1993). These easy-to-read, zany adventures take the trio—Joe, Sam, and Fred—back in time to face such foes as evil knights and burly pirates. Witty dialogue enlivens these bizarre tales, though they are not as rich as Scieszka's masterful picture books. *The Stinky Cheese Man and Other Fairly Stupid Tales* (1992), a Caldecott Honor Book, encapsulates all of Scieszka's wild and whimsical techniques of parody. The narrator, Jack, states that these stories "are almost Fairy Tales. But not quite." Individual tales such as "The Princess and the Bowling Ball," "Little Red Running Shorts," and "Cinderumpelstiltskin" capture Scieszka's original playfulness. Who would ever imagine that the ugly duckling would grow up to be a really ugly duck? Though his books are ageless, the traditional picture-book audience would have to be familiar with the classic tales to thoroughly enjoy Scieszka's parodies.

One cannot discuss Scieszka's writing without mentioning the illustrations of LANE SMITH, who shares the author's quest for the truly absurd. The unbreakable connection between text and illustration makes these hilarious picture books a complete and unified package. Scieszka's seriously silly characters coupled with his genuinely goofy stories are perfect for any reader who just wants to have fun. ❧ C.H.

SEBESTYEN, OUIDA

AMERICAN AUTHOR, B. 1924. When twenty-year-old Ouida Sebestyen submitted the manuscript for her first novel to a publisher, she naively assumed the book would be published within a few weeks. But the manuscript was rejected, and it would be thirty-five years before the author discovered the field of children's literature, wrote a novel with a young protagonist, and finally published her first book.

The daughter of a schoolteacher, Sebestyen grew up in Vernon, Texas. She pursued her childhood goal of becoming a writer as she briefly attended the University of Colorado and worked repairing airplanes during World War II. A divorced mother of one son, Sebestyen did housecleaning and other odd jobs while amassing several hundred rejection slips for her plays, poetry, and stories. She found success in the field of children's books when she expanded one of her few published stories to novel length.

Words by Heart (1979) concerns an African American family living in a small Texas town during the early twentieth century. Twelve-year-old Lena uses her intelligence to win a Scripture-reciting contest, but also learns to use her heart in dealing with the prejudice she encounters in the classroom, at her housekeeping job, and in the community. The headstrong young protagonist, who moves slowly toward emotional maturity, her gentle father, and their selfish, coarse employer, Mrs. Chism, are particularly well-defined characters in this excellent first novel. Sebestyen's prose sensitively explores the bonds of family love and assumes a surreal, nightmarish quality as an inevitable tragic conclusion approaches. Tater Haney, the teenage boy whose act of violence changes Lena's life, is featured in *On Fire* (1985), an examination of family dynamics in a Colorado mining town.

Another historical novel, *Far from Home* (1980), concerns Salty, a thirteen-year-old orphan who finds a job at Tom Buckley's boardinghouse. Superb, multilayered characterizations of the boardinghouse inhabitants and evocative details of Depression-era life are neatly woven into the story, which concerns Salty's realization that Tom is actually his father. Like all of the author's work, *Far from Home* contains tragic scenes and hints at dark secrets in the characters' pasts, but it also shows the inner strength and goodness of society's disenfranchised. These themes are in the forefront of Sebestyen's shocking novel *The Girl in the Box* (1988), which concerns a teenager abducted off the street and locked in a dark room where she desperately types pages of notes, letters, and memories while awaiting her fate. As a story of contemporary random violence, the book is harrowing. Yet because the basic situation is so unlikely—Jackie just happened to be carrying a typewriter and paper when abducted—and because she has recently suffered the painful dissolution of a close friendship, the reader confronts the equally frightening possibility that the novel is actually a troubled teenager's dark fantasy of dissociation. In either case, the emotional content is heartbreakingly real and Jackie's courage in the darkness is a testament to the human spirit. Sebestyen has also written *IOU's* (1982), a fine novel about a teenage boy who meets estranged relatives for the first time, and *Out of Nowhere* (1994), the story of thirteen-year-old Harley and the makeshift family he forms with a group of social outcasts.

Sebestyen's novels consistently explore the intrinsic goodness of humanity in a sometimes unsettling world. ❦ P.D.S.

Segal, Lore

AMERICAN AUTHOR AND TRANSLATOR, B. 1928. Renowned for her masterful translations of tales from the Brothers Grimm in *The Juniper Tree* (1973), Lore Segal is accomplished in many genres: PICTURE BOOKS, novels for adults, and TRANSLATION. Her writing is elegant, restrained, and witty, yet it is also filled with a healthy respect for life's trials.

Born in Vienna, the only child in a prosperous Jewish household, Segal was ten years old when her family fled the Nazis for England. Impoverished as a result, her parents couldn't afford to raise her, so she lived variously with five English families before earning her degree from the University of London in 1948. She then, reluctantly, followed her mother to the Dominican Republic, where her grandparents were living. She stayed for three years, finding work as a teacher, and then moved to New York City in 1951 to start over yet again. In time, she married, gave birth to two sons, was widowed, and established both a writing and an academic career. She has taught at Columbia, Bennington, Princeton, Sarah Lawrence, and, for many years, the University of Illinois in Chicago,

The Juniper Tree and Other Tales from Grimm, which she produced in collaboration with MAURICE SENDAK, is an indispensable volume for all admirers of literature, children's or otherwise. The two-volume collection includes twenty-seven tales selected by Segal and Sendak from the Grimms' complete tales. Four were translated by RANDALL JARRELL and the remainder by Segal, with each translator keeping faithfully to the original German texts and assiduously avoiding abridgment, retelling, and bowdlerization. The result is an astonishingly fine book, by turns hilarious and harrowing, beautifully illustrated and designed, and exquisitely written.

On her own, Segal has written several picture books. They are all funny and spry; even so, they have an edgy, slightly wary tone. *Tell Me a Mitzi* (1970) and its companion, *Tell Me a Trudy* (1977), each contain three stories of ordinary family life that trace the thin line separating anxiety and hilarity: a terrible cold that stalks the whole family; a visit to Grandma and Grandpa's that proves to be hopelessly hard to complete; a superhero who chases a robber from the bathroom. *The Story of Mrs. Lovewright and Purrless Her Cat* (1985) tells of a chilly person who woefully miscalculates the warmth of her cat.

The Story of Old Mrs. Brubeck and How She Looked for Trouble and Where She Found Him (1981) chronicles the fears of a grandmother who is convinced, without much evidence, that Trouble is stalking her and her granddaughter, little Beatrix. Though the old woman's paranoia is comically portrayed, her fears may not be totally groundless. For Trouble, which Grandmother decides has found shape as a shadow, really is always nearby. The trick, this story and much of Segal's work seems to be suggesting, is not to go looking for it. ❦ A.Q.

Selden, George

AMERICAN AUTHOR, 1929–1989. George Selden Thompson, one of the best contemporary authors of animal FANTASY, crafts breezy, entertaining tales of pure imagination in which his brilliantly conceived animal characters often provide shrewd and subtly satiric glimpses into human behavior.

Thompson, who wrote under the name Selden, was born in Hartford, Connecticut. He attended the Loomis School in Windsor and in 1951 received his B.A. from Yale, where he was a contributor to the literary magazine. Selden was working as a freelance writer when his first book, *The Dog that Could Swim under Water* (1956), was published. The adventures of a dog named Flossy Thompson revealed Selden's facility with fantasy, wit, and knack for inventiveness, distinguishing traits in all of his later work.

Selden eventually wrote more than fifteen books, but *The Cricket in Times Square* (1960), one of those rare works both critically applauded by adults and beloved by children, secured him a place of acclaim among writers of animal fantasy. The book has earned frequent comparisons with E. B. WHITE's *Charlotte's Web* for animal characters who are brought vividly to life and for its parallel themes of loyal and enduring friendship. Selden, a New Yorker, said of the creation of his best-known book, "One night I was coming home on the subway, and I did hear a cricket chirp in the Times Square subway station. The story formed in my mind within minutes." A devotee of opera, Selden wove his own love of melody into the engaging, urbane story of Chester, a musical cricket from Connecticut, and his streetwise friends Harry Cat and Tucker Mouse. The unlikely trio share a home in the Times Square subway station, where a boy named Mario Bellini and his family barely eke out a living from a newsstand. After the compassionate Chester befriends Mario, his operatic talents earn the cricket celebrity and salvage the Bellinis' failing business; but Chester, longing for the country, gives up his fame and returns home. *The Cricket in Times Square* was named a Newbery Honor Book in 1961. Eventually, the "Cricket" series grew to seven titles, including *Tucker's Countryside* (1969), *Chester Cricket's New Home* (1983), and *Harry Kitten and Tucker Mouse* (1986). Warm-hearted, beguiling pen-and-ink drawings by the well-loved American illustrator GARTH WILLIAMS accompany all of the "Cricket" stories.

Two biographies of famous archaeologists, *Heinrich Schliemann: Discoverer of Buried Treasure* (1964) and *Sir Arthur Evans: Discoverer of Knossos* (1964), mesh Selden's talents as a writer with his lifelong interest in archaeology. Selden's other imaginative works, such as *The Garden under the Sea* (1957) and *The Genie of Sutton Place* (1973), never achieved the enormous popularity of *Cricket*. Almost thirty-five years after his debut, the wise, compassionate, and irresistibly charming Chester Cricket and his friends continue to pay tribute to friendship and entertain legions of readers. For that noteworthy achievement alone, Selden's work will endure as a touchstone in the field of children's books. ❧ C.S.

SELSAM, MILLICENT E.

AMERICAN AUTHOR, B. 1912. Equally drawn to the arts and sciences, Millicent E. Selsam found a creative way to satisfy both interests in writing books on scientific topics for children. As an undergraduate, she was planning to pursue a theatrical career, but a course that she took in botany sent her on a new path. Many years later she still was able to recall the first time that she was shown the intricate relationship between a flower and the insect that pollinated it and how the perfection of the adaptation made her want to learn as much as she could about the wonders of the natural world.

Born Millicent Ellis, the youngest of eight children, she grew up in New York City and received her B.A. in biology from Brooklyn College and M.A. in botany from Columbia University. In 1936 she married Howard Selsam and taught in New York City schools until the birth of her son, Robert. At that time, she decided against returning to teaching, but wanting to continue to tell children about the excitement of science, she turned to writing. Fascinated with embryology, she chose as her first subject the development of a chicken, an animal familiar to most children, and *Egg to Chick* came out in 1946. From then on she published regularly, always looking for ideas that she could connect with the interests of young readers. Few juvenile writers had her background in botany and biology during those years, and she quickly became known for this specialty.

To appeal to children's natural curiosity, Selsam used the technique of suggested activities and experimentation in her books whenever she could. In 1949, for example, she published *Play with Plants*, a book that discussed different types of plants and encouraged readers to grow them. The approach was immediately successful, and she used the words *play with* as a peg for a loosely connected series that included *Play with Trees* (1950) and *Play with Vines* (1951). A houseplant and garden lover herself, she could write from the heart about the pleasures of growing things and enable others to share her enthusiasm. The summers she spent at her house on Fire Island, off the south shore of Long Island, provided an ideal setting for this hobby, and she became the neighborhood plant doctor as friends brought her their ailing plants to nurse back to good health.

Even more important to Selsam than passing along the essential facts of a single subject, however, was conveying an appreciation and understanding of the meaning of scientific method. Concepts of careful observation and controlled experiments capable of being reproduced were always central to her work. In her view, techniques that undermined this standard such as anthropomorphism in the portrayal of animals were condescending to a child's intelligence, and she avoided them with passion. Not surprisingly, a scientist whom Selsam revered was Charles Darwin, and in 1959 she published an edition of Darwin's *The Voyage of the Beagle*, especially prepared for young people so they could see for themselves the "process of creative science at work."

After writing more than sixty successful titles in twenty-five years, Selsam broadened her work to include the role of science editor as well. In 1972 she joined the staff of Walker and Company, where she launched a science list for children headed by the "First Look" series, which she wrote with Joyce Hunt. Throughout her career, Selsam received many awards, but perhaps the one that most recognizes the range of her accomplishments is the Nonfiction Award given to her by the Washington Post/Children's Book Guild in 1977 "for a total body of creative writing." ❧ C.C.E.

SENDAK, MAURICE

AMERICAN ARTIST AND WRITER, B. 1928. In the early 1960s, Brian O'Doherty, then the art critic for the *New York Times*, called Maurice Sendak "one of the most powerful men in the U.S." because of his ability to "give shape to the fantasies of millions of children—an awful responsibility." It is a challenge Sendak has continued to meet in a career that has spanned four decades and has led to Sendak's creation of the texts and illustrations for more than seventy books, which have sold tens of millions of copies in more than a dozen languages. But though Max in his wolf suit and the monsters he tames in Sendak's classic *Where the Wild Things Are* (1963) have taken a permanent place in American popular culture and the global mythology of childhood, Sendak confesses to being baffled by the acclaim his books have won. "It's amazing I've had success," he reflects, "because my books are so idiosyncratic and personal and striving for inner things rather than for outer things."

The "inner" subject that Sendak has explored in many of his books—and what he calls his "obsession" as a writer and artist—are the fantasies that children create "to combat an awful fact of childhood." In accepting the prestigious Caldecott Medal for *Where the Wild Things Are*, Sendak explained this fact: "From their earliest years, children live on familiar terms with disrupting emotions. . . . They continually cope with frustration as best they can. And it is through fantasy that children achieve catharsis. It is the best means they have for taming Wild Things."

Before *Where the Wild Things Are* was published, Sendak had illustrated nearly fifty books written by others, many of them remarkable in their own right, like ELSE HOLMELUND MINARIK's "Little Bear" books, a memorable series of early readers. Sendak's first major group of pictures appeared in *A Hole Is to Dig* (1952), RUTH KRAUSS's path-breaking collection of "first definitions" that children themselves had invented to describe their world. Buttons, one definition explained, are "to keep people warm"; others reasoned that "steps are to sit on," and rugs, of course, "are so dogs have napkins." To capture these fresh perceptions, Sendak set them dancing with dozens of small pen-and-ink drawings of children.

But these were not what Sendak described as the "all-American, white-toothed" children that were so common in children's books at the time. Instead, Sendak depicted the "hurdy-gurdy, fantasy-plagued kids" he remembered from the Brooklyn neighborhoods of the 1930s in which he spent his childhood, the son of immigrant Jewish parents who had left little villages in Poland to come to America just before World War I. These "little greenhorns just off the boat" that Sendak drew for *A Hole Is to Dig* effectively began the revolution in children's literature that Michael di Capua, one of Sendak's editors, thinks "turned the entire tide of what is acceptable, of what is possible to put in a children's-book illustration." Or, he might well have added, in a children's book as a whole.

Through the 1950s Sendak went on, like his favorite composer, Mozart, to play variations on the one theme that, he believes, runs throughout his books: "how kids get through a day, how they survive tedium, boredom, how they cope with anger, frustration." It is a subject close to his own experience in which he struggled through what he has called a "miserable" childhood. As a young boy, he was frequently ill, often desperately so—with measles, pneumonia, scarlet fever—and stuck indoors for weeks on end. But the positive effect of this isolation was that he was forced to develop his own imaginative resources; while his older siblings, Natalie and Jack, were out playing with the other kids, he "stayed home and drew pictures."

In *The Sign on Rosie's Door* (1960), Sendak gave this theme another variation when he introduced, as the book's main character, an eight-year-old girl named Rosie. Sendak had watched and sketched the real-life Rosie from the window of his family's Brooklyn apartment building during the summer of 1948. Recently graduated from high school, he was unemployed and trapped at home, all the while wishing he could be living across the river in Manhattan. He identified with Rosie: "She had the same problem that I had as a child in that she was stuck on a street that was probably inappropriate for her, but she'd have to make do. So, in a sense, she became the prototypical child of all my books." In fact, this "Fellini of 18th Avenue" transformed her daily task of survival into an art form, and herself into a superstar by creating elaborate dramas and movie scripts that she "hoaxed" the neighborhood kids into acting out with her.

Sendak's fascination with this child impresario and genius of improvisational play led him, in 1974, to do an animated television special about her (*Really Rosie, Starring the Nutshell Kids*), with music by another kid from Brooklyn, Carole King. And in 1981, he gave Rosie her ultimate star vehicle in the off-Broadway musical *Really Rosie*, which drew its characters from those who made their first appearance in Sendak's perennially popular boxed set of four small books, *The Nutshell Library* (1962). Among them were Johnnie, a little boy obsessed with lurid stories he picks up about kidnappings (as it happens, one of Sendak's own childhood fears), and Pierre, "who only could say 'I don't care.'" Then, of course, there is Rosie herself, who, by this time in her twenty-one-year career, can quip about how "you have to make peace with your crummy past."

Where the Wild Things Are, though, would be Sendak's breakthrough book. It was the first full-color picture book for which he both wrote the text and drew the pictures, and it took up, uncompromisingly and forcefully, one of those "inner things" that have continued to preoccupy Sendak's creative life. In Max, the tantrum-tossing wolf-child, Sendak portrayed what he regards as an ordinary but also "a very crucial point in a child's life," a dark moment when only a leap of faith into fantasy can help him find release from his rage.

Today, we are used to having around various furry, befanged descendants of the Wild Things—gobbling cookies, teaching the alphabet, or advising children about how they can cope with the dark. But when Sendak's monsters first appeared, they were revolutionary, unexpected creatures who had sprung out of the unconscious of a child. Ordinary children were not supposed to behave that way, at least not in the public pages of a picture book. Yet Sendak asked the reader to accept Max's behavior as just that—ordinary—and in doing so Sendak reminded us that the world of children's fantasies is one of their best-kept secrets. Dr. Seuss's Cat in the Hat had warned children about upsetting their parents by telling them what really went on "inside" while the adults were out. But Sendak let the cat out of the bag.

Other books that followed *Wild Things* took Sendak farther into the territory that the psychologist James Hillman refers to as "the dark side of the bambino." *In the Night Kitchen* (1970) spun the reader through the surreal fantasy of a child's dream, like Alice into Wonderland or Dorothy into Oz. Mickey, the hero of this voyage into the unconscious, is popped into an oven by three giant, Oliver-Hardy bakers before he can escape in an airplane that he fashions from dough and fly off to find the missing ingredient for morning cake.

While the book was, in part, Sendak's homage to New York City and the movies of the 1930s that had so affected him as a child (among them Disney's early Mickey Mouse cartoons, *King Kong*, and Busby Berkeley's musicals), it was also a celebration of the primal, sensory world of childhood and an affirmation of its imaginative potency. The jubilant point that Sendak makes about our naked human nature continues to transcend the controversy that may arise as a result of Sendak's having let Mickey fall out of his bed and out of his pajamas across the pages of his adventure.

About ten years later, *Outside Over There* (1981), the third book in what Sendak considers is his trilogy of works that deals specifically with that "inner" theme, took up the fantasy of a little girl, Ida, who is stuck looking after her baby sister. For an instant, Ida ignores the infant and plays her wonderhorn instead. In that brief moment, the baby is stolen by goblins and Ida must imagine a way to recover the infant. Sendak chose the late eighteenth century as the setting for the book, the time of the Brothers Grimm (whose tales Sendak has illustrated in his 1973 collection, *The Juniper Tree* done with translator LORE SEGAL) and of Sendak's favorite artist, Mozart. But though he places the book in the past, Sendak is again dealing with the complex emotional life of children in the present, as they try to cope with the mysteries of feeling through their fantasies.

Sendak believes that "his most unusual gift is that [his] child self seems still to be alive and well" and that he can continue to remain closely in touch with this source of creative energy. But there are some risks, he notes: "Reaching back to childhood is to put yourself in a state of vulnerability again because being a child was to be so. But then all of living is so—to be an artist is to be vulnerable."

Sendak has continued to take these creative chances himself, beginning a second career in the 1980s as a designer for ballet and opera, gathering rave reviews for this new work that now ranges from Mozart's *Magic Flute* and Tchaikovsky's *Nutcracker* to a double bill of two short fantasy operas based on *Where the Wild Things Are* and another Sendak book, *Higglety-Pigglety Pop!* (1967). There also have been other book projects, including his powerful paintings for a hitherto unpublished Grimm's tale, *Dear Mili* (1988), and his spirited, playful drawings (reminiscent of those that began his career) for the children's folklore collected by IONA AND PETER OPIE in *I Saw Esau* (1992).

Sendak has continued to draw on the rich interpretative possibilities of folk rhymes in his most recent picture book, *We Are All in the Dumps with Jack and Guy* (1993). The text for this work comes from two obscure Mother Goose rhymes whose meaning had puzzled Sendak, he reports, since the 1960s when he first came across them while working on a possible collection of nursery rhymes. He was finally able to make sense of these verses when he saw that they could be used to illustrate the problem of the homeless, impoverished, violent conditions in which so many children today are forced to live. In the book that has emerged from this fusion of the archaic with his impassioned, contemporary vision, Sendak finds the happiest ending that he can for his abandoned kids: in a world that is indifferent—indeed, hostile—to their needs, they end up taking care of one another. In the process they claim for themselves a moving, transcendent power—one based on compassion and community.

The 1990s are offering Sendak other new directions for his creative drives, taking him to Hollywood, where he is in the process of developing a number of his projects as films, and back to the dramatic stage, as the founding force, with ARTHUR YORINKS, of the Night Kitchen Theater. The innovative national touring

Voices of the Creators

Maurice Sendak

I was the youngest of three children growing up in Brooklyn, and when I got a book from my sister, about the last thing I did was read it. A book, to me, was for sniffing, poking, chewing, licking. The first real book I ever had was Mark Twain's *Prince and the Pauper,* illustrated by Robert Lawson, whose work I still admire. I treasure that book, although I don't know if I ever actually read it.

Children have a sensuous approach to books. I remember one letter I received from a little boy who loved *Where the Wild Things Are.* Actually, I think the letter was written by the boy's mother, and he sent me a picture he had drawn. So I wrote him back and sent him a picture. Eventually, I received another letter, this time from his mother: "Jimmy liked your post card so much he ate it." That letter confirmed everything I'd ever suspected.

I seem to have been blessed, or cursed, with a vivid memory of childhood. This is not supposed to happen. According to Freud, there's a valve that shuts off the horrors of childhood to make room for the horrors of adolescence. I must have a leaky valve, because I have these torrential memories. From a career standpoint, I guess that's been a good thing. Socially, it's been nothing short of disaster.

I profited as a child from the dynamics of my family. My brother was a writer, and I was allowed to illustrate his stories. With alarming regularity, our home would be invaded by these galumphing people called relatives. My brother would be called upon to read his latest opus, and I would hold up illustrations that I had done on shirt cardboard.

I remember one story called "They Were Inseparable." It was about a brother and sister who loved each other so much that they planned to get married. You see, Freud never came to Brooklyn. At any rate, I could understand my brother's feelings. Our sister was very beautiful, in a Dolores del Rio way. But he must have had a hint that this would never work, because his story ended with a terrible accident in which the brother was permanently damaged. I did very well at illustrating the blood and bandages, but not nearly so well at creating the kissing scenes.

I was a sickly child and spent a lot of time looking out the window. There was a little girl across the street named Rosie, and I must have forty sketchpads filled with Rosie pictures and Rosie stories. She was incredible. She had to fight the other kids on the block for attention, and she had to be inventive. I remember one time, when she came up with the explosive line: "Did you hear who died?" Rosie started telling the kids that she had heard a noise upstairs—a noise like someone falling, furniture breaking, and gasping, choking sounds. She went to investigate, and her grandmother was on the floor. Rosie had to give her the kiss of life—twice. Her grandmother managed to whisper "Addio Rosie" before dying. While Rosie was talking, her grandmother came up the street, carrying groceries from the market. The kids waited until she had gone into the house before turning to Rosie with the request: "Tell us how your grandma died again."

Rosie's stories became the basis of *Really Rosie,* an animated film. Then Arthur Yorinks and I formed The Night Kitchen, a children's theater company, and we cast Really Rosie for the stage. Then we planned to collaborate on a production of *Peter Pan.*

J. M. Barrie left the copyright of the play with a children's hospital in London, so I visited the hospital to ask for permission to produce the work. While I was there, I visited some of the children. You might be surprised to learn that most of the children who are terminally ill know that they are. I was asked to go see a little girl who's dying. She had heard I was in the hospital, and since her favorite book was *Where the Wild Things Are,* she had asked to see me.

I sat down by her bed and started drawing. Before long, she was sitting so close to me that her face was practically on my elbow. She was saying "Put the horns on; put the teeth in" and ordering me about. She was wonderful and funny, and I drew very slowly to give her as much pleasure as possible. But after a while I became aware of something. I saw a look on her mother's face. The girl was engrossed in the drawing, and the mother was watching her child with a look that said "How can she be so cheerful and lively when we all know . . ." It was a puzzled, confused, lonely look. Suddenly, without glancing up, the girl reached out until her hand touched her mother's. Without looking, she took her mother's hand and squeezed it. Children know everything.

My books are written for and dedicated to children like Rosie and this little girl. Children who are never satisfied with condescending material. Children who understand real emotion and real feeling. Children who are not afraid of knowing emotional truth.

company has begun to produce original dramatic works by, among others, Yorinks and Sendak.

Though Sendak does not have any actual children, he remains extremely close to those creative offspring who have appeared in his books. Every year, Sendak reports, dozens of schools and children's groups ask him for permission to stage their own versions of *Where the Wild Things Are*, often with a girl playing Max, a gender-breaking change in his text that delights him. And every year, he says, he can hardly hold back the tears when "parents who were little people when I wrote the book present their children to me. And here are these new human beings with their eyes beaming, and they are again in wolf suits." ❦ JOHN CECH

Seredy, Kate

AMERICAN AUTHOR AND ILLUSTRATOR, 1899–1975. Kate Seredy arrived in the United States knowing very little English, but within fifteen years was writing award-winning children's books in her new language. As a child, the Budapest-born author often accompanied her schoolteacher father as he visited peasants on the Hungarian plains; these experiences instilled the love for nature and traditional culture found in many of the author's books. Seredy attended the Academy of Arts in Budapest, where she received an art teacher's diploma, then studied in Berlin, Paris, and Rome. After serving as a nurse during World War I, she visited the United States in 1922 and stayed for the rest of her life.

At first she could only find employment painting lampshades and greeting cards. When she sought free-lance artwork at a publishing company, an editor suggested she write a story based on her childhood. Although she had never attempted creative writing before, Seredy began a picture-book text, which quickly blossomed into a middle-grade novel. *The Good Master* (1935) is the warm, appealing story of Kate, a somewhat wild girl, who comes to live with her cousin Jancsi on his family's ranch. Both children are well-realized characters in a book that contains humor, adventure, and a vivid sense of rural Hungarian life. A sequel, *The Singing Tree* (1939), relates the World War I experiences of the cousins. Although it includes a few melodramatic scenes, this strong and moving narrative was especially timely, as it was published when the world was on the verge of a second major war. Both novels were named Newbery Honor Books and are still popular with young readers. Seredy won the Newbery Medal for *The White Stag* (1937), which is based on Hun and Magyar legends and includes such renowned historical figures as Attila. Powerful, poetic prose and stunning illustrations combine to make the book one of Seredy's best, although it lacks the child appeal of her other work.

One of the author's most consistent themes is an appreciation for rural living, displayed in *The Tenement Tree* (1959), the story of a city boy exposed to country life for the first time, and *The Open Gate* (1943), in which a family leaves New York City for a rural farm during World War II. Another book concerning that war, *The Chestry Oak* (1948), tells of a young Hungarian prince sent to live on an American farm. Seredy's books do not shy away from social issues such as war or poverty but present a basic belief in humanity's goodness. *A Tree for Peter* (1941) shows how a boy from Shantytown helps transform the area into a thriving community. This sentimental story is poorly structured but contains some of Seredy's finest illustrations. The author claimed that all of her novels began as picture books that grew too large to be contained within that format, yet ultimately she published only one picture book, *Gypsy* (1951), the life story of a cat. Seredy continued to illustrate other authors' books throughout her writing career, including CAROL RYRIE BRINK's *Caddie Woodlawn* (1935) and *The Wonderful Year* (1946) by Nancy Barnes. Her ornate color illustrations for RUTH SAWYER's *The Christmas Anna Angel* (1944) received a Caldecott Honor award. As both an illustrator and an author, Seredy's appreciation for nature and ability to create appealing characters resulted in many vibrant books. ❦ P.D.S.

Series Books

They have been decried by critics and most librarians, but series books have always found a ready audience among young readers. A children's book series can be defined as a succession of related stories that usually focus on a continuing lead character. Perhaps the books should be termed "formula series" to distinguish them from *literary* works that also follow a continuing character through several volumes. LAURA INGALLS WILDER's "Little House" series and BEVERLY CLEARY's "Ramona" books have three-dimensional characterizations, thought-provoking themes, and high-quality writing that sets them far above the series label. The literary series is guided by an artistic vision, while the formula series seems to be driven by commercial considerations. Quantity, rather than quality, is the key for most formula series. Characterization and thematic concerns are usually sacrificed for formulaic, plot-driven adventures and surface insights.

At the turn of the century, HORATIO ALGER was the foremost practitioner of formula series. His "rags to riches" story lines feature plucky, industrious boys who rise from humble beginnings to great success. Among his many series are "Boys' Home," "Rise in Life," and the "Alger Series for Boys."

Laura Lee Hope directed her efforts at a somewhat younger audience when she began her "BOBBSEY TWINS" series in 1904. These overly sweet stories concern the mild adventures of two sets of twins in the same family, older siblings Nan and Bert, and their preschool counterparts, Flossie and Freddie. Like Alger's dated series, the Bobbsey Twins books are seldom read by contemporary children.

The various series produced by the STRATEMEYER LITERARY SYNDICATE are among the best known of the twentieth century. Edward Stratemeyer created and wrote the initial volumes of the "NANCY DREW" series, the "HARDY BOYS" series, and the "Tom Swift" series before assigning the bulk of the workload to commissioned writers for whom he provided detailed plots. Nancy Drew (written by "Carolyn Keene") and the Hardy Boys (written by "Franklin W. Dixon") are junior sleuths, noted for their exciting adventures and crime-solving techniques. Tom Swift stories were written by "Victor Appleton" and concern a scientific genius who uses his inventions for fighting crime and pursuing adventure.

Traditionally, series books have been published in inexpensive editions, so it is not surprising that the most popular series of the late twentieth century have been published in paperback. In 1982 Francine Pascal began the "Sweet Valley High" series, which focuses on teenage romance in a small-town school. The "Baby-Sitters Club" series by ANN M. MARTIN concerns a group of girls who work as baby sitters. The books on various periods in the "American Girls" series, published in both hardcover and paperback, are written by different authors, such as Connie Porter and Valerie Tripp. The books are part of a marketing empire that produces expensive, well-made dolls representing girls from different historical eras, including the Civil War and World War II.

There have been a huge number of series books published in the twentieth century. Many, such as the "Rover Boys" series, the "Elsie Dinsmore" series, the "Trixie Belden" books, and Enid Blyton's "Famous Five" adventures, have faded from popularity. Some, like "Nancy Drew," remain successful for decades. With prose that ranges from competent to downright awful, very few series books can be considered great literature. But these light, escapist books are appealing to children who find comfort in reading story after story about their favorite, familiar characters. ❦ P.D.S.

SERVICE, ROBERT W.

BRITISH POET AND NOVELIST, 1874–1958. Robert Service, the "Poet of the Yukon," was born in England and raised in Scotland. Growing up, he felt a special affinity for the poems of Robert Burns; he also absorbed the romantic and adventure-filled works of Robert Louis Stevenson and Sir Walter Scott. But reading about adventure wasn't enough for this literary-minded young man—he wanted to live it and write about it. After working for the Commercial Bank of Scotland, Service headed for Canada in 1894 to collect experiences and impressions. He worked for a time as a farmer and rancher in British Columbia. Then wanderlust again set in and his travels took him as far as Mexico.

An article Service happened to spy in a California newspaper told of the gold strike in Canada's Klondike. Service headed back to British Columbia, where he eventually resumed the banking career he had left behind in Scotland. Service subsequently found himself transferred to Whitehorse and then Dawson, Yukon: the heart of gold rush territory. There, Service found the inspiration to pen the verses for which he would quickly become famous.

Service's first collection of verse, *Songs of a Sourdough*, retitled *The Spell of the Yukon* in the United States when it was reprinted in 1915, was published in 1907. Although some contemporary critics were lukewarm about the literary quality of Service's work, it quickly found its public. Especially in his melodramatic monologues, Service captured for the rest of the world the heightened life of a gold rush town, with its rugged men, barrooms, and dance-hall girls. As Service himself wrote in the first volume of his autobiography, *Ploughman of the Moon* (1945), "Vice seemed to me a more vital subject for poetry than virtue, more colourful, more dramatic, so I specialized in the Red Light atmosphere."

The verses of this free-spirited adventurer have been loved and recited continually around the world since their publication. His two best-known works (both originally published in *Songs of a Sourdough*) have been brought to renewed prominence in picture-book versions accompanied by stunning and remarkably appropriate full-color illustrations by Canadian artist TED HARRISON: *The Cremation of Sam McGee* in 1986 (both an American Library Association Notable Book and a

New York Times Best Book Selection) and *The Shooting of Dan McGrew* in 1988.

In 1912 Service left the Yukon behind, traveling to Europe, where he worked both as a journalist and for the Red Cross during the First World War. Through the years he wrote seventeen collections of verse, popular fiction, and a two-part autobiography. Eventually, he made his home in Monte Carlo, where he died in 1958.

Service's success lies in his firsthand understanding of the part of the human psyche that craves adventure and drama. He seems almost to have been born to chronicle an exciting time of history, and Canada's gold rush filled the bill. Are the verses of Robert Service great literature? Perhaps not. But they have lived on because readers of all ages cannot resist reciting them, whether in barrooms, living rooms, or classrooms. M.B.

Seton, Ernest Thompson

CANADIAN ARTIST, NATURALIST, AND AUTHOR, 1860–1946. As a child, Seton felt an attraction to wildlife and early displayed an artistic gift. Later in life, Seton recounted a story about saving his money to buy a much coveted book on Canadian birds—the so-called authoritative text on the subject—only to be disappointed when he discovered the book's numerous flaws. He filled in the margins with his own notes and drawings.

From childhood, Seton took copious notes and made meticulous drawings on what he observed in nature. His beautifully rendered wildlife drawings and paintings exemplify that attention to detail. He won praise from his art teachers and eventually went to study in England. In the early 1890s Seton studied in Paris, where he was known for carrying carcasses of dogs home from the pound so that he could dissect them and study their anatomy. Ironically, Seton's struggle to paint realistically took place in the midst of the Impressionist movement in France. Nevertheless, one of his paintings, "The Sleeping Wolf," was accepted at the Paris Salon in 1891.

Seton moved often, living in New York City, Toronto, Paris, and the Canadian prairie province of Manitoba. Although he loved the wilderness, he could better earn a living in the city, and arthritis and failing eyesight impaired his ability to enjoy the out-of-doors and work at his art. By the time *Two Little Savages* was published in 1903, Seton had turned completely to writing, at which he believed he could make a better living, and, indeed, he did. His books sold well, and he was a popular speaker, enthralling his audiences with stories about wildlife.

Seton was committed to preserving nature, but like so many of the naturalists of his day, he was also an avid hunter. His most famous story, "Lobo, King of the Currumpaw" (1894), describes how Seton successfully hunted down and killed a wolf. Later he came to understand the contradiction inherent in pursuit of the two activities, and he put down his rifle and picked up a camera.

Seton is best known for his works of fiction on wildlife, which he called animal biographies. At the time of their publication, books such as *Wild Animals I Have Known* (1898) and others were extremely popular; they remained so for years. Seton was among the first to write about animals as they really lived—not dressed up and behaving like humans—establishing the true animal-story genre.

Though Seton wrote most of his works in the twentieth century, his realism was tinged with romanticism: He did not write about ordinary beasts in the woods. His animal characters, such as Wohl in *Biography of a Grizzly* (1900), were outstanding representatives of their species. He elevated them to the level of "noble beasts." Today's critics often view his work in a different light. Seton, who claimed to understand the language of the animals about which he wrote, attributed thoughts and conversations to them in his stories—a subjective approach not far removed from anthropomorphism. Still, Seton's animals always behaved naturally.

Today, Seton's stories are not widely read. By current standards, the stories are sentimental and the prose plodding. They are important historically, but modern naturalist writers, while they have benefited from Seton's break with the earlier tradition of ANIMAL STORIES, have advanced the stories both in terms of their realism and their avoidance of sentimentality. Seton's wildlife drawings, sketches, and paintings, however, do not suffer from age. Today they continue to be admired for their precision, accuracy, and beauty. T.H.

Seuss, Dr.

AMERICAN AUTHOR AND ILLUSTRATOR, 1904–1991. Writing under the pseudonym "Dr. Seuss," Theodor Seuss Geisel was a publishing phenomenon, an author of unique nonsense books for children who gained unprecedented acclaim outside the children's book field. Two of his picture books, *The Butter Battle Book* (1984) and *Oh, the Places You'll Go* (1990), broke records for the number of weeks they appeared on the *New York Times* adult best-seller list. Since 1937, his books have sold more than two hundred million copies and have been translated into some twenty languages as well as Braille. Yet Geisel never compromised his own artistic impulses, creating original, iconoclastic books that were at one time considered "too different" to be marketable.

Geisel's versatile creativity earned him three Academy Awards, including one for the animated cartoon "Gerald McBoing-Boing," and two Peabody Awards for the television specials "How the Grinch Stole Christmas" and "Horton Hears a Who," adapted from his children's books. His recognition within the children's book field was marked by two Caldecott Honor Awards, for *McElligot's Pool* (1947) and *Bartholomew and the Oobleck* (1949); in 1980 he was awarded the prestigious Laura Ingalls Wilder Award from the American Library Association for the body of his work.

Geisel was born in Springfield, Massachusetts, where his father was curator of public parks, including a small zoo. He spent much of his happy childhood with his father, learning about animals and storing that knowledge for the fantastic creatures that would later populate his picture books. In 1925 Geisel graduated from Dartmouth College, where he was editor of the school humor magazine—the first outlet for his freewheeling, zany humor. Geisel then attended Oxford University, intending to earn a Ph.D. in English literature; he found his studies "astonishingly irrelevant," however, and returned home. He soon found success—but not fulfillment —as an advertising illustrator and as a cartoonist for such national magazines as *Vanity Fair, The Saturday Evening Post,* and *Judge.*

A couplet he made up to the relentless pulse of an ocean liner's engines—"And that is a story that no one can beat/when I say that I saw it on Mulberry Street"—developed into Geisel's first children's book. In the cumulative tall tale *And to Think That I Saw It on Mulberry Street* (1937) a little boy's imagination transforms an ordinary horse and wagon into an increasingly outrageous parade of rajahs, elephants, brass bands, and magicians. The innovative, aggressively rhythmic *Mulberry Street*—the first of forty-six children's books written by Dr. Seuss—was reputedly turned down by twenty-eight publishers before it was finally accepted.

Mulberry Street was followed in 1938 by *The Five Hundred Hats of Bartholomew Cubbins,* an original, Seussian fairy tale in which a hapless boy's hats keep reproducing as he doffs them, desperate to obey the mandate "Hats off to the King!" The story's traditional fairy-tale structure contains pointed digs at pompous adults and spoiled children as well as the first glimmerings of Geisel's joyous experimentation with the English language.

Another beloved Seuss character was introduced in *Horton Hatches the Egg* (1940), about an elephant who agrees to sit on a bird's egg while the flighty, irresponsible mother takes a long vacation. Horton's brave constancy is rewarded when a tiny winged elephant hatches from the egg; his refrain, "I meant what I said, and I said what I meant/An elephant's faithful, one hundred percent," has become a classic line in children's literature. The sequel, *Horton Hears a Who!* (1954), finds the kind elephant doggedly protecting a complete, microscopic world that exists on a speck of dust. The moral, "A person's a person, no matter how small," reflects Geisel's great respect for the world's underdogs—including its children.

During World War II, Geisel worked as a political cartoonist and as a filmmaker for the army (two of his wartime documentaries, *Hitler Lives!* and *Design for Death,* won Academy Awards). His concern for social and political issues found continuing outlets in many of his children's books, which explore such topics as the commercialization of Christmas, in *How the Grinch Stole Christmas* (1957); totalitarianism, in *Yertle the Turtle* (1958); pollution, in the ecological allegory *The Lorax* (1971); discrimination, in *The Sneetches and Other Stories* (1961); and nuclear disarmament, in *The Butter Battle Book.*

Many of his books are simply celebrations of invention. Books such as *There's a Wocket in My Pocket* (1974), *Oh, the Thinks You Can Think* (1975), and *Oh, Say Can You Say* (1979) sparkle with wordplay and tongue-twisters. Geisel's imagination runs rampant in extravaganzas such as *If I Ran the Zoo* (1950) or *On Beyond Zebra* (1955) with their impossible, fantastic, funny creatures and wildly imaginative situations.

Perhaps Geisel's greatest contribution to children's literature, however, came with the publication of *The Cat in the Hat* and its companions. In a 1954 article in *Life* magazine, novelist John Hersey decried the dullness of the "pallid primers" used in schools to teach reading, complaining that they featured "abnormally courteous, unnaturally clean boys and girls" that bored real children and discouraged them from learning to read. Geisel responded with *The Cat in the Hat* (1957), published simultaneously as a trade book and a textbook; in it, Geisel used just 223 words to tell a decidedly unpallid story about what happened one rainy day when a completely conscienceless, mischievous, mayhem-making cat came to play. The book's open acceptance of children's misbehavior (subversive for that time), its wildly imaginative pictures and situation, and its spontaneous humor combined to give children a compelling incentive

Voices of the Creators

Dr. Seuss: an interview

How do you get your ideas for books?
This is the most asked question of any successful author. Most authors will not disclose their source for fear that other less successful authors will chisel in on their territory. However, I am willing to take a chance. I get all my ideas in Switzerland near the Forka Pass. There is a little town called Gletch, and two thousand feet up above Gletch there is a smaller hamlet called Uber Gletch. I go there on the fourth of August every summer to get my cuckoo clock repaired. While the cuckoo is in the hospital, I wander around and talk to the people in the streets. They are very strange people, and I get my ideas from them.

How do you handle the nonsense words in translation?
The books have been translated into about fifteen foreign languages. I have no idea how they handled it in the Japanese. Oddly enough, the Germanic and Nordic languages are much more successful for translating the nonsense words than the romance languages are. Why that is, I don't know. The Germans will take a name like *Bartholomew Cubbins* and turn it into *Bartel Lugepros,* which I think is a very beautiful approximation.

Do your characters live with you all the time?
Well, I hope not . . . If I were invited to a dinner party with my characters, I wouldn't show up.

Was your first book, And to Think That I Saw It on Mulberry Street (1937), *rejected by many publishers before it was accepted?*
Twenty-seven or twenty-nine, I forget which. The excuse I got for all those rejections was that there was nothing on the market quite like it, so they didn't know whether it would sell.

How much has your own early childhood influenced your work?
Not to a very great extent. I think my aberrations started when I got out of early childhood. My father, however, in my early childhood, did, among other things, run a zoo, and I used to play with the baby lions and the antelope and a few other things of that sort. Generally speaking, I don't think my childhood influenced my work. I think I skipped my childhood.

Do your ideas for books spring forth from free drawing you might be doing?
Mine always start as a doodle. I may doodle a couple of animals; if they bite each other, it's going to be a good book. If you doodle enough, the characters begin to take over themselves—after a year and a half or so.

Sometimes you have luck when you are doodling. I did one day when I was drawing some trees. Then I began drawing elephants. I had a window that was open, and the wind blew the elephant on top of a tree. I looked at it and said, "What do you suppose that elephant is doing there?" The answer was: "He is hatching an egg." Then all I had to do was write a book about it. I have left that window open ever since, but it's never happened again.

How do you shut out the reality of the world when you're creating your books? Do nuclear weapons, cancer, unemployment, and pollution affect you?
They're all there, but I look at them through the wrong end of the telescope. I change them in that way.

Excerpt from *The Horn Book Magazine.* Vol. 65. pp. 582-588.

to read. *The Cat in the Hat* became the first of the Beginner Books, a division of Random House of which Geisel was president; seventeen more limited-vocabulary books followed, including the immensely popular *Green Eggs and Ham* (1960), which contained just fifty words—and, as one critic noted, "unlimited exuberance."

Although he received some criticism for a repetitive sameness of rhyme and illustration style, Dr. Seuss remains a favorite of children of all ages—so beloved, in fact, that his name is "synonymous with laughter," according to critics May Hill Arbuthnot and Zena Sutherland. He gave children stories of great originality accompanied by pictures "characterized by a strange, wild grace, with their great heights and depths" and bright, clear colors. He inspired generations of children to explore the infinite possibilities of language and of their own imaginations.

The late Bennett Cerf, the publisher of the Dr. Seuss books, once said: "I've published any number of great writers, from William Faulkner to John O'Hara, but there's only one genius on my authors' list. His name is Ted Geisel." ✣ MARTHA V. PARRAVANO

Sewall, Marcia

AMERICAN ILLUSTRATOR, B. 1935. Marcia Sewall's warmly humorous illustrations are character-driven in much the same way a story is; the artist's sense of the character is the motive force behind her choice of medium, the composition of each piece, and the pacing of the illustrations throughout the work. Sewall says that as soon as she receives a manuscript, "I begin to immediately struggle with a sense of character, the movement of character onto believable space." In *The Story of Old Mrs. Brubeck and How She Looked for Trouble and Where She Found Him* (1981), Sewall had great difficulty in seeing Mrs. Brubeck, until she realized her character should be wearing clogs that clumped and clacked, almost an auditory accompaniment to the woman's fussing and worrying.

Sewall's work on Richard Kennedy's books, such as *The Rise and Fall of Ben Gizzard* (1978) and *The Song of the Horse* (ALA Notable Book, 1981), shows the illustrator at her most characteristic: people with strong features—impressive noses and determined chins—and clothing and landscape with a distinct folk quality about them. "I love the wisdom, the character, and the tradition in folk people, so I often choose books with that sort of quality," Sewall explains.

Sewall frequently adapts folktales herself to illustrate; in these her humor is in full effect. In *The Wee, Wee Mannie and the Big, Big Coo* (1977), Sewall sees the "wee, wee mannie," not as a child, as is usually the case in adaptations of this Scottish cumulative verse tale, but as a very small man, with an even smaller mustache.

Sewall drew on a continuing source of inspiration, the landscape of southern New England, for her two most honored books, *The Pilgrims of Plimoth* (1986), and the companion piece, *The People of the Breaking Day* (1990). Both books were critically acclaimed for their simple yet evocative descriptions of the lives of the first European settlers in Plymouth Colony and the people of the Wampanoag tribe that inhabited the area when the settlers came. In a seeming departure from her usual style of deftly drawn characters, Sewall used color and composition to dominate the paintings in the books. The landscape is the primary character in both books, and it is the differing relationships between the Pilgrims and the land, and the Wampanoags and the land, that provide the narrative tension for each book and the linking theme between them. So her breathtaking paintings in which the people are merely faceless elements, equally but no more important than the skies or the trees, are character studies of the land.

Sewall was born in Providence, Rhode Island, and spent summers in rural Maine with her father's family, times, she says, that "filled me with an appreciation for people who could survive close to the earth. . . . It also gave me a deep appreciation for a fresh and beautiful landscape." Sewall passes on this love for the land, and the people who live close to it, in her books. ✣ S.G.K.

Sewell, Anna

BRITISH AUTHOR, 1820–1878. Anna Sewell stayed at home for much of her life, but her only book, *Black Beauty,* traveled throughout the world. Since its publication in 1877, a year before Anna Sewell's death, this account in the first person of the ups and downs of a horse's life has fueled the fervor of animal rights activists and inspired numerous filmmakers, including Thomas Edison, and illustrators, such as Charles Keeping and SUSAN JEFFERS. At one time the book was reputed—truthfully or not—to have a distribution second only to that of the Bible.

Such a distinction might have overwhelmed its unpretentious Quaker author. A fall during a rainstorm left fourteen-year-old Sewell with a sprained ankle that never quite healed. She could never afterward walk very far, but she could drive her parents' carriage, and presumably on those drives she witnessed the cruelties about which she later wrote. Confined to her couch for the last six years of her life, Sewell created a new breed of animal stories—of which Canadian writer Margaret Marshall Saunders's sentimental dog story, *Beautiful Joe* (1894) is a direct descendant—that treated animals as animals instead of as stand-ins for humans or human vices. She set out to show that a horse would work harder in response to kindness than in response to abuse. Black Beauty changes hands several times during the course of the novel, and some of his owners don't share Sewell's conviction. They make him haul excessively heavy loads and hold his head up unnaturally high for hours, causing his neck to stiffen and his mouth to foam. He hears another horse tell how his owner ordered his tail cut off because it was "the fashion," rendering him permanently unable to swat the flies off his back.

Most of the cruelty in *Black Beauty* is inflicted by those under the influence of fashion or excessive drink.

Some have felt that Sewell's preaching fatally flaws her narrative. The stable man who ruins Black Beauty's knees—and gets himself killed in the process—would have been a model horseman if not for the drinking bouts that transformed him into "a disgrace to himself, a terror to his wife, and a nuisance to all that had to do with him." Those who are model horsemen are model in every respect. Black Beauty records faithfully how they dote on their families, keep the Sabbath holy, and speak out whenever they see someone (most likely a drunkard) mistreating a horse.

Yet sturdier than Sewell's soapbox, thankfully, is the empathy she demonstrates and evokes for her equine characters, an empathy that has raised her "little book," as she once dubbed it, to the stature of a classic. Because Sewell's careful descriptions let readers feel the bit tearing into Black Beauty's mouth or the chills caused by a stable boy who doesn't know enough to throw blankets on an overheated horse, the book made a real difference in the treatment of horses in Europe and America. The founder of the Massachusetts Society for the Prevention of Cruelty to Animals, George T. Angell, promoted the book's distribution and used its emotional impact to lobby for U.S. laws against the mistreatment of horses.

No longer needed as a tool of propaganda, *Black Beauty* still captivates children today through its strong story and characters, as publishers continue to reprint it in new, often adapted, editions. It has succeeded far beyond Sewell's modest goal of making men treat horses with a little compassion. C.M.H.

Illustration by George Ford Morris from a 1950 edition of *Black Beauty* (1877), by Anna Sewell.

Sewell, Helen

American artist, 1896–1957. One of the busiest artists at work in the field of children's illustration during the 1930s, 1940s, and 1950s, Helen Moore Sewell had a lifelong interest in depicting the world around her that was rooted in early travel experiences. By the age of seven, Sewell had circumnavigated the globe. She cited such disparate images as volcanoes glowing in the night, camels near the Suez Canal, and the varying colors of the oceans as stimulating her first artistic tendencies.

Sewell spent a portion of her early childhood on Guam, where her father was governor. Orphaned at the age of eight, she lived with a large, extended family that provided her lifelong support and continuous contact with children, which was essential to her career as an illustrator. Sewell was the youngest student to be admitted to art classes at Pratt Institute in New York City and continued to study art intermittently, including a stint with the Russian sculptor Aleksandr Archipenko. The result was Sewell's distinctive, highly stylized illustration technique, which often utilized hard-lined ink sketches, no shadowing, and close-in focus on characters.

Sewell first earned her living as a designer of Christmas and greeting cards. Her stark black-and-white drawings, often with highly detailed content, became her trademark when she began illustrating books for other authors in 1924. More than sixty assignments followed. Her work appeared in books by such authors as Carol Ryrie Brink, Alice Dalgliesh, Langston Hughes, Elizabeth Coatsworth, and Frances Clarke Sayers. By 1932 Sewell had illustrated nine books and she was asked to produce art for Laura Ingalls Wilder's *Little House in the Big Woods*. She continued to illustrate two more "Little House" titles, but was eventually in such demand that Mildred Boyle assisted her for the remainder of the series. In her art, Sewell usually drew from memories of familiar landscapes and children within her family circle and only occasionally used live models. For the "Little House" books, she consulted photographs of Wilder's family.

In addition to illustrating children's stories, Sewell provided drawings for many adult books, including works by Emily Dickinson and Jane Austen. Sewell's own writings and compilations were self-illustrated, starting with *ABC for Everyday* (1930). Among the other books she wrote and illustrated are *Blue Barns: The Story of Two Big Geese and Seven Little Ducks* (1933), *Peggy and the Pony* (1936), *Jimmy and Jemima* (1940), *Peggy and the Pup* (1941), and *Belinda the Mouse* (1944). In 1947 Sewell collaborated with Elena Eleska for *Three Tall Tales*, stories based on Eleska's experiences in Asia and Africa. The book was innovative in its use of comic-strip-style graphics.

Throughout her career, Sewell's illustrations appeared in a number of award-winning books, including the Caldecott Medal Honor Book *The Thanksgiving Story* (1955) by Alice Dalgliesh and five "Little House" titles, all of which were Newbery Honor Books.

Sewell's work was best known from the 1930s through the 1950s. Her body of art makes her an interesting historical example of children's book illustration during that era. ❧ W.A.

Shannon, George

AMERICAN AUTHOR, B. 1952. A professional storyteller whose picture books are often based on tales he has told young audiences, George Shannon is also the author of literary criticism and a young adult novel. Born in Caldwell, Kansas, and raised in small towns in both Kansas and Kentucky, Shannon began writing in grade school and submitted stories for publication during his teenage years. After receiving a bachelor's degree from Western Kentucky University and a master's degree in library science from the University of Kentucky, he spent five years as a children's librarian at school and public libraries. Sharing books and telling stories to young library patrons provided further training for the aspiring author, and in 1978 he left his library job to work full-time as a writer and storyteller.

Shannon's first picture-book text was *The Gang and Mrs. Higgins* (1981), which takes place at a pioneer trading post in Kansas. The author's storytelling skill is evident in a number of picture books that encourage movement, response, or activity from an audience. Throughout *Lizard's Song* (1981), a happy amphibian tries to teach Bear the words to a nonsense song; a song also runs through the author's tongue-in-cheek tall tale, *The Piney Woods Peddler* (1981). In *Dance Away* (1982), the instructions for Rabbit's dance are incorporated into the story of how the dance helps Rabbit and his friends evade a hungry fox. *O I Love* (1985) is based on the folksong "My Little Rooster." In Shannon's adaptation, a little girl celebrates her stuffed animal friends; young readers may add to the lyrics of the song by including their own special friends and daily activities. *Bean Boy* (1984) is a less joyful reading experience. This tale of an orphan searching for food contains moments of humor and a happy ending, but both the tone of the writing and PETER SIS's illustrations are cold and depressing.

Shannon's best-known work may be his volumes of folktales, which involve riddles or puzzles. Beginning with *Stories to Solve* (1985) and continued with *More Stories to Solve* (1990) and *Still More Stories to Solve* (1994), the books contain brief folktales from a variety of places, including the United States, Kashmir, Ethiopia, and China. The reader is invited to solve the puzzle presented in each tale.

Shannon has also written a fine young adult novel, *Unlived Affections* (1989), in which college-bound Willie Ramsey discovers a cache of old letters and learns that his father left Willie's mother when he fell in love with another man. This mature and thoughtful novel contains Shannon's most accomplished writing, as he makes effective use of symbol and metaphor and capably balances the framing story of Willie's isolation with the contents of his father's letters. It is the only Shannon book driven by characterization, and it leaves the reader thinking about the characters long after they finish the book and hoping for a sequel in which Willie will finally meet his father.

In addition to his works for children, the author has published several studies of folklore and a 1989 monograph surveying the life and career of ARNOLD LOBEL. Much of Shannon's work has been based on folktales and storytelling, but his young adult novel shows his ability to move in interesting and diverse directions in his writing. ❧ P.D.S.

Shannon, Monica

AMERICAN AUTHOR, 1905?–1965. In a writing career that spanned less than ten years, Monica Shannon wrote fairy tales, poetry, and novels and won the 1935 Newbery Medal for her finest achievement, *Dobry*.

Shannon was born in Ontario, Canada, but immigrated to the United States as an infant. The daughter of a cattle importer, Shannon grew up in Washington, Idaho, Montana, and California. Although her earliest writing efforts won school prizes, the hours she spent exploring nature and visiting her family's Bulgarian ranch hands would prove equally significant. While working at the Los Angeles Public Library, Shannon began to write stories incorporating California's natural history with fanciful tales. *California Fairy Tales* (1926) established Shannon's reputation as a poetic stylist. Shannon next wrote a second volume of fairy tales, a book of verse, and the pirate story *Tawnymore* (1931).

Finally, using the Bulgarian tales she had learned as a child and the reminiscences of illustrator Atanas Katchamakoff, Shannon wrote *Dobry,* the evocative story of an artistic peasant boy in Bulgaria. Dobry lives in a small village with his kindly grandfather and strong mother. As the seasons change, Dobry matures from an impulsive youngster to a young man preparing to leave home for art school. Bulgarian customs and philosophies are smoothly woven into the story, showing the villagers' intense appreciation of nature. *Dobry* is a wise and poetic book, unforgettable for its beautiful writing. Although its quiet plot, measured pace, and vaguely historical Bulgarian setting have prevented *Dobry* from achieving popularity among today's readers, the distinction of being a Newbery winner has kept the book in print, and it remains a true gem waiting to be discovered by special readers. ❧ P.D.S.

Sharmat, Marjorie Weinman

AMERICAN AUTHOR, B. 1928. Marjorie Weinman Sharmat's first picture book, *Rex,* the story of a little boy who runs away from home to live with an elderly neighborhood man and pretends to be his dog, launched her career as a children's author in 1967. Her dream of becoming a writer arose tangentially from a childhood desire to become a detective. The eight-year-old Marjorie and a friend decided to incorporate and publish their surreptitious gleanings in a newspaper aptly named *The Snooper's Gazette,* but a lack of subscribers brought the paper to an untimely end. Undaunted and determined to become a writer, she went on to hone her craft on poetry, diaries, and school newspapers. In high school she followed her parents' encouragement and sent stories to national magazines, never letting her optimism be deterred by rejection slips. Because "it was practical," she majored in merchandising when she attended Westbrook Junior College in Portland, Maine, her hometown. Nevertheless, writing remained her love. Her first published works were a four-word advertising slogan for the W. T. Grant Company, a short story for adults, and an article about Yale, which merited assignment to the Yale Memorabilia Collection.

From the publication of *Rex* until 1982, Sharmat concentrated on books for preschool to middle-school children. Among these are her "I Can Read" and "Easy Reader" series, the most popular being the "Nate the Great" detective series, which began in 1972. Nate the Great is a nine-year-old pancake-eating sleuth who dresses in a trench coat and a Sherlock Holmes deerstalker. He confidently and methodically goes about solving neighborhood mysteries with his faithful dog, Sludge. Within the limited vocabulary of this format, Sharmat has created a classic of her own. The stories are clever and witty, written in traditional deadpan detective style. A film of *Nate Goes Undercover* (1974) won a Los Angeles International Children's Film Festival Award. Among her stories about friendship, such as *Sophie and Gussie* (1973), *I'm Not Oscar's Friend Anymore* (1975), *Uncle Boris and Maude* (1979), *Mooch the Messy Meets Prudence the Neat* (1979), Sharmat shows that ingenuity can resolve real and imagined wrongs that arise between friends with opposing personalities.

Memorable in her stories for older readers are those about sixth-grader Maggie Marmelstein, which include *Getting Something on Maggie Marmelstein* (1971). As this self-assured, dynamic, opinionated child faces daily trials, she finds that even perceived enemies can be loyal friends and that winning the battle can result in losing the war; tact and saving face are as important as being right. The "Olivia Sharp, Agent for Secrets" series follows a wealthy eleven-year-old's adventures as she either secures or uncovers secrets for her clients, while the "Kids on the Bus" series involves mysteries and clever

Illustration by MARC SIMONT from *Nate the Great and the Lost List* (1975), by Marjorie Weinman Sharmat.

problem solving for children seven to nine years old. Of less literary merit, although enjoyable recreational reading, are Sharmat's entertaining situation comedy young adult stories, such as *I Saw Him First* (1983) and *How to Meet a Gorgeous Guy* (1983). Many of Sharmat's books have been Junior Literary Guild selections and others have been chosen as Books of the Year by the Library of Congress, while several have been made into films for television.

In all her work, Sharmat examines the entire gamut of children's emotions and fears with humor and understanding. She has done this successfully in over seventy books ranging from picture books through young adult novels. ❧ S.R.

Sharp, Margery

British author, 1905–1991. Creator of the beloved "Miss Bianca" series—nine books of fantasy featuring the elegant and dauntless white mouse Miss Bianca and her stalwart companion Bernard—Margery Sharp turned to writing for children after thirty years of publishing popular and witty adult novels, "because," she said, "they are a complete release of the imagination." Her invention of the MPAS, or Mouse Prisoner Aid Society, provided fertile ground for her special brand of tongue-in-cheek grand adventure on a mouse-sized scale.

Lovely, artistic, brave, and, above all, well-bred, Miss Bianca must rank as one of the great heroines of children's literature. Along with the gentle satire and precise writing of the series, it is the joy of watching Miss Bianca rise to every occasion that sustains book after book. She grows from the pampered and flighty young gentlemouse of *The Rescuers* (1959)—where, as part of her reluctant participation in the rescue of a captive Norwegian poet, she draws a map that strongly resembles a garden party hat—to the ever-resourceful Perpetual Madam President of the MPAS at the height of her career in such books as *Miss Bianca in the Salt Mines* (1966) and *Miss Bianca and the Bridesmaid* (1972). The valiant Bernard, at Miss Bianca's side in every adventure, while "lacking in personality" (according to his creator), more than makes up for it in his dedication to Miss Bianca.

Bernard comes into his own in the last two books of the series, *Bernard the Brave* (1976) and *Bernard into Battle: A Miss Bianca Story* (1979), in which Miss Bianca has retreated into a rather unsatisfying (to her and to her fans) retirement and keeps well in the background. The unresolved romantic tension between Bernard and Miss Bianca hangs in the air of every adventure, and readers are left wondering if the two will ever be able to put aside their class differences in order to marry. And yet their relationship seems perfect as it is, with Bernard playing chivalrous knight to Miss Bianca's lady fair—he forever adoring, she forever adored.

Books in the series have been variously illustrated—by Garth Williams, Erik Blegvad, Faith Jacques, and Leslie Morrill—but always in a highly complementary style. The illustrations perfectly capture the combination of swashbuckling adventure and miniature detail (walnut-shell chairs, postage-stamp rugs) that have enthralled and delighted children. ❧ S.G.K.

Shaw, Charles

American author and illustrator, 1892–1974. Foremost as an abstract artist, then as a writer, Charles Green Shaw helped usher in a thoroughly contemporary look and sound in the images and words of the American PICTURE BOOK for the very young. During the late 1930s and 1940s, an extremely creative and expansive period in juvenile book publishing, Shaw, along with notable children's book illustrators Leonard Weisgard and Esphyr Slobodkina, introduced nonrepresentational art to picture-book illustration in America. Shaw also crafted books whose words were among the early instances of interactive texts written for children. His best and most famous work, the inimitable *It Looked Like Spilt Milk* (1945), represents one of the finest picture-book examples of abstract art and participatory text. It is a renowned American classic that continues to engage young readers with its absolute graphic strength and verbal dialogue between craftsman and child.

Born in New York City, Shaw was graduated from Yale University and studied architecture at Columbia University. From an affluent family, he first dabbled in journalism; as a freelance writer, he contributed to *Harper's Bazaar, Vanity Fair, Town & Country,* and *The New Yorker.* Shaw lived for several years in Paris and London, began to paint while abroad, and in 1936 returned to New York, where he joined the American Abstract Artists. This avant-garde group sensed the universal appeal that nonobjective art held for people and helped popularize the movement. Shaw combined his literary and artistic talents in the late 1930s when he created several manuscripts of children's books, hopeful of their publication. With rejections from many of the larger, well-known publishing houses, Shaw, in 1939, inquired at William R. Scott, a small, progressive company just establishing its reputation as a publisher of daring, distinctively new kinds of books for very young children. There he met MARGARET WISE BROWN, Scott's first children's book editor and a burgeoning, innovative force in American picture books. Brown's discerning eye and ear for young children's literature gave the Scott titles their characteristic large pictures and brief texts that were exclusively about the real world of small children.

Brown saw potential in Shaw, and with her encouragement, his first children's book, *The Giant of Central Park*, was one of eight Scott titles in 1940, while his second, *The Guess Book*, appeared a year later. More important, as a talented and prominent picture-book writer herself, Brown helped further Shaw's career in children's books when she spoke of him to her own editor at Harper's, URSULA NORDSTROM. Harper's 1947 fall list included, among others, Brown's *Goodnight Moon* and RUTH KRAUSS's *The Growing Tree;* another Nordstrom choice was Shaw's *It Looked Like Spilt Milk.*

"Sometimes it looked like Spilt Milk. But it wasn't Spilt Milk," begins the text, which continues with a dozen other examples young children recognize and respond to; rabbit, bird, ice-cream cone, flower, birthday cake, squirrel, and angel are some possibilities, but not what "it" really is. To conclude, the text comes full circle and finally divulges the answer: "It was just a Cloud in the Sky." Different from the interactive books that typically pose queries inviting reader involvement, Shaw's luminous gem contains no questions. The repetition of the phrase "Sometimes it looked like a..." when paired with a single image demands a reply from children, who derive great pleasure from the recognition of the picture. Although their answers are initially correct, they are ultimately incorrect. Therein lies the fun and the desire to read the book again and again. Such interaction also makes the book experience a child's very own, with little adult intervention. For every double-page spread, Shaw employed just two colors: the rich royal blue background that suggests sky and the pristine white of the typeface and fluid fluff of cloud forms. Both colors stunningly contrast to achieve a visual effect that is at once simple and powerful. With a single title, *It Looked Like Spilt Milk*, Charles Shaw lent modern shape and active participation to the graphic and literary art form of the American picture book. S.L.S.

SHEPARD, E. H.

ENGLISH ILLUSTRATOR, 1879–1976. Although Ernest Howard Shepard is best known as the illustrator of works by A. A. MILNE, the 1931 edition of KENNETH GRAHAME's *Wind in the Willows* also helped to establish him as one of the foremost illustrators of humorous books for children.

Shepard's mother, the daughter of a well-known watercolor artist, encouraged his early efforts and pointed him toward a career as an artist. She died when he was only ten, but Shepard's architect father continued to foster his son's artistic talent. By the time he was fifteen, Shepard had definitely decided that he would become an artist and, at age eighteen, was admitted to the Royal Academy Schools, where he met his future wife, Florence Chaplin. The Shepards had two children, Graham and Mary, and Mary followed in her father's footsteps, becoming an artist known for her illustrations for the *Mary Poppins* books.

Quite early in his career, Shepard began drawing for the magazine *Punch*. His association with that magazine gave him experience in depicting comic themes. He was particularly adept at exposing the humor lying just beneath the surface of a situation and was able to capture the subtlest expression with an economy of line. Although Shepard made color plates somewhat late in his career, he is chiefly known for his pen-and-ink illustrations that are rich in detail and alive with the personalities of his characters. His expert use of this medium allowed him to create memorable scenes that capture a sense of place as well as a sense of character. Shepard's success as an illustrator was also due to an intuitive feel for motion in a picture, along with the elements of surprise and the unusual in his portrayal of characters. These attributes contribute to his success in capturing perfectly the childlike quality of Christopher Robin and the naiveté of Pooh in *Winnie-the-Pooh* (1926) and creating an unforgettable portrait of the witty but naughty Toad in *The Wind in the Willows.*

Shepard began his illustrations for *The Wind in the Willows* with great enthusiasm, though he had previously considered it a book that ought not to be illustrated. He had several meetings with Grahame, who showed him the nearby river that had inspired him to describe the lives of Mole, Badger, Rat, and Toad. Guided by Grahame's request that he treat these characters kindly, Shepard spent an afternoon beside the river with his sketchbook, searching for Rat's boathouse and examining the holes that were home to some of the animals and the meadows where Mole retired for the winter. Though Grahame did not live to see the finished work, he did express approval of the drafts that Shepard was able to show him. Later in his life, Shepard also tried his hand at writing, producing two autobiographies, *Drawn from Memory* (1957) and *Drawn from Life*

Illustration by E. H. Shepard from *When We Were Very Young* (1924), by A. A. MILNE.

(1961). He also wrote and illustrated two children's books, *Ben and Brock* (1965) and *Betty and Joe* (1966).

In all his work, Shepard encouraged readers to appreciate the humor in the stories he illustrated. Near the end of a long and immensely productive artistic life, Shepard received the Order of the British Empire in 1972, an honor he richly deserved for his contribution to the world of art and, in particular, to children's book illustration. ❧ D.L.M.

Sherlock Holmes Books

Sherlock Holmes was born on January 6, 1854, in Yorkshire, England, and solved his first case while a twenty-year-old student at Oxford University. He was an excellent boxer and fencer and published several books on subjects ranging from tobacco ash to bee raising. He moved to 221B Baker Street in London in 1881, sharing his quarters with Dr. John Watson. The two men became friends, and Watson chronicled the adventures of his roommate. But for the fact that Sherlock Holmes is a literary character, his biography is as full and detailed as that of any Englishman of his time. Arthur Conan Doyle first wrote about Sherlock Holmes's detective skills in *A Study in Scarlet* (1887) and proceeded to write three more novels—*The Sign of Four* (1890), *The Hound of the Baskervilles* (1902), and *The Valley of Fear* (1915)—and fifty-six short stories featuring Holmes.

At the time of Holmes's birth, Edgar Allan Poe's detective M. Dupin epitomized the fictional sleuth; his unofficial status, his bewildered friend and narrator, and his cold logic were his major traits. Conan Doyle altered not only the existing story formula by substituting crisp dialogue for Poe's psychological introductions, but he also added new dimensions to the detective personality. Influenced by Joseph Bell, a surgeon at the Edinburgh Infirmary famous for spotting minute and revealing details of his patient's lives during examinations, Conan Doyle gave Sherlock Holmes an omniscient knowledge of a huge variety of subjects and a mastery of the science of deductive reasoning.

Subjected to a purely technical analysis, the Sherlock Holmes stories are painfully Gothic, depending on the obvious or trite treatment of the revenge motif. It has never, however, been the complexity or intricacy of the mystery that captivated Conan Doyle's readers. Rather it is the "romantic reality" of nostalgic England—the hansom cabs and gas lamps, the wet cobblestones and the reek of tobacco, the dressing gown and the violin case—that has led us to imagine Holmes as the prototypical late Victorian Londoner. So powerful was the lure of Holmes's character that his death at the hands of his nemesis, Professor Moriarty, at the Reichenbach Falls in Switzerland left England devastated. The mourning and protest led Conan Doyle, who had begun to feel constrained by his famous creation, to revive his hero, claiming that Holmes had not really been killed in the fall. Sherlock Holmes is one of the few literary creations who has passed into the life and language of his readers—his name is synonymous with the profession of detective. As T. S. Eliot said, "Every writer of detective fiction owes something to Holmes." ❧ M.I.A.

Shulevitz, Uri

POLISH-BORN AMERICAN AUTHOR-ILLUSTRATOR, B. 1935. After living through the 1939 Warsaw blitz, young Uri Shulevitz wandered with his family for eight years, eventually settling in Paris and finally Israel. He moved to New York City as an adult, attended the Brooklyn Museum Art School, and in 1963 created his first picture book, *The Moon in My Room* (1963). Since then he has illustrated numerous folktales and fantasies as PICTURE BOOKS and CHAPTER BOOKS, taught at several art schools, and published an invaluable resource called *Writing with Pictures: How to Write and Illustrate Children's Books* (1985).

Voices of the Creators

Uri Shulevitz

It was my good luck, when I began toting my portfolio around to publishers in 1962, that the first editor I saw was Susan Hirschman. But when she suggested I try writing my own picture book, I was horrified. Write my own story? Impossible. I was an artist, not a writer. I could imagine myself in various activities, but never in my wildest dreams had I imagined myself a writer. Writing seemed a mysterious activity, suited to those who had magical ways with words. To me, using words was like taming wild tigers.

I told Susan that I had been speaking English for less than four years. "Don't worry," she reassured me, "we'll fix your English." There was nothing to do but try. And try I did, many times. I went back to her office for months, bringing my awkward writing efforts. After many unsuccessful attempts, I finally came up with a picture book. With minor changes, it became *The Moon in My Room,* my first book. If it were not for those many unsuccessful attempts, I don't think I could have written it.

My initial fear that I could not write was based on a preconception that writing was strictly related to words and to spoken language. I had assumed that using many words skillfully was central to writing. I was overlooking what was of primary importance—*what* I had to say. I was overwhelmed by what was of secondary importance—*how* to say it.

Once I understood that *what* I had to say was of primary importance, I began to concentrate on what would happen in my story. First I visualized the action, and then I thought of how to say it in words. I realized that all I had to do was communicate the action as simply as possible. It also dawned on me that I could channel my natural inclination to visualize into my writing. That is how I wrote my first book; the story unfolded in my head, like a movie. Years later, I learned that, when writing, C. S. Lewis saw pictures, too; with Lewis, "images always come first."

The approach I used for illustrating my first book was derived from drawings I did one day while talking on the telephone. As I talked, I doodled, and I noticed that the doodles had a fresh look—the lines appeared to be moving across the page. In addition to my preconception about writing, I also had a preconceived idea of how the illustrations for that book would evolve. I had assumed they would require much effort. But instead, while my mind was busy with the phone conversation, I let the lines flow effortlessly through my hand onto the paper; they seemed to have a life and an intelligence of their own. Of course, it subsequently took considerable work and effort to develop the doodles into appropriate illustrations, but that process took place at a later stage.

When asked why they want to write children's books, many people reply, "I love children." Sentimentality, unfortunately, is no help; in fact, it is a hindrance. Sentimentality does not replace the craft that is essential in making good children's books. My first obligation is to the book, not to the audience. Only by understanding the book's structure and how it functions can I make a good book.

Rather than asking whether I am happy with a book, I ask, "Is the book happy? Are the illustrations happy?" In other words, I want to know if the story is told with clarity. Are the characters unique? Is the setting specific? Is the ending consistent with the beginning? Are the scale, size, and shape of the book suited to its content and mood? Are the parts of a book coordinated into a coherent whole?

After I consider these questions, I understand the needs of the book, and I can begin to know if the book is happy. The integrity and clarity of that book are my primary concerns.

In this profusely illustrated book, Shulevitz covers the technical aspects of creating a picture book and expounds his philosophies of writing and drawing, giving clear, concise examples. When conceiving a story idea, he "writes" the story with pictures. Shulevitz believes that technique must be an "organic extension of content," and he suits his artistic style to the story's content and feeling. Detailed pen-and-ink drawings or stridently bright colors are equally within his grasp, but most of his books are done in watercolors or pen-and-ink. Shulevitz develops a text that does not repeat the pictorial details but expands story elements that cannot be told visually, an approach that leads to a tight blending of text and art.

Rain Rain Rivers (1969) displays Shulevitz's view that picture books are "closer to theater and film, silent films in particular, than to other kinds of books." After showing a girl in her room, the "camera" takes the reader through the city and into the countryside, all the way to the ocean. The artist also uses the size and shape of the pictures to enhance the cinematic movement from close-up to expansive horizon. Shulevitz's characters tend to have a firm, sculpted appearance, and architecture, frequently the Eastern European cities of his youthful travels, is often a strong presence in his pictures. Yet he also masters evocative landscapes, as in *Dawn* (1974), in which a spare Oriental influence can be seen as the simple story unfolds. From a soft-edged oval of nighttime blue, successive images gain light and clarity, revealing a mountain lake with two figures who wake in darkness and experience the dawn's sudden yellow-green illumination of their surroundings. The oval pictures with their soft edges keep the mood quiet until the color breaks forth, flowing off the page in the loud visual climax.

Shulevitz has won awards for *Dawn* and other books, including the Caldecott Medal for *The Fool of the World and the Flying Ship* (1968), a Russian folktale retold by ARTHUR RANSOME. This is a "story book"—in Shulevitz's definition—a book in which the text can stand alone. In his illustrations, Shulevitz adds humor, details of the Russian landscape and architecture, even the sensation of flying a ship through the air. In this book, too, is evident the strong composition Shulevitz considers necessary for excellent illustration. One's eye is always drawn back to the main element of the picture after it has discovered the secondary elements. Because of Shulevitz's thoughtful approach to illustration, his pictures have integrity, depth, and beauty. His child readers, he says, are never far from his thoughts: "I try to suggest and evoke rather than state rigidly, in order to encourage the child to participate actively, filling in with his own imagination. This approach is based on the belief that my audience is intelligent and active rather than passive." ❧ S.S.

SIDNEY, MARGARET

AMERICAN AUTHOR, 1844–1924. Harriet Mulford Stone Lothrop, writing under the pseudonym Margaret Sidney, was a prolific writer of family stories, best known for *The Five Little Peppers and How They Grew* (1881). In the first book of a series, the five Pepper children and their mother try to survive in the face of extreme poverty and hardship. Mrs. Pepper's husband has died, and she must work part-time, but the self-reliant children have many adventures in their "Little Brown House." In spite of the hardship in their lives, the family manages to be cheerful and good. This goodness becomes their financial salvation when the children become friends with Jasper King, a lonely, wealthy boy, and win over his brusque father. The novel first appeared serially in *Wide Awake* magazine; Sidney used a pseudonym because she feared failure, but the story was immensely popular, contributing to the magazine's success. Sidney continued the series, eventually publishing another eleven books about the Pepper family. The subsequent stories are set in the wealthy King household, where the Peppers live as Jasper's companions and friends. These stories are pleasant but lack the tension in the original book created by the Peppers' poverty. When they no longer worry about surviving, the Peppers reminisce about past pleasures in the Little Brown House. The sequels are no longer widely read.

Margaret Sidney grew up in New Haven, Connecticut. As a child she longed for life in the country, and, later, with her husband, Daniel, the founder of Lothrop Publishing Company, she moved to Concord, Massachusetts. Her stories reflect her love for rural New England life. The *Five Little Peppers and How They Grew* is filled with cheerful characters and details of late-nineteenth-century life. The gentle adventures, in this first volume, continue to appeal to children who enjoy innocent amusements and stories that end happily. ❧ M.V.K.

SILVERSTEIN, SHEL

AMERICAN AUTHOR/ILLUSTRATOR, POET, AND SONGWRITER, B. 1932. Born and raised in Chicago, Silverstein says that he "couldn't play ball, couldn't dance, and the girls didn't want me. So I started to draw and write." While serving with the United States forces in Japan and Korea in the 1950s, Silverstein was a cartoonist for the *Pacific Stars and Stripes*. A cartoonist for *Playboy* magazine, a composer, and a lyricist—one of his most famous songs was the Johnny Cash hit "A Boy Named Sue"—Silverstein is best known for his humorous poetry, innovative drawings, and allegorical stories.

The Giving Tree (1964), Silverstein's most successful book, was initially rejected by his future editor, who believed that "it was a nice book, but it would never sell." Despite an initial lack of interest, the book eventually brought Silverstein national acclaim. "Once there was a tree . . . and she loved a little boy," begins the simple tale, illustrated in graceful cartoon style and touched with sadness. As a small child, the boy played in the shade of the tree, loving her as a friend; as he grew older, he began to want more from the tree than just her love. She gave him her apples, her branches, and her trunk. When he returns as an old man, she can only give him her stump upon which to rest—she has nothing left to give him, but she is happy. While some interpret this story as a parable about giving and taking, loving and being loved, others see it as a "dressed-up version of the 'happy slave' myth" and a tale of "man's selfish plundering of the environment." The danger does exist that young readers will identify with the greedy, exploitative boy/man rather than with the generous, devoted tree.

The Missing Piece (1976) and its sequel, *The Missing Piece Meets the Big O* (1981), two books that revolve around simply drawn geometric shapes, have been accepted as tales of adaptation, growth, and the quest for self-fulfillment. In the first book, "it," a pie-shaped circle, searches for its missing piece only to realize that the piece isn't needed; in the sequel, it is the missing piece that arrives at the realization that it, too, can survive by itself. With just a few lines and circles, Silverstein anthropomorphizes his inanimate objects, giving them individual personalities and human traits and allowing them to discover the gift of independence.

Silverstein's poetry collections, *Where the Sidewalk Ends: The Poems and Drawings of Shel Silverstein* (1974) and the William Allen White Award winner *A Light in the Attic* (1981), provide a showcase for over 250 poems, some of which have been adapted from Silverstein's earlier song lyrics, and almost as many black-and-white line drawings. The poems, ranging from serious to silly, from philosophical to ridiculous, allow the reader or listener—the rhyme and rhythm of these nonsensical poems make them perfect for reading aloud—to discover Silverstein's greatest gift: his ability to understand the fears and wishes and silliness of children. From the list of frightening "whatifs" that plague children at night ("Whatif my parents get divorced?" "Whatif nobody likes me?") to Mrs. McTwitter, the baby sitter who actually sits on the baby, the poems are eerily attuned to the natural joy and playfulness of childhood. Allusions to belching, nose-picking, and the disruption of parental authority can be found in the poems as can statements of friendship and tolerance: "We're all worth the same/When we turn off the light" and "I will not play at tug o' war/I'd rather play at hug o' war."

Silverstein says that he doesn't believe in happy endings or magical solutions in children's books. Nevertheless, with his hilarious poetry, expressively simple drawings, and provocative fables, he has succeeded in creating some magic of his own. ❧ M.I.A.

Simon, Seymour

AMERICAN AUTHOR, B. 1931. From paper airplanes to optical illusions, from outer space to the ocean floor, from anatomy to computers, there are few subjects that award-winning science writer Seymour Simon hasn't covered in his over one hundred and fifty INFORMATION BOOKS for children.

Born and raised in New York City, Simon was fascinated with finding out about the world from an early age. He attended the Bronx High School of Science, earned a B.S. from City College in New York, and began teaching science in New York City public schools in 1955 while taking graduate courses in subjects as varied as psychology, philosophy, literature, and history. Frustrated by the lack of good science books for children to use in the classroom, Simon began his writing career in 1968 with *Animals in Field and Laboratory: Projects in Animal Behavior,* which contains ideas for experiments to help readers learn more about aspects of animal behavior such as communication and migration. He continued to write and teach until 1979, when he turned his attention to writing for children full-time.

Simon draws on his teaching experience in writing; his over twenty years in the classroom are reflected in his ability to know what will interest children and to understand how to present new information in a straightforward and fascinating way. His books do not merely answer questions, they teach children how to think about a problem and encourage them to become involved in discovering answers on their own. Simon takes this approach because, he says, "Many of the books I write are guidebooks to unknown territories."

Simon has written a number of outstanding series, including the "Discovering" books, which introduce readers to common and popular animals such as frogs, goldfish, and puppies; the "Einstein Anderson" fiction series, which features a whiz-kid sleuth; the "Let's Try It Out" series, which teaches readers about physical properties such as hot and cold and about how the heart and senses function; and photo essays about animals, earth science, and the solar system. The photo essays are Simon's most successful books, as the consistently spectacular photographs, accessible text, and strong, clear design work together to present mind-stretching concepts in a lively and engaging format.

His gift for clarity and for making the complex fathomable is what raises his books above the ordinary, often uninviting science book. In *Oceans* (1990), for example, Simon tells readers that the amount of water in all the oceans on Earth is one-and-one-half quintillion tons. To most readers, this figure is probably difficult to grasp, but Simon puts it in perspective: "That's 100 billion gallons for each person in the world." The information is immediately much more manageable and useful.

His series of photo essays about the planets also presents the unimaginable in language we can easily understand. In *Mars* (1987) Simon compares the size of that planet to Earth, saying that if Earth were hollow, seven planets the size of Mars could fit inside. Or from *Our Solar System* (1992), a companion to the "Planets" series: "If the sun were hollow, it could hold 1.3 *million* Earths." His animal photo essays, such as *Whales* (1989), a *New York Times* Best Illustrated Book, combine fascinating facts and lively photographs to make beautiful and factual volumes.

For his contribution to children's science literature, Simon was awarded the Eva L. Gordon Award from the American Nature Society, and over one third of his books have been named Outstanding Science Trade Books for Children by the National Science Teachers Association and the Children's Book Council. Although he is no longer teaching in a classroom, Simon feels that as long as he continues to write, he won't ever really stop being a teacher. His books capture children's imaginations and encourage them to use science as a way to wonder and learn about the world. ❧ K.F.

Simont, Marc

French-born American illustrator, b. 1915. The prolific creator of pictures for nearly one hundred children's books over a span of six decades, Simont was born in Paris, France, to parents from the Catalonian region of Spain. His childhood was spent in France, Spain, and the United States. While the repeated relocations were detrimental to his schoolwork, traveling served to sharpen the observational skills that became so important to him as an artist—Simont often claims that how his teachers looked fascinated him more than what they said. As a young boy, Simont taught himself to draw by studying *El Ginesello,* a Spanish picture book, and drawing remained his foremost interest during his school years. While Simont never finished high school, he studied art at the Académie Julien and the Académie Ranson in Paris, as well as at New York's National Academy of Design. Despite his formal training, he considers his father, Joseph, a longtime illustrator for *L'Illustration* magazine, his most influential art teacher.

Before creating pictures for children's books, Simont painted portraits, designed visual aids, and produced work for magazines and advertising firms. Since providing the art for a collection of Scandinavian fairy tales in 1939, his work has consisted mainly of illustrating children's stories. While he has both written and illustrated a number of stories, it is Simont's illustrations for stories by well-known children's book authors like Meindert DeJong, Margaret Wise Brown, Charlotte Zolotow, Jean Fritz, David McCord, and Marjorie Wienman Sharmat that form the bedrock of his success. The charming, soft charcoal pictures for Ruth Krauss's *The Happy Day* (1949), which capture the coziness of animals denned for winter and their joyful awakening at the first scent of spring, earned Simont a Caldecott Honor in 1950. In 1957 he was again honored when Janice May Udry's paean to trees, *A Tree Is Nice* (1955), was awarded the Caldecott Medal. Color-saturated pages alternate with loose-lined black-and-white drawings; Simont's watercolors perfectly complement the poetic simplicity of the text, allowing the reader room to engage in his or her own imaginative embroiderings about trees.

Other notable titles include *The Thirteen Clocks* (1951), *The Wonderful "O"* (1957), and *Many Moons,* written by James Thurber. *Many Moons* (1943), originally illustrated by Louis Slobodkin, won a Caldecott Medal in 1944, but Simont's 1990 reinterpretation adds fresh life through dreamy, elegant watercolor renderings of Thurber's richly imagined story of a princess who must have the moon to recover from an illness due to a "surfeit of raspberry tarts." Simont's inspired and invitingly humorous art provides a brilliant foil for the wit, wordplay, and nonsense of these three much-loved tales, now considered contemporary classics.

Two books by Karla Kuskin, *The Philharmonic Gets Dressed* (1982) and *The Dallas Titans Get Ready for Bed* (1986), also underscore Simont's strengths as an illustrator. The former is an antic inside look at one hundred and five members of the Philharmonic Orchestra as they bathe, dress, and prepare for an evening's performance; the latter is a hilarious locker-room peek at what goes on after a football team wins a big game. In both, Simont deftly renders a large cast of characters of varied ages, genders, colors, and physiques with distinct personalities. Simple, almost cartoonlike drawings belie in style their richness of content as they convey humor, movement, and convincing emotion.

Whether painting scenes limpid with delicate watercolors and resonant with childlike sensibility or using sure brushstrokes to capture characters brimming with life and humor, Simont has a remarkable ability to connect emotionally with the child reader. His visual interpretations of stories have insured him a place as a much-loved illustrator in the world of children's books. ❧ C.S.

Singer, Isaac Bashevis

Polish-born American Yiddish author, 1904–1991. Isaac Bashevis Singer was awarded the Nobel Prize for Literature in 1978 for his stories drawn from Jewish life and traditions in the ghettos of eastern Europe prior to World War II. Most of these stories were written in Yiddish, the language of a vanished culture in which rabbis, thieves, merchants, and chedar boys existed side by side with imps, goblins, angels, and saints. In his stories for children, Singer distills this culture into a microcosm where the mystical and fantastic become commonplace and everyday life assumes cosmic dimension.

Singer was brought up in a Hasidic household. His father was a rabbi, his mother the daughter of a rabbi, and the often-heated family discussions centered around such topics as whether or not proof of God's existence could better be found in the supernatural shrieking of dead geese or the stubborn pride of a Gentile washerwoman. The worldly and the otherworldly clashed continually in Singer's life, and he found the resolution to that conflict not in the religion of his father but in his own writing.

The stories in two of his best-known books for children illustrate the blending of the real and the imaginary that Singer makes so resonant. Singer's first book for children, *Zlateh the Goat and Other Stories* (1966), a Newbery Honor Book illustrated by Maurice Sendak, is filled with tales of fools, magicians, witches, and saints. Yet the title story is an intensely realistic account of the love a young boy feels for his goat. Singer's National Book Award–winning *A Day of Pleasure: Stories of a Boy Growing Up in Warsaw* (1969) is a collection of autobiographical stories of a childhood saturated with wildly improbable events and characters in which the mysteries of the universe could be unlocked at any moment and heaven hung down very low.

Many critics of Singer's work were uneasy with the mix of "the mythic and the colloquial" in his work; others lauded the way he "captured the poetic power of folktales" with "a quality of timelessness in the wisdom imparted and a feeling for the essence of human nature." Singer himself felt the importance of his work lay in its ability to entertain, to "intrigue the reader, uplift his spirit, give him the joy and escape that true art always grants." ❧ S.G.K.

Sis, Peter

American illustrator and author, b. 1949. Peter Sis came to the United States in 1982, and that act both changed his life and informs his work. He was born in Czechoslovakia and grew up in Prague in the 1950s and 1960s during the height of Soviet rule and remembers the world outside his family's home as bleak and oppressive: "It's amazing, though, even within that very undesirable world, we had time to play our games and have fun and everything as children do. So now, in retrospect, I think I had a wonderful childhood, mostly thanks to my parents." Sis's parents actively encouraged his artistic growth, actually giving the budding artist assignments with deadlines, creating an atmosphere of creative discipline that Sis credits as one of the most powerful influences on his professional career. Once in formal art school, however, Sis found the lack of freedom of expression difficult: "It was very hard because there was really no space for fantasy or individuality." Despite this obstacle, Sis credits this academic experience with exposing him to the great European art traditions, traces of which can be seen in his pointillist, somewhat formal style.

Sis received his master's degree from the Academy of Applied Arts in Prague in 1974 and attended the Royal College of Art in London. When he arrived in the United States in 1982, he had found success in Europe as an artist and filmmaker and came to Los Angeles to do a film connected with the 1984 Olympics that were to be held there. When the Soviet-bloc countries withdrew from the games as the result of a political imbroglio, Sis remained behind. The isolation, loneliness, confusion, joy, and newfound freedom of the immigrant experience show up in his work again and again.

Sis was launched in his American career with the help of Maurice Sendak and began by illustrating works written by others, gaining praise for his ability to capture the story's mood and the writer's intent. His illustrations of Sid Fleischman's work in particular garnered much critical attention, in books such as *The Whipping Boy* (1986), the Newbery Award winner, and *The Scarebird* (1988). The first book that he both wrote and illustrated is *Rainbow Rhino* (1987), the story of a rhinoceros who lives on a vast plain ringed by mountains. The rhino climbs the mountains with three bird friends, leaving them behind one by one in a series of lovely new environments and collecting them all again when he heads home. The image of an isolated figure on a vast, empty expanse that is repeated throughout *Rainbow Rhino* has become a trademark of Sis's work.

In *Follow the Dream: The Story of Christopher Colum-*

Illustration by Peter Sis for "A Dragon's Lament" from *The Dragons Are Singing Tonight* (1993), by JACK PRELUTSKY.

bus (1991), the tiny, determined figure of Columbus is repeatedly shown as dwarfed by the limitless sky, the trackless ocean, or a detailed map of the known world. Another theme that intrigues Sis, the tension between confinement and freedom, is central to *An Ocean World* (1992), the poignant story of a baby whale who grows too large for the aquarium that holds her and is released to the ocean. Sis's 1992 book, *Komodo,* which won a Society of Illustrators Gold Medal, once again centers around a small figure in a large world. A young boy travels by boat with his family to see a Komodo dragon. The boy escapes the crush of tourists to explore on his own and is the only one to come face to face with the beast.

Sis's concept books, *Waving: A Counting Book* (1988), *Going Up! A Color Counting Book* (1989), and *Beach Ball* (1990), feature a solitary little girl amidst busy, detailed double-page spreads filled with visual puns and puzzles, another Sis hallmark.

In his work for children, Sis has sought to foster the personal courage and creative freedom that have shaped his own life. "I think children should have choices, and I would like to participate in their growth," he says. "It's sort of a civic responsibility, but it's also a romantic thing. I would like to re-create something from child-hood—create something wonderful, some sort of magic." S.G.K.

SLEATOR, WILLIAM

AMERICAN AUTHOR, B. 1945. William Sleator is acclaimed for his YOUNG ADULT NOVELS that explore scientific theories such as black holes, cloning, and time travel in an accessible manner.

Sleator was born in Maryland but grew up in University City, Missouri. Sleator's father was a college professor and his mother a physician. The author's volume of autobiographical stories, *Oddballs* (1993), presents an entertaining picture of life in an unconventional family, where the children were encouraged to pursue a variety of interests. Sleator's interests included playing the piano, composing music, and writing stories of the supernatural. He attended Harvard, planning to major in music, but graduated with a degree in English. He then spent time in London, studying musical composition and working as an accompanist with the Royal Ballet School. He continued to work with the Boston Ballet Company as a rehearsal pianist for much of his writing career.

Sleator's first book was *The Angry Moon* (1970), a retelling of a Tlingit Indian legend. This picture book received praise for the high quality of Sleator's writing and for BLAIR LENT's outstanding illustrations and was named a Caldecott Honor Book. The following year Sleator published his first young adult book. A gothic novel about an English schoolboy living in a haunted cottage, *Blackbriar* (1972) is based on the author's experiences in a similar English cottage. Sleator's gift for provoking shivers and maintaining suspense is evident in this first novel; subsequent novels have been even stronger due to tighter plotting and faster pacing. An early science fiction novel, *House of Stairs* (1974), is among Sleator's best. It is the story of five orphaned teenagers unknowingly participating in a psychological experiment. They live in a world without walls, ceilings, or floors. Their environment contains only endless stairways and a machine that dispenses food. Suspenseful and thought-provoking, this fascinating novel explores issues of conditioning, behavior modification, and survival.

Although Sleator has written a handful of books for younger readers, he is best known for his young adult science fiction, in which everyday teenagers stumble into extraordinary adventures. Barney, in *Interstellar Pig* (1984), finds himself playing a board game with his new neighbors and slowly comes to realize that they are aliens and the game has intergalactic consequences. In *The Green Futures of Tycho* (1981), a boy travels back and forth in time, ultimately meeting his own future self.

Sleator is greatly skilled at incorporating current scientific theories into his fiction, resulting in stories such as *Singularity* (1985), in which two brothers discover a time warp, and *The Boy Who Reversed Himself* (1986), which concerns travel to other dimensions. He is also extremely successful at setting tone in his novels. Some are bone-chilling throughout; others have a tongue-in-cheek quality behind the suspense.

A consistent weakness in Sleator's writing, however, is characterization. His protagonists seem to fall into two groups: blandly likable or downright disagreeable. And almost always, his teenagers behave and speak like children much younger than their stated ages. Nevertheless, Sleator has continued to show growth as a writer, and his skillful translation of scientific theories into entertaining fiction has resulted in an important body of work. P.D.S.

Slepian, Jan

American writer, b. 1921. Janice B. Slepian's first career, in speech therapy, led eventually to her second career in writing. After a number of years as a speech therapist, she and her colleague Ann Seidler designed the six "Listen-Hear" picture books (1964) to help young children master various sounds. A second series, the "Junior Listen-Hear" books, followed in 1967. *The Hungry Thing Returns* (1990), also written with Seidler, continues the amusing wordplay of *The Hungry Thing* (1967), one of the "Junior Listen-Hear" books.

In 1979 Slepian discovered the field of young adult literature and decided to write a young adult novel featuring a character based on her mentally retarded, epileptic, hemiplegic brother, Alfred. The resulting story, *The Alfred Summer* (1980), earned praise from critics. Since then, Slepian has continued to create characters and settings from people and places she knows. Set in Brighton Beach, New York, in 1937, *The Alfred Summer* relates how Lester, a bright boy with cerebral palsy, breaks out of his isolation through friendship with Alfie and two other out-of-the-ordinary young people. Slepian acknowledges how difficult it can be for people to know one another; nevertheless, connecting—not only making contact with others but also participating in life—is a recurrent theme in her novels. In *Lester's Turn* (1981) Lester, unwilling to confront his future, devises an unrealistic plan to get Alfred out of the hospital and care for him on his own. Lester finally realizes that he has used his concern for Alfie as a shield and that he must take his own turn at life.

At the beginning of *The Night of the Bozos* (1983), George, a boy with a passion for music, prefers to keep his distance from other people, and he wants his Uncle Hibbie, who stutters, to do the same. Like Lester, the imaginative Berry, in *Getting On with It* (1985), runs the risk of being sidetracked, in her case by her parents' divorce. She must give up her daydreams of bringing her parents back together and get on with her own life. The cousins Linny and Hilary in *Back to Before* (1993) also find themselves stuck, yearning for the year before, when Linny's mother was still alive and Hilary's father was still at home. An apparent slip in time enables them to relive several days in the past with the benefit of an extra year of maturity.

In addition to dealing with the challenges presented by mental and physical handicaps, divorce, aging, and death, Slepian also explores the ambivalent relationship between parents and children. In *Something beyond Paradise* (1987), Franny is torn between her desire to study dance and her sense of responsibility toward her mother and her aging, disoriented grandmother. The death of her grandmother places extra stress on Sara's family after they move temporarily to Hawaii in *The Broccoli Tapes* (1988). Feeling cut off from friends and her parents, Sara uses the tapes to record her experiences. Skip, the protagonist of *Risk N' Roses* (1990) struggles not only with her role as the "normal" daughter but also with the conflict between her longing for friendship and her loyalty to her retarded sister.

At her best when describing the complexities of family dynamics, Slepian tells stories that communicate enthusiasm for life while offering a realistic view of its vicissitudes. M.F.S.

Slobodkin, Louis

American author and illustrator, 1903–1975. A sculptor and award-winning artist, Louis Slobodkin is best remembered for writing a series of humorous science fiction stories. Growing up in Albany, New York, Slobodkin displayed an early artistic talent. He dropped out of high school and worked as a bellhop and dishwasher to fund his education at the Beaux Arts Institute of Design in New York.

Slobodkin was a professional sculptor for several years before ELEANOR ESTES asked him to illustrate her first book, *The Moffats* (1941). His sketchy, whimsically humorous illustrations received critical praise and established his reputation in the children's book field. He illustrated stories by MARK TWAIN, Charles Dickens, and several books by his wife, Florence, including *Too Many Mittens* (1958). He received the Caldecott Medal for JAMES THURBER's 1943 fairy tale *Many Moons;* although the pale-color artwork lacks detail and vibrancy, it is alive with movement and emotion.

Slobodkin also wrote and illustrated picture books, such as *Magic Michael* (1944), and nonfiction, including *The First Book of Drawing* (1958). His most lasting contribution to children's literature is the series that began with *The Space Ship under the Apple Tree* (1952) and continued with *The Space Ship Returns to the Apple Tree* (1958), *The Three-Seated Space Ship* (1962), *Round Trip Space Ship* (1968), and *The Space Ship in the Park* (1972). The stories concern the friendship between eleven-year-old Eddie Blow and Marty, an alien from the planet Martinea. Their fast-moving adventures are filled with futuristic gadgetry and fun, as the two tour the United States, England, and other parts of the galaxy in a variety of space vehicles. The books are hugely popular with intermediate readers and remain Slobodkin's best-known work. ❧ P.D.S.

SLOBODKINA, ESPHYR

RUSSIAN-BORN AMERICAN ILLUSTRATOR, B. 1908. Amusing children for more than fifty years, Esphyr Slobodkina's *Caps for Sale* (1940) has become one of the most popular children's PICTURE BOOKS ever published. As an author and innovative illustrator of other notable titles, this prominent and multitalented painter, textile designer, and sculptor first entered the field of children's book publishing in the late 1930s, a time known as the golden age of the American picture book. Along with leading artists Leonard Weisgard and CHARLES SHAW, Slobodkina helped bring modern art to children's book illustrations.

Slobodkina, born in Siberia to a family with considerable artistic ability, was a frail child often confined to bed for lengthy periods; there she entertained herself with materials on hand and learned to cut out paper dolls and doilies. Immigrating to New York in 1928, Slobodkina brought with her a thorough knowledge of Russian modern art. She continued her schooling as an abstract artist for several years, observing the Russian influence on the American avant-garde movement during the postdepression thirties.

Early in 1938 a friend suggested that Slobodkina prepare a portfolio for another friend of his, a famous writer and editor of children's books: MARGARET WISE BROWN. Slobodkina resorted to her childhood pastime of cut-paper dolls as she constructed nineteen paper-collage storyboards for her portfolio. This paper-doll technique favorably impressed Brown, and soon after the artist and editor's meeting, their first collaboration, *The Little Fireman* (1938), was published. The paper-collage originals, in brilliant, bold, and arbitrary colors, shared qualities of absolute flatness and simplicity. Slobodkina firmly asserted that using scissors enforced a "simplicity of line which cannot be achieved by a pen." She crafted the firemen with no countenances so that all children could easily identify with the characters. Slobodkina was in the vanguard of the cutout-collage method of illustration in American picture books, with many currently prominent illustrators following her example.

Although she illustrated the sequels, *The Little Farmer* (1948), and *The Little Cowboy* (1948), in collaboration

Illustration by Esphyr Slobodkina from her book *Caps for Sale* (1940).

with Brown, Slobodkina alone retold and illustrated in 1940 what proved to be her greatest success: *Caps for Sale*. A troop of monkeys relieves a napping street peddler of his stock of caps. Unwittingly, the peddler retrieves his goods as the amusing, imitative monkeys respond to his tantrum. Her inspiration for these illustrations was the late-nineteenth-century naive painter Henri Rousseau; this influence accounted for a mustachioed face on the peddler and mischievous faces on the monkeys. First published in just three primary colors, *Caps for Sale* improved its looks with a second edition in 1947. Slobodkina's subsequent palette of ocher, red, and robin's-egg blue watercolors softened her cutout collage technique. The highly repetitive and comic text possessed interactive qualities that encouraged participation from even the very youngest of audiences: Children mimic the furious antics of the flummoxed peddler and delight in retorting with the monkeys' laughably annoying "Tsz,tsz,tsz." Still in print, and with eight foreign-language editions, *Caps for Sale* is an enduring picture-book classic.

Slobodkina's career in writing and illustrating children's books has also endured, as she created more than twenty titles in the ensuing four decades. And with the 1993 reissues of earlier books such as *The Little Fireman* and *The Wonderful Feast*, many of Slobodkina's picture books continue to enjoy popular and critical acclaim. ❧ S.L.S.

Smith, Doris Buchanan

AMERICAN AUTHOR, B. 1934. The publication of *A Taste of Blackberries* in 1973 was significant for two reasons. It was one of the first children's novels to explore realistically the topic of death, and it served to introduce a talented new writer to the field of children's literature.

Doris Buchanan Smith was born in Washington, D.C., and grew up in a Maryland suburb. She always loved reading and writing, but did not consider becoming an author until a grade school teacher suggested the idea. During World War II, when Smith was nine years old, her family moved to Atlanta; her autobiographical novel, *Salted Lemons* (1980), relates these experiences. She attended South Georgia College, then married and began to raise a large family, which eventually included over twenty foster children.

Although her life was filled with young people, Smith knew nothing about children's literature. She wrote poetry and adult fiction with little success until it was suggested that she rewrite one of her adult pieces as a children's story.

A Taste of Blackberries is narrated by a nameless boy whose fun-loving best friend dies after being stung by bees. Long considered the "last taboo" of children's literature, the issue of death had been addressed in a number of books by the early 1970s, but Smith's brief, tightly focused novel broke new ground in its realistic depiction of a child's death. The narrator's experiences as he attends the funeral, grieves, and slowly begins to recover from his loss are presented in simple, forthright prose that achieves moments of great poignancy. The book raises a distracting and unnecessary issue by hinting that another, earlier family death was a suicide; otherwise, Smith's first novel is a small gem.

Smith's reputation was further enhanced when she published two exceptionally fine novels in 1974. Like much of her writing, the stories take place in Georgia and deal with troubled young people. *Kick a Stone Home* features Sarah Jane Chambers, a multifaceted teenager interested in sports and veterinary medicine, who comes to accept her parents' divorce, begins dating, and learns to take an interest in others. *Tough Chauncey* concerns an undersized, illiterate thirteen-year-old juvenile delinquent. Both books have generally happy endings, though several concerns and issues are left unresolved.

This type of realism is one of the strongest aspects of Smith's writing. Her greatest strength may be her ability to create believable characters who often face nearly insurmountable problems, but always persevere and grow. Smith has demonstrated a great versatility in characterization, writing about protagonists of both sexes and varying ages, from an eleven-year-old whose family problems cause her to seek refuge under a neighbor's porch in *Best Girl* (1993) to the male high school track star in *Up and Over* (1976). The author has made one foray into fantasy with *Voyages* (1989), but most of her books are firmly grounded in reality, such as *Last Was Lloyd* (1981), the story of an overprotected twelve-year-old boy, and its sequel, *The First Hard Times* (1983). *Laura Upside-Down* (1984) concerns a ten-year-old girl who explores various religious traditions; the book has been criticized for being too didactic and heavy-handed, but it remains interesting because religion is seldom explored in children's fiction.

Smith has earned a fine reputation as an author of realistic books filled with insightful characterizations. ❧ P.D.S.

Smith, E. Boyd

AMERICAN ILLUSTRATOR, 1860–1943. E. Boyd Smith was born in St. John, New Brunswick. Raised in Boston,

Illustration by E. Boyd Smith from his work *The Seashore Book* (1985).

he lived for many years in France, traveled through the West, settled in Wilton, Connecticut, and died there—the illustrator of more than seventy books for children and adults. Of his personal life, he left few traces. Once asked his "Recreations, Amusements, Hobbies," he answered "Work."

For some years he worked for The Riverside Press, the manufacturing arm of Houghton Mifflin, a preeminent American printer. But it was in France, where he lived according to differing accounts from twelve to twenty years, that Smith acquired what he considered his education. During his years in France, Smith spent the summers outside Paris in little Valombre, whose everyday life, "with all its good and bad, its light and shadows," he celebrated in *My Village* (1896). In the book he drew the villagers, reaping and tying and stacking grain, with a vigor and precision that give weight to each gesture. He spoke of them in the sly, grave, almost courtly manner that would be a hallmark, later, of his writing for children. Whatever his subject or his audience, Smith didn't sentimentalize or condescend.

In January 1898, Smith came back to Boston, competing with A. B. Frost to illustrate Joel Chandler Harris's *Tales of the Home Folk in Peace and War.* Smith won that commission and became a publishing mainstay. After traveling through the West and sketching various Western subjects, he created his first two children's picture books, *The Story of Noah's Ark* (1905) and *The Story of Pocahontas and Captain John Smith* (1906). The latter was prompted by the three hundredth anniversary of the Jamestown settlement and was executed in the same grand manner as Boutet de Monvel's *Jeanne d'Arc.*

In an age when cities meant excitement and progress, while farming was for hayseeds, Smith published *The Farm Book* (1910). Brooklyn children's librarian Clara Hunt hailed him for bringing out a book that would teach children respect for what the farmer did and show them the satisfaction of doing things for themselves. Hunt had agitated for the radical change in juveniles—from the fanciful to the honest and true. To today's reader *The Farm Book* is a unique pictorial record of a bygone, envied way of life—a round of shared labor and shared pleasure.

Smith followed this highly successful title with *The Seashore Book* (1912) and *The Railroad Book* (1913). In these volumes he gave many child readers some of their first pictures of American life. One contemporary teacher and critic called them "the best pictures of American life available."

His *Chicken World* (1910) is more fully a picture book than anything Smith had done before or would do again. The pictures are by far his boldest. The brilliant reds, the coal blacks, the cool, clear greens were printed from separate plates, whether or not the nine plates that Smith once stipulated were employed. There is a vitality and vividness in the illustrations; here was a life of the chicken in pictures that spoke for themselves.

Before the end of his career, Smith created a few more books—*The Early Life of Mr. Man Before Noah* (1914), *They Came Out of the Ark* (1918), *The Story of Our Country* (1920), and *So Long Ago* (1944). But his style of illustrating became too expensive, and he retired to a French house and garden in the backwoods of Wilton, Connecticut.

Early in his career Smith had some imitators, but he had no followers. His were distinctly American picture books; they combined delicate, subtle colorations with clear definition, striking details, and often complex, dramatic compositions. ❧ B.B.

This essay was adapted by Barbara Bader from her introduction to *The Farm Book,* reprinted in 1982, and from her book *American Picture Books: From Noah's Ark to the Beast Within* (1976).

SMITH, JESSIE WILLCOX

AMERICAN ILLUSTRATOR, 1863–1935. During the early 1900s paintings by Jessie Willcox Smith illustrated handsome editions of children's classics, including *Little Women, The Water-Babies, At the Back of the North Wind, The Princess and the Goblin, Heidi, A Child's Garden of Verses,* and *'Twas the Night before Christmas.* Smith was a pupil of HOWARD PYLE, and, like many artists in the late 1880s, she began her career illustrating stories in magazines. This led to her doing cover illustrations for *Good Housekeeping,* and until Norman Rockwell came along in more recent times with his paintings for *The Saturday Evening Post,* she was the only artist whose work was used consistently on the cover of a national magazine—over 180 paintings in fifteen consecutive years. Her subjects were children, playing, dreaming, doing—often in family and school scenes—and were presented for the most part without sentimentality. Her compositions, while less painterly than those of Mary Cassatt, conveyed the same realistic look at the tenderness of mother and child together.

Smith brought a strong sense of storytelling to her illustrations, and in ROBERT LOUIS STEVENSON'S *Child's Garden of Verses,* the paintings of the little girl dressing by yellow candlelight, the small boy in bed with his toy soldiers strewn about the counterpane, and the child on the seaside rock contemplating his shadow are as evocative and memorable as the poems. Memorable, too, are her depictions of the frightening Mrs. Bedonebyasyoudid and the comforting Mrs. Doasyouwouldbedoneby in *The Water-Babies.* In that book her decorative line drawings and colorful paintings of naked, potbellied babies innocently preceded MAURICE SENDAK'S later and more controversial nude babies. Smith presented illustrations with simplicity, making the story's actions and emotions clear, but her use of detail and texture enriched them just as it enhances fine paintings. In the frontispiece of *A Child's Book of Old Verses,* for example, the little boy and girl saying grace at the table are flanked by a fine still life of jug, bread, and plate, while the curtained window behind them recalls those in Dutch paintings.

Illustration by Jessie Willcox Smith from *Twas the Night Before Christmas* (1912), by CLEMENT MOORE.

Jessie Willcox Smith was born in Philadelphia and in 1879 was studying to be a kindergarten teacher when a chance remark awakened her interest in art, and she discovered her natural ability for it. She then studied at the School for Design for Women, the Pennsylvania Academy of the Fine Arts, and the Drexel Institute of Arts and Sciences, all in Philadelphia. Looking today at the reproduction of her work in various books, one senses that the inadequate processes of preparing and printing color plates before the use of offset lithography in children's books in the 1920s failed to capture the freshness and brilliance of her original full-color oil paintings and watercolors. ❧ L.K.

Voices of the Creators

Lane Smith

There seem to be two factions, two schools of thought, in children's books. One faction nests high atop a pillar made of "educational," "socially acceptable," "moralistic" books; the other, a smallish army of wackos and ne'er-do-wells, attempts constantly to dislodge them with well-aimed lobs of zany, irreverent thirty-two pagers.

I am a bit of a schizophrenic. Some days I can empathize with the former group. In fact, some days I am thankful that they are out there. But on other days—well, on most days—I find myself lining up with my little bag of waggish ammo.

I am a great admirer of the school whose alumni include Dr. Heinrich Hoffman, Florence Parry Heide, James Marshall, Remy Charlip, Peter S. Neumeyer, and Maurice Sendak—Folks who really seem to know kids and what they like to read, not what they think they *should* read.

Occasionally I am asked by adults, "Why *is* your work so dark?" I am not quite sure why myself. All I can say is when I was a child, I *liked* dark things. I liked the night. I liked being indoors with my family and listening to the sound the wind made outside. I liked the scratching of the clawlike branches against the roof. I liked thunderstorms. I liked building tents and castles out of blankets and chairs, then crawling in under them. I liked telling ghost stories. I liked Halloween.

When I wrote *The Big Pets,* a surreal nighttime journey of a little girl and her giant cat, I was expanding on my own childhood fantasies of slipping out into the night for fantastic adventures while always knowing there was a home base of security to come back to. Of course, the paintings had to be dark. All of the action took place at night!

As for the books on which I've collaborated with Jon Scieszka, particularly *The True Story of the Three Little Pigs* and *The Stinky Cheese Man and Other Fairly Stupid Tales,* I knew the palette had to be one of rich oil colors: the palette of the original fairy tales. If I had gone too light and cartoony, I would have taken the satiric edge off of Jon's sly text.

Often I am asked how I get "that mottled texture" in my illustrations. I use acrylic spray varnishes in conjunction with oil paints. Naturally, the water-based acrylic and the oils react to one another, and the result is tiny beads of color. I build up a gradual surface of thin glazes—transparent glazes. Eventually, the paint becomes more opaque and monochromatic, but all the little beads remain intact.

I have always been attracted to weathered surfaces, old crackled paint, organic wear and tear, rot, grunge, oxidation of metals. My mother was an antiques dealer. I was fascinated by the different grains of the wood and the natural decay of the furniture and the minute cracks in the dolls and folk art figures. Later in college, I discovered the great Czech puppet-animated films of Jiri Trnka and Jan Svankmajer. Like their fine-artist brothers Joseph Cornell, Paul Klee, and Kurt Schwitters, Svankmajer and Trnka seemed to revel in the various layers of a surface. The more confident I become with my own work, the more these influences emerge. Today, I will try anything to achieve an interesting effect. I might use sandpaper directly on the paintings to get a scratchy rough feel, or I might collage in intriguing bits of ephemera or sticks or leaves.

Design is one of the most crucial aspects of book making and sadly one of the most overlooked and abused. Most children's books suffer from mediocre "cookie cutter" design. I have been fortunate to work with Molly Leach. In *Glasses, Who Needs 'Em?,* in order to quickly place the story in its proper framework, Molly designed the opening lines of the story in the form of an eye chart with the words literally shrinking down to the size of the type used throughout the rest of the book. Not only did this device draw the reader into the story and establish the proper framework, it also looked smashing! At least one third of the humor in *The Stinky Cheese Man and Other Fairly Stupid Tales* relies on the execution of the type. At one point the Stinky Cheese Man's malodorous vapors drift up from the illustration, reach the text, and cause the words to actually wilt on the page.

All in all, I am grateful that I have been given the opportunity to create books that I think offer somewhat of a different voice—books that just a few years ago were sometimes dismissed as being too sophisticated for young minds. Of course, whenever I start to feel even slightly confident about my work, I only have to pull out Ruth Krauss and Crockett Johnson's *Carrot Seed,* a masterpiece of understated writing, or Florence Parry Heide and Edward Gorey's *Shrinking of Treehorn,* in my opinion one of the most brilliant books ever, to send me back to the drawing table.

SMITH, LANE

AMERICAN ILLUSTRATOR AND AUTHOR, B. 1959. Lane Smith created a sensation in the picture-book world in 1989 with his illustrations for JON SCIESZKA'S *The True Story of the Three Little Pigs.* This zany story, told from the wolf's point of view, is perfectly complemented by oil paintings of the bespectacled Alexander T. Wolf and his exploits. Scieszka and Smith's second picture-book collaboration, *The Stinky Cheese Man and Other Fairly Stupid Tales* (1992), was also inventive in format, design, text, and illustration. This book, a 1993 Caldecott Honor recipient, contains ten fractured fairy tales that are interrupted by Jack the Narrator and the screeching of Little Red Hen. Smith's dark palette and use of collage highlight the surreal nature of tales such as "The Princess and the Bowling Bowl" and "Little Red Running Shorts" (whose wolf will look familiar). Teachers delight in using these books to teach about point of view, parody, and book design.

Scieszka and Lane also created a series of CHAPTER BOOKS for third- to fifth-graders about three boys who go back in time. *Knights of the Kitchen Table* (1991) and *The Good, the Bad and the Goofy* (1992) are two titles in this funny "Time Warp Trio" series. Unlike his collaborations with Scieszka, Smith's first book, *The Halloween ABC* (1987), was just a set of spooky pictures until EVE MERRIAM composed equally creepy poems to match the mood of the pictures.

Smith, a graduate of the Art Center College of Design in Pasadena, has written as well as illustrated some books in addition to his magazine, newspaper, and album-cover illustration work. *The Big Pets* (1991) is a fantasy in which children frolic with their huge pets in a dreamlike night world, and in *Glasses: Who Needs 'Em?* (1991), a ghoulish optometrist convinces a boy that he needs glasses. Both books feature Smith's complex process of using oil paints and acrylic sprays with collage and his characteristically bizarre-looking animals and people with their rows of tiny teeth. In his hilarious *The Happy Hocky Family* (1993), however, Smith uses childlike drawings on brown paper to parody, with a relentlessly upbeat family and short, choppy sentences, the "Dick and Jane" readers.

Smith's books are groundbreaking works that have received much recognition. They have been influential in expanding the readership of PICTURE BOOKS to older children and adults. Many baby boomers are thrilled to have books to share with their children that they enjoy as much—if not more—than their children do. Smith's books have also encouraged experimentation with book design. From the endpapers to the copyright notice to the author information on the dust jackets, surprises abound. Critics may say that, like MAIRA KALMAN, Lane Smith is too adult, too offbeat, and too much of a 1990s phenomenon to endure. But his many fans will continue to anticipate with glee every new book he publishes. P.O.B.

SNYDER, ZILPHA KEATLEY

AMERICAN AUTHOR, B. 1927. Whether she is writing a fantasy for middle-grade readers or a realistic novel for the young adult audience, there is a sense of magic and wonder in most of Zilpha Keatley Snyder's books.

Born in Lemoore, California, the author grew up in Ventura County, where she played fantasy games and read constantly. At an early age she determined that she would someday become a writer but, upon graduating from Whittier College, opted to teach instead. Although Snyder soon married, had children, and moved around the country with her husband as he attended school and served in the military, she always continued her teaching career, whether in California, New York, Washington, or Alaska. Teaching gave Snyder an understanding and appreciation for children that naturally found its way into her writing.

Recalling a childhood dream, she wrote her first book, a fantasy about a girl who uses a magic amulet to conjure up a herd of ponies. Accepted by the first editor who saw it, *Season of Ponies* was published in 1964. Snyder then quit teaching to write full-time and the following year published *The Velvet Room,* a Depression-era story of a homeless family finding work on a California fruit farm. Robin, the young protagonist, makes new friends and gains access to a mysterious book-filled room on a nearby estate. *The Velvet Room* is representative of many Snyder novels in its sure sense of setting, intriguing plot, evocative writing, and well-defined cast of characters. There is also a sense of magic and mystery hovering around the edges of the realistic story.

Although Snyder has written several books that deal directly with the supernatural, even her realistic novels seem to contain an elusive hint of magic. *The Egypt Game* (1967) concerns a group of children who play a highly imaginative game in the yard behind a junk shop. At the time of its publication, this inventive novel was unusual for its multicultural group of playmates; even now the book is somewhat daring for its matter-of-fact handling of a stalking child killer. *The Egypt Game* was named a Newbery Honor Book, as was Snyder's excellent *The Headless Cupid* (1971), the first of four books about the "Stanley Family," five stepbrothers and stepsisters who become involved in humorous, occasionally dangerous situations. Snyder received a third Newbery Honor designation for *The Witches of Worm* (1972), a spooky story about a girl who believes her cat is possessed by a witch.

In *The Changeling* (1970), a girl makes up a story about a place called "The Land of the Green Sky." Several years later, Snyder wrote *Below the Root* (1975), the first in a fantasy trilogy about Green-sky. This series, which continued with *And All Between* (1976) and *Until the Celebration* (1977), is intriguing but may not appeal to fans of the author's more realistic novels. Snyder's work is popular, but it is unfortunate that her best-known and most honored books were published rather early in her career. As good as those titles are, later books such as *Libby on Wednesday* (1990), *And Condors Danced* (1987), and the beautifully written young adult novel *A Fabulous Creature* (1981) show an artist at the peak of her powers.

Snyder has written in a variety of genres, including poetry, picture books, and an adult gothic novel. In addition to her typically solid plots, three-dimensional characterizations, and rare ability to evoke mood, Snyder has matured in her handling of language. She continues creating books that linger in the imagination. P.D.S.

Sobol, Donald J.

American author, b. 1924. Leroy Brown's vast reading background and keen memory have earned him the nickname "Encyclopedia." This boy detective cracks criminal cases for his police-chief father and helps neighborhood kids solve mysteries in a series of books that are exceptionally popular with intermediate readers. The author, Donald J. Sobol, was born and raised in New York City. After serving with the Army Corps of Engineers in World War II, he attended Oberlin College in Ohio, where he became interested in writing. He worked as a reporter for the *New York Sun* and the *Long Island Daily Press* before becoming a full-time writer. His children's books include historical novels, such as *The Lost Dispatch* (1958), which concerns an incident from the Civil War; a fictionalized biography, *The Wright Brothers of Kitty Hawk* (1961); and nonfiction works, including *The First Book of Stocks and Bonds* (1963), which he wrote with his wife, Rose.

Encyclopedia Brown: Boy Detective was published in 1963 and followed by more than a score of volumes, including *Encyclopedia Brown Finds the Clues* (1966) and *Encyclopedia Brown Saves the Day* (1970). Each book contains ten plot-driven stories that the reader is invited to solve using observation, deduction, and logic; Encyclopedia Brown's solutions are found at the end of each volume. Lacking literary pretensions, the stories have minimal characterization but are fast-moving and humorous, making them especially appealing to reluctant readers. Although each book follows a similar formula, there is enough diversity in subject matter and in the method of solving the individual cases that readers eagerly return to the shelves for another volume in order to again match wits with Encyclopedia Brown. P.D.S.

Soto, Gary

American author, b. 1952. Born and raised in Fresno, California, Gary Soto is a prize-winning poet and essayist who teaches at the University of California, Berkeley. *Baseball in April and Other Stories* (1990), Soto's first juvenile work, was highly acclaimed. Drawing on his memories of growing up Mexican American, Soto brings veracity and authenticity to these short stories about children and teenagers living in California's Central Valley. The stories tell vividly of the yearnings, disappointments, and joys of childhood and adolescence. In "The No-Blues Guitar," Fausto, guilt-ridden over a lie that brings him money for the guitar he desires, drops the cash in the collection plate at church and is later rewarded when his mother gives him his grandfather's old bass *guitarron*. Soto uses small but telling details to give life to his characters: Alfonso's attempts to straighten his teeth leave him with pink and wrinkly thumbs; and Veronica, searching so long for her beloved Barbie doll's missing head, loses concentration and has to remind herself what she is looking for. Winner of the 1990 Beatty Award, the collection was named an American Library Association Best Book for Young Adults.

Already known for his adult poetry, Soto proved with *A Fire in My Hands: A Book of Poems* (1990) that he is also a young people's poet. In the foreword, the writer explains how, as a college student, he decided to give up geography to study poetry. Anecdotes precede each poem, and a concluding section answers questions young readers may have about Soto the poet and about the writing of poetry in general.

Those moved by the brief glimpses of people in Soto's short stories and poems can fully acquaint themselves with one of his characters in the novel *Taking Sides*

Voices of the Creators

Gary Soto

For me, streets have always mattered. When I'm ready to write, ready to sit down, usually at our kitchen table, I conjure up inside my head an image of our old street in south Fresno, one that was torn down in the name of Urban Renewal at the beginning of the 1960s. It was, as one might imagine, a blighted area: a junk yard to the left of our house. Coleman Pickle across the street, a broom factory with its nightly *whack-whack* of straw taking shape and warehouses humming with machinery down the alley, and the almighty Sun-Maid Raisin factory in the distance. These are pictures that I take into my work, both in poetry and prose, pictures that stir the past, which I constantly haunt with an inventory list. They muster up a power inside me, a delicious feeling of memory, imagination, and the willingness to care for the smallest of objects—shards of glass, taps on my shoes, a chicken claw that I worked like a lever, a bicycle part, and an inner tube I rolled from one end of the yard to the other. In short, all the raw and discarded elements of the world.

When I work, I divide up this world, this street that I speak of. In my book *A Summer Life,* I was able to part the memories in such a way that I didn't yawn over these simple objects. One object was the ceramic Buddha we kept on a stand near the telephone, a gold-splotched Buddha with a large belly and laughter on his face. My uncle "El Shorty" had brought him home from the Korean war. Just as I'm ready to write, it's not unusual for me to close my eyes for a moment and remember the Buddha and other symbols of childhood. I see people and things in their place, from my father, dead now, and an uncle, also dead, to our dusty-white house, the bean plants, the almond tree where I hung, ridiculously, by an army belt, the fishless pond, my uncle back from Korea sleeping in the sun porch. Nothing much happened. No one pushed ahead; no one got rich and jingled coins in his or her pockets. We leaned our sadness on fences, sat in twos or threes on porches. We all faced the street, that river of black asphalt embedded with bottle caps, and followed with a curious gaze every car that passed.

I spent my first six years running like a chicken from one dirt yard to another, and I can't think of a more curious or unadorned childhood. I kept busy running around, a flag of shirt tail waving in the wind of my own doing. I was hot for action. I stole butt-faced plums from our neighbor on Van Ness Avenue. This was my favorite fruit. But when fall arrived and the turn of earth tugged at reddish leaves, my loyalty changed in favor of pomegranates, which I cracked like skulls on the curb, a sticky juice dripping from my chin. I was greedy for this fruit, treasure that glowed in the faintest light. Recently a young reader asked, "How come you have so many fruits in your poems?" I wanted to provide a large, complex metaphorical answer that would deepen my work. But I smiled and answered, "I'm a pig for fruit. Toss me an orange!"

How much memory is enough? How much can a writer siphon from the gorged heart of experience and yet have the heart still pump? If one cares about the mystery of childhood, then it's amazingly deep and long. The subjects come back again and again, sometimes effortlessly and sometimes with the stubbornness of a toad that won't leap. In one recollection from *A Summer Life,* I wrote about a handbrake. If I can reduce the narrative to a simple sentence, it's about my five-year-old self who discovers a discarded bicycle handbrake while looking about in an alley for something to do on a summer day. Its use? I tied the cable around my waist and raced about, whistling the sounds of an on-coming train. When I wanted to stop, I pulled on the lever, which worked like a chicken claw. I came to a stop in clouds of dust, blinked, and continued on, "the cable jumping on my waist, the lever shining with sunlight and God's forgiving stare."

It's these images from our old street that I take to the page, whether the subject is that street or another street from a time when I was older. It's these first images—these first losses when our street was leveled to the height of yellow weeds—that perhaps made me a writer. We lose family, deep friends, our place in childhood, and finally ourselves in the haunted end, when we'll lay on a rack of blackness in our graves. In short, as with other writers, I wish to restore these losses, first with private, closed-eyed moments in which I see our lives as they were, simple and full, and later in the shape of poems and prose, which may or may not live on the page. It depends on the luck we draw when I open my eyes, blink, look around, and take up a pencil.

Adapted from an article that appeared in *CMLEA,* Fall 1992 (Vol. 16, No. 1).

(1991) and its sequel, *Pacific Crossing* (1992). In the first book, Lincoln Mendoza deals with racism when he and his mother move from the barrio to the suburbs and he is the only Latino on the school's basketball team. In the sequel, fourteen-year-old Lincoln is chosen to be an exchange student in Japan because of his interest in a Japanese martial art. The story is moving and humorous, as Lincoln, responding to his host family's questions, tries for the first time to express what his identity as a Mexican American means to him.

Soto is also a perceptive writer for younger children, as evidenced by the brief novel *The Skirt* (1992). While tracing fourth-grader Miata's attempts to retrieve the *folklorico* skirt she has left on the school bus, the story highlights a family's success in combining old and new traditions. In *Too Many Tamales* (1993), a picture book, Soto tells about a young girl who fears she has lost her mother's diamond ring while kneading the cornmeal for their holiday tamales. The amusing story presents a loving look at one middle-class family's Christmas celebration.

Glossaries are provided in most of Soto's books to define the Spanish words and phrases that are smoothly and naturally interjected throughout his writing. Though his characters are Mexican American, and many are economically disadvantaged, Soto's stories contain universal experiences of childhood that will be recognized by readers of every background. J.M.B.

Southall, Ivan

Australian author, b. 1921. In the 1960s and 1970s no other Australian children's books were better known or more frequently discussed than those by Ivan Southall. With the publication of *Josh* in 1971, he became the only Australian to win the Carnegie Medal. This renowned writer has managed his literary accomplishments despite rather extraordinary family circumstances that didn't even allow him to complete an average sort of education.

Southall's early years were normal enough. He grew up in a Melbourne suburb, the son of a Presbyterian home missionary and the elder of two sons. Southall has described his family as "church people," and he had a childhood saturated with church activities. Although he won a scholarship to the well-respected Box Hill Grammar School—partly in recognition of his writing talent—his father's death from tuberculosis forced him to leave school at the age of fourteen to support his mother and younger brother. He initially got a job as a copyboy. From there he moved on to become an apprentice process engraver and photographic plate maker for the Melbourne *Herald* and managed to write a few articles and short stories on the side. His first article was published when he was only sixteen. World War II arrived, and Southall found himself serving in the Australian army and then in the RAAF, where he became the captain of a Sunderland flying boat. The material in his wartime diaries eventually provided fodder for at least ten different books, including his "Simon Black" series of adventure books and *Blackbird* (1988).

Southall married in 1945 and returned to Australia, where he took various jobs to support his family of one son and three daughters until his writing income could do so sufficiently. He became a Methodist lay preacher for a time and has commented that he regards his "writing as worship. . . . I've striven to do the very best work I can for that purpose . . . as an act of worship." Although Southall's books are frequently criticized for using themes that are too pessimistic or too adult, his titles have nevertheless collected an enormous amount of critical acclaim over the years. Not only have they won many prizes in Australia—Southall has received the Children's Book Council's Book of the Year Award four times—but they have been translated into twenty languages and received awards in Austria, the Netherlands, Japan, and the United States.

Internationally, he is best known for about nine books, starting with *Hills End* in 1962 and including such titles as *Ash Road* (1965) and *To the Wild Sky* (1967), in which young characters must call on strength from within themselves. Southall pokes and prods against the expected parameters of language, topic, and style. He doesn't necessarily provide relaxing reading experiences, but he does challenge. And over the course of his writing career, he has continuously set high standards for his fellow writers as well. K.J.

Speare, Elizabeth George

American author, 1908–1994. Many writers of historical fiction for children are adept at crafting fairly authentic historical settings for their novels, but what separated Elizabeth George Speare from the vast majority of these writers was her ability to create complex, full-blooded characters within the historical setting.

Born and raised in Melrose, Massachusetts, the author began writing as a child. After a year at Smith College, Speare attended Boston University, where she

Voices of the Creators

Elizabeth George Speare

Forty years ago, I happened, by sheer chance, upon the occupation which was to happily fill the remaining years of my life—the writing of historical fiction. I cannot remember when I first decided that I would be a writer. At the age of eight, I filled a brown notebook with my first novel, an incredibly dull imitation of my much-loved *Bobbsey Twins.* But somehow, with teaching and raising two children, it was many years before I attempted a second novel, finding time only for short stories, articles, and one-act plays. Then, by chance, I happened upon a somewhat forgotten story from the history of New England. It was written in 1807 by Susanna Johnson, who recalled in vivid detail the terrifying morning in 1754 when she and her husband, their three young children, and a teenaged sister were dragged from their beds in a surprise Indian attack and forced to march, scantily clad, through the wilderness toward Canada. Susanna was a brave and gallant woman, who well deserves to have her story retold, but it was the young sister, who was given slight mention in the narrative, who sprang to life, in my imagination, a girl torn from a life that had seemed so full of promise and faced suddenly with who knew what terrible fate.

I could not forget this girl, and day by day her adventures began to grow in my mind. Her story, remaining true to Susanna's brief narrative, expanded to include imaginary people, Indian and French, as I tried to relive her experience as it might have been. Slowly, these adventures grew into a book and became *Calico Captive,* and I had discovered the most absorbing and rewarding occupation of my life.

Twice again, in the years to come, I have borrowed from history true characters around whom to fashion my own story. For *The Sign of the Beaver,* I found in the history of Maine, a boy who, with the help of an Indian friend, survived for many months in a lonely cabin. For an adult novel, *The Prospering,* I chose a girl who was barely mentioned in the history of Stockbridge, Massachusetts, and through whose eyes I re-created the founding of that town.

For my second venture, I decided to visit the very old town of Wethersfield, Connecticut, and to imagine it as it was three hundred years ago, when it was a busy little river port. I did not find in history a girl who captured my imagination, but instead an imaginary girl began to walk and talk in my mind. Once again, she was an outsider, coming this time from the lush and sunny British island of Barbados to the harsh Puritan town where I hoped she would find, though she was bound to make many mistakes, a welcoming family, new friends, a place for herself, and a love for this narrow hard country.

Young readers write to me, "How did you learn about Indians?" or about life in colonial times? The answer, of course, is *research,* a word most students seem to find forbidding. To me, it is an ever-fascinating game which I have likened to a scavenger hunt. I go to the library with a long list of items I must find. And turning the pages of some long-forgotten book in a dusty corner, I come upon unexpected treasures, bright bits of history. Museums are a priceless source, and there are ancient houses that have been restored and opened to the public. There are faded old letters that speak as clearly as though they had arrived in this morning's mail.

Not all the discoveries are in libraries. At a local fair, I watched a woman demonstrating the art of spinning. The colonists, she told me, used a mixture of wool and flax, and, she said, it was the scratchiest clothing you could imagine. I thought of boys sitting for hours on school benches, in their homespun linsey-woolsey clothes, waiting patiently for a turn to read from the book held in the teacher's hand.

At the end of a day of my game of research, I return from my hunt with a bag stuffed with odd and brightly colored pieces. Most of these pieces I will never use, but in some way each piece that is chosen gains authenticity from all that is left behind.

I have always loved to read historical fiction. A novel possesses an immediacy which is impossible in a textbook. It involves us totally. It draws us into an event so that for a time we are present in some remote time and place, and by some magic, the event becomes part of our own experience. And this is even more true of writing a historical story, when I am involved for weeks and months, even for years, leading all this time a sort of double life in which the people and places I am writing about often seem more real than the room in which I am working. Far from escaping the problems of today, I find that I return from my adventures in "olden times" with a renewed appreciation and understanding of the present world. This is one of the great gifts that historical fiction can give to all of us, old and young. I am grateful to have had a share in it.

received bachelor's and master's degrees. She then embarked on a teaching career in Massachusetts high schools, leaving the profession in 1936 when she married and moved to Connecticut. When her two children were in junior high school, Speare began writing articles for magazines such as *Woman's Day* and *Better Homes and Gardens.* One article, in which Speare retold an incident from Connecticut's past, appeared in *American Heritage* magazine and was later adapted for television.

Her first novel also had its origins in New England history. Speare came across a diary published in 1807 by a woman named Susanna Johnson, who, with her family, was taken prisoner by Native Americans and forced to walk from New Hampshire to Montreal, Canada, where they were held for ransom. Among the captives was Johnson's teenaged sister, Miriam, but the narrative included scant information about her. Speare was intrigued by this character and began to imagine what life had been like for her. The resulting novel, *Calico Captive,* was published to great acclaim in 1957.

The following year, Speare published *The Witch of Blackbird Pond,* the story of sixteen-year-old Kit Tyler, born and raised in Barbados, who arrives in Connecticut to live with relatives in 1687. The impulsive, independent heroine feels constrained by the Puritans' way of life, and her restlessness leads to an accusation of witchcraft against her when she befriends an outcast Quaker woman. With its strong story and vivid characters, this portrait of Colonial America was awarded the Newbery Medal, reportedly winning by a rare unanimous vote.

Three years later, Speare won a second Newbery Medal, for *The Bronze Bow* (1961), a novel set in Palestine at the time of Jesus. The protagonist is Daniel bar Jamin, a bitter Jewish youth seeking vengeance against the Romans. The novel contains wonderfully real characters, strong action, intrigue, and a scene in which Daniel meets Jesus. Unlike the popular *Witch of Blackbird Pond,* which has achieved near-classic status, *The Bronze Bow* has never been a widely read book, probably because of its remote setting and its religious content. Yet it is precisely these factors that underscore the book's greatness. Neither time nor distance prevents the author from bringing historical Palestine breathtakingly alive for modern readers. The religious material is handled with great delicacy: The author's presentation of Jesus is particularly masterful. *The Bronze Bow* is equal to, perhaps better than, *The Witch of Blackbird Pond.*

A nonfiction children's book, *Life in Colonial America,* and a historical novel for adults followed, but it was over twenty years before Speare's next work of fiction for children appeared. *The Sign of the Beaver,* based on the true story of a boy who spent the summer alone in Colonial Maine, is vivid historical fiction and a compelling survival story. Speare once again received Newbery recognition when it was named a Newbery Honor Book. In 1989, Elizabeth George Speare won the Laura Ingalls Wilder Award for her fine body of work. Filled with memorable, strongly individualized characters, authentic details of setting, speech, and manners, Speare's work represents historical fiction at its best. ❧ P.D.S.

Sperry, Armstrong

AMERICAN AUTHOR AND ILLUSTRATOR, 1897–1976. Armstrong Sperry grew up listening to his great-grandfather spin yarns about his experiences as a sailor in the South Pacific, so it was perhaps inevitable that Sperry would someday create his own stories about Polynesia, New Guinea, and Bora Bora.

Born in New Haven, Connecticut, the author displayed an early interest in art, filling the margins of his school assignments with drawings. Although his education was interrupted by naval service during World War I, he attended the Yale School of Fine Arts, the Art Students League in New York, and Colorassi's Academy in Paris. He found work as an illustrator at an advertising agency, but left his job to join an expedition sponsored by the Bishop Museum of Honolulu. As assistant ethnologist, he collected languages, stories, and music from the South Sea Islands, returning to the United States two years later with plans to write and illustrate his own island stories.

Sperry's early efforts were storybooks filled with color illustrations. *One Day with Manu* (1933) and *One Day with Jambi in Sumatra* (1934) depict the daily lives of boys growing up in the South Pacific. The author also wrote a number of historical novels set in the United States, including *Wagons Westward* (1936), a fifteen-year-old boy's account of traveling the Sante Fe Trail in the 1840s, *Storm Canvas* (1944), a story about the War of 1812, and *Black Falcon* (1949), in which a shipmaster's son encounters pirate Jean Lafitte. Although sometimes lengthy and overly detailed, Sperry's historical fiction provides a vivid picture of the past and includes well-rounded male protagonists who achieve emotional maturity through their adventures.

All Sail Set (1935) was named a Newbery Honor Book and remains one of Sperry's best novels. Although a work of fiction, it concerns an actual clipper ship from the 1840s, the *Flying Cloud.* Narrator Enoch Thacher relates his teenage experiences assisting shipbuilder Donald McKay, then serving as an apprentice on the ship's maiden voyage around Cape Horn. Sperry's evocative prose and meticulous pen-and-ink illustrations have a fine nautical flavor, as Enoch acquires his sea legs, suffers through initiation rites as he crosses the equator, observes a mutiny, and survives terrible storms in a book flawed only by a distracting overuse of dialect.

The author returned to a South Seas setting for many of his books, most notably the Newbery Award–winning *Call It Courage* (1940). This brief volume concerns a Polynesian boy shunned by his people because he fears the sea. Mafatu leaves his island by canoe and is shipwrecked on a deserted isle, where he survives by finding food and shelter; killing a shark, an octopus, and a wild boar; making a spear and a new canoe; and escaping a tribe of cannibals on his grueling journey home. The tightly focused writing and blue-ink illustrations combine to tell a story with mythic qualities.

Although Sperry wrote several nonfiction books, including *Pacific Islands Speaking* (1955), and biographies such as *John Paul Jones, Fighting Sailor* (1953), which unfortunately contains invented characters and dialogue, today he is best remembered for his coming-of-age stories that feature young men encountering adult situations and the forces of nature as they mature and grow. § P.D.S.

Spier, Peter

DUTCH-AMERICAN PICTURE-BOOK AUTHOR AND ILLUSTRATOR, B. 1927. Peter Spier's more than fifty PICTURE BOOKS cover a range of subjects that reveal both his pride in America and his childhood in Holland, where his lifelong love of boats and water began. His style is recognized for its descriptive black line drawings with color wash. While Spier excels at casual humor, he does not shy away from the harsher realities of the stories he illustrates. This combination of humor and integrity seems to account for his success with both child and adult audiences.

Born in Amsterdam in 1927, Spier spent his childhood in Broek-in-Waterland, a small village where boats passed by outside his window. His father was a well-known journalistic artist, and Spier grew up surrounded by books and exposed to current events, theater, and concerts. While in school, he considered careers in architecture, publishing, the navy, and the law, but at eighteen he enrolled in the Royal Academy of Art in Amsterdam. After art school, he joined the navy, where, he says, "I liked the service a lot and almost signed on for a couple of decades. The discipline, the ships, the water, the people—everything about it pleased me." A job in publishing soon sent him to the United States, where he began his career as a children's book illustrator in 1953. In 1958 he became a U. S. citizen and married, later settling on Long Island, where he and his wife raised their two children.

Spier's earliest books, produced with color separations, use traditional, bright colors in pleasingly vivid combinations. His later books employ a lighter touch to show atmospheric effects of night and day, stormy skies, and other uses of a more refined palette. In all, he has illustrated close to one hundred books, though not all of them are children's picture books. His other work includes nonfiction for children and adults for Golden Books, Time-Life, and *Reader's Digest.* While Spier began his career by illustrating books by others, by the mid-1960s he was almost exclusively illustrating either his own writings or preexisting song texts. Many of his books are wordless, but when he wrote, he kept his texts as simple as possible. He says, "Writing and drawing are two of the same art forms. What you say in the text, you no longer need to say in the pictures and vice versa. The ideal picture book doesn't need any text. I realize that this doesn't apply to all picture books. Some stories need to be told in words as well as in pictures." Spier has won several awards for his wordless or nearly wordless picture books and for his illustrated folk songs, among them the Caldecott Medal and the Lewis Carroll Shelf Award for *Noah's Ark* (1977); a Caldecott Honor for *The Fox Went Out on a Chilly Night* (1961); and the Boston Globe–Horn Book Award for illustration for *London Bridge Is Falling Down* (1967).

Spier spends about six months on each picture book. After sending a dummy to his publisher, he embarks on an extensive research that includes quickly rendered sketches from life. In planning *The Erie Canal* (1970), he drove the length of the canal twice, stopping to draw frequently. Although his books appear to include pen-and-ink, he actually draws his final art in pencil, which the printer overexposes to print black. After his line drawings are photographed, Spier colors them on a light blue print. He says, "I am integrally involved in every phase of production. I do my own mechanicals, spec type, paste-up, work with the printer and handle foreign rights."

Noah's Ark displays Spier's qualities at their apex. In this mostly wordless book, his palette is full of warm browns and sky blues and he pays acute attention to pleasing juxtapositions of cool and warm colors. As the book progresses, the interiors become grayer and

Illustration by Peter Spier from his book *Tin Lizzie* (1975).

browner as the ark becomes dirtier. Both humans and animals are drawn with love and empathy mixed with humor, while the well-paced visual impact seesaws between pages full of detail to spreads of calm atmospheric beauty. The most rewarding aspect of the book comes from examining the details in the busy scenes inside the ark. Hundreds of small dramas occur involving interactions of the animals, the never-ending job of the humans to feed and clean up after the animals, and the overcrowding that begins almost immediately as the animals reproduce. Finally, the later spreads showing an increasingly dark, gray-brown, dilapidated interior give way to the final spread, which uses colors not seen since the beginning of the book: spring-green fields with orange wheat, blue mountains, and, of course, the rainbow.

Spier's books have been published in twenty-four languages and include a variety of subjects. Each book demonstrates his sense of fun, a consistently sharp yet benevolent eye, a confident color sense, and a gift for knowing which details are indispensable. ❧ L.R.

Spinelli, Jerry

American author, b. 1941. In his many successful books for middle readers and young adults, Jerry Spinelli proves that he has accomplished what is perhaps the most important aspect of writing for children: He has stayed in touch with childhood. With this gift he has produced a series of provocative stories that remain true to the language, the joys and sorrows, and the often difficult situations of children and young adults.

Spinelli and his wife, Eileen, also a writer of children's books, have seven children. Their lives and the author's own memories serve as inspiration for his lively tales, which focus around universal and sensitive issues—

Voices of the Creators

Jerry Spinelli

If the visiting author to a school stays long enough, three questions are sure to be asked: (1) "How much money do you make?" (2) "How old are you?" and (3) "Where do you get your ideas?" There is another question, asked not quite so often, which I find especially interesting. The question comes in different forms, but what it boils down to is this: "Why do you write books?"

What a befuddlement must an author be to the questioner, who probably doesn't read or write beyond the assignments made by a teacher. In a world of video games, slam dunks, and obliterator movies, why would anyone want to write a book? I imagine I must appear to such a kid as the wasp appeared to young Dylan Thomas, whose consideration thereof was reduced to a single word—*why?*

But it's a good question, an excellent question. Before I first heard it, I'm not sure I had ever asked it of myself. I frame my answer in a context familiar to most of my audience. "Suppose you're riding to school on the bus," I say, "and you look out the window, and for just a couple of seconds as the bus zooms by, you see something really incredible. It may be strange, funny, tragic, poignant, whatever—the point is, it touches you, it smacks you. Now," I say, "when the bus drops you off at school, what is the first thing you're going to do?"

Hands go up. The right answer always comes on the first or second try: "Tell somebody."

"Bingo!" I say. "You already understand in a general way why I write. It has to do with this desire, this need to communicate our experiences to others. Life itself is kind of like taking the bus to school, except that you get to experience it from all sides. Sometimes you're just going along for the ride; sometimes you're in the driver's seat; sometimes you're left waiting at the corner; and sometimes the wheels roll right on over you.

"When I write a book, you can think of it as my way of telling you what I saw—and felt, feared, wished, imagined, remembered—on the way to school. So you see, I'm not nearly as different from you as you thought."

It's a good thing there's no Late Room beyond school, because life's bus ride is a long one. Years, decades, all but a lifetime can pass between the experiencing and the telling. I was just a few years old when I accompanied my mother one day to the dentist. His name was Dr. Winters. His skin was Hershey Bar brown. I must have been acting jealous of the attention my mother was getting, because when he finished with her teeth, he put me in the tilt-back chair and gave me my very own check-up. It's one of the first moments I remember about my life: Dr. Winters's brown fingers inside my mouth. Nearly fifty years later that memory, tailored to the story, finally landed in *Maniac Magee:*

> He especially loved the warm brown of Mrs. Beale's thumb, as it appeared from under the creamy white icing that she allowed him to lick away when she was frosting his favorite cake.

Only then, when I wrote down those words (longhand, ballpoint pen, yellow copy paper) did the experience that began half a century before complete itself.

With the chicken bones, however, fulfillment was only hours away. Early one morning in 1979, I took from the refrigerator a paper bag. The night before, I had placed in it the fried chicken that I would take to work for lunch the next day. I opened the bag to find chicken bones—*only* chicken bones. Obviously, one of our six kids had eaten the meat. Obviously, too, the culprit would not confess. So I went to work that day fried-chickenless, and when lunchtime arrived I decided to use the morning's incident as the starting point for a story. I made a second decision, one whose import to my future I never suspected. I decided to write not from my point of view, but from the culprit's, the kid's:

> One by one my stepfather took the chicken bones out of the bag and laid them on the kitchen table. He laid them down real neat. In a row. Five of them. Two leg bones, two wing bones, one thigh bone....
>
> Was this really happening? Did my stepfather really drag me out of bed at seven o'clock in the morning on my summer vacation so I could stand in the kitchen in my underpants and stare down at a row of chicken bones?

Those words open what became my first published novel, *Space Station Seventh Grade.* There is one sense, however, in which that particular experience may never be completed. The culprit has yet to confess. I wish he or she would. I'd like to say "Thank you."

sibling rivalry, maturity, love, friendship, death, prejudice—while maintaining a balance through humorous dialogue and often comic situations. Many adults have objected to Spinelli's use of language, considering attribution to young adult protagonists of references to drinking, flatulence, and sexual situations, as well as profanity, to be crude and inappropriate. Others, including his growing audience, appreciate the honesty of these characters and recognize in them a mirror of reality. Spinelli's early book *Space Station Seventh Grade* (1982) is chiefly the story of the irrepressible Jason Herkimer, who with an assortment of equally hormonal friends grapples with the difficult transitional period of seventh grade. In chapters organized under one-word titles such as "Hair," "Punishment," "Mothers," and "Girls," Spinelli tracks the ups and downs of Jason's year with a galloping hilarity sprinkled with reflection, and no topic is off-limits. A sequel, *Jason and Marce-line* (1986), probes the subject of relationships through earthy locker-room dialogue and adolescent escapades while successfully tackling the issues of male dominance and respect for women.

The most successful of Spinelli's works for middle-grade readers is *Fourth Grade Rats* (1991), a brief, lighthearted tale of a boy's struggle to make the transition into the fourth grade and to master requisite courageous tasks such as defying his mother and giving up his favorite lunchbox.

Content aside, all of the author's books demonstrate a true genius with words. Using a spare, evocative prose resplendent with imagery and metaphor to create narrative that often borders on the poetic, Spinelli can bring the most remote setting or situation to life. Nowhere is this more evident than in the half-realistic, half-mythical tale *Maniac Magee* (1990), for which Spinelli was awarded both the Newbery Award and the Boston Globe–Horn Book Award. The story of a homeless boy with extraordinary talents who takes on the very real issues of racial tension, illiteracy, and family strife, this novel represented a new direction for Spinelli and became a testament to the substantial and multifaceted abilities of this gifted writer. C.C.B.

Sports Stories

Sports make up an integral part of teenage life. Even for nonathletes, sports seem to dominate a school's social life, to determine its pecking order, and to define the cliques. It is no surprise, then, that sports stories have always been an important genre in young-adult literature. Most young-adult literature deals with the basic problems of adolescent development, such as building character. Sports, because they are about winning and losing, are about character building and about values. The heart of sports fiction isn't even about playing or winning the game, but about the heroes that sports create and the values that sports instill.

Such a hero is Roy Tucker. Tucker is the creation of the 1940s author John Tunis. Tucker is introduced in *The Kid from Tompkinsville* (1940) and patrols center field in several other novels. Tunis's books were quite successful at their original publication and were repackaged in the late 1980s for a new audience, one that was probably eager to escape the idea of the athlete as a millionaire superstar and return to a simpler time when only the game mattered. The details of the game are the strength of Tunis's work. He is a novelist but has a sportswriter's gift for making every crack of the bat sound authentic and even beautiful. His attention to the details of the game and the character that it builds made Tunis the forefather of contemporary young-adult sports fiction.

After Tunis, there were many years without significant sports fiction. The genre was loaded down with collections of stories for girls, for boys, and about every sport. Books like John Carson's *The Coach Nobody Liked* (1960), Joe Archibald's *Right Field Rookie* (1967), and Tex Maule's *The Receiver* (1968) tried to recapture the Tunis touch. Writing about baseball and other sports, these authors worked the same field but just weren't in Tunis's league in terms of quality. Books by these authors and others during this period were often bogged down by formula elements, usually finding the athlete overcoming the odds to win the "big game."

Matt Christopher and Alfred Slote also began writing sports books in the 1960s, but for the preteen audience. While faults can be found in both authors' books, Christopher and Slote realized that sports are supposed to be fun and brought some of that feeling to their works. Christopher, in particular, wrote books that were just enjoyable to read—such as *The Team That Couldn't Lose* (1967)—in which he mixes a couple of characters, lots of action, and a likable and unheroic hero.

The breakthrough modern sports novel was very different from those of either Tunis or Christopher. Robert Lipsyte's *The Contender* (1967) introduced a new hard edge to sports fiction. Early sports fiction was concerned primarily with what happened on the field, but the heart of *The Contender* took the action off the field and out of the ring. The boxing scenes are realistic yet also poetic as Lipsyte demonstrates his sportswriting

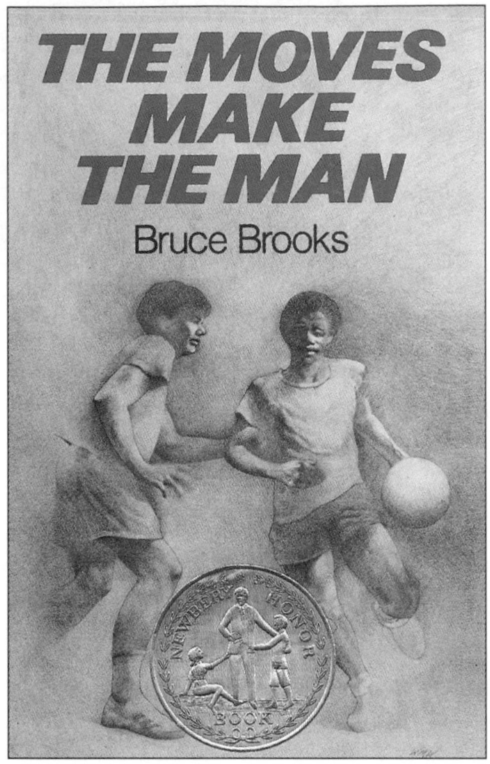

Jacket illustration by Wayne Winfield for *The Moves Make the Man* (1984), by BRUCE BROOKS.

skills. But as the title says, the book isn't just about being a winner or champion; it is about the importance of being a contender. In and out of the ring, Lipsyte's Alfred Brooks showed young readers the true meaning of being a hero.

With *The Contender* the sports story was transformed into what Jack Forman called the "sports metaphor novel." Writing in the *Horn Book*, Forman explained that this new breed of novel has "no formula, no uplifting moral, no climactic heroics, just the turbulence of adolescent life." Forman also points out that the focus of these novels is no longer the sport itself, but rather the character who just happens to have an interest in sports.

Another example of this trend was Robin Brancato's *Winning* (1977). In this novel the protagonist's life is shattered by a sports injury. Gary Madden is a high-school football player left a quadriplegic from an accident during a game. Like Alfred Brooks, Gary has the goal no longer just to win but to survive with dignity. *Winning* is one of the few sports novels to deal with the often tragic consequences of violent high-school athletics.

The other big 1970s breakthrough novels were those of R. R. Knudson concerning female athlete Suzanne Hagen. Knudson is the Tunis of girl's sports fiction. She gets the characters and the action right as superwoman athlete Zan Hagen competes in several different sports in books like *Zanbanger* (1977). These titles opened the way for more realistic women's sports books. ROSEMARY WELLS's *When No One Was Looking* (1980) and CYNTHIA VOIGT's *Tell Me If the Lovers Are Losers* (1982) use sports—tennis and volleyball respectively—as backdrops for novels looking at character-building through athletics. A more recent trend in books like JERRY SPINELLI's *There's a Girl in My Hammerlock* (1991) and Paul Baczewski's *Just for Kicks* (1990) finds female athletes competing in boys' sports. Both novels are comic, yet the seriousness of the issue is also explored.

The 1980s brought a renewed interest in sports fiction. Paperback publishers attempted to create popular sports series, such as Bantam's *Varsity Coach* and Ballantine's trio *Blitz, Rookies, and Hoops,* but the books failed to catch on. These books ignored the fact that sport is more than just a game: As Tunis proved in his novels, it is also beauty.

The 1980s also produced several powerful first novels by male writers, who used sports as a backdrop for complicated coming-of-age stories. In just a few years such accomplished works as *Vision Quest* by Terry Davis (1980), *Football Dreams* by David Guy (1980), *A Passing Season* by Richard Blessing (1982), *The Throwing Season* by Michael French (1980), *Juggling* by Robert Lehrman (1982), *Running Loose* by CHRIS CRUTCHER (1983), and *The Moves Make the Man* by BRUCE BROOKS (1984) were all published. Covering a variety of sports, all these novels present a new kind of sports protagonist who uses sports as a method to achieve self-realization and sort out competing values: the biggest challenges are off the field.

But what makes these novels so successful as sports fiction is that the authors, like Tunis, get the details right. Brooks writes about basketball with the same grace and style that Tunis brought to the national pastime. While the actual amount of football played in *Running Loose* is minimal, Crutcher's writing brings the reader onto the field to feel the hits and catch the passes. Of all these writers, Crutcher has continued to use sports as his primary subject. Three of his later books, *Stotan!* (1986), *Crazy Horse Electric Game* (1987), and *Athletic Shorts* (1991) were all "Best Books for Young Adults," and deservedly so. In particular, the story collection *Athletic Shorts* merges the beauty of sportswriting à la Tunis with the modern realistic novel in a powerful fashion. During the same time, WALTER DEAN

MYERS produced hard-hitting basketball novels such as *Hoops* (1981) and its sequel, *The Outside Shot* (1984), featuring African American characters. The books of Myers, Brooks, and Crutcher also place the issue of sports into large societal concerns, such as racism and the exploitation of athletes in high school and college.

Sports fiction has grown continually from the simple days of dime novels to the beauty of John Tunis, from the simple joy of Matt Christopher to the power and the glory of Chris Crutcher. The genre has evolved, following closely the evolution of young-adult literature. As long as young adults are interested in sports, the literature will reflect this passion. In today's sports fiction, there are still winners and losers and heroes, but the heroes aren't perfect. They are human beings just like their readers, who are grappling with the same challenges of maturing, sorting out their values, and becoming contenders. PATRICK JONES

Spyri, Johanna

SWISS AUTHOR, 1827–1901. Johanna Heusser Spyri began writing at age forty-three, donating the proceeds from her short stories to help refugees of the Franco-Prussian War. She went on to write more than forty children's books, but it is her first full-length novel, *Heidi*, originally published in 1880, translated from German to English in 1884, and rendered in numerous illustrated editions and screen interpretations since, that earned her lasting international renown.

Born in the village of Hirzel, Switzerland, near Zurich, Spyri infused all her writing with her love of the Swiss countryside. Readers experience Heidi's delight in the sound of wind rustling the fir trees outside her grandfather's Alpine hut or in the wildflowers carpeting the higher pastures where the goats graze. What distinguishes *Heidi* from the rest of Spyri's writing, however, is the character of Heidi herself. Although she plays a role found repeatedly in literature of the period, that of a child reformer whose innate goodness spiritually revives almost everyone she meets, this does not diminish the strength and appeal of her personality. When taken to live with her gruff, reclusive grandfather, called the Alm-Uncle by the villagers who speculate on his reputedly shady past, Heidi shows no fear—only tenacious curiosity, then infectious enthusiasm for his simple way of life.

Critics over the years have found fault with the book's interludes of religion, used, some have said, to resign poverty-stricken characters to their fate. Children apparently overlook these elements, enthralled with the story of a little girl who, they feel, would make a marvelous friend. C.M.H.

Stanley, Diane

AMERICAN AUTHOR AND ILLUSTRATOR, B. 1943. Born in Abilene, Texas, Diane Stanley grew up in New York City among writers, artists, actors, and musicians—friends of her mother, writer Fay Stanley. Diane Stanley and her mother read books together and even created their own, with Diane drawing the pictures to accompany her mother's stories.

Diane Stanley's path to illustrating award-winning picture books, however, was a circuitous one. She developed her talent for drawing while attending Trinity University in San Antonio, Texas, and after graduating in 1965 with a B.A. in history and political science, she did postgraduate work at the University of Texas and the Edinburgh College of Art in Scotland. She began her career as a medical illustrator, thinking that her detailed, realistic drawing style was well suited to that type of work. It was, but Stanley discovered she wasn't. She obtained a master's degree in medical and biological illustration from Johns Hopkins University in 1970 and worked for some years as a medical illustrator, but she felt the field didn't offer her the freedom of creativity she had known as a child. It wasn't until she was visiting libraries with her own children that she became interested in picture books and saw an opportunity to express herself creatively. After taking a year to compile a portfolio, she illustrated her first book, *The Farmer in the Dell* (1977), under the name Diane Zuromskis. Finally, she had found her niche, and she began to concentrate on illustrating children's books, primarily in gouache, an opaque watercolor, and on working in publishing as a graphic designer and an art director. *The Conversation Club* (1983) was the first book she both wrote and illustrated.

The illustrations in her early works are characteristically detailed and finely rendered, but it was with the publication of *Peter the Great* in 1986 that Stanley was able to employ her talents to their best advantage. She embarked on a series of picture-book biographies that combine accurate, exquisitely detailed illustrations and thoroughly researched stories of some of history's great men and women. The blending of art and text is masterful, as the illustrations and the story enhance one another. In *Peter the Great,* Stanley presents a brave reformer and leader who brought czarist Russia into the modern world. Her illustrations allow readers to see for themselves the contrasts between the old, archaic Russian society and modern eighteenth-century Europe with rich details in costume, architecture, and interiors. Complex issues are simplified in the text, but Stanley still manages to convey volumes about the man of vision and his times. *Shaka, King of the Zulus* (1988), written with her husband, Peter Vennema, is about another great leader, but one who ruled with brutal force and fear instead of concern about social reforms. Vennema and Stanley give a thoughtful, unflinching portrait of this nineteenth-century South African military genius. As in all her books, Stanley maintains a keen sense of the overall design: From the intricate borders and the costumes to the use of full-color spreads to convey a sense of the awesome beauty of the African countryside, all the elements work together to give the reader a feel for the culture and times in which this story takes place. Other titles in this exceptional series are *Good Queen Bess: The Story of Elizabeth I of England* (1990), *Charles Dickens: The Man Who Had Great Expectations* (1993), and *The Bard of Avon: The Story of William Shakespeare* (1993), all written with Peter Vennema, and *The Last Princess: The Story of Princess Ka'ialani of Hawai'i* (1991), written by Fay Stanley.

Stanley has published over twenty titles since 1977, and several of her books were named Notable Children's Trade Books in the Field of Social Sciences by the National Council on Social Studies and the Children's Book Council. Her lively texts and sumptuous illustrations invite the reader to share adventures and encourage further study of the past. K.F.

Staples, Suzanne Fisher

American author, b. 1945. Suzanne Fisher Staples, born in Philadelphia, spent eight years as a United Press International correspondent and news editor in Hong Kong, India, Afghanistan, and Pakistan. She worked as a part-time editor for the foreign desk at the Washington *Post,* then as a consultant to the U.S. Agency for International Development. Since 1988 Staples has devoted herself to writing fiction and lecturing on the status of women in the Islamic republic of Pakistan.

While in Pakistan, Staples became engrossed with the nomads of the Cholistan desert, who inspired *Shabanu, Daughter of the Wind* (1989), named a Newbery Honor Book in 1990. Staples felt that journalism seemed an "inadequate" means of portraying "the essential humanness of us all" and decided that fiction would enable her to express her passion for these generous and courageous people. *Shabanu* is a stark, uncompromising story of a spirited, intelligent Cholistani girl's coming of age in a culture where childhood is all too brief. Eleven-year-old Shabanu lives in a close-knit extended family of camel traders. One is struck by the manner in which Staples conveys, within a culture "profoundly different" from our own, the universality of Shabanu's life. *Haveli* (1993) follows eighteen-year-old Shabanu, now the favored fourth wife of the wealthy and influential Rahim. Fighting against the rigid rules and traditions of Islam, Shabanu slowly builds a future for herself and her daughter.

Staples captures all the color and cruel beauty of the desert in an unsentimental style. Both books offer a vividly drawn portrait of the Islamic way of life, its beliefs and traditions. The portrayal of the role of women is, however, disturbingly accurate, and sometimes violent. M.O'D.H.

Steele, Mary Q.

American author, 1922–1992. Mary Q. Steele published a wide variety of children's books under her own name and as Wilson Gage. Born in Chattanooga, Tennessee, the author was raised in a family that valued the written word. Her mother, Christine Govan, wrote children's books; her father was the book review editor for a local newspaper and a librarian at the University of Chattanooga. While studying physics at that university, the author met and married William O. Steele. She briefly worked for the Tennessee Valley Authority as a map editor, but devoted most of her time to raising a family while her husband pursued a literary career. After William Steele established his reputation as a writer of historical fiction for children, Mary Steele also began writing for young people, using the pseudonym Wilson Gage.

Her first book, *Secret of the Indian Mound* (1958), is a mystery about two cousins helping their uncle excavate an ancient Indian burial mound. The entertaining, fast-paced story contains elements central to much of the author's work. The characters are original and well developed. Uncle Zan is the first of many unconventional or eccentric Steele characters. The author's deep appreciation for nature is also apparent; almost all of her books contain evocative descriptions of flowers, birds, and wildlife, whether they are central or peripheral to the main story line. The most popular Wilson Gage novel is *Miss Osborne-the-Mop* (1963), a humorous fantasy about a magical pair of eyeglasses that change magazines into layer cakes, sassafras leaves into chocolate sodas, and a kitchen mop into a strange, living creature.

A strikingly imaginative writer, Steele published several fantasies that are decidedly offbeat. In *Journey Outside* (1969), the Raft People have traveled on a dark underground river for generations, believing they are headed for a better place, but actually circling endlessly. When young Dilar jumps from his raft and climbs through a crevice in a rock wall, he discovers the outside world. Dilar's experiences in this new environment can be read as a fantasy, an adventure story, or an allegory. Written in hypnotic prose, this stunning work was named a Newbery Honor Book; it is also the first title Steele published under her own name. Much less successful is *The First of the Penguins* (1973), an esoteric fantasy with a nearly impenetrable plot.

The author's talent for exploring the unusual extends to her realistic novels as well. *The Life (and Death) of Sarah Elizabeth Harwood* (1980) tells of Sarah's flirtation with suicide as she despairs over losing a valuable item borrowed from a neighbor. Readers may feel uncomfortable to find such a serious issue at the core of a rather lighthearted book, but the story is ultimately life affirming and reassuring. The characterizations of Sarah and her eccentric family are particularly impressive because Steele shows the thought processes and emotions behind their strange behavior.

Steele's other works include volumes of poetry, a series of easy readers about a spirited older woman named Mrs. Gaddy, an adult book of nature essays, and *The Eye in the Forest* (1975), a children's novel about the Adena Indians that she wrote with her husband. Versatility and originality distinguish the work of Mary Q. Steele. P.D.S.

STEELE, WILLIAM O.

AMERICAN AUTHOR, 1917–1979. William O. Steele's childhood interest in the past resulted in a career as a highly regarded author of historical books for young people. Born in Franklin, Tennessee, he spent his early years searching for arrowheads and other Indian artifacts. He explored historical landmarks and studied pioneer life, hoping someday to incorporate this material into fiction. The author graduated from Cumberland University in Lebanon, Tennessee, where he worked on the school newspaper. Steele served five years in the military during World War II; before being sent overseas, he met and married MARY Q. STEELE, who would also become a distinguished author of children's books. After the war, William Steele returned to Tennessee and supported his family by doing clerical work. When one of his children was ill, Steele read historical stories to her and was prompted to write one of his own.

The Buffalo Knife (1952) was the first book he wrote, although it was preceded in print by another, lesser effort that he wrote afterward, *The Golden Root* (1951). *The Buffalo Knife* is the exciting story of young Andy Clark and his family as they travel down the Tennessee River in 1782. The thousand-mile flatboat journey includes Indian attacks and a dangerous passage over the rapids. After this initial success, Steele quit his office job to become a full-time author. Most of his fiction deals with frontier life in the southeastern United States. Notable titles include *Wilderness Journey* (1953), which describes a ten-year-old boy's trip over the Tennessee Wilderness Trail during the late eighteenth century, and *Tomahawks and Trouble* (1955), the story of three young people who are taken prisoner by Shawnee Indians, then must endure a forced march through the wilderness before escaping from their captors.

Steele's historical novels are well researched and filled with vivid details of frontier life. Colorful, colloquial dialogue contributes to this feeling of authenticity. The protagonists are realistically portrayed, but seldom developed in great depth; they are occasionally upstaged by more engaging supporting characters. Steele's early works have been criticized for their stereotyped treatment of American Indian cultures. The author publicly noted this flaw in his work and later made attempts to remedy the situation by writing more sympathetic accounts of Indian life in *The Man with the Silver Eyes* (1976), in which a Cherokee boy learns of his mixed parentage, and books such as *The Magic Amulet* (1979), which deal with ancient Indian cultures. Steele's best-known novel, *The Perilous Road* (1959), is a Civil War story about a Tennessee farm boy whose older brother joins the Union Army. Young Chris supports the Confederacy but comes to realize the futility of war when he witnesses a violent attack on a Yankee wagon train.

Steele published nonfiction about historical events, as well as biographies of Daniel Boone, Leif Ericson, and Hernando De Soto, among others. He also authored a number of rollicking tall tales involving real-life figures such as Davy Crockett and Andrew Jackson. But the author remains best known for his historical novels, which, although dated in their treatment of American Indians remain rousing adventure stories. P.D.S.

Voices of the Creators

William Steig

I grew up in the Bronx. Lamplighters lit the old gas lamps; people sat on the stoops; gypsies wandered through the streets. Among the things that affected me most profoundly as a child were certain works of art: Grimms' fairy tales, Charlie Chaplin movies, Humperdinck's opera *Hansel and Gretel,* the Katzenjammer Kids, and *Pinocchio.* I can still remember the turmoil of emotions, the excitement, the fears, the delights, and the wonder with which I followed Pinocchio's adventures.

I didn't spend many years in school. I graduated from high school when I was fifteen and spent two years in the City College of New York where my biggest interest was not learning but playing—water polo. Then I went to the National Academy of Design. There was a time that I wanted to go to sea, and I had the necessary papers. If I'd had it my way, I'd have been a professional athlete, a sailor, a beachcomber, or some other form of hobo. When I was an adolescent, Tahiti was a paradise. I made up my mind to settle there someday. I was going to be a seaman, like Melville, but the Great Depression put me to work.

My father didn't want us to become laborers, because we'd be exploited by businessmen, and he didn't want us to become businessmen, because then we'd exploit the laborers. Since he couldn't afford to send us to school to become professionals, the arts were the only thing that remained. Now we were always poor. My father made six dollars a week and supported a family on that. Many years later came the Depression, and my father couldn't find work—nor could my brothers. My father said, "It is up to you to do something." So I started peddling cartoons. I flew out of the nest, with my family on my back.

I would have liked to become a writer. Since I had to make a living, I turned to cartooning. Cartooning is a kind of writing. I worked for a magazine called *Life* and a magazine called *Judge.* I started selling my pieces in 1930. *The New Yorker* was founded in 1925, so I felt I had come five years late. I'm not the oldest contributor, but the lengthiest.

I got into children's book writing by accident. Robert Kraus, who was a colleague at *The New Yorker,* started a company, Windmill, and asked me to write a children's book. I actually even liked creating the color separations—the old method—because you have to imagine how the stuff is going to look. If you keep the color very simple, the results are usually good.

I like working on the longer books better, because the process is more like writing. *The Real Thief* is my favorite. I enjoyed writing *Dominic,* my first long book. I read my wife, Jeanne, a bit from the book every night, and she encouraged me to go on.

My books always evolve from a character. I decide who the chief character is, and once I have made him, say, a dentist, the story is on its way. I do as little drawing as possible in the beginning; I imagine the character. I draw when I create the dummy; then when I illustrate, I try to get the spontaneous quality of the drawing in the dummy.

My best drawing doesn't appear anywhere, although it does occasionally in books. My biggest pleasure is just drawing. Sometimes I'm referred to as a doodler. I was flattered by someone's comment that "Steig is a sublime doodler." With illustration you have to repeat the same characters again and again, make sure they don't change. My unconscious is more intelligent than my conscious. I often ask myself, "What would be an ideal life?" I think an ideal life would be just drawing.

The child is the hope of humanity. If they are going to change the world, they have to start off optimistically. I wouldn't consider writing a depressing book for children.

This article is based on an interview with William Steig conducted by Anita Silvey in September 1992.

Steig, William

American author and illustrator, b. 1907. William Steig has been deservedly praised for both his writing and his illustrating, receiving the Caldecott Medal for *Sylvester and the Magic Pebble* (1969), a Caldecott honor for *The Amazing Bone* (1976), and two Newbery honors for *Abel's Island* (1976) and *Doctor De Soto* (1982).

Steig grew up in the Bronx, where his father was a house painter and his mother a seamstress. He started painting at an early age. Among his influences, Steig credits the Grimms' fairy tales, Charlie Chaplin's movies, the Katzenjammer Kids, the opera *Hansel and Gretel,* and *Pinocchio.* He says, "If I'd had it my way, I'd have been a professional athlete, a sailor, a beachcomber, or some other form of hobo, a painter, a gardener, a novelist, a banjo-player, a traveler, anything but a rich man." During the Depression, when his father could not find work, it was up to young Steig to support his family, which he did quite successfully by selling cartoons to *The New Yorker* and other magazines. He has published several volumes of these drawings, which are often enigmatic, thought-provoking doodles. Steig attended City College in New York for two years, then spent four years at the National Academy of Design. In the 1940s he began carving in wood, and his sculptures are in several museum collections. He came to children's books late, when he was sixty, at the suggestion of ROBERT KRAUS, a *New Yorker* colleague, and found immediate success. Since then he has written and illustrated more than twenty books and provided illustrations for eight more. He married his fourth wife in 1969 and has three children.

Describing his creative process, Steig says, "I usually start a picture book by selecting a main character—donkey, mouse, or perhaps human. Then I decide what his or her occupation is and take it from there. I make a very rough dummy and afterward try to get the spontaneous quality of the rough drawings. . . . I like drawing, but not illustrating, because basically I'm a doodler. My best work is spontaneous and unconscious, as someone once pointed out, calling me a 'sublime doodler'—the best compliment I ever had." Once an idea is accepted by his editor, Steig works quickly, taking about a week to write the text and a month to illustrate.

Steig's illustrations are instantly recognizable, as he uses a consistent style involving a fairly thick sketchy black line with watercolor added loosely, often including stripes, polka dots, and flowered patterns in his characters' clothing and in the backgrounds. His prose has a forthright style, and he uses precise, often surprising language, which some adults fear is too challenging but which children love. He is serious about his characters and their situations. This is real life, even if it involves a mouse dentist or a donkey with a magic pebble, and the humor comes from the believable situations and characteristics the reader recognizes from his or her own experiences. In even his most fantastical stories, the problems his characters face are universal and their solutions are never didactic. Steig says, "I feel this way: I have a position—a point of view. But I don't have to think about it to express it. I can write about anything and my point of view will come out. So when I am at work my conscious intention is to tell a story to the reader. All this other stuff takes place automatically."

Steig's books provide serious situations factually illustrated with familiar settings and characters with intensely real emotions. His humor, alternately silly and poignant, and his integrity regarding his characters and his readers should ensure his popularity for many years. ❧ L.R.

STEPTOE, JOHN

AMERICAN ILLUSTRATOR AND AUTHOR, 1950–1989. The publication of Steptoe's first book, *Stevie* (1969), commanded notice by the children's book world, first, because its creator was only nineteen and, second, because it depicted a black city child's experiences in simple, bulky illustrations and black dialogue, both unprecedented at that time. The title received instant recognition as a Notable Book from the American Library Association, the Gold Medal from the Society of Illustrators, the Lewis Carroll Shelf Award, and other honors. Clearly, Steptoe not only achieved his desire to provide a book that black children would relate to, but reached children of all races.

Growing up in the Bedford-Stuyvesant section of Brooklyn, Steptoe was out of step with peer activities because he preferred to stay home to paint and draw. At sixteen he attended New York's High School of Art and Design but quit three weeks before finishing his senior year. Before that abrupt departure, a program at the Vermont Academy for minority artists provided the opportunity for Steptoe to apply his creative talent; three years later his first book was published.

Following *Stevie* came two more picture books expressing the experience of black inner-city children, *Uptown* (1970) and *Train Ride* (1971), which formed the trilogy that established Steptoe's career and reputation. The births of his son and daughter were the next influences on his work. In *My Special Best Words* (1974) and *Daddy Is a Monster . . . Sometimes* (1980) were voiced the strong relationship between father and child. The foreboding, compact illustrations in *Stevie* were replaced with prismatic paintings in airier hues.

Published at an early age, Steptoe also died at an early age—thirty-nine. During his twenty years in children's book publishing, he wrote and illustrated eleven books and illustrated six books written by other authors. In the last phase of his work, he experimented with his style, reaching for new dimensions. For *The Story of Jumping Mouse: A Native American Legend* (1984), he used black-and-white pencil drawings to convey both the sensitivity and strength of light and dark. In *Mufaro's*

Beautiful Daughters: An African Tale (1987), he added vivid coloration to his skillful patterns of light and dark, creating beautiful landscapes and beautiful people. Both books earned him Caldecott Honors, and *Mufaro* won a Boston Globe–Horn Book Honor Award.

The range of Steptoe's work embodies the growth of an illustrator: from densely formed shapes to delicately lined faces, from condensed composition to delicate, free-flowing lines. Throughout his books, Steptoe left readers with a specific image, message, and sensitivity, and a universal theme of self-pride in cultural heritage speaks loudly. Steptoe's interest in ethnic folk stories in his last years reinforced his belief in self-discovery through cultural esteem. In his acceptance speech for the Coretta Scott King Award for *Mother Crocodile* (1982), which he illustrated, he stated: "I'm gratified sometimes by the positive social effect my work may have had. But an effect comes after the aesthetic statement." His work has poignantly achieved both. J.C.

Sterling, Dorothy

AMERICAN AUTHOR, B. 1913. At the outset of her career as a juvenile author, Dorothy Sterling wrote books of three different kinds that were both very good and very popular. There were crisp and enthusiastic nature studies for early exploration like *Insects and the Homes They Build* (1954), *Creatures of the Night* (1960), and *Caterpillars* (1961); lively stories of neighborhood sleuthing—*The Cub Scout Mystery* (1952) and *The Brownie Scout Mystery* (1955)—that also immerse the reader in 1950s Scouting customs and speech ways; and, beginning with *Freedom Train: The Story of Harriet Tubman* (1954), notable books about African American history and life that made Sterling's name.

The books were to an unusual extent a fulfillment. As a child in Central Park and at summer camps in Maine, Sterling "preferred bugs to baseball" and sought in vain for answers to her questions. Graduating from college during the Depression, she was glad to find work eventually with the Federal Writers Project, where she got to know people less protected from adversity than she, marched on picket lines to save the arts projects ("The Movement of our day"), and met her husband, Philip Sterling, who would also later write juveniles of natural history and African American interest. Twelve years at Time Inc. taught her how to collect, assemble, and verify information and present it in readable form, skills she herself cites as significant. When she was ready to begin writing on her own, the Sterlings were living in the suburbs, where their two children brought home assorted wildlife specimens and belonged to the Scouts, and Sterling herself took an active role in local civil rights organizations.

Harriet Tubman was hardly an unsung hero when Sterling wrote about her in *Freedom Train*. But other juvenile treatments, whether fiction or nonfiction, concentrate on Tubman's role in spiriting away slaves to the neglect of her Civil War service as a nurse, community organizer, and Union Army spy. Along the way, in Sterling's sturdy full-length account, the legend became a leader of her people, only to be hurled into a baggage car en route home from Washington.

The year of *Freedom Train*, 1954, was the year the Supreme Court outlawed school segregation. In 1955 Sterling traveled through the South interviewing black children entering the first desegregated schools, as reported in an adult book, *Tender Warriors* (1958), and recaptured for all time in *Mary Jane* (1959). Carefully dressed and groomed to resemble "them," twelve-year-old Mary Jane and fellow pioneer Fred pass through a gauntlet of screams and insults to enter Wilson Junior High; on the premises they endure petty harassment, open hostility, and constant gawking from schoolmates and stereotypical reactions from teachers. Mary Jane's old friends cut her out, and her reliable, sympathetic parents can only suggest that she backtrack. Despite crushing loneliness and the difficulties of building a new friendship with a white classmate, Mary Jane is not about to give up. Direct and undoctrinaire, the book is still moving, decades after the historic events.

In 1955 came the Montgomery, Alabama, bus boycott, the start of the civil rights movement; in 1968 Martin Luther King, Jr., was assassinated and the civil rights movement was more or less over, transformed into a new impetus toward black nationalism.

Four Sterling books, two biographies and two histories, span the period of renewal and revolution. *Captain of the Planter: The Story of Robert Smalls* (1958) brought to notice the Charleston pilot who stole a steamboat (with his family and other black women and children aboard) from under the guns of Fort Sumter and later served in the House of Representatives, a fighter to the bitter, post-Reconstruction end. By contrast, *The Making of an Afro-American: Martin Robison Delany, 1812–1885* (1971) deals with a man hailed in the 1960s as "the father of black nationalism" for his pride in black endowments and ancestry but subsequently tarnished by attention to his lifelong elitism and post–Civil War collusion with Southern planters. Sterling, if not incisive, lays out the evasions and contradictions in a challenging biography for older teens.

The two books of African American history, *Forever Free: The Story of the Emancipation Proclamation* (1963) and *Tear Down the Walls! A History of the American Civil Rights Movement* (1968), were both important in their time and neither is obsolete today, in part because neither is what its title implies. *Forever Free* is an account of the black struggle for freedom from the first expropriation of a master's chicken through outbreaks of rebellion, the abolitionist movement, and outright flight to military enlistment and presidential emancipation. *Tear Down the Walls,* in turn, recounts another, longer black struggle—for education, voter registration, use of public facilities, personal safety—both before the 1954 landmark decision and after, in the modern civil rights movement.

What most distinguishes Sterling's work in the area and what makes her books still recommendable is a combination of two factors: Her African Americans think and act for themselves; they are not supinely or resentfully acted upon, nor are they preoccupied with white reactions. She never fails to note, moreover, what remains undone and indefensible, from Harriet Tubman's mistreatment by a train conductor to the walls that have not yet come down.

With some fine feminist- *and* black-oriented work to her credit, too, including *Lucretia Mott* (1964), a biography of the abolitionist leader, and a collective portrait of Ellen Craft, Ida B. Wells, and Mary Church Terrell, entitled *Black Foremothers* (1979), Sterling's strong skills are put to high purpose. B.B.

Stevenson, James

American author and illustrator, b. 1929. While spending half his time contributing cartoons and features to *The New Yorker,* the prolific James Stevenson creates as many as five children's books each year, most of which he both writes and illustrates himself. With a devoted following for each of his careers and a long list of highly acclaimed and widely read books to his credit,

Voices of the Creators

James Stevenson

A big influence on my life was my elementary school—Hessian Hills in Croton-on-Hudson, New York—a wonderful place that was alert to the social and political issues of the day. I remember writing letters to Roosevelt when I was seven, asking him to lift the arms embargo on Spain. I did political cartoons about Hitler and Mussolini and Chamberlain later on. In one of the school plays, I was a banker foreclosing mortgages on farmers in the dust bowl. The school taught everybody that they could do everything: sing, dance, act, play musical instruments, write stories, make pictures—and change the world.

I worked one summer before college as an office boy at *The New Yorker.* I learned that cartoon ideas were bought from outsiders, so I began to sell them. I was a full-time employee at *Life* when I got an offer from the art editor of *The New Yorker* to think up cartoons full time. I was elated. They paid me to sit at a desk and do ideas that the regular cartoonists could draw. I wasn't allowed to tell people what I was doing. The cartoonists liked the readers to think the ideas were their own, I guess, or the editors thought that might be the case. It was a good job, but when people asked me what I did at *The New Yorker,* I had to say, "I don't know." I assumed they figured that I was unemployed.

Cartoon ideas and children's books are not really that similar. A cartoon is a formalization of a certain situation; it might be political or reflect the news. The challenge is to take an issue and reduce it to simple form. A children's book, on the other hand, is like making a movie. I often use the comic strip form because it's cinematic. You get to write the story, produce it, direct it, cast it, choose the costumes, and direct the cinematography. You're not waiting for any set-up or lights. You don't have to deal with weather changes or personalities. You can create the entire thing.

My editor, Susan Hirschman, has a superb sense of what is necessary and what is not. We've never disagreed. Susan's ideas come as fresh, welcome surprises. You need to trigger a story with something specific. If the idea is too universal, then you have nothing.

Most people have a limited number of stories to tell—maybe only one story—and we keep telling it in different ways. A theme of mine might be reassurance, telling children that things are not so bad and that they are going to be all right. I have tried to reassure my own children. Now they reassure me.

Illustration by James Stevenson from *Grandaddy and Janetta* (1993), by Helen V. Griffith.

Stevenson ranks among today's top picture-book producers in both popularity and excellence.

Born in New York City, Stevenson graduated from Yale University in 1951 and spent several years in the U.S. Marines, followed by two years as a reporter for *Life* magazine. He joined the *New Yorker*'s art department in 1955, creating cartoon ideas for other artists, until writing aspirations drove him to begin reporting in addition to his artistic duties. By the time his first children's book, *If I Owned a Candy Factory,* was released in 1968, he had already published three novels and a book of his own cartoons.

Stevenson is best known for his highly appealing PICTURE BOOKS, which combine fast-moving stories with gentle humor and a keen interpretation of childhood. His illustrations, usually rendered in a cartoon-like style and often making use of the traditional frame sequences and dialogue bubbles, frequently give the impression of being breezy and effortless; however, through his careful use of line Stevenson provides his characters with a remarkable depth of emotion. Aside from many individual books centering on child-related themes such as fear, boredom, family issues, and holidays, Stevenson has developed several long-running series of popular books featuring a wide assortment of winsome characters. The best known of these series, launched with *Could Be Worse!* (1977) and continuing with *What's Under My Bed?* (1983), *Worse Than Willy* (1984), and more than ten additional titles, focuses on the imaginative and hilarious Grandpa, whose stories of youthful escapades with his brother Wainwright make for breathtaking, laugh-aloud reading. Stevenson's witty drawings, including the famous mustache apparently affixed to Uncle Wainey since his birth, double the appeal created by the books' already enjoyable texts. Other favorite series' characters include Emma, the benevolent little witch who, from her debut in *Emma* (1985), has proven that she can easily foil her two less kindly witch colleagues in their hilarious attempts to outwit her; and The Worst, the crusty star of *The Worst Person in the World* (1978) and *The Worst Person's Christmas* (1991), a miserable grouch who somehow cannot escape his yearning for human interaction.

In a departure from his traditional style, Stevenson has also created a set of critically acclaimed autobiographical picture books, each featuring an episode from his youth. In addition to their subject matter, the books, including *When I Was Nine* (1986), *Higher on the Door* (1987), *July* (1990), and *Don't You Know There's a War On?* (1992), are distinguished from Stevenson's other work by their artistic style. Unlike his traditional watercolor washes enclosed by black line, here the artist uses only watercolors, creating a soft, blurred visual effect designed to emulate the hazy recollection of past events. This style, which Stevenson calls minimalist art, is designed to encourage readers to supply their own images from memory or imagination. In addition to his own writings, Stevenson has also illustrated books by such well-known authors as JACK PRELUTSKY and CHARLOTTE ZOLOTOW and has received several important awards, including the 1987 Christopher Award.

Stevenson has become a favorite with children everywhere because he can make them laugh, but his true gift lies beyond the humor. Whether the subject is a rainy day, a nightmare, or the terrible realities of war, Stevenson imbues it with a powerful understanding of children, of what is important and meaningful to them, and of how to fill even the most difficult situation with warmth, comfort, and joy. C.C.B.

STEVENSON, ROBERT LOUIS

BRITISH AUTHOR, 1850–1894. Known primarily for his swashbuckling adventure stories such as *Treasure Island* (1883) and *Kidnapped* (1886), it is the romance of Robert

Louis Stevenson's life as much as the novels he wrote that has captured the imaginations of generations of readers. From a sickly, bedridden child, confined to the nursery much of the time, Stevenson grew up to travel the world and live out the adventures he had dreamed of as a child. He never outgrew his ill health, but he refused to let it stop him from venturing forth from the cold, bleak climate of Scotland to savor the air of the gold mines of California and the beaches of the South Seas.

Stevenson's father was a religious and strong-minded man who was determined that his son would follow the family tradition of designing and building lighthouses. While certain aspects of the job appealed to the young Stevenson, primarily visits to isolated islands and promontories and the "hanging about at harboursides, which is the richest form of idling," writing was the only craft that ever truly appealed to him. After making a final stab at respectable employment as a barrister, Stevenson settled down to the life that pleased him most—rubbing shoulders with people from all walks of life, traveling, and writing about everything he saw and said and did.

Stevenson had made a name for himself as an essayist, poet, and travel writer when he began his first novel, *Treasure Island.* Like many other CLASSICS of children's literature, this book grew out of an attempt to entertain a particular child—in this case, the author's stepson—and ended up capturing the imagination of not only its boyish author but children the world over. Inspired by a detailed map of an island that Stevenson and his stepson drew one rainy day, with hidden treasure and cryptic instructions reverently included, the author and his stepson vowed that any book about such a place must be "a story for boys, no need of psychology or fine writing . . . [and] Women were to be excluded." Viewed as one of the highest examples of its genre—the boys' story—*Treasure Island* is best enjoyed as its author intended, simply as a good tale well told. The strengths of *Treasure Island* are Stevenson's strengths as a writer in general: vivid descriptions of place—the malarial Treasure Island itself looms as large and palpable a physical presence as any human character—pell-mell pacing, plot construction that is almost architectural in its blending of necessity and art, and lively, fully realized characters. In Long John Silver, in particular, the arch-villain of the piece, Stevenson created a personality that jumps off the page for the reader and lingers long in the mind.

Illustration by Henriette Willebeek Le Mair for "The Land of Counterpane" from *A Child's Garden of Verses* (1926), by Robert Louis Stevenson.

Treasure Island, Kidnapped, The Black Arrow (1888), a romantic account of the War of the Roses, and *A Child's Garden of Verses* (1885), a collection of poems about childhood from a child's point of view, stand to this day as brilliantly evoked slices of the imaginative life of Victorian childhood and have become part of the imaginative heritage of our culture. S.G.K.

STEWART, MARY

ENGLISH AUTHOR, B. 1916. Best known for her adult novels of romance and suspense, Mary Stewart has also written works of FANTASY for children. The author was born in Sunderland, Durham, England, and graduated from the University of Durham, where she taught for several years. Stewart did not begin writing fiction until she was in her mid-thirties. *Madam, Will You Talk?* (1955) was followed by several successful novels, including *The Moon-Spinners* (1962), which was made into a DISNEY film, and a popular trilogy about Arthurian England: *The Crystal Cave* (1970), *The Hollow Hills* (1973), and *The Last Enchantment* (1979).

Stewart entered the field of children's books with *The Little Broomstick* (1971), a gently amusing fantasy about a girl who is suddenly transported to a school for witches. Stewart's subsequent fantasies have a more European flavor. *A Walk in Wolf Wood* (1980) concerns two English children visiting the Black Forest who time-travel to a medieval era and meet a werewolf. In the inventive *Ludo and the Star Horse* (1974), a Bavarian boy journeys through the houses of the Zodiac with his horse.

Like many authors who write primarily for adults, Stewart tends to use a condescending, occasionally sentimental style in her children's books, often interrupting her stories to include first-person commentary—most distractingly in *Ludo and the Star Horse*, in which remarks and asides are consistently directed at a particular reader named Amélie. Nevertheless, Stewart's novels are comfortable and appealing to younger fantasy readers; even during the occasionally frightening scenes, a happy ending always seems assured. ❧ P.D.S.

Stockton, Frank R.

AMERICAN AUTHOR, 1834–1902. Although hugely popular during the late nineteenth century, most of Frank R. Stockton's works had faded into obscurity until MAURICE SENDAK helped revive the author's reputation with newly illustrated editions of two Stockton stories during the 1960s.

Born in Blockley, Pennsylvania, Stockton wrote fiction throughout his early years. After high school he became a wood engraver, but continued writing and eventually published his first book, *Ting-a-Ling* (1870), a collection of literary fairy tales. Stockton then worked as an editor at several magazines, including *Hearth and Home, Scribner's Monthly,* and *St. Nicholas,* where he served as assistant editor to MARY MAPES DODGE. His writing career flourished with short-story collections, novels, and works of history for young readers, as well as both fiction and nonfiction for adults. His most enduring adult story, "The Lady or the Tiger?" (1882), is notable for its open-ended conclusion; it has been widely anthologized and was included in the 1966 Broadway musical *The Apple Tree*.

The 1960s also saw a reissue of Stockton's 1898 book of true sea stories for children, *Buccaneers and Pirates of Our Coasts* (1960), and, most notably, the Sendak editions of two Stockton stories. *The Griffin and the Minor Canon* (1963) tells of a griffin who visits a town to see a sculpture, develops a fondness for a cleric, and becomes involved in the lives of the townspeople. *The Bee-Man of Orn* (1964) concerns an elderly man who sets out to discover his true origins. Highlighted by Sendak's memorable color illustrations, these spirited, satirical tales are perfect for reading aloud and may lead modern readers to seek out other works by this highly imaginative author. ❧ P.D.S.

Stolz, Mary

AMERICAN AUTHOR, B. 1920. Mary Stolz first won acclaim as a gifted writer of young adult novels but later achieved equal success with her middle-grade books and animal fantasies. The Boston-born author was raised in New York and attended the progressive Birch Wathen School, where her interests in reading and writing were encouraged. Later she was a student at Columbia University. Stolz always wanted to be a writer, but after leaving school, she sold books at Macy's, did secretarial work, married, and gave birth to a son. In the late 1940s, Stolz became ill for several months. Her physician suggested that she pursue an interest while recovering, so she began writing. The physician became her second husband; the manuscript, *To Tell Your Love,* published in 1950. Stolz based the story on her own teenage years, and the resulting novel was praised as a sensitive depiction of first love. It was the first of many young adult books that the prolific author would write.

Stolz's young adult novels are mature, thought-provoking, and sensitive. Romance always plays a key role, usually as a catalyst for growth and change in the protagonist. The novels reflect their era and contain some sex-role stereotyping, but since the real focus is on the heroine's personal growth as a human being, there is also a modern sensibility that seems not at all dated. In light of the realism that young adult novels later achieved, Stolz's romances may now be considered cautious and chaste, but they cannot be described as immature. The typical Stolz protagonist is unusually intelligent and analytical; her conversations and opinions evoke the image of a thoughtful, eloquent college student rather than a fourteen- or fifteen-year-old girl. There is also realism in the unflinching way Stolz presents her characters. One of her best books, *Because of Madeline* (1957), concerns a lower-class nonconformist who affects the lives of everyone she meets when she begins attending private school. Madeline is not particularly sympathetic, and many of the upper-class characters she encounters are presented as well intentioned but shallow. The characterizations are extremely perceptive in this stimulating novel about class and conformity.

Stolz credits Ursula Nordstrom, the legendary Harper's editor, with providing writing guidance throughout much of her career, but Stolz herself can be credited with writing some of the most sophisticated young adult books of the fifties, which paved the way for the "new realism" that arrived in the 1960s. During that new decade, Stolz continued to write the occasional young adult novel, but switched her main focus to early-reader and middle-grade books. Her "Barkham Street" stories, particularly *The Bully of Barkham Street* (1963), are extremely popular, and her love of nature is evident in several animal tales, including *Cat Walk* (1983). Her outstanding middle-grade novel *The Noonday Friends,* concerning underprivileged Franny's friendship with a Puerto Rican girl, was named a Newbery Honor Book in 1966. An earlier Newbery Honor title was *Belling the Tiger* (1961), an enjoyable, if somewhat bland, tale about two mice. Stolz has written many other award-worthy novels, including *The Edge of Next Year* (1964), a haunting, poetic study of a family's recovery after the mother's accidental death, and the splendid time-travel fantasy *Cat in the Mirror* (1975). Stolz's work is notable for its diversity and general excellence. P.D.S.

Stratemeyer Literary Syndicate

The Stratemeyer Literary Syndicate, founded by Edward Stratemeyer (1862–1930), is a writing organization responsible for the development of over sixty-five juvenile series. The syndicate is credited with having produced more than 1,300 books with sales estimated at over 200 million copies.

In 1889 Stratemeyer wrote his first story on sheets of wrapping paper from his father's drugstore. During the next few years, he continued to write juvenile serialized stories, became editor of three children's magazines, and was the ghostwriter for Horatio Alger after Alger's death. With the outbreak of the Spanish-American War in 1898, Stratemeyer realized the importance of the link between historical events and market trends, which could be exploited to create juvenile series and sell books. The "Old Glory" and "Soldiers of Fortune" series were quickly developed, as were books featuring boys in the American Revolution, the French and Indian War, and the Mexican War. Realizing that the attraction of contemporary war stories was likely to be temporary, Stratemeyer created another series—the "Rover Boys," under the pseudonym Arthur M. Winfield in 1899—which depicted youthful adventures, games, and hijinks and featured elements of melodrama and detective fiction. The series was an immediate success and continued to be published until 1926. The popularity of the "Rover Boys" encouraged Stratemeyer to design similar series, each of which he wrote with a different pseudonym.

When his ideas outstripped his writing capabilities, he began to hire freelance writers to develop his outlines into full-length books. By 1906 he had established the Stratemeyer Literary Syndicate, an organization that incorporated his marketing and writing ideas into a "literary assembly line." From this factory emerged such perennial favorites as Tom Swift (first introduced in 1910), the Hardy Boys (1927), and Nancy Drew (1930). New series were constantly being developed, from 1912 to 1931, and the syndicate had no fewer than twenty-five series in progress at any one time. Every type of series imaginable was offered, from fantasy and science fiction to school, career, and travel adventures. If one series failed, another would quickly replace it. Critics tended to compare Stratemeyer to Ford and Rockefeller, derisively calling him a master of mass production.

The official history of Stratemeyer criticism begins in 1914 with the publication of an article called "Blowing the Boy's Brains Out," written by Franklin Mathiews, the chief Scout librarian of the Boy Scouts of America. Mathiews suggested that the poor quality of syndicate-type fiction, its lack of moral purpose and uncontrolled excitement, could cripple a young reader's imagination: "The result is that [their] imaginations are literally 'blown out,' and they go into life, as though by some material explosion they had lost a hand or foot." A 1934 *Fortune* magazine article stated, "Tripe [the books] were in the beginning, tripe they are now, and tripe they will always be." In 1956 librarians in South Carolina, Kansas, and Mississippi took up the battle cry, calling Stratemeyer an "arch-fiend" and his books "devices of Satan." Even today, when most libraries allow "Nancy Drew" and the "Hardy Boys" series on their shelves, Stratemeyer and his syndicate are noticeably absent from many children's literature reference books.

Stratemeyer's death in 1930 marked the end of his syndicate's "golden age" and the beginning of its "maintenance and renovation" period. Control of the syndicate passed to Stratemeyer's daughters, Edna Squier and Harriet Stratemeyer Adams, and Adams continued to run the syndicate until her death in 1982. During this period, the syndicate dropped many series and created few new ones. By 1954 there were only six syndicate series in production. Early volumes in these series were updated—racist and sexist stereotypes were removed—and new volumes were added. In the 1980s, "Nancy Drew," "Tom Swift," the "Hardy Boys," and the "Bobbsey Twins" were rereleased to reflect contemporary concerns. In a changing world, the Stratemeyer Literary Syndicate has survived two world wars, the Great Depression, television and the electronic revolution, and numerous attacks by critics. The history of the series-book empire Stratemeyer created can be summed up best in one word—*success*. M.I.A.

Streatfeild, Noel

English author, 1897–1986. Noel Streatfeild drew on her personal experiences as the daughter of a country vicar and a professional actress to develop novels about professional children—the "Shoes" series—that give young readers an in-depth look at intriguing, unusual experiences. The genre is called the career novel, and

Streatfeild's first novel for children, *Ballet Shoes* (1936), was also the first British career novel.

After attending the Royal Academy of Dramatic Art and working for several years as an actress with a traveling repertory company in England, Streatfeild began her writing career. Initially, she published novels for adult readers, many under the pseudonym Susan Scarlett; then, at her publisher's suggestion, she wrote *Ballet Shoes.* The story concerns the discovery of the talents of three sisters, who must become professional performers in order to contribute to the household income. The reader is drawn into the story through sympathy for children who must earn a living and through the pleasure of learning about the details and rigors of professional training. The novel was an immediate success in England and the United States, and Streatfeild continued to write fiction and nonfiction for children, achieving critical and popular acclaim in both countries. *The Circus Is Coming* (1938), published in the United States as *Circus Shoes* (1939), won the 1938 Carnegie Medal in England and both *Ballet Shoes* and *Tennis Shoes* (1937) were runners-up for the Carnegie Medal.

Skating Shoes (1951) details the training involved in preparing for a life as a competitive figure skater. The reader follows Lalla, the daughter of a famous skater, who is being forced into skating by her aunt. The story is told through Lalla's companion, Harriet, who has natural talent but lacks the resources to devote her childhood to training as a skater. Each of Streatfeild's career novels includes a character with no special talent or inclination toward a professional lifestyle. These characters allow the reader, who is presumably just such a normal child, an entrance into the story. Mark Forbes fills this role in *Theatre Shoes* (1945). His two sisters are talented and enjoy the chance to attend theater school in London. Mark, forced to attend the same theater school, longs for his boarding school and hopes to join the navy.

Each of these career novels includes realistic details about training and performing. Characters must memorize dance steps, prepare for auditions, and suffer the indignity of being turned down for a coveted role. Streatfeild successfully turns these collections of details into unified novels about children who overcome adversity and become strong individuals. Streatfeild's novels are family stories as well as professional stories. Many of her characters are orphans, but they create strong family ties with the children and adults with whom they live. The orphaned Fossil sisters in *Ballet Shoes,* for example, depend upon their adopted sisters for support and give each other tremendous love and encouragement. Margaret Thursday, the indomitable orphan in *Thursday's Child* (1970), gets strength from the mother she does not remember and defines herself as an individual because her "family" sets her apart from her peers. Streatfeild wrote popular radio stories about the Bell family and their life in a vicarage. These stories became the novel *Family Shoes* (1954).

Streatfeild's novels are not all equally successful, as her later books follow formulas that she developed in early stories, but she continues to be read by children intrigued by the inner workings of the professional training of children. M.V.K.

Survival Stories

When children or adolescents are first introduced to literature, they are taught that conflict makes a story work. One such conflict is "man versus nature," which often shows up as the theme of survival stories. From the early days of literature with *Robinson Crusoe* (1719) by Daniel Defoe to JACK LONDON's novels and stories, especially "To Build a Fire," the survival genre has been read, studied, and enjoyed by children and young adults over centuries. Unlike other genres, there is a timelessness to survival tales because of the basic conflict. They are also normally easy to read—the very nature of the tale means there will be few characters, lots of action and adventure, and the question: "Will this person survive?" Teens might also enjoy survival tales for deeper, more emotional reasons. Survival tales can be seen as a metaphor for adolescence itself: an endless series of obstacles for which they are often unprepared and which leaves the teen, and many a parent, asking: "Will I survive?"

Although there are some survival stories with a female protagonist such as the Newbery Award winner *Julie of the Wolves* (1972) by JEAN CRAIGHEAD GEORGE, most survival tales involve young men in danger. Reading interest surveys show that survival and adventure fiction is the most popular genre for teenage boy readers. A classical survival novel, Robb White's *Deathwatch* (1972), tells of a young man stalked in the wilderness by a crazed hunter. Although published as an adult title, *Deathwatch* has become a young adult staple and has been reprinted over twenty-five times. Arthur Roth has written several survival novels, *The Iceberg Hermit* (1975) being his best. This work of historical fiction with a 1757 setting tells the story of a shipwreck survivor in the frozen north. *Snowbound* by Harry Mazer (1973) traps two unlikable characters in a car during a snowstorm. Mazer also wrote a Robinson Crusoe variation, *The Island Keeper* (1981), and a war story, *The Last Mission* (1979), with survival elements.

The island survival theme is explored in THEODORE

TAYLOR's award-winning *The Cay* (1969), which tells of a young boy and an older black man stranded together. BROCK COLE's *The Goats* (1987) is a brilliant novel about two social misfits left on an island as part of a nasty prank. GARY PAULSEN in *Hatchet* (1986) strands his youthful protagonist in the Canadian north woods to fend for himself. *Hatchet* was an immediate sensation, earning rave reviews, winning a Newbery Honor Award, and inspiring a sequel, *The River* (1991). P. J. Petersen has also written several books in this genre; *Going for the Big One* (1986) has the best elements: teenage campers not only face nature's fury but also a "bad guy" drug dealer. Although many of these books are similar with their stock settings of islands, mountains, and wilderness, there are enough differences in characters and challenges to make each one interesting.

Some authors have attempted to expand the genre even further. *Slake's Limbo* (1974) by FELICE HOLMAN tells the tale of urban survival, as a thirteen-year-old boy makes a home for himself inside the New York City subway tunnels. Julian Thompson's *The Grounding of Group Six* (1983) presents radical new ways of telling a story, as Thompson's slam-bang, one-liner style is a far cry from the straight narrative of most survival tales. Finally, Art Spiegelman's *Maus* (1986) and *Maus II* (1991) examine Holocaust survival using comic-book storytelling. These acclaimed graphic novels demonstrate that while survival stories may be old and the theme basic to literature, enough new ways still exist to tell the tale.

Nonfiction survival books like Piers Paul Read's *Alive* (1974) and Stephen Callahan's *Adrift* (1986) have proven popular, especially with older teenage readers. Part of the appeal, especially in a book like *Alive*, is the lurid elements and tactics people will take to survive. The survival theme doesn't just supply action, but also psychological insight. The theme is the undercurrent of horror and thriller fiction also popular with teens. Finally, most good young adult fiction is really a survival tale, not teens surviving against the elements so much as surviving through the changes and pain of growing up. ❦ P.J.

SUTCLIFF, ROSEMARY

BRITISH AUTHOR OF HISTORICAL FICTION, 1920–1992. Rosemary Sutcliff's fiction brings history to life. A prolific writer, Sutcliff immersed herself in the facts and details of historical periods and emerged with stories that carry readers into the past and bring them back to the present with a broader view of the world and of human nature. Her work spans the ages from the myths and legends of Beowulf, Tristan and Iseult, King Arthur, and Finn MacCool through Roman Britain to the seventeenth century. In her novels based on folklore, Sutcliff fleshes out the legendary characters, weaving a whole out of the threads of story but preserving, at the same time, the sense of the mysterious and the magical. No other author rivals Sutcliff's achievement in terms of breadth within a single genre and consistency of quality.

Afflicted with juvenile arthritis, called Still's disease, ever since she could remember, Sutcliff spent a great part of her childhood undergoing operations and treatment for the crippling condition. Filled with battles and voyages, intrigue and swashbuckling adventure, Sutcliff's novels also display an uncommonly perceptive depiction of individuals from all ages of time who exist on the fringe of their society or who feel alienated. *The Witch's Brat* (1970), for which Sutcliff received a Lewis Carroll Shelf Award, features a character with a physical handicap, but sometimes the scarring is emotional, as in *The Lantern Bearers* (1959), winner of the 1959 Carnegie Medal, in which Aquila, a young man in a Roman family, survives a murderous attack on his father's home, years as a slave to his captors, and grave disappointments and disillusionment.

Although some of her characters have cause for bitterness, Sutcliff ultimately affirms humanity in her work; no matter how bleak the situation, how impossible the odds, always some character breathes hope and life. In *Blue Remembered Hills* (1983), Sutcliff recollects her youth, her family, and her first years as a writer with the same matter-of-fact dignity found in her fiction. No great student, she left school at age fourteen and began art school, which she attended for three years. Because of her disability, her parents believed miniature portraiture would be her most successful work. She felt constricted by this genre, however, and secretly took to writing because it allowed her to express herself in full.

Indeed, Sutcliff's work never bends to accommodate the reader; instead, her facility with the written word and her mature, sometimes dense prose challenge readers even as the action-filled plots draw them in. Sutcliff's enthusiastic representations of numerous eras of British history are the finest historical novels for children of their time. ❦ A.E.D.

T

TAFURI, NANCY

AMERICAN ILLUSTRATOR, B. 1946. When Nancy Tafuri started illustrating picture books, she provided the very youngest readers with a new, imaginative world of visual playfulness. Tafuri's 1984 Caldecott Honor Book, *Have You Seen My Duckling?* is representative of her distinctive, artistic style. A master of visual storytelling, Tafuri creates illustrations in bright, flat colors that feature large, clearly limned characters set against accurate, intricately detailed backgrounds. Each picture, many of them double-page spreads, is the result of precise, often playful, placement of shapes on a page. Tafuri's books often feature simple hide-and-seek games, puzzles, and even visual jokes, which are scaled to the level of the picture-book audience. The artist's visual ingenuity piques a child's interest, stimulates imagination, and encourages observation and discussion.

Illustration by Nancy Tafuri from her book *Have You Seen My Duckling?* (1984).

Tafuri studied illustration at the School of Visual Arts in New York City. While developing her portfolio, she and her husband opened a studio and began doing jacket illustrations for hardcover books. In 1981, Tafuri illustrated her first book, *The Piney Woods Peddler,* written by GEORGE SHANNON. The text, a repetitive, cheerful rhyme, uses elements of traditional American swapping songs. The pictures are large and humorous, and their exaggerated style gives the book a folktale quality. Tafuri then illustrated *The Song* (1981), written by CHARLOTTE ZOLOTOW, and *If I Had a Paka* (1981), by Charlotte Pomerantz, a book of poems that incorporates words and phrases from eleven languages. In 1983, Tafuri wrote and illustrated two books of her own; they were acclaimed critically for their imagination and child-appeal. *All Year Long* is an artfully simple, artistically logical concept book explaining cycles—days of the week and months of the year; and *Early Morning in the Barn* (1983) follows three inquisitive baby chicks as they make their way around the farm greeting other animals. Small children enjoy pointing to the easily recognizable barnyard friends and imitating the *moos, oinks, cheeps,* and *quacks* that constitute the book's text. The clever format used in *Spots, Feathers, and Curly Tails* (1988) is a favorite with preschoolers. A question and a clue is on one page: "What has spots?" The answer is found on the next: "A cow has spots."

Tafuri spends much time working the sense into the pictures, as she feels too much print confuses younger readers. *The Ball Bounced* (1989) provides an imaginative example of the care she takes balancing the narrative and artwork. In only thirty-three words, Tafuri creates a beguiling tale about a small boy whose random toss of a ball sends it on an adventure. Each page discloses the next tumble of the brilliant red, white, and blue ball. Young readers, who enjoy predictability, return repeatedly to this charming book.

Tafuri has illustrated a number of books written by other authors. *All Asleep* (1984), by Charlotte Pomerantz, is a soothing combination of rhymes and pictures and a guaranteed soporific. Tafuri's stylized illustrations in Patricia Lillie's *Everything Has a Place* (1993) are equally as assuring to toddlers, who are just learning to bring order into a bewildering world. S.L.

Voices of the Creators

Nancy Tafuri

Until the age of ten, I was an only child, and I had a lot of time to myself. My mother read to me and encouraged my drawing. She thought I would make a great interior decorator, but the more I thought about it, the more I realized that decorating really wasn't the profession for me. Then in the late 1960s, I enrolled in the School of Visual Arts in New York City and majored in children's book illustration. At school I met my future husband, Tom, who was studying graphic and jacket design.

After graduation I worked in the adult trade department of Simon and Schuster as an associate art director. Several years later Tom and I opened up our own studio, One Plus One, and started doing jackets for hardcover books. During the first ten years, while we worked to make the studio a success, I continued to create drawings for my children's book portfolio. My artistic vision drew me to large shapes. I always felt that, for very young children, large shapes would be an attractive form of art. At first, publishers felt my images were too graphic, and I got a lot of rejections. But in 1980 Ava Weiss and Susan Hirschman of Greenwillow gave me a book to illustrate, *The Piney Woods Peddler* by George Shannon, and I have been working with them on projects ever since.

Twenty-four or thirty-two pages may seem like a small number, but when you are putting a book together, they can seem endless. At some point, however, you can create all the final details—fixing the paws and putting the whiskers in. At that point, working on a book is real pleasure. Putting it together—the what-am-I-going-to-do-with-the-last-four-pages stage—is hard work!

I also work a great deal on getting all the facts correct in illustrations. Each animal or rock formation should be correct. Even though my books aren't nonfiction, they must be accurate. I research all my animals and plants, and I then reduce them to their basic, fundamental shapes. I often use four-by-five snapshots as reference for my drawings.

When I start a book, I only have a rough idea about what I want to create. So when I start illustrating, I rely a lot on tissues. I draw out the format of the page and then keep putting pieces of tissue over the drawing, until I get the final effect that I want. Basically, I work on one double-page spread at a time.

When I'm designing a book, I usually make a dummy first. I cut up the text, if there is to be any, and draw around it. I enjoy working with type in combination with my illustrations. I find working images around type a challenge. I also enjoy the way the printed letter form complements the colorful images.

In 1989 our daughter Cristina was born, and since then my books have taken on a different feel. Now I have a model to work into my drawings—and a very patient one. I do find that I need to plan ahead more and put some things on hold. But when I place myself at the drawing table, I'm a different person than I was before. I feel that what I'm doing is more important; what I'm trying to say means more. My life has more depth, more responsibility, more meaning.

I feel honored to be creating literature for young children. Working on children's books, whether totally my own or another author's, is one of my life's joys. I love to be able to take short lines of text, or little or no text, and turn that into a package that can be held by small hands.

Being involved in children's literature has been a special part of my life. I encourage anyone who feels they might want to create children's books to enter the world of books for the young. My books have made me grow and become aware of the natural world around me; in turn, I hope I can help young children do the same.

Tarkington, Booth

AMERICAN NOVELIST, SHORT-STORY WRITER, AND PLAYWRIGHT, 1869–1946. Booth Tarkington's portraits of small-town, Middle American life won him a huge following during the early and central decades of this century. Brought up in Indianapolis, a "quiet, lovely town," as he once recalled it, he considered himself a resident of the city for most of his long life. He was, however, educated at Exeter Academy in New Hampshire and at Purdue and Princeton universities. As an adult he lived for periods in New York, Paris, Rome, and the island of Capri and in his later life resided virtually year-round in Kennebunkport, Maine.

After an early career as an illustrator failed (his lone success was one drawing sold to *Life* magazine) and his first three novels attracted little attention, he was elected to the Indianapolis legislature in 1902, where he spent one term. His writing fortunes turned around soon thereafter, and his prodigious outpouring of novels, stories, and plays established him as one of the most successful and popular American writers of his era. He was twice awarded the Pulitzer Prize: in 1919 for *The Magnificent Ambersons* and 1922 for *Alice Adams*.

Children's book publishing was in its infancy during Tarkington's heyday and books marketed specifically for young adults were still far in the future, but the author merits attention as a writer for children for two of his most popular works: *Seventeen* (1916) and the Penrod stories, which were published in three separate volumes, *Penrod* (1914), *Penrod and Sam* (1916), and *Penrod Jashber* (1929), and then in a collected volume, *Penrod: His Complete Story* (1931).

Seventeen follows the trials of a lovesick adolescent, William Sylvanus Baxter, and his passion for Lola Pratt, a beauty who devotes herself to lavishing excruciatingly coy baby talk on her dog, Flopit, and to stringing along her many admirers. The Penrod stories recount the small-town adventures of a high-spirited twelve-year-old, Penrod Schofield. The books' many admirers compared William Baxter and Penrod Schofield to latter-day Huck Finns and Tom Sawyers. Detractors thought the books sophomoric, sentimental, and sometimes cynical, faithful to the many details of daily life but lacking insight.

Neither the Penrod stories nor *Seventeen* is likely to engage most modern young readers. While both are undeniably gracefully written and engagingly told, the books are often both out of synch and at odds with current sensibilities. Their plots tend to unfold in a very leisurely fashion; the vocabulary is sometimes archaic. More disturbingly, a dark strain of offhanded racism runs through the books. The servants are often dismissed as "niggers," characterized as slow-witted and filthy, given to forgetting how many children they have fathered. While it is unfair to impose the standards of one generation on a writer from another long past, these books nevertheless sometimes read like genial apologies for provincial life that was as close-minded as it was lighthearted. The result is almost claustrophobic storytelling, offering current readers little more than set-piece humor and social insights that have long passed their shelf life. A.Q.

Taylor, Mildred

American novelist, b. 1943. Mildred Taylor was born in Jackson, Mississippi. When she was a child, her father decided that he could not stand living in the segregated South any longer and left for Ohio, sending for his family three months later. Taylor grew up in Toledo, but made return trips to the South with her family. During these travels, they reencountered segregationist signs such as those forbidding black people to drink from the same water fountains as whites, and, as they were not allowed to stay in hotels or motels, they had to drive straight through without stopping. Often, their car was stopped by police anyway, particularly because they drove expensive new cars with Northern license plates. Such incidents later appeared in Taylor's books.

Taylor excelled in school but from an early age realized that the history books she read did not represent the dignity, the courage, and the achievements of the people she knew about from stories told in her family. She considers herself one in a line of these family storytellers, and the one who put the words to paper. She tried and failed to become a published writer many times before entering a Council on Interracial Books for Children contest with the story she told in *Song of the Trees*, which was published in 1975. In this book she introduced a vivid family of characters, most of whom were based on people in her own family. The Logans owned land in the South, as her family did. The main character, Cassie Logan, combined the feisty natures of her sister and an aunt, but Cassie's feelings were those of Mildred Taylor, who was a quieter child.

Taylor has stated that she wants children of all colors to walk in the shoes of the Logan family and understand the value system within the family. She strives to convey how the strong black men and women she knew persevered, retained hope, and fought for what they believed in. She recounts true incidents such as beatings and near-lynchings from real life.

Taylor's second book, *Roll of Thunder, Hear My Cry*, her best-known work, won the 1977 Newbery Medal from the American Library Association, and was also a nominee for the 1977 National Book Award. The third book in the Logan series, *Let the Circle Be Unbroken*, was the winner of a Coretta Scott King Award in 1982. Additional books about the Logans followed: *The Friendship* was published in 1987, and both *The Road to Memphis* and *Mississippi Bridge* were published in 1990. *The Gold Cadillac* (1987) is drawn from Taylor's childhood experiences during her family's first years in Toledo and in 1987 was named an Outstanding Book by the *New York Times*, an honor several of her other novels have earned.

Taylor is a graduate of the University of Toledo. After college she joined the Peace Corps and was sent to Ethiopia, where she taught English and history. After her return, she became a recruiter for the Peace Corps and

Illustration by Max Ginsburg from *The Friendship* (1987), by Mildred D. Taylor.

received a master's degree in journalism from the University of Colorado. Before she became a full-time writer, she worked as a study-skills coordinator in a black education program she helped structure. Two documentaries have been produced about Taylor, including *Meet the Newbery Author: Mildred Taylor.*

Mildred Taylor's novels are excellently written, suspenseful stories of a strong, resourceful family. They serve to introduce readers, primarily children in elementary school, to the tragic history of injustice and violence against blacks in America. S.H.H.

Taylor, Sydney

American author, 1904–1978. Sydney Taylor began her career as an actress and professional dancer with the Martha Graham Dance Company. Also a student of dramatics, Taylor wrote, directed, and choreographed original plays in addition to writing books for children.

Taylor's native New York City provides the setting for the well-loved "All-of-a-Kind Family" series, which evolved from Taylor's own childhood on Manhattan's Lower East Side in the early 1900s. At the request of her daughter, Taylor finally began to record her adventures with her five sisters, and the "All-of-a-Kind Family" books were born. *All-of-a-Kind Family* (1951) introduces a close-knit family of five girls, ranging in age from four to twelve, Mama, and Papa, who operates a junk shop. It is a difficult life; money is hard-earned and precious, but there is no shortage of love in the girls' family. Mama is hardworking and wise, dispensing discipline and love with an even hand and a good deal of humor. Papa is the spiritual guide for the family, providing the foundation for a deep and abiding faith in Judaism. Joyous family celebrations, with the significance of each holiday often interpreted in a personal manner for a particular child, furnish an underlying theme throughout the series. Within the girls' extended family of relatives, friends, and neighbors there is a wonderful sense of community and vibrancy. In adventure after adventure, the girls come in contact with an engaging array of characters. In response to positive letters from children around the country about her first book, Taylor continued the saga with *More All-of-a-Kind Family* (1954), in which a much-awaited son, Charlie, is born; and *All-of-a-Kind Family Uptown* (1958), which chronicles the family's move to the Bronx at the start of World War I; and *All-of-a-Kind Family Downtown* (1972), which records yet another move and a change in the family's financial status.

Taylor deftly establishes warm, congenial relationships between the sisters that are sustained through each volume, and skillfully develops characters so the reader gains a sense of the unique personality of each girl. The last book in the series, *Ella of All-of-a-Kind Family* (1978), focuses on one particular child as it follows Ella, the eldest, on her career as an aspiring singer. After being discovered, Ella joins a vaudeville troupe and, disillusioned after months of training and hard work, faces a difficult decision regarding her future. This book is of particular interest because the first stirrings of the women's movement are felt both by Ella, who must choose between the man she loves and her blossoming career, and by Henny, her younger sister, who faces an uphill battle for a class office against the boys in her class.

Taylor was honored for her work by the Jewish Book Council's National Jewish Book Award in 1951 for *All-of-a-Kind Family,* an award given for the work that "combines literary merit with an affirmative expression of Jewish values." She was also honored posthumously in 1979 by the Association of Jewish Libraries for her entire body of work. In addition to the series, Taylor's other books include *A Papa Like Everyone Else* (1966) and, for younger children, *Mr. Barney's Beard* (1961), and *The Dog Who Came to Dinner* (1965). Taylor's books may seem dated to the modern reader, yet they are still appreciated as a valuable retrospective of family life in the early part of this century. ❧ M.O'D.H.

Taylor, Theodore

American author, b. 1921. Theodore Taylor's earliest exposure to the printed word was an illustrated volume of Bible stories for children. His favorite tales, such as David and Goliath, were strong in action and adventure. Many years later, Taylor would be acclaimed for writing his own action-filled stories for children.

When he was thirteen years old, Taylor's family moved from Statesville, North Carolina, to Portsmouth, Virginia, where he soon acquired a job on the local newspaper, writing a column about high school sports. He continued his journalism career at the *Washington Daily News* as a copy boy, served as sports editor at two newspapers, and reported on the early space race for the *Orlando Sentinel-Star*. He has also worked as a merchant marine, press agent, and prizefighter manager. Taylor published two nonfiction books for adults before he entered the children's field with *People Who Make Movies* (1967), which was inspired by his own children's interest in the film industry. He has since written several nonfiction books for young people, often focusing on World War II themes, as in *Air Raid—Pearl Harbor!* (1971). But Taylor is best known for writing fiction that is filled with vivid characterizations and strong action.

His first novel, *The Cay* (1969), is the story of eleven-year-old Phillip, who is shipwrecked on a Caribbean island with an elderly black sailor during World War II. Blinded by a torpedo attack, Phillip must overcome his prejudices and learn survival skills from Timothy, who teaches the boy how to hunt for food, signal for help, and weather a hurricane. The theme of racial harmony is powerfully explored in a series of suspenseful, tightly focused scenes. The book has achieved great popularity among young readers but has also been a source of controversy. Amid charges that Timothy's background is underdeveloped, that his Creole dialect is undignified, and that his deference to the young white boy is offensive, Taylor was asked to relinquish the Jane Addams Children's Book Award that the novel received in 1970. Much of the controversy seems unfounded, since Timothy is clearly the hero of the novel and functions as a teacher to Phillip throughout. His early subservience seems more a product of his historical era than a reflection of his own self-worth. Taylor addresses the subject of Timothy's past in a volume he terms a "prequel-sequel." In alternating chapters, *Timothy of the Cay* (1993) parallels the story of Timothy's nineteenth-century youth with Phillip's post–World War II experiences.

Taylor has written other multivolume stories, including a pair of books about Helen's blind dog, *The Trouble with Tuck* (1981) and *Tuck Triumphant* (1991), and a trilogy about a mysterious girl who is rescued from a shipwreck on the Outer Banks of North Carolina, *Teetoncey* (1974), *Teetoncey and Ben O'Neal* (1975), and *The Odyssey of Ben O'Neal* (1977). Among Taylor's other novels of adventure are *Sniper* (1989), the story of a teenager guarding lions and tigers on his family's private nature preserve, and *The Weirdo* (1991), which concerns young people trying to protect wild bears in a North Carolina wildlife refuge. *Walking Up a Rainbow* (1986) is a rousing frontier story about an orphaned teenage girl, memorable for its colorful first-person narration.

A fine sense of dramatic action propels Taylor's fiction, making his fast-paced novels exciting and readable. ❧ P.D.S.

Tenniel, Sir John

British illustrator, 1820–1914. With the illustrations of only two children's books to his credit, Sir John Tenniel has nevertheless well earned his place as one of the great names in children's literature. His illustrations for Lewis Carroll's *Alice's Adventures in Wonderland* (1865) and *Through the Looking-Glass* (1872) have been termed the most perfect marriage of text and illustration in a children's book, with the illustrator's style complementing and expanding the scope of the author's story and, with time, becoming virtually inseparable from it.

Thought by many to have been the epitome of the Victorian gentleman, Tenniel was born the year before Queen Victoria ascended the throne and died on the eve of the First World War, when the world order with which he had been so comfortable changed forever. In between, he lived a solid, steady life of respectability and satisfactory personal achievement, and his strong, literal artistic style captured and reflected his times. He was primarily a self-taught artist, having quit the Royal Academy School "in utter disgust of there being no teaching" and spent long hours at the British Museum and the Tower of London studying and copying suits of armor and books on medieval costume. He hoped to make his living as a painter, and he viewed the illustrating work that came his way as incidental.

But in 1848 he was asked to illustrate *AESOP's Fables,* a retelling by the Reverend Thomas James. The book met with wide success, and as a result he was invited to become the primary illustrator for *Punch,* a satirical magazine that set the political and social tone of the day. Tenniel's political cartoons for *Punch* form the other half of his enduring body of work, and they greatly influenced British political life for the half century he drew them. His early studies of knights and ladies loomed large in Tenniel's artistic vocabulary, as did his interest in animals (particularly lions and eagles) and his very Victorian love of whimsy, which frequently expressed itself in drawings of anthropomorphic animals: rabbits in waistcoats and fishes in knee breeches.

When Charles Dodgson, as Lewis Carroll, decided to publish the story about a little girl named Alice he had written for some of his young friends, he knew his own amateurish drawings would not do. He was taken with Tenniel's work in *Punch* and asked a mutual friend to introduce them. Thus began an extremely contentious, wearing, and ultimately fruitful collaboration. The two gentlemen met in 1864, and over the next eight years and through two books, they conducted a very courteous, highly restrained, but deadly serious battle over artistic control of Wonderland. Carroll had very definite ideas about how the illustrations for his books should look, having illustrated himself the first, unpublished version of *Alice,* called *Alice's Adventures Under Ground.* Tenniel felt himself to be little more than an employee of Carroll's, a position at which his independent nature balked. He had his own strong vision of the works, and occasionally, especially for the second book, Carroll incorporated his suggestions into the text. Carroll's mania for detail was matched only by Tenniel's, and the two drove each other to the ultimate reaches of patience with their competing fastidiousness.

Illustration by Sir John Tenniel from *Alice's Adventures in Wonderland* (1865), by LEWIS CARROLL.

The drawings were done in the manner of the day. This involved sketches followed by finished pen-and-ink drawings on paper; transferred by the artist onto wooden blocks, the drawings were then engraved by an engraver and handed over to a printer. It was a long, laborious process, with many opportunities for mistakes and misunderstandings. In fact, Tenniel and Carroll recalled the first printing of *Alice* because they felt it had been improperly printed, to the detriment of the illustrations. Ultimately, however, the two men produced books that have been celebrated for their beauty, wit, fantasy, and uncommon harmony between text and art. Tenniel diplomatically claimed, "It is a curious fact that with *Through the Looking-Glass* the faculty of making drawings for book illustrations departed from me," and he spent the rest of his career focused on his cartoons for *Punch.* When he died, a few days before his ninety-fourth birthday, his contemporaries mourned the passing of an era, along with the man who exemplified and captured it so well. ❧ S.G.K.

TERHUNE, ALBERT PAYSON

AMERICAN AUTHOR, 1872–1942. Albert Payson Terhune was born in Newark, New Jersey. His mother, Mary Virginia Hawes Terhune, was a professional writer who used the pen name Marion Harland. His father, Edward Payson Terhune, was a minister. "Bert" Terhune graduated from Columbia University in 1893 and the next year began a twelve-year stint writing for the New York *Evening World.* A practitioner of participatory journalism, the burly, six-foot-three Terhune boxed with some of the leading prizefighters of his day in order to write about these experiences. Terhune did not like newspaper work and during his newspaper career sought relief by writing novels, plays, and many magazine short stories. "His Mate," a short story published in *Redbook* in 1915 went on to become the opening chapter of his first book, *Lad: A Dog* (1919), the work that helped carve out Terhune's niche as a leading writer of ANIMAL STORIES for children.

Terhune's most beloved and well-remembered book, *Lad: A Dog* tells in episodic fashion the story of Lad, an eighty-pound collie who lives on a New Jersey country estate called Sunnybank. Like the typical Terhune dog, Lad has nearly human intelligence, and his phenomenal courage leads him to commit frequent acts of bravery. Catching crooks, killing poisonous snakes, fighting wicked enemy dogs, and saving the lives of humans (especially children) is the stuff of Lad's everyday life. Though lesser humans frequently suspect Lad of criminal behavior, his Godlike master and mistress have complete faith in their dog, and for this they are repaid with worshipful devotion from Lad.

Capitalizing on the success of *Lad: A Dog,* Terhune went on to publish nearly twenty children's books featuring dogs, including *Further Adventures of Lad* (1922) and *Lad of Sunnybank* (1929). The success of Terhune's dog stories allowed the author to live and write full-time at his family's New Jersey estate, also called Sunnybank. In the 1920s Terhune's books were so popular that he was making close to $100,000 a year, and his once idyllic estate became clogged with admiring tourists hoping to catch a glimpse of the famous author and his collies.

Today Terhune's work is neither widely known nor much appreciated. Collectively, Terhune's books are repetitive in their emphasis on dog heroics, and even within a single work Terhune often repeats the same bits of description and pieces of dog lore again and again. Also, the flow of a Terhune story is frequently broken as the author steps in to sermonize on the foibles of human and canine nature. Despite such literary shortcomings, Terhune's stories can be well told and exhilarating, and the author's love and understanding of dogs shines through. In life an avid outdoorsman and hunter, Terhune cared deeply about the treatment of dogs and used his stories to speak out against both vivisection and the lesser cruelties inflicted by show-dog trainers and breeders. The encroachment of the city on the countryside was also a concern of Terhune's, and he opposed such despoiling in his books as well as through his role as a New Jersey parks commissioner, a position he held until his death from cancer in 1942. ❧ D.A.B.

THRILLERS

The teenage MYSTERY, a staple of young adult literature since the days of NANCY DREW, contains suspense, but is more a detective story than an exercise in terror. CHRISTOPHER PIKE's *Slumber Party* (1985) changed that equation, creating the genre of teenage thrillers. Subsequent books by Pike, such as *Chain Letter* (1986), R. L. Stine's *Babysitter* (1989) and his "Fear Street" series (1990–), and Richie Cusick's *Lifeguard* (1988) developed the genre, and paperback thrillers became the best-selling books for teenagers in the 1990s.

While owing something to the traditional mystery story, thrillers have unique elements. The "whodunit" aspect remains, but thrillers incorporate elements of horror and the supernatural. Rather than responding to a crime with detective work, the teenaged protagonists encounter acts of random violence, usually in a suburban setting such as a mall or high school, or in some faraway place such as the ski-lodge setting of *Slumber Party.* Adults rarely appear, as the novels take place in a teenage world filled with secrets and slang and run by its own set of rules.

In many ways thrillers resemble horror movies more than they resemble other teenage mystery novels. The covers and titles reflect movie promotion tricks, and the books themselves often read like novelizations for unmade slasher films. Bold use of black, blue, and blood red dominates the covers, which feature illustrations of teenagers in danger or graphic emblems such as a bloody knife. While less violent than horror movies, teenage thriller novels are more violent than detective novels for the same age group. Most of the violence is inflicted by teenagers on other teenagers for revenge. The book typically ends with the killer revealed and declaring something like "you chose him over me" as a motive for his brutal acts.

It is easy to understand the basic reasons for the runaway success of thrillers: their paperback format and their appeal to both boys and girls. Big issues, such as trust, loyalty, acceptance, and betrayal, figure heavily. More than merely providing thrills, these novels speak to developmental needs. The scary parts allow teenagers to enjoy the excitement of being terrified while still feeling in control. The violence puts teenagers out on the edge of danger without pushing them over. Like rollercoaster rides, thrillers provide an enticing mix of danger and fun and keep readers coming back for more of the same.

The emphasis is on plot, not character; most of the books are told in the third person rather than in the first-person narration standard in young adult literature.

Plots move quickly with lots of twists and turns. Most books are under two hundred pages and have short chapters, usually ending with a cliffhanger or some other jolt to the reader. Like MTV, the repeated shock images keep the reader constantly stimulated.

All these factors made *Slumber Party* and other titles successful. By 1994, every major publisher of teenage paperbacks had at least one series: "Nightmare Club" (Zebra), "Nightmare Hall" (Scholastic), and "Nightmare Inn" (Harper), to name just a few. Other publishers released non-series titles, such as *The Cheerleader* by Caroline Cooney (1991), *Party Line* by A. Bates (1990), and *The Photographer* by Barbara Steiner (1989). To keep up with demand, publishers pushed sequels, such as Pike's *Chain Letter II: The Ancient Evil* (1992), and republished old titles, such as Stine's *Broken Date* (1988), originally part of a romance series. Dell repackaged LOIS DUNCAN's titles to make them look like the genre, although they contain much less violence and much better writing. Several books that were not really thrillers in hardback were marketed as part of the genre when reprinted as paperbacks. Spurred on by the success of the "Fear Street" series, Stine created the "Goosebumps" series (1992–) aimed at the preteen market. In 1994, each new "Goosebumps" title became the best-selling paperback in the country. Other publishers then developed their preteen series, such as "Shadow Zone" (Random House) and "Phantom Valley" (Minstrel).

This burgeoning has not gone without notice, including negative articles in *Time* and the *New York Times Book Review.* Most local newspapers carried "do you know what your children are reading?" stories, as did magazines such as *Family Life.* While violence in youth fiction always draws attention from concerned adults, the popularity of these titles, coinciding with a rapid increase in the public awareness of teen violence, perhaps explains the high-profile hatchet jobs done on the genre.

The two main complaints stem from the genre's content and from its repetitive, formulaic nature. Certain devices, among them stalkers with knives, car accidents, faked deaths, and other tricks are used time and time again. The basic plot established by Pike is hauled out for each new title; the setting and the characters' names may change, but results remain the same. Objections have also been raised to the supernatural content, including the use of ouija boards. While thrillers offer recreational reading, the escape they provide is not into the intellectual innocence of a Nancy Drew mystery story but into a world made cynical by violence and danger. Yet perhaps inevitably, fiction for the teenagers of the 1990s was bound to reflect the world in which they live, a world that is indeed more violent and more dangerous than that of the Nancy Drew generation. ♘

PATRICK JONES

THURBER, JAMES

AMERICAN AUTHOR, 1894–1961. Celebrated for his mordant sketches of contemporary life in the 1940s and 1950s, James Thurber's five works that have been classified as children's books show a lover of words at play. The books, starting with *Many Moons* (1943) and ending with *The Wonderful O* (1957), are filled with wordplay, allusions, rhymes, alliteration, snatches of song and poetry, wild flights of fancy that veer into the absurd, and—in the greatest departure from his work for adults—happy endings.

Many Moons is considered his best book for children, and it shows a tenderness and charm that his writing for adults does not. In its first incarnation, with illustrations by LOUIS SLOBODKIN, it won the Caldecott Medal for 1944. Slobodkin's illustrations emphasize the theatrical, light-opera quality of the tale, depicting a tiny and seemingly frail Princess Lenore nearly overwhelmed by the soaring castle surrounding her, making the solution to her problem all the more satisfying. MARC SIMONT reillustrated the story for reissue in 1990, putting the fantasy of the piece on a more magical plane and calling forth a greater awareness of the King's love for his ill daughter. In *Many Moons* Thurber succeeded in corralling his acid wit and penchant for the absurd with a silken halter of sweetness and pure storytelling skill; in his subsequent books for children, he was less successful at controlling his natural pessimism. *The Great Quillow* (1944), *The White Deer* (1945), and *The Thirteen Clocks* (1950) are highly colored, extravagant fairy tales in which his wonderfully dark humor and basic disgust with the human race become more and more apparent. In his final children's book, *The Wonderful O,* the melancholy and sharpness that was a hallmark of his writing for adults overwhelms this slim tale of pirates who ban the letter O from the language of a small, mythical island.

Thurber's absurd view of his own childhood certainly influenced his writing for children. Born in Columbus, Ohio, the second of three boys in a "family of eccentrics," as he termed it, Thurber grew up amidst a large cast of unlikely characters. His father was a political animal whose employment in various appointed capacities lent an uncertain and peripatetic air to the Thurber household. His mother, Thurber wrote, was "an aspiring actress," and "deprived of a larger audience, the frustrated comedienne performed for whoever would listen." A childhood accident while playing "William Tell" with his brothers left Thurber with permanently impaired eyesight, which gradually deteriorated over his lifetime, eventually blinding him, a handicap that would cause him great pain, both physically and spiritually. Upon graduation from Ohio State University in 1919, he worked as a newspaper reporter in Columbus, Paris, and New York.

It was at a cocktail party in New York City in 1927 that he met E. B. WHITE and began the firm friendship (and sometime literary collaboration) that was to last the rest of his life. White introduced Thurber to Herbert Ross, founding editor of the *New Yorker,* which was then in its infancy. Ross hired Thurber as managing editor, and while Thurber was uncomfortable with executive authority and eventually demoted himself down to staff writer and then off the magazine entirely to become a contributing writer, he nevertheless had much to do with setting the tone and style that made the *New Yorker* such a literary high-water mark during its halcyon days.

Thurber's writing took many forms—all of them short. Essays, sketches, fables, satires, parables, fantasies, and reminiscences all share his bleak view of an overwhelming, chaotic world. But in the best of his writing for children, Thurber felt free to let good triumph over evil, love overcome hate, virtue gain its just reward, and hope hold fast. S.G.K.

TOLKIEN, J.R.R.

BRITISH SCHOLAR AND WRITER, 1892–1973. John Ronald Reuel Tolkien's *The Hobbit or, There and Back Again* (1937), with illustrations by the author, is a captivating FANTASY with wide appeal for both children and adults. It concerns the quest of Bilbo Baggins, a comfort-loving, ordinary, and unambitious hero. The *New York Herald Tribune* awarded it a prize as the best book published for young children in the spring of 1938. That year, Tolkien's friend and colleague, C. S. LEWIS, wrote, "*The Hobbit* may well prove a classic." *The Hobbit,* in fact, has proved to be the most popular of all twentieth-century fantasies written for children. Tolkien was so well grounded in ancient legend and saga, medieval literature, his own original languages, and philological study of the connections between language and literature, that there was, as Lewis said, "a happy fusion of the scholar's with the poet's grasp of mythology."

According to Tolkien, his stories "arose in the mind as 'given' things, and as they came, separately, so too the links grew . . . always I had the sense of recording what was already 'there,' somewhere, not of 'inventing.'" At a time when fairy stories were considered childish, Tolkien claimed in a 1939 lecture, "On Fairy-Stories," collected in *Tree and Leaf* (1964), that, "If fairy-story as a kind is worth reading at all it is worthy to be written for and read by adults." According to Tolkien, children were not a race or class apart from adults, but fellow humans of fewer experiences, and thus, usually, had less need for the fantasy, recovery, escape, and consolation provided by fairy stories. He had enjoyed fairy stories during his own childhood, but it was not until "the threshold of manhood," when his philological studies had made clear to him the connections between the origins of stories, language, and the creative human mind, that he developed a real taste for them. Fantasy, he said, is a natural human activity and is not in opposition to reason. We make or create from our imagination "because we are made; and not only made, but made in the image and likeness of a Maker." The storymaker is a successful subcreator when his secondary world can be entered by the reader who is convinced by the inner consistency of the laws of that world that his experiences are "true." Later twentieth-century writers of fantasy for children, such as LLOYD ALEXANDER, SUSAN COOPER, ROBIN MCKINLEY, and others, reflect some Tolkien influence.

As reprintings of *The Hobbit* continued, there followed many requests for more about hobbits. But it was not until seventeen years later that the long-awaited "sequel" finally appeared. It was *The Lord of the Rings* (1954–55), published in three volumes: Part I, "The Fellowship of the Ring"; Part II, "The Two Towers"; and Part III, "The Return of the King." Some of the delay was caused by the author's need to ensure that the geography, chronology, and nomenclature were perfectly consistent within the sequel; with its predecessor, *The Hobbit* (which required a revised edition, published in 1951); and with the foundation "history," a large body of unpublished original legends and many-layered mythologies of Elven lore of the "First Age of the World."

Since early adulthood, Tolkien had been engaged in the process of inventing variants, revising, and finely tuning integrations of this material, and he continued to do so until his death. (Much of this "history" was published posthumously as *The Silmarillion* [1977] and additional volumes have appeared since the early 1980s, all edited by Christopher Tolkien, who had worked closely with his father.) When the first part of *The Lord of the Rings* appeared, C. S. Lewis again gave Tolkien's work generous praise: "This book is like lightning from a clear sky. To say that in it heroic romance, gorgeous, eloquent and unashamed, has suddenly returned at a period almost pathological in its anti-romanticism is inade-

Illustration by J. R. R. Tolkien from his book *The Hobbit* (1938).

quate . . . it makes . . . an advance or revolution: the conquest of new territory." In a short six weeks the first edition had sold out, demonstrating its popularity for a wide age range. Several years later, when a pirated paperback edition of *The Lord of the Rings* (and later an authorized one) became available, both works soared to the best-seller lists.

The sequels, similarly structured, share the time frame of "The Third Age of Middle Earth" and both are purported to have roots in the events of "The First Age"; but they differ in complexity and tone. The narrative tone is more relaxed and humorous in Bilbo's story, where there are occasional asides to children, and there are only a few fleeting glimpses of "the older matter." In *The Lord of the Rings,* however, Tolkien claimed that he was "discovering" the significance of these "glimpses" and expanding on their relation to his "Ancient histories." The primary link between the sequels is the Ring of Power, treacherously forged by Sauron to control Elven-kings, Dwarf-lords, and Mortal Men.

Central to a deeper understanding of Tolkien's life and mind are two short allegories, *Leaf by Niggle* (1947) and *Smith of Wooton Major* (1967). Both can be enjoyed by children, but in each case the stories have deeper meaning for adults. The first represents the author's fear of dying before he had completed the *Lord of the Rings,* and in the second the author recognizes that the gift that permits his visits to the land of faery must be relinquished and passed on to another generation. A humorous dragon story with more child appeal is *Farmer Giles of Ham* (1949). *The Adventures of Tom Bombadil* (1962) contains entertaining verses from "The Red Book," also the alleged source of *The Hobbit.* This collection, as well as *Bilbo's Last Song* (1974), is illustrated by Pauline Baynes, whose work greatly pleased Tolkien. *The Father Christmas Letters* (1976) and *Mr. Bliss* (1982) are both illustrated by the author and are evidence of his special joy in creating stories for his children.

The enormous popularity of Tolkien's work on American campuses during the 1960s may have slowed the Academy's appreciation of his fiction. His academic reputation was well established. He had occupied two chairs as Professor of Anglo-Saxon and Professor of English Language and Literature, had lectured far more than was required, and had produced valued research publications. An authorized biography by Humphrey Carpenter (1977) and the appearance of Tolkien's letters (1981) stimulated academic attention. By the 1990s, his works had found their place in the canon of English literature and are now the subject of hundreds of critical and scholarly books, essays, dissertations, theses, and journal articles. He received many honors in the last two decades of his life, including honorary doctorates from University College, Dublin, and from Liege in 1954, and for his work in philology from Oxford University, in 1972. The same year he was awarded the Order of the British Empire. J.R.R. Tolkien's books have been translated into more than twenty-six languages and have reached annual worldwide sales of several million copies. ❧ ELIZABETH C. HOKE

Tomes, Margot

AMERICAN ILLUSTRATOR, 1917–1991. Becoming an artist seemed natural to Margot Ladd Tomes, since her mother enjoyed drawing and her cousins included Guy Pène duBois, the painter, WILLIAM PÈNE DUBOIS, the illustrator, and Raoul Pène duBois, the theatrical designer. Nonetheless, Tomes detested taking art training at Pratt Institute. She never found it easy to paint and draw and disliked the isolation of working alone.

After years of designing fabric and wallpaper, she tried illustrating children's books and felt more at ease with these cherished objects of her childhood. Tomes illustrated dozens of stories over the years, and the list of authors she worked with includes many familiar names: FRANCES HODGSON BURNETT, BEATRICE SCHENK DE REGNIERS, WANDA GÁG, JAMES CROSS GIBLIN, and MILDRED PITTS WALTER, to name a few. Some of the prizes awarded her books include the *New York Times* Choice of Best Illustrated Children's Books of the Year for *Jack and the Wonder Beans* (1977) and the Society of Illustrators Certificate of Merit for *The Sorcerer's Apprentice* (1979).

Illustration by Margot Tomes from *The Sorcerer's Apprentice* (1979), adapted by WANDA GÁG.

Pen and ink forms the foundation of Tomes's work, and many of her illustrations are strictly black-and-white. She employed flat-toned paint in muted colors as subtle enhancement to her drawings. In some of her work, she used more painterly techniques, but the recognizable Tomes style centers on animated characters rendered with crookedly quaint but purposeful outlines. Human beings were Tomes's forte, wonderfully quirky characters drawn with delightful exaggeration, usually with small feet and heads and long, large bodies. Delicate, spare, scratchy lines reveal evocative facial expressions that run the gamut of emotions. Tomes used crosshatching liberally and was expert at making the page's white space an integral part of a picture. Movement is a natural part of her work, whether it is a long skirt swinging as a girl turns or a lad's hair being tossed about by a breeze.

The books Tomes illustrated were most often historical stories or fairy tales. She started being widely recognized after illustrating JEAN FRITZ's *And Then What Happened, Paul Revere?* (1973) and *Where Was Patrick Henry on the 29th of May?* (1975).

As crisp and sparkling as Fritz's prose, Tomes's art vivifies individuals and small details, keeping the books perennially compelling. Incidentals like a broom resting against a brick wall or a lantern sitting on a high shelf give her illustrations a ring of truth and a spark of interest. The architecture, clothing, and surroundings have a charming, Old World feeling, whether they depict the Revolutionary War story *Phoebe the Spy* (1977), originally *Phoebe and the General,* by Judith Berry Griffin, or the silly tale of a magic cooking pot and a clever hat in Tony Johnston's *The Witch's Hat* (1984). Tomes's strong line and composition and the intriguing minutiae draw the reader's attention and keep it, while the reader enjoys the tension, humor, or emotion within her narrative art. ❧ S.S.

TOWNSEND, JOHN ROWE

BRITISH AUTHOR OF FICTION AND CRITICISM, B. 1922. In 1961, after many years as a journalist, John Rowe Townsend published the urban adventure story *Gumble's Yard* (American title: *Trouble in the Jungle*), the first in a trilogy that also includes *Widdershins Crescent* (1965, American title: *Good-bye to the Jungle*) and *Pirate's Island* (1968). The first book tells how four children, deserted by their guardians, find temporary refuge in a canal-side abandoned building. Townsend has explained that he wrote *Gumble's Yard* not only because of his own childhood in the city of Leeds, but also because of his conviction that realistic stories about inner-city children were missing from the children's literature of the time. Without ignoring its problems, Townsend found the industrial city "extraordinarily beautiful in its own strange way," and he communicates his enthusiasm in several other books, including *Hell's Edge* (1963) and *Tom Tiddler's Ground* (1986, American title: *The Hidden Treasure*), another adventure story.

Townsend has noted that "dens and refuges" appeal to him; in fact, the need for refuge and the desire to secure one's own place appear quite often in his work.

Set many years earlier in the same city as *Gumble's Yard*, *Dan Alone* (1983) chronicles the adventures of a child who, longing for the ideal family he envisions in his daydreams, runs away from his ailing grandfather's house to avoid being sent to a children's home. *The Intruder* (1969), a suspenseful novel for older readers, tells how a sinister newcomer to an isolated village almost deprives Arnold of his place in the community. Townsend also speculates on what happens when a refuge becomes a stronghold against the rest of the world. During a severe economic crisis in the near future, the narrator of *Noah's Castle* (1975) struggles with the knowledge that his father is illegally hoarding supplies for his family. Projecting further into the future, Townsend wrote *The Xanadu Manuscript* (1977, American title: *The Visitors*), about twenty-second-century visitors to the twentieth century, and *King Creature, Come* (1980, American title: *The Creatures*), about a colony of aliens living segregated from the Earth people they have subjugated. He invented an island kingdom for *The Golden Journey* (1989, American title: *The Fortunate Isles*), a story in which two friends seek out the Living God in an attempt to stop the excesses of their warmongering king.

Townsend has also created several novels about contemporary young adults in keeping with his commitment to representing their concerns. In *Downstream* (1987) Alan, infatuated with his tutor, reacts violently to the discovery that his father is having an affair with her. *Good Night, Prof, Love* (1970, American title: *Good Night, Prof, Dear*) and *Cloudy-Bright* (1984) provide sensitive, sometimes humorous stories of encounters between very different young men and women.

Beginning with his work as children's book editor for the Manchester *Guardian*, Townsend has produced a considerable volume of literary criticism, including *Written for Children: An Outline of English-Language Children's Literature* (1965), now in its fourth revised edition, *A Sense of Story: Essays on Contemporary Writers for Children* (1971), and *A Sounding of Storytellers: New and Revised Essays on Contemporary Children's Writers* (1979). With his years of experience as critic and writer, Townsend offers a rich and varied contribution to children's literature. M.F.S.

Translation

Although the term *global community* has become a part of today's vocabulary, the concept has not carried forward in children's books, at least not in books originating in other countries and appearing here in translation. The recent trend toward multicultural books has certainly increased the number of titles about children in other countries, but the majority of these books are written and illustrated in the United States.

Of the thousands of books that originate abroad, very few make the oceanic crossing successfully. In addition to poor sales and low profits, factors cited by publishers include the necessary editorial work prior to publication, editors' inability to read other languages, translators' fees, librarians' hesitancy to purchase possible "shelf sitters," and resistance on the part of children to reading books that are "different."

In the nonfiction area, the peculiarities of terminology, the use of metric measurement, and children's possible lack of familiarity with a subject (wildlife native to a country, for example) keep many nonfiction books from reaching U.S. shores. Novels, which would seemingly translate more easily, tend to be either abstract fantasies or long historical books, which U.S. children, whose reading preferences tend toward short, contemporary realism, often avoid. And when they *are* translated and published here, these books usually go out of print after a short time.

PICTURE BOOKS in translation make up the greatest numbers; not only can the artwork help hurdle gaps in understanding the story, but it attracts publishers who buy the rights. Picture books are also more readily accepted by purchasers and by children because of the visual elements.

To encourage more publication of translated books and to help promote their importance, the American Library Association (ALA) created, in 1966, the Mildred L. Batchelder Award, named for a former executive director and long-time advocate of children's books. The citation is awarded annually to an American publisher for a children's book considered to be the most outstanding book originally published in a foreign language in a foreign country and subsequently published in the United States. Since 1968, a committee of member librarians from the ALA's Association of Library Service to Children selects a worthy title. In 1993, the committee found no deserving book and the award was not granted. A survey of the past twenty-five winners reveals some interesting points. Among them, seventeen come from the Germanic languages (Danish, Dutch, German, Norwegian, Swedish) and only one from a non-Western language (Japanese). Eight titles had German origins.

Geographic settings are more representative, although more than half take place in Europe. Except for *Hiroshima No Pika* (1982), which was written and published in Japan, others, with such far-flung settings as

Ethiopia, Colombia, and Mesopotamia, were written by a Dane, a Dutchman, and a German, respectively. Of the two Hebrew winners, one is set in Warsaw and the other in Syria, while the three books set in Greece are all by the same author (Aliki Zei) and the same translator (Edward Fenton). This European concentration undoubtedly results from many countries' lack of high-quality books worthy of translation as well as a lack of qualified translators working in languages less well known in the West. Time is equally one-sided: historical settings account for fifteen of the titles, with World War II being the time period tapped for the sole nonfiction winner as well as for eight of the novels. URI ORLEV's *The Man from the Other Side* (1991), the story of fourteen-year-old Marek, who after learning that his father, a Jew, was killed in prison comes to terms with his own prejudice by helping a young Polish doctor hide from the Germans, and PETER HÄRTLING's *Crutches* (1988), which tells of the developing friendship between a lost boy and an embittered soldier as they search for the boy's mother through war-ravaged Europe, are outstanding examples of this genre. A much needed balance has recently surfaced with the increasing number of humorous and lighthearted books being brought into the United States. For example, Milos Macourek and Adolf Born's *Max and Sally and the Phenomenal Phone* (1989), translated from the Czech, finds two children enjoying a number of fantastical experiences when they acquire a magic telephone, and Christina Björk and Lena Anderson's *Linnea in Monet's Garden* (1987) follows a young girl as she happily visits the artist's homes in Paris and Giverny with her friend Mr. Bloom.

A continued interest in translated books is found among virtually all the major publishers. In the twenty-seven years since the inception of the Batchelder Award, more than seventeen publishers have been named winners, with Dutton capturing top honors with four separate awards. This continuing interest bodes well for the genre and indicates that despite translation difficulties and economic problems, books from a variety of countries around the world are finding their way into American schools, libraries, and homes.

For a complete picture of the genre, however, one must also know that not all translated books brought into the United States are eligible for Batchelder consideration. For example, books translated and published first in another English-speaking country and then brought to the United States are ineligible. These books, along with the Batchelder titles, should be introduced to children as an avenue for an exchange of ideas.

This promise of communication—and the hope that it would lead to peace and cooperation between peoples—undoubtedly underscored Mildred Batchelder's statement that "when children of one country come to know and love the books and stories of many countries, they have made an important beginning toward international understanding." ❧ BARBARA ELLEMAN

Travers, P. L.

BRITISH AUTHOR, CRITIC, LECTURER, B. 1906. Pamela Lyndon Traver is as unwilling to "explain" herself as a writer as she is to explain the staunch and unbendable character for whom she is so well known—a British nanny in a 1930s household. *Mary Poppins* was published in 1934 and has since been translated into twenty-five languages and sold copies in the millions. It was the basis for a 1964 Disney film that had tremendous success despite its lack of favor with those loyal to the original book. Travers went on to write eight more books about Mary Poppins, including *Mary Poppins Comes Back* (1935), *Mary Poppins Opens the Door* (1943), *Mary Poppins in Cherry Tree Lane* (1982), and *Mary Poppins and the House Next Door* (1988). Critics have praised Travers for continuing to expand and explore her themes in the later books and for the enduring liveliness and unpredictability of her main character.

Mary Poppins has confounded critics over the years by being full of contradictions and impossible to characterize in a few simple words. She has been called stern, vain, proud, no-nonsense, unsentimental. She has the complete loyalty of her charges—Jane and Michael Banks and their younger brother and sister. In the series of episodes that make up *Mary Poppins*, she takes the children on adventures that both delight and amaze them. Whether she is gluing stars to the sky, having a tea party on the ceiling, or dancing under a full moon at the zoo, she leaves the children baffled and perplexed by her actions—never ceasing to deny that anything out-of-the-ordinary has taken place.

Travers draws her themes from a childhood rich in fairy tale and myth, a love of Shakespeare and the Bible, and later study of Eastern religion and philosophy. She grew up in Australia, daughter of an Irish father and a mother of Scottish and Irish descent. At eighteen, she traveled to England, determined to discover her roots—and has made her home there ever since. As a young woman she worked as a dressmaker, a dancer, an actress, and a reporter—first to help support her family in Australia after her father died and later to support herself in England, where she became established as a drama critic, travel essayist, and reviewer. She also wrote poetry and was taken under the wing of the Irish writer-editor

George Russell, who published her work in the *Irish Statesman* and encouraged her literary growth and development for the rest of his life. Travers has written several other children's books, including *I Go by Sea, I Go by Land* (1941), *The Fox at the Manger* (1962), and *Friend Monkey* (1971), as well as adult books—*Moscow Excursion* (1934) and *About the Sleeping Beauty* (1975). Although these titles haven't achieved the acclaim or success of the Mary Poppins books, they have continued faithfully to explore the themes and ideas that intrigue their author.

Illustration by Mary Shepard from *Mary Poppins Opens the Door* (1943), by P. L. Travers.

In her writing Travers has a strongly mystical bent; she has often said that she didn't create Mary Poppins at all; rather Mary Poppins found her way into Travers's consciousness and demanded that her story be told. Just as the character of Mary Poppins has continued to occupy the mind and writings of Travers over several decades, so the books have continued to be rediscovered by new generations of readers. § K.M.K.

Trease, Geoffrey

British author, b. 1909. Geoffrey Trease's prolific career spans more than sixty years, and his work reflects the growth and innovation in children's books during this century.

Born in historical Nottingham, England, Trease became enchanted with history. He won a scholarship to Oxford but, weary of scholarly study, left after one year. He chose instead to travel, delving deeply into the history of a place while gathering material for his books. From *Bows against the Barons* (1934), his first book, to *Follow My Black Plume* (1963) and beyond, Trease's masterfully written historical novels offer young readers a glimpse of another time and place. Trease began writing for children, he says, "in revulsion against the sentimental romanticism [then] pervading historical fiction." Continually striving for the "modern relevance" of a historical event or a period in history, Trease's novels have grown steadily in competency and scope. *Bows against the Barons* portrayed Robin Hood as a left-wing revolutionary. Brimming with self-righteous emotion, the book was less than historically correct, and Trease admits its inaccuracies made him wince for years. From that point on, however, Trease conducted meticulous research for his books.

Trease confesses to a lifelong passion for theater, which profoundly affects his work. His books are fast-paced adventures, with pervading themes of injustice against individuals and the unveiling of sinister plots. His writing is crisp and sure.

Drawing inspiration from a variety of sources, Trease asserts, "I always said I could write about any period if I could figure out what made those people laugh." Since Trease's books are historical, they frequently deal with armed conflict, yet the conflict serves as a backdrop for stories that are really about people. *Web of Traitors: An Adventure Story of Ancient Athens* (1952), whose plot is immersed in intrigue, presents a colorful illustration of family life. It is the minutiae of people's lives—the pastimes that occupied their days, their thoughts, and their dreams—that make Trease's books so accessible, even to contemporary readers. He managed to break free of many conventions, creating, for example, a credible female heroine in the English civil war story *A Cue for Treason* (1940). Trease felt frustrated with societal restrictions concerning suitable topics and their treatment in children's books. At a time when serious discussion of children's books was virtually unheard of, he wrote *Tales Out of School: A Survey of Children's Fiction* (1949). This book was influential in asserting that books be accessible to children first and foremost.

Trease has actively avoided didacticism, and his books are very informative and are valuable aids to teaching history. His biographies of Lord Byron, *Byron: A Poet Dangerous to Know* (1969), and D. H. Lawrence,

The Phoenix and the Flame (1973), bring these authors to life for children and were the result of a request to write "teenage" biographies of these unusual writers. Above all, and perhaps most important, Trease's books satisfy that urge for a good yarn. ❧ M.O'D.H.

Treece, Henry

British writer, 1911–1966. Henry Treece is known primarily for his historical novels for children. Treece had a particular interest in the crossroads of history. He recalled that, as a child, he had only historical books to read and credited those books and their illustrations with his taste for historical subjects. In his writing, although the context was the historical past, his focus was on human behavior. Treece was, above all, a fine storyteller, able to create characters who made the tales come alive. As a writer, his poetic ability influenced his use of language, investing it with precision and grace.

Treece was born in Staffordshire, England. After earning a B.A. from Birmingham University, he received a degree in education and spent his early career as a teacher. At the time he began to write for children, he was already an established poet and was developing a reputation for his adult novels. Treece was able to write for children and adults concurrently, taking the same care with his novels for children as with his adult books. He adopted somewhat different styles of writing for the two audiences, however, describing settings more explicitly and stating the historical facts more clearly in his books for children.

Treece's early work as a schoolmaster and his understanding of children may have been the reason he included a section entitled "About This Book" in many of his children's books. He chose as characters people who might have lived during important historical times. In notes written during the last month of his life, Treece identified the theme of the son seeking a father as important to much of his writing, a theme that may have been influenced by sorrow over the death of his youngest child. The use of that narrative device is evident in many of his novels, including two books set in England during Roman times, *The Eagles Have Flown* (1954) and *Legions of the Eagle* (1954).

As a historian, Treece was attracted to the migrations that have taken place over centuries. It is not surprising that the Vikings interested him, for "Viking" in Norse means "wanderer," and their voyages played out the sort of quest that fascinated Treece. Treece used the Vikings as a basis for the trilogy *Viking's Dawn* (1955), *The Road to Miklagard* (1957), and *Viking's Sunset* (1960). The journeys of the fictitious central character, Harold Sigurdson, take him from the fjords of Scandinavia to Scotland, Ireland, Miklagard, and Kiev, and finally to Iceland, Greenland, and Finland. Though most of the adventures are fictional, they are based to some extent on history and on sagas.

Treece's last book, *The Dream-Time* (1966), bridges the ages by creating a story around people of prehistoric times who lived with the same universal fears and joys that we know today and whose lives were governed by the struggle to defend themselves from aggressors. The book is an eloquent cry for peace in a wartorn world, expressing a hope that people might care enough about one another not to make war.

Treece was developing as a writer to the very end of his life. *The Dream-Time* was a provocative novel and different enough from his earlier work so that we can only guess what may have followed had his life not been cut short. Certainly, Treece's historical novels for children deserve a special place among the fine books of that genre. ❧ D.L.M.

Tresselt, Alvin

American picture-book author, b. 1916. From the beginning of his writing career in the 1940s, Alvin Tresselt exhibited a knack for introducing young children to nature. His first picture book, *Rain Drop Splash* (1946), won Caldecott honors for Leonard Weisgard's illustrations and received praise for its cadenced text, which follows raindrops on a journey from sky, to puddle, to pond, to sea. Along the way the rain splashes a bear, flows through a brook from which deer drink, helps create a pond beside which red-winged blackbirds live, and thus Tresselt, as he would in succeeding picture books, gives children a manageable glimpse into entire ecosystems.

The Caldecott Award–winning *White Snow, Bright Snow* (1947) is the first of Tresselt's mood picture books to evoke the sights, sounds, and feel of a particular event. This poetic account of a snowstorm and how grown-ups and children respond to it also marks Tresselt's first collaboration with illustrator Roger Duvoisin, with whom he would go on to create more than fifteen picture books. Duvoisin's bold use of line and color matches the childlike exuberance that Tresselt's texts often convey.

Tresselt's own very tactile childhood memories help explain the freshness of the images in his writing. From his first visit to a farm at age nine, he remembers his excitement over the smell of mown fields and the feel of a cow licking his face. Readers experience such vivid sensations in *Hide and Seek Fog* (1965), a Caldecott honor winner illustrated by Duvoisin that describes three foggy days ay the beach during which the fog "twisted about the cottages like slow-motion smoke" and "hung, wet and dripping, from the bathing suits and towels on the clothesline." Remembering his love of words as a child, Tresselt never limits his vocabulary for his young audience, but lets them appreciate the fun and beauty of language.

Many of his books make readers aware of life's cycles. He has written frequently of the changing seasons, as in *Hi, Mr. Robin!* (1950), a boy's search for signs of spring, and *It's Time Now!* (1969), a look at what people in the city do during different times of the year. The building of beaver dams starts a chain of events in *The Beaver Pond* (1970) that turns a stream to a pond to a stream again, consequently affecting the creatures living nearby.

As editor of *Humpty Dumpty's Magazine* from 1952 to 1965, Tresselt sought material that would expand young children's minds, and he instituted an ecology feature that continued after he left the magazine. He went on to work as editor at Parent's Magazine Press while continuing to write. He tried his hand at retelling folktales from around the world, mainly from Japan, but his own work remains his most popular.

In the early 1990s, Tresselt revised several of his texts for a new generation of readers, and new illustrators gave each a more modern look. Carolyn Ewing provided realistic paintings in soft colors for *Wake Up, City!*, *Wake Up, Farm!*, and *The Rabbit Story*—all three originally published in the 1950s. *The Dead Tree* (1972), Tresselt's lucid account of an oak tree's contribution to the forest in life and in death, was renamed *The Gift of the Tree* (1992) and given new sun-drenched illustrations by Henri Sorensen. ❧ C.M.H.

Tripp, Wallace

AMERICAN ILLUSTRATOR, ANTHOLOGIST, AND AUTHOR, B. 1940. Lively pen lines and a strong sense of humor characterize Wallace Tripp's illustrations. He has more than forty books to his credit, and although he has written three PICTURE BOOKS, he primarily illustrates the works of others. He is best known for his collections of nonsense verse. Drawing from MOTHER GOOSE, folk rhymes, and well-known poets such as Alexander Pope and Emily Dickinson, these books include humorous POETRY and visual jokes.

Tripp grew up in rural New Hampshire and New

Illustration by Wallace Tripp from his book *Marguerite, Go Wash Your Feet!* (1985).

Voices of the Creators

Wallace Tripp

After my 1940 Boston debut, we moved to Westchester, New York, which, with its abundance of kids, was a rouser of a place to grow up in. But I've come down on the side of the country mice, and since age fourteen have lived in New Hampshire, where my wife Marcy and I have raised three kids. It's a scribbling sort of household: our older son and daughter are professional artists; our younger son shows the unmistakable signs.

Yellowing clumps of my childhood pictures suggest that though I have improved my drawing and color over the years, the work's substance has changed little. The focus then and now is on anatomically correct comic people and animals—individualized as much as possible—almost always in bygone settings. Hardly a picture of mine exists that I did not set out attempting to be funny. Giving fair value is important to me. That's one reason my pictures are so detail-packed. Besides, I hate to waste a joke.

People ask, "Did you always draw?" Yes. Early on most kids draw a lot, but only a few persist. An illustrator is just a kid who hung on to his pencils.

Kids ask, "Do you put people you know in your books?" Hardly ever. Our daughter is on the dedication page of *Granfa' Grig Had a Pig,* and our older son gets a haircut on a later page. Our younger son is on the dedication page of *Marguerite, Go Wash Your Feet!* Otherwise, except for historical people like Toscanini, Groucho Marx, and Robert Frost, nearly all the characters are imaginary.

Occasionally people point out the good fortune of being born with talent, sometimes with hints of "You got a free lunch, and I didn't." Genius is rare as turtle fangs, but talent is common enough. Complementary capabilities are often critical to success. A. A. Milne said, "If we make use of a talent it is only because we make use of another talent, a talent for using talents." The great conductor, Sir Thomas Beecham, famed for his musicianship and matchless wit, complained in a rare serious moment, "I never receive recognition of the one gift which I command beyond any other—a gift for industry, patient industry." If I'm fortunate it's because my wife, aside from being a boffo girl and a talented painter, is a business whiz. Since artists practically epitomize lack of business sense, this is luck.

The experienced illustrator subscribes to the principle of the application of the seat of the pants to the seat of the chair. Should inspiration whisk down your chimney, be at your table. The first ten thousand drawings are the hardest. Put another way, you have ten thousand bad drawings within and should expel them as quickly as possible. Lest you imagine me a sour pragmatist, know that I once imagined my work was energized by a Muse. Kindergarten, Crestwood, New York. Enchanting girl named, happy chance, Rijn (as in Rembrandt), a surname to twangle the aestheticals and set the paint glands raging. She moved away. The loss, the pain. Bereft, hollow-eyed, I became the wraith of PS 15 and wandered the halls croaking, "My Precious." One day I absently picked up a pencil, and before I could think I was drawing. "Bother Muses and other mythological claptrap," I said. "Looks like I'm to do it on my own."

Speaking of pencils, I use 4B to 2H plus forests of Berol Electronic 350 Scorer pencils. Sketches are made on tracing paper, transferred to cold press illustration board, and inked with Gillott 170 pens supplemented by the temperamental Gillott 659 and the docile Hunt 102. Color is courtesy of Winsor & Newton watercolors and Series 7 brushes. I also rely on the usual 6,000 research books.

Grant me one wish, and it would be a time machine: extinct animals; early man; the Trojan Horse; Cleopatra's nose; King Arthur (please let him be there), authentically costumed; history's most unlikely hero, Joan of Arc; Shakespeare at the Globe; Vermeer at his easel; travels with Dürer; secrets of the Cremona violin makers; hanging out with Hogarth; Mozart conducting *The Magic Flute.*

Perhaps my biggest problem as an artist has been the distracting range of my interests. My hobbies are never casual and always time-consuming and only tolerated because my wife believes they enrich my work. Aviation, Indians, history, herpetology, music, you name it, I jump right in like Stephen Leacock's Lord Ronald who flung himself upon his horse and rode madly off in all directions. The only comfort is that Leonardo da Vinci was a bit like that too. Horses and all animals delight me. With apologies to our dachshund, Tessie, and our cat, Chelsea, lions are my favorites. I wish they made more reliable pets.

Illustrators are word people who happen to draw. We work with one foot in a book, the other stuck in a paint pot. Our shoes are a disgrace.

York. After receiving a degree in graphic arts from the School of the Museum of Fine Arts, Boston, he returned to New Hampshire to earn a bachelor's degree in education from Keene State College. He then taught English for three years. In addition to illustrating books, Tripp ran a publishing house, Sparhawk Books, during the 1980s, and he designed greeting cards for Pawprints, his successful, family-owned card company.

Tripp uses a fine black pen line for his illustrations, often with only two additional colors. In *Catofy the Clever* (1972), a Russian folktale adapted by Cynthia Jameson, Tripp's illustrations add to the humor of the story about a cat who outwits the other forest animals. His energetic lines dance across the page, providing texture and interest, and compensate for the limited palette. But Tripp's greatest strength lies in his ability to provide his animals with personality and in conveying a wide range of feelings. As Casey steps up to the plate in Ernest Lawrence Thayer's *Casey at the Bat: A Ballad of the Republic, Sung in the Year 1888* (1978), Tripp draws him as a large smug bear, overly confident of his ability to hit the needed home run. The variety of emotions—from hope to despair—in this classic poem are portrayed delightfully by the body language and expressions of the ballplayers and fans.

After Tripp and his family spent a year in England, he wrote *Sir Toby Jingle's Beastly Journey* (1976). Sir Toby, who has fought many a fearsome beast, takes one final journey to rid the forest of its evil creatures. This time, however, the aging knight uses his wits rather than his strength to trick the animals into submission. In addition to the text, Tripp uses dialogue balloons in his pen-and-ink illustrations to create humor and add another dimension to the story.

Tripp's anthologies of humorous verse have received a number of awards. *A Great Big Ugly Man Came Up and Tied His Horse to Me: A Book of Nonsense Verse* (1973) was named an American Library Association Notable Book, and *Granfa' Grig Had a Pig and Other Rhymes without Reason from Mother Goose* (1976) won the Boston Globe–Horn Book Award for illustration. In these titles, as well as in his most recent one, *Marguerite, Go Wash Your Feet!* (1985), Tripp's illustrations are filled with jokes and references to the larger world. For example, in illustrating the poem "A hedge between,/ keeps friendship green," included in *Granfa' Grig,* Robert Frost stands on the far side of the hedge. *Marguerite* in particular contains such humorous allusions to art, entertainment, politics, and children's literature.

Whether he illustrates stories or poetry anthologies, Tripp's pictures are peopled with a marvelous assortment of animals, full of character and emotion. ❧ P.R.

Tudor, Tasha

American artist and author, b. 1915. Tasha Tudor, gifted artist beloved by generations of readers, published her first book, *Pumpkin Moonshine,* in 1938. Since then, she has written, illustrated, and edited over seventy-five books for young children. Born Starling Burgess in Boston, Massachusetts, the daughter of a naval architect and his independent artist wife, Tudor was nicknamed "Natasha" by her father after Tolstoy's heroine in *War and Peace* and she eventually changed her name to Tudor, her mother's maiden name. When Tudor was nine, her parents divorced and she went to live with family friends in Connecticut while her mother pursued her a career in art. Tudor embraced the family's unconventional lifestyle and credits them with liberating her creativity. Convinced that she had a past existence in 1830, Tudor has lived a simple, serene life in accordance with that time in rural Vermont, surrounded by animals, children, and breathtaking gardens.

In books characterized by delicate illustrations and simple prose, Tudor presents an unashamedly sentimental view of childhood. She outfits her characters in old-fashioned attire and places them in pastoral settings. In *A Is for Annabelle* (1954) the charming sepia-toned illustrations create a mood of nostalgia, as two little girls play dress-up with their grandmother's doll. The companion book, *1 Is One* (1956), alternates pages of soft black-and-white sketches with glowing watercolor illustrations. At the time, *1 Is One* was a unique sort of counting book, using elements in nature to teach numbers. The pages are bordered with the intricate garlands of flowers, birds, and animals that have become a Tudor trademark, reflecting her lifelong love of nature.

Tudor's work repeatedly expresses a realism afforded only by close interaction with her subjects. Animals, children, and situations, she says, are "done from actuality, not imagined." Even in books of fantasy, such as *A Tale for Easter* (1941), which describes a magical ride on Easter eve, Tudor's depictions of animals associated with Easter are thoroughly lifelike. Tudor's favorite book is *Corgiville Fair* (1971), a bucolic tale centered around her beloved corgi dogs. In matter-of-fact, conversational prose and busy, action-filled pages, Tudor tells a rollicking tale of feline scoundrels, prize "race goats," and mischievous, troll-like "boggarts." *The Tasha Tudor Book of Fairy Tales* (1961) is a compilation of Tudor's favorite tales, presented in uncomplicated language, with beautifully bordered pages.

Tudor has illustrated numerous works by other authors, including *The Secret Garden* (1962) and *A Little Princess* (1963) by Frances Hodgson Burnett. For her edition of RUMER GODDEN's *The Dolls' House* (1962), Tudor looked to her own handcrafted dolls and marionettes for inspiration.

Efner Tudor Holmes inherited her mother's gift for storytelling, as seen in *Amy's Goose* (1977), the moving story of the rehabilitation of a wounded goose. Tudor's warm, sensitive pictures for her daughter's book are evocative of a New England autumn. Awarded the Regina Medal in 1971 for her body of work, Tudor has also been the subject of both a biography, *Drawn from New England* (1979), by another daughter, Bethany Tudor, and a beautiful photographic celebration, *The Private World of Tasha Tudor* (1992), by Richard Brown.

To the modern child, Tudor's books may appear idealized and dated; however, they celebrate the ageless wonder of childhood and reflect Tudor's belief in a creative, warm, and nurturing home. ❧ M.O'D.H.

Tunis, Edwin

AMERICAN ARTIST AND NONFICTION AUTHOR, 1897–1973. "For the whole family" is a favorite catch phrase of overly optimistic publishers, but the term does, indeed, apply to the handsome social histories written and illustrated by Edwin Tunis. His books can be read by schoolchildren in the middle grades and enjoyed by history buffs long past their school years.

Born in Cold Spring Harbor, New York, and brought up in North Carolina (where he spent the first grade in a one-room schoolhouse), Maryland, and Delaware, Tunis developed a lifelong passion for American history and culture during his peripatetic early years. Trained at the Maryland Institute of Art, he was an artist with a prodigious capacity for detail. His most ambitious undertaking, a mural depicting the history of spices, was 145 feet long, and two and a half years in the painting. The work required extensive research into ancient ships and prompted Tunis to write and illustrate his first book, *Oars, Sails, and Steam* (1952). Two other pictorial histories soon followed: *Wheels* (1955) and *Weapons* (1955).

Tunis proved to be as fine a writer as he was an artist. His books have an engaging, almost infectiously enthusiastic tone. They are simply written and astonishingly thorough. *Colonial Living* (1957) is representative of both his ambition and his skill. The subject is enormous: everyday living in seventeenth- and eighteenth-century America. From the fragile beachhead settlements to the highly structured society of Virginia at the dawn of the Revolutionary War, this is a vivid panorama of how the colonists really lived—what they ate, how they slept, how rich men tended their wigs, and how criminals were punished; the stuff of daily life is portrayed in simple prose and scores of finely crafted drawings.

Tunis's books were frequently favored by award committees. *Frontier Living* (1961), which tracks the manners and customs of American frontier life from the Revolutionary War through the nineteenth-century migrations, was a Newbery Honor Book. *Oars, Sails, and Steam* was chosen by the American Institute of Graphic Artists as one of their Fifty Books of the Year. *The Young United States: 1783–1830* (1969) was nominated for the National Book Award.

Like the topics they explore, Tunis's books are themselves of a time now long past. Few nonfiction books for children look like this anymore. The illustrations are black-and-white; the design is simple and elegant. The texts, even in his picture books, are long, helpfully broken down into topics, but not split by sidebars of historical oddities or trivia. His respect for history, and for his readers, distinguishes every page. ❧ A.Q.

Tunis, John R.

AMERICAN AUTHOR, 1889–1975. A native of Boston, Massachusetts, John R. Tunis is considered by many to be the dean of American juvenile sports novelists. Beginning with *Iron Duke* in 1938, he wrote more than twenty-one books for adolescents, striving to tell an authentic, exciting sports story while simultaneously weaving in his own perspective on competition.

Tunis believed in clean-cut, intelligent, honest young men, playing games with the spirit of teamwork and sportsmanship. He opposed coaches, players, and fans who believed in winning at any cost. He advocated opportunity for all and boldly tackled the issue of racial and religious discrimination in the athletic arena.

Success as a writer of juvenile sports novels came later in his versatile fifty-year writing career. Beginning as a struggling freelance writer in the early 1920s after graduation from Harvard and a stint in the army, his first year as a writer netted him $81 from Boston newspapers. Moving to Connecticut to be closer to the New York market, he continued to pound the pavement with proposals for magazine and newspaper articles.

"It was like working for the Fuller Brush Company, and in many magazine offices I must have been no more welcome," he said in his 1964 autobiography, *A Measure of Independence*. His perseverance paid off, however, and his skills were recognized. Landing a job as a sportswriter for the *New York Evening Post* in 1925, he held that position for seven years. While a freelance writer, Tunis had over 2,000 articles printed and became a household name in respected publications such as *The New Yorker, The Saturday Evening Post, Esquire,* and *Reader's Digest.*

During the Depression, with magazines folding and his earnings not assured, Tunis, at age forty-nine, turned his attention to completing a novel. In 1938, confident that he had a marketable story, he delivered *Iron Duke* to Alfred Harcourt, founder of Harcourt, Brace. Within ten days, Tunis had a response. Harcourt would publish his story of a midwestern boy entering Harvard who struggles with loneliness but finds his niche through sports. Initially shocked at the suggestion that he publish with a juvenile imprint, Tunis was convinced by his editor to accept the contract and the novel went on to win the *New York Tribune*'s Spring Book Festival award in 1938, launching him in this genre; by 1970 the book had sold over 70,000 copies.

Twenty novels for young readers followed over the next thirty years, and Tunis's firsthand experience as an athlete combined with his knowledge of the sports world gave his books authenticity and appeal. The majority of his stories are concerned with the inner struggles of realistic adolescents involved in sports who often were losers on the field but became heroes in life. Whether writing about basketball, baseball, football, track, or tennis, he uses dialogue that is colorful and descriptive and settings that are plausible.

The essence of Tunis's research was experience. From the crowd at a high school basketball game in Indiana to baseball training camp in Florida, Tunis spent time at the scene. His readers can smell the odor in the locker room, feel a runner's aching legs, or hear the crowd roar. Central to his books are the values of persistence, hard work, sacrifice, and commitment to the team. When Duke Wellington in *Iron Duke* outruns a Yale track star, his elation is clear: "Despite his weariness he almost felt he could run across the river. Fellows were speaking to him who had never noticed him before, calling him 'Duke,' men he didn't even know. . . . It took three years, but he'd arrived."

When corruption taints parents and the community in *Yea! Wildcats!* (1944), the team's basketball coach risks the state championship in order to uphold the values he thinks are worth upholding. The newspaper editor in town thinks, "Basketball is wonderful as long as it's a game. But here, now, in this region it's sort of a disease."

The lessons from Tunis's minister father and teacher mother—to educate and reform—stayed with him in all of his novels. Only two of his later juvenile books take readers outside the sports scene and into World War II. Clearly, all of Tunis's books speak to the struggles of teens. They have been read for the past fifty-five years.

L.G.S.

Turkle, Brinton

American illustrator and author, b. 1915. Brinton Cassady Turkle's books are notable for their well-researched settings and memorable characters. Those books he has illustrated for others, like Monjo's *Poor Richard in France* (1973) and Clifton's *The Boy Who Didn't Believe in Spring* (1973), have so perfectly captured the stories' location and characters that readers can imagine historical Ben Franklin and contemporary King Shabazz in no other way. Books he has both written and illustrated, like *Deep in the Forest* (1976) and *Do Not Open* (1981) are even richer for coming from a single hand.

With characteristic modesty, Turkle has remarked, "I feel that I have had only marginal success with the [picture book] ideal [of unity], but I do keep trying and I think I am getting better." But Turkle's four Obadiah books, beginning with *Obadiah the Bold* (1965), attest to success that is far from marginal: *Thy Friend, Obadiah* (1969), was named a Caldecott Honor Book. The series's nineteenth-century Nantucket is both historically accurate and lively, full of warmth and gentle humor. In the four books Obadiah Starbuck, a young Quaker, and later his sister (*Rachel and Obadiah,* 1978) successfully engage contemporary readers with timeless adventures like friendship with a bird and a sibling foot race.

In *Do Not Open* the deft interweaving of text and art create page-turning tension between Miss Moody, her cat, and the "voice" inside the bottle on the beach. Readers of wordless *Deep in the Forest* know the story of "Goldilocks and the Three Bears," upon which it is based, but Turkle maintains suspense through the little bear's engaging personality. *The Fiddler of High Lonesome* (1968) is longer, darker in mood, and intended for older readers, but it, too, blends its black-and-white art with the story to heighten suspense and deepen character.

Despite the fact that Turkle was "always drawing" as a child, he received little encouragement to become an artist, so in college he studied theater. He did, eventually, study art and work in advertising, but most of his adult life has been spent illustrating books—first he illustrated an adult book and, he recalls, "after that I worked on college texts, gradually coming down through the grades to picture books." At the same time he worked on local theatrical productions—directing, acting, and designing—and occasionally employing his skill with marionettes. Consequently, Turkle's books for children not only have a strong sense of character, but of drama.

Turkle may use simple charcoal sketches or more detailed drawings; his work may be unadorned or shaded, tinted by wash or aglow with layers of color. But it is his combination of artistic skill, well-researched setting, and fully conceived character that creates high drama of ordinary life and makes his books memorable. ♘ S.A.B.

Twain, Mark

American author, 1835–1910. Born Samuel Langhorne Clemens in Florida, Missouri, the youth who would become Mark Twain undertook careers as a printer, riverboat pilot, and prospector before turning to writing for his livelihood. First as a journalist and then as a writer of short stories, novels, and nonfiction, Twain was one of the nineteenth century's most successful writers. Since his death, young and adult readers around the world have continued to enjoy Twain's work, though the suitability of his writing for children has always been a subject of debate. In his own time Twain's work was attacked as too coarse for children; more recently, it has been criticized as too racist.

Perhaps the best explanation for Twain's reputation as a children's writer comes from Justin Kaplan's *Mr. Clemens and Mark Twain* (1966), a seminal biography that explores the split between Samuel Clemens, the man who strove for respectability and acceptance among America's eastern literary and social establishments, and Clemens's alter ego, Mark Twain, the earthy, funny, frontier-formed rough who loved attacking the hypocrisies of his era. Just as there is this split between Mr. Clemens and Mark Twain, there is a split between the fun-loving Mark Twain, much-loved children's author, and the dark Mark Twain, revered by adults—including many scholars—as one of the world's great literary geniuses.

As an author writing for adults, Twain imbues his works with irony and barbed social criticism that escapes most young readers, traits apparent even in such traditionally child-pleasing works as *The Prince and the Pauper* (1881), *The Adventures of Huckleberry Finn* (1884), and *A Connecticut Yankee in King Arthur's Court* (1889). Bitter disillusionment is another adult element that runs through Twain's work, dominating such late-period writings as "The Mysterious Stranger" (1898), *Mark Twain's Burlesque Autobiography* (1906), and "The War Prayer." Though Twain's works (with the exception of the notorious but insignificant *1601*, published in 1876) are not *adult* in the modern sense, they can include violence and language that many find inappropriate for children.

On the other hand, Twain's suitability as a children's author is attested to by his perennial popularity among young readers. Twain's marvelously accessible sense of humor—his sense of fun—has always been appreciated by the young. There is a nearly universal appeal to classic Twain humor, whether it is in the form of Tom Sawyer tricking his pals into paying for the honor of painting Aunt Polly's fence or of King Arthur's armored knights clanking to the rescue on their newly invented bicycles. Besides enjoying his sense of humor, young readers also appreciate the fact that Twain writes about children in a realistic way. Twain's best young characters are neither miniature adults nor stock symbols of innocence but rounded human beings. They are frequently in conflict with adult authority and can be, in turn, as disobedient, sweet, frightened, brave, serious, and playful as real children. It is the realistic completeness of Twain's child characters that makes them live long after the reading world has forgotten the countless one-dimensional children born of the dime-novel tradition that flourished during Twain's lifetime.

Twain's two greatest works featuring child characters are *The Adventures of Tom Sawyer* and *The Adventures of Huckleberry Finn*. Set in the fictional, pre–Civil War river town of St. Petersburg, *The Adventures of Tom Sawyer* (1875) is the story of a boy on the edge of adolescence, living a life that alternates between the restrictions imposed by the respectable adult-dominated society of St. Petersburg and the freedom offered by the Mississippi River wilderness surrounding the town. Acting out Everybody's fantasy, Tom gets to live wild on Jackson's Island, explore the labyrinths of McDougal's Cave, defeat the ominous Indian Joe, discover a treasure in gold, and woo Becky Thatcher, the girl of his puppy-love dreams. Tom also enjoys the sport of pulling practical jokes against such enemies of the State of Boyhood as the schoolteacher and the Sunday-school superintendent. Younger readers enjoy *The Adventures of Tom Sawyer* for its pranks and adventures of boyhood glory, but adults are more likely to appreciate the novel's nostalgic re-creation of the pleasures of boyhood. Twain's third-person narrative, detached and distant from the action, reinforces the nostalgic aspect of the novel, particularly when he bathes boyhood incidents in an irony that only adults can appreciate. Always a popular character, Tom would reappear in *The Adventures of Huckleberry Finn* as well as in two of Twain's least-satisfying books, *Tom Sawyer Abroad* (1894) and *Tom Sawyer, Detective* (1896). Twain also attempted to revive Tom in "Huck Finn and Tom Sawyer among the Indians" and "Tom Sawyer's Conspiracy," two unpublished fragments.

Huckleberry Finn has attracted young readers who delight in Huck, the book's picaresque narrator, as well as his adventures. Huck's adventures are amusing and thrilling enough to hold the attention of young readers, while his journey down the Mississippi strikes a deeper chord by representing the delightful—and terrifying—possibilities inherent in any attempt to escape the tyranny of adult society. Besides attracting young readers, *The Adventures of Huckleberry Finn* has attracted debate over its suitability for children. Certainly its irony eludes many young readers, and the book's plot includes such "unsuitable" elements as theft, murder, running away from home, child abuse, human slavery, and mob violence. Furthermore, the text is spiced with dialect speech that many younger readers have trouble deciphering and contains language that many children and adults find offensive. The book's language has generated accusations of racism. These accusations have, in turn, generated hot denials from those readers who see the book as a testament to racial tolerance. Although there is no denying that some of Huck's words are racially offensive, he does, however, avow that he will "go to hell" rather than see his friend Jim remain enslaved. Despite this, the controversy over *Huckleberry Finn* continues to swirl like a Mississippi back eddy, just as the book itself continues to roll on with all the force of Huck's "monstrous big" river. Having appeared in over 850 editions published in some sixty-five languages, *The Adventures of Huckleberry Finn* remains a reading rite of passage for much of the literate world.

Twain's image as an author for children has been shaped not only by his own talent for writing about children but also by the various ways in which his works have been packaged. For years publishers have abridged, bowdlerized, and illustrated Twain's work expressly for the children's market. His work has also been packaged for children via feature films, television programs, stage plays, musicals, animated films, and comic books. Frequently, such child-oriented packaging has resulted in many freckle-faced and barefoot interpretations that omit or gloss over Twain's darker intentions.

As far as Twain's intentions go, his *Slovenly Peter,* a translation of a German fairy tale, is his only work indisputably intended for children alone, and it was not published until 1935. Twain's later attempts to revive the character of Tom Sawyer, as well as the largely forgotten *Personal Recollections of Joan of Arc* (1896), might be argued to have been intended for young readers, but it is clear Twain hoped they would be read by adults as well as children. On the other hand, his large body of nonfiction, including all of his immensely popular travel books, was not intended for young readers—though there is no reason a young adult reader could not enjoy the hilarious *Innocents Abroad* (1869) or the rousing *Roughing It* (1872). Similarly, such popular novels as *The Adventures of Huckleberry Finn, The Adventures of Tom Sawyer, The Prince and the Pauper,* and *A Connecticut Yankee in King Arthur's Court,* were not written with children in mind—at least not exclusively so. It is largely these novels' enthusiastic appropriation by the young that has earned them their reputations as children's novels.

Despite LOUISA MAY ALCOTT's unfriendly recommendation that the coarse Mark Twain should not write for children, the fact is that most often Twain's intended audience was the entire family, not just its younger nor just its older members. Like all popular writers of his time and station, Twain tried (if not always successfully) to observe those nineteenth-century standards of taste and decorum that held that good writing should be fit for consumption by men, women, and children alike. So conscious of these standards was Twain that he willingly allowed his upright and proper wife, Olivia, to censor from his work anything that might prove offensive to young or old.

That Twain could successfully write for both young and old at the same time is as much a mark of his greatness as the fact that his work is as popular now, among both young and old, as it was when first published. And while the list of those who write for children but manage to appeal to adults is long, Twain is among the very few writers who have managed to find an audience of children without writing specifically for them.

DONALD A. BARCLAY

U

Uchida, Yoshiko

American author and author-illustrator, 1921–1992. Yoshiko Uchida, author of more than twenty-five books for children, was born in Alameda and grew up in Berkeley, California, where she attended the University of California. During her senior year of college, in 1942, Uchida and her family, along with 120,000 other Japanese Americans, were imprisoned in U.S. concentration camps following the bombing of Pearl Harbor. *The Invisible Thread* (1992), a moving memoir of Uchida's childhood and her time in the prison camps, describes the influence this experience had on her writing.

In 1952 Uchida received a Ford Foundation research fellowship that allowed her to visit Japan for two years. Three collections of folktales resulted from her research there, the first of which was *The Dancing Kettle and Other Japanese Folk Tales* (1949), a book that received a warm welcome, especially since older translations of tales were out of print at the time. A glossary, pronunciation guide, and source notes on the folktales are included in this and each of her later collections. Among the stories retold in *The Dancing Kettle* are "The Tongue-Cut Sparrow," "Momotaro: The Peach Boy," and "The Wedding of the Mouse."

Uchida's best-known books are her five historical novels about Japanese Americans, all written for middle-grade readers. *Journey to Topaz: A Story of the Japanese-American Evacuation* (1971), which was named an American Library Association Notable Book, and its sequel, *Journey Home* (1978), tell what happens to eleven-year-old Yuki Sakane and her family during and following their internment in the prison camps in World War II. Based on Uchida's own experiences, *Journey to Topaz* conveys—with an astonishing lack of bitterness—the quiet dignity and strength demonstrated by the prisoners, especially the first-generation Japanese, the Issei. The sequel depicts the difficulties individuals and families faced in rebuilding their lives amid a climate of distrust and fear.

A Japanese-American girl growing up during the Depression is the heroine of three more acclaimed books: *A Jar of Dreams* (1981), *The Best Bad Thing* (1983), and *The Happiest Ending* (1985). The first of these novels depicts eleven-year-old Rinko's changing attitude about her heritage during the summer her aunt from Japan visits. Aunt Waka gives Rinko and her family the courage to follow their dreams despite the prejudice they must endure. Filled with details of Japanese-American life in the 1930s, the book contains humor, sensitivity, and drama.

Uchida retold Japanese folktales and wrote stories about children living in Japan in order to share with American children the beauty of that country's culture and to dispel racist stereotypes. She wrote historical fiction about Japanese Americans to give children of Japanese descent pride in their ancestry and to inform all children about the past. She told about her wartime experiences as a testimony to those who survived the internment and to prevent the same tragedy from ever occurring again. But in all of her writing, Uchida hoped to show that people are the same, no matter where they live or what they look like—a goal she has admirably fulfilled. § J.M.B.

Ungerer, Tomi

American illustrator, b. 1931. His heroes are boa constrictors, bats, vultures, robbers, moon men, and octopi. His supporting cast is Dickensian. His style is both tender and satiric. His illustrations are both charming and frightening. He is not sweet. He is never pretty. He is, at the very least, Jean de Brunhoff and Eugène Ionesco, together, in one body.

Born in Strasbourg, France, Tomi Ungerer grew up in the shadow of death and poverty. His father, Theodor, died when Tomi was three years old. During the Depression, his mother was forced by economic hardship to move the family into her mother's home in nearby Colmar. The onslaught of World War II and the subsequent

German occupation of Alsace formed a perilous and confusing backdrop for Ungerer: "My whole childhood was a schooling in relativity, in figuring out for myself who were the good guys and who were the bad." For three months, as the Allied Front moved over Colmar, Ungerer and his family lived in their cellar, bombs having destroyed their house. "There was plenty to see and remember," he notes, "and my taste for the macabre certainly finds its roots there." When the war ended, the disillusioned Ungerer set out on foot across Europe. Though he studied briefly at the Ecole des Arts Décoratifs in Strasbourg, Ungerer feels that the greater part of his education "came from travels through Europe, walking and hitchhiking, earning my way by odd jobs, and of course painting, drawing, and working in the graphic arts."

In 1956 Ungerer immigrated to the United States. Arriving in New York, he looked for work as a freelance illustrator. His first professional assignment came from *Sports Illustrated,* and soon after he received a children's book contract for *The Mellops Go Flying* (1957), the first of four humorous books about a resourceful pig family and their entertaining adventures. Among Ungerer's early improbable protagonists were Emile, the octopus; Adelaide, the flying kangaroo; and Rufus, the bat. Crictor, the clever boa constrictor, of the book by the same name, has earned, in children's eyes, the status of Babar and Curious George.

"I want to amuse myself and in the same process amuse children. I use a lot of satire because I find satire more digestible and I think it has less hypocrisy. Satire points out the foolish aspects of society and the absurdity," Ungerer explains. In *The Beast of Monsieur Racine* (1971), an elderly gentleman befriends the beast who has been pilfering prize pears from his garden, only to find that the beast is actually two children in disguise. When the man in the moon, in *Moon Man* (1967), is jailed by the authorities after crash landing on Earth, he wanes to his third quarter, slips through the bars, and escapes. A scientist, residing in a remote castle, launches him back into the air, where, his curiosity satiated, he remains "curled up in his shimmering seat in space." *The Three Robbers* (1962), graphically bold with dramatic color contrasts, is the story of three hoodlums converted to philanthropy by a young orphan. Only Ungerer would have robbers steal away a child named Tiffany. He elucidated the use of intense black in the book: "This book is really a book of darkness. It's a book of shadows. It reflects the fears I had as a child." Many of Ungerer's books, in the tradition of European fairy tales, offer darkly satiric details, both graphic and literal, which may appall adults' sensitivities, but children take gleeful delight in his sometimes gruesome humor.

Ungerer, who in recent years has been living in Canada, Ireland, and France, is also known for his sophisticated adult books and poster art. He can draw blood with an incisive stroke of his pen, but he also displays a keen understanding of, and affection for, the human condition. His *Moon Man* looks down on us all.

M.B.B.

VAN ALLSBURG, CHRIS

AMERICAN ILLUSTRATOR AND AUTHOR, B. 1949. The publication and subsequent success of Chris Van Allsburg's *The Polar Express* (1985) clearly established the illustrator-author as one of the premier creators of PICTURE BOOKS in twentieth-century children's literature. *The Polar Express,* immediately taken to heart by children and adults alike, was a phenomenon in children's publishing. It won the Caldecott Medal for illustration, appeared on the *New York Times* best seller list, sold more than a million copies in its first five years of publication, and achieved the status of a contemporary classic.

The story chronicles the adventures of a boy who boards the Polar Express, travels to the North Pole, meets Santa Claus, and is given a silver bell. Its sound can be heard only by those who believe in the impossible—that is, in Santa Claus. Rich pastel illustrations, in blues and purples, are accompanied by a narrative that achieves an exceptional sense of story. The story appeals because Van Allsburg touches a universal chord—faith. The simple truth of the story is perceptively conveyed through a felicitous blend of pictures and narrative; the combination radiates with childlike wonder while reverberating with mysterious intensity.

Born in Grand Rapids, Michigan, Van Allsburg received his B.F.A. from the University of Michigan. He attended graduate school at the Rhode Island School of Design and received his M.F.A. in sculpture. In 1977, Van Allsburg's sculptures, described as "fastidiously crafted, surreal, enigmatic and whimsical," were exhibited in New York galleries. Originally, he began drawing as a casual diversion from sculpting, and his early black-and-white drawings contained elements of sculpture—heavy, solid forms, which appear to be built with even, controlled lines and architectural perspectives.

While *The Polar Express* unquestionably ranks as Van Allsburg's most popular book, it is only a part of his contribution to children's books. His first book, *The Garden of Abdul Gasazi* (1979), met with a variety of critical responses. The striking, pointillistic graphite drawings were hailed as "intriguing and refreshing." The story, about a young boy pursuing a dog into the topiary gardens of the magician Gasazi, was labeled ominous and disquieting by some. The book won the Boston Globe–Horn Book Award for illustration; it was considered an auspicious beginning.

Van Allsburg has stated that stories begin as fragments of pictures in his mind. "Creating the story comes out of posing questions to myself. I call it the 'what if' and 'what then' approach. What if two bored children discover a board game? What then . . . ?" That was the beginning of *Jumanji* (1981). As the protagonists, Judy and Peter, play the game, their house is transformed into a jungle—complete with a hungry lion, marauding monkeys, a menacing python, and an erupting volcano. The children know they must finish the game, and in a chaotic final moment all is set right when one player reaches the end. Readers are spellbound by this cautionary adventure and delight in the final page when they witness the game being discovered by two more curious children. Masterly use of light and shadow and exaggerated changes of perspective create a bizarre and mythical world that leaves one wondering whether the adventure was real or imagined.

In *The Wreck of the Zephyr* (1983), a story about the disasters wrought by youthful pride, the artist leaves the dramatic tonal range of grays and black and white—characteristic of previous books—and bursts into color. Using pastels, he creates vibrant, luminous landscapes. The sharp delineation of figures and objects found in earlier work is more diffused here, imbuing the illustrations with a mysterious light.

This softening of line is carried into *The Mysteries of Harris Burdick* (1984), where richly shaded charcoal drawings intrigue and tantalize the imagination. The book is composed of fourteen illustrations, labeled with captions. Pictures range from whimsical to frightening, and are linked by unexplained elements or the supernatural. The book's enigmatic premise and the exquisite drawings, which speak eloquently without text, represent

Voices of the Creators

Chris Van Allsburg

Over the years that have passed since my first book was published, a question I've been asked often is "Where do your ideas come from?" I've given a variety of answers to this question, such as "I steal them from the neighborhood kids" or "They are beamed to me from outer space."

It's not really my intention to be rude or smart-alecky. The fact is, I don't know where my ideas come from. Each story I've written starts out as a vague idea that seems to be going nowhere, then suddenly materializes as a completed concept. It almost seems like a discovery, as if the story were always there. The few elements I start out with are actually clues. If I figure out what they mean, I can discover the story that's waiting.

When I began thinking about what became *The Polar Express,* I had a single image in mind: a young boy sees a train standing still in front of his house one night. The boy and I took a few different trips on the train, but we did not, in a figurative sense, go anywhere. Then I headed north, and I got the feeling that this time I'd picked the right direction, because the train kept rolling all the way to the North Pole. At that point the story seemed literally to present itself. Who lives at the North Pole? Santa. When would the perfect time for a visit be? Christmas Eve. What happens on Christmas Eve at the North Pole? Undoubtedly, a ceremony of some kind, a ceremony requiring a child, delivered by a train that would have to be named the Polar Express.

These stray elements are, of course, merely events. A good story uses the description of events to reveal some kind of moral or psychological premise. I am not aware, as I develop a story, what the premise is. When I started the book, I thought I was writing about a train trip, but the story was actually about faith and the desire to believe in something. Creating books is an intriguing process. I know if I'd set out with the goal of writing a book about faith, I'd still be holding a pencil over a blank sheet of paper.

Santa Claus is our culture's only mythic figure truly believed in by a large percentage of the population. Most of the true believers are under eight years old, and that's a pity. The rationality we all embrace as adults makes believing in the fantastic difficult, if not impossible. Lucky are the children who know there is a jolly fat man in a red suit who pilots a flying sleigh. We should envy them. And we should envy the people who are so certain Martians will land in their back yard that they keep a loaded Polaroid camera by the back door. The inclination to believe in the fantastic may strike some as a failure in logic, but it's really a gift. A world that might have Bigfoot and the Loch Ness monster is clearly superior to one that does not.

The application of logical or analytical thought may be the enemy of belief in the fantastic, but it is not, for me, a liability in its illustration. When I conceived of the North Pole in the book, it was logic that insisted it be a vast collection of factories. I don't see this as a whim of mine or even as an act of imagination. How could it look any other way, given the volume of toys produced there every year?

I do not find that illustrating a story has the same quality of discovery as writing it. As I consider a story, I see it quite clearly. Illustrating is simply a matter of drawing something I've already experienced in my mind's eye. Because I see the story unfold as if it were on film, the challenge is deciding precisely which moment should be illustrated and from what point of view.

A fantasy of mine is a miraculous machine, a machine that could be hooked up to my brain and instantly produce finished art from the images in my mind. Conceiving something is only part of the creative process. Giving life to the conception is the other half. The struggle to master a medium, whether it's words, notes, paint, or marble, is the heroic part of making art.

qualities that have become hallmarks of Van Allsburg's work.

Magic and the supernatural in *The Widow's Broom* (1993) are tempered by the practical, kindly nature of the widow, who assists a witch and is given her broom. Good versus evil is the theme, but the story bubbles with humor and affection when the protective, magic broom and the widow become fast friends.

Van Allsburg's artistic style is often described as surrealistic fantasy. Van Allsburg states that "he is intrigued by a setting of a normal, everyday reality, where something strange or puzzling happens"; he also enjoys "creating impossible worlds." So, it is not surprising that visual illusions, created by the dramatic use of scale and perspective, are a common thread running through his books. Also characteristic of Van Allsburg's illustrations are forms and figures that—to varying degrees—appear sculptured and frozen in time. But the breadth and sophistication in his style also allow for fluid, subtle nuances in human figures and detailed facial expressions, which reflect deeper psychological interpretations of character. Whether executed in black and white or in color, Van Allsburg's illustrations never fail to fascinate the intellect, pique the senses, and emphasize the power of imagination. ♠ STEPHANIE LOER

VAN LOON, HENDRIK WILLEM

AMERICAN WRITER AND ILLUSTRATOR, 1882–1944. Born and raised in the Netherlands, Hendrik Willem van Loon immigrated to the United States in 1902. After graduating from Cornell University in 1905, he began his career as a journalist in Washington and later continued this profession in Russia. In 1911 he earned a doctorate in history from the University of Munich. Upon his return to the United States he taught at various colleges, continued his journalistic activity, and wrote books that received little attention.

In 1919 publisher Horace Liveright asked van Loon to write a series of eight history books for children. The first, *Ancient Man,* was published in 1920. Its success and the success of H. G. Wells's two-volume *Outline of History* (1920) gave Liveright the notion to have van Loon combine the ideas for the series into a single volume of history for children. The result, *The Story of Mankind* (1921), received fine reviews, sold well, and brought van Loon his first real measure of literary fame. In 1922 the book was the first recipient of the John Newbery Medal, given by the American Library Association for the most distinguished contribution to American children's literature. Van Loon's apparent delight in telling history, his exceptional ability to speak directly to his readers without condescension, and his lively storytelling style were all factors that made the book of interest to adults as well as to his intended child audience. Van Loon illustrated the book profusely, including a pictorial history at its end. For many years the book continued to sell well, and it was translated into several languages.

The Story of Mankind was not universally accepted, however, and several libraries chose not to purchase it, apparently because of van Loon's discussion of evolution. Today the book is seldom read and is subject to criticism because of racial and cultural slurs and because parts contain outdated information or interpretation despite van Loon's and later various publishers' updates to add later events. Despite these problems, with this book van Loon set a standard of what good nonfiction can do—engage the reader and impart its content in a lively fashion.

Following the success of *The Story of Mankind,* van Loon gave up teaching and turned his attention more fully to writing and illustrating. Among his other books for young readers are *The Story of the Bible* (1923), *Van Loon's Geography* (1932), several biographies, and a few picture books. In addition van Loon worked on three song books for children with Grace Castagnetta and illustrated other authors' books, such as Lucy Sprague Mitchell's *Here and Now Storybook* (1936). Besides the books he wrote for children, van Loon wrote many books for adults in the areas of history, the arts, biography, and autobiography. He also wrote magazine and newspaper articles, was associate editor of the Baltimore *Sun* in 1923–24, and was a prolific letter writer. In need of intellectual stimulation and change, van Loon moved often and sought out interesting people, but it is said he preferred to be the center of attention. He continued to lecture, often using the dramatic style that had engaged his college students. He also did radio commentary on arts and news events and during World War II broadcast to the Netherlands as part of the war effort.

In 1944 van Loon died of heart failure. Despite his success in several fields, it is *The Story of Mankind* that remains his best-known and most important contribution. ♠ B.J.P.

VERNE, JULES

FRENCH AUTHOR, 1828–1905. A lawyer by training and a scientific interpreter by inclination, Jules Verne revealed a world based on scientific reality, full of wonder and delight. Such themes established the SCIENCE FICTION genre introduced by Mary Shelley and Edgar Allan Poe. Verne described possibilities based on nineteenth-century explorations and events in *Journey to the Center of the Earth* (1864), *A Trip to the Moon* (1865), and *Around the World in Eighty Days* (1873).

The popular *Twenty Thousand Leagues under the Sea* (1870) impressed adults of the time with the wonderful reality of undersea travel. Today, young adult readers prefer the compelling adventure the story offers. Based on a French inventor's steam-driven submarine, Verne's story features three characters (Professor Aronnax; his servant, Conseil; and the Canadian harpooner, Ned Land) who find themselves captured and residing on a powerful undersea craft, the *Nautilus.* The mysterious Captain Nemo—a rigid individualist who has decided to live in the oceans of the world—leads the adventurers on their journey. Verne's text resonates with contemporary beliefs about preservation of natural resources, although his instincts tend toward nineteenth-century exploitation, with animals seen as sources of protein and gustatory delight. Verne weaves science lessons throughout the story: geography, as the *Nautilus* visits each of the continents; physics, in discussions of submarine air displacement; biology, with descriptions and classifications of marine organisms; geology, as the submarine explores rock formations. Verne's facts, while yellow with age and brittle with incorrect information, make fiction appear real. By the end, with the fate of Captain Nemo and the *Nautilus* unclear, Verne's power is such that we dismiss photographs from space and exhaustive ocean exploration for the imaginative possibility that the *Nautilus* remains afloat and continues its adventures. B.C.

Viorst, Judith

American author and poet, b. 1931. Judith Viorst became well known first through her column in *Redbook,* which was witty, stylish, and self-deprecating. Her strong family orientation emerged in that forum and gracefully led her into writing children's books. Her books could win awards for title length alone, witness *My Mama Says There Aren't Any Zombies, Ghosts, Vampires, Creatures, Demons, Monsters, Fiends, Goblins or Things* (1973). In this case her collaboration with illustrator Kay Chorao is a marriage of one clean, direct style with another, no excess baggage in either one. In *Alexander and the Terrible, Horrible, No Good, Very Bad Day* (1972), Viorst teamed with illustrator Ray Cruz in an effective partnership that carries poor Alex through a day of being ignored, harassed by his peers, and harshly judged.

Viorst always knew she would be a writer and is emphatic that her family has provided inspiration and encouragement for her efforts. Born in Newark, she married political writer Milton Viorst in 1960. Both write at home, and Judith Viorst has said her husband encourages her efforts and provides constructive criticism. Viorst's writing began with odes to dead parents (who were still alive and annoyed, she says), but it is Viorst's children whom she is writing about and writing for, even down to using their real names. She has three sons, Anthony, Nicholas, and Alexander, now grown, who have given her material for her work. She says she wrote *I'll Fix Anthony* (1969) to reflect how her oldest son used to torment his brother Nick.

The Tenth Good Thing about Barney (1971) has become a classic in helping children deal with grief. In this book, the children in the family try to find positive things about their cat who has just died, from his value as a playmate to his worth as garden compost. *The Good-bye Book* (1988) is about a young boy who tries everything to talk his parents out of going out that evening—whining, threatening, begging—while they calmly get dressed through all of it. When the unfamiliar baby sitter arrives, the boy is pleasantly surprised to find a friendly teenage boy who may not be so bad after all.

Viorst's work is valued for her sensitivity to children and her slightly irreverent sense of humor, which can be appreciated by readers of any age. A.C.

Vivas, Julie

Australian illustrator, b. 1947. While *Possum Magic* (1983) unquestionably ranks as one of Australia's most popular contemporary picture books, its enchanting illustrations comprise just a small wedge of Julie Vivas's contribution to children's literature. Her distinctive rounded shapes and sense of character and motion have made her one of Australia's most beloved illustrators.

Vivas was born in Adelaide and grew up in Melbourne and later Sydney. After studying interior design and film animation at the National Art School, she worked briefly in a veterinary clinic and then joined a film-animation studio for a few years. Although she spent that time on assembly-line work—painting cells, mixing colors, and filling in artwork—the experience left its mark, as it helped shape the strong sense of flowing movement in so many of her illustrations. Between 1968 and 1972 she lived in Spain, where she "drew and drew"—mostly people in the streets and markets. That artwork formed the basis of an exhibition when she returned to Australia. One visitor to the event, author Libby Hathorn, was particularly impressed and approached Vivas about illustrating her text for *The Train to Bondi Beach* (1980), the story of a young paper boy with larger aspirations. After a year and a half of meticulously drawing and redrawing and designing and redesigning, the book was completed and in 1981 won a

Highly Commended Award medal from the Australian Children's Book Council.

In the meantime Vivas had done a set of illustrations for a story written by a children's literature student about some mice traveling around the world. Six years later, when the student, a young woman by the name of MEM FOX, had rewritten the story with possums instead of mice and set it in Australia, the publisher asked Vivas if she would reillustrate the story. She did, and *Possum Magic* was born. As the book swept through Australia, delighting thousands of readers with its ingenuous possum characters, the artist turned her attention to a variety of other titles. *The Nativity* (1986), an earthy, warm depiction of the Christmas story, took her some years to complete, partly, she says, because the characters drove her "mad" and partly because she put the book aside to illustrate *Wilfrid Gordon McDonald Partridge* (1985), about a little boy's understanding of memory through his friendships with the elderly, and the *Grandma Poss Cook Book* (1985). Other titles followed, including *I Went Walking* (1989) by Sue Machin, a rhythmic book for very young readers; the award-winning title *The Very Best of Friends* (1989) by Margaret Wild, about friendship, understanding, and coming to terms with grief; and her most controversial title, *Let the Celebrations Begin!* (1991), also by Wild, which is set in Belsen concentration camp and shows women inmates making toys for the children to have as a celebration when they are released. The book has caused some adult readers to criticize it severely for softening a harsh chapter of history and others to applaud it for providing a positive vehicle for discussion.

Whatever text Vivas turns her hand to, her gentle, muted watercolors, comfortably flowing lines, and perceptive interpretations make a distinguished and fitting accompaniment. Her paintings have a wonderful tendency to move the eye right across the page, and it is no wonder that her work has met with both popular and critical acclaim in both hemispheres. ❧ K.J.

VOIGT, CYNTHIA

AMERICAN AUTHOR, B. 1942. In just over a decade—since 1981, when her first book, *Homecoming*, was published—this prolific writer has produced almost twenty books in a wide range of genres. Best known for her Crisfield novels—seven books set in a small town on Maryland's Eastern Shore that center around the Tillerman family and their friends—she has also written, among others, a Gothic mystery, *The Callendar Papers*, for which she won the 1984 Edgar Allan Poe Award for Best Juvenile Mystery; a medieval FANTASY, *Jackaroo* (1985), featuring a strong, swashbuckling heroine, and two sequels, *On Fortune's Wheel* (1990), set two generations later, and *The Wings of a Falcon* (1993); a PICTURE BOOK, *Stories about Rosie* (1986); and several YOUNG ADULT NOVELS, including *Izzy, Willy-Nilly* (1986), about a "nice" teenager who loses a leg in an accident and must face the effect on her life of her disability.

Voigt's books are noted for their vivid descriptions, strong sense of place, memorable characters, and distinctive rhythm in both language and plot. A unique stylist, Voigt often employs unorthodox punctuation or sentence structure to establish character or mood. Her settings—whether the real world of the Chesapeake Bay in the Crisfield novels or the imaginary feudal world of *Jackaroo*—are fully realized and convincing.

Born in Boston, Voigt decided in ninth grade that she wanted to become a writer. Following a long family tradition, her parents sent her to boarding school, Dana Hall in Wellesley, Massachusetts, an experience that Voigt says encouraged her independence. She attended Smith College in Northampton, graduating in 1963. After working for a time in New York City for a large advertising agency and earning her teaching accreditation at St. Michael's College (now the College of Santa Fe), Voigt eventually settled in Annapolis, Maryland, where she taught English for many years at the Key School, a small independent primary and secondary school. There she met Walter Voigt, whom she married in 1974; the Voigts have two children, Jessica and Peter.

It was while teaching fifth-graders at Key that Voigt discovered children's literature: "As a reader, I was delighted and excited. As a writer, it was as if somebody had opened a window for me, to show me a whole new landscape." Her flexible teaching schedule and the relaxed atmosphere of the school—she taught classes carrying her infant son in a Snugli—allowed her space to write.

She began working on *Tell Me If the Lovers Are Losers* (1982), a young adult novel that she calls an attempt to capture the tone and feeling of her years at college. One day while shopping she saw a car full of children left to wait alone in the parking lot. She asked herself what would happen if nobody ever came back for them, and the result was the first of Voigt's Crisfield novels, *Homecoming*. As she says, "Writers only need to see the edges of a situation to be inspired to make it come alive." In *Homecoming* thirteen-year-old Dicey Tillerman, tough and resourceful, must take charge of her three younger siblings after the children's despairing mother, unable to cope with the overwhelming pressures in her life, abandons them in a shopping-center parking lot in Connecticut. In an odyssey down U.S. Route 1, Dicey leads James, Maybeth, and Sammy to Maryland in the hope of finding a home with their grandmother, whom they have never met. On the journey Dicey must not only struggle with their physical survival but also grapple with moral choices and fight for the Tillermans' survival as a family. *Dicey's Song*, winner of the 1983 Newbery Medal and the sequel to *Homecoming*, follows the Tillerman saga as the children begin tentatively to make a home for themselves with their eccentric Gram. The bonds grow tighter after their momma, who has been in a catatonic state in a Boston hospital, dies, and Dicey must learn how to reach out to people, hold on to those she loves, and let go when necessary. The book is a powerful and moving story of an unusual family.

A Solitary Blue, a 1984 Newbery Honor Book and a companion book to *Dicey's Song*, tells the story of Dicey's classmate and friend Jefferson Greene, who, almost irrevocably wounded by his manipulative mother's abandonment and betrayal, eventually finds himself through music, a new and honest relationship with his father, his friendship with the Tillermans—and his gift for seeing the truth. Other Crisfield novels include *The Runner* (1985), which, centering on seventeen-year-old Bullet, Dicey's uncle, details the grim disintegration of the previous generation of the Tillerman family, and *Seventeen Against the Dealer* (1989), the final book about the Tillermans, in which Dicey's obsession with her long-dreamed-of boat-building business almost causes her to lose everything of importance to her. As the *Horn Book* said of *The Runner*, the book is "about connections—severed, denied, sustained, treasured," and indeed this human and deeply resonant theme is at the core of the entire Tillerman family saga. In addition, the books all reflect Voigt's love of music, the Eastern Shore landscape, and the waters of the Chesapeake Bay.

After many years of living in Maryland, Voigt and her family now make their home in Maine. Voigt says that she has always considered herself a New Englander, and "real New Englanders live in Maine," which is the setting for *Tree by Leaf* (1988), a mystical novel exploring a twelve-year-old girl's communication with an omnipotent being, and *The Vandemark Mummy* (1991), an unusual—but accessible—MYSTERY featuring Egyptian antiquities and classical languages. In addition to her Newbery Awards, Voigt is the recipient of the 1989 ALAN Award, given by the Assembly on Literature for Adolescents by the National Council of Teachers of English for significant contributions to the field of adolescent literature. Although some of her young adult novels, notably *David and Jonathan* (1992) and *Orfe* (1992), have received mixed reviews from critics, Voigt continues to challenge herself and her readers, breaking new ground with every distinctive, original book.

MARTHA PARRAVANO

W

Waber, Bernard

American picture book author and illustrator, b. 1924. The best known of Bernard Waber's characters, Lyle, the lovable anthropomorphic crocodile, has delighted and won the hearts of readers since appearing in 1962 in *The House on East 88th Street.* The cartoon reptile has shared his madcap antics in a half-dozen picture books, benefiting from Waber's adroit ability to blend fantasy and reality in credible and reasonable stories always beset with conflicts that parallel those of humans. Armed with a clear understanding of the anxieties, taunts, and humor that go hand in hand with childhood, Waber provides the readers of his more than twenty-four books with a mirror of their childhood experiences. From Arthur the anteater, to Legs the octopus, to a dog named Bernard, his protagonists lightheartedly cope with situations familiar to us all.

Waber, born in Philadelphia to immigrant parents, had a transient childhood. The failure of family businesses uprooted the Wabers frequently during the Depression, and they often moved just ahead of the bill collectors. With each move, young Bernard had two priorities—finding the neighborhood library and finding a movie theater—both significant elements in his survival kit. The youngest of four children, he was a constant recipient of hand-me-downs, the best being the books his siblings had read and loved. For Waber, the key to getting hooked on a book is its physical appearance and the opening paragraph. In his works, both are distinctive. His readers quickly turn the opening pages to discover who was making the "swish, swash, splash, swoosh" on East 88th Street and to discover Ira's conflict in *Ira Sleeps Over* (1972). In appealing to youngsters, Waber deliberately makes his books colorful and easily manipulated by small hands.

Waber's first job enhanced his ability to devise a plausible plot. Working in a movie theater after school at age eight stretched his imagination. His ushering duties allowed him only a glimpse at the final ten minutes of the big screen, so he began inventing plots: Having seen only endings, he reconstructed the beginnings and the middles. This cinema background continues to help him create plots for young readers.

While his childhood drawings—copies of film star photos—didn't lead him directly to an art career, a tour of duty during World War II gave him a change of scenery and time to reflect on his future. He reconsidered his original plan of a career in finance and when he returned from the service he enrolled at the Philadelphia College of Art.

With a degree in commercial art and newly married, he headed to New York City for a job in the promotions

Illustration by Bernard Waber from his book *Lyle, Lyle, Crocodile* (1965).

Voices of the Creators

Bernard Waber

In my book *Nobody Is Perfick*, a little girl doing homework tries desperately not to slip into daydreaming. She resists daydreaming with gargantuan will. She gulps down glasses of water. She chews bubble gum furiously. She stands on her head. She somersaults. But in the end she succumbs to a perfectly lovely daydream.

True confession: That was me, or in the words of Flaubert's reference to *Madame Bovary*, "C'est moi." I was that kid, a hopeless, chronic daydreamer. Everyone told me it was bad—bad, bad, bad—to daydream. "Wake up! Snap out of it!" These were the admonitions of my childhood. And don't think I wasn't worried. I tried everything to cure myself of this pernicious affliction. If a support program were available to cure daydreaming, I would have rushed to sign up. The problem deviled me all through my maturing years. Even in the army, sergeants constantly bellowed at me to wake up.

True confession: I still suffer from the same affliction. The only difference is, now I'm encouraged to do it. Now, it's quite proper for me to do it. Now, I'm even expected to do it. So, when I am asked where I get my ideas, I'm tempted to say, "I'm only doing what I've always done—daydreaming."

True confession: Wordplay tops my list of greedy pleasures, just after fudge sundaes and M&Ms. The idea and plot for *But Names Will Never Hurt Me* came to me while shaving one morning. The story has nothing to do with shaving; it has to do with a little girl named Alison who has the unfortunate surname of Wonderland. Get it? Alison Wonderland. Often, my ideas begin with just such musings. An absurd name like Alison Wonderland tickled me. But digging deeper, I was moved by the burden of troublesome names, and that burden became the central theme. Similarly, in *Ira Sleeps Over*, a little boy's dilemma on whether or not to take his teddy bear along on his first sleepover seemed like a funny idea. But probing the idea's underside revealed tantalizing complexities—peer pressure, separation, self-belief, even sibling rivalry.

True confession: Among the really pleasurable dividends of writing for children are the letters children send to authors. In their letters, children talk freely about family, friends, school, pets, sports, everything crucial to their lives. They also want to know about their authors—absolutely everything. Sometimes I think kids want more personal information than my health insurance plan. My age and other vital statistics are matters of keen interest. I always tell the truth about my age because I love to astonish children. A frequent question from children is, "What made you become a writer?" Early environment had much to do with it. My siblings, a sister and two brothers, all older and all artistic, were a major influence. My sister played piano and wrote poetry. She also wrote love letters, in the fashion of Cyrano de Bergerac, for love-stricken, but less poetically expressive, friends. She read her love letters to the family for critical comment and hearing them made us all fall in love just a little. My brothers wrote and drew, and I spent a major chunk of my childhood hanging over their shoulders, observing words and pictures emerge on paper.

True confession: I did not set out to be an author. I began professionally as a designer and illustrator for magazines. My illustrations tended toward whimsy, and my love of drawing animals led to this fatal attraction—children's books. Quality time, for me, meant hanging out in bookstores—looking, looking, looking at picture books. And looking wasn't all that easy way back then. Unlike today's mammoth book chains, where one could literally spend the day reading *War and Peace* unnoticed and unmolested, back then I could scarcely begin browsing without an overzealous clerk offering unsolicited assistance. I did, however, buy lots of children's books, mostly as gifts, but many for myself to satisfy an insatiable appetite for them. Children giggle when I tell them I fell in love with picture books. One even asked, "Did you marry one?"

Later, as the father of three, I had three compelling reasons for giving children's books close scrutiny. I loved reading aloud and, as many parents do, began inventing stories. I probably caused my children some self-consciousness as I constantly trailed after them into the children's room of our library. Once, they suggested that I might find more appropriate books in the grown-ups department. True confession: It was too late to change a habit—especially one so possessing. Besides, I had already begun to write my first children's book.

department of Condé Nast, publisher of several fashion magazines, where artists worked quickly to achieve a fresh and spontaneous effect. A whimsical style of drawing, developed while working for the fashion magazines, became embedded in his art.

Waber claims that a wastebasket became a necessity. He draws quickly and discards the "completed" product several times. His main characters, rendered in strong lines, appear within an environment resplendent with background details. Subtle watercolors, enhanced family portraits, patterned curtains, and significant details have become Waber's trademark in the homes into which he invites his readers. His own home has become a memorial to the Primms and Lyle, a museum of crocodilia laden with artifacts sent by his readers and friends.

While Waber may not have been seeking a career creating children's books, several art directors who saw his portfolio told him his drawings were perfect for children's books. His own love of reading aloud to his three children encouraged him further, and his career was launched. *Lorenzo* (1961), his first book, was published after multiple rejections.

For thirty-three years, Waber has continued his anthropomorphic adventures. From Lyle's zoo escape to the relationship between an anteater and his mother, readers have been able to suspend their disbelief and casually accept the existence of his characters' situations. ❧ L.G.S.

Waldo Books

Where's Waldo? The diminutive star of Martin Handford's wordless PICTURE BOOKS is usually cleverly concealed and surrounded by hundreds of similarly sized figures densely packed into a double-page spread. Although dismissed as "game books" by some critics, and not likely to appear on any list of award winners, the Waldo books have nevertheless been embraced not only by young children but by their older siblings and parents as well.

Handford, the talented artist responsible for creating Waldo, was born on September 27, 1956, in London, and developed an early interest in art and drawing, particularly historical scenes rendered in minute detail and scale. After a three-year stint selling insurance, Handford was able to win a government grant that enabled him to attend the Maidstone College of Art. Freelance work followed, until a meeting with David Bennett, the art director for Walker Books in England, led to the creation of Handford's first children's book, featuring his distinctive "crowd" art and with the inspiration of hiding the Waldo figure in each spread. Taking up to a year to create each book, Handford hides his Waldos in scenes featuring undersea life, outer space, historical battles, pirate ships, or more prosaically in department stores full of tiny shoppers. The enormous popularity of the series has led to merchandising on a grand scale; Waldo has even been embraced as the Halloween costume of choice by many young trick-or-treaters. Although enjoyed by many as simply an entertaining fad, the Waldo books will be remembered for making wordless picture books interesting to adults and thus bringing them into mainstream popular culture. ❧ E.H.

Walsh, Jill Paton

See PATON WALSH, JILL.

Walter, Mildred Pitts

AMERICAN AUTHOR, B. 1922. "I didn't want to do it," recalls Walter, referring to the writing of her first children's book, *Lillie of Watts: A Birthday Discovery* (1969). Nevertheless, this novel was the product of two of her major interests: her career as an educator and her desire to improve the lives of African Americans.

Walter worked for a number of years as an elementary school teacher and as an activist in the California civil rights movement. When she complained to a publisher about the scarcity of books by and about African Americans, he persuaded her to create such a book herself. Walter soon became involved in the craft of writing. Since *Lillie of Watts* and its sequel, *Lillie of Watts Takes a Giant Step* (1971), she has published a wide variety of works, from picture books to novels to nonfiction for older readers. Her native state of Louisiana provides the setting for *Ty's One-Man Band* (1980), a picture-book retelling of a childhood memory, and for the skillfully realistic *Trouble's Child* (1985), in which an African American girl from an isolated island struggles to compromise between serving her community and finding her own way.

Not surprisingly, in several of her novels one can follow the recent history of African Americans in schools in the United States. Alternating between the viewpoints of two girls—one black and one white—*The Girl on the Outside* (1982) reveals the complex emotions involved in the integration of a Southern high school in the 1950s. In *Because We Are* (1983) Emma, unjustly transferred from an integrated high school to an all-black one, declares her own independence but also finds courage and pride in her solidarity with a group of fellow black students. The title comes from an African proverb: "Because we are, I am."

Other aspects of African American history and culture permeate Walter's work. In the award-winning *Justin and the Best Biscuits in the World* (1986), Justin's cowboy grandfather helps him explore the family history of their "Exoduster" forebears, who left Tennessee in 1880 to start a ranch in Missouri. Walter's informational book *Mississippi Challenge* (1992) chronicles the complicated history of voting rights in Mississippi through the mid-1960s. *Brother to the Wind* (1985), an original folk tale in picture-book form, resulted from Walter's desire to give an African flavor to a story written with an American audience in mind. African ideas also figure in *Have a Happy . . .* (1989), in which the principles behind the African American holiday Kwanzaa, including faith and unity, help Chris's family survive the crisis brought on by his father's unemployment.

Family, like community, plays an important role in Walter's work; the picture books *My Mama Needs Me* (1983) and *Two and Too Much* (1990) provide sensitive portraits of contemporary family dynamics, as do the Mariah novels—*Mariah Loves Rock* (1988) and *Mariah Keeps Cool* (1990).

Walter's interest in education and human rights continues to inspire her work as a writer. In her books, readers can find characters who experience the truth of the proverb "Because we are, I am" as they strive to balance their own needs with the needs of family and community. ❧ M.F.S.

Ward, Lynd

AMERICAN GRAPHIC ARTIST, ILLUSTRATOR, AND AUTHOR, 1905–1985. Lynd Kendall Ward was born in Chicago, son of Harry F. and Daisy Kendall Ward. Educated at Teachers College, Columbia University, he received his B.S. in 1926 with a major in fine arts. While in college Ward met MAY MCNEER, a writer, and they married during graduation week. The Wards traveled to Germany where Lynd studied at the National Academy of Graphic Arts in Leipzig (1926–27). Returning to the States, Lynd turned his talents to graphic arts and illustration while May McNeer embarked on her career as a children's author. They took great pleasure in working together. Ward illustrated several children's books written by his wife.

Illustration by Lynd Ward from his book *The Biggest Bear* (1952).

Childhood experiences influenced Lynd Ward's life and work. Lynd's father was a Methodist minister whose first ministry included Chicago's "back of the yards" neighborhood, its abject poverty, and the legendary Jane Addams. His family's lasting struggle to better the lot of abandoned people dominated Ward's conscience and his spirit. The code of conduct for children of a Methodist minister did not permit reading funny papers on Sunday. In this "extremity" young Lynd turned to books. A volume of Bible stories with little text but absorbing pictures became his favorite. His addiction had begun. Throughout Lynd's growing years the family spent summers in a log cabin on Lonely Lake in the Canadian wilderness. These summers nurtured his enduring respect and love for nature. His mature work reflects this childhood world.

Ward's career began in 1929 with his first book, *God's Man: A Novel in Woodcuts*. Five more books, engravings without words, established his reputation as a wood engraver. Not wishing to be relegated to one medium, Ward experimented with a variety of techniques for book illustration. He worked in watercolor, oil, lithography, in full color, and in black and white. His artistic versatility and his interest in children's books deepened as his career in illustration flourished.

An amazing collection of illustrations now poured from this inspired artist. His prodigious body of work includes more than two hundred books for children and adults. There is depth and variety of subject and style. Adult classics and scholarly editions stand beside children's fiction, BIOGRAPHY, and PICTURE BOOKS. Some enduring favorites are *The Biggest Bear* (1952), winner of the 1953 Caldecott Award, the beloved tale of Johnny and his bear in which both story and cub grow dramatically through the humor and pathos of the illustrations; *The Silver Pony* (1973), a powerful wordless FANTASY of a boy and his magical pony, which won the Lewis Carroll Shelf Award and the Boston Globe–Horn Book Honor Award; *America's Ethan Allen* (1949) by Stuart Holbrook, recipient of a 1950 Caldecott Honor Award; *The Cat Who Went to Heaven* (1930) by ELIZABETH COATSWORTH, winner of the 1931 Newbery Award; *Johnny Tremain* (1943) by ESTHER FORBES, winner of the 1944 Newbery Award; and *The Little Red Lighthouse and the Great Grey Bridge* (1942), by Hildegarde Swift, a gentle story enlivened by Ward's winsome pictures. Among the many biographies written by his wife that Ward illustrated were *America's Abraham Lincoln* (1957) and *America's Mark Twain* (1962).

During his lifetime Ward was widely recognized for his distinguished contribution to children's literature. He clearly relished his life work as artist and illustrator. He believed that children's books offered great opportunities for "the best that artists can produce." In his Caldecott acceptance speech Ward opined that, more than any other artist he knew and "without punning," his life had been an open book, for "the things that I have learned are all there on the pages of the books on which I have worked." ❧ P.W.

WATSON, CLYDE

AMERICAN POET, B. 1947. Clyde Watson was just three years out of Smith College when she and her older sister, artist WENDY WATSON, collaborated on *Father Fox's Pennyrhymes* (1971). That book, her third, was nominated for a National Book Award and immediately established her as a worthy and very American successor to MOTHER GOOSE.

Jaunty and saucy, the rhymes are told by old Father Fox, who entertains his enormous brood around the fire on a stormy winter night. Each verse is short, keeps to a simple and irresistible rhythm, and bounces with playful nonsense. The joy (and the sorrow) of eating too much is chronicled, as are the satisfaction of love, the high spirits of family life, and the value of song. The illustrations, pen-and-ink with watercolors, extend the rhymes with their energetic detail and often wiseacre cartoon-style captions. The result is both cozy and irreverent, deftly recognizing the contrary streak in even the sweetest-mannered small child.

The daughter of Aldren and Nancy Dingman Watson, an accomplished artist and writer respectively, Clyde Watson was born in New York City and grew up on a farm in Vermont with her seven brothers and sisters. In all her work, especially *Father Fox's Pennyrhymes,* one finds echoes of that childhood. The rhythms of New England rural life—how each season demands various jobs and makes possible various play—and the joyful chaos of life are among her favorite themes. More subtly evident is Watson's musical background—she was a music major in college and has played the violin professionally with various orchestras. Read aloud, her rhymes automatically suggest melodies, and, not surprisingly, she has set a number of her poems to music of her own composition.

Catch Me & Kiss Me & Say It Again (1978) is another collection of NURSERY RHYMES, also illustrated by Wendy Watson. The scope here is somewhat narrower than that of its predecessor, focusing on the everyday play of a little girl and her toddler brother. Beginning with the sun kissing "my poppet on the nose/With a How-do-you-do-today?" and ending with "All tucked in & roasty toasty" the energetic verses and gently colored illustrations follow the pair as they wash, practice counting, dance until they drop, and march around their yard at night by firefly and candlelight. Some of the verses borrow phrases from traditional rhymes, others are wholly original, yet all are satisfyingly rounded and familiarly shaped, as if they have always been part of our folklore.

Genuinely silly and unabashedly romantic, Watson's verses give purpose, form, and most of all rhythm to the eager wordplay of the very young. Her poem's celebrate the possibility of language, its ability to surprise, delight, and comfort, and present a rosy world rich with possibilities, everyday marvels, and reassuring truths. ❧ A.Q.

WATSON, WENDY

AMERICAN AUTHOR AND ILLUSTRATOR, B. 1942. Wendy Watson was born in New Jersey but grew up in Putney, Vermont. Her cheerful, homey illustrations reflect this rural upbringing.

Watson attended Bryn Mawr College and studied drawing and painting at the National Academy of Design. After working as a book designer, she began illustrating children's books. She began by collaborating with her sister CLYDE WATSON, and they received much attention for their National Book Award nominee, *Father Fox's Pennyrhymes* (1971). This collection of rhymes, which were originally songs written by Clyde, are illustrated by Wendy with detailed, cartoonlike panels. The humorous, childlike verses are American MOTHER GOOSE rhymes, full of references to ginger beer, country fairs, and other bits of Americana. The pen-and-ink and watercolor illustrations of a large family of foxes depict the changing seasons of rural New England life and the chaos and warmth of family life.

Clyde and Wendy Watson followed this success with other collaborations, including the story of *Tom Fox and the Apple Pie* (1972) and another book of verse, *Catch Me & Kiss Me & Say It Again* (1978), both of which reflect the Watsons' love of family and an appreciation for the humor and details of childhood. The poems can be instantly memorized, and each is paired with a simple scene picturing toddlers throughout the day—having their fingernails clipped, their hair brushed, and so on. "Phoebe in a rosebush, / Phoebe in a tree, / There's many a Phoebe in the world, / But you're the one for me" is matched with a watercolor and pencil illustration of a mother swinging her child out of her perch in a tree.

In addition to illustrating the work of others, Wendy Watson has written and illustrated her own PICTURE BOOKS and become recognized for her unpretentious stories and gentle humor. She creates an inviting setting for *Tales for a Winter's Eve* (1988) in which Freddie Fox hurts a paw skiing and family and friends tell stories around the fire to ease his discomfort. Watson brings to her children's books a heritage of folklore and an appreciation for old-fashioned pursuits.

Characters, as likely to be foxes as humans, are often dressed in overalls and sit around a hearth or collect sap for maple syrup. Children pinch their fingers cracking nuts and tease each other with childlike insults.

In many of her illustrations, Watson uses cartoonlike balloons for her characters' speech, and she encourages her readers to pore over her illustrations by filling them with details not told in the text. Her honest, often wise stories and detailed country illustrations are full of joy and life. ❧ M.V.K.

WEBSTER, JEAN

AMERICAN AUTHOR, 1876–1916. It is not surprising to learn that the heroine of *Daddy Long-Legs* (1912) changed her name from dreary Jerusha to Judy, for Jean Webster herself set the precedent. Discovering that her boarding-school roommate shared the name Alice, Alice Jane Chandler immediately changed hers to the more sprightly "Jean," discarding "Jane" as too plain—even though she had been given it in memory of her great-grandaunt Jane Clemens, mother of MARK TWAIN. This show of independence reveals much about Jean Webster's character.

Brought up in comfortable circumstances, Webster rejected the status quo. Born in Fredonia, New York, she attended the Lady Jane Grey School in Binghamton, New York, and graduated from Vassar in 1901. In the course of her studies, Webster visited orphanages, prisons, and other institutions meant to cope with social problems. Such experiences had a profound influence on her thinking, leading to her belief that anyone—given encouragement and a proper education—could become a successful, productive individual. This premise served as the underlying theme for her most acclaimed novels, *Daddy Long-Legs* and *Dear Enemy* (1915). Her first book, *When Patty Went to College* (1903), however, consisted of short stories garnered from the weekly columns that she wrote for the *Poughkeepsie Courier* describing student life at Vassar. Webster wrote several other adult novels, including a mystery story, but her lasting fame rests on *Daddy Long-Legs,* the story of Judy, an orphan girl, and her exciting adjustment to college life.

Judy, whose education is sponsored by an unknown benefactor, is required to write a monthly letter detailing her activities. She chooses to address her correspondence to Daddy Long-Legs, her description of the lanky character she suspects to be her patron. The letters are piquant, amusing, honest observations of a girl who welcomes the challenges of her new setting. Eventually, Judy meets her mysterious sponsor, the scion of an established, upper class family, who has a social conscience and a sense of humor. Over the course of Judy's correspondence he becomes increasingly taken with her. This Cinderella romance, along with the epistolary storytelling form and the charm of an orphan story, has delighted girls for nearly a century. The book was an immediate success, going on to become a Broadway play, an early talking film, a Hollywood musical, and a movie starring Shirley Temple.

Dear Enemy, its sequel, is also written as a series of letters and is illustrated with Webster's own whimsical cartoonlike drawings. It recounts the daily battles waged by Sallie McBride (Judy's former roommate), who has grudgingly accepted the responsibility of running the orphanage where Judy grew up. Her letters are written to Judy and to a dour Scottish doctor, the Dear Enemy of the title, a no-nonsense physician who provides medical services to the home. *Dear Enemy* reveals Webster's progressive views on caring for orphans while providing an illuminating picture of the social structure and strictures of the times. The book was her final publication, for Jean Webster died in childbirth the following year.

When *Daddy Long-Legs* and *Dear Enemy* were first published, they reached an enormous audience, who read them as lighthearted entertainment. They served a dual purpose, however; along with providing enjoyment they also did much to enlighten readers on important issues dealing with the care of dependent children. Times have changed, but the books have retained their appeal and become classics. P.S.

WEIL, LISL

AMERICAN ILLUSTRATOR AND AUTHOR, B. 1910. Lisl Weil, who was born in Vienna and immigrated to the United States when she was in her early twenties, has created books from a wide range of her interests and presented them in her distinctive style. Although she has worked with well-known writers, Weil herself has written many of the 139 books she has illustrated. Her strong style, whether expressed by an apt black pen line or by a flourishing brush stroke, seems totally spontaneous, yet with that line she captures both motion and emotion.

Weil's pictures can be read as clearly as her text. Many of her books are done primarily in black, with washes in one or two colors used for ground or emphasis. Her pages bustle with action and detail. She sets a scene with decorative, often architectural, embellishments, conveying a strong sense of place, whether it is an Austrian village or New York City. Humor, too, adds to the character and drama of her drawings, from the dog with a toothache in *Bill the Brave* (1948) to the futuristic apartment complex on the jacket of *The Houses We Build* (1985).

Weil's texts range through folktale-like fiction for the very young, as in *Jacoble Tells the Truth* (1946); to retellings of operas in *The Story of Smetana's "The Bartered Bride"* (1966); to an adaptation, *Donkey Head* (1977), based on the character of Bottom in *A Midsummer Night's Dream;* to retellings of Biblical stories, among them *The Very First Story Ever Told* (1976) and *Esther;* to the narration of historical events as specific as *I Christopher Columbus* (1983) or as epic as *Our World to You with Love* (1983). In *To Sail a Ship of Treasures* (1984), she gives an autobiographical glimpse of her childhood and family life in Vienna and her journey to the United States in 1939. *Wolferl* (1991), which is about Mozart as a child, completes a circle that began when, at age fourteen, she first sold her drawings in a bookshop in Vienna. During her late teens her drawings and caricatures appeared in several Viennese newspapers.

Illustration by Lisl Weil from her book *Mimi* (1961).

As a child Weil studied ballet and performed in a famous Viennese children's dance group. This love of dance and music, combined with her ability to draw so spontaneously, led to her remarkable performances for more than twenty years with the Little Orchestra Society of New York and other major orchestras. During the playing of such pieces as *Petrouchka* and *The Firebird* Weil drew the characters and their stories—in perfect time and with dancelike gestures—on huge panels stretched across the stage. A film of her performance in *The Sorcerer's Apprentice* was made by the Weston Woods Studio.

Weil has made New York City her home. Though she has no children of her own, she has an ease and a keen rapport with them. Her desire to pique their interests has led her to create a fascinating, varied group of lively books throughout her long and productive career. L.K.

Wells, Rosemary

AMERICAN ILLUSTRATOR AND AUTHOR, B. 1943. Although best known for her PICTURE BOOKS about the inimitable rabbit Max and his older sister, Ruby, Rosemary Wells is a versatile storyteller with more than forty picture books and YOUNG ADULT NOVELS to her name. Wells, a gifted illustrator, began her career as an artist at the Museum School in Boston. There she was derided as no more than an illustrator, and she decided to leave school.

She worked first as an editor at Allyn and Bacon and later as an art designer at Macmillan in New York, where she presented the editor-in-chief with illustrations for a Gilbert and Sullivan song. This book became her first published work, *A Song to Sing, O!* (1968), and Wells has produced high-quality, award-winning books ever since.

From the beginning, her books have been lauded for their strong sense of humor and realism. Even when she is writing about mice or rabbits in human clothing, Wells is able to create very realistic interactions among siblings, parents, or neighbors. *Benjamin and Tulip* (1973) is a physically small book that tackles a large topic: bullies. Tulip beats up Benjamin each time he passes her. The two raccoons seem caught in their respective roles until Benjamin accidentally lands on Tulip when the two fall out of a tree. Benjamin, surprised into action, courageously confronts Tulip, and the two end up amiably sharing a squashed watermelon. The story is told with very few, but very expressive words, and its success is due to Wells's direct and funny approach to a perennial childhood problem. Tulip and Benjamin do not talk out their differences, but act them out with watermelon juice dripping and overalls askew.

As with *Benjamin and Tulip,* much of the appeal of Wells's "Max" books comes again from her gently rebellious approach to childhood. Wells's characters do not conform to adult ideals, but rather act as human children. *Max's First Word, Max's New Suit, Max's Ride,* and *Max's Toys* (all 1979) were published simultaneously as the first funny BOARD BOOKS for very young children. Each of the brief books is a complete interaction between Max, a toddler bunny, and his older sister, Ruby. Wells writes that the books were inspired by her own two daughters. In each adventure, Ruby hopes to control Max and is sure she knows what is best for him. In *Max's First Word,* for example, Ruby is intent upon teaching Max words beyond "BANG," but Max reveals his strength of character and outsmarts his older sister. The books are elementary concept books, bright art objects in vivid red, blue, and yellow, and early lessons in individuality. Most importantly, they express humor that is understandable to young children and hilarious to the adults asked to read the books again and again.

The successive adventures of Max and Ruby are no less winsome than the early ones as Max grows older and his adventures become more complex. *Max's Chocolate Chicken* (1989) tells of Max and Ruby's Easter egg hunt. Ruby is so busy giving Max advice and gloating over the eggs she finds that she notices too late that Max has helped himself to the grand prize, a chocolate chicken. With chocolate smeared around his mouth, Max declares "I love you," leaving the reader to decide if he is talking to his sister, the Easter Bunny, or the chocolate. The "Max" books succeed because Max and Ruby are unforgettable characters—Ruby is bossy and sure of herself, Max is independent and curious. But in each one Max always manages to get the better of his sister. In these books the illustrations are created from pen and ink and watercolor. Max and Ruby, portrayed as squat, stylized rabbits, are sharply outlined in black. Wells uses bright watercolors to fill in background, clothing, and limited details of setting. She develops character through minute changes in expression: Max's eyes and sly smile give the reader a tremendous amount of information about his feelings and motives.

Max and Ruby are only two in the long list of Wells's irrepressible characters, each an individual and each a part of a small, childhood drama. Wells claims that she learned to write picture books by modeling her stories after comic theater. This theatrical construction is evident in *Hazel's Amazing Mother* (1985), the story of a small badger who loses her way and is the victim of an attack by bullies. Hazel is saved by her mother, who literally flies to her rescue, blown by the wind and the power of love. Wells's emotionally satisfying fantasy was named a New York Times Best Illustrated Children's Book of 1985. *Shy Charles* (1988), the tale of a shy mouse who eludes his parents' attempts to socialize him but does overcome his shyness in a crisis, won the Boston Globe–Horn Book Award. The story is, like Wells's other picture books, emotionally satisfying and empowering to children. The trilogy *Voyage to the Bunny Planet* (1992) spins out fantasies in which small rabbits are granted true quality time with parents in peaceful days filled with attention and delicious food.

While Rosemary Wells's art is often recognizable for her strong use of line, her humorous stocky mammals, and her love of vivid color, her writing style is not so clearly identifiable. Many of her picture books are written in a spare, almost laconic style, while others include rich details and lyrical prose. *Waiting for the Evening Star* (1993), illustrated by SUSAN JEFFERS, is a quiet, historical picture book set on a Vermont farm in the

Voices of the Creators

Rosemary Wells

Many of the stories in my books come from our two children, Victoria and Beezoo. Ruby and Max are Victoria and Beezoo. They appeared on my drawing board in the summer of 1977. Victoria was then five and Beezoo nine months. Victoria had taken it upon herself to teach her baby sister about the world and dragged her, like a sack of flour, because she was too heavy to really carry, from object to object, shouting, "Table, Beezoo! say table, TA-BLE!" Beezoo did not cooperate at all and was always off in a world of her own.

Victoria tried to teach Beezoo how to get dressed—another complete failure, as Beezoo preferred to be undressed at all times. Victoria attempted to instruct vocabularyless Beezoo to share and not to take toys that didn't belong to her. This was like talking to the wind. Victoria took pride in wheeling Beezoo's stroller along the boardwalk. Beezoo had to be harnessed into it, with the zipper put on backward and pinned in four places, or she would immediately escape and crawl like a racing crab right into the ocean or the traffic or wherever danger lay.

These simple incidents from childhood are universal. The dynamics between older and younger sibling are also common to all families. What is funny is not the events, but Victoria's dogged insistence on leading Beezoo in the paths of righteousness and Beezoo's complete insouciance in the face of slightly skewed authority.

In part I wrote the board books because there were no funny books around for very young children. But mostly I wrote them because the characters materialized on paper in front of me, under my hand, so to speak. The characters were alive; the stories were going on all around me. Other books come from other episodes in my life, in the children's lives. Victoria, in first grade, came home the day of the Christmas concert in bitter tears. She had selected a blouse and kilt to wear that morning. One of her classmates, Audrey, had told her she was supposed to wear a dress, not an everyday kilt. We patched up the day with conventional wisdom, but I used Audrey's remark as the basis for *Timothy Goes to School.*

Benjamin and Tulip was written before we had any children. It is partly a story of my best friend and me, wheeling our bicycles up a steep hill every day after school and being regularly ambushed by the boys who lived at the top of the hill. I changed the lead bully boy into Patty Gerardi, queen of the second grade, who was heard to say only two things in her career: "I'm captain," and "I'm gonna beat you up." I changed a boy to a girl here because a female bully was much funnier.

Once the story is there, the drawings just appear. I feel the emotion I want to show; then I let it run down my arm from my face, and it goes out the pencil. My drawings look as if they are done quickly. They are not. First they are sketched in light pencil, then nearly rubbed out, then drawn again in heavier pencil. What appears to be a confident, thick ink line is really a series of layers of tiny ink lines intensifying all day until the drawings are ready for color.

Most of my books use animals rather than children as characters. I draw animals more easily and amusingly than I do children. Animals are broader in range—age, race, time, and place—than children are. They also can do things in pictures that children cannot. All of my stories are written with deeply felt emotional content. Animals express this best most of the time for the same reason that a harpsichord expresses certain concertos better than an organ does. As I work on a book I try to keep a few very simple things in mind. In order to stand up to hundreds of readings-aloud, a good picture book must be fresh, intelligent, and succinct. The words must spin out like song lyrics, and like song lyrics there must not be one syllable too many or too few.

We live in a curious time. Our people used to recognize that culture must enlighten as well as entertain. Now culture does one thing only. It sells via entertainment, and in so doing to children, the child's sense of privacy, individuality, and intellect is numbed. There is a vast market basket of merchandise aimed at the late twentieth-century consumer-child. In it I know only one commodity still able to enlighten as well as entertain. It is a children's book.

To hold a cutting edge in this cultural wasteland of products, many of which abet everything from attention deficiency to gang violence, a children's story must have great integrity and staying power. The hand of the artist—a little stained with paint around the fingernails—must be seen. The voice of the writer—passionate and idiosyncratic—must be heard. And whether it is through adventure or humor or pathos, the story and pictures must always touch the heart.

early twentieth century. It illuminates a way of life, as it recounts the tale of a boy learning to accept change as he grows older.

Wells also writes for young adults. Her novels are characterized by an ability to weave together several stories and to faithfully reproduce the emotional lives of and interactions between adolescents. *The Fog Comes on Little Pig Feet* (1972), Wells's first novel, concerns a disaffected college dropout, a character based loosely on Wells herself. *The Man in the Woods* (1984) and *Through the Hidden Door* (1987) are both mysteries peopled with highly realistic characters who struggle with ethical dilemmas. Barney Penniman, the unlikely protagonist of *Through the Hidden Door*, works to extract himself from the grip of malevolent classmates. In order to escape, he teams up with an emotionally crippled, secretive boy, and the two uncover a buried ancient village. Wells tells both a contemporary boarding school story, in which Barney matures as he recognizes the perfidy of classmates and headmaster, and a fantasy, in which two misfits discover an improbable, private world that becomes their salvation. As in her picture books, Wells creates extremely realistic characters who struggle to develop independence against outside pressures.

Rosemary Wells faithfully re-creates child and adolescent behavior in her picture books and novels. The highly skilled author and illustrator fashions a fictional world in which both humor and individuality have saving powers. ❧ MAEVE VISSER KNOTH

Wersba, Barbara

AMERICAN AUTHOR, B. 1932. Although she began her career writing whimsical stories for children, Barbara Wersba is best known for her young adult novels that focus on sensitive teenage loners. The Chicago-born author was herself a loner while growing up in California. At age eleven she became enchanted with the stage and joined a community theater, quickly graduating from backstage gofer to onstage performer. After her parents' divorce, she moved to New York City with her mother and continued her theater training. She received a degree from Bard College and embarked on a career as a professional actress, despite the fact that she suffered stage fright and did not really enjoy acting.

Although she had always written stories and poems, she never considered writing a viable career option. But while recuperating from an illness, Wersba wrote a fantasy story about a boy who decides to live under the sea. With the publication of *The Boy Who Loved the Sea* (1961), Wersba left acting behind and began a new career as a writer. She published several short fanciful books for younger children before writing her landmark young adult novel, *The Dream Watcher* (1968), which concerns teenage loner Albert Scully and his relationship with an eccentric elderly woman. Praised by critics and popular with readers, the book firmly established Wersba's reputation as an author; she later adapted the book for a stage production starring Eva Le Gallienne. *The Dream Watcher* is a thoughtful and sensitive novel, but its impact has lessened over the years. The theme of youth receiving self-esteem and direction from an older person has been somewhat diluted by the huge number of young adult novels on the same topic, including some of Wersba's later works. Topical references to Lady Bird Johnson, "happenings," and a fair amount of 1960s jargon don't place the events in a historical perspective as much as they date the novel.

Wersba wrote two serious teenage novels, *The Country of the Heart* (1975), about a college student's love affair with a dying poet, and *Run Softly, Go Fast* (1970), a father-son story steeped in the sixties drug culture, as well as several more lyrical, dreamy children's stories, including the oblique *Let Me Fall Before I Fly* (1971). But Wersba's forte has been the young adult novel in which she presents painfully real characterizations of teenage outsiders who are intelligent, wisecracking, interested in art and nature, yet out of step with family and peers. They bond with animals, street people, and other outsiders. Although romance and unrequited love often play a part in their lives, Wersba's protagonists—both male and female—are frequently androgynous. Their romantic attachments sometimes don't work out, but the characters are always left with a newfound sense of self-worth.

These young adult novels are not strong on plot. Some, like *The Best Place to Live Is the Ceiling* (1990) and *You'll Never Guess the End* (1992), are almost preposterous and can only be viewed as parodies; others are more grounded in reality yet include elements that stretch credibility. But this is not a major flaw since the books can most accurately be described as character studies, and Wersba has proven herself a master of delineating teenagers who feel like misfits because they are different. In her books she shows the value of being different. ❧

P.D.S.

Westall, Robert

BRITISH AUTHOR, 1929–1993. Robert Westall was born in Tynemouth, Northumberland, in England. He admired his father, a gasworks manager, for always being able to handle the most difficult task confidently and fearlessly, even if it meant the nearly impossible job of going out alone to repair crucial equipment in the middle of an air raid during World War II. Westall treasured the wonderful gifts his father made for him, such as model ships and a full-size model machine gun. The region in which he grew up, the loving memories of a father and his son, and the beautifully crafted models all figure in Westall's career as a writer.

Westall studied fine art at Durham University, receiving a B.A. degree in 1953. He also received a diploma in 1957 from the Slade School at the University of London. After serving in the British army from 1953 to 1955, he taught art to children and was Head of Art and Head of Careers at Sir John Deane's College, a secondary school in Chester. He once wrote that he was "not really a writer, but a teacher who writes."

Westall, recalling the model machine gun his father made for him, prominently featured one in his first novel. Set in wartime, in 1940, in a British industrial area, a schoolboy named Chas McGill competes with other children in scrounging for war souvenirs among the bits and pieces of shot-down Nazi airplanes he and his acquaintances find. He discovers an astonishing prize when he is the first to find a German plane that has crashed: there is an intact, working machine gun in the hands of a dead Nazi soldier. He steals it before adults find the site and, with several other intense grammar school children, constructs a fortress for it, hidden and unknown to the adults. Recommended for junior high school students, the book is written with Briticisms that could be difficult for some American readers, yet its pace and vitality minimize the obstacle. The publication of *The Machine Gunners* (U.S. 1976) was a great success, earning critics' accolades and prestigious awards in England and the United States. It won the 1975 Carnegie Medal and was runner-up for the 1976 Guardian Award.

In both this book and its sequel, *Fathom Five* (U.S. 1980), Westall made his father a character. Later, in *The Devil on the Road* (U.S. 1979), Westall wrote about his son, Christopher, who died in a motorcycle accident at the age of eighteen. In the novel, the main character, John Webster, sets off on a motorcycle trip and travels in time; in the past, he meets a young woman accused of witchcraft, and he attempts to use time shifts to save her from execution. In the book, the author considers themes of guilt and innocence, fate and chance. In *The Wind Eye* (U.S. 1977), a family buys a house on the shore of the North Sea and travels back to the seventh century by means of a boat that they find there. They restore it to look like a Viking ship. *The Scarecrows* (U.S. 1981), a ghost story, tells of a boy whose father dies in the war; the young man feels fury toward his mother and stepfather, and he begins to relate that anger to the presence of the several ghosts who begin to haunt him. Westall won his second Carnegie Medal for the book. Westall, who has also written short stories for adults, remains best known in the children's book field for the gritty realism of *The Machine Gunners,* in which he creates a tense atmosphere around children who become participants in war. ❦ S.H.H.

White, E. B.

AMERICAN ESSAYIST, POET, AND CHILDREN'S BOOK AUTHOR, 1899–1985. More than once, Elwyn Brooks White pretended ignorance of literary affairs. In fact, when one critic sent him an exhaustive scholarly exegesis of White's children's classic, *Charlotte's Web* (1952), the wry essayist, poet, and novelist replied, "It's good I did not know what in hell was going on. To have known might well have been catastrophic."

Actually, there can be little doubt about E. B. White's literary sophistication. He wrote virtually all his life, breaking into print for the first time in 1909 with a prize-winning poem in *Woman's Home Companion.* Eleven years later, at the university, White was elected editor of the *Cornell Daily Sun.* Having tried a stint at newspaper reporting and advertising, White, in 1925, submitted some short sketches to the newly founded *New Yorker* magazine. He joined the staff in 1926, and soon wrote for the magazine full-time, turning out countless pithy, ironical articles, squibs, and observations. Although, over the years, White contributed to other magazines as well, his primary allegiance for almost half a century was to *The New Yorker,* on which he left an indelible stamp. Playwright Marc Connelly observed that it was White's distinctive style that "gave the steel and music to the magazine."

For children, however, White is of interest primarily as the author of three children's novels: *Stuart Little* (1945), *Charlotte's Web,* and *The Trumpet of the Swan* (1970). These do nothing to dispel the notion of White as a consummate stylist whose sentences put him clearly in the literary tradition of Henry David Thoreau and Mark Twain, and whose manuscripts testify to the infinite pains he took to research his materials and to hone his text.

As a novelist, White showed himself a deft deviser of plots, a keen observer of character, a virtuoso in the rendering of emotion—whether porcine or human. Few

Illustration by GARTH WILLIAMS from *Charlotte's Web* (1952), by E. B. White.

can read *Charlotte's Web* for the first time without shedding a tear at the death of the arachnid heroine. And, indeed, while making a commercial recording of the book, White himself choked as he read those elegiacal words about Charlotte—"and no one was with her when she died"—so that the taping session had to be stopped.

But *Charlotte's Web* was not White's debut in the world of children's books. That honor goes to *Stuart Little,* the episodic, picaresque adventure story of a two-inch creature who, in White's words, "looks very much like a mouse," but who "obviously is not a mouse [but rather] a second son."

The story had been brewing with White for years as a disconnected series of bedtime tales for his nieces and nephews by the time it came to Harper. There, shepherded by the distinguished editor Ursula Nordstrom and felicitously illustrated by GARTH WILLIAMS, the book was eventually published—generally to high acclaim, but not without violent objection from the influential Anne Carroll Moore, head of the Children's Department of the New York Public Library, as well as from a number of librarians who objected to what was perceived as the hero's "monstrous birth."

The adventures of the Lilliputian hero are inherently funny—as he loosens stuck piano keys, fetches a ring from a drain, gets rolled up in a window shade, and sails a toy boat through a storm in Central Park. But quite beyond these surface amusements, the book sounds a resonant note as Stuart undertakes his quest for the beautiful bird, Margalo. And that quest, as White himself noted, "symbolizes the continuing journey that everybody takes—in search of what is perfect and unattainable. This is perhaps too elusive an idea to put into a book for children, but I put it in anyway."

It is, however, White's second book, *Charlotte's Web,* which has drawn the most widespread admiration. Essentially a pastoral comedy in which a little girl, Fern, saves the life of the runty thirteenth pig of a litter, the novel operates on two planes. On the first, we follow life in the barnyard, in which the animals converse with each other and empathetically enter into the mercurial emotions of the pig, Wilbur. We meet the eponymous heroine, Charlotte, an articulate sophisticate, a lover of words, who—*by* the word, as it were—saves the life of Wilbur. On the second, we have the story of the little girl, Fern, richly rendered by White, memorably drawn by Garth Williams. It was the poignant story of a girl in one fleeting moment of her life. In the beginning she has an empathy for and understanding of the animals she loves; at the book's end, she has grown into a world of Ferris wheels, of boys—and will be, forever, beyond "childish things."

The book is resonant, lyrical, serious, profound. It is one of the very few books for young children that face, squarely, the subject of death. And above all it is celebratory. White called it "pastoral, seasonal . . . concerned with ordinary people," "a hymn to the barn, an acceptance of dung," a "story of friendship, life, death, salvation."

White's last book for children, *The Trumpet of the Swan,* published almost twenty years after *Charlotte,* is the unlikely tale of Louis, a mute trumpeter swan (named for Louis Armstrong), who compensates for his muteness by becoming a virtuoso player of a real trumpet. Louis is befriended by a young boy, Sam Beaver, a male counterpart to Fern of *Charlotte's Web,* with the significant difference that, at book's end, Sam remains loyal to the bird and, in a manner, keeps the faith.

White wrote the book in old age and under the impression that he was in financial need. As he had done with *Charlotte's Web,* he researched his material thoroughly—making inquiries about everything from the annual migration of trumpeter swans to the workings of the swan boats in the Boston Public Garden, and he wrote the text with the same scrupulous attention to detail. Nonetheless, with the striking exception of John Updike, who praised the author's "sense of the precious instinctual heritage represented by wild nature," most critics responded coolly to the implausible swan who flies through the world encumbered with a trumpet and a slate on which to write.

E. B. White has a firm place in American letters as a distinguished essayist, a man who expressed his wry view of the world in exquisitely chiseled sentences. Applying that same craft to three books for children, E. B. White has won a place in the hearts of the young forever. ❧ PETER F. NEUMEYER

WHITE, T. H.

BRITISH NOVELIST, 1906–1964. Born in Bombay, India, Terence Hanbury White, known to his acquaintances as Tim, suffered an unhappy childhood and, for his entire life, had trouble escaping his deep loneliness. His manipulative mother vied for his undiluted love, and his parents fought bitterly and constantly until their divorce in 1920. The breakup of his family had a profound effect on White, who, from then on, felt a need to excel in all areas of life in order to feel secure. He earned first class honors at Queens' College, Cambridge, and became head of the English Department at Stowe School, but at age thirty he resigned to write full-time.

In 1938, after achieving some prominence as a writer of novels for adults, he published *The Sword in the Stone,* which was later revised and included as the first section of White's classic version of King Arthur's life, *The Once and Future King,* finished twenty years later. Inspired by Malory's *Morte d'Arthur, The Once and Future King* brings together the legend, White's vision of an ideal childhood, and his views on human interaction, particularly war.

In *The Sword in the Stone,* made into a motion picture in 1963 by WALT DISNEY Productions, the young Wart, a fosterling with no notion of his regal birth, receives special tutoring from Merlyn, who transforms him into a fish, a hawk, an ant, a goose, and a badger to teach him lessons about society and life. Without mincing words or leaving out unsavory details, the subsequent books relay the story of King Arthur's reign, Guenever's devastating affair with Lancelot, Arthur's fatal seduction by his half sister, Morgause, and his relationship with Morgause's children—among them his son. With humor and wit, White delves into motivation and character as he retells the epic story, but, threaded throughout is the serious theme of the futility of war. As a young king, Arthur sets out to create a new code of chivalry, in which knights fight for morality and truth rather than individual gain, but age and experience give him an understanding of the waste of war of any kind. White's personal perspective informs Arthur's growth in wisdom, and his own loneliness as a bachelor brings a keen understanding to Arthur's pain at his wife's betrayal. When White wrote *The Book of Merlyn,* which reunites Arthur with his magician teacher after his final defeat, he intended it to be the fifth book in the volume, but after much editing and arguing with his publishers, the piece was instead published posthumously as a separate book in 1972.

Mistress Masham's Repose (1946), White's other novel for children, also had as inspiration a classic work of literature. Upon the premise that some of the Lilliputians from Swift's *Gulliver's Travels* ended up in England, White built a charming fantasy, filled with details about life in miniature. Orphaned Maria finds the tiny community on an abandoned island on her estate and must prevent the Lilliputians' exploitation when their existence is discovered by Maria's evil guardians. The characters are delightfully drawn to illustrate the farce, showing off White's skill in stretching the boundaries of humor and caricature.

White's work received positive critical attention on both sides of the Atlantic. *The Once and Future King* inspired *Camelot,* the acclaimed and much beloved musical in which Julie Andrews and Richard Burton starred. Although disappointed by much in life, T. H. White left a lasting legacy. ❧ A.E.D.

WIESE, KURT

AMERICAN ILLUSTRATOR AND AUTHOR, 1887–1974. Kurt Wiese, one of the most prolific illustrators known in the field of American children's literature, illustrated over three hundred books during a highly respected career that spanned more than four decades. Best known for having illustrated MARJORIE FLACK's *Story about Ping* (1933) and CLAIRE HUCHET BISHOP's timeless retelling of a Chinese folktale, *Five Chinese Brothers* (1938), Wiese was a versatile artist who imparted vitality, emotion, and a keen design sense to the variety of media in which he worked.

Published in the late 1920s and early 1930s, Wiese's first books were among the titles that established the genesis of the American picture book. Wiese worked for the three preeminent juvenile book editors of the time, Louise Seaman of Macmillan, May Massee of Doubleday, and Ernestine Evans of Coward-McCann. So productive was he that he had more books than any other artist published in the fall of 1930. Wiese and colleagues WANDA GAG BERTA and ELMER HADER, and LOIS LENSKI were some of America's first prominent author-illustrators for children. Their creative talents shifted the focus of picture books from Europe to the United States.

Born and schooled in Germany, Wiese later lived in China for six years, Australia for five years, and Brazil for four years. In 1927 a well-traveled Wiese arrived in America looking for work. He soon found employment with *Collier's Weekly* and shortly afterward illustrated one of his first books for Louise Seaman. As one of twelve small picture books that constituted Macmillan's "Happy Hour" series, Wiese's *Three Little Kittens* (1928) contained innovative book design elements and lively lithographs that launched his successful career.

In another of his notable picture books, *Liang and Lo* (1930), Wiese made new and exhilarating use of the interplay between two facing pages to picture the story of the young boy Liang and his newfound friend, Lo, who lives on a buffalo's back, and their encounter with a dragon. Knowledgeable in commercial color lithography, Wiese had a direct hand in creating his five-color illustrations for *Liang and Lo*. As a result, he achieved dramatic effects with color, making it serve both his drawings and the book's design.

Wiese's years in China also helped create his illustrations for *The Story about Ping*. Sincere and straightforward, Wiese's memorable pictures are a perfect match for Flack's words, rich with imagery, about the young Chinese duck who lives with his large extended family on a wise-eyed boat on the great Yangtze River. The resplendent lithographs, in predominant hues of yellow and blue, convey a cheerfulness touched by serenity, an appropriate mood that makes Ping's misadventure away from home palatable and universal to very young children. Developmentally significant to American picture books, *The Story about Ping* was one of the earliest collaborative efforts between a well-known writer and an accomplished illustrator. This important change in the making of picture books took hold, flourished, and came to fruition years later during the Golden Age of children's book publishing.

In spite of some criticism for his stereotypic depiction of the Chinese in *Five Chinese Brothers,* Wiese's choice of the long and narrow horizontal format, his animated two-color drawings of the clever brothers who possess unique magical powers, and the comic-strip feel imparted by the turning of the pages combine to make an exemplary picture book.

Among the several series of children's books Wiese illustrated were the tremendously popular "Freddy, the Pig" stories by Walter Rollin Brooks. Other noteworthy titles in Wiese's vast body of work include two Caldecott Honor books that he wrote and illustrated, *You Can Write Chinese* (1945) and *Fish in the Air* (1948).

Wiese's global experience gave young American children some of their first glimpses of other cultures and countries in picture-book form; his masterful, artistic interpretations of words have enlarged, enriched, and enchanted the children's book world. ❧ S.L.S.

WIESNER, DAVID

AMERICAN PICTURE BOOK AUTHOR AND ILLUSTRATOR, B. 1956. Things in David Wiesner's books tend to "fly": from flying frogs to giant floating vegetables, his amusing inventiveness takes wing.

Born and raised in Bridgewater, New Jersey, Wiesner was known in school as "the kid who could draw." The youngest of five children, Wiesner had an artistic older sister and brother, so art supplies were abundant in the house. Ink bottles, tubes of paint, and boxes of pastels held an exotic appeal for him, and relatives always gave him art-related presents. His fascination with drawing and painting led him to copy all forms of illustration from COMIC BOOKS to reference books. In a history book he discovered dinosaurs, and the hazy but realistic black-and-white renditions, which he believed were actual photographs, became favorite subjects, which he drew over and over.

Wiesner's artistic pursuit led him to the Rhode Island School of Design and a B.F.A. in 1978. His first book contract came a year later, after he made the rounds of publishers. An editor offered him the manuscript for *Honest Andrew* (1980), an otter family story written by Gloria Skurzynski. The books that followed were a variety of fictional stories written by other people: Nancy Luenn's *The Ugly Princess* (1981) and Dennis Haseley's *Kite Flier* (1986). In 1987 Wiesner and his wife, Kim Kahng, retold *The Loathsome Dragon,* which he illustrated with watercolors. A year later he wrote and illustrated *Free Fall* (1988), for which he received a Caldecott Honor Medal. In *Free Fall* the dream sequences are evoked, as Wiesner has described them, through a series of "metamorphosing landscapes through which the characters walk, float, fly and ride." The wordless adventure allows each reader to interpret the dream individually. In his next three books, Wiesner combined humor and creativeness with a playfulness and a wry use of perspective, which solidified into a detailed, imaginative style of telling stories with pictures. As flying appeared frequently as a motif in these books, Wiesner's illustrative style began to soar. Based on one of Wiesner's childhood experiences, *Hurricane* (1990) relates how two brothers share their fright during the storm and afterward when they pretend a toppled tree is a jungle, a galleon, and a spaceship. Then came *Tuesday* (1991), in which an eerie flotilla of floating frogs flies through a sleeping town leaving a lily-pad trail of suspicious doings. The subtleties and delightful humorous details in this picture book garnered the Caldecott Medal in 1992. In *June 29, 1999* (1992) Holly Evans's science project sends seedlings aloft into the ionosphere, creating skies filled with giant vegetables: lima beans loom over Levittown, artichokes advance on Anchorage, and parsnips pass by Providence.

In his picture books, Wiesner visually explores the improbable with good humor and lively ingenuity. His hypothetical situations are the perfect beginning for his colorful, wittily depicted stretches of the imagination. ❧ J.C.

Wiggin, Kate Douglas

American author, 1856–1923. When Kate Douglas Wiggin wrote *Rebecca of Sunnybrook Farm* (1903) over ninety years ago, she created a child who stepped into that elite group of book characters whose names are familiar to each new generation of readers. Rebecca, a spirited and lively ten-year-old, was not the child her two spinster aunts had invited to live with them. They had offered to educate Rebecca's more placid older sister, but with seven children to raise, Rebecca's widowed mother could not spare the dependable Hannah. In spite of the no-nonsense discipline in her aunt's home, Rebecca has many adventures, among them her meeting with the kindly man she nicknames "Mr. Aladdin" when she sells him three hundred cakes of soap in order to secure a beautiful oil lamp for a poor family. After leaving school, Rebecca is able to rescue her family from the poverty of Sunnybrook Farm when her Aunt Mirandy dies and wills her neat brick house to Rebecca.

Like Rebecca, Kate Douglas Wiggin spent the formative years of her childhood in a small Maine village, moving there from Philadelphia when her widowed mother married a country doctor. Hollis, Maine, was an enchanting place to Wiggin, her sister Nora, and their half brother, Philip. She fondly remembered the culmination of their frog-singing school, when all twenty-one frogs sat in a row, neatly graded by size. Wiggin joked that this clearly foretold her interest in being an educator. Reading was an early passion for Wiggin, and Charles Dickens was a family favorite—nearly all the pets and farm animals were named after Dickens's characters. As a child, she chanced to meet her revered author on a train, and, like Rebecca, whose candor and articulate enthusiasm charmed adults, the young Kate entertained Dickens with her reviews of the "long dull parts" in his novels.

With the decline of the stepfather's health, the family moved to Santa Barbara, and after his death, as they experienced financial worries for the first time, Wiggin submitted a story to *St. Nicholas* magazine. When a letter of acceptance and a check for $150 arrived, Wiggin considered writing more stories, but she felt she had little to say and was more suited to teaching young children. At this critical moment, she met Mrs. Caroline M. Severance, a passionate believer in the new kindergarten movement. Wiggin rapidly became one of her disciples; in 1878 she and Felix Adler opened the Silver Street Free Kindergarten in San Francisco. By 1880 Wiggin and Nora had opened their own Kindergarten Training School. Wiggin devoted herself to her profession and spent many years speaking and writing about the education of young children.

With a thought to raising money for the movement, she wrote a story called *The Birds' Christmas Carol* (1887) and had it privately printed. Later, after the death of her young husband, Wiggin felt the need of new directions and sent the book off to a publisher, who accepted it. This short and sentimental story was received enthusiastically by the public, inspiring Wiggin to write *Polly Oliver's Problem* (1893) and other stories.

But it was *Rebecca of Sunnybrook Farm* that most captivated the public—so much so that Wiggin was persuaded to adapt it as a play. In 1917 Mary Pickford starred in a movie version of *Rebecca,* and in 1938, several years after Wiggin's death, Shirley Temple starred in another film version. Less substantial than Louisa May Alcott's landmark novel, *Little Women,* which also centered on spirited sisters struggling to preserve their family in the face of poverty, *Rebecca of Sunnybrook Farm* might have slipped from memory had it not been for the two famous movie treatments. ❧ P.H.

Wild, Margaret

Australian writer, b. 1948. Rapidly establishing a reputation as one of Australia's most talented and prolific writers for children, Margaret Wild spins a carousel of topics, including the controversial, throughout the pages of her books.

This intrepid writer grew up in South Africa—Johannesburg for the most part—where she was one of twin girls in a family with five children. She stepped into the world of employment as a reporter on a country newspaper, then later moved on to the Johannesburg *Star.*

As so often happens, her journalism experiences required her to turn her hand to a huge range of topics, even—she is quick to point out—to a subject as enigmatic to her as cricket, logical and solid preparation for someone who later was to become such a diverse writer of fiction. After moving to Australia in 1973, she continued to contribute to newspapers until she enrolled at the Australian National University to complete her formal education. Then, following a move to Sydney in 1980, her life became a combination of child rearing and freelance work. It was when her first child was young that she began to take a keener interest in children's literature, discovered the treasures she had missed as a child, and considered turning her hand to writing for the young, although she admits that she never "consciously set out to write children's books. Increasingly," she says, "what interested Daniel [her son] interested me."

Even in some of her first writing, *There's a Sea in My Bedroom* (1984), for example, an imaginative exploration of a child's fear of the sea, she proved her ability to please young readers. Her titles rarely concern themselves with conventional topics; she is far better known for her courageous and numerous forays into less conventional territory. *Let the Celebrations Begin!* (1991), for instance—illustrated by JULIE VIVAS and short-listed for the Australian 1992 Books of the Year Awards—takes place at the end of World War II and tells of a group of women and children in a concentration camp. The book created a fair amount of controversy in Australia and in other countries when it was published, as critics complained that it painted too rosy a portrait of the situation. *The Very Best of Friends* (1989), also illustrated by Vivas and named the 1990 Australian Picture Book of the Year, concerns friendship but also tackles, with grace and beauty, issues of death and loss. *My Dearest Dinosaur* (1992), copes intriguingly with the unusual subject of a dinosaur writing letters to her missing, beloved spouse and raises haunting questions about extinction.

Although Wild has become internationally well known for her enormous and worthy contributions to the picture-book genre, her first novel for young people, *Beast,* appeared in 1992. It displays just as strongly Wild's talent for creating fresh, believable characters and following them through challenging and unusual situations. With her sensitivity to human nature and her ability to communicate it with quiet drama, she creates books that leave readers with plenty to contemplate. K.J.

Wilder, Laura Ingalls

AMERICAN AUTHOR, 1867–1957. Laura Ingalls Wilder's Little House books chronicle life in the Midwest from 1870 to 1894. Written in the third person, with Wilder as principal protagonist, the books are rich in the social history which surrounds the effects of the Homestead Act and last phase of American westward expansion. Readers of the Little House books learn the intricacies of frontier house-building, agriculture, home economics, entertainment, schooling, and railroad and town building. In addition to Wilder's vivid descriptions of daily life in the pioneer era, her books recount the necessity of family solidarity versus an uncertain wilderness and the virtues of independent living far removed from government control.

Wilder's career as a children's author started in 1932, when at sixty-five she published her first book, *Little House in the Big Woods.* The book described the Ingalls family's life in the forest near Pepin, Wisconsin, where the first two children, Mary and Laura, were born. The parents, Charles and Caroline Ingalls, were infected with the "go west" spirit of the post–Civil War period. They took their family to the area near Independence, Kansas, described in *Little House on the Prairie* (1935), but later returned north to Walnut Grove, Minnesota, in *On the Banks of Plum Creek* (1937). Wilder omitted two years from her saga (1876 to 1878), but resumed the story with her family's journey west to Dakota Territory in 1879 in *By the Shores of Silver Lake* (1939). *The Long Winter* (1940) and *Little Town on the Prairie* (1941) document homesteading and the building of the town of De Smet, South Dakota.

While the early books of the Little House series are written for middle-grade children, the later ones show a decidedly more complex plot structure and character development as Laura Ingalls enters young adulthood. The last of the series, *These Happy Golden Years* (1943), relates Laura's teaching career, courtship, and marriage to Almanzo Wilder in 1885. Chronologically, Wilder's second published book was *Farmer Boy* (1933), which is the story of her husband's boyhood near Malone, New York. The Wilder boys, Almanzo and Royal, reappear as homesteaders in the last four books, with Almanzo assuming the male protagonist role, in place of Pa Ingalls.

Illustration by GARTH WILLIAMS from *Little House in the Big Woods* (1953), by Laura Ingalls Wilder.

As farmers, Laura and Almanzo Wilder homesteaded near De Smet from 1885 to 1889. Their hardships with weather, disease, and other disasters make up the plot of *The First Four Years* (1971), published from an unpolished first draft fourteen years after Wilder's death. Its worth is largely informational, and it pales in comparison to the detailed, skillfully told earlier books in the series. The book introduces the only Wilder child to survive to adulthood, Rose (1886–1968). Rose Wilder Lane edited her mother's travel diary of her 1894 journey from South Dakota to Mansfield, Missouri, in *On the Way Home* (1962). The Wilders moved to the Missouri Ozarks, settling on Rocky Ridge Farm, which became the permanent family home. Laura Wilder's activities, in addition to her role as a farm wife, included the management of the Mansfield Farm Loan Association in the 1920s, numerous community betterment projects, and approximately fifteen years (1911–1926) as a country journalist. Wilder's essays, features, poetry, and interviews were printed regularly by *The Missouri Ruralist* and also appeared in *McCall's, Country Gentlemen,* and other regional publications. Some of these contributions are gathered in *A Little House Sampler* (1989).

Rose Wilder left the family farm for a more liberating career in business and journalism. Her influence on her mother's writing is evident in *West from Home* (1974), which consists of letters Wilder sent to her husband while visiting their journalist daughter in San Francisco in 1915. The Wilder-Lane writing collaboration has been examined with use of their manuscripts, letters, and the daughter's diaries.

In addition to her own work as a biographer, short story writer, foreign correspondent, and novelist, Lane successfully managed and promoted her mother's Little House books during the 1930s and 1940s. She alternated between tutor, publicist, intermediate agent, and editor through the twelve-year writing process of the Wilder titles. Wilder was accurate in later describing the books as truthful and autobiographical in content, but her daughter's skilled hand helped greatly in transforming memoir into compelling fiction. Editorial staff at Harper and Brothers found little need for revision on the Wilder manuscripts; essentially, that role was assumed by Lane, *sub rosa.*

The Little House books brought immediate accolades to their author; although none earned Newbery Medals, five were runners-up for that honor. The books enjoyed a grassroots popularity, and, because of their value as Americana, they quickly became entrenched in school curricula, where they show no signs of diminishing popularity. In 1993, a conservative estimate of Little House book printings topped forty million copies. They are also widely translated into foreign languages. Following World War II, the United States State Department ordered the translation of Wilder titles into German and Japanese for inclusion in education programs in those countries. The books have remained perennially popular in Japan. Although Wilder's meticulous, descriptive prose style diminishes the need for illustrations, GARTH WILLIAMS's 1953 drawings for the Little House series provided sensitive, graphic, and authentic art to enhance the author's words. His artwork replaced that of HELEN SEWELL and Mildred Boyle, which had appeared in earlier editions.

In 1954 the American Library Association created the Laura Ingalls Wilder Award, first to honor Wilder, and later to recognize creators of children's books whose cumulative work represents significant contributions to the field. Wilder was widely honored for her work during her lifetime and beyond. Libraries, schools, parks, highways, and streets bear her name. The settings of her books and her former homes are all preserved or memorialized. But Wilder's greatest tribute is the continued reading of her Little House books, which seem to cross all barriers of age, language, or nationality. Her life and writings make her perhaps the quintessential American pioneer. ❧ WILLIAM ANDERSON

Wildsmith, Brian

British illustrator and author, b. 1930. Brian Wildsmith is foremost a painter; he consistently employs vivid color and intricately patterned designs in his art for the picture book. Throughout the past three decades, Wildsmith has published more than fifty books in fourteen languages, and nearly eight million copies have been sold. Wildsmith burst into the literary arena with the publication of his first picture book, *Brian Wildsmith's ABC*, in 1962. His bold colorations offered a fresh and exciting perspective following a relatively tranquil decade in the field of children's publishing. Graced with the esteemed Kate Greenaway Award, *Brian Wildsmith's ABC* launched his career as a picture-book artist and author.

Wildsmith was born in a small mining village in Yorkshire. As a young child, he developed an appreciation of art from his father, who enjoyed painting after his day's work in the coal mines. Wildsmith was awarded a scholarship to the Slade School of Fine Art at the University of London, where he refined his passion for both music and art, two talents that permeate his work as an illustrator.

Initially, Wildsmith illustrated book jackets for several publishers. Mabel George, the former children's book editor of Oxford University Press, recognized and fostered Wildsmith's artistic talents. George recalls her first impressions of his art when he came to her in 1957: "Looking at the abstract paintings, I saw how boldly, yet delicately, the color was used, how poetically and simply the imagination behind the painting was expressed." In 1961, she asked Wildsmith to make fourteen color plates for a new edition of *The Arabian Nights*. Eventually, George discovered a talented fine art printer capable of reproducing Wildsmith's brilliantly colored pictures; she then invited Wildsmith to create Oxford's first children's picture book. *Brian Wildsmith's ABC* represents the simplest type of alphabet book, pairing one word with one picture. To depict the letter *L*, he pictures a fiery orange lion regally posed against a royal-blue matte finished background. The contrast in colors and texture energizes the simple format.

Realistic about the high cost of reproducing color, George and Wildsmith sought to captivate the international market with picture books that would have universal appeal. They settled on Jean de La Fontaine's fables, which had never been issued in picture-book form. Wildsmith filled his illustrations for La Fontaine's classic tale *The Hare and the Tortoise* (1967) with a panoply of multicolored wild creatures. Among others, he illustrated La Fontaine's *The Lion and the Rat* (1963), *The Rich Man and the Shoemaker* (1965), and *The Miller, the Boy and the Donkey* (1969). In addition to the fables, Wildsmith illustrated *The Oxford Book of Poetry for Children* (1963), edited by Edward Blishen.

Wildsmith believes an artist, like a musician, must be able to work in the whole range and scale; his trademark illustrations reflect a sweeping spectrum of color. He achieves a strong sense of texture and design by combining bold complementary colors and expressing each in a full range in tones. His penchant for the animal figure is seen in several picture books that thematically group the animal kingdom. In *Brian Wildsmith's Birds* (1967) he playfully combines a menagerie of archaic and familiar expressions—a "sedge of herons" or a "gaggle of geese"—with brilliantly rendered ornithological specimens. The wide-eyed owls feathered with soft yellow, burgundy, teal, and black-and-white colors stare at the reader. He presents *Brian Wildsmith's Wild Animals* (1967), *Brian Wildsmith's Fishes* (1968), and other titles in a similar format. Wildsmith experimented with the split-page image during the 1980s. Using this intricate format, he illustrated and wrote *Pelican* (1982), a story about a misplaced bird with a mistaken identity. This technique added the element of surprise to Wildsmith's highly visual narrative.

In both his art and his prose, Wildsmith has realized the personal goals that he envisioned as a young man. He recalls, "From the beginning, what I wanted to do above all for children's literature was to try and span the whole spectrum from an ABC to counting—through puzzles, myths, nursery rhymes, and stories." He has succeeded in doing just that. ❧ S.M.G.

Wilkinson, Brenda

American novelist, poet, and short story writer, b. 1946. Brenda Wilkinson is best known for her books about Ludell Wilson, the protagonist of *Ludell* (1975). Ludell Wilson lives in Waycross, a small town in Georgia, with her grandmother, whom she calls "Mama." Ludell's own mother, who was not married, left her in Mama's care when Ludell was a baby and then moved to New York. Ludell is intelligent and observant, and with her writer's sensibility she portrays her black society: The mothers work for white families as domestic servants during the week, then struggle to do the same work for their own families when they return home at night and on weekends, butchering their own chickens and washing clothes by hand. Through Ludell's narrative, the reader resents the employer who forces her neighbor, Mrs. Johnson, to leave her children and work most of Christmas Day. The more childlike problems and dramas of grade-school classrooms are vividly described, as are the indignities that Ludell and her acquaintances suffer because of their poverty. Though just in the fifth grade, Ludell is one of the first to comprehend the activities of Mrs. Johnson's daughter, an unwed mother, as she begins dating a married man.

One of the most noteworthy aspects of Wilkinson's work is her use of language. Descriptive prose and Ludell's thoughts are set down in standard English, but in her characters' speech, the authentic syntax, vocabulary, and pronunciation of the time and place of Wilkinson's own upbringing are lovingly employed, lending a distinctive voice to the sympathetic protagonist. *Ludell* was nominated for a National Book Award.

Ludell and Willie (1977) was the first sequel to *Ludell*. This book follows the teenage romance of Ludell and Willie Johnson, their goals in writing and in sports respectively, and her employment as a domestic worker. In *Ludell's New York Time* (1980), Ludell goes to New York City to join her mother, who tries to introduce her to a new life so she will forget Willie, whom Ludell wants to marry. Wilkinson introduces the social activism of the civil rights movement in the early 1960s into the story, and Ludell encounters prejudice in the workplace in New York as she did in her hometown.

Wilkinson was indeed brought up in Waycross, Georgia, though she was born in Moultrie, Georgia. After high school she attended Hunter College in New York City, where she settled.

Wilkinson is a poet and short story writer, and a member of several writers' organizations including The Harlem Writers Guild. Her novels about Ludell present the lives of rural black children prior to the civil rights era. Through her lively and forthright protagonist, she succeeds in delineating the joy she felt in her southern upbringing in the 1950s and in exploring the choice of staying in the South and resettling in the North. Among her other writings is *Jesse Jackson: Still Fighting for the Dream* (1990). S.H.H.

Willard, Nancy

American author and poet, b. 1936. A writer of stories for adults as well as young people, Nancy Willard enjoys a reputation as an author with versatility, good humor, and, most of all, a gift for storytelling.

Born in Ann Arbor, she holds a bachelor of arts and a Ph.D. from the University of Michigan and an M.A. from Stanford University.

Illustration by Alice and Martin Provensen from *A Visit to William Blake's Inn* (1981), by Nancy Willard.

Willard's books often deal with homey topics: family, food, the hearth. Her touch is loving and gentle, but she does not gloss over the anxieties of childhood or the essential sadness that is part of growing up. She is not limited, however, to the close-to-home, as demonstrated by her fascination with fantasy and British poet William Blake, affinities she developed in childhood. Willard received the Newbery Medal for *A Visit to William Blake's Inn: Poems for Innocent and Experienced Travelers* (1981), a collection of poems illustrated by Alice and Martin Provensen, which exhibits Willard's talent for bringing the literary world to children in poetry form. Her fantasy trilogy—*Sailing to Cythera and Other Anatole Stories* (1979), *The Island of the Grass King* (1979), and *Uncle Terrible: More Adventures of Anatole* (1982)—contains some of her best writing.

Willard's picture books vary in look, as she collaborates with different illustrators: Ilse Plume in *Night Story*

(1986), Tomie dePaola in *Simple Pictures Are Best* (1977), and David McPhail in *The Nightgown of the Sullen Moon* (1983). Angels often figure into the Willard formula, never more so than in *The High Rise Glorious Skittle Skat Roarious Sky Pie Angel Food Cake* (1990), an enchanting story of a nine-year-old who wants Mom to have a heavenly birthday present, illustrated by Richard Jesse Watson.

Willard grew up in Michigan and spent summers at a cottage on a lake, the setting of her first book, *Sailing to Cythera,* sketching and making up stories with her sister. Encouraged by her parents to write and draw, Willard and her sister put out a little newspaper. To collect news, they visited neighbors, hoping for a newsworthy bit of gossip.

Willard is married to photographer Eric Lindbloom, and they have one son, James. A lecturer at Vassar, she lives in Poughkeepsie, New York. ❧ A.C.

Williams, Garth

American illustrator and author, b. 1912. Garth Williams, best known as the illustrator of Laura Ingalls Wilder's "Little House" books and E. B. White's *Stuart Little* (1945) and *Charlotte's Web* (1952), illustrated more than eighty books and wrote seven picture books, including *The Rabbit's Wedding* (1958), unintentionally controversial because of its depiction of the wedding of a black rabbit and a white rabbit.

Williams was born in New York City, but his family soon moved to a farm in New Jersey; his earliest memories of this time include riding with the farmer on his tractor. From there the family moved to Ontario and, in 1922, to England. His father was a cartoonist and his mother a landscape painter, and Williams has said, "Everybody in my house was either painting or drawing, so I thought there was nothing else to do in life but make pictures." He attended the Westminster School of Art and went on to win a painting scholarship to the Royal College of Art; there he discovered sculpture. Williams's affinity for weight and texture in his illustrations seems to come from his sculpting. He applied for and received the British Prix de Rome, allowing him to study art in Italy, France, and Germany, where he met and married the first of his four wives. While driving an ambulance during World War II, he was wounded in the spine and went to the United States, where he continued to work for the war effort. In 1943 he began looking for work as an illustrator and cartoonist and was eventually accepted by *The New Yorker.* His first children's book illustrations appeared in *Stuart Little* in 1945, followed in 1946 by Margaret Wise Brown's *Little Fur Family,* which was bound in rabbit fur. This title began a collaboration with Brown that would eventually include eleven books.

When he works with pen and ink, Williams combines a classical style of flowing lines and crosshatching with humorous, loving depictions of his characters, as in the novels he illustrated for White, George Selden, and Margery Sharp. When he uses pencil, as in Russell Hoban's *Bedtime for Frances* (1960) and Wilder's *Little House in the Big Woods* (1932) and the other books in this series, his lines are fewer and softer, yet still recognizable for the caring, understated facial expressions. Williams excels at textures, particularly animal fur and the tall waving grasses in Wilder's books. When he works with color, as in his picture books with Brown and Jack Prelutsky, he opts for deep colors to add warmth to his lines. About his animal drawings, he says, "I start with the real animal, working over and over until I can get the effect of human qualities and expressions and poses. I redesign animals, as it were."

Williams worked on the "Little House" books for nearly six years, meeting Wilder and traveling to the locations of all but one of her books. Though he was not the first illustrator for this series, his images quickly became the definitive ones. When he was approached about the job, he was uncertain about his ability to draw people. It is true that the faces and proportions of people in these books sometimes lack consistency, but Williams so closely matches the spirit of each character and setting that any flaws become irrelevant.

Williams's long career has allowed him to work with some of the most respected children's authors. He is recognized for his uncanny ability to show realistic animals whose thoughts we can read because of their subtle human qualities, but he should be known equally for his evocative yet solid settings for both animal fantasies and Wilder's realistic books. ❧ L.R.

Williams, Vera B.

American author and illustrator, b. 1927. A striking element in the award-winning books Vera Williams creates is the wealth of strong female characters. An active supporter of both peace and feminist issues, Williams writes about confident girls and women who live amicably with other people and with the environment. Also expressed in her books is the holistic

Illustration by Vera B. Williams from *Stringbean's Trip to the Shining Sea* (1988), by Vera B. Williams and Jennifer Williams.

philosophy taught at Black Mountain College in North Carolina, where Williams earned a degree in graphic art. Keenly aware of interdependence, her characters strive together toward goals—as families, neighbors, and friends. Most prominent in her stories, though, is the emphasis on people and simple pleasures rather than on money and material goods.

Williams, who was raised during the Depression, tells of families discovering beauty and joy in the simple things in life. *Three Days on a River in a Red Canoe* (1981), for example, describes a no-frills, but fun-filled, family vacation. When two young cousins are taken on a camping trip by their mothers, both knowledgeable campers and canoeists, they experience the inexpensive but rewarding adventure of the great outdoors. Another low-budget but exciting journey is described in *Stringbean's Trip to the Shining Sea* (1988), a joint effort created by the author-illustrator and her daughter, artist Jennifer Williams. This innovative book is an album of the postcards and pictures young Stringbean sends home while traveling by truck with his older brother from Kansas to the Pacific. The unpretentious descriptions of the trip are down-to-earth and authentically childlike. In *"More More More," Said the Baby: Three Love Stories* (1990), gentle vignettes depict toddlers having fun, not with fancy toys but with family—a father, mother, and grandmother—hugging, playing, and kissing. Exuberance and joy are depicted in this Caldecott Honor Book's lively art that depicts African-, Asian-, and Anglo-American children and adults.

The sincere enjoyment of simple things is also evident in the trio of books about Rosa and her mother and grandmother, a close-knit, working-class family. In the first, the Caldecott Honor Book *A Chair for My Mother* (1982), Rosa's mom, a waitress, needs a comfortable chair in which to relax after work, so daughter, mother, and grandmother save coins in a big jar until the long-awaited day when the jar is filled and the three can have the fun of shopping for the perfect chair. In *Something Special for Me* (1983) and *Music, Music for Everyone* (1984), Rosa discovers the pleasures of music. The art in these and Williams's other picture books is unique and instantly recognizable. Multicultural communities and families people her stories, and spontaneity and energy—family love and deep joy—are all expressed in the brightly colored illustrations. When Williams utilizes borders, they serve as extensions of the story rather than mere decorations. Though her art is reminiscent of children's drawings and the appearance of her books is deceptively simple, together the pictures and stories evoke strong emotions that still move both young and old readers. ❧ J.M.B.

Voices of the Creators

Vera B. Williams

Those fairies that presided at my birth did not bring the gift of security. We had a struggle keeping jobs, family, and places to live. But I was given the promise that life, however rocky, would be an adventure. And just as my parents believed that material goods should be distributed equably, so they also believed in an equable distribution of culture and a chance at creative expression. Bread *and* roses. They found the free places where my sister and I might paint and sculpt, dance, and act. And that was a blessing, for I was a child with a lot to say. When people grew tired of my talking, I drew pictures. But then I had to tell about the pictures. Even with acting and dancing, I couldn't get it all told.

I still can't. Of course all stories aren't equally important to tell. I distinguish between natural and synthetic stories, by which I mean something about the depth from which a story springs. I admit it's a delight to make up stories and pictures, whatever their source. It flexes the muscles of the imagination. But it takes about a year for me to bring a book from its first shadowy glimmerings to a completed work in which each element is rooted in the tale to be told: type (sometimes hand lettering); paper; format; even the flaps and back cover. Naturally, I desire to embark only on projects with "serious consequences." But "serious" most certainly includes the colorful, playful, and humorous.

Take my book *Stringbean's Trip to the Shining Sea.* In it are the postcards and snapshots that Stringbean Coe and his brother Fred sent home to their family from the long trip they made one summer in Fred's truck. I did this book with my adult daughter Jennifer Williams as co-illustrator. Despite rough spots, we shared the pleasure of a beguiling, childlike project creating stamps, picture postcards, postcardese descriptions of places, including a restaurant in a cowboy boot. We could have gone on inventing cards and stamps for years. I had, in fact, no ending for the story for a long time. Yet something of deep importance to me was working its way.

Tied with a string in my drawer was a collection of postcards. I had sent them to my mother as I traveled across Canada in my late forties to make a canoe voyage down the Yukon River. She too had traveled through the West when she was young. I knew the snapshots of her trip well, and I wanted to provide her with a vicarious trip for her late years. My canoe trip led to my book *Three Days on a River in a Red Canoe.* But more importantly, it was a prelude to the main adventure of my fifties and sixties: creating picture books. I well remember a day on the trip when I turned down a hike to stay in camp and wash up. But my real desire was to be left alone with myself as storyteller. I spent my time sketching equipment, making a storyboard.

I had had many adventures: parenthood, the organizing of a cooperative community and experimental school, arrests in anti-nuclear demonstrations, jobs as cook, baker, and teacher. I had been caught up in nature study, canoeing, and hiking—and love. But the time had come to fill that other promise of my childhood, to somehow tell my stories.

My mother died when I was on the threshold of this career. I had told her I was on my way to being an author/illustrator. She had said, "Hurry up! I'm not going to live much longer." After she died, I retrieved the postcards I had sent her. They became, in time, the mysterious engine of *Stringbean's Trip to the Shining Sea.* My mother used to call me Stringbean back when I was a skinny kid driving her crazy with my need to report on everything. In the book, Stringbean finally gets to "tell" until he is content with it. He has had his say, but still he longs for his parents to hang on to his every word. And he looks forward to all those marvelous things he might yet do and see. For him it was a true trip to his own shining sea.

For me, its author and main character, it became a tightly condensed autobiography in which the enthusiasms of my or my daughter's life appear on the different cards—a great device for an autobiographical novel in forty-eight pages! I had been helped in this by a study of the postcard tradition and its history. I saw that geography, history, personal events, and entertainment combined tidily on those little cards. I developed a friendly regard for the vanished writers and readers of the cards I read. Then, as I wrote my own cards, I began to feel that same affectionate bond with all the unknown readers-to-be of my and Jennifer's made-up cards. Now when I sign the book for people, I sometimes write, "Have your own wonderful trip to the shining sea."

Wojciechowska, Maia

American author, b. 1927. Maia Wojciechowska's *Shadow of a Bull* was a somewhat surprising choice to win the Newbery Medal in 1965. Not only did the book concern the unusual topic of bullfighting, but it was the first novel by an unknown Polish immigrant. Yet Wojciechowska had created what many readers consider a stunning story about courage, choices, and pride. Several other inventive books followed, proving the initial success of this naturalized American citizen was not just a fluke.

Wojciechowska was born into a Warsaw military family but left Poland during World War II. She spent several years in France, which she later recorded in her autobiographical *Till the Break of Day: Memories 1939–1942* (1972). She also attended schools in England, Washington, D.C., and ultimately Los Angeles, where her family settled after the war. In 1947 Wojciechowska moved to New York to become a writer. She immediately visited a publisher with a manuscript of short stories, fully expecting a contract. When the manuscript was rejected, the resilient author tossed all her remaining money—a dime—over the Brooklyn Bridge and set off to find other employment. The adventurous spirit that led the young Wojciechowska to parachute from airplanes and become a junior tennis champion in Poland served her well over the next few years. She assisted a famous tennis coach and worked as a private detective, broadcaster, and beautician. She married poet Selden Rodman, had a daughter, and later divorced. She wrote a picture book and another on hairstyles. She rode a motorcycle through Europe and learned to bullfight.

A chance encounter with a young girl on a New York City bus inspired Wojciechowska to turn a thirteen-page bullfighting story she had written into a book for young people. It took her only two weeks to transform the short story into *Shadow of a Bull,* but this first novel received rave reviews. The story of young Manolo Olivar, forced into the same career as his deceased bullfighter-father, was acclaimed for its strong Spanish setting, its unusual topic, and its theme of a boy's struggle toward manhood. Some readers feel the writing is too stylized and the protagonist too remote, but there is no denying the power of the stark prose. The topic of bullfighting is well handled, and a great deal of technical information is well integrated into the plot through Manolo's mentors and acquaintances, who almost function as a Greek chorus.

Wojciechowska's subsequent books were further proof of her unique talent. *Don't Play Dead Before You Have To* (1970) is the novel-length monologue of a teenage boy; *A Single Light* (1968) is written from the point of view of a deaf-mute girl. *Tuned-Out* (1968), one of the first young adult novels about drug abuse, was extremely popular with readers. As Wojciechowska continued to experiment with literary forms, she wrote the odd but rewarding *Through the Broken Mirror with Alice* (1972), an updating of Lewis Carroll's *Through the Looking Glass,* about a modern African American chess-playing Alice. Critics reacted negatively to the almost plotless *The Rotten Years* (1971), which functions mainly as a forum for the author's liberal philosophies, but even this strange book is fascinating as a polemic.

In the 1970s Wojciechowska became disillusioned with publishing trends and took a five-year sabbatical during which she raised a second daughter before finally writing a well-received adult novel in 1980 about Ernest Hemingway. P.D.S.

Wolkstein, Diane

American author, b. 1942. Storyteller Diane Wolkstein has published many of her best-liked tales as children's books. Born and raised in New York, Wolkstein attended Smith College and received a master's degree from the Bank Street College of Education. She studied acting and pantomime in Paris and later used these skills when she became a fifth-grade teacher and performed stories for her classes. A summer job as a storyteller in city parks led to a professional career in the field. She has traveled throughout the world telling stories at festivals and has hosted a New York radio program, "Stories from Many Lands with Diane Wolkstein."

Most of the author's books are based on stories that are audience favorites. In *8,000 Stones: A Chinese Folktale* (1972), a second-century story, a little boy discovers a method for weighing an elephant. Like many of Wolkstein's books, it was published in a picture-book format, although the text may be too intricate for the youngest audience. Other picture books include *The Cool Ride in the Sky* (1973), which has its origins in the story and song "Straighten Up and Fly Right," *The Red Lion: A Tale of Ancient Persia* (1977), and *The Magic Wings: A Tale from China* (1983). In a slightly longer format, *Lazy Stories* (1976) contains tales of idleness gathered from Japanese, Mexican, and Laotian cultures. *The Magic Orange Tree and Other Haitian Folktales* (1978) is a spirited collection filled with rhythm and song. Prefatory remarks provide background information about each of the tales and relate the author's experiences gathering stories in Haiti.

Wolkstein's works are commendable for their diversity and sure-handed storytelling. ♘ P.D.S.

Wood, Audrey
Wood, Don

AUDREY: AMERICAN AUTHOR AND ILLUSTRATOR, B. 1948; DON: AMERICAN ILLUSTRATOR, B. 1945. Don and Audrey Wood are an acclaimed husband-and-wife author-and-illustrator team who produce exuberant PICTURE BOOKS for young children. While Audrey has written and illustrated books on her own, Don has worked as an illustrator exclusively on his wife's texts.

Audrey descends from a long line of artists that dates to the fifteenth century, and she claims to have broken the mold by being the first female working artist in the family. She was born in Little Rock, Arkansas, and raised with two younger sisters in a free-spirited childhood that included travel, intriguing people, and a broad exposure to the arts. She attended the Arkansas Art Center, an art and drama institute whose founders included her father and grandfather. Don was brought up on a working farm in California's central San Joaquin Valley with little time to pursue his passion for art. After deciding to leave the family business and become an artist, Don graduated from the University of California at Santa Barbara in 1967 and received a Master of Fine Arts degree from the California College of Arts and Crafts in 1969. He married Audrey the same year and worked at a number of jobs until, at his wife's request, he submitted sample drawings for a manuscript that she had written but not yet illustrated, and their successful collaboration was born.

The result of this merger, *Moonflute* (1980), was an admirable but flawed first effort. The lustrous oil paintings demonstrate Don's mastery, yet they are somewhat static, and the text, while appropriately lyrical and dreamlike for this tale of an airborne nighttime journey, is a bit wordy. A more successful book is *The Napping House* (1984), named a New York Times Best Illustrated Book. In this cumulative tale about an unlikely heap of nappers, perfect for reading aloud at bedtime, Don's fresh, inventive style provides the perfect accompaniment to the rhythmic text that began as a melody in Audrey's head.

For Don, each book represents a particular artistic challenge with respect to dynamics of light and dark, point of view, perspective, or narrative slant. In *The Napping House,* Don's subtle, expert use of light brings the reader from the dim, blue glow of night to sunny, riotous color as day breaks.

The Woods stage elaborate performances of their work for artistic inspiration and refinement at various points in the creative process. *King Bidgood's in the Bathtub* (1985), a Caldecott Honor Book, demonstrates the Woods' collective sense of drama and reaps the benefits of this practice. *King Bidgood* resembles an extravagant opera about a robust king who refuses to leave his bath.

An admitted "fiddler and doer-over," Don prefers oil because it is easily changed. His paintings for *Heckedy Peg* (1987), a tale based upon an old English game, are reminiscent of the sixteenth-century Flemish masters. In *Piggies* (1991), a COUNTING BOOK, spare text spotlights the humorous antics of the frisky piggies as they cavort on colorful double-page spreads. *Elbert's Bad Word* (1988) is a satire of haughty high society upset by a particularly noxious, corporeal bad word. The Woods' fondness for the outrageous is apparent in their collaborations as well as in Audrey's lighthearted illustrations for *Tugford Wanted to Be Bad* (1983) and *Weird Parents* (1990), which she wrote and illustrated. The couple maintain a shared sense of fun while exploring each other's individuality for the perfect marriage of art and text. ♘ M.O'D.H.

World War II Books

Few subjects have captured the interest of readers and writers of children's books during the second half of the twentieth century as has World War II. Virtually every major children's trade publisher releases at least one novel and perhaps an informational book about some aspect of World War II during each publishing season. Virtually no reading audience or genre has been neglected. BIOGRAPHIES, INFORMATION BOOKS, PICTURE BOOKS, and novels examine all aspects of the war from every angle imaginable. Readers seeking background material about one of the twentieth century's most compelling events will want to refer to Miriam Chaikin's *A Nightmare in History* (1987), a well-organized, chronological survey of the war.

Why do books about World War II continually fascinate young readers? Maybe it is the thrill of reading about the dangers of war with the safety of vicarious experience. The real events featured in many of the books may also seem more suspenseful than any survival or adventure story an author could imagine. Certainly, the reader who knows something about World War II can easily predict the general plot and outcome of novels set during this period. Perhaps these books have the same appealing predictability as do SERIES BOOKS: children can easily discern who is good and who is evil, and find comfort and reassurance in books that follow the pattern.

The perennial popularity of these books helps many to remain in print long after others of the same generation have disappeared. One of the earliest entries into the now-crowded field is Marie McSwigan's *Snow Treasure* (1942), a highly suspenseful story about Norwegian children who use sleds to smuggle gold bullion past the Germans. Another book that made an early appearance and has stood the test of time is *Twenty and Ten* by CLAIRE HUCHET BISHOP (1952), which takes place in a country boarding school where French evacuees shelter ten Jewish orphans.

World War II books fall into certain general categories. Some of the most captivating describe the lives of children and families who leave their homes and go into hiding or assume other identities in order to survive Nazi persecution. Many of these are written by World War II survivors. *Anne Frank: The Diary of a Young Girl* (1952) has emerged as a touchstone against which other memoirs of Jewish families in hiding are measured. A similar memoir is *The Upstairs Room* (1972) by JOHANNA REISS. In this Newbery Honor Book, the author gives a moving autobiographical account of the three years she and her sister spent hiding in the upstairs room of a remote farmhouse owned by a Gentile family in Holland. A companion book, *The Journey Back* (1976), describes how members of the author's family attempted to rebuild their lives after the war. Howard Greenfeld's *The Hidden Children* (1993) weaves together firsthand accounts of Jewish men and women who survived the Holocaust. Some people relate how they posed as children of non-Jewish families; others describe life in orphanages or religious institutions. All these children endured deception as a way of life. Numerous photographs of the contributors make the horrifying descriptions even more real. In *Behind the Secret Window: A Memoir of a Hidden Childhood during World War Two* (1993) by Nelly S. Toll, the author describes the terror and boredom she and her mother endured when they spent thirteen months in a secret room in Poland, sheltered by a Christian couple. Toll's propensity for painting helped her pass the time productively; her memoir includes twenty-nine reproductions of the lighthearted watercolors she created as a distraction during her captivity.

Many children did not go into hiding but were relocated from an area under siege in an attempt to ensure their safety. In her autobiography, *Kindertransport* (1992), Olga Levy Drucker describes the six very difficult years she spent in England, where she was sent to avoid persecution in Germany; the book ends in 1945 when she is reunited with her parents in the United States. Often, stories about evacuees are adapted and told as fiction, such as *Good Night, Mr. Tom* (1981) by MICHELLE MAGORIAN. In this enormously affecting story, an abused boy who is evacuated to the English countryside finds a world of friendship and love in the household of a seemingly gruff old man. Sheila Garrigue's autobiographical novel, *All the Children Were Sent Away* (1976), describes her evacuation from England to Canada as a child in wartime. Despite the war, most children did not want to leave their homes and sometimes made their way back after evacuation, as did Bill and Julie in Jill Paton Walsh's *Fireweed* (1969); these two teenagers secretly returned to London and survived the Blitz of 1940. Robert Westall puts an interesting twist on the plight of refugees in *Blitzcat* (1989), a riveting story about the war seen through the eyes of a displaced cat trying to find its way home. In *When Hitler Stole Pink Rabbit* (1971) by Judith Kerr, Anna's father, an outspoken Jewish journalist, finds that his views are not welcome in Nazi Germany; the whole family manages a sudden escape to Switzerland and eventually establishes a new life in England. Two other books, *The Other Way Around* (1975) and *A Small Person Far Away* (1979), complete the trio of novels that follows Anna until she is married and working as a writer for the British Broadcasting Corporation.

Another basic theme in books that take place during wartime is friendship; in World War II fiction, plots often center around maintaining relationships between friends of differing religions. DORIS ORGEL's autobiographical novel, *The Devil in Vienna* (1978), tackles this problem: two thirteen-year-old Viennese girls, one Jewish and one not, manage secretly to maintain their friendship even when the narrator's friend is forced by her Nazi father to join the Hitler Youth. The Newbery Medal winner *Number the Stars* (1989) by LOIS LOWRY deals with similar issues. Annemarie and her family, who are not Jewish, shelter Ellen Rosen, Annemarie's best friend, after the German troops attempt to remove all Jews from Denmark. The two ten-year-olds must do some quick thinking when German soldiers arrive one night to question them.

Many books about World War II recount almost superhuman feats of survival. In *Along the Tracks* (1991) by Tamar Bergman, Yankele and his family flee Nazi-occupied Poland. When their refugee train is bombed, they are separated. The boy struggles to survive on the streets of war-torn Europe as he searches for his parents. Another riveting story is *The Kingdom by the Sea* (1991) by ROBERT WESTALL. In this British novel, twelve-year-old Harry Baguely searches for a new home after his is destroyed in a bombing raid. Joan Lingard's *Tug of War* (1989) describes the trials of the Peterson family as they flee their native Latvia in 1944. The Russians are advancing, and the Petersons find themselves refugees in Germany. The fourteen-year-old twins Astra and Hugo become separated early in their desperate exodus; suspense over whether they will be reunited drives the novel's narrative at a breathless pace. *Between Two Worlds* (1991) continues the family's saga as the Petersons arrive in Canada to start a new life. Carol Matas has written a variety of novels that take place during World War II. *Daniel's Story* (1993), published in conjunction with the United States Holocaust Memorial Museum, presents a horrifyingly typical course of events for a German Jewish family in the 1930s and 1940s, a period of ever-narrowing rights and privileges; deportation and imprisonment in a concentration camp. Survival is also the theme of ESTHER HAUTZIG's *Endless Steppe: Growing Up in Siberia* (1968), one of the earliest books to describe the deplorable conditions of life in a concentration camp—in this case, a German prison camp in Siberia.

Stories about resistance movements that arose in the various countries under Nazi control fuel some of the most action-packed plots. Carol Matas writes about the Danish resistance movement in the engrossing *Lisa's War* (1987) and its sequel, *Code Name Kris* (1989). In *Bright Candles: A Novel of the Danish Resistance* (1974) by Robert Benchley, readers follow the dangerous sabotage work of a sixteen-year-old boy in Nazi-occupied Denmark. Resistance is also a main theme in Christa Laird's *Shadow of the Wall* (1990), a historical novel that includes the heroic Dr. Janusz Korczak, who unselfishly refused to leave the Warsaw Ghetto orphanage in which he sheltered large numbers of Jewish children. In *Waiting for Anya* (1991) by Michael Morpurgo, residents of Vichy, France, find themselves involved in a plot to smuggle Jewish children over the border to safety in Spain.

Another popular genre of World War II books comprises those told from the viewpoint of non-Jewish participants. In *War Boy* (1989), Michael Foreman effectively combines a brief narrative with watercolors and black-and-white drawings that offer an evocative portrait of his wartime childhood on the Suffolk coast in England. Ever-present soldiers, frequent air raids, and the deprivations of rationing punctuate his memories. *The Man from the Other Side* (1991) by URI ORLEV is a suspenseful story about fourteen-year-old Marek, who lives on the outskirts of the Warsaw Ghetto in Poland. With his grandparents, he shelters a Jewish man who has escaped from inside the ghetto walls. Hilda von Stockum's *Borrowed House* (1975) is a novel about Janna, a member of the Hitler Youth, who must deal with her feelings when she realizes that the house into which she has just moved had been confiscated from a Jewish family that had a child near her own age. *Mischling, Second Degree: My Childhood in Nazi Germany* (1977), Ilse Koehn's autobiography, describes the tactics, including enrolling her in the Hitler Youth, that her family used to hide the fact that she had one Jewish grandparent. *The Little Riders* (1963) by Margaretha Shemin tells the story of eleven-year-old Johanna, whose father gives her the responsibility of taking care of the little riders, twelve metal figures on horseback that appear each hour on the old church tower in the Dutch town where she lives. Her task becomes much harder when a German soldier is quartered in her home and she must risk her life to protect the riders. Rachel Anderson's *Paper Faces* (1993) takes place in 1945, just after the war has ended. Preschooler Dot and her mother have spent the war living in wretched conditions in London slums and are waiting for the return of Dot's father. Dot's life has been one continuous adjustment to wartime, and she is consequently fearful of his imminent return. *Transport 7-41-R* (1974) by T. Degens is a novel with an unusual point of view, having as its protagonist a German girl who is an ex-member of the Hitler Youth, who must adjust to the aftermath of war and defeat.

The events of World War II affected people outside of the arena of combat. Children in America had their own terrors and problems to confront, and these experiences have been described in a variety of children's books. One of the most affecting is *Summer of My German Soldier* (1973). In this novel by BETTE GREENE, Patty Bergen, a twelve-year-old Jewish girl, forms an unlikely friendship with a young German soldier brought to the prisoner-of-war camp outside her Arkansas town. *Morning Is a Long Time Coming* (1978) describes Patty's trip to Europe after the war to find her friend's mother. Mary Downing Hahn's sensitive novel *Stepping on the Cracks* (1991) examines events in a small Maryland town in 1944, when two girls confront their previously unquestioned patriotic feelings about the war after learning that a classmate's brother is an army deserter. JAMES STEVENSON deals with the subject in an entirely different fashion in *Don't You Know There's a War On?* (1992). A companion to his two other charming picture-book autobiographies, the author-illustrator illuminates the efforts of a ten-year-old on the home front to help win the war and bring home his father and brother. Alternately humorous and poignant, the picture book succeeds marvelously at capturing the flavor of life in the United States during the war: victory gardens, air raid wardens, collecting tinfoil, and looking for spies all became a temporary part of his life. The lingering horror of the war is explored in Myron Levoy's moving *Alan and Naomi* (1977). Alan, who has lived his whole life in the security of the United States, attempts to make friends with the pathologically withdrawn Naomi Kirshenbaum, a refugee who has just arrived in Brooklyn, New York, after having seen her father brutally murdered by the Gestapo in her native France. Michele Murray, in *The Crystal Nights* (1973), tells the story of the Josephs, a family of Jewish refugees who help bring other family members to Connecticut, and the difficult adjustments this merged household must make. In *Molly Donnelly* (1993) author Jean Thesman describes the disruption in a twelve-year-old's life when her best friend, who is a Japanese American, is interned in a U. S. version of a concentration camp.

Clearly, the horrific experiences suffered by men, women, and children in many parts of the world during the war continue to capture the interest of readers in the latter part of this century. Many authors of books about World War II believe that through their writing they can help to illuminate and make sense of an incredibly dark period in modern history. They insist on revealing the destructive hatred, bigotry, and racism that fueled the Nazis' cruel and barbaric actions. They use the atrocities of the war as a reminder of a situation that they hope will never be repeated. In appealing to children's innate sense of optimism and their developing understanding of good and evil, the authors of books about World War II work to encourage peaceful solutions for the future. ❧ ELLEN G. FADER

Worth, Valerie

AMERICAN AUTHOR, 1933–1994. Readers who happen upon Valerie Worth's *Small Poems* (1972) are usually impressed by the volume's compact design and attractive layout but may be taken aback by the table of contents, which lists each poem's unassuming title in lowercase print: "dog," "frog," "cat," "crickets." Can a modern poet find anything fresh and exciting to say about such prosaic subjects? The answer is a resounding yes. Worth's POETRY is alive with minute observations recorded in precise, vivid language.

Many of the author's childhood loves and memories found their way into her work. Born in Philadelphia, Pennsylvania, Worth developed an early interest in reading, writing, and nature. As the smallest child in her class, she learned to appreciate the power of the diminutive in the natural world. Exploring the nearby woods, she observed the insects, flowers, and wildlife that became the subjects of her poems. Worth attended Swarthmore College, worked at Yale University Press, married, and began a family before publishing her first book.

Small Poems contains two-dozen brief free-verse poems that examine common objects and animals. A dog is described as sleeping "in his loose skin." A duck "speaks wet sounds, / Hardly opening / His round-tipped wooden / Yellow-painted beak." Daisies "seem wide celebrations— / As if earth were glad / To see us passing here." Delicately illustrated by NATALIE BABBITT, herself an outstanding author of children's books, the tiny, simply written volume alerts readers to the extraordinary world of ordinary things, using evocative imagery and beautifully chosen language. *More Small Poems* (1976), *Still More Small Poems* (1978), and *Small Poems Again* (1986) utilize the same format and are equally expressive in tone. The four books were collected in a single volume, *All the Small Poems* (1987). In *At Christmas Time* (1992), with customary skill and excellence, the author celebrates the season from early December's expectations to the hanging of stockings and opening of presents. Worth captures the joy of Christmas Eve, as well as the melancholy of Christmas afternoon, ending the cycle of poems with a springtime verse in which "By the muddy path / Glints a single / Crumpled strand / Of Christmas tinsel."

In addition to her poetry, the author has written several works of prose. *Curlicues: The Fortunes of Two Pug Dogs* (1980) is a brief tale of two dogs raised in very different homes. The fussy Victorian setting, heightened literary style, and lack of child characters reduce the story's appeal for young readers. Worth's two young adult novels have been praised for their fine sense of language, but criticized for their somewhat slender plots. *Gypsy Gold* (1983) concerns a girl who joins a troupe of gypsies and discovers her talent for fortunetelling; *Fox Hill* (1986) is a Gothic novel about an orphaned teenager who becomes intrigued by stories of a long-dead body.

The author remains best known for her volumes of poetry. Although she occasionally describes giraffes, telephone poles, and other oversized objects, Worth is most concerned with small, everyday items such as safety pins and marbles. A recurring theme is expressed in the poem "compass": "Wherever you happen / To stand, /

Voices of the Creators

Valerie Worth

I did lots of reading, all kinds of reading, as a child: myths and Bible stories and fairy tales, Beatrix Potter, Thornton Burgess, the "Honey Bunch" series, reams of comic books—and poetry. I had two anthologies, *One Hundred Best Poems for Boys and Girls* and *Sung under the Silver Umbrella,* both of which I read over and over. They were full of variety, highly appealing and accessible, and they taught me to think of all poetry as a great delight.

My parents were poetry lovers, too, and I went on to read some of their favorite poets. They were often more difficult to understand but, in some cases, even more rewarding and, ultimately, inspiring. These "harder" poets—among them Carl Sandburg, Emily Dickinson, Amy Lowell, Alfred Tennyson, T. S. Eliot, Rupert Brooke—used language in a way that seemed to me mysterious, almost miraculous. They were able to create out of words and sounds and images an extraordinarily vivid world, a world filled with sights and experiences that were either new and fascinating to me, or else familiar but never before shown to me with such clear and intense reality.

The ability to capture the essence of things in words struck me as something marvelous, and I found it irresistible to try doing the same thing myself. In fact, I discovered that just to write anything down—even a single noun, *moon* or *rabbit* or *flowerpot*—had a kind of magic about it: there something was, out in the world; but at the same time it was here, at my fingertips, caught hold of and set down on paper.

The trick, of course, was to capture it whole and alive, to make its word-self as true to its actual self as possible. That process needed the help of other words, too. That is where the language of poetry came into play, creating a unique, complex reality out of a wide array of adjectives and verbs, as well as nouns. But they had to be the *right* verbs, the *right* adjectives, or else the object, the image, the subtle truth would fade away and be gone, and the magic would be gone as well.

So this is what I have been doing ever since, trying to catch hold of things and put them into poems: poems that would somehow express the essential qualities of an object or an experience, so that somebody else could read what I'd written and think, "Yes, that's right. I've seen that myself." So many poets have done this for me. I've tried to do the same for others, especially for children, who are encountering so much for the first time and are responding to what they see so directly and intensely—the way I remember doing when I was a child.

Such poems can offer much to adults, too. I think most people enjoy remembering their childhood perceptions, and poetry is certainly one of the best avenues through which the first, freshest experiences can be recaptured and relived. For me, at any rate, childhood and poetry are profoundly connected. I feel very fortunate to have found ways of bringing them together in my own writing.

North, south, / East and west, / Meet in the palm / Of your hand." With fresh perceptions and language, Worth's poems describe entire worlds that can be held in the palm of one's hand. P.D.S.

Wrightson, Patricia

Australian author, b. 1921. As the only Australian novelist who has won the Hans Christian Andersen Medal, Patricia Wrightson may rightfully be called Australia's most distinguished writer for children. Ever since her first book, *The Crooked Snake* (1955) appeared—and subsequently won the 1956 Australian Children's Book Council Book of the Year Award—her titles have consistently garnered much critical acclaim.

Wrightson grew up in a country environment on the north coast of New South Wales. The middle child in a family of six, she attended a variety of schools, including a two-teacher country school and the State Correspondence School for Isolated Children. As she has commented however, "My most profitable year of schooling was the one in which I abandoned the syllabus altogether and spent the year, without permission or guidance, in discovering Shakespeare."

It was not until she had been married and divorced and had two children that Wrightson began writing. She created *The Crooked Snake* especially for her children, not expecting it to be published and certainly not expecting it to win awards. But her titles, which ripple with her understanding of and trust in the land, immediately established her as part of the group of authors responsible for the emergence of the modern Australian children's novel. She went on, in such books as *The Rocks of Honey* (1960), *An Older Kind of Magic* (1972), and The Wirrun Trilogy, to incorporate aboriginal land spirits and motifs into her writing. The Wirrun books, which include *The Ice Is Coming* (1977)—winner of the 1978 Australian Children's Book Council Book of the Year Award—*The Bright Dark Water* (1978), and the highly commended *Behind the Wind* (1981), focus on the adventures of the Wirrun: a mythic hero who also portrays characteristics of an Aborigine. In her well-loved fantasy *The Nargun and the Stars* (1973), spirits and human beings combine forces to help protect the land from the Nargun, an ancient stone creature. Many of her novels positively pulse with the rhythms of nature while reflecting a true faith in people themselves. But other titles, such as *A Racecourse for Andy* (1968) and *Down to Earth* (1965), bustle and hum with the energy of the city. She spent a number of years working in Sydney as a hospital administrator and also as editor for the New South Wales *School Magazine,* a literary publication for primary school children. She finally left in 1975 to move to the country, which she prefers. There she has continued to produce a solid, evocative body of literature, including her first book for younger readers, *The Sugar Gum Tree* (1991), a title that demonstrates her understanding of the human spirit, regardless of age.

Wrightson won Australia's 1984 Dromkien Medal for distinguished contributions to children's literature. Numerous other distinctions have been heaped upon her work the world over as readers in an array of places step into her intriguing Australian worlds. Indeed, when she received the Hans Christian Andersen Medal in 1986, the jury officially recognized "the contribution she has made to Australian literature and, by extension, to literature everywhere, by giving shape to that country's underlying myth, the spirits that are the living land, and thereby making her country known to the world in the most fundamental way." ❦ K.J.

Writing for Children

A generation ago anyone interested in writing for children learned to do it by haunting library children's rooms, writing and rewriting in isolation, and adapting resources intended for the adult market. It was a profession self-taught, by trial and error. Now children's books are in demand; their publication is big business; and the professional resources are both sophisticated and abundant.

One of the oldest handbooks is still one of the most pleasant ways for a beginner to learn about the range of material called children's books. First published as *Writing Books for Children* in 1973, JANE YOLEN's *Guide to Writing for Children* uses an anecdotal style to sketch the broad view of children's book publishing, the wide range of children's books, and the many opportunities for those who would write for children. Along the way this author of over 125 books for children also explains the profession's conventions, jargon, and "unwritten rules." An excellent companion volume is one of the newest resources, JAMES CROSS GIBLIN's *Writing Books for Young People* (1990). Unlike Yolen, who is primarily a fiction writer, Giblin draws on his experience as a nonfiction writer and, before that, an editor of children's books. The two books work together to inform and entice the novice, but they also provide a hefty dose of the reality of hard work involved in becoming a children's book professional.

Although there are over five thousand children's books being published every year, the competition is keen; only one percent of the manuscripts annually submitted to publishers become a book. Writers in the successful one percent are original, skilled, and professional. This is the thrust of *How to Write a Children's Book and Get It Published* (1984) by Barbara Seuling. Drawing on experience as both a writer and editor, Seuling ends every chapter with specific activities for developing writing skills. In addition, the book provides details about marketing and extensive resource appendices.

Some would-be writers feel they need better skills. One of the most unique books on the craft of writing for children takes a philosophical approach. JOAN AIKEN's *The Way to Write for Children* (1982) has a lively text punctuated by quotations from such diverse writers as Pascal, Dickens, and Wordsworth. Discussions of audience, technique, and genre use questions to frame sage advice: "What can be done to hasten the creative process?" "How do you go about building and maintaining the reader's interest?" and "What to put in, what to leave out?"

There are other, more traditional books. One of the oldest is *Writing for Children and Teen-Agers,* written by Lee Wyndham and revised by Arnold Madison. First published in 1968, the book has been made increasingly detailed with revisions. Flaws in point of view, achieving a sense of place, ending a chapter, and transitions are some of the hundreds of fine points laid out for writers looking to hone their craft.

Jane Fitz-Randolph's *How to Write for Children and Young Adults* (1980; revised with Barbara Steiner, 1987) is more academic. After a brief overview it examines plot patterns, the tools of character and dialogue, and the special demands of various genres and forms. Like a textbook, every chapter concludes with "Points to Remember" and "Questions and Answers" to challenge the student. Although every professional knows that success does not come without apprenticeship, this is one of the few current books to examine the magazine market, the logical career starting point.

Editors remain one of the profession's mysteries; their remoteness endows them with power. Two books published in the early 1990s are especially welcome because they provide an editorial perspective.

Writing for children requires the same skills as writing for adults: a diverse and interesting vocabulary, a grasp of conventional grammar, and lively expression. What sets children's book writers apart is their sense of audience, and, in particular, their awareness that their primary purpose is to provide pleasure. In *The Art of Writing for Children: Skills and Techniques of the Craft* (1991), Connie C. Epstein sets forth these and other basic principles of good writing. Each chapter weaves examples and exercises to encourage a writer's development. Her introductory chapter, "Children's Books Then and Now," is a particularly fine summary of the historical attitudes toward and the current publishing of children's books.

Children's book publishing is a business—the business of selling books. Yet the only guide devoting itself to the business relationship between writer and editor is Olga Litowinsky's *Writing and Publishing Books for Children in the 1990's: The Inside Story from the Editor's Desk* (1992). Written for the active writer, Litowinsky's book focuses on the current markets, the kinds of books that have emerged in the past fifteen years, and the conventions evolving from the enormous volume of submissions and increased use of the computer.

One indication of the popularity and growth of children's books is that it now has its own specialties. One of the most popular is the picture book.

Although directed to the author-illustrator, any writer will benefit from studying *How to Write and Illustrate Children's Books* (1988), edited by Treld Pelkey Bicknell and Felicity Trotman. Using an open, abundantly illustrated page, the book contains essays that cover a variety of aspects, from "Art of the Storyteller" to "Making the Book—Technique and Production." The English origins of the book are evident in references to authors and illustrators, but the contents are, nonetheless, accessible.

Ellen E. M. Roberts's *The Children's Picture Book: How to Write It, How to Sell It* (1981) is more general. In addition to exploring the craft of writing for this specialty, Roberts devotes about one third of the book to submitting the manuscript, dealing with contracts and agents, assisting in production and promotion, and life after publication. Writers for all age levels will find the information valuable.

Hadley Irwin and Jeannette Eyerly demystify the business of writing for teenagers in *Writing Young Adult Novels* (1988). As books for this age level are the most stylistically varied and complex, this book provides the most complete resource on plotting and other writing skills.

Just as the "how to" books are specialized, so are the marketing tools. The annual *Children's Writer's and Illustrator's Market,* like its parent volumes, *Writer's Market* and *Illustrator's Market,* provides introductory essays (including "Portfolio Power" for the illustrator), listings of more than six hundred publishers of children's material, "Young Writers/Illustrator's Markets," and "Contests and Awards." The glossary is particularly helpful to those new to the field.

Children's book editors spend only about ten percent of their time reading submissions and no longer provide written critiques. But children's book writers now find support through specialty conferences, college courses, and a network of critique groups. The Society of Children's Book Writers and Illustrators (22736 Vanowen Street, Suite 106, West Hills, California 91307), founded in 1968, has over nine thousand members around the world and is the largest writer's organization in the country—the only one devoted to supporting children's book creators.

Clearly, writing for children is not for the faint-hearted, and few in the field become rich or famous, but there are rewards. Writers often speak of their joy at discovering one of their books in a store or on a recommended reading list. They take pleasure in talking with children and reading their letters.

Most successful children's book creators share a love of books, an appreciation for language, and a respect for children. For many there is no greater reward than knowing their book has made a difference in a child's life. ❧ SUSAN A. BURGESS

WYETH, N. C.

AMERICAN ILLUSTRATOR, 1882–1945. HOWARD PYLE's most famous pupil and closest follower, Newell Convers Wyeth (known professionally by his initials) had an artistic personality quite distinct, in style and substance, from the Master's. Raised on a Massachusetts farm staked out by the Wyeths in 1730, he was a vigorous outdoorsman and a keen observer of nature's contours and shadings. (His letters, otherwise banal, come alive in reference to "mellow, beseeching hills," to a large blue-black butterfly "lazying his way through the soft air.") The boy who drew horses and other real-life things became, at an art teacher's suggestion, a student of illustration. But the training, with its emphasis on cleverness and stunts, rankled; and when word reached Wyeth of Pyle's new school in the Brandywine Valley, he was an eager, anxious applicant. The ensuing interview was the pivotal event of Wyeth's life: though he sometimes criticized Pyle in later years and rued concentrating on illustration, Pyle remained the fountainhead of his aspirations, the impetus to "the *unattainable* in art."

Everything about the Pyle studio-school, then at full throttle (see BRANDYWINE SCHOOL), agreed with Wyeth: the summers at Chadds Ford on the Brandywine; the student camaraderie; the intense effort and inspired teaching; the manifest results. Spurred on by the advanced students' magazine work, Wyeth painted an oil in the flamboyant Wild West manner—a wild bronco, pitching and twisting to unseat his rider—and submitted it to the *Saturday Evening Post*; on February 21, 1903, Wyeth's first professional effort was the *Post*'s cover illustration, heralding a story by Western writer Emerson Hough, and the young artist, at twenty, was on his way.

The direction was plain. Further Western assignments led to a sketchbook-and-saddle trip through the Southwest, jointly sponsored by the *Post* and another Wyeth patron, *Scribner's Magazine*. Officially a student no longer, Wyeth stayed on at Wilmington, joining other professionals in the Pyle orbit. One slight adjustment remained. Wyeth's heart was in the gentle, historic Brandywine countryside, so like and unlike his beloved New England, and once married he settled permanently in Chadds Ford.

Through the World War I years Western illustration and magazine illustration flourished—boosted by full-color photographic reproduction—and Wyeth was swamped with assignments. By nature he was a painter of broadly rendered, richly colored and textured oils, not a linear artist like Pyle. With the advent of the four-color half-tone process, Old Master paintings, reduced to the size of a printed page, came into wide circulation; Wyeth, in turn, made illustrations, on large canvases, that were indistinguishable from full-blown paintings. His compositions not only crackled with action (his mother once begged him for quieter scenes), they made dramatic use of isolated figures, of light and shade, of odd, arresting angles. They had ambiguous depths. Pyle, who mastered every step in the transition from wood-engraved reproduction to half-tone to full color, had also produced some memorable illustrations in oil; Wyeth, however, was to the medium born.

Full-color reproduction had an allure, as well, for publishers of children's books. The House of Scribner capitalized on its potential by launching a new series of elaborate reprint editions, Scribner Illustrated Classics. Wyeth's first contribution to the series was ROBERT LOUIS STEVENSON's *Treasure Island* (1911). Printed on coated stock and tipped-in, Wyeth's fourteen illustrations form a gallery of powerful images, from the explosive action of Billy Bones taking "one last tremendous cut" at the fleeing Black Dog to the doom-laden menace of Blind Pew, "tapping up and down the road in a frenzy."

Treasure Island was "a phenomenal success," as Wyeth wrote his mother, and a landmark in children's book publishing. Scribner's quickly commissioned Wyeth to illustrate Stevenson's *Kidnapped* (1913), putting the Illustrated Classics on a sure course, and other publishers weighed in with similar series, some of them virtually identical in appearance to the Scribner model. This stream of publication is hardly conceivable without Wyeth's affinity for romantic adventure. For the Scribner series he illustrated fourteen other titles, including *The Boy's King Arthur* (1917) and the two most popular Leatherstocking Tales of JAMES FENIMORE COOPER, *The Last of the Mohicans* (1919) and *The Deerslayer* (1924), as well as two additional Stevenson titles, *The Black Arrow* (1916) and *David Balfour* (1924). For Harper he illustrated MARK TWAIN's *Mysterious Stranger* (1916); for McKay, *Robin Hood* (1917) and *Rip Van Winkle* (1921); for Cosmopolitan, Arthur Conan Doyle's *White Company* (1922), Daniel Defoe's *Robinson Crusoe* (1920), and *Legends of Charlemagne* (1924); for Houghton Mifflin, two dubious choices, HENRY WADSWORTH LONGFELLOW's *Courtship of Miles Standish* (1920) and Homer's *Odyssey* (1929). Sometimes Wyeth's contribution was crucial. Published for adults in 1925, James Boyd's Revolutionary War novel *Drums* became a children's book in the Scribner series with the addition—the added attraction—of illustrations by Wyeth, and MARJORIE KINNAN RAWLINGS's 1938 Pulitzer Prize winner, *The Yearling*, achieved instant children's-classic status the following year in the same fashion. Successful as interpretations or not, Wyeth's illustrations lent a glamour to CLASSICS that lured even indifferent readers and kept some of the titles in print for generations. Recently the best of the Scribner series, beginning with *Treasure Island*, have been reprinted in facsimiles of the first editions.

By the 1920s Wyeth had largely ceased doing magazine illustration, switching for supplementary income—he was very well paid for his book work—to advertising design, calendar illustration, and other commercial art. Color prints of his famous illustrations, displayed in parlors and classrooms, provided still further exposure and income. Most gratifying to him were mural commissions, and in the 1930s he also fulfilled his yearning to paint easel pictures. His son Andrew, also a painter and a partial influence on his father, and others of the talented Wyeth brood were already renewing the Brandywine tradition. ❧ BARBARA BADER

Wynne-Jones, Tim

Canadian writer and poet, b. 1948. Tim Wynne-Jones came to the writing of children's books sideways. He took fine arts degrees, at York University and at the University of Waterloo, where he also studied to be an architect. A detour into book illustration and design led to writing, but it was only after the publication of two successful adult mystery novels that he sat down one morning and wrote *Zoom at Sea* (1983), the story of a cat who follows his seafaring Uncle Roy to an adventure on the dancing main.

Since his first appearance Zoom has starred in two more adventures, a trip to the North Pole in *Zoom Away* (1985) and a sojourn in ancient Egypt in *Zoom Upstream* (1992). The "Zoom" stories are Wynne-Jones's best-known books for children, and they typify his strengths as a writer—the ability to shape a plot and pare it to its essentials, gentle child-centered humor, a palpable pleasure in words, and a musician's sense of rhythm and cadence.

The sense of music is also evident in Wynne-Jones's collection of poetry, *Mischief City* (1986), a set of lively, celebratory poems in the first person: "Don't drink the bathwater! / Don't feed it to the cat. / Your sailboat's mucky / And poor rubber duck / He got stuck in the guck where he sat." The poems have been set to music and produced as a recording and as live theater.

Wynne-Jones's continuing interest in architecture can be seen in *The Builder of the Moon* (1988), his fantasy adventure about David Finebloom, who travels to the moon on his homemade spaceship to answer the moon's plea for help. David's rebuilding of the moon, "course upon course, layer upon layer," can be seen as a metaphor for writing, or indeed any creative activity, and his confidence, competence, and pluck are typical of Wynne-Jones's child heroes.

There is a darker side to Wynne-Jones's writing, a side seen in his chilling adult novels. He plays with this darker, scary-story genre in *The Hour of the Frog* (1990), a single illustrated poem about the goings-on at the late-night frog hour: "Thlump. Thlump. He's at the foot of the stairs."

Wynne-Jones lives in the country with his wife, writer/calligrapher/director Amanda West Lewis, and their three children. When he is not writing novels, short fiction, picture books, reviews, poems, or song lyrics, he sings with the local operetta company. Such versatility informs all Wynne-Jones's work which, in its quirky humor and distinctive voice, reflects a mind of wide-ranging enthusiasms. ❧ S.E.

Wyss, Johann David

Swiss author, 1743–1818. Johann Wyss served as an army chaplain and cathedral pastor, factors contributing to his sense of order and piety. *Der schweizerische Robinson* was written for the entertainment and edification of his four sons. In 1812–1813 Wyss's son Johann Rudolph edited and published the eight-hundred-page manuscript, omitting the illustrations by brother Johann Emmanuel. English and French editions were published next. Prominent editors such as William Dean Howells, Felix Sutton, and Georgina Hargreaves and such noted illustrators as Charles Folkard, Lynd Ward, and Fritz Kredel are among those who have interpreted the story's drama.

The Swiss Family Robinson is filled with moralizing, lecturing, and errors in natural science; its characters reflect dated social attitudes; its plot depends on unbelievable good fortune. Why, then, are several editions still in print? An adventure story patterned after the Robinson Crusoe theme, this period piece is filled with nonstop action, inventiveness, close calls, and strange encounters. Each new situation is an opportunity for a lesson in problem solving. Readers often forgive the unlikely combinations of plants and animals because survival, not science, is paramount. Family relationships, typical of the early 1800s, reflect a harmonious ideal, with the role and rights of each member clearly delineated. In its well-ordered existence the industrious family works, plays, and prays and is rewarded with good fortune and a glimpse of Eden. So the story has remained popular, despite its drawbacks, and nonprint media has brought the annals of the Robinson family into the modern age. ❧ J.E.G.

Y

Yates, Elizabeth

American author, b. 1905. Born and raised in Buffalo, New York, Elizabeth Yates spent summers on a family farm, where she wrote her earliest stories in a vacant pigeon loft. At age twenty, she moved to New York, determined to become a writer. She wrote poetry, book reviews, and articles while holding a series of odd jobs, including comparison shopping for Macy's. Marriage took the author to London for ten years, where she began selling articles and celebrity interviews to both English and American publications.

When a friend suggested that she write a book about a topic that she understood better than the average reader, Yates recalled her experiences mountain climbing in Switzerland, and wrote *High Holiday,* which was published in England in 1938. This children's book established the author's practice of writing novels based on real-life incidents. She used her experiences as a visitor in Iceland for the sequel, published in the United States as *Quest in the North-land* (1940). At the start of World War II, Yates and her husband returned to the United States, where they purchased and restored a home in New Hampshire. Stencil designs hidden behind the wallpaper gave Yates the idea for her next book, *Patterns on the Wall* (1943), which concerns a young painter during the early nineteenth century. A neighbor's remark about a sheep that became a family pet led to the Newbery Honor Book *Mountain Born* (1943), the touching story of young Peter and the lamb he raises. Against a backdrop of changing seasons and passing years, a vivid portrait of farm life emerges as the sheep are born, shorn, bred, and die. The crystal-clear prose demonstrates a love of nature and a strong awareness of the human heart. The author also wrote about Peter and his family in *A Place for Peter* (1952) and the Christmas story *Once a Year* (1947).

Yates was awarded the Newbery Medal for *Amos Fortune, Free Man* (1950), the biography of an eighteenth-century black man who was born a prince in Africa, shipped to America as a slave, and bought his own freedom in middle age. Based on historical fact, the book might best be termed fictional or speculative biography because manufactured dialogue and thoughts are attributed to the characters. Nevertheless, every word rings true in this moving story, written with obvious respect for and a sense of the dignity of Amos Fortune. Yates wrote other strong biographies, including *Prudence Crandall: Woman of Courage* (1955) and *Pebble in a Pool: The Widening Circles of Dorothy Canfield Fisher's Life* (1958), and several notable works of nonfiction, including *Rainbow 'round the World: A Story of UNICEF* (1954) and *Skeezer, Dog with a Mission* (1973), which was adapted as a movie for television. Yates's adult novels include *Hue and Cry* (1953), which continues the story begun in her children's book *Patterns on the Wall,* and several religious stories stemming from the Christian faith that informs most of her work. Her most personal writing can be found in *The Lighted Heart* (1960), which relates how her husband met the challenges of blindness, and a series of autobiographies: *My Diary—My World* (1981), *My Widening World* (1983), and *One Writer's Way* (1984). Written with clarity and grace, each volume displays the love of humanity found in all of the author's books. P.D.S.

Yep, Laurence

American author, b. 1948. At age eighteen, Laurence Yep launched his writing career with the publication of a science fiction story, and his first novel, *Sweetwater* (1973), takes place on a planet called Harmony. Subsequently, his acclaimed works for children have spanned the genres from science fiction and fantasy to historical and realistic fiction to collections of Chinese folktales. Yep's historical novels bring the Chinese and Chinese American cultures alive and brilliantly convey not only the settings but also the internal lives of the characters. Yep introduces readers to life in China in *The Serpent's Children* (1984) and its sequel, *Mountain Light*

Voices of the Creators

Laurence Yep

There are two sources of history for anyone who writes historical fiction for children. The first source is the adult version of history with facts and dates and statistics; the second source is a child's version of history.

Had I only read the first type, I probably would never have written *Dragonwings, Serpent's Children,* or *Mountain Light.* However, I grew up with stories about China. It was not the China of the travelogues though, nor was it the China of vast, ancient monuments. It was the China my father knew before he came to America at the age of ten. So it was China as perceived by a child and colored by memory over the years.

My father has never seen the Great Wall or the Forbidden City. His China consisted of small villages where each village had its own distinctive architecture (based on whatever overseas country its menfolk had worked in). The difference, however, between my father's China and the China of the travelogues is the difference between a child's version of history and an adult's. Adult history thunders on a grand scale like a movie in Cinemascope, but for all of its size, it is still flat and its actors are like ants except for a few close-ups of the stars. On the other hand, a child's history is like a hologram that can be held in the palm, quiet and small but three-dimensional. It treats its subjects with an immediateness that makes them seem to live and breathe.

I first began thinking of the difference between a child's version of history and an adult's when I finally made a pilgrimage to West Virginia. In our family's own personal story West Virginia is as much a mythical homeland as China, for my mother was born in Ohio and then raised in West Virginia, where my maternal grandfather had started a Chinese laundry. Since my mother had left West Virginia for California when she was a child, West Virginia was a homeland constructed from children's histories. So in her stories my mother's town was full of houses with big porches that were perfect for children to jump from—even if that was forbidden. In fact, a good deal of what my mother did was forbidden to children. Mischief was a year-round activity. In summer she escaped the heat by wading in the "crick" in her underwear while looking for arrowheads.

Though I haven't been to China yet, I did decide to go to the second of my mythical homelands, West Virginia. When I did my research for the trip, it was strange to go from a child's history—what my mother had told me—to the history of adults. I found the bare facts buried in books like bones in the dirt: wedding licenses, birth certificates, and wills full of dates and lifeless statistics.

Above all, I was dealing with the process of acculturation. It is useful to see what happened some sixty years ago to other Asian children. But acculturation is an abstract concept spawned by adult history, and abstractions are not necessarily useful for writing stories that children will want to read.

My family also had to deal with acculturation. My mother's family tried to juggle elements of both the Chinese and American cultures. My grandmother not only learned how to speak English but how to cook and bake American dishes. Her specialty was apple pies. She once bragged to me that her pies always fetched the best price at church auctions—Methodist or Baptist. I think my grandmother's ecumenicism helped win acceptance in that small West Virginia community.

When my aunt visited her family home in 1951, the occupants asked her about a tenacious weed they could not get rid of. They had chopped it with hoes, dosed it with herbicide, and dug up its roots with spades. But the plant kept growing back as if it were determined to stay. It turned out to be a Chinese vegetable that my grandparents had planted so long ago.

It may be something as simple and yet as indestructible as a weed that links us to our past and binds us to our dreams. Seed, cast into strange soil, may thrive and grow—just like children and just like their history. In fact, a child's history is about growth itself, not only in terms of the body but also in terms of consciousness. Despite all of its limitations, a child's version of history is more useful for writing than adult history.

A child's history, like magic, never quite goes away. It is there, only hidden, like the laughter of unseen children in a garden. It is like the sound of a "crick" heard on a dusty summer afternoon decades ago in West Virginia. It is all the sweeter for never being seen, only heard about.

(1985), which depict the struggles of Cassia and Foxfire, the children of a Chinese family in rebellion against the conquering Manchus.

Dragonwings (1975), which explores Yep's Chinese American heritage, garnered a Newbery Honor award as well as numerous other prizes. Moon Shadow is called to America, "the land of the Golden Mountain," to be with his father, Windrider, who dreamed that he was a dragon in a previous life and now wants to fly again—this time in a handcrafted aeroplane. As the years pass, Moon Shadow learns not only that life in San Francisco at the turn of the century is more challenging and perilous than he had imagined but that his father can be unreasonable, proud, and full of a fighting spirit, as well as so driven by his passion to fly that he jeopardizes all that they possess and care for.

Similarly, Otter, in *Dragon's Gate* (1993), also a Newbery Honor Book, discovers the human side of his father and Uncle Foxfire, who are considered heroes back home in the Chinese village, when he joins them in the Sierra Nevada Mountains during the winter of 1867 on the construction site of the transcontinental railroad. Even as Otter and Moon Shadow grow in their understanding of their families, they gain experience in surviving in two cultures simultaneously, which is a common theme in much of Yep's fiction. *Child of the Owl* (1977), winner of the 1977 Boston Globe–Horn Book Award for fiction, details a young girl's growing awareness of her Chinese American background due to her grandmother's storytelling.

Having grown up in an African American neighborhood in San Francisco, Yep lacked a true understanding of Chinese traditions, so he began to record the stories his relatives told about their early experiences living in the United States. *The Star Fisher* (1991) is a fictionalized account of his mother's adolescence as a member of the only Asian family in a small West Virginia town.

In addition to writing historical and realistic fiction, Yep composed several mysteries, yet he never lost his love of fantasy, and his fantasy novels have been well received by critics and readers. *Dragon of the Lost Sea* (1982), *Dragon Steel* (1985), *Dragon Cauldron* (1991), and *Dragon War* (1992) relay the adventures of a deposed Chinese dragon-princess named Shimmer and two children as they attempt to regain Shimmer's kingdom. Not only a much-respected creator of fiction, Yep has selected and retold Chinese folktales in *The Rainbow People* (1989) and *Tongues of Jade* (1991), and picture books such as *The Man Who Tricked a Ghost* (1993), and edited a collection of Asian American fiction and poetry entitled *American Dragons: Twenty-Five Asian American Voices* (1993).

By drawing from his own cultural inheritance, Yep has written exemplary books that introduce to all children and young adults specific eras of history and universal themes while providing for Chinese American readers a literature of their own. A.E.D.

YOLEN, JANE

AMERICAN AUTHOR, B. 1939. With a confident writing style and inexhaustible imagination, Jane Yolen has proven herself one of the most prolific and diverse creators in the field of children's literature.

Born in New York City, Yolen spent her early years in Virginia and California, but returned to New York, where she attended grade school and wrote the script, music, and lyrics for school plays. She continued to develop her writing and musical skills while attending high school in Connecticut and Smith College in Massachusetts. After graduation, she worked in publishing for several years, then settled in Massachusetts with her family and embarked on a full-time writing career.

Yolen's first book for children was *Pirates in Petticoats* (1963), a factual work about female pirates. Although she has continued to publish an occasional volume of nonfiction, including the biographical *Friend: The Story of George Fox and the Quakers* (1972), Yolen has concentrated on fiction and POETRY. She has published several volumes of verse, beginning with *See This Little Line?* in 1963 and including *How Beastly!: A Menagerie of Nonsense Poems* (1980) and *The Three Bears Rhyme Book* (1987). Although her PICTURE BOOKS include such lighthearted narratives as *No Bath Tonight* (1978), the story of Jeremy's attempts to avoid bathing, her best-known picture-book texts are sensitive free-verse poems. *Owl Moon* (1987) received the Caldecott Award for JOHN SCHOENHERR's watercolor illustrations, but Yolen's story of a father and child walking in the woods on a winter night is equally masterful. *All the Secrets in the World* (1991), *Letting Swift River Go* (1992), and other prose poems are distinguished by their lyrical, evocative writing and the sense of wonder that imbues much of the author's work. Yolen's literary fairy tales, such as *The Girl Who Cried Flowers and Other Tales* (1974), combine traditional FANTASY motifs, including magic, giants, and animals transformed into human beings, with themes of death, kindness, and love to create memorable, original stories.

As Yolen's children grew, she extended her talents to writing books for young adults. *The Gift of Sarah Barker* (1981) is a historical novel about two teenagers who fall in love, although they belong to a celibate Shaker community. Their emerging sexuality is sensitively and tastefully explored, despite some unlikely plot twists. Yolen sometimes includes an implausible element of fantasy in her realistic fiction for older readers. This has a detrimental effect in *The Stone Silenus* (1984), which concerns a girl coping with her father's death, but works extremely well in *The Devil's Arithmetic* (1988), the moving story of a contemporary Jewish girl magically transported to a Nazi death camp. Yolen's first foray into young adult high fantasy was the well-received Pit Dragon Trilogy, consisting of *Dragon's Blood* (1982), *Heart's Blood* (1984), and *A Sending of Dragons* (1987). Writing for a younger audience, she has published the humorous "Commander Toad" SCIENCE FICTION series, which includes *Commander Toad in Space* (1980).

Yolen has written well over a hundred books, has edited anthologies, continues to write stories and nonfiction for magazines, and oversees her own imprint of children's books for a major publishing house. Considering her prodigious output, Yolen's sure-handed writing is consistently high in quality and child appeal. An occasional volume may be considered slight or facile, but the majority are sensitive, poetic, and imaginative. ❧ P.D.S.

Yorinks, Arthur

AMERICAN AUTHOR, B. 1953. Arthur Yorinks has one of the most distinctive prose styles in children's literature. His picture-book texts are spare, precise, and almost staccato in their rhythm. He favors short phrases and ironic turns of plot. No matter where his stories are set, his characters speak in the clipped cadence of New Yorkers. They are often a bit world-weary, nagged by unfulfillment, and eager for whatever transforming miracle comes their way.

Brought up in suburban New York, Yorinks was a teenager when he found himself drawn to picture books, especially the work of Tomi Ungerer, William Steig, and above all MAURICE SENDAK. At sixteen, he appeared on Sendak's doorstep, handed his somewhat-taken-aback idol some manuscripts, and began an unlikely friendship. Sendak later introduced Yorinks to Richard Egielski, setting into motion a long and successful collaboration.

The author-and-artist team is best known for *Hey, Al* (1986), for which Egielski won the 1987 Caldecott Medal: "Al, a nice man, a quiet man, a janitor," lives with Eddie, his ambitious dog. When an exotic bird flies into their minuscule apartment and offers them a new life in a terrific place, Eddie is ready to take flight immediately and Al soon concurs. They are ferried up to a lush island in the sky, where all at first is bliss, until they discover its too-high price. They then make a harrowing retreat to the city, where they happily discover that "Paradise lost is sometimes Heaven found."

As in much of Yorinks's work, there are no children anywhere. The predicament is adult and so are many of the longings—for release from dreary work, escape from a dreary home. Yet there is also an offhand and childlike acceptance of the magical in this very earth-bound fantasy. Dogs talk, birds do too, and men can sprout wings. The central dilemma is common to readers of any age. When push comes to shove, what matters most? How much are you willing to give up for your dreams? The story provokes and challenges while at the same time offering considerable comfort. Maybe heaven really is close to home.

Yorinks's inspirations come from many sources, including, a bit unexpectedly, Franz Kafka's *Metamorphosis*. In *Louis the Fish* (1980), also illustrated by Egielski, a third-generation butcher is profoundly unhappy with his lot in life. Poor Louis loathes meat but loves fish. He is obsessed by them. And one morning, miraculously, he becomes one and finally finds bliss. For "after a hard life, Louis was a happy fish."

Idiosyncratic and often unabashedly strange, Yorinks's picture books are neither cozy nor sweet, but they are kindhearted and knowing, providing their own perspective on the measure of a life well lived. ❧ A.Q.

Young, Ed

AMERICAN ILLUSTRATOR AND AUTHOR, B. 1931. Mice, elephants, wolves, and rabbits are among the many animals brought vividly to life by picture-book illustrator Ed Young, whose career began with lunch-hour sketches at New York's Central Park Zoo. A former architecture student, Young switched to art, graduating from the Art Center College of Design in Los Angeles before moving to New York to work in advertising. While working, he continued to take art and design classes at Pratt Institute in Brooklyn and was urged by friends who saw his animal sketches to try illustrating children's books. When Young illustrated *The Mean Mouse and Other Mean Stories* (1962) by JANICE MAY UDRY, he expected it to be his first and last book, but it won an American Institute of Graphic Arts award and launched a career that has resulted in over fifty books, including a few he wrote himself.

Voices of the Creators

Ed Young

I read a fable about a naturalist who was visiting a farm and was surprised to find an eagle feeding among the chickens. The farmer said, "Since I raised it from the beginning and fed it chicken feed, it never learned to fly or act as an eagle." "Still," insisted the naturalist, "it has the heart of an eagle and can surely learn to fly." They put the eagle on a tall fence so that he could stretch his wings and fly. The eagle was confused. Seeing the chickens feeding, he gladly jumped down to join them again. Undeterred, the following day the naturalist took the eagle up on the roof of a house and urged him again saying, "You are an eagle. Stretch forth your wings and fly!" But the eagle was afraid of the unknown and jumped down once more with the chickens. Still determined, the naturalist rose early the third day and took the eagle to a high mountain. There he raised the eagle high above his head saying, "You are an eagle. King of all birds. Stretch out your wings and fly!" The eagle began to tremble. Slowly he stretched his wings. At last, with a triumphant cry, he soared into the heavens.

I identify myself with that eagle in many ways. Because of ill health, I was kept home an additional year before my schooling. When I did go to school, everyone in my class was a head shorter than me. I sat in the rear of the classroom, where there were plenty of distractions for all my school years in Shanghai and, later, in Hong Kong. It was not great for my self-esteem—as the oldest and the biggest student in class, I was not also the smartest. I had no incentive to excel and whiled my time away drawing or simply daydreaming. Heaven only knows how I managed to graduate from high school, and it was even more puzzling that I was admitted by an accredited college in the United States.

As my parents were still in communist China, my guardian uncle in Hong Kong took me aside before I embarked on the boat to America. "You will soon be on your own, Ed. If there is something in you to make your life a success, this is now your chance. This opportunity may not come your way again." I took stock of myself and was surprised to find that all the years of drawing and playing were considered wasted time in a world of measurable assets, of which I had none. So, once I landed in the United States, I took up every avenue of menial work offered to me—janitorial jobs, pot- and dishwasher, paper cutter, houseboy, cook, busboy, bellhop, waiter, soda jerk—with a great sense of newness and adventure far beyond the expectation of my superiors. In my studies I saw that architecture was not exactly where my strength lay. So, against the advice of my advisers at the University of Illinois, I transferred into a professional art school in Los Angeles. In another three years, I began my career focused totally on success. Although I was proud of my skills in what I call "the art of visual persuasion," I was not pleased with the advertising world—in which the norm is to exploit the public. It was then I received word from my father behind the Bamboo Curtain. Although the letter was addressed to all his offspring, I suspected that he had my new profession in mind: "You may put down as rule number one that life is not rich, not real, unless you partake of life with your fellowmen. A successful life and a happy life is one measured by how much you have accomplished for others and not one measured by how much you have done for yourself." I understood then that to realize my potential as an artist was subservient to my worth as a human being. To be truly successful, I needed to find a place where my work would also inspire others to fuller and happier lives. Luckily my enthusiasm about nature led me into the world of children's literature.

I also began my study of Tai Chi Chuan with a Chinese master, who cured a knee injury I had had for many years. With him I also returned to Chinese calligraphy. The brush exercise was done by sitting squarely on a stool and drawing equally spaced horizontal and vertical lines with a thin brush on newsprint paper with the least amount of tension in my arms and body. He told stories of how, as a boy, he did this with diluted ink on newspaper, gradually darkening the spaces in between strokes until each sheet was completely covered with crisscross lines. Every morning his desk would be filled by stacks of blackened paper. As I practiced and thought I was improving with each executed line, I noticed that the lines were actually correcting something in me. Although I had not resisted work in the United States, I now realize that it is not just labor, but a love of labor that opens our innermost potential.

I wish to share with everyone my father's words about success and my teacher's brush lesson: work can, in fact, be the rooftop from which we launch ourselves to higher places. §

Born in Tientsin, China, Young spent his childhood in Shanghai and attended high school in Hong Kong before moving to the United States in 1951, where he has lived since. He has illustrated numerous stories set in his native China, including the Caldecott Honor Book *The Emperor and the Kite* (1967), edited by JANE YOLEN, and his own folktale retelling, the Caldecott Medal winner *Lon Po Po: A Red-Riding Hood Story from China* (1989). Skilled in the use of a variety of media, Young is also skilled in choosing the best medium with which to illustrate a particular story; one example is the ancient Chinese paper-cutting technique used in *The Emperor and the Kite,* which perfectly suits the poetic beauty of Yolen's narrative. In *Lon Po Po,* Young's illustrations reveal his interest in the panel art found in a number of cultures. The drawings are split into sections that give the art the appearance of Chinese decorative panels; however, strong color and dramatic angles transform the art, giving it a thoroughly contemporary look.

Young has illustrated many tales from lands other than China, among them *Seven Blind Mice* (1992), another Caldecott Honor Book. In Young's version of the Indian fable, blind mice make humorously incorrect judgments about an object they encounter; only the seventh mouse, who examines the entire object, guesses rightly that it is an elephant—the moral is "Knowing in part may make a fine tale, but wisdom comes from seeing the whole." Another moral—"A change in circumstances can make the strong weak and the weak strong"—is illustrated in Young's rendition of *The Lion and the Mouse* (1979), the AESOP fable of the small creature who promises to one day repay the lion if he will spare him. A Jataka tale adapted by Rafe Martin, *Foolish Rabbit's Big Mistake* (1985), is a version of the Chicken Little story. Young's large, brightly colored illustrations in the amusing tale differ from his earlier art, much of which resembles Indian miniatures. The striking and powerful figures—in one case, a lion's paw fills an entire double-page spread—add impact to the story by placing readers at the center of the drama.

The stories, folktales, fables, and myths Young illustrates impart simple but significant truths about people and the world. The age-old technique of using animal stories to teach spiritual lessons is given new life by this versatile and talented artist. J.M.B.

YOUNG ADULT NOVELS

In 1967 and 1968 three books were published that established the form of literature we now term the realistic young adult novel or the problem novel—S. E. HINTON's *The Outsiders* (1967), PAUL ZINDEL's *The Pigman* (1968), and ROBERT LIPSYTE's *The Contender* (1967).

Though these three novels clearly set the young adult novel on a new path, they did not just appear "ex nihilo." They were an outgrowth of the twenty-year post–World War II period when authors such as Henry Gregor Felsen and Maureen Daly directed their storytelling talents exclusively to the American adolescent. Felsen's *Hot Rod* (1950) and Daly's *Seventeenth Summer* (1942), for example, were involving and inspiring junior novels geared to the narrow and very special interests of adolescents as seen by authors who reflected society's stereotypical views of teenagers. For one thing, they believed that boys will be boys—and girls will be girls; novels for males were about cars and sports, and those for females were about dates and dances. The world in which the teen characters lived seldom extended further than the home and the high school, and the plots dealt with the challenges the teen protagonists faced within this limited, white, middle-class environment.

While even the best of these novels were often didactic, they created sharply etched, highly individual characters with whom teen readers could easily identify. And, for the first time, they treated adolescents as entities with social and psychological needs separate from those of children.

During this same postwar period, another phenomenon took place that influenced the development of what we now call the young adult realistic novel. A small number of provocative novels, put out by trade publishers for adult audiences, filtered down slowly to the more sophisticated teen readers who found the junior novels too limiting and too remote from their everyday lives. These stories—such as J. D. SALINGER's *Catcher in the Rye* (1951), William Golding's *The Lord of the Flies* (1955), and John Knowles's *A Separate Peace* (1959)—all possessed coming-of-age themes and youthful protagonists whose relationships with peers and the outside adult world highlighted moral and social concerns ignored by junior novels.

By 1967 the teenagers of the 1960s had witnessed the assassination of a youthful, popular president and had seen the hopeful promises of the Great Society and of the newly created Peace Corps dissipate as a result of an uncertain war in Southeast Asia. They had also witnessed the bravery of many of their older brothers and sisters in Martin Luther King Jr.'s campaign of nonviolent civil disobedience against segregation laws, and they had seen the violent reactions to it. Television was thrusting the turbulence of the outside world into the relatively confined world of teenagers that Felsen and Daly had so effectively portrayed in their novels. In addition, rock music had matured into a creative form of expression that communicated the needs and aspirations of American teenagers in the sixties. Fewer and fewer teen readers believed that the worlds created by Felsen and Daly had any relevance to their own worlds.

It is therefore not surprising that the young adult novel would try to reflect some of the changes taking place in the sixties. Like the junior novels of the post–World War II period, *The Outsiders, The Pigman,* and *The Contender* were about teenagers and were directed exclusively to teen readers. And like the earlier stories, they attempted to deal with the social and psychological needs of the adolescent: social identity; personal identity; peer relationships; independence from family; and social responsibility. But the milieu had changed—radically. Bolstered by the surprising success of Salinger's, Golding's, and Knowles's novels among teen readers and influenced by the fast-moving and intrusive political and cultural events of the sixties, Hinton, Zindel, and Lipsyte moved the center of their fictional setting from the family and the school to places beyond—the street, the community, and the adult world.

In *The Outsiders,* S. E. Hinton wrote about a socially stratified high school society based not on personality differences but on socioeconomic backgrounds. The conflicts between the Socs and the Greasers were different from the ethnically stratified gangs of *West Side Story* (written in the early sixties) and from later stories dealing with youth gangs in the seventies and eighties. In *The Outsiders* one group (the Socs) represented the establishment and one (the Greasers) represented the "outsiders"; the Greasers' lifestyle, clothing, and families' socioeconomic background set them apart from the middle-class mainstream of the high school. Into this stratified setting, Hinton interjected highly individualistic teen characters who get caught up in a gang fight, with tragic consequences. Likewise, in Paul Zindel's *The Pigman,* tragic consequences result from the attempt of two disaffected teens to exploit the goodwill of a lonely old man whose wife has recently died. Here, however, the focus was not on what happens when teenagers are prisoners of social strata, but what happens when teenagers focus on satisfying their immediate needs at the expense of what they are doing to others. And with a more positive outcome, Robert Lipsyte's *The Contender* mixed the themes of personal success and social responsibility in a racially stratified setting that itself created pressures on a young and talented black would-be boxer.

The realistic young adult novel also parted company with the post–World War II junior novel in its refusal to accept gender pigeonholes. *The Pigman,* for example, has coequal protagonists—a boy and a girl who share the successes and the failures of their ill-fated relationship with Mr. Pignati. And, although *The Outsiders* is about boys, S. E. Hinton is female—and the story appeals equally to both genders of teen readers.

The characters in most post–World War II junior novels were white, Protestant, and middle class. The realistic young adult novel changed all that by developing characters with a wide variety of ethnic, racial, and religious backgrounds. The major characters in *The Contender* are black, Italian, and Jewish—representing an accurate microcosm of New York City, where the story takes place.

As these three novels quickly found acceptance with teen readers, more books followed that built on the strengths of this new genre. JOHN DONOVAN's *I'll Get There. It Better Be Worth the Trip* (1969) dealt with a teenager, raised by his grandmother, who is forced to live with his alcoholic mother in New York City. VERA AND BILL CLEAVER's *Where the Lilies Bloom* (1969)—and its sequel *Trial Valley* (1977)—related the story of a gritty and tenacious Appalachian teenager, orphaned with her younger brothers and sisters, who struggles to keep her family together under adverse conditions. Glendon Swarthout's *Bless the Beasts and the Children* (1970) created a bond between five "misfit" children at a summer camp and a herd of hunted buffalo. *Go Ask Alice* (1971), published as a true diary of a runaway girl's involvement with street drugs and prostitution, was actually a fictionalized account based on a true story; the book shocked parents, teachers, and librarians because it was about a white, middle-class girl who, thirty years before, could have been the lead character of *Seventeenth Summer.*

Following the lead of the above-mentioned novels, other authors published books, but many did not meet the high standards established by Hinton, Zindel, and Lipsyte. In these inferior stories, fully developed characters became predictable stereotypes, imaginative writing and critical examination became clichés and pieties, and original plots were turned into derivative story lines. Even the later stories of Zindel, Hinton, and Lipsyte, all of whom wrote other novels in the 1970s, were vulnerable to these criticisms. But the 1970s also saw the publication of perhaps the most discussed and controversial young adult novel of the century—ROBERT CORMIER's *The Chocolate War* (1974). It is an intriguing, gripping, and tightly written story dealing with a variation of "the outsider" theme: what happens when a lone teenager in a private school refuses to sell boxes of chocolate. When the teenager says no, he bucks not only the morally bankrupt leadership of the school, led by power-hungry, cynical Brother Leon, but also the intense and violent peer pressure of the established school gang that has been co-opted by the school administration to enforce its dictates. The reason why the novel was so controversial was not the cynicism of the school nor the violence of the gang but the story's pessimistic ending and ostensible message. "Don't disturb the universe," the physically beaten and spiritually drained teen rebel tells his one remaining friend. Parents, teachers, librarians, and even a few teen readers assailed this message of defeatism, but Cormier and his defenders claimed the novel was a description of the real world, not a prescription for passivity. *The Chocolate War*'s controversial ending, however, highlights a major feature of realistic young adult novels: Like the best of adult fiction, the novels end celebrating the human spirit or depicting the depths of human depravity. *The Chocolate War* indicated that teenagers were no longer going to be protected from the dark side of life.

Nonetheless, many of these books emphasized the light at the end of the tunnel, often with humor and wit. Three of WALTER DEAN MYERS's most popular novels—*The Young Landlords* (1979), *Motown and Didi* (1984), and *It Ain't All for Nothin'* (1978)—are about young teens in Harlem who transform their bleak inner-city environment into successful business projects, overcome their disruptive family lives while making close friends and falling in love, and turn street problems into adventurous challenges. M. E. KERR's *Dinky Hocker Shoots Smack* (1972) parodies a mother who tries to do good for others but neglects her overweight daughter, and her *If I Love You, Am I Trapped Forever?* (1973) humorously shows the surprise and confusion of the self-proclaimed "most popular" boy in school when an unlikely nonconformist newcomer challenges his leadership role. RICHARD PECK, a former high-school teacher, wrote many successful novels about personal and social problems teens face, but three of his most popular stories—*The Ghost Belonged to Me* (1975), *Ghosts I Have Been* (1977), and *The Dreadful Future of Blossom Culp* (1983)—revolve around an unforgettable character named Blossom Culp, whose encounters with ghosts and other unworldly forms of life create some of the most down-to-earth and humorous situations in young adult fiction. Peck's imaginative satire of suburban life in *Secrets of the Shopping Mall* (1979) and his parody of beauty pageants in *Representing Super Doll* (1974) reflect the realistic novel's concern with societal issues even as it tries to entertain its intended teen readership.

Between 1967 and the late seventies, the realistic novel constituted the mainstream of young adult literature. A serious challenge to the realistic novel's dominant position arose in the second half of the 1970s because of a decision by publishers to package fiction for teenagers in genre series in order to appeal to the interests and enthusiasms of young adult readers. This change in publishing strategy was a result of a variety of factors: the increasing success of the juvenile and young adult paperback market in retail bookstores; the influence of television and movies on what teens read; the realization that many teens were graduating from high school unable to read at the twelfth-grade level; and the success of the "hi-low" (high-interest, low-reading level) books packaged for this increasingly large group of young problem readers. However, although the genre packages that the publishers developed—such as "Sweet Valley High," "Sweet Dreams," "Wildfire," and "Confidentially Yours"—were initially profitable for publishers, they did not adversely affect the influence of the realistic novel. In fact, it could be argued that the realistic novel co-opted the genre stories.

The genre of sports novels, for example, combined sports action with predictable characters, who existed largely to make baskets, score touchdowns, or hit home runs—and to leave readers with hackneyed homilies and positive feelings. However, in the late seventies and the eighties when the genre packages were flourishing, well-written and provocative realistic novels with teen characters involved actively in sports were published for young adults. The function of the sports action, however, was not to drive the plot but rather to serve as a metaphor for the real action of the story that was taking place off the playing field. *Juggling* (1982) by David Lehrman, *Football Dreams* (1982) by David Guy, *A Passing Season* (1982) by Richard Blessing, *The Moves Make the Man* (1984) by BRUCE BROOKS, and *Running Loose* (1983) by CHRIS CRUTCHER are five of the best such stories, all of which featured teenagers whose athletic pursuits paralleled their life away from sports.

It is a far cry from the formula-driven saccharine plots of "Sweet Dreams" and "Wildfire," but many quality realistic young adult novels published during this same period dealt with teen romance. ROBERT LIPSYTE's *Jock and Jill* (1982) mixed broad humor, a dash of politics, some sports action, and a lot of romance into a novel about love under even the most improbable of circumstances. JUDY BLUME's *Forever . . .* (1975) sketched a sexual love affair between two innocent teenagers that emphasized the humor of sexual activity and the impermanence of love. Harry Mazer's *The Girl of His Dreams* (1987)—a sequel to *The War on Villa Street* (1978)—was about a young high-school graduate who dreamt of the perfect girl to meet. *Annie on My Mind* (1982) by Nancy Garden sensitively portrayed a teen lesbian relationship that paralleled the physical and emotional aspects of teen heterosexual relationships. In all of these novels about love, romance was used as a backdrop in order to develop a rich, entertaining, unpredictable story peopled with colorful, complex unstereotypical teen characters to whom teen readers could easily relate.

In addition to enriching literature published specifically for young adult readers, the realistic young adult novel has raised the standards and broadened the parameters of all the fiction teenagers read. By successfully fighting the battles to tear down subject taboos and by introducing sophisticated literary devices and techniques such as foreshadowing, metaphors and similes, irony and allegory, and alternate first-person narratives and omniscient third-person narratives, the realistic novel paved the way for the quality contemporary adult novel to be considered desirable reading material for young adults. Among the more prominent of these novels were: Ernest Gaines's *A Gathering of Old Men* (1983), Chaim Potok's *The Chosen* (1967) and *My Name Is Asher Lev* (1972), James Baldwin's *If Beale Street Could Talk* (1974), and William Wharton's *Birdy* (1979), all of which were published originally for adult audiences. It is largely because of the influences of the successful realistic young adult novel that serious fiction gained such a wide readership among teenagers.

During the past five years, one young Los Angeles novelist has emerged whose work promises to push the young adult novel into a very new direction. In four novels—*Weetzie Bat* (1989), *Witch Baby* (1990), *Cherokee Bat and the Goat Guys* (1991), and *Missing Angel Juan* (1993)—FRANCESCA LIA BLOCK has created a cast of memorable teen characters whose lives reflect a bizarre mixture of campy fairy-tale and punk reality. Her interconnected short novels are told in a richly lyrical and often allusive prose that portrays Block's sensitive but alienated adolescents as they make their way through L.A.'s often eerie and very real fantasyland.

What about the future of the realistic young adult novel? Rock music changed the direction of American popular music irrevocably in the fifties and sixties; although it has undergone changes of form and style since then, the core of the music is what it was at its birth. No one can safely predict the shape it will take in the next decade, but few are predicting its demise. Similarly, the realistic young adult novel changed young adult literature irrevocably in the sixties. Although it has changed forms and extended in many directions since then, it is as strong and influential as ever. It has made young adult literature honest, and it has kept the teenage reader honest. And the realistic young adult novel will probably continue to be the mainstream force in young adult literature, as long as it reflects life in a truthful way and keeps faith with the young adult's needs and aspirations. ❧ JACK FORMAN

Z

Zelinsky, Paul O.

American illustrator, b. 1953. Paul O. Zelinsky was born in Evanston, Illinois. His father, a college professor, taught in various places, so the family moved often; Zelinsky, forced to make new friends, found that his predilection for drawing made him the "class artist" wherever he lived. When he was in high school, he learned printmaking and made etchings and linoleum cuts to illustrate stories and poems that others wrote. In college, he was introduced to children's books in a class taught by author-illustrator Maurice Sendak on the history and making of children's books. He graduated from Yale University in 1974 and received an M.F.A. degree in painting from Tyler School of Art in 1976.

Zelinsky's first picture book was Boris Zhitkov's *How I Hunted the Little Fellows* (1979), a Russian story that allowed him to research late nineteenth-century Russian interiors. He then illustrated a novel by Avi, *The History of Helpless Harry: To Which Is Added a Variety of Amusing and Entertaining Adventures* (1980), which was set in 1845. He was pulled ahead to the current century with *Ralph S. Mouse* (1982), his first assignment to illustrate a novel by Beverly Cleary. Cleary's Newbery Medal-winning *Dear Mr. Henshaw* came next, in 1983. These books brought Zelinsky's work to the attention of the widest possible audience in the field of books for children, so that when his magnificent *Hansel and Gretel* appeared in 1984, many adults in the children's book field knew his name. Rich paintings with details redolent of a more romantic and a more rustic time limn the familiar tale of two children who best a witch. The book was named a Caldecott Honor Book by the American Library Association, as was his *Rumpelstiltskin* (1986). The latter was exhibited in an American Institute of Graphic Artists show, as were several other of his books, and was also named a Bratislava Biennale selection by the International Board on Books for Young People.

A completely different picture-book style is used in *The Maid and the Mouse and the Odd-Shaped House* (1981), which is based on a late nineteenth-century "tell-and-draw" story designed to be created on a school blackboard, with each child adding to the picture. Zelinsky's mastery of book design is evident in the deceptively simple, whimsical, and clever book. The book was chosen by judges to appear in the *Horn Book* "Graphic Gallery" as an example of admirable illustration and design criteria, and it was a New York Times Best Illustrated Children's Book of 1981. Another picture book, *The Story of Mrs. Lovewright and Purrless Her Cat* (1985), is a story by Lore Segal, illustrated to full comic effect. It too was named a New York Times Best Illustrated Children's Book.

Illustration by Paul O. Zelinsky from his book *The Maid and the Mouse and the Odd-Shaped House* (1981).

Voices of the Creators

Paul Zelinsky

I fell short in my art school training because I never quite believed in Quality of Edge or Color Relationship as a painting's only reason for being; I was, and still am, happier trying to put these abstract qualities in the service of something else, such as a story.

Every story is a different experience, carries its own feelings and associations. When I read a story to illustrate it, I want to capture the feelings—grab them and hold on, because they can be fleeting—and figure out how to make pictures that support and intensify them. This problem demands abstract solutions (a quality of line, a kind of space, a color relationship), which often means playing with new and different mediums: pencil, pastel, oils, on paper, canvas, drafting film, wood. But increasingly, I spend time just thinking about the feelings in the story.

Often these feelings come to me as a sort of flavor. I know that when I call up my earliest memories, what I remember seeing and hearing is accompanied by a flavor-like sense of what it felt like to be *there* and see *that.* It is usually a wonderful sense, belonging to the whole experience the way the smell of a room can become the whole experience of the room. Some years ago I was reading my daughter a Babar book for the second or third time when suddenly an illustration (of the monkeys' tree-houses) sparked a lost memory. It was simply the memory of that same page, but as I had seen it as a young child. Not only did the crudeness of the drawing fall away in this child's-eye view, and the sketchy detail blossom into something incredible, but the whole scene was enveloped in a kind of air, had a particular quality. Suddenly I could breathe, smell, and taste this world. So, too, with each new text I take on, I want to grasp what its taste is, and bring it out in the pictures.

When I first learned the song "The Wheels on the Bus" I knew I wanted to illustrate it some day (I was well out of kindergarten, and already illustrating books). My literal-minded mind immediately suggested a book where the bus's moving parts would really move. But what should the pictures look like? The song reminded me a little of bubble gum: it was sweet and bouncy. The pictures needed plenty of rhythm, and the sense of sinking your teeth into something. I thought thick oil paint might give that chewy feeling. And the palette of colors I eventually came up with does, I think, give some of the same kind of pleasure as sweets. There was also a physical pleasure in the laying down of paint and the way colored pencil lines would sometimes plow through the wet oils. Altogether the flavor is strong and full of energy. I hope the pictures are more nutritious, though, than bubble gum.

Lore Segal's marvelous ear for language gave *The Story of Mrs. Lovewright and Purrless Her Cat* a tangy quality. I think perhaps of dill pickles, which are sour, deliciously flavorful, and somehow unintentionally funny. Looking for ways to make these feelings visual, I saw all stretched-out shapes and sharp angles. (Not how a pickle looks, certainly, but how I think the *taste* of a pickle would look.) Mrs. Lovewright was so uncomfortable a person—a chilly woman, trying vainly to make things cozy by cuddling with an unwilling cat. The drawings were in colored pencil; its line has a fittingly edgy quality, unlike, say, watercolor.

I used watercolor as well as opaque watercolor and pastels for Mirra Ginsburg's good-night book *The Sun's Asleep Behind the Hill.* This chant-like text seemed to breathe the smells of a summer night. Soft and darkening by degrees, the watercolor pictures took on a filmy haze of color, consisting of pastels rubbed onto the thumb and smeared over the paper. The best pictures were done while house-sitting for friends in the country, where night came on slowly and I was alone to sense the changes of color and the sounds and smells in the air. That was an attempt to bring some real-life experience into the illumination of a text. Drawing *Rumpelstiltskin* was an effort to create a purely imagined world. It called for a sort of perfect beauty: smooth surfaces placed in a clear light, reminiscent of the paintings of the Northern Renaissance. These were painted in many transparent layers of carefully applied oil paint, and I worked out my own version of the technique. I would have liked to paint what it's like on the inside of a jewel—bright and still, perhaps with no smell at all.

It seems I give myself the task with every book of inventing a new way of working toward a different effect. Three-quarters of the way through each project, I wonder why it has taken so very long before the drawing started to flow. It is hard to remember after the fact how much trial and error—and error and error—goes into the earliest stage of the work of illustrating: sensing the flavor of a text, and figuring out how to capture it for the eyes.

Zelinsky is capable of humor and an almost cartoonish style as in *Mrs. Lovewright* and of geometrically drawn, clean lines and innovative design as in *The Maid and the Mouse.* He can paint sumptuous pictures for traditional tales, such as the forest scenes and the gingerbread house in *Hansel and Gretel,* with lush detail and intricate composition. Clearly, this artist is capable of completely changing his approach to design and his style of illustration with practically every book and with repeated success. ❧ S.H.H.

Zemach, Margot

American illustrator and author, 1931–1989. Since the publication of *A Small Boy Is Listening* (1959), a collaboration with Harve Zemach, Margot Zemach has ranked among the finest of contemporary children's book illustrators. Zemach's strong graphic language—animated drawings, comic high spirits, and impeccable design—inform all her work.

Zemach was born in Los Angeles. Her mother was an actress and her stepfather a dancer and choreographer, thespian influences that helped Zemach prepare for her future career. As Zemach detailed in *Self-Portrait: Margot Zemach* (1978), "When there is a story I want to tell in pictures, I find my actors, build the sets, design the costumes and light the stage . . . when the book closes, the curtain comes down."

Pursuing her childhood ambition to become an artist, Zemach studied at the Los Angeles County Art Institute and other Los Angeles art schools. After receiving a Fulbright scholarship, she attended the Vienna Academy of Fine Arts. There she met Harvey Fischstrom, a fellow Fulbright student who became her husband and collaborator using the name Harve Zemach. Zemach's early career was characterized by collaborations with Harve as storyteller. These joint productions included *Nail Soup: A Swedish Folk Tale Retold* (1964), *Salt: A Russian Tale* (1965), and *Too Much Nose: An Italian Tale* (1967). These tales, like much of Zemach's work, resonate with a distinct European sensibility. Zemach's tenure abroad, first in Vienna and later in Italy, Denmark, and England, imbued her work with an understanding of, and appreciation for, other cultures.

Using the folktale as a vehicle, Zemach's portrayal of human foibles and absurdities is recognizable for its comic warmth and clear-eyed yet sympathetic vision of humanity. Zemach's human comedy is fully developed in *The Judge: An Untrue Tale* (1969), a Caldecott Honor Book, in which a lusty cast of characters are successively imprisoned for attempting to warn a judge that "a horrible thing is coming this way, creeping closer day by day." *Duffy and the Devil: A Cornish Tale* retells the Rumpelstiltskin story. The lazy girl Duffy bargains with the devil to do all her knitting, with the proviso that at the end of three years he'll take her away unless she can guess his name. Rich with the authentic flavor of England, the book won the 1974 Caldecott Medal. Both books burst with antic wit, robust line drawing, and incandescent color. After Harve's death in 1974, Zemach continued to interpret and revitalize tales from traditional sources, including Grimm. With the exception of *Jake and Honeybunch Go to Heaven* (1981), an adaptation of an African American folktale disparaged for promoting stereotypes, Zemach's work has won wide critical acclaim. Besides illustrating nine American Library Association Notable Children's Books, Zemach herself was twice selected as a United States candidate for the Hans Christian Andersen Award, honoring the body of an artist's work. Zemach's matchless talent for creating graphic interpretations—whether explosively energetic, broadly comic, or purposefully understated—brought exuberant new life to a varied body of stories. Margot Zemach died of Lou Gehrig's disease. ❧ C.L.S.

Zim, Herbert S.

American author, b. 1909. One of the first writers to recognize that many children enjoy reading narrative nonfiction as much as and sometimes more than fiction was Herbert S. Zim. A man of many interests, he started his long and varied career as a science teacher at the elementary level, and though his work led him out of the classroom to the desk of the writer and editor, he always considered himself primarily an educator. From his contact with young pupils, he learned that the most effective way to arouse their curiosity in a subject was to present them with concrete information. Applying this insight to writing for them, he deliberately chose specific topics for his information books—snakes, for example, rather than a survey of reptiles—and so developed the concept of the "single-species" title. Highly successful, the form was widely adopted by other writers and came to exert a lasting influence on the juvenile nonfiction that followed.

Born in New York City, Zim spent much of his childhood in California but returned east at the age of fourteen. In 1928 he became a science instructor for the Ethical Culture Schools in Brooklyn, moving in 1930 to Manhattan, where he remained teaching science and science education until 1950. During that time he developed the first elementary science laboratories and received his B.S., M.A., and Ph.D. degrees from Columbia University. In remarks about himself, Zim has told of the impression made on him by a grade-school teacher who did not punish him for passing a note written in his own invented code in class but instead praised him for his creativity. Years later, as related in a *New Yorker* profile on Marvin Minsky, the MIT professor renowned for his work on artificial intelligence, Zim apparently made the same kind of impression on *his* pupil, when he seemed to cooperate with (though cleverly foiled) a lab experiment that Minsky devised to produce a terrible stench. As a teacher, Zim believed first and foremost in letting a child satisfy his natural curiosity, and he held to this principle in his writing as well.

While with the Ethical Culture Schools, Zim conducted a study titled "Science Interests and Activities of Adolescents," and he has said that what he learned from it produced a lifetime of book ideas. His first, *Mice, Men, and Elephants,* dealing with intelligence and reproduction, appeared in 1942, and seven books later, in 1946, he presented some of the material in a short, highly illustrated format as *Elephants,* his first single-species book. There followed more than fifty titles in this format in a range of fields that included zoology, astronomy, oceanography, and physiology. As Zim noted, the subjects gradually became more complex, some of the more far-reaching being *The Universe* (1961) and *Life and Death* (1970), but with his ability to select key essentials and connect them to a child's world, he was always able to make them accessible.

At the same time that Zim was writing these individual trade titles for the school and library market, he was also originating a mass-market series of Golden Guides, pocket identification books designed for inexpensive rack sales. The first was *American Birds and Wildflowers* (1949), and it was followed by a host of others in botany, geology, and zoology. So successful were these guides, soon selling in the millions, that the publisher set Zim up as editor of the program in his own office in the Florida Keys, where he lived, with a staff of a half dozen or so working for him.

Always the restless innovator, Zim left a long-lasting mark on each field that drew his attention: teaching, writing, editing. C.C.E.

Zindel, Paul

American author, b. 1936. Pulitzer Prize–winning author of the brilliant, emotionally devastating play *The Effect of Gamma Rays on Man-in-the-Moon Marigolds* (1965), Paul Zindel was first inspired to write novels by Charlotte Zolotow, an editor who had seen the play and recognized the enormous potential of this talented writer. His first young adult novel, *The Pigman* (1968), is the story of John and Lorraine, two high school students who befriend a lonely old man, with disastrous consequences. Funny, poignant, and believable, *The Pigman* firmly established Zindel's reputation as a major author of literature for adolescents, and it is considered a classic in the field of realistic teenage novels.

Zindel grew up on Staten Island. His parents were divorced when he was young, and he had an unhappy childhood, characterized by poverty and isolation. Zindel has documented many of his childhood and teenage experiences in his autobiography for young people, *The Pigman and Me* (1991). As an adult he spent ten years as a chemistry teacher. His early experiences and his firsthand knowledge of teenagers and life in a public high school are reflected in his work. Staten Island serves as the backdrop for most of his novels, although they could easily be set anywhere in suburban America. His books are generally written in the first person, and he captures the teenage vernacular with amazing accuracy. His characters are troubled teenagers, trying to cope with real-life problems in a hostile world.

In *My Darling, My Hamburger* (1969), Zindel's second novel, a beautiful and intelligent young woman named Liz becomes pregnant in her senior year of high school. How she and her boyfriend, Sean, and their two best friends, Dennis and Maggie, cope with the catastrophic effects of an unwanted pregnancy is a subject young people still find relevant more than twenty years after the book's first publication. Yvette and Dewey, the unlikely protagonists of *I Never Loved Your Mind* (1970), seem to be polar opposites. Although they are both high school dropouts, Dewey is a beer-guzzling cynic and Yvette an idealistic vegetarian. The story of this mismatched couple's attempts to love each other is an insightful, if depressing, commentary on the sense of alienation many teenagers feel when confronted with the emptiness at the heart of our materialistic culture.

Many of Zindel's books, including *The Pigman* and its sequel, *The Pigman's Legacy* (1980), *Confessions of a Teenage Baboon* (1977), and *A Begonia for Miss Applebaum* (1989), center on the relationship between teenagers and one remarkable, sympathetic adult. *Confessions of a Teenage Baboon* is the story of a lonely boy dominated by his mother, a kleptomaniacal private nurse. When Chris and his mother go to live with Lloyd Dipardi, a middle-aged alcoholic, Chris takes some important steps forward in achieving independence from his mother and taking responsibility for himself. In *A Begonia for Miss Applebaum* Henry and Zelda learn invaluable lessons about the meaning of life and love when they become the companions of their beloved science teacher, a woman dying of cancer.

Zindel has been criticized for frequently portraying the parents of his characters in an extremely negative light. But as Zindel himself has written, "Kids don't like to admit how strong an influence parents have on them, and it's natural to have to reject them . . . in order to find themselves." The enduring popularity of Zindel's novels is testimony to his ability to speak directly to adolescents. ❧ K.T.

Zion, Gene

American author, 1913–1975. Few picture-book writers have as light or as sure a comic touch as Gene Zion did. Born in New York City and raised in New Jersey, he studied at the New School of Social Research, graduated from Pratt Institute, and spent the early part of his career as a designer and art director at various magazines. In 1948, he married artist Margaret Bloy Graham, and it was she, along with Ursula Nordstrom, the legendary children's book editor at Harper and Brothers, who encouraged him to try his hand at writing. Together, he wrote and his wife illustrated more than a dozen books, but their collaboration, and his publishing career, ended upon their divorce in 1968.

His first book, *All Falling Down* (1951), is a gently witty tribute to things that fall down (rain, sand castles, and snow among them) and one very important thing that doesn't fall (a baby tossed up and then caught in his father's arms). Spare and tidy, the text is just right in its reassuring tone.

Beginning with *Harry the Dirty Dog* (1956), Zion's wit was turned up several notches. The first of several stories about a strong-minded white dog with brown spots, it offers a clear-eyed perspective on the horrors of being washed. Representing every child who has ever howled at bathtime, Harry hides his scrubbing brush and richly enjoys one totally dirty day. In *No Roses for Harry!* (1958), he finds a way to unload the rose-covered sweater that Grandmother brings him. *Harry and the Lady Next Door* (1960) tracks Harry's effort to silence a singing neighbor. *Harry by the Sea* (1965) takes him to the shore, where seaweed transforms him into a sea monster.

Zion's genial comedies also included *Dear Garbage Man* (1957), in which Stan, a new garbage man, encourages his customers to help themselves to their neighbor's discards. Poor Stan soon discovers that people don't really want other people's rejects, but that's fine, too. For, as a real garbage man, he takes pleasure in helping fill the dump. Though hardly a tribute to recycling, it is an amiable story about work and community, with illustrations that take clear delight in city life. In *The Plant Sitter* (1959), the title character is a little boy whose little business of taking in and tending the plants of vacationing neighbors nearly grows out of control.

Zion's best books portray a world that few children can resist. Funny and kind, filled with caring family, close neighbors, and plucky pets, his stories are distinguished by their playful pleasure in the comic richness of everyday life. ❧ A.Q.

Zolotow, Charlotte

American author, b. 1915. A Virginian who attended the University of Wisconsin before coming to New York, Charlotte Zolotow would have attained professional distinction had she been only a writer of picture books or only an editor, but she has made signal contributions in both areas. She is the author of more than seventy picture books. Unusual in their laser-beam perception of a child's emotions, they are written with a deceptive simplicity that is in fact polished prose.

Zolotow's first book, *The Park Book* (1944), was published by Harper when she was an assistant to children's book editor Ursula Nordstrom; Zolotow in fact wrote it in response to Nordstrom's encouragement. Nordstrom was one of a legendary group of pioneer editors in the field of children's literature; Zolotow credits her as the major influence in her writing and editing career and has pointed out that it was from this mentor that she learned to differentiate between her role as an author and her role as an editor.

Some of Zolotow's writing is in verse, and often her prose has a poetic quality. Almost all her picture books are explorations of personal relationships cast in story form and given depth by humor and tenderness. *The Storm Book* (1953), illustrated by Margaret Bloy Graham, and *Mr. Rabbit and the Lovely Present* (1963), illustrated by Maurice Sendak (and one of the author's few fanciful tales), were Caldecott Honor Books.

In *The Hating Book* (1969) a small girl learns that it may not always be easy to be a friend but that it's worth the effort. Two books about parent-child relationships, *When I Have a Little Girl* (1965) and *When I Have a Little Boy* (1967, originally published under the title *When I Have a Son*), express children's plans for their own future progeny, plans that do not include having to take piano lessons (boy) and not being allowed to eat snow (girl). There weren't many people taking a stand against stereotyped sex roles in children's books in 1972, but in her quiet way Charlotte Zolotow struck a blow for common sense in *William's Doll*, the story of a boy who wanted a doll so he could practice being a father.

Zolotow's understanding of children's emotional needs and problems and her ability to express them at a young child's level of comprehension, leavened with a gentle, affectionate humor, have made her one of the major contemporary writers of realistic books for young children. She has edited books for older readers with courage and percipience and has produced two excellent anthologies for adolescent readers, *Early Sorrows: Ten Stories of Youth* (1986) and *An Overpraised Season: Ten Stories of Youth* (1973).

Zolotow became editorial director of Harper Junior Books in 1976, and in 1981 was appointed vice president of Harper and Row. Six years later she resigned these positions to become editorial consultant to Harper Junior Books and editorial director of her own imprint, Charlotte Zolotow Books. In 1986 she received the University of Minnesota's Kerlan Award for "her singular attainments in the creation of children's literature." The University of Mississippi presented her, in 1990, with the Silver Medallion, awarded annually for the body of an author's or an artist's work, and in 1991 the American Library Association adopted a resolution acknowledging "her far-reaching contribution to children's literature." ❧ Z.S.

Zwerger, Lisbeth

Austrian illustrator, b. 1954. In 1990 Lisbeth Zwerger was awarded the Hans Christian Andersen Medal for lifetime achievement and contribution to the field of children's literature. Just sixteen years earlier, she had dropped out of art school, frustrated and disillusioned. None of her teachers had encouraged the art of illustration nor felt it was a worthwhile endeavor. Around the same time, Zwerger met an English artist, John Rowe, who later became her husband. They lived in Vienna, where Zwerger had grown up, and struggled to support themselves as artists. At one point, Rowe showed Zwerger a book of illustrations by Arthur Rackham. This was a turning point for Zwerger, who found in Rackham's work both the inspiration and the direction she had lost.

She began to illustrate stories and to sell individual pieces, and eventually her work caught the eye of an Austrian publisher, who gave her a contract for her first book, *The Strange Child* (1984) by E. T. A. Hoffman. Zwerger has now illustrated more than fifteen books, all fairy tales, folktales, or classic stories such as O. Henry's *Gift of the Magi* (1982), Oscar Wilde's *Selfish Giant* (1984), and Charles Dickens's *A Christmas Carol* (1988). Although Zwerger's artwork is immediately recognizable, she acknowledges her great debt to Rackham and other English illustrators. Accustomed to working in black-and-white, she used a very limited palette in her earlier work, such as *Thumbeline* (1980), *The Swineherd* (1982), and *The Nightingale* (1984). Her characterization was superb, as seen in the ghostlike witch of *Hansel and Gretel* (1979) and the simple and informal portrayal of Marie in *The Nutcracker* (1987).

During her developmental years, Zwerger concentrated on composition, technique, and accuracy of detail. Her backgrounds were open and vague—almost dreamlike—creating a wonderful dramatic contrast. The reader's eye focuses immediately on her characters and on significant objects in a scene.

While her pictures have elegance and an often breathtaking beauty, Zwerger also shows respect for great storytellers; her art never overwhelms the story. Over the years, she has added more color to her work, as in Heinz Janisch's *Till Eugenspiegel's Merry Pranks* (1990), in which the pictures are gay and light compared with her earlier work and are framed in handsome decorative borders, and in her 1992 collection *Hans Christian Andersen Fairy Tales*, which includes "The Sandman" and "The Naughty Boy" along with such old favorites as "The Princess and the Pea" and "The Emperor's New Clothes."

Zwerger has said that the most difficult task for her now is choosing material to illustrate; at first she gravitated toward childhood favorites, but later she tired of traditional fairy-tale endings, which often seemed sexist or overly moralistic. Her work has continued to be published in Austria; in addition, she is published in more than sixteen other countries, and her work has been exhibited worldwide. Zwerger has been honored several times at the Bologna International Children's Book Fair, at the Biennial of Illustrators at Bratislava, and by library organizations and literary publications in the United States. She is among the best illustrative artists to have emerged in this century. ❧ K.M.K.

Notes on the Contributors

Lauren Adams has worked in children's publishing for several years and is currently managing editor of *The Horn Book Magazine.* She has an M.A. in children's literature from Simmons College.

Vivien Alcock, London, England

Lloyd Alexander, author of many award-winning books for children, lives in Drexel Hill, Pennsylvania, with his wife, Janine, and assorted cats. An amateur violinist, his musical hero is Mozart.

A graduate student in English literature and women's studies at the University of Virginia, **Mara Ilyse Amster**'s work has been published in *Engaging Feminism: Students Speak Up and Speak Out.*

After several years as a library/media specialist in Lexington, Massachusetts, **Lois F. Anderson** now resides in Chapel Hill, North Carolina. She reviews children's books for *The Horn Book Magazine* and enjoys reading to young children as a volunteer.

William Anderson, educator and author, specializes in American studies and children's literature. He has written several books about Laura Ingalls Wilder and helped establish the historical sites and memorials at "Little House" book locales.

Gillian Avery, writer for children and historian of children's books, lives in Oxford, England. Her *Behold the Child,* a history of American children and their books from 1621 to 1922, was published in 1994.

Natalie Babbitt is the author and illustrator of thirteen books for children, some for the youngest and some for the older ones, but fifth-graders are her favorites. She is the mother of three, the grandmother of three, and lives in Providence, Rhode Island.

Barbara Bader is a former editor and juvenile editor of *Kirkus Reviews* and the author of *American Picturebooks from Noah's Ark to the Beast Within.* She currently lives and works in rural Connecticut, among stacks of adult and children's books.

Donald A. Barclay is a reference and instruction librarian at New Mexico State University Library, and he and his wife, Darcie Reimann-Barclay, live in Las Cruces, New Mexico. He has published in the areas of children's literature, the literature of the American West, and library science.

Mary Brigid Barrett, writer, illustrator, and mother of three, is the author of *Sing to the Stars* and the forthcoming *Shoebox Sam,* both picture books. She resides in Franklin, Massachusetts.

Barbara M. Barstow is a children's librarian. Coauthor of *Beyond Picture Books: A Guide to First Readers,* she is actively involved in both the Association for Library Service to Children and the United States Board on Books for Young People.

Barbara Baskin, State University of New York at Stony Brook

Nina Bawden writes for children, for adults, and for her own amusement. She has four children and nine grandchildren and lives in London and in Greece.

Margo Beggs is a writer and editor living in Toronto, Ontario, Canada. Specializing in children's literature, she is a contributing editor to *Quill & Quire,* Canada's book trade periodical.

Christine C. Behr is the children's librarian at the Wayland Public Library in Wayland, Massachusetts, and a regular reviewer for *The Horn Book Guide.*

Quentin Blake, London, England

Michael Bond, of London, England, author of children's fiction, including *Paddington Bear, Olga da Polga,* etc., also writes mystery novels for adults about a French gourmet detective called Monsieur Pamplemousse.

Jane Botham, Coordinator of Children's Services for the Milwaukee (Wisconsin) Public Library, is a speaker and lecturer on children's literature.

Susan Boulanger, Cambridge, Massachusetts

A freelance writer in Providence, Rhode Island, **Jennifer M. Brabander** is a graduate of the Simmons College Center for the Study of Children's Literature.

Paula Overland Brandt is the coordinator of the Curriculum Laboratory in the College of Education at the University of Iowa, Iowa City, Iowa.

Beverly J. Braun, director of library and instructional services at Hartnell College, lives in Monterey, California. A speaker and reviewer of children's literature, she is owner of Authors and More, a service bureau for authors and illustrators.

An alumna of the Boston Museum School, **Jan Brett**'s books are often identified by borders and a detailed style. She uses her favorite animal, the hedgehog, in *The Mitten* and many of her picture books.

Bruce Brooks, Silver Spring, Maryland

Marc Brown, author and illustrator of the popular "Arthur Adventure" series, lives in Hingham, Massachusetts, where he is constantly on the lookout for subjects and characters to amuse children of all ages.

Former teacher, librarian, and three-time Caldecott medalist **Marcia Brown** studied painting with fine artists Judson Smith, Yasuo Kuniyoshi, Stuart Davis, and Julian Levi. Her work reflects her interest in storytelling, folklore, and travel.

Ashley Bryan, Islesford, Maine

Susan A. Burgess is a Westwood, Massachusetts, children's literature consultant and Framingham (Massachusetts) State College graduate faculty educator. The numerous children's literature professional resources are Sue's area of expertise.

John Burningham, London, England

Constance Burns is a librarian and reviewer. She holds a master's in library science from Simmons College and a master's of art in New England studies from the University of Southern Maine. She lives in Cape Elizabeth, Maine.

Coordinator of the Curriculum Library at Framingham (Massachusetts) State College, **Mary Mehlman Burns**, a former children's librarian and secondary school teacher, teaches about, lectures on, and reviews books for children.

Margaret Bush, associate professor of library science at Simmons College, has also been a long-time children's librarian, book reviewer, and selector of science books for *The Elementary School Library Collection* (Bro-Dart).

A public television producer for many years, **Terri Payne Butler** is now a national reviewer of video for families and children and a member of the Horn Book advisory board.

Betsy Byars writes contemporary realistic fiction. She is a licensed pilot and lives with her husband on an airstrip in South Carolina.

Marie C. Campbell is Books for Young People editor at *Quill & Quire*, Canada's book trade magazine. Her M.A. thesis examined L. M. Montgomery's Emily of New Moon trilogy.

Eric Carle has written and illustrated over forty highly honored books for children, including *The Very Hungry Caterpillar, Do You Want to Be My Friend?, Papa, Please Get Me the Moon,* and many others. He lives in Northampton, Massachusetts.

Dudley B. Carlson, Princeton, New Jersey

Marilyn Carpenter is a consultant on children's literature and integrated instruction. Residing in Tucson, Arizona, she has conducted professional development for teachers at hundreds of schools throughout the nation.

Betty Carter teaches children's and young adult literature in the School of Library and Information Studies at Texas Woman's University. She is the coauthor of *Nonfiction for Young Adults.*

John O. Cech, writer and scholar, is the author of *Angels and Wild Things: The Archetypal Poetics of Maurice Sendak,* and the children's books *My Grandmother's Journey* (1991), *First Snow, Magic Snow* (1992), and *Django* (1994). He teaches children's literature at the University of Florida in Gainesville.

Barbara A. Chatton is an associate professor at the University of Wyoming, where she teaches courses in children's and young adult literature and library science. Her *Using Poetry Across the Curriculum: A Whole Language Approach,* has recently been published.

Bill Clark is a freelance writer who obtained a master's degree in technical and professional writing from Northeastern University. He lives in Boston and writes about natural history subjects.

Beverly Cleary, a former children's librarian, writes the sort of books she wanted to read as a child but which she could not find on the library shelves at that time.

Andrea Cleghorn, a journalist and children's book editor at the *Boston Herald*, reviews children's books for newspapers nationally. She especially enjoys reading with her own kids—Abby, 14, and Alex, 12.

Brock Cole, Buffalo, New York

Barbara Cooney lives in midcoast Maine, where she writes and illustrates books for children. Two of these have earned Caldecott Medals, a third the American Book Award.

Susan Cooper writes books for children, screenplays, plays, verse, songs, and very occasional lectures. She is British but lives in Cambridge, Massachusetts.

Robert Cormier, a former reporter and newspaper editor, has written several young adult novels. Born in Leominster, Massachusetts, he still lives there with his wife, Connie.

Margaret N. Coughlan, Library of Congress, Washington, D.C.

Julie Cummins supervises children's services in the 82 branches of the New York Public Library, has edited *Children's Book Illustration and Design*, and has held major offices in library associations.

Donnelyn Curtis is a reference/information technology librarian at New Mexico State University in Las Cruces. Her personal interest in children's literature is encouraged by her three children.

Ann-Marie Davis, Boston, Massachusetts

Managing editor of *The Horn Book Guide*, **Anne E. Deifendeifer** holds a master's degree in children's literature from Simmons College.

Dominique Demers, journalist and writer, teaches children's literature at l'Université du Québec à Montréal. She has written many novels for children as well as a book on children's literature: *Du Petit Poucet au Dernier des Raisins*.

Tomie dePaola, New London, New Hampshire

Michael Dorris, Kalispell, Montana

A university professor and school district administrator in Madison, Wisconsin, **Eliza T. Dresang** provides literary leadership through speaking, writing, and research. She has served on the Newbery and Caldecott Award committees.

Eden K. Edwards has worked in a children's bookstore, reviewed for *The Horn Book Guide*, and manages the marketing and advertising department of The Horn Book, Inc.

Sheila A. Egoff of Vancouver, Canada, is author of *The Republic of Childhood*, the first full-length critical study of Canadian children's literature, now in its third edition. She is also compiler of *Canadian Children's Books, 1799–1939*.

Lois Ehlert, children's book author and illustrator/designer, graduated from the Layton School of Art and the University of Wisconsin. She lives in Milwaukee, Wisconsin, and loves gardening and collecting folk art.

Barbara Elleman, editor of *Book Links*, served on the board of directors for the United States Board on Books for Young People and was formerly children's editor for *Booklist*.

Sarah Ellis is a Vancouver writer, librarian, and storyteller. She writes a regular column on Canadian children's books for *The Horn Book Magazine*.

Former editor in chief of Morrow Junior Books, **Connie C. Epstein** is the author of *The Art of Writing for Children*, reports on the publishing scene, and conducts workshops for aspiring writers.

Librarian **Ellen G. Fader** reviews for *School Library Journal* and *The Horn Book Magazine*. She has been on the Newbery Medal Committee twice and has served as a Boston Globe–Horn Book Award judge.

A former professional magician and newspaperman, **Sid Fleischman** won the Newbery Award for his comic novel *The Whipping Boy*. He lives in Santa Monica, California.

Katherine Flynn, a freelance editor specializing in children's books, has worked for *The Horn Book Magazine* and as an editor for Morrow Junior Books. She lives in Maine.

Author of *Presenting Paul Zindel* and articles and book reviews in library publications, **Jack Forman** is a librarian at the San Diego Community College District's Mesa College Library.

Paula Fox is the author of twenty-one books for young people and six other novels. She lives and writes in Brooklyn, New York.

Russell Freedman is the author of *Lincoln: A Photobiography*, the 1988 Newbery Medal Book, and many other nonfiction books for children on subjects ranging from American history to animal behavior.

Jean Fritz, winner of the 1986 Laura Ingalls Wilder Award, writes historical fiction and biography. She has also written *Homesick*, the story of her childhood in China.

Leon Garfield, London, England

Jean Craighead George, writer and illustrator, lives in Chappaqua, New York. She is a naturalist and writes about North American wildlife and the children who venture into nature. She won the 1973 Newbery Medal.

A parent, critic, and children's bookseller in Marblehead, Massachusetts, **Sheila McMorrow Geraty** received her master's degree from Simmons College Center for the Study of Children's Literature. She contributes regularly to the *Boston Parents' Paper* and reviews for *The Horn Book Guide*.

Bernie Goedhart reviews children's literature for the Montreal *Gazette* and, as a bibliophile in her own right, has a particular passion for picture books.

Carol Goldenberg has designed many award-winning books for children. Formerly art director for a major children's book publisher, she is now a freelance designer and consultant living in Newton, Massachusetts.

Annette Goldsmith takes pleasure in her work as a Toronto children's librarian, book reviewer, and storyteller. Her specialty is Canadian children's literature in both English and French.

Jane Granstrom has thirty years of public library service to children. Her efforts to promote children's literature include teaching, writing, committee work, but especially talking and listening to children.

M. Jean Greenlaw is Regents Professor at the University of North Texas. She is an author of professional and trade books, a critic, and the recipient of the Arbuthnot Award.

Virginia Hamilton, Yellow Springs, Ohio

Carrie A. Harasimowicz holds a master's degree in children's literature from Simmons College and works at The Horn Book, Inc.

Karen Harris, professor of library science and confirmed bibliophile, has written extensively about books and children in fortuitous combinations.

Crystal C. Haynes-Smith, Dorchester, Massachusetts

Kevin Henkes, writer and illustrator, lives in Wisconsin.

Christine Heppermann has a master's degree in children's literature from Simmons College. She manages a children's bookstore in San Antonio, Texas, and reviews children's books for *The Horn Book Guide* and the San Antonio *Express-News*.

A children's librarian for the Toronto Public Library, **Theo Hersh** is active in the children's literature community, reviews children's books for professional journals, and edits the *IBBY-Newsletter*.

Maryclare O'Donnell Himmel is a freelance writer and reviewer who has contributed essays to *The Sixth Book of Junior Authors and Illustrators* and *Twentieth-Century Young Adult Writers*.

A former teacher, children's bookstore manager, and publishing house marketing manager for children's books, **Peggy Hogan** is now publishing gift books for children and adults at the Museum of Fine Arts, Boston.

Elizabeth C. Hoke, coordinator, children's services, Montgomery County (Maryland) Public Libraries (1979–89), served on ALA Newbery, Caldecott, Batchelder, and Notable Books committees and has coordinated five annual Montgomery College Children's Literature Celebrations.

Sally Holmes Holtze, series editor of the H. W. Wilson Company's *Junior Authors* volumes, wrote *Presenting Norma Fox Mazer* and also writes for film (*Meet the Author: Louisa May Alcott*).

Lyn Littlefield Hoopes is the author of several picture books, including *Wing a Ding* and *My Own Home*. She teaches creative writing to elementary school children and lives in Marion, Massachusetts.

Shirley Hughes illustrated around two hundred books by other authors before concentrating on her own picture books. She has won several awards in England and is widely published abroad.

Mollie Hunter, children's author, folklorist, and lecturer, winner of the Carnegie Medal, Arbuthnot Lectureship, Phoenix Award, and many others, lives in the Scottish Highlands, the inspiration for most of her work.

Elizabeth Hurd coordinates children's services at the main library in Greensboro, North Carolina.

Trina Schart Hyman has been illustrating children's books for thirty-two years. Some of them have even won awards. She was also the first art director for *Cricket* magazine.

Anne Irish is the owner of Pooh Corner Bookstore in Madison, Wisconsin, which was established in 1976. She is vice president of the Association of Booksellers for Children and a reviewer for *The Horn Book Guide*.

An expert in children's and young adult literature, **Cyrisse Jaffee** has been a trade book editor, librarian, and lecturer. The author of many reviews and articles, she is currently a freelance editor, writer, and book consultant in the Boston area.

J. Alison James writes novels (*Sing for a Gentle Rain, Runa*), translates children's books (from Swedish and German), and plays with her husband and daughter in their little house in Vermont.

Karen Jameyson, a former managing editor of *The Horn Book Magazine*, moved to Australia in 1989. A critic and reviewer, she also works for the New South Wales *School Magazine.*

Susan Jeffers graduated from Pratt Institute and now lives in New York State, where she continues her lifelong study of drawing, painting, and dressage.

Patrick Jones is the author of *Connecting Young Adults and Libraries* and over twenty articles on young adult library services and literature. He is a librarian in Fort Wayne, Indiana.

William Joyce lives in Shreveport, Louisiana, with his lovely wife, Elizabeth, and their daughter, Mary Katherine, the Wonder Baby. He is currently adapting several of his children's books into motion pictures. He has a cat named Doris Day, who lost her tail in an automobile accident.

Amy Kellman is district coordinator for children's services of the Carnegie Library, a book reviewer for *School Library Journal* and *The Horn Book Guide,* and past president of the Association for Library Service to Children and the United States Board on Books for Young People.

As a child **Steven Kellogg** told stories and drew pictures to entertain his two younger sisters. He went on to attend the Rhode Island School of Design, graduated in 1963, and has been an enthusiastic author and illustrator ever since.

M. E. Kerr, winner of the American Library Association's Margaret A. Edwards lifetime achievement award (1993), is the author of eighteen young adult novels. Under another pseudonym, Mary James, she writes middle-grade books.

Barbara Kiefer is an associate professor at Teachers College, Columbia University, where she teaches courses in children's literature and reading.

Dick King-Smith, children's author, lives in Queen Charlton, near Bristol, England. His fictional works are mainly, though not exclusively, about animals, adventure stories in which unlikely heroes often overcome terrible odds.

Lee Kingman lives in Gloucester, Massachusetts, has written books for children and young adults, edited books about art and writing in children's literature, and been a director of The Horn Book, Inc.

Karen M. Klockner is a children's book editor who has been on the staff at Little, Brown and Orchard Books. She currently freelances from her home in Shaker Heights, Ohio.

A children's librarian for the Cambridge, Massachusetts, Public Library, **Maeve Visser Knoth** reviews for *The Horn Book Magazine* and has worked as an elementary school teacher and a children's bookseller.

Dr. Beverly Kobrin, author of *Eyeopeners!* and publisher of the *Kobrin Letter* on children's nonfiction, lives in California with two serious cats and a whimsical husband.

Sarah Guille Kvilhaug holds a master's degree in children's literature and is the mother of two children. She is a freelance writer specializing in children's literature.

Retired Sonoma County Schools librarian **Mildred Lee** works as a library consultant when not traveling to see the world she found in books. She lives in Santa Rosa, California.

Robert Lipsyte, TV journalist and *New York Times* sportswriter, is the author of eight young adult novels, including *The Contender,* and a new biography series, "Superstar Lineup," of twentieth-century sports figures.

Jean Little, the blind author of over twenty children's books, lives a tumultuous but creative life in an Ontario farmhouse with her sister, her great-niece, four dogs, and a cat.

A school librarian in Westbrook, Maine, **Deborah M. Locke** also holds a master's degree in children's literature from Simmons College, has chaired Maine's Intellectual Freedom Committee, and currently reviews books on tape for *AudioFile.*

Stephanie Loer, children's book editor of the Boston *Globe*, is also the author of a quarterly newsletter about children's books. She has written several guides about teaching children to read.

Claudia Logan, Cambridge, Massachusetts

Like the family in her novel *Anastasia Krupnik,* writer **Lois Lowry** lives in Cambridge, Massachusetts. She shares with Anastasia's father a love of pro football, Billie Holiday, and *Casablanca.*

David Macaulay, Warren, Rhode Island

Patricia MacLachlan, Leeds, Massachusetts

Susan M. Maguire, Canton, Massachusetts

Margaret Mahy, Christchurch, New Zealand

Leonard S. Marcus is the author of *Margaret Wise Brown: Awakened by the Moon* and *75 Years of Children's Book Week Posters.* He lives with his wife and son in Brooklyn, New York.

Barbara A. Marinak is a founder and past president of the Children's Literature Council of Pennsylvania. She enjoys reviewing for a number of publications, including *The Horn Book Guide.*

Jill P. May is professor of literacy and languages at Purdue University, where she teaches courses in children's literature. She wrote *Films and Filmstrips for Language Arts* and *Lloyd Alexander* (1991) and edited *Children and Their Literature.* She works with elementary school teachers to create literary studies programs in their schools.

Juliana McIntyre, La Jolla, California

Amy J. Meeker, Newton, Massachusetts

Associate director and assistant professor at the Simmons College Center for the Study of Children's Literature, **Cathryn M. Mercier** chaired the 1993 Boston Globe–Horn Book Award Committee and served on the 1994 Caldecott Committee. She reviews children's and young adult books for *Five Owls* and *The Boston Parents' Paper.*

Sara Miller teaches children's and young adult literature at Manhattanville College in Purchase, New York, and is currently library director at the Rye Country Day School in Rye, New York.

Dianne Monson is professor of children's literature at the University of Minnesota. She has served as president of the United States Board on Books for Young People.

Barry Moser has illustrated nearly two hundred books. A member of the National Academy, he has received the American Book Award, the Boston Globe–Horn Book Award, and the New York Times Best Illustrated Book of the Year Award.

Walter Dean Myers has been fortunate enough to spend a great deal of his life doing just what he wants to do, write.

Former teacher and school director and cofounder of the Cheshire Cat children's bookstore, **Helen Green Neuburg** lives in Princeton, New Jersey, and is a children's book buyer and consultant.

Helen Snell Neumeyer, former children's book editor and teacher of grades K through graduate school, is author/editor of several language arts texts. Presently she reads, walks, and plays the violin in California.

Peter F. Neumeyer is a professor, writer, and reviewer. He has published over ten books for children and adults, and his *Annotated Charlotte's Web* was published in 1994.

Zibby Oneal lives in Ann Arbor, Michigan. Besides writing for young people, she has taught courses in children's literature and in creative writing at the University of Michigan and at Simmons College in Boston.

Jan Ormerod, Cambridge, England

Helen Oxenbury, London, England

Martha Vaughan Parravano is associate editor of *The Horn Book Magazine* and teaches children's literature at Wheelock College in Boston, Massachusetts.

Katherine Paterson was born in China, raised in the American South, has worked in Japan, and now lives and writes in Barre, Vermont. She and her husband, a Presbyterian minister and sometime coauthor, have four grown children.

Richard Peck, who won the 1990 Margaret Edwards Author Achievement Award, is at work on a novel on censorship, to be called *The Last Safe Place on Earth.*

Bette J. Peltola is professor of education at the University of Wisconsin–Milwaukee, where she teaches children's literature. She chaired the 1975 Newbery–Caldecott Awards Committee and the 1988 Caldecott Award Committee.

Jerry Pinkney, illustrator-designer, studied at the Philadelphia Museum College of Art, Pennsylvania, has illustrated over sixty books for children, and is married to author Gloria Jean Pinkney.

As a columnist and freelance journalist, **Gail Pool** has written about the editorial, financial, cultural, and ethical aspects of magazines for many publications. She lives in Cambridge, Massachusetts.

Amy E. Quigley, librarian, writer, and reviewer, is currently designing a database for the National Center for Death Education and discovering the joys and perils of gardening with her young daughter.

Anne Quirk lives in Cambridge, Massachusetts. She has worked for a number of children's book publishers and now runs her own consulting and advertising agency.

Sandra Ray reviews for *The Horn Book Guide* and writes articles about children's authors for both Ungar Publications and Salem Press. She holds a master's degree in children's literature from Simmons College.

Tim Retzloff, Flint, Michigan

Patricia Riley, who has master's degrees in children's literature and social work, cofounded Connections: Children's Literature Consultants. She also reviews books and teaches writing children's books in Boston and Providence.

Lolly Robinson, Cambridge, Massachusetts

Sarah L. Rueter, a Boston-area librarian long involved with children's books, has served as chair of the Boston Globe–Horn Book Committee and is a charter member of The Wildflowers.

Grace W. Ruth is children's book selection specialist for the San Francisco Public Library. She chaired the 1988 and 1989 ALA Notable Children's Books and the 1995 Caldecott Award committees.

Cynthia Rylant, Eugene, Oregon

Of her diverse duties as a children's services librarian in Washington, D.C., **Maria B. Salvadore** most enjoys introducing children and adults to children's literature.

Sheryl Lee Saunders, Chatham, Massachusetts

Australian **Maurice Saxby**'s *Proof of the Puddin': Australian Children's Literature, 1970–1990* is the third volume in his history of Australian children's literature, a subject on which he has written and lectured internationally.

Allen Say, San Francisco, California

A freelance children's literature reviewer from Minnetonka, Minnesota, **Suzy Schmidt** is also a contributor to *From Sea to Shining Sea: A Treasury of American Folklore and Folk Songs.*

Dr. Isabel Schon, founding director of the Center for the Study of Books in Spanish for Children and Adolescents at California State University, San Marcos, has written extensively about books for and about Latino young readers.

Maurice Sendak, Ridgefield, Connecticut

Uri Shulevitz, author of *Writing with Pictures* and author-illustrator of over thirty children's books, lives in New York City. He has received the Caldecott Medal and the Christopher Award.

A content research editor and freelance writer, **Carolyn L. Shute** has taught courses on children's literature in the United States and Canada. She holds a master's degree in children's literature from Simmons College.

Martha F. Sibert, who has a master's degree in children's literature, is a book reviewer and former children's coordinator for a public library system. She also cofounded Connections: Children's Literature Consultants.

Phyllis Gibbs Sidorsky, National Cathedral School Lower School librarian (retired), enjoys designing needlepoint, painting, cooking, and traveling, along with growing herbs in her walled city garden and native plants at her West Virginia cabin.

Peter D. Sieruta grew up in Detroit, Michigan. He has had several plays produced, has reviewed children's and young adult books, and is the author of *Heartbeats and Other Stories.*

Anita Silvey, editor-in-chief, *The Horn Book Magazine,* Boston, Massachusetts

A 1981 graduate of Simmons College Center for the Study of Children's Literature, **Cooki Slone** is the children's book reviewer for the *Middlesex News* in Framingham, Massachusetts.

Jill A. Smilow, currently a consultant in the field of children's literature, has been professionally associated with *The Horn Book Magazine,* Scholastic, Inc., Candlewick Press, and The Massachusetts Corporation for Educational Telecommunications.

Henrietta M. Smith, professor emerita, University of South Florida, Tampa, teaches storytelling and children's literature and is a reviewer for *The Horn Book Guide.* Smith is particularly interested in research related to literature and the African American child.

Lane Smith illustrated the Caldecott Honor Book *The Stinky Cheese Man and Other Fairly Stupid Tales.* He is the author/illustrator of *The Happy Hocky Family, The Big Pets, Glasses—Who Needs 'Em?,* and *Flying Jake.* He lives in New York City.

Gary Soto was raised in Fresno, California, and now lives and teaches in Berkeley, California. He has produced films and numerous books, including *Baseball in April* and *Living Up the Street.*

Elizabeth George Speare, Tucson, Arizona

For story material **Jerry Spinelli** often draws on his

childhood in Norristown, Pennsylvania. He is married to fellow author Eileen Spinelli.

William Steig, Boston, Massachusetts

James Stevenson, Guilford, Connecticut

Jewell Stoddard is co-owner of The Cheshire Cat Book Store in Washington, D.C. She serves on the Library of Congress selection committee and was a member of the 1994 Caldecott Committee.

Zena Sutherland, professor emerita, University of Chicago, is author of *Children and Books* and was editor for *Saturday Review* and *Bulletin of the Center for Children's Books.*

A children's bureau director, **Lynn Sygiel** lives in Indianapolis, Indiana.

Nancy Tafuri is the author-artist of the Caldecott Honor Book *Have You Seen My Duckling?* She lives and works in Roxbury, Connecticut, with her husband, Tom, and her daughter, Cristina.

Katrin Tchana has been an avid reader of children's literature for twenty-seven years. She works as a teacher, writer, and mother in Burlington, Vermont.

Wallace Tripp, illustrator of *Granfa' Grig Had a Pig,* other funny animal books, and Pawprints greeting cards, lives in a yellow house on a hill in New Hampshire.

Chris Van Allsburg, Providence, Rhode Island

Formerly an editor of children's books, **Nancy Vasilakis** is currently librarian at the Tower School in Marblehead, Massachusetts. She has been reviewing for *The Horn Book Magazine* since 1987.

Bernard Waber is the author-illustrator of the "Lyle" (the Crocodile) series, *Ira Sleeps Over,* and other titles for children. He lives in Baldwin Harbor, New York.

Caroline Ward is the youth services consultant for New York's Nassau Library System, where she examines and evaluates over four thousand new children's books each year. She has taught at Long Island University and served as chairperson of the 1990 Newbery Committee.

Rosemary Wells has written over fifty books for children, including *Noisy Nora* and the "Max and Ruby" board books. She lives in Briarcliff Manor, New York.

Vera B. Williams, New York, New York

Melanie Millis Wissel is a children's program librarian for the Indianapolis–Marion County Public Library. She works at the historic central library, built on land donated by James Whitcomb Riley, beloved Hoosier poet.

In 1991 **Valerie Worth** received the NCTE Award for Excellence in Poetry for Children. She lives with her husband in upstate New York.

Patricia Wroclawski, Winnetka, Illinois

Laurence Yep is a writer and teacher. His stage adaptation of *Dragonwings* played at Lincoln Center and the Kennedy Center. In 1990 he won an NEA fellowship.

Ed Young, New York, New York

Hanna B. Zeiger is editor of *The Horn Book Guide* and reviews for *The Horn Book Magazine.* She was a school librarian in Brookline, Massachusetts, and adjunct professor at Boston University.

Paul O. Zelinsky has illustrated some twenty children's books, including the mechanical book *The Wheels on the Bus,* the Caldecott Honor Books *Rumpelstiltskin* and *Hansel and Gretel,* and Carl Sandburg's *More Rootabagas.*

Credits

BLACK AND WHITE ILLUSTRATIONS

AHLBERG, JANET AND ALLAN. From The *Jolly Postman; or, Other People's Letters,* by Janet and Allan Ahlberg. Copyright © 1986 by Janet and Allan Ahlberg. By permission of Little, Brown and Company. ALEXANDER, LLOYD. Illustration by Evaline Ness from *The High King* © 1968 by Lloyd Alexander. By permission of Henry Holt and Co., Inc. ALIKI. Interior illustration by Aliki Brandenberg from her book *Feelings.* Copyright © 1984 by Aliki Brandenberg. By permission of Greenwillow Books, a division of William Morrow & Company, Inc. ANDERSON, C. W. Reprinted with the permission of Macmillan Publishing Company from *Billy and Blaze,* by C. W. Anderson. Copyright 1936 Macmillan Publishing Company; copyright renewed © 1964 C. W. Anderson. ASBJORNSEN, PETER, AND JORGEN MOE. Reprinted by permission of Grondahl Og Dreyers Forlag from *Norwegian Folk Tales* (1960). From the collection of Peter Christen Asbjornsen and Jorgen Moe, illustrated by Erik Werenskiold and Theodor Kittelsen. Translated by Pat Shaw Iversen and Carl Norman. ATWATER, RICHARD. From *Mr. Popper's Penguins,* by Richard & Florence Atwater. Copyright 1938 by Florence Atwater and Richard Atwater; © renewed 1966 by Florence Atwater, Doris Atwater, and Carroll Atwater Bishop. By permission of Little, Brown and Company .

BESKOW, ELSA. Illustration from *Tomtebobarnen (Children of the Forest)* by Elsa Beskow. Copyright © 1966 by Elsa Beskow. By permission of Bonnier Carlsen Förlag AB, Stockholm, Sweden. BOND, MICHAEL. Illustration by Peggy Fortnum from *Paddington Abroad* by Michael Bond. Illustration copyright © 1972 by Peggy Fortnum. Reprinted by permission of Houghton Mifflin Co. All rights reserved. BOSTON, L. M. Illustration from *An Enemy at Green Knowe* by Lucy M. Boston and illustrated by Peter Boston, copyright © 1964 by Lucy Maria Boston and renewed 1992 by Peter Boston, reproduced by permission of Harcourt Brace & Company. BOUTET DE MONVEL, MAURICE. From *Joan of Arc* by Maurice Boutet de Monvel, English translation by Gerald Gottlieb. Copyright © 1980 by Gerald Gottlieb. Used by permission of Viking Penguin, a division of Penguin Books USA Inc. BRETT, JAN. From the *Twelve Days of Christmas,* illustrated by Jan Brett. Copyright © 1986. By permission of The Putnam & Grosset Group. BRIGGS, RAYMOND. Illustration by Raymond Briggs from his book *Father Chirstmas.* Copyright © 1973 by Raymond Briggs. By permission of The Putnam & Grosset Group. BRITISH CHILDREN'S BOOKS TO WORLD WAR II. Illustration reprinted with the permission of Charles Scribner's Sons, an imprint of Macmillan Publishing Company from *The Wind in the Willows,* by Kenneth Grahame, illustrated by Ernest H. Shepard. Copyright 1933, 1953 Charles Scribner's Sons; copyright renewed © 1961 Ernest H. Shepard. BROWN, MARCIA. Reprinted with the permission of Charles Scribner's Sons, an imprint of Macmillan Publishing Company from *Cinderella or the Little Glass Slipper* by Marcia Brown. Copyright 1954 Marcia Brown; copyright renewed © 1982 Marcia Brown. BROWN, MARGARET WISE. Illustration by Garth Williams from *Little Fur Family* (1946), by Margaret Wise Brown. Selection reprinted by permission of HarperCollins Publishers. BROWNE, ANTHONY. From *Gorilla* by Anthony Browne. Copyright © 1983 by Anthony Browne. Reprinted by permission of Alfred A. Knopf, Inc. BURKERT, NANCY EKHOLM. Picture by Nancy Ekholm Burkert from *Snow-White and the Seven Dwarfs* by the Brothers Grimm, translated by Randall Jarrell. Pictures copyright © 1972 by Nancy Ekholm Burkert. Reprinted by permission of Farrar, Straus & Giroux, Inc. BURNFORD, SHEILA. Illustration by Carl Burger from *The Incredible Journey,* by Sheila Burnford (1961). By permission of Knox Burger. BURTON, VIRGINIA LEE. Illustration from *The Little House* by Virginia Lee Burton. Copyright © 1942 by Virginia Lee Burton. Reprinted by permission of Houghton Mifflin Co. All rights reserved.

CALDECOTT, RANDOLPH. From *The Randolph Caldecott Treasury* by Elizabeth T. Billington, editor. Copyright © 1978 by Elizabeth T. Billington; Foreword copyright © 1978 by Maurice Sendak. Used by permission of Frederick Warne Books, a division of Penguin Books USA Inc. CHASE, RICHARD. Illustration from *The Jack Tales* by Richard Chase. Copyright 1943, © renewed 1971 by Richard Chase. Reprinted by permission of Houghton Mifflin Co. All rights reserved. CLEARY, BEVERLY. Illustration by Alan Tiegreen from *Ramona and Her Father,* by Beverly Cleary. Copyright © 1975, 1977 by Beverly Cleary. By permission of Morrow Junior, a division of William Morrow and Company, Inc. CLIFTON, LUCILLE. From *Everett Anderson's Year* by Lucille Clifton. Illustrations copyright © 1974 by Ann Grifalconi. Reprinted by permission of Henry Holt and Company, Inc. COLE, WILLIAM. Illustration by Tomi Ungerer from *Beastly Boys and Ghastly Girls,* by William Cole. Copyright © 1964 by Diogenes Verlag AG Zürich. By permission of the publisher. COLLODI, CARLO. Reprinted with the permission of Macmillan Publishing Company from *The Adventures of Pinocchio,* by C. Collodi with illustrations after Attilio Mussino. Illustrations copyright © 1969 Giunti Marzocco S.P.A. CONRAD, PAM. Illustration copyright © 1989 by Richard Egielski from *The Tub People,* by Pam Conrad. Selection reprinted by permission of HarperCollins Publishers. COUNTING BOOKS. Illustration from *Moja Means One: Swahili Counting Book* by Muriel Feelings, pictures by Tom Feelings. Copyright © 1971 by Tom Feelings, pictures. Used by permission of Dial Books for Young Readers, a division of Penguin Books USA Inc. CRAIG, HELEN. From *Angelina's Birthday Surprise* by Katharine Holabird, illustrations by Helen Craig. Text copyright © 1989 by Katharine Holabird. Illustrations copyright © 1989 by Helen Craig. Reprinted by permission of Clarkson N. Potter, Inc., a member of the Crown Publishing Group. CREWS, DONALD. Illustration by Donald Crews from his book *Parade.* Copyright © 1983 by Donald Crews. By permission of Greenwillow Books, a division of William Morrow and Company, Inc.

DAUGHERTY, JAMES. From *Andy and the Lion* by James Daugherty. Copyright 1938 by James Daugherty, renewed © 1966 by James Daugherty. Used by permission of Viking Penguin, a division of Penguin Books USA Inc. D'AULAIRE, EDGAR AND INGRI PARIN. From *D'Aulaires' Trolls* by Ingri & Edgar Parin d'Aulaire. Copyright © 1972 by Ingri & Edgar Parin d'Aulaire. Used by permission of Doubleday, a division of Bantam Doubleday Dell Publishing Group, Inc. DE LA MARE, WALTER. From *Come Hither* by Walter de la Mare, decorations by Warren Chappell. Copyright 1923, 1928 by Walter de la Mare. Copyright 1957 by Alfred A. Knopf, Inc. Reprinted by permission of Alfred A. Knopf, Inc. DEPAOLA, TOMIE. From *Tomie dePaola's Mother Goose* by Tomie dePaola. Copyright © 1985. By permission of The Putnam & Grosset Group. DILLON, LEO AND DIANE. From *The People Could Fly* by Virginia Hamilton, illustrated by Leo and Diane Dillon. Text copyright © 1985 by Virginia Hamilton. Illustrations copyright © 1985 by Leo and Diane Dillon. Reprinted by permission of Alfred A. Knopf, Inc. DRESCHER, HENRIK. Illustration by Henrik Drescher from *Simon's Book.* Copyright © 1983 by Henrik Drescher. By permission of Lothrop, Lee & Shepard Books, a division of William Morrow and Company, Inc. DU BOIS, WILLIAM PENE. From *The Twenty-One Balloons* by William Pène du Bois. Copyright 1947 by William Pène du Bois, renewed © 1975 by William Pène du Bois. Used by permission of Viking Penguin, a division of Penguin Books USA Inc.

EICHENBERG, FRITZ. Illustration from *Ape in a Cape,* copyright 1952 and renewed 1980 by Fritz Eichenberg, reproduced by permission of Harcourt Brace & Company. ESTES, ELEANOR. Illustration from *Ginger Pye,* copyright 1951 and renewed 1979 by Eleanor Estes, reproduced by permission of Harcourt Brace & Company. FARJEON, ELEANOR. Illustration by E. H. Shepard from *The Glass Slipper* (1946), by Eleanor Farjeon. Copyright E. H. Shepard. Reproduced by permission of Curtis Brown London. FITZGERALD, JOHN D. From *The Great Brain* by John D. Fitzgerald, illustrated by Mercer Mayer. Copyright © 1967 by John D. Fitzgerald. Used by permission of Dial Books for Young Readers, a division of Penguin Books USA Inc. FLEISCHMAN, SID. From *Humbug Mountain* by Sid Fleischman; illustrated by Eric von Schmidt. Copyright © 1978 by Albert S. Fleischman. By permission of Little, Brown and Company. FOX, MEM. From *Wilfrid Gordon McDonald Partridge,* by Mem Fox. First American edition published by Kane/Miller Book Publishers 1985. Text copyright © Mem Fox 1984. Illustrations copyright © Julie Vivas 1984. Originally published in Australia by Omnibus Books 1984. FRITZ, JEAN. From *And Then What Happened, Paul Revere?* by Jean Fritz, illustrated by Margot Tomes. Copyright © 1973. By permission of The Putnam & Grosset Group.

GAG, WANDA. From *Millions of Cats,* by Wanda Gág. Copyright © 1928. By permission of the Putnam & Grosset Group. GANNETT, RUTH CHRISMAN AND RUTH STILES. Illustration by Ruth Chrisman Gannett from *My Father's Dragon* (1948), by Ruth Stiles Gannett. GEISERT, ARTHUR. Illustration from *Pigs from A to Z* by Arthur Geisert. Copyright © 1986 by Arthur Geisert. Reprinted by permission of Houghton Mifflin Co. All rights reserved. GEORGE, JEAN CRAIGHEAD. From *My Side of the Mountain* by Jean Craighead George. Copyright © 1959 by Jean Craighead George renewed 1987 by Jean Craighead George. Used by permission of Dutton Children's Books, a division of Penguin Books USA Inc. GIBBONS, GAIL. Copyright © 1991 by Gail Gibbons. All rights reserved. Reprinted from *Whales* by permission of Holiday House, Inc. GOREY, EDWARD. Copyright © 1971 by Edward Gorey. All rights reserved. Reprinted from *The Shrinking of Treehorn* by Florence Parry Heide by permission of Holiday House, Inc.

HADER, BERTA AND ELMER. Reprinted with the permission of Macmillan Publishing Company from *The Big Snow,* by Berta and Elmer Hader. Coyright 1948 Berta Hader and Elmer Hader; copyright renewed © 1976 Berta Hader. HAYWOOD, CAROLYN. Illustration by Carolyn Haywood from *Eddie the Dog Holder.* Copyright © 1966 by Carolyn Haywood. By permission of Morrow Junior, a division of William Morrow & Company, Inc. HENKES, KEVIN. Illustration by Kevin Henkes from *Julius, the Baby of the World.* Copyright © 1990 by Kevin Henkes. By permission of Greenwillow Books, a division of William Morrow and Company, Inc. HILL, ERIC. Illustration by Eric Hill from *Spot Goes to the Beach* (1985). By permission of The Putnam & Grosset Group. HISTORICAL FICTION FOR CHILDREN. Illustration from *Johnny Tremain* by Esther Forbes Hoskins. Copyright © renewed 1971 by Linwood M. Erskine, Jr., Executor for the Estate of Esther Forbes Hoskins. Reprinted by permission of Houghton Mifflin Co. All rights reserved. HOBAN, LILLIAN. Illustration by Lillian Hoban from *Bread and Jam for Frances* (1964), by Russell Hoban. Selection reprinted by permission of HarperCollins Publishers. HOLLING, HOLLING C. Illustration from *Minn of the Mississippi* by Holling C. Holling. Copyright © 1951 by Holling C. Holling. Reprinted by permission of Houghton Mifflin Co. All rights reserved. HOUSTON, JAMES. Illustration from *Songs of the Dream People: Chants and Images from the Indians and Eskimos of North America.* Edited and illustrated by James Houston. Atheneum, New York. Copyright © 1972 by James Houston. HUGHES, SHIRLEY. Initial sketch for *Alfie's Feet* reproduced by permission of Shirley Hughes. HUGHES, SHIRLEY. Illustration by Shirley Hughes from *Alfie's Feet.* Copyright © 1982 by Shirley Hughes. By permission of Lothrop, Lee & Shepard Books, a division of William Morrow & Company, Inc. HURD, CLEMENT. Illustration by Clement Hurd from *The Runaway Bunny* (1942), by Margaret Wise Brown. Illustration copyright © 1972 by Edith T. Hurd, Clement Hurd, John Thacher Hurd, and George Hellyer as trustees of the Edith and Clement Hurd 1982 Trust. Selection reprinted by permission of HarperCollins Publishers. HYMAN, TRINA SCHART. From *King Stork* by Trina Schart Hyman. Copyright © 1973 by Trina Schart Hyman. By permission of Little, Brown and Co.

INFORMATION BOOKS. From *Dinosaurs to the Rescue* by Laurie Krasny Brown and Marc Brown. Copyright © 1992 by Laurene Krasny Brown and Marc Brown. By permission of Little, Brown and Company.

KELLOGG, STEVEN. Illustration from *How Much is a Million?,* by David Schwartz, illustrated by Steven Kellogg. Copyright © 1985 by Steven Kellogg. By permission of Lothrop, Lee & Shepard Books, a division of William Morrow and Company, Inc. KING-SMITH, DICK. From *Babe the Gallant Pig* by Dick King-Smith, illustrated by Mary Rayner. Text copyright © 1983 by Dick King-Smith. Illustrations copyright © 1983 by Mary Rayner. Reprinted by permission of Crown Publishers, Inc. KRASILOVSKY, PHYLLIS. Illustration by Peter Spier, copyright © 1957 by Peter Spier. From *The Cow Who Fell in the Canal* by Phyllis Krasilovsky. Used by permission of Doubleday, a division of Bantam Doubleday Dell Publishing Group, Inc. KRAUSS, RUTH. Illustration copyright © 1945 by Crockett Johnson from *The Carrot Seed,* by Ruth Krauss. Selection reprinted by permission of HarperCollins Publishers. KROEBER, THEODORA. Illustration by Ruth Robbins from *Ishi: Last of His Tribe* by Theodora Kroeber. Illustration copyright © 1964 by Ruth Robbins. Reprinted by permission of Houghton Mifflin Co. All rights reserved. KUSKIN, KARLA. Illustration copyright © 1982 by Marc Simont from *The Philharmonic Gets Dressed,* by Karla Kuskin. Selection reprinted by permission of HarperCollins Publishers.

LAWSON, ROBERT. From *Ben and Me,* by Robert Lawson. Copyright 1939 by Robert Lawson; © 1967 by John W. Boyd. By permission of Little, Brown and Company. LENT, BLAIR. Illustration from *Pistachio,* copyright © 1964 by Blair Lent. Reprinted by permission of the author. LINDGREN, ASTRID. From *Pippi Longstocking* by Astrid Lindgren, translated by Florence Lamborn. Copyright 1950 by the Viking Press, Inc., renewed © 1978 by Viking Penguin Inc. Used by permission of Viking Penguin, a division of Penguin Books USA Inc. LIONNI, LEO. From *Alexander and the Wind-Up Mouse* by Leo Lionni. Copyright © 1969 by Leo Lionni. Reprinted by permission of Pantheon Books, a division of Random House, Inc. LOBEL, ANITA. Illustration from *On Market Street,* by Arnold Lobel and Anita Lobel, illustrated by Anita Lobel. Copyright © 1981 by Anita Lobel. By permission of Greenwillow Books, a division of William Morrow and Company, Inc. LOBEL, ARNOLD. Illustration by Arnold Lobel from *Whiskers and Rhymes.* Copyright © 1985 by Arnold Lobel. By permission of Greenwillow Books, a division of William Morrow and Company, Inc. LOWRY, LOIS. Illustration from *A Summer to Die* by Lois Lowry. Illustration copyright © 1977 by Jenni Oliver. Reprinted by permission of Houghton Mifflin Co. All rights reserved.

MACAULAY, DAVID. Illustration from *Pyramid* by David Macaulay. Copyright © 1975 by David Macaulay. Reprinted by permission of Houghton Mifflin Co. All rights reserved. MACLACHLAN, PATRICIA. Jacket illustration by Marcia Sewall for *Sarah, Plain and Tall* (1985), by Patricia MacLachlan. Selection reprinted by permission of HarperCollins Publishers. MCCLOSKEY, ROBERT. From *Make Way for Ducklings* by Robert McCloskey. Copyright 1941 by Robert McCloskey, renewed © 1969 by Robert McCloskey. Used by permission of Viking Penguin, a division of Penguin Books USA Inc. MIDDLE GRADE FICTION. Illustration by Louise Fitzhugh from *Harriet the Spy* (1964). Selection reprinted by permission of HarperCollins Publishers. MILNE, A. A. From *Winnie-the-Pooh* by A. A. Milne, illustrated by E. H. Shepard. Copyright 1926 by E. P. Dutton, renewed 1954 by A. A. Milne. Used by permission of Dutton Children's Books, a division of Penguin Books USA Inc. MINARIK, ELSE HOLMELUND. Illustration by Maurice Sendak from *Little Bear* (1957), by Else Holmelund Minarik. Selection reprinted by permission of HarperCollins Publishers. MUNSINGER, LYNN. Illustration from *A Zooful of Animals* by William Cole. Illustrations copyright © 1992 by Lynn Munsinger. Reprinted by permission of Houghton Mifflin Co. All rights reserved.

NASH, OGDEN. From *Custard and Company,* selected and illustrated by Quentin Blake. Copyright © 1980 by Quentin Blake. By permission of Little, Brown and Company. NESS, EVALINE. From *Sam, Bangs, and Moonshine* by Evaline Ness. Copyright © 1966 by Evaline Ness. Reprinted by permission of Henry Holt and Company, Inc. NORTON, MARY. Illustration from *The Borrowers* by Mary Norton and illustrated by Beth and Joe Krush, copyright 1953, 1952 by Mary Norton and renewed 1981, 1980 by Mary Norton, Beth Krush, and Joe Krush, reproduced by permission of Harcourt Brace & Company. NURSERY RYHMES. Illustration from *The Annotated Mother Goose* by William S. Baring-Gould and Ceil Baring-Gould. Copyright © 1962 by William S. and Ceil Baring-Gould. Reprinted by permission of Bramhall House, published by Clarkson N. Potter, a member of the Crown Publishing Group.

O'BRIEN, ROBERT C. Reprinted with the permission of Atheneum Publishers, an imprint of Macmillan Publishing Company from *Mrs. Frisby and the Rats of NIMH,* by Robert C. O'Brien, illustrated by Zena Bernstein. Copyright © 1971 Robert C. O'Brien. O'DELL, SCOTT. Illustration from *Island of the Blue Dolphins* by Scott O'Dell. Illustration copyright © 1960 by Evaline Ness. Reprinted by permission of Houghton Mifflin Co. All rights reserved. ORMEROD, JAN. Illustration by Jan Ormerod from *Moonlight.* Copyright © 1982 by Jan Ormerod. By permission of Lothrop, Lee & Shepard Books, a division of William Morrow and Company, Inc.

PARRISH, MAXFIELD. From *The Annotated Mother Goose* by William S. Baring-Gould and Ceil Baring-Gould. Copyright © 1962 by William S. and Ceil Baring-Gould. Reprinted by permission of Bramhall House, published by Clarkson N. Potter, a member of the Crown Publishing Group. PEET, BILL. Illustration from *The Wump World* by Bill Peet. Copyright © 1970 by Bill Peet. Reprinted by permission of Houghton Mifflin Co. All rights reserved. PERRAULT, CHARLES. Illustration by Gustave Dor from *Perrault's Fairy Tales* (1921), translated by A. E. Johnson. PEYTON, K. M. Illustration by K. M. Peyton from *Fly-by-Night.* Copyright © 1968 by K. M. Peyton. By permission of The Putnam & Grosset Group. POLITI, LEO. Reprinted with the permission of Charles Scribner's Sons, an imprint of Macmillan Publishing Company from *Song of the Swallows* by Leo Politi. Copyright 1949 Charles Scribner's Sons; copyright renewed © 1977 Leo Politi. PRELUTSKY, JACK. Illustration from *The New Kid on the Block* by Jack Prelutsky, illustrated by James Stevenson. Copyright © 1984 by James Stevenson. By permission of Greenwillow Books, a division of William Morrow and Company, Inc. PRESCHOOL BOOKS. Illustration from Max's Bedtime by Rosemary Wells. Copyright © 1985 Rosemary Wells. Used by permission of Dial

Books for Young Readers, a division of Penguin Books USA Inc. PROVENSEN, ALICE AND MARTIN. From *Our Animal Friends at Maple Hill Farm* by Alice and Martin Provensen. Copyright © 1974 by Alice and Martin Provensen. Reprinted by permission of Random House, Inc. PYLE, HOWARD. Reprinted with the permission of Charles Scribner's Sons, an imprint of Macmillan Publishing Company from *The Story of the Champions of the Round Table* written and illustrated by Howard Pyle. Copyright 1905 Charles Scribner's Sons; copyright renewed 1933 Anne Poole Pyle.

RASKIN, ELLEN. From *The Mysterious Disappearance of Leon (I Mean Noel)* by Ellen Raskin. Copyright © 1971 by Ellen Raskin. Used by permission of Dutton Children's Books, a division of Penguin Books USA Inc. REY, H. A. Illustration from *Curious George* by H. A. Rey. Copyright 1941 and © renewed 1969 by Margaret E. Rey. Copyright assigned to Houghton Mifflin Company in 1993. Reprinted by permission of Houghton Mifflin Co. All rights reserved. RICE, EVE. Illustration by Eve Rice from her *Goodnight, Goodnight.* Copyright © 1980 by Eve Rice. By permission of Greenwillow Books, a division of William Morrow and Company, Inc. ROBERTSON, KEITH. From *Henry Reed's Baby-Sitting Service* by Keith Robertson, illustrated by Robert McCloskey. Copyright © 1966 by Keith Robertson. Used by permission of Viking Penguin, a division of Penguin Books USA Inc. ROBINSON, BARBARA. Illustration by Judith Gwyn Brown from *The Best Christmas Pageant Ever* (1972), by Barbara Robinson. Selection reprinted by permission of HarperCollins Publishers. RODGERS, MARY. Jacket illustration by Edward Gorey from *Freaky Friday* (1972), by Mary Rodgers. Selection reprinted by permission of HarperCollins Publishers. ROJANKOVSKY, FEODOR. From *Animals in the Zoo* by Feodor Rojankovsky. Copyright © 1962 Feodor Rojankovsky. Used by permission of Tatiana R. Koly. ROUNDS, GLEN. Copyright © 1989 by Glen Rounds. All rights reserved. Reprinted from *Old MacDonald Had a Farm* by permission of Holiday House, Inc. RUBEL, NICOLE. Illustration from *Rotten Ralph* by Jack Gantos and Nicole Rubel. Illustration copyright © 1976 by Leslie Rubel. Reprinted by permission of Houghton Mifflin Co. All rights reserved.

SAINT-EXUPERY, ANTOINE DE. Illustration from *The Little Prince* by Antoine de Saint-Exupéry, copyright 1943 and renewed 1971 by Harcourt Brace & Company, reproduced by permission of the publisher. SANDBURG, CARL. Illustration by Maud Petersham and Miska Petersham from *Rootabaga Stories* by Carl Sandburg, copyright 1923, 1922 by Harcourt Brace & Company and renewed 1951, 1950 by Carl Sandburg, reproduced by permission of the publisher. SAY, ALLEN. Illustration from *Grandfather's Journey* by Allen Say. Copyright © 1993 by Allen Say. Reprinted by permission of Houghton Mifflin Co. All rights reserved. SCHOENHERR, JOHN. From *Rascal* by Sterling North. Copyright © 1963 by Sterling North, renewed © 1991 by David S. North and Arielle North Olson, text. Used by permission of Dutton Children's Books, a division of Penguin Books USA Inc. SEWELL, ANNA. From *Black Beauty,* by Anna Sewell, illustrations copyright 1950 by George Ford Morris. Illustrations copyright renewed 1978 by Sidney M. Morris. Selection reprinted by permission of HarperCollins Publishers. SHARMAT, MARJORIE WEINMAN. Illustration by Marc Simont from *Nate the Great and the Lost List* (1975) by Marjorie Weinman Sharmat. By permission of The Putnam & Grosset Group. SHEPARD, ERNEST H. From *When We Were Very Young* by A. A. Milne, illustrated by E. H. Shepard. Copyright 1924 by E. P. Dutton, renewed copyright 1952 by A. A. Milne. Used by permission of Dutton Children's Books, a division of Penguin Books USA Inc. SIS, PETER. Interior illustration from *The Dragons Are Singing Tonight,* by Jack Prelutsky, illustrated by Peter Sis. Copyright © 1993 by Peter Sis. By permission of Greenwillow Books, a division of William Morrow and Company, Inc. SLOBODKINA, ESPHYR. Illustration by Esphyr Slobodkina from *Caps for Sale* (1940). Selection reprinted by permission of HarperCollins Publishers. SPIER, PETER. From *Tin Lizzie* by Peter Spier. Copyright © 1975 by Peter Spier. Used by permission of Doubleday, a division of Bantam Doubleday Dell Publishing Group, Inc. SPORTS STORIES. Jacket illustration by Wayne Winfield for *The Moves Make the Man* (1984), by Bruce Brooks. Selection reprinted by permission of HarperCollins Publishers. STEVENSON, JAMES. Illustration from *Grandaddy and Janetta,* by Helen V. Griffith, illustrated by James Stevenson. Copyright © 1993 by James Stevenson. By permission of Greenwillow Books, a division of William Morrow and Company, Inc. STEVENSON, ROBERT LOUIS. Illustration by Henriette Willebeek le Mair from *A Child's Garden of Verses* by Robert Louis Stevenson. Copyright © 1926. By permission of The Putnam & Grosset Group.

TAFURI, NANCY. Illustration by Nancy Tafuri from her book *Have You Seen My Duckling?* Copyright © 1984 by Nancy Tafuri. By permission of Greenwillow Books, a division of William Morrow and Company, Inc. TAYLOR, MILDRED. From *The Friendship* by Mildred D. Taylor, pictures by Max Ginsburg. Copyright © 1987 Max Ginsburg for pictures. Used by permission of Dial Books for Young Readers, a division of Penguin Books USA Inc. TENNIEL, SIR JOHN. Reprinted with the permission of Macmillan Publishing Company from *Alice's Adventures in Wonderland,* by Lewis Carroll, illustrated by Sir John Tenniel (Macmillan, NY, 1963). TOLKIEN, J. R. R. Illustration from *The Hobbit* by J. R. R. Tolkien. Copyright © 1966 by J. R. R. Tolkien. Reprinted by permission of Houghton Mifflin Co. All rights reserved. TOMES, MARGOT. Illustrated by Margot Tomes from *The Sorcerer's Apprentice* (1979), adapted by Wanda Gág. By permission of the Putnam & Grosset Group. TRAVERS, P. L. Illustration from *Mary Poppins Opens the Door* by P. L. Travers and illustrated by Mary Shepard and Agnes Sims, copyright 1943 and renewed 1971 by P. L. Travers, reproduced by permission of Harcourt Brace & Company. TRIPP, WALLACE. Illustration from *Marguerite, Go Wash Your Feet* by Wallace Tripp. Copyright © 1985 by Wallace Tripp. Reprinted by permission of Houghton Mifflin Co. All rights reserved.

WABER, BERNARD. Illustration from *Lyle, Lyle Crocodile* by Bernard Waber. Copyright © 1965 by Bernard Waber. Reprinted by permission of Houghton Mifflin Co. All rights reserved. WARD, LYND. Illustration from *The Biggest Bear* by Lynd Ward. Copyright © 1952, renewed 1980 by Lynd Ward. Reprinted by permission of Houghton Mifflin Co. All rights reserved. WEIL, LISL. Illustration from *Mimi* by Lisl Weil. Copyright © 1961 by Lisl Weil Marx. Reprinted by permission of Houghton Mifflin Co. All rights reserved. WHITE, E. B. Illustration by Garth Williams from *Charlotte's Web* (1952), by E. B. White. Illustration copyright renewed © 1980 by Garth Williams. Selection reprinted by permission of HarperCollins

Publishers. WILDER, LAURA INGALLS. Illustration by Garth Williams from *Little House in the Big Woods* (1953), by Laura Ingalls Wilder. Pictures copyright 1953, renewed © 1981 by Garth Williams. Selection reprinted by permission of HarperCollins Publishers. WILLARD, NANCY. Illustration from *A Visit to William Blake's Inn* by Nancy Willard, illustrations copyright © 1981 by Alice Provensen and Martin Provensen, reproduced by permission of Harcourt Brace & Company. WILLIAMS, VERA. Illustration by Vera Williams from *Stringbean's Trip to the Shining Sea,* by Vera B. Williams and Jennifer Williams. Copyright © 1988 by Vera B. Williams. By permission of Greenwillow Books, a division of William Morrow and Company, Inc.

ZELINSKY, PAUL O. From *The Maid and the Mouse and the Odd-Shaped House* by Paul O. Zelinsky. Copyright © 1981 by Paul O. Zelinsky. Used by permission of Dutton Children's Books, a division of Penguin Books USA Inc.

COLOR ILLUSTRATIONS

Illustration from *Little Tim and the Brave Sea Captain,* by Edward Ardizzone. Copyright © Edward Ardizzone 1955. First published 1936 by the Oxford University Press. Reprinted by permission of the Ardizzone Estate. From *Madeline* by Ludwig Bemelmans. Copyright 1939 by Ludwig Bemelmans, renewed © 1967 by Madeleine Bemelmans and Barbara Bemelmans Marciano. Used by permission of Viking Penguin, a division of Penguin Books USA Inc. Illustration by John Burningham from his book *Mr. Gumpy's Outing* (1973). By permission of HarperCollins Publishers. From *The Very Hungry Caterpillar* by Eric Carle. Copyright ©1969. By permission of The Putnam & Grosset Group. From *Thirteen,* copyright © 1975 by Remy Charlip and Jerry Joyner. Reprinted by permission of Remy Charlip. From *Miss Rumphius* by Barbara Cooney. Copyright © 1982 by Barbara Cooney Porter. Used by permission of Viking Penguin, a division of Penguin Books USA Inc. From *The Travels of Babar* by Jean de Brunhoff. Copyright 1934 and renewed 1962 by Random House, Inc. Reprinted by permission of Random House, Inc. Illustration copyright © 1947 by Clement Hurd from *Goodnight Moon,* by Margaret Wise Brown. Selection reprinted by permission of HarperCollins Publishers. From *The Snowy Day* by Ezra Jack Keats. Copyright © 1962 by Ezra Jack Keats, renewed © 1990 by Martin Pope. Used by permission of Viking Penguin, a division of Penguin Books USA Inc. Illustration by Arnold Lobel from *Frog and Toad Are Friends* (1970). Reprinted by permission of HarperCollins Publishers. Illustration from *Miss Nelson Is Missing!* by Harry Allard and James Marshall. Illustration copyright © 1977 by James Marshall. Reprinted by permission of Houghton Mifflin Co. All rights reserved. From *The Tale of Squirrel Nutkin,* by Beatrix Potter. Copyright © Frederick Warne & Co., 1903, 1987. Reprinted by permission of Frederick Warne & Co. From *Where the Wild Things Are,* by Maurice Sendak. Reprinted by permission of HarperCollins Publishers. Illustration from *Many Moons* by James Thurber, artwork copyright © 1990 by Marc Simont, reproduced by permission of Harcourt Brace & Company. Picture from *Doctor De Soto* by William Steig. Copyright © 1982 by William Steig. Reprinted by permission of Farrar, Straus & Giroux, Inc. Picture from *The Beast of Monsieur Racine* by Tomi Ungerer. Copyright © 1971 by Tomi Ungerer. Reprinted by permission of Farrar, Straus & Giroux, Inc. Illustration from *The Polar Express* by Chris Van Allsburg. Copyright © 1985 by Chris Van Allsburg. Reprinted by permission of Houghton Mifflin Co. All rights reserved. Illustration from *Possum Magic* by Mem Fox, illustrations copyright © 1983 by Julie Vivas, reproduced by permission of Harcourt Brace & Company. Reprinted with the permission of Atheneum books for Young Readers, an imprint of Simon & Schuster Children's Publishing Division from *Treasure Island* by Robert Louis Stevenson, illustrated by N. C. Wyeth. Picture from *Duffy and the Devil,* retold by Harve Zemach with pictures by Margot Zemach. Copyright ©1973 by Farrar, Straus & Giroux, Inc. Reprinted by permission of the publisher.

TEXT PERMISSIONS

KENNEDY, X. J. Excerpts from "Brats" from *Drat These Brats* by X. J. Kennedy. Copyright 1986 by X. J. Kennedy. Reprinted with permission of Margaret K. McElderry Books, an imprint of Simon & Schuster Children's Publishing Division. MCCORD, DAVID. Excerpts from "The Pickety Fence" and "Runover Rhyme" from *One at a Time* by David McCord. Copyright 1952 by David McCord. By permission of Little, Brown and Company. POETRY. Excerpt from *This Same Sky: A Collection of Poems from Around the World,* edited by Naomi Shihab Nye, originally published in *Leaf and Bone, African Praise Poems,* edited by Judith Gleason (Penguin Books, 1980, p. 121); translated by Judith Gleason. Reprinted by permission of the translator. WORTH, VALERIE. Excerpt from *At Christmastime* (1992) by Valerie Worth. Reprinted by permission of HarperCollins Children's Books. Excerpts "dog," "duck," and "daisies" from *Small Poems* by Valerie Worth with pictures by Natalie Babbitt. Poems copyright 1972 by Valerie Worth. Excerpt from "compass" from *Still More Small Poems* by Valerie Worth with pictures by Natalie Babbitt. Poems by copyright 1978 by Valerie Worth. Reprinted by permission of Farrar, Straus & Giroux, Inc.

Index of Contributors

General Index

Page numbers in **boldface type** refer to the major article for an entry. Page numbers in *italics* refer to illustrations.